FACILITIES MANAGEMENT

A Manual for Plant Administration

Second Edition

FACILITIES

MANAGEMENT

A Manual for Plant Administration

Second Edition

Rex O. Dillow, Editor-in-Chief

The Association of
Physical Plant Administrators
of Universities and Colleges

Alexandria, Virginia

Association of Physical Plant Administrators of Universities and Colleges
1446 Duke Street, Alexandria, Virginia 22314-3492

Printed in the United States of America
Library of Congress Catalog Card Number: 89-84403
International Standard Book Number: 0-913359-50-5

*Mention of companies and products are for information or illustrative purposes only and are not
intended by the publisher as an endorsement of any kind. The Foreword and Chapter 30 originally
appeared in* Facilities Manager.

Editor: Steve Glazner
Assistant Editor and Production Manager: Fran Pflieger

Typography: Applied Graphics Technologies, Inc.
Printing: R.R. Donnelley & Sons Company

Printed on acid-free paper

CONTENTS

SECTION III: BUSINESS MANAGEMENT

SECTION IV: FACILITIES OF HIGHER EDUCATION

CONCLUSION

ACKNOWLEDGMENTS

Thousands of hours, most of it contributed by volunteers from the facilities management profession, have gone into the writing, editing, and publishing of this second edition. The Association of Physical Plant Administrators of Universities and Colleges (APPA), whose purpose is to promote excellence in higher education facilities management, gratefully acknowledges the dozens of individuals who participated in the preparation of this comprehensive reference manual. We sincerely regret any omissions.

Our first thanks must go to Rex O. Dillow, who agreed to serve as editor-in-chief of this second edition after having served in the same capacity on the first edition, which was published in 1984. His professional judgment, technical expertise, strong leadership, and unflagging energy have kept this project's many components firmly focused and directed. Without his diligent efforts this manual would not have been possible.

Within APPA, this second edition has come under the oversight of the Professional Affairs Committee. We thank Norman H. Bedell, Pennsylvania State University, who chaired the committee and coordinated the initial efforts in 1986 to develop the second edition when it would have been easy to rest on the success of the first edition. We also thank the members of the committee and their subsequent chairs: Philip G. Rector, University of Arizona, and Alan D. Lewis, Colby College. Additional acknowledgments must go to APPA's Board of Directors and Executive Committee for their support.

We extend our thanks to the members of the Editorial Board, which was created solely for the purpose of producing this manual. They are responsible for the structure, content, and quality of this book and found that their greatest difficulty was in determining how to include the vast amount of excellent information contributed by the authors. Chaired by Rex Dillow, APPA member emeritus (University of Missouri-Columbia), the Board also included Gene B. Cross, University of California at Berkeley; Steve Glazner, APPA staff; H.C. Lott Jr., University of Texas at Austin; and William D. Middleton, University of Virginia.

Each major portion of the manual had a designated Section Leader who discovered authors, communicated progress to the Editorial Board, and kept the chapters in their sections on schedule. The following Section Leaders deserve our thanks and congratulations on a job well done: Harley A. Schrader, APPA member emeritus (University of Nebraska-Lincoln), for Section I: General Administration; Norman H. Bedell, Pennsylvania State University, for Section II: Human Resources Management; William A. Daigneau, University of Rochester, for Section III: Business Management; Herbert I. Collier, University of Houston, for Section IV: Facilities of Higher Education; William D. Middleton, University of Virginia, for Section V: Facilities Planning, Design, and Construction; Paul F. Tabolt, University of California at Berkeley, for Section VI: Work Management and Control; and James T. Mergner, University of North Carolina at Chapel Hill, for Section VII: Physical Plant Operations. We also gratefully acknowledge Ernest L. Boyer, president of the Carnegie Foundation for the Advancement of Teaching, for his foreword, and Gene B. Cross, University of California at Berkeley, for his conclusion.

Sixty-two facilities professionals wrote or cowrote the fifty-seven chapters included in this manual. We cannot thank them enough for the many hours spent researching, writing, and rewriting their drafts; we also extend our appreciation to the authors' institutions for their support. Additional contributions were made by Kirk Campbell, Dennis Cesari, Bob Early, Fred Plant, William Rose, and Howard Wilson.

Many people were involved in the production of this manual. Steve Glazner served as editor of the entire manuscript. Fran Pflieger served as assistant editor and production manager. Primary copyediting was done by Stephanie Gretchen, Candis Johnson, and Fran Pflieger, with additional copyediting by Mary Burke and Ann Petty. Thanks to Bita Lanys and Communicators Connection, Inc. Anita Blanchar provided most of the word processing required on the project; Peggy Ann Brown, Colleen Conner, Wayne Hilburn of Hilburn Communications, and Patti Saylor also provided word processing assistance.

Many thanks to Jill Pflug and her coworkers at Applied Graphics Technologies for their tremendous effort in typesetting text, developing figures, and preparing the book for the printer. Figures for Chapter 21 were drawn by the Graphic Arts Department, Academic Support Center, of the University of Missouri-Columbia. Editorial Experts, Inc. provided the indexing services of Catherine Dettmar and Martha Sencindiver, coordinated by June Morse. Thanks also to Shirley Schulz and Karen Richards of R.R. Donnelley & Sons.

FOREWORD

Facilities and the Academic Mission

Ernest L. Boyer
President
Carnegie Foundation for the
Advancement of Teaching

S everal years ago the Carnegie Foundation completed a study of American higher education, and we discovered that colleges in America are still highly prized. Only in America is the decal from almost any college displayed proudly on the rear window of the family car, and the message is, "Here's a family on the move."

We talked to a student who said, "I want a better life for myself, and that means college." We have in this country the aspiration in the hearts of our citizens that we want our children to do better, and that means a college education. Today about 57 percent of all high school graduates go on to college. But when we interviewed the parents of one thousand high school students, *95 percent* said that they want their children to go to college some day. In this country higher education is the door of hope, the ladder to success. I think those of us who are engaged in this enterprise should understand that in a fundamental way we are contributing, not only to the quality of the nation's life, but also to the aspirations of almost every citizen.

During the past few years since our report, *College: The Undergraduate Experience in America*, was released, I have visited a hundred colleges or more and found four themes being discussed from coast to coast. First, in the search for excellence in higher education, almost all campuses are inquiring about what we should be teaching. That is, what is the best curriculum for the year 2000 and beyond?

Second, there's a great and renewed interest in the quality of instruction. We've had a long period in which faculty were rewarded primarily for research, but there's a growing interest in the matter of how we can increase the quality of teaching, too.

Third, there's a renewed interest in the quality of campus life, something I know touches the commitments of facilities managers at most colleges and universities. The truth is, students don't just learn in the classroom. They learn a great deal outside the classroom as well. I am increasingly convinced that twenty or thirty years after students leave college, what they remember has less to do with the twelve or so hours every week they spend in classrooms, than with what happens in the dormitories and in the "rathskellers" late at night.

How to improve that quality outside the classroom will be one of the most important agenda items for higher learning in the days and years ahead. We've gone from the colonial parent-child model—*in loco parentis*—when student life was tightly regulated, to *in loco clinician*, with students left largely on their own unless there's a crisis. Now we have to ask ourselves how we can develop a means of support for student life outside the classroom that is something other than low-grade decadence.

This leads me then to the fourth issue that is being discussed—how to measure the outcomes of higher education. What, in fact, does it all add up to? We've been having a big debate in the United States on the quality of schools, and some gains indeed have been achieved since *A Nation at Risk* was first released in 1983. But now we are beginning to say that four years of college education—a huge investment—must be evaluated, too.

Those issues, then, are the ones that I hear debated: the curriculum, teaching, the quality of campus life, and how to measure the outcomes. But I should like to add issue number five. I am convinced that in the days ahead, the quality of education also must be measured by the quality of the facilities on the campus.

Over one hundred years ago, James Garfield during a speech at his alma mater, Williams College, said that the ideal college is Mark Hopkins on one end of the log and a student on the other. Garfield went on to become the twentieth President of the United States; he was soon shot, and nothing that he said in his short term of office was as well remembered as that statement.

There aren't many colleges today that could be conducted on a log. Twelve million students need much more than that. They need libraries, research facilities, residence halls, and classrooms. What we need today is not a log, but the equivalent of a modern city to carry on the enterprise of higher learning. Without a campus with facilities that are both adequate and aesthetic, we could not carry on this magnificent enterprise of higher education that is the envy of the world.

The simple truth is that if we did not have facilities that functioned well, we would have loud complaints from one end of the campus to the other. But since they are available, somehow they're not noticed. It's time to recognize that facilities provide the centerpiece around which all other functions take place.

First, facilities are vitally important in the recruitment of students to the campus. During our study of higher education we surveyed a thousand high school graduates who planned to attend college, and we asked them what they considered most important in their choice. You may have seen the data: over 60 percent said the appearance of the campus most affected their decision. And that's why we said in our report that when it comes to recruiting students, the director of facilities is far more important than the academic dean.

I visit dozens of colleges and universities every year, and the moment I step on campus I have a strong sense of the quality and the priorities of the institution. The president or chancellor may meet my plane and give me a speech about excellence in teaching and brag about the quality of research; the public relations director may hand me a nice brochure and show me the new videocassette they have prepared to recruit students. But in the end, if facilities are neglected and the campus is not well maintained, those actions speak much louder than words. You cannot have a core of excellence if you don't demonstrate a commitment to facilities.

We studied about thirty catalogs to see what colleges were promoting and we discovered that from that standpoint, about 60 percent of all classes in America are held outside, underneath a tree, usually with autumn leaves at their peak, and almost always by a lake. In fact, one of the public relations directors said to us, "Water's very big this year. You just can't recruit students without some water."

No matter what presidents and administrators say on campus, when they want to present their image to the public and say something about quality, they turn to facilities. They want it understood that excellence has to touch every aspect of the institution.

What I've said about recruiting students applies to faculty, too. I've heard some stories about colleges and universities offering big salaries and lots of fringe benefits to top ranking scholars. All goes well until the future candidate comes to visit the campus and is turned off because the facilities are inadequate to the function.

I'm suggesting that the priorities of the university are dramatically revealed by the way facilities are maintained and the importance that is assigned to the plant itself. If the grounds and buildings are neglected, it suggests a carelessness in administration that cannot be concealed by glossy brochures or by the inspirational speeches that the president gives to the Rotary Club on Wednesday afternoon.

This leads me to priority number two. Not only are the facilities crucial to attracting and holding outstanding scholars and students, they're also critical because they relate to fiscal efficiency as well. I was at the State University of New York during the 1960s when we had perhaps one of the largest higher education construction programs in history. During that period every campus in the SUNY system was expanding, and buildings were going up at the rate of one a week.

Construction costs approached $3 billion, which was managed by a separate corporation in New York called the State University of New York Construction Fund. We had to make decisions about facilities literally every single day.

All of this, in my judgment, was a spectacular achievement, and what we did in New York in the 1960s occurred in many states from coast to coast. Towns and villages in New York State were enormously enriched. But it is much easier to erect buildings than to maintain them. When we had a deep recession in New York in the 1970s, it was the facilities budget that was hardest hit, and maintenance was endlessly postponed.

The APPA/NACUBO/Coopers & Lybrand study, *The Decaying American Campus: A Ticking Time Bomb*, estimates that if we were to add up all of the urgent deferred maintenance needs in higher education, it would total more than $20 billion. By neglecting these precious resources, we are stacking up a staggering debt that will catch up with us later on. Several years ago I returned to one of the SUNY campuses and, quite frankly, was shocked to see the peeling paint, the tattered rugs, and the sidewalks that were already cracked and crumbling. The good news is that I returned to that very same campus recently and saw tremendous improvement. But the president told me they were probably paying double the amount for maintenance they would have paid if the projects had not been delayed.

I am suggesting that maintenance, like health, cannot be deferred. We can pretend that we are saving money by delay, but that simply means there will be a far greater investment later on. We must find a way to convince state governments that maintaining buildings not only makes sense for education; it reflects sound fiscal management as well.

Third, I'd like to say a word about how good facilities relate to good education. The quality of education is related to the quality of the teaching materials and facilities on the campus. Those of you who maintain the plant, supply the equipment, and seek to keep the buildings working well are, in my judgment, educators, too. The physical plant administrators should not be the last to know the academic plans of the institution; they should be among the first to know. They should be involved intimately in helping to set priorities of the institution because, in the end, they must see that those priorities can be implemented every single day. While the facilities may be taken for granted, just try closing them for a day and you'll find out what faculty revolution is like.

This leads me then to priority four. I am convinced that good facilities are needed to enrich the educational experience on the campus and help build a spirit of community as well. Rebuilding community is perhaps one of our most important responsibilities in higher education, and that certainly has to do with the quality of the campus and how one *feels* about the place.

In the award-winning Broadway play *Fiddler on the Roof*, the peasant dairyman who has raised five daughters with considerable help from scriptural quotations—many of which he himself invented—says the old laws, the old customs, and the feasts and traditions handed down from one generation to another are what makes life tolerable to the hard-working Jewish families. Without them, the dairyman declared, life would be as shaky as a fiddler on the roof.

So it is with colleges. While professors do their research in isolation and students worry about their careers, and while administrators fight for budgets, I still believe that life is made tolerable by the shared rituals, remembrances, and sense of community on campus. Yet during our study of the undergraduate college, we found that this spirit is not very well sustained. Almost half of the students we surveyed said that they feel like they are treated like a number in a book. We also found that only 20 percent of the faculty said they feel loyalty to their campus, while 70 percent said they feel more affinity for their academic discipline nationwide.

How can one not have a sense of allegiance to a place where one lives every day? We are close to our families, I assume. How can we not feel loyalty to the place that nurtures us, provides friendships, and gives us facilities for support, comfort, and protection from the wind?

One professor captured the spirit that prevails on many campuses when he said, "My community is the WATS line, not my colleagues down the hall." I don't wish to romanticize the notion of community in higher education, and yet we say in our book *College* that a university should be held together by something more than a common grievance over parking.

I do believe that facilities are a part of affirming community on the campus. They give dignity and status to the institution and allow it to function. When we rebuild our cities, we rebuild our facilities. The building of community in the city means new banks, hotels, and shopping malls; but it also means new parks and pedestrian walkways. That's what we mean by rebuilding a sense of urban community.

We build facilities in order to make a statement about what we prize. And while the spirit of community in higher education is sustained by good teaching and good communication, it's also sustained by facilities of quality that are well-maintained and provide warmth and intimacy on the campus.

The buildings we erect reflect our priorities as a people because they define the functions that we carry on. The physical plant administrators of colleges and universities perform an essential function on behalf of education, not only for the students of today, but also for the coming generation. James Agee once wrote that every child born, under no matter what circumstance, reaffirms the future of the human race. I believe that as we invest in higher education, as we build our cathedrals of learning, we are, in fact, making a statement about the future generation and the potentiality of every student.

INTRODUCTION

Second Edition

Rex O. Dillow
APPA Member Emeritus
Columbia, Missouri

Higher education facilities management has been subjected to more forces for change in the last thirty-five years than in all prior history.

In the 1950s and 1960s, the profession was primarily concerned with the enrollment-driven expansion in physical plants. The end of the expansion period in the early 1970s saw the onset of rapidly rising fund requirements. A series of new governmental regulations established stringent building codes, required accessibility for the handicapped, environmental protection, and other health and safety standards, adding fund requirements for new buildings as well as for bringing existing structures into compliance. Energy consumption increased and building mechanical and electrical systems were designed to provide year-round optimum conditions of comfort. The increased usage, combined with unprecedented increases in fuels and energy prices, caused energy to suddenly become a major item in the operating budget.

It is difficult to comprehend the extent of growth in technologies in higher education facilities that was occurring during the same time period. This growth led to changes in teaching, research methods, and equipment, which necessitated alterations to buildings, special features such as stable voltages and close control of environmental conditions, and special research facilities. Meeting these needs added costs and increased training requirements for operation and maintenance personnel.

With the end of the expansion period and escalation in fund requirements, higher education came under special stresses at both private and public institutions. As needs outstripped income and as state support dwindled, college and university administrators often deferred the maintenance and renewal needs of their facilities.

The net result of these interacting forces was vastly expanded physical plants of higher technologies, infinitely higher operating and maintenance costs, and limited fund availability.

The facilities management profession responded with superior efforts to meet the situation. Temperature and humidity control systems were installed to limit energy usage; building heating and cooling plants were converted to more efficient types, and to central plants with campus distribution systems; thermal and electrical requirements were coordinated through cogeneration; new technologies improved power plant efficiencies; building heat recovery systems were installed. Professional maintenance programs, with emphasis on preventive maintenance, were developed to keep equipment in optimum operating condition and extend its life to the maximum extent possible.

New equipment and technologies were adopted for more effective management, especially in the areas of fiscal, work, and personnel management. Improved cost accounting and control contributed to more valid and accurate budgeting and more effective coordination of resources and expenditures. Centralized work management better coordinated work capabilities and priorities. Added emphasis was given to the development and maintenance of an attractive and functional campus, contributing to the recruitment and retention of students, faculty, and staff.

Perhaps the most serious challenge facing the profession, affecting the quality of the facilities for which it is responsible, is the $60 to $70 billion total backlog of capital renewal/deferred maintenance needs recently documented in the APPA/NACUBO/Coopers & Lybrand research report, *The Decaying American Campus: A Ticking Time Bomb.* Despite a persistent effort by physical plant administrators to reverse a decades-long accumulation of backlogs, funding at many institutions continues to fall short of even partial requests for CRDM funding.

As we move into the 1990s and beyond, the economic pressures on higher education are projected to continue, even intensify. Facilities standards can be expected to be progressively elevated, while resources will be limited. The profession must continue to grow and develop, to make even more effective and economical use of funds, to ever seek new methods and materials to provide the best possible physical environment within which learning takes place.

Decision making in the allocation of resources will surely be more and more centralized. The line of demarcation between educational goals and facilities management objectives will become more indistinct. The inability to fund all perceived needs requires that available resources be used for greatest effectiveness in carrying out the teaching, research, and public service missions. Physical plant administrators must continue to identify fund needs in the facilities area, but must also participate with other top administrators of the institution in evaluating these needs relative to other institutional requirements. Few facilities fund requirements are absolute; all must be weighed on the basis of economy with regard to timeliness, and their contribution to the quality and suitability of the facilities. The physical plant administrator must be teaching and research oriented, capable of seeing the role of facilities management in true perspective relative to the mission of the institution. This not only broadens the role, but makes more critical the traditional facilities management functions.

Perhaps the most dominant single influence in the growth of the physical plant profession has been the Association of Physical Plant Administrators of Universities and Colleges (APPA). During the thirty-five years of accelerated evolution of the profession, APPA has developed from an all-volunteer organization serving the membership primarily through the promotion of the informal exchange of information between members to a dynamic association with permanent staff, administering comprehensive education and publication programs, and coordinating and directing programs of research and study for the advancement of the profession. This manual is one element of the publications program and serves as the basic text of the APPA Institute for Facilities Management, the association's basic training and development program for the profession.

A Basic Manual for Physical Plant Administration, edited by George Weber, was published in 1974. The first edition of *Facilities Management: A Manual for Plant Administration*, published in 1984, continued the effort to provide a comprehensive manual for the profession. Completed in about one year, it had shortcomings in both detail and comprehensiveness for that time, and the profession has further developed in the ensuing years. No work is infallible, but sufficient effort has been expended on this latest edition, building on the prior efforts, that it is considered to be of inestimably greater value.

Every effort has been made to maintain objectivity and a healthy skepticism, even of personal observations. Also avoided has been the presentation of specific procedures and solutions to continuing problems. In these days of tremendous technological developments, and with the political, economic, and demographic environment of higher education continually changing, facilities management must be adaptable to change. The intention has been to thoroughly research all subjects and present factual information for use by professionals in future problem solving.

Because of the greater complexity and detail inherent in some subjects, the depth of coverage varies between chapters. In many cases a bibliography is provided for further study. Additionally, other APPA publications are available on many of the subjects covered herein.

The facilities management profession is so diverse that it embodies a vast profusion of information. The organization and classification of information, which may well be one of the principal values of this manual, is organized into four functional areas:

1. Sections I-III address the support functions of the organization, as well as business and personnel management.
2. Section IV, a new section, is devoted to the description of the types and characteristics of the facilities of higher education.
3. Sections IV-VII address the mainstream functions of the construction, maintenance, and operation of facilities.
4. The concluding section summarizes the salient elements of success in tying it all together as an essential component of the total higher education institution.

This second edition of *Facilities Management: A Manual for Plant Administration* represents the best collective knowledge of today's professionals in the facilities management and related professions. It is recommended with confidence by the Association of Physical Plant Administrators of Universities and Colleges to all members of the profession, and to other higher education officials with an interest in facilities management.

August 1989

INTRODUCTION

First Edition

Rex O. Dillow
APPA Member Emeritus
Columbia, Missouri

Postsecondary education has never been a unified system under effective centralized control. It is, instead, a composite of public and private institutions in fifty states and territories, each developing in response to unique requirements and varying types and degrees of organization and control. Yet the major forces affecting postsecondary education in the past thirty years have required sweeping and national adaptations. These influences have demanded solutions more universal than at any time in the past. These forces for change have contributed to the growth and development of professionals who manage education facilities. The magnitude of the requirements and functions assigned to the profession have enhanced the value and stimulated the development of the Association of Physical Plant Administrators of Universities and Colleges.

Four factors have contributed most to the current state of education facilities: 1) expanding enrollments of the 1950s and 1960s required extensive additions to physical plants, 2) increasing complexity of new facilities, 3) proliferation of government regulations pertaining to facilities, primarily regarding public safety and welfare, and 4) unprecedented increases in energy costs.

The GI Bill of Rights significantly increased the numbers of students attending college after World War II. This influx broke a stereotype—that a college education was just for the elite—and led to higher percentages of high school graduates continuing their education. Combined with the subsequent population growth, colleges and universities experienced an explosive growth in enrollment. The 1957 launching of Sputnik created a crisis of confidence in U.S. leadership in many academic fields, and brought about greater federal support of institutional research and teaching.

The growth in enrollment and increased emphasis on research created a demand for more facilities. Lawmakers responded with a largess without precedent. An "edifice complex" developed that linked growth with funding. Increasing enrollments served as the most persuasive arguments for additional funds. The plant value of all postsecondary education more than doubled in the 1950s; it increased almost fourfold in the 1960s.

In this period of adequate public funding and low operating and maintenance costs, little attention was given to operating efficiencies in the design of new buildings, or to timely maintenance and/or renovation of existing structures to modern standards of adequacy and suitability. Funds were devoted to meeting the most demanding requirement at the time—the addition of maximum floor space to handle growing enrollments and added research. Rooftop heating and cooling units, then inefficient in energy use and exposed to the worst possible maintenance conditions, were used in order to increase usable interior space. Mechanical systems were designed to furnish high ventilation rates and close year-round temperature control. Buildings contained vast expanses of glass and had flat roofs with little insulation. Lighting standards were scaled upwards, beyond what were subsequently determined to be optimum levels. Energy consumption in buildings constructed in the 1950s and 1960s ran 400 to 500 percent higher than that of pre-World War II buildings.

The 1970s produced a series of federal and state mandates establishing stringent building codes and standards. In 1977 the Department of Health, Education and Welfare published regulations for implementing Section 504 of the Rehabilitation Act of 1973, requiring program accessibility for handicapped students. Other governmental regulations pertaining to facilities management and operation were enacted. Most of them were concerned with health and safety, including environmental protection. All added funding requirements, not only for new structures, but also for bringing the vast existing plants into compliance.

The energy crisis arrived suddenly in 1973, precipitated by developments in international relations. Long neglected because of its ready availability and low cost, energy suddenly became a major factor requiring careful management. The large increases in cost, and shortages or threatened shortages of certain fuels, dictated changes in operating procedures and building alterations for improved energy efficiency. Universities had typically provided their own heating and cooling while purchasing electric power, potable water, sewage treatment, and solid waste disposal services from sources in the community. Economic advantages developed for integrating utility systems independently or in conjunction with the community, such as on-site electric power generation with use of residual heat for space heating and cooling, incineration of solid waste for its heat content, and partial re-use of effluent from sewage treatment for equipment makeup water and irrigation.

The late 1970s ushered in two new developments: an end to the period of sustained growth, and a faltering of traditional revenue sources. The force for expansion ceased to dominate at about the same time as the comfortable conditions promoted by the growth environment ended. Postsecondary education came under the same stresses that were affecting the rest of society—rising costs and dwindling resources. With declining enrollments and the competing claims of cities, public highways, the elderly, and environmental problems, education received a reduced share of the tax dollar.

In order to maintain quality education with diminished real dollar resources, college and university governance began to try to reduce administrative expenses in order to increase funds available for instruction, research, and academic support. Plant departments, the largest single unit in the managerial, administrative services area, often received the largest percentage of fund reductions. Many plant administrators came to realize that they were confronted with a new set of problems, problems for which they had developed no criteria for determining or justifying needed funds. This gave immediate rise to an admixture of crash methods such as average cost-per-square-foot, square-feet-per-employee, formula budgeting, etc.—all valuable comparative data but hardly adequate justification in support of fund requests.

Education is in transition, facing administrative problems that can only be solved by professionals. No requirement looms greater than that of providing a suitable physical environment for the teaching and research of postsecondary institutions. As we look forward, facilities administration in the rest of the 1980s may be characterized by five features.

Fund reductions.   Rising costs, further reductions in the percentage of tax dollars assigned to education, and priority consideration to maintaining high quality in the primary institutional functions of teaching, research, and public service will further erode facilities funding.

Emphasis on existing facilities.   Shift from new construction to existing facilities—preservation, renovation to modern standards of quality, alterations to meet changed program requirements, and space management including removing excess facilities from use to improve operation and maintenance efficiencies.

Professionalism in budgeting and administration.   Professional programs and systems must be used for the operation, maintenance, and management of facilities. Funding requirements for the various functions must be determined and supported by factual information. Those requirements must be articulated clearly to funding authorities.

Close integration of academic, fiscal, and facilities planning.   Institutional requirements cannot be met by simply dividing funds between academic and facilities needs. All facilities fund requirements relate directly to the effectiveness of the facilities in supporting the institution's teaching and research missions. A planning climate and system must exist to evaluate all fund requirements in light of that mission, and to maintain the unity of final decisions.

Greater emphasis upon leadership.   Governmental mandates on collective bargaining, working conditions, health and safety, affirmative action, and equal opportunity have made personnel administration more complex and difficult. At the same time the need for greater productivity has made effective management of human resources most important. The requirement for technical competence has not lessened, but new administrative responsibilities and obligations have been added.

In the stable environment of education before World War II, physical plant functions emphasized trades methods and responded to customer requests. There was no commonly accepted definition of the responsibilities of a plant administrator, nor was it even considered a distinctive profession. Recent developments in education levied vast new requirements on facilities administration. The future will surely bring requirements even more difficult and perplexing. A common, though by no means universal, response to the changing demands has been to assign the new responsibilities to the physical plant department and upgrade the capabilities of the department. Sometimes, however, the physical plant department has been splintered into separate specialist roles. Construction departments were created with central roles in new construction and other facilities projects, but without defining those roles relative to the maintenance and operation functions. Safety offices have been treated outside the physical plant, with ill-defined roles for compliance with codes and standards. Other offices such as facilities management and energy management have been created. Lack of coordination has humorous, if not tragic, results. New buildings were constructed with incandescent lighting that physical plant replaced with fluorescent, for greater energy efficiency, immediately upon occupancy.

The situation in postsecondary education points toward centralization of all facilities management functions under one chief administrator. This central administration will result in more economical operations, more efficient and comprehensive facilities planning, and better integration of facilities planning with academic and fiscal planning. A facilities administrator on a par with other top administrators can help plan for the most effective utilization of physical resources and for the most economical use of facilities funds in support of the institution's mission. This comprehensive facilities administration could not have been met by physical plants of the past, using antiquated methods and ideas, but we are entering a new age of expanded capabilities. In its present state, automation can contribute to more effective control of operations, as well as provide accurate and timely information for decision making.

The industrial sector is aware of the unique requirements of education institutions and will respond with improved technologies and processes for managing energy, utilities, and maintenance. The profession is attracting well-educated young people experienced in the latest technologies. The physical plant can now hire personnel with outstanding professional qualifications and can purchase the most sophisticated management assistance equipment. An objective of facilities professionals for the immediate future should be to identify and describe the functions and responsibilities that should be assigned to the physical plant department in order to achieve effective facilities management. As a corollary we need to describe the professional qualifications required to implement those functions and responsibilities. Our professional association, APPA, can then develop and administer programs addressing these defined responsibilities. APPA will advise and encourage the proper physical plant role in its liaison with other educational associations and individual institutions.

This publication is an effort to provide comprehensive coverage of the major aspects of the physical plant profession today. Organized and outlined by the Professional Affairs Committee and the APPA staff in 1981, it is a work prepared by members for members and others associated with plant administration. It presents basic principles and considerations that will help individuals meet the requirements unique to their situation. Descriptions of successful systems or methods are intended as examples, not as recommendations.

This book should be viewed as a continuing project. New developments in the profession will necessitate changes. As it is used by members, requirements for additional information will become apparent; however, it is intended as a basic, long-lasting document. Elaborations on elements of the contents, tentative new methods, special problems requiring timely emphasis, and other short-term matters can best be handled by supplementary publications.

Facilities Management: A Manual for Plant Administration represents the best collective knowledge and efforts of the membership today. It is recommended to all members with confidence by the Professional Affairs Committee, the APPA officers, and staff.

July 1984

SECTION I

GENERAL

ADMINISTRATION

Section Leader:
Harley Schrader
APPA Member Emeritus
Lincoln, Nebraska

CHAPTER 1

The Facilities Organization

William D. Middleton, P.E.
Assistant Vice President, Physical Plant
University of Virginia

1.1 INTRODUCTION

The objective of a physical plant department, as for any organization, is the performance of its assigned mission and functions with optimum effectiveness and economy. Achieving this requires maximum individual productivity and coordination of the efforts of all personnel. The organizational structure reflects the activities of physical plant staff; it establishes the channels through which these activities are administered.

It is important to distinguish between organization and administration. Organization is the instrument; administration is the method of using the instrument. The central object of administration is coordination, through ensuring a common understanding of objectives, a knowledge of individual tasks and their interrelationships, and the enforcement of efficient work standards. Administration is an important element of leadership. But the importance of organization cannot be overlooked. A good organizational structure facilitates effective performance. Without a good organization, it can be exceedingly difficult to provide responsive, efficient, or effective services.

This chapter discusses the basic principles of effective organization and their application to the special needs of a physical plant department. Typical physical plant functions and their interrelationships will be reviewed. Several concepts of organization will be discussed, as well as methods of organizing in accordance with basic principles and these concepts. Recommendations will be presented for a "model" facilities organizational structure based upon the organizational principles presented, together with several variations of the model structure adapting it to typical situations.

1.2 UNIQUE PHYSICAL PLANT CHARACTERISTICS AFFECTING ORGANIZATION

A physical plant department is typically a large organization with responsibility for a multitude of diverse functions. It is composed of a large number of people with diverse educational and professional backgrounds, organized into as many as four or five levels of line authority. Many of its functions require quick response, preventing deliberate planning of individual projects. The size and diversity necessitates decentralization of control of functions, yet close coordination between component units is mandatory.

A physical plant department has a mission and functions that relate to virtually all other departments of the institution. Perhaps no other department has such frequent working relationships with so many other departments. These contacts and working relationships, including certain decision-making authority, must exist as each level, from the director to individual tradesmen. Yet all must be coordinated to achieve unity of effort and consistency in policies and procedures.

The mission and functions of the physical plant department are in the service support area and therefore outside the mainstream of the institution's teaching, research, and public service missions. Its organization and functioning are unique within the institution, unlike that of any other department. This, together with the magnitude and diversity of its functions, creates special problems and requirements in establishing and maintaining effective liaison and communications with the campus community.

1.3 PURPOSE OF THE PHYSICAL PLANT ORGANIZATION

The basic objective of the organizational structure of a physical plant department, as for any service organization, is to arrange functional resources in a way that permits the organization to effectively and efficiently deliver services in support of the overall mission of the institution. In an effective physical plant organization, there will be clear and orderly procedures for the receipt or generation of the work load; priorities will be established in an effective and consistent manner; materials will be procured expeditiously; work will be planned and scheduled efficiently; and the actual performance of work will be done by divisions with a clear understanding of their responsibilities and effective procedures for coordinating their work with other components of the organization.

1.4 PRINCIPLES OF EFFECTIVE ORGANIZATION

The following principles are generally accepted as having high validity in any organization.

1. *Every necessary function is assigned to a unit of the organization.* The organization exists to accomplish all required functions. This includes not only the assigned end-functions, but component tasks included in the functions.
2. *The responsibilities assigned a unit of the organization must be clear-cut and understood.* Standing instructions should be checked periodically to ensure adherence to this principle and to guard against overlapping responsibilities.
3. *The type of organizational structure should be consistent throughout the department.* Deviations will be necessary due to different assigned tasks, but to the maximum extent possible the organizational structure should be consistent.
4. *Each member of the organization reports to no more than one supervisor, and each member knows to whom they report and who reports to them.* Adherence to this principle eliminates the confusion caused by conflicting instructions and overlapping responsibilities.
5. *Responsibility for a function must be matched by the authority necessary to perform the function.* Nothing is more destructive to morale than having to check continually with a supervisor, or to obtain widespread concurrence, before taking action to carry out a function for which one is responsible.
6. *Individuals reporting to a supervisor must not exceed the number that can be effectively coordinated and directed.* The specific number will vary with the function. One supervisor can effectively supervise a far greater number of custodians performing repetitive work, for example, than can a chief engineer supervising engineers and engineering technicians involved in creative design.
7. *Line channels must not be violated by staff members.* The line channels run from the director through succeeding echelons—for example, director to superintendent to supervisor to foreman. It is through these channels that the assigned functions of physical plant are accomplished. Staff personnel carry out specialized functions in support of the line organization. Although staff members must confer with line supervisors at all echelons, care must be exercised that they do not circumvent line channels of authority by issuing instructions or otherwise exercising direct supervision over subordinate units in their specialized areas.
8. *Authority and responsibility for action must be delegated to the lowest level commensurate with the personnel available and qualified to assume*

such responsibility. Each decision should be made at the lowest level at which there exists a full understanding of the factors involved, including relevant policy considerations.

9. *Organization should be as simply constructed as the tasks assigned to the unit will permit.* Consistent with span of control considerations, supervisory and management levels should be held to the minimum. Organizational structures should not become so cumbersome or intricate as to hinder the accomplishment of assigned functions.

Leadership styles and capabilities can greatly affect the way organizations function. Strong, autocratic leaders tend to centralize authority and decision-making, while authority and decision-making tend to flow to the next level below or above a weak or indecisive leader. To some extent, these trends are inevitable in organizations, but the structuring of organizations around the leadership styles of individuals should be avoided.

1.5 ORGANIZATIONAL CONCEPTS

There are several concepts of organization that should be kept in mind when designing an effective organizational structure.

Line and Staff Functions

Every organization has certain primary, or line, functions associated with the actual performance of work in support of the organizational mission. Some examples of line functions in physical plant include operation and maintenance of utilities plants and distribution systems, facilities maintenance and repair, custodial services, grounds maintenance, and facilities planning, design, and construction.

In addition to its line functions, every organization will also require the performance of various functions that are not directly involved with the execution of these line functions, but which advise, assist, or otherwise support them in some way. These are commonly referred to as staff functions.

Staff functions in a physical plant organization include personnel and training administration, budgeting and cost accounting, facilities inspection, work reception, material procurement, and computing services, among others.

Organization Structure

In designing an organization, the scalar or "stair-step" principle commonly is used. This refers to the delegation of authority through a series of organizational steps or levels, as represented by an organization chart.

In establishing the organization, particular attention should be paid to striking a balance between the "span of control" at each managerial level, and "layering" of the organization.

If the span of control for a manager is too great, inadequate direction and coordination will result. As a general rule, the number of interdependent positions reporting to a single manager should be limited to about five or six. This number can be substantially greater if there is little or no interdependence among the reporting units, or if relatively simple, repetitive tasks are supervised.

On the other hand, if managers are limited to too narrow a span of control, an excessive number of organizational layers is created, which tends to make an organization sluggish and inflexible, and makes top-to-bottom communication more difficult.

1.6 FUNCTIONS OF A PHYSICAL PLANT ORGANIZATION

Following are the broad functional groupings that may be part of a physical plant organization:

- Facilities space administration
- Facilities planning
- Facilities design and construction
- Utilities services
- Facilities maintenance
- Renovations
- Custodial services
- Grounds maintenance
- Transportation
- Other services
  — Solid waste collection and disposal
  — Fire protection and safety
  — Security
  — Risk management
  — Environmental health and safety
  — Mail and messenger service.

Together with internal staff and support services, the organizational components required for effective delivery of this wide variety of services fall into several broad functional groupings.

Management and Control

An effective physical plant program requires a strong management control group, clearly separated from the work performing component of the organization. Some of its principal functions may include:

- External relations
- Planning for the organization
- Establishment of goals and objectives
- Establishment of policies and procedures
- Resource allocation
- Work-load planning
- Priority setting
- Assurance of coordination and cooperation among operation components
- Inspection and monitoring of performance
- Support services
  — Administrative services
  — Budget and cost accounting
  — Personnel
  — Training
  — Procurement.

An important organizational consideration is that the management and control component of the organization provides overall direction to the organization, plans and assigns the work load, sets overall priorities and schedules, and monitors and evaluates the results. The performing component trains, directs, and coordinates the work force to carry out the planned organizational work load.

In organizational terms, these functions can be organized as follows.

Executive Head of the Physical Plant Organization

The head of the physical plant organization typically will be titled a director of physical plant, or an assistant vice president for physical plant or facilities management. This position should function as the principal external representative of physical plant. It should provide broad, general policy and management guidance for physical plant, and should coordinate the work of its individual divisions.

Business Services

This grouping of physical plant management functions can include the following:

- Administrative services
- Cost accounting and budget
- Personnel and training
- Procurement
- Computing.

Work Management

This central management component of the physical plant organization should be responsible for work identification, planning, management, coordination, control, and reporting. Among its principal functions are:

- Work reception (i.e., telephone service calls or written requests for services)
- Planning and estimating
- Inspection
- Work assignment (i.e., service calls, preventive maintenance work orders, general work orders)
- Priority assignment
- Work load planning
- Maintenance service contracting
- Performance monitoring and evaluation
- Reporting.

Facilities Management, Planning, and Construction

A major grouping of functions normally included within a physical plant department, but sometimes organized separately from physical plant, is concerned with the overall facilities planning and programming of the institution, the architectural and engineering planning of new construction, and construction project management. The principal functions include the following:

- Facilities planning and administration
  — Facilities master planning
  — Space management and utilization
  — Capital program planning
  — Real estate management
- Architectural and engineering services
  — Design by staff or through architectural and engineering contracts
  — Architectural and engineering consulting services
- Construction contract administration.

Physical Plant Operations

These include the operating components of a physical plant organization that actually perform work. In establishing an organization for an operating division, particular attention should be paid to the following principles:

- Establish clear responsibilities for each functional group.
- Avoid overlapping responsibilities between operating groups.
- Minimize coordination requirements.
- Provide for necessary coordination at the lowest possible level.
- Minimize supervisory layering.

There are eight major groupings of operations activities.

Utilities Services   This is the organizational component responsible for operation of utilities plants and systems, and for the performance of preventive and routine maintenance for the plants and systems. Major maintenance and repair tasks usually can best be performed by the basic facilities maintenance organization or by contract. The principal utilities services divisions may include the following:

- Utilities plant operations
  — Heating plants
  — Chiller plants
  — Electric power generating plants
  — Water purification plants
  — Sewage treatment plants
- Utilities distribution systems
  — Steam or hot water heating
  — Electrical
  — Potable water
  — Sewage
  — Chilled water
- Energy management and control system operation
- Heating, ventilating, and air conditioning operation and maintenance
- Communications.

Facilities Maintenance   This component of the operating organization is responsible for the performance of scheduled preventive and other continuing maintenance, unscheduled minor maintenance, and major maintenance and repair of facilities and facilities systems. Principal divisions can include the following:

- Service work center
- Preventive maintenance section
- Maintenance trades
  — Building trades
  — Mechanical and electrical trades
  — Heating, ventilating, and air conditioning
  — General services.

Renovations   If a physical plant organization is responsible for carrying out a significant and continuing volume of minor construction and renovation, a separate division for this purpose usually will prove more effective than assigning this work to the basic maintenance organization. A separate renovation division can be organized more effectively for performing this type of work, and keeping such work separate from the maintenance division avoids disrupting scheduled maintenance activities.

Custodial Services   A separate division to provide the custodial function is usually most effective. A typical custodial organization can be organized along a shift and area basis. If some custodial work is done by contract, contract administration and supervision usually can best be provided by the custodial services division.

Grounds Maintenance   This division is responsible for the institution's outside maintenance, including lawns, plantings, and tree care. Maintenance of roads, walks, and miscellaneous grounds structures may also be assigned to this division. Snow and ice removal is a common winter task for the grounds maintenance division. Their responsibilities can also include such tasks as solid waste collection and disposal, and general labor support (i.e., hauling and demolition).

Transportation   Responsibility for the transportation function is sometimes assigned to physical plant and can best be accommodated by a separate operating division with the following responsibilities:

- Maintenance
- Operations
  — Scheduled and unscheduled bus or other transportation services
  — Motor pool.

Other Services   Such other services as may be assigned to physical plant can be handled by separate operating divisions, or branches of other divisions, depending upon the nature and scope of these services.

Branch Components   Dependent upon geographic dispersal, branch operating components of physical plant may provide optimum effectiveness and economy. Generally, these branch components should consist of the minimum organization sufficient to provide for the continuing preventive and routine maintenance and operational requirements of the areas they support. It is usually more advantageous and cost-effective to provide major maintenance and repair, renovation, and shop fabrication support to outlying areas from central physical plant shops.

1.7 PHYSICAL PLANT ORGANIZATIONAL CONCEPTS

The specific organizational structure will vary greatly with the needs, size, and character of the institution, and will depend upon the specific range of responsibilities assigned the physical plant organization.

Organization Placement

The placement of the physical plant organization in the overall institutional organization, and the specific responsibilities assigned to it, can be of extreme importance to the department's overall effectiveness.

The physical plant, or facilities management, mission should encompass the full range of facilities planning, construction, management, maintenance, and operations functions. A comprehensive facilities organization such as this can administer a facilities program in which all of the elements are well balanced and coordinated and closely integrated with the functioning of the institution. The head of this comprehensive organization should be a facilities professional who functions as the chief facilities officer of the institution.

In institutions with a comprehensive facilities organization, the chief facilities officer may be an assistant or associate vice president, vice chancellor for physical plant or facilities management, or executive director or director of physical plant or of campus facilities. Most often the reporting relationship is to a vice president or vice chancellor for business and finance, or for administration. In some institutions the chief facilities officer is at the vice president or vice chancellor level.

Sometimes the facilities planning and construction and physical plant maintenance and operations functions are performed by separate departments, typically headed by a director. These separate departments may report to a vice president or vice chancellor through an intermediate assistant or associate vice chancellor. The ever-increasing emphasis on cost-effectiveness and economy throughout institutions of higher education has brought about a trend toward centralization of control and allocation of resources. This recommends that all facilities functions be grouped into one organization headed by a facilities management professional who participates in the highest levels of governance of the institution.

A "Model" Physical Plant Organization

Actual physical plant organizations vary widely among colleges and universities of differing types and sizes, and depend upon the specific functions assigned to the facilities organization. Specific requirements and conditions will vary widely among institutions and the physical plant organization that can most effectively support an institution will vary just as widely. Therefore, there can be no "standard" physical plant organizational structure that will work well in all situations. However, based upon the organizational principles and concepts discussed in this chapter, a suggested model physical plant organization has been developed (see Figure 1-1) that provides a logical starting point. Tailored to actual conditions and requirements, it could provide a sound basis for building an effective organization structure. This model organization can be adapted easily to the specific needs of institutions of various sizes by adding or deleting functional groupings, or by combining separate or related functions as appropriate.

Chief Facilities Executive   As discussed earlier, this position should be filled by the facilities professional who functions as the chief facilities officer of the institution with responsibility for broad general policy and management guidance for the organization. In large organizations, a deputy can be an extremely important member of the overall management team. Typically, the chief facilities executive will be concerned primarily with questions of external relationships and broad policy and management direction, while a deputy will be concerned primarily with more detailed day-to-day direction and management of the various components of the facilities organization.

Staff Support Functions   These business services and work management functions provide a variety of support services, organizational planning, and management control for the organization. In a medium-sized or small organization, these two functional groupings can be combined, with individual managers or staff members responsible for several support areas.

Line Functions   The principal line functions of a comprehensive facilities organization may be organized into two overall groups: facilities planning management and construction, and facilities operations.

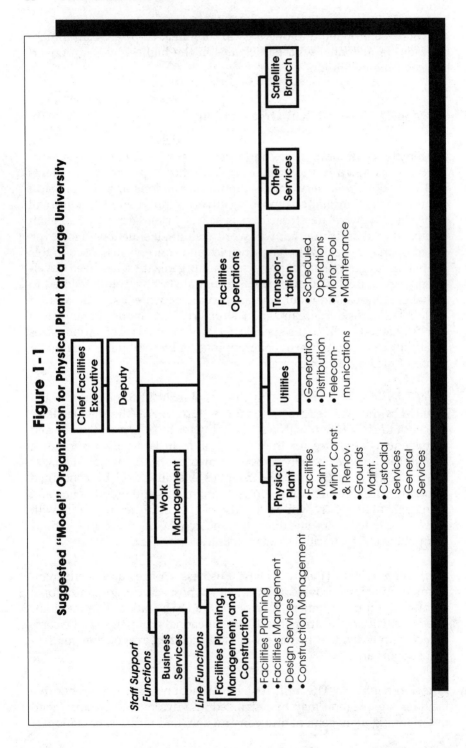

Figure 1-1

Suggested "Model" Organization for Physical Plant at a Large University

Chief Facilities Executive

Deputy

Staff Support Functions

Business Services

Work Management

Line Functions

Facilities Planning, Management, and Construction
- Facilities Planning
- Facilities Management
- Design Services
- Construction Management

Facilities Operations

Physical Plant
- Facilities Maint.
- Minor Const. & Renov.
- Grounds Maint.
- Custodial Services
- General Services

Utilities
- Generation
- Distribution
- Telecommunications

Transportation
- Scheduled Operations
- Motor Pool
- Maintenance

Other Services

Satellite Branch

In a large facilities organization, grouping of *facilities planning management and construction* functions frequently is headed by an overall director of planning and construction, while in many organizations the heads of the individual functional areas report directly to the chief facilities executive. In smaller organizations, two or more of these functions can be combined into a single unit. In many organizations, the design services group is concerned with design or management of design contracts for both major capital projects and the smaller minor construction and renovation projects that typically are carried out by physical plant forces. In other organizations, this minor renovation design is performed by a separate group that might be part of either the work management group or the minor construction and renovation group in physical plant operations.

The *facilities operations* grouping of line functions comprises the area of facilities operations traditionally associated with physical plant departments. In large organizations, this grouping of functions might be headed by an overall director of operations, while in others the individual functional areas might report directly to the chief facilities executive. Following are subdivisions within the facilities operation.

- *Physical Plant.*   This functional grouping is concerned with the basic facilities maintenance, minor construction, and renovation services provided by the building, mechanical, and electrical trades, grounds maintenance, custodial services, and general services. If a physical plant organization carries out a significant and continuing volume of minor construction and renovation work, a separate branch of this unit specifically staffed and organized for construction and renovation work probably is warranted. However, if work of this kind is intermittent and limited in scope, construction and renovation work may be best assigned to the maintenance branch.

- *Utilities.*   In any institution with a large volume of utilities generation and distribution, or a significant telecommunications system, establishment of a separate utilities division usually is warranted. This division may be responsible for operation of utilities plants and systems and, perhaps, minor and preventive maintenance, with major maintenance work assigned to the basic physical plant organization. An extremely large utilities organization, however, may have its own separate and complete maintenance and repair capability. In colleges or universities with only limited utility plants and systems, utilities operations and maintenance functions typically are combined into the basic facility maintenance division.

- *Transportation.*   A separate division typically is warranted if a significant transportation operation is a physical plant responsibility. In a small institution with only limited transportation assets, this function may be consolidated into the basic physical plant division.
- *Other Services.*   One or more separate divisions may be required to provide other services that may be a responsibility of physical plant.
- *Satellite Branch.*   As may be required to support geographically remote units of the institution, or highly specialized components such as a hospital or medical center, a separate branch may be required, with a partial or full capability for providing basic physical plant services. This might be a branch operating component as indicated in Figure 1-1, or it could be a much larger unit incorporating staff support, facilities planning, and construction capabilities of its own, in which case it would be more appropriately established as a branch unit reporting directly to the chief facilities executive.

Figure 1-2 shows an adaptation of this model organization for a hypothetical medium-sized institution. In this example, the business services and work management staff support functions have been combined into a single management division. Line functions concerned with facilities planning, design, and construction are combined into a single division under a director of planning and construction. Utilities and transportation functions, because of limited scope, have been combined with other physical plant functions under a director of physical plant operations. Because of the specialized facilities support requirements of a medical institution, a separate medical center physical plant division has been established; this includes a small work management group of its own and a facilities maintenance organization staffed to handle routine and preventive maintenance requirements. Facilities planning and construction, major maintenance and repair, utilities services, minor construction and renovation, grounds maintenance, and transportation services are provided as required from the parent physical plant organization.

Figure 1-3 shows a typical physical plant organization at a small college. While at first glance there appears to be little resemblance to the model organization shown in Figure 1-1, the essential elements are in place. In this case the staff support functions provided by the business services and work management divisions in Figure 1-1 are combined into single administration division. Since this small college does not have a continuing requirement for facilities planning or construction activities, these functions are managed directly by the director of physi-

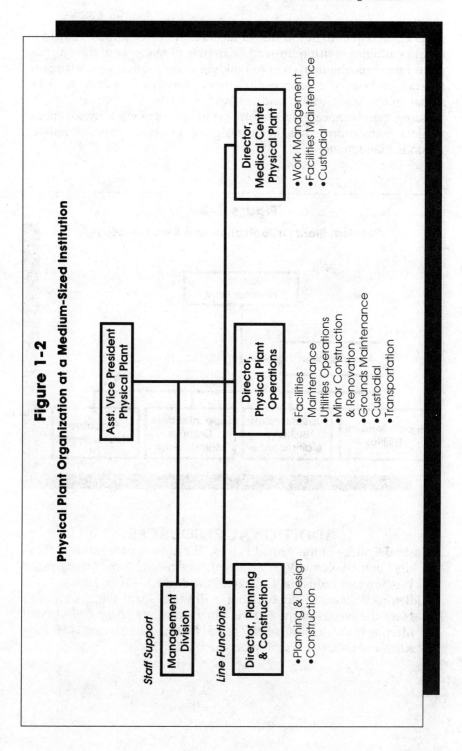

Figure 1-2

Physical Plant Organization at a Medium-Sized Institution

Asst. Vice President
Physical Plant

Staff Support

Management
Division

Line Functions

Director, Planning
& Construction

•Planning & Design
•Construction

Director,
Physical Plant
Operations

•Facilities
 Maintenance
•Utilities Operations
•Minor Construction
 & Renovation
•Grounds Maintenance
•Custodial
•Transportation

Director,
Medical Center
Physical Plant

•Work Management
•Facilities Maintenance
•Custodial

cal plant as required. In the area of facilities operations, there remains a separate utilities division. Instead of an overall manager of the physical plant functions, the managers of building maintenance, grounds maintenance, and custodial services each report directly to the director. Occasional minor construction and renovation work is performed by the building maintenance organization, while the responsibility for motor vehicle maintenance has been assigned to the superintendent of grounds maintenance.

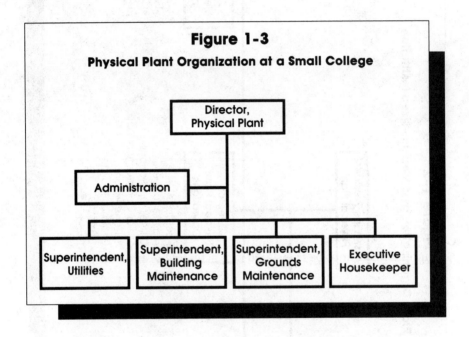

Figure 1-3

Physical Plant Organization at a Small College

ADDITIONAL RESOURCES

Industrial College of the Armed Forces. *The Economics of National Security Course*, Volume IV, *Principles of Administration and Management.* Washington: Industrial College of the Armed Forces, 1960.

Middleton, William D. "Rebuilding a Physical Plant Organization to Meet the Needs of the Future." In *Proceedings of the 69th Annual Meeting of the Association of Physical Plant Administrators of Universities and Colleges.* Washington: APPA, 1982.

CHAPTER 2

Staffing for Physical Plant

Assistant Vice President, Physical Plant University of Virginia

2.1 INTRODUCTION

Accomplishing the physical plant mission requires both individual productivity and coordination of the efforts of all department personnel. Many factors influence the effectiveness of the organization, but none is more essential than appropriate staffing—having the appropriate skills in optimum numbers.

The specific skills, number of personnel in each skill, and supervisory requirements depend upon the funded work load. Perceived work requirements cannot be translated into actual work projects without the necessary funding. Staffing is therefore dependent upon year-to-year funding. Yearly variations in funding will affect not only the total staffing level, but will necessitate continuing evaluations of the mix of skills. Changes in the facilities themselves will change staffing patterns. For example, increased use of air conditioning over the past forty years has changed the mechanical trades requirements. Similarly, the installation of a central chiller plant, replacing multiple building systems, could be expected to change trades requirements.

Effective staffing of a physical plant in today's changing higher education environment is difficult. It is not an isolated function, but involves all functions and operations. This chapter will review alternative approaches to determining required staffing levels, including methods for accommodating changing work loads.

2.2 STAFFING CRITERIA AND STANDARDS

Staffing needs for continuing repetitive maintenance tasks, such as custodial services or grounds care, often can be projected effectively through the use of staffing standards based upon area of coverage per employee. The area per employee will vary with the nature of the buildings or grounds, the level of utilization, and the service level or quality to be provided. A review of actual custodial staffing at small, medium, and large institutions compiled from the APPA *Comparative Costs and Staffing Report for College and University Facilities* indicates that custodial staffing may vary from as high as one custodian for each 10,000 gross square feet of building space, to as low as one custodian caring for an average of more than 40,000 gross square feet. On average, most institutions utilize about one custodian for each 25,000 gross square feet of space requiring custodial care.

A preferred method for assessing staffing needs, however, is to utilize some form of industrial engineering standards based upon work measurement techniques and productivity standards. One widely used set of standards is the Engineered Performance Standards (EPS), originally developed for facilities maintenance functions by the Department of Defense.[1] EPS employs quantities of work to be performed, unit standards for specific tasks, and such variables as travel time to determine the labor hours a productive employee needs in order to perform work. Based upon the quantity of work to be done and the level of

Figure 2-1

Schedule of Staffing Arrangements for Various Size Hypothetical Facilities

Organizational Level	Number of Positions			
	Small	Medium	Large	Huge
Facility Size GSF	100,000	500,000	1,500,000	5,000,000
Administrative	1	1	2	3
Administrative Staff	1	1	2	10
Mid-Supervisory	0	1	3	5
Supervisory Staff	0	1	6	15
First-line Supervisory	2	6	18	67
Employees	8	50	144	500
Total Positions	12	60	175	600

Source: *Comprehensive Maintenance and Repair Program: Guidelines and Standards for the Maintenance and Repair of State-Owned Facilities.* State of Maryland, Department of General Services, December 1978.

service to be provided, staffing needs for continuing maintenance tasks can be determined accurately with EPS. Similarly, trade labor hours for each specific maintenance, repair, or renovation project can be assessed this way. On a long-range basis, labor analysis, by trades, of the continuing maintenance work load by EPS or similar techniques can be an effective way to analyze staffing needs in a physical plant organization.

2.3 STAFFING GUIDELINES

Another approach to staffing is to use guidelines that are based upon the scope of the facilities to be maintained. An example of these guidelines can be found in the State of Maryland, Department of General Services publication, *Comprehensive Maintenance and Repair Program*. Figure 2-1 shows a schedule of staffing arrangements for various sized facilities from that publication.

A similar approach to developing staffing requirements based upon gross square feet of building space was developed by the State of Florida for its institutions of higher education, and is described in a paper presented by a panel at APPA's 57th Annual Meeting in 1970.

2.4 COMPARATIVE STAFFING DATA

Actual staffing data for institutions of comparable type and size can be helpful in establishing an approximation of the appropriate staffing level. An excellent source for current data of this type is APPA's *Comparative Costs and Staffing Report*, developed every two years by APPA's Research and Survey Subcommittee.

For comparison with the State of Maryland guidelines in Figure 2-1, Figure 2-2 summarizes the actual range of staffing for a number of institutions of comparable size, in facilities gross square feet, as reported in the *1984-85 Comparative Costs and Staffing Report*. Comparisons of the range of *total* staffing for various types of institutions, by Carnegie classification and by size, from the *1987-88 Comparative Costs and Staffing Report*, are shown in Figure 2-3. Generally, the actual data from APPA member institutions indicates a lower level of staffing than the Maryland guidelines suggest.

Such guidelines are useful only as general indicators. In any institution, actual staffing needs will vary greatly, depending upon the nature of the facilities, their age and condition, level of use, standards of care, and other variables.

Figure 2-2

Range of Staffing for Institutions of Various Sizes

Number of Positions (Range)

Facility Size GSF	Small 100,000+	Medium 500,000+	Large 1,500,000+	Huge 5,000,000+
Administrative	1- 3	1- 8	3- 10	8- 38
Engr/Arch.	0	0- 1	0- 4	3- 17
Building Maintenance	2- 6	4-17	9- 39	33-194
Custodial	1- 8	8-41	49-107	79-166
Grounds	0- 2	2- 8	11- 23	22- 45
Utilities	0- 1	0-10	0- 12	15- 50
Staffing Range	5-14	28-74	91-174	292-418
Average	11	37	122	346

Source: *1984-85 Comparative Costs and Staffing Report for College and University Facilities.* Association of Physical Plant Administrators of Universities and Colleges, 1986.

Figure 2-3

Total Staffing for Institutions of Various Sizes, by Carnegie Classification

Number of Positions (Range)

Facility Size GSF	Small 100,000	Medium 500,000	Large 1,500,000	Huge 5,000,000
Type of Institution (Carnegie)				
Research	4	32-54	74-242	270-878
Doctorate	-	26-49	105-207	288-370
Comprehensive	-	35-82	71-207	-
Liberal Arts	-	20-74	65-164	-
Two-year	4-14	24-120	46-213	-

Source: *1987-88 Comparative Costs and Staffing Report for College and University Facilities,* Association of Physical Plant Administrators of Universities and Colleges, 1989.

2.5 MATCHING STAFFING WITH NEEDS

Given all of the variations in physical plant work load imposed by periodic peaks, seasonal requirements, special projects funded by other departments, or budget fluctuations, actual staffing needs are rarely constant or predictable. In order to avoid over-staffing, a prudent management approach is to staff the organization only to the level needed to meet the continuing base work load, and then employ measures to adjust the work force capacity to meet periodic changes in requirements.

To meet intermittent or temporary requirements, the use of overtime or temporary employees can be effective. Work load beyond the capability of permanent staffing usually can be accommodated through the use of maintenance and repair, construction, or maintenance service contracts. The award of contracts for the provision of labor at established rates can be an effective way of meeting peak or special requirements.

Many physical plant organizations operate under financial procedures that provide for direct funding of staff salaries. This approach does not relate staffing levels to actual annual needs. An alternative method used by many large facilities organizations is some form of revolving or industrial fund, under which employee salaries are earned through rates charged to reimbursable or functional accounts. This procedure requires that staffing be commensurate with actual needs. If painters are available in excess of the number needed for funded painting work, for example, it will not be possible to generate sufficient salary funding, and the work force will have to be reduced to match the available work.

NOTES

1. EPS handbooks that address a variety of facilities maintenance and service tasks are available from the Superintendent of Documents, U.S. Government Printing Office, Washington, D.C. 20402.

ADDITIONAL RESOURCES

Association of Physical Plant Administrators of Universities and Colleges. *1984-85 Comparative Costs and Staffing Report for College and University Facilities*. Alexandria, Virginia: APPA, 1986.

—————. *1987-88 Comparative Costs and Staffing Report for College and University Facilities*. Alexandria, Virginia: APPA, 1989.

Greene, Calvin C. "Physical Plant Budgeting Standards for the Florida University System." In *Proceedings of the 57th Annual Meeting of the Association of Physical Plant Administrators of Universities and Colleges*, 1970.

State of Maryland, Department of General Services. *Comprehensive Maintenance and Repair Program: Guidelines and Standards for the Maintenance and Repair of State-Owned Facilities.* Washington: Association of Physical Plant Administrators of Universities and Colleges, 1983.

CHAPTER 3

Communication

Edward C. Bogard, P.E.
Director of Physical Plant
University of Nebraska Medical Center

3.1 INTRODUCTION

A college or university physical plant department has responsibility for a wide variety of functions, the accomplishment of which requires diverse skills ranging from unskilled labor to complex engineering technologies. Effectiveness and efficiency in carrying out assigned functions necessitate unity of effort—the coordination of the efforts of all personnel towards the common goals of the institution. Communication is essential to achieving this coordination. The more diverse the functions and skills, the more difficult it is to achieve coordinated effort; thus, the more critical is the role of communication.

Words have different meaning to people with different experience and training. In transmitting policies and instructions to employees, the supervisor must interpret instructions at different levels. The supervisor must therefore listen to staff members to understand the language that is meaningful to them, as well as to transmit their ideas up the chain of supervision.

All coordination cannot be formal and vertical between succeeding levels. Much of the coordination must be lateral within the physical plant department.

Effective communication is not only the lifeblood of any organization, but the larger the organization the more complex will be the communicating network. Everyone in the business of facilities management knows that good public relations and communication are inherently important to a large and diverse service organization such as the typical college or university physical plant department. These departments typically provide a greater range of services than most other campus service organizations. The extent and quality of service affects almost everyone in the institution.

This chapter discusses methods of communication, both internal within physical plant as well as external with the organizations served.

Communication for the Organizational Structure

The importance of communication is underscored in the management newsletter *Bottom Line Personal*, which noted that, as an executive reaches middle management and beyond, the primary criteria for advancement are communication skills with superiors and motivational skills with subordinates. Communicating effectively involves understanding the structure of the organization, the problems that exist in the organization, and the personalities of those involved in the organizational structure.

If the organizational structure is basically horizontal, it becomes important to form alliances or positive working relationships with a number of peers. This arrangement requires compromise, the ability to understand the motivating factors of a large cross section of the institution, and an understanding of conflict resolution. Serious problems can result when coalitions within the group report conflicting information or ideas to supervisors.

In a vertical organizational structure, there are fewer peers to coordinate and communications up and down the organization are more singular and carry more weight. Ideas tend to stand more on their own merit and depend less on compromise and negotiation.

Any problems within an organization have a dramatic effect upon efforts to promote successful communication. If the organization is saturated with problems, it may seem impossible to accomplish effective communication. If continual effort is needed to "put out fires," little opportunity remains to develop and sustain a communication network, either internally or externally. In this environment, the department will find itself under criticism. Problems are solved by people, and it is imperative that the information communicated be accurate and adequate for the required decision making.

Individual personalities affect interpersonal relationships. Understanding those we communicate with permits the development of strategies for effective communication. Feelings are at the very foundation of human motivation. If a topic is raised knowing how others feel about it, there is a better than 50-50 chance that the ideas will be communicated. The effective manager often can prevent misunderstandings by visiting with peers or supervisors to obtain their opinions and reactions. Initial impressions are very difficult to change, and misunderstandings due to faulty communication can doom efforts from the start.

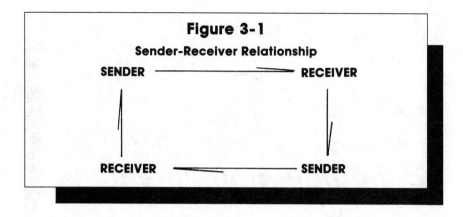

Figure 3-1

Sender-Receiver Relationship

SENDER ⟶ RECEIVER

RECEIVER ⟵ SENDER

Effective communication necessitates empathy—seeing things from the viewpoint of others. During communication there is selective filtering by the receivers, and the information that makes it through the filter is subject to two types of translation that give the words meaning. There is the denotative meaning, which is the dictionary definition, and the connotative meaning, in which all the bits of information that circle a word come together to personalize it. The connotative meaning determines how the word is applied and is based on individual experience. Words take on different meanings to different people. Emphasis and inflections give connotation to words.

During the communication process, the initiator implies something by words and the receiver infers something from the words. Inference is drawing a conclusion about something that is unknown from something that is known. Facts are the other side of inference, since they are verifiable. During the communication process, there is no time to wait for all of the facts, so the gaps are filled in with inferences.

The exact form of communication depends upon which public is being addressed. In general there are three main categories:

1. Outside of the institution—the public and private community that is not a part of the corporate structure of the campus community.
2. The university community—the faculty, staff, and students within the corporate structure of the institution, but outside of the physical plant department.
3. The physical plant department—the physical plant staff and the next higher division in the organizational chart.

There are a number of basic principles and concepts that can impact the effectiveness of the physical plant public relations program, and

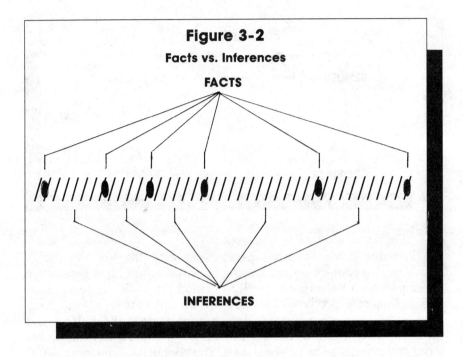

Figure 3-2

Facts vs. Inferences

FACTS

INFERENCES

they depend to a great extent upon the nature of the audience. The form the public relations program takes will reflect the style of management within the physical plant department, and should be structured to capitalize on the strengths while minimizing weaknesses. The smaller, more compact department may find an individualized personal approach most successful, while a large, diversified organization may find it more effective to develop a formal and highly structured public relations division within the physical plant department.

Effective communication requires perseverance and a dedication to detail in order to assure that all of the many resources within physical plant are adequately and accurately described. If communication were easy, there would not be approximately one million words in the English language today. The message must be clear, concise, and accurate, and it must be packaged so that the intended receiver will be interested and motivated to act.

Communication and the Public Relations Philosophy

Large organizations need public relations divisions, or a staff member with that responsibility, and a formalized public relations program.

Truly successful public relations, however, depends upon the awareness and involvement of all members of the organization.

Some of the most important public relations work is performed by members of the department in their day-to-day work. There are numerous accounts of parents visiting the campus for the first time and forming their impression of the institution based on the appearance of the buildings and grounds. The perception of the competency of a medical center is often related to the condition of the restrooms. All of these activities are associated with how well everyone in the physical plant department does their job.

In a physical plant environment, any program of public relations and communication must be founded upon a truly service-oriented organizational frame of mind. The public relations program must accurately represent the type of organization that the particular institution promotes. It must reflect the level of service available and the responsiveness of the department.

In support of this program, every employee in the physical plant department, from the newest custodian to the most senior accountant or engineer, must have a positive and professional feeling about themselves and their work. They must be convinced that they are, in fact, professionals in their area of responsibility and that they represent the institution's chief administrative officer. This attitude must originate with the physical plant director. There is a tendency for physical plant employees to become overawed by the academic credentials of so many of the people physical plant serves, and to assume a self-deprecating attitude. Whether an office worker or a tradesperson, the typical physical plant employee has the requisite educational training, experience, and qualifications to carry out his or her duties to the complete satisfaction of those served.

It is even more important to the success of a physical plant program, and the maintenance of good public relations, that there be a good understanding of the needs and attitudes of those the department supports, as well as a real appreciation and respect for their qualities and achievements. An academic career in higher education is intensely competitive, and success is dependent upon excellent credentials and experience as well as significant achievement in scholarly pursuits and research. Academicians are not only extremely devoted to their profession and areas of specialization, but success or failure in a research project can affect their careers. Thus, physical plant's failure to meet a schedule or performance requirements for a laboratory renovation will bring about a strong reaction. An understanding is necessary of the intense pressures and demands in patient care and teaching that are placed upon the medical faculty in order to understand and appreciate why they expect from physical plant the same level of performance that they demand of themselves.

The objective should be to achieve a mutual respect between physical plant personnel and those they support. Physical plant operations should be conducted so as to command respect for performance and for a professional attitude. Physical plant personnel should be aware of the high quality of the institution's programs, the academic credentials and achievements of the faculty, and take pride in being a part of the achievements of the institution.

Physical plant employees tend to think of their institution in terms of the buildings and grounds that make up the physical facilities and not enough in terms of the academic, research, and public service programs within the institution. These activities are driven by the student body and faculty—the real heart of any college or university. To be a part of this process and provide the necessary physical environment should be a source of pride for all physical plant employees.

Developing a Public Relations Plan

The development and maintenance of a successful public relations program is difficult in settings as large and complex as a college or university campus. It involves effective communication between the physical plant department and a diverse public dedicated to teaching, research, and public service. The commitment must be sufficient to assure a continuous effort with identifiable results. Intense bursts of activity followed by prolonged intervals of inactivity will result in a loss of public confidence and support.

It is better not to undertake a highly visible program until adequate resources are available to assure its continuation. A service organization must give a great deal of thought and effort to building an effective public relations program that is based upon a clear understanding of communication needs, as well as an understanding of the audience.

Purpose

It is becoming increasingly critical to develop effective communication procedures through a formal public relations program. As institutions feel the effects of fewer applicants, reduced financial resources, an aging physical plant, and competing demands for funds, every opportunity must be utilized to inform potential users of the services available from the physical plant.

The physical plant department public relations program is concerned with the following:

- Physical plant services
- Special services
- Regulatory compliance
- Professional competency
- Feedback.

Physical Plant Services

It is necessary to inform all potential clients of the many services available both from and through the physical plant department. Explanations should be provided for all the services available, how each service may be obtained, who is authorized to secure the service or item, cost obligations, sample order forms, and the requirements or authorizations for outside vendors or services.

It is helpful to describe the physical plant structure and the responsibilities of each major component. An organizational chart helps explain departmental responsibilities and alleviates a number of jurisdictional questions. In certain cases it may be appropriate to provide information about campus-wide policies and procedures that directly affect physical plant operations.

Special Services

It is important to provide information about specific physical plant functions to members of the campus community, including specifics about maintenance of building utility systems that fall within the routine maintenance activities of the physical plant department. Any activities that require special funding—such as capital construction projects or the installation, maintenance, and operation of special departmental equipment—should be outlined. Special cases involving building systems, limitations, and areas of responsibilities should be well defined.

Regulatory Compliance

Institutions are subject to more complex and restrictive rules and regulations each year. Local code enforcement agencies, insurance inspections, federal funding agencies, and other legislated authorities have generated a proliferation of rules and regulations governing waste disposal, chemical storage, smoking, and more. Most of these regulatory bodies require special reporting, notifications, and testimonials that are available only through physical plant. Physical plant activities that are of a general interest or that have widespread impact within the institution should be distributed widely.

Professional Competence

There is a critical need to develop a general public awareness of the nature and scope of physical plant activities and accomplishments. A general public awareness of what physical plant does, its capabilities, and its professional competence can help develop a positive and supportive attitude within the institution. This should include descriptions of the professional qualifications achieved by the physical plant staff.

Recognition of special accomplishments and abilities should be publicized in order to emphasize the professional nature of the physical plant staff. This category will help to publicize special skills to those with whom physical plant comes in contact.

Feedback

The communication process involves the exchange of information, both sending and receiving. If there is a break anywhere along this loop, there is incomplete communication; if physical plant does not receive a signal from the public, or receives an incomplete signal, it is unaware of the success or failure of its service operations. An assumption that no news is good news can result in learning about a problem too late to correct it. There is no way to determine the quality or responsiveness of physical plant services without some feedback mechanism.

It is important to know not only how well physical plant is performing, but also the perception of the campus community as to how well it is performing. Many frustrations and inaccuracies about services can be corrected if feedback is gathered, followed by a mechanism to follow through on suggestions and problems.

3.2 THE MANY PUBLICS OF PHYSICAL PLANT

There are three publics with which the physical plant must communicate:

- External community
- Institutional departments
- Physical plant.

Each of these publics represents a group of individuals with a different set of needs and perceptions. The type of information, the format for presentation, and the mechanism for delivery is quite different in each case. Consequently, it is of prime importance that the composition of each public be evaluated carefully to understand particular biases, stumbling blocks, strengths, and weaknesses. It has been said that the successful politician, among other things, knows the audience even better than the audience knows itself. Effective communication is dependent upon "talking the same language." Each individual tunes into a different part of the signal, and the important signal should be the one they hear even if it must be repeated many times. For some, it is difficult to filter the substance of the message, and it is important to make certain the message is repeated often enough and in a form that will encourage appropriate filtering.

The diversity of the communication requirement, and the extent and diversity of the many publics, necessitates multiple channels of communication. An effective public relations and communications program must employ many methods to build effective two-way communication. Combinations of techniques that have proven successful should be zealously guarded and improved through practice and experimentation. Area anomalies must be integrated into each public, since a great deal of the success is dependent upon capitalizing upon the strengths of the physical plant department and its leadership. A good understanding of the tools of communication is as important as the message. This can be better appreciated by a review of the three audiences.

External Community Communications

The external community consists of the public beyond the institution's surrounding neighborhood and includes parents of students, campus visitors, vendors, suppliers, governmental agencies, and other members of the general public who may be affected by actions of the college or university. Also included in this category are people who receive a service from the institutions, such as the patients in a university medical center.

In most colleges and universities, formal communication between the institution and outside public occurs through a public relations or public affairs office. Many institutions insist that all external public relations and communications be handled in this manner in order to ensure consistency and adherence to guidelines. Physical plant can assure that its public relations interests are best served by working closely with the campus public relations staff to furnish newsworthy information on physical plant activities. This includes information on things that are going wrong, so that a response can be made to public inquiries.

Sooner or later, most physical plant administrators will need to deal directly with the press. The best way to communicate with the press is to be honest, factual, and concise, and to focus on solutions. Open and frank communication, both when the news is good and when it is bad, will best serve public relations and communication needs by building trust and confidence with the press. It is important that a plan be established in advance so that when the time arrives for the release of information, one person will handle the interview for the department. This process must be established ahead of time so that when a boiler blows up in the middle of the night, each individual knows his or her role.

In developing a strategy for communicating with the external community, it is best to have a written policy. A physical plant department manual could contain the policy. For larger institutions, a formal policy and procedures manual may be more appropriate. A factor to consider is the degree of autonomy given to physical plant for public relations.

Public relations is best served if the public information releases are professional, honest, and reflective of the institution's stated goals. Many outside organizations and individuals form their opinion of the institution solely on their contact with the physical plant department.

Institutional Communications

The most important public is the campus community external to physical plant, which includes students, faculty, and staff. This group includes those involved with physical plant on a close and continuing basis, those who utilize support services on an occasional basis, and still others who probably will never utilize support services but who are affected by the quality of the general support services that physical plant provides. Because of the broad and diverse nature of physical plant's public within the institution, a variety of methods is needed to maintain effective two-way communication.

Of prime importance is the need for recognition of the physical plant director. The fact that the department touches almost every segment of the campus community makes it imperative that administrators throughout the campus have recognition of the director. The director often has the opportunity to become acquainted with other university officials, which will promote and facilitate subsequent communications.

Developing Communication Opportunities

The Physical Plant Director   The successful physical plant director will seek opportunities to meet with groups to discuss physical plant services and needs. Faculty meetings, college and department meetings, research faculty gatherings, and meetings of student groups all provide opportunities for healthy two-way communication between physical plant and its public. Whenever appropriate, physical plant directors can arrange for special meetings to present information of interest to the university community. For example, on the occasion of a major remodeling project affecting several departments, good will can be created by holding a "town hall" meeting to allow everyone to hear from the director and construction team about how the project will be coordinated, who will be affected, and when it will be completed. People appreciate hearing about problems up front, and many times they can offer prospective solutions that would have been impossible to promote if dictated from the construction team. A director can develop support and recognition through this type of informal meeting.

Building the Informal Network   A physical plant director can enhance his or her effectiveness simply by becoming as well acquainted and as widely known as possible among university faculty and staff. Participation in university social and official functions, serving as a fraternity adviser, and similar activities not only serve the institution but also help develop a sense of trust and confidence within the campus community.

The Responsive Manager   No amount of public relations and communications work will be effective if the organization is not responsive to the problems and questions that are presented. It is absolutely essential that managers return all telephone calls promptly, answer their mail, or just get out of the office to see someone who has an urgent problem. The physical plant department must be sensitive to problems. The area that is consistently too hot or too cold, the leak that never seems to get fixed, or the faculty office that is bothered by noise may deserve a visit by the director. The people affected will know that their problems are being addressed and not just filed for future reference.

A successful manager will recognize that everyone who deals with the department is a customer. Every successful enterprise recognizes customers as the lifeblood of their existence. In his book *In Search of Excellence*, Tom Peters testifies time and time again to the success of those who put the customer first. Communicating this fact and making everyone in the organization aware of its importance will assure a vote of confidence from every segment of the campus community. The mark of a professional is concern for those who depend upon his or her response to a request for assistance.

Department Image

Public perception is an important part of what is communicated about physical plant. Consequently, it is extremely important that the organization convey an image of a competent, professional organization. It is essential that every publication, letter, and memorandum from physical plant be professional in appearance, tone, and style, and grammatically correct. Every phone call should be handled in a professional manner, so that callers know they have contacted an organization that is service-oriented and concerned with details.

Physical plant vehicles should be kept clean and in a good state of repair, and they should be identified in a professional manner. Many institutions provide uniforms for their service and trades employees; it is important that the uniforms be kept clean and worn correctly. Employees should be aware that a good image reflects on the entire department. Wearing the uniform should be considered the mark of a professional person belonging to a professional organization.

The public image of the department can be enhanced greatly by letting others know of special accomplishments. Professional and technical achievements of the physical plant staff should be published. Since many physical plant employees are actively involved in community programs, there should be a conscious effort to learn of these activities and make them known to the campus community.

Written Communication

The Physical Plant Services Guide   Some form of published guide to physical plant services can be the single most important item in an effective communication program. The manual should be a catalog of physical plant services and how they can be obtained.

A good services guide typically covers departmental policy, services available, the project priority system, and financial policies. It summarizes the capabilities and services available in each of the department's major functional areas, such as facilities planning and design, maintenance, repair and renovation, utilities services, and departmental organization and functions, with an organization chart. A useful feature of a services manual can be an alphabetical quick-reference guide to physical plant services. An appendix can include samples of forms and reports, and a directory of key physical plant personnel, their titles and main area of responsibility. To be effective, the services guide must be widely publicized and distributed throughout the college or university, and it should be revised and reissued periodically to keep it up to date.

The following is a general outline for what might be included in a table of contents for a physical plant services guide. Specific content will depend upon the scope and nature of the services provided by the individual physical plant organization.

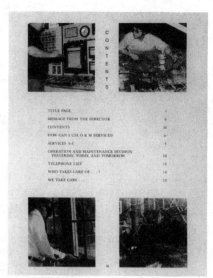

Figure 3-3
Services Guides

Table of Contents

Foreword.
1. *General Information.*   This can be a brief summary of basic information about the mission of the physical plant organization, institutional and departmental policies related to physical plant, and other material of general interest to users of physical plant services.
2. *Work Management Procedures.*   This section should deal with definitions of the various categories of work provided by physical plant, procedures for the receipt and authorization of work, procedures for requesting services, any system in effect for establishing project priorities, status reporting procedures, budgeting responsibilities for work performed by physical plant, and other information related to rates and charges for work and billing procedures.
3. *Facilities Planning and Construction.*   To the extent that they are provided by physical plant, this section can discuss services provided and procedures concerned with facilities planning, space management, architectural and engineering design, renovation or new construction project development, and construction management.
4. *Maintenance, Repair, and Renovation Services.*   This section should cover the services available and procedures related to facilities

maintenance and repair, renovation, and improvement construction, grounds maintenance services, refuse collection services, custodial services, or other basic maintenance services provided by physical plant.

5. *Utility Services.*   This section can discuss the utilities services provided by physical plant and any related procedures.

6. *Transportation Services.*   This section could discuss transportation services provided by physical plant together with related procedures.

7. *Other Services.*   One or more additional sections may be appropriate to cover other services provided by physical plant that do not logically fit under one of the foregoing general categories of service.

8. *Physical Plant Organization and Functions.*   This section could provide a departmental organization chart and a summary of the functional responsibilities of each component of the department.

9. *Quick Reference Guide to Services.*   A valuable feature of a services guide can be an alphabetical guide to different categories of service available from physical plant. Each item can provide users with a brief summary of useful information concerning that category of service, and a cross-reference to other sections of the services guide where these services are discussed in greater detail. This section might also include referral to other college and university departments for services that are not provided by physical plant, but are often requested from the department.

Appendix.   This appendix could include copies of sample forms required for physical plant services or reports provided by physical plant together with instructions explaining how to use them.

Glossary.   This section could include definitions of key terminology often misunderstood by users of physical plant services.

Directory.   The inside front and back covers of a services guide can be a good place for providing directories of key departmental telephone numbers and principal management and supervisory staff of the department.

A services guide may be an expensive and handsome publication in a major college or university, or it can be a modest publication in a smaller institution. Regardless, it is important that a great deal of thought and care go into its preparation. It must be well-written and well-organized if it is to be used properly. In deciding what goes into such a guide, it might be beneficial to talk to a variety of users of physical plant services to find out the kind of information they would desire in such a guide.

As an alternative to a single services guide, several universities have developed a series of service bulletins, each of which provides informa-

Figure 3-4
Service Bulletins

tion about the specific services provided each major component of physical plant (such as transportation, maintenance and repair, custodial services, and security). (See Figure 3-4.)

Physical Plant Service Notices   In addition to a basic services manual, many physical plants publish periodic notices that provide short-range information supplementing the basic information in the manual. These notices or bulletins might announce new services or service changes, and provide seasonal service notices or an annual rate schedule. Often such bulletins, notices, or newsletters are published on a fixed schedule, but it may prove more advantageous to publish them as required.

Status Reports   Every physical plant organization typically works on a number of projects of continuing interest to members of the college or university public. These range from maintenance and repair projects to laboratory renovations, landscaping, and major new construction.

Keeping people who have a need to know well informed can have enormous public relations benefits. It is important that reports be distributed on a regular basis and that they provide accurate, current, and adequate information about project status. A good report might summarize the current status of each project and compare actual progress against projections. An important item of information on a status report is the name and telephone number of a manager who can provide additional information if needed. This type of information normally is published on a weekly basis.

University Publications   Almost every college or university has some form of newspaper or magazine, typically prepared by the institution's public information section. Informing the editors of appropriate physical plant news items and stories of general university interest can help build a greater awareness of physical plant. A campus radio station is another avenue for providing information to the campus community; sponsoring a regular radio program may increase campus awareness of physical plant services.

Annual Report   Many colleges and universities require each department to prepare and submit to the administration an annual report of their operations. By going beyond the bare essentials required, a departmental annual report can be a comprehensive review of each year's operations and achievements and a summary of plans and objectives for the coming year. Carefully and professionally prepared, such an annual report can be distributed widely within the college or university community as a means of building awareness of physical plant accomplishments.

Organization Procedures

Facilities Representatives   Communication between physical plant and the many departments or components of the university or college can often be enhanced greatly by asking each department to appoint a facilities representative who will act as a continuing central point of contact for his or her department with the physical plant organization. Working closely with these representatives to keep them well informed can improve the business relationship between physical plant and individual university departments and enable physical plant to identify service problems earlier and respond to critical conditions. The departmental facilities representative can keep physical plant informed of any special activities that may have an impact on building services, thus enabling physical plant to take corrective action in advance. It can also serve as a mechanism to advise users of potential violations of regulatory codes, as well as to alert users of planned building service outages.

Customer Service Representatives   Almost any service organization that serves a large number of users has some kind of customer service representative responsible for managing and coordinating the delivery of services to a specific customer or group of customers. These should be senior professional level managers who are responsible for providing advice and assistance concerning any kind of services, and for coordinating and resolving any kind of physical plant problem.

Project Managers   Many organizations that carry out a large number of projects for various customers employ the project manager system as a means of providing coordinated management of individual projects. This can be a useful technique for any physical plant organization with a large number of maintenance and repair, renovation, or new construction projects to manage. For each project, a project manager should be responsible for cradle-to-grave management, coordination, and customer liaison. These individuals should visit each assigned project on a regular basis to personally acquaint themselves with progress or problems. They must develop a routine of informing occupants, or those departmental individuals for which the work is being done, of the progress made or problems that have developed. They must be sensitive to the questions and concerns of those affected by the project. It is easy to forget that physical plant personnel deal with project disruptions and schedule changes on a daily basis, while customers deal with these things less frequently. It should be remembered that each project is the most important project for those who are involved in it.

Physical Plant Advisory Board   Getting good feedback from the many users of physical plant services can be one of the most important communication channels. A physical plant advisory board can be an extremely useful tool for providing this kind of two-way communication. Its membership should represent a broad cross section of the university's faculty, staff, and student body. It should meet regularly and set its own agenda. There must be a mechanism to obtain feedback from the appropriate clientele. One means is an evaluation form provided to every customer who uses physical plant services (see Figure 3-5).

This form is used to determine the actual, as well as the perceived level of competency. Complaints can be answered quickly and potential problems stopped before they start. The thought of asking someone how well you perform can be frightening the first time, but it holds a real potential for improvement and personal satisfaction in a job well done. The advisory board can use this information to help stop unwarranted

Figure 3–5

Services Questionnaire

**DEPARTMENT OF PHYSICAL PLANT
HOW DID WE DO?**

To: _____   Dept.:_____

Work Order Number _____   Trade:_____

Date Requested _____ Date Completed:_____

Work Performed

1. Was our response time to your work request acceptable?
   Yes ___, No ___. If no, why not?
2. Once started, was the work done promptly?
   Yes___, No ___. If no, in your opinion what was wrong?

   Upon completion, was the area cleaned up properly?
   Yes ___, No ___.
3. If it was necessary for the job to be delayed, was this communicated
   to you? Yes ___, No ___.
4. Were the workers pleasant? _____
5. Was the work done professionally? If not, what, in your opinion, was
   unprofessional? _____
6. When you have a facilities management related problem, do you
   call Work Control ___, the foreman ___, a supervisor or manager ___,
   or other _____.
7. What is your overall perception (or other comments) of the Department of Facilities Management?

8. Do you think communication between Facilities Management and
   the campus community is good ___, fair ___, poor ___? How do you
   think it could be improved?
9. Would you like a representative from Facilities Management to
   ___visit with you, ___call you to answer questions?

Signed: _____ Phone: _____

   THANK YOU FOR HELPING PHYSICAL PLANT SERVE YOU BETTER.

Our mail location is preprinted on the reverse side. . . . simply fold in half
and drop into the campus mail.

Supervisor: _____ Phone: _____

criticism that can develop occasionally. The advantage in using an advisory board will be a boost in communication and a greatly improved professional image throughout the entire campus community.

3.3 PHYSICAL PLANT COMMUNICATIONS

If physical plant is going to convey the correct attitudes and information to the external public, personnel in the department must be kept informed. A well-established program of internal communication is just as necessary as the program for external communication. Managers and supervisors must understand policies and goals, and they in turn must convey these to all employees.

Perhaps in no other area is the influence of the director more evident and influential than in the physical plant department. He or she sets the tone and character of how communications will be formulated and promoted. An effective, professional organization begins with the director and, regardless of written policies and procedures, the effectiveness of the public relations effort to promote effective communications will depend to a great extent on the priority it receives within the top management group of physical plant.

This effort can take many forms. There are a number of methods that have proven effective:

- Staff meetings
- Physical plant council
- Meetings with employees
- Suggestion program
- Newsletter.

The degree of effort and number of options that an institution employs depends on the size, complexity, and management style of the particular physical plant organization.

Staff Meetings

Staff meetings enable managers to disseminate and collect information. When properly formulated, meetings serve as a means to develop and encourage communication throughout physical plant. Senior managers should make a point of meeting periodically with the department's managers and supervisors in small groups that extend to the first level supervisor, to provide opportunities to discuss current developments in the department and to respond to questions and comments. Many times erroneous rumors can be short-circuited and incorrect information replaced with more productive and accurate facts. Minutes of these meetings should be recorded and sent to all attendees, as well as to the next higher level supervisor. Staff meetings also provide a good forum to promote professionalism and professional development.

Physical Plant Council

A physical plant council allows direct dialogue between members of the physical plant administrative staff and the service workers. It promotes communication and acts as a conduit for delivery of information between the two groups. In most administrative organizations there is a natural filtering that takes place in the communications process. Too often, important information is filtered out.

The council structure provides a means of sampling how much information is being delivered and at what level of accuracy. This type of sounding board can defuse potential problems by providing a means to get accurate information in a relatively short period of time. Employees often feel they have an opportunity to participate in the management of the department if they are asked for input relative to decision making. Council meetings should be formal with a prepared agenda, a set time frame, and minutes kept for distribution to the council members.

Meetings With Employees

In his book *In Search of Excellence,* Tom Peters gives many examples of how employees are encouraged to go beyond "just getting by" through simple examples of leadership. He describes a leadership technique with the nonglamorous acronym MBWA—Management By Walking Around. It is a simple technique wherein the manager meets the people he or she supervises in their work environment, takes a few minutes to visit and learn what they are doing, and compliments them when appropriate.

This setting provides a perfect opportunity to talk about professional pride and how physical plant is built on the concept of a team effort. People feel more like sharing ideas when they are in familiar and comfortable surroundings. The face-to-face, one-on-one opportunity is a simple and positive way to develop communications and at the same time learn about those people who are the best emissaries for the department.

Suggestion Program

In large organizations, people often feel alienated and lost in the crowd, thinking that their input is of little value. A suggestion plan is one way to overcome this feeling. There must be a formal process for receiving, evaluating, and then implementing suggestions. Suggestion forms may be simply note paper that employees can drop into a suggestion box, or special forms that require a complete description and a formal presentation of the suggestion. This latter form also requires a formal procedure on the part of the organization so that appropriate credit is given to the suggestor when the merits of the suggestion are evaluated. In either case, there should be a procedure allowing all suggestions to be evaluated in an unbiased environment. If the author of the suggestion is identified, appropriate recognition should be made. The most effective suggestion program gives some type of formal recognition or reward for suggestions that produce measurable results.

As with any recognition program, there must be a commitment of adequate resources on the part of the administration to assure that the program will continue. If the suggestions are evaluated only when someone thinks of it, resentment will result and the opportunity to develop a communications conduit will be lost.

Newsletter

Everyone likes to see their name in print. Most like to read about others they know and work with, and about what is happening in the department. The newsletter is an instrument that can provide this type of information. It can be a simple one-page document typed in the department office and printed on the office copy machine, or an elaborate multi-page newspaper with many stories, detailed reports, social schedules, and information about institutional activities (see Figure 3-6).

A physical plant newspaper can include articles covering new departmental procedures; proposed changes in operating routines; employee news items such as births, weddings, and promotions; safety hints; new employee profiles; and selected news briefs from the campus. The newsletter should be upbeat, positive, and occasionally humorous—but not at anyone's expense. Bad news does not belong in a departmental publication. Information must be accurate—every piece of information needs to be verified before it is included.

A number of physical plant publications are received and retained at the headquarters of the Association of Physical Plant Administrators of Universities and Colleges. A new publication can get a head start if time is taken to review successful examples.

A good newsletter can be a source of departmental pride and a prime communications tool, not only within the physical plant department, but throughout the entire institution. There are many examples of physical plant newsletters that are the envy of other campus departments.

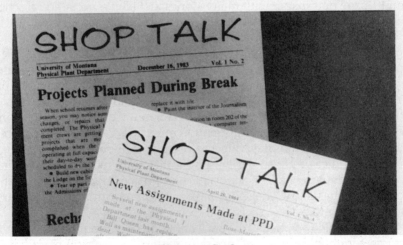

Figure 3-6

Physical Plant Newsletters

In some cases, it may be appropriate to include a physical plant column or page in the campus-wide news publication. This will alleviate the problem of trying to secure adequate information for an entire issue each week or month.

The "Grapevine"

One of the greatest opportunities to communicate within any organization is through the informal structure commonly known as the grapevine. This network knows no boundaries, respects no authority, and responds with a speed that surpasses any formal communications tool. Wherever people congregate, the grapevine is close at hand. It can penetrate the tightest company security and is accountable to no one, which contributes to its vitality within an organization. There are numerous accounts of promotions or demotions that have spread throughout an organization to the very people affected even before they have been officially informed.

The grapevine is a natural part of any healthy organization and is a dynamic force that helps to build teamwork, motivate people, and create institutional identity. The extent and degree of grapevine activity is a measure of the vitality of an organization—it is a reflection of the need for people to talk about their organization or department and share a significant part of their life with those who are involved just as deeply. People have a common interest in what is being carried on the grapevine. The absence of a grapevine indicates major problems within the department, because it signals that people no longer have an interest in any of the activities or other people. No matter how strange or humorous the stories on the grapevine, they all have an origin and are representative of some activity within the institution. The grapevine affords an opportunity for feedback about what is going on in the organization, and it also can serve to help translate formal communication into the language employees understand best.

One of the unfortunate characteristics of the grapevine is its reputation as a rumor mill. Rumors must be stopped because they are not founded on fact. Employees accept rumors because correct information is not available, and they tend to distort all information relating to the rumor in order to support the rumor.

Most managers can attest to the problems that rumors can cause. There was the case of an individual who left without any prior notification, and the rumor was that he had been fired. The director posted a notice in all shops that the employee had left to take advantage of a research grant, which was the case. No matter how hard departments try, it is not possible to stamp out the grapevine. The harder one tries the more prolific the grapevine becomes and it soon consumes a vital part of the productive day. Therefore, the good manager recognizes the advantage of the grapevine as a communications tool and takes advantage of it. It must be accepted as a part of institutional life, respected for its ability to communicate information and to serve as open channel into this communications network.

When both the formal and informal communication networks are working together, they complement each other. Each network carries information that is suited to its need and audience.

3.4 CONCLUSION

Each physical plant department has unique characteristics that accurately reflect the institutions they serve. If physical plant is to remain one of the premier departments on campus, there must be a concerted effort to develop a good, effective public relations program that stresses the need for effective communications. This program must be designed to promote the service nature of the department and reach as wide a constituency as possible. It must promote the professional nature of physical plant and be as user friendly as the most modern computer software program.

It is not intended that institutions undertake all of the possible communications techniques that have been presented. On the contrary, it is intended that each physical plant organization choose the elements that will emphasize its strengths, minimize its weaknesses, and utilize a minimum of the institution's resources. The best program for any department will be the one tailored to fit the size, administrative structure, and complexity of the college or university which it serves. It should be structured to bring out the professional competence and abilities of the individuals who staff the department. This effort is not something that can be done once and then forgotten; good public relations and communications demand a continuing effort and a commitment from the top management of the organization. It must become an integral, conscious part of our daily activities as physical plant managers.

ADDITIONAL RESOURCES

Davis, Keith. "The Care and Cultivation of the Corporate Grapevine." *Dunn Review,* July 1973.

Ferguson, Stewart and Sherry Devereaux Ferguson. "The Physical Environment and Communication." *The Open Organization.*

Goleman, D. "People Who Read People." *Psychology Today,* July 1979.

Moine, D. J. Herd. *Modern Persuasion Strategies.* Prentice-Hall, 1984.

Peters, Thomas and R.H. Waterman Jr. *In Search of Excellence.* New York: Harper & Row, 1982.

Richardson, Jerry and Joel Margulis. *The Business of Negotiation.* Avon, 1984.

Rogr, M. D'Aprix. *How's That Again.* Dow Jones-Irwin, 1971.

SECTION II

HUMAN

RESOURCES

MANAGEMENT

Section Leader:
Norman H. Bedell
Assistant Vice President for Physical Plant
Pennsylvania State University

CHAPTER 4

Overview of

Human Resources Management

Philip G. Rector
Director of Physical Plant
The Colorado College

4.1 INTRODUCTION

T he most important element in any physical plant department is its people. The staffing requirements will vary with the responsibilities assigned and the size of the institution, but a common dominant characteristic of all physical plants is that they are "people intensive." Well over 50 percent of the department's budget is for personnel.

There are few organizations of comparable size that have the diversity of professional, trades, and skills requirements as does a physical plant department. Department personnel include engineers and architects with knowledge of the latest technologies; engineering technicians; fiscal and personnel specialists; computer programmers and operating personnel; most of the construction and mechanical trades classifications; transportation and material moving occupations; the range of administrative, managerial, and administrative support occupations; and lesser skilled personnel such as groundspeople, custodians, and laborers. The organizational structure and the techniques of leadership vary among these classifications of workers.

In recent years, increasing emphasis has been placed on achieving ever-higher productivity from personnel—to do more with fewer people—necessitated by limited fund availability.

The comparatively large number of employees in a physical plant department, the diversity of training and skills required, and the need for maximum productivity makes personnel administration and leadership both critical and difficult. Many, perhaps most, of the top officials in college and university facilities management have backgrounds in engineering or architecture, but their major responsibility is managing human resources.

4.2 SCOPE OF PROFESSIONALS RELATIVE TO THE ROLE OF THE DEPARTMENT

In smaller institutions, the head of the physical plant department usually is expected to be competent in technical areas as well as in financial, personnel, and administrative management. Submanagers commonly are found in custodial and grounds services, building maintenance/ utilities, business and financial management, planning, and engineering. In many cases, submanagers' capabilities are limited to operational expertise. When professional consulting assistance is required, outside architects, engineers, construction managers, and planners must be utilized. In some instances, this expertise can be obtained efficiently and effectively from vendors of the services needed. If the size and breadth of the department's responsibilities are large enough, highly specialized professionals can be added to the department staff, with the benefits of lower cost and greater familiarity with the problems and needs of the campus. When these professionally trained personnel are a part of the management of the organization, their professional capabilities will transfer effectively into the management and operations of the department.

The organization and staffing of a physical plant department is discussed in Section I, General Administration.

4.3 PROFESSIONAL STAFF

In any organization there is a cost-effective balance of in-house professionals with professional services provided from outside the organization. The determination of how best to obtain these services is based on very practical factors such as cost, response time, and quality of services. Contracts for outside professional services on an hourly basis can effectively supplement in-house staff when work loads are too small to justify a particular staffing level, or when work loads fluctuate significantly. See Chapter 40, Contracting for Services.

4.4 POSITION DESCRIPTIONS

The position description should clearly delineate the overall purpose and specific components of the position. It outlines the type and level of work, the hours, specific tasks, levels of authority and responsibilities, reporting relationships, and criteria for measurement of performance, as well as the training and education required for the job.

Since work conditions and requirements change, position descriptions should be reviewed periodically and revised when necessary. The revision process can be coupled with an annual employee evaluation, which can result in reclassification of the job or regrading of the employee position.

4.5 JOB CLASSIFICATION/EVALUATION

Typically, the institution's personnel department develops job classification structure that groups positions in the same salary range with others having similar education, experience, and responsibilities.

This structure should reflect organizational reporting relationships and identify the sequence of positions available to employees for career mobility and advancement. Classifications need to be viewed as more than just titles; they should be part of a system that helps establish and clarify wage and salary levels, as well as levels of authority and responsibility. Classifications show salary ranges for each position (from starting salary to maximum salary) and step increases, if applicable. If employees belong to a union, the classification lists the wage levels established in the union contract.

Evaluation

In evaluating individual positions within a job category framework, administrators should consider these factors carefully:

Exempt positions (supervisory with hiring/firing authority)

- Knowledge
- Planning
- Creative thinking
- Financial responsibility
- Working relationships (contacts)
- Supervisory responsibility

For nonexempt positions (nonsupervisory)

- Prior experience
- Education and training
- Complexity

- Physical demand
- Mental/visual/oral demand
- Responsibility for records and reports
- Relations with others
- Confidential data
- Equipment and supplies
- Safety of others
- Working conditions
- Unavoidable hazards

These elements can be used in an informal evaluation, or they may be included in some type of formalized point-factor analysis procedure.

4.6 SUMMARY

The foregoing is intended as an introduction to the subject of human resources management. The following chapters include more detailed discussions of recruitment and employment, employee relations, training and development, and motivation and leadership—all critical to success in this important realm of physical plant administration.

CHAPTER 5

Recruitment and Employment Practices

H.R. Patterson Jr.
Associate Vice President for
Campus Planning and Plant Operations
Southern Methodist University

With additional contributions by Philip G. Rector.

5.1 RECRUITMENT AND EMPLOYMENT

People are the most important asset of an organization. The recruitment process either opens or slams the door to people, and for this reason it is essential that recruitment be done on a systematic and well-informed basis.

Recruitment may be viewed as the attempt to match the needs of the organization with the skills and aspirations of the individual applicant in an optimal way. People do their best work when they have a strong expectation of being well-adjusted to their work and their environment.

Job Descriptions

To begin the process of recruitment, the job to be filled first must be analyzed. A job is a collection of tasks that comprise the work of one person. A task is a major element of work intended to achieve a specific result. A job may be analyzed most effectively with a written job description that includes the following elements:

- The purpose of the job.
- The position of the job within the organization.
- Principal duties and responsibilities.
- Specific tasks.
- Working relationships.

The job description provides the basis for identifying those qualifications needed to do the job. The qualifications must be realistic; over- or underqualified people have a low success rate. Qualifications have to be stated in specific terms: level of education, prior work experience, specialized skills, level of intelligence, and essential personality characteristics relating to the job.

Candidate Search

After determining specific qualifications, the next step is to attract a field of applicants. Normally, it is best to attract a large number of qualified applicants from which to make selections. Selection standards should never be compromised. An underqualified applicant will not be satisfied and will become a problem for the organization. Common recruitment sources are:

- Recommendations and referrals by college or university employees.
- Newspaper advertising.
- Advertising in trade, professional, or business journals.
- Private employment agencies.
- Public employment agencies.
- High school, trade, and technical services.
- Professional sales and business organizations.
- Recruiting at conventions and professional society meetings.
- College recruitment.
- Executive search firms.
- Unsolicited applicants.
- Minority and women career centers.

Screening Process

There is little purpose served in spending time interviewing unqualified applicants. Applicants can first be screened on the basis of their application and/or resume. Further screening can be accomplished by a short initial interview to determine whether the applicant has the necessary qualifications.

Any employment or skills assessment test must be professionally developed and validated and be based on abilities needed for the job. It must not discriminate, nor may it continue the results of past discrimination.

Most companies no longer check employment references because of Equal Employment Opportunity (EEO) compliance problems (see Section 5.3, Equal Opportunity Legislation). There are three methods of checking references—by mail, in person, and by telephone. The use of a structured and sequential questionnaire administered over the telephone is generally considered the most effective and expeditious method.

For EEO compliance, the following facts about each applicant must be recorded and kept for one year:

- Date of application.
- Name of applicant.
- Minority group, if any.
- Sex.
- Position applied for.
- Appropriate EEO classification category.
- Disposition of application.
- Specific recruiting source that referred applicant.

One of the best indicators of an applicant's future job performance is their record of past performance.

Interviewing Techniques

The basic guidelines for conducting interviews are: 1) establish rapport with the applicant; 2) have a plan of questions and discussion; 3) devote appropriate time for the interview (not too much or too little); 4) know your biases and do not rely on intuition—first impressions should not be overemphasized.

The job interview may be broken into six separate parts:

1. Introducing yourself and welcoming the applicant.
2. Engaging in small talk to establish rapport.
3. Obtaining relevant interview information.
4. Providing the applicant with information about the organization and the job.
5. Responding to the applicant's questions.
6. Concluding the interview.

After conducting the job interviews, the final step is to rate each applicant on each selection standard. This provides an objective view of each applicant and helps in selecting the best person for that particular job.

5.2 PROMOTION POLICIES

General

There are three essential ingredients to successful promotion of staff: 1) establishing career ladders, 2) announcing and posting all promotional opportunities, and 3) thoughtfully choosing the selection criteria. Also affecting promotion policies may be local civil service regulations, union-negotiated agreements, affirmative action plans and goals, local school policies, and settlements of grievances.

Promotions for staff should be done objectively, fairly, and openly. The staff should be acquainted with promotion policies and individual requirements. Objectivity in selections for promotion helps to ensure that the most qualified people are promoted, and creates a general confidence in the fairness of the process.

Career Ladders

Career ladders refer to the relationship between jobs, wherein experience gained in a job on the career ladder will qualify that person for consideration for one of the next higher jobs. This enables an individual to come into the organization at an entry-level position and, through time and experience, progress through various related jobs. For example, it may be possible for an individual to join a physical plant department as a crafts helper, and through experience and competent performance be promoted progressively to craftsperson, senior craftsperson, foreman, superintendent, and perhaps even to director.

Job Announcements and Postings

All promotional opportunities should be announced and posted where all personnel can see them. Announcements should include instructions for making an application and the selection criteria. Job announcements generally are posted for seven to ten days, but the specific time is governed by local policies. Procedures for filling positions in an emergency must also be included in local policies.

Selection Criteria

The selection criteria describe the qualifications a person must possess to perform the job, and are derived from the written job description. For example, the job description for the director's secretary might read, "Provides rapid typing support and types accurately; takes dictation and minutes of meetings; maintains director's files." The selection criteria might read:

1. Able to type 60-75 words per minute with 2 percent or less error rate.
2. Able to take shorthand or speedwriting at 120 words per minute with 2 percent or less error rate.
3. Knowledge of filing systems, and able to file 50 documents per week with no errors.

From this description of specific job duties, the candidates' qualifications are compared.

There are several objective methods of rating applicants. A weight may be assigned to each criterion, then each applicant rated on each criterion. Another method is to evaluate each individual's percentage of meeting 100 percent of each criterion, which rates each criterion of equal value.

5.3 EQUAL OPPORTUNITY LEGISLATION

There are four federal legal sources that prohibit discrimination in all aspects of employment (hiring, firing, promotions, and training of employees). Equal opportunity is guaranteed by: 1) the U.S. Constitution, 2) federal laws, 3) Executive Orders, and 4) court interpretations and decisions.

U.S. Constitution

The Fifth Amendment (1791) prohibits the federal government from engaging in discriminatory actions or policies and ensures that "no person shall . . . be deprived of life, liberty, or property, without due process of law." The Fourteenth Amendment (1868) applies the provisions of the Fifth Amendment to state and local governments.

Federal Laws

Before 1963, there were only two statutes concerning employment discrimination. The 1960s and early 1970s saw a proliferation of federal legislation dealing with all areas of employment discrimination. The following are the current federal laws with which employers must comply.

The Civil Rights Act of 1866 (Section 1981 U.S. Code, Title 42) was enacted to enforce the Thirteenth Amendment prohibiting slavery. This law specifically mentions the right to contract and later was interpreted to mean the right to contract for employment.

The Civil Rights Act of 1871 (Section 1983 U.S. Code, Title 42) was enacted to enforce the Fourteenth Amendment. State and local governments cannot deprive any person of any rights secured by the Constitution and laws. Violators are liable for prosecution by the injured party.

The Equal Pay Act of 1963 prohibits wage discrimination based on sex. It applies to both the public and private sectors and is administered by the Department of Labor. It was enacted as an amendment to the Fair Labor Standards Act of 1938.

Title VI of the Civil Rights Act of 1964 prohibits employment discrimination in federally assisted programs. It also prohibits discrimination against the beneficiaries of federal assistance programs.

Title VII of the Civil Rights Act of 1964 as amended by the Equal Employment Opportunity Act of 1972 prohibits all forms of employment discrimination on the basis of race, color, religion, sex, or national origin. It covers both public and private employers, employment agencies, labor unions, and joint labor-management apprenticeship committees. It also bans discrimination against individuals who file a Title VII complaint. The law is administered by the Equal Employment Opportunity Commission (EEOC).

The Age Discrimination in Employment Act of 1967 prohibits employment discrimination based on age. It applies to public and private employers, employment agencies, and labor unions. The protected class is employees age 40 and older. Legislation has recently has been passed by Congress which states that there is no mandatory age for retirement.

The Civil Rights Act of 1968 (Title I—Interference with Federally Protected Activities) provides criminal penalities for interference with an individual's employment rights because of race, color, religion, or national origin.

The Intergovernmental Personnel Act of 1970 provides for intergovernmental cooperation in the administration of grant-in-aid programs, grants for improvements in state and local personnel administration, federal assistance in training employees, and federal grants for training. To qualify for technical and financial assistance, the employer must comply with certain merit principles, such as fair treatment.

The Public Health Service Act of 1943, as amended in 1971, prohibits funding to any medical school or health-training facility unless the Department of Health receives satisfactory assurance that the school is not, or will not, discriminate on the basis of sex in employment or admission of individuals to training programs.

Vietnam Era Veterans Act of 1972 requires special emphasis be given to the employment of qualified disabled veterans or veterans of the

Vietnam era by those employers receiving federal funding or under federal contract. It is administered by the Department of Labor.

Title IX of the Education Amendments of 1972 prohibits sex discrimination in employment, admissions, and treatment of students in all federally funded education programs.

The State and Local Fiscal Assistance Act of 1972, commonly known as the General Revenue Sharing Act, prohibits discrimination in any program or activity funded in whole or in part with revenue sharing funds. It is administered by the U.S. Treasury department.

Section 503 of the Rehabilitation Act of 1973 provides that any contractor or subcontractor (fulfilling a contract worth more than $2,500) shall take affirmative action to employ and advance in employment qualified handicapped individuals.

Section 504 of the Rehabilitation Act of 1973 prohibits discrimination based on handicap by providing that any recipient, public or private, of HEW (now HHS and ED) funds must take positive steps to employ and promote qualified handicapped persons through reasonable accommodations and services. Programs and activities of the funded organization must be made accessible to the handicapped. Executive Order 11914 extends this section to all federal agencies granting assistance.

The Immigration Reform and Control Act of 1986 makes it unlawful to "hire, or to recruit or refer for a fee an alien knowing that he is an unauthorized alien." It also provides penalties for failing to comply with the documentary and records requirements of the Act. Penalties became effective on or about June 1, 1987. The Employer Sanction provisions *do not apply* to the hiring or continued employment of any alien hired prior to November 7, 1986. Anyone hired prior to that date may continue to be employed without the employer being penalized in any way.

Executive Orders

Executive Orders are directives issued by the President to clarify, extend, or explain existing federal legislation. There are three Executive Orders that relate directly to equal employment opportunity.

- Executive Order 11141, issued by President Lyndon B. Johnson on February 3, 1964, prohibits federal contractors and subcontractors from discriminating based on age "except upon the basis of a bona fide occupational qualification, retirement plan, or statutory requirement."
- Executive Order 11246 as amended by 11375, signed by President Lyndon B. Johnson on September 24, 1965, prohibits discrimination by nonexempt government contractors and sub-

contractors on the grounds of race, color, religion, sex, or national origin. It applies to hiring, upgrading and promotion, apprenticeship programs, testing procedures, wage and fringe benefits, cosponsored training programs, education, tuition assistance, transfers, layoffs and seniority practices, and other related conditions of employment. This order also established the Office of Federal Contract Compliance (OFCC) within the Department of Labor to administer and enforce the order.

- Executive Order 11478, signed by President Richard M. Nixon on August 8, 1969, prohibits discriminatory practices in federal government employment on the basis of race, color, religion, sex, or national origin.

The courts have interpreted these laws to mean that all groups in the labor force are entitled to equal employment opportunity throughout all levels and subdivisions of the organization, unless business necessity precludes such consideration. The burden of proof rests clearly upon the employer to justify any exception to the general rule of nondiscrimination.

Griggs v. Duke Power Company (401 U.S. 424-1971) held that the results and the consequences of an employer's actions must be considered rather than its intent not to discriminate. If an employer's action has a "disparate effect" (an uneven or numerically disproportionate impact) on members of a protected class, or perpetuates the effect of previous discriminatory practices, then such action shall constitute unlawful discrimination unless the employer can prove business necessity. Further, the courts have held that where barriers to equal employment opportunity exist, positive and affirmative action is required by all organizations, regardless of whether or not they hold a government contract.

Additional cases since *Griggs v. Duke Power Company* include the following:

- *Meritor Savings Bank v. Vinson*, June 19, 1987, in which the court ruled that sexual harassment is a form of unlawful sex discrimination under Title VII of the Civil Rights Act.
- *U.S. v. Paradise*, February 25, 1987, in which the court upheld the use of a racial promotion quota, or a "one-for-one" promotion ratio for blacks and whites to the rank of corporal in the Alabama State Police.
- *School Board of Jassau County v. Airline*, March 3, 1987, in which the court said having a contagious disease does not necessarily remove an employee from protected status under the Rehabilitation Act. This decision could have significant impact of employment on persons with AIDS.

5.4 AFFIRMATIVE ACTION

Affirmative action is a set of written, specified, and result-oriented procedures designed to achieve equal employment opportunity within an organization. To develop an acceptable affirmative action plan, the employer first must analyze its employment of minority groups and women, and determine where it is deficient. Next, the employer must develop goals and timetables to which good-faith efforts may be directed to correct the deficiencies and increase the use of minorities and women at all levels of the work force where deficiencies exist.

Affirmative Action Plan

There are eight steps in the development of a written affirmative action plan.

1. Top management must write a policy statement in support of affirmative action and its intent to follow such a plan.
2. Top management must appoint an official to direct and implement the program.
3. The employer must publicize the program both internally and externally. One common method of publicity is to include a statement about being an equal opportunity employer on the organization's stationery.
4. The employer must analyze its employment of minorities and women by department and job classification.
5. The company must develop specific affirmative action goals and timetables for reaching those goals.
6. The employer must develop and implement the program.
7. The appointed official must develop internal audit and reporting systems to evaluate the effectiveness of the program.
8. The company must organize appropriate additional supportive training and development programs. Affirmative action plans do not work unless first-line supervisors understand their responsibilities.

5.5 WAGE AND SALARY ADMINISTRATION

Although there are other significant motivators, wages and salaries are the most tangible rewards that employees receive. Wages and salaries are important to employees as indicators of their personal value to the employer, and as a reference for comparison among themselves. Consequently, wage and salary relationships can lead to employee dissatisfaction. A well-planned program of wage and salary administration is important in minimizing potential employee dissatisfaction.

Typically, employees of the physical plant department comprise a small part of an institution's nonacademic staff and are subject to overall institutional personnel and fiscal management programs. However, since the plant manager ultimately is responsible for employees' performance, it is important that the manager take a prime role in assuring fair and equitable wage and salary relationships. Personnel departments usually are objective, but the success of an organization depends upon administrators adapting standard procedures to their organizational units.

5.6 WAGE AND SALARY RELATIONSHIPS

The most sensitive salary relationships generally exist among employees within their own organizations or departments. This sensitivity to compensation is higher within the group than with comparable positions outside the institution. Generally, administrators find that the greater the physical and organizational distance between employees, the less compensation sensitivity there is.

Three Levels of Salary Relationships

Wage and salary relationships must be considered on at least three levels:

- Among employees of the same classification, e.g., electricians.
- Among employees of a larger work group who work side by side, e.g., technical shops (electricians, plumbers, HVAC mechanics).
- Among employees of the same major organizational unit, e.g., physical plant department.

Longevity and Other Factors

In addition to hourly wages and fringe benefits, employees are often sensitive to salary relationships that exist due to differences in longevity, and increases due to merit or economic factors. Administrators often unconsciously bring these differences to the attention of the employees. For example, the manner in which administrators present annual wage adjustments can emphasize salary differences rather than personal progress. Upper-level administrators and financial and personnel officers frequently view and fund annual increases on a percentage of the salary base. While this is logical and practical during the budget-cycle discussion, it can cause administrative problems, since percentage increases tend to increase the differential between employees.

Salary Increase Programs

Salary structures in the education sector follow the long-established trend of recognizing that merit and longevity are the primary factors in setting salaries for a particular classification. Percentage increases tend to insert an extraneous factor, frequently causing unnecessary concern among the employees. This extraneous factor can be eliminated by administering merit increases to employees of similar classifications on a standardized cent-per-hour basis. For example, all electricians performing satisfactory work can be awarded the same amount-per-hour increase at annual salary review time. Likewise, those having better than satisfactory or less than satisfactory performance can be awarded a different, but standardized, increase.

To administer this principle in a large physical plant organization that utilizes both unskilled and skilled trades, it may be necessary to develop different increase standards for different classifications. Normally, different standardized increases will work, due to traditional differences in salary between the skilled and unskilled classifications. Administrators can use the average percentage increase (upon which funding is based) as a guide to providing employees having identical performance with approximately the same percentage increase in each of the classifications. The key to the success of the program is to discuss increases in terms of amount-per-hour increases for each unit, not percentages.

If physical plant administrators want to reinforce departmental unity, then a standard economic adjustment (cost-of-living) factor (equal-amount-per-hour) can be considered and applied to the entire department. In this case, the salary increase program could be made up of three parts:

- Economic adjustment (same for everyone).
- Merit adjustment (equal-amount-per-hour based on classification).
- Other adjustment (to compensate for salary misalignments, etc.).

In this system, standard salary relationships exist among employees and controversy is reduced. However, union contracts may preclude this flexibility to adjust salary relationships.

Equal Pay for Equal Job Description

Another factor of interest and concern to employees is the practice by unions outside the institution to establish equal pay for the same job description. Historically, the education community has rewarded employees for longevity, although longevity is now becoming less important to all workers, particularly younger ones. In the past, workers readily accepted differences in salaries based on ten years difference in longevity; it is now important to consider equating salaries with as little as a five-year differential in longevity. Thus, employees of a single classification with over five years satisfactory service would earn the same hourly rate. While this may ease the concern of the employee who has come from union membership, it does occasionally run counter to the standard university practice of rewarding for merit.

It is possible to have a grouping of experienced employees at one rate and still provide a system of justification where employees with exceptional merit can earn salaries above a standard maximum rate. Such a system must be administered carefully, however, so that supervisors do not inadvertently move all employees to the higher rate within a few years and thus dilute the true merit implications of the rate. By adapting these guidelines to specific situations, the facilities administrator can address and remove many employee concerns that interfere with their maximum effectiveness.

5.7 PAY POLICIES AND PROGRAMS

Two primary criteria beyond the requirements of basic federal or state law need to be used in determining pay policies and pay rates: labor market considerations and internal equity. Within these broad guidelines, it probably will be necessary to adopt specific programs, different in detail, for the exempt and nonexempt employee groups.

Comparative Surveys

Administrators need to conduct comparative market surveys, at least annually and occasionally more often in an active labor market, to maintain the institution's relative position in the marketplace. If the organizational salary philosophy is to be rated consistently in the top 10 percent of the defined labor market in the geographic area, the market survey data will show what changes, if any, are necessary to maintain salary levels according to the philosophy.

The physical plant administrator, not the personnel administrator, needs to monitor the results of market surveys for the facilities staff. It is important for the plant manager to be vitally interested in all aspects of the pay policies and programs, since the effectiveness of the staff and the administrator's performance are at stake. Through close relationships with the personnel department and staff, plant administrators can maintain the desired external and internal salary and benefits relationships.

5.8 SALARY INCREASE GUIDELINES

It is common to establish salary increase guidelines for outstanding, above-average, satisfactory, and unsatisfactory performance. The guidelines relate to the average and to percentage increases that will fit within the budgeted or available funds each year. As these funds change from year to year, the actual amount of increase will vary.

An exempt salary program should:

* Maintain a performance-drive (merit increase) program.
* Maintain expanded salary ranges to ensure the potential for salary movement for individuals with outstanding long-term performance.
* Establish salary ranges allowing for competitive hiring and retention.

The non-exempt wage program should be evaluated periodically to ensure its simplicity with a minimum number of wage classification scales. In addition, the scales already established should be sufficiently broad to accommodate most salary requirements.

Pay and related policies need to be stated specifically for:

* Overtime
* Shift differential
* Holiday pay
* Hazardous-duty pay
* Out-of-title work
* Work week definition
* Meal periods
* Rest periods

These policies should be given to employees at the initial department orientation, and records should be maintained in each employee's folder stating that the employee received and signed a copy of the policies. Updated copies should be posted at major employee bulletin boards so that employees can refer to them easily. Supervisors need to review the policies periodically in the work unit staff meetings.

None of the policies and procedures described in this chapter will be completely effective if the employees do not understand them. Therefore, these policies should be developed to serve the best interests of both the employees and the institution, and then sold through good communication and fair administration.

5.9 EMPLOYEES' PERCEPTIONS

Employee perception of salary relationships is an important factor. Each employee should feel secure that the external and internal salary relationships are the best the institution can provide, and that both plant management and the institution are interested in these relationships. To establish and maintain credibility with employees, it may be desirable to include responsible and respected employees in the sample wage surveys and interviews conducted by the personnel department. Often the question arises as to whether real comparability exists between job classifications at one institution and those sampled at other institutions.

It is important that the comparisons be equitable. Generally, the personnel department is not as closely attuned to a department's specific needs as is the physical plant manager. The facilities department can provide valuable assistance to the personnel department and to itself by evaluating and comparing job descriptions of the department's employees with those surveyed.

Internal equality of salary relationships is even more important than equality with external employees. The process of determining internal equality can be informal or can be based upon a validated job analysis system that is appropriately ranked and rated by positions, in such a way that a nondiscriminatory structure exists for the different positions within the organization. The personnel department should be able to help evaluate the equality of physical plant employees among themselves and with other employees of the institution.

5.10 PAYROLL PRACTICES

Some physical plant employees work unusual hours and occasionally accumulate considerable overtime. Custodians, plant engineers, and security police often work night shifts. Maintenance workers, moving crews, and groundskeepers work overtime for several weeks at the beginning and end of each academic period. As a standard procedure, the interviewer should warn applicants for these positions that such conditions are part of the job, and that supervisors accept no excuses for not complying with overtime requirements.

Pay Differentials

The physical plant organization can compensate for differing work conditions and requirements in various ways. All night work should qualify for some night differential premium, either a flat hourly increase or a percentage of the worker's normal rate. State and local government employees may use compensatory time for overtime at 1.5 hours for each hour of overtime worked. This is important and applicable to state colleges and universities only. According to many state laws, work performed beyond forty hours per week must be paid at the overtime rate in institutions that receive any federal funds (i.e., grants, student loan funds, capital building funds, etc.).

Overtime

Overtime should be distributed as equally as possible among qualified employees. If an employee refuses overtime on one occasion, he or she should not be excluded from future opportunities.

For more traditional services such as maintenance and groundskeeping, it may be more efficient to have employees report for work prior to the commencement of classes. In drawing up work schedules, facilities managers should consult with supervisors and employees to determine the most appropriate work times. A simple change, such as moving the reporting time fifteen minutes to coincide with local bus schedules, may ease transportation problems and improve worker morale.

Standby

Another common scheduling problem is the standby roster. For some essential services, it is necessary to place skilled employees on call in case an emergency requires immediate work. While on standby status, the workers must remain accessible for immediate recall. One method of handling standby is to require all employees to take turns. The rotation need not be inflexible; individuals willing to trade can arrange switches among themselves. To justify the disruption of leisure, it is traditional and advisable to provide a small premium for remaining on standby alert. Institutions generally pay travel expenses and a minimum of two hours of pay, or at least four hours of pay without travel expenses, to the employee who is called back.

5.11 RECORDKEEPING

It may be a duplication of effort for the physical plant office to maintain a set of employee records when those records are also maintained in the institution's personnel office. However, this duplication provides two benefits. First, employees can find any information they need in their home offices, a benefit that helps develop a sense of departmental identity and loyalty. Second, the director who keeps complete records on hand retains management authority that otherwise might fall by default to another office. Following are items that should be kept in an employee's personnel file in the physical plant office.

Application Form

The basic document is the job application form. It provides information such as name, social security number, local address, birthdate, marital status, education, previous work experience, military service, job title, date of employment, and salary.

Photographs and Fingerprints

There are advantages and disadvantages to keeping pictures and fingerprints in the personnel file. The photographs may create fears about racial discrimination. Fingerprints may be objectionable if a potential employee has a police record that has not been reported in the application, but fingerprints discourage omissions and falsifications of previous police records. They can also protect employees from unwarranted suspicion in the event of thefts. Many schools participate in rehabilitation programs by hiring people with previous police records. Few schools, however, tolerate deliberate concealment of such information.

Performance Memos

One of the most important uses of the employee file is as a repository for memos of commendation and criticism. The awareness that commendatory and deficient performances are recorded can be an incentive to employees. Performance appraisals also should be included in the file.

Payroll Card

A payroll card with a complete financial account of the individual's tenure at the institution is a service to the employee. The essential data on such a form are date of employment, original job title, starting salary, increases earned, reclassifications, and present salary. From this card the secretary or personnel clerk can quickly answer most questions an employee might ask.

Attendance Records

As a backup to payroll cards, the department should maintain complete attendance records. For tradespeople, laborers, and others on hourly wages, time cards generally are used. For supervisors, office personnel, and others on straight salaries, a daily attendance sheet notes any absences. These documents help resolve disputes about sick leave taken, amount of annual leave earned, and similar fringe benefits.

Many employers ask employees to request time off in writing in advance. If the time off is for unanticipated sick leave, the request form should be completed immediately after the employee returns.

5.12 SEPARATION PAPERS

The final item in the employee's file is his or her separation papers. These papers include all information pertinent to accrued benefits, such as leave and retirement pay. To ensure that the separation proceeds smoothly, the director should compile a checklist of all required actions. The statement of cause of separation should specify whether the employee resigned to take another job, relocate, advance her or his career, or was terminated. This information is valuable to employees, since they may want a reference letter from the institution, and to the institution, since planners can use this data in formulating future personnel policies. The statement of cause of separation may also provide insight to possible unemployment compensation claims and equal opportunity discrimination hearings.

5.13 PERFORMANCE APPRAISAL PROCESSES

The performance of each employee should be evaluated, and the evaluation documented, at least annually. Figure 5-1 is a sample evaluation form. Following are general guidelines for making performance evaluations.

Preparing for the Rating

1. Become familiar with the contents of the evaluation form. Analyze its general scope as well as the general instructions.

Figure 5-1
Staff Performance Evaluation

Employee's Name _____   **Evaluation Date** _____

Department _____   **Job Title & Code** _____

Evaluating Supervisor _____   **Date of Employment** _____

Instructions: Supervisor should prepare form entirely before holding the conference with the employee. This is a time for positive comments first, followed by constructive criticism. A frank and cordial atmosphere should be fostered that should result in a helpful dialogue between supervisor and employee. At the end of the conference employee should take the form to study, write reactions, and sign. Upon request, a copy may be made for employee.

Rating Scale: 1 = Superior   4 = Marginal
                   2 = Commendable   5 = Unsatisfactory
                   3 = Satisfactory

Factors

Cooperation   1   2   3   4   5

1. In relationship with other employees   ☐   ☐   ☐   ☐   ☐
2. In relationship with supervisor   ☐   ☐   ☐   ☐   ☐
3. In relationship with the public   ☐   ☐   ☐   ☐   ☐
4. In working toward departmental objectives   ☐   ☐   ☐   ☐   ☐

Initiative

1. Resourcefulness   ☐   ☐   ☐   ☐   ☐
2. Fidelity to established procedures   ☐   ☐   ☐   ☐   ☐
3. Creative   ☐   ☐   ☐   ☐   ☐
4. Constructive thinker   ☐   ☐   ☐   ☐   ☐

Productivity

1. Speed of work   ☐   ☐   ☐   ☐   ☐
2. Steady worker   ☐   ☐   ☐   ☐   ☐
3. Task persistence   ☐   ☐   ☐   ☐   ☐
4. Gets things done   ☐   ☐   ☐   ☐   ☐

Quality

1. Degree of errors   ☐   ☐   ☐   ☐   ☐
2. Faithfulness to standards   ☐   ☐   ☐   ☐   ☐
3. Appearance of finished work   ☐   ☐   ☐   ☐   ☐
4. Supervision required to ensure quality   ☐   ☐   ☐   ☐   ☐

Job Knowledge

1. Understanding of duties   □ □ □ □ □
2. Ability to handle equipment used   □ □ □ □ □
3. Versatility in varied tasks   □ □ □ □ □
4. Capable of complex assignments   □ □ □ □ □

Dependability

1. Gets to work on time   □ □ □ □ □
2. Attendance record   □ □ □ □ □
3. Can be trusted with money, valuable
   equipment   □ □ □ □ □
4. Trustworthy with confidential information   □ □ □ □ □

General

1. Conduct helps institution meet EEO
   commitment   □ □ □ □ □
2. Supportive of institution's objectives   □ □ □ □ □
3. Understands public relations aspect of job   □ □ □ □ □
4. Aware and observant of institution's policies   □ □ □ □ □

Supervisor's comments on strengths and weaknesses of employee's job performance and steps employee must take to improve:

_____

_____

_____

_____

          Supervisor's signature   **Date**

Employee's comments about this evaluation, the job, the supervisor, and in general about work at the University:

_____

_____

_____

_____

          Employee's signature   **Date**

Department Head's signature   **Date**

2. Understand thoroughly the duties and requirements of the particular position held by the employee to be rated.
3. Use a process of objective reasoning, eliminating personal prejudice, bias, or favoritism. Do not allow your own personal likes or dislikes of certain mannerisms to influence the rating.
4. Do not assume that excellence in one factor implies excellence in all factors. Observe and analyze the employee's performance in each factor individually.
5. Base your judgment on demonstrated performance, not on antici-pated performance. The evaluation is to be based on what has hap-pened, not on what might happen.
6. Evaluate on the basis of the entire rating period. It is better not to consider only single accomplishments or failures, or the most recent performance. Achievements or failures should be considered in con-text with the total performance for the period.
7. Consider seniority apart from performance. An employee with a short service record may not necessarily be less effective than one with a longer term of employment.
8. Consider the requirements in terms of the level of the position. An individual in a lower classification may be meeting the requirements of his or her job more effectively than the immediate supervisor does in his or her position in a higher classification.
9. Include any additional factors that are important enough to be in-cluded in the overall appraisal of the employee.

The Evaluation Interview

1. Review your initial evaluation of the employee's performance and consider why you evaluated the work as you did.
2. Plan to meet in private. If this is the employee's first evaluation interview, anticipate tension, anxiety, or curiosity.
3. Create the impression that you have time for the interview and that you consider it important.
4. Make the employee feel that the interview is a constructive, cooper-ative one by placing primary interest upon his or her development and growth.
5. Be open-minded to the opinions and facts presented by employees. Be willing to learn about them. Don't dominate or cross-examine. Avoid argument. Employees must do most of the talking at some time during the interview,

  - In bringing opinions and feelings to the surface and to your at-tention.
  - In gaining a better understanding of themselves.

- In identifying their own areas of needed or potential improvement, and in making plans for their accomplishment.

6. Talk about the employee's strengths first, covering each point in some detail. This practice helps start the interview off on the right foot. While building upon the employee's strengths, do not fail to discuss weaknesses or failures and how to prevent or curtail them in the future. At this point introduce your suggestions for a specific improvement program.

7. End the interview when you have made clear whatever points you intended to cover, when the employee has had a chance to review his or her problems and release any emotional tensions that may exist, when plans of action have been cooperatively developed, and when a natural stopping point has been reached. Reassure employees of your interest in their progress and indicate willingness to take up the discussion again at any time. It may be appropriate to schedule a follow-up meeting to monitor progress.

8. Secure the employee's signature, then date and sign the report. Forward it to the department head who will review and sign the report and forward it to the personnel department. The report is kept in the employee's personnel file, available to both employee and supervisor, but not available to anyone else.

CHAPTER 6

Employee Relations

Patrick J. Cunningham
Manager, Transportation Services
University of Michigan

With additional contributions by Armando Lopez.

6.1 INTRODUCTION

Perhaps the single most important personnel service is that of employee relations. The fair and consistent treatment of employees, whether they belong to a union or not, is the objective of this function, and the responsibilities usually include the following:

- Development, revision, and communication of personnel policies or rules, including negotiations of labor contracts that are consistent with the goals of the organization, applicable federal and state laws, and modern management practices.
- Interpretation and administration of personnel policies, including administration of labor contracts.
- Peaceful resolution of grievances or complaints arising out of the interpretation or application of policies and labor contracts.
- Administration of corrective discipline for misconduct. These responsibilities of the employee relations function can be met only through the cooperation of all staff members, especially those in management or supervisory roles.

6.2 ESTABLISHING AND COMMUNICATING PERSONNEL POLICIES

Most universities and colleges have established written personnel policies and procedures to assure the consistent and equitable treatment of employees. For employees who belong to a union, the labor contract defines most policy standards. Labor contracts are established through collective negotiations with the union representing the employees. This process is described in more detail later in this chapter. Personnel policies pertaining to nonunion employees generally are developed unilaterally by management, but care should be taken to assure conformance with organizational goals and applicable state and federal laws and regulations. Appendix 6-A is an example of a university policy guide pertaining to vacation time.

Labor Costs

The largest single expenditure for the facilities manager is labor. How administrators deal with employees has a significant impact on the institution's operating budget.

With a commitment to nonunionism, managers must look seriously at employee groups and prepare job descriptions that are meaningful for the organization, incorporating the flexibility needed to administer the department effectively. When each of the individual job categories and probable assignments have been made, market surveys must be made for each position. Two factors of primary concern are wage levels and supplementary benefit packages. Normally, these are enumerated in a union contract and are matters for negotiation.

Once surveys are completed, the facilities manager must determine where within the range of responses each item will fall. The physical plant budget cannot be excessive, and the facilities manager's goal is to provide an employee package that will attract good candidates and keep them in a college or university environment. An institution cannot offer extremely large compensation, but to offer too little would be noncompetitive, and the organization would be unable to attract or retain effective personnel.

A manager should know the available market of each employee group and should determine the combination of real benefits (wages, fringe benefits, insurance, etc.) and intangible benefits equal to that of organized groups in the immediate labor market. Educational assistance is a good benefit often found in colleges and universities.

Personnel Policies and Procedures

Once the wage rates are established and employees recruited, managers must try to remain nonunionized in order to be cost-effective. This does not come automatically. An effective grievance procedure must be developed, and the physical plant administrator must concentrate on the first step of the grievance procedure—how to avoid it.

The director must spend time with the crews and become sensitive to their needs, frustrations, and job-related problems. Employees need to know that the boss cares. Directors should look for potential grievance situations, and correct them before they become problems. If the director sees an employee violating safety procedures, for example, he or she should correct the employee privately, not in order to exercise authority, but to demonstrate genuine concern for the employee. The director must show interest and concern.

A labor agreement establishes the general framework of labor relations in the organization. It spells out in broad language the rights and benefits of employees, the obligations and rights of management, and the protection and responsibilities of the union. In institutions without a union, a similar book on policies, procedures, and benefit programs should be supplied by the personnel office.

Established policies and procedures should be kept current. Some existing policies and/or procedures may be obsolete or confusing. They should be periodically reviewed and updated to embody what is important and relevant today. They should be described simply and clearly.

After the policies and procedures are updated and realistically presented, they should be distributed to all employees and supervisors. This is a good time to meet with supervisors to make sure they understand their content and application, including limits on supervisor authority in applying policies. Flexibility in the application of policies is not advisable; fairness and consistency are the most important factors.

Given the complexity of operating a physical plant department, the establishment of written personnel policies and procedures specific to the department also should be considered. These should cover areas not included in institution-wide personnel policies. Appendix 6-B is an example of a departmental policy concerning sick time.

Policies established through labor contracts are reviewed in subsequent negotiations and may be revised then. A periodic management review of personnel policies applied to nonunion employees is recommended. Most policies should be reviewed at least once every three years. Changes in methods of operation or applicable state and federal laws may require review and revision of a particular policy on a more frequent basis, and may at that time be revised.

Communicating personnel policies is a major consideration. Without adequate communication, policies will not be applied consistently. Various ways to communicate policies and procedures include the following: institution and departmental handbooks, institution and departmental newsletters or papers, management memoranda, and staff meetings.

6.3 UNION RELATIONS

History and Legal Issues

Unionization and collective bargaining have taken place in the United States for more than 100 years. The National Labor Relations Act of 1935 and its subsequent amendments have formalized procedures for employees in the private sector to organize and choose an exclusive bargaining representative (union) for the purpose of bargaining collectively with the employer over the "terms and conditions of employment." The law also allows employees to engage in concerted activities, principally strikes.

The five-member National Labor Relations Board (NLRB) interprets and enforces the law. The regional offices of the board conduct representation elections (union or nonunion) and certify the results. They also investigate Unfair Labor Practice charges (allegations of violations of the law.)

Public Employees

Public employees are specifically exempted from the National Labor Relations Act (NLRA). However, few states now prohibit union participation and collective bargaining, and many states have adopted laws similar to the NLRA for their public employees. Most states prohibit strikes. However, several have granted a limited right to strike. Public universities and colleges should look to their particular state laws for further information.

Union Organizing

As mentioned before, employees of private institutions covered by the NLRA and those employed by public institutions with state laws patterned after the NLRA have the right to organize a union.

Union organizing efforts are initiated by interested employees who must file a petition with the NLRB (or the state agency, in the case of public employees) for a certification election. Under NLRA rules, at least 30 percent of the employees of the intended bargaining unit must sign the petition showing their interest in an election.

If a 30 percent show of interest is obtained, the NLRB or state commission orders an election. First, however, an appropriate bargaining unit must be determined. This determination, which ultimately is made by a federal or state agency, establishes which classifications will be represented by a union if it wins the election. The employer should look at this question carefully and negotiate with the NLRB or state agency to assure that the intended bargaining unit does not encompass too many or too few classifications.

If the intended bargaining unit contains employees with diverse interests, e.g., skilled trades and custodians, these employees are said to have no "community of interest." Bargaining over wages and working conditions with employees who have no "community of interest" is particularly difficult since disagreements within the union will occur often.

On the other hand, if the intended bargaining unit covers employees with limited interest (e.g., all electricians) and excludes the other building trades, a fragmentation of bargaining units can occur, and the employer can be negotiating with as many as fifteen to twenty different unions. Obviously this would cause a labor relations nightmare.

The employer must strive for a balance between these two extremes and prevent introduction of either a fragmentation of bargaining units or an all-encompassing bargaining unit with no community of interest. Temporary and student employees should be excluded from the intended bargaining unit, as these employees rarely have a community of interest with the other employees.

When an appropriate bargaining unit is determined, the election will normally occur on the employer's premises. All employees within the intended bargaining unit are eligible to vote. A majority of those who vote determine the outcome, which is certified by the NLRB or state agency. Should the majority vote against unionizing, another petition for an election cannot be submitted for one year.

Once a petition is filed and accepted, management may decide to wage a campaign against unionization. This should be done only after legal consultation, since strict rules apply. A violation of these rules (the commission of an Unfair Labor Practice) could result in the election results being overturned and another election held.

Perhaps the most important thing for management to do is encourage participation in the election. Experience has proven that a large turnout usually favors management. Other tactics include keeping union organizing efforts and information out of work areas, and informational mailings to employees from management that discourage unionization. Again, these activities are strictly regulated. Always seek legal advice before acting.

Decertification Elections

Employees (not management) who are dissatisfied with their union can petition the NLRB (or state agency) for a decertification election. A 30 percent show of interest is required before an election will be ordered. Similar to a certification election, the decertification election is determined by a majority of those who vote. If a union is decertified, and the unit becomes nonunion, no further unionization attempts can be made for one year.

Collective Negotiations

When a union becomes certified as the exclusive bargaining representative of a group of employees, management must then negotiate with the union over "terms and conditions of employment." Failure to bargain or "bargain in good faith" is a violation of the NLRA and/or state law if it was patterned after the federal law. This constitutes an unfair labor practice.

As result of collective negotiations, agreements usually are written and a contract specifying the rights and responsibilities of both parties is executed. Contracts vary in length, but most often cover time periods of one to three years.

When the union makes a demand, management must respond to it if it is a mandatory subject of bargaining. Legal rulings have now identified approximately seventy mandatory bargaining items under the National Labor Relations Act. Many state laws, however, are more restrictive. Those issues that are not mandatory are either voluntary bargaining items or illegal items. Illegal bargaining items are those forbidden by law. For instance, several states prohibit union shops or clauses in a contract that make membership in the union mandatory. Voluntary bargaining items also have been identified by both federal and state laws and are subjects about which management may either agree or refuse to bargain. One example is benefit increases for past retired employees. Legal advice should be sought when disputes over mandatory or voluntary bargaining subjects occur.

Under no circumstances does the duty to bargain equate with the duty to concede to, or even compromise on, a union demand. Even on mandatory bargaining items, management may bargain but decide not to agree on any contract language.

First-time contracts are important because they set the stage for future agreements. Therefore, management should obtain outside assistance in negotiating a first contract if no one within the organization has previous experience in this field.

Management's strategy during negotiations is usually to preserve as many management rights as possible and keep the overall costs of the contract within specific boundaries. A strong "management rights" clause is of utmost necessity to assure that subjects not discussed or agreed to during the negotiations remain firmly within management's discretion.

Failure to reach an agreement over a contract may result in a strike or the withholding of services by the union employees. Strikes by public employees are technically illegal in most states in this country. In 1978, 409 public employee strikes were reported, most of them illegal under the law. Management may decide to seek a court order to return illegal strikers to work, especially if the strike can be shown to be against the public interest.

Why Employees Join Unions

Traditionally, workers have sought a voice in their treatment on the job. History bears witness to several examples of worker actions intended to dramatize their concerns. Union organizing is one. When workers view management as impersonal and unresponsive to their needs, it is not surprising to see them turn to unions for support and representation.

Moreover, workers have traditionally been unwilling to relinquish full control of the organization to management. Workers view themselves as having a vested interest in the enterprise and entitled to a voice in the day-to-day activities that affect them most: transfers, work assignments, and wages, for example.[1]

Many factors lead workers to unions. Sloan and Witney summarize research that suggests that employees form unions when they feel their basic need to protect themselves—safety—is threatened; to preserve or enhance their self-esteem; and to fulfill their need for association— belonging to a group focused on common interests and purposes.[2]

Safety, in the hierarchy of individual needs, broadly means protection from danger. In the work place, safety translates to protection against the arbitrary or capricious actions of management. Safety also implies some safeguard against the unfair or biased decisions of management.

In labor agreements, protection against the feared arbitrary actions of management is usually afforded through seniority provisions. Seniority becomes the single most important factor influencing management decisions on transfers, promotions, work and shift assignments, and layoffs.

Seniority functions as the great equalizer among the rank and file. Seniority provides the objective, measurable criterion that ensures the uniform treatment the workers and the union seek.

Even in times of concession bargaining, workers are unwilling to give up strong seniority provisions. They recognize that job tenure-longevity—translates into job security. They also recognize that seniority forces management to reward tenure, not disregard it.[3]

As workers seek guarantees against job deprivation and the arbitrary demands of the organization, they also desire a voice in the decisions that affect them. This is not new, as we have already noted. Unions, however, by virtue of their bargaining position, provide workers with a formal and safe mechanism to express their views about how they should be treated.

Internal union structures encourage the participation of the workers in the formulation of bargaining strategy and demands. Issues affecting the working lives of the rank and file thus receive expression, backed by an organization that has management's ear at the bargaining table and during the administration of the agreement. Negotiated provisions, such as job bidding and posting processes, are examples of procedures in which workers may have a role in determining. Frequently based on seniority, these procedures are expressions of how the rank and file prefer to be treated by management, and rules by which the workers are willing to live. The degree to which workers participate in the decisions that affect their lives on the job influences the level of satisfaction and achievement they feel.

Unions also offer leadership opportunities. Through elected union offices, such as president, steward, or bargaining committee representative, members find added means of influencing the processes that affect their lives, a chance for advancement, and recognition by their peers and management.

Unions are not unlike social clubs. Clubs and unions allow for the formation of relationships based on common interests or purposes. Unions, however, are labor organizations. They focus on the real and perceived concerns of their members and the similarity of their jobs to create worker solidarity and a sense of identity with the union.

The strength of unions rests, in part, on their ability to develop and nurture a strong sense of fellowship among their members. Unions capitalize on the workers' "social" needs—the workers' desire to belong to a group. The members benefit from friendships, recreational and social activities, and educational opportunities that otherwise might not be available.

Impact on Physical Plants

A physical plant operation is labor intensive. Because of the variety of functions a physical plant department performs—from equipment repair and maintenance to facilities renovations—its work force is typically employed in the skilled and semi-skilled jobs characteristically represented by bargaining units. Therefore, it may not be unusual to find that about 80 percent of the physical plant work force is unionized.

Thus, the immediate impact of unionization on employee salaries and fringe benefits is obviously great and the first factor to be recognized.

The presence of a union also imposes limitations on plant management's ability to manage its operations freely. Actions such as employee transfers and job assignments, for example, may be restricted by seniority provisions of a bargaining agreement. This is not news. But what of the less evident, more subtle impacts?

Jack Hug, writing in *Collective Bargaining In Higher Education*, identifies three areas that are compromised by the presence of a union: the management team, departmental organization, and intraplant communications.[4]

The existence of a union results in an increased reliance by management on a central personnel function because of the need to ensure consistency in the administration of the labor agreement. Matters relating to discipline, e.g., disciplinary layoffs and discharges, may require the review and approval of the employee relations unit of personnel before they can be affected by management. There will be an increasing need, as well, for management to maintain closer liaison with personnel services as the terms and conditions of the agreement change as a result of successive contract settlements.

The presence of a union may pit employees against management, particularly if supervisors and managers are insufficiently acquainted with the terms of the bargaining agreement. In such cases, the authority and credibility of the management team are severely compromised. Management can expect increasing challenges from the union officers whenever they perceive that management's decisions or actions have violated the contract.

Problems for management compound when the physical plant work force is represented by more than one union. This may not be uncommon. Skilled craftspeople, for example, may be represented by one labor organization, boiler operators by another, and mechanics and custodians still by a third. Preunion methods of intraplant-subunit communication and cooperation may require revision because of the need to keep the departments well informed of upper management decisions and to coordinate the delivery of services to the customer. A task as simple as repairing a malfunctioning heating unit, for instance, could require the combined services of workers from the different bargaining units, considerations of different contractual terms and requirements, even jurisdictional disputes about the nature of the work.

The composition of the union can affect the management and structure of the physical plant department. A bargaining unit that includes first-line supervisors in the definition of the union drives a wedge through the very heart of a management team. Upper management can expect a conflict of loyalty and interests in such events. The effective assignment of work—even the administration of corrective discipline—is severely compromised. As a result, management should always lobby vigorously to have supervisors excluded from a bargaining unit that seeks to represent the rank and file.

The number and scope of the unions will affect the total departmental organization. Whether the employees are represented by a single union or by several, according to specialty areas or crafts, will require a rethinking by management of such factors as lines of authority, response to work stoppages or other employee actions, management style—including management-employee communications—and the costs associated with the administration of the agreements.

"Management is communication, and employee relations management is communicating with employees."[5] Good employee communications should never end. The need for good employee communications is intensified by the presence of a union.

Employees need to be properly informed of management's expectations. Clearly delineated work rules, policies, and procedures need to be fully communicated to employees and supervisors alike to assure consistent treatment and results. Employees want to know how their behavior and productivity will be measured and the consequences of any deviations from expressed norms.

Unions can and do, unfortunately, create pitfalls for management's communications processes. Management should keep in mind that one of the union's purposes is to maintain a low level of agitation among the rank and file to legitimize the union's existence. Management should be continuously aware of distortions of fact and rumors. It should immediately respond to clarify the issues and to keep the lines of communication open and accessible.

An effective management-union communication device is the joint labor-management committee. Joint committees typically discuss items of mutual interest—safety and productivity, for example. See Appendix 6-C for an example of relevant contract language in a memorandum of understanding on an advisory committee.

6.4 IMPASSE RESOLUTION

When collective negotiations fail to reach an agreement or contract, with little or no movement expected from either side, negotiations are said to be at an impasse. Impasses may be resolved in one of three ways.

Federal or State Mediation   The federal and state governments offer, and in some cases mandate, assistance in breaking impasses and settling contracts without a strike. A federal or state mediator may come in, as a third party, to assist the parties in resolving the impasse. A mediator's only power is the power of persuasion. While he or she may make recommendations toward a settlement, the recommendations are not binding. The mediator's primary purpose is to keep the negotiations going and avoid locked positions by either party.

Interest Arbitration   Interest arbitration on the other hand, is the use of an arbitrator to settle the contract, where the arbitrator (a third party) actually determines what the settlement will be. Some states have mandated interest arbitration for public employees engaged in crucial services, e.g., police and fire, to prevent strikes.

In several states, the arbitrator must settle the impasse on the basis of the last best offer of the parties. Under this scheme, each party is encouraged to come up with a "reasonable" last offer.

Experience with interest arbitration has, at best, been mixed. Where procedures for interest arbitration exist, meaningful bargaining often stops with one or the other party opting for arbitration. Interest arbitration is considered by many labor relations experts as a circumvention of the bargaining process and against the public interest, since an outside party ultimately may settle the issue without regard to the public interest or settlement costs involved.

Fact-Finding   A third technique of impasse resolution in the public sector has been fact-finding. In fact-finding, a third party, analyzes the final positions of both parties and issues a public report based on his or her findings with or without recommendations for settlement.

This is another technique designed to cause the parties to establish reasonable positions on the issues, since their positions would be scrutinized by the public. As in interest arbitration, fact-finding has produced mixed results, at best. Many labor relations experts have criticized this process for many of the same reasons argued against interest arbitration.

6.5 GRIEVANCE PROCEDURES

The grievance procedure is a systematic, peaceful way to resolve an actual or alleged contract violation. The objective of all grievance procedures includes:

- Intention to settle an alleged contract violation case in a friendly and orderly manner.
- Specification of a series of definite steps to follow in the processing of grievances.
- Staying within time limits placed on each step.

- Answering a grievance within the allotted time (as specified in the contract).[6]

The majority of all grievances are resolved in the first two steps. Most of the remaining grievances are resolved in the third step; however, a few grievances go to arbitration.

Most collective bargaining agreements outline procedures whereby the union or the employee may adjust grievances. A grievance procedure can act as a stabilizing force in the work place, since it establishes a peaceful and orderly procedure for resolving disagreements. For this reason, many organizations have adopted grievance procedures for their nonunion or professional staff as well.

A grievance procedure is usually designed to assure a progressively higher level of review as the grievance moves from step to step. The concept is to encourage resolution of grievances at the lowest level (between the supervisor and employee), while allowing upper-level management review if the grievance is appealed. Time limits are usually established for each step to assure a timely resolution of the grievance.

In most cases, grievances begin with an employee requesting a steward to discuss a problem. The employee, now the grievant, meets with the steward and supervisor (as arranged by the supervisor) and presents his or her grievances. Should the employee fail to gain satisfaction, the grievance is appealed to the next level. Appendix 6-D is a grievance procedure used by a university for its nonunionized staff members. A grievance procedure should be available to all employee groups, whether they belong to a union or not. All employers need a means of resolving actual or perceived injustices. Failure to address injustices is counterproductive and lead to employee problems of the greatest magnitude.

Complex variables control the nature and frequency of grievances. Those variables are:

- The policies and discipline specified in the labor contract.
- The political environment and militancy of the local union.
- The caliber of the company's personnel administration and supervision.
- The nature of the existing union-management relationship.
- Economic and related variables affecting employment and working conditions.[7]

Supervisors and managers often find handling grievances a stressful and unrewarding experience. Because grievances are often filed against a supervisor or as a result of a supervisor's judgment, the supervisor may feel personally threatened. Employees, in many instances, also look upon the grievance as a struggle between them and the supervisor. This conflict between the supervisor and the employee can be greatly reduced, if not eliminated, if a supervisor remembers the following principles of grievance handling:

- Think of a grievance hearing as an investigatory interview. The object is to gather enough facts to understand and solve a problem.
- Let the employee and/or steward present the grievance. Managers must not assume knowledge of the grievance. Let the grievant and the steward tell their stories. Look for underlying reasons why the grievance was filed.
- Never argue with the grievant or steward. Even if managers disagree with what is being said, they should not comment. This principle defuses the conflict and shortens the length of the hearing.
- Ask for a citation of the specific violation of the contract or policy and a remedy.
- Ask questions to clarify the issue and gather essential facts.
- End the hearing after collecting all the facts. A gracious way to end a hearing is simply to say, "Do I have all the facts I need to make my decision?"
- Never answer the grievance at the hearing, even if you know the answer or have reached a decision. Take time to consider the facts before responding to the grievant.
- Sell the answer to the grievant. A manager should tell the grievant the reasons for a decision. Allow the grievant some dignity even when the grievance is denied.

6.6 ARBITRATION

Arbitration is a process by which union and management agree to select an impartial person from a local, state, or federal list of arbitrators. Both groups agree that the arbitrator's decision is binding. An arbitrator views all pertinent material presented by the union and management and makes a determination on the *facts* presented.

An arbitration decision must be accepted. The decision to go to arbitration is a serious one. The results cannot be predetermined. Either side can lose. Sloan and Witney summarize arbitration this way.

> Arbitration cases are not won on the basis of emotional appeals, theatrical gestures, or speechmaking.

> The arbitrator is interested in the facts, the evidence, and the parties' arguments as they apply to the issues of the dispute. Such material should be developed in the hearing through careful questioning of witnesses and the presentation of relevant documents.[8]

Agreement to use an arbitrator's binding decision has made drastic, costly measures such as strikes and lockouts unnecessary. Peaceful settlements can be reached without disrupting the entire organization.

Some collective bargaining agreements specify that a grievance not resolved through the grievance procedure can be appealed to arbitration by the union. Arbitration is a costly procedure (usually over $1,000 per case) that calls for a disinterested party (the arbitrator) to decide the outcome of the grievance. Arbitrators use the collective bargaining agreements, past arbitration decisions, and their considerable experience in the field to make their determinations. The selection of arbitrators is a topic to be determined through contract negotiations. A popular method is to adopt the American Arbitration Association rules.

Almost all arbitration cases fall into two categories. The first category includes those questions about the interpretation or application of the bargaining agreement. These disputes arise when the union disagrees with management's administration of specific contract provisions. Management's preparation for this type of case should involve a thorough research of past negotiation minutes or notes. What was said during prior negotiations will be of primary importance, so detailed minutes or notes of each negotiation session should be kept indefinitely. In this type of case, the union has the burden of proof and presents its evidence and testimony first.

The second type of arbitration case involves the administration of discipline. Most contracts specify that discipline must be for "just cause." If the union disagrees with a disciplinary action taken by management and the grievance goes to arbitration, an arbitrator will decide whether the discipline was for "just cause" or if it was excessive. In these cases, the credibility of the witnesses is of prime consideration. Therefore management's witnesses should be well prepared by an attorney prior to the hearing. In cases involving questions of discipline, management has the burden of proof and must proceed first.

Arbitration for Non-Bargained-For Employees

Arbitration need not be limited to represented employees. Indeed, as a mechanism for the peaceful and cost-effective resolution of employee complaints, arbitration for nonunion employees is finding increasing use, particularly in the private sector. Several factors favor adopting an arbitration procedure for non-bargained-for workers.

- The erosion of the doctrine of employment-at-will has placed players at risk and exposure to costly wrongful discharge law suits. The associated legal expenses, liability, expenditures of time and effort, and unfavorable publicity are great. It makes good business sense to consider the adoption of less costly and reasonable alternatives to conflict resolution.
- The organization's employee relations climate is enriched because the arbitration procedure signals to the entire enterprise management's added commitment to resolve issues peacefully and objectively. It communicates to the employees the perception that management values the employees and cares about their concerns.
- The risks to the employer are fewer in arbitration than they are in a jury trial. Moreover, an arbitration award could preclude an action at law. Depending on the circumstances, an arbitration decision could have the effect of a verdict. (Seek legal advice to determine the applicability of the law in your specific jurisdiction.)

Generally, management's resistance to an arbitration procedure for nonunion employees has centered around its reluctance to voluntarily have its decisions reviewed, modified, or reversed by a third party. As already noted, arbitration is risky; anyone can win or lose. When the alternatives are considered, however—the uncertainty of a jury trial and the tendency toward high jury awards—arbitration becomes more attractive. The authority of the arbitrator can be limited by the arbitration procedure, as well.

Appendix 6-E is an example of an arbitration procedure for non-bargained public employees. The procedure specifically provides for a review of decisions governing lost time discipline, i.e., disciplinary layoffs and discharge.

Generally, because of the varying interpretations of relevant law across the country, arbitration procedures for nonrepresented workers are most effective in the resolution of discharge cases. The effectiveness of such a procedure in cases involving complaints of discrimination, for example, remains generally unsettled.

6.7 CORRECTIVE DISCIPLINE PROCEDURES

An important factor for maintaining good employee relations is the consistent application of discipline standards. When misconduct occurs in the work place, it disrupts the orderly and efficient operation of the organization. The supervisor must restore order to the work place by administering discipline to the employee(s) involved.

Most modern organizations follow what is called a philosophy of corrective discipline. Discipline is administered to correct the behavior, not punish the employee for his or her misconduct.

Discipline for common misconduct, such as attendance and work performance problems, begins with an oral warning or reprimand, then a written reprimand, a disciplinary layoff, and ultimately discharge/ termination.

Most serious forms of misconduct, such as insubordination, may begin at a higher level with a written reprimand or a disciplinary layoff, and misconduct constituting uncorrectable behavior, such as theft and fighting, may result in immediate discharge.

Some employers choose to define, and even negotiate with, their union's discipline standards, thus determining specific penalties for specific infractions of the rules. Others do not favor this "cookbook" approach and prefer to base the discipline on the facts of the individual case, taking into account any extenuating or mitigating circumstances. Either way, it is important to administer discipline consistently when similar situations exist.

Regardless of the size or nature of the institution, all organizations should use a corrective discipline procedure for misconduct. Employees who are unionized usually come under a "just cause" provision in their contract that more or less states that employees will not be disciplined or discharged without just cause.

Corrective discipline helps assure that discharged employees were adequately warned and given a chance to correct their misconduct, thus documenting "just cause" for the discharge. This helps management win arbitration cases. The same care is suggested for nonunion employees. Although they do not have the protection of a labor contract, they may decide to file discrimination charges or claim unemployment benefits for "wrongful discharge." Appendix 6-F is an example of a university's discipline policy for nonunion employees.

Last Chance Agreements

Unfortunately, despite the best efforts of management and the imposition of well intended corrective procedures, some employees fail to make the necessary adjustments in their behavior to justify continuing their employment. In those cases, discharge is the only option.

The decision to discharge an employee is neither a pleasant nor an easy one for management. Many variables influence the decision, including the employee's past record of service to the organization, seniority, and work performance. Those factors must be weighed against the nature of the employee's misconduct before the discharge is effected. Management's action may also have to be defended in arbitration—a risky and costly process at best.

There may be occasions when discharge may be appropriate, just, and fair, but "penny wise and pound foolish" for some reason. In those instances, the "last chance agreement" provides a reasonable alternative.

Last chance agreements are written arrangements between the organization, the employee, and the union, if any. Last chance agreements, as their title implies, are used to give the employee one more opportunity to preserve his or her employment.

Last chance agreements may be affected following disciplinary review conferences in which the employer's rationale for recommending discharge is given to the employee and the union; to settle final step grievances prior to arbitration; and to settle grievances already in arbitration.

The value of last chance agreements is that they:

- Clearly summarize the unacceptable behavior that has imperiled the employee's job.
- Outline management's expectations of the employee's behavior.
- Spell out in detail what behavior will result in the employee's immediate discharge.
- Are useful with nonbargained employees as well.
- Save the costs associated with any final step grievance processes and arbitration when the agreement contains a provision that any discharge subsequent to the affirmation of the agreement will be neither grievable nor arbitrable.
- Convey to the employee and the union that management may not be so heartless after all.

Last chance agreements are particularly effective in situations involving excessive sick time and unexcused absenteeism. Appendix 6-G contains several examples of a last chance agreement.

Release of All Claims

A release of all claims is a written agreement in which an employee agrees to relinquish certain interests in the employment relationship. Typically used in termination cases, the release of all claims is a settlement. In exchange for monetary consideration, the employee agrees effectively to depart peacefully and to relieve the employer from any additional claims or demands.

A properly drafted and executed release of all claims may generally bar a terminated employee from prevailing in a wrongful discharge suit. It can also save management the time, costs, and unfortunate publicity associated with wrongful discharge suits. Such suits strain management's resources and create unnecessary stresses for the entire organization.

A release of all claims is a type of contract; its terms are negotiated. In this regard, a release that reflects some compromises is more likely to be enforceable than one that is forced upon the employee. In addition, the employee may be less inclined to try to "break" the release and to seek other remedies.

A terminated employee may seek to "break" or overturn a release of all claims on several grounds.[9]

- The release was hastily executed. Insufficient time was allowed for deliberations.
- The language of the release was unclear or the employee did not understand English.
- The employee was under the influence of drugs, "dazed or shocked" at the time the release was executed.
- The employer failed to pay more than "nominal consideration" in exchange for the release.
- The employer and employee both shared a "mistake of fact."
- Fraud, concealment, or duress were attendant factors at either the inducement or execution of the release.

Legal advice should be sought when negotiating and drafting a release of all claims to ensure that the terms of the agreement are reasonable, the interests of management are preserved, and there is a complete meeting of the minds. The employee should also be encouraged to consult with an attorney. A release generally is considered stronger if it has been approved by a lawyer representing the discharged employee.

Even with legal help, the guidelines for executing releases are fairly simple. For example:

- Provide an adequate opportunity for the employee and his or her attorney to read and understand the release. Do not conceal any pertinent information.
- Put the release in writing, in clear and concise language. Be sure the employee understands the language and is neither shocked, dazed, nor under the influence of drugs.

- Provide more than nominal consideration. The payment of benefits already due, such as accrued vacation pay or vested pension benefits, does not constitute consideration.

Appendix 6-H contains two examples of releases of all claims.

6.8 TOWARD A POSITIVE EMPLOYEE RELATIONS ENVIRONMENT

The key to an enriching employee relations climate is simple: workers want to be treated with respect and dignity, as human beings with intrinsic qualities and abilities.[10]

Workers do not labor solely to buy bread. They work to satisfy a variety of needs—such as achievement, self-fulfillment, recognition—which are uniquely human. The employment relationship is not just economic; it is social as well.

Workers need to be recognized as the most important resources of the organization. Their importance needs to be communicated to them as well as the value of all their work to the goals and mission of the enterprise. In this regard, employees need to have a clear understanding of the organization's goals, how their work contributes to the realization of the corporate mission, and the standards by which their performance will be measured. This serves two purposes: it enhances the likelihood the employees will act in support of the corporate mission, and it reinforces the employees' sense of importance to management.

Communication is perhaps the most important element of any employee relations effort. Effective communication crosses traditional employee boundaries; encourages, solicits, and rewards worker viewpoints; and reflects openness and receptivity on the part of management to the concerns and ideas of the workers. Employee ideas also contribute to overall goals.

Listening is the crucial activity. It requires skill and the greatest expenditure of time and effort. Management should listen carefully to rumors. Rumors surface when group expectations of behavior are perceived as having been violated. Rumors serve as unsanctioned controls to identify troublesome behavior and to obtain compliance with established rules.

Are the rumors in the work place critical of management's actions or decisions? Then management is failing to live by the rules as perceived by the rank and file. Management is failing to meet the employees' expectations in some way.

Similarly, management should listen to employee humor. Sick humor reflects a sick organization in the eyes of the employees.

Responses to employee concerns or suggestions should be prompt. They should be as thorough as necessary to allay any employee's fears or doubts about management's decisions or actions, particularly in difficult situations when the employees may view management's move in an unfavorable light. A good explanation goes a long way toward boosting worker confidence in management, but keep in mind, that employees only want to know what affects them directly.

Skilled and effective leadership from supervisors and managers is fundamental to a positive employee relations climate. Skilled leadership continually stresses the importance of goals of the enterprise to strengthen the employees' sense of importance and to engender trust in the process.

Skilled leaders practice open-mindedness. They are consistent in the application of policy, but flexible at the same time. Above all, good leaders are impeccably honest. They realize that once their credibility is impugned, employee confidence in the entire organization's abilities and commitments can drop to abysmal lows.

In healthy employee relations climates, leaders are visible and approachable. Supervisors and managers practice "management by walking around." Similarly, management's doors are always open to employees.

Good leadership establishes realistic expectations of the employees, takes a sincere interest in their welfare, supports the employees when they are right, and helps them learn from their mistakes.

Effective leadership believes attitudes are self-fulfilling. Good leaders say "it can be done" and "you are the best," because they realize these attitudes are contagious.

In the positive human relations climate, goals and standards are clearly and positively defined. They are set by employees as well as by management, and properly communicated. Employees are evaluated regularly to measure progress toward goals and compliance with standards. The evaluation serves as a teaching technique as well as a means of providing constructive criticism. The evaluation also provides clues to employee dissatisfaction.

Finally, a supportive employee relations climate offers more than economic rewards. It provides incentives and opportunities for individual growth, positive feedback, recognition, opportunities to learn, and career development. On-the-job training, formal class work and preparation, and mentoring provide means of developing employees for greater responsibilities and growth.[11] Formal and informal recognition systems, from employee awards programs to a simple pat on the back, respond in part to the employees' need to be seen not as a cog in the immense organizational machinery, but as a human being.

NOTES

1. John A. Fossum, "Strategic Issues in Labor Relations,"*Strategic Resources Management.*
2. Arthur A. Sloan and Fred Witney, *Labor Relations,* 2nd Ed., Prentice-Hall, Inc., Englewood Cliffs, New Jersey, 1972 (4th Ed., 1981).
3. See note 1.
4. Jack Hug, *Collective Bargaining in Higher Education,* Washington: College and University Personnel Association.
5. See note 4.
6. Arthur A. Sloan and Fred Witney, *Labor Relations,* 4th Ed., (Englewood Cliffs, New Jersey: Prentice-Hall, Inc., 1981).
7. See note 6.
8. See note 6.
9. Robert M. Vercruysse, "Releases: The Effect of a Terminated Employee's Execution of a Release of All Claims," 1986 Midwest CUPA Regional Conference, Ann Arbor, Michigan, April 1986.
10. Keith Davis, *Human Behavior at Work,* 4th Ed., McGraw-Hill, New York, 1972.
11. Charles Fombrun, Noel Tichy and Mary Ann Devanna, "A Framework for Strategic Human Resources Management," in *Strategic Human Resources Management,* Fombrun, Tichy and Devanna, ed., John Wiley & Sons, New York, 1984.

Appendix 6-A

Standard Practice Guide

SECTION: Personnel
SUBJECT: Vacation
APPLIES TO: Regular Office and Technical Staff Members

I. Policy

To provide time off from work with pay for rest and personal convenience, the university provides regular staff members with paid vacation. Vacation time must be approved by the staff member's supervisor.

II. Regulations and Definitions

A. Accrual

1. Regular full-time staff members accrue paid vacation at their rates of compensation as follows:

First 5 years service (0–60 months)	1 day/month
Over 5 through 8 years service (61–96 months)	1½ days/month
Over 8 years service (97 months or more)	2 days/month

2. Part-time regular staff members normally scheduled to work eight (8) or more hours per week, accrue vacation time on a proportionate basis. Staff members normally scheduled to work less than 8 hours per week do not accrue paid vacation.

3. Vacation time accrues during time worked and during absences covered by Sick Time and Vacation.

4. Vacation days may not be accumulated in excess of twice the annual accrual.

5. Accrued time is available for use during the calendar month in which it is accrued.

6. Vacation accrual for partial calendar months of employment, (which can occur during first or last month of employment and during the month in which a leave of absence begins or ends) is calculated on the basis of the effective date of said occurrence according to the following table:

Effective Date	Start of Employment or Return from Leave	End of Employment or Start of Leave
1 through 10	100% accrual	no accrual
11 through 20	50% accrual	50% accrual
21 through end of month	no accrual	100% accrual

7. Except as provided in 6 above, staff members will not accrue any paid vacation time during any leave of absence or during any calendar month in which they are absent without pay for fifteen (15) or more working days. During any calendar month in which absence without pay is less than 15 but more than seven work days, the staff member will accrue 50 percent of the accrual provided in 1.

8. Increases in rate of accrual are effective on the first day of the month following completion of working time equivalent to five and eight years of continuous service.

9. Leaves of absence will be counted as time worked for the purpose of determining the appropriate rate of vacation accrual.

10. Time worked as overtime will not be counted when calculating accrual or rate of accrual.

B. Scheduling

Each department is responsible for scheduling vacations so as not to interfere with the operation of the department and so that each staff member receives his or her accrued vacation time each year, if he or she so desires. Vacations must, therefore, be scheduled to meet the work requirements of the department, but every effort will be made to satisfy the staff member's request. Units that experience "slack" or "down" periods may require that vacations be taken during these times. When practical, staff members should be informed of such requirements in advance.

C. Compensation for Vacation Time Off

A staff member who meets these regulations will receive regular compensation (rate at the time of absence plus shift premium, if applicable) times the number of hours of accrued paid vacation time scheduled and used based on his or her regular work schedule.

D. Pay in Lieu of Vacation

Actual time off work must be taken in order to receive compensation for accrued vacation time except upon:

1. Retirement.
2. Start of a military leave of absence.
3. Termination for any cause.
4. Quit without notice.
5. Resignation.
6. Death.
7. Layoff.
8. Reduction in hours (fraction) of appointment: If the hours (fraction) of an appointment are reduced, payment is made for all accrued vacation hours in excess of the maximum accrual eligibility for the reduced appointment. In the case of an interdepartmental transfer, the previous employing department will pay the excess accrual.

E. Advance Vacation Pay

Staff members who are paid monthly may request up to 50 percent of their regular gross monthly pay in advance. Staff members who are paid biweekly may request up to two weeks regular gross pay in advance. Complete the Vacation Payroll Advance Request form and obtain the signed approval on the form by the supervisor and/or the authorized signer for the department or organizational unit and present it to the payroll office. Supervisors and authorized signers cannot approve their own requests for advance vacation pay. To be eligible for an advance vacation payment, a staff member must—

1. Have accumulated the amount of vacation time being requested.
2. Request and take no less than ten (10) consecutive working days (holidays may be included).
3. Agree to have the advance deducted in one sum only from the next regular paycheck if paid

monthly, or one-half from each of the next two regularly scheduled paychecks if paid biweekly. (No other repayment plan can be arranged.)

Where applicable, supervisors may wish to double-check the amount of a staff member's accrued vacation time with the appropriate timekeeping office, e.g., Compensation Section, Personnel Office, Hospital Payroll, etc. (See sample form, Figure 6-1, attached.)

F. Probationary Period

Vacation time may not be granted during the probationary period.

G. Neither vacation time nor pay in lieu of vacation can be granted prior to the calendar month in which it accrued.

H. Holiday

A university holiday falling during a scheduled period of vacation will not be charged against accrued vacation unless it is one for which an employee has substituted a day of personal significance. In this case the university's designated holiday may be charged as vacation or excused absence without pay at the employee's option.

I. Vacation Time Substituted for Sick Time

At a staff member's request, absence due to illness or injury (as defined in Sick Time Policy) may be charged as vacation time in place of sick time. The time absent should be recorded as "S" (sick time) not "V" (vacation time) on the appropriate timekeeping document, and the box authorizing this substitution should also be checked.

J. Transfers

Unused vacation allowances will be transferred with an individual when transferring from one position, budget, or operating unit to another.

Staff members transferred from 12-month instructional staff appointments retain their accumulated vacation upon transfer based on maximum of one month less vacation actually used in the fiscal year in which the transfer occurs. They accrue vacation time from the date of their new appointment at the rate applicable to their new appointment. Staff members transferred to instructional staff appointments will receive pay in lieu of unused vacation.

Staff members involved in transfers should be encouraged to take their accumulated vacation prior to beginning their new appointments.

K. Vacation Benefits Phased Retirement

1. Staff members who are participating in Phased Retirement by reducing their hours of appointment will be paid for all accrued vacation in excess of the maximum accrual eligibility for the reduced appointment.

2. Staff members who are participating in Phased Retirement by taking a leave of absence for a fixed period of time will maintain vacation hours accrued, but not to exceed the maximum eligibility. Vacation hours do not accrue during the absence.

L. Long-Term Disability Plan

In order to be eligible for long-term disability benefits staff members must first exhaust their accrued vacation time, which will not be paid in a lump sum.

III. Procedure

A. Maximum Accrual Record

Responsibility	Action
Office maintaining permanent vacation accrual records.	1. Inform supervisor when staff member is approaching maximum accrual.
Supervisor	2. Assist staff member in scheduling time off in an effort to avoid reaching maximum accrual.

B. Vacation Accrual Records Maintenance

Responsibility	Action
Staff Member	1. Report all attendance as follows:

    a) If paid from account 20XXXX, report on Hospital Payroll Time Sheets to Hospital Payroll.

    b) If employed on an 090000 blanket account, report on prepared Accounting Time Sheet to Research Administration Accounting Timekeeping.

    c) If paid from non-20XXXX or non-090000 account and employed in the Medical Center, report on pre-punched card to Medical Center Staff Records.

    d) If employed in the Plant Housing, Student Union, Intercollegiate Athletics, University Library, Plant, Extension, Lawyer's Club, Alumni Association, or Student Publications, report to operational unit.

    e) If paid biweekly, follow departmental procedure.

    f) All other staff members report on pre-punched cards to Central Staff Records.

C. Transfer of Vacation Accrual Between Units

Responsibility	Action
Old department or office maintaining vacation accrual records.	1. Send an interunit transfer request to the Personnel Office in the office in the receiving unit.

D. Requesting Vacation Pay Advance

Responsibility	Action
Staff Member	1. Initiate the Vacation Payroll Advance Request and complete necessary information for supervisor.

Supervisor	2. Check salary and accrued vacation of staff member.
	3. Check if amount of advance is 50 percent of gross salary or less.
	4. Check if vacation days requested are 10 or more consecutive working days.
	5. Sign form authorizing the Cashier's Office to pay the advance.
	6. If not an authorized signer for the organization unit, route the form to such person for signature.
	7. Retain supervisor's copy and give staff member his or her copy.
Staff Member	8. Take authorized form and University Identification Card to the Central Payroll Office or the Hospital Cashier's Office for payment.
Central Payroll Office or Hospital Cashier's Office	9. Pay staff member amount requested.
	10. Retain appropriate copy of the form. Hospital Cashier's Office: forward Payroll Copy to the Payroll Office.
Payroll Office	11. Deduct amount of the advance from staff member's next regular paycheck.
	12. Reimburse Hospital Cashier's Office.

Figure 6-1
Vacation Pay Advance Request

_____
Last Name   First   Initial   Social Security No.

_____
Salary Account   University Department or Unit

_____
Vac. Pay Advance Amt*   Consecutive Working Days
(See below)

*MONTHLY PAID—Cannot exceed 50 percent of monthly gross pay.
*BIWEEKLY PAID—Cannot exceed two weeks gross pay.

SIGNATURE REQUIREMENTS—Two (2) different signatures are required as the requestor cannot also certify as the Supervisor or Authorized Account Signer.

SUPERVISOR/AUTHORIZED SIGNER: I certify that this staff member has accumulated the vacation days requested and is eligible for a Vacation Pay Advance in accordance with University policy.

_____
Signature   Date

STAFF MEMBER: I acknowledge the receipt of the Vacation Pay Advance Amount and hereby agree that the Advance Amount will be repaid by payroll deduction(s) from my subsequent salary payment(s) in accordance with University policy. If paid monthly, the deduction will be from the next regular paycheck. If paid biweekly, ½ of the Advance Amount will be taken from the next two (2) regularly scheduled paychecks. No other repayment plan can be arranged.

_____
Signature   Date

Appendix 6-B

Plant Department
Sick Time Usage Guidelines

All Plant Department employees are expected to meet a regular schedule of attendance. Employees who are unable to meet their employment obligation of regular and reasonable attendance and are excessively absent due to illness or injury shall be (1) counseled, (2) required to provide physician's evidence of disability, (3) provide a general medical evaluation of their ability to work, (4) attend a Sick Time Conference, and (5) may ultimately be discharged.

Absenteeism due to illness becomes excessive when it adversely affects our ability to maintain efficient service. It is the supervisor's responsibility to determine when an employee's absenteeism becomes excessive, but standards have been established to assist the supervisor in this effort.

Sick Time Standards for Plant Department Employees

Each separate or distinct absence is considered an occurrence. An absence of two or more consecutive days is still considered to be one occurrence. In determining whether an individual's sick time usage is excessive, the number of occurrences within specified time periods is used. Other factors to consider are total hours lost from work; patterns of absences, such as before and after weekends; preventive medical appointments; and on-the-job injuries.

The following chart may be consulted to determine whether an employee's absences are excessive based on Plant Department standards and what corrective action is recommended. Please note that occurrences of longer length (three or more consecutive days) require special consideration. Any unusual absences or factors should be discussed with your supervisor before taking action.

OCCURRENCES (of 1 or 2 days)   CORRECTIVE ACTION

3 or more occurrences in last 5 months — Counsel employee about employment obligation of regular attendance.

4 or more occurrences in last 6 months — Counsel employee again about problem and require employee to furnish physician's proof of disability for future

absences. Employees covered by the AFSCME agreement will be given a copy of "Notice and Proof of Disability" (see Figure 6-2) with bottom box checked.)

6 or more occurrences in last 12 months

Employee will be required to provide a general evaluation of their health on a one-page Physician's Statement (see Figure 6-3). A form letter and a record of their attendance is also attached.

After receipt of physician's statement

A Sick Time Conference will be held. Please contact the personnel officer before scheduling a Sick Time Conference. This conference is followed with a letter to the employee that confirms his or her employment obligation of meeting a regular and reasonable standard of attendance.

7 or more occurrences in last 12 months

Discharge. A Disciplinary Review Conference will be held prior to discharge in the case of AFSCME and trades employees.

These standards are guidelines only, and each employee's record should be discussed with your supervisor prior to taking any corrective action.

Physician's Excuse Guidelines

A supervisor or foreman may require an employee to provide a physician's statement under the following circumstances:

1. **When the supervisor has a reason to doubt that an employee is legitimately ill or injured.** Evidence of disability should be required when an employee has shown a pattern of frequent one- or two-day absences due to illness. Other examples include before or after a holiday or vacation, or when a vacation day is requested but denied. Please note that an employee can be required to provide a physician's excuse for absences of any length, even one day or less. However, this must be requested before the employee returns to work.

2. **When the supervisor needs additional information on the nature or length of disability.** When extended (three or more days) absences occur, a supervisor may require a physician's evaluation to determine what action should be taken, if any. This must be requested before the employee returns to work.

3. **To ascertain an employee's general health and ability to maintain his or her employment obligation of regular attendance.** Employees who are frequently absent will be required to provide a general evaluation of their health (one- or three-page medical statement, Figure 6-3). After this provided, a Sick Time Conference will most likely be scheduled. Please refer to Plant Department Guidelines regarding sick time usage.

Those employees who are required to provide medical evidence of their disability or general health *shall do so at their own expense* unless we require them to see a physician of our choice. The Occupational Health Coordinator should be contacted to arrange those examinations where we require the employee to see a particular physician.

All physician's statements must include the following information:

1. **Name and signature of attending physician.** A nurse, secretary, or office manager cannot certify an employee's disability or general health.

2. **Date of examination.** An employee must provide evidence that he or she was seen by the physician on the date of the disability.

3. **Nature of illness or injury.**

4. **Duration of disability.** The statement must indicate that the employee was unable to work and for what duration.

Physician's excuses that do not provide the information listed should not be accepted. When a supervisor questions the validity of a doctor's excuse, he or she should contact the Personnel Manager immediately. Falsification of a physician's statement is grounds for discharge. Employees who are unable to provide the required evidence of disability shall receive an unexcused absence, which is subject to disciplinary action. Medical statements are to be submitted by the employee on the first day of his or her return to work. A copy of the statement should be sent to the Occupational Health Coordinator.

Special contractual requirements must be met when an employee covered by the AFSCME or Trades Agreement is required to provide proof of disability.

AFSCME

Employees covered by this agreement can be required to provide physician's evidence of disability by checking the box at the bottom of Form "Notice and Proof of Disability." This is done after an employee returns from a disability and has shown a pattern of frequent one- and two-day absences due to illness.

Trades

Employees covered by this agreement can only be required to provide a physician's proof of disability once prior to a Sick Time Conference. After an employee is asked to provide a physician's excuse, a Sick Time Conference can be held, and a six-month requirement to provide evidence of disability may be established. Please contact the personnel manager when this problem arises.

Preventive Medical Appointment Guidelines

Employees are encouraged to schedule their preventive medical appointments before or after work time. In those cases where this is not possible, sick time may be used.

Preventive medical treatment includes any medical treatment that is not an emergency and can be scheduled at the convenience of both the employee and the department. Routine medical or dental checkups, preventive treatments for a post-operative or ongoing medical condition, and cosmetic or minor corrective surgery are all considered examples of preventive medical care.

Employees may request sick time for preventive medical treatment by giving written notice of an appointment, name of the physician and duration of the appointment to their supervisor based on work requirements. In the event that emergency work requirements make it infeasible to release an employee for preventive medical treatment (even if appointment was scheduled five or more days in advance), the supervisor may require the employee to reschedule the appointment.

Employees who abuse this privilege will not be allowed to use sick time for preventive medical purposes.

Figure 6-2

Notice and Proof of Disability

(To be completed by employee upon return to work.)

NAME _____ DATE _____

(Please print)

SOCIAL SECURITY NUMBER_____

I certify that I was unable to work because of a disability resulting from personal SICKNESS ☐   INJURY ☐

From: _____   Date _____   Time_____
To: _____   Date _____   Time_____

Total time lost from work in hours:_____

Nature of Disability:_____

_____

_____

☐ I was under the care of a physician._____

Physician's Name

☐ I was not under the care of a physician.

☐ I gave advance notice to:_____

☐ Time and date notice given:_____

☐ I did not give advance notice because:_____

_____

_____

_____

Signature of Employee

☐ Approved   ☐ Disapproved Date_____ By_____
                                   Signature of Supervisor

Reasons for disapproval or other comments_____
_____
_____
_____

☐ A physician's statement will be required as verification that you are unable to work because of personal sickness or injury prior to being considered for any future sickness or injury pay.

Figure 6-3

Employee's Authorization for Release of Medical Information

Doctor _____   Date _____

You are hereby authorized to supply (name of institution) with requested information regarding your findings as to my sickness or injury.

_____   _____
(print name)   (sign name)

(Detach for retention with patient's medical records)

PHYSICIAN'S STATEMENT

1. I examined_____ on_____
        (patient's name)   (date)

   My diagnosis is:

   (a) Date of injury or onset of illness_____

   (b) Date first consulted_____

2. Based on this diagnosis* I believe that this patient is *able/unable* to perform his or her usual work on a full-time basis.

   If the patient is currently unable to perform his or her regular work, when do you believe the patient will be able to do his or her usual work?_____

_____

3. Other comments with respect to the patient's health as it may relate to his or her occupation?_____

_____

4. I would be willing to be called at _____ for further information or clarification of this patient's status. ☐ yes   ☐ no

Signed _____
(Attending Physician)

Please return the completed form as soon as possible to:

*Note: If disability is the result of pregnancy and childbirth, the patient must be *physically unable* to do her usual work in order to be eligible to receive *paid sick leave*. If she is able to work but wishes to stay home with her newborn child, she will be granted a child care leave of absence.

— **Appendix 6-C** —

MEMORANDUM OF UNDERSTANDING

Advisory Committee

The parties recognize that productivity, the quality of work performed and the standards to be met, and matters concerning the application of this agreement as it pertains to employees and the operations of the University are, and have been, matters of mutual concern, and that improvement to these functions is in the best interest of employees and the University. In this connection and during the term of this agreement, an advisory committee is established, which shall be composed of six (6) members, three (3) of which shall be University representatives and three (3) of which shall be Trades Board representatives. The University and the Trades Board shall each designate one (1) of their members as co-chairperson, who shall be responsible for the conduct of meetings. Either party may identify matters to be discussed and, thereafter, request a conference. At least one (1) week prior to such a conference, the requesting party shall submit an agenda of matters to be discussed. If no agenda is submitted, there shall be no conference. Matters brought before the committee will be discussed and reviewed and the committee may prepare recommendations concerning such matters. Such recommendations may be presented, in writing, to appropriate University and Trades Board officials, when a general consensus of the committee is reached regarding specific matters considered. Such recommendations shall be advisory only and not be binding on either party, unless otherwise agreed upon by the University and the Trades Board.

This understanding shall not be construed as adding to or detracting from any part of this agreement, nor shall it limit or otherwise interfere with the right of the University to determine the work to be done; to assign work; to determine work schedules, standards, methods, processes, and means; or to meet with employees.

Appendix 6-D

Standard Practice Guide

SECTION: Personnel
SUBJECT: Grievance Procedure
APPLIES TO: Regular Office and Technical, Professional, Administrative and Primary Staff Members except those covered by Approved Unit Grievance Procedures.

I. Policy

A staff member shall be afforded the opportunity to file a grievance on matters directly associated with the staff member's employment relationship with the university. Filing of a grievance will not cause any reflection on the individual's status as a staff member nor will it affect future employment, compensation, or work assignments. An allegation that a staff member's rights under this policy have been violated also will be subject to review under the grievance procedure.

II. Regulations and Definitions

A. Pre-Grievance Counseling

A representative of the Personnel Office or, in cases dealing with discrimination, a representative of the Affirmative Action Program Office will be available to counsel staff members who believe they have a grievance. Pre-grievance counseling is not judgmental. The role of the counselor is to help the grievant identify the source of the problem.

A Personnel Office representative provides the grievant with information concerning university policies and Standard Practice Guides, as well as protective laws and regulations related to the potential grievance. In cases dealing with a potential discrimination grievance, an Affirmative Action Program Office representative may also inform the grievant concerning university policies as well as protective laws and regulations as they may apply.

B. Pre-Grievance Resolution

The university will make a good-faith effort to seek resolution of a problem informally brought to the attention of the Personnel Office representative (in the case of alleged discrimination, to an Affirmative Action Program Office representative) through discussion and communication with the department or unit involved and with appropriate university officials.

C. Definition

The Grievance Procedure is a three-step review process whereby a staff member may exercise the right to address matters directly associated with his or her employment in accordance with the procedures set forth in this Standard Practice Guide.

D. Time Standards

Time limits set forth for filing and appealing grievances, holding review meetings, and issuing answers must be strictly followed. Mutually agreeable adjustments in holding a review meeting and in issuing an answer may be made due to the unavailability of a necessary party. In any event, such time limit adjustments shall not be in excess of five days beyond the stated limits. The grievance is considered withdrawn if the grievant fails to appear at a scheduled review meeting or does not appeal on a timely basis.

E. Modification

The university may modify the orderly progression from Steps 1 through 3 by reducing the number of steps for grievance resolution where the origin of the grievance, the operational unit involved, or the content and scope of the grievance makes the usual progression impractical.

F. Assistance in Review Meetings

A staff member may select any individual (except a staff member who is included in a university collective bargaining unit or the grievant's immediate supervisor) to assist in the review meetings at Steps 2 and 3. If the assistant is a university staff member, the assistant will not lose time or pay for attending meetings held during the assistant's normal working hours.

G. No Loss of Time or Pay

A staff member's attendance at a grievance review meeting held during normal working hours shall be with pay. Any other time spent in formulating or preparing a grievance shall be done outside the regular work schedule and shall be without compensation.

H. Discipline Grievances

Grievances concerning discharge or disciplinary layoff will be heard directly at Step 3.

I. University Grievance Review Committee

The University Grievance Review Committee will consist of the University Personnel Director, or Assistant to the Vice-President for Academic Affairs (or their designated representative) as Chairperson, the head of the operating unit in which the grieving staff member works (or a designated representative), and other staff members who may be deemed appropriate in the review process by the chairperson because of their special sensitivity or expertise. A representative of the General Counsel's Office will be available to advise the Review Committee.

When unlawful discrimination is alleged, the University Grievance Review Committee also will include a representative from the University Affirmative Action Programs Office.

J. Failure to Appeal

If a staff member does not appeal a grievance within the time requirement set forth in the procedure below, the grievance shall be considered settled on the basis of the university's last answer.

K. Liability
Except as otherwise specifically provided, the university shall not be liable on a grievance claiming back wages or other financial reimbursement for any period prior to thirty (30) calendar days prior to knowledge of the facts giving rise to the grievance.

III. Procedure

Responsibility	Action
Staff Member	Consider involvement in Pre-Grievance Counseling and Pre-Grievance Resolution.
Representative of the Personnel Office/Affirmative Action Program Office	Counsel the employee concerning university policies, practices, Standard Practice Guides, and protective laws and regulations.
Representative of the Personnel Office/Affirmative Action Program Office	Work to informally resolve a grievance. In no event shall this effort void the time limits established in the procedure outlined in this Standard Practice Guide.
Staff Member (Step 1)	1) Within 15 calendar days (30 calendar days if the grievant works with a representative of the Personnel Office/Affirmative Action Program to informally resolve a grievance) of knowledge of the facts giving rise to the grievance, discuss grievance with immediate supervisor.
Supervisor	2) Reply orally to staff member within three (3) mutual working days from date of discussion.
Staff Member (Step 2)	3) If not satisfied with oral answer, or none received within three (3) mutual working days, may appeal in writing to department head. a) Complete the grievance form. Obtain advice as needed from Staff and Union Relations.

b) Present the grievance form to department head (or equivalent level of supervisor) or his/her designated representative within seven (7) calendar days following a timely, but unsatisfactory answer or no answer at Step 1.

Department Head 4) Upon receipt of written appeal—

a) Notify Personnel Office representative and send copy of grievance.

b) Schedule review meeting and hear oral presentation of grievance within seven (7) calendar days of receipt of written grievance.

c) Provide staff member with a written response to grievance within seven (7) calendar days of review meeting.

Staff Member (Step 3)

5) If not satisfied with the answer may appeal to the University Grievance Review Committee within fourteen (14) calendar days after receipt of Step 2 answer. If no Step 2 answer is received within seven (7) calendar days of review meeting, may appeal to the University Grievance Review Committee (grievance involving lost time, discipline, or discharge begins at Step 3).

a) Present the grievance form (including Step 2 answer) to the University Grievance Review Committee.

Chairperson—
University
Grievance Review
Committee

6) Upon receipt of written appeal—

   a) Schedule review meeting within fourteen (14) calendar days of receipt of written grievance.

   b) Review the record and any additional pertinent new information.

   c) Answer grievance in writing within sixty (60) days from date of hearing [thirty (30) days when the grievant is appealing a discharge or a lost time disciplinary action]. If the grievance involves alleged unlawful discrimination, the answer will be reviewed by the president, with no extension of time, before being issued.

Staff Member

7) No further appeal is available unless unlawful discrimination is alleged (in which case appeal, if timely, may be to an external agency).

Appendix 6-E

Sample Arbitration Procedure

SECTION: Personnel
SUBJECT: Arbitration
APPLIES TO: All Regular Non-Bargained Staff Members

I. Policy

A grievant who is dissatisfied with his or her Step 3 grievance answer concerning lost time discipline or discharge, and who is not alleging unlawful discrimination, has the right to request a hearing before an impartial arbitrator for the final and binding resolution of the grievance.

II. Regulations

A. Time standards for the pre-arbitration conference, the hearing and final decision may be adjusted by mutual agreement between the parties.

B. The grievant is encouraged though not required to obtain competent representation.

A grievant may select any individual to assist him or her in the process except staff members who are included in a collective bargaining unit. If a staff member is selected to represent the grievant, such staff member will not lose time or pay while presenting the arbitration.

C. An employee who loses time from work during the employee's assigned working hours when testifying during any arbitration shall do so without loss of time or pay.

III. Procedure

A. Time Limits

Following receipt of the University Review Committee's Step 3 answer, a grievant who is dissatisfied with such answer may appeal it to arbitration. The appeal must be made in writing on the form provided by the University, and submitted to the Chairperson of the University Review Committee within seven (7) calendar days from the date of the Step 3 answer.

B. Arbitrator Selection and Pre-Arbitration Conference
1. Upon receipt of the appeal to arbitration and the initial administrative fee, the University will request a list of five (5) qualified arbitrators from the American Arbitration Association, none of whom may be an employee of the University.
2. Upon receipt of the list of arbitrators, the chairperson of the University Review Committee and one other University Representative will schedule a Pre-Arbitration Conference within five (5) calendar days with the grievant and his or her representative. At the conference the parties will consider means of expediting the hearing by, for example, stipulating facts and authenticating proposed exhibits. Further, the parties will select an arbitrator by alternately striking names from the list of arbitrators until one remains.
3. The University shall be responsible for contacting the arbitrator and requesting a date mutually agreeable to all parties. Included in the request will be a copy of the grievance, the Step 3 answer, and the arbitration policy.

C. Arbitrator's Authority
1. The arbitrator's authority shall be limited to the evaluation of whether or not misconduct occurred.
2. The decision of the arbitrator must either sustain or deny the lost time discipline or discharge based upon proof of a violation of University rules, policies and/or regulations, whether written or unwritten.
3. The decision of the arbitrator when made in accordance with his or her jurisdiction and authority established by this procedure shall be final and binding upon all parties involved.
4. The arbitrator shall issue an expedited answer within fifteen (15) calendar days.

D. Fees and Expenses
1. The initial administrative fee charged by the American Arbitration Association is due and payable at the time of filing.
2. A fee is payable by the party causing a postponement of any scheduled hearing.

3. All other fees and expenses of the Arbitrator shall be paid jointly by the University and the grievant.

E. Liability

Awards sustaining the grievance shall *not* exceed wages the grievant otherwise would have earned, less any remuneration or payment the grievant received during the period of suspension from employment with the University.

F. Transcripts

Either the grievant or the University may arrange at its own expense, unless the parties mutually agree to share the expense, a court reporter to record and/or transcribe the hearing. The transcript or a copy thereof shall be available to the arbitrator. In the event that the party which did not arrange for the court reporter wishes a copy of the transcript, the cost of the court reporter and the transcripts shall be shared equally.

Appendix 6-F

Standard Practice Guide

SECTION: Personnel
SUBJECT: Discipline
APPLIES TO: Nonprobationary Regular Professional/Administrative, Primary, Office, Technical, and Service/Maintenance Staff Members

I. Policy

When staff conduct interferes with the orderly and efficient operation of the university, the university—when practical—will take corrective action that provides an opportunity for the staff member to change his or her conduct or attitude to avoid termination of employment.

II. Regulations and Definitions

A. Corrective Discipline

The purpose of the discipline procedure is to provide a means of correction, not punishment.

B. Just Cause

No disciplinary action, including discharge, will be taken without just cause.

C. Misconduct

Misconduct means conduct, whether by act or omission, that interferes with or affects in any way the orderly and efficient operation of the university. This includes any violation of rules and regulations or unsatisfactory work performance that is caused by other than a lack of capacity or ability, and off-duty behavior that adversely affects the employment relationship.

D. Suspension

Suspension is the interruption of active employment status (without compensation) pending investigation and a decision as to the extent of disciplinary action. Time off during a suspension may be considered part of a disciplinary layoff. The suspension should not be given for a predetermined period of time, but should last only long enough in the supervisor's judgment to permit time for investigation or cooling off or for the formulation of his or her decision after the investigation.

E. Oral Counseling

Oral counseling is discussion between the staff member and supervisor about the staff member's undesirable or unsatisfactory conduct or performance, including specific deficiencies or problems, corrective action required of the staff member, and the consequences of not complying with the expected standards of conduct.

F. Written Reprimand

A written reprimand should be in the form of a memorandum from the supervisor to the staff member, and a copy should be sent to Staff and Union Relations of the Personnel Office for the employee's personnel file. It will state the nature of the misconduct, what is required to change the conduct, by when the change must be made, and the consequences if the change is not made.

G. Disciplinary Layoff

Disciplinary layoff without compensation is a serious form of corrective action. It should only be used when supervision believes that by its use the staff member will correct his or her misconduct. In contrast to the suspension, the disciplinary layoff should be for a stated period of time but only of a duration sufficient to correct misconduct. It may range from the balance of a shift to several weeks. The staff member will be given a written statement of the reasons for the disciplinary layoff.

H. Discharge

Discharge is used when attempts to correct the employee's conduct have failed or when the improper conduct is of such a serious nature that the employment relationship should not be continued.

I. Grievances

Grievances processed by employees in the bargaining unit, which concern disciplinary layoff or discharge of nonprobationary employees, are subject to specific contract provisions. Complaints processed by non-bargaining staff members that concern disciplinary layoff or discharge of nonprobationary employees must be submitted directly at Step 3 of the complaint procedure.

J. Approval for Disciplinary Layoff or Discharge
No disciplinary action involving lost time and pay may be taken without the approval of the Staff and Union Relations section of the Personnel Office.

K. Staff Benefits if Discharged

When a staff member is discharged, the following conditions will apply to his or her staff benefits:

1. Staff members will be paid for vacation accrued at the time of discharge. In the case of staff members represented by a particular bargaining unit, specific contract provisions apply.

2. Sickness or injury disability income (sick time) that may have been accrued is canceled upon discharge.

3. Group life insurance will terminate the later of 31 days after the date of termination or at the end of the period through which premiums have been paid. During this period of time the discharged employee has conversion privileges.

4. Health insurance coverage will terminate at the end of the period for which the employee's payroll deduction pre-paid the insurance premium. During that period of time arrangements can be made to convert health insurance to individual billing.

5. Travel accident insurance ceases upon discharge.

6. The same provisions of the retirement plans apply for terminations by resignation or discharge.

III. Procedure

The Disciplinary Process

Responsibility	Action
Supervisor	

1. Investigate the circumstances surrounding the alleged misconduct and its consequences as completely as possible. Include discussion with the staff member if practicable.

2. Give a clear explanation to staff member concerning what he or she should have done, not done, or done differently, and how it should have been done.

3. If misconduct involved a violation of university rules and regulations, explain to the staff member what rules or regulations were violated and how.

4. If misconduct involved off-duty behavior adversely affecting the employment relationship, tell the staff member your understanding of the nature of the misconduct and how it adversely affects his or her employment relationship.

5. Determine appropriate disciplinary action in consultation with Staff and Union Relations Section.

6. If you decide after investigation that the unsatisfactory work performance of the employee is caused by his or her lack of capacity or ability rather than by misconduct, discuss transfer with the Staff and Union Relations Section.

7. If immediate removal of the
staff member from university
premises is necessary to prevent injury to himself, herself
or others, disruption of work
or other serious consequences,
suspend him or her indefinitely without compensation during investigation.

a. If the staff member is
represented by a particular
bargaining unit, specific
contract provisions may
also apply.

Appendix 6-G

Last Chance Agreement

This will confirm our agreement respecting the discharge and subsequent reinstatement of ___employee's name___, ___title___, ___unit___.

The University discharged ___employee's name___ effective ___date___, for ___description of misconduct___. Employee's name ___ has admitted the misconduct, and has acknowledged his awareness of ___unit___ policy prohibiting its employees from the ___misconduct___.

The union and the University agree that ___employee's name___ misconduct justifies discharge; however, the University agrees to reinstate ___employee's name___ to a ___title___ position at ___unit___ effective ___date___. The period from ___date___ through ___date___ remains as a disciplinary layoff without compensation.

This agreement constitutes full and final settlement of ___grievance number___. It is further agreed that there will be no arbitration of the matter.

This agreement does not constitute a precedent, and is without prejudice to the position the University may have taken in the past or may take in the future in cases with similar circumstances.

Date: _____

_____
Employee
Title

Date: _____

_____
For the Union
Title
Union

Date: _____

_____
For the University
Title

Grievance No. _____
Submission to Arbitration

Request for Arbitration Hearing

Date: _____

I hereby request a hearing under the arbitration provisions of Standard Practice Guide No. _____ on the following grievance:

_____

_____

_____

My share of the initial administrative fee in the amount of $_____ is attached. I understand all other fees and expenses of the Arbitrator shall be paid jointly by the University and me, except the postponement fee which is to be paid by the party causing a postponement of any scheduled hearing.

I agree to accept the decision of the arbitrator as final and binding.

_____
Employee Signature

_____
University Department

_____
University Phone Number

_____
Home Address

_____
Home Telephone Number

Last Chance Agreement—Illness

This confirms our agreement regarding the employment of _____ employee's name _____ , _____ title _____ , _____ unit _____ .

Employee's name _____ has an extensive record of absenteeism due to illness which necessitated our convening a Sick Time Conference on _____ date _____ , and a Disciplinary Review Conference on _____ date _____ .

Employee's name _____ record of absenteeism due to illness has been reviewed with you and him during the Sick Time Conference of _____ date _____ . His continuing absenteeism due to sickness, which includes an additional ___ # ___ hours of absenteeism since then, has been reviewed in the Disciplinary Review Conference of _____ date _____ .

Presently, the University agrees not to discharge _____ employee's name _____ ; however, the parties agree that should his absenteeism due to personal illness continue, he will be discharged and there will be no Disciplinary Review Conference, grievance or arbitration of such discharge.

Additionally, it is understood that this action is without prejudice to the University in the future interpretation and application of the terms of our collective bargaining agreement, or actions the University may or may not have taken in the past or may or may not take in the future in cases with similar circumstances.

Date: _____

_____
Employee

Date: _____

_____
For the Union
Title
Union

Date: _____

_____
For the University
Title

_____

Last Chance Agreement—Misconduct

This will confirm our agreement of ___date___, regarding the employment of _____employee's name_____
_____, ___title___, _____unit_____.

The University suspended _____employee's name_____
on ___date___, and subsequently conducted a Disciplinary Review Conference on ___date___, to investigate his misconduct of ___date___ when he engaged in an
_____description of misconduct_____.

The Union and _____employee's name_____ recognize that such behavior constitutes serious misconduct, justifying discharge from the University; however, in recognition of employee's name service to the University and work record, the University agrees not to discharge employee's name at this time, but to convert the period of his suspension to a disciplinary layoff without pay effective ___date___.

The Union and _____employee's name_____ agree that this agreement serves as full and final settlement of this matter, and that there will be no grievance or arbitration of _____employee's name_____ suspension or disciplinary layoff.

Additionally, it is expressly understood that should _____employee's name_____ engage in similar misconduct in the future, he will be discharged, but only following a thorough investigation of the facts by Staff and Union Relations and there will be no grievance or arbitration of his discharge.

This agreement is without prejudice to the University in the application or interpretation of our bargaining agreement, or any actions the University may or may not have taken in the past or may or may not take in the future in cases of similar circumstances.

Endorsed in full agreement:

Date: _____   _____
                                    Employee

Date: _____   _____
                                    For the Union
                                    Title
                                    Union

Date: _____   _____
                         For the University
                         Title

Appendix 6-H

Full and Final Release
for Severance Pay

FOR AND IN CONSIDERATION of the sum of
_____ paid to _____ as sever-
ance pay by the University, receipt of which is hereby acknowledged, _____ for himself/herself,
his/her heirs, administrators and executors, does hereby fully
and forever release, acquit and discharge the University, its
agents, servants and representatives, of and from any and all
claims, demands, actions and causes of action of every kind,
nature and description which _____ may
have had, may now have or may hereafter have by reason of
any matter, cause, act or omission arising out of or in connection with _____ 's employment and/or ter-
mination of employment by _____ _____.

IT IS UNDERSTOOD AND ACKNOWLEDGED that
this Release is executed and the aforementioned payment is
made in final settlement and compromise of any disputed
claims and shall not be, and shall not be construed to be, an
admission of any obligation or liability by the University, its
agents, servants and representatives, or related companies by
whom any obligation or liability is expressly denied.

IT IS FURTHER UNDERSTOOD AND ACKNOWL-
EDGED that _____ has no right to severance
pay under any policy and that the payment received pursuant
to this Release is consideration for _____ 's
final release of all claims.

IT IS FURTHER UNDERSTOOD AND ACKNOWL-
EDGED that the terms of this Release are contractual and not
a mere recital and that there are no agreements, understandings or representations made by the University, its agents,
servants and representatives, except as expressly stated
herein.

_____ represents and acknowl-
edges that before signing this Release he/she has read the
same, that he/she fully understands its terms, content and
effect, that he/she has had the benefit of advice from an
attorney of his/her own choosing and has relied fully and

completely on his/her own judgment and the advice of his/her attorney in executing this Release.

IN WITNESS WHEREOF, _____ has executed this FULL AND FINAL RELEASE as his/her free act and deed this _____ day of _____, 199__.

Full and Final Release
of All Claims

FOR AND IN CONSIDERATION of the payment of
_____ ($_____) Dollars gross wages, less
appropriate withholding, paid to _____ as
severance pay by _____, receipt of which is
hereby acknowledged, _____ for him/her-
self, his heirs, administrators and executors, does hereby fully
and forever release, acquit and discharge _____
_____, its agents, servants and represen-
tatives, of and from any and all claims, demands, actions and
causes of action of every kind, nature and description which
_____ may have had, may now have or may
hereafter have by reason of any matter, cause, act or omission arising out of or in connection with
_____'s employment and/or termination
of employment by _____.

IT IS UNDERSTOOD AND ACKNOWLEDGED that
this Release is executed and the aforementioned payment is
made in final settlement and compromise of any disputed
claims and shall not be, and shall not be construed to be, an
admission of any obligation or liability by _____
_____, its agents, servants and representatives, or related
companies by whom any obligation or liability is expressly
denied.

IT IS FURTHER UNDERSTOOD AND ACKNOWL-
EDGED that _____ has no right to severance
pay under any _____ policy and that the
payment received pursuant to this Release is consideration
for ___ _____'s final release of all claims.

IT IS FURTHER UNDERSTOOD AND ACKNOWL-
EDGED that _____ does not now, and rep-
resents and warrants that he/she will not in the future, seek
reemployment, employment or independent contractor status with or by _____, or any company,
agency or entity controlled, owned or operated by it or any
parent or controlling entity of it. He/she agrees that such is
fair and just under all of the relevant facts and circumstances.

IT IS FURTHER UNDERSTOOD AND ACKNOWL-
EDGED that the terms of this Release are contractual and not

a mere recital and that there are no agreements, understandings or representations made by _____ , its agents, servants and representatives, except as expressly stated herein.

_____ represents and acknowledges that before signing this Release he/she read the same, that he/she fully understands its terms, content and effect, that he/she has had the benefit of advice from an attorney of his/her own choosing and has relied fully and completely on his/her own judgment and the advice of his/her attorney in executing this Release.

IN WITNESS WHEREOF, _____ has executed this FULL AND FINAL RELEASE OF ALL CLAIMS as his/her free act and deed this _____ day of _____, 199__.

CHAPTER 7

Training and Development

Jack Hug
Assistant Vice Chancellor
Physical Plant Services
University of California, San Diego

7.1 INTRODUCTION

The recognition that people are our most valuable resource and that they are a great storehouse of knowledge has given emphasis to training and development programs in our college and university physical plant departments. Participation in these programs by physical plant staff is at an all-time high, and includes employees who are required to learn new skills, those who have changed careers, those who have new job responsibilities, as well as a variety of other participants.

The type of programs and degree of participation is as broad and as varied as the population of colleges and universities themselves. As a form of "continuing education" in our physical plant departments, the training and development activities are being fueled by changing technologies, individual desires for self-improvement, and an ever-widening gap between existing skills and knowledge and the required performance.

Generalization is always risky, but experience shows that a high percentage of our college and university physical plant departments (large and small) regularly participate in training and development programs of one kind or another. The choice of programs differs greatly and is appropriately influenced by a variety of factors, some of which include:

- Department structure, size, and responsibility
- Department demographics
- Available skills and knowledge

- Department mission
- Policy
- Resources
- Management commitment
- Individual interests.

A variety of forms and practices are utilized. Some are structured, formal, and well thought out, while others are unstructured, informal, and randomly approached.

The training and development function is a complex task that, requires careful planning, professional guidance, and knowledge of the human resource.

The physical plant department provides a unique environment in which work, in the variety of daily activities, provides an excellent opportunity for staff growth and development.

Physical plant department training and development needs differ greatly from one campus to another. Most organizations are complex and multifaceted, with widely varying organizational purposes, priorities, programs, and orientation practices. To prescribe programs to meet all circumstances would be foolish and impractical. We cannot provide effective "one-stop shopping" for a department's total training and development needs. Department training and development programs must be tailored to meet each department's unique circumstances and needs.

Physical plant departments meet their training needs in various ways. Some have developed in-house training programs, others utilize ready-made programs produced by commercial and professional training companies, while still others use a combination of in-house and commercial programs. Given the variety of choices, it can be difficult to select the best. APPA provides quality training and development programs for physical plant staff. These programs can be recommended without hesitation as a source for physical plant department staff training and development.

The human resource professionals working in staff development offices often do not have the resources nor the expertise to cover the broad arena of physical plant human resource training and development needs. Some universities met this need by incorporating a full-time position as part of the physical plant organization to work with department managers in developing and coordinating training and development programs.

Other universities have hired or contracted with a professional trainer for a specific program, on a one-time or ongoing basis (quarterly or semi-annually). Still others have used the committee approach, often to complement a professional contract, consultant, or full-time staff person. Training and development committees are usually advisory in nature and comprise a cross section of department members. The committee's charge varies but encompasses the responsibility to develop, assess, locate, and recommend training and development programs that fit departmental needs.

As with many other decisions, in order to be effective the choice of a training and development program requires careful thought, planning, and preparation.

7.2 THE MANAGER'S RESPONSIBILITY

There are few management responsibilities that are more important than for training and development. This does not mean managers themselves should personally conduct training programs. However, they should know what training is needed by the department, where to get this training, and how to plan and provide the resources required to manage an effective program for the training and development of physical plant staff.

It is understood that a primary and related responsibility of the physical plant department at colleges and universities is effective management of assets. If it is agreed that the assets include the physical facilities as well as the human asset (often referred to as the most valuable asset), then it follows that the training and development of physical plant staff are among the primary responsibilities of the physical plant manager.

Managers are expected to know the department mission. The questions of "what is our business?" and "what should our business be?" will continue to be asked by physical plant managers who are faced with keeping pace with demands for department services. The effective renewal of our human resource skills, knowledge, and performance is management responsibility.

Choosing appropriate and effective training and development programs is a difficult task that requires the application of professional human resource management principles, supported by management through policy, planning, and allocation of resources.

It has been accurately stated that all development is self-development: That a department of physical plant can assume total responsibility for the development of an individual is an idle boast. No department is obligated to substitute its efforts for the self development efforts of individuals. However, every manager in the organization has an opportunity to encourage or discourage individual self-development. The manager should be assigned the specific responsibility of helping assigned staff to focus, direct, and apply self-development efforts. To aid in this, an effective and vital physical plant department will make available to its managers development challenges and development experiences. Says management expert Peter Drucker: "Just as no one learns as much about a subject as someone who is forced to teach it, no one develops as much as the one who is trying to help others develop themselves."[1]

Policy

In order to establish a meaningful training and development program, management must make its direction clear to those who must apply its policies. See Figure 7-1 for an example of a training and development policy.

Figure 7-1
PHYSICAL PLANT SERVICES
POLICY ON EMPLOYEE DEVELOPMENT

Physical Plant Services actively supports the policy of the University concerning employee development as identified by the Staff Personnel Policy Manual. You are encouraged to read the Staff Personnel Policy Manual and identify those areas where, as a manager/supervisor, you have specific responsibilities.

Our primary emphasis is:
    Training directed toward the position related programs. We must develop and have available the needed skills to meet our department's primary purpose.

An important secondary emphasis is:
    To provide development and educational opportunities (Career Related Programs) for career advancement within the organization.

Before any request for career related training will be considered, a training plan, specific to the individual requesting the training, must be developed and approved by the appropriate supervisor/manager.

A companion document to this Physical Plant Services Policy, "Training and Development Guidelines for Supervisors and Managers," has been prepared for your use in application to this policy.

Some physical plant departments have published a resource guide to assist in communicating department policy and programs to the staff. Several of the key points include:

- An overall university policy concerning employee training and development is supported.
- The program's primary and secondary emphasis is identified.
- The policy must be easily understood and communicated throughout the department to *all levels* of the organization with plenty of opportunities and encouragement for discussion.
- To ensure success, department managers must be thoroughly familiar with the policy and be prepared to answer questions and to implement the policy when appropriate.
- The policy must include a "user-friendly" participation process to facilitate training and development; in other words, a "no hassle" method of participation.
- The policy must support and reinforce the department mission.

A well-considered training and development policy for physical plant staff will provide strong support for management's commitment, will keep programs proactive and focused as well as greatly reduce or eliminate ad hoc requests. It clearly establishes that training and development is not reserved for a select few, but rather is available wherever appropriate to support previously identified needs.

Human Resources

The primary purpose of human resource development is to improve organizational and individual performance in achieving institutional goals. Training and development are essential elements of human resource management responsibilities that enable managers to examine the mission's effectiveness, to fine tune it, or move the mission forward. The term "training" usually refers to learning to increase effectiveness in doing one's job. "Development" generally connotes learning that prepares the individual for increased or new responsibilities.[2]

The fact that physical plant departments are composed of adults, dictates that successful training and development programs adopt many features of the tried and proven methods of adult education (continuing education), and requires that we have some understanding of how adults learn.

Stephen Brookfield provides a summary of the principles of adult learning taken from years of study and the experience of nine other leading authorities on adult learning.

> Adults learn throughout their lives, with the negotiations of the transitional stages in the lifespan being the immediate causes and motives for much of this learn-

ing. They exhibit diverse learning styles—strategies for coding information, cognitive procedures, mental sets—and learn in different ways, at different times, for different purposes. As a rule, however, they like their learning activities to be problem centered and to be meaningful to their life situation, and they want the learning outcomes to have some immediacy of application. The past experiences of adults affect their current learning, sometimes serving as an enhancement, sometimes as a hindrance. Effective learning is also linked to the adult's subscription to a self-concept of himself or herself as a learner. Finally, adults exhibit a tendency toward self-directedness in their learning.[3]

7.3 NEEDS ANALYSIS

Purpose

A needs analysis of training and development within the physical plant department can aid in identifying specific goals for a program. Experts advise that managers begin with an analysis of what the department is currently doing in this area, since many times managers are not totally aware of all of the programs already in existence. It is important to catalog existing formal and informal programs, and to develop a status inventory to provide a starting point.

Most physical plant departments actively participate in some form of training and development, without formal programs. Ray Fortunato and Dennis Kaiser make an excellent point in emphasizing that managers should look at existing programs and start from there in performing a needs analysis of department training and development needs.[4]

Data on current training and development activities should be analyzed and evaluated to determine the best aspects of existing programs and to develop a plan for a more comprehensive approach to assessing departmental needs. The identification of the department's training and development needs through a needs assessment will serve as the cornerstone for a comprehensive program for the physical plant department.

Process/Methods

An effective needs analysis requires some preliminary work, including the following steps.

Front-end Analysis   Begin with what is already being done. Look at the formal programs. Look at the informal programs. Keep the best. Catalog the programs in order to assess training needs.

Methods commonly used for needs assessment include surveys/questionnaires, review of records and documents, interviews, and observations.

Surveys   There are many methods of conducting surveys to determine training and development needs. One popular method is called the "perception" method, in which specific staff members are asked what types of programs interest them in meeting perceived problems connected with their work. Since people sometimes find it difficult to be objective when it comes to assessing their own strengths and weaknesses, the perception concept of surveying also can be used for that individual's immediate supervisor. A comparison can be done between the individual's perceived need and that of the individual's supervisor.

A sample needs assessment for a supervisory management training and development program, patterned on the perception method, is found in Figure 7-2.

Review of Records and Documents   A review of accident reports, grievances, performance evaluations, new policy releases, supervisor reports, purchase requisitions for new equipment and special tools, literature concerning the job, and other such records can give clues to training needs.

Interview   The interview is a common method of determining needs, and can be performed effectively one-on-one or in small groups. Frequently, these interviews will generate requests for many training needs that can be easily identified. A good question to ask staff is, "What do you need to help you do your job better?" Often overlooked is the need for basic training, especially for those employees who have not had the opportunity of working with a solid "mentor" as a first boss.

Observation   Observation is another method that can be used for determining training and development needs for the physical plant. Simply observing work activities, inspecting and reviewing the work performed, and identifying the cost to perform specific functions can provide valuable information.

For most jobs in the department, relatively standardized procedures can be followed to obtain satisfactory needs assessment. On the other hand, an analysis of a manager's job is not as simple. The complex and ambiguous nature of the manager's job makes it difficult for the man-

Figure 7–2

Needs Assessment—Supervisory Management Training and Development

I have the following perceptions of my training and development needs in order to improve my performance as a supervisor:

Perceived Level of Need

	Important	Moderate	Little	Don't Know
Skills in Interviewing				
Speaking to Groups				
Time Management				
Motivation				
Delegating				
Dealing With Stress				
Creating Teamwork				
Planning				
Alcohol & Drug Usage				
Managing Difficult Personalities				
Performance Appraisal Discussions				
Making Discipline Productive				
Making Decisions				
Writing (Letters & Reports)				
Oral Communications				
Speed Reading & Understanding				
Other (Specify)				
Other (Specify)				
Other (Specify)				

My department is: _____

ager to describe just what it entails and how it is done. Much of the manager's time is spent in interpersonal interaction and in thinking. One way to assess a manager's need for training and development is to use what Stephen Brookfield describes as the Critical Incident Method.[5]

Critical Incident Method   An example of a do-it-yourself approach for determining a manager's training and development needs is called a critical incident method. This method is good for use with one or one hundred staff persons and is especially effective for use with managers and supervisors. The critical incident method begins with a brief written statement that is requested from each person. The written statement forces them to think about specific happenings. This exercise provides the director with a series of one-paragraph statements from each manager regarding their feelings and perception of the problems they face doing their job.

An example of a critical incident exercise is as follows. Think back over the past six months and identify a job-related incident that you remember as one that caused you the greatest discomfort, that caused pressures and/or difficulty. Write a brief description of no more than half a page, including the following details about the incident.

1. Where and when it occurred,
2. Who was involved (you can use roles rather than names), and
3. What was so significant about the incident to cause you problems.[6]

7.4 TRAINING GROUPS

It is important to keep in mind during the needs assessment process that there are many different "training groups" in the physical plant department. A good place to begin in identifying training groups is to review the department's organization chart. A typical physical plant organization has managers, professionals, supervisors, and support staff, and each of these groups has different training and development needs. Before proceeding, it is helpful to consider the consequences of training and development for each of these four groups.

Managers

Peter F. Drucker, often referred to as the founding father of the science of management, has noted that the years since 1950 have been a veritable management development boom, within the wider management boom. In the mid-1940s, only two companies that had given serious thought to the development of managers—Sears Roebuck in America, and Marks and Spenser in England. At that time, there were only three university programs in America for the continuing advanced education of managers: the Sloan Program at the Massachusetts Institute of Technology; the programs at New York Graduate Business School for the Continuing Education of Managers and Young Professionals; and the Advanced Management Program at the Harvard Business School.

By the mid-1950s, the number of these programs had increased to 3,000 and a great many of the universities in the United States had incorporated all kinds of advanced management programs.

Today, it is impossible to count the number of companies that in some way address the development of management and managers. In addition, an untold number of organizations, such as trade associations and consulting firms, have gone into the management development business.

The task of managing a physical plant department has become increasingly complex. In addition to rapidly changing technology, managers must be able to handle "relations" problems—relations with faculty, staff, suppliers, customers, labor unions, and others. On top of this are demands to be creative and innovative; to manage knowledge and the information worker; to understand multi-cultural staff management; and to take responsibility for the environment that produces and provides what has become known as the quality of work life. These factors and others increase the complexity of the standards against which managers are measured.

Professionals

Personnel classified as professional in the physical plant organization usually include engineers, architects, analysts, or individuals working in an area of specialty or expertise. More and more, the staff professional in the physical plant needs a broad-based exposure to other areas in the department and to other departments. In some instances professionals act as a group leaders, managers, or supervisors.

An excellent starting point and source for broad-based training and development for the professional is the APPA Institute for Facilities Management. The Institute, consisting of a standard three-track program plus timely specialized courses, provides the highest level of comprehensive professional instruction for physical plant managers of all levels.

Professional staff have specific needs, and as a training group may need a program more tailored to those specific needs. Most certainly, the professional employees' specific needs will vary greatly from one physical plant department environment to another. It is important that the department training and development program recognize specific needs of this group and incorporate them in planning the department's comprehensive training and development program.

Supervisors

Just as other groups have different goals, purposes, and objectives associated with their work, supervisors have specific needs as a training and development group. There have been more training and development books, courses, seminars, and programs available for supervisors than any other group of physical plant employees. A multitude of programs are available, from basic supervision for the new supervisor to advanced supervision and management development for the more experienced supervisors. The challenge for the physical plant manager is not in finding a program, but in finding a good program that meets the individual needs of the particular supervisor. A tailor-made program for supervisors, designed for the best fit, is in order, especially for training and development of physical plant supervisors.

In physical plant departments, it is the support staff that carries out most of the work of the organization. The supervisory role in physical plant is extremely demanding and is most often characterized by ambiguous or uncertain authority. The supervisory training group represents a significant segment of the department organization—it is not uncommon to find supervisory to support staff ratios averaging 1:10 or 1:15.

The supervisor is required to prepare, instruct, translate, direct, and otherwise communicate management's concepts and priorities to the work force. "Make no doubt about it; an organization's policies and procedures stand or fall on the competency of its supervision. This competency, in turn, depends in large measure on the quality of training and development its supervisors receive."[7]

Because of the unique position of the supervisor in the organizational structure, supervisory training is considered different and separate from the training of managers. The role of the supervisor, functioning as a dual interface between management and workers, is the only role of its kind in the organization. In addition to their special role, nearly 75 percent of all supervisors rise from the lower ranks rather than entering their position directly from college or from a high level professional occupation. Bittel wrote, "The unique nature of the supervisory job creates a supervisory segment of managers that is distinct from other managers."[8]

Few supervisors have the inclination, knowledge, or resources to provide for their own development. Thus, most physical plant supervisors depend upon the guidance, instruction, and structural support that only top management and the human resources professional can provide.

Supervisory training is extremely popular in the United States. Nearly 1 out of every 6 organizations offer some form of program for first-line supervisors—providing an average of 32 hours of training.[9]

Support Staff

Support staff in the physical plant department can be defined as non-supervisory workers. This staff generally consists of skilled, semi-skilled, and minimally-skilled employees. Many jobs that require minimal skill (at entry level) and some semi-skilled jobs fall within the categories of custodial services, grounds, and landscape operations. Frequently, minimum formal education is required, with no previous experience. A willingness to report for work and to work hard are the basic criteria for employee selection into this group. On most campuses, these positions comprise the majority of the physical plant department.

A standard training program for this group does not exist. Some of the reasons for this are the variety of assignments, duties, and responsibilities given to this group; the changing nature of their work; newer methods, materials, machinery, and equipment; wide variances among institutions in level of program commitment; geographic conditions affecting the campus, and ethnic makeup of the personnel. Some colleges and universities have developed certified programs and require all new employees to participate in and successfully complete a training program before they are given a regular work assignment. Such a program for custodial services has been successful in maintaining quality control and for maintenance of standards.

For the semi-skilled and skilled support staff, many universities actively participate in apprenticeship programs. Such programs are usually offered in the trades such as plumbing, painting, carpentry, air conditioning, sheetmetal, electrical, electronics, and automotive mechanics. Some institutions have a formal apprenticeship program maintaining an adequate supply of skilled employees. The particular market and geographic area of the institution has a major influence on a physical plant department's approach and emphasis in participating in apprenticeship programs. Apprenticeship programs can be certified and established in conjunction with the Federal Bureau of Apprenticeships and Training, through equivalent state agencies, or independently. However, when employees in an apprentice trade in a college or university are members of a union, by law the union's cooperation must be solicited. Both parties covered by the collective bargaining agreement must approve the program if it is to be certified by the U. S. Department of Labor.

Most apprenticeship programs involve 4,000 to 8,000 hours of specific training in two parts: self-study and on-the-job training. The self-study part of the training covers both theoretical and practical training. Frequently, such training is taken through correspondence study, in which case tests are administered and certified as part of the formal program.

Specified work performed on the job, under supervision, is the second important part of the apprenticeship process. Both parts of the apprenticeship program must be carefully monitored and graded. Performance evaluations are made regularly and a log is maintained of work successfully completed.

Most apprentices prefer to receive an official certificate indicating their satisfactory completion of a governmental-sanctioned apprenticeship program. Thus, while informal apprenticeship programs may be feasible for some physical plant departments, they usually are not as well received by the participants. Colleges and universities that consider formal apprenticeships for skilled tradespeople are encouraged to seek advice from those who have had experience in structuring such programs. A list of colleges and universities with apprenticeship programs for physical plant staff is available through the APPA office.

7.5 PLANNING A COMPREHENSIVE PROGRAM

The cornerstone of any effective training and development program is an accurate, high-quality needs assessment. When planning a training and development program, some of the questions that need to be answered include Who, What, and How. It is essential to establish where you are now as a starting point, with an eye toward where you want to be in order to determine what must be done in the meantime. (See Figure 7-3.)

Ingredients of a Quality Program

Who needs training?   Who needs development? Who needs training and development? In physical plant departments, the answer is that practically everyone needs some level of training and development. It is recommended that a detailed review of the department organizational structure be conducted to identify the specific training group, or person, for whom the training and development is intended. This may sound quite elementary, but in approaching training and development as a

Figure 7-3

Needs-Inventory Format

Respondents rate each item according to a scale of 3 "extremely important," 2 "fairly important," and 1 "not too relevant."

_____ Ability to set realistic goals and standards, define performance requirements, and develop action plans for achieving and for controlling (tracking) performance.

_____ Skill in communicating effectively in face-to-face situations—with subordinates, peers, superiors, customers, etc.

_____ Ability to conduct selection interviews in a way that produces the information needed to make sound hiring decisions consistent with company policy and the law.

_____ Skill in balancing daily activities between the demands of the task (production-oriented side) and of the employees (people-oriented side).

_____ Ability to challenge and motivate subordinates, thereby increasing their job satisfaction and developing a team of "turned-on" employees.

_____ Skill in giving on-the-job training and counseling relating to behavior at work.

_____ Ability to appraise performance objectively and to conduct regular, constructive performance reviews that are two-way dialogs.

_____ Skill in writing letters, memos, and reports that are clear, concise, complete, and compelling—writing that gets action.

_____ Ability to manage time (of self and others) effectively by prioritizing, controlling interruptions, measuring cost-effectiveness, investing rather than spending time, etc.

_____ Skill in cutting costs through methods improvement, work simplification or reallocation, flow charting, analysis of procedures, etc.

_____ Ability to hold meetings, briefings, conferences that are well-organized, crisp, and results-oriented.

_____ Skill in negotiating and resolving conflict as it arises in interpersonal relations.

_____ Facility in interviewing in depth, drawing out what is and isn't said, summarizing and clarifying, and organizing the speaker's message so that it can be acted upon.

_____ Ability to identify problems, to separate causes from symptoms, to evaluate evidence, to weigh alternatives, and to select and implement appropriate solutions.

_____ Ability to make effective presentations and to sell ideas in a persuasive, well-documented manner—to management, to subordinates, to users.

Source: Adapted from Scott B. Parry and Edward J. Robinson, "Management Development: Training or Education?" _Training and Development Journal_ (July 1979):9–10

comprehensive plan for the entire physical plant, it is necessary to take this first step.

Identifying the four training groups, as identified earlier in this chapter, can serve as a good starting point. These training groups should represent everyone in the organization. The needs of each member of each group will be different, but some significant similarities will emerge in training needs among the individuals within each particular group.

When looking at the various training groups, it is important to pay attention to the numbers in each group; this will be helpful in structuring the comprehensive program. Keep in mind that the program should be pertinent to the participants' needs in relation to their job within the organization.

What kind of training and development is needed?   Applying this question to each specific training group and by applying the needs assessment techniques mentioned earlier, will provide important information for planning for the department's specific training and development needs.

A needs assessment will produce a lot of information and may appear overwhelming; a seemingly insurmountable list of needs for each group will be assembled. Take heart, because this is the objective. Critical issues and training needs will surface within each group, and the needs can be ranked in priority order: 1) the must do, 2) the need to do, and 3) the important but not urgent. These are all good starting points for sorting training and development needs. In addition, identify the difference between those programs that will "produce success" and those that are "failure preventers" will become obvious.

Information obtained from the needs assessment can be refined to carve out the appropriate match between who to train and what training is needed.

Methods and Applications

Once there are answers to who is to be trained and what training is needed, it is time to address how to package the training program. The choice of methods are many and varied, ranging from a one-hour lecture and film package to a five-day retreat in the mountains.

It is helpful to separate the choices into two general headings—on-the-job training and off-the-job training.

On-the-Job Training

On-the-job training programs generally require no special space or equipment and are a common way for physical plant personnel to receive instruction. This is a practical approach, since often the trainee can learn and produce some work at the same time. It is estimated that 60 percent of training in most companies occurs on the job.[10] On-the-job training may be formally scheduled and planned and can include lectures, demonstrations, simulations, and practice, or may be informal and conducted by first-line supervisors or managers. Several important points concerning on-the-job training are supported by research and are important to keep in mind when choosing training methods.[11] Research has shown that:

- Skills learned in the work place, and tied directly to the job to be done, are learned faster, retained longer, and result in greater productivity gains than skills learned in the classroom.
- The immediacy of the task, and the idea that it yields the same output as that for which the employee was hired, make the "event of training" salient to the employee.

When the supervisor turns to the employee and says, "Okay, now you do it," the motivation to learn and the mechanism of learning are clearly established. Thus, two factors play an important role in the success of on-the-job training: the relevance of the task itself, and the fact that the person doing the training will be holding the worker accountable for the result.

On-the-job training usually involves a supervisor or manager showing an employee what to do and how to do it, in order to produce some specific output or process. Common practices of on-the-job training include:

- Job orientation
- Apprenticeship training
- Job rotation
- Coaching
- Internship.

A word of caution: charging supervisors/managers with becoming trainers in addition to their many other responsibilities is no guarantee of a successful on-the-job training program. There is a wide degree of difference in the capabilities of supervisors/managers to effectively present information and conduct the training. Some are good at it and others are not.

Off-the-Job Training

In most off-the-job training programs, the training process cannot be as closely related to the job as in on-the-job training. Off-the-job training varies greatly, but is generally considered to be a formal training program that has as its chief advantages:

- It lets the trainee get away from the pressures of the job.
- It provides resource people and resource material—faculty, colleagues and associates, and books—that contribute suggestions and ideas.
- It presents a challenge to employees that, in general, enhances their motivation to learn.

The major weakness of many off-the-job programs is their failure to incorporate materials that will facilitate transfer of training back to the job. A great deal of potential benefit to the individual and to the department is lost unless a departmental plan exists for capturing the new perspectives and ideas to reinforce on-the-job learning with off-the-job.[12]

Descriptions of the most common types of off-the-job training follow.

The Lecture   The lecture is, of course, the old standby—the traditional method of transmitting information to others in a classroom setting. It is the most widely used of all the techniques, both on and off the job.

Special Study   Suitable reading matter for trainees often serves the same aims as the lecture, but with greater success. A reader is able to stop when necessary, make notes, check back on earlier portions of materials to clarify meaning, and consult other books as the program progresses. A department library is an important training and management aid. Special study programs also include special university programs for supervisors and managers and executive management programs.

Films/Videotapes/Videodiscs   Films offer some unique advantages over other off-the-job techniques. Skillful editing can increase the extent that the film conforms to a particular point of emphasis or need that has been identified in the department. Films allow subject matter to be organized optimally and utilized with a skillful lecturer. Films are most effective if they are planned from the trainees' viewpoint by considering their current level of readiness to learn, their interest in learning, and the difficulties encountered in the process.

Television   While television permits no interaction between trainee and trainer, like films it can make use of the most skillful instructor and can be the most efficiently organized way to present material to large numbers of people. Video teleconferencing has become popular and is an effective way to use the television media.

Conferences/Workshops/Seminars   Training in conferences, workshops, or seminars involves a carefully planned meeting with a specific purpose. This method has proven particularly suitable for teaching conceptual data and for developing modifications in attitudes and outlooks.

Case Study   The case study method is based on the belief that managerial understanding and confidence can best be attained through the study, contemplation, and discussion of concrete cases and examples rather than through other common training methods. Many variations are possible in the specific application of case studies, but generally, trainees are presented with a written case describing a concrete example of an organizational problem and are asked to study it and propose the best solution. The case study method is designed to promote the trainees' discovery of underlying principles; rather than seeking a single answer, trainees ferret out appropriate and useful questions that may suggest several alternative solutions.

Role Playing   Role playing involves participants assuming specific roles and acting out significant events. Instead of just talking about solving the problems at hand, trainees spontaneously play out solutions to these problems as they think the person whose role they are playing might view them.

Programmed Instruction   More than in any other training technique, programmed instruction materials are constructed to ensure that at a particular moment in the learning process, trainees are ready, willing, and able to deal with the material confronting them and to take an active part in the learning process. The material is planned so that trainees receive immediate knowledge of the results of their response and that their learning occurs in an optimum sequence of the separate steps.

Computer-Based Training

Computer-based training is one of the newest methods of training and development utilized for physical plant staff. The rapid proliferations of the personal computers in physical plant departments is providing much interest in computer-based training delivery systems. Computer-based training replaces the instructor with a computer software program. Although in its infancy, improvements in the courseware available are encouraging and more and more useful programs for physical plant departments are on the way.

The single most dramatic impact of training and development is realized when departments become more effective in providing physical plant services. Today's environment requires appropriate training and development programs to increase performance effectively against the backdrop of ever-changing conditions.

7.6 IMPLEMENTING THE PROGRAM

A successful program begins with careful planning and the application of the principles and practices outlined in this chapter. Paramount in importance is:

- *The starting point*—management commitment.
- *Coupled to*—a carefully planned program that is based on a needs assessment, matched with the organization's mission, goals, and objectives.
- *Backed by*—a training and development policy that is easily understood, communicated throughout the department, and supported by a user-friendly process for employee participation in the training programs.
- *Reinforced through*—an organizational climate and work environment on the job that encourages and rewards the continuing education, training, and development process.
- *Matched to*—realistic and achievable resources available for training and development.

It is not practical to expect one person to train all areas of the physical plant department. But, one individual—whether full-time, part-time, or contracted consultant—can function as a program creator or coordinator. The coordination of training and development resources, with this responsibility clearly identified, will go a long way toward implementing an effective training and development program.

7.7 SPECIAL PROGRAMS

Managers and supervisors are made, not born; they need opportunities to acquire the skills necessary to manage today and to be effective tomorrow.

Management Development

Managing a physical plant department is a complex undertaking, and the development of managers must be taken seriously. Management development starts by asking, "What kind of manager do we need in order to carry out the department mission?" Quality training programs for managers can be useful tools, but the development of the manager requires more than just taking courses. Training programs need to be matched to the job.

Looking at the general characteristics of a manager's job can provide a clue as to why management development may require special attention. Typically, the physical plant manager must solve constantly changing and must deal with many unknowns. The manager's tasks include planning, coordinating, evaluating, negotiating, supervising and investigating. These tasks require skills in gathering information, solving problems, and making decisions. An effective development program for a manager must reflect these functions and be matched to the skills required of each individual manager.

Drucker has written, "The development of managers focuses on the person. Its aim is to enable the manager to develop abilities and strengths to the fullest extent and to find individual achievement."[13] As with other training programs, the starting point for any management development program is performance appraisal and needs assessment. The selection of courses, seminars, and programs can then follow much more easily with some assurance that the manager's needs will be met through a specific program. This tailoring of the development program also encourages the manager to assume a share of the responsibility for personal as well as institutional development.

It is no longer appropriate in the physical plant profession to contend that manager development is a luxury afforded only to the large universities. The demand for good managers has increased faster than even the most successful programs can supply them.

An excellent example of a management development program designed to meet the needs of the physical plant manager is the Executive Development Institute for Facilities Managers, offered annually by APPA in conjunction with the University of Notre Dame College of Business Administration.

Supervisory Development

The physical plant manager who wants to recognize the challenge of supervisory development is well-advised to read the following books by Lester R. Bittel: *What Every Supervisor Should Know* and *The Complete Guide to Supervisory Training and Development*. These two books provide extensive and detailed coverage of all the basics of supervisory training, from determining supervisory training needs and developing a training curriculum and its specific programs, to issues of supervisor selection and career development.

For further reference in preparing a program for supervisory training and development, Bittel has also included an invaluable collection of twenty-five model course outlines and actual training materials, from a productivity improvement program to a listing of supervisory audio tapes, films/videos, and packaged programs.

7.8 SUMMARY

Human resource management in a physical plant department is a complex and ever-changing job. To be effective, management commitment is required and a professional approach to this subject must be taken. Training and development for physical plant staff at all levels is a life-long process; it is constantly in motion and changing. Managing a program with such a profound effect on this most important physical plant asset is a worthwhile and challenging endeavor for the physical plant professional.

NOTES

1. Drucker, Peter. *Management Tasks, Responsibilities, Practices*, 1985.
2. Fortunato, Ray T., and Dennis W. Keiser. *Human Resource Development in Higher Education Institutions*, College and University Personnel Association, 1985.
3. Brookfield, Stephen D. *Understanding and Facilitating Adult Learning*, 1986.
4. See note 2.
5. See note 3.
6. See note 1.
7. Bittel, Lester R. *Supervisory Training and Development*. Addison-Wesley Publishing Co., Inc, 1987.
8. See note 7.
9. See note 7.
10. Wehrenberg, Stephen B. "Supervisors as Trainers: The Long-Term Gains of OJT," *Training*, April 1984.
11. See note 10.
12. Bass, Bernard M. and James A. Vaughan. *Training in Industry: The Management of Learning*, Brooks/Cole Publishing Company, Belmont, California, 1966.
13. See note 1.

ADDITIONAL RESOURCES

American Society for Training and Development. *Supervisory Training: Approaches and Methods*. Alexandria, Virginia: ASTD.

Apps, J.W. *The Adult Learner on Campus: A Guide for Instructors and Administrators*. New York: Cambridge Books, 1981.

Argyris, C. *Reasoning, Learning, and Action: Individual and Organizational*. San Francisco: Jossey-Bass Inc., 1982.

Arms, D., B. Chenevy, C. Karrer, and C.J. Rumpler. In *Andragogy in Action: Applying Modern Principles of Adult Learning*, by M.S. Knowles. San Francisco: Jossey-Bass Inc., 1984.

Association of Physical Plant Administrators of Universities and Colleges. *Personnel Management and Development*. Critical Issues in Facilities Management No. 3. Alexandria, Virginia: APPA, 1988.

Bass, Bernard M. and James A. Vaughan. *Training in Industry: The Management of Learning*. Belmont, California: Brooks/Cole Publishing Company, 1966.

Bauer, B.A. In *Self-Directed Learning: From Theory to Practice*, ed. by S. Brookfield. New Directions for Continuing Education, no. 25. San Francisco: Jossey-Bass Inc., 1985.

Beder, H.W. and G.G. Darkenwald. "Differences Between Teaching Adults and Pre-Adults: Some Propositions and Findings." *Adult Education*, 32 (3), 1982.

Bittel, Lester R. *The Complete Guide to Supervisory Training and Development*. Reading, Massachusetts: Addison-Wesley Publishing Company, 1987.

————. *What Every Supervisor Should Know*, third edition. New York: McGraw-Hill Book Company, 1974.

Brookfield, Stephen D. *Understanding and Facilitating Adult Learning*. San Francisco: Jossey-Bass Publishers, Inc., 1986.

Craig, R.L., ed. *Training and Development Handbook*, second edition. New York: McGraw-Hill, 1976.

Daloz, L. *Teaching Adults*. San Francisco: Jossey-Bass Inc., 1986.

Drucker, Peter. *Management Tasks, Responsibilities, Practices*. New York: Harper & Row, 1985.

Fortunato, Ray T. and Dennis W. Keiser. *Human Resource Development in Higher Education Institutions*. Washington: College and University Personnel Association, 1985.

Gardner, James E. *Training the New Supervisor*. New York: AMA COM, 1983.

Kirkpatrick, Donald L. *A Practical Guide to Supervisory Training and Development*, second edition. Reading, Massachusetts: Addison-Wesley Publishing Company, 1983.

Knox, Alan B. *Helping Adults Learn*. San Francisco: Jossey-Bass Inc., 1986.

Lambert, Clark. *The Complete Book of Supervisory Training.* New York: John Wiley & Sons, 1984.

Wehrenberg, Stephen B. "Supervisors as Trainers: The Long-Term Gains of OJT." *Training,* April 1987.

CHAPTER 8

Motivation and Leadership

Desmond D. Martin
Professor of Management
University of Cincinnati

8.1 INTRODUCTION

This chapter looks at leadership and motivation in the physical plant environment and suggests specific tested techniques that, when applied, should improve the performance of the organizational unit.[1]

Recently, there has been considerable pressure in this country in both public and private enterprise for increased productivity among existing employees. In manufacturing firms these pressures have been nurtured by the dramatic inroads made by foreign competition, particularly from the Far East—Japan, Korea, and Taiwan—in American markets. Many corporations have gone through streamlining efforts to become lean and mean as a way of surviving in this new competitive environment. Efficiency trends have carried over from private enterprise into the public sector. State and local governments, for example, have found shrinking tax bases that suggest efficiency is the key to success. Many universities and colleges, therefore, are adopting this same philosophy; namely, a need for greater output from existing or fewer resources. Unfortunately, facilities management is often particularly hard hit. This department is usually seen as a support area for the academic side of the institution.

Since top administrators in most universities and colleges are usually drawn from the academic ranks, they tend to look to the support areas for initial reductions; consequently, many facilities management units are under constant pressure from budgetary limitations. The end result of this trend is that the modern physical plant supervisor cannot afford an ineffective or poorly motivated employee at any level in the organization. These real pressures place difficult and challenging demands on supervisors. Through proper management techniques, cost reductions and efficiency, improvements of the people resource can be realized. Physical plant leadership needs to accept people as a vitally important resource to organizational effectiveness. Also, with the application of state-of-the-art management techniques, these employees represent an asset that offers considerable potential for cost reduction and efficiency improvement.

The competitive pressures alluded to earlier are causing many organizations to either change their management style or fail. It is that simple. Although most universities and colleges are not facing total failure or putting a going-out-of-business sign on their campus doors, they are dramatically affected by how organizations are managed. Although people-oriented techniques usually involve high levels of involvement and participation that have been taught in colleges of business administration for several decades, it has only been in recent years that organizations have seriously recognized the need to apply them. Management styles and trends tend to permeate all organizations as they become more widely used and create a set of expectations on management. These expectations are increasingly taking on a professional tone that includes involvement in decision making and general participation in the affairs of the organization at all levels. As Professor Edward Lawler has pointed out, the time for involvement management has come.[2] The future is now.

8.2 KEY FACTORS THAT DETERMINE EMPLOYEE BEHAVIOR

There are several common elements that directly affect the behavior patterns of people in facilities organizations. The three most important elements are culture, perception, and status.

Culture

Culture can be defined as a value system or mode of behavior to which people in a given geographical area subscribe. Much behavior is culturally bound. Since the United States' culture is, generally, heavily characterized by individual competition and has historically been an achievement-oriented society, workers tend to expect opportunities to advance, and they respond to rewards for individual accomplishments.

Paternalistic management practices have been accepted in certain cultures, but may not work well in the United States. These practices are particularly questionable in those areas of plant management where highly trained engineering functions are involved or where employees have other trained specialties. Individual accomplishment and achievement flourishes in an environment that fosters recognition and reward.

Plant managers also need to recognize that subcultural differences dictated by varying geographical locations can affect management style and motivation. For example, employees in small colleges and rural areas may respond more favorably to paternalistic management than will employees in large universities located in urban environments.

Perceptions

Perceptions relate to how we see the world around us and how we see ourselves. People tend to behave in accordance with their perceptions. For example, if physical plant employees see themselves and their role in the university or college environment as considerably less important than the role of faculty or other administrative groups, their motivational potential and actual performance is likely to be affected. The facilities manager must continually stress the important role of the department to the overall institution's goal and mission. The facilities manager must favorably influence the perception of employees with regard to the importance and contributions both their work and job performance make to attaining the institution's mission.

Behavior is determined by what each employee sees as relevant in his or her environment and is not greatly affected by what outside observers perceive as reality. Managers are often more sensitive to the perceptions of outsiders with regard to their environment rather than to the perceptions of their own employees. If this sensitivity is directed more towards individual employee perceptions, managerial action can be adjusted to correct problems before they become serious.

Status

An important factor that influences behavior in the facilities environment is the perceived status of individuals relative to each other. Americans are particularly sensitive to status perceptions, and most employees want to be ranked higher rather than lower. A primary source of status in the American culture comes through both one's work assignment and organization.

Several useful points can plant managers understand the status variable. First, employees wanting high status try to protect that status from outside threat. As a result, any managerial action that is perceived to be lowering one's status will meet resistance. Conversely, managerial action that tends to increase status will be accepted. Since status relates directly to one's self esteem, and research shows that self esteem is clearly related to motivational potential, supervisors who act to raise the status of employees increase the motivational potential for each of them.

Since status perceptions differ, it is not always true that managers see actions as affecting one's status the same way that nonmanagers do. For example, a manager changes the work assignment of an employee and moves that employee from one university building to another. That manager may be unable to explain why this particular employee is so resistant to such a change in job assignment. In fact, the manager may feel the new job assignment is actually easier to accomplish than the old one. However, the employee may perceive the new building assignment to be a lower status part of the institution than the old building assignment. And even though the job duties may be more interesting or easier to perform, these factors may not be enough to offset the perceived lowering of status. Thus, resistance to change, poor performance, and other symptoms of maladjustment may occur.

Threats to status are much more severe if they are visible to one's peers. Management authorities agree that one of the biggest single mistakes a manager can make is to reprimand or insult a subordinate in the presence of others, particularly his or her peers. When one's status is lowered in the eyes of others, the severity of this problem often leads to serious performance deterioration and interpersonal conflict between the superior and the subordinate.

A manager who understands the complexities of behavior as dictated by the basic variables outlined above is in a much better position to make the right kinds of management decisions.

8.3 MOTIVATING PHYSICAL PLANT EMPLOYEES

Managerial views and understanding of motivation have undergone several changes in recent years. The dominant management philosophy prior to the 1930s was that employee motivation at all organizational levels was a function of two basic factors, wages and working conditions. Managers commonly believed that regular increments in wages and improvements in working conditions would lead to corresponding increases in productivity. The results of the Hawthorne Studies conducted at the Western Electric plant near Chicago in the 1920s and early 1930s did not support this widely held view. In contrast, these classic studies suggested that the social system was a key determinant of worker performance. Moreover, the Hawthorne Studies revealed that employee motivation was a complex process and provided much impetus for ensuing research. Since the mid 1940s, our understanding of motivation in American organizations has revolved around three basic factors.

First, in the 1940s and 1950s, considerable attention was paid to employee needs and how the satisfaction of these needs at work, related to motivating behavior. In the 1960s, need theory became widely accepted and much attention was given to the refinement of existing needs applications models to the motivation process.

Second, in the 1970s, attention was being paid to the impact of goals and the goal-setting process on employee behavior and performance. For example, the mere presence of goals or objectives in a typical work environment, e.g., physical plant, has been shown to have a positive effect on worker performance. Importantly, the process used to establish these goals, namely the extent of worker involvement and participation in goal setting, can either enhance or detract from their motivational impact. As a related point, as foreign competition became more pronounced and threatening to American manufacturing markets, particularly in the late 1970s, organizations began to look at how foreign companies were managing their employees. In this time period, the Japanese represented the most significant foreign threat; and examination of Japanese management practices became wide spread throughout the United States. As knowledge of Japanese management increased, it was clear that heavy reliance was placed on employee involvement, particularly group involvement, through such techniques as quality circles and other types of decision-making teams in Japan. It was also clear that for these teams to work effectively in moving the organization forward in a unified direction, both clear goals and an understanding of these goals needed to exist.

Third, there has been a recent emphasis on perceived equity within the organization.[3] Perceived equity is a product of a ratio of inputs to outputs; namely, an employee will look at input (effort) in relation to output (rewards) achieved from performance within the organization. Equity is upset when an employee feels that other people making lesser inputs are receiving greater relative rewards from the organization. This approach to motivation suggests that when employees encounter these inequities they will adjust their performance downward accordingly. Thus, they reestablish a sense of equity by making less input, which they feel is commensurate with their perceived level of reward. Since rewards are often closely tied in to when and how one's performance is appraised, the equity component of motivation is closely integrated into the performance appraisal system.

There are several important conclusions that today's facilities manager can draw from these foregoing points. First, wages and working conditions do impact on levels of performance. Also, the approaches to motivation widely used in the early part of this century that were primarily based on remuneration and discipline have relevance to today's supervisors. However, these approaches are overly simplistic and do not take into account the complexities of human behavior. The effective physical plant supervisor needs an understanding of the employees' psychological makeup and need orientation if he or she is to be motivated.

While an understanding of an employee's needs is certainly a vital link in the motivation process, this understanding alone is insufficient for today's supervisor. For example, employees not only internalize how well their needs are being met through work, but they respond to directives from the organization as well. If that direction is not provided, one may be a happy employee but not a very productive or motivated employee. It is through the goal and objective process that the manager can link employee performance and need satisfaction to productive effort for the physical plant department.

Finally, if this productive effort is not rewarded in a manner that is perceived to be equitable by the employee, then his or her future performance will be effected. As previously pointed out, perceptions determine reality, and although the supervisor may feel equity is present, it is the employee's perception that is a vital determinant of his or her response to future assignments. Wages, working conditions, employee need structures, the presence or absence of goals, and perceived equity are all important components of motivation; and the physical plant supervisor's application of knowledge about these factors is an important component of his or her leadership style. In fact, the art of leading is a determinant of motivational levels among followers in many physical plant settings. The remainder of this chapter will put these complex variables into a systematic framework designed to help a physical plant manager or supervisor increase employee performance within his or her department.

8.4 SUPERVISORY STEPS IN THE MOTIVATION PROCESS

Successful applications of employee motivation steps are particularly challenging in the complex academic environment. At colleges and universities plant personnel exercise their maintenance and operation profession and skills in an environment where it is not unusual for them to be perceived by themselves and others as less important than the faculty or some of the other staff. When members of the campus community including the president, administrators, staff, and the students acknowledge and recognize their work and contribution, plant personnel become part of the total institution. This valued, inclusive attitude needs to be developed and fostered by plant mangers. Managers can build this acceptance by soliciting written acknowledgements, when justified, and by getting appropriate media coverage in the school newspaper and broadcast station, as well as the local community press. Good managers seek out valid recognition for their employees.

Capable employees at all levels grow and achieve if given challenges and not just orders. Those that achieve the most consistently, become obvious when given opportunities to perform and succeed at their level of capability. When a deserving employee receives a promotion, everyone in the organization benefits. Everyone is assured that the organization has the potential to benefit each worthy individual.

Understanding the Supervisory Function

The first step needed to motivate a physical plant employee is to understand that the supervisor should manage the work for the employee and not actually do the employee's job. Increasingly, the effective supervisor's role is seen as a facilitative role involving planning, organizing, and providing support to employees so they can properly carry out assigned tasks. This is a much more complex function than it appears.

Many physical plant supervisors are promoted from the ranks or hired from other jobs that are nonmanagerial in nature. In first managerial assignments there is a tendency to want to do hands-on activities rather than planning and organizing activities, because hands-on activities are perceived to be more productive and useful by the new manager. The problem with performing many hands-on activities from the supervisory standpoint is that it lowers the status and image of the supervisor. Doing the same work side by side with subordinates and performing similar tasks to theirs encourages perceptions of organizational equality. It is important that supervisors respect their bosses and see them in a superior organizational role; performing the same duties as a subordinate tends to alter this perception in a nonconstructive or negative manner.

The second problem with performing the work of the subordinate is that his or her learning stops because the job is being done for them and often they are not given the opportunity to learn by doing. Developmental and challenging assignments are often handled by the supervisor. Routine and menial assignments are handled by the subordinate, which impedes employee growth, works contrary to a higher level need of satisfaction, and is essentially nonmotivational in nature.

Facilitation on the part of the supervisor is highly valued by subordinates for a number of reasons. Goal accomplishments are often more effectively realized, interference with one's work is minimized, and the process of getting the job done by the employee is made easier by the manager. Of course, these benefits of facilitation also have an equally positive impact on individual motivation.

Agreeing on Job Expectations and Goal Setting

Each supervisor should have established goals which are understood by all employees that report to that supervisor. As stated earlier, the presence of these goals or objectives in itself has a positive effect on motivational levels for the unit. These goals should be congruent with the goals of the upper-level management hierarchy, including the physical plant director and the top level goals of the school administration as a whole. Upper-level objectives provide guidance for the supervisor in working to mutually establish goals with subordinates regarding specific jobs. As indicated previously, involvement of subordinates in the establishment of job objectives has a positive motivational impact.

Job expectations, then, should revolve around goal accomplishment. Studies have shown that the first job assignment is important in long-term career growth and development for individual employees; namely, more difficult and challenging first assignments tend to lead to employee growth and foster a more positive career orientation then simple job assignments.[4] Ideally, first job assignments and expectations should be rather difficult and challenging but achievable to subordinates, and supervisors should avoid making simple assignments that have no challenge or inherent satisfaction in their accomplishment.

In summary, supervisors could ask themselves the following questions in order to make a self-assessment of how they are likely to be perceived by their subordinates.

- Am I planning work activities so that it is easier for my subordinates to accomplish their assigned tasks?
- Have I helped them organize their work?
- Have I organized the relationships in the physical plant unit so that they have access to people and equipment that they need to help them perform their assigned tasks?
- Do they understand how their work relates to the total goals and objectives of the physical plant department?
- Am I taking an interest in my employees as people and not simply treating them as instruments of production?
- Do the decision-making processes in use support their self image and reflect positively on their values as employees?

If the preceding questions can all be answered affirmatively, then this aspect of the motivation process is being handled quite well.

Understanding Employee Needs

Much has been written in the last quarter century about employee needs and how these needs interact to shape individual behavior within the organization. This chapter does not attempt to develop in great detail all the various ramifications of need theory, but will condense these approaches into a most usable pattern for the physical plant supervisor. As Abraham Maslow suggested, needs can be broken down into categories, which include physiological, safety, social, and ego needs.[5] Physiological and safety needs are powerful motivators when frustrated because they involve the survival of individuals.

However, most jobs' wages and benefits enable physiological needs to be handled satisfactorily; and governmental regulations, including OSHA and EPA requirements, safeguard against hazardous work assignments. Similarly, social needs are often quite easily handled in the facilities management setting because physical plant personnel tend to be supportive of one another and provide opportunities for employee socialization. Accepting Maslow's view, that satisfied needs do not motivate employees, there is little room for need satisfaction applications in the area of physiological, safety, and social needs to increase individual or departmental performance. However, the remaining upper-level category of ego needs does have great potential for improving motivation and performance.

Ego needs revolve around status, recognition, esteem, and self actualization. These needs are often frustrated in modern work settings. Therefore, supervision that pays great attention to satisfaction of these needs, and links that satisfaction to employee performance, is likely to note positive changes in performance outcomes.

Employees' self esteem can be fundamental to their motivational behavior. When managers take action that reduces one's self esteem, they tend to make motivation of those employees more difficult. As an example, if a physical plant supervisor puts down a worker for not painting properly or not cleaning buildings well with phrases like "Can't you do anything right?" or "I learn everyday more about your stupidity," these kinds of comments reach deeply into the employee's self image and tend to lower his or her self-perception. Since supervisors are seen as leaders by many subordinates, these comments are often taken personally and seriously.

The bottom-line point is that motivation becomes much more difficult because lowered self image results in lowering motivational potential. Conversely, statements like "I know you can do a good job; you have done it in the past" or "You're a very bright person, and you can learn these things and be one of our top performers" raise self image and make other motivation techniques more effective.

One of the more difficult aspects of applying needs theory to the motivation process is to be able to link those needs to the performance results desired by the organizational unit. The physical plant supervisor that can make interesting and rewarding work assignments, and then recognize good performance periodically, has taken a giant step toward motivating that subordinate to higher levels of work performance and effectiveness. Uninteresting work or the absence of recognition for good performance leaves employees to seek higher level need satisfaction outside the work environment or with coworkers in nonwork activities, and the end result is a reduction in the department's motivational score.

Behavior Modification

The importance of relating rewards to performance as a motivational tool cannot be overemphasized to physical plant managers. In fact, the behavior modification approach to motivation focuses heavily on this concept. Simply stated, this approach suggests that worker performance can be improved using reward structures to reinforce desired outcomes. Successful behavior modification requires that work performance or standards must be both set and understood so that accomplishments can be specifically recognized and rewarded. Punishment or criticism is not recommended because of its tendency to have a negative impact on performance.

If behavior modification is to work, the physical plant manager must exercise rather tight-knit control over both the work environment and reward contingencies. Tight-knit control assumes the following characteristics:

- Continuous feedback that recognizes both good and bad performance.
- Differentiating rewards among employees so the better performers receive measurably more value for their good work.

In order to fulfill these requirements, physical plant managers need the courage to confront poor performance, both verbally and tangibly, and they will need strong support from their respective bosses. If their subordinates do not see a clear relationship between performance and rewards, they are not likely to increase performance. Also, the supervisor must not be perceived as coercing or manipulating the employee, because resentment will surface, which offsets positive benefits. Thus, punishment meted out by supervision is not recommended. Additionally, the complex social environment found in most physical plant settings may upset the reward performance relationship. If implemented carefully and diligently, however, this approach can offer help to physical plant departments that are experiencing employee-related motivation problems.

One study of several well-known organizations that were using behavioral modification concepts found that many of these firms credited this approach with improving morale and increasing profits.[6]

Goal Setting and Equity Theory

There is an important link between needs, goal setting, and equity. The challenging question to the physical plant supervisor is, "How do I link employee needs to desired performance outcomes for the organization?" One of the ways to do this is to set realistic goals with the subordinate that, when accomplished, will benefit the organizational unit, and then to utilize a performance appraisal system that will provide regular feedback to the employee that suggests that the performance is both recognized and valued. In the absence of specific job objectives and standards, it is difficult for employees to measure performance adequately. The ensuing problem is that the better performing subordinates do not feel they are adequately recognized for their work which also leads to perceptions of inequity. Perceived inequity is most likely when high performers see that other employees doing much less are getting the same or more recognition from management. If this type of conflict and adverse motivational impact is to be avoided, supervisors need to regularly use an effective performance appraisal system.

Often personnel departments in universities and colleges can offer considerable help to facilities management in setting up and implementing effective performance appraisal systems. One of the big problems with appraisals is that honest appraisals may have negative overtones for some employees. Many supervisors avoid giving appraisals because they do not want to get involved in the negative aspects of identifying problems for their poor performing employees. It is important that upper-level supervisors in physical plant actively encourage regular appraisals for subordinate employees by their supervisor. One method that has helped in many departments to overcome this resistance to giving good appraisals is to make the conducting of regular performance appraisals an important part of the evaluation of supervisors in physical plant.

Since the passage of the Equal Employment Opportunity Act in 1972, there have been several court decisions that have gone against organizations that have based appraisals on nonobjective job criteria. It is important that the entire management team work hard to establish criteria that can be defended as job related in any kind of affirmative action or discrimination suit. The personnel department within the university or college can usually help assure that adequate attention has been given to EEO requirements through the establishment of specific performance criteria or guidelines. The establishment of a clear relationship between reward and performance is the most important element in the modern expectancy theory of motivation, which has been given considerable credibility in research studies.[7]

Specifically, research supports the contention of expectancy theory that motivation is related to productivity in those situations where the acquisition of desired goals is related to one's individual productivity and performance.[8] Fortunately, two of the most popular approaches to motivation, expectancy theory and motivation hygiene theory, are remarkably complementary in their proposed solution to the motivation problem. While expectancy theory focuses on a definitive relationship between reward and performance, motivation hygiene theory, as developed by Frederick Herzberg, emphasizes interesting and challenging work coupled with reward and advancement for good performance as a key to motivation.[9] Thus, when jobs are both interesting and good performance is tangibly rewarded, the ingredients are there for a highly motivated employee.

Today's physical plant manager should help design jobs that contain intrinsic value and are not boring to employees performing them. Notable researchers such as J.R. Hackman have given modern supervisors clues as to what constitutes a well designed job from the motivational standpoint.[10] Among the more important components of a well-designed job are those that contain a variety of tasks for successful performance. These tasks should be perceived as related to some kind of final product or service output that is seen as significant by the employee performing the work. Regular feedback on good performance should be provided, and as already alluded to, a formal performance appraisal should be conducted on a regular basis.

The presence of established and understood objectives for the job will minimize the need for close supervision of employee performance. Increased autonomy given to employees will result in intrinsic satisfaction associated with performing the task. If these foregoing variables have been effectively integrated into the supervisory-subordinate relationship and made an important part of the assigned task, the ingredients are present for a positive motivational climate.

Pay and Equity

The pay equity component is another vital factor in the motivation process. The early approaches to motivation that emphasized wages and working conditions as performance determinants were not completely fallacious. Wages play a role in the satisfaction of all need levels. They provide the opportunity to purchase food, clothing, and shelter, and they are a major measure of factors that are identified as ego related. For example, expensive cars or elaborate homes serve as success signals to others and they measure for others, one's level of esteem and accomplishment. Thus, wages are not totally separate from higher level need satisfaction.

Wages are also a major factor in an employee's assessment of his or her personal worth. The establishment of personal worth criteria usually involves a comparison with other employees within the organization. Wages are a tangible factor in that comparison, particularly in open-salary systems where incomes become known. Since it is difficult to keep wage levels totally secret, there is the potential for wage comparisons to exist in almost any organization. If the physical plant employee is able to make a pay comparison with other comparable employees and concludes that there is an inequitable relationship, motivation levels are likely to fall. Moreover, if that employee is female or a member of a minority, perceptions of discrimination may be fostered. Supervisors and upper-level managers should continually monitor wage and salary administration to ensure that high levels of perceived pay equity exist. Unfortunately, complaints about pay inequities often cause managers to distribute pay more evenly among employees, thereby reducing merit increments or wage differentials to reduce conflict. Effective supervisors resist this tendency and retain control over a dollar pool for merit increases that is distributed to physical plant employees for good performance. Additionally, managers and supervisors should clearly communicate to these employees the criteria that will be used in the distribution of merit increases. It is desirable to solicit input from physical plant personnel in the development of wage distribution criteria. In addition to good performance, seniority, job difficulty, and working conditions are pertinent elements to the determination of pay raises. It is essential, however, that when pay differentials exist, and they should exist, that supervisors and managers be able to justify these differentials on the basis of clearly measurable and agreed upon factors.

The proper use of wages and salaries increases managerial effectiveness and is an important step in the motivation process. Summary points and suggestions about the constructive management of the remuneration process follow.

- The physical plant director should retain control over some dollar pool for merit increases that are distributed periodically among subordinates for good performance.
- Facilities managers should communicate to subordinates the criteria that will be used in the distribution of merit increases. Opinions from subordinates in the development of these criteria will aid their acceptance.
- Effective wage and salary administration is a continuous process. Managers should constantly try to have wage and salary

equity in the entire plant organization. Equitable wage and salary conditions have two fundamental characteristics. A direct relationship exists between perceived skill requirements, job difficulty, and pay scales; and good performance is recognized with salary increments.

- Most employees see wage reductions as seriously threatening their self esteem and resist any action that reduces pay. Consequently, it is often best to handle overpaid employees through normal attrition and to reduce rates of pay when new employees are moved into these jobs.
- It is important to remember that the demand for wage increases by employees may be symptomatic of other problems associated with the organizational climate. This is true because wages are tangible, easy to measure, and they are a direct way of expressing dissatisfaction. Thus, managers should look beyond demands for wage increases by employees to see if there are other more basic causes of the problem.

Variables contained in Figure 8-1 help to illustrate the incremental factors that raise output in both the traditional and modern views of motivation. These incremental factors are represented by movement up the vertical axis of each chart, while corresponding output improvements are identified with movement across the horizontal axis. As indicated previously, the traditional approaches were based on simple assumptions about employee behavior, but today's approaches emphasize the complexities of individual need fulfillment. However, as just noted, wages are still important to motivation because they often serve as a measure of need fulfillment and perceived equity.

8.5 LEADERSHIP STYLE

Leadership style can be viewed as a continuum—from highly controlling leadership practices where employees are permitted practically no discretion, to highly participative leadership practices where employees are permitted great discretion. The two extremes of this continuum are generally identified as autocratic and democratic styles, while the middle of the continuum is usually termed a consultative style of management.

When overall organizational success is related to leadership qualities and style, it is clear that effective leadership can and does make a difference in motivation and performance. For example, when high-ranking managers are asked to identify key factors that they attribute to their success in rising to top levels in their respective organizations, they

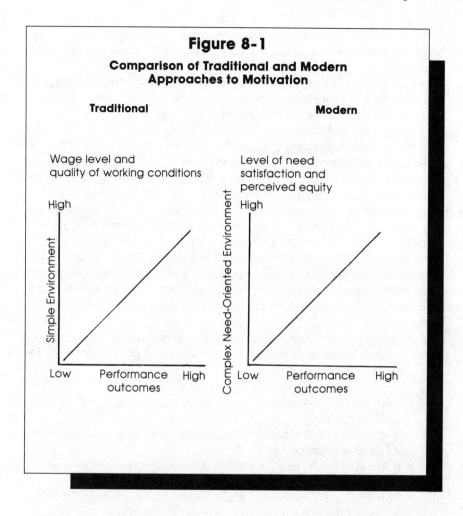

Figure 8-1

Comparison of Traditional and Modern Approaches to Motivation

often attribute their success to specific leadership qualities. Physical plant employees are highly sensitive to how they are lead and strong leadership practices can greatly enhance the entire motivational process.

Leadership and Motivation

As pointed out at the beginning of this chapter, the time for involvement management is here. It seems to be no longer a question or choice between democracy and autocracy, but rather an issue of how much democracy should be instituted in the leadership climate of the organization. However, simply stating that democratic leadership should be practiced in physical plant settings is an oversimplification of a complex process and problem. Research is continually showing that leadership style is greatly affected by the situation in which the supervision is being practiced.

Crisis situations or other situations that involve immature employees with highly programmed work tasks tend to work well with autocratic leadership styles. As the training and maturity of employees increase, and the situation is not in crisis, the evidence clearly indicates that more democratic approaches that involve employees in decision making are most motivational and effective.[11] Although it may sound like a simple choice, deciding which style is most useful is not easy. Maintaining tight control over employees often raises productivity levels. These increases, however, tend to be short-lived and are attained at the expense of long-term costs, reflected in deteriorating human relationships. Yet, some kinds of problems tend to be particularly suitable for tight-reign control and any other style is clearly inappropriate. While democratic styles produce good human relationships, they usually will only work if employees are knowledgeable of the problem, feel it is important, and strongly support the overall goals of the plant department.

A useful guide to follow in determining how democratic you should be in a situation can be reflected in the number of yes responses to the following specific statements.[12]

- I do not have enough information to make a high-quality decision on my own.
- Acceptance of the decision I make by subordinates is critical to its implementation.
- If I make the decision myself, it is unlikely that it will be accepted by my subordinates.
- Subordinates share in the goals of physical plant management.
- Subordinates have sufficient information to make a high-quality decision or at least to help in this process.

If each of these statements is answered affirmatively, the democratic style is called for. Of course, this has to be coupled with the fact that there is sufficient time to involve subordinates in the decision-making process. Emergency and crisis decisions needing an answer in a short period of time preclude using the democratic approach. Decisions that involve reduction in force, allocation of merit awards, and disciplining employees are among those that normally are handled best on an autocratic basis.

Successful operations exist along the spectrum of management styles. There are three universal elements that have been found to exist in any successfully managed organization:

- The management philosophy is known and understood.
- The leadership style is consistently applied.
- It is flexible enough to meet change and emergencies.

These elements say a great deal about human behavior and what is important. However, given these three principles, the organization that more fully maximizes the potential of its individual members falls on the democratic side of the management spectrum.

Physical plant supervisors should fully understand that democratic management is not giving up control and decision-making power to the subordinates, and it is not necessarily making decisions by majority vote among subordinates. Democratic management works best when goals and objectives are clear for the organization in the departmental unit. Goals and objectives allow subordinates to become more involved within the context of direction and thrust.

The absence of a clear direction or thrust as identified by goals for a department can cause democratic techniques to be destructive. Physical plant supervisors that choose democratic management must recognize that this process requires continuous development of subordinates. The democratic supervisor should help to provide a work climate that fosters the development of objectives, stimulates employees' capacity and desire to become involved, and includes employees with varying levels of technical knowledge. As a related point, one of the biggest obstacles to adopting a sound democratic approach to management is the natural tendency to want to keep doing those tasks and duties that are particularly interesting, or for those who are promoted into management to want to continue to perform those activities they did well on in their previous job.

Good, democratic leadership is based on a willingness to delegate to subordinates those activities that will aid their development and are challenging and interesting to perform. When challenging tasks are delegated, subordinates may have to struggle with these tasks for awhile in order to master them. This is a normal part of the developmental process and should be encouraged within prescribed limits by the facilities manager. When a manager jumps in too quickly to bail out a subordinate struggling with an assigned task, the creative development of that subordinate is stifled, learning is impeded, and the subordinate becomes more dependent as other tasks are assigned. In most instances, these are all negative consequences of helping a subordinate too quickly.

There are many situations in physical plant where a lack of knowledge among subordinates or short time constraints make democratic principles inappropriate. Organizations are strengthened when the occurrence of these kinds of situations is minimized. Reducing the occurrence of crisis, time constraints, and developing subordinates' knowledge of decision-making situations is an important part of a positive motivational climate.

In fact, climate is such an important factor in motivation that supervisors and upper-level managers should work together to periodically assess the organizational climate within physical plant and take corrective action when climate factors are having adverse effects on motivation and performance. Figure 8-2 illustrates positive and negative factors in the physical plant environment that can lead to either high or low motivation.

One-on-One Leadership

Leader-member exchanges, often called vertical dyad linkages, play an important role in leadership effectiveness. Exchanges of challenging and interesting work assignments for valued rewards can have a positive long-term effect on individual performance and satisfaction. A knowledge of dyadic relationships may offer the key to individual levels of performance. For example, leader-member exchanges can help explain the value of mutual goal setting to performance improvement. Some researchers suggest that participation in goal setting is a critical factor in determining individual performance.[13] The important point appears to be that.participation leads both to understanding specificity and negotiation regarding performance goals. The ultimate acceptance of a goal is tied to complexities involved in the leader-follower dyad. If goals are dictated to subordinates with little participation, the positive motivational effect of the presence of goals appears to be lost. Communication style and language affects the entire motivation process.[14]

Other important factors influencing employees' physical plant supervisory perceptions in this area of leader-member exchange include trust, presence of upward influence with the supervisor, and continual two-way dialogue with each subordinate. Trust is established by supporting words with action and promoting equity in the pay-performance relationship. Upward influence is determined by the acceptance of supervisory management to the upper levels in the physical plant hierarchy. Overruling lower-level supervisors on any points, particularly in the eyes of their subordinates, substantially weakens their self image and makes it more difficult to motivate employees who report to them.

Since it is important for supervisors to be supported by their bosses and be able to demonstrate that they have influence with these bosses to their subordinates, if situations are occurring with regularity that undermine this support from upper levels in the physical plant hierarchy, then dramatic changes are called for. If these supervisors cannot be supported because of their poor judgment, or just outright incompetence, then it is

Figure 8-2

Motivational Impact of Alternative Physical Plant Work Environments

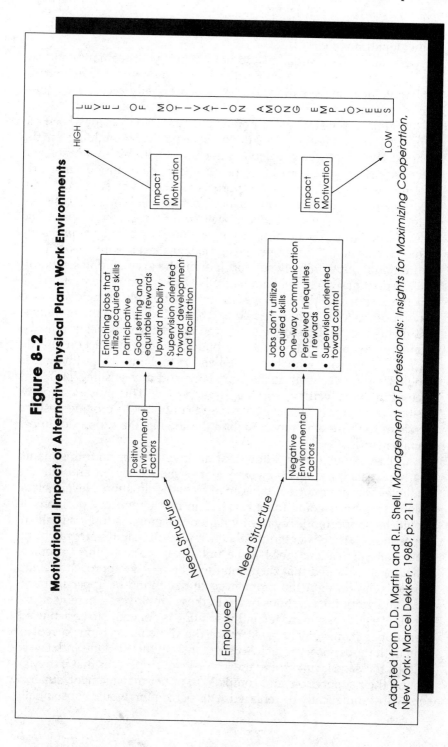

LEVEL OF MOTIVATION AMONG EMPLOYEES

HIGH

Impact on Motivation

Positive Environmental Factors
- Enriching jobs that utilize acquired skills
- Participative
- Goal setting and equitable rewards
- Upward mobility
- Supervision oriented toward development and facilitation

Negative Environmental Factors
- Jobs don't utilize acquired skills
- One-way communication
- Perceived inequities in rewards
- Supervision oriented toward control

Impact on Motivation

LOW

Employee

Need Structure

Need Structure

Adapted from D.D. Martin and R.L. Shell. *Management of Professionals: Insights for Maximizing Cooperation,* New York: Marcel Dekker, 1988, p. 211.

necessary to take documented steps so these employees can be replaced in the department.

Assuming these situations do not happen with regularity and supervisors can generally be supportive, how should upper-level managers handle negative situations that may occasionally occur? This question may best be answered through the use of a work example.

Assume a physical plant nonmanagerial employee has been assigned a job of painting the interior of a particular building on the campus. This employee is obviously in conflict with his supervisor, and there are several questions being raised about the quality of his work. This non-managerial employee approaches his supervisor's boss with the following statements, "John is incompetent. He's unfair in his work assignments, and I just can't work well with him as a supervisor. You must do something about John, or you're going to have bigger problems in our department." An upper-level manager faced with this kind of confrontation must initially support John in the eyes of John's subordinate. To do otherwise would dramatically weaken John's perception as a superior by not only the employee in question but other employees who may report to John. While it is acceptable to indicate to the employee that this matter will be looked into, the upper-level manager must be careful not to imply that he will go around John and take action directly with the employee who has raised the complaint. This situation is handled most effectively if the complaint and any ensuing problems uncovered are solved by working through John. This preserves John's position of authority as a supervisor and continues to provide positive messages to those who report to John that he has the support of upper management.

Occasionally, it may follow that an investigation into this matter clearly reveals that John is incompetent as the supervisor and that the employee was quite correct in his analysis of the situation. Nevertheless, as long as John is going to be retained in his supervisory position, he should be supported if organizational effectiveness is to be sustained. Consequently, if he is not immediately replaced, training programs and other communications need to be utilized to correct John's problem behavior. It is hoped that then, John will be able to approach the employees who brought the problem to the attention of upper management and work the solutions out with these employees, thereby ensuring his integrity as a manager. If this solution is not going to be achieved, then upper management must make the difficult decision to replace John in the supervisory role. It is important that this be done with tact so that the message is not sent to the lower-level employees that if they go around their supervisors and complain to upper management, supervisors will automatically be replaced. This perception would substantially weaken the ranks of first-level supervision in the entire facilities management organization.

8.6 MOTIVATING PHYSICAL PLANT EMPLOYEES: A POINT OF VIEW AND A METHOD

Material contained in this chapter suggests that managing employees involves specific techniques that, when applied, can raise levels of motivation. It also suggests that motivation is more than the application of techniques but involves a philosophy of leadership associated with a particular manager. Physical plant personnel need to be perceived as a resource, of equal value to other factors, such as technology and capital, within the organization. The United States is a status-conscious society, and employees in all organizations including physical plant are sensitive as to how work assignments and organizational communications of all types affect their status. The application of most of the managerial concepts discussed in this chapter has an impact either positively or negatively on an employee's perceived self worth.

For example, supervisors who practice involvement management techniques derive positive motivational benefits in two specific ways. First, employee participation in important decisions improves self image and identification with the job in the organization; and second, this same involvement builds commitment to task through ownership. When an employee tells a supervisor "I will do it" through an involvement process, the probability of that task being performed well increases considerably. Conversely, although contrary situations where the supervisor tells the employee, "You will do it because I am your boss," may have been acceptable to employees thirty to forty years ago, they are now likely to fail. In fact, many organizations now find employees are simply turned off by such direct orders and supervisory effectiveness is reduced.

An important by-product of building self image among subordinates by supervisors is the extension of positive values to clients served by physical plant throughout the college or university community. In dealing with others at any level, if self esteem is sustained and that sense of importance is communicated to clients served by physical plant, the responsiveness, support, and department image will improve. There is little doubt that when an employee is being put down by his or her boss, he or she has additional trouble dealing with clients in performing services in a positive and supportive manner. Since many physical plant departments, particularly those associated with universities in urban environments, face competition from suppliers outside the university for many of their services, it is important that clients are confident of the services received from physical plant employees. Thus, the double pay-off of applying effective supervisory techniques is that motivation is sustained and often improved, and increased self esteem enables employees to deal more constructively with their clients.

Studies of emotional profiles of individuals who assume leadership positions suggest that some people by nature of their personality are more comfortable with involvement-management processes than others. One's previous experience as a supervisor with particular supervisory techniques coupled with his or her educational and cultural background tend to shape their views of how people should be managed. Supervisors who are trained to practice involvement techniques and have observed successful application of these techniques are more likely to use them. Conversely, supervisors who lack the training or have seen few successes with applications of involvement-management practices, need additional training and support from upper management. Also, lower-level supervisors who are managed autocratically by their own bosses find it difficult to utilize involvement management with their own subordinates.

8.7 SUMMARY AND CONCLUSIONS

Principles of effective supervision must permeate the entire organization, and in many instances they, in fact, start with the vice president or director of physical plant and promulgate downward throughout the management hierarchy. Facilities management personnel should be encouraged to continue their education either through formal academic degree work or professional development training programs, which will enable them to constantly monitor both new and useful management techniques as well as change values and attitudes among physical plant personnel. This type of activity can have high payoffs as exemplified by the fact that some of the most successful and best managed organizations in the United States, e.g., G.E., IBM, and 3-M, devote considerable organizational resources to managerial development activities.[15] Good supervision and attendant motivation of physical plant employees does not just happen, but is a product of training and study, critical self analysis for managers, and courageous application of supervisory techniques and rewards systems.

The key to motivation is found in the characteristics of the organization climate. Facilities managers should strive to develop a climate that supports democratic leadership, straightforward two-way communication, and is perceived by subordinates to recognize and reward good performance. Employees who do not respond to this type of environment may have low-achievement needs. These individuals should be identified in the preemployment screening process as not suited for the organization. Physical plant managers who inherit large numbers of these employees from previous administrations should make it clear that this is a new ball game and explain how rewards will be distributed. A few of these employees will probably adjust to the new environment and offer improved levels of motivation. Others will become disgruntled and leave. The unsatisfactory employees that remain may be small in number or placed in positions with minimum negative impact on the rest of the organization.

High levels of performance among employees is usually catching. Poor performers are encouraged to do better by good performers. A good organizational climate moves employees in the direction of solving the motivation problems that confront the plant manager. Also, proper climates attract good employees and put pressure on weaker employees to perform better or leave.[16] Although the managerial task in building a strong climate is a difficult one, once accomplished the rewards are great to both the manager and the employee.

Current population statistics and economic conditions confronting colleges and universities promise even tighter budgetary constraints and increasing pressure to get more from fewer resources. Many facilities managers will find a deep reservoir of untapped potential among their workers. The application of motivational tools and the use of sound leadership practices can result in substantial improvements in motivation that will release much of the potential in that untapped reservoir.

NOTES

1. Many of the concepts and ideas contained in this chapter are adopted from Desmond D. Martin and Richard L. Shell, *Management of Professionals: Insights for Maximizing Cooperation.* (New York: Marcel Dekker, 1988).
2. E. Lawler III. *High Involvement Management.* (San Francisco: Jossey-Bass, 1986), p. 1.
3. For a discussion of equity theory, see M.R. Carrell and J.E. Dittrich, "Equity Theory: The Recent Literature, Methodological Considerations, and New Directions." *Academy of Management Review,* No. 3, 1978, pp. 202-210.
4. E.E. Berlew and D.T. Hall. "The Socialization of Managers: Effects of Expectations on Performance." *Administrative Science Quarterly,* Vol. II, 1966, pp. 207-223.

5. Abraham H. Maslow. "A Theory of Human Motivation." *Psychological Review,* Vol. 50, 1943, pp. 370-396.
6. W. Clay Hamner and Ellen P. Hamner. "Behavior Modification and the Bottom Line." *Organizational Dynamics,* Spring 1976, pp. 8-21.
7. For a detailed discussion of expectancy theory, see Victor H. Vroom. *Work and Motivation.* New York: John Wiley & Sons, 1964.
8. J.M. Ivancevich and J.T. McMahon. "The Effects of Goal Setting, and Self Generated Feedback on Outcome Variables: A Field Experiment." *Academy of Management Journal,* Vol. 25, No. 2, June 1982, pp. 359-372.
9. For a concise discussion of motivation hygiene theory, see Frederick Herzberg. *Work and the Nature of Man,* Chapter 6. Cleveland: World Publishing, 1966.
10. J.R. Hackman, G. Oldham, R. Janson, and K. Purdy. "A New Strategy for Job Enrichment." *California Management Review,* Vol. XVII, No. 4, 1975, pp. 55-71.
11. For a detailed discussion of these issues, see Paul Hersey and Kenneth Blanchard. *Management of Organizational Behavior.* Englewood Cliffs, New Jersey: Prentice Hall, 1982, pp. 150-192.
12. For a discussion of these questions and their meaning, see Victor H. Vroom and Philip W. Yetton. *Leadership and Decision Making.* Pittsburgh: University of Pittsburgh Press, 1973.
13. Jay S. Kim. "Effect of Behavior plus Outcome Goal Setting and Feedback on Employee Satisfaction and Performance." *Academy of Management Journal,* Vol. 27, No. 1, March, 1984, pp. 139-149.
14. Jeremiah J. Sullivan. "Three Roles of Language in Motivation Theory." *Academy of Management Review,* Vol. 13, No. 1, January 1988, pp. 104-115.
15. For an effective discussion of well managed companies, see T.J. Peters and R.H. Waterman Jr. *In Search of Excellence.* New York: Harper & Row, 1982.
16. Support for this position is offered by S.M. McEvoy and W.F. Cascio. "Do Good or Poor Performers Leave? A Meta Analysis of the Relationship Between Performance and Turnover." *Academy of Management Journal.* Vol. 30, No. 4, December, 1987, pp. 744-762.

SECTION III

BUSINESS

MANAGEMENT

Section Leader:
William A. Daigneau
Director of University Facilities
University of Rochester

CHAPTER 9

Overview of Accounting Systems

Raymond Degenhart
Budget Officer
University of Northern Colorado

9.1 PURPOSE OF FUND ACCOUNTING AND REPORTING

Service, not profits, is the objective of the college and/or university. The primary purpose of accounting and reporting is one of accounting for resources received and used, rather than the determination of profits. In some cases, fees charged do not necessarily cover actual expenditures of program services. For example, philanthropic sources often specify a particular program, service, or fund to which the contributions are to be applied, and nonexpendable gifts must sometimes be provided to generate income for general or specific programs. The principles and practices of fund accounting have developed through the years in order to properly account for these resources and their varied uses.

Fund accounting provides the means by which a college or university controls the use of money or other assets in accordance with the laws, regulations, or contract terms that govern the school's expenditures. Through the use of funds, the school can verify that it has complied with these restrictions.

Description of Fund Groupings

A fund is an accounting entity with a self-balancing set of accounts for recording assets, liabilities, a fund balance, and changes in that fund balance. Separate accounts are maintained for each fund to ensure observance of any limitations and restrictions placed on the use of these resources. Funds having similar characteristics are combined and recorded into fund groups.

The fund groups typically used in higher education are as follows:

- Current funds (restricted and unrestricted)
- Loan funds
- Endowment and similar funds
- Annuity and life income funds
- Plant funds
- Agency funds

A brief explanation and identification of each of these fund groups follows.

Current funds account for assets available for general unrestricted or restricted current purposes. Loan funds account for assets that may be loaned to students or, in some cases, faculty or staff. Endowment and other similar funds are used to account for assets the income from which may be expended whereas the principle may not. Annuity and life income funds handle those assets the income from which must be used to pay annuities. Plant funds is a generic term used for the four types of funds: unexpended plant fund, repair and replacement fund, retirement of indebtedness fund, and invested in plant fund (a separate group of accounts is necessary to account for each of these four types of assets). Agency funds are those held by the college or university in the capacity of agent or trustee.

The Accounting Equation   The accounting equation involves the balanced relationship among three kinds of economic representations: assets, liabilities, and net worth. Assets are economic values that are owned by or are under the control of the institution. They are of two kinds. The first type is cash and that which can be converted into cash, such as investments and accounts receivable. The other type of asset is represented by costs incurred at an earlier date that have not yet been attributed to a given fiscal period. Examples of this second type of asset are capital costs, depreciable equipment, buildings, inventories, prepaid expenses, and deferred charges.

There also are two kinds of liability accounts. The first type represents amounts that are owed to organizations or individuals who are outside the institution itself. In general, liabilities represent amounts owed to others, including creditors, for a variety of reasons. Some liabilities may be amounts that are owed and must be paid in the near term or immediately; other liabilities may be paid out over a period of many years. The second type of liability account is used to record deferred credits or deferred revenues. These liabilities represent amounts that have been collected in cash or whose collection is anticipated but for which an earnings process has not yet occurred. Until such a process begins, the institution carries these items as a liability.

The relationship between assets and liabilities, or the difference between them, produces the third kind of account, generally referred to as net worth, equity, or proprietorship. Net worth is also net assets, which represent the net difference between assets and related liabilities. In fund accounting, the fund balance equals assets minus liabilities.

The accounting equation is the relationship among these three kinds of accounts and is expressed by the statement that assets minus liabilities equals net worth, or by an algebraic transposition of that equation (i.e., assets equal liabilities plus net worth). Another way of interpreting the accounting equation is to state that equities are claims by an owner against assets.

Real and Nominal Accounts   The accounts used in the accounting system to record asset values, liability values, and net worth or fund balance values are referred to as real accounts. These balances carry forward from the beginning of the organization until its end or until the particular type of asset, liability, or net worth no longer exists. Nominal accounts, on the other hand, expire at the end of a given fiscal period (e.g., the fiscal year) and are created anew at the beginning of the next period. Such accounts—called income and expenses—classify the increases and decreases in net worth and provide more detailed information about the sources and uses of net worth throughout the year. For example, increases in net worth may result from sales, gifts, endowment income, or contributions to capital; decreases may reflect expenses or losses in investments, among other possibilities.

In most cases, financial statements deal exclusively with either real accounts or nominal accounts (special types of reports may deal with elements of both at the same time). In examining financial statements, it is helpful to remember that net worth or fund balances are changed by increases or decreases in assets or liabilities (such as by income and expenses).

The concept of double-entry bookkeeping is built on the accounting equation. Thus, for each economic event that is recorded there is a balanced set of entries to record the event (i.e., a debit and a credit). At all times the system must balance so that debits equal credits. The total of assets likewise must equal the total of liabilities and net worth in the system.

The accounting equation and the principles of real and nominal accounts underlie all accounting and apply to fund accounting as well as to other forms of accounting.

Fund Classifications   Resources received by institutions are labeled in several ways to indicate the nature of any pertinent restrictions.

- *Ownership versus agency relationship.* When an institution receives new monies, the first question is whether the resources actually belong to the institution. Funds that do not belong to the institution are called agency funds and represent assets held by the institution on behalf of others. Alternatively, agency funds represent liabilities for amounts due to outside organizations, students, or faculty that will be paid out on their instructions for purposes other than normal operations. Institutions have on occasion used the agency fund classification inappropriately for funds that officials would like to use outside the constraints of the budget process.
- *Restricted versus unrestricted.* If the monies received by the institution are indeed owned by the institution, the next question is whether the monies are restricted or unrestricted. As noted earlier, the specific nature of the restrictions must be stated clearly.
- *Expendable versus nonexpendable.* If the monies received by the institution are restricted, it must be determined whether the monies are expendable or nonexpendable. If the monies are expendable (i.e., can be spent), one must ask for what specific purpose, function, activity, or object they are to be spent. If the purpose or character of the expenditure is such that it is a part of normal operations, it is classified in a category that relates it to current operations. If, on the other hand, the restriction is such that the monies must be spent to acquire land, buildings, equipment, or other types of capital assets, the expenditure is classified as a part of plant funds.

Nonexpendable funds can be distinguished by several types of restrictions. For example, endowment funds cannot be spent; they must be invested and only the income can be used. It should be noted that the income from the endowment represents a new source of funds, and the nature of this money must be determined by the same series of questions outlined earlier. It is possible for a donor to restrict both the principal (the endowment monies) and the investment income.

Certain other funds cannot be spent but must be loaned to students or faculty. Under this arrangement the monies will be loaned, the borrowers will repay the loans, and the same resources will be reloaned to other borrowers.

A third nonexpendable fund is the annuity fund or life income fund. Here, the donor provides money to the institution with instructions to pay to an outside party for a period of time either a certain amount of money (in the case of an annuity fund) or the investment income (in the case of a life income fund).

All funds not restricted by the donor are by definition unrestricted. Generally, all unrestricted funds are to be used first as revenue for current operating purposes. A governing board also may designate unrestricted funds for long-term investments to produce income (in the manner of endowment funds), or for plant acquisition purposes (for which restricted funds normally are used).

Thus, certain unrestricted funds are intended for the same purpose as certain restricted funds. In the reporting of college and university financial matters, as evidenced in financial statements, funds that are either restricted or designated for similar types of activities are classified in a group that has a name indicating the purpose. However, within each one of the groups it is necessary to distinguish between those amounts that are in the group by reason of restrictions imposed by donors, and those amounts that are in the group by reason of designation by a governing board.

Funds and Fund Groups   A fund is an accounting entity with a self-balancing set of assets, liabilities, and a fund balance account, in addition to nominal accounts that measure increases and decreases in the fund balance. Separate funds are established to account for financial activity related to a particular restricted donation, source of restricted funds, or designated amount established by the governing board. These accounting entries are set up to ensure the observance of restrictions imposed by donors and of limitations on the use of unrestricted funds that have been established by the governing board. In many cases, however, funds of similar designation and restriction are grouped together for reporting purposes and for purposes of efficient management. Often the assets of like kinds of funds are placed in one set of asset accounts. Similarly, liability accounts related to those assets may be merged. Nevertheless, there still will be a series of individual fund balances for which a separate accounting will have to be performed. The total of all such assets should equal the total of all such liabilities and the total of the fund balances to which they relate. This grouping together for accounting and reporting purposes yields what is termed a fund group. It is important to note that within each fund group it is necessary to continue to distinguish between the balance of funds that are unrestricted and those that are externally restricted. Within the restricted subgroup it is necessary to account for each separate restricted fund balance.

Accrual Basis of Accounting   Accrual-basis accounting is often defined in comparison to cash-basis accounting. In the latter, the only transactions recorded are those in which cash comes into the organization or goes out. Thus, an asset or an increase in the fund balance would be recognized only when cash is collected. Similarly, the assets and fund balance would be reduced only when a cash payment is made. Almost nothing else would be accounted for, making the cash basis of accounting rather unsatisfactory for most reporting and management purposes.

Accrual-basis accounting was developed in response to this shortcoming in the cash-basis method. The accrual basis recognizes fund balance increments (such as revenue) when the amount is earned. Expenses and other types of deductions are recognized when the goods or services have been used up. An asset is recognized as an amount that has been received and has continuing value (such as unexpired costs), although a payment may not have been made for this amount. The measurement of revenues and expenses is called the accrual basis of accounting because accruals are used to convert cash receipts into revenue and cash disbursements into expenses.

The objective of accrual-basis accounting is to provide a more satisfactory matching of revenues and other fund balance additions with expenses and other fund balance deductions in the accounting period to which the financial statements relate. In other words, the accrual basis attempts to determine the real economic impact of what has occurred during a given period of time rather than simply determining how much cash was received or disbursed.

Interfund Accounting   The concept of interfund accounting relates to maintaining the integrity and self-balancing characteristics of the individual funds. Problems arise, for example, when cash used for the benefit of one fund actually belongs to another fund. To illustrate, assume that an institution has a scholarship fund of $10,000 and has $10,000 in the bank for that fund. Also assume that in the institution's unrestricted current fund is another $10,000 that is available for any purpose. Assume that the institution makes a payment of $1,000 to a scholarship recipient out of the unrestricted current fund bank account, whereas the intent was to use the restricted scholarship fund. If the fund balance of the scholarship fund is reduced along with the amount of cash belonging to the unrestricted current fund, both funds would be unbalanced. That is, their assets (when examined separately) would not be equal to their liabilities and fund balances. In the fund that has made the disbursement (that has given up the cash), an asset account would be established representing the amount due from the fund that ultimately is to finance the activity. This arrangement puts the unrestricted current fund back in balance. In the restricted fund that is to be used for scholarship, a liability account would be established for the $1,000 paid on behalf of the restricted fund, and the fund balance would be charged the same amount. Again, the restricted fund now would be in balance and there would exist an interfund receivable and payable. The asset and liability at some point would be extinguished by a transfer of cash between the funds.

Chart of Accounts   The chart of accounts in an accounting system is used to classify each transaction accounted for in the system, facilitating easy and accurate retrieval. It is based on the accounting principles for proper classification of economic phenomena and the reporting needs of management and external parties, calling for segregation of different kinds of transactions so that later those transactions may be aggregated and reported by type.

Accounting systems in higher education usually involve both an alphabetical designation of the account name, which can be read, and a numerical or alphanumeric designation of the account, which can be used for encoding purposes. This arrangement allows the system to work with a numerical or shortened reference rather than a long rational name.

It is important to remember that the purpose of the chart of accounts is to assist in the locating of discrete kinds of transactions. The only rules are those that make sense in terms of how much information and what kinds of categories should be reported. The information needs of many colleges and universities are the same in certain areas, particularly with regard to the production of basic financial statements. (For more information, see Appendix 12-A for the APPA/NACUBO Classification of Accounts.)

Accounting Needs for Auxiliary Enterprise/Service Departments

Auxiliary enterprises are recorded in the current unrestricted fund group of accounts. Auxiliary enterprises are operated primarily for service to students and staff and are required to be self-supporting. Included in this group are residence halls, dining halls, student unions, bookstores, motor pools, and certain physical plant services.

An auxiliary enterprise furnishes a service directly or indirectly to students, faculty, or staff, and charges a fee related to, but not necessarily equal to, the cost of services. Traditionally, these services have encompassed food services, student housing, and college stores. On many campuses, services have expanded to include motor pools, minor alterations, concessions, and others.

The distinguishing characteristic of most auxiliary enterprises is that they are managed essentially as self-supporting activities, although sometimes a portion of student fees or other support is allocated to assist these activities. Services provided by auxiliary operations are important elements in support of an institution's educational program.

Auxiliary enterprises should contribute to and relate directly to the mission, goals, and objectives of a college or university. They should not be regarded merely as service activities or as businesses, but as active expressions of an institution, reflecting its history, style, and relation to its various constituencies. Such enterprises should reflect the quality of service that a college or university desires for its students, faculty, staff, alumni, and the public. Auxiliary enterprises are recognized vehicles for attracting and retaining students, faculty, and staff.

Auxiliary enterprises are charged for a share of general administrative expenses as well as their direct operating expenses, including debt service and provisions for renewal and replacement. Self-supporting auxiliary enterprises also provide working capital to finance accounts receivable and inventory. To generate sufficient operating revenue, auxiliary enterprises attempt to set selling prices, rents, fees, and other charges at a level adequate to support the operations.

Types of Financial Statements

A college or university's financial statement is generally composed of four segments: 1) balance sheet; 2) statement of changes in fund balances; 3) statement of current fund revenues, expenditures, and other changes; and 4) footnotes to the other three segments.

The balance sheet reflects the financial resources of the institution at a given time. The balance sheet contains the assets of the institution, the liabilities, and the fund balances. Thus, the status of the institution is generally expressed in terms of its real accounts. The assets can be viewed as the forms of the institution's financial resources, whereas the liabilities and fund balance are the sources.

The statement of changes in fund balances summarizes the activity within each group of funds during a specific fiscal period. This statement is comparable to the income statement and statement of changes in the stockholders' equity in the for-profit sector. For nonprofit organizations, however, the statement of changes in fund balances covers each set of funds.

The statement of current funds revenues, expenditures, and other changes is a detailed accounting of changes in the current funds column that are included in the statement of changes in fund balances. Sometimes this statement is referred to as the statement of changes in financial position. In fund accounting, most useful information already is contained in the balance sheet and the statement of changes in fund balances, often making redundant the information contained in the statement of current fund revenues, expenditures, and other changes. On the other hand, there may be some activity that should be reported and that has not been disclosed in any of the statements; this often can be taken care of by enhancing the statements with another presentation summarizing the changes in financial position or by adding footnotes to the financial statements. Footnotes summarize the significant accounting principles used to prepare the statements and provide other information essential to a full understanding of the institution's particular financial environment. No examination of an institution's financial statement is complete without a thorough perusal of the footnotes.

Selected Accounting Principles   Accounting principles are the standards that define how economic transactions are to be classified and reported. Recognition of proper accounting principles is important in establishing a college or university accounting system. Most institutions adhere to the accounting principles set forth by the American Institute of Certified Public Accountants (AICPA). These principles should be reflected in an institution's financial statement. When studying a financial statement that has been audited, one should see in the auditor's report a statement as to whether the financial statement has been prepared in accordance with generally accepted accounting principles. If the auditor notes an exception or denies that proper accounting principles have been followed, it will be difficult to evaluate the financial statement in a meaningful fashion.

9.2 COST ACCOUNTING AND REPORTING

Needs of Management Analysis versus Financial Reporting

Cost accounting is concerned with measuring the performance of the various functional subunits of a firm or university, whereas in financial accounting the income statement serves to measure the performance of the total firm or university.

The usefulness of cost accounting in higher education is the ability to understand alternate courses of action and to evaluate these alternatives and predict within reasonable accurateness the effects on the university objectives.

University administration requires not only post-determination, but predeterminations of costs so that it can most effectively direct the university. This cost behavior within a university function is a prerequisite for any type of planning. Intelligent analysis of experience is a major method of seeking improvement in the university's programs. Cost accounting must provide administration a measurement of past results and also information to assist in current control and future planning.

Classification Costs

Some of the more useful classifications and concepts of cost accounting are identified as follows.

1. Classification of Investment Cost Data:
   - Fixed   — Semi-fixed   — Semi-variable
   - Variable   — Differential   — Marginal
   - Common   — Indirect   — Joint
   - Traceable   — Uncontrollable   — Controllable
   - Sunk   — Out-of-pocket   — Direct
2. Classification of Potential Data Useful in Control, Planning, and Decision-Making:
   - Future replacement costs
   - Future counterpart of all the classifications of invested cost data as future fixed cost, future variable cost, and future traceable cost
3. Classification of External Economic Data Useful in Planning and Decision-Making, plus Measurement of Performance:
   - Present replacement cost
   - Opportunity cost related to the present
   - Opportunity cost related to the past
   - Imputed costs related to the present
   - Imputed cost related to the past
   - Changes in general or specific levels used to prepare statistical interpretation of invested cost

Variable costs tend to vary proportionately in total amount with changes in the function involved. Direct materials, direct labor based on rates, and the cost of operating supplies are examples of variable costs.

Semi-variable costs include a substantial segment of fixed costs and a substantial segment of variable costs. As an example, a certain minimum amount of costs will be incurred for internal building maintenance and repairs even if the function or facility is shut down, assuming that the administration intends to resume operations. When productive activity resumes and increases, the accompanying internal wear and tear will tend to cause a steady increase in this cost.

Semi-fixed costs are those that are not fixed over the entire range of capacity of the function, but are fixed over substantial segments of the total range of productive activity of a department or function.

Fixed costs are constant in total amount regardless of changes in production and volume or level within the limits of the existing capacity of a function. A prime example of fixed costs is salaries of operating supervisors.

Differential costs are the difference in total cost at one level of volume and the total cost at another level of volume. Differential costs are helpful in making certain pricing decisions; in deciding whether to make or buy certain equipment, parts, or material; and in comparing different production methods.

Directly traceable costs are those costs that can be traced directly to a job or product, a cost center, an operation, a department, or an operating division of a firm or unit. These can also be referred to as direct costs.

Indirect costs are those that cannot be traced directly to a job or a product, a cost center, an operation, a department, or an operating division. These also are often referred to as common or joint costs.

Controllable costs are those costs whose level of incurrance can be influenced substantially by immediate or longer term management action at some level of authority.

Uncontrollable costs are those whose level of physical incurrance or dollar incurrance cannot be influenced by management action at a given level of authority and in a given period.

Sunk costs are those costs invested in a tangible productive asset, an intangible right, or some extended contract for service that cannot be recovered only by use of the asset over its service life or by use of the service over the term of the contract. Sunk cost is an invested cost or recorded cost.

Out-of-pocket costs are those elements of cost that have required or will require cash disbursement in the period. Some fixed costs, insurance, supervisory salaries, as well as most variable, semi-variable, and semi-fixed costs are out-of-pocket costs.

Replacement costs may be selected from a current market or some anticipated future market. The market usage is practiced widely within financial accounting through the application of the "lower of cost or market" rule to obtain current evaluation of certain assets. The cost of replacement projected two or more years into the future may become important for management purposes, especially capital budgeting.

Standard costs are predeterminations of what specific elements of cost should be under projected conditions. Standard costs usually are set for the basic elements of cost such as material, labor, and overhead, in each operation. They represent the cost that needs to be utilized.

Opportunity costs represent measurable advantage foregone or that may be sacrificed as a result of the rejection of alternative uses of material, labor, or facilities. In the private sector, opportunity costs often are used as an imputed cost in comparing certain proposals for improving profits.

Imputed costs are certain costs that need to be imputed in order to get a more complete or adequate cost for certain comparisons. An imputed cost is the amount of dollars assigned for the use of any productive service that has not been a subject of an independent transaction between a supplier and user to establish a liability or to cause a disbursement of cash. Imputed costs can be inferred or estimated for similar situations outside the university or organization. Opportunity costs are often imputed in certain comparisons to give a proper presentation of different alternatives. Planning and decision-making costs involve primarily directly traceable, differential costs priced on a replacement dollar basis. Certain imputed costs, or opportunity costs, often must be included to make proper cost construction for assisting management.

It should be noted that an individual cost term may have different definitions because different purposes call for different concepts. Carefully defined concepts are extremely useful to the manager in the management process. They enable the manager to distinguish those factors he seeks to measure from those that are extraneous to a particular problem.

A cost accounting system does not exercise managerial control. Management must assume the responsibility for acting on the information furnished. The purpose of a cost accounting system is to help administration make decisions and take actions that result in the control of the university. To do their job well, administration requires facts. Supplying the factual basis for control is a function of an accounting system.

Summary of Applications

The purpose of the cost accounting system is to help administrators make decisions and take actions that result in the control of the university.

Higher education should make a continuous critical evaluation of costing methods of analysis and reporting. It is important to verify that cost centers conform to the assigned areas of responsibility. An appropriate analysis of cost data has been made so that costs can be tracked on a valid basis and that the cost reports are providing the type of cost data required by administration at the time they need it. An obvious fact is that colleges and universities consist of human beings. People, not figures, get things done. Anything that the university accomplishes is the result of the action of these people. It is a fact of life that problems must be solved, decisions must be made, and often the decisions cannot be delayed until all the pertinent information is available.

Cost accounting should relate the results of service evaluation to cost elements in a clear, timely manner and should be used to identify, analyze, and compare costs with commercial providers of similar services.

9.3 PLANT FUND ACCOUNTING SYSTEMS

Types of Plant Funds

The plant fund group consists of four types of funds as follows:

- Unexpended plant funds
- Funds for renewal and replacements
- Funds for retirement of indebtedness
- Funds invested in plant.

Several comments can be made about the four subgroups of the plant fund group.

Unexpended. Unexpended plant funds arise from restricted grants, gifts, and appropriations that can be used only for the acquisition of plant.

When an expenditure of these funds is made, there is 1) a reduction in the fund balance and in cash, and 2) an equal increase in the plant funds subgroup labeled "investment in plant," where the cost of the asset acquired and the increase in net investment in plant are recorded.

Borrowings are an important source of funding for capital outlay. Monies borrowed for acquisition of new plant and equipment are accounted for in this unexpended plant funds subgroup. When the borrowed money is spent, the charge is against the liability account rather than the fund balance. In the investment in plant subgroup, the credit is not to net investment in plant but to the reestablishment of a liability.

Construction in progress may be accounted for in unexpended plant funds until the project is complete. Accountability is then established in the investment in plant subgroup. The procedure most commonly followed is to remove the accountability for construction in progress from the unexpended subgroup as quickly as expenditures are made and to carry the construction in progress in the investment in plant subgroup.

Renewals and replacements. This subgroup represents monies set aside to renew or replace plant assets presently in use. Here, too, the fund balances are subdivided between restricted and unrestricted. One of the sources of renewal and replacement funds is a portion of the mandatory transfer; when mandatory transfers are received, they are classified as restricted funds. The assets consist of cash, investments, and amounts of money that have been turned over to a trustee in accordance with an indenture. These assets are classified as deposits with trustees. Expenditures of these monies result in the reduction of assets and fund balances in this subgroup. Simultaneously, an equal amount is recorded as an increase in net investment in plant and in the investment in plant subgroup. These expenditures often do not result in the acquisition of a capitalizable asset. The amount of such expenditures not capitalized should be disclosed, usually in a parenthetical note.

Retirement of indebtedness. Funds for this subgroup may come from contributions or grants that are made for this explicit purpose and are restricted. Most frequently, the monies for this subgroup come from a mandatory transfer. Amounts so received are classified as restricted fund balances. If the governing board sets aside excess funds for the retirement of indebtedness, such amounts in excess of what is required would be nonmandatory transfers and would be classified as unrestricted. Funds for retirement of indebtedness are used to meet two kinds of obligations: 1) interest expense, which should be shown separately, and 2) amortization of the debt. Amortization of the debt results in another set of entries in the investment in plant subgroup.

Investment in plant. The assets of this subgroup consist of the carrying values of land improvements, buildings, equipment, library books, museum collections, and other similar capital holdings with a long-term life. Some of these are depreciable.

These assets are to be carried at their historical cost until disposed of. In earlier years, some institutions carried such assets at some other amount (such as periodic appraisal value), either out of preference or because the original cost records had been lost or destroyed. When historical cost information is not available, it is permissible for an institution to obtain a professional estimate of the historical costs and to use the estimate as the basis for reporting.

Rules must be established by the institution to determine when a particular expenditure results in the acquisition of a capital asset. For example, items of movable equipment should be capitalized, provided they have a significant value and that they have a useful life that extends beyond at least a year (otherwise the items do not have capital value). The value thresholds vary widely from institution to institution. The Cost Accounting Standards Board established costing rules for all contractors employing federal funds and set certain limits beyond which an expenditure is classified as a capital addition. Another rule must be made to determine when a renovation becomes a capital asset. For example, a minor renovation probably has little value associated with it and would not be considered a capitalizable asset. On the other hand, a renovation that extended the life of the asset or permitted an entirely new use of an existing facility probably will be capitalized. Finally, new assets are added to the carrying values of the asset section of this subgroup, and assets that have been sold, destroyed, stolen, lost, or otherwise eliminated from the possession of the institution should be removed from the records (that is, their carrying values should be removed).

If debt is incurred by the institution to finance working capital, it should not be carried in the plant fund but rather as a liability of current funds. This rule holds even though plant assets may be pledged as collateral against the loan. The reader of financial statements needs to know a great deal about the liabilities of a long-term nature that may appear in other fund groups. Some disclosure requirements in this regard are therefore illustrated in the notes to the financial statements.

The fund balance of the investment implant subgroup is referred to as net investment in plant. It is not classified as restricted or unrestricted because it is simply the accountability for the net asset values carried in this section. No further future use is intended. Thus, any restrictions that may have been imposed on the funds used to finance these assets generally have been met. There are, however, some instances of gifts that carry restrictions of a second-generation nature. For example, the initial restrictions may require that the funds be used for the acquisition of a building. An additional restriction might require that, in the event the building is later sold, the proceeds of the sale be used for a replacement building. This situation is rare, however.

In the statement of changes in fund balances, increases in the net investment in plant arise from the expenditure of unexpended plant funds and renewal and replacement funds. Increases also arise from debt reductions (reflected in the decrease in funds for the retirement of indebtedness) and from contributions-in-kind such as a building, land, or equipment.

Decreases in the net investment in plant represent the elimination from the capital assets inventory of those assets that are retired, sold, disposed of, or destroyed. When such assets are eliminated, the total carrying value of the asset is deducted from the asset category and from the net investment in plant. Any cash proceeds received as a result of this retirement are taken in the unexpended plant fund, and, in the absence of any of the secondary types of restrictions mentioned earlier, are classified as an addition plant funds. Thus, the net gain or loss from the sale or disposal of the capital asset does not appear separately. Another major deduction would be the depreciation of capital assets (if such a practice is followed).

Net investment in plant can increase for a reason that is linked to the peculiar operations of colleges and universities. Many institutions include in the operating budgets of the various departments a provision for minor items of equipment. In some cases, there is a policy of equipment replacement with respect to certain types of assets. For example, typewriters may be replaced on a scheduled basis. The amount that will be expended annually for this purpose is budgeted in that department. Therefore, the expenditure for this purpose becomes part of the functional expenditures set forth in the statement of current funds revenues, expenditures, and other changes in the statement of changes in fund balances for unrestricted or restricted current funds. Another kind of capital outlay that might be financed in a similar manner from current funds expenditures is library books. These expenditures of current funds for the replacement of capital assets are reported first as expenditures of current funds, and then are picked up as assets and as additions to the fund balance of the investment in plant subgroup.

Capital Improvement Recording Procedures

The university will have in place written guidelines pertaining to recording costs of major repairs, maintenance, replacement, remodeling, and other capital additions.

Appendix 9-A is a sample set of procedures and guidelines that highlight the coding requirement associated with recording costs of capital improvement on the books of the university. Appendix 9-B is a glossary of financial terms designed to assist facilities managers in their budgeting and accounting efforts.

Sinking Funds

A sinking fund is a group of assets that have been accumulated to provide for the retirement of term bonds. Since the objective of the fund is to permit the debtor to accumulate a large sum by means of smaller periodic payments, the sinking fund should not be used for the payment of interest nor for the retirement of serial bonds. A sinking fund typically has two sources of revenue: contributions, or in some cases a special tax levy, and earnings on the invested assets of the funds. Since the latter are dependent in part on the size of the funds, they may be expected to increase over the life of the funds. In order to equalize the costs of replacement, it is desirable for the contributions to be the same amount each year. The typical bond agreement takes the above factors into account and establishes the amount of the contribution on an actuarial basis. The procedure requires estimation of interest which the fund assets will earn and the establishment of the contributions at an amount which, made periodically and invested for the life of the fund, will accumulate to the amount of the debt.

Issues Related to Depreciation in Higher Education

In December 1986, the Financial Accounting Standards Board published an exposure draft of a proposed standard that would require depreciation in accounting for all not-for-profit organizations. Most higher education institutions have not used depreciation accounting. However, depreciation accounting appears to be an inevitable consequence of accrued accounting, and accrued accounting is essential to determine whether net assets have been maintained.

Under the proposed statement, nonprofit organizations can be required to disclose depreciation expense for the period, balances of major classes of depreciable assets at the balance sheet date, accumulated depreciation at the balance sheet date, and a general description of the method used in computing depreciation.

The Financial Accounting Standards Board's draft proposal on depreciation received many negative replies on accounting for depreciation. The majority of the respondents returning comments to the Board stated that the use of depreciation in higher education financial statements would not be usable to outside interests such as contributors, lenders, or state governments in evaluating the needs of the institution.

A large number of the respondents also declared that implementation of the depreciation concept would not be worthwhile to the institution in cost benefit terms. They contend that the administrative and operational costs of developing and maintaining a computerized depreciation system for buildings, and hundreds or thousands of pieces of equipment would be burdensome, and the information provided would not necessarily represent the value or actual physical condition of the assets.

The respondents also expressed their concern about the impact of the decision on smaller, struggling institutions that can least afford to pay for the necessary adjustments in their financial reporting requirements. These institutions face significant pressures, such as declining enrollment and rising costs, and therefore cannot easily afford the administrative expense of complying with the ruling.

A number of other comments provided in their responses reaffirm the strong support for NACUBO's long-standing position against recording depreciation, including the inappropriateness of applying the concept to art and collections. Among other comments are the contention that contributions are intended for use and the generation of capital assets and not for depreciation expense, and also the belief that the proposed implementation date does not allow sufficient time to prepare for this major change in procedure.

While it is expected that the Financial Accounting Standards Board will establish requirements for depreciation, its effect should be understood by both the business and facilities officers of the institution.

ADDITIONAL RESOURCES

Meisinger, Richard J. Jr., and Leroy W. Dubeck. *College and University Budgeting*. Washington, D.C.: National Association of College and University Business Officers, 1984.

National Association of College and University Business Officers. *College and University Business Administration*, third edition. Washington, D.C.: NACUBO, 1974.

————. "FASB Proposes Requiring Recognition of Depreciation Costs." *Business Officer*, February 1987.

————. "Issues in Accounting Depreciation." *Business Officer*, March 1987.

————. "FASB Receives Negative Replies on Depreciation Accounting." *Business Officer*, May 1987.

Simons, Harry, and Wilbert E. Karrenbrock. *Intermediate Accounting—Comprehensive Volume*, fourth edition. Southwestern Publishing Company.

Silvoso, Joseph A., and Royal D. M. Bauer. *Auditing*, second edition. Southwestern Publishing Company, 1965.

Tenner, Irving, and Edward S. Lynn. *Municipal and Governmental Accounting*, fourth edition. Englewood Cliffs, New Jersey: Prentice-Hall.

Wixon, Rufus, and Walter G. Kell. *Accountant's Handbook*, fourth edition. New York: The Ronald Press Company.

Appendix 9-A

UNIVERSITY OF NORTHERN COLORADO

Guidelines for Use of Repair and Replacement Funds

The Series 1963 Bond Resolution (UNC Housing System) defines current operating expenses of the Housing System as all necessary operating expenses, current maintenance charges, expenses of reasonable upkeep and repairs . . . and all other expenses incident to the operation of the Housing System. The language in the Series 1972 Bond Resolution (Trustees of State Colleges Housing System) is similar in intent to the above. Therefore, *cost of repairs, maintenance and upkeep occurring annually or more frequently in each unit will be considered as ordinary and normal expenses* of the system and charged to the Revenue Fund as operating expense.

The Resolution states that *funds in the Repair and Replacement Account may be drawn . . . for the purpose of paying the cost of unusual maintenance or repairs, renewals or replacements and the renovating or replacement of furniture and equipment not paid as part of the ordinary expense.* The language in the Series 1972 Bond Resolution (Trustees of State Colleges Housing System) is similar in intent to the above. *Major items of repairs, maintenance and renovating (remodeling) costing $1,000 or more that are non-recurring, not required annually or more frequently, in relation to an individual unit are, therefore, chargeable to the Repair and Replacement Reserve.*

Renovating or replacing furniture and equipment shall be charged to the Repair and Replacement Reserve if the unit cost is $1,000 or more, or if like items having an aggregate cost of $1,000 or more are acquired on a single order.

Major non-recurring repairs, maintenance and renovating costing less than $1,000 will be considered ordinary and normal expenses of the system and charged to the Revenue as operating expense.

Replacement or renovating of furniture and equipment costing between $200 and $1,000 will be charged to the Revenue Fund and coded as capital outlay in accordance with established University procedures, and will not be considered current operating expense.

The following table is intended as a summary of the requirements of the various bond resolutions pertaining to costs of repairs, maintenance, replacement, remodeling and capital additions.

	Will be charged to Revenue Fund		
	Operating Expense	Capital Outlay	Repair and Replacement Fund
1. Cost of repairs, maintenance and upkeep occurring annually or more frequently regardless of cost.	X		
2. Major items of repairs, maintenance and renovating (remodeling) not required annually or more frequently			
Costing $1,000 or more			X
Costing less than $1,000	X		
3. Additions or improvements to buildings			
*Costing $1,000 or more		X	
Costing less than $1,000	X		
4. Replacement or renovating of furniture and equipment			
Costing $1,000 or more			X
*Costing more than $200 but less than $1,000		X	
Costing less than $200	X		
5. New or additional furniture and equipment			
*Costing $200 or more		X	

Costing less than
$200   X

*NOTE: The following will be coded as capital outlay on the
University's records regardless of the fund charge.

1. Renovating, remodeling, additions or improvements to
buildings costing more than $1,000.

2. Replacing, renovating, new or additional equipment, if
the unit cost is $200 or more.

Project No. _____
(Assigned by General Accounting)

UNIVERSITY OF NORTHERN COLORADO
Construction Project Request/Authorization
(Proposed or Approved Projects)

Work Order No. _____
(Assigned by F & O)

(Use for all planning, remodeling, new construction, or major
repair/replacement exceeding $1,000)

1. Name of Project: _____
2. Requested by: _____
                       Name   Phone   Date
3. Project Description:

4. Program Justification (Need as related to University Mission and Master Plan):

5. Project Budget: Prepared by: _____ Date: _____
    Preliminary Planning
    A/E Design & Construction Doc (6-10%)   _____
    Construction   _____
    Equipment   _____
    Occupancy (Move-in Services)   _____
    Construction Supervision (4-8%)   _____
    Other (Specify _____)   _____
    Contingency (5-10%)   _____
          TOTAL PROJECT BUDGET   _____

6. Source of Funds:
   Account Name _____
   Account # _____
   (Assigned by General Accounting)

7. Proposed Project Schedule:
   Preliminary Planning _____
   Board Approval (if necessary) _____
   Design Specifications _____
   Construction Start _____
   Construction Completion _____
   Occupancy/Close-out _____

8. Approvals:
   Requestor: Signed _____ Date _____
   Area Vice President _____ Date _____
   Budget Office _____ Date _____
   V.P. Administration _____ Date _____
   Board of Trustees (if necessary) Date of Approval ____

9. Additional information for accounting distributions if needed.

Data revised and accounting codes assigned.
Signatures: _____ Date: _____
                    Fund Accountant

_____ Date: _____
            Manager of General Accounting

10. Distribution of Completed Form
    Original Filed in General Accounting Office
    Copy to Facilities and Operations
    Copy to Budget Office
    Copy to Requestor

Appendix 9-B

Glossary of Financial Terms

Compiled by John C. Romer
Controller
Guest Services, Inc.

Abatement—A complete or partial cancellation of a levy imposed by a governmental unit. Abatements usually apply to tax levy, special assessment, and service charges.

Accounting procedure—The arrangement of all processes that discover, record, and summarize financial information to produce financial statements and reports as well as to provide internal control.

Accounts receivable—Amount owed an open account from private persons, firms, or corporations for goods and services furnished by an organization.

Accrual basis—The basis of accounting under which all items are recorded when incurred. Revenues are recorded when earned and expenditures are recorded as soon as they result in liabilities even though the actual receipt of the revenue or payment of the expenditure may take place, in whole or in part, in another accounting period.

Acquisition adjustment—Premium paid for a physical asset over and above original cost less depreciation.

Agency funds—Resources held by an institution as custodian or fiscal agent for individual students, faculty, staff members, and organizations.

Aging of receivables—An analysis of individual accounts receivable according to the time elapsed after the billing or due date—usually the former.

Allocate—To divide a lump sum into parts that are designated for expenditure by a specific organizational unit and/or for specific purposes, activities, or objects.

Amortization—The gradual reduction, redemption, or liquidation of the balance of an account according to a specified schedule of times and amounts.

Annuity agreement—An agreement whereby money or other property is made available to an institution or individual on the condition that the institution bind itself to pay stipulated amounts periodically to the donor or other designated individuals. The payments are to terminate at a time specified in the agreement.

Annuity funds—Funds acquired by an institution that are subject to annuity agreements.

Appraise—To make an estimate of value, particularly of the value of property.

Appropriation—An expenditure authorization with specific limitations as to amount, purpose, and time; a formal advance approval of an expenditure from designated resources that are available or estimated to be available.

Audit—Examination of documents, records, reports, systems of internal control, accounting and financial procedures, and other evidence to ascertain whether financial information is presented fairly in its entirety.

Auxiliary enterprise—An entity that furnishes a service directly or indirectly to students, faculty, or staff and charges a fee directly related to, but not necessarily equal to, the cost of the service. The public may be served incidentally by some auxiliary enterprises. The services are essential elements in support of the institution's program and conceptually should be regarded as self-supporting.

Balance sheet—A historical summary for a given economic entity of the assets, liabilities, and owner's equity (or fund balance).

Bequest—Property or funds received through a will. Restrictions may or may not attach to use of the property or funds.

Bond—A written promise to pay a specified sum of money, called the face value or principal amount, at a specified date or dates in the future, called the maturity dates, together with periodic interest at a specified rate.

Bond discount—The excess of the face value of a bond over the price for which it is acquired or sold.

Book value (of assets)—Purchase price of an asset less any accumulated depreciation. In the case of an asset received as a gift, it is the appraised market value of the asset as of the date donated less any accumulated depreciation.

Budget—A plan of proposed expenditures for a fixed period or for a specific project or program along with the proposed means of financing the expenditures.

Capital budget—An expenditure plan for adding to or improving plant or equipment. The means for financing for the current fiscal period are included. If a capital program is already underway, the capital budget will be first year of the program. A capital program is sometimes referred to as a capital budget.

Cash—Currency, coin, checks, postal and express money orders, and bankers' drafts on hand or on deposit with an official occasionally designated as custodian of cash and bank deposits.

Cash basis—The basis of accounting under which revenues are recorded when received in cash and expenditures are recorded when paid.

Cash discounts—An allowance received or given when payment is completed within a stated period of time.

Clearing account—An account used to accumulate total charges for credit for the purpose of either distributing them later among applicable accounts or of transferring the net difference to the proper account.

Contingent fund—Assets or other resources set aside to provide for unforeseen expenditures or for anticipated expenditures of uncertain amount.

Contingent liability—Items that may become a liability as a result of conditions undetermined at a given date such as guarantee, pending law suits, judgment under appeal, unsettled disputed claims, unfilled purchase orders, and incomplete contracts.

Continuing appropriation—An appropriation that, once established, is automatically renewed without further legislative action, period after period, until altered or revoked.

Control account—An account in a general ledger in which the aggregate of debit and credit postings for a number of identical or related accounts called subsidiary accounts are recorded.

Cost accounting—That method of accounting which provides for the assembling and recording of all the elements of cost incurred to accomplish a goal, to carry on an activity or operation, or to complete a unit of work for a specific job.

Cost ledger—A subsidiary record in which each project, job, production center, process, operation, product, or service is given a separate account to which all items entered into its cost are posted in the required detail. These accounts should be arranged and kept so that the result shown in them may be reconciled and verified by a control account or an account from the general book.

Coupon rate—The interest rate specified on the interest coupon attached to a bond. The term is synonymous with nominal interest rate.

Credits—The term "credit" relates to the basic accounting equation of "assets equal liabilities and owners' equity (or fund balance)." Credits, on one hand, increase liabilities and owners' equity (or fund balance) and, on the other hand, decrease assets and expenses. The "credit" is the recording entry to the right column in the double-entry accounting records.

Current assets—Those assets that are available or can be made readily available to meet the cost of operations or to pay current liabilities.

Current funds—Resources to be expended in the near term and used for operating purposes.

Current liabilities—Liabilities that are payable within a relatively short period of time, usually no longer than a year.

Debits—The term "debit" relates to the basic accounting equation of "assets equal liabilities and owners' equity (or fund balance)." Debits, on one hand, increase assets or expenses, and, on the other hand, decrease revenues and owners' equity (or fund balance). The "debit" is the recording entry to the left column in the double-entry accounting records.

Debt—An obligation that results from the borrowing of money or from the purchase of goods and services.

Debt financing—Acquisition of an asset by borrowing money, thereby creating a liability. Typical forms of debt financing are loans and mortgages.

Debt service—All payments in connection with funds borrowed by an institution: principal payments, interest charges, payments to sinking funds to ensure future principal and interest payments, payments to reserves to ensure proper upkeep and maintenance of the facilities, trustees' service charges, legal expenses, and other items related to indebtedness.

Deferred charges—Expenditures that are not chargeable to a fiscal period in which they are needed but are carried on the asset side of the balance sheet pending amortization or other disposition.

Deferred (or unearned) revenue—That portion of receipts for which services have not been completely performed such as food service payments. Until such services are performed in their entirety, that portion of the receipts is considered a liability.

Deficit—The excess of the liabilities and reserves of a fund over its assets. It is also the excess of expenditures over revenues during an accounting period.

Depreciation—Expiration in the service life of fixed assets other than that attributable to wear and tear, deterioration from physical elements, inadequacy, obsolescence, or waste of assets.

Designated funds—Unrestricted monies expendable only for purposes designated by the governing board.

Direct expenses—Those expenses that can be charged directly as a part of a cost of a product for service, of a department, or of an operating unit. They are to be distinguished from overhead and other indirect costs that must be prorated among several products or services, departments, or operating units.

Direct labor—The cost of labor directly expended in the production of specific goods for rendition of specific services.

Direct materials—The cost of materials that become an integral part of a specific manufactured product or that are consumed in the performance of a specific service.

Disbursements—Payment in cash.

Double-entry system—A system of bookkeeping that requires, for every entry made to the debit side of an account or accounts, an entry for a corresponding amount or amounts to the credit side of another account or accounts.

Effective interest rate—The rate of earning on a bond investment based on the actual price paid for the bond, the coupon rate, the maturity date, and the length of time between interest dates. This is in contrast to the nominal interest rate.

Encumbrances—Obligations in the form of purchase orders, contracts, or salary commitments that are chargeable to an appropriation and for which a part of the appropriation is reserved. They cease to be encumbrances when paid or when the actual liability is recorded.

Endowment funds—Funds that a donor or other outside agency has stipulated, as a condition of the gift, that the principal is to be maintained inviolate and in perpetuity and that only the income from the investments of the fund may be expended.

Endowment income—Yield, usually in the form of interest and dividends, that occurs as a result of investing the principal of an endowment fund. Capital gains and losses are not a part of endowment income.

Entry—The record of a financial transaction in its appropriate book of accounts. An entry is also defined as an act of recording a transaction in the books of account.

Expendable fund—A fund whose resources, including both principal and earnings, may be expended.

Expenditures—Where accounts are kept on the accrual or modified accrual basis, this term designates the cost of goods or services received, whether or not payment has been made. Expenditures also include provision for debt retirement not reported as a liability of the fund from which retired as well as capital outlay. Where accounts are kept on the cash basis, the term designates only actual cash disbursements for these purposes.

Expenses—Charges incurred—whether paid or unpaid—for operations, maintenance, interest, and other charges that are presumed to benefit the current fiscal period.

Face value—As applied to securities, the amount of liability stated in the security document.

Fidelity bond—A written promise to indemnify against losses from theft, defalcation, and misappropriation of funds.

Fiscal year—A twelve-month period of time to which the annual budget applies. At the end of this period an organization determines its financial position and the results of its operations.

Fixed assets—Assets of a long-term character that are intended to continue to be held or used such as land, buildings, machinery, furniture, and other equipment.

Fixed charges—Expenses, the amount of which are more or less fixed. Examples are such items as interest, insurance, and contributions to pension funds.

Floating debt—Liabilities other than bonded debt and time warrants that are payable on demand or at an early date.

Full-time equivalent (FTE)—A means for expressing part-time students, faculty, or employees in terms of full-time students, faculty, or employees. The formula for determining an FTE is generally based on credit hours. For example, an institution may define full time as being 12 credit hours. Thus a student (or faculty member) taking (or teaching) 3 credit hours would be a .25 FTE. The same applies to staff based on the number of hours in the normal work week for the job.

Fund—An independent fiscal and accounting entity with a self-balancing set of accounts recording cash and/or other resources together with all related liabilities, obligations, reserves, and equities that are segregated for the purpose of carrying on specific activities or attaining certain objectives in accordance with specific regulations, restrictions, or limitations.

Fund accounting—A sum of money and other assets that constitute a separate accounting entity, created and maintained for a particular purpose and having transactions subject to legal or administrative limitations. Its double-entry accounts are self-balancing, and from there a balance sheet and operating statement may be prepared.

Fund balance—The excess of the assets of a fund over its liabilities and reserves. An exception is in a case of a fund subject to budgetary accounting prior to the end of a fiscal period. In this instance a fund balance is the excess of the fund's assets and estimated revenues for the period over its liabilities, reserves, and appropriations for the period.

General fund—A fund used to account for all transactions of an organizational unit that are not accounted for in another fund.

General ledger—A book, file, or other device that contains the account needed to reflect, in summary and in detail, financial position and result of financial operations.

Grant—A contribution by one unit to another unit. The contribution is usually made to aid in the support of a specified function, but is sometimes also for general purposes.

Indirect costs—Costs that have been incurred for purposes common to some or all of the specific programs or activities of an institution but that cannot easily be identified and charged directly to them with a reasonable degree of accuracy and without an inordinate amount of accounting. Examples include such items as heating, lighting, air conditioning, and janitorial services of buildings plus administrative services such as accounting, purchasing, personnel, and library services.

Internal auditing—A review of operations within established policy guidelines that provides managers with reports, conclusions, and recommendations of the results of the review. It is used to measure and evaluate the effectiveness of the organization.

Internal control—A plan whereby employees' duties are arranged and records and procedures are designed in a way that permits effective accounting control over assets, liabilities, revenues, and expenditures. Under such a system the work of employees is subdivided so that no single employee performs a complete cycle of operations. Thus, for example, an employee handling cash would not post accounts receivable records. Under such a system the procedures to be followed are delineated and require proper authorization by designated officials in order for all actions to be taken.

Inventory—A detailed list showing quantities, descriptions, and values of property and, frequently, units of measure and unit prices.

Investments—Securities and real estate held to produce income in the form of interest, dividends, rentals, or lease payments.

Journal voucher—A voucher for recording certain transactions or information in place of or supplementary to the journals or registers. The journal voucher usually contains an entry or entries, explanations, references to documentary evidence supporting the entry or entries, and the signature or initials of one or more properly authorized officials.

Land—A fixed asset account that reflects the value of land owned by an organization. If land is purchased, this account shows the purchase price and costs such as legal fees and excavation costs incurred to ready the land for its intended use. If the land is acquired by gift, the account reflects the proposed value at the time of acquisition.

Leasehold—The right to the use of real estate by virtue of lease, usually for a specific term of years, for which a consideration is paid.

Liabilities—Debt or other legal obligations arising out of past transactions that must be liquidated, renewed, or refunded at some future date.

Life income agreement—An agreement by which a donor makes assets available to an institution under the condition that the institution will, for the donor's lifetime, pay the donor the income earned by the assets.

Life income funds—Funds acquired by an institution subject to life income agreements.

Loan funds—Funds to be lent to students, faculty, or staff. When both principal and interest on the loans are lendable, they are included in the loan funds group. If only the income from a fund is lendable, the principal is included in the endowment and similar funds group. The cumulative income, however, constitutes the loan fund.

Long-term debt—Debt with a maturity of more than one year after the date of issuance.

Maintenance—The upkeep required on physical properties to make them fit for use or occupancy. Examples are inspecting equipment to detect defects and making repairs.

Mandatory transfers—Transfers arising out of binding legal agreements related to the financing of the educational plant such as amounts for debt retirement, interest, and required provisions for plant renewals and replacements that are not financed from other sources. Also, transfers arising out of grant agreements with federal government agencies, donors, and other organizations to match gifts and grants to loan funds or other funds.

Net income—The term used in accounting for designating the excess of total revenues over total expenditures for an accounting period.

Net revenue available for debt service—Gross operating revenues of an enterprise less operating and maintenance expenses but exclusive of depreciation and bond interest.

Nominal interest rate—The contractual interest rate shown on the face and in the body of a bond that represents the amount of interest to be paid. This is in contrast to the effective interest rate.

Nonoperating expenses—Expenses incurred for nonoperating properties, or expenses incurred in performing activities not directly related to supplying the basic service of an enterprise.

Notes payable—Generally, an unconditional written promise signed by the maker to pay a certain sum in money. The money is payable on demand or at a fixed or determinable time either to the bearer or to the order of a person designated on the note.

Object classification—Grouping expenditures on the basis of goods or services purchased. For example, expenditures would be grouped under personal services, materials, supplies, equipment, etc.

Obsolescence—The decrease in the value of fixed assets relating to economic, social, technological, or legal changes.

Operating budget—A budget that applies to all outlays except capital outlays.

Operating statements—A statement that summarizes the financial operations for an accounting period. This is to be contrasted with a balance sheet that shows financial position at a given time.

Original cost—The total of assets given and/or liabilities assumed to acquire an asset.

Overhead—Those elements of cost necessary to produce an article or to perform a service that cannot be easily or accurately charged to the product or service. Overhead items usually relate to those objects of expenditure that do not become an integral part of the finished product or service. Examples are rent, heat, light, office supplies, and insurance.

Perpetual inventory—A system in which the inventory of units of property at any date may be obtained directly from the records without resorting to an actual physical count.

Petty cash—A sum of money set aside for the purpose of making change or paying small obligations. The money is used for cases in which issuing a formal voucher and check would be too expensive and time consuming.

Plant funds—Funds to be used for the construction, rehabilitation, and acquisition of physical properties for institutional purposes; funds already expended for such properties; funds set aside for the renewal and replacement of properties; and funds accumulated for the retirement of indebtedness on these properties.

Prepaid expenses—Expenses entered in the accounts for benefits not yet received.

Prepaid expenses differ from deferred charges in that they are spread over a shorter period of time and are regularly recurring costs of operations. Examples of prepaid expenses are prepaid rent, prepaid interest, and premiums on unexpired insurance.

Pro forma—A term used in conjunction with a noun to denote a sample form, document, statement, certificate, or presentation. The contents may be either wholly or partially hypothetical or factual and may be estimates or proposals.

Program budget—A budget in which expenditures are based primarily on programs of work and secondarily on character and object budget. A program budget is a traditional type of budget that falls between the traditional character and object budget, on one hand, and the performance budget, on the other.

Project—A plan of work, job, assignment, or task.

Purchase order—A document that authorizes the delivery of specified merchandise or the rendering of certain services and the making of a charge for them.

Quasi-endowment funds—Funds that the governing board, rather than a donor or other outside agency, has determined are to be retained and invested. The governing board has the right to decide at any time to expend such funds. These monies are sometimes referred to as funds functioning as endowment.

Receipts—A term that, unless otherwise qualified, means cash received.

Recoverable expenditures—An expenditure made for or on behalf of another fund—or for a private individual, firm, or corporation—that will subsequently be recovered in cash or its equivalent.

Refund—An amount paid back or credit allowed because of an overcollection or due to the return of an object sold.

Reimbursement—Cash or other assets paid back for work or services performed; repayment for expenditures made for or on behalf of another individual, firm, or corporation.

Replacement cost—The cost, as of a certain date, of a structure that can render similar service—but need not be of the same structural form—as the structure to be replaced.

Requisition—A written demand or request, usually from one department to the purchasing officer or from one department to another department, for a specified article or services.

Reserve—An account that records a portion of the fund balance that is allocated or set aside for some future use and is thus not otherwise available.

Resources—The actual assets of an entity, such as cash, land, and buildings plus contingent assets such as estimated revenue applying to current fiscal year not accrued or collected.

Restricted funds—Funds limited to a specific use by outside agencies or persons. These are to be distinguished from funds over which the institution has complete control or freedom of use.

Retained earnings—The accumulated earnings of an enterprise that have been retained in the fund and that are not reserved for any specific purpose.

Schedules—The explanatory or supplementary statements that accompany the balance sheet or other principal statements that are periodically prepared from the accounting records.

Securities—Bonds, notes, mortgages, or other forms of negotiable or non-negotiable instruments.

Short-term debt—Debt that matures one year or less after the date of issuance.

Sinking fund—Cash or other assets, and the interest or other income earned from it, that are set apart for the retirement of a debt or for the protection of an investment in depreciable property.

Spending policy—In investing for total return, the portion of earnings allocated for current operating purposes. It is expressed as a percentage of market value and is sometimes called the "pay-out rate." The term "earnings" includes the sum of net realized and unrealized appreciation or shrinkage in portfolio value plus dividend and interest income. A prudent spending policy would protect the endowment from loss of purchasing power before appropriating gains.

Standard costs—A predetermined cost of performing an operation efficiently under reasonable and normal conditions. Normal conditions exist when there is an absence of extraordinary factors affecting the quality or quantity of the work performed, or the time or method of performing it.

Stores—Goods on hand in storerooms, subject to requisition and use.

Surplus—See fund balance or retained earnings.

Suspense account—An account that carries charges or credits temporarily, pending the determination of the proper account or accounts to which they are to be posted.

Temporary loans—Short-term obligations representing amounts borrowed for a short period of time and usually evidenced by notes payable or warrants payable. They may be unsecured or secured by specific revenues to be collected.

Term endowment—Funds which donors or other outside agencies have contributed to an institution with certain terms or conditions attached and that, only upon the occurrence of a particular event or upon passage of a stipulated date, can be expended.

Total return—The sum of net realized and unrealized appreciation or shrinkage in portfolio value plus yield (dividend and interest income).

Transfers—The moving of assets, liabilities, and balances from one fund group to another.

Trial balance—A list of the balances of the accounts in a ledger kept by double entry with the debit and credit balances shown in separate columns. The totals of the debit and credit columns are equal.

Unappropriated budget surplus—If the fund balance at the close of the preceding year is not included in the annual budget, the term designates that portion of the current fiscal year's estimated revenues that has not been appropriated. If the fund balance of the preceding year is included, the term designates the estimated fund balance at the end of the current fiscal year.

Undesignated funds—Unrestricted monies available for any purpose.

Unearned or deferred revenue—See deferred or unearned revenue.

Unencumbered appropriations—That portion of an appropriation not yet expended or encumbered.

Unit cost—A term used in cost accounting to denote the cost of producing a unit of product or rendering a unit of service.

Unrestricted funds—Monies provided to the institution with no restrictions on their use.

Voucher—A written document that evidences the propriety of transactions and usually indicates the accounts in which they are to be recorded.

Work in process—The cost of partially completed products manufactured or processed. An example would be a partially completed printing job. This term is sometimes referred to as "work in progress."

Work order—A written order, authorizing and directing a certain task to be performed, that is issued to the person who will direct the work. Among the items of information shown on the order are the nature and location of the job, specifications of the work to be performed, and a job number that is referred to in reporting the amount of labor, materials, and overhead.

Work unit—A fixed quantity that will consistently measure work effort expended in the performance of an activity or in the production of a commodity.

Working capital—Current fund cash, or current fund assets converted to cash, that will be used to liquidate current fund liabilities in a normal operating cycle—typically one year.

CHAPTER 10

Plant Finance

Mohammad H. Qayoumi
Associate Executive Vice President
Facilities Development and Operations
San Jose State University

10.1 INTRODUCTION

College and university business and financial management has undergone change, in both method and emphasis, over the last thirty years. During the expansion period of the 1950s and 1960s, there were adequate funds to meet all needs. This availability of funds, and the persistent urgency to expand physical facilities to meet the needs of constantly escalating enrollments, resulted in limited emphasis on economy studies. Decisions sometimes were made on the basis of what was most expeditious, what engineers and architects considered the best technology, personal preference, tradition, and similar considerations, without evaluating long-term economies.

Commencing in the early 1970s, economy became a major, even dominant, consideration in business and financial decision-making. Nationwide enrollments leveled off, then fell. Costs increased in all facets of plant construction, maintenance, and operation, especially the purchase of fuels and energy. Governmental mandates on accessibility and safety added costly new requirements. Simultaneously, there was a faltering of revenue sources. Requests for funds had to be justified and prioritized by individual project.

It has become mandatory that optimum economies be achieved in facilities management, and that fund requests be accompanied by a showing that they are limited to that needed to satisfy requirements with the greatest long-term economy. This necessitates economy studies in decision-making. An economy study is a comparison between alternative solutions in which the differences are expressed as far as practicable in money terms. Where technical considerations are involved, such a comparison is called an engineering economy study.

Nearly all facilities management problems involve alternatives, and their resolution requires considerations and comparisons of the costs of alternatives. What levels of electric power should be purchased and produced? Should a heating or power plant be converted to a different type fuel? Should building cooling systems be converted to a central chiller plant with a chilled water distribution system? There are alternatives in the replacement of building components and equipment, such as absorption chillers, compressors, components of a steam distribution system, roofs, and roof drainage systems. The choice between alternatives often is not simple; machines and structures generally are parts of a complex plant, and this creates difficulties in determining the effects of alternatives. Many alternatives embody subsidiary alternatives. Satisfaction of the engineer's sense of technical perfection is not normally the most economical alternative; imperfect alternatives are sometimes the most economical.

In most cases, costs to be compared are not immediate costs but rather long-term costs. Initial cost, operating and maintenance costs, life expectancy, and replacement cost must be considered. This involves determining the time value of money. The time value of money is a factor and should always be considered. The business manager who is not technically trained must rely on the physical plant director for advice as to the difference between technical alternatives. Physical plant management must translate the differences between alternatives into money terms, both for internal decision-making as well as to justify requests to higher authorities for funds.

This chapter addresses basic financial principles and methods with which physical plant professionals must be familiar in order to participate competently and effectively in college and university financial management.

10.2 SOURCES OF FUNDS

The principal sources of funds for colleges and universities are tuitions and fees, governmental appropriations, gifts, grants and contracts, endowments, sales, and auxiliary enterprises. The percentage breakdown differs widely among institutions. Private universities receive roughly 35 to 45 percent of their total revenue from tuition, while most public institutions receive only 13 to 18 percent from this source. Federal funding accounts for about 15 percent for both private and public institutions.

Private colleges and universities receive less than 3 percent of their revenues from state and local governments, while public institutions receive 40 to 45 percent from this source. Gifts, grants, contracts, and endowments provide less than 5 percent of the funding for public institutions; for private institutions this source provides about 15 percent. Sales and auxiliary enterprises provide roughly the same percentage for both types of institutions—15 to 20 percent.

From the foregoing, it is apparent that public institutions are more dependent upon state or local governments for funds, and therefore that political and economic changes can directly affect appropriations. This adversely affects long-term planning. For any institution, the accurate projection of future enrollments is essential for effective planning. Sponsored research funds have seen major fluctuations in recent years, and the value of most endowment funds fluctuates with the overall business and investment climate.

By becoming acquainted with the funding plan of the institution, the director and other physical plant management personnel can better understand and anticipate funding problems, and, most importantly, contribute to constructive public relations with regard to institutional funding.

10.3 TIME VALUE OF MONEY

Where a choice is made between alternatives that involve different receipts and disbursements, it is essential that interest be considered. Economy studies in facilities management generally involve decisions between such alternatives. When evaluating alternative solutions to a problem, the dollar values must be made comparable. This requires computations of interest.

Interest may be defined as money paid for the use of borrowed money. The rate of interest is the ratio between the interest payable at the end of a period of time, usually a year or less, and the money owed at the beginning of the period. If $8 interest is paid annually on a debt of $100, the interest rate is $8/$100 or 8 percent per annum. Simple interest refers to interest that is paid each year of the loan period. Interest that each year is based on the total amount owed at the end of the previous year, an amount which includes the original principal and accumulated interest, is called compound interest. Compound interest is the general practice of the business world; simple interest usually applies to loans for periods of a year or less.

10.4 USE OF INTEREST FORMULAS

Interest tables are used to obtain multiplication factors for compound amount, present worth, sinking fund, and capital recovery. These tables can be found in most managerial finance textbooks.

In comparing various alternatives, each scenario may have different types of costs. The simplest method in making comparisons is to compute the present worth or future value of each alternative. For example, two machines proposed for a given service are to be compared, using an interest rate of 6 percent.

Machine A has a first cost of $7,000, an estimated life of ten years, and an estimated salvage value of $1,000. The estimated annual expenditure for operation and maintenance is $2,500.

Machine B has a first cost of $10,000, an estimated life of ten years, and an estimated salvage value of $1,500. The estimated annual expenditure for operation and maintenance is $2,000.

Machine A

First cost	$7,000.00
Present worth of annual expenditure of $2,500 for ten years	18,400.00
	25,400.00
Present worth of $1,000 salvage value ten years hence	558.40
Present worth of cost of ten years of service	**$24,841.60**

Machine B

First cost	$10,000.00
Present worth of annual expenditure of $2,000 for ten years	14,720.00
	24,720.00
Present worth of $1,500 salvage value ten years hence	837.40
Present worth of cost of ten years of service	**$23,882.60**

Machine B shows a prospective savings of $959 in present worth of the cost of ten years of service.

10.5 RISK AND RETURN

It is impossible to project future economic developments with certainty. Risk is defined as the probability of the occurrence of an unfavorable outcome. There are two types of risks, systematic and unsystematic. Systematic risk is the variability of outcome due to causes that simultaneously affect the general market—such as economical, political or social changes, international conflicts, and securities markets. Unsystematic risk is the variability of outcome unique to a firm or an industry—such as labor strikes, management errors, new inventions, advertising campaigns, shifts in consumer tastes, and new government regulations.

The major sources of systematic risk are as follows:

1. Operating risk, due to variations in operating earnings before interest and taxes (such as fluctuations in ratio of fixed cost to variable cost).
2. Financial risk, due to variations in earnings per share due to use of leverage in the capital structure.
3. Market risk, due to external elements that affect the economy in general and that will impact the earnings.
4. Purchasing power risk, mainly due to inflation reducing the purchasing power of savings or invested wealth.

Return is defined as benefit received from incurring a certain cost. It is intuitively obvious that a financial venture is attractive only when the benefit is greater than the cost. Rate of return is defined as:

$$R = \text{Rate of return} = \frac{\text{Net benefit}}{\text{Cost}}$$

When capital is invested in any financial venture, the rate of return must be high enough to compensate for systematic and unsystematic risks in addition to the pure interest rate.
Therefore:

$$R = r_p + r_i + r_b + r_f + r_{pp} + r_t + \text{——}$$

Where:
r_p = Pure interest rate solely due to the use of money; it is about 2 to 2.25 percent.
r_i = Interest rate risk due to variations in the present rate.
r_b = Business risk associated with an individual firm, due to the business cycle, technological change, availability of materials, etc.
r_f = Financial risk.
r_{pp} = Purchasing power which accounts for inflation.
r_t = Tax-related issues.

Risk and return are tied together closely and one cannot be calculated without the other. If the rate of return increases, so will the risk and vice versa.

10.6 FINANCIAL PLANNING AND CONTROL

Break-even Analysis

A major task for every manager is to choose financial alternatives. The motivation behind analyzing various alternatives is to utilize the funds available for getting a particular job done in the most cost-effective manner. Some typical problems might be:

1. The decision to contract certain services such as elevator maintenance, or to use in-house crews.
2. The decision to buy certain equipment that will make maintenance more productive.
3. The decision to generate any of the utilities, or to buy from a utility company.
4. The decision to purchase computers and other equipment, or lease from a third party.
5. The decision as to how frequently and in what quantities stock items should be ordered.

A technique that can be used in making such decisions is called breakeven analysis. The methodology can be illustrated with item 5 in the preceding list, commonly referred to as the economic order quantity, or EOQ.

Economic Order Quantity

There are many costs associated with maintaining an inventory, such as carrying costs, ordering costs, and stockout costs. Carrying costs refer to the cost of capital tie-up in inventory, storage costs, insurance, depreciation and obsolescence costs. Ordering costs refer to the cost of placing an order (including production setup costs, if appropriate), shipping and handling costs, and loss of quantity discount savings. Stockout costs include added expenses that might be incurred because of loss of good will. The idea is to minimize the total cost as shown below:

$$TC = 1/2\ QC_1 + \frac{P}{Q} + Co$$

Where:
TC = Total cost
Q = Quantity to be ordered
C_1 = Annual holding cost per unit
D = Annual demand for the part
Co = The cost of placing an order

To minimize total cost, take the first derivative of TC with respect to Q and put it equal to zero.

$$\frac{dTC}{d\ Q} = \frac{1}{2}\ C_1 = \frac{D}{Q^2}\ Co = 0$$

$$Q^2 = \frac{2D\ Co}{C_1}$$

$$Q^* = \sqrt{\frac{2D\ Co}{C_1}}$$

Where Q^* is equal to the economic order quantity.

Financial Ratios

Financial ratios are one of the ways to determine how well an institution is living within its own means, in comparison with similar institutions and with itself over time. Based on the trends of these ratios, they also can predict if trouble lies ahead or if the institution is on solid ground. Financial ratios can be a useful tool for both internal and external management. One of the potential pitfalls of using ratios, especially when making comparisons with other institutions, is failing to assemble comparable data. To illustrate, imagine that you want to know how the performance of your institution compares with another institution in maintenance dollars spent per-square-foot. You find that the cost at your institution is twice that of the other institution. After further research, you find that in the other organization the custodial service is part of another department and all maintenance items costing over $1,000 come from capital budget, rather than operating budget as in your institution. You also find that the other campus has a higher ratio of scientific space. Failure to include adjustments for these differences would render any comparison invalid.

The biennial APPA *Comparative Costs and Staffing Report for College and University Facilities* provides valuable data that can be used for ratio analysis in comparing similar institutions, or for analyzing the trend within the same institutions through the use of historical data from past reports.

Financial Forecasting

One of the important uses of financial ratios is in financial forecasting. The objective is to determine how changing external factors will affect the financial health of the institution. For example, most institutional funding is enrollment driven. When enrollment decreases, the campuses that have a higher fixed operation cost to total cost ratio will be hurt; or when federal funds for research drop, campuses that have a higher research revenue to total revenue ratio will suffer.

The key for financial forecasting is the ability to project factors for a period of five years or more with a reasonable degree of accuracy. This will determine whether the changes in these factors are linear, curvilinear, cyclic, or simply due to temporary fluctuations of conditions beyond management's control. Statistical methods can provide better insight in this case. Some of the common tools are the use of scatter diagrams and regression techniques.

Debt Financing

Debt financing is becoming a viable method of financing a capital project. There are two types of debt financing: short-term and long-term. For short-term debt, the essential factors in selecting a source are the effective cost of credit, availability of credit, and the influence of a particular credit on the availability and cost of other sources. The decision to finance an asset using short-term or long-term debt is made by hedging principal, which means that permanent assets should be financed with long-term debt and temporary investments should be financed with short-term debt. Therefore, the most common form of debt financing encountered by a physical plant administrator is long-term, and the most common form of long-term debt is bond financing.

Bond Evaluation

A bond is a long-term promissory note issued by the federal government, state or local government, or an individual firm. It usually is issued for a period of more than ten years in denominations of $1,000. The par value of the bond is the face value appearing on the note to be redeemed by the bondholder at maturity. The market value of the bond varies with the market interest rate. When the interest rate increases, the market value of bonds drops below par and vice versa. The bond's selling price is quoted as the percentage of par value. For instance, if one sees that a bond is selling at 65-1/2, it means the market price is $655; but at maturity the bondholder will receive $1,000.

The coupon interest rate indicates the percentage of the par value to be paid to the bondholder on an annual basis. For example, if the coupon interest rate of a bond is 11 percent, it means the bondholder receives $110 annually, regardless of the market interest rates. Bond interest usually is paid semiannually. Therefore, it can be deduced that when the coupon interest rate is more than the market interest rate, the market value of the bond will be more than par value and vice versa.

The current yield of a bond is the ratio of the annual interest payment to the bond market price, while the yield to maturity refers to the internal rate of return (IRR) of the bond. If a bond is callable, it means the issuing agency can repurchase the bonds from their holders at a stated price over a predetermined period. Since this feature gives the issuing agency flexibility to pay the indenture before maturity, the bondholder must be paid a premium. The difference between the call price and the par value is known as the call premium.

Bond Rating

Bond rating is a debt quality measurement of a firm based on both subjective and objective assessments of the relative degree of risk associated with the timely payments required by the obligation. The role of debt-rating agencies is to assist those responsible for primary debt issues in setting the price and fixed rate of return. The quality assessment often is expressed as a number or a letter and is based on a scale that expresses the highest quality to the lowest quality relative to prior quality assessments of the rater. The analysis is based on a review of financial ratios and a comprehensive analysis of the issue, including the issuer's industry.

The evaluation looks into the adequacy of issuers' cash flow for servicing the predetermined interest and principal payment obligations. Therefore, ratios relating to cash flows and debt service, companies' earning power, financial resources, and predictability of earning are essential elements of the rating process. It is important to note that the stability of earnings is more important than the level of earnings. Academic research strongly suggests that between 50 and 70 percent of many bond ratings can be determined by the following key variables:

* Subordination status of the issue
* Size of the company
* Degree of financial leverage
* Profitability of the issuer
* Interest coverage
* Stability of issue's dividends and earnings

A rough estimate can be made of a bond's rating from the issuer's stock quality rankings. Although ratio analysis influences about 50 percent of a rating decision, the process is subject to qualitative analysis.

A study performed in January 1976 reveals that, while each rating grade category has a certain "financial center of gravity," there is considerable overlap. Therefore, rating procedure is not mathematically weighing or ranking the quantitative data because the importance of every factor is a function of the particular industry. For instance, in consumer goods industries the marketing strategy carries great weight, while for public utilities the regulatory environment, the geographic area served, and the companies' construction program are major factors in the analysis.

Another factor that determines the debt rating is the quality of the firm's management. This is related to the nature of the company's managerial quality, strength, and depth in the following areas:

1. Company's performance compared with competitors.
2. Upper management turnover and hiring from the outside versus internal promotions.
3. Company's decision-making structure—centralization versus decentralization.
4. Types and relations of different activities with which the firm is involved.
5. Public sentiment toward the company.
6. Geographic location of the company as it relates to firm's ability to attract top-quality managers.
7. How management plans to achieve stated goals and objectives.
8. Management's ability to define financial and operating policies.
9. Management's past track record.
10. Management's ability to deal with unforeseen events.
11. Management's strategies for replacing itself over time.

Bond quality measurements are subjective and based on the rating agency's comprehensive approach. This implies that it would be difficult to replicate precisely the ratings of a rating agency. A number of researchers have attempted to predict bond ratings by simulating the rating agency process and have developed statistical models based on quantitative variables. Although these researchers recognize the importance of the qualitative variable, they believe that a reliable gauge of potential agency ratings can be determined from certain financial data.

The key variables considered by the researchers were indenture, size, leverage, profitability, coverage, stability, turnover, asset protection, liquidity, marketability, management, industry, and competitive analysis. Depending upon the particular model, they were able to predict properly 66 to 80 percent of the ratings. It is important to note that the aforementioned models attempt to predict a prediction, inasmuch as the agency ratings themselves are projections of the future credit experience and are not based on deterministic knowledge of future performance of a firm. Thus, even in the face of apparently limited financial ratios, a firm might have opportunities to build an effective debt quality management strategy both in the long term, and short-term, or vice versa.

The first formal bond rating was begun by John Moody in 1909. Presently, two other agencies rate bonds in addition to Moody's—Standard & Poor and Fitch Investor Services. Standard & Poor's rating starts with a AAA rating as the highest assigned, followed by AA, A, BBB, BB, B, CCC, CC, C, and D. The AAA refers to bonds with the least amount of risk and D to ones in default. Therefore, AAA bonds normally have the lowest yield because of the relatively low level of risk associated with them, and, of course, the opposite is true for D-rated bonds. The other two types of ratings are basically similar to Standard & Poor's.

10.7 CAPITAL BUDGETING TECHNIQUES

Capital budgeting deals with the planning and investment of a fixed asset where the expenditure and expected return extend beyond one year. Capital budgeting is an important function of plant management because today's decisions will have an impact for many years to come, and reversing or modifying decisions will be costly. Moreover, in most of these situations the size of the investment requires careful analysis. There are a number of different techniques to use in comparing various project alternatives. Descriptions of the most common ones follow:

Payback Method

This method determines the number of years over which the initial capital outlay will be recovered. A project is accepted if the payback period is less than or equal to a predetermined desired period. The advantage of the payback method is its simplicity. It also emphasizes the early years' cash flow, which is more certain than that of later years. The drawback of the payback method is that it does not take into account the time value of money. In addition, revenues beyond payback years are not considered. Despite these serious shortcomings, however, this method usually is used as a prescreening technique.

Net Present Value (NPV)

This technique is the accumulation of the future contribution of the project profit to the firm, less the initial capital outlay. It is important to note that every year's profit is discounted using the present value technique. The rate of return usually is set by the institution as the opportunity cost of capital. In formula expression, the net present value is given by:

$$NPV = \sum_{t=1}^{n} \frac{R_t}{(1+r)^t} = I_o$$

Where:
r = Discount rate
n = Expected useful life of the project
R_t = Net revenue (income minus expenses) for year t
I_o = Initial capital outlay

For a project to be investigated further, the NPV must be larger than zero; if it is minus, it will be rejected. When various project options are compared, the one with the highest NPV is the most attractive. This is a much better technique for analyzing capital budgeting options than the payback method for the reasons mentioned earlier, but there also are some potential problems associated with NPV.

First, the discount rate has a significant role, not only in providing a go/no-go solution, but in comparing various investment options, especially if different options have diverse income streams. In other words, the method discriminates heavily against options that provide larger revenues in later years versus first years. This intuitively makes sense, because the returns in the first years are more certain than returns in later years. To illustrate this, assume two investment options, A and B, have the same NPV at a discount rate of 10 percent. Option A has a uniform revenue stream during the project life, while Option B has small revenues in the first year but gradually increases toward the end of the project. Now, if the discount rate is changed to 12 percent, Option A will be more attractive than B. Conversely, if the discount rate is dropped to 8 percent, the opposite will be true.

Secondly, the NPV technique assumes that any cash flow created by the project can be invested almost instantaneously at the discounted rate. In reality, this is hardly the case. Therefore, the NPV resulting might be a bit skewed; but even with these shortcomings NPV is preferred to the payback method in capital budgeting.

Internal Rate of Return (IRR)

This is a variation of the NPV method in which a discount rate on the project is calculated using an NPV of zero. If the calculated discount rate is equal to or greater than the institution's discount rate, the project is accepted; otherwise it is rejected. If different options are compared, the project with the highest IRR is favored. The internal rate of return is given by the following formula:

$$I_O = \sum_{t=1}^{n} \frac{R_t}{(1 + IRR)^t}$$

Where:

n = Expected useful life of the project

R_t = Net revenues for year t

I_o = Initial capital outlay

IRR = Internal rate of return for the project

Although IRR is a better technique, it has two main disadvantages. First, finding an analytical solution involves solving a polynomial of degree "n." Usually, IRR is calculated by trial and error. Second, because the above formula is a polynomial of degree "n," then, mathematically speaking, there are "n" solutions to the polynomial. Generally this is not a problem if the net revenues for every year are positive; i.e., there is not any period where the operating expenses exceed revenues. The polynomial will have only one positive root, and all the other roots will be negative or imaginary. Naturally, the positive root is the true solution, but if there is at least one period where net revenue is negative, there will be more than one positive root. This sometimes can create a problem, although in most instances, the correct root will be pretty obvious. One of the appropriate uses of IRR is in capital rationing situations, in which only a fixed amount of funds is available for all projects. Here, the projects can be ranked by IRR in descending order. The projects will be selected, starting from the top of the list, until the funds are depleted.

Third-Party Financing

There are many occasions when lack of funding prevents accomplishing many desired capital projects. During the past decade, third-party financing has become a viable option for funding certain types of capital outlay projects, mostly in the areas of central utilities and energy projects.

Cogeneration projects have been the most common type of third-party financing in the central utilities area. During the first half of the 1980s many universities entered into such contracts due to some lucrative incentives by PURPA on tax credits, liberal depreciation schedules for cogeneration projects, and projected escalations caused by energy crises. In most of these projects, the institutions either received better electrical rates than the local utility, or paid the same rate as before but received revenues in terms of land lease and labor reimbursement benefits. As some of the tax incentives disappeared and energy prices dropped during in the mid-1980s, many of these enterprises encountered financial problems for not meeting the projected revenue stream.

Third-party financing also has been applied in central plant projects other than or combined with cogeneration. There have been cases in which a campus has leased its existing chillers and boilers to a third party and entered into a contract to provide a certain quantity of steam and chilled water at predetermined costs. The third party in turn has expanded the plant, adding new chillers and boilers to meet the projected load, recovering their investment through guaranteed buy-back contracts for unit cost and quantity. In this scenario, the campus has abdicated its responsibility to produce steam, chilled water, and/or electricity to the third party. The campus does not have to be concerned about financing any equipment upgrades or labor problems associated with running the central plant; but in losing control of the central plant their operational flexibility also is limited. In such situations it is paramount that the physical plant administrator have major input in writing the contract between the third party and the university.

Third-party financing for energy projects has occurred mostly in the area of installing more energy-efficient hardware, such as new lamps, variable frequency drives, or energy management systems. Independent financing companies as well as equipment vendors have provided this service. In such a project, the third-party financier will perform a preliminary audit. If the project appears to be financially attractive, they will fund the purchase and installation of the hardware; the savings or cost-avoidance resulting from the project will then be shared between the third party and the host institution.

One of the biggest problems experienced in such projects is in determining the savings attributed to the modification. For instance, if installing an energy management system will reduce the heating cost for a building by so many MMBTU from the baseline year, what happens if there is an extremely severe or a mild winter, or if changes occur in building occupancy? Sharing the savings between the third party and the host institution, although simple in theory, can become involved in actual practice.

In summary, third-party financing has offered another potential savings mechanism. It needs to be understood that, since the third party is assuming the risk and funding the project, they will want to be compensated for that risk. Generally speaking, third-party financing is less attractive for nonprofit institutions since the tax implications usually are moot. But for institutions that have limited capital funding for the needed levels, it can be a viable funding mechanism.

Capital Budgeting Under Uncertainty

In the previous section it was assumed that perfect information is available when capital outlay decisions are made. Naturally, this is very far from reality. In every situation there is uncertainty associated with net revenue stream and the useful life of the project. The intent of this section is to find ways to account for this uncertainty. One technique is called the certainty equivalent approach, in which the projected cash flow is discounted by a certain factor known as the certainty equivalent coefficient "a" where:

$$a = \frac{\text{Certain cash flow}}{\text{Risky cash flow}}$$

Thus, "a" will vary between zero and one. It can also be viewed as a probability number, since "a" is close to zero in cases of extreme risk and close to one in cases of certainty.

In this approach, after the risky cash flow has been discounted by the certainty equivalent coefficient, then any of the capital budgeting discussed earlier will be applicable. For instance, using net present value the formula will be:

$$NPV = \sum_{t=1}^{n} \frac{a_t\, R_t}{(1 + r)^t} = I_o$$

Where a_t = Certainty equivalent coefficient for the year t.

A second approach to account for uncertainty is to use a risk-adjusted discount rate. Here, the risk-free rate of return is increased to compensate for the uncertainty, so the NPV equation discussed earlier can be used and the only difference will be that a higher rate of return is used. Either of these methods can be used effectively, the main difference being that the second method makes an implicit assumption that cash flow risk is greater for later years than early years.

10.8 DEPRECIATION

The balance sheet and other main financial statements normally have an annual cycle, but the fixed cost elements usually have more than one year of useful life. Depreciation is an accounting mechanism used to allocate that cost over the use of major fixed assets, with the goal of determining the true operational cost of the plant where a portion of the cost is derived from utilization of the fixed assets. For business enterprises, depreciation also is viewed as a source of working capital and a means of deferring portions of income tax for a period of time. For nonprofit institutions, it is equally important to recognize depreciation as a means of calculating true operating cost to top administration and funding agencies, thus reducing occasional major capital outlays as replacement costs. Ideally, every year the actual wear and tear of fixed cost (such as buildings, boilers, chillers, and switchgear) should be charged against depreciation, but in reality this is not usually practical. Therefore, one of the following acceptable depreciation techniques is used.

Straight Line

This is the simplest depreciation technique. Here the cost of the asset reduced by the salvage value is uniformly allocated over its useful life. For example, if a boiler costs $1,030,000 and has a salvage value of $30,000 after twenty years of useful life, the annual depreciation is

$$\frac{1,050,000 - 30,000}{20} = \$ 50,000$$

Units of Production

The useful life of some assets can be quantified by the number of hours of operation. Every year, based on the number of hours used, that percentage of the asset cost less the salvage value is allocated. For example, if the aforementioned boiler has a useful life of 100,000 hours and in one year it ran for 4,500 hours, then the depreciation cost for the year is (1,030,000 - $30,000) (4,500/100,000) = $45,000. Although this method is a more accurate technique in determining the true level of wear and tear, projecting the depreciation cost prior to the end of the fiscal year might be difficult. In addition, this method is not suitable for some assets, such as buildings.

Sum of Years Digits

This is an accelerated depreciation method which provides a more rapid rate of expanding the asset than the straight-line technique in the first years. The annual depreciation cost is determined as follows, using the boiler example.

1. Calculate the sum of the year digits, namely

$$(1 + 2 + - - - + 18 + 19 + 20) = 20 \left(\frac{20 + 1}{2} \right) = 210$$

2. Divide the number of years of remaining useful life of the asset by the sum of years' digit and multiply this fraction by the cost of the asset less the depreciation. Therefore, the depreciation schedule will be:

Year 1 $\dfrac{20}{210}$ ($\$1,030,000 - \$30,000$) = $\$95,200$

Year 2 $\dfrac{19}{210}$ ($\$1,030,000 - \$30,000$) = $\$90,500$

. . .

Year 19 $\dfrac{2}{210}$ ($\$1,030,000 - \$30,000$) = $\$\ 9,500$

Year 20 $\dfrac{1}{210}$ ($\$1,030,000 - \$30,000$) = $\$\ 4,800$

Double Declining Balance (DDB)

This is another accelerated method that allows the maximum depreciation cost in the first years of the life of the asset. In the other three methods, the depreciation cost was calculated using the asset cost less salvage value, multiplied by the appropriate factor. Here, the same DDB factor is multiplied by the asset cost less accumulated depreciation. The DDB factor is twice the straight-line method. Therefore, a simple way of looking at the DDB method is depreciating the undepreciated value of the asset at twice the rate of the straight line method.

To illustrate this technique using the boiler example:

Useful life = 20 years
Straight-line factor = 1/20 = 0.05
DDB factor = 2 (0.05) = 0.1
Year 1 depreciation = (0.1) ($1,030,000) = $103,000
For year 2 asset book value = ($1,030,000 - 103,000) = $927,000
    year 2 depreciation = (0.1) ($927,000) = $92,700
For year 3 asset book value = $927,000 - $92,700 = $834,300
    year 3 depreciation = (0.1) ($834,300) = $83,430 etc.

In this technique, unlike other methods, the salvage value usually is not subtracted from the asset when the depreciation cost is calculated. Theoretically speaking, the method does not end and the asset is never fully depreciated; but the Internal Revenue Service allows any company to switch from DDB to straight-line technique. Usually, companies switch over when the annual depreciation allowance falls below that of the straight-line method.

Depreciation Summary

Regardless of the depreciation technique, one can only charge the value of the asset less than salvage value over the entire useful life of the asset. The above techniques are accepted ways of allocating the depreciation cost. One of the problems in plant finance is determining the useful life of an asset. Although there might be general agreement of an acceptable range for useful life of plant equipment, the operational conditions and environment will have significant impact on the actual useful life.

Since accounting deals with historical cost, in a period of high inflation it cannot fully account for the replacement value of the fixed assets. This always has caused concern for many institutions, and to date, the Financial Accounting Standards Board has not addressed it satisfactorily. Therefore, for internal accounting purposes, it is prudent to use a replacement cost of the asset as the basis of depreciation.

10.9 FINANCIAL ACCOUNTING STANDARDS BOARD STATEMENT NO. 93

Generally accepted accounting principles always have recognized depreciation expense in financial statements. Some nonprofit organizations, such as health-care institutions and foundations, have recognized depreciation costs, while universities have not. In August 1987, the Financial Accounting Standards Board issued its Statement No. 93, which states:

"Not-for-profit organizations shall recognize the cost of using up the future economic benefits or service potentials of their long-lived tangible assets—depreciation—and shall disclose the following:

- Depreciation expense for the period
- Balances of major classes of depreciable assets, by nature or function, at the balance sheet date
- Accumulated depreciation, either by major classes of depreciable assets or in total, at the balance sheet date
- A general description of the method or methods used in computing depreciation for major classes of depreciable assets."

It is too early to know the impact of Statement No. 93, but it is the first step for fiscal officers to recognize and disclose the backlog of deferred maintenance items and the first step in looking for a solution.

10.10 LEASE FINANCING

Leasing provides an alternative way to acquire the services of an asset instead of purchase. Prior to the 1950s, leasing was associated mostly with land and buildings, but now one can lease practically any type of fixed asset. One of the advantages of leasing over debt financing is that it does not reduce the credit rating of the lessee. There are different types of leases, namely sale and lease back, operating lease, and financial lease. In a sale and lease back arrangement, the firm owning the asset will sell the asset to the financial institution and simultaneously lease it for a certain period of time. In this way, the lessee receives the purchase price dollars and may use them any way they see fit, and they continue to utilize those assets.

With an operating lease, both financing and maintenance costs are included. Usually such a lease is for a relatively short period of time where the asset is not fully amortized. In contrast to this, in a financial lease the asset is fully amortized and is not cancellable. Usually maintenance service is not provided by the lessor. According to the Internal Revenue Service, a lease must be for less than thirty years, have a reasonable rate of return to the lessor (between 7 and 12 percent), the renewal option must be bona fide, and, in a purchase option, the lessee should only be given parity with an equal outside offer.

According to *State of Financial Accounting Standards No. 13*, on "Accounting for Leases," any lease that meets one or more of the following criteria must be included in the body of a balance sheet:

- Ownership is transferred to the lessee by the end of the lease term.
- The lessee has an option to purchase the asset below the fair market value.
- The lease term is equal to or more than 75 percent of the fair value of the asset.
- The present value of the minimum lease payment exceeds 90 percent of the fair value of the asset at the beginning of the lease.

Since leasing is an option, the decision that managers face is whether to purchase or lease an asset. Sometimes, even if the net present value of purchase is less than zero with optimal financing mix and purchase is rejected, leasing might still be an attractive option. To determine this the net advantage of leasing (NAL) should be calculated and NPV compared. For example, if NPV of a project is $2,000 and NAL is $5,000, then the net present value of the asset if leased is $3,000. The net present value (NPV) can be computed as discussed earlier, and NAL can be calculated as shown below (Petty 1986):

$$n = 1$$

$$NAL = \left| {}_{t=1}^{n} \right| O_t (1-T) + \frac{R_t(1-T)}{(1+r)^t} - T \cdot I_t - T \cdot D_t - \frac{V_n - 1}{(1+K_s)}$$

Where:
O_t = Yearly operating expenses paid by the lessor
T = Marginal tax rate for period t
R_t = Annual rental for period t
I_t = Tax-deductible interest expense lost by the firm when leasing is adopted
D_t = Depreciation expense for period t
V_n = After-tax salvage value at year n
K_s = Discount rate used to find present value of V_n
I = Purchase price of the asset
r = Interest rate before taxes on borrowed funds

When NAL and NPV are computed, the following decision tree is utilized:

1. If NPV and NAL are positive, lease the asset.
2. If NPV is positive but NAL is negative, purchase the asset.
3. If NPV is negative and NAL is positive, lease the asset if NAL = NPV; otherwise reject the project.
4. If both NPV and NAL are negative, reject the project.

In conclusion, leasing offers additional financial options and opportunities for an institution. Although the results might not be as dramatic and attractive for nonprofit institutions as they are for business enterprises, there are many occasions when it can be a viable alternative for a university.

ADDITIONAL RESOURCES

Anderson, P. and J. Martin. "Leasing vs. Purchase Decisions: A Survey of Current Practices." *Financial Management*, Spring 1977.

Cissel, R., et al. *Mathematics of Finance*. Boston: Houghton-Mifflin, 1978.

McKeown, M. and K. Alexander. *Values in Conflict, Funding Priorities in Higher Education*. Cambridge: Ballinger Publishing Company, 1986.

Petty, J. W., et al. *Basic Financial Management*. Englewood Cliffs, New Jersey: Prentice-Hall, 1986.

Weston, J. F. and E. F. Brigham. *Managerial Finance*. Hinsdale, Illinois: Dryden Press, 1981.

CHAPTER 11

Budget Development

William S. Gardiner
Vice President
The Colonial Williamsburg Foundation

11.1 INTRODUCTION

The development of a comprehensive annual operating budget and a capital improvements budget is one of the most important aspects of good facilities management; these budgets represent management's plans for maintaining and improving the college or university's physical assets, both now and in the future.

Unlike industry, colleges and universities' physical assets are here to stay, and they must be maintained with that premise in mind. Like industry, colleges and universities are in competition, yet all provide the same product—education.

Their consumers are students who must pay substantial sums for the opportunity to obtain this product; however, because of many options, the students can select the college offering the best value. That value includes the quality of course offerings, faculty, and facilities.

In today's college world, students can usually obtain the same general level of quality of course offerings and faculty from several colleges or universities. The choice, then, may come down to the quality of the physical assets of the college—the campus and its buildings. The space in which the student will spend at least four years becomes a critical factor in the students and parents' decision-making process.

For the parent, about to make a major expenditure for a child's education, what was seen on the campus visit greatly influences the decision. Are the facilities well-maintained? Is the school investing its money (my money) wisely? Do I want my son or daughter spending four years in this place? The selection process is based on the total value the student or parent expects to receive for his or her investment.

Likewise, colleges and universities are often in competition for faculty and staff. Employees are interested in their work environment and, given an option, they are likely to select the employer with the best facilities.

To preserve the physical facilities and to provide the best physical environment in which to teach and learn, the administration and managers of the college must ensure that an adequate amount of the college's limited operating funds is spent wisely for the maintenance of these facilities. It is the responsibility of the director of the college's facilities maintenance organization to obtain these funds through the budget process. This job can only be accomplished through thoughtful planning and careful administration of the department's annual operating budget by the staff and through an understanding of these plans and needs by the funding authority of the college or university.

Good budgeting reflects good planning. Too often this is not understood. Either the staff puts insufficient effort into the budget development process or the funding authority (the state, the board of trustees, the president, or the administrative officer to whom the director of facilities reports) makes arbitrary decisions affecting the budget request. In the worst case, both occur.

Good budgeting should not be ignored. All should view the process as an opportunity to develop plans for the current and future maintenance of the facilities, protecting and nurturing them so that they continue to be a viable resource for education and development.

11.2 OVERVIEW OF HIGHER EDUCATION BUDGETING METHODS

Many budget processes exist in higher education. Various states have established their own format for bringing the education budget to the legislature. Some use formulas to assure equitable allocation of funds. Others use more traditional methods.

Private colleges and universities tend to develop their own format, some basing it on the zero base method of budgeting and others on a more traditional line item system, such as the APPA Classification of Accounts developed by a joint APPA/NACUBO commission (see Appendix 12-A).

The process often varies considerably between large and small colleges. The former often requires voluminous, complex documentation while small colleges tend to simplify the process as much as possible.

Incremental Budgeting

Unfortunately, regardless of the format and documentation required by colleges and universities, most use a form of incremental budgeting.

Under this method, the funding authority, when establishing the guidelines for the coming fiscal year, dictates that budgets will increase (or decrease) by a certain percent. Usually this percentage increase (or decrease) is passed along to each department.

Little thought is given to the changing needs of the college from one year to the next, which may require the transfer of full-time equivalent (FTE) positions from one unit to another. The increased demand for staff created by expanded facilities may not be recognized. Some colleges do allow for consideration of added costs due to necessary increases in staff. The emphasis is often on these packages rather than the ongoing level of maintenance required to keep the facilities in good repair.

Incremental budgeting encourages the same misallocation of funds to be repeated from one year to the next. It is an expedient, simple process that allows the funding authority to exercise fiscal control even though the method may not enable the college to meet its long-range needs.

The management of the facilities department does, of course, have the option to employ its own method for preparing their budget within the incremental budget guidelines. It should seize this opportunity and apply the best principles of budget preparation even though it ultimately conforms to the overall college budget format. Likewise, once the funding has been approved, implementation and control can be left to the discretion of the facilities manager and, again, good principles should be applied.

Formula Budgeting

Shortly after World War II, with the cost of labor and materials at a premium because of shortages, many states sought to develop a method of budgeting that would ensure equity to all the institutions within the state and provide adequate levels of funding based on quantifiable data.

Walter W. Kraft, writing in the May 1950 issue of *College and University Business*, was one of the first to propose formula budgeting. He reasoned that formula methods based on gross square feet or cubic feet would not be valid because building types varied widely. Instead, he argued, the cost of maintenance would vary over time according to building type. This concept would become the basis for the formula that would establish the maintenance budget. The formula is as follows:

Maintenance budget = (Maintenance cost factor) X
(Current replacement cost of the building)

The replacement cost of the building can be calculated by multiplying original cost by a construction cost index such as the Engineering News Record Index or the Turner Construction Company Cost Index.

In addition, Kraft evaluated various building types and established the following maintenance cost factors:

Construction Classification	Factor (%)
Wood Frame Construction	1.75
Masonry-Wood Construction	1.30
Masonry-Concrete or Masonry-Steel	1.10

These factors, developed in 1950, did not reflect the added cost of maintaining buildings with air conditioning systems, as they were not common at the time. Subsequently, some states that adopted formula budgeting added .5 percent to the factors to allow for the added cost of maintaining these systems.

Other states have applied variations of these formulas to custodial and grounds maintenance to establish the level of funding for these accounts. Some states have developed formulas that take the number of FTE students and other factors, such as acres of land to be maintained, into consideration.

States that allocate funds on this basis often do not require the institution to apply these funds to the line item accounts, such as custodial or grounds maintenance. Individual institutions are allowed the flexibility of assigning the funds to the line item accounts of their choosing.

Normally, utility budgets are not prepared by a formula. They are established independently, based on historical cost data and the anticipated increases due to inflation, world markets, added facilities, and other factors.

Zero Base Budgeting

Many have criticized zero base budgeting, some of whom have never used the method. However, it is the one budgeting method that incorporates all the good principles of budgeting including preparation, implementation, and control. The process is simple in concept; the college's resources are allocated to the various departments on the basis of projected results. The underlying principle requires a periodic (not necessarily annual) reevaluation of the department's goals, objectives, plans, and operations.

Zero base budgeting:

- Forces good management practices to be followed and integrates them into the budget process.

- Forces order into thinking and planning as it emphasizes work to be done and priorities. It focuses upon measuring workloads and other input sources and emphasizes measuring performance and stress in accomplishing the task.
- Identifies the consequences of adding incremental amounts of funding and of not funding activities.
- Recognizes the budget-making activity is critically important in the decision-making process and vice versa.

The process requires the identification of all cost centers in the department that are then designated "decision units." Each decision unit is required to submit "decision packages" that describe the activity, the personnel involved, the funding required, and the benefits and consequences of funding or not funding the activity. Decision packages are broken down into incremental units that require management to think of alternative ways of accomplishing the tasks. The decision packages are submitted to a central authority; the director or manager or a committee appointed by the director then ranks them in order of importance.

The ranking process offers the managers an opportunity to recognize the relative importance of the activities they are responsible for versus the other activities competing for funding. This process can thus result in a much closer working organization.

If budget reductions are subsequently necessary, the process enables management to implement the reductions on a priority basis and eliminate decision packages in the order of least importance. Theoretically, this is easily understood and agreed upon once the ranking committee has determined the priorities.

Zero base budgeting systematically evaluates the activities of a facilities organization to accomplish effective planning, resource allocation, and management control. Activities can be analyzed in terms of their benefits, costs, and consequences of performing or eliminating them. Pros and cons, in effect, can be weighed with more ease and certainty. The process is a planning and decision-making technique in which the end product is sound resource allocation for the next year.

Finally, zero base budgeting is a process that forces planning by determining what to do, how to do it, why it is being done, and the cost associated with the task. It is an excellent method, incorporating the best principles of budgeting and producing a financial plan that assures the institution that its funds will be spent wisely in maintaining its facilities. Appendix 11-A illustrates a step-by-step application of zero base budgeting.

11.3 PRINCIPLES OF GOOD BUDGETING

Good budgeting reflects good planning and represents a continuing, year-round process. It consists of three phases: preparation, implementation, and control.

Preparation of Budgets

The key to the preparation of good budgets is good planning coupled with the team approach. The department's entire staff, including field employees, should be involved in the planning process if only to be asked for their comments and opinions.

A field employee represents the smallest element of a cost center. Employees actually expend the budgeted funds in the field when they perform their assigned tasks. Asking for their suggestions and using their participation in the planning process serves as an opportunity to communicate with them and explain the concerns and limitations that may be imposed on the department.

The department's director and senior staff must establish the goals for the department based on knowledge of the college's plans and the facility's needs gained through the above process and through directives issued by the funding authority. Once they have established these goals and objectives, the staff can evaluate the way in which the department can best organize to achieve these goals. Staffing levels can be reviewed and adjustments made to assign the appropriate number of employees for each section of the department.

If, regardless of the final format the college requires for submission of budgets, the staff chooses the zero base budgeting method or its own variation of that method, individual sections of the department can develop packages to represent incremental staffing required to meet the goals and objectives. The process can include the following:

- Use whatever format best enables the organization to clearly set forth the financial requirements necessary to accomplish its basic responsibilities and goals.
- Transfer these requirements to the college's required budget format for submission to the funding authority.
- Document and support these requests with professional reports and estimates, photos, video presentations, and other devices that clearly state your needs.

It is important to recognize and cultivate the relationship between the facilities maintenance department and the funding authority. If the funding authority is an individual (the president or the vice president for administration), attempt to keep him or her informed about the plans and needs of the department by taking the person on-site to see the problems firsthand.

If the funding authority is the board of trustees, consider showing the problems to them via videotape or photographs. A presentation to the board or to its buildings committee can be effective if done well.

All facilities managers should remember that many interests compete for the available funds. The funding authority must make hard decisions with regard to relative funding of departments.

Despite what we have said earlier about their importance, a college or university does not exist for its facilities. It exists to educate students. However, when dealing with budgets, fitting the facilities maintenance department into a perspective of the whole institution is critical.

Budget Implementation

A facilities manager must recognize that the final approved budget may not resemble the budget submitted to the funding authority. The funding authority may incorporate changes without explanation. The manager must communicate these changes to the staff and all employees who participated in the budget preparation. Each team member needs to know what was changed and why in order to understand and respond to the new challenges created by such reductions.

The final format adopted by the department should provide a clear breakdown of personnel, material, equipment, and contract labor. Specific budget assignments must be made to all management staff accountable for controlling budgets in their departments. They must understand their responsibilities and manage their departments within the available funds.

Budget Control

In addition to charging each manager with the responsibility for keeping within the available funds, other measures of control can be implemented.

Spending Limits   Each manager or staff member should be assigned a spending limit beyond which the manager must obtain approval from the next higher level of authority. This procedure allows the staff member to act independently while retaining control of the overall budget.

Establish a Contingency   Withhold a portion of funding from initial approval to establish a contingency. These funds can be allocated only upon the approval of the director. If the department is well within budget limitations at the end of the third quarter (or at other appropriate points throughout the year), funds can be reassigned to the appropriate cost centers.

Budget Amendments   Often circumstances beyond the manager's control change, necessitating a full budget amendment. Under such circumstances, the funding authority will authorize a budget increase that must be incorporated into the department's budget.

Communication   The most effective way to control budgets is through continuing communication among managers, staff, and employees. Review and discussion of budget performance and resultant changes on a regular basis allows management a current view of the department's performance.

Cost Accounting   Good control also depends on accurate cost accounting that provides current cost data. It is more important to know what commitments to expend funds have been made, rather than the actual expenditures. The latter often lag commitments due to the delays encountered in performing work and processing invoices.

Cyclical Costs   Expenditures for insurance, interest, snow removal, and other seasonal expenditures often are incurred on a cyclical basis. These costs must be included when analyzing budgets for conformance and to evaluate performance to date.

Budget preparation is important in securing adequate funding to properly operate and maintain the installation. However, budget control is equally important once funding has been allocated as this is the basis for measurement of performance. A year-long process, it must be a major part of every effective manager's routine.

11.4 BUDGETING FOR CAPITAL ITEMS

Most colleges and universities continue to either replace antiquated, outdated facilities or add new facilities to meet the needs for more sophisticated laboratories, computer facilities, athletic facilities, and other buildings. These additions to the physical assets are considered capital improvements. They are usually funded through contributions and special gifts or by special allocation from state legislatures. Capital assets may also include vehicles, equipment, and either new or improved systems.

Capital Budgeting

Capital budgeting can take many forms. Some institutions have taken an open approach to try to identify all potential capital needs of the faculty and staff. Administrators developed and circulated a questionnaire designed to elicit all needs so the staff could categorize and prioritize them. Obviously, this process generates more requests than an institution can fund. It does, however, allow everyone to clearly state his or her needs.

As an alternative, a committee representing faculty and staff can assess the capital needs of the campus. This results in a list of prioritized projects having the support of both groups. In either case, it is essential that facilities' needs are well-stated and documented so they receive equal consideration with academic needs.

Renewal and Replacement

It is important an institution recognize that it must invest in ongoing maintenance of its facilities. Many institutions neglected this aspect during the 1960s and 1970s. As a result, a backlog of deferred maintenance occurred, and institutions now have to correct these deficiencies. In addition, facilities become outdated; they must be modernized even if they have been well-maintained. Each institution should establish a renewal and replacement program, beginning with a survey audit of each facility to determine the extent of the necessary upgrades.

Funding

Deferred maintenance, renewal and replacement, and capital improvement programs should be funded separately from operating budgets.

Depreciation

Although some controversy exists, a college's physical assets should be depreciated so that faculty, staff, and the funding authority understand that these assets deteriorate and require maintenance.

Depreciation does not require any outlay of funds as it is primarily an accounting procedure. However, if funds are actually set aside at the depreciation rate, the institution usually does not have to be concerned about finding adequate funds for maintenance.

ADDITIONAL RESOURCES

Buchannon, A. Dean. "Budget Control and Analysis in the Small College." In *NACUBO Professional File*, Vol. 9, No. 8, August 1977.

Clawson, Robert H.. *Capital Planning for Physical Plant Administrators.*
Fundamentals of Finance and Accounting for the Non-Financial Executive.
Philadelphia, Pennsylvania: The Wharton School.

Jones, Regwald L. and H. George Trentin. *Planning and Administering the*
Company Budget. American Management Association.

McClintook, David L. *Formula Budgeting: An Approach to Facilities Fund-*
ing. Washington: APPA, 1980.

National Association of College and University Business Officers. "A
System for Accounting for Physical Plant Costs." In *NACUBO Ad-*
ministrative Services/Supplement, April 1975.

Robinson, Daniel D. and Frederick J. Turk. "Cost Behavior Analysis for
Planning in Higher Education." In *NACUBO Professional File,* Vol.
9, No. 5, May 1977.

Appendix 11-A

Application of the Zero-Base Technique

Ronald R. Blickhahn
Assistant Vice President
Facilities Planning and Management
Duke University

THE CONCEPT AND COMPARISON

Zero-base budgeting was first introduced in 1970 by Texas Instruments, Inc.[1] The firm initially applied the technique to develop its staff and research budgets and then in 1971 extended its use to all nonmanufacturing budgets. Since that time both private and government bodies throughout the country have also successfully employed this technique.

A system that requires each function, activity, or program to be justified on the basis of its own merit to the organization, zero-base budgeting calls for resource allocations to be committed only after each activity or program is analyzed and justified from "scratch" or "base zero." Thus the term "zero-base budgeting." This approach requires all activities to be identified in decision packages which are then evaluated by systematic analysis and rank ordered according to importance. While it can be demonstrated that zero-base budgeting is a form of comprehensive budgeting, it can also be shown that it goes much further in the demand for analysis and proof of funding need than do other budgeting methods.

The technique focuses on those activities most fundamental to achieving the organization's goals and objectives. It specifically requires that all activities be reviewed in their entirety each budget cycle.

Because the process is a structured and formalized one, it requires management to plan and analyze activities and programs more carefully than may otherwise be done. Management must take the following eight steps:

- Define goals and objectives.
- Identify assumptions necessary to facilitate planning and budgeting.
- Identify decision units within the organization.
- Develop decision packages for activities within the decision units.
- Review the decision packages and rank them in priority order. Ranking is based on how closely the item meets the organization's objectives.

- Develop alternatives and consider their results.
- Prepare and authorize the budget. Allocate the resources.
- Monitor and evaluate the results.

The process, which employs in-depth planning and analysis, emphasizes the importance of the budgeting activity in the decision-making process. It forces numerous levels of managers to become substantially involved as they identify specific activities associated with decision packages. In addition, the process identifies the consequences of committing or not committing resources to an activity and the results of considering incremental allocations above the base zero. Thus, each additional increment is considered on the basis of its specific cost and associated benefit to the organization compared to other activities also vying for resource allocations.

Zero-base budgeting reorients the traditional thinking about the budgeting process. Traditionally, managers accepted the previous year's budget amount as the base and then simply attempted to justify increments above that level. The focus was upon individual types of expenditures rather than those programs the expenditures helped to accomplish. The zero-base budgeting method, however, requires managers at all levels to take a fresh look each budget cycle at how they are going to manage their operation and at what activities and programs will accomplish the results they desire.

The underlying assumption of zero-base budgeting is that simply because a program was funded in the past does not mean that the program should automatically be funded in the future.

Traditional budgeting does not provide an impetus to reexamine activities or programs on a regular, in-depth basis. The assumptions are that the activities are necessary and decisions are usually made to either maintain the allocation at the previous year's level or, if funding is available, add to it. If funds are limited, allocations are usually kept at the same as the previous year or are cut without a detailed investigation and insight into the anticipated impact that zero-base budgeting demands. It is often the case with the traditional method that management imposes across-the-board increases or reductions because adequate details and substantiation for selective allocation simply do not exist.

Zero-base budgeting is truly a management-oriented tool. Identifying the individual activities and programs, the resources required by each, and the prospective results require substantial time and effort. As a result, staff members who are most knowledgeable about the intricacies of the activities are drawn into the analysis. This involvement buoys morale and prompts a commitment for success. It also forces individual managers to consider different ways of performing activities or to weigh alternative methods of attaining specific results.

Perhaps its greatest asset to plant managers lies in its usefulness as a decision-making device. For even if a budget is approved based on the traditional approach—which uses last year's figures as reference—the manager can use zero-base budgeting with its prioritization to quickly determine which programs to eliminate and which to retain.

In sum, zero-base budgeting can be defined as a technique that allocates resources according to intended results. Managers specify the results they expect to obtain within each organizational unit and then allocate the resources needed to achieve them.

SPOTLIGHT ON THE PROCESS

The eight steps for preparing a zero-base budget were presented earlier as a generalization for the user's convenience. What follows is an expanded description of the procedure. Throughout the chapter a building maintenance operation associated specifically with painting will be used as a concrete example to explain the concept.

Step 1: Define Goals and Objectives

Basic to effective management is the definition of goals and objectives so that all concerned understand what must be accomplished. In other words, it is essential to know one's destination before planning the travel route. Goals, therefore, should be formulated in terms of both general application and specific definition. Using the building maintenance painting operation as an illustration, what follows are appropriate goals.

General Goal: Provide a maintenance service that will result in an environment conducive to the education of students. This would include providing residence hall and food service facilities.

Specific Goal: Paint building interior walls once every seven years with semigloss latex paint to maintain an attractive and protected structure.

Step 2: Identify Planning Assumptions

It is here that the real substance of zero-base budgeting begins. It is essential at this stage for managers to define assumptions relating to such considerations as the inflation rates, salary increases, level of service—much as is done when developing traditional budgets. The more comprehensive the development of the assumptions, the more easily the process will proceed and the more accurate the budget will be.

For example, differing inflation rates may have to be assigned depending on whether or not the considerations are material or labor. Furthermore, different rates may have to be assigned according to the type of material or the classification of the labor. When considering the painting function, one may wish to consider one inflation rate keyed to petroleum-based products and a different inflation rate for synthetic materials that are more readily available and less sensitive to the world's supply and demand. The same holds true for salary increases. Different employee groups may be associated with different bargaining groups, which result in different pay percentage increases.

Step 3: Identify Decision Units

A decision unit is a single activity or group of activities which a single manager has responsibility to carry out in line with prestated goals and objectives. A decision unit must be one for which the manager has sole control. It cannot be an activity such as training if that is the responsibility of numerous managers in many departments. A typical decision unit is a specific cost center, project, program, or service provided.

Regardless of how the decision units are identified, they must be units that will lend themselves to quantifiable measurement. It is essential to be able to regularly measure the resources employed and consumed and to determine that tangible progress is being made toward meeting objectives.

Step 4: Identify Decision Packages

Decision packages can be thought of as components within decision units. The packages provide further detail or elaborate on the decision unit. For example, when dealing with a plant operation, the plant division could be considered the decision unit and the painting department within the plant division could be considered the decision package. Similarly, a business office could be considered the decision unit while its components of accounts payable, accounts receivable, student collections, and payroll could be considered decision packages.

Step 3 makes clear the importance of involving managers who are intimately knowledgeable about the specific decision units. Using the painting operation as an example, the decision packages should, at a minimum, include the following components:

- Description of the cost center or service to be provided. Example—painting of all buildings and equipment.
- Goals or objectives. Example—paint building interior walls once every seven years.
- Specific measures of performance. Example—paint 300 square feet of wall surface per productive workhour.
- Benefit derived from funding the activity. Example—will not only result in a more attractive environment but will also protect the wall.
- Consequences of not funding the activity. Example— attractiveness of the facility would deteriorate to the point that faculty, staff, students, and visitors would prefer to go elsewhere for education or other activities; building would physically deteriorate.
- Projected costs of funding the activity. Example—$300,000 for in-house materials and labor.
- Alternative ways of performing the activity. Example—contract the service to a commercial painting contractor.

Decision packages are formulated either as mutually exclusive or incremental packages. Alternatively, the packages can be developed by using both techniques. Mutually exclusive packages require the development of alternative methods of performing the same function. Each alternative is considered and ranked, and the best chosen for implementation. The procedure compels managers to think creatively and to identify more efficient methods of performing functions rather than simply stating different ways of performing the same function.

Incremental packages are developed by identifying the most basic or minimum service that can be provided. The specific increments are devised, including the benefits and costs that they entail. They are evaluated increment by increment until a total package is eventually formulated.

One advantage of this method is that it forces managers to carefully consider the absolute minimum that can produce a meaningful result. If a more thorough approach is desired, both exclusive and incremental packages can be used. For example, alternatives can be developed and then increments devised for each alternative. While this combined approach results in a thorough evaluation process, it does demand more time and effort.

This step in the process requires the greatest effort on the part of staff. It is also the most time consuming. Since organizations are seldom able to assign to the task additional personnel who are adequately knowledgeable in specific substantive areas, the regular staff members are responsible for carrying out the effort. The first year that zero-base budgets are developed and implemented requires the most attention. Subsequent years become easier as the staff becomes familiar with the process. It is essential, however, that zero-base budgets be prepared with the input of the most knowledgeable first-line managers as well as higher-echelon managers. That means that sufficient time and effort must be allocated. For without the appropriate commitment and support, the resulting budget will fall short of the desired results.

Step 5: Analyze and Rank Decision Packages

Ranking can be accomplished in a couple of ways. It is most commonly performed at various management levels. For instance, the supervisors who developed decision packages must carefully consider those packages and rank them from most important to least important for their area of responsibility. A written explanation should accompany the ranking that details the associated costs and benefits. If incremental packaging is used, the package should be proposed with both an "absolute essential base" and individual increments. Each increment must include a statement of costs and benefits that would be keyed to the effort.

Step 6: Develop Alternatives and Consider Their Results

Alternatives should also be developed and presented for each package. They should be presented by stating the different ways a function can be performed and by identifying the different levels of effort at which each function can be performed. The decision-making process is two-pronged: selecting the particular way the result will be achieved and determining what resources are to be used to achieve that result. In arriving at a decision, the incremental technique at times affords a better opportunity to garner support for a package, while the mutually exclusive method may result in an all-or-nothing situation.

The decision packages are then passed up to the next level of management for consolidation with those from managers of other functions. Generally, the rankings are then reviewed by a committee. The committee focuses most of its attention on those packages at the margin of being funded or not funded as defined by the group's criteria. It is unlikely that those packages designated "absolutely essential" will have to be considered unless budgetary retrenchment is severe. For this reason it is important that criteria for ranking be well defined so that only those packages that are "absolutely essential" are labeled as such.

During the rating process, the highest level manager from each unit should have an opportunity to present to the committee the rationale for prioritization. A question-and-answer period should be set aside so that each committee member obtains a thorough understanding of the packages.

Committees will often use a cutoff point or payback criteria to assist in the ranking process. Final ranking can be achieved simply by assigning a numerical priority.

Step 7: Prepare and Authorize the Budget and Allocate Resources

Once the final ranking is completed, preparing the budget and allocating financial resources is quite straightforward. A cutoff line is drawn at the point where the package costs above the line add up to the total sum available for that budget period. Decision packages above that line will be funded while those below it will not. For monitoring purposes, the final budget can be formatted in the same way as traditional budgets.

Step 8: Monitor and Evaluate the Results

A budget is only as effective as its monitoring and control. Zero-base budgeting is no exception. While it had been important to identify priorities for funding allocation during the budget formulation stage, it later becomes important to operate effectively within those funding limits.

Individual unit managers should be authorized to monitor and control their staff's performance and budget allocations. Continual general review should be left to the manager of the subunit. Involving subunit managers instills a sense of pride in these persons. It also requires them to focus attention on their functions in a way that stimulates them to perform well and operate within the confines of their budgets.

The zero-base budgeting process provides financial and performance measurement data that are useful for monitoring purposes. Examples of statistics that are recommended are—

- Basic monthly data comparing actual expenditures against budgeted projections.
- Monthly workload and performance data to assure that the subunits are accomplishing their projected results.

Performance feedback will indicate if personnel are appropriately productive, who is the most efficient, and if work time is being used effectively. It will also show if staff performance results are in line with expenditures for materials or if personnel assignments should be modified to meet the objectives. For example, if standards were developed to identify specifically what was expected of painters, the supervisor could—

- Compare the actual painter's performance against the standard.
- Compare painters' productivity to encourage competition. The most productive staff would be rewarded.
- Measure painters' nonproductive time against productive periods to determine if improvements should be made such as scheduling more effectively, minimizing travel time, or adhering more closely to break periods.
- Evaluate the most cost-effective way to assign painters, either individually or in teams, based on the individuals' productivity.

With these data in hand, the supervisor can take whatever action may be needed to improve the efficiency of the painting staff.

This information provides a tool for the subunit managers to evaluate their staff and gives upper level managers a means of evaluating the effectiveness of the subunit managers.

PHYSICAL PLANT APPLICATION

How does zero-base budgeting apply directly to plant operation? It can be applied most readily to personnel. For purposes of illustration we will use an example of a painting operation, a typical decision package.

We will assume that the college or university has already defined its goals and general planning assumptions and has expressed interest in the plant project. The plant manager would then meet with the supervisors of subunits to identify the decision packages. A briefing to explain why the budget is being prepared by the zero-base method would be in order. At the meeting it is important for the plant administrator to walk the participants through the process. Emphasis should be placed on the need for furnishing solid documentation in order to evaluate how well goals are being met. It should be made clear that the viability of each subunit depends upon meeting measurable performance goals. Each supervisor would then be asked to assemble a resource needs document using incremental analysis.

At that point the painting supervisor would begin to develop a decision package. First, general and specific goals would be stated.

General Goal: Provide a maintenance service that will result in an environment conducive to the education of students. This would include providing residence hall and food service facilities.

Specific Goal: Paint building interior walls once every seven years with semigloss latex paint to maintain an attractive and protected structure.

It would then be necessary to identify planning assumptions. Examples are—

- Productivity rates for interior walls.
- Productivity rate for ceilings.
- Definition of what constitutes a productive workhour (pwhr).
- Statement as to whether productivity rates include moving furniture, removing electrical wall plates, taping cracks where necessary, caulking, and working in occupied or unoccupied areas.
- Statement as to whether productivity rates should be determined based on the texture of surface to be painted or whether all surfaces are to be considered equal.
- Productivity rates for each painting method—brush, roller, and sprayer. A statement should note whether all methods are to be considered equal.
- Productivity rates for unique circumstances such as staining stair railings with numerous spindles, door frames, miscellaneous metal, etc.
- Statement declaring whether painters work independently or as a team.
- Statement of material coverage (square feet per gallon).
- Statement noting the frequency of interior painting.

It is advisable to record any special notes. The notes may pertain to how the amount of interior wall area in each building was determined, how the total amount of window sash was calculated, and how the frequency rates were derived. Thus if future modifications need to be made, such documentation not only assures that the same method will be used for determinations but also serves as a help in making accurate comparisons.

Once the necessary data are accumulated, the painting supervisor then begins to formulate the budget. Since it is generally most desirable to use the incremental technique, the supervisor would define the base and the increments needed to reach the established goal. The base may simply suggest that it is essential to paint all interior metal surfaces once every 8 years and all interior nonmetal surfaces once every 12 years.

Increments should then be determined and funding levels assigned to each. The increments should be arrayed from the base activity level all the way up to the goal level. In the example given above, a decision simply may be made to shorten the intervals between painting.

The benefit to be derived from performing the base activity should be identified. In addition, benefits should be keyed to each increment. Whenever possible, a benefit should be stated in terms of actual dollars. Intangibles, however, should not be ignored though they are not always easily quantified. For example, what is it worth to have an unmarked, bright surface as opposed to a marred, dull, deteriorated one?

The consequences to be expected if an activity is funded or not funded must be presented. Thus, both dollar and intangible values must be developed. Using a painting example, the statement of consequences could take the following form:

> If a specific piece of equipment were not painted once every four years, the surface protection would deteriorate such that in six years it would cost twice as much to return it to a satisfactory condition. When metal is not adequately protected it will rust. As a result, it not only requires more time for surface preparation but also requires applications of primer and finish coats of paint. A well-maintained surface, on the other hand, will likely require only one coat of paint or possibly only touchup.

Such information should be well substantiated and clearly defined to promote understanding of this budget item. Calculations could then be made of how many dollars would be needed for labor and materials in order to maintain the facilities at the identified minimum level as well as at each incremental level.

Finally, alternative ways of performing the activity should be identified and considered. Costs must be determined and benefits and consequences analyzed. An example of an alternative way to carry out an activity would be to consider outside contracting for some or all of the institution's painting needs.

Once this were done, supervisors would then prepare and present their budget requests with justification to substantiate each claim. They should be made aware that their presentations have an impact on the upcoming year's budget since they are competing with other subunits for resources.

BENEFITS OF ZERO-BASE BUDGETING

Organizations can benefit greatly by preparing their budgets in this fashion. Since the budget is not pro forma, it forces organizations to think through their needs and objectives afresh. Some of the benefits to be reaped are described.

- Participants in the process become better informed about their specific operations as well as more aware of the operations of other divisions. This fosters improved interdepartmental relations and mutual reliance.
- Managers improve their communications skills since they are called upon to present their case for human and financial resources. Equally important, they must sharpen their analytical skills since those skills are essential to determining how resources are allocated.
- The method shifts the focus of budgeting from performing numerical calculations to decision making at all levels.
- The budget, once it has been developed, provides managers with a systematic means to evaluate the efficiency and cost-effectiveness of their activities.
- The process provides a way of identifying for consideration new programs or new ways of performing ongoing activities and having them compete for funding on their merits rather than being relegated to secondary status. Thus, it consistently forces participants to be creative and to challenge the status quo.
- Efficiency improves as a result of considering alternative operations methods. Monetary savings can be a subsequent byproduct.
- The method allows tradeoffs between long-term goals and short-term objectives or needs based upon the projected costs and benefits.
- The budget preparation steps simplify the identification of similar functions or tasks in different departments for comparison, evaluation, and establishment of common work measurements.
- The process draws operating managers into the planning and implementation phases and forces a commitment to the programs they recommend.
- The process encourages administrative efficiency. Decision packages that do not change in subsequent budget cycles need only be reranked with the other packages submitted for consideration.
- The practice shifts the responsibility for recommending activities to the operating managers, for evaluating their priority to all levels of the organization, and for funding to top management.
- The procedure shifts the focus from the amount of the expenditure to its effectiveness as measured by prestated standards.
- The procedure simplifies and systematizes the follow-up on the performance as measured against the projected costs and benefits.

- The method provides flexibility for periodic reevaluations of progress with possible reallocations of resources based on performance or to accommodate changes in revenues generated.
- The process can lead to better budgeting because it is a joint effort that draws on collective wisdom.

OBSTACLES IN IMPLEMENTING THE BUDGET

Probably the greatest problem faced when developing a zero-base budget is to establish and retain commitment to see the process through to completion and implementation. It becomes important, then, for top management to fully support the activity. To ensure success, upper-echelon managers must also build in accountability.

For the process to work well, first-line managers who are likely to be most familiar with the day-to-day details of an operation should be drawn into the process. All levels of managers, however, should participate. And, in the end, the final product must emerge as a useful tool for managers or it will not be used effectively.

Knowing the value of a good budget, management should approach budget preparation with the view that many workhours must be expended in order to harvest the benefits. Budget preparation will be time consuming, particularly during the first year, since staff will have to gear up for the effort while holding down their regular responsibilities. It is essential, therefore, that adequate time be devoted to thinking creatively and accurately.

It would be a mistake to present the process as a totally new and innovative concept that will solve all problems. Instead, it must be identified as another tool to educate and assist staff. If expectations are too great and are not met (or perceived to be met), employees may become frustrated over the long hours of effort they contributed. As a result, management has a vested interest in making the process pay off. Some obstacles are commonly experienced during the process.

For example, deciding on what activities are appropriate for decision packages and then sorting out the "optional" activities from the "essential" ones can be quite involved.

There may be a tendency on the part of managers to establish the minimum effort level at the current operating level and justify expansions beyond that point in incremental effort levels. It is highly unlikely that the current level is the minimum one, and managers who present this case should be asked to justify the claim.

A natural tendency exists to protect positions. Care must be taken to ensure that an appropriate reduction in personnel is related to the reduction in service or support.

Inertia may have built up to judge personnel on past performance rather than on what should be expected. Standards of performance, consequently, must be established carefully and fairly. While various standards may already exist for numerous tasks, it often becomes necessary to adjust the standards to more accurately reflect specific conditions unique to a setting.

At the same time, it is important to guard against arbitrary modifications to nationally established standards simply because one individual does not believe their accuracy. It is a good policy to analyze the basis on which various standards were developed to judge their applicability. If none can be found, which is quite unlikely, an organization can develop its own. Care should be taken to test and substantiate what is developed. A number of states such as Maryland have spent a great deal of effort and money to establish standards. Additionally, corporations, consultants, and the federal government have developed standards suitable for adoption.

Managers may have a tendency to overbudget in order to build in leeway for inflation or bad predictions. If the tendency to pad is not overcome, inaccurate budgets will result.

Finally, high-priority items do not always receive the close scrutiny they should. In organizations there is sometimes a tendency to pay a minimal amount of attention to the content of these decision packages since management realizes their importance and automatically backs them. High-priority packages, therefore, may reflect costs that, though not deliberately overstated, have not been subjected to careful examination.

SUMMARY

Zero-base budgeting is not an altogether new concept. It has been in existence, though seldom applied, for many years. However, its acceptance has been growing steadily since Texas Instruments, Inc. effectively introduced and applied this management tool in the early 1970s.

It is a technique that, when introduced and supported fully by upper-level management and given adequate time and personal commitment during preparation, can result in a myriad of benefits. It can encourage managers to analyze their operation with a critical eye, measuring them against other goals of the organization. Further, it can help managers prioritize needs in order to make difficult budget decisions. The outcome can be to direct both manpower and monetary resources to the activities that will be most beneficial to the organization.

END NOTE

1. Peter A. Pyhrr, *Zero-Base Budgeting* (New York: John Wiley and Sons, 1973), p. ix.

CHAPTER 12

Cost Accounting

David J. Gojdics
Director of Physical Plant
Emory University

Jesse C. Nipper, CPA
Assistant Director for
Business Management
Physical Plant Department
Emory University

12.1 INTRODUCTION

Most physical plants rely on two separate accounting systems for virtually all of their financial and operating data. One is the college or university's overall financial accounting and budgeting system, which is designed to handle the complex and assorted financial needs of the departments, schools, and affiliates. Its functions are generally too broad to provide adequate operating data for physical plants, aside from its usefulness as a spending record and budget compliance tool.

Because of this, the second accounting system is needed—physical plant's internal cost accounting system—which meets two needs: 1) to gather and record cost and operating data needed for day-to-day plant operation, and 2) to report certain cost information back to the college or university system. The two systems should be compatible. Additional management information is also generated, making the system the primary planning and control tool of the physical plant department.

This chapter discusses the purpose, design, operation, and principal features of physical plant cost accounting systems. Chapter 13 discusses the use of the information produced in decision making and cost control.

12.2 PURPOSE OF COST ACCOUNTING

The objective of the cost accounting system is to provide management information that is not otherwise produced by the college or university accounting system in a timely manner. Included are maintenance and capital project costs, as well as reimbursable costs to be charged back to users of physical plant services. The cost information provided to plant management is the basis for control of recurring plant activities and for decision making.

12.3 COST ACCOUNTING CONCEPTS IN PHYSICAL PLANT

Cost is the acquisition price of an asset. The costs classified and reported by cost accounting systems are the acquisition prices of assets consumed. Thus, as maintenance and upkeep efforts are ongoing, the cost accounting system is measuring and reporting, in acquisition price terms, the labor, materials, administration, and other assets being consumed by those efforts.

Cost accounting is the means by which expenditures for assets are applied to individual units of work or production, to shops, or to departments. The application process is the essence of cost accounting.

The application process is dependent upon the establishment of relationships between expenditures and operations. These relationships for some expenditures are easily determined. Clearly, the expenditures for fuel in the steam plant are related to the steam produced. For other expenditures, however, the relationships are not so simple.

Consider the accounting department, which supports the operations of all sections in the plant. How much of the expenditures for accounting are related to steam production? Custodial services? Grounds maintenance?

The end products of a cost accounting system are unit costs. The units may be a pound of steam, a month's production of steam, a repair job, the operating cost of a shop, or the operating cost of the entire physical plant. The accuracy and comparability of unit costs are totally dependent on accurate and consistent applications of expenditures.

12.4 TYPES OF COSTS

The term "cost" is extremely broad. Listed and defined below are types of cost with which physical plant managers are concerned.

Direct and Indirect Costs

The word "direct" infers a physical tracing of a cost to a given unit of work or production. It is not necessary to have an intervening basis of allocation of direct cost to the work or production. Materials that are an integral part of a finished product or job, labor of a craftsperson doing a job or making a product, and fuel used in steam production are examples of direct costs.

Indirect costs are much more difficult to trace. There is no direct physical relationship between the incurrence of these costs and units of work or production. These costs must be applied through an intervening basis of allocation.

The determination of whether a cost is direct or indirect is often difficult. For example, fuel cost is directly related to steam production. But what about payroll and supervisory costs of plant operators? Whether these are direct or indirect depends upon the specific cost information being developed. If a report on the cost of operation of the steam plant is being developed, certainly these costs are direct. If, however, the unit cost of production is being determined, they may be indirect. Thus, the classification of cost as direct or indirect is often dependent on the end use of the cost information.

A general rule of thumb in determining whether a cost is direct or indirect is to establish whether the cost is related to production or to the ability to produce. The craft labor and materials used in maintenance and upkeep are direct, whereas supervisory, materials-handling, and administrative costs are related to providing the craftspeople with the necessary support and are generally indirect. The distinction between direct and indirect costs will be discussed in greater detail in Section 12.5.

Overhead

It is generally accepted that all indirect costs are overhead. However, due to the unique structure of physical plant, overhead includes those costs incurred in support of the operating functions of the plant, such as maintenance, construction, grounds and landscape, and custodial. Supervisory personnel, an accounting office, a personnel and payroll office, and an engineering staff support these functions and serve the entire physical plant operation. The cost of these support functions must be allocated to the operating departments and to the units of work or production so cost information for all general uses will be available.

Standard Costs

Standard costs are predetermined target costs. They are of three types.

- Basic standard costs, which are unchanging costs. They provide a basis for comparison of actual to standard through the years.

Basic standard costs are seldom used because changes in products and methods necessitate changes in standards.

- Ideal (theoretical) standard costs, which are the absolute minimum costs possible under the best operating conditions.
- Currently attainable standard costs, which are standard costs that should be attained with efficient operations. They are difficult, but attainable. It is important that the managers and operating personnel accept the standard costs as fair and that the standards be high enough that their achievement gives a sense of accomplishment.

Most physical plant departments establish currently attainable standard costs, which are closely related to the operating budget. For example, most institutions allocate or bill plant costs to users of plant services. The use of a valid standard cost per square foot is a method of establishing physical plant cost budgets for the different users.

Comparisons of actual costs to standards is also a useful analytical tool in the management of plant operations. The mechanics of comparative methods will be covered in Chapter 13, Cost Control.

Fixed and Variable Costs

Fixed costs are not expected to change over a given time period and a given range of activity. Physical plant's fixed costs include management salaries, clerical and secretarial support, and insurance. Variable costs are those costs that change directly in proportion to changes in output or activity.

Fixed and variable costs are terms that are closely related to indirect and direct costs. Cost accounting covers the direct and indirect concept whereas the economic evaluation of alternative courses of action involves the fixed and variable concept.

Controllable and Noncontrollable Costs

These are classifications of cost linked to the concept of responsibility accounting. Controllable costs can be directly influenced by a manager within a given time span. The difference between controllable and noncontrollable costs cannot be distinguished without specifying a level and scope of management authority.

Closely linked are the concepts of full (absorption) and partial (direct) costing. Full costing means that units of work or production are fully burdened with applicable indirect and overhead costs. Partial costing means that the units would include only direct costs as defined previously.

The reporting to be done determines the costing application utilized. If, for example, a performance report is to be prepared to evaluate the effectiveness of the management of the different craft shops, the first determination is what costs are controllable at that level of management. The managers in the shops have no control over the amounts allocated for the director's office, payroll and personnel, and warehouse overhead on materials used. A report analyzing only those costs over which the managers have control would be appropriate. If, however, a report of the total cost of building and equipment maintenance is being developed, a full cost report would be required.

12.5 OVERHEAD ALLOCATIONS

In attempting to accurately determine the cost of work done or product produced, it is important to account for all costs involved. Consider again the production of steam. For a month of production, the fuel consumed is directly related to the volume produced. This direct cost per unit of production can be easily calculated; however, indirect costs exist.

Indirect costs in the steam production include maintenance and repair of the steam plant, insurance, custodial and grounds service, lighting, payroll and benefits of operators, and all the other costs associated with operation. It appears that the payroll and supervisory cost of plant operators is directly related to the units produced during the month. However, operators and supervisors are most likely paid at a fixed rate over a year or other personnel-related cycle, whereas periodic production of steam varies with weather and other factors over the same cycle. Thus, the staffing of the plant is based on the ability or need to produce at a given level. Actual production may vary widely from month to month, but the plant staff, most likely, will not.

Overhead must be considered. Most physical plant departments have a director, an accounting office, a personnel and payroll office, an engineering staff, and possibly other functions that serve the entire physical plant operation (see Chapter 1, The Facilities Organization). The administrative offices require upkeep, office supplies, equipment, and other necessary expenditures in order to accomplish their functions. The identification of the portion of these costs related to the steam plant is difficult. Generally, an allocation base or allocation bases are derived to spread these costs to the different plant activities, one of which would be the steam plant. Figure 12-1 shows several, though by no means all, bases of allocation of these costs to physical plant.

Whatever bases of allocation of these administrative costs are selected, two generally used procedures exist for allocation to production departments, depending on the preference of management. They in-

Figure 12-1
Typical Bases of Allocation

Function	Allocation Bases
Director's Office	1. Number of employees 2. Labor hours available 3. Percentage of director's time devoted to departments 4. Department's percentage of the physical plant budget
Accounting Office	1. Number of transactions processed for each department 2. Department's percent of the physical plant budget
Payroll/Personnel Office	1. Number of employees 2. Payroll hours 3. Transactions processed by department
Engineering	1. Percentage of engineering time devoted to departments 2. Dollar volume of engineering projects by department

clude: 1) allocate the administrative departments to the production departments only; and 2) allocate the administrative departments to other administrative departments as well as production departments.

Under the first procedure, each administrative department is allocated, using the selected basis, to the production departments. The second procedure is more complicated as it entails an analysis of the services administrative departments render to each other. Administrative departments must be ranked based on the amount of service rendered to other administrative departments.

When the ranking is completed, each administrative department is allocated to the administrative departments ranked below it and to the production departments. Figures 12-2 and 12-3 show a graphic representation of this procedure.

The second procedure has two advantages: the actual costs associated with the production departments are more accurate, and the process produces a more accurate picture of expenditures for administrative departments.

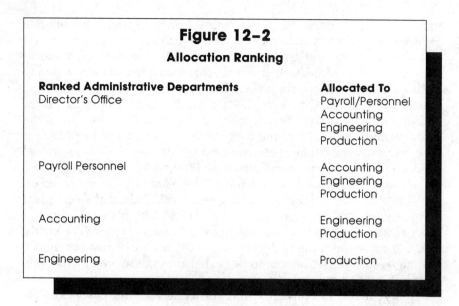

Figure 12-2

Allocation Ranking

Ranked Administrative Departments	Allocated To
Director's Office	Payroll/Personnel Accounting Engineering Production
Payroll Personnel	Accounting Engineering Production
Accounting	Engineering Production
Engineering	Production

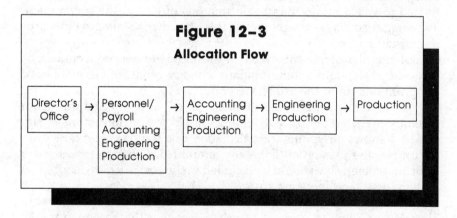

Figure 12-3

Allocation Flow

Director's Office → Personnel/ Payroll Accounting Engineering Production → Accounting Engineering Production → Engineering Production → Production

12.6 ESTABLISHING RATES

Continuing the steam production example, three levels of cost have been identified. These are direct costs (fuel), indirect costs related only to steam production, and overhead. This manner of presentation illustrates the factors that must be considered in establishing the rates at which steam will be billed or allocated to the various users.

It would be theoretically correct to establish a bill rate for each month that would include all costs associated with production during that period. It would also be theoretically correct to establish a bill rate for each month that would include fuel, actual indirect costs related to steam production, and an allocated overhead. However, such allocations are generally infeasible due to fluctuations of expenditures during a budget cycle. For example, an expensive roof repair or painting project may be budgeted for the steam plant during one of the summer months. To burden the steam produced during that month with the cost of the repair would cause an extreme fluctuation in the allocation or bill rate. Also, to establish a bill rate based on each month would, due to seasonal production volumes, produce rates that differ widely with seasons.

As stated previously, the staffing of the plant is generally based on the ability or need to produce at a given level. Unless physical plant management establishes a layoff policy or uses the plant operators in other areas during low volume seasons, the personnel costs will be fairly constant throughout the budget cycle. To use an actual cost per month bill rate would cause the rate to be higher during low volume periods than in high volume periods.

It is generally desirable to determine a rate such that cost per unit is seasonally smooth, and variations in billing or allocations to users are related to usage rather than to fluctuations of cost at the steam plant. Two suggested ways can accomplish this objective: a standard bill rate or a semistandard bill rate.

Standard or semistandard bill rates should, for nonprofit entities, be the same as standard or semistandard cost. For-profit entities would add the profit margin to the established rate.

An annual standard cost for steam must be performed through a carefully prepared annual budget and annual production estimate. Figure 12-4 shows a hypothetical calculation of a standard cost for steam. Of course, the illustration is greatly simplified. Other factors that are difficult to determine should be included in the cost, such as distribution system losses and metering costs.

For most facilities operations, the total costs of plant operations are allocated or billed to users of plant services. For this reason, a purely standard rate might leave fairly large amounts of unallocated or overallocated cost. A semistandard rate would help to alleviate this problem. It can be derived to allocate fuel cost on an actual basis and indirect and overhead on a standard basis. This would entail calculating the fuel cost per unit based on the metered period actual cost and adding the indirect and overhead as shown in Figure 12-5.

The concepts and principles for developing cost rates for steam apply as well to developing rates for labor, material, or other costs that must be applied to units of work or production. It must be kept in mind that calculated rates, no matter how carefully prepared, will, for a variety of reasons, vary from actual cost. The analysis of these variances

Figure 12-4

Preparation of a Standard Steam Budget

Annual Budget

Fuel	$2,240,000
Labor and Fringes	450,000
Operating Supplies and Expenses	250,000
Overhead Distribution	300,000
Budget Cost of Production	$3,240,000
Annual Production Estimate	500,000,000 lbs

Standard Annual Cost Per Pound of Production:
$3,240,000 ÷ 500,000,000 = $0.00648/lb

Standard Annual Cost Per Thousand Pounds of Production:
$0.00684 × 1,000 = $6.48/Thousand

between actual and calculated costs is essential in order to identify cost trends and efficiences. Variance analysis also points out the need to readjust rates to ensure that all costs are allocated.

12.7 COST CENTERS

A cost center is the smallest segment of activity or area of responsibility for which costs are accumulated. Because cost centers are actually responsibility centers, this definition implies that each level of management within the plant requires different accumulations of cost. For example, the foreman of the electric shop has responsibility for the individual work projects of the craftspeople under his or her control, and for overall cost of operations for the shop. The head of maintenance has responsibility for all projects and overall cost of operations of all shops under his or her direction. The director has responsibility for all projects and overall cost of operations for the entire department. The costing system must provide the costs in a suitable format that meets the needs of all levels of management and the other needs and uses for cost information.

The objectives of the plant costing system will dictate proper structuring of the cost centers for physical plant. The costing system has at least four objectives:

Figure 12-5

Preparation of a Semistandard Steam Cost Rate

Annual Budget for Indirect & Overhead

Labor & Fringes	$450,000
Operating Supplies & Expenses	250,000
Overhead Distribution	300,000
	$1,000,000

Annual Production Estimate 500,000,000 lbs.

Standard Annual Indirect and Overhead Cost Per Pound of Production:
$1,000,000 ÷ 500,000,000 = $.002/lb.

Standard Annual Indirect and Overhead Cost Per Thousand Pounds of Production:
$.002 × 1,000 = $2.00/Thousand

Calculation of a Monthly Cost Rate

Monthly Actual Fuel Cost	$285,000
Monthly Metered Production	60,000,000

Monthly Fuel Cost Per Pound:
$285,000 ÷ 60,000,000 = $.00475

Standard Annual Indirect and Overhead Cost Per Pound: $.00200

Monthly Bill Rate Per Pound: $.00675

Monthly Bill Rate Per Thousand: $6.75

- Financial Accountability—to satisfy such needs as controlling expenditures within budgeted allocations and accounting for expenditure transactions, purchasing transactions, personnel and payroll obligations, materials, inventories, and funding requirements.
- Unit Cost Information—to provide information at points where costs can be measured and compared, historically and laterally, such as physical plant functional areas, work orders, physical facilities (structures and vehicles), and benefiting activities.

- Management Reporting—to create labor utilization reports, vehicle utilization reports, job status reports, budget-versus-actual cost and utilization reports, and budget-versus-actual work order funding reports.
- System Integration—to integrate data from the financial accounting system (payroll and operating expenses) and feed data (billings and allocations) into the financial accounting system of the institution.

To achieve these objectives, the organizational cost centers should be established such that the expenses of operation can be charged to the cost centers through the central accounting of the institution. The cost centers should represent units of activity, usually the plant offices and the different shops.

A work order system is essential to cost accounting. The cost accounting purposes of the work order system are:

- Provide the capital costs of projects in which the plant is involved.
- Collect the ongoing maintenance, upkeep, and operating costs for individual facilities, equipment, and landscape.
- Identify the costs to be allocated or billed to the operating units of the institution.
- Provide management with reports of asset utilization and utilization variance reports.

Each work order is itself a cost center. The work orders must capture all costs of the plant, both direct and indirect.

Work orders are of two types: 1) standing, blanket, or perpetual work orders; and 2) specific or project work orders. A standing work order is generally established for collection of ongoing maintenance, custodial, landscape, and utilities of individual facilities, vehicles, or major components. The costs gathered can include preventive maintenance, service calls, scheduled service, and any other costs management wants to include in the standing work order. If more detail is needed, standing work orders can be established for the different types of service for each entity on which costs are kept by standing work order. More and more data processing systems are being developed to provide various levels of detail.

It may be that management might want a specific work order for any job requiring an estimate or any job estimated to cost more than $500, with jobs falling outside these parameters being charged to a standing work order. Whatever the guidelines, the policy must be clearly understood by those having input into the costing system.

12.8 WORK ORDER SYSTEM OPERATION

The work order system used by physical plant must provide the cost accounting detail necessary to meet the costing system requirements. The work orders are the basic building blocks of the cost information. It is imperative that the work order system be properly structured and effectively operated.

Whether the system is automated or manual, the individual work orders must contain sufficient detail to identify the type and location of the work (maintenance, grounds, custodial, and building or project). Accounting nomenclature must be included for billing and allocation purposes. More sophisticated systems might include estimates in desired levels of detail, classification of work as preventive or corrective maintenance, and other useful management information. Systems are available that generate preventive maintenance work orders automatically.

A daily reporting of labor hours worked against work orders by the craftspeople assigned must be produced; materials and supplies drawn from stores must be properly charged to the project.

The accuracy and comparability of the costs reported against the work orders depend on conscientious attention to detail by craftspeople and material handlers. Management must always check that accurate cost data is being furnished.

The cost shown on the work order reports is the labor hours extended at the calculated rate with applicable indirect and overhead, materials at purchase price or inventory value with applicable indirect and overhead, utilities with metered usage extended by the appropriate rate, and other costs such as contracts that the individual work orders are established to capture.

The output of the system is the basis for service and utility billings to auxiliary enterprises and other self-supporting entities, and for allocations of cost to the operating departments of the institution.

12.9 CLASSIFICATION OF COSTS

To assure comparability among institutions, APPA and NACUBO have endorsed a classification of costs to serve as a general model for physical plant accounting. Six classifications or accounts categorize all costs incurred by physical plants. A reprint of the APPA/NACUBO Classification of Accounts appears in Appendix 12-A. The classifications are:

- Physical plant administration
- Architecture and engineering

- Utilities
- Maintenance and operations
- Major repairs and renovations (MR&R)
- Other services.

Physical Plant Administration

This classification should include all costs necessary to carry out the duties of management and administration of all areas under the jurisdiction of the physical plant division. These costs would include all payroll and personnel, operating supplies and expenses, equipment, and travel related to the director, assistant directors, office and accounting personnel, clerical and data processing personnel, purchasing and materials handling personnel, and work dispatching and control personnel.

Architecture and Engineering

This classification includes all payroll and personnel, operating supplies and expenses related to drafting, design, technical, and engineering services. Illustrative of types of activities to be included are major capital design and construction management, minor project design, maintenance of project files, space management, and long-range development and master planning. In many instances, some or all of these activities may be funded in other operating units of the institution. Those funded in the physical plant division should be included in this classification.

Utilities

This classification includes all energy costs for heating, cooling, light, power, gas, water, and other utilities necessary for physical plant operation. These costs would include all payroll and personnel; operating supplies and expenses; and repairs and maintenance related to central power, heating, and cooling plants. Also, the maintenance costs of utility distribution, not to include building interior distribution systems, would be included in this classification. Contractual costs for purchase of utilities would be included here.

Maintenance and Operations

This classification includes all payroll and personnel, operating supplies and expenses, equipment, and tools related to maintenance and upkeep of buildings and grounds. Categories of this classification follow.

Building Services   Building services involve all costs related to repair and maintenance of buildings and building equipment to include contracted maintenance services and interior utility distribution.

Grounds Services   Grounds services include all costs related to the institution's grounds and landscape, including grass, trees, flowers, shrubbery, roads, walks, open ditch drainage, fences, and all other landscape features. Parking areas, playing fields, irrigation systems, and signage are also included in grounds services.

Custodial Services   Custodial services include all costs related to housekeeping. These costs would include the cleaning of all interior surfaces and fixtures, cleaning of exterior window surfaces, custodial supplies to include chalk, trash removal to the exterior of buildings, and snow removal around building entrances.

Major Repairs and Renovations

This classification includes costs for major nonrecurring repairs, major deferred maintenance, and renovations. These projects should include only those with a predetermined cost threshold. The costs reported for each project would include all personnel and payroll, planning, design, administration, and contracting related to the project.

Other Services

This classification is used for other essential services not consistently within physical plant, yet frequently assigned. Among these are automotive repair, facilities planning and inspection, telecommunications, fire protection, mail service, insurance, public safety, and possibly others.

12.10 OTHER CONSIDERATIONS

To set the plant operating budget, two actual budgets for each organizational cost center usually exist: gross and net budgets. This is one of the reasons physical plant cannot effectively operate without a work order costing system. Much of the gross costs of utilities, maintenance and repair, custodial, and grounds are incurred for the benefit of self-supporting entities such as auxiliary enterprises, hospitals, and funded research facilities. These costs, though paid through physical plant, must be regularly and accurately billed to the benefiting activities for their interim financial information to be meaningful.

Separately funded projects also exist, such as plant funds and MR&R projects, which are generally ongoing at any point in time. The costing system must provide a means to accurately move the costs related to these projects from physical plant operating cost centers into the cost centers established for these projects.

It is also necessary, on a periodic or annual basis, to allocate the maintenance, utilities, custodial, and other costs incurred by physical plant to the various schools and departments of the institution. This is generally done on a space-occupied or similar basis, and may be automated or manual. The costing system of physical plant must provide those costs to be allocated.

It is of utmost importance that charges be made to work orders on an accurate and timely basis and the cost accounting techniques be consistently applied. Fairness of billings and comparability of current and prior period reports are totally dependent on accuracy and consistency.

Management will also be frequently confronted with the decision to pay a cost through an operating cost center of physical plant or charge it directly to a separately funded project. This is frequently a difficult decision. Suppose, for example, that the engineering department of the plant does the precontracting studies to accomplish a separately funded project, and actually negotiates the contract. Should the contract be charged directly to the separate funding, with engineering making a charge against the separate funding for services? It would appear so; however, the engineering cost may be included in the overhead rates by which administrative costs are allocated to work orders, in which case a direct charge against the project would be erroneous.

This dilemma, and others equally perplexing, occur with regularity in the administration of physical plant cost accounting systems. The complexities involved are frequently not understood outside the department. Such problems make the guiding principles of consistency and accuracy difficult to maintain.

12.11 ADVANCED SYSTEMS

Automated systems that greatly enhance the cost information available to plant management are currently available. These systems allow the budget structure of physical plant to be arranged in cost centers that match the various functions or shops. In this way each shop can have its own cost and recovery budget. This amounts to a great advance in the provision of management information. These systems carry the capability to summarize cost and budget data in the NACUBO/APPA reporting formats. Thus, the required comparative data can be made available on an automated basis when required.

ADDITIONAL RESOURCES

Anderson, Henry R. and Mitchell H. Raiborn. *Basic Cost Accounting Concepts.* Boston: Houghton Mifflin Co., 1977.

Bierman, Harold Jr. and Allan R. Dubin. *Managerial Accounting: An Introduction,* third edition. New York: The Macmillan Co., 1968.

Dearden, John. *Cost and Budget Analysis.* Englewood Cliffs, New Jersey: Prentice-Hall, 1978.

Horngren, Charles T. and George Foster. *Cost Accounting: A Managerial Emphasis,* sixth edition. Englewood Cliffs, New Jersey: Prentice-Hall, 1987.

Welzenbach, Lanora F., ed. *College & University Business Management,* fourth edition. Washington, D.C.: NACUBO, 1982.

Appendix 12-A

Operations and Maintenance of Physical Plant

Reprinted with permission by the National Association of College and University Business Officers.

In 1965 the Association of Physical Plant Administrators of Universities and Colleges (APPA) and NACUBO recommended a classification of accounts designed to serve as a general model for physical plant accounting and to provide a standard base for the development of comparative data. It is used by APPA as a base for studies of comparative unit costs and staffing for the operation of physical plant. Although minor adjustments have been made in this classification of accounts since its introduction, until now the general format has remained the same.

Since the classification of accounts was originally formulated, the organization and responsibilities of physical plants have changed drastically because of such developments as the air conditioning of facilities, the installation of sophisticated research equipment and computers, and the adoption of environmental regulations. In addition to these influences has been the rapid rise in the cost of energy combined with the accountability for the utilization of institutional resources, including those allocated for the use of the physical plant.

The new classification of accounts has been divided into six major sections: Administration, Architecture and Engineering, Utilities, Maintenance and Operations, Other Services, and Major Repairs and Renovations.

Because it is generally a sensitive area, Administration is treated as a separate item; it is always easy to criticize any organization for having too much administration. The previous classification of accounts included architectural and engineering costs under Administration. In many institutions in which the architectural and engineering function is much larger than the administration function, however, a false indication is given of the high costs of administration expenses. In addition, architectural and engineering services in many institutions are allocated to other cost centers, which reduces the allocation to the main section.

Utilities is also treated as a separate item because it generally represents a large expenditure not only for the physical plant but for the entire institution. The Maintenance and Operations section comprises the building maintenance, grounds, and custodial services included in the previous classification of accounts. These sections have been combined into one because in most institutions they are closely related and generally under the direction of a single assistant director or manager. Other Services and Major Repairs varied significantly from institution to institution, and cost comparisons in staffing are not reliable.

The use of the classification of accounts for comparison on a yearly basis among institutions has proved to be highly reliable for the Maintenance and Operations area only. This is because the functions of this section do not vary significantly among institutions. The cost data from the other sections are not as reliable, however, and it is the intent of this classification of accounts to define more accurately the cost data that are to be included in these sections, with the hope that better and more consistent data will be generated.

PART A:
A Classification of Accounts for Operation and Maintenance of Physical Plant

I. MAJOR ACCOUNTS

1. Administration
2. Architecture and Engineering
3. Utilities
4. Maintenance and Operations
5. Other Services
6. Major Repairs and Renovations

OUTLINE OF COSTS INCLUDED UNDER MAJOR ACCOUNTS

1. Administration

Activities necessary for the general management and administration of all functions under the jurisdiction of the physical plant division are included unless the activity is predominantly related to another major account. This section will generally be used to collect all costs associated with the director's/assistant director's offices of the division. It will include functions that are organized specifically to provide support services (i.e., purchasing, personnel) for the operation of the physical plant division. It should not include general university service units (purchasing and property insurance) that serve the entire campus and are more appropriately classified under the section entitled Other Services if assigned to physical plant. Generally, foremen and other supervisory personnel will be assigned to the major account classifications that most nearly reflect the principal responsibility of these personnel. The total cost of this major account should be considered an indirect or overhead item in determining rates to be used in a cost-accounting system for specific projects and activities. The following subaccounts (cost centers) are illustrative of the activities that may be included in the major account entitled Administration.

A. *Administration*

B. *Work Control Center*
   1. Estimating
   2. Scheduling

C. *Purchasing*

D. *Managerial and Fiduciary Accounting*
   1. Fund accounting
   2. Payroll

E. *Personnel/Labor Relations*

F. *Data Processing*

G. *Clerical Pool*

Section II describes the objects of expenditure that can be used with the major account or subaccounts to more completely describe the type of expenditure transactions.

2. **Architecture and Engineering**
   This major account can be used for those in-house drafting, design, technical, and engineering services necessary to perform functions assigned and funded in the physical plant division. The following subaccounts (cost centers) are illustrative of the activities that can be included in this major account.

   A. *Major Capital Design and Construction Management*
      1. Programming
      2. Major project coordination
      3. Construction management

   B. *Minor Project Design*

   C. *Project and "As Built" Records for Major and Minor Projects*

   D. *Space Management*

   E. *Long-Range Development and Master Planning*

Some institutions may be organized in a manner in which this function is assigned as a separate organizational unit or carried as a subaccount within another unit of the institution. If this is true, then a cost comparison between institutions should recognize this fact. Some expenditures included in this section may be allocated and capitalized under plant funds. Individual institutional policies will control this consideration.

Section III defines various activities that can be used by some institutions to describe programmatical expenditures within the physical plant division. These institutions may wish to include in the chart of accounts structure a coding scheme that will identify those programs. If this is done, the individual transaction of the Architecture and Engineering account can then be identified by subaccount (cost center), object of expenditures, and activities (program) type.

3. **Utilities**
   This major account is structured to capture all costs associated with fuel and purchased utilities, central plant operations (if applicable), utility distribution systems exterior to the buildings, energy management operations, and all types of waste and refuse disposal. The intent is to be able to compare institutional costs for the conversion of energy to a building-usable form (for example, natural gas to steam), the delivery of the utility to the individual facilities, and those expenditures that are used to avoid future energy use. The following cost centers are illustrative of the activities that can be included in this major account:
   A. *Fuel and Purchased Utilities*
      1. Natural gas
      2. Coal
      3. Fuel oil
      4. Other fuels (e.g., propane)
      5. Chilled water
      6. Steam
      7. Sewer
      8. Electricity
      9. Water
   B. *Central Plant Operations (heating, cooling, and electricity generation)*
      1. Personnel services
      2. Plant operation, supplies, and expense

    3. Fuel handling (unless charged to Fuel, see A)
    4. Plant maintenance
C. *Utility Distribution Systems (maintenance and line losses)*
D. *Energy Management Systems*
E. *Waste Disposal and Refuse Systems*

Some institutions may be organized in a manner that separates the various functions among other physical plant departments or other institutional departments. If this is true, then cost comparisons between institutions should recognize this fact. Or, for reporting purposes, those costs can be identified in the chart of accounts by using a code scheme to identify the subaccount (cost center) to the object of expenditure and activities type. This may occur most often for energy-management systems; waste disposal is distinguished in that hazardous and nonhazardous categories are accounted for under separate university departments.

4. **Maintenance and Operations**

Activities necessary for the management, supervision, and execution of all functions relating to the maintenance and operation of buildings and grounds (excluding utilities, covered in section 3) are included in this category. This section will generally be used to collect all costs, including personnel compensation, supplies and expenses, travel. contractual services, and equipment. Also included are all costs for the maintenance of buildings (including interior utility distribution systems). structures and pertinences, maintenance of grounds and landscape, and custodial services in building interiors.

A. *Building Services*
    1. Plumbing, heating, air conditioning, and ventilation
    2. Electrical repairs
    3. Carpentry and cabinetmaking
    · 4. Painting and glazing
    5. Hardware and locks
    6. Roofing
    7. Sheet metal, downspouts, and gutters
    8. Masonry and other structural components
    9. Filters
    10. Controls
    11. Refrigeration
    12. Elevators

B. *Grounds Services*
1. Plant materials
2. Lawns
3. Streets
4. Walks
5. Athletic fields, unless operated as auxiliary enterprises
6. Physical education and intramural fields
7. Open-ditch drainage, fences, retaining walls, and other landscape features
8. Signs
9. Benches and other fixed equipment
10. Litter

C. *Custodial Services*
1. Cleaning interior building surfaces
2. Cleaning interior and exterior window surfaces
3. Cleaning interior fixtures, including toilets, blinds, chalkboards, and so forth
4. Trash removal to exterior of buildings
5. Snow removal on building steps and short distances of walks
6. Paper towels, soap, chalk, and other custodial supplies

Many institutions will maintain both the building and the utility systems with the same craft shops and personnel. It is recommended that a cost-accounting system be used to separate costs between buildings and utilities in order to reflect more accurately the cost of each of these facilities. Personnel compensation and expenses of administrative personnel (such as assistant directors and managers whose function is to administer and manage this section only) should be included in this section. In many institutions, architectural and engineering services will be a direct charge to this section or included as an overhead item. When architectural and engineering services are included in this section, the cost-accounting system should separate those costs because they should be reported there.

5. **Other Services**

The physical plant organization affects all segments of the institution and must provide for necessary levels of service in a manner that is effective and compatible with institutional objectives. The physical plant that is organized primarily along functional lines requires that each of the appropriate categories have its own budget. However, often functional categories that are not consistently within the physical plant division are assigned there in light of their functions.

Examples include:

> Motor pool/fleet management
> Transportation/bus service
> Construction/planning and inspection
> Telecommunications
> Public safety
> Parking
> Environmental health and safety
> Fire protection
> Mail and messenger service
> Property insurance
> Purchasing and stores
> Security
> Hazardous waste treatment, storage, and disposal
> Typewriter and business machine repair
> Storage and warehousing
> Traffic
> Trucking and moving

Such services are assigned to the physical plant as a means to facilitate use by all institutional entities and avoid duplication of purchases or services.

6. **Major Repairs and Renovations**
This major account includes expenditures for those major jobs or projects that must be accomplished but are not funded by normal maintenance resources received in the annual operating budget cycle. The following subaccounts (cost centers) are illustrative of the type of projects that would be included in each cost center with a potential for subaccount costing. (The descriptions given in A.1, A.2, and A.3 also apply to cost centers B and C.)

A. *Renewal and Replacement Maintenance*
    1. Buildings (work on or within the building walls)
    2. Grounds (plantings, site, roads, parking)
    3. Utilities (all utility distribution systems from the central plant or property line to the individual building exterior wall)

B. *Unscheduled Major Maintenance (requires immediate action to restore)*

   1. Buildings
   2. Grounds
   3. Utilities
C. *Alteration and Renovation*
   1. Buildings
   2. Grounds
   3. Utilities

For cost center A, some institutions may submit project listings to the appropriate administrative units or the board of trustees, board of regents, or legislative bodies. The resources may come in the form of capital appropriation, reserve account release, or supplemental appropriation from specific fund sources. Sources of funding may not come from existing operating budget allocations.

Because of the emergency nature of need for cost center B, the fund source could come from annual operating accounts, reserve accounts, or other institutional sources. The data in this category would provide institutional comparisons of the level of resources needed to meet emergency needs.

For cost center C, the distinction is to segregate and identify those projects that are required because of a change in the use of a facility or a change in program requirements, or both. This cost center would normally not include those projects received through the institution's major capital improvement program or those funded by annual operating budget allocations.

II. CLASSIFICATION OF EXPENDITURES BY OBJECT

The object classification of expenditures identifies what is received in return for the expenditures. Object classification is important as a tool for internal management, but should be considered complementary to the classification of expenditures by function and by organizational unit and should not replace these classifications in the various schedules of current funds expenditures. The value of object classification will depend on the usefulness of the information it provides to management. The classifications may be omitted from published financial reports or they may be used to any degree considered desirable by the institution. The use of object classification and the related identifying codes and symbols should not be carried to an extreme: the number of categories should be limited to those that will be of significant value to management.

For the division of physical plant operations and maintenance, five major objects of expenditure have been identified. Breakdowns of objects within these major categories may be necessary or desirable in some situations.

Personnel Compensation

This classification includes salaries, wages, and staff benefits. In the various salary and wage expense accounts, it may be desirable to distinguish between staff members, such as full-time and part-time personnel; student and nonstudent workers; and professional, secretarial, clerical, skilled, and nonskilled employees. Appropriate code numbers and symbols within this category will aid in identifying, collecting, and summarizing information. Fringe benefits may be stated separately as an object of expenditure, if desired.

Travel

Contractual Services

Supplies and Other Expenses

Equipment Expenditure

This classification includes expenditures for low-cost equipment purchased for less than a specific dollar limit set by the institution. For example, the Office of Management and Budget (OMB) Circular A-21 stipulates an acquisition cost of $500 or more per unit and a useful life of more than two years as the threshold at which tangible personal property must be considered a capital asset. As a rule of thumb, therefore, acquisitions costing less than $500 may be considered noncapital expenditures.

III. DEFINITIONS

Activity Definitions

Each of these activities would be included in one of the functional categories outlined in section I (Major Accounts).

1. *Normal maintenance* is a systematic day-to-day process funded by the annual operating budget to control the deterioration of the college or university plant facilities, e.g., structures, systems, equipment, pavement, and grounds. Planned maintenance includes the following:
   a. Scheduled repetitive work, such as housekeeping activities, groundskeeping, site maintenance, and certain types of service contracts.

b. Periodic scheduled work (preventive maintenance) that has been planned to provide adjustments, cleaning, minor repair, and routine inspections of equipment to reduce service interruptions.

c. Call-in requests for service.

2. *Renewal and replacement maintenance* is a systematic management process to plan and budget for known future cyclic repair and replacement requirements that extend the life and retain the usable condition of campus facilities and systems and that are not normally contained in the annual operating budget. This includes major items that have a maintenance cycle in excess of one year, e.g., replacing roofs, painting buildings, resurfacing roads, replacing equipment (boilers, chillers, transformers, and so forth).

3. *Unscheduled major maintenance* is work requiring immediate action to restore service or remove anticipated problems that will interrupt agency activities. Unscheduled major maintenance should be included if expenditures are made from current funds. Examples include a loss of electrical power, water, or refrigeration, and building failures creating hazards to personnel or equipment.

4. *Alteration and renovation* is work that is required because of a change in the use of the facility or a change in program.

5. *New construction* includes in-house planning for new construction and small construction projects if funded out of current funds.

Space Definitions

1. *Gross area*

The area reported is the total area maintained by the division and for which the division has a budget. Any area for which the division is reimbursed should not be included. Areas and costs should be included only if the physical plant division is responsible for them.

Gross area is determined in accordance with the following guidelines from Publication 1235 of the National Academy of Sciences, National Research Council (Classification of Building Areas, Federal Construction Council Technical Report no. 50). In the event that gross area is already calculated on some other basis, it should be reported as such, but a footnote should indicate the basis or reference for calculation.

a. *Gross area* is construed to mean the sum of floor areas included within the outside faces of exterior walls for all stories, or areas, having floor surface.

b. *Basis for measurement*
Gross area should be computed by measuring from the outside face of exterior walls, disregarding such extensions as cornices, pilasters, and buttresses.

c. *Description*
In addition to ground-to-top-story internal floored spaces covered in (a) above, gross area should include basements, garages, enclosed porches, penthouses and mechanical equipment, floors, lobbies, mezzanines, functional balconies—inside and outside—and corridors, provided they are within the outside face lines of the building. Roofed loading or shipping platforms should be included whether within or outside the exterior face lines of the building.

d. *Limitations*
Open courts, light wells, or portions of upper floors rising above singlefloor ceiling height should not be included in the gross area. Neither should unenclosed roofed-over areas or floored surfaces with less than six feet, six inches clear head room be included, unless they can be designated and used as net-assignable, mechanical, circulation, or custodial areas.

e. *Part-year occupancy*
When new buildings become operative during a year or if an existing building is in service for only part of a year, the area reported is the gross area multiplied by the fraction of the year the building was in service.

An example: The fiscal year ends June 30. A new building of 100,000 gross square feet is accepted for beneficial occupancy April 1. The area reported is 3/12 x 100,000 square feet, or 25,000 square feet, for the year of first occupancy. The following year the area reported is 100,000 square feet.

IV. DEFINITIONS OF COST CENTER AND COST OBJECTIVE

Cost Center
This refers to the smallest unit of activity or area of responsibility into which an operating organization is divided for con-

trol and accountability purposes and to which costs are assigned or allocated.

Cost Objective

This refers to which costs can be attributed. It can be a service provided by an organizational unit, a project, a responsibility center, a function, a program, or any other identifiable activity. Cost objectives can be composed of one or more cost centers.

PART B:
Management Information for Operations and Maintenance of Physical Plant

I. CAPITAL USAGE CHARGE

Many institutional managers want to collect information on the full costs associated with providing educational services. An important element of an institution's total operating cost is the cost of using its physical facilities. Although colleges and universities do not currently recognize depreciation of capital assets in current operating accounts, depreciation or use charge for the consumption of facilities or capital equipment must be included in costing data in order to obtain the full costs associated with a cost center or cost objective.[1]

Depreciation charges should be based on the useful life of the assets and should take into consideration such factors as the type of construction, potential obsolescence, and the institution's renewal and replacement policies.

In *Procedures for Determining Historical Full Costs*, an alternative to depreciation is presented in the form of an annual use charge on buildings and land improvements.[2] The use charge may be one overall rate that an institution applies to the total cost of all its buildings and land improvements, or it may be a combination of rates that reflects the remaining lives of capital assets. An important difference between the use-charge rate and depreciation is that a usecharge rate can be applied to a particular building or group of buildings as long as that building exists, whereas under the depreciation method the time period is limited to the estimated useful life of the building. NACUBO recommends an overall annual rate of 2 percent, based on an estimated useful life of 50 years for buildings and land improvements. For capital equipment, a 10 percent rate reflecting an estimated useful life of 10 years is recommended, although this may vary depending on the type of equipment.[3]

An example of the application of an annual use charge is as follows:

Original cost of all buildings and land improvements	$10,000,000
Multiply by annual use factor	.02
Annual use charge for buildings and land improvements	$ 200,000

For more information on collecting, analyzing, and using cost information for internal decision making, see *A Cost Accounting Handbook for Colleges and Universities* (NACUBO, 1983).

II. DEFERRED MAINTENANCE

Part A, section III provides definitions for normal maintenance, renewal and replacement maintenance, unscheduled major maintenance, alteration and renovation, and new construction. Institutional managers may want information on how much of the maintenance that should have been done in a year or budget cycle was deferred. NACUBO and APPA recommend the following definition for *deferred maintenance*.

Deferred maintenance consists of maintenance projects that were not included in the maintenance process because of a perceived lower priority status than those funded within available funding. Deferred maintenance comprises two categories of unfunded maintenance: first, the lack of which does not cause the facility to deteriorate further; and second, the lack of which does result in a progressive deterioration of the facility for the current function.

Less frequent painting of interior walls would be an example of unfunded maintenance that does not cause a facility to deteriorate. One the other hand, less frequent painting of building exterior trim may indeed contribute to building deterioration at some point. Roof repairs or replacement would be the most glaring example of unfunded maintenance that, if not attended to, inevitably leads to deterioration from leaks within the building.

Note: The use of this definition requires a clear understanding and acceptance of the definition by the institutional administration.

NOTES

1. For definitions of *cost center* and *cost objective*, see part A, section IV.
2. NACUBO/NCHEMS, *Procedures for Determining Historical Full Costs. Technical Report 65* (Washington, D.C., 1977), 2.44-2.47.
3. Office of Management and Budget Circular A-21, Section J9, sets the use allowance for buildings at 2 percent of acquisition cost and the use allowance for equipment at 6.67 percent, based on an estimated useful life of 15 years.

CHAPTER 13

Cost Control

David J. Gojdics
Director of Physical Plant
Emory University

Jesse C. Nipper, CPA
Assistant Director for
Business Management
Physical Plant Department
Emory University

13.1 INTRODUCTION

Chapter 12, Cost Accounting, described the cost accounting system and how it operates to collect cost information and allocate certain costs to establish unit costs and rates for the services provided by the physical plant. This chapter addresses the use of the information generated by the cost accounting system in cost control. Many of the techniques involve technical concepts that are of primary concern to the financial specialist. Our purpose here is to provide a basic understanding of cost control methods to general facilities management personnel.

13.2 CONTROL CONCEPTS

Control is so closely interlinked with planning that they are virtually inseparable. Planning is the process of deciding what needs to be done and anticipating the steps needed to produce the desired outcome. Control involves implementing the planning decision, comparing actual results with what was planned, and taking corrective action if there is an unacceptable deviation. This close relationship is illustrated by the planning and control cycle, which continues until goals are achieved:

- Goals are set.
- Steps to achieve the goals are chosen.
- Actual performance occurs, either according to plan or with variation.
- Performance is monitored through feedback mechanisms.

- Adjustments are made in either goals, plans, or actions.
- Additional feedback is received.
- Additional adjustment takes place.

To control, it is necessary to have a way of measuring performance and a standard to which that performance will be compared. The cost accounting system, when properly structured, provides the means of measuring cost performance. The standards for comparison can take many forms.

13.3 GENERAL COST CONTROL TECHNIQUES

Many actions of physical plant managers influence cost, but all are not dependent upon the use of cost accounting information. For example, one of the most powerful cost control techniques available is a manager's personal observations as he or she travels the campus, the shops, and the job sites. These observations may provide more information about the effectiveness of the physical plant than any accountant's cost report.

However, there are many excellent techniques that rely on cost accounting information.

Present Versus Past

Even the most rudimentary accounting systems permit a comparison of present to past costs for the same time period. If conditions are generally the same and the account breakdown is sufficiently detailed, this can be an effective control method. Even in the presence of other more sophisticated techniques, a present versus past comparison is usually useful. Its usefulness is enhanced if trend lines are established which depict performance over a series of time periods.

The chief difficulty with using past performance as a standard is that there is no indication of what performance should have been. Historical data could represent excellent or poor performance. Unless past conditions are known, a standard may be adopted that contains inefficiency and extraordinary costs.

While present versus past comparisons should not be dismissed entirely, they should be used with extreme caution and skepticism. They are most valuable when used in conjunction with other indicators.

Actual Versus Budget

Comparison of actual costs to budget is perhaps the most important technique available to the physical plant manager. It is generally superior to comparisons against past performance, due to the characteristics of budgets in general and from the unique role they play in nonprofit organizations.

When properly prepared, budgets represent the plan, stated in monetary terms, that has been formulated to meet the objectives of the organization. As such, they force the manager to anticipate changes.

In nonprofit organizations, budgets play an even more important role in management control. In such organizations, control is generally viewed to be more difficult because of the absence of profit as an objective, as a criterion for appraising alternative courses of action, and as a measure of performance. This shifts the focus from profits to plans and budgets and makes the budget the principal means of overall control.

When budgets are used, cost control will be much more effective if the cost accounting system is designed to be consistent with the budget, and vice versa. Unless the two are stated in the same terms and structured similarly, there is no way of determining whether spending occurred according to the budget plan. This does not mean that a budget should be set for each detail account, but it does mean that there should be accounts in the cost accounting system that match each line item in the budget so that a direct comparison can be made.

Responsibility Accounting

Organizations are composed of units and subunits, each responsible for some phase of its operation. The unit is a responsibility center. Responsibility accounting refers to a system designed to measure the performance of each responsibility center, including that of the person in charge of its operation. The general philosophy is to assign responsibility for controlling costs to the supervisory head at the point where the costs originate. It is a way of setting up the cost accounting system and establishing budgets to correspond with the organization's structure. Thus, ideally, there is three-way consistency among the budget, the accounting system, and the organization. The organization reflects what is needed to get the job done, and the budget and accounting systems are structured in harmony with it.

Responsibility accounting systems recognize that organizations and their subunits are made up of people and managers with well-defined jobs. Cost control is accomplished by virtue of the motivation and accountability usually inherent in a system in which people know what is expected of them.

Under ideal conditions, responsibility accounting systems should either exclude all uncontrollable costs from a manager's performance report, or they should segregate them from those that are controllable. This results in maximum accountability and cost control.

It is difficult to achieve the ideal state described here because change can easily upset the three-way consistency among the organization, the budget, and the accounting system. However, application of these principles can produce excellent results even when only approximations of the ideal can be maintained.

Performance Measurement

Performance measurement seeks to establish other standards besides budgets against which to measure and compare actual performance. These standards are frequently nonmonetary but are intended to complement, not replace, budgets. In many cases these standards provide the detail upon which budgets are built.

Performance standards may be generated internally or they may come from outside sources. Both are useful. Internal standards usually relate to the budget in some way, or to an individual department's unique goals and objectives. Examples of internal standards might be:

- A twenty-day backlog of work should be maintained at all times.
- Actual job costs should be within 10 percent of the estimates.
- Actual labor performance should be from 95 to 105 percent of standard labor.
- Energy use should not exceed 100,000 Btus per square foot per year.

The most effective standards are those tailor-made to the institution's needs, which will vary among institutions.

Most managers are interested in how their operations compare to physical plants at other universities, or to the average of universities, and seek performance measures common to all physical plants. For example, the time required to run 100 feet of electrical conduit can be measured on an absolute basis. It should take the same amount of time anywhere, assuming workers of equal ability do the job and similar conditions exist. Few absolute measures exist, however, against which actual performance can be compared. Most measurements are relative to past performance, are in index or ratio form, and are most meaningfully analyzed using trend lines and charts.

Following are discussed performance measures that are 1) published and generally accepted and 2) more specific and generally developed by individual institutions.

Published Performance Indicators   The most comprehensive and useful publication for plant administration is published by APPA. Every two years APPA surveys its members and publishes the results in its *Comparative Costs and Staffing Report for College and University Facilities.* The information reported by each participating institution includes the following:

- Full-time equivalent (FTE) student enrollment.
- Total gross square footage of all buildings.
- Gross square footage maintained in physical plant budget.
- Ground acreage.
- Administrative cost per gross square foot (GSF).
- FTE administrators.
- Engineering cost per GSF.
- FTE engineering personnel.
- Maintenance cost per GSF.
- FTE maintenance employees.
- Custodial cost per GSF.
- FTE custodial personnel.
- Landscape and grounds cost per GSF.
- FTE landscape and grounds personnel.

The report presents this information in a format that permits comparisons. Managers can compare their performance to that of institutions of similar size, type, and educational purpose.

Other information, although not nearly as comprehensive as APPA's report, is published periodically in various trade journals. For example, *American School and University* annually publishes a maintenance and operations cost survey with costs analyzed as follows:

- Custodial salaries stated in dollars per student and per square foot.
- Maintenance salaries stated in dollars per student and per square foot.
- Heat, other utilities, and other costs stated in dollars and per square foot.
- Average custodial and maintenance salaries.
- Square feet per custodian.
- The above data is presented for each of ten regions of the United States, including Alaska and Hawaii.

At best, published indicators can only serve as a guide. Large differences are often noticeable, even among similar organizations. These wide variations reflect not only the differences in costs but also in methods of accounting for costs. For this reason, caution is required in using such comparative data.

Internal Performance Indicators   Even though meaningful comparisons of one organization to another are difficult, there are remarkable similarities in the items organizations measure. In one way or another, measurements usually relate to labor productivity, materials usage and cost, energy usage, quantity of work done, quality of work, timeliness of service, and job cost.

Performance measures are usually expressed in index (ratio) form. In establishing indexes, managers must carefully consider two questions: What do I want to control? and What index will indicate the performance? After selecting appropriate indexes, target values of desired performance must be selected. These will probably be based upon budgets, past history, or future goals and objectives.

Performance measures are specific to each institution, so it would not be possible to list those measures applicable to individual organizations. It can be noted that many are specific and obviously tailor-made to certain industries and organizations.

Variance Analysis

Thus far, it has been noted that the essential element of control is repeated comparison of actual performance to a standard. The standard may be historical data; comparable data from another university; or a predetermined yardstick such as an estimate, a labor standard, or a budget. Deviations from the standard, called variances, will usually occur. Note that a variance is the *difference* between a standard and an actual quantity or result.

For cost control, it is of little use to know only the dollar amount of the variance, especially if many factors are at work to influence cost. To take effective action, it is necessary to break down the total difference into its individual elements using variance analysis.

There are basically two types of variances: price and quantity. Several other variances can be developed for specialized purposes, but each one will be ultimately traceable to variations in price, variations in quantity used, or a combination of price and quantity variations.

Any cost can be stated in terms of price and quantity, as follows:

Cost = Price x Quantity

If two costs are involved, one can be considered the standard, and the other the actual. The difference between them represents the variance. As shown in Figure 13-1, the variance consists of the area marked V_P plus the area V_Q.

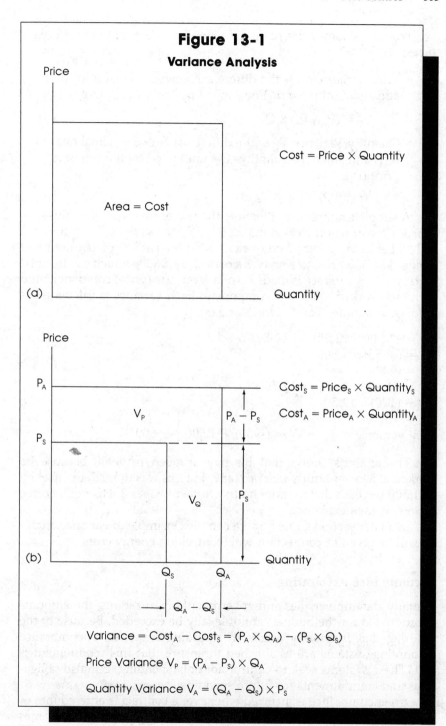

Figure 13-1

Variance Analysis

(a) Cost = Price × Quantity

Area = Cost

(b)
$$\text{Cost}_S = \text{Price}_S \times \text{Quantity}_S$$
$$\text{Cost}_A = \text{Price}_A \times \text{Quantity}_A$$

$$\text{Variance} = \text{Cost}_A - \text{Cost}_S = (P_A \times Q_A) - (P_S \times Q_S)$$

$$\text{Price Variance } V_P = (P_A - P_S) \times Q_A$$

$$\text{Quantity Variance } V_A = (Q_A - Q_S) \times P_S$$

From this comes the basic definitions of price and quantity variances:

- Price Variance V_P = the difference between actual price (P_A) and standard price (P_S) multiplied by the actual quantity (Q_A).

$$V_P = (P_A - P_S) \times Q_A$$

- Quantity Variance V_Q = the difference between actual quantity (Q_A) and standard quantity (Q_S) multiplied by the standard price (P_S).

$$V_Q = (Q_A - Q_S) \times P_S$$

A simple example will illustrate the use of this type of analysis. In Year 1 a construction worker makes $21,000 by working 1,680 hours at $12.50 per hour. In Year 2 he works 1,800 hours at $12.00 per hour and makes $21,600. His total pay increased by $600, which is the total variance. This variance is made up of a wage rate (price) component and an hours-worked (quantity) component. Each variance is calculated as follows, assuming Year 1 is the standard:

$$
\begin{aligned}
V_P &= (12.00 - 12.50) \times 1{,}800 \\
&= (-0.50) \times 1{,}800 \\
&= -900 \\
V_Q &= (1{,}800 - 1{,}680) \times 12.50 \\
&= (120) \times 12.50 \\
&= +1{,}500
\end{aligned}
$$

Total variance $= V_P + V_Q = (-900) + 1{,}500 = +600$

The analysis shows that his pay dropped by $900 because he worked at a lower hourly rate in Year 2, but this was more than offset by a $1,500 increase due to more hours worked in Year 2. His net increase of $600 is thus explained.

In a later section a much more complex example of variance analysis will be given in connection with controlling energy costs.

Encumbrance Accounting

In many state universities and government organizations, the amounts appropriated for the budget cannot legally be exceeded. Because of the time lag that frequently occurs in recording expenses, encumbrance accounting systems are established to ensure that this requirement is met. These systems seek to control not only spending, but also obligations and commitments for future spending.

An encumbrance is incurred whenever a contract is entered into or when personnel perform work. At that time the organization becomes obligated to the other party in the contract, or to its personnel for their salaries and related benefits. Systems are established for keeping track of each obligation when it is made as well as when it is satisfied (liquidated). Control is achieved when the aggregate total of these encumbrances plus the actual spending is kept at or below the authorized budget level.

Management by Exception

The essential ingredients of control systems are standards, feedback on how actual results compare to the standards, and corrective action. Control applied in this manner makes possible the practice of management by exception.

A cost control system operated on the exception principle is one in which management's attention is focused on the relatively small number of items in which actual performance is significantly different from the standard. This principle acknowledges that management time is a scarce resource which should be applied to problems having the greatest impact on the organization. The relatively large number of minor variances from standard are either ignored or left to become the priority concern of a lower level manager in the responsibility accounting hierarchy.

Management by exception is implicitly based upon "Pareto's Law." Vilfredo Pareto (1848-1923), an Italian economist and sociologist, first proposed the theory that, in any type of activity, a small percentage of forces will influence a large percentage of results. This is also known as the 80-20 rule: 80 percent of any result is controlled by 20 percent of that which is producing the result. Management by exception focuses on the 20 percent of the deviations from standard that account for 80 percent of the problems.

Organizing for Control

Care in establishing the organizational structure and individuals' job duties can go a long way toward providing cost control that is "built-in." A number of internal controls follow that can be designed into the accounting system and the organization:

Separation of Duties   No one should have complete control over a given asset. This is accomplished by keeping operational responsibility separate from record-keeping responsibility. For example, the employee who authorizes purchases should not be the sole person approving invoices for those purchases. The purchaser, knowing that someone else will be reviewing the transaction, will not be inclined to misappropriate it, and the person approving the invoice has no incentive to falsify the records.

Authorization Controls   Spending authority limits should be established for each level of supervision and management in the organization. For example, the maintenance superintendent may have to approve overtime, rather than the shop foreman. Another example is to set higher approval levels for larger dollar value purchase requisitions.

Physical Security of Assets   It may seem that physical protection of assets has little to do with accounting, yet without protection proper accounting cannot be accomplished. Controls should be established that detect losses of cash, supplies, inventories, and records. However, first priority is to guard against the possibility of losses by providing proper physical protection a well as policies, procedures, and staffing to ensure operation as intended.

The list of control measures could go on. The point is that as many safeguards as possible should be designed into the organization and its basic systems rather than added on later.

13.4 SPECIFIC COST CONTROL TECHNIQUES

The cost control techniques thus far have been general. In the subparagraphs that follow, specific techniques for controlling the various types of costs are discussed. The following are the principal types of costs to be controlled:

- Labor, including hourly, salaried, part-time, and temporary.
- Purchased goods and services, which include:
  —Materials and supplies
  —Equipment
  —Service and construction contracts.
- Utilities.

Labor

Labor (salaried, hourly, part-time, temporary, and contract) can account for one-fourth to one-third of physical plant's entire budget.

A number of familiar controls are outside the scope of this chapter. These relate to personnel management and wage and salary administration. Briefly, these controls consist of matching people to jobs, maintaining wage rates that are competitive in the job markets, properly classifying employees within jobs and labor grades, merit rating and other wage incentive systems, and training. Important as these systems are in cost control, they are not considered a part of cost accounting.

Our concern here is with specific techniques that relate directly to the control of the amount of labor used. The most useful of these are position control; overtime control; use of temporary, part-time, or contract labor; and labor productivity standards and measurement.

Position Control   Position control refers to strict management of personnel headcount. The personnel budget should be traceable to an exact list of positions (jobs) with known labor grades and based upon current wages. Furthermore, allowances for overtime, wage increases, promotional increases, and contract labor should be budgeted. Positions, which are often numbered, are tracked and controlled separately from the employees who are incumbent in them. Personnel cannot be added unless a budgeted position with sufficient budgeted dollars is open to receive him or her. If a position is available, a person must be hired within the budgeted amount for that position or additional budget dollars must be identified elsewhere.

In organizations with sophisiticated position control methods, budget dollars for vacant positions may be withdrawn from the unit's budget allocation and pooled centrally in a contingency fund, or reallocated to another organizational unit. Sometimes the unit may be allowed to retain these savings.

Position control recognizes that personnel may represent the single largest cost to an organization. It also recognizes that additional people cause other expenses to increase, such as fringe benefits, desks, tools, uniforms, supplies, telephones, travel, and so forth.

Overtime Control   It is difficult for physical plant to operate without overtime. Unavoidable emergencies and planned work during the customer's off-hours make it almost impossible to avoid all overtime. There are theories that overtime below about 3 to 5 percent of regular hours indicates excess staffing, and overtime above this percentage indicates an organization's inability to plan and schedule work.

The first step in control of overtime is to produce reports showing the amount of overtime being spent by shop, cost center, department, or individual. If a budget amount has been established for overtime, a comparison can be made and the reasons for any differences explored. The key to control, as we have seen in the discussion of other techniques, is in establishing a standard (budget, in this case) and monitoring actual performance compared to it.

Use of Temporary, Part-time, or Contract Labor   Many physical plants appear to be discovering anew the advantages of using temporary, part-time, or contract labor for seasonal and peak-load work. Typical examples include seasonal grounds work, use of retired personnel during peak periods, and the traditional use of temporary agencies for secretarial and clerical needs.

Labor Productivity Improvement   Two main techniques are available for productivity improvement: use of labor standards and analysis of labor utilization. The most common and useful labor standard in physical plant work is the estimate, one of the basic foundations for planning and controlling construction and maintenance work. Its importance can be better understood by considering some of the ways in which estimates are used:

- To determine whether a job is large enough for formal planning and scheduling activities.
- To determine the size of the work backlog.
- To schedule work on a daily, weekly, or longer-term basis.
- To measure performance on an individual or shop basis.
- To quote costs to customers or other requestors of service.
- To compare in-house costs with contractor costs.
- To plan staffing increases or decreases.
- To establish budgets.

Some uses of estimates require more accuracy than others. For this reason many estimating methods are in use, and most managers use some combination of them depending upon the estimate's purpose.

The most common estimating methods involve use of 1) historical records, 2) estimator's experience, 3) commercial data, 4) contract data, and 5) predetermined time standards. Some of these sources contain data on both material and labor, but most focus primarily on labor as material is easier to define.

Each estimating technique has its advantages and disadvantages. While historical records can be useful for budget estimates or cost quoting, they are not usually adequate for scheduling or performance measurement. Too many variables are unknown. What kind of worker was assigned to that last job? Was he or she fast, slow, skilled, or unskilled? Were the working conditions normal? The best estimate that can be obtained using historical records is one that averages several similar jobs, if such information is available.

An estimator's experience can be an accurate estimating method that serves most purposes. Its major failing, however, is that estimators usually know only one or two trades well. In complex multitrade jobs, only certain phases will be accurately estimated.

Commercial data are generally developed on new construction work. They are frequently based upon repetitive tasks such as installing a number of new doors in a new building. New construction tasks differ from maintenance or renovation work. For example, the time to install a new door in a new building will usually be less than installing a new door in an old building. Thus, commercial data are useful for new work, but not particularly applicable for intermittent maintenance work.

"Contract data" refers to developing estimates for in-house work by analyzing completed contracts for similar work. This has the same advantages and disadvantages as using historical records with the added problem of translating contractor prices into work hours.

Using predetermined time standards is potentially the most useful and accurate method of estimating. It has the advantages of consistency, accuracy, and universality. It is based on engineering studies that attempt to determine an absolute, not relative, level of performance. Its main disadvantage is that more time is required to develop an estimate because the data are usually somewhat detailed and complex.

The most comprehensive body of data developed for maintenance work is Engineered Performance Standards (EPS) published by the United States Navy. Other predetermined time standards exist, but none covers as many trades or the variety of maintenance tasks as EPS.

Notice that the use of time study to develop one's own standards has not been mentioned as a viable estimating technique. Time study is too expensive for most organizations' budgets. Standards established by time study would require about one time-study employee for every ten maintenance employees whose work was to be estimated. With EPS the ratio is closer to one estimator for every twenty-five to thirty mechanics, and with historical estimates and commercial data the ratio is much higher—about one estimator to every fifty mechanics.

Most facilities managers begin by using a combination of the estimator's experience and historical records. As their overall systems develop and the need for control increases, they begin using some form of engineered predetermined standards. Few organizations, if any, rely solely on one estimating method. The method chosen is usually the least expensive one that will serve the purpose.

Even though estimates are an important labor cost control tool, they do not help much in the control of indirect labor—that is, the time workers spend in delays, travel, illness, meetings, training, and other nonproductive activities. This nonproductive time can easily amount to 30 to 50 percent of an employee's day, while only the remaining 50 to 70 percent is spent doing work covered by the estimate.

Control of these lost-time hours begins with labor utilization analysis and reports. A labor utilization report is simply a breakdown of how physical plant's total hours are spent. The report divides total payroll hours (or dollars) into various predetermined classifications such as productive work, rework, lost time, vacation, paid sick leave, training, meetings, and breaks. In the best systems complete reconciliation exists between this data and the payroll.

This report is prepared from the daily time sheets filled out by each employee. The labor utilization report does not show productivity per se; it simply shows how employees are spending their time, without relating this to work output. The report is nevertheless useful for determining:

- Proportion of total hours spent on work orders. (This can be compared to the planned proportion.)
- Amount of lost time occurring.
- Actual workhour capacity for productive work (for use in scheduling).

A number of other reports can be developed as aids to productivity measurement and control. The principal ones are the job cost report and the backlog report.

Job cost reports show all actual material and labor charges made to individual jobs. They also show the estimated material and labor so that an actual versus estimated comparison can be made.

The job cost report is frequently prepared in two formats. One format, called work in progress or jobs in progress, shows all the charges made to each job as of a certain date. This information helps supervisors know, while the job is still progressing, whether the work will be accomplished within the estimated time.

The other common job cost report format is a periodic report on completed jobs. This report gives the final comparison of actual versus estimated charges. All jobs appearing on this report are completed and no additional charges can be made to them. Reports such as this are usually issued monthly and contain all jobs closed out during a given month. At large institutions with a high volume of work orders, it may be necessary to prepare this report more often than monthly.

Both of these job cost reports are effective aids for control. For example, the jobs in progress report is useful in the following ways:

- There is a relationship between the number of jobs being performed and the number of new jobs issued each month. If 15 new jobs are issued each day and the average time for completion from date of issue is twenty-five days, then the number of jobs in progress at any time should be 375 (15 x 25). If 600 jobs appear on the report, something is wrong or at least abnormal. Possibilities are a bottleneck in one or more shops, an abnormally high influx of jobs, slow processing of paperwork in closing out jobs, or a disproportionately high number of large jobs that raise the average time for completion above twenty-five days. Whatever the cause, use of this report for control begins when managers and supervisors start questioning the high number of jobs in process.

- The appearance of many old jobs on the report could mean there is a problem with shop capacity, material delivery, change orders, or lost paperwork.
- A review of actual charges to date versus the estimates can be an early warning of jobs that are in trouble. If a job is 50 percent complete, but 90 percent of the money or estimated hours have been spent, something is probably wrong.

The job cost report for completed work is also an effective control tool.

- This report identifies the relationship between the number of new jobs issued and the number of jobs completed. Obviously, over a period of time, the number of jobs completed should equal the number of jobs issued. This is elementary but can be overlooked if reports are not available. If fewer jobs are being completed than being issued, a bottleneck exists somewhere in the system that needs management's attention.
- The completed jobs report is the main source of information on actual job performance versus estimate. Large variances can mean poor performance, poor accounting for charges, poor estimating, or insufficient planning.
- The completed jobs report can also serve as a fundamental data base on the characteristics of the plant's work flow. The report can help managers classify work into different systems for the different types of jobs encountered. Analysis of completed jobs might show that 75 percent of a shop's workforce is spent on jobs that have a labor content of twenty-four to thirty-two hours or more. This factual information could affect the design of a scheduling system or allocation of a shop's workforce.

Backlog reports try to measure how much known work remains undone at any point in time. The amount of known work remaining is stated in terms of total workhours.

While it is important to be able to track the total workhour backlog, managers usually find it more meaningful to think of backlog in terms of the number of days, weeks, or months worth of work represented by the total workhour backlog figure. To do this they relate the workhour backlog to their workhour capacity.

If a shop has 5 employees, its work-hour capacity (in simplest terms) is 200 work hours per week (5 employees x 40 work hours/week/employee). If the total work remaining unfinished for that shop is estimated to be 6,000 work hours, the backlog is 30 days (6,000 work hours ÷ 200 work hours/week). If one employee goes on extended sick leave, the shop capacity drops to 150 work hours per week and the backlog increases to 37.5 days (6,000 ÷ 160).

In more refined systems, managers are not satisfied with calculations as simple as these. The main adjustment they make is in calculating shop capacity. They know that employees are not productive 40 hours a week, so they attempt to determine what percentage of time is actually productive in their organization. Managers usually settle on a capacity per employee of 6.0 to 7.5 hours per day, or 30 to 37.5 work hours per week per employee. Using the lower figure in the above example, the 6,000 work hours backlog would now represent 40 days worth of work (6,000 ÷ 150 work hours/week).

More accurate backlog calculations do not become vitally important until schedulers begin using backlog figures to quote promise dates for starting jobs. Until that time, it is best to keep the calculations simple and consistent so that trends can be seen.

In more complex systems, additional detail on the composition of the backlog is contained in the report. For example, managers would know that the 6,000 work-hours backlog in the preceding examples had the following breakdown:

Jobs in progress	1,500 work hours
Jobs awaiting material	2,500 work hours
Jobs awaiting scheduling	2,000 work hours
Total	6,000 work hours

The true backlog of available work is now known to be 3,500 work hours (jobs in progress plus jobs awaiting scheduling); 2,500 work hours of the 6,000 work-hour backlog is awaiting materials on order.

Backlog reports can be a control tool in the following ways:

- They let management know if the shops are getting ahead, getting behind, or staying current with the work.
- They guide decisions on which shops are over- or understaffed.
- They help determine when outside contracting is needed, and how much.
- They assist schedulers in informing customers when new jobs can be started.

- They point out bottlenecks such as slow material specification, ordering, or delivery.

While the labor utilization reports discussed earlier are useful for showing how time is spent, they may not contain enough detailed data for corrections of problem areas. A technique called work sampling is available for gathering additional detailed information in an economical way.

Work sampling gathers data through sampling rather than through more detailed recording of actual time spent.

Purchased Goods and Services

Materials, supplies, noncapital equipment, and services which are purchased from outside suppliers are a major part of the physical plant budget—possibly the largest category if services such as grounds and custodial are contracted. Methods for controlling the actual purchase price of these goods and services are the domain of the purchasing function and are thus outside the scope of this chapter. Our interest is in the use of cost accounting data and techniques in the control of the cost of goods and services. Three of the most useful are make versus buy analysis, inventory control, and estimates.

Make Versus Buy   Every physical plant must decide whether to use its own skills to operate and service the campus, or whether to buy all or part of this capability. Frequently these decisions have been made in the distant past and they are being perpetuated out of habit instead of current choice. From the standpoint of cost control, large amounts of money can hinge on these decisions. Make versus buy, a technique for making such decisions, relies heavily on cost accounting data plus other cost information.

If a product or service can be bought cheaper than it can be made or performed in-house, it should normally be bought. However, there is often confusion in making cost comparisons. The confusion usually relates to which costs are relevant and which are not.

In a make-or-buy decision, the only costs that are relevant are incremental costs. These are also referred to as differential costs in some texts. Incremental costs are those which differ with the alternatives being considered, and only those. If certain costs stay the same regardless of which alternative is chosen, they are irrelevant. Thus, we must ask the question: If we buy this product or service, which costs are eliminated, and are these reductions in costs greater than the costs that we assume by buying the product or service?

Figure 13-2 gives a simplified guide to which costs are relevant in a make or buy decision:

- When "buy" costs are less than the sum of direct material plus direct labor plus variable overhead, the decision is to buy.
- When "buy" costs are greater than the sum of direct material plus direct labor plus variable overhead plus fixed overhead plus general and administrative expenses, the decision is to make.
- When "buy" costs fall between these two extremes, the question of make or buy requires further evaluation. This evaluation centers on whether any of the fixed overhead and general and administrative expenses will be increased or reduced in actuality.

Note that in this simplified illustration it is assumed that no large investments or one-time start-up expenses are required to "make" the product or to perform the service in-house. If significant front-end expense is required, then a payback or return on investment must be calculated, based upon the ongoing savings expected by doing the work in-house, before the decision can be made.

We have not attempted to give an exhaustive treatment to all the factors in make versus buy analysis. However, this brief introduction shows the use of cost accounting data in this type of cost control decision.

Inventory Control   An important aspect of material cost control is control over inventory. This includes both physical control to minimize theft and spoilage, and accounting control to ensure that funds are used wisely and that costs are kept low consistent with acceptable service. Our concern here is with cost controls.

Inventory control is always a balancing act—having enough stock on hand, but not too much. An unnecessarily large investment in inventory ties up resources that could be put to better use. The cost to the university of idle inventory is not limited to the cost of the materials themselves. To this must be added such additional costs as storage space, stock-keeping personnel, insurance, and other costs related to buying and holding the excess portion. On the other hand, too little inventory can be costly. In physical plant work the largest of these costs is the wasted time of service personnel when work is interrupted because materials are not available.

The following is a listing of some of the most useful inventory control methods and techniques:

Figure 13-2
Make versus Buy Guidelines

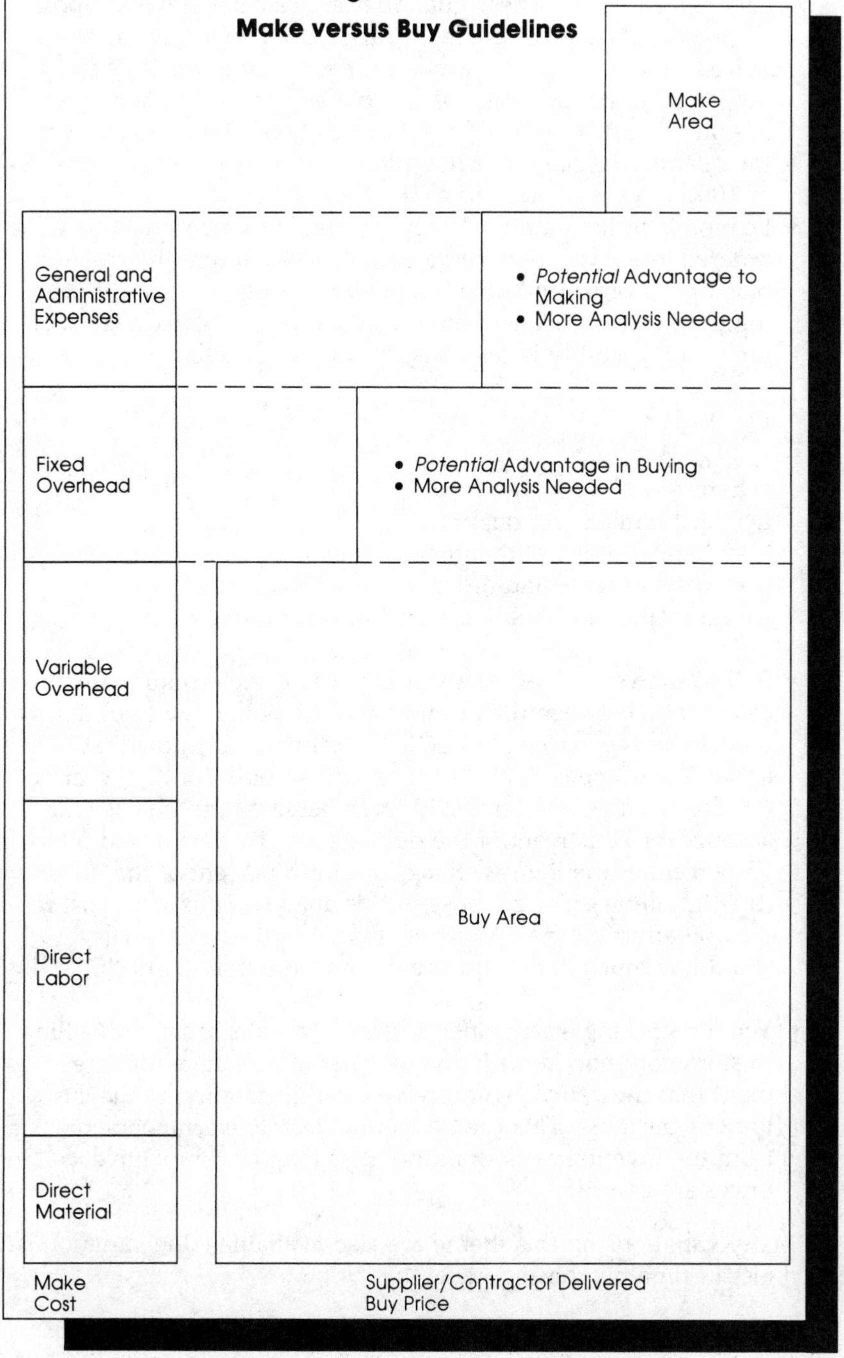

Make
Area

General and
Administrative
Expenses

- *Potential* Advantage to
  Making
- More Analysis Needed

Fixed
Overhead

- *Potential* Advantage in Buying
- More Analysis Needed

Variable
Overhead

Buy Area

Direct
Labor

Direct
Material

Make
Cost

Supplier/Contractor Delivered
Buy Price

- Order point. Maximum and minimum quantities are set for each item stocked. These quantities are calculated based upon the expected usage of the item during the period of time required to obtain delivery on an order. For example, if delivery time is 30 days and usage of 100 pieces is expected during a 30-day period, a replenishment order should be placed when the quantity on hand reaches 100 pieces. The inventory level of 100 pieces is referred to as the order point.
- Economic order quantity. When an inventory item must be reordered, the quantity ordered should be such that the costs of placing the order and obtaining delivery plus the costs of keeping the item in stock are minimized over a stipulated period of time. This quantity is calculated from the formula:

$$Q = \frac{2RS}{i}$$

Where:
Q = Economic order quantity
R = Annual usage of the item in units
S = Costs to write and order
i = Annual cost of holding a unit in inventory

- A-B-C analysis. A-B-C analysis is a way of determining the relative ratios between the number and the dollar values of items repeatedly purchased for stock. Typically, it will show that about 5 to 10 percent of the items will account for 75 percent of the dollars (the "A" items); 20 to 25 percent of the items will account for 20 percent of the dollars (the "B" items); and 50 to 75 percent of the items will account for 5 percent of the dollars (the "C" items). The purpose of this analysis is to focus cost reduction effort on the "A" items. Inventory turnover goals should be much higher for them than those for "B" or "C" items.
- Vendor stocking arrangements. Many vendors today are willing to stock common items for a customer in exchange for agreement that the vendor will receive a certain portion of the customer's business. This can be a quite desirable arrangement from the inventory cost standpoint as long as competitive prices are assured.

Many variations on this theme are also available. One variation is called just-in-time purchasing, whereby:

- Smaller and more frequent purchase orders are issued.

- The number of suppliers for each item is reduced and longer-term contracts are established.
- Minimal paperwork is used for each transaction (e.g., a telephone call or a computer entry).
- Payment to suppliers is made for batches of deliveries rather than for each item delivery.

Material Estimates   The control principles discussed earlier can be applied to material costs as well. All work orders with a material content above some policy amount should contain material estimates in addition to labor estimates discussed previously. A comparison of actual to estimated cost can then be done on a job-by-job basis and also in aggregate. Variances can be analyzed by the methods discussed earlier.

Life-Cycle Costing   The techniques discussed so far (make versus buy, inventory control, and material estimates) are not usually applicable for purchases of large and expensive pieces of equipment such as chillers, boilers, air handlers, pumps, office furniture, lawn mowers, vehicles, and other such items. Yet cost control is needed on these beyond that provided by basic manufacturer selection and competitive bidding.

Life-cycle costing, which should be considered in every major purchase of equipment, is an analysis of the total cost of owning and operating a specific piece of equipment over its expected life. The life-cycle cost is obtained by adding the total lifetime operating cost to the initial purchase price. When this is done on competitively bid items, a different decision will frequently result than if bid price alone is used as the only economic factor.

Life-cycle costing calculations must include adjustments for the time value of money. This assumes that money received today is more valuable than the same amount received at some time in the future. For example, one dollar received today is more valuable than one dollar received one year from now, because the dollar received today can be put in the bank at 5 percent interest.

Future operating costs of a piece of equipment behave in the same way. A cost five years from now is not as bad as the same cost three years from now. The two-year delay allows the money that would have been spent to be invested or put to some other use until Year 5.

Utilities

The cost of utilities can easily account for 20 to 40 percent of the entire physical plant budget, which usually makes them a continuous target for cost control. Our concern is with the use of cost accounting information and techniques to help in tracking and analyzing energy use.

Some of the most difficult accounting questions for the plant utilities manager are: How effective are energy management efforts, and how can I determine and explain what is happening to energy usage and cost, and why. These questions can be answered if energy data is accumulated and analyzed properly. The key technique is variance analysis. Recall that variance analysis is one of the most powerful tools available for explaining differences between two numbers. The following example is based upon actual data from a southeastern university:

Over a four-year period, total energy cost rose from $7,392,097 to $7,741,181 per year, an increase of $349,084. Energy use is predominantly electricity (one substation), natural gas (central heating plant), and #2 fuel oil (used as backup fuel in heating plant). During this same period, total building area increased by almost 15 percent (from 3,805,316 to 4,368,996 sq. ft.). Total energy used remained virtually unchanged (1.1592×10^{12} Btus versus 1.1575×10^{12} Btus) while the unit cost of energy increased 4.6 percent (from 6.3861×10^{-6} $/Btu to 6.6781×10^{-6} $/Btu). Variance analysis shows that the $349,084 increase in cost is actually composed of a $1,094,989 increase due to additional square footage, a $338,493 increase due to higher unit cost of energy, and a $1,084,398 decrease as a result of energy conservation efforts. These variances net to the total increase of $349,084 as follows:

1,094,989 + 338,493 - 1,084,398 = 349,084

Actually, there was a fourth factor at work—weather—which affected the total amount of energy used. However, we will not complicate this example with a fourth variance even though in practice it gives useful information. Once variance analysis is mastered, the weather variance can be calculated. As an indication to the weather effect in the above example, heating degree days decreased by 7 percent and cooling degree days increased by 26 percent from the base year to the current year.

The preceding example does not give any of the definitions and calculations; it only gives the results. For those interested, complete step-by-step calculations are supplied in Appendix 13-A.

As can be seen, variance analysis avoids the use of theoretical calculations that cannot be proven. It uses actual data and reconciles the results that come directly from accounting system data.

13.5 MANAGING FISCAL CONTINGENCIES

Most physical plant departments encounter fiscal contingencies sooner or later. Some contingencies can be considered routine in that facilities managers know they will occur; they just do not know when. Examples of these include emergency equipment replacements, high utility costs because of weather, and overspending.

Other contingencies can come as a complete surprise, or start out minor and become protracted. For example, low tax revenues in state systems or below-expected gift and endowment income can occur at any time and may continue indefinitely.

Low enrollments are yet another fiscal trauma. Demographic changes, such as those affecting the 1988-1993 period, can mean that there simply are not enough college-age young people available to fill existing classrooms.

The key to dealing with fiscal contingencies is planning. Contingency plans should be reflected in the budget structure as well as in the spending plans. A discussion of actions that can be taken in both of these areas follows.

Budgeting Actions

If the possibility of financial hardship is recognized during the budgeting process, several steps can be taken. One possibility is to include a contingency allowance as part of the budget. The contingency fund absorbs either the unexpected emergency spending or the overspending that may occur if budgets must be cut.

Another approach is to structure budgets in two or three levels. Level One represents the highest priority needs, Level Two the next highest, and Level Three the lowest. As the financial situation tightens, the lower-priority budget levels are reduced or eliminated.

A third approach, similar to budget levels, is to release somewhat less than the proportionate amount of funds in the early part of the year. For example, only 20 percent of the funds might be authorized for the first quarter rather than 25 percent, which would be the proportionate amount.

A fourth possibility is line item budget control. This means that overspending will not be allowed on any budget line item even though a corresponding amount of underspending may occur in another line item.

Another issue always surfaces when management is faced with budget cuts—whether to enact an across-the-board cut that affects all cost centers equally, or to cut on a selective basis. The first approach has the appearance of fairness and impartiality, but it impairs the strong units as well as the weak. It is usually better to reduce budgets on a selective basis, with substantial participation by unit managers. In this way, lower-priority services and programs can be reduced without immediate impact on the more crucial ones.

Spending Actions

Even if contingency plans are built into the budget structure, it will still be necessary to have in mind specific actions that can be taken on the spending side. The following are typical kinds of actions that have been used successfully by many organizations.

- Forego all but the most necessary expenditures.
- Reduce spending authority limits at all supervisory and managerial levels.
- Separate expenses into those that are controllable and uncontrollable.
- Delay or cease filling vacant positions, or fill on a selective, must-do basis.
- Use temporary or contract personnel in selected areas to avoid fringe benefit costs.
- Lease or rent equipment rather than buy to avoid high initial outlays of funds.
- Install temporary encumbrance accounting measures to control obligations.
- Reduce inventory purchases.
- Reduce the frequency of noncrucial services and drop unnecessary or marginal programs.
- Lay off personnel.
- Install quick payback, low-cost energy reduction measures.

The above actions will not be appropriate in all organizations and situations, but they do illustrate effective measures under most circumstances.

ADDITIONAL RESOURCES

American School and University. "Maintenance and Operations Cost Study," annual feature.

Anthony, Robert N. and David W. Young. *Management Control in Nonprofit Organizations,* third edition. Homewood, Illinois: Dow Jones-Irwin, 1984.

Association of Physical Plant Administrators of Universities and Colleges. *Comparative Costs and Staffing Report for College and University Facilities.* Alexandria, Virginia: APPA, biennial.

Buffa, Elwood S. *Basic Production Management,* second edition. New York: John Wiley & Sons, 1975.

Dearden, John. *Cost and Budget Analysis.* Englewood Cliffs, New Jersey: Prentice-Hall Inc., 1978.

Heintzelman, John E. *The Complete Handbook of Maintenance Management*. Englewood Cliffs, New Jersey: Prentice-Hall Inc., 1976.

Horngren, Charles T. and George Foster. *Cost Accounting: A Managerial Emphasis*, sixth edition. Englewood Cliffs, New Jersey: Prentice-Hall, 1987.

Lewis, Bernard T. *Developing Maintenance Time Standards*. Boston: Farnsworth Publishing, 1967.

Lewis, Bernard T., ed. *Management Handbook for Plant Engineers*. New York: McGraw-Hill Book Co., 1977.

Loopo, L. Paul. "Work Sampling: What, Why, and Especially, How." Presentation at APPA Institute for Facilities Management, 1982. Alexandria, Virginia: Association of Physical Plant Administrators of Universities and Colleges.

Maintenance Management of Shore Facilities. Publication Number NAVFAC MO-321. Philadelphia, Pennsylvania: Naval Publications and Forms Center, November 1977.

Newbrough, E.T. *Effective Maintenance Management*. New York: McGraw-Hill Book Co., 1967.

Planner and Estimator's Workbook. Publication number NAVFAC P-700.2. Philadelphia, Pennsylvania: Naval Publications and Forms Center, March 1980.

Suber, L. Terry. "Work Sampling: What, Why, and How." In *Proceedings of the Sixty-Eighth Annual Meeting of the Association of Physical Plant Administrators of Universities and Colleges*. Washington: APPA, 1981.

Syska and Hennessy, Inc. *A Guide for Improved Maintenance Management*. New York: Syska and Hennessy, Inc.

Welzenbach, Lanora F., ed. *College and University Business Administration*, fourth edition. Washington: National Association of College and University Business Officers, 1982.

Appendix 13-A

USE OF VARIANCE ANALYSIS
FOR ENERGY ANALYSIS

Following are the complete definitions and calculations for the sample problem given in Section 13.4.

A. Step 1—Definitions

Terms	Units	Base Year	Current Year
		Symbols	
Total energy cost	Dollars	TC_B	TC_C
Unit price of energy	$/BTU	P_B	P_C
Energy efficiency	BTU/sq. ft.	E_B	E_C
Total building square footage (Avg.)	sq. ft.	F_B	F_C
Total energy usage	BTU	B_B	B_C
Total natural gas usage	therms	T_B	T_C
Total electricity usage	KWH	K_B	K_C
Total #2 oil usage	gallons	O_B	O_C
Total cost variance	Dollars		V_T
Variance due to price	Dollars		V_P
Variance due to energy efficiency	Dollars		V_E
Variance due to square footage	Dollars		V_F

Definition of Variances

$V_T = TC_C - TC_B = V_E + V_P + V_F$

$V_E = (E_C - E_B) \times P_B \times F_C$

$V_P = (P_C - P_B) \times E_C \times F_C$

$V_F = (F_C - F_B) \times E_B \times P_B$

B. Step 2—Given Data

$TC_B = 7,392,097$　　　　　$K_C = 136,072,800$

$TC_C = 7,741,181$　　　　　$O_B = 20,736$

$T_B = 8,024,878$　　　　　　$O_C = 45,741$

$T_C = 6,884,597$　　　　　　$F_B = 3,805,316$

$K_B = 103,188,000$　　　　　$F_C = 4,368,996$

Also given are the following energy conversion factors.

1 therm = 100,000 BTU

1 KWH = 3413 BTU

1 Gal #2 oil = 138,000 BTU

C. Step 3—Calculations Using Given Data

$B_B = 10^5 T_B + 3413 K_B + 138,000 O_B = 1.1575 \times 10^{12}$ BTU

$B_C = 10^5 T_C + 3413 K_C + 138,000 O_C = 1.1592 \times 10^{12}$ BTU

D. Step 4—Calculations Using Given Data + Step 3 Results

$P_B = TC_B/B_B = 7,392,097 \div 1.1575 \times 10^{12} = 6.3861 \times 10^{-6}$ \$/BTU
$P_C = TC_C/B_C = 7,741,181 \div 1.1592 \times 10^{12} = 6.6781 \times 10^{-6}$ \$/BTU
$E_B = B_B/F_B = 1.1575 \times 10^{12} \div 3,805,316 = 304,188$ BTU/sq. ft.
$E_C = B_C/F_C = 1.1592 \times 10^{12} \div 4,368,996 = 265,321$ BTU/sq. ft.

E. Step 5—Calculation of Variances

$V_P = (P_C - P_B) \times E_C \times F_C = (6.6781 \times 10^{-6} - 6.3861 \times 10^{-6}) \times 265,321 \times 4,368,996 = +338,493$ Price Variance
$V_F = (F_C - F_B \times E_B \times P_B = (4,368,996 - 3,805,316) \times 304,188 \times 6.3861 \times 10^{-6} = +1,094,989$ Square Footage Variance
$V_E = (E_C - E_B) \times P_B \times F_C = (265,321 - 304,188) \times 6.3861 \times 10^{-6} \times 4,368,996 = -1,084,398$ Efficiency Variance

It can be seen that,
$V_T = TC_C - TC_B = 7,741,181 - 7,392,097 = +349,084$ Total Variance

Which also equals,
$V_T = V_P + V_F + V_E = +338,493 + 1,094,989 - 1,084,398 = +349,084$

F. Graphical Representation

From the above definitions and calculations, it can be seen that,

$TC_C = P_C \times F_C \times E_C$
$TC_B = P_B \times F_B \times E_B$

The product of these three factors can be represented by the volumes shown in Figure 13-A.1 on the next page. Illustration shows base year total energy cost (TC_B) represented by the inner volumetric figure. The variances combine with TC_B to produce the current year total energy cost (TC_C). It also shows through the three different cross-hatchings how the variances are defined.

Figure 13-A.1 does not coincide exactly with the example calculated above in that the Efficiency Variance V_E is shown as a positive quantity in the illustration and a negative quantity in the example. This is done for graphical clarity.

Figure 13-A.1

Graphical Representation of Energy Costs and Variances

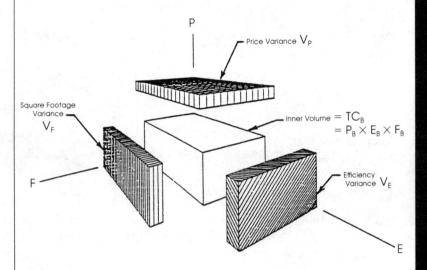

(a) Base Year Energy Cost and Variances

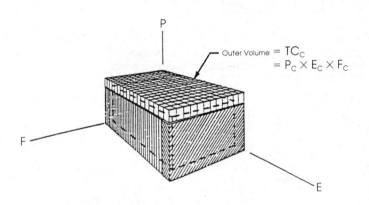

**(b) Current Year Energy Cost with
Variances Shown as Defined**

CHAPTER 14

Information Management and
Computerization

Dennis P. Cesari
Director, Facilities Planning and Development
University of Missouri System

With additional contributions by Two Crows Stacy.

14.1 INTRODUCTION

The development of computers and data management systems over the last few years has been staggering. Keeping pace with the development in computerization has been the growth and development of the facilities management profession to ever higher standards of efficiency and excellence. Both these developments—computer technologies and the standards of the facilities management profession—are continuing at a rapid pace. The cost effectiveness of computers in large organizations has been widely recognized for several years. Recent developments in both hardware and software have lowered the size threshold of organizations where computerized management systems may be cost effective. It is becoming more difficult for a physical plant department to perform traditional functions, in keeping with today's standards, without extensive use of computers.

The uses of computers in facilities operations are unlimited. As facilities managers introduce computers into their organizations, they typically continue to find new and innovative uses. Some of the known applications are:

Office Automation

- Word processing
- Personnel records
- Payroll records
- Spreadsheet applications

- Electronic mail
- Fax communications
- Presentation graphics
- Desktop publishing
- Financial data management
- Payments
- Capital budgeting

Plant Automation

- Work scheduling
- Stock management and inventory control
- Key control
- Energy management
- Life safety monitoring
- Deferred maintenance
- Construction management
- Bar coding
- Equipment inventory

This chapter describes the methodologies for identifying those operations that can be more effectively and efficiently managed through the use of computer systems, and reviews the characteristics of the various systems available.

14.2 IDENTIFICATION OF COMPUTER APPLICATIONS

Itemize Physical Plant Functions and Operations

The initial task in the process is the identification of operations that will benefit from computerization. To accomplish this, all existing operations and functions of the department must be reviewed. The first step is to develop a comprehensive and detailed list of all functions being performed, without evaluation as to their suitability for computerization. There should be input from all staff members throughout the planning and implementation phases of computerization, both to develop the system efficiently and to achieve a feeling of ownership and acceptance of the new system.

It can be beneficial to briefly outline the functions of the key areas within the department, then expand each area by more detailed descriptions of the tasks. Listing the activities in chronological order also assists in creating flow diagrams of operations and determining interactions between areas of the physical plant department as well as with other departments. The importance of the completeness of this initial list of functions cannot be overemphasized.

Updating Operations and Functions

Once the comprehensive list of functions has been developed, it should be reviewed for the following:

1. Is the function required?
2. Can the function be improved?

The computerization evaluation can serve the useful subsidiary purpose of reviewing and updating all operations. Overtime functions tend to become compartmentalized and are sometimes continued when no longer needed, or unduly complicated through incremental changes over time. All functions should be updated before computerization.

Once developed, the itemized list of functions can be organized into a few functional areas such as budget management, including accounting; work management, including scheduling; management information; and office operations.

Evaluation of Functions for Computerization

Once the functions and operations have been identified, updated, and classified by functional groupings, they can be evaluated for computerization. This step is critical and outside assistance may be advisable. The use of computer consultants is discussed later in this chapter.

Various approaches are used in the evaluations. One identifies functions for which computerization would most improve the overall productivity of the physical plant department. Another option selects the most labor intensive operations, typically tracking, accounting, and record keeping. Whatever the approach, the objective is to determine specifically what would be accomplished through the computerization of each function, then to prioritize with regard to the value to be derived.

14.3 CONDUCTING A DETAILED INFORMATION REQUIREMENT STUDY

Before proceeding, parameters affecting the development of the system should be identified. Included are the following:

1. Responsibility and authority for specific actions that must be incorporated into the programming of an operation—for example, who ap-

proves the purchase of material or authorizes a work project; who approves construction documents before bidding.
2. Budget restrictions.
3. Need for restructuring the organization for the use of computers—it is usually beneficial to train current personnel to use the new computer systems in the areas of their existing responsibilities. But, as computerization progresses, some restructuring may be needed.
4. Time phasing of computerization—it is difficult for members of the physical plant staff to implement computerization while carrying out current duties. A progressive implementation schedule facilitates the transition.

Having now identified those functions that appropriately warrant automation, the final step in the planning and pre-implementation phase involves conducting a thorough and detailed information requirement study.

Simply stated, the purpose of the requirement study is the complete identification of all the management, financial, and statistical information needs that exist within the organization. The typical requirement study is a lengthy, time-consuming, and necessary process involving every generator and user of information within the organization, from the chief executive officer to the data input technician and everyone in between.

Typically, the identification and accumulation of these information needs takes the form of detailed interviews, conducted by appropriately qualified personnel, of each user and generator of information as to their needs for operating information. The interviewing process can be conducted by qualified university or outside personnel. It is recommended that the process be closely supervised by individuals who are, at the least, technically qualified as a systems analyst, systems engineer, or systems architect.

It is of the utmost importance that it be understood by senior management personnel within your organization that the eventual configuration of your management and financial information system, the "final product," is a direct result of how thoroughly you conduct the requirement study. As is said in the computer field: garbage in, garbage out. It is precisely at this step where you exercise complete control of your information environment. Once you have gone beyond this point, it becomes difficult, time-consuming, and costly to reconfigure your system to include information needs that were overlooked before.

Therefore, this step is not where corners, dollars, or time are cut. This step should be viewed as a long-term investment that, while costly on the front end, will nonetheless yield a greater return in the near and distant future.

14.4 IMPLEMENTATION

Once the operations are prioritized and parameters established, the decision must be made whether to implement the computerization with university personnel or to use consultants. If outside consultants are to be used, they should be hired at this time in order to assist in the selection of hardware and software. If university personnel are to be used, they should be hired or assigned to the physical plant department at this time.

Gaining Acceptance

The system should be directed at solving the problems of the working-level managers and their staffs. Unless the physical plant personnel are convinced of the value of computerization, it will be difficult to implement effectively. The personnel who will be using computers must be involved throughout the implementation phase. Planning and implementation must recognize the importance of acceptance.

Training and Maintenance Requirements

Before proceeding with the implementation of computerization, consideration must be given to the training requirements, which necessitates determining specifically who will have access to the systems. In addition, it must be determined who will take care of maintenance, physical plant personnel, other university personnel, or maintenance service contract.

Projection of Future Requirements

Even if initially limited computerization will be used, the possibility of further computerization must be evaluated so future additions can be compatible with the initial systems and equipment.

14.5 TYPES OF HARDWARE

Systems Definitions

1. *Microcomputers* are considered personal computers (PCs) that can either stand alone and be connected to an electrical outlet or can be linked together with several other microcomputers to establish computer networks. The most common microcomputer is the IBM PC

and its variations such as the XT and AT. The IBM PC is the basic microcomputer offered by IBM; the XT incorporates a disk drive within the computer; and the AT offers much faster computing time and disk drive. Many other manufacturers produce IBM PC clones or compatibles that are based upon IBM architecture and can run its disk operating system, DOS.

2. *Minicomputers* are somewhere between a microcomputer and a mainframe. These computers are usually quite expensive but have more memory and larger capacities than the microcomputers. Typically, these computers are used by a department or are shared with other departments in a university system. Major vendors for these systems include IBM, Digital Equipment Corporation, Hewlett-Packard, Perkin Elmer, Prime, Honeywell, and Data General.

3. *Mainframes* are usually extremely large computer systems; many colleges and universities have one mainframe system for the entire campus. These systems are capable of handling large data, such as payroll and other campus computing systems needs. IBM is a major manufacturer of mainframes along with Amdahl, Digital Equipment Corporation, Honeywell, and Unisys.

Microcomputers

The most affordable and commonly used computer system in a typical facilities operation is the microcomputer. If a microcomputer is a stand-alone, the user has access only to data in a program that resides on his or her own disks and has no link to another microcomputer in the same office, the central mainframe, or a central minicomputer. Fewer microcomputers are standalone as networking and terminal emulation become the standard.

Networking of microcomputers allows a microcomputer user to be linked to another microcomputer and peripherals in his or her office, department, or building. The linking of these microcomputers is known as local area networks (LANs). A network of computers is economical because all files may be shared since they reside on one central disk called a file server. This removes the need for a hard disk in every machine. Expenditures for printers are also reduced since each work station has access to a printer attached to the network. There is no need for each employee to have a copy of each software package; the department has one copy that can be used on the network by many people. Multiuser software is also becoming more plentiful. Networks enhance data and system security since a LAN system supervisor may decide which employees are allowed access to individual systems and sets of data.

There are different types of network configurations (topologies) available for LANs. These configurations are usually a star, linear, ring, or modified ring.

1. *Star* configuration is characterized by having a central file server with direct cabling to each work station, as shown in Figure 14-1. Several directional communication paths are in place from the work station to the file server, and from the file server back to the work station. Additional communication can take place from one work station to a file server to another work station. An advantage of the star system is the short response time caused by each work station being directly connected to the file server. Of all network configurations, the star lends the most flexibility to the user.

2. *Linear,* or as commonly referred to as bus topology, is characterized by a single communication line, called a trunk, serving several work

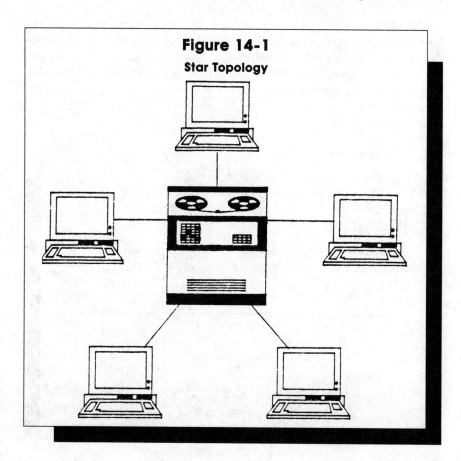

Figure 14-1

Star Topology

stations (see Figure 14-2). In this configuration a work station may serve as a file server or a dedicated file server may be used. With this topology each work station must share the common trunk back to the file server. This type of configuration is usually advantageous if there are six or fewer work stations connected to the LAN. The main disadvantage to this system is the poor response time as additional work stations are tied to the network.

3. *Ring* and *modified ring* configurations are characterized by a circular or semicircular communications link between work stations (see Figure 14-3). Again, the file server may be a work station or a dedicated file server may be incorporated. Communications from the work stations with this system circulate around the ring back to the file server. A common ring system in place today is the IBM token ring. Although this system is capable of handling more PCs than the linear system, it does not have the flexibility inherent in the star system.

Whichever configuration is chosen for a LAN, all systems have the inherent advantage of having software developed and maintained locally in the physical plant department. The hardware exists in the department and programs can be easily written to incorporate requirements. Costs for operating the LAN is virtually nonexistent, except for maintenance costs of software and hardware. There is no connect time

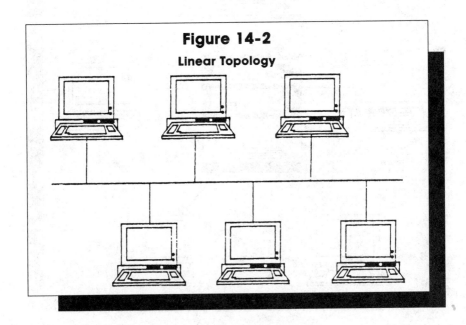

Figure 14-2

Linear Topology

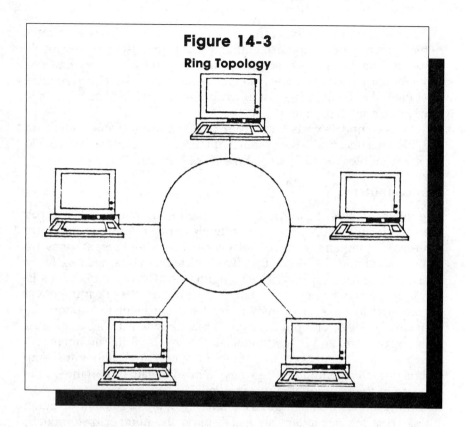

Figure 14-3

Ring Topology

or CPU costs as normally incurred when the department is connected to the campus mainframe.

It is usually advantageous that one or more of the work stations within the LAN have the capability of access to the mainframe for transmission of data. Terminal emulation allows the user to be linked to the central mainframe or minicomputer through a cable attached to a communications controller. With this configuration, the user may use any software facilities available on the larger machine, and still have the flexibility and speed of a microcomputer applications. Many computer systems use the microcomputer to enter data that is then sent up to the mainframe or minicomputer via the terminal emulation. Once this data is on the mainframe, faster disk, tape, and high speed printer units can be used, which in effect will save time on the LAN for development of reports and voluminous calculations. Terminal emulation can also be achieved through the LAN using a LAN gateway. This system eliminates the need for each work station of the LAN to have an emulation board, and the file server has one emulation board through which all work stations communicate with the mainframe.

Support for the microcomputer connection to the mainframe computer is increasing as more mainframe data processing professionals recognize the capabilities of microcomputers and ways they can improve employee productivity. Mainframe professionals also recognize the inherent cost advantages of microcomputers and the flexibility they offer individual departments.

Microcomputer costs vary from $1,500 for one work station, to $12,000 for a linear network system with three work stations, to $18,000 for a star topology system with three work stations.

Minicomputer

The microcomputer has, through its continued development, reduced the need for the middle-of-the-road minicomputer. Minicomputers are more powerful than the micro; however, software for these systems are more limited and the use is usually restricted to users needing faster speed and greater capacity. Minicomputers may have applications in physical plants of large college campuses; however, the department will be required to have programmers in the department to support the software. In 1988, one out of every three computer dollars expended was on software, and it was predicted that by 1990 the numbers will increase to four out of every five.[1] Since most new applications are being written for microcomputers, they have tended to gain importance at the expense of the traditional minicomputer.

Minicomputers range in cost from $20,000 to $200,000 or more. These costs are dependent, as usual, upon the number of terminals, drives, memory, and peripherals required. Due to the high cost and reduced flexibility of the minicomputer, it is not recommended for most facilities operations, except for the very large ones.

Mainframe

Mainframe computers are not practical for physical plant departments; costs can easily run $100,000 and more. Mainframes can be used by a department if the campus mainframe is available. Each time a user logs on to the mainframe, there is CPU cost, run time cost, and printer charges each time a printout is made. It is extremely difficult for a physical plant department to obtain programming support for a mainframe. Because of their speed, mainframes are valuable in running reports that are uploaded from a LAN; however, they are generally not recommended for use in physical plant automation due to the high cost and inflexibility of the system.

One of the highest hurdles facilities managers have had to jump within the last several years is convincing central computing operators of the need for stand-alone microcomputers. Where microcomputers have been brought on campus, mainframe users are beginning to recognize their advantages. In many cases, central processing departments are now supporting microcomputers in both software and hardware maintenance.

Hardware Summary

There is always a trade-off when selecting a computer system. If a manager does not want to hire at least one computer professional, purchase of the minicomputer should probably not be considered because these systems will require professional hardware and software maintenance and support. This is true even if packaged software is found that meets the department's needs. The use of the central mainframe computer is similarly limited, although it is usually easier to find computer programmers who have mainframe computer experience and it is not necessary for them to have hardware experience. Stand-alone microcomputers often need little trained, technical support. It is usually to a departments advantage to hire at least one staff member to be responsible for the hardware maintenance and supervision activities.

DATAPRO Research Corporation publishes a series of unbiased reviews and recommendations about computer hardware and software that are updated monthly. These guides also give model numbers, capability, prices, and peripherals available for each major vendor. A subscription to one or more of these services allows a manager to keep up to date on current availability and prices. These guides are usually available at the central computing site of large organizations.

Computing guides published by Ziff/Davis Publishing Company include *Data Sources Software Edition* and *Data Sources Hardware Edition*. These guides are well received by computer professionals who oftentimes subscribe to both.

It is also important to have access, through a private subscription or the organizational library, to one or more of the publications that help the manager and his or her staff stay up to date in the computer area.

14.6 SOFTWARE

Depending on the computer hardware purchased, there are many software products available for use on the various systems. In addition to prepackaged software products available from various companies, the facilities manager should give serious consideration to the development of programs by in-house personnel. The complexity of the facilities operations and the requirements for computerization previously identified will heavily influence the decision of whether to purchase prepackaged programs or to develop custom software.

If the facilities manager has limited applications and requires immediate implementation of a computerized system, the purchase of prepackaged programs may be appropriate. Typically, prepackaged programs address certain areas within physical plant, such as a work order system, preventive maintenance system, and key control system. It is rare, however, to find a prepackaged program that will encompass all the areas within physical plant and meet the requirements of the department. If prepackaged programs are purchased there are several things that should be taken into consideration.

Many companies provide prepackaged software with the option to customize the software if desirable. Typically, some customizing is necessary, and the services of the software company can be purchased to provide this service. Software companies may provide the software and rights to the physical plant department to make modifications with in-house personnel. In any case, the facilities manager should obtain rights to modify the software.

It is important in the overall management of the physical plant department to obtain software that will communicate with various systems within the university, as well as within the department. For instance, if there presently exists a building inventory on either a mainframe system or a local system, the new software for work order systems should communicate with this building information data base. The goal of every department should be to have a comprehensive facilities management system with data bases that are accessible by all programs within the department. It is also important for physical plant to be able to manage these programs and update them as necessary as new policies and procedures are implemented within the department. To this end, it is usually necessary for each facilities operation to have at least one, and possibly more, computer programmers on staff.

After the facilities manager has reviewed software systems available and compared these systems to the requirements of the department, it may be decided to develop all software in-house with in-house personnel. It will usually take at least one full-time computer programmer to develop software for a physical plant department. There are several software packages that can be used to assist in the development of the detailed programming. It is possible to develop complete computerized systems for facilities operations using these prepackaged software programs as a basis for the development of the detailed programming. The biggest advantage to developing in-house programs is the programs will be tailored to suit the requirements of the department and can be easily changed in the future as facilities requirements are changed.

It is difficult to assign cost values to prepackaged programs versus in-house personnel. Obviously, the cost of programming varies depending on the nature of the program that is required and the size of the facilities operation. Facilities managers must recognize that regardless of whether software is purchased or developed in-house, there will be a requirement for in-house computer staff to support the systems, both from a software and hardware perspective.

To aid the facilities manager, the following are several examples of data entry screens that can be used in a university facilities setting.

Figure 14-4 is a data entry screen for a key control record. The screen indicates the basic information required for tracking the issuing of keys to campus personnel. This program can be developed in-house, but there are several key control systems readily available from hardware manufacturers.

Figure 14-5 is a data entry screen for accounting information for a work order system. This program summarizes critical project information and is updated as the project progresses and is completed. Additional work order information would include: type of craft assigned,

Figure 14-4

Key Record Data Entry Screen

Keys

```
       Key#  _____ -____
  Last Name  _____
 First Name  _____
       SSN  _____-_____-_____

   Building  _____  _____
      Room  _____
 Department  _____
      User  _____   1-Faculty  2-Staff  3-Student
 Assignment  _____        P-Permanent   T-Temporary
Current Status _____       L-Lost           S-Stolen
     Issued  ____/ ____/ ____
       Due  ____/ ____/ ____

 Key Level  _____
   Core ID  _____

Physical Plant ____/ ____/ ____
   Updated  ____/ ____/ ____
     Batch  _____
```

number of hours allocated, number of hours actually used, and additional feedback reporting which would indicate to the user when a project would be started and include followups asking for comments after completion. Feedback information is usually beneficial in establishing credibility for physical plant with the use of automated work order systems; work order notification information can be issued to the user departments to keep them informed of the project status.

Use of automated facilities system for construction management can prove extremely beneficial. Computer programs can be developed to track projects from initial conception, architect/engineer selection, project design, bidding, construction, and project closeout.

The use of bar coding can reduce staff time in logging information and improve record keeping on facility equipment. The bar coding concept is in wide use in merchandising companies where each item is assigned a code. This same concept is now available in the facilities area where each piece of equipment is assigned a code and a permanent record is maintained on the equipment indicating servicing dates and types of service. Field personnel are usually equipped with hand-held computers that scan the equipment code from which information is loaded onto the department computer.

Figure 14-6 provides initial information regarding a construction project and is used to initially set up a project. Figure 14-7 is used to establish the perimeters and architect/engineer's agreement, and Figure 14-8 establishes the original project budget. Once construction bids are received, Figure 14-9 establishes the contractor information and basic contract information. Figure 14-10 is used to enter the contractor's breakdown of costs, which is provided to the contractor for use in his monthly periodic payments. Figure 14-11 is a contract payment summary used by the contractor to request monthly payments.

Facilities managers interested in pursuing automation, but who are having difficulty understanding all the potential uses, are encouraged to contact computer software companies or other facilities managers with computer systems. There are many colleges and universities that have successful, computerized operations and, typically, facilities managers are eager to share their systems with other college and university administrators.

14.7 SUMMARY

Computerization results in a more efficient department which will gain credibility within the university. Managers become more knowledgeable and are better equipped to serve upper-level management.

Figure 14–5
IDO Directory Data Entry Screen

IDO Directory

IDO W-_____.   IDO Date ___/___/___   Priority ___   Bldg. ___

Type ___   E-Emergency   P-Project   B-Blanket   K-Key Shop   S-Sign Shop   M-Misc.

Account Charged ___-___-___   Amount Approved ___.___

Dept. ___   W-___

Previous IDO ___   ___.___

Prev. S&W Charges ___   ___.___

Prev. Total Installed ___   ___.___

Attn: ___

Ready to Schedule? (Y/N) ___   Split Funded? (Y/N) ___

Coordinator ___   Date Approved ___/___/___

Estimator ___   Date Estimated ___/___/___

Date Started ___/___/___   Date Completed ___/___/___

Description ___

___

___

___

Physical Facilities ___/___/___   Last Update ___/___/___

Figure 14–6
Project Directory Data Entry Screen

Project Directory

PROJECT _____

Campus ____ Status ____ Type ____

Coordinators ____

Funding _____

Description _____

Today __/__/__   Last Save __/__/__   Batch ____

Figure 14-7

Consultant Agreements Data Entry Screen

Consultant Agreements _____

PROJECT _____

AGREEMENT _____ Dated ___/___/___
Print on Planning? ___ Per month? ___
Construction? ___

A/E Site Visits _____
Extra Visits Charge _____
Insurance _____
Board Presentation? ___ Brochures _____
Rendering? ___
Life Cycle Cost St.? ___ Energy Performance? ___

Fee Description _____
_____
_____
_____
_____

Letter Agreement ___ Payment Type ___ Includes Reimbursables ___ Complete ___/___
Other Consultant ___
Today ___/___/___ Last Save ___/___/___ Batch ___.

Figure 14–8

Preliminary Cost Estimates Data Entry Screen

Preliminary Cost Estimates

PROJECT _____ .

A/E AGREEMENT _____

Contract Amount	_____ . _____	
A/E Fees	_____ . _____	%
CM Fees	_____ . _____	%
Consultant	_____ . _____	%
Surveys/Tests	_____ . _____	
A/E Reimbursables	_____ . _____	
CM Reimbursables	_____ . _____	
Movable Equip.	_____ . _____	
Telephone	_____ . _____	
Landscaping	_____ . _____	
Contingency	_____ . _____	%
Advertising	_____ . _____	Paper(s)
CPM	_____ . _____	%
Administration	_____ . _____	%
Reproduction	_____ . _____	%
Microfilming	_____ . _____	
Moving	_____ . _____	

Total _____ . _____

Today ___ / ___ / ___   Last Save ___ / ___ / ___   Batch _____ .

Figure 14–9
Contract Directory Data Entry Screen

Contract Directory

PROJECT _____ .

CONTRACT _____ .

Construction Project Manager _____   Contract Status ___

Architect/Engineer _____ :

Cert. Letter Rcvd ___ / ___ / ___   Percent Work Complete ___ .

Notice to Proceed ___ / ___ / ___

Contracted Days ___ / ___ .

Contract Completion ___ / ___ / ___

Authorized Exts. ___ .

Revised Completion ___ / ___ / ___

Estimated Completion ___ / ___ / ___   Substantial Completion ___ / ___ / ___

Comments _____

_____

_____

Today ___ / ___ / ___   Last Save ___ / ___ / ___   Batch ___ .

Figure 14–10
Breakdown of Costs Data Entry Screen

Breakdown of Costs

PROJECT _____

CONTRACT _____ : _____

TASK _____ : _____

Quantity _____ : _____   Unit _____   Start _____ / _____ / _____   Finish _____ / _____ / _____
Unit Cost _____ : _____

Contract _____ : _____   Subtask _____ / _____

Material _____ : _____   Material _____ / _____
Total _____ : _____   Total _____ : _____

Today _____ / _____ / _____   Last Save _____ / _____   Batch _____ .

Figure 14–11

Contract Payment Summary Data Entry Screen

Contract Payment Summary

PROJECT _____

CONTRACT _____
Original Contract Amount
Plus Authorized Change Orders
Adjusted Contract Amount
Less Direct Purchases of Materials
Net Adjusted Contract Amount

Original Contract Earned Value to Date
Plus Change Order Work Performed to Date
Total Earned Value to Date

Less _____ % Retainage
Net Earned Value to Date
Plus 90% Materials Stored at end of Period
Total Earned Value and Materials

Less Previous Payments
Balance Due this Payment

Today ___ / ___ / ___   Last Save ___ / ___ / ___   Batch _____

The implementation and enhancement of computers within the physical plant department should be a well-considered process using step-by-step procedures. Administrators should use the greatest asset available within facilities operations, and that is to contact similar institutions and find out what they are using and ask how well their systems work.

Computers do cost money. However, no college or university facilities operations can afford not to computerize. The future is now, and the failure of an operation to computerize will keep it in the past.

NOTES

1. McCellan, Stephen T., "The End of the Hardware Era." *Datamation*, Vol. 30, No. 6, May 1, 1984, Pg. 122t.

ADDITIONAL RESOURCES

Berity, John W. "Upstarts Optional in the Stars." *Datamation*, Volume 30 Number 19, November 15, 1984. Discusses new software development for micro-systems.

Durr, Mike Judson, "Mini vs. LAN: And the Winner is . . . ." *LAN Times*, April 1987. This article discusses the comparison between mini-computers and LAN.

Forbes, Jim and Beth Freedom. "IBM to Debut Products Linking Mainframe Mid-Range System." *PC Week*, Volume 4 Number 21, May 19, 1987. Discusses inner connection and capability of PCs to mainframes.

Judson, Mike. "Minis vs. LANs: A Question of Flexibility." *LAN Times*, May 1987. This article discusses the philosophical viewpoint of the move to LANs.

———. "Mini vs. LAN: Making Sense Out of Wonderland." *LAN Times*, July 1987. This article discusses the minimal gap between LANs and minicomputers.

Kramer, Matt. "Use of Controllers, Processors, Forges Stronger Host LAN Link." *PC Week*, Volume 4 Number 15, April 14, 1987. Discusses how new controllers increase capabilities of different LANs.

CHAPTER 15

Procurement and Materials Management

James K. Marshall
Director, Buying and Contracting
University of Colorado, Boulder

With additional contributions by G. Don Shepherd.

15.1 INTRODUCTION

E ffective materials management is essential to the economical accomplishment of the facilities management mission. Every physical plant operation spends a considerable portion of its budget on materials, ranging from inexpensive common-use items to highly technical and expensive equipment. Expenditures for materials can constitute as much as 25 percent of the total physical plant operating budget. The success of materials management is largely dependent upon top level management's support of and involvement in the process. It is a major business operation that interacts with most physical plant functions and therefore requires centralized control and direction.

This chapter describes three materials management functions: purchasing, storage, and distribution. The interrelationships between these functions are illustrated in Figure 15-1.

15.2 THE PROCUREMENT PROCESS

The Purchasing Cycle

Figure 15-2 illustrates the purchasing cycle, a model of a fictional general purchasing transaction. Each purchasing transaction is unique and must be considered individually. Before preparing a purchase request and forwarding it to the purchasing agent, consideration must be given to the nature of the demand for the item. Is it a one-time need? What is the usage rate for the item, if there is a continuing need? Approximately

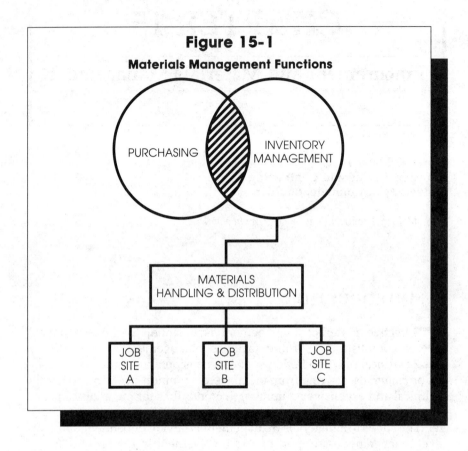

Figure 15-1

Materials Management Functions

how much will the item cost? Consulting with the purchasing agent who handles physical plant business can answer these and other questions that affect the process. Bearing in mind the uniqueness of each transaction, we turn to a description of the general process.

A Felt Need   The purchasing cycle begins with a "felt need" on the part of a physical plant worker or supervisor. This need generally occurs as the result of having to perform a particular task. It is always desirable to anticipate materials requirements prior to assignment of jobs to individual workers. Supervisors can plan the need for materials in advance and make work assignments that take into account material lead times. Otherwise, there is a risk of lost worker productivity, resulting in excessive labor charges.

Creating the Request   Once the need has been felt, someone in physical plant must generate a requisition. Ordinarily this is controlled

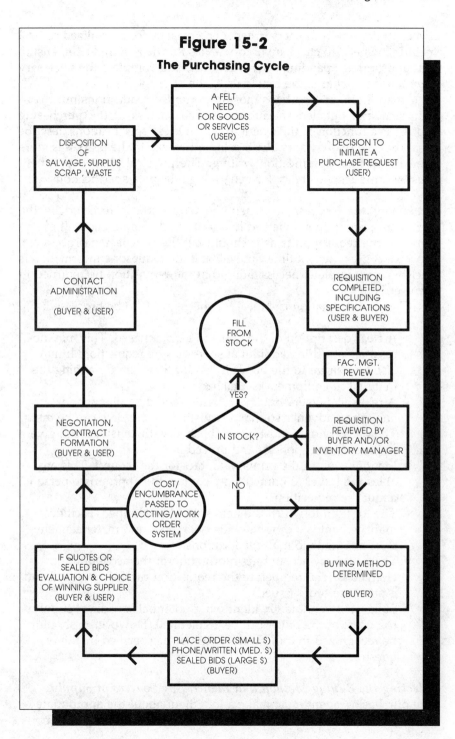

Figure 15-2
The Purchasing Cycle

at a central point in the department. The reasons for centralized control include the need to check inventory levels for the required item, ensure that appropriate spending approvals exist, and complete the necessary transactions to charge the materials to the appropriate job.

In addition, and perhaps most importantly, requisitions must contain clear and detailed specifications. The success of the purchasing process is a function of the extent to which these specifications describe what the user really wants. Perhaps no other step in the process is more user-driven than specification writing. The physical plant department must assume responsibility for generating adequate specifications.

Reviewing the Request   When the requisition is received by the purchasing agent, it is reviewed for clarity and completeness. If everything on the requisition is as it should be, the purchasing process can proceed. A great deal of time can be lost if the requesting information is unclear or incomplete, necessitating that the requisition be returned to the user.

Certain information is critical for the requests to be processed:

- A clear description of the items to be purchased. This may necessitate attaching additional sheets to the requisition. It may also be helpful to the buyer if vendor literature describing the material or equipment is attached.
- A realistic delivery date. Purchases should be planned far enough in advance so that a realistic delivery date can be met. The delivery date must be established with consideration given to procurement policies and procedures.
- Identification of the primary contact for the request. This enables the buyer to immediately contact the appropriate person about the requisition.
- The location to which the item should be shipped. Facilities management is a campus-wide operation, and materials deliveries are made to multiple locations.
- The necessary accounting information of the account to be charged is required before the requisition can be processed and a purchase order issued.
- Suggested vendors. By identifying potential sources of supply, the work of the buyer can be accelerated. However, it should be recognized that the vendor cannot be specified by the requestor.

Selecting the Buying Method and Identifying Sources of Supply
The purchasing agent must make a judgment about the appropriate buying method to use. The buying method chosen will depend upon

the cost and the nature of the market for the item in question. Depending upon the buying method chosen, the order is placed with a vendor suggested by physical plant (if the dollar value of the purchase is small), verbal telephone quotes may be taken (for medium dollar value purchases), or a sealed bidding process will be utilized (if the dollar value is large or if market conditions warrant).

Sealed Bid Evaluation   If the sealed bid method is used, then the buyer and appropriate members of the physical plant staff must evaluate the responses and determine which bid is most responsive to the need in question, price and all other relevant factors considered. The physical plant representative chosen to work with the purchasing agent must be knowledgeable about the goods or services requested, as well as unbiased and open-minded. Each sealed process should have as its primary purpose the selection of a responsible vendor whose bid is most responsive to departmental requirements. If committee members are known to favor or dislike a particular vendor, the process is likely to be compromised. The risk of bias in vendor selection includes vendor protests, which not only harm vendor relations but consume a great deal of time. Valid protests may have serious legal implications for the individuals involved, the physical plant department, and the college or university. Worse, bias in this regard may often result in unsatisfactory products and services.

Contract Negotiation   Before goods can be received for use by the facilities management department, some kind of written contract is established between the purchasing department and the vendor. For small purchases, contract negotiations are generally unnecessary, and the written agreement between the parties takes the form of a purchase order created by the buyer.

For larger purchases, however, especially those made as a result of competitive bidding, some kind of formal contract negotiations occur. These negotiations take place for two major reasons. The first is simply a logical extension of the sealed bidding process, where all the details of the agreement between buyer and seller cannot be known in advance. After all bids or proposals are received and the apparent successful bidder has been identified, the final details of the contract must be determined.

For example, large construction projects will be tentatively awarded to the apparent low bidder and the details of the construction project will be specified in contract negotiation sessions. If an agreement cannot be worked out with the apparent low bidder, then the second low bidder is contacted and negotiations reopened. The facilities management and purchasing departments must make sure that they work together during contract negotiations. This includes determining, in advance of meetings with vendors, their preferred objectives and their "fall-back" positions.

The second reason for undertaking contract negotiations is in the event that one party objects to the other party's terms. While interdepartmental teamwork is important, the actual negotiations will probably be carried out by representatives from the purchasing department or the university's legal counsel.

Contract Administration   A common and costly mistake is to assume that the job is done once the contract has been signed. Physical plant administrators must assume responsibility for ensuring that vendors supply what they promise to supply, delivered when they promise to supply it. Thus, delivery schedules are an important aspect of contract administration. To ensure performance compliance, inspection and testing of goods is critical. If vendors do not live up to expectations of performance and delivery, it is up to physical plant to determine the cause of the problem and initiate appropriate corrective action, in conjunction with the purchasing agent.

Contract administration includes the responsibility for ensuring that the university lives up to its promises as well. The contract embodies a promise to pay the vendor for goods and services rendered, assuming proper vendor performance. Nothing is more detrimental to relationships with a vendor than delayed payment. Everyone who makes purchases must see to it that vendors are paid promptly, and rectify payment problems as quickly as possible.

Receiving and Inspection   This step in the purchasing cycle involves making sure that what has been purchased fulfills the requirements. If the physical plant department has a stores operation on site, this is a good place for most receiving and inspection to be performed. Except when specialized inspection procedures are necessary, the stores staff should be able to inspect shipments and work with the buyer in case a rejection is necessary. If no central stores exists, then groups of items requiring inspection should be assigned to engineers and managers as part of their job descriptions.

Disposing of Salvageable Materials   Many materials and equipment have economic value even after their replacement is warranted. A good salvage management program can be beneficial to the physical plant department.

- The sale of scrap and used items can generate substantial revenue.

- Many items have a trade-in value that can be used to offset the cost of new equipment.
- Overstocked and slow-moving inventory items, which can be costly to carry, should be purged regularly.
- Some items may be excessive to the needs of the physical plant department, but be of use to another department within the university. Transfering these items can generate good will.

It is important to keep in mind that the purchasing cycle has implications for the physical plant department's inventory and job cost (work order) systems. At some point, once the cost of a purchase is known, it must be passed through the job cost accounting system and charged to the appropriate job/account and expense classification. If the items purchased are to be stored in physical inventory, then the appropriate inventory account must be credited with the items and their cost. It is often convenient to initiate the transactions necessary for these accounting entries as part of the purchasing cycle. (See Chapter 12, Cost Accounting.)

Purchasing Methods

A number of factors determine the purchasing methods used in each case, including the following.

- The dollar amount of the purchase.
- State and federal laws and regulations.
- The nature of the market for the item being purchased.
- Whether the item represents a one-time or continuing need.

The following summarizes various purchasing methods, based primarily on cost of the item. While this general framework is useful, it should be kept in mind that it is up to the buyer to make a determination of the appropriate method to use in each case. Even relatively inexpensive items may be secured by competitive bidding if the market for the item is highly competitive.

Small-Dollar-Value Purchases   Most of the purchasing transactions made by physical plant and other departments are for items costing less than $500. These purchases may represent up to 80 percent of the transactions, but generally will represent less than 20 percent of total expenditures. Many purchasing operations have recognized the benefits of sharing the responsibility for managing these voluminous small purchases with user departments. Following are examples of small-dollar-value purchasing methods to simplify the purchase of small items, reduce paperwork, decrease delivery time, and process payments more easily and quickly.

Limited Purchase Orders. Many colleges and universities have some form of limited purchase order that can be initiated directly by the using department without purchasing department involvement. These purchase orders go by various names—memorandum purchase orders, small dollar orders, request for payment, and others—but they share the common characteristic of enabling a campus department to make a direct purchase from a vendor, and generally are only reviewed by the purchasing department after the fact to determine compliance with applicable rules and statutes. A sample of such an order is shown in Figure 15-3.

Checkable Purchase Orders. Another alternative for handling small-dollar-value purchases is to use a checkable purchase order, or check with order. This type of order includes a check on the face of the order. At the time of purchase, the check is filled out and given to a vendor as payment for the goods. Since no invoice needs to be sent, the accounts payable department's involvement in the process is eliminated. In addition, vendors appreciate the prompt payment. The persons authorized to make purchases with this type of order must be trustworthy, since they will write a check on behalf of the institution.

Limited Purchasing Authority Delegation. This method decentralizes the purchase of small-dollar-value items to the user departments. Purchasing managers add little to the purchasing process for such small items. In addition, the principle behind limited purchasing authority delegation is that departmental users, whose budgets are relatively small, will act in their own best interest and seek those suppliers that provide the best value. Naturally, the purchasing department will ensure that appropriate procedures are followed, usually by performing a post-audit of purchases made under the delegated authority arrangement.

If limited purchasing authority delegation is an alternative, physical plant administrators should pursue it. Both the physical plant and purchasing departments benefit from this kind of arrangement.

Blanket Orders with Limits on Individual Purchases. Nearly all university purchasing operations have a mechanism to allow repetitive purchases of small dollar-value-items from a given supplier. These come under various names, including standing purchase orders, blanket orders, master orders, and others. All share the common characteristic of making frequent small purchases more convenient, obviating the need for an individual purchase order for each transaction. Often, these types of orders carry limits on individual transactions (such as $200 to $500), particularly if they have been established without competitive bidding. If competitive bidding is used, it may be possible to increase or remove

Figure 15-3

Memorandum Purchase Order

RECORD THIS MPO NUMBER ON ALL
INVOICES AND CORRESPONDENCE

MPO 008924

VENDOR
NAME _____ (40)

ADDRESS _____ (40)

_____ (40)

CITY _____ STATE ___ (2) ZIP ___ (10) DATE: _____

QUANTITY	COMPLETE DESCRIPTION OF ITEM AND/OR ITEMS (ITEMIZED)	ESTIMATE	PRICE
	(20)		

TOTAL DOLLAR AMOUNT FOR THIS TRANSACTION MUST NOT EXCEED $ . . 200.00 . . . : . . . . TAX EXEMPT ___ TOTAL

I N F O R M A T I O N

ACCOUNT NO.	AMOUNT	DESCRIPTION
(10)	(6) (23)	
(10)	(6) (23)	
(10)	(6) (23)	

SPECIAL
HANDLING ___

TELEPHONE _____

DUE DATE _____

WARRANT NO _____

MEMO TO VENDOR —
1. This MPO is invalid without Departmental approval.
2. Mail original invoice plus copy to
3. MPO number must be included on invoice to ensure payment.
4. _____

UNIVERSITY DEPARTMENTAL INSTRUCTIONS —
1. Provide vendor with original copy (white).
2. In the FRS information area, enter the account number (including object code), the amount and the description of the item(s) purchased. (The size of each field, including spaces, is indicated by the number in parenthesis below the field.)
3. Attach receipt or other documentation showing description, quantity, price of item(s), and send to Accounts Payable.
4. If invoice is received by the department, forward it to Accounts Payable.
5. Retain fourth copy (blue) of MPO to reconcile the FRS statements.

Department Name _____

Contact _____ Ext. _____

By _____ Date _____
   Departmental Approval

VENDOR COPY

these limits. For example, it may be reasonable for physical plant to take bids to establish a blanket order for lumber. This would allow lumber vendors to bid competitively for the university's business for a specified time period, such as a year. In addition, with competitive bidding the individual transaction limits could be set at a level that allows physical plant the flexibility to make routine purchases.

Competitive Bidding   For purchases exceeding the small-dollar-value limit but still too small for sealed bidding, an informal bidding process can be used. The most common procedure involves contacting some minimum number of vendors, usually at least three, by telephone or in writing, for quotations. You may be required by law to request bids from or award contracts to a certain number of women- or minority-owned businesses. The university or college legal counsel can provide information on this topic.

The quotes, submitted by telephone or letter, are tabulated and the lowest responsive bidder is contacted. This procedure works well for medium-dollar-value items ($1,000 to $5,000) when specifications are uncomplicated and easy to communicate. It retains some of the simplicity of the small-dollar-value methods, and adds some of the desirable aspects of competition while taking less time than formal bidding.

For those goods and services having a substantial cost, and for items whose specifications cannot be completely described before a vendor is selected, formal sealed bidding is used. This type of bidding requires the active participation of the facilities management staff to a greater extent than the other buying methods. The procedure generally includes the steps outlined in Figure 15-4.

The importance of establishing an objective evaluation committee and creating good specifications was discussed previously. Once the committee and specifications have been established, a major decision must be made. That is, whether to use a Request for Bid (RFB) process or a more detailed Request for Proposal (RFP). The main difference between the two options is that the vendor selection decision under a Request for Bid process is primarily determined by the price of the item to be acquired; whereas the Request for Proposal process allows for additional evaluation factors to be considered explicitly in the evaluation process.

If the specifications for the item to be acquired are well known and price is the primary consideration, then an RFB process can be used. For example, if the grounds crew needs small lawn mowers, we may specify in detail what the design of those lawn mowers should be (e.g., gas powered, twenty-inch cutting path, safety shutoff on handle, controls mounted on handle). Using the RFB method, these specifications would be stated as mandatory. That is, the mower offered either meets the

Figure 15-4
Request for Bids/Proposals Process

1. Initiation of Request
2. Committee of facilities management users appointed to work closely with the purchasing agent. Purchasing agent reviews procedures with committee.
3. Determine which alternative to use: Request for Bids or Request for Proposals.
4. Clarify Specifications and Scope of Work
   a. Statement of work to be performed.
   b. Definition of vendor responsibilities.
   c. Create questions to be included in RFP.
   d. Define mandatory (pass/fail) items which must be present for a bid to be considered responsive.
5. Identify evaluation criteria and scoring methods.
6. Create a clear statement of how vendors are to respond.
7. Send out the Request for Bids/Proposals, ensuring that items 4 through 6 above are included.
8. Evaluate bid/proposal responses.
   a. Clarify vendor responses if necessary.
   b. Each committee member assigns point values to responses independently, at first.
   c. Committee members assemble their scoring and negotiate a consensus.
9. Notify apparent successful respondent of award.

specifications or it does not. The award is made to the offeror with the lowest priced mower that meets all the mandatory specifications.

In addition to its simplicity, an RFB generally requires less lead time for potential bidders to respond. These advantages, however, are somewhat offset by the requirement to make the award to the lowest responsive bidder. RFBs should only be used when all of the specifications for an item are well known and no surprises are likely regarding the design or performance of the lowest cost product.

A Request for Proposal is generally used when the exact specifications of a desired product or service are unknown. For example, if a cogeneration facility is to be built, it is unlikely that all the details of the facility will be determined in advance. Under these circumstances, factors in addition to price will be important in the selection of the general contractor. Experience in similar projects, willingness to meet a construction schedule, guarantees that the facility will perform at a certain level of output, and so on, would be evaluated individually. An overall score for each offeror is obtained by adding up the score achieved for each of the criteria, including price. The award is made to the offeror with the highest score.

One of the most difficult aspects of RFP preparation is creating the right kind of questions to ask and the scoring methods that will be used to rate responses. For each question to be included in the solicitation, a test should be conducted to make sure that the question is understandable. A way to test questions is to ask someone from outside the process to read the questions and provide feedback.

Closely related to the creation of questions is anticipating the range of answers the questions will elicit from respondents. Creating objective, defendable rating scales to assign points to responses is as much an art as a science. As much as possible, questions should be quantitatively oriented. For example, years of relevant experience, number of individuals who will be dedicated to a project, and cost are relatively straightforward and easy to evaluate. Other questions, such as background of vendor personnel, are more difficult to evaluate objectively.

Rating scales can take on many forms. Regardless of the type of scale used, it should allow for an unequivocal assignment of points to the response. It should also allow for the assignment of points to all potential responses. Finally, the rating scale should ensure that the most desirable responses receive the most points.

The evaluation criteria and rating scales are created before the RFP is sent to prospective vendors. This allows the evaluation committee to establish the objectivity of its evaluation process. While it is possible, through an addendum, to change a question after the RFP has been sent to vendors, doing so often creates confusion and requires an extension to the proposal opening date and thus should be avoided. At many institutions it is unacceptable to change a rating scale once the evaluation of responses has begun. Changing the rules during the competitive process is seen as unfair to vendors and is extremely difficult to defend. Other institutions allow a change in the scale under certain conditions.

Once responses have been received, it may be necessary to clarify information provided by vendors. It is acceptable to hold individual discussions with respondents to help to interpret their answers, as long as no information about the scoring of a response, or about another vendor's response, is revealed. Physical plant representatives should work closely with the buyer if clarification is necessary.

The actual process of scoring RFP responses should be monitored closely by the buyer. While each individual on the evaluation committee ranks the responses, the committee as a whole must ultimately reach a consensus. It is up to the buyer to bring about such a consensus.

Competitive Negotiations   In some circumstances, quality is the most important aspect of a service, while price is of lesser importance. In such cases, some states allow for competitive negotiations based on factors such as the professional competence of the offerors, the technical merits of the offers, and the price for which the services are to be rendered, in that order. Competitive negotiations are generally conducted in two stages. During the first stage, offers are evaluated to determine the competence of the offerors and the quality of their offers and are rank-ordered based on these and/or other critiera.

During the second stage, the cost of the services to be performed is negotiated with the highest ranked offeror from stage one. If an agreement regarding price can be reached, the process is concluded. If physical plant and the highest ranked offeror cannot reach an agreement regarding price, then negotiations are undertaken with the second highest ranked offeror, and so on, until an acceptable agreement is reached. This process is often used when acquiring professional services such as those of architects, engineers, surveyors, lawyers, and consultants.

Sole Source Purchases   The term sole source, while self-explanatory, is often misunderstood. There is a subtle distinction between a true sole source and one that simply reflects the preference of the individual requiring the item in question. In the latter case, the justification for the sole source rests on shaky ground. A legitimate sole source exists when only one company or individual in a reasonable subset of the universe is capable of supplying a particular good or service. While this is sometimes the case (as with most public utilities), a sole source acquisition should only be made when this condition is met. The most important reason for being cautious about purchasing from a single source is related to the price to be paid for the item in question.

In the absence of competition, how are we to know if the price we are paying is reasonable? Many times, a user will be convinced that a sole source is justified on the basis of the price alone. Price should never be used as a rationale for a sole source purchase, because of the differential pricing schedule vendors will use when they understand that they face a competitive environment versus, effectively, having a monopoly. Aside from the likelihood of paying more, there is a risk that other potential suppliers will be unhappy if they perceive that one vendor is receiving preferential treatment. In some cases, a sole source acquisition may be necessary to match existing equipment or acquire replacement parts. Even in these cases, vendors' claims about the uniqueness of their products should be thoroughly investigated before a purchase is made.

Timing of Purchases and the Bid Calendar

The cycle of activities for most university facilities operations follows a predictable seasonal pattern. For items used throughout the year in a relatively level pattern, needs are filled by competitive bids when a contract term expires. Especially for large volume purchases of items like air filters, bedding plants, grounds and custodial equipment repair parts, and plumbing and electrical supplies, reasonably accurate estimates of needs can be made. An effective method of reminding both the purchasing and physical plant departments of such recurring needs is the use of a bid calendar (see Figure 15-5).

Working together, a purchasing agent and physical plant representatives can formulate a bid calendar in a few hours. The calendar is then distributed within physical plant and to the buyer(s) responsible for physical plant purchases.

Vendor Relations

Good vendor relations should be a priority concern for those involved in managing materials. Vendors can be valuable sources of information about products and services utilized by physical plant. It also is important to recognize that the reputation of a college or university is affected by all contacts. Marketing representatives have many contacts, so they can have a significant impact on others perception of the institution. It is especially important that an institution maintain a reputation of fairness to potential suppliers. This not only fosters a competitive environment, but also makes it easier to resolve the inevitable disputes that occur as part of the purchasing process.

Physical plant representatives often deal directly with vendor salespersons. The following guidelines promote good vendor relations, as well as serve the interests of physical plant.

- Contact more than one vendor whenever possible. The more alternatives considered, the better the prospects for the most advantageous business deal. You may want to develop a means to prequalify the bidders.
- Keep an open mind; do not make hasty decisions. Regardless of how outstanding a material or piece of equipment may seem, a better or less costly alternative may be available.
- Be sure to convey how the product is to be used. This can have important implications with respect to the warranties offered by a vendor. "Vendor seminars" may be useful for the benefit of vendors and physical plant alike.
- When obtaining information about the cost of a product, make sure the life-cycle cost is considered. The analysis should include not only the initial product cost, but also installation, maintenance, operating and utilities costs, as well as salvage or trade-in value.

Figure 15-5

Sample Facilities Management Bid Calendar

JANUARY	FEBRUARY	MARCH
• NSS floor machine parts • Windsor & Kent floor • Machine parts • Service & repair buffers • Tree spade & operator • Freon refrigerant • Repair small John Deere tractors & parts for garden tractors • Concrete for delivery • Roadbase for delivery	• Electrical contract • Nuts & bolts • Compressor parts • Rubbish disposal • Pyr-a-larm parts • Bowl cleaner • Deicer • Plastic sheet, etc. • Glass	• Sheet copper & steel • Trane replacement parts • Natural gas • Grader, operator & supt • Buchner irrigation parts • Roofing materials • Valves-Nibco/ Stockham • Control cutter hammer • Deicer • Elevator repair
APRIL	**MAY**	**JUNE**
• Paper towels • Repair & parts Hotsy pressure washer	• Controls & parts (even years) • Strainers & steam traps • Fuel oil • ASCO valves • NIBCO • Parts Rockwell & Porter • Cable Tools • Asbestos Count & Ident. • AMF CUNO filters & cartridges	• Wooden doors • Abs & PVS pipe fittings • Fuseal • Sheet copper & steel • Drywall framing studs • Carpeting • Venetian blinds • Honeywell energy control parts • Duct tape • Rags
JULY	**AUGUST**	**SEPTEMBER**
• Construction contractors • Builder's HDW • Soil & mixes	• Gloves & boots • Large fire extinguisher system	• Asphalt equip. & oper. • Bearings • Sheet copper & steel • Taco pump parts • V-belts

OCTOBER	NOVEMBER	DECEMBER
• Flooring & cove base	• Skill tool parts	• Air filter-disposable
• Doors - metal frames	• Fire extinguisher fill	• Sheet copper & steel
• Asbestos coatings & encapsulants	• Terry Turb repair parts	• Sealant
• Misc. Hand tools	• Parts for Western traffic gates	• Credit S.O. metals
• Metalizing service	• Service & parts floor buffer	• Electric motor repair
	• Drills & blades	• Repair service for Sterling generator
	• Honeywell energy system maintenance	• Towing service
	• Plumbing supplies	• Parking lot striping

- Do not mislead sales representatives by making statements that might lead them to believe that their product is the only one you are considering.
- Avoid statements that might make vendors think they will receive an order. Unless physical plant has been delegated specific responsibility for making purchases, physical plant staff cannot make such commitments. Generally, only the purchasing department can issue valid purchase orders.
- Do not reveal the budgeted or estimated cost of the purchase.
- Avoid accepting gratuities from vendors. Not only can favors such as dinner or gifts cloud decision-making, they may also unduly raise vendors' expectations. Also, acceptance of gratuities can destroy the reputation of the physical plant staff person responsible for the procurement and, in some states, can result in termination for a conflict of interest.
- Do not accept everything a sales representative might say as factual or correct. While few sales people intentionally mislead, some have been known to tightrope the boundaries of the truth. Do not overreact to a vendor-created crisis. Phrases such as "the price goes up after the first of the month," or "this is the last one left in stock," are intended to induce hasty decisions.
- Once a competitive bidding process has begun, avoid contact with vendor representatives until after the bid has been awarded. Be especially careful not to reveal anything to a vendor that might give an unfair advantage.

Specifications

The National Institute of Governmental Purchasing (NIGP) defines a specification as

> a concise statement of a set of requirements to be sat-
> isfied by a product, material or process; indicating
> whenever appropriate the procedures to determine
> whether the requirements are satisfied. As far as prac-
> ticable, it is desirable that the requirement be ex-
> pressed numerically in terms of appropriate units to-
> gether with their limits.[1]

Specifications are physical plant's responsibility. Engineers and managers who complain about "having to take the low bid" and not getting the goods or services they really want often have not created a complete and concise statement of product requirements.

There are two basic kinds of specifications: design and perfor-mance. Design specifications are most often used for one-of-a-kind items. Physical plant must determine when the product is needed, and describe it adequately so that potential suppliers can reasonably esti-mate the cost to produce it. Design specifications are often used for building construction where dimensions, materials, and physical re-quirements are spelled out in detail, along with the quality tests that will be used to determine that requirements are met. Design specifications have the advantages of giving physical plant control over the final product and a clear understanding of what is expected from that prod-uct.

Performance specifications generally are used for items that are commonly available. Since there are many different types and brands of lawn mowers, for example, there is no need for the grounds supervisor to design a new mower; but it is essential that the performance expecta-tions for the kind of mower desired be communicated clearly. The super-visor should indicate, for example, the desired output for the mower in terms of cutting swath and speed. In addition, desired functions, such as attachments for snow removal or sweeping, must be carefully enumer-ated. Performance specifications generally are easier to write than de-sign specifications. In addition they have the advantage of allowing more flexibility by suppliers.

In some situations it is possible to use a combination of design and performance specifications. Regardless of the type used, all specifica-tions must accomplish four things:

- Identify minimum requirements.
- Allow for a competitive bid process.
- List reproducible test methods to be used in determining compliance with specifications.
- Provide for an equitable award at the lowest possible cost.[2]

One way to avoid "having to take the low bid" and "not really getting what we want" is for engineers and managers to work closely with the purchasing agent to compile specifications that meet the above criteria.

Disposition of Surplus Property

Physical plant operations generate a tremendous amount of excess or otherwise unneeded material. An effective program to manage these materials can reduce inventory investment, free up scarce storage space, and realize revenue from their sale. The following are alternative methods of surplus property management.

Recycling   Many states require that property excess to the needs of one department or agency be offered to other state agencies before it is offered for sale to the public. Some items, like furniture and movable partitions, often can be sold by advertising them via a memorandum or in the campus newspaper. Purchasing departments can advise of equipment or material recycling requirements. Generally, these regulations do not require that items be given away, but only that they be offered at a reasonable price.

Trade-ins   When buying replacement equipment, a determination should be made as to whether the items being replaced can be traded in to offset part of the cost of the new items. For capital equipment such as vehicles or construction equipment, a trade-in often can be negotiated as part of the purchase agreement. Or it may be better to sell the used equipment separately from the procurement transaction.

Sale to the Public—Auctions   Another option may be to dispose of excess property by holding periodic public auctions. Many colleges and universities have an established auction program. Auctions work well for items that can be easily stored and inspected by the potential buying public, such as automobiles, garden equipment, typewriters, and personal computer components.

Scrap   Nearly every facilities operation generates some salable scrap, such as scrap metal—copper, brass, and steel—generated in the plumbing, electrical, and machine shops. Scrap recycling is not without cost. The materials must be separated and stored, and bids taken. The pickup and weighing of scrap must be monitored. But the return can be substantial.

Waste   Physical plant operations also generate a considerable amount of waste products. Custodial, grounds and building maintenance, as well as construction and energy management operations all create some waste products as part of their daily operations. Waste should be immediately identified and disposed of in a timely manner. Hazardous waste must be disposed of according to university, state, and federal regulations.

Uniqueness of Facilities Operations

Facilities management operations are unique among campus administrative and academic departments. Perhaps its most important characteristic with regard to materials management is the breadth of services. No other campus department has as many functional responsibilities. The result of this diversity is the need for thousands of different equipment items, tools, office supplies, and repair and replacement parts. Physical plant is the purchasing department's largest customer on most campuses.

Many colleges and universities have been built over long periods of time, reulting in a variety of building types. Mechanical, electrical, and other building systems vary widely, and this variety affects the physical plant/purchasing relationship in a number of ways. Training costs increase and productivity suffers because individual tradespeople and engineers must be able to service many different types and brands of equipment. This means that the purchasing agent assigned to work with physical plant must be equally well trained in these broad material requirements. Standardization of building components and repair parts is discussed later in the context of inventory management. One aspect of this issue is cooperation with the purchasing agent. As long as all buying activity is coordinated at a central point, the buyer is in a position to review purchases for compliance with established standards.

Physical plant workers often are frustrated by their inability to justify the purchase of a certain type or brand of repair parts that they think is best. An experienced purchasing agent can provide the necessary assistance to determine the costs associated with alternative steam traps or air filters, for example. A systematic analysis can often substantiate the experience of the worker and can help to identify the most cost-effective items.

For the reasons identified here, physical plants require special attention. Their procurement decisions affect not only the cost of providing maintenance, but also the quality of campus life. Directors of purchasing and physical plant can benefit by working together to devise a program that provides the dedicated, specialized procurement support needed. At a minimum, the purchasing department should identify a buyer whose primary responsibility is satisfying the procurement requirements of physical plant, and physical plant should identify an individual who can serve as the chief liaison with purchasing. The benefits of dedicated support include large potential cost savings by selecting appropriate purchasing and negotiating techniques, faster turnaround of purchase requests, professional analytical support for materials management decisions, and help in finding flexibility within the myriad purchasing statutes, rules and regulations applicable to most colleges and universities. The National Association of Educational Buyers can provide additional information and assistance on purchasing practices.

15.3 STORING MATERIALS—INVENTORY MANAGEMENT

This treatment of inventory management is concerned primarily with the practical problems of ordering, storing, and controlling inventories. Ordering formulae and automated inventory control systems are not ends unto themselves. While familiarity with these tools is important, they do not guarantee that the materials to do the job will be there when needed at a reasonable cost. Three basic problems of inventory management are addressed here: providing good customer service, managing the cost tradeoffs, and maximizing operational efficiency.

Customer Service

The facilities management stores operation is a key component in the department's effectiveness with respect to customer service. The stores operation has at least two types of customers: those that make direct withdrawals from the inventory, and those for whom maintenance or project work is being performed, such as campus departments. If the stores operation fulfills the needs of the direct customer group, it can enhance the service provided to the ultimate customers. Among the major factors that promote the goals of the organization are:

- The breadth and depth of the items stocked.
- The experience and customer orientation of the stores staff.

- The stores location and layout.
- The ease with which items not in stock can be obtained on short notice.

What To Stock   Determining which items and how many of each to stock is one of the most important decisions inventory managers face. Because of the impact on customer service and the cost, physical plant must make wise decisions about what is stored as inventory. Too often only the cost tradeoffs are considered, and inventory managers maintain a lean inventory at the expense of customer relations. For example, some compressors may be so reliable that they rarely break down, and so require infrequent repairs. The inventory manager, based on the cost of spare parts for the compressor, may decide not to stock these parts. If one of the compressors breaks down in the psychology building in mid-July, however, hundreds of research animals may be threatened. The implications for the research activities of the psychology faculty could be so severe that the decision is made to maintain some spare compressor parts in inventory, even though the economics would not justify it. Effective customer service plays an important role in what is stored in inventory.

Organization and Staffing   The stores stock must be under the control of a manager who is not involved in the maintenance function. At a small college, the stores manager may handle this responsibility singlehandedly. At larger institutions the manager will require a staff to handle various parts of the work. Clerical staff in the stores office handle all records, reordering of stock, receiving documents, invoices, and inquiries. In the stockroom stock clerks are responsible for the issue counter(s). They also stock the shelves with incoming goods, count the stock, write issue tickets to record stock being issued, and do all of the labor associated with the operation of the storeroom. In large storerooms a foreman or storekeeper may supervise the stock clerks and oversee the operation of the storeroom.

Stores Personnel and Customer Service   Working with the customers of the facilities stores operation is an important responsibility. Personnel assigned to this function need to be familiar with the basic principles of stores and inventory management, as well as have experience in a maintenance or construction organization. Because college and university facilities operations are so diverse, individuals employed in stores should be given the opportunity to become familiar with the types of work being performed. Whether they come to the organization with this background or must be trained, they cannot provide effective customer service without understanding the work the department does.

Standards for customer service should be established and made a part of each staff member's performance plan. Among other issues, these standards should address the time necessary to fill individual customer requests for materials, and a maximum acceptable number of customer complaints in a period of time.

Centralized and Decentralized Stores   On large university campuses it may be necessary to decentralize the stores operation. This is true if the maintenance organization itself is decentralized. There are various ways to do this. For example, maintenance and nonmaintenance items may be kept at one stores location, while custodial supplies are at another location. Stores might be decentralized by trades groups. Or there could be a major storeroom and a minor one located on a branch campus, each containing the same general variety of supplies. Another option is the open stock store, a "supermarket" that allows workers to use shopping carts and check out their supplies.

While there may appear to be strong justification for decentralized stores, this option should be carefully considered. If the stores operation is decentralized, all locations must remain under the same manager and common control system.

Some of the limitations of centralized stores can be overcome without decentralizing the operation. Delivery service can be provided. This requires high levels of cooperation, coordination, and communication between maintenance staff and stores personnel. On college campuses telephones are everywhere, and many physical plant organizations are now equipped with sophisticated radio systems, thus alleviating communication problems. If used effectively, a delivery system can save staffing in the maintenance function. Maintenance personnel should keep the appropriate section of the stores catalog in their tool kits. They can order supplies by phone using the exact stock numbers(s). The delivery van must be equipped with a radio.

Central Stores Location and Layout   Materials distribution will be discussed in detail in a later section. An important aspect of this function is related to the stores location and its layout. A good location will provide easy access to facilities management workers as well as for deliveries from suppliers. A central campus location may satisfy physical plant access, while a perimeter location works best for deliveries. If the central campus area is already densely developed, using scarce space for a stores operation may not be a popular alternative. The size of the inventory to be stored is a primary factor in determining the size of the stores area. The customers of the stores operation will also influence its location. If their only customers are physical plant workers, the stores can be located to best meet their needs. If other customers use facilities stores, accessibility for them must be considered. Administrative control of the stores operation is facilitated if it is close to administrative offices.

The overall maintenance organization must also be considered. At some colleges and universities, the work force is organized into several units, each with responsibility for an area or zone of the campus. This kind of program may require a decentralization of the stores operation.

As used here, the layout of the stores operation refers to what it looks like on the inside and to its location relative to the work areas or shops of the facilities operation. The objective of the layout is to minimize the cost of distributing individual items from inventory to workers and work sites, commensurate with the goal of providing satisfactory customer service. Layout is a function of the demand for items stored, the administrative procedures necessary to process a withdrawal from inventory, and the space available for the warehouse. In this context, ease of access for physical plant workers is the primary concern.

Figure 15-6 shows two alternative designs that allow easy access in a high-demand, full-service facilities operation. Alternative 1 is a "mirror image" layout. It locates inventory in a controlled area directly behind the facilities divisions that consume the inventory. Alternative 2 is a "drive-thru" design that allows for both walk-up and vehicular access.

Obtaining Non-stock Materials Quickly   Physical plant stores staff provides an important link with the purchasing department. Stores customers (physical plant tradespeople and other workers) generally need items "on demand." If an item is not in stock, purchasing through the normal cycle would probably mean an unacceptable delay. A better alternative is for stores staff to identify those items for which it should have "blanket" or "standing" purchase orders. This may include most, if not all, of the items carried in inventory. Blanket orders allow for quick purchases of items from local vendors in the event that a needed item is out of stock. The stores staff may also be a logical place to utilize the other small-dollar-value payment methods mentioned earlier in this chapter. By working with the buyer responsible for physical plant purchases, procedures can be developed for acquiring out-of-stock materials quickly.

Managing the Cost Tradeoffs

It is a simple fact that inventories are costly (lack of inventories can also be costly, which will be discussed later). Some of these costs, known as carrying or holding costs, vary directly with the size of inventories. The larger the inventory order quantity and the resulting average inventory amount held, the greater the carrying costs. Other costs, known as

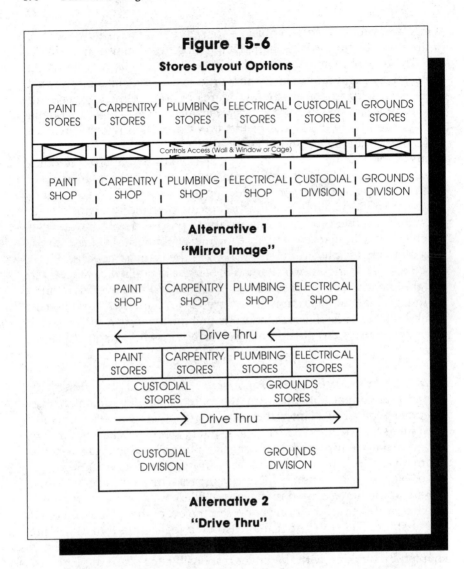

Figure 15-6

Stores Layout Options

| PAINT STORES | CARPENTRY STORES | PLUMBING STORES | ELECTRICAL STORES | CUSTODIAL STORES | GROUNDS STORES |

Controls Access (Wall & Window or Cage)

| PAINT SHOP | CARPENTRY SHOP | PLUMBING SHOP | ELECTRICAL SHOP | CUSTODIAL DIVISION | GROUNDS DIVISION |

Alternative 1

"Mirror Image"

| PAINT SHOP | CARPENTRY SHOP | PLUMBING SHOP | ELECTRICAL SHOP |

← ———— Drive Thru ←————

| PAINT STORES | CARPENTRY STORES | PLUMBING STORES | ELECTRICAL STORES |
| CUSTODIAL STORES | | GROUNDS STORES | |

———→ Drive Thru ————→

| CUSTODIAL DIVISION | GROUNDS DIVISION |

Alternative 2

"Drive Thru"

ordering costs, vary inversely with the size of inventory order quantities. The objective is to determine the inventory order quantity that minimizes the sum of these costs.

Carrying Costs   Inventory carrying costs are those that result from owning inventory. Many of these costs are hidden in that they do not involve a cash outlay. Among the costs associated with holding inventory are storage, investment and spoilage, and obsolesence costs.

Storage Costs. These include all costs associated with the physical storage of inventory. A stores operation requires a warehouse with attendant utilities, maintenance, and perhaps rental costs. Thus, there is an opportunity cost associated with the ownership of warehouse space. Part of the salaries of the stores staff are associated with tasks related to holding inventory, such as the periodic physical count required to adjust inventory book value to its actual value. Another storage cost is insurance premiums for the warehouse and its contents. If all these costs are added together, they can easily constitute 5 percent of the value of the inventory carried. This means that it can cost $50 or more for every $1,000 of average annual inventory.

Investment Costs. Purchases of inventory require an outlay of working capital. If the college or university treasurer charges interest on working capital balances, this is a direct cost to the physical plant department. Even if explicit interest charges are not made for inventory balances, there is still an implicit opportunity cost associated with the funds tied up. Instead of investing in inventory, the institution would have the option of revenue producing investments.

Spoilage and Obsolesence Costs. Some items stored in inventory are not used before they outlive their shelf life. Paint, for example, if stored for too long will harden and become unmixable. Lumber stored improperly can warp and become unusable. Such spoilage and deterioration costs are largely avoidable, but they still occur.

Some inventory items do not move out of inventory as quickly as anticipated. Other items can become obsolete as a result of major technological improvements. Installing an automated energy management system, for example, can mean that many replacement parts for pneumatic control systems are no longer necessary. Periodically, and at least as often as physical inventory is taken, obsolete and slow-moving items should be disposed of as discussed previously or written off and added to the cost of goods sold for the period.

Ordering Costs   Each time an order is placed costs are incurred. Ordering costs decrease as the number of orders decrease; fewer orders for greater quantities incur smaller ordering costs than many orders for small quantities. Ordering costs are due to the effort required to process a requisition, create a purchase order, receive and inspect the goods, and process payment to the vendor. These costs vary widely, depending on the purchasing method used (e.g., telephone quotes or sealed bids) and the items being purchased.

Acquisition Costs   The acquisition cost of an order is simply the unit price of the items multiplied by the number of units ordered. If the unit price of an item is unaffected by the size of the order, then acquisition

cost will not affect the order quantity. Acquisition costs become important when quantity discounts are available for order sizes greater than a
supplier-determined minimum. In such cases acquisition costs would
decrease at order levels above the discount quantities. Determining the
appropriate order quantity is slightly more complicated when quantity
discounts are available, but the underlying framework is the same.

Out-of-Stock Costs   Occasionally there may be measurable dollar
losses associated with not having a part in stock in an emergency. When
the freezer malfunctions in mid-summer and there are no back-up parts,
valuable research projects can be lost or buildings may become unusable
due to high temperatures.

The economic risks of being out of stock vary inversely with order
quantity. If out-of-stock costs are important, it may be desirable to carry
more than the optimum inventory amount in safety stock. Safety stocks
of critical parts can provide a buffer to reduce the impact of variations in
lead time (the time between ordering and receiving inventory items) and
usage rates.

Summary—Balancing the Cost Tradeoffs   Some costs increase as
the order quantity and average inventory increase (holding costs), and
other costs decrease as the order quantity and the size of average inventory increase (ordering and out-of-stock costs). The optimum balance
between the two is known as the economic order quantity. Figure 15-7
illustrates the tradeoffs graphically. The vertical axis of the graph is
measured in dollars—the cost of having inventory. The horizontal axis
measures the order quantity of an inventory item. The curve sloping
downward to the right measures ordering and out-of-stock costs, assuming that acquisition costs are constant for all order quantities. The
curve that slopes upward to the right represents the various components
of carrying costs. The upper curve represents the sum of ordering and
out-of-stock costs and holding costs. The lowest point on this total cost
curve (Q*) is the optimal order quantity for the item under consideration.

Operational Efficiency

Since one of the goals of inventory management is operating efficiency,
it is important that the function be supervised and coordinated at a high
level within physical plant. Operational efficiency is affected by usage
rates, the type of inventory control system used, the degree to which
automation is employed, and inventory standardization.

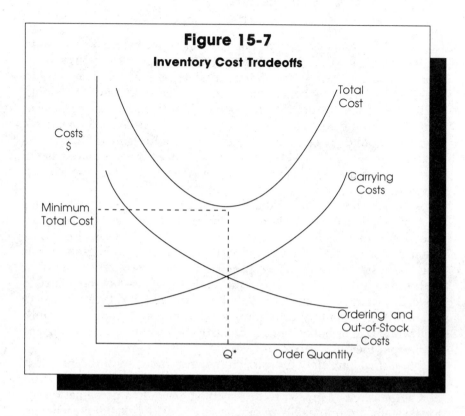

Figure 15-7
Inventory Cost Tradeoffs

Measuring Usage Rates   The most important variable in designing and implementing inventory control systems is the usage rate, or demand, for the items in question. Irrespective of the inventory control system utilized, it is impossible to calculate appropriate order quantities and reorder points without knowing item-by-item usage rates. The direct method for determining usage of an item is to record to receipts to and distributions from inventory as they occur. Usage rates can then be estimated from stores records.

It is possible to estimate usage where item-by-item issues are not recorded. The following formula can be used to determine usage rates: beginning inventory balance + purchases during the period - ending inventory balance = usage rate during the period.

This formula requires two inputs: a periodic physical inventory, and records that indicate the number of items purchased that can be inventoried. The purchasing department should be able to provide the data regarding the volume of purchases. While the initial work to establish usage rates for the many items used by facilities management can be formidable, it is possible.

Inventory Control Systems

Two-Bin System. In the two-bin inventory system, two bins are used for the storage of goods in inventory. The first, or primary, bin is used to store the order quantity less an amount determined to be necessary to meet usage during the item's lead time. The lead time quantity is stored in the second bin. In addition, the second bin may contain a safety stock, that allows for fluctuations in demand and variations in lead time. Items used as part of daily operations are drawn from the primary bin. When all the items in the primary bin have been used, an order is placed. Items are used from the second bin until the ordered quantity is received and the primary bin and secondary bins are replenished.

The advantage in using this kind of a system is its simplicity. It can be easily operated manually and requires only the most rudimentary knowledge about demand for the items being stored. Its use also avoids the need for maintaining detailed records. The disadvantages in using two-bin systems are that they produce no records of stock-on-hand, without a physical count. The result is that they are not very flexible under lead-time or demand variability, and make it difficult to detect unauthorized inventory withdrawals. A two-bin system does not work well with large or bulky items because of the need to segregate regular stock from the safety stock.

Perpetual Inventory Systems. Somewhat more sophisticated than two-bin systems, perpetual inventory systems provide more information at the cost of a greater record-keeping effort. In a perpetual inventory system, a running tally of purchases and sales is kept for each item stored. Figure 15-8 shows an example of the type of records maintained in such a system.

Perpetual inventory systems are also known as "min-max" systems. The records kept as part of the system allow for continuous balances of individual items to be known at all times. When the inventory balance reaches a predetermined minimum, an order is initiated by stores personnel. This minimum quantity consists of the expected demand during lead time and any safety stock. The maximum quantity that would be on hand at any point in time is, in theory, equal to the safety stock plus the order quantity. This amount may be determined based on the desired turnover rate for the item, taking into account the cost tradeoffs.

The perpetual inventory system requires a great deal of labor to maintain the necessary records for individual inventory items and a great deal of records storage space. A typical medium-sized facilities operation may require hundreds or thousands of items to be stored in inventory, and several filing cabinets for the records.

Economic Order Quantity (EOQ) Systems. The simple control systems

Figure 15-8
Perpetual Inventory System Record

STORES INVENTORY RECORD						
ITEM DESCRIPTION			STOCK NUMBER			
REORDER POINT		REORDER QUANTITY	LEAD TIME		UNIT OF MEASURE	
DATE	ACTION	PURCHASED	QUANTITY SOLD		ON ORDER	IN STOCK

described above can be enhanced by calculating reorder quantity using a formula known as the economic order quantity:

$$EOQ = \frac{2fS}{cP}$$

Where:
f = Cost of placing an order (ordering costs)
S = Annual usage rate for the item
c = Percentage that reflects the aggregate holding costs of inventory
P = Price per unit (assumed to be constant)

The economic order quantity formula is an attempt to incorporate the cost tradeoffs discussed previously into a calculation of the optimal order quantity for individual inventory items. Notice that the formula indicates that if ordering costs increase and all other variables remain constant, the EOQ will increase. Conversely, if holding costs increase the EOQ will tend to decrease. The economic order quantity formula should be used with caution, however, since it requires a great deal of data to calculate and makes several other assumptions. For example, the formula assumes that usage is constant and predictable, and that the purchase price is constant regardless of the quantity being purchased.

All of the systems discussed so far focus on individual items of inventory. Reorder points and order quantities are calculated one at a time. Aggregate inventory management systems focus on groups of items or the total inventory. They require a great deal of data and require several assumptions that must be tested before such systems can be used. More information about these alternatives can be found in the suggested readings at the end of this chapter.

Automated Inventory Control Systems. All of the systems described previously can be automated. While automation involves tradeoffs, it can reduce labor costs associated with record keeping and, more importantly, can provide improved information for decision making. Figure 15-9 shows an inquiry screen that provides important, on-line information about an individual stock item. Another primary advantage of an automated system is that it can be used to automatically generate a listing of items that are at their minimum stock levels or below. Information of this nature can be used to automatically generate order documents when reorder points are reached, or a stores staff member can manually create an order.

An important asset of automated systems is that they provide an electronic link between the facilities inventory and job cost accounting, or work order systems. Figure 15-10 is a document that, when data entry is performed, will automatically charge the appropriate work order number for the cost of items drawn from inventory. Figure 15-11 shows a specialized version of the inventory material ticket that can be used for custodial supplies.

Improved management reporting is a further advantage of automated systems. Figure 15-12 shows how data generated from an automated system can be used to generate information about inventory purchase, sales, and turnover activity in a decentralized inventory management system.

Automation is not without cost, however, and certain key elements must be present for it to be successful. First, there must be a felt need for automation by the staff members of the facilities management department. Nothing will doom a systems development effort faster than an unwilling group of users. Second, a structured systems development method must be used that collects and responds to input from all con-

Figure 15-9
Stores Inventory Status Report

STORES INVENTORY STATUS REPORT

02/21/89

PAGE- 36

PHYSICAL PLANT DIVISION

STOCK NO.	DESCRIPTION	U/M	CUR BAL	MIN BAL	MAX BAL	12-MO ISSUE	STK T/O	UNIT COST $	CURRENT INV VL $
03 046 0121	SWITCH, TUMBLER, 'JUNIOR QUIET SWITCH', FOUR WAY, 15 AMP, 120-277 VOLT, AC ONLY, IVORY, HUBBEL #1184-I	EA	5	2	5	4	0.75	6.187	30.93
03 046 0123	SWITCH, TUMBLER, DOUBLE POLE, INTER-CHANGEABLE QUIETTE, 15 AMP, 120-277 VOLT, BROWN, HUBBELL #1162, ARROW #QST-2	EA	4	3	5	4	0.86	5.151	20.60
03 046 0125	SWITCH, TUMBLER, DOUBLE POLE, INTER-CHANGEABLE QUIETTE, 15 AMP, 120-277 VOLT, IVORY, HUBBELL #1162-I, ARROW #QST-2-I	EA	4	3	5	0	0.00	3.640	14.56
03 046 0127	SWITCH, TUMBLER, 'QUIETTE' TYPE, SINGLE POLE, BROWN, 15 AMP, 125-277 VOLT, AC ONLY, A-H #189I	EA	57	45	90	107	1.62	3.434	195.73
03 046 0129	SWITCH, TUMBLER, 'QUIETTE' TYPE, SINGLE POLE, IVORY, 20 AMP, 125-277 VOLT, AC ONLY, A-H #1991-I	EA	43	30	60	235	4.36	6.097	262.17
03 046 0131	SWITCH, TUMBLER, 'QUIETTE' TYPE, THREE WAY, 20 AMP, 120-277 VOLT, AC ONLY, BROWN, ARROW #1993, HUBBELL #1223, LEVITON #5523	EA	14	10	20	31	1.46	5.857	81.99

Item	Description	Unit							
03 046 0133	SWITCH, TUMBLER, 'QUIETTE' THREE WAY, 20 AMP, 120-277 VOLT, AC ONLY, ARROW #1993-I, HUBBELL #1223-I, LEVITON #5523-I. IVORY	EA	11	10	20	40	2.87	4.061	44.67
03 047 0001	TAPE, FILAMENT, ¾" x 60"	ROLL	17	12	24	73	4.59	2.828	48.07
03 047 0006	TAPE, FRICTION, ¾" x 60"	ROLL	39	20	50	49	1.40	.889	34.67
03 047 0013	TAPE, ELECTRICAL SEMI-CONDUCTING EPR. SCOTCH 13, ¾" x 15'/ROLL	EA	47	10	20	9	0.39	2.942	138.27
03 047 0014	TAPE, ELECTRICAL SHIELDING BRAID, ALL METAL, OPEN WEAVE, SCOTCH #24, 1" x 15'/ROLL	EA	25	10	20	21	1.22	5.702	142.55
03 047 0015	TAPE, ELECTRICAL GROUNDING BRAID, FLAT TINNED-COPPER, SCOTCH #25, 1" x 15'/ROLL	EA	4	3	5	2	0.42	23.373	93.49
03 047 0016	TAPE, PLASTIC, ELECTRICIAN, #33	ROLL	334	175	350	547	2.35	1.372	458.24
03 047 0018	TAPE, 3M SCOTCH 23 ELECTRICAL TAPE, HIGH VOLTAGE	ROLL	121	80	170	237	2.43	3.692	446.73
03 047 0020	TAPE, CABLE PREPARATION KIT, SCOTCH #A-2	EA	11	5	10	16	1.88	4.265	46.91
03 047 023	TAPE, UNDERGROUND LINE IDENTIFICATION (BRADY #UT20-Y3, 3" WIDTH, 1056 FOOT LENGTH, YELLOW, NAED 63012	ROLL	6	1	6	8	2.34	29.485	176.91

Figure 15–10
Inventory Material Ticket

N⁰ S 30189

WORK ORDER # __W__

ZONE _____

SALES DATE _____

SEQUENCE NUMBER _____

	STOCK NUMBER					DESCRIPTION	FUNCTION CODE	UNIT OF MEASURE	QUANTITY SOLD	EXTENDED AMOUNT
1										.
2										.
3										.
4										.
5										.
6										.
7										.
8										.
						TOTALS				.

RECEIVED BY _____   ENTERED BY _____

Figure 15-11

Custodial Stock Order for Work Order

№ S 03411

WORK ORDER # _____   BUILDING _____

SHOP _____   CLUSTER # _____

DATE ORDERED _____   DELIVERY DATE _____

	STOCK NUMBER	ITEM DESCRIPTION	UNIT OF MEASURE	FNC	QUANTITY REQUESTED	QUANTITY ISSUED	EXTENDED AMOUNT
1							
2							
3							
4							
5							
6							
7							
8							
9							
10							
	12-13-179	SPRAY BOTTLE, PLASTIC	EACH				
	12-13-189	DUSTER HEAD, WEDGE, 101A	EACH				
	12-13-193	DUSTER HEAD, SPLIT	EACH				
	12-13-195	18" DUST MOP HEAD, BIG MIKE	EACH				
	12-13-199	24" DUST MOP HEAD, BIG MIKE	EACH				
	12-13-205	36" DUST MOP HEAD, BIG MIKE	EACH				
	12-13-221	16-OZ. WET MOP HEAD, RAYON	EACH				
	12-13-225	20-OZ. WET MOP HEAD, RAYON	EACH				
	12-13-229	24-OZ. WET MOP HEAD, RAYON	EACH				
	12-13-233	MOPSTICK 92	EACH				
	12-13-235	MOPSTICK 93	EACH				
	12-15-101	AMMONIA	½ GAL/CASE				
	12-15-103	BLEACH	GAL/CASE				
	12-15-104	BOWL CLEANER	GAL/CASE				
	12-15-131	TEMP. CLEANER	CAN				
	12-15-157	CLEANSER (AJAX)	CAN				
	12-15-158	CLEANER, AJAX CREAM	BOTTLE				
	12-15-171	GLASS CLEANER (CRYSTAL)	GAL/CASE				
	12-15-174	VINEGAR	GAL.				
	12-15-215	BAR SOAP (DIAL)	CASE				
	12-15-223	POWDER SOAP (BORAXO)	BOX				
	12-15-225	LAVA	BAR				
	12-13-279	TURKISH RAGS	BAG/POUND				
	12-13-277	GLASS RAGS	BAG/POUND				
	12-19-121	LINER, HIGHBOY WASTE CAN, 16x14x37	CASE				
	12-19-123	LINER, WASTEBASKET, 15x9x27	CASE				
	12-19-125	LINER, TRASH CAN, 29x20x48	CASE				
	12-19-127	LINER, LARGE TRASH CAN, EX HEAVY	CASE				
	12-17-101	TOILET PAPER	CASE				
	12-17-103	PAPER TOWELS, FLAT	CASE				
	12-17-104	PAPER TOWELS, ROLL	CASE				
	12-21-009	RUBBER GLOVES, SMALL	PAIR				
	12-21-010	RUBBER GLOVES, MEDIUM	PAIR				
	12-21-013	RUBBER GLOVES, LARGE	PAIR				
	12-15-122	GRAFFITI REMOVER	CAN				

TOTAL _____ _____ _____

OF LINES

OPERATIONS MANAGER _____   ENTERED BY/DATE _____

Figure 15-12
Automated Inventory System Reporting

Inventory Purchases, Sales, and Balances by Shop   Preparation Date:
For the Month of July

Shop Name	06-30 Balance	Purchases		Sales		07-31 Balance	Inventory Turnover Ratio August–July	
		Reporting Month	To Date	Reporting Month	To Date		Yearly	# of Days
Construction Stores	$189,888	$3,223	$3,223	($13,491)[1]	($13,491)	$179,620	1.35 X	271.37 days
Carpentry Shop	$9,022	$0	$0	($157)	($157)	$8,865	2.10	173.97
Paint Shop	$2,259	$164	$164	($437)	($437)	$1,985	5.24	69.67
Custodial/Grounds	$19,088	$2,948	$2,948	($5,487)[2]	($5,487)	$16,549	6.93	52.68
Sheetmetal Shop	$15,029	$0	$0	$0	$0	$15,029	0.54	671.27
Total	$235,287	$6,335	$6,335	($19,573)	($19,573)	$222,048	1.97 X	185.50 days

$222,048

Comments: 1. Includes inventory adjustment of ($2.95), to date inventory adjustment ($2.95)
2. Includes inventory adjustment of ($.12), to date inventory adjustment ($.12)

cerned parties, from individual workers to departmental users to the campus controller's office. Finally, the systems analysts assigned to the task should be familiar with facilities management operations in general, and must be willing and able to work with all facilities management staff members, utilizing a participative approach.

Basic Concepts

As discussed earlier, carrying inventory means that costs are incurred. As a result of these costs, it is in the best interest of the facilities management organization to minimize its inventory holdings, subject to meeting customer needs. Two ways in which inventory balances can be reduced include a program of standardization and negotiating with local suppliers to shift to them the responsibility for carrying inventory.

Standardization   Many college and university physical plant organizations face the difficulties associated with variations in types of building built over long periods of time. The result is many different types of building components, requiring a tremendous variety of repair equipment and parts. This has a direct impact on the total quantity of inventory that facilities management organizations must have on hand.

Facilities operations suffer other effects of a lack of standardization in building components. Training costs are increased because workers must be able to perform maintenance on many different kinds of equipment. A program of standardization is desirable. Engineering standards should be established for new construction and major repair and renovation. Preventive maintenance programs can help to identify building component types and make recommendations. Once the appropriate engineering guidelines have been established, the purchasing agent assigned to facilities management becomes the key to successful program implementation.

Shift of Inventory Responsibility   Many maintenance items are used at a stable rate, and the usage for such items can be forecast accurately. For these items, e.g., custodial supplies, it may not be necessary to carry large inventory quantities on campus. Rather, it may be possible to shift the responsibility for inventory management to the supplier by negotiating an appropriate delivery schedule. It may be possible to reduce the facilities inventory balance considerably by using this strategy. While the supplier will want to pass along its inventory carrying costs to the user, this approach may still be attractive. By working with the purchasing agent to review those items for which the usage rate is well known, and making the necessary delivery schedule part of the Request for Bid/Proposal criteria, it may be possible to relieve the facilities management operation of a considerable inventory management burden.

15.4 MATERIALS DISTRIBUTION SYSTEMS

The choices among the many alternatives for getting materials to the job site are determined by a number of factors:

- How large is the campus?
- How many vehicles does the facilities operation have available?
- How is physical plant organized? Do all workers operate from a central facility, or are they assigned to decentralized locations across campus?
- Is inventory storage centralized?

Alternative Distribution Methods

Pickup on a Job-by-Job Basis   The most common method of acquiring materials from inventory is a combination of picking up materials on a job-by-job basis and rolling stock. While workable, this can be very costly. If individual workers are given the responsibility for acquiring their own materials, the operation will suffer significant losses in productivity as a result of frequent trips to central stores, the possibility that a stockout for a needed item exists, plus time spent waiting in line.

Supervisory Involvement   The responsibility for acquiring materials for individual jobs should be assumed by the same supervisor responsible for work assignments and scheduling. The supervisor, before finalizing job assignments, can review inventory on hand to determine if materials are available to complete individual jobs. If so, that person needs to arrange for materials to be assembled and staged so that a worker can make one pickup of all materials needed for that day's work. If materials are not available, an order can be initiated and the job delayed until the necessary materials are received.

Rolling Stock   Rolling stock refers to items stored in vehicles for use by workers as needed. This distribution method offers a number of advantages, the principal one being its convenience for small, frequently used items. Rolling stock works particularly well for electricians, plumbers, and carpenters who commonly have such usage patterns. It is also effective in emergencies, allowing workers to pick up a vehicle and proceed directly to the job site.

Rolling stock should be used with caution, however. First, the method for replenishment of the stock must be controlled carefully so that unnecessary trips to stores are minimized. Second, the amount of materials carried in individual vehicles must not be allowed to become excessive. There is a tendency to carry so many items in a vehicle that it becomes useless for moving other items, such as specialty tools and components that are removed from their permanent locations for repairs. Finally, a well-developed method for charging the items to individual jobs or an overhead account must be established and monitored closely. Will all items moved to rolling stock be charged to an overhead account immediately, or will they be charged to individual work orders as they are used?

Taxi Service   If the facilities operation does not own many vehicles relative to the size of the work force, and if campus traffic patterns allow it, a taxi may be used to deliver materials to individual job sites. The use of a delivery van as a taxi for materials can work for many applications in which usage is easily predictable. Scheduling is a critical aspect of this distribution method and requires careful planning and monitoring to ensure that workers' and customers' needs are met.

Remote Storage   It may be desirable to establish remote storage locations for certain items. HVAC system filters, for example, may be stored in mechanical rooms to be used as needed. Light bulbs can be stored in individual buildings, if appropriate storage facilities are available and secure.

Remote storage locations can mean a loss of administrative control over the accounting mechanisms for charging items to cost centers, and procedures for monitoring usage must be established and monitored. In addition, judgment must be exercised to prevent remote storage of materials from becoming safety hazards. Finally, the security of these locations must be established and maintained.

Custodial Closets. These small storage areas provide a way to store the most commonly used items—cleansers, mopheads, and small quantities of toilet tissue and paper towels. Rather than acquiring these items from a central storage area each day, regular deliveries can be made to custodial closets to keep necessary items at the job site. Again, controls must be established to ensure that the costs of all items are allocated to their ultimate end use and that pilferage is kept to a minimum.

Grounds Field Storage. Particularly when workers are assigned to specific areas of the campus, it may be possible to establish small storage boxes or sheds for hand tools and small quantities of fertilizer, irrigation system replacement parts, and other items. This may allow workers to report directly to the job site at starting time rather than using time to secure needed materials.

The location of these storage areas must be planned carefully so that they are unobtrusive and secure. In addition, the usual caveat about cost accounting for these materials applies.

Construction Projects   Prior to the beginning of construction, storage locations for materials should be planned carefully and, for large projects, fenced and secured. If outside contractors will be performing the work, the contract should specify where and how materials will be stored and assign responsibility for managing materials to the contractor, if possible.

Supplier Delivery Services   It may be possible to negotiate delivery by materials suppliers directly to job sites. Campus accessibility to vehicular traffic will be a major factor in determining the workability of such an arrangement. Direct supplier delivery to job sites may complicate the receiving and accounting functions, and can probably be used most effectively when usage of materials is stable and predictable.

NOTES

1. National Institute of Governmental Purchasing, *The Dictionary of Purchasing Terms.* (Falls Church, Virginia: NIGP, 1986, p. 28).
2. National Institute of Governmental Purchasing, *General Public Purchasing.* (Falls Church, Virginia: NIGP, 1985, p. 3).

ADDITIONAL RESOURCES

Ammer, Dean S. *Materials Management and Purchasing.* Homewood, Illinois: Irwin, 1980.

Baker, R. J., R. S. Kheune, and L. Buddress. *Policy and Procedures Manual for Purchasing and Materials Control.* Englewood Cliffs, New Jersey: Prentice-Hall, 1981.

Bennet, Richard, ed. *Small Order Handling Guide.* Woodbury, New York: National Association of Educational Buyers, 1986.

Cohen, Herb. *You Can Negotiate Anything.*

Dobler, D. W., L. Lee Jr., and D. N. Burt. *Purchasing and Materials Management,* fourth edition. New York: McGraw-Hill, 1984.

Janson, R. L.. *Handbook of Inventory Management.* Englewood Cliffs, New Jersey: Prentice-Hall, 1987.

Leenders, M. R., H. E. Fearon, and W. B. England. *Purchasing and Materials Management,* eighth edition. Homewood, Illinois: Irwin, 1985.

National Institute of Governmental Purchasing. *General Public Purchasing*. Falls Church, Virginia: NIGP, 1987.

————. *Public Purchasing and Materials Management*. Falls Church, Virginia: NIGP, 1983.

Welzenbach, L. F., ed. *College and University Business Administration*. Washington, D.C.: National Association of College and University Business Officers, 1982.

CHAPTER 16

Risk Management

Raymond Degenhart
Budget Officer
University of Northern Colorado

16.1 INTRODUCTION

R isk is uncertainty concerning the probability of an occurrence—in the context of higher education, the occurrence of financial loss not offset by opportunity for gain. Such loss may include loss of or damage to property, loss of use of property, additional expense caused by such losses or by use of substitute property, loss of money or securities, employment-connected employee injuries, and monies legally owed to other parties because of bodily injury, other personal injury, or property damage arising from the operations of an institution. Each loss would include costs of investigation, adjustment, and claim defense.

A primary objective of a program of risk management is to identify and analyze loss potential and prevent the occurrence of loss to the maximum practical extent. Risk management is further concerned with funding predictable losses and financing risks undertaken but not predictable as to actual loss outcome. A program of risk management typically includes insurance, which is the sharing of risk of possible losses from specified hazards by a group of individuals.

The cost of risk management includes funding expected or predictable losses, financing risks and potential loss, preventing loss, and administering the program. A program employing techniques of risk management can be more cost-effective than a program limited to insurance purchase. The ultimate evaluation of a program of risk management is the degree of success in preventing personal injury and property loss, while reducing the cost of risk to a minimum.

The study of loss funding and risk financing principles and techniques is relatively new in higher education administration. The property insurance crisis in the late 1960s and early 1970s caused some concern about traditional methods of providing financial protection; this prompted evaluation of loss, risk retention, and self-insurance. The strongest impetus for study and evaluation resulted from the medical professional liability insurance crisis, the "wrongful acts" situation, and legal actions concerning discrimination, in the mid-1970s. Later, the general liability insurance market deteriorated, a situation aggravated by reinsurance problems.

Continuing crises promoted the growth of risk management education and sophistication among college and university administrators. Traditional insurance-buying approaches are, to some extent, being discarded and alternative approaches are being studied, tried, and adopted. New methods of retention, self-insurance (including captive insurance companies), and other funding and financing techniques are available to the risk manager. The cost of traditional techniques is making them impracticable, and in some cases old insurance sources and methods have disappeared.

16.2 STATEMENT OF POLICY

Every institution has a risk management policy, whether tacit or stated. Such a policy should be flexible and general enough to permit prompt response to unusual situations. It is best to have a written policy that states the risk management objectives and describes the responsibilities of the risk manager; this policy should be approved by the governing board. The policy serves to inform the governing board and the institution's officers of the limits within which the risk management program is defined and operates. The policy augments the effectiveness of the risk manager, and promotes efficiency of the function. A written policy should include the following: 1) a general statement of the need, purpose, and goals of the risk management program, 2) general information regarding the risks that are to be insured and those that are to be uninsured or self-insured, 3) a statement identifying the dollar level of risk retention per occurrence and the aggregate per year, and 4) a statement concerning the authority and responsibilities of the risk manager.

16.3 THE RISK MANAGER AND THE FUNCTION

In smaller institutions, the chief business officer is usually the risk manager. So many individuals in an institution are affected by risk management that the task of coordinating this function cannot satisfactorily be assigned, referred, or transferred from the chief business officer to another person except in a large institution. There, the function may warrant a specialist or even an entire department devoted to managing risk. In the latter cases, the risk manager typically reports to the chief business or finance officer, whether the manager's position is staff or line. The risk manager should have clear and open lines of communication with every department head. He or she should enjoy sufficient independence and authority, within the overall scope of risk management, to make effective decisions relating to identification and evaluation of risk, loss control and prevention, and avoidance, retention, and transfer of risk.

Risk management is an integral part of the financial management of the institution, so should most appropriately be assigned to the department with responsibility for fiscal affairs. Location in another administrative area adds a requirement for interdepartmental coordination between risk management and financial management.

The risk manager should be involved in the decision-making process in all functions relating to risk control: environmental health and safety, health physics (radiation safety), fire prevention, property protection, claims administration, and insurance. In addition, the risk manager should have ready access to the chief business officer.

16.4 IDENTIFICATION OF RISK

Whether the risk manager is the chief business officer or a specialist on the staff, identification of risk is the first task. A review of financial statements, property, and other records will indicate physical assets to be preserved, although an up-to-date evaluation for risk management purposes is often necessary. The manager and an agent or broker must be informed of new building plans and changes in space utilization. Accounting officers, legal counsel, physical plant directors, and academic administrators are among those to be consulted. Outside the staff are external auditors, insurance brokers, and insurance company specialists in various fields. The identification process is never ending; the lines of communication must be kept open, but the risk manager should exercise initiative to keep abreast of changes that might affect risk handling.

16.5 RISK CONTROL

Following are some established techniques by which risks may be controlled:

Avoiding Risk

A risk may be avoided by not accepting it or by not entering into a risk situation. This method has limitations because such a choice is not always possible, or if possible, it may require giving up certain advantages. However, in some situations risk avoidance is both possible and desirable.

Spreading Risk

It is possible to spread the risk of loss for both money and other property. Duplication of records and documents, with copies stored in separate facilities, is an example of spreading risk. A small fire in a single room can destroy many records.

Loss Prevention or Reduction of Risk

The adage, "An ounce of prevention is worth a pound of cure," provides a guide for the control of risk. Risk may be reduced, eliminated, or at least controlled by using a well-planned loss-prevention program.

Retention, Assumption, or Acceptance of Risk

These methods should be of particular concern to every institution. Constant vigilance is necessary to avoid unintentional acceptance of risk through unawareness of an exposure. Some risks must be retained because insurance for them cannot be purchased or because the cost of such insurance is not economically sound. Examples of risk that may have to be retained, assumed, or accepted are earthquake, war, flood, and accidental glass breakage. The importance and economic value of risk are reviewed in relation to the size of the institution's operations and the probability and severity of loss. These must be considered before accepting a risk.

Transfer of Risk to Insurance Carriers or Others

Risk may be transferred contractually to others. For example, when leasing facilities from others, the lease could require the lessor to assume all property and liability losses including departments, directors, officers, employees, and agents as additional insureds. Contracts to be entered into by the institution must be reviewed by legal counsel and, in some cases, the purchasing department. Only properly designated persons should sign contracts or obligate the institution through a written agreement. Many risks can and should be transferred to an insurance company. Such action reduces that part of the risk to a certainty—the amount of the premium (and deductible).

16.6 RISK FUNDING

Identified risks that cannot be eliminated or transferred by contract, must be deliberately noninsured, self-insured, or insured commercially. The risk management concept dictates that all three approaches—no insurance, total self-insurance, or retention through use of deductibles—be weighed carefully in light of the budget, peculiar financial needs, investment policy, and experience of the administrator. Before a decision is made among the alternatives, a careful analysis of risk, including a history of losses, is necessary. A decision for no insurance or self-insurance, without an adequate program of loss prevention or control, can be a costly error.

In a normal situation, glass breakage is a noninsured risk. Physical damage to vehicles and theft of movable equipment are other risks that might not lend themselves to insurance, depending on the cost and the loss history. The probability factor must be considered. This can be done by studying and analyzing the frequency and severity of past losses and then applying inflationary factors to those losses in order to predict what future loss experience may be.

Business interruption, long-term disability, worker's compensation, liability, direct property damage up to a given level, and limited crime loss may lend themselves to self-insurance. Self-insurance offers several advantages over not insuring. It produces a record of risk cost, including administrative cost, that is otherwise lost.

Self-insurance may be funded from the annual operating budget as losses are incurred or through reserves arising from appropriation or allocation of the institution's fund balance and adjusted from year to year, depending on the capability and needs of the institution. Generally acceptable accounting principles do not allow for the establishment of a reserve for self-insurance arising through charges to current year operating expenditures, since an identifiable loss has not, as yet, occurred. However, the allocation or appropriation of a portion of the fund balance as a reserve for self-insurance is permissible.

The level of self-insurance retention will naturally vary among institutions. A general guide is a self-insurance retention of one-tenth of 1 percent of total budget (or expenditures) per occurrence, with an annual aggregate retention of 1 percent of total budget (or expenditures).

Some states and institutions have examined the feasibility of pooling certain risks. A state may self-insure most risks and provide a self-insurance program to its entire college and university system. A combination of self-insurance and retention through deductibles may offer significant savings, but risk managers should carefully study such a program before adopting it.

16.7 SELF-INSURANCE

Self-insurance requires the establishment of reserves for losses, the charge of premiums to subsidiary units to support the reserves, systematic accounting for losses, and loss prevention and claims control services. The insured acts as its own insurance company. Traditionally, self-insurance has been considered to be most valid in a relatively stable and predictable area of losses, where the aggregate level of self-insurance exposure can be capped by excess catastrophe insurance that is purchased commercially. In such an arrangement, the area of self-insurance operates as a funded deductible to commercial insurance.

In the past, the use of self-insurance was restricted largely to property and worker's compensation exposure. Some institutions are now considering some form of self-insurance program for liability risks.

Advantages of Self-Insurance

1. Reduced premium costs resulting from the elimination of low-value, high-premium units from commercial insurance policies.
2. Reduction in commercial carrier administrative costs by eliminating high-frequency, low-severity claims.
3. Reduction in internal administrative costs by eliminating the need for written and oral communications with commercial carriers, reduction in the number of coverage and claim-supporting documents, and simplification of record keeping.
4. Flexibility in coverages and claims handling.
5. Retention of premium dollars and investment income and, in the case of worker's compensation and liability, retention of reserves for losses until losses are actually paid.
6. Elimination of commercial insurance carrier profits, premium taxes, and agents' or brokers' commissions.

Disadvantages of Self-Insurance

1. Loss of cost stabilization—the spread or risk among many insureds—that is provided by commercial insurance premiums.
2. Administration and expense of an "insurance company" within the institution, which may not be desirable.

3. Possibly less objective claims handling (where personal bias can affect settlements) than by commercial companies.
4. Claims-handling complaints arising against the institution rather than against an insurance carrier.
5. Possibly less efficient subrogation and collection from other parties at fault.
6. Possible lack of integrity of self-insurance loss reserves.
7. Difficulty in charging unfunded claims to government indirect cost recovery system.

Where an exposure is not a deductible but is totally self-insured without a cap of commercial insurance, other disadvantages occur.

8. Possibly less effective inspection and loss-prevention services.
9. Poorer planning because of loss of insurance-carrier engineering information as used in new construction and remodeling.
10. Less effective efforts to keep administrators and supervisors loss-conscious because of insurance-carrier absence.

Keys to the Successful Administration of a Self-Insurance Program

1. Written policy—It is essential that self-insured protection be defined with insuring agreements, conditions, and exclusions so that it will be understood by all parties and so that arbitrariness in claims handling can be avoided.
2. Adequate reserves—Funds must be available to cover both normal, expected losses and unexpected losses to the extent of the agreed-on level of coverage-per-loss and to the aggregate.
3. Integrity of reserves—Self-insurance coverage exists only to the extent of the loss reserves. Accumulated reserves must be inviolate from invasion of purposes other than the self-insurance program. Ideally, interest on invested reserves would be retained within the reserves, and a self-insurance premium charge formula would be developed to insure the adequacy of the reserves and provide for the administrative operating expenses of the program.

Self-insurance as a loss-funding mechanism has taken on significance in areas where its use was formerly considered inappropriate. These new areas include general liability and medical professional liability. The primary reason for this development is that commercial coverage has become unavailable, or unavailable within familiar premium frameworks.

Self-insurance is not suitable for all institutions. Some simply are not large enough, do not have sufficient reserves or endowment, or have inadequate loss-prevention programs. There may also be difficulty in persuading an institution's officers to use risk assumption as a means of risk control. In addition, each institution must be aware of limitations on the use of self-insurance for educational and medical facilities because of accountability, cost distribution, and other regulations developed by federal agencies such as the Financial Accounting Standards Board, the Cost Accounting Standards Board, Medicare, and others.

16.8 CAPTIVE INSURANCE

A self-insurance program can be formalized into a "captive" insurance company, which is a device used to fund losses and finance risks of the organizing parent enterprise or enterprises. In the strictest sense, a captive is a wholly-owned insurance subsidiary designed solely to insure the parent's exposures. It is a formalized self-insurance program operating as an insurance company, meeting the same legal requirements as any other insurance company organized within the same jurisdiction. Variations include insurance companies formed by groups of individuals, organizations, trade associations seeking to mutually solve a common exposure problem, and senior captives established originally to serve only the needs of the parents, but further developed into organizations insuring the risks of others as well.

In the formalized, self-insurance concept, a captive would be formed for direct underwriting of the parent's risks, for the purchase of stop loss and aggregate excel loss insurance, and for the purchase of excess or reinsurance (this is sometimes not included). In practice, all university captives at this writing have used the fronting approach, whereby a conventional insurance company licensed to operate within the parent's jurisdiction issues an insurance policy and provides loss prevention and claims-handling services. The parent pays a premium directly to the fronting insurance company. The latter then purchases reinsurance from the parent's control. The cost of such a program includes a fronting fee based on the original gross premium, the expense of financial guarantees to cover the full exposure of the fronting carrier, and the expense of any other required services not provided by the fronting company.

The reasons why a college or university may form a captive include:

- Coverage for exposures not insurable in the commercial markets.

- Broader, more flexible, and more permanent coverage than is available commercially.
- Possible lower cost of insurance protection.
- Integrity of self-insurance reserves.

It usually is far easier to obtain excess coverage over a self-insurance program if it has been formalized into a captive insurance company, especially if it is fronted by an established commercial carrier. Further, the reinsurance and excess markets are directly accessible to a captive, where they would not ordinarily be so to a self-insured.

Whether or not a college or university uses the fronting approach will be governed largely by the insured exposure itself. Worker's compensation and automobile liability are statutory and must be insured by a domestically licensed carrier in all jurisdictions. Reimbursement of medical malpractice premiums, depending largely on federal regulations, may be more secure in a fronted operation, although the applicable regulations are not clear.

Captives have been established in many states and in foreign countries. Factors to be considered when deciding on a site include:

- Ease and speed of formation of the captive.
- Capitalization requirements.
- Tax rates, if any.
- Regulation of premium rates.
- Reserves and investments.
- Amount of paperwork required.
- Flexibility in underwriting.
- Participation in guaranty funds (if required).
- Assigned risk pools and FAIR plans (Fair Access to Insurance Requirements: the federal government provides riot reinsurance to insurance companies that participate in FAIR plans).
- Availability of necessary professional services.

At this writing, Colorado offers the greatest captive formation incentives among the states. Some foreign locations (off the East Coast) offer attractive incentives: lack of taxation; excellent communications; free currency convertibility; low capital and surplus requirements; flexible underwriting ratios; lack of language problems; and economic, social, and political stability. Proximity and accessibility place Bermuda and the Cayman Islands at the top of the foreign-site list.

It should be emphasized that sound reasons must determine the establishment of a captive, and that sound insurance and risk management principles must govern its operations. The captive must serve the risk management needs of the parent and control must not be surrendered to anyone outside the parent organization. Ideally, the university risk manager would serve as president and chairman of the board of the captive. Other directors should be chosen from institutional areas that can be of assistance to the risk manager, such as legal, investment, and loss prevention.

As with self-insurance, the captive program is not suitable for every institution. Formation of a captive requires careful analysis and study; there are legal requirements and implications (which vary by state and charter), tax consequences, and liability and financial considerations that must be addressed before making the decision to form a captive.

16.9 INSURANCE

In managing risk by insurance, each member, or policyholder, within a group agrees to pay a portion of the losses suffered by other members of that group. In that way, the annual cost of such contingencies to each policyholder is reasonably predictable. At the same time, uncertainty is removed about having the higher costs of individually assuming the results of a catastrophe. The larger and more widespread the risk-sharing group, the more mathematically predictable are the anticipated losses in any given period.

In exchange for the benefits gained by spreading the risk among many individuals, the policyholder must pay a share of the estimated cost of catastrophes predicted to occur to members of the group during a future period, as well as the appropriate share of the operating costs of the organization.

Several factors affect the amount of insurance premiums. The total amount collected in premiums must cover 1) anticipated claims for losses of policyholders during a designated period, determined on mathematical and statistical bases; 2) operating expenses of the company; 3) agents' commissions; and 4) any amounts retained by the company or paid to stockholders. The total cost is reduced by earnings on investment of reserves and other funds of the insurance company.

No insurance company escapes the economics of this formula. Lower costs to educational institutions can be realized only by purchasing insurance from companies that operate economically. Companies that have selected risks wisely and that have held down operating expenses may offer satisfactory protection to colleges and universities at minimum cost. Insurance should be purchased on the basis of these factors—not because of friendship, patronage, or reciprocity.

16.10 AGENTS AND BROKERS

Although agents work on behalf of insurers and brokers work on behalf of insureds, the terms are used synonymously in this section. The largest insurance volume on a national scale is placed through agents and brokers, and indeed, some of the largest insurance companies will underwrite risks only through an agent or broker. There are advantages in dealing with an agent or broker having available within his or her organization marketing skills, as well as claim and loss prevention engineering services that can be used directly or coordinated with an insurance company.

Agents and brokers traditionally have been compensated by a commission paid by the insurance company, which varies with the line of insurance. This is changing. More brokers are willing to perform services for a specified fee on large accounts, rather than to rely on commission. In smaller institutions, the percentage commission is undoubtedly a fair means of compensating the broker for his or her knowledge and skill. The risk manager must determine in each instance what the commission amounts to and whether fair services are received for the money spent. It is important to learn all the services that an agent or broker has to offer in order to request those that are desired.

To assure serious and efficient consideration of the specifications by the carriers, it is suggested that a limited number of qualified brokers be invited to market the portfolio. This affords effective competition and, since professional services are essential to the entire process, it is not inappropriate. Selecting brokers to compete is an exacting process. A demonstrated interest in the account, scope of services offered, and experience and qualifications of personnel are important considerations. Proximity of a service office is desirable. If possible, the broker should know something about a similar institution's risk management and insurance problems. Finally, the broker should demonstrate familiarity with the concepts of risk management.

From time to time, any insurance program should be reviewed by one of several methods, such as peer review by risk managers at similar institutions, or by an independent consultant. Some institutions operate on the assumption that they have a lasting broker relationship, which dictates that the broker participate in designing specifications and solicit all proposals from insurance companies.

16.11 THE CONSULTANT

On occasion, the use of an independent insurance or risk management consultant may be desirable in order to obtain knowledge to suit special needs and for the objectivity that a consultant can give a client. A consultant's income is derived entirely from fees, resulting in freedom from influence caused by the placement of insurance coverage. Tasks that may be performed by a consultant include: 1) audits to determine the adequacy of insurance coverage and whether costs are reasonable, 2) designing of a risk management program, and 3) special studies such as those involving preparation of specifications, evaluation of proposals, self-insurance, staff resources, appraisal of a risk manager, and pooling or captive insurance.

Fees may range from $35 to $90 per hour or more. In most cases, a maximum fee will be quoted, to which will be added any out-of-pocket expenses. A few firms work on a percentage of savings; however, many believe this may not be entirely professional since it places heavy emphasis on cost rather than on coverage, service, and other factors that could be more important.

16.12 THE UNDERWRITER

The insurance company's decision on accepting the risk and on the price to charge is the function of the underwriter. Although many types of insurance are priced from a manual, it is generally true that there are numerous variables or credits possible. The underwriter's analysis of the risk is an essential point; in many instances he or she receives information from the agent or broker or, in the case of a direct writing company, from a salesperson. It is desirable to invite the underwriter to the institution, as a full understanding of the local situation is valuable.

16.13 CONSIDERATIONS IN SELECTING A COMPANY

The relationship between an institution and an insurance company should be long-term. Assuming that the quality of service is satisfactory, an accepted minimum guideline is three to five years of continuous coverage before testing the market. Different timing could be appropriate, depending upon market conditions.

For the large insurance purchaser, competitive positions between stock insurance companies and direct writers, including many mutual companies, probably are indistinguishable. A thorough survey of prospective companies by the insurance purchaser or broker should include direct writing and mutual companies. Brokers have access to these types of firms as well as all others, even though mutual companies do not pay a commission. It is anticipated that the purchaser will pay a fee to the broker for his or her services if a company other than one offering a commission is selected.

Another school of thought suggests competition among agents and brokers as well as insurers. This generally requires that the specifications be designed by the institution. Sometimes this complex job is best done by a consultant. Design of specifications should produce a clear, insurance-term description of coverages desired. These specifications should enable production of proposals that may be compared fairly, and yet should be flexible enough to permit an innovative insurer to do the best job possible. Insurers should be required to present a comprehensive illustration of services to be provided, by whom they will be performed, and what personnel are present at each servicing location.

To facilitate a service-after-the-sale inquiry and to evaluate familiarity with the field, it is not out of order for any insurer not previously known to the institution to name other institutions of higher education serviced by that company. Price and breadth of protection are critical factors. In view of market cycles (restricted markets or a highly-competitive environment) it may be desirable to include a provision that the bidding arrangement may require the right to negotiate. In addition, there may be a need to specify the extent or limits of markets to be explored.[1]

Adequate time should be allowed from issuance of specifications until proposals are due. This should be at least thirty days, and up to ninety days if the risk is large and complex. It is best to allow at least a month to evaluate proposals.

16.14 PUBLIC BIDDING

Public bidding is designed to eliminate corruption in the purchasing process and to prompt the acquisition of coverage at the lowest available cost. As permissible by public law, selection should be based on the bid having the best match of cost to coverage and services to be provided, credentials of the bidder, not solely on price. The objectives of public bidding can be frustrated by several factors.

- Many colleges and universities package numerous coverages under a single bid. Since the final premium cost of many items of insurance is based on audits during the term or after expiration, the bidding may be looked on as a quote of what deposit premium costs will be. To the uninitiated or to the careless reviewer of quotations, a bid may be accepted because it is attractively low. Yet when the final audit is made, a higher net cost could result from this low bid than that from other, more completely prepared initial quotations. In other words, a quotation may be unrealistically low because it represents merely a deposit against future audit.

- Public bidding does not necessarily produce the lowest available cost. Often contract changes are needed during the policy term and require negotiations with the carrier. If there has not been continuity with the market source over time, these negotiations can be difficult and costly.
- In a public bidding situation, the large, full-service agencies with facilities to provide the broad range of services needed by an educational institution may not be available. This may happen because, in open bidding, a single carrier may submit identical bids through a number of agencies representing the full spectrum of the capability and the desire to provide services. The pressures of local politics may favor an agent who cannot provide full services. If permitted by law, this may be prevented by the qualification of a limited number of agents and the assignment of markets.
- Public bidding at each renewal period has an upsetting effect on the market. Every carrier is well aware that it may win this year but lose next year over a relatively insignificant difference in premium cost. This leads to reluctance of carriers over time to be aggressive in preparing quotations. Some may submit only token bids. Further, the risk manager may have difficulty in establishing a satisfactory relationship over a period of years with a single carrier or agency.
- Availability of reinsurance can be, and often is, restricted as insurance markets collide in the uncoordinated search for coverage. Some reinsurers may withdraw completely.

Classifying agents according to ability and desire to provide needed services may be difficult, but well worth the effort. Instead of a broad public bidding program, it may be more appropriate to select a limited number of agents who can perform best to meet the institution's needs. In this way, the institution can be sure that the agency has the capabilities and services needed, in addition to responsible insurance and reinsurance markets will be available for its use.

16.15 PROPERTY INSURANCE

In general, insurance coverages should be thought of and discussed in terms of the types of risks. The two major divisions are property insurance and liability insurance (including worker's compensation).

Most institutions are insured by fire, lightning, and extended coverages for replacement value of buildings and contents. This represents the total cost to repair, rebuild, or replace on the same or another site with new materials of like kind and quality. Extended coverages usually include damage caused by wind, hail, some explosions, smoke, riot, civil commotion, and vandalism. Other coverages may be included for an additional premium.

In the event of loss or damage to property that is not repaired, rebuilt, or replaced, recovery is usually limited to the extent of actual cash value (ACV), or replacement cost less depreciation, rather than replacement cost value. Some institutions insure all property for actual cash value, although their number is declining. Many institutions now arrange for their property insurance to cover replacement cost (new for old); that is, the insurance recovery is not depreciated.

The inadequacy of fire and extended coverage policies becomes evident when other property perils are considered, such as earthquake, flood, water damage, or collapse. A difference-in-conditions (DIC) policy can be negotiated to cover these and other perils. It is wise to cover all risks of physical loss by DIC, without specific, named perils.

Building and Content Valuations

Valuation of institutional property is difficult, especially on a building-by-building basis. There is frequent shifting of contents from building to building, acquisitions, new construction, and demolition. Traditionally, financial reports have shown original construction or acquisition costs. These reports are of little value to the risk manager, whether coverage is on a replacement or an actual cash value basis. The risk manager may wish to have a complete appraisal made as a basis for a statement of property values, updated each year by increased value factors. It is essential that the risk manager be notified promptly of any acquisitions, dispositions, and demolitions, and of any remodeling or alterations that would affect property values substantially. Where possible, there should be coordination of existing records and consideration should be given to maintaining automated records of insurable values. Institutions with frequent or continuing construction projects may wish to include builder's risk coverage in basic property policies, and an automatic acquisition clause would be valuable in covering new properties.

An agreed-amount clause (where losses are paid in proportion to the amount insured) is considered essential, thereby eliminating any penalty that might be assessed if a policy has an average or coinsurance clause.

Additional components of the property insurance package may be transit insurance, covering merchandise and purchases while in commercial movement, and other types of floater (or movable property) coverage on institutional assets, either in movement or on premises. College or university property located off-campus should also be covered; this could include art objects on loan, property in storage, or gift properties. Special property insurance is available on data processing systems and can apply to both hardware and software coverage, which refers to processing loss as a result of direct damage.

Deductibles

The deductible amount of an insured loss is that portion borne by the insured before he or she is entitled to any recovery from the insurer. The deductible may be for each loss, an annual amount of losses, or a combination of both. The purpose of the deductible is to eliminate relatively small and frequent losses from insurance coverage. The business officer should carefully appraise the ability of the institution to fund loss through increasing deductibles. As large a risk as is feasible should be retained, based on history of loss, present efforts at loss prevention, and market requirements. Sometimes premium savings may be possible for a relatively small increase in the deductible.

16.16 BOILERS, PRESSURE VESSELS, AND MACHINERY

Colleges and universities use a wide variety of pressure vessels and machines, from which loss can occur through accidental bursting or breaking. Although these accidents rarely happen, they have great loss potential, and are therefore excluded from most property insurance policies. Boiler and machinery insurance, a specialty contract, was developed to overcome this deficiency. To avoid confusion and assure smooth settlement of losses, boiler and machinery coverage should be coordinated with the insurer used for property coverage.

The primary purpose of boiler and machinery insurance is to prevent loss. Thus, its inspection service is as important as its indemnity function (approximately one-third or more of the premium goes toward loss prevention). The value of inspection services is enhanced by the statutory inspection requirement of most states.

Boiler and machinery insurance generally covers the following:

- The insured's property.
- Expediting expenses.
- Property damage liability.

- Bodily injury liability.
- Defense and legal services.

Additional protection against indirect losses also may be purchased. These involve the loss of use or occupancy, spoilage, and power outages both at the institution and at any public utility serving the institution.

A contract of this kind will be technical. To insure adequate handling of the coverages, a risk manager should seek expert advice, such as that of a boiler engineer underwriter or outside consultant. A generally accepted practice is to delete the coverages for liability as well as for property already protected under a fire policy and extended coverages. Although the savings may be small in relation to the total premium, it is unwise to duplicate coverages.

Finally, the concept of maximum loss potential is an important guide in setting limits. Due in large part to good inspection services, boilers are subject to low-loss frequency. However, when occasional loss does occur, it is likely to be of serious magnitude. Protection should therefore be the kind in which a certain loss (a deductible) is substituted for an uncertain loss (exposure beyond the insurance coverage). As a result, it is preferable that boiler and machinery contracts include a high limit of coverage above a high deductible. The machinery coverage may include such items as electrical equipment and distribution systems, utility systems, air tankers, air conditioning, motors, and furnaces.

16.17 LIABILITY INSURANCE

In recent years, the market for conventional forms of liability insurance policies has become more restricted and premium costs have increased substantially as the size and variety of liability claims increase. Some institutions have therefore assumed part of the risk through self-insurance programs or large deductibles.

Changes in state laws have affected colleges and universities. An example is legislation, passed by some states, that limits the amount that can be collected in a claim resulting from negligence. At the same time, the traditional concept of sovereign immunity for public institutions has become eroded. Even in most of those states where institutions still enjoy statutory immunity from suit, employees can be sued. It is imperative that individual faculty and staff members be protected from litigation directed against them. All liability policies should contain an endorsement prohibiting the insurance company from invoking the defense of immunity without specific written consent.

The chief purpose of liability insurance is to protect the institution from liability imposed by law for bodily or other personal injury or damage to property. Legal liability normally results from negligent acts or omissions. A comprehensive general liability policy offers the broadest protection and can be tailored to fit the needs of colleges and universities. Certain extensions of coverage are essential. One such extension is contractual liability on a broad-form basis. This protects the insured from liability assumed under a contract other than a lease of property, which is already covered under the basic liability form. Extensions of coverage include protection for owned and nonowned automotive liability risks, products liability, and liability arising out of construction projects. Another extension is the personal injury endorsement, which provides coverage in such areas as libel, slander, and false arrest. Professional liability and errors and omissions coverage should be strongly emphasized; these coverages may be a part of an institution's comprehensive general liability policy or may be written separately.

Insurance companies may insist on writing the medical professional liability as a separate policy. This coverage should have a specifically worded definition of the insured to include all employees in the hospital, medical school, and allied health professions as well as the students in these schools while they are completing their clinical experience. If the medical school has a clinical practice plan for the medical doctors, those activities that generate income that is returned to the medical school should be covered by the institution.

The errors and omissions coverage should extend to all professional employees of the institution, including architects, engineers, lawyers, and fringe benefit counselors. Usually a separate endorsement is necessary to provide this coverage. Extreme care should be taken to make sure that the insurance company provides a written commitment that the policy covers professional errors and omissions outside the medical area. There is some confusion within the insurance industry itself as to what should be done to properly provide this coverage.

There are two new areas of concern involving liability insurance. One is the need of independent institutions for fiduciary liability protection for those employees who administer pension and welfare plans and benefits. The Employee Retirement Income Security Act of 1974 (ERISA) imposes strict requirements on the trustees of pension plans. Public institutions are exempt from the Act at this writing, but many are complying on a voluntary basis.

The second area of concern is protection for the trustees or regents for any wrongful acts they may have committed in that capacity. A special policy called Trustees Indemnity or Directors and Officers Liability has been designed to meet this need. The coverage may be extended to all institutional employees. Existing general liability insurance may cover the directors and officers, but such insurance is limited to bodily injury and property damage; the special policy referred to above would cover claims such as suits by faculty members whose contracts are not renewed, students who are expelled, donors who claim their gifts were mismanaged, and others.

Other types of liability insurance that may require the purchase of separate or special coverages include owned and nonowned aircraft; airports; watercraft; nuclear reactors or special nuclear materials; broadform coverage for property of others while in the institution's care, custody, or control; fire legal liability for leased premises; liability of use, sale, or distribution of liquor; and overseas operations. Punitive damages may not be insurable in every state but, wherever possible, coverage for such damages should be included in the institution's liability policies.

16.18 UMBRELLA LIABILITY

The umbrella policy is often regarded as the most important device available to the risk manager. In its best form, it provides excess coverage over underlying liability policies, including all the terms of those underlying coverages, as well as protection covering liabilities that underlying policies do not cover, usually subject to a deductible of $10,000 or more. High limits provide protection against catastrophic legal actions, and a wider range of coverage is available.

If an umbrella liability policy is to indemnify, it is important that a pay-on-behalf-of endorsement be added to prevent a situation in which the institution would be required to pay a large claim and then be reimbursed by the carrier. A following form agreement or endorsement should be used to make sure that the umbrella policy is not more restrictive than the underlying primary coverages.

If primary coverage contains aggregate limits, it is advisable that an umbrella provide further primary coverage after primary policy limits have been exhausted. Depending on institutional policy and financial resources, the risk manager may wish to have umbrella coverage include defense costs in the absence of primary coverage as well as defense costs after primary limits are exhausted. It is important that the anniversary date of the umbrella policy coincide with the anniversary dates of underlying coverages. Wherever possible, exclusions such as "care, custody, and control," professional services, and oral contractual obligations should be deleted.

Worker's Compensation

Each state requires an employer to indemnify an employee against certain types of losses resulting from a work-connected injury. Some consider this a staff benefit, but most authorities agree it more closely resembles liability insurance in terms of its financial effect on the institution.

This effect varies with the benefit level of each state. In some jurisdictions, such as California, New Jersey, and New York, the financial effect of compensation liability can be substantial. Many larger institutions now partially self-insure this risk. Even in those cases where self-insurance programs are maintained, it is wise to reinsure upper-level liability for catastrophic losses.

When an institution chooses to insure its entire liability, several forms are available. For the smaller institutions, the manual rates are applied to the payroll. The premium is set by experience of similar employers in the state. Larger institutions may secure experience-rated policies. These contrast the individual institution's experience over a three-year period with similar employers and provide a credit or debit factor to manual rates. Larger institutions that do not self-insure generally find it advantageous to insure under a retrospective rating plan in which roughly 20 percent of the experience-rated premium is retained by the insurance company. The balance of the premium is determined by the actual claim payout, modified by certain additional charges for claim cost and taxes; thus, an institution pays its own way.

All such plans have a maximum annual premium. The 20 percent retention includes the cost of pure insurance for exposures that the insurance company cannot pass back to the policyholder in the retrospective premium plan. For an institution large enough to qualify for a retrospective plan, this is usually an excellent vehicle for securing the proper credit for a good safety program and other efforts aimed at curtailing employee injury.

In some jurisdictions, a state monopoly is the only source of insurance. This form of insurance is regulated carefully everywhere. Still, it is essential that experts be employed to evaluate the most advantageous plan for a given institution, and the insurance company best able to furnish the invaluable loss-prevention engineering and claims services must be a part of the worker's compensation program. This protects both the institution's finances and the rights of employees to prompt and fair treatment after injury. Many compensation insurers operate in only one state and due to efficient, specialized operations, offer substantial dividends to selected policyholders. This coverage deserves complete investigation, since worker's compensation often represents a significant cost.

It is important that possible endorsements to the compensation policy be evaluated. Examples of these are voluntary compensation endorsements, all-states coverage for employees subject to a jurisdiction outside the state of primary work, foreign coverage for faculty members who may be abroad, coverage under the Jones Act, longshoremen and harborworkers' compensation program, or federal maritime jurisdiction.

Defense Base Act Insurance (DBA)

The section on worker's compensation insurance under provisions of the Defense Base Act of the United States, Public Law 208, 77th Congress, as amended, requires that:

1. The contractor shall provide and maintain worker's compensation insurance as required by the Act with respect to, and prior to, the departure for overseas employment under this contract of all employees hired in the United States, are U.S. citizens, or are bona fide residents of the United States.

2. The contractor shall provide compensation benefits for all employees who are nationals or permanent residents of the country in which services are being rendered (if the contract authorizes their employment), pursuant to the applicable law of such country for injury or death in the course of such employment, or the employer's liability insurance in the absence of such law. For all other authorized employees not hired in the United States or who are not U.S. citizens or bona fide residents of the United States, the contractor shall provide the necessary employer's liability insurance.

The Act discusses various insurance claims. The "liability to third persons" clause is of major concern to colleges and universities having contracts with government agencies covered under the provisions of the Act. The Agency for International Development (AID) is the chief government unit concerned with this clause, but other government agencies also may require it. The clause provides that the contractor must procure and maintain worker's compensation insurance, employer's liability, comprehensive automobile liability (bodily injury and property damage) insurance in connection with the performance of the contract in amount of form required by the contracting officer. Self-insurance programs may be approved. Self-insured worker's compensation programs must be qualified under statutory authority.

16.19 CRIME INSURANCE

Careful attention should be given to covering all employees to prevent financial loss due to their activities. Two basic types of policies, Comprehensive 3-D (dishonesty, disappearance, and destruction) and Blanket Crime are available. A brief description of the two contracts follows.

The comprehensive 3-D policy differs from a blanket bond in that it does not provide a single amount of insurance to cover loss from any insured hazard, or any combination of hazards. Instead, it has eighteen insuring clauses, with a separate amount of insurance and a separate premium for each. None of the coverages is mandatory and the insured may carry protection under any or all. The first five are printed in the policy form and the others can be added by separate endorsements.

Division of the comprehensive 3-D policy

1. Fidelity insurance.
2. On-premises coverage.
3. Off-premises coverage.
4. Money orders and counterfeit paper currency coverage.
5. Depositor's forgery insurance on outgoing instruments.
6. Forgery insurance on incoming instrument.
7. Burglary coverage on merchandise.
8. Paymaster robbery coverage.
9. Paymaster broad-form coverage.
10. Burglary and theft coverage on merchandise.
11. Warehouse receipts forgery coverage.
12. Securities of lessees of safe-deposit boxes coverage.
13. Burglary coverage on office equipment.
14. Credit card forgery coverage.
15. Extortion coverage.

The blanket crime policy is a package contract that, with a single, overall limit, provides five major crime coverages.
1. Fidelity insurance.
2. Premises coverage.
3. Outside coverage.
4. Money orders and counterfeit paper currency coverage.
5. Depositor's forgery insurance.

The contract closely resembles the 3-D policy, differing in two important ways: 1) the blanket crime policy is written at a single limit of liability, while the 3-D policy establishes separate limits for each of its insuring agreements, and 2) the blanket crime policy may be written for as little as $1,000 (subject to the applicable minimum premiums from the appropriate sections of the burglary and bond manuals). The minimum permissible amount of fidelity coverage under the comprehensive 3-D policy is $10,000. Separate policies or bonds providing some or all of the features of the blanket crime policy may be purchased as excess over the initial policy.

These policies, including their limits of liability, must be tailored to the needs of the institution. This requires careful scrutiny by financial officers, auditors, and the agent or broker.

16.20 UNEMPLOYMENT COMPENSATION

When an employee is dismissed without being at fault, he or she is entitled under law to unemployment compensation benefits. In part, this is intended to discourage unnecessary expansion and contraction of staff and can be costly if not well-managed. Students usually are not covered; faculty contracts should be so written that faculty members with contracts for teaching in the subsequent fall are not eligible to claim unemployment compensation benefits during the summer months.

Management of this risk dictates prudent personnel practices, especially in larger institutions, which may be laying off employees in one department while hiring in another. Close coordination and rethinking of the economics of some summer layoff practices are necessary. Careful documentation of discharge for cause is elementary in controlling this risk. Funding generally permitted includes either reimbursement to the state for actual benefits paid to former employees or payment of a payroll tax, which is usually experience-modified. Thoughtful but prompt attention must be paid to each claim for unemployment compensation when notice is received from state employment offices.

For institutions having low-employee termination, significant cost savings may result from self-insurance through reimbursement to the state for actual benefits paid. In addition, some institutions have determined through feasibility studies or by using consultants, that self-insurance is a less expensive method of funding this risk.

16.21 STUDENT ACCIDENT AND HEALTH INSURANCE

Many institutions have a program to provide such group insurance to its students. It may be mandatory or optional. In a few instances, student groups administer and purchase such coverage; in others, the institution itself directly purchases the coverage on behalf of its students. Many innovations are being made in the type of insurance coverage available in this complex, competitive market. The choice varies with the amount spent and the size of the institution.

Statistics is the key to effective student health insurance. The agent or broker handling this coverage should provide detailed claim statistics for joint analysis of the price structure. This insurance usually is written on a low company overhead compared to liability or property insurance and has all the advantages of mass-merchandising economies. It behooves the institution, on behalf of its students, to make sure the price is fair.

16.22 OTHER INSURANCE

Business Interruption   Insurance to cover both lost income and continuation of salaries in the event that buildings, contents, boilers, or machinery are damaged or destroyed, thereby resulting in curtailment of part or all of the institutions activities.

Extra Expense   Coverage for the extra expenses incurred (above normal operating expenses) to continue operations in the event that property or equipment is damaged or destroyed. These expenses would include overtime payments, temporary rental of facilities, auxiliary equipment, and others.

Builder's Risk   Insurance to cover buildings during course of construction. Such coverage should be arranged to include the insurable interest of the owner, contractor, and subcontractor.

Valuable Papers and Records   Coverage of the cost to restore the damage to, or replace the loss of, papers and records. Usually, a general property policy will cover the cost of blank paper and transcribing, but not the cost of redevelopment of the information in institutional records. A microfilm program (with copies stored in a separate building) could be better protection than insurance.

Accounts Receivable Insurance   Coverage of damage to or loss of accounts receivable that results from the inability to collect on receivables in the event that records cannot be reconstructed.

Miscellaneous Bonds   Examples of the types of bonds institutions may require are notary, performance, and payment bonds provided by contractors for construction projects, tax-free alcohol users' bonds, and post office operators' bonds.

Nuclear Risks   Radioactive contamination insurance, available for covering the cost of decontaminating buildings and controls, and nuclear pool coverages for both property damage and liability exposures for institutions that own or operate nuclear reactors or that use special nuclear pool coverages for both property damage and liability exposures for institutions that own or operate nuclear reactors or that use special nuclear materials, as defined by federal agencies.

Travel Accident   Should be provided for faculty and staff while they are traveling on business for the institution.

Athletics Insurance   Covers accidental death, dismemberment, disability, and medical insurance provided for athletes, cheerleaders, and band members. Such insurance should include protection for travel, play, and practice.

Personal Automobile and Homeowner's Insurance   Made available by some institutions or their credit unions to faculty and staff on a payroll deduction basis.

16.23 SUMMARY

For humanitarian, social, legal, and financial reasons, an institution must make every reasonable effort to protect the health and safety of the campus community and the public from any hazards incidental to its operations. Colleges and universities must protect their resources against possible losses, thus assisting accomplishment of the goals of providing instruction, research, and public service.

To meet these objectives in a cost-effective manner, a professional risk management program is required. Following are the necessary steps to control risks:

- Identify and appraise all risks.
- Estimate the probability of loss because of risks.
- Select the optimum method of treating risk, that is avoidance of risk, spreading risk, loss prevention or reduction of risk, retention, assumption or acceptance of risk, or transfer of risk to insurance companies or others.

- Implement a plan to carry out and monitor the selected methods of treating risks.

For many institutions, self-insurance may be a less expensive way to fund certain risks; nevertheless, insurance programs continue to play a vital role in protecting an institution's resources.

Care must be given to selection of an insurance company intermediary and the competitive marketing of an institution's insurance. Coverage is best bought on the broadest possible basis after the assumption of maximum risk. Insurance may be grouped into property coverages, liability coverage (including worker's compensation), crime coverage, and insured benefits.

For further information or assistance, contact the University Risk Management and Insurance Association.

NOTES

1. Further information on insurance companies may be obtained by consulting *Best's Insurance Report: Property-Casualty* or *Best's Insurance Report: Life-Health*, published by the A.M. Best Company, Inc., Oldwick, New Jersey.

SECTION IV

FACILITIES OF

HIGHER

EDUCATION

Section Leader:
Herbert I. Collier
Director of Physical Plant
University of Houston

CHAPTER 17

Classification of Facilities

Rex O. Dillow
APPA Member Emeritus
Columbia, Missouri

17.1 INTRODUCTION

Many factors have combined to shape the facilities of higher education today, including changing enrollment patterns which necessitate flexibility in functional use, proliferation of codes and standards, increasing operation and maintenance costs, and austere funding. These factors often conflict with the overriding requirement that facilities satisfactorily serve the mission of the institution. Facilities managers are continuously faced with the need to meet this requirement economically and effectively with available funds. The collective studies in meeting this responsibility have brought higher education facilities management to a new high as a unique and distinctive profession. They have also promoted close coordination with the industrial sector in developing new technologies and methods.

The first three sections of this manual pertain to the supporting functions of administration, personnel management, and fiscal management; the last three sections address the construction, maintenance, and operation of facilities. This section describes the various components, equipment, and systems that constitute the facilities of higher education. It is intended to give organization to the vast variety of facilities and to describe their purpose and basic functional characteristics, and to compare alternatives when appropriate. Their construction, operation, and maintenance will be addressed in the final three sections.

17.2 SCOPE AND ORGANIZATION

In addition to the campus infrastructure of roads, walks, lighting, street furniture, and other such features, higher education facilities can be grouped into three broad classifications:

1. The *buildings*, which must provide a suitable, safe, and healthful environment for carrying out the assigned functions.
2. The *central plants*, which convert fuels to energy, and energy to different utilization forms.
3. *Utility distribution systems*, which transport utilities from central plants, or from where purchased utilities are received into the college or university system, to the building or point of utilization.

17.3 BUILDINGS

Modern buildings can be compared roughly with machines; the building shell of roof, floor, walls, windows, and doors keeps out the elements and provides insulation, while the mechanical and electrical systems provide an interior environment for carrying out the assigned functions. Building heating and cooling systems must be designed to add or remove heat from all building spaces at the rate it is lost or gained. The type of construction, including the insulation, directly influences the design capacities of the heating and cooling systems. Meanwhile, the interior of a building—including floor covering, walls, lighting, and furniture—must be designed to be aesthetically pleasing, functional, durable, and maintainable.

Heating is provided most often by the delivery of a heating media from a central plant to a building system, although heat pumps and building boilers are not uncommon, especially in the more moderate climates. Cooling may be provided by a building air conditioning system, or by the delivery of a cooling media from a central plant. A variety of building HVAC systems are available, each with distinctive characteristics and applications.

Building electrical systems are designed to provide the right amount of current at the right voltage to the point of utilization, with protection from fire and accident and with built-in flexibility for changing requirements. The building electrical system extends from the low side of transformers, after reduction to utilization voltages. The growing use of ever more sophisticated electric and electronic equipment continually raises new requirements, such as for stable voltages.

Many college and university buildings house processes that require the maintenance of special environmental conditions and special measures for the removal of toxic or inflammable vapors. Meeting these requirements requires special equipment and special considerations in the design of the building heating, cooling, electrical, and fire protection systems.

Building fire protection equipment is governed largely by codes and standards, which are based on occupancy and construction classifications. Since most college and university buildings are people-intensive and frequently house highly combustible materials and processes, strict compliance must be given to the installation and maintenance of the required fire protection equipment.

Chapters in this section describe the types of building construction, building interiors, and mechanical and electrical systems. It is important to note that virtually all energy purchased by a college or university finds its ultimate end use in the buildings' mechanical and electrical systems.

17.4 CENTRAL PLANTS

Many colleges and universities have had central heating plants for several years. Most came into existence because coal was the available fuel, and it required special facilities for handling, storage, burning, and disposal of the residue. The concentration of this bulky, dirty, and noisy operation in one large plant separated from the rest of the campus met an obvious need. The growth in central plants in recent years has been due to three quite different factors:

1. The greater efficiencies of central plants. The vast increases in energy use and unit cost have given emphasis to energy efficiency. Central plants, though costly to construct, generally realize greater efficiencies, especially through cogeneration and the balancing of electric and thermal loads through the year.
2. The more demanding standards for building interior environments, which can be better met by removing industrial equipment, such as boilers and air conditioning equipment, from the building.
3. The increasingly stringent emission standards, which can be met more efficiently and economically in a central plant.

Many plants built before the mid-1970s did not have maximum attainable efficiencies. All components are very expensive, and many technologies that previously were not cost-effective require periodic re-evaluation.

Nowhere is there a greater education gap, a difference between the technologies taught in colleges and universities and the up-to-date knowledge of specialists, than in central plants. Chapter 26, Heating and Power Plants, and Chapter 27, Central Chiller Plants, are designed to enable facilities managers to better evaluate efficiency improvement and stack gas clean-up options, and to more effectively discuss systems and equipment modifications with consultants and manufacturers.

17.5 UTILITY DISTRIBUTION SYSTEMS

Underground heat distribution systems are assemblies of one or more fluid-carrying pipes to convey a given quantity of fluid from one point to another without undue fluid leakage or loss/gain of heat. Over the years, many capable people have devoted a lot of time and effort to this requirement—with questionable success. An underground heat distribution system has a lot going against it:

- Unfavorable economics. Underground systems are very costly, resulting in frequent compromising of sound engineering in order to hold down construction costs.
- Hostile underground environment. All systems are exposed to underground water, and this promotes corrosion and destroys the insulating properties of most materials. In addition, soils, especially where disturbed during installation, can settle and shift, putting additional structural loads on underground equipment.
- Difficulty in conducting timely maintenance due to the relative inaccessibility of most components.

Electrical distribution systems deliver power from central plants (or where received into the college or university system, in the case of purchased electricity) to the low side of building transformers. These systems must deliver the power safely, reliably, and economically. Economics require an optimum balance between current, transmission voltage, and the sizing of conductors and other transmission equipment. The growth in building electrical equipment increases the consumption of electric power. This in turn requires frequent reevaluation of the distribution system's efficiency. The chapters on heating and cooling media distribution and electrical distribution systems describe the type of systems and equipment that are available to meet distribution requirements.

17.6 SUMMARY

This section is intended to provide a comprehensive understanding of the types and characteristics of the facilities of higher education, to which all physical plant functions must be oriented. A knowledge of these facilities will in itself assist in decision making; but its primary value is in a better understanding of the facility construction, maintenance, and operation processes in the last three sections of this manual.

CHAPTER 18

The Campus Infrastructure

Frederick W. Mayer
University Planner
The University of Michigan

18.1 INTRODUCTION

In a recent study of entering college freshman conducted by the Carnegie Foundation, it was reported that

> The appearance of the campus is, by far, the most influential characteristic during campus visits, and we gained the distinct impression that when it comes to recruiting students, the director of buildings and grounds may be more important than the academic dean.[1]

It is clear that in addition to the normal aesthetic, cultural, and psychological values associated with an attractive environment, there are hard, practical reasons for devoting special attention to the physical appearance of the campus. In addition to attracting students, a physically attractive campus can contribute significantly in recruiting outstanding faculty and staff members, and certainly plays an important role in alumni support and fund-raising. Thus, the quality of the physical environment of the campus has a direct relationship to the ongoing operations and fundamental mission of the university. Furthermore, in many communities the campus itself serves as a focus for community life and a point of pride for the residents of the municipality that plays host to the university. As such, it is a positive force in the area of town-gown relations and one which can help promote a positive interaction between the two. Therefore, the quality of the physical campus environment is an issue in which the university should be prepared to invest a reasonable level of intellectual and economic capital.

When one thinks about the quality of the built environment, one naturally tends to think first about the architecture of the individual buildings. To be sure, this is a significant aspect of the campus setting, but the issue of environmental quality goes well beyond the mere matter of architectural design. The word "campus" derives from the Latin word for "field," indicating a concern with the area between the buildings and the interrelationship between them as opposed to the actual design of the buildings themselves. Over the years, the popular image conjured up by the word "campus" is one of green lawns and tall shade trees surrounding a series of buildings related to one another in a rational manner, all contributing to a harmonious and aesthetically pleasing environment.

It is true that a most attractive environment can be created by careful attention to the landscape and plant materials and other site design elements, even on a campus characterized by mediocre buildings. No matter how great the architectural statements may be, if they are set in an environment of chaos with scarce or unattractive landscaping, the overall result will not be pleasing. Thus, if one is sincerely committed to the creation of a physically inviting campus environment, it is necessary to pay as much attention to the spaces between the buildings and to the nonarchitectural elements of campus design as it is to the architecture of the individual buildings.

It is to these nonarchitectural elements of campus design that this chapter is devoted. It attempts to provide the appropriate university decision makers with the information they need to direct the development and operation of a successful system of campus infrastructure. It identifies the issues to be considered when addressing the various areas discussed, and identifies the resources available to solve problems or to develop appropriate proposals for each element of campus infrastructure. It is not an attempt to recommend individually "best" solutions in each area, nor to provide a design handbook for professionals undertaking the actual development of the various elements; there is no one "right" solution. Campuses vary in terms of climatic conditions, campus traditions, organizational patterns, and intellectual philosophies, and the right solution for one campus will not necessarily be the right solution for another. Options always exist, and the best one will vary from place to place. An understanding of the issues involved and the resources available should enable the decision maker to arrive at an intelligent and effective decision for each area that must be addressed.

The Importance of the Master Plan

The starting point for the development of any system of campus infrastructure should always be the master plan. This is the document that sets forth the basic guidelines for providing continuity in the overall development of the campus. Specific elements of campus infrastructure must be developed in a manner consistent with the overall objectives of the master plan if they are to contribute to the development of coherent and consistent environmental expression. No matter how good an individual element may be, if the campus becomes a chaotic mixture of unrelated elements, the result often will be the exact opposite from what one sought to achieve in the design and selection of the elements themselves. The importance of continuity and compatibility in the evolution of the overall campus environment cannot be overemphasized. Each individual decision must be related back to the fundamental principles set down in the master plan in order to assure compatibility and consistency.

However, the master plan provides only the basic framework and guidelines that must be followed in the development of a system of campus infrastructure; few master plans go into great detail on the design and selection of individual elements. Therefore, many individual decisions will have to be made by plant and planning administrators in developing and implementing a coherent system of campus infrastructure. The following discussion seeks to identify the major areas of concern which must be faced, to outline some of the key issues relating to each particular area, and to identify resources available to develop appropriate solutions in each case.

18.2 CIRCULATION

An efficient and effective system of circulation is an absolute necessity for the proper functioning of any campus. The basic concept for such a circulation system should be spelled out clearly in the master plan. The general elements of vehicular, pedestrian, bicycle, and other circulation systems should be defined in their general principles and established as a basic pattern on which to build. Detailed decisions, however, will have to be made on a day-to-day basis as various elements of the system need to be implemented, upgraded, expanded, or redone. In attempting to deal with these specific issues, professional assistance should be employed. For example, traffic and parking consultants can provide valuable information in areas such as capacity, utilization, signalization, and general analysis of system problems and solutions. In addition, civil engineers have considerable expertise in the design of roadways, walks, and drainage systems.

Some specific issues that need to be addressed when designing a circulation system are as follows.

General Vehicular Circulation

This system provides access to campus for general vehicular traffic via a regional circulation system and allows it to circulate to major destinations (particularly parking structures and major campus arrival points) via a campus circulation system. It also may be used by service and delivery vehicles and by mass transit vehicles. The system often takes the form of a major peripheral circulation ring, with secondary roads onto the campus to allow access to various major destinations (see Figure 18-1).

Service and Delivery Access

This system often utilizes the general vehicular system, but it also provides additional designated service drives and service dock areas to allow delivery and service vehicles to appropriately access the campus.

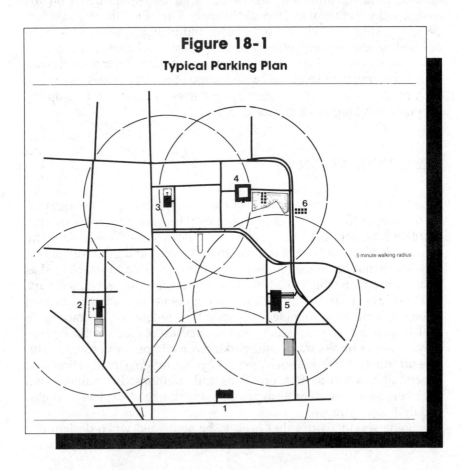

Figure 18-1
Typical Parking Plan

Mass Transportation

As with delivery and service vehicles, mass transportation often makes use of the general vehicular circulation system, since it is primarily provided by means of buses. However, exclusive bus lanes sometimes are employed, as are other forms of mass transportation such as monorails and jitneys. Penetration is crucial for the success of mass transportation systems.

Pedestrian Circulation

One of the most significant aspects of movement on campus is pedestrian flow to and from the campus and between buildings. This is accomplished by a system of pedestrian walkways that both parallel the major roadways and serve interior areas of the campus to connect major destinations such as parking structures and major academic facilities. Specific aspects of walkway design will be addressed later in this chapter.

Bicycles

The bicycle is a popular form of transportation on campus and must be accommodated in the circulation system. In many cases, bicycle circulation is combined with either walkway or vehicular circulation systems, through designated lanes or simply by providing additional capacity in the right-of-way. In some cases, specifically designated bicycle circulation paths have been created, and bicycle transportation is treated as a separate circulation system.

18.3 PARKING

Perhaps no area of the physical campus environment generates more complaints and more dissatisfaction than the parking system. Therefore, it is extremely important that a rational system be conceived by the institution stating the policies to which the system must respond; the system then must operate within those policies. Transportation and parking consultants can be extremely valuable in the definition of the system and in analyzing the consequences that flow from it. However, the decisions as to the nature of the basic system will have to be made by the institution. These decisions include such things as:

- Population to be served (faculty and staff, students, visitors, or patients).

- Type of management system (zone parking, reserved spaces, or a combination).
- Financing mechanism (self-supporting, subsidized, or a combination).
- Method of providing spaces (surface lots versus structures).

In addition to automobile parking, consideration must be given to providing appropriate parking for motorcycles and other nontraditional vehicles.

Finally, appropriate parking must also be provided for bicycles on the campus. The challenge here concerns the form of storage, the number of spaces required, and their appropriate distribution throughout the campus. Racks, shelters, or lockers are available options, and within the general category of racks, a variety of types are available. In general, the simpler racks are the best, and moving parts should be avoided in exterior use. Racks are most efficiently grouped near building entrances and other destinations where people wish to change from the bicycle mode to the pedestrian mode. But they should be located in areas where there is a high level of safety and security and where the bicycles can be viewed from inside adjoining buildings.

The type of parking solution chosen can have a major impact on the character of the campus (see Figure 18-2). There are serious tradeoffs involved in the use of land for buildings, parking, or open space and plazas. Nothing can do as much harm to the physical appearance of a campus as a decision to utilize large areas of campus land for surface parking, or to convert small bits of open space to surface parking as demands present themselves.

18.4 CAMPUS PLACES

Campus places are the major open spaces that play a significant role in shaping the campus image in the mind of faculty, staff, students, and visitors. They take a variety of forms:

Open Spaces

Open spaces are the natural green spaces where landscape is the dominant element. Open spaces provide the major elements of landscape image that characterize the campus. They can be characterized in one of several ways.

Natural Areas   These may be open space preserves around the edge of the campus, arboreta, botanical gardens, gorges, river edges, or other

Figure 18-2
Alternative Parking Solutions
Top: Urban Setting; Bottom: Rural Setting

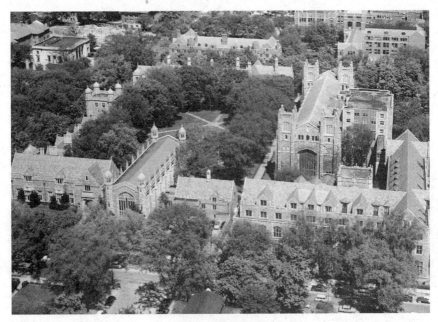

Figure 18-3

A Classic Academic Quadrangle

major natural features encompassing the campus. They often are left in a natural state and require less intense maintenance.

Visual Areas   These are more formal and highly maintained green areas such as the interior of quadrangles, courtyards, or malls that retain a predominantly green and landscaped image.

Recreational Areas   These are the playing fields, golf courses, or other forms of natural open space areas used in conjunction with athletic and recreational activities.

Plazas

Plazas are campus open spaces that are subjected to heavy pedestrian traffic and are characterized by hard surfaces. They often are associated with major campus destinations such as the library, the student union, or major academic buildings.

Malls

Malls are organized along a long, linear, axial pattern and tend to provide structure on many campuses. They may take the form of a landscaped alleé or a hard surfaced esplanade but they serve to provide powerful, organizing spatial elements.

Linkages

Linkages are the smaller spaces that serve to connect the major places on campus. They are often little more than passages between buildings or minor forecourts to building groupings. Linkages play an important role in maintaining the continuity of visual images between the major spaces and deserve careful treatment in the development of the campus.

18.5 PAVING AND HARD SURFACES

The specific design of individual campus plazas, major open spaces, or circulation systems is best left to professionals such as planning and landscape architecture firms for the design aspects and civil engineers for the technical aspects. These professionals are well-equipped to execute attractive and functional designs for such areas, and their advice should be sought in the design of any major campus space. A number of key issues must be addressed while designing hard surface areas.

Figure 18-4
Campus Walkways

Materials

A wide variety of materials are available, and each has certain characteristics that should be considered.

Stone   This most elegant of the materials available provides a highly attractive walking surface and works well with traditional architecture, particularly Gothic or Colonial buildings. It is, however, the most expensive of the options and the most difficult to install. Stone requires major care and maintenance, particularly in areas where winter ice and snow is a problem, but it has a long life expectancy. Stone often can be used in conjunction with other materials such as concrete to highlight building entrances or major gathering places on the campus.

Brick   Brick has many of the same characteristics as stone in terms of its attractiveness and compatibility with traditional architecture. It is also a relatively expensive material, but like stone it can be used effectively in combination with less expensive materials such as concrete. Brick is a relatively long-lasting material and if properly installed will outlast most of the less expensive paving materials.

Precast Pavers   These are made of less expensive materials such as concrete or asphalt and are shaped to produce attractive patterns that are normally associated with brick or stone paving. They can be obtained in a variety of colors and shapes and tend to be a reasonable compromise between the more elegant brick and stone materials and the less expensive concrete or asphalt.

Concrete   A less expensive material than the modular units referred to earlier, concrete can be poured in place and positioned in such a way as to achieve relatively good control in terms of drainage and design continuity. Concrete is appropriate in formal campus areas and often is used in conjunction with brick or stone in large paved areas.

Asphalt   Like concrete, asphalt is a relatively inexpensive material often used on normal walking surfaces as well as streets and parking lots. Edge control and grading with asphalt is more difficult than with other materials, and this can lead to deterioration at the edges of the walks or drives and uneven drainage. This in turn can cause ponding, which creates unsafe icy conditions in cold climates. Higher quality asphalt paving can be obtained by using edging or curbing and more stringent control measures, but this increases the cost of the installation. Asphalt walks are particularly compatible with natural areas and in less formal areas of the campus.

Wood   While boardwalks rarely are used except in swampy areas or botanical gardens, wood decking and seating areas often are employed in conjunction with recreation buildings or in housing areas. Treated lumber, which is now widely available, makes the cost and life expectancy of wood decks quite attractive.

Gravel   This is a traditional walkway material in English quadrangles and is sometimes employed on American campuses, particularly in building complexes endeavoring to duplicate the character of English quadrangles. Gravel has a low initial installation cost, but often requires a high level of maintenance to keep it looking attractive and free of weeds.

Bark Chips   Shredded or chipped bark often is employed in natural areas to provide walkways through woodlands, botanical gardens, and arboretums. It also is used in conjunction with playground equipment. It is inexpensive to install but requires constant refurbishing in order to keep it attractive and functional.

Size

Walkways on college campuses must accommodate large numbers of students utilizing the walks at the same time (the ten-minute break period between classes). The five-foot walk that is common along city streets is not adequate to handle the loads imposed by a campus. An eight-foot walk provides a comfortable minimum width for snow removal in northern climates, but wider walks often are necessary along main circulation routes.

The exact dimensions required must be determined on the basis of the individual campus population and movement patterns, but it is important not to undersize walkways on the campus; adjacent lawn areas will bear the brunt of a poor decision. By the same token, roads must be sized to accommodate the vehicular traffic demands placed upon them.

Placement

The appropriate location of walkways and roads on campus is essential in providing access to major campus destinations. Basic guidelines for the placement of walkways and streets should be a part of the master plan, but many minor decisions will need to be made, such as whether to place walks adjacent to the curb or maintain a green planting strip between the walk and the curb.

These questions should be studied carefully with design professionals in order to arrive at an appropriate decision for the individual campus. The proper location of walkways and roads has major implications in terms of the overall maintenance impact on the campus, and therefore on the visual appearance.

Intersections

College students tend to take the shortest distance between two points; therefore, walks that intersect with sharp points and narrow angles often result in worn-off corners that provide constant maintenance headaches for the grounds department. Proper design of the walkways should allow for natural pedestrian movement or provide a protective device (such as curbs or seat walls) to separate the walking surface from adjacent landscaped areas.

Scoring

Proper scoring of walkways and other hard surface areas not only provides attractive patterns and designs for the surfaces themselves, but is essential to control cracking and settling of the materials. A well-engineered scoring pattern is not only a structural necessity, but can be designed in an attractive way that enhances the campus.

Drainage

It is extremely important that walkways and roads be properly drained so that people do not have to trudge through mini-lakes on their way from one campus destination to another. This is of particular importance in northern climates where poorly drained areas are likely to freeze in the winter and produce hazardous icy surfaces.

18.6 LANDSCAPE[2]

No other single element plays as important a role in the development of a positive campus image as the landscape. Mature trees and well-maintained lawns provide a sense of permanence and quality. Plants are invaluable on campus because of their attractiveness and because they often can solve design problems more easily and less expensively than architectural solutions. Trees and lawns should be employed whenever possible since their use is flexible and they have comparatively low maintenance and natural aesthetic value.

Figure 18-5
Landscaping

Vegetation issues on campus include:

- Maintenance. Plants should be chosen for minimum mainte-nance. Zones can be established so that high-visibility areas re-ceive more intensive maintenance than low-visibility areas. Careful consideration must be given to the type of maintenance appropriate for each plant species. Proper plant selection and design can significantly reduce maintenance.
- Physical Conditions. Careful consideration of the soil and cli-matic conditions is necessary in the selection of plant species. Species prone to disease or insects should be avoided or used sparingly.
- Security. Issues of security must be considered in any planting design. Visual access should be maintained in areas immedi-ately adjacent to circulation routes, and large masses of tall ev-ergreens in housing areas can cause problems.
- Circulation. Movement can be regulated, reinforced, and clari-fied with vegetation.
- Microclimate. When used correctly, vegetation helps regulate wind, create shade, decrease runoff, and establish "sun pock-ets."
- Aesthetics. The general appearance of the campus can be greatly improved by the appropriate use of plant materials in the institutional setting. The best effects are achieved when plants are used with boldness and simplicity. When chosen for form and seasonal color, plants enhance year-round interest and appeal.
- Education. Whether established separately or incorporated into the overall campus landscape, an arboretum on campus pro-vides plant specimens for study and research and for attracting wildlife.
- Historical context. Vegetation used on campus provides histori-cal associations. The history of the campus or the region can be recalled by preserving remnants of groves and mature or his-torically significant trees, and by using native plant materials. Plantings also may be used as memorials to significant people or events in the institution's history.

Use of Plant Types

Various plant types, such as deciduous and evergreen trees and shrubs, ground covers, and vines are suitable for different areas and can be used to perform specific functions on campus. Careful consideration should be given to the intention of any new planting. The plant type should then be carefully chosen.

Deciduous Trees   Deciduous trees, together with buildings, should provide the framework for the campus image. While other elements die or are removed, deciduous trees and architecture age gracefully, providing continuity in the design. Deciduous trees have a transparency at eye level which emphasizes spatial continuity and conveys a human scale. They also provide a canopy or "roof" for the exterior of the campus. Careful spacing can express the character of the site, and impart a consistency between the tree pattern and the surrounding order. Deciduous hardwood species can be used throughout the campus wherever physical conditions (soil and drainage) meet their requirements.

Evergreen Trees   Evergreen trees can live as long as deciduous trees but function differently in a design. They have an opaqueness rather than transparency at eye level which makes them more useful as backdrops to other features or as focal points. They function well in groups at the edge of campus where their stiff forms can be appreciated from a distance, and where they will not create dense shade and security problems. They provide winter color and, when used among several rows of vegetation, are valuable as part of a windbreak. They also can be used to screen unattractive views or features.

Evergreen and Deciduous Shrubs   Shrubs can be used to organize pedestrian routes and play a supporting role for trees in campus design. They can reinforce entrances and focal points and enhance small spaces. From both a maintenance and safety standpoint, shrubs work best in masses or hedges rather than as individual specimens. Dwarf shrubs eliminate many pruning and security problems, while larger ones can be used in much the same way as dwarf trees to provide scale, fragrance, and seasonal color.

Annuals and Perennials   Flowers provide a highly attractive splash of color that is greatly appreciated by students, staff, and visitors. Annuals may require complicated and continuous maintenance to keep from looking neglected; perennials require less continuous care and only need to be divided occasionally for optimum growth. Many perennials are taller than annuals, and often are more suitable for larger institutional settings because they are more noticeable from circulation routes. Annuals can be used in front of the taller perennials and in large planters (five to ten feet long) for the greatest visual impact. These should, however, be concentrated in a few highly visible areas in order to minimize maintenance. The use of mulch in these areas also will decrease maintenance.

Ground Covers   Grass is the best ground cover for general use on campus. Modern mowing equipment makes it unnecessary to replace grass with other ground cover species in most areas. Allowing grass and wildflowers to grow tall in wet or swampy areas reduces maintenance and the need for costly drainage systems while adding variety and color to the landscape. When allowed to evolve naturally, these areas also attract wildlife and are valuable for use by the academic units as a teaching and research tool. Broadleaf evergreen ground covers are best planted in deeply shaded areas where grass will not grow, and in raised planters under trees where they will add color and interest and eventually end the need for weeding. They also can be useful on slopes too steep for mowing. Invasive ground covers such as crownvetch should be limited to remote areas such as drainage ditches, where they can spread without crowding out other desirable vegetation.

Vines   Vines are commonly associated with a college image. They often are used to cover large unbroken expanses of masonry and brick or to unify incompatible styles of architecture and building materials by providing consistency of color and texture. Vines require pruning and nonclinging ones need strong trellises. Clinging vines can sometimes accelerate the deterioration of masonry.

Institutional versus Residential Design

Careful consideration should be given to the appropriateness of any new design. Many plant species used in a residential design are not appropriate in an institutional setting because of their small size, short life spans requiring frequent replacement, disease susceptibility, and high maintenance requirements. Though attractive, annuals commonly are overused on campus. They are short-lived, and often too small for the campus setting. Annuals also require vast amounts of intensive maintenance time (planting, watering, weeding, and fertilizing) that could be better spent on more valuable vegetation such as trees. When correctly chosen, perennials are a viable alternative because of their larger size and easier care. Structures such as railroad ties and oak barrels, which look attractive at home, are too informal and visually inappropriate for the formal campus setting.

18.7 CAMPUS FURNITURE

One of the major physical design challenges facing the university is how to create a consistent image for the campus—a design continuity that ties together the various parts of the campus and which distinguishes it as a unique element within its larger community environment. Considerable attention has been focused on how some of the major building blocks of the campus can be utilized to further this overall environmental design objective. Subjects such as continuity of architectural style or materials and of landscape elements have been examined in great detail by both professionals and laypersons who are involved in the overall development of the campus. Less attention, however, has been focused upon the smaller elements of "campus furniture" that are necessary for the proper functioning of all campuses but that all too often are acquired and placed in an uncoordinated, haphazard fashion. Items such as waste receptacles, benches, and lighting standards often contribute not to a sense of design harmony on the campus, but rather to a sense of aesthetic chaos.

Many campuses have endeavored to tackle this problem by developing a unified system of campus furniture based on well-formulated design criteria. The nature of materials utilized and the design solutions selected vary from campus to campus depending upon differences in climatic conditions, student lifestyle, campus traditions, budget, and maintenance requirements. But the existence of a conscienciously developed, well-designed system of campus furniture is of great importance.

Again, the starting point for the development of any system of campus furniture should be the master plan. This document will set forth general campus design objectives that should be applied in selecting individual elements of campus furniture. It should address the crucial subject of how the elements should be placed on the campus and related to other design elements, such as buildings, walks, and roads. The predominant architectural material on the campus or the architectural style may influence the choice of individual items of campus furniture, as will external elements such as walkways and plazas, tree masses, and open space. This fact can be capitalized upon and strengthened by the development of unified, campus-wide systems of outdoor lighting, signage and graphics, and campus furniture and detailing.

Accepting the basic master plan objectives, the university and its retained consultants can proceed to identify the performance characteristics required of the elements to be used on the campus and to develop designs that embody these basic characteristics. One important characteristic may be that the units must lend themselves to a program of implementation to be carried out incrementally over a period of years. Others may include such things as durability (particularly in harsh climates), stability, cost, low maintenance, resistance to vandalism, and attractiveness. By applying these basic criteria and respecting the basic objectives set forth in the master plan, it should be possible to identify a system of campus furniture appropriate for each individual institution.

The following is a brief inventory of the major items of campus furniture now in use on most American university campuses.

Figure 18-6

Typical Campus Furniture

- Benches and seat walls
- Movable planters
- Storage structures
- Partitions (fences, railings, post and chain, walls, and gates)
- Bollards
- Telephone booths
- Outdoor sales booths
- Drinking fountains
- Newspaper vending machines
- Outdoor tables
- Bus shelters
- Hydrants
- Vents for underground utilities
- Tree guards and grates
- Parking meters
- Mailboxes

All of these and any similar objects on campus should be included as part of a comprehensive, integrated system of campus furniture.

18.8 WAY-FINDING AND SIGNAGE

In order for people to use a campus effectively, they must be able to find their way, first to the campus itself and then to various destinations within it. In order to accomplish this, it is necessary to create a system of way-finding with appropriate signage at several levels.

- Freeway identification at appropriate exits for the campus.
- Trailblazer signs along the routes from the freeway to the campus.
- Identification signs signifying arrival at the campus.
- Detailed information via "You Are Here" maps and other devices.
- Building identification signs on individual buildings.
- Subsidiary information signs to designate such things as visitor parking, loading zones, and other information for drivers and pedestrians.

In addition to way-finding signs, a variety of regulatory and warning signs also are necessary. These include stop signs, "no parking" signs, and fire zone signs. These are often dictated by federal and state traffic control manuals that must be followed in order to secure appropriate enforcement from law enforcement and judicial agencies.

One last category of signage and graphics to be considered concerns formal and informal facilities to allow students, faculty, and other appropriate groups to present messages of meetings, events, and activities to the campus community. Such facilities can include kiosks for the informal posting of notices, posters and handbills; formal advertising billboards; display boards which can be used by campus theater, lecture, and musical organizations in a more formal manner; and other devices such as banners and flags that can be employed by various campus and student organizations.

Each of these elements should be thought out carefully and planned so that appropriate facilities will be provided for legitimate informational requirements in a way that enhances the aesthetic character of the campus and reduces maintenance problems. If posting of notices and information is allowed to take place in a haphazard or scattered manner, it can be extremely detrimental to the appearance of the campus, and taken to its worst extreme can constitute nothing more than campus graffiti.

When designing a system of campus way-finding and graphics, some basic principles should be kept in mind.

- Hierarchy. A logical progression of signs is essential to effective way-finding.
- Campus Orientation. This should be provided through the use of "You Are Here" or verbal messages.
- Consistency. High-quality materials and uniform colors and type styles should be used throughout the campus.
- Visibility. Signs should not be visually obstructed by vegetation or other objects and should have adequate lighting for night viewing.
- Placement. Signs that are located inappropriately can present an obstacle or a hazard. Signage should be placed an adequate distance from the road or path and high enough off the ground so that it does not interfere with traffic.
- Message Length. Informational overload can be avoided by providing only vital, concise information on signs.

A successful signage system meets the needs of its users with clarity and strategic placement. It can make a first-time experience or a daily routine hassle-free.

18.9 LIGHTING

A well-designed system of exterior lighting is essential to the safe use of the campus after dark. In addition, lighting fixtures affect the appearance of the campus both during the day and at night, and may affect surrounding residential and business areas in the evening. Therefore, careful design of the campus lighting system is essential. Electrical engineers and lighting consultants have detailed expertise in this field and should be employed in developing the lighting system for the campus. In addition, if lighting is to be supplied by a local utility rather than by the university itself, the fixtures will have to conform to the standards established by the utility company. Many types of lighting fixtures are employed on the typical campus.

- Roadway Lighting provides well-lighted pathways for vehicular circulation and adjacent pedestrian walkways.
- Pedestrian Lighting provides clear visibility and security along campus walkways.
- Athletic Field Lighting allows for extended use of recreation facilities during evening hours. Great care should be taken in selecting athletic field fixtures to assure that the relatively high levels of light required for these facilities are directed primarily at the playing area and do not spill into adjoining residential areas. In addition, the appearance of such fixtures during the day when they are not in use often is unsightly and can have a negative impact on the overall campus. Well-designed exterior athletic field lighting is available and, if care is taken in the selection of the fixtures, it can be employed on the campus in a way that meets the requirements of recreation field users without harming the aesthetics of the campus or the surrounding area.
- Landscape Lighting. Special lighting to highlight landscape features such as flower beds, attractive trees, fountains, and art work often is used on campus for special effects. This has a secondary benefit of increasing security and visibility on the campus.
- Architectural Lighting. It is common on campuses to highlight the face of prominent buildings or architectural features such as towers and clocks. Again, this enhances the aesthetic appearance of the campus and assists in security.
- Security Lighting. In some areas, such as plant department complexes, service areas, or less visible campus areas, there may be a need for simple security lighting. This can be provided from building-mounted fixtures designed primarily to illuminate the area surrounding a building with relatively little concern for the fixtures' aesthetic impact. This type of fixture should be employed with great care and only in areas of a

utilitarian, functional nature where its impact on the overall campus will not be detrimental.

18.10 REFUSE AND WASTE REMOVAL

In order to keep the campus clean, attractive, and free of litter it is essential that an effective system of trash collection and removal be developed. Such a system will contain a number of elements.

Movable Trash Receptacles

Receptacles should be placed near major walkway intersections, plazas, food centers, and building entrances. They should be located for convenient use, but should be as visually unobtrusive as possible. The design of these receptacles should be attractive and compatible with the overall design framework of the campus, but they should be built in a sturdy manner that will stand up to the rugged wear and tear they will receive in outdoor campus use.

Smoking Urns

With the advent of the smoke-free environment movement, it is becoming necessary to provide smoking urns at all major building entrances and at other locations on the campus to allow for the extinguishing of cigarettes, cigars, and pipes before entering university buildings. These urns should be designed in a manner that is compatible with the rest of the outdoor furniture employed on the campus but, as with trash receptacles, they should be of a sturdy construction that can withstand the heavy use they will receive.

Built-in Trash Receptacles

In areas of heavy use where constant emptying of small containers becomes a maintenance problem, it may be necessary to build larger trash receptacles that can hold greater volumes of refuse. These should be designed in a way that will be compatible with the other elements of campus refuse collection and outdoor furniture.

Dumpsters and Compactors

These elements commonly are employed throughout campuses to allow for the collection and disposal of waste materials from inside the individual buildings. Typically, these are large and relatively unattractive units that if placed adjacent to each building on the campus can have a negative aesthetic impact. Wherever possible, dumpsters and compactors should be designed into the architecture of the building so as to provide as little impact on the campus as possible. When such integration is not possible, effective screening via screen walls, berms, or plants should be provided to reduce the negative impact.

18.11 ART AND ARTIFACTS

The overall appearance of the campus can be enhanced greatly by the addition of various design elements to mark the focal point of major campus spaces or simply to provide an attractive embellishment to the campus.

Fountains and Pools

The use of water in an artistic manner on the campus can provide visual and auditory delight. Such adornments are used widely on American campuses and are particularly appropriate in warmer climates where concerns about freezing and thawing do not exist.

Artifacts and Memorabilia

Often collected by various academic departments, these can be used in ways that enhance the design of the campus. Boulders used by the geology department as instructional media, obelisks or other elements collected by the archaeology department, memorial benches, and other such items can be placed in such a way as to contribute to the overall appearance of the campus.

Memorials and Plaques

Various classes or individuals may wish to memorialize an individual, group, or event by constructing various elements on campus or installing memorial plaques. Again, if properly designed these memorials can contribute to the attractive character of the campus.

Sculpture and Fine Art

By far the most instructive and enriching element that can be added to the campus is fine art. This can be done on either an individual building-by-building basis (where donors are available) or by assembling collections of art, such as the Murphy Sculpture Garden at UCLA. Numerous campuses have undertaken highly successful programs of this nature. In

Figure 18-7

Use of Sculpture as a Campus Focal Point

states that have enacted a "1-percent-for-art program," these funds have been extremely influential in bringing fine art to the campus. The introduction of fine art into the campus not only enhances the visual character of the environment, but provides an instructive day-to-day experience for students.

18.12 ACCOMMODATING THE PHYSICALLY HANDICAPPED

The permanently or temporarily disabled deserve special consideration on campus. At some time most of us will experience a temporary physical impairment necessitating crutches or a wheelchair. The needs of the visually impaired and those with emotional or learning disabilities must be considered as well. Even baby strollers require curb cuts and ramps. It is important to plan for all these groups in order to facilitate their movement on campus.

When planning for those with special physical needs, important considerations are:

- Physical Dimensions. Standard dimensions are required for ramps, walkways, doorways, halls, and parking spaces that are to be used by those with physical disabilities.
- Convenient Access. Access should be considered between buildings and parking areas. Convenient access must be facilitated to all important parts of the campus.
- Sensory Cues. Cues must be provided for the visually and physically impaired. Blind persons rely on tactile cues such as paving, grade changes, and braille signs; auditory cues such as street sounds; and olfactory cues, such as plant aromas. The physically impaired, including those in wheelchairs, need cues located where they can see them. Signs must be low enough to

Figure 18-8

Accessibility for the Handicapped

read from a wheelchair, and building entries and alternate routes must be marked clearly.

Planning for those with special needs is not merely a matter of traveling around campus and looking for places where curb cuts are needed. Such decisions should be approached systematically and comprehensively, and should always allow input of the users who best understand their physical limitations and requirements.

18.13 CAMPUS/COMMUNITY INTERFACE

The boundary where the campus and the community meet is an extremely important one, both in terms of the overall image of the campus and the nature of the relationship between the campus and the host community. The form this boundary takes depends upon the nature of its origin and the manner of its growth. Urban universities often began on a small parcel of land and expanded on a parcel by parcel basis so that their boundary is relatively indistinguishable from the surrounding community. Land grant institutions, on the other hand, often were given large expanses of land that enabled them to develop a green belt surrounding the campus. Some urban universities benefited from sizable initial land acquisitions and have developed a well-defined, attractive campus in the heart of the community.

The exact form of the boundary, however, is less important than the image it conveys. Some universities have chosen to construct buildings in such a way as to create a fortress-like wall, thereby saying "keep out" to the community. Others have achieved a similar separation, but by means of a landscaped green belt that relates in a more pleasant and inviting way to the surrounding neighborhood. Other campuses have surrounded themselves with low, nonthreatening walls that do not send a negative message to the neighborhood, and still others have chosen to keep their boundaries loosely defined so that the campus and the neighborhood blend together. A number of successful solutions have been devised utilizing a number of these approaches. The goal is to create an image of positive interaction between the campus and the community while establishing an identity for the campus. Thus, the identity of the campus can be preserved in a way that the community perceives as inviting rather than hostile.

18.14 OTHER CONCERNS

In addition to the areas already covered in this section, a variety of other issues may present themselves on a given campus. Issues such as the presence of overhead wires and what to do about them, or the necessity to screen unsightly or inappropriate elements on the campus such as pad mount transformers, cooling towers, and outdoor storage areas may present themselves from time to time. It is impossible in one chapter to cover every contingency. However, it is clear that whatever issue of campus infrastructure may arise, it is important to develop a well-conceived and integrated solution that conforms to the overall objectives of the master plan and is consistent with the other elements of campus infrastructure. The talent to solve these problems is available through various consultants and in-house professionals, and, if this objective is kept clearly in mind by decision makers, the result can be an attractive and well-integrated system of campus infrastructure that serves to enhance the overall appearance of the campus.

The final challenge as the campus attains the environmental and aesthetic qualities it seeks will be that of preserving a quality environment in the face of various day-to-day pressures. Developing methods to keep university vehicles, contractors, outside vendors, and others from abusing the landscaped areas or misusing the walkways is critical.

The ongoing operation of the campus must become oriented to respecting the environmental qualities that have been created and to preserving and enhancing them as the campus continues to grow and develop.

18.15 CONCLUSION

The importance and interrelationship of campus infrastructure can be overlooked easily in the design of the campus, but its importance should not be underestimated. For a campus to project a clear, unified image, the introduction of any new elements into the environment—from buildings to trash receptacles—must be viewed in the context of the existing campus and the master plan for future development. By repeating materials, forms, scale, and other characteristics, a great many aesthetic and functional problems can be solved and a unified image for the campus created.

People are most aware of the elements they come in close contact with. This is why attention to detail is so critical in the design of a campus environment. Efforts and resources expended upon the development of an integrated system of campus infrastructure will pay benefits not only in terms of the aesthetic and psychological impact on those who come in contact with the campus, but also in the functional and operational aspects of the institution.

NOTES

1. Ernest L. Boyer, *College, the Undergraduate Experience in America.* (New York: Harper & Row, 1987).
2. The material presented in this section and the sections "Way-Finding and Signage" and "Accommodating the Physically Handicapped" is drawn heavily from a report entitled *Campus: A Compendium of Planning and Design,* prepared by State University of New York Environmental Improvement Program in 1988.

ADDITIONAL RESOURCES

Center for Design Planning. *Streetscape Equipment Sourcebook.* Washington: The Urban Land Institute, 1979.

Lynch, Kevin. *The Image of the City.* Cambridge, Massachusetts: Harvard University Press, 1960.

McLendon, Charles B. and Mick Blackstone. *Signage: Graphic Communication in the Built World.* New York: McGraw-Hill, 1982.

Robinette, Gary O. *Barrier Free Exterior Design.* New York: Van Nostrand Reinhold Co., 1985.

Robinette, Margaret A. *Outdoor Sculpture.* New York: Whitney Library of Design, 1976.

Simonds, J. O. *Landscape Architecture.* New York: McGraw-Hill, 1983.

CHAPTER 19

Types of Construction

Warren Corman
Director of Facilities
Kansas Board of Regents

19.1 INTRODUCTION

Thousands of buildings exist on college campuses and all appear to be different. Their outward appearance is limited only by the designer and builder. Buildings also vary according to their primary structure. The following sections describe these basic types of structure.

19.2 BUILDING FRAMING TYPES

The basic structure or framing types are:

1. Wall bearing
2. Reinforced concrete
3. Structural steel
4. Combination of types

Wall Bearing

Wall bearing refers to a building type which contains thick exterior masonry walls that support the floor and roof joists. Such structures are usually only one or two stories. In earlier days, before the widespread use of skeletal framing, it was not unusual for wall bearing buildings to have many stories, but the walls at the first floor were necessarily very thick (three or four feet) to withstand the unit pressures on the masonry. A typical one-story wall bearing structure might consist of a twelve-inch exterior wall made up of four inches of face brick and eight inches of concrete block with the roof framing constructed of steel open web bar joists.

Wall bearing construction is usually found in fairly simple structures in which no major modifications are anticipated. They are rather easy to construct but are not as flexible in floor plan as the other building types because of the heavy bearing walls. Since masonry and mortar cannot be laid in wet weather or freezing temperatures, such cold or inclement weather can slow the masonry construction, thus delaying the completion.

Reinforced Concrete

Reinforced concrete framing is different from wall bearing construction in that it consists entirely of free-standing columns, braced by horizontal beams at each floor level. Skeletal framing is necessary for high-rise construction, as the columns and beams can be designed to carry almost unlimited loadings from the dead load of the building weight and the live loading of the occupants and the wind. Skeletal framing provides a wide flexibility for future change to the layout, as there are few, if any, solid masonry bearing walls to remove or relocate.

Reinforced concrete frames are usually formed on the job and poured floor by floor as the structure rises. If beams are a real problem, either functionally or aesthetically, a flat slab floor system can be designed that eliminates beams by thickening the floor construction.

Reinforced concrete is an ideal material for structures as it is fireproof and does not have to be protected. This is especially important in high-rise structures because the fire safety and exit codes are more stringent.

Precast concrete framing is ideal for some situations. The beams, columns, and even units of the floor slab may be cast in a factory and delivered to the job already cured and ready for erection. The connecting joints are usually welded to steel plates precast into the concrete. One of the most common uses of precast concrete structures is for multistory parking garages.

Structural Steel

Steel framed buildings have similar characteristics to concrete framed buildings in that the structural frame is freestanding and constructed before the exterior walls are erected. Steel is erected more quickly and is easier to work with in winter weather than concrete. Steel framed buildings range from the relatively simple Butler- and Armco-type prefabricated metal buildings to the more complex and sophisticated "superdomes," the sports arenas and high-rise structures. Steel structures are shop fabricated and field erected using either rivets, bolts, or welds.

Steel framing must be fireproofed for certain types of occupancies and for multi-story construction. If a steel structure is not properly insulated it will suddenly collapse in a fire if the temperature of the steel rises well over 1,000°F. Steel construction is lighter in weight, more quickly erected, and usually costs less initially than concrete framing.

Combinations of Types

Some of the more simple buildings are combinations of framing types. It is not uncommon for one- or two-story structures to have exterior walls that are wall bearing masonry while the interior supports are all steel columns with steel beams or trusses.

Some portions of the country are highly suitable for wood frame construction and wood siding. This is particularly true in California, Oregon, and Washington where the native woods are abundant and the products of the giant redwoods, firs, and cedars weather well.

19.3 FOOTINGS AND FOUNDATIONS

Spread Footings

Spread footings are simple concrete footings bearing on the ground to support concrete foundation walls or grade beams above them. They are commonly used on simple and low-rise structures, but they are usually not adequate for tall buildings or for poor or unstable soil conditions. Tall buildings create large unit pressures that spread footings cannot accommodate. Poor soils cannot safely support spread footings without settlement and cracking.

Pilings

The most common and best substitute for spread footings is piling. Piling can be made of treated timber, steel, or concrete. Concrete piles may be precast or cast in place. Piles are also either friction or point bearing. Friction piles carry their loads from the friction generated along their surface between the pile and the soil. Point bearing piles usually sit on a stiff stratum of shale, rock, gravel, or other bearing strata capable of carrying large unit pressures.

Piles are usually placed in groups and capped with a heavy concrete top. Some piles in each group are driven at a slight angle off of the vertical to provide batter, thus creating more stability within each individual pile grouping. They are driven into the soil by a large free-falling, or double-acting hammer weight. The pile driver guides the pile as it is driven.

Poured-in-place piles are created by drilling large holes into the ground and filing them with concrete after the bottom of the hole has reached a suitable bearing stratum. Pilings vary in diameter from twelve inches to as much as five or six feet and sometimes reach sixty feet in depth. In very shifty soils or where water is present, the pile drilling may have to be lined with a steel casing as it is being drilled and the hole may have to be pumped full of concrete as the steel wall is withdrawn.

Pilings are more expensive than simple spread footings but the footing is a critical part of the building design and must last for the life of the building. It cannot be revised or replaced or even maintained without a huge expenditure of funds, thus it is not an item to gamble with in the overall design of the building.

19.4 FLOOR SYSTEMS

Monolithic Concrete

Many concrete framed buildings have concrete floor systems that are poured in place as a part of the overall structural system. This is called a monolithic concrete system. Monolithic systems are usually solid and stable and tend to reduce sound transmission problems.

Precast Concrete

Many companies manufacture a precast floor unit that can be set in place by a crane and anchored to the supporting beams. Precast units have the advantage of quick erection in all types of weather and the same solid and noise-reducing characteristics as monolithic concrete.

Some units are also prestressed and may have hollow cores to reduce weight. A typical unit might be six inches thick and twelve inches wide. Precast units do not have quite the same flexibility as poured-in-place concrete when it comes to designing special openings through the floor.

Steel Systems

Steel systems consist of lightweight steel joists or trusses with steel decking spot welded to them. Sometimes a thin layer of concrete is poured on top of the decking to add strength and stability, reduce noise transmission, and improve fire resistance.

Steel units can be erected quickly and are usually more economical than concrete. Many steel deck units are designed with compartments or cells to carry wiring for power, computers, telephones, and other uses.

Composite Systems

Many types of floor systems are on the market and in use. One such system is called a composite system because it uses steel beams for the main support with a poured concrete floor on top of the beams. The concrete and steel are designed to act together as a single unit to carry the loads by rigidly securing the top flange of each beam to the concrete slab. This anchoring is achieved by a series of steel studs welded to the top flange of the beam and encased into the concrete when the slab is poured. This type of system tends to have the advantage of a lighter weight yet provides the advantages of a concrete floor.

19.5 EXTERIOR WALL TYPES

Solid Masonry

Exterior walls composed of masonry units have been used for centuries. Still in common use today are facings of brick and native stone with a backup material made of concrete block or lightweight cinder masonry units. Such walls are usually twelve to sixteen inches thick and are relatively easy to maintain. They have a poor insulation value and should be insulated in the core or on the interior face with high-quality, permanent insulating materials.

Masonry Veneers

One of the more common exterior wall systems consists of an exterior wythe (one thickness) of brick or stone masonry anchored to wood or metal stud framing behind it. This system can be heavily insulated in the stud cavities, but extreme care must be taken in making sure that the exterior veneer is solidly and permanently anchored and that water entering the core of the wall is swiftly and surely routed back to the exterior.

Curtain Walls

The term "curtain wall" is used to describe any exterior wall suspended from floor to floor on the structural frame of the building. This is a direct opposite of the term "wall bearing." One type of curtain wall, popular since the 1950s, is the system composed of metal (usually aluminum) extrusions anchored together to form an exterior grid of vertical and horizontal mullions. The spaces formed by these mullions are filled with windows and opaque insulated panels. The number of designs, shapes, colors, and materials are almost unlimited.

High-quality curtain walls are relatively easy to maintain and have performed well. The major concern involves keeping them well-caulked to avoid leakage in heavy rains and strong winds.

Precast Units

Curtain walls faced with precast concrete units provide a good, permanent exterior building face. Concrete units can be formed into any shape and texture and are usually of a size that can be easily transported and erected. Steel anchors are embedded into the concrete units so that the units can be welded or bolted to the building structure. The precast units can be backed with steel studs and gypsum board for insulation. This assembly makes an excellent exterior wall and is extensively used for university building projects. The stone and brick industries have developed and promoted prefabricated panels of brick or stone that can be erected in large sections similar to precast concrete units.

Miscellaneous Types

Tilt-up wall construction is sometimes used for warehouse and other simple utilitarian-type structures. Tilt-up wall panels are made of concrete and poured in a flat plane on the job site, preferably next to the wall location. After curing, each panel is tilted up into place and is anchored to the building structure. This is an economical method of construction but is not used widely on college campuses.

Wood facades are normally used on wood-framed structures. Redwood, cedar, and fir weather well in their natural state and can be utilized in many shapes such as lap siding, shakes, board and batten, tongue and groove, and shiplap siding.

19.6 ROOFING

Nothing in the building industry has gained more attention than roofing and the problem of leaking roofs. Roofs generally fall into two basic categories: flat (or nearly flat) or steep. Older buildings tend to have steep roofs or roofs with an adequate slope. Newer structures, being larger in floor plan, are often topped with flat roofs or roofs with little slope.

Steep roofs are usually made of shingles (slate, asphalt, wood, asbestos, or clay tile) or standing seam metal sheets. Dead level roofs are built up with layers of felt and hot moppings of asphalt or coal tar pitch and then capped with a flood coat of the hot liquid material.

Built-up Roofs

A built-up roof is constructed by placing alternate layers of saturated felt paper and moppings of hot asphalt or bitumen; it is then flood coated on the top surface of the last felt with the hot liquid asphalt or bitumen. Sometimes a rock or gravel aggregate is embedded onto the hot pour to form a protective surface. The number of layers is usually four or five. Such a roof is expected to last at least fifteen to twenty years.

Such a roof should have at least a 1/2-inch-per-foot slope to readily allow water drainage. One should expect to receive at least a ten-year guarantee on the roof against leakage. The guarantee should include the flashings and counterflashings in addition to the roof itself. Flashings and counterflashings are usually made from galvanized steel or copper.

On older roofs with a slope of less than 1/2 inch per foot, it is necessary to use coal tar pitch instead of asphalt. Pitch flows at a lower temperature and tends to seal itself in warm weather. Thus, it will flow off a sloping roof in hot weather and clog the gutters and downspouts. Four grades of asphalts exist; their use depends on the roof slope that can vary from almost flat to six inches per foot.

The installation of a built-up roof is extremely labor-intensive in the field and requires strict control of workmanship and attention to the weather. Built-up roofs are flexible and can adapt to almost any roofing problem.

Single-Ply Roofs

The term "single-ply" describes a factory-made sheet system from one material or a laminated material. The sheets are shipped in a large continuous roll and are cut to fit field conditions on the roof. The top surface of a single-ply sheet may be factory coated or may be field coated. Single-ply roofs can be grouped into many classifications: type of installation, material type, chemical composition, or manufacturing process. The usual installation types are adhered or externally ballasted. Joints between sheets are sealed by contact cements or welding by solvents or heat.

Single-Ply (Adhered)   A fully adhered system is usually attached to the top surface of the roof insulation by contact cements spread by hand or sprayed. The partially adhered system uses mechanically attached plates spaced over the roof surface or other types of individual mechanical fasteners. Adhered sheets are fairly easy to maintain as rips, tears, or holes are apparent and can be repaired.

Single-Ply (Ballasted)   A different installation method involves laying the single-ply onto the roof deck without any direct adhesion except at roof edges or penetrations. The loose-laid membrane is then held down by rounded, smooth, clean rocks with a diameter of about two inches.

Other Roofing Types

Steep roof slopes are readily compatible with various types of shingles or with standing seam metal sheets. Conventional shingles are composed of asphalt, clay tile, cement tile, wood, or slate. Standing seam roofs are made of long, narrow sheets of metal and are joined by a raised, interlocking watertight joint called the standing seam.

Also on the market are foamed coatings that spray on and provide insulation and waterproofing. They are usually used on reroofing and not for new construction.

Roof Protection

It is important to protect roofs from damage from pedestrian traffic. If equipment on the roof requires regular maintenance, roof walkways or stepping stones must be installed for the maintenance people. Special units are made for this purpose.

19.7 WINDOWS

The basic material for window frames is primarily metal or wood, although new high-strength plastics are appearing on the market. The most popular windows for university buildings are of aluminum or nonferrous alloys. They are long lasting, do not rust or rot, can be extruded into intricate shapes to receive good weather stripping, and require very little maintenance. Factory applied permanent finishes are very popular; they coat the raw aluminum with a rich dark bronze color that blends well with brick and stone facades. Many of these coatings are chemically or electrically applied and will last for many years.

It is important to compare air infiltration tests provided by the window manufacturers as a measure of the amount of tempered air within the building that may be lost to the outside on a windy day. Some of the more expensive windows provide a nonconducting thermal break barrier or joint built into the window in an attempt to prevent frost buildup on the interior in extremely cold weather. Good windows should be designed to allow the installation of factory-sealed dual glazing which can be 3/4-inch thick or even thicker for extremely large panes of glass. For multistoried structures it may be important to select a window that can hinge or pivot so that the exterior pane of glass can be cleaned from the inside of the building.

Wood windows require more maintenance, primarily painting, but some window manufacturers are providing a factory applied plastic facing for the exterior portion of the window that does not require painting. Wood windows conserve more energy than metal windows because of the difference in density and conductance between wood and metal. In addition, naturally finished wood windows contribute to the aesthetic beauty of a project. If wood windows are considered, it is important to select the better windows on the market as they are usually made of better materials and hardware and have a more acceptable appearance and longer life cycle.

19.8 DOORS AND FRAMES

Doors and frames for institutions are usually categorized as wood or hollow metal. Hollow metal doors and frames are fabricated from sheet steel and are strong and durable. The doors and frames are reinforced to fit all types, styles, and sizes of hardware. They are custom-fabricated and require a certain amount of lead time for shop drawings, manufacture, and delivery. This is important if the frames are to be in place before the masonry work is to be laid, so that the frame anchors can be built into the masonry joints. Special attention should be given to entrances with heavy traffic to make them durable enough. Wood doors should be solid-core to withstand abuse, provide better fire protection and noise control, and serve as a substantial receiver of the various anchoring devices for hardware.

The selection of high-quality hardware for lock sets, panic devices, closers, and butts is important to provide security, service, and low maintenance costs. Institutions should select a good hardware company and use the same keying system for all buildings, if possible, to reduce the number of keys and master keys. Cheap hardware is quite costly over a long period of time.

19.9 EXTERIOR INSULATION

Roof and exterior wall insulations are manufactured of many types and materials. They can be classified as loose fill, batts, boards, or poured-in-place lightweight material. Hollow cells in masonry units are usually filled with a pourable, granular material that is delivered to the job in sacks. It is important to select only materials that will not settle or decay and will not be eaten by termites or rodents.

Insulation boards are commonly used as roof insulation and as the vertical joint between masonry wythes in exterior walls. Again, this material should be permanent and not attractive to insects or rodents. Many materials are on the market and it requires the services of an expert to select the proper board or plank insulation from the available organics, inorganics, plastics, and synthetics.

Some roof boards are preformed to install on a flat roof to provide a sloping top surface. This requires special attention to the location and height of roof drains, curbs, scuppers, and flashings. An option to roof board insulation is a poured-in-place lightweight concrete-like type material that is very flexible and can solve many roof slope problems. Care must be exercised in allowing sufficient cure time for the wet materials before roofing or vapor barriers are installed.

Batt insulation is quite effective in joist or stud space. It should be permanently anchored to avoid future slipping or sagging. Fiber glass material is common but other good inorganic materials also exist on the market.

ADDITIONAL RESOURCES

Edward, Allen. *Fundamentals of Building Construction.*
1988 Handbook of Commercial Roofing Systems. Cleveland, Ohio: Edgell Communications, Inc., 1988.
TEK Information Series. Herndon, Virginia: National Concrete Masonry Association.

CHAPTER 20

Building Interiors

Grace C. Kelley
Manager, Interior Design Services
The University of Texas at Austin

20.1 INTRODUCTION

Interior design as a profession, a specialized branch of architecture, is a relatively new field. Graduates in this field have a thorough education with strong architectural emphasis, and many are finding careers in facilities management. Simultaneous with the development of the interior design profession, and perhaps related to it, has been the growing emphasis on creating and maintaining a higher education environment conducive to learning. Until recently, the principal concerns with interiors were that they were kept painted, clean, adequately lighted, and contained serviceable furniture. Choices of interior colors often were left to the occupants, and economy dominated the choice of furniture and interior materials. Today, the value of professional interior design in creating an effective interior environment is widely recognized. Several large institutions now have interior designers on their physical plant staffs. However, many physical plant departments do not have the resources to include a professionally trained interior designer.

This chapter provides fundamental information that will be useful to the physical plant director. It includes extensive information on interior issues—interior materials and systems, space planning, acoustics, and lighting. It also includes information on standardization of furniture, flammability regulations, and facilities for the handicapped. Some effort is made to provide a sense of the aesthetic issues with which the interior designer is faced.

All information is tailored to the requirements of the institutional environment. Within this environment, a design solution must first be functional, then cost-effective. It must be aesthetically pleasing and commensurate with other factors such as durability, maintainability, and safety.

20.2 BASIC PRINCIPLES OF DESIGN

All interior design schemes endeavor to relate functionally and aesthetically to the existing environment. The more appropriate the design scheme, the clearer the perception that it was created as an integral part of the whole. Fads that prevail over what is functionally appropriate generally will be perceived as cluttered, disjointed, or dysfunctional. The designer must distinguish good design from inappropriate design.

Good design does not refer to taste. Taste is a matter of preference. Good design has a basic, lasting quality. Most people will recognize a design scheme that works well, even though they may be unable to fully appreciate why it works.

It is relatively simple to state the basic principles of good design: proportion, balance, rhythm, focus, and harmony. Once these principles are understood, they can be applied almost without effort.

Proportion

Proportion in design is the harmonious relationship of one part to another or to the whole. The early Greeks discovered the secret of good proportion and established rules that have been accepted and followed by designers for centuries. Their standard for good proportion was a rectangle with its sides in a ratio of two parts to three. This is called the "golden rectangle." The "golden section" involves the division of a form so that the ratio of the smaller proportion to the larger is the same as the larger to the whole. The progression 2, 3, 5, 8, 13, 21, 34, and so on, in which each number is the sum of the two preceding numbers, provides an approximation of this relationship. For example, 2 to 3 is the same ratio as 3 to 5; 5 to 8 is the same ratio as 8 to 13. These proportions should be applied when planning the dimensions of a room or selecting a piece of furniture for a particular area. Classical rules of proportion also dictated that the division of a line somewhere between one-half and one-third was most pleasing. This concept was called the "golden mean" and can be applied in interiors when hanging pictures or tying back draperies.

An object is perceived in relation to the area around it. Objects that are too large will crowd a small room, while furniture that is too small will seem even smaller in a large room. In addition, a large piece of furniture will seem even larger when surrounded by small furniture.

Form, color, texture, and pattern all influence our perception of scale and proportion. Coarse texture, large patterns, and bold colors will make an object appear larger, while smooth textures, small patterns, and light colors will make it appear smaller. Whatever attracts the eye appears larger. These principles can alter the apparent size and proportion of spaces and objects.

Balance

Balance provides a sense of equilibrium and repose, a feeling of the weight of an object. Three types of balance exist: bisymmetrical, asymmetrical, and radial.

Bisymmetrical, or formal balance uses identical objects arranged similarly on either side of an imaginary line, such as a sofa with identical end tables and matching lamps on both ends. Every arrangement needs some bisymmetry.

Asymmetrical, or informal balance is more subtle. This type of balance requires more thought, but remains interesting longer than completely symmetrical arrangements. In asymmetrical arrangements, objects of different sizes, shapes, and colors may be used in an infinite number of ways. Two small objects may balance one large one; a small shiny object may balance a larger dull one; or a spot of bright color may balance a large neutral area.

Radial balance is an arrangement that radiates from a central point. A round conference table or a dining table with chairs around it is an example of radial balance.

The architectural features of a room, such as doors and windows, should be located to give this feeling of balance. A pleasing distribution of highs and lows and large and small features give a room a well-balanced feeling.

Rhythm

In interiors, rhythm is something that allows the eye to move smoothly around the room. It may be achieved by repetition, gradation, opposition, transition, and radiation. By repeating color, pattern, texture, line, or form, a rhythm of a repetitive nature is achieved. Gradation is the succession of the size of objects from large to small, or of colors from dark to light. Opposition occurs wherever lines come together at right angles, or wherever a horizontal line of furniture meets a vertical architectural member. Transition is the rhythm of a curved line which carries the eye over the room, as occurs with an archway. Radial rhythm is a result of lines extending outward from a central axis.

Focus

This is a feature of the room to which the eye is drawn—the focal point. It creates a feeling of unity and order in the room. A prominent architectural feature commonly serves as a focal point, but if no architectural feature exists, an important piece of furniture can substitute.

Harmony

Harmony involves fitting together parts to form a cohesive whole. Completeness and order are established when the furnishings of a room harmonize in their relationships with other items within the space and with the background. If the room is large or small, furniture should be scaled accordingly. Floor coverings should be selected with a theme or purpose in mind. Fabrics and colors should be appropriate to the style of furniture. Accessories should be appropriate to the style of the other furnishings and should reflect the personality of the space.

20.3 CHARACTERISTICS OF OBJECTS

The basic principles of proportion, balance, rhythm, focus, and harmony are achieved by considerating the characteristics of the elements in the interior landscape. Much as one looks at a park-like landscape and perceives the characteristics of trees, shrubs, grass, flowers, sky, water, and pathways, one can look at the interior landscape and perceive the characteristics of desks, chairs, files, carpet, walls, and ceilings. These characteristics include the following elements: texture, pattern, line, form, space, color, and light.

Texture

Texture refers to the surface quality conveyed by objects within a space, and the dominant texture the architectural background establishes. For example, a room paneled in polished wood or papered in a traditional wall covering will require furniture woods and fabrics with smoother textures than a room paneled with rough-hewn wood or constructed of masonry.

Pattern

Pattern forms the simplest method of surface embellishment. Too much pattern can make a room too busy. Although the total arrangement of the components of a room create an overall pattern, the more obvious patterns are in carpet, fabric, and wallpaper. These should be appropriate to the general feeling of the room.

Line

Line is expressed by the sense of composition, direction, and whether motion or repose is felt within a space. Line can seemingly alter the proportion of an object or of an entire room. Vertical lines cause the eye to travel upward, causing the area to seem higher. Horizontal lines direct the eye across the area, making it appear wider. Curved lines are graceful and feminine. Diagonal lines give a room a feeling of action; staircases and slanted ceilings are examples of this. Too much line movement gives an unsettled feeling. A proper balance of the various vertical, horizontal, and curved lines achieves harmony.

Form

Form is a major concern in planning interiors. The shape or mass of objects within a space causes a sense of confusion if an excessive variety is used. A lack of variety creates monotony.

Space

Basic rules govern the use of space. Anthropologist and father of proxemics, Edward T. Hall, observed that people have specific, culturally prescribed distances in their daily activities. Designers must be aware of these personal and public space relationships and allow for them in their designs.

Color and Light

Color and light are the most interrelated elements of interior design. Color is a quality of light reflected from an object to the human eye. When light strikes an object, some of it is absorbed, the rest is reflected. The wave length of the light an object reflects determines its color.

To use color effectively in planning attractive rooms or in selecting furniture, draperies, or floor coverings, it is necessary to consider these factors:

- The relationship of colors to each other, and how light affects the apparent color.
- The characteristics of colors and their psychological effects.
- Which colors harmonize, and which contrast.
- What combinations are appropriate and practical for the specific project.

Color Schemes

Red, yellow, and blue make up the three primary colors or hues. The secondary colors (a combination of two primary colors) include orange, green, and violet. Numerous shades result when one of the primary colors dominates the mixture, as in the case of yellow-green or green-yellow.

Three basic color schemes exist: analogous, complementary, and monochromatic.

- Analogous—Colors harmonize with each other when they share a common element. Blue, for example, is a basic element of green, blue-violet, purple, and red-violet.
- Complementary—Too many harmonizing elements can become tiresome. It is therefore desirable to introduce contrast by adding a complementary, or contrasting color. The complement of red is green, which is a color containing no red, but made up of blue combined with yellow.
- Monochromatic—Color schemes that use various shades or values of a single color are called monochromatic. Monochromatic can be monotonous unless other elements such as pattern or texture are used.

The color to dominate the room should be the first one selected. This selection is based on the client's preference or the room's size and light conditions. After choosing the dominant color, the related or harmonizing colors are selected. Most rooms should be decorated in an ascending scale from dark to light; rugs or floors should be darkest, walls lighter, and ceilings lightest. Efforts should be made to avoid pure white in favor of off-white shades. Another style of decorating involves a descending scale of values, with colored walls and ceilings of greyed or darkened hues and light-hued floor covering.

Colors should be distributed throughout the room, avoiding the spotty effect of isolated splotches of color concentrated in one area. One way of distributing colors is to upholster at least one piece of furniture in a fabric containing all the colors in the room.

The main areas of a space usually should be the most neutral in value. As areas are reduced in size, the chromatic intensity can be proportionately increased.

In a color scheme small touches of bright hues are called accents. Accessories or an occasional chair can supply the accent color to heighten the effect of a color scheme.

Cooler shades such as blue or green, for example, will make small rooms look larger, while yellow, orange, and red can make larger rooms more intimate and cozy. Cool tones are quiet and restful. Warm colors are friendly and cheery.

20.4 INTERIOR MATERIALS AND SYSTEMS

Floor Coverings

This section primarily concerns rugs, carpeting, and resilient tiles. However, flooring is not limited to these materials. Terrazzo, wood, ceramic tile, and marble are flooring materials whose initial high cost can be justified under the appropriate circumstances. The best approach to flooring design entails considering the specification of flooring in the initial phases of construction and not as an afterthought, limiting it to surface decoration.

Rugs   In the seventeenth and eighteenth centuries, carpets and other floor coverings were rarely found in the homes of ordinary people; textiles were considered precious and were not used on the floor. The word "rug" referred to a handmade coverlet, and "carpet" referred to a table cover. Woven or hand-knotted rugs did not become common as floor coverings until the early eighteenth century, when Oriental carpets became popular among the wealthy.

The hand-knotted type is the best rug or carpet, the Oriental rug being a fine example. However, the demand for Oriental rugs has increased to such an extent that their manufacture has become commercialized. Although Oriental rugs are still made on hand looms, quantity production in factories—with less experienced craftspeople, cheaper materials, and aniline instead of vegetable dyes—has become common.

In the university environment, the designer may have an opportunity to specify such a rug in a special setting, perhaps the office of the president or an important public area. In this case, the designer should depend on the advice of an expert or reputable dealer.

Custom-designed tufted rugs also create a rich effect. For those with a tight budget, manufacturers in Puerto Rico, Hong Kong, and Japan produce fine hand-tufted rugs to specification. In addition, the larger mills in this country serve as a source of custom-designed products.

A less expensive way to achieve this custom look is to use broadloom carpet and border it with another broadloom, cut to the desired width. Several borders of varying widths and coordinating colors or patterns can be used. After the border is added by attaching it to the field carpet with seaming tape, the seams can be beveled for a sculptured look.

Carpet   Carpets and rugs represent beauty, luxury, or status, regardless of the actual function of a space. Perhaps the most important question when considering carpeting is, What will the use of the space be? The following is a list of properties carpets can be expected to provide.

- Acoustical privacy
- Ease of maintenance
- Cost effectiveness
- Design flexibility
- Feel of luxury.

The type and quantity of fiber and the carpet's construction determine the quality. The determining factors in manufacturing are the pitch (number of face yarns per inch), the pile height (the height of the yarn above the backing), the ply of the yarn (number of individual ends of yarn twisted together), and the method of weaving or tufting. Ultimately these factors are reflected in the price, and a reputable manufacturer's price is a good indication of its quality.

To make an intelligent decision when specifying carpet, one must have at least a basic knowledge of carpet fibers and how they perform. The following summarizes the types of natural and man-made fibers used in commercial carpet manufacturing.

Carpet Fibers
Natural fibers include wool, cotton, and flax. Wool carpet has reemerged in prestigious contract interiors and still represents the standard against which all carpet fibers are measured. The surface of wool scatters optical light, thus improving its appearance by diffusing soil visibility. Because of its scaly character, crevices in the carpet do not hold surface dirt and dust readily. Below-surface particles release with ease and resilience is outstanding. The significant characteristics of wool fiber are as follows:

Advantages	*Disadvantages*
Consumer appeal	Initial cost
Appearance	Stain removal
Feel	Abrasion resistance
Resilience	Styling versatility
Flame resistance	
Soil resistance	
Cleanability	
Solvent resistance	

Economics and technology have resulted in the displacement of wool by man-made fibers. Man-made fibers are in liquid form before solidifying at room temperature. Essentially, they are manufactured by heating the polymer (chemical material) and blowing it through a perforated plate called a spinnerette. Fine streams of liquid become solid strands of filament as the material cools in a liquid or air bath.

Nylon leads petrochemically derived face fiber materials, followed by acrylics and olefins. Made of chemicals from the polyamide group, nylon is the most widely used carpet fiber. The synthetic yarn is not resilient but is crimped, bent, and twisted to create resilience. Nylon tends to retain its shape because it is nearly 40 percent harder than, for example, olefin. This means that nylon made to the same specifications as olefin and used in the same area will show wear at a lesser rate. However, nylon absorbs and holds limited amounts of moisture, so is not as stain resistant as olefin even when solution dyed. This capillary characteristic enables nylon to be dyed in many ways, increasing its manufacturing and styling flexibility.

Nylon's hard, smooth surface reduces the tendency of soil particles to cling to the fiber, so they can be easily removed during vacuuming. The fiber cross section, with its modified triangular shape, breaks up and scatters light rays and tends to hide the soil on the back side of the fiber, making the carpet appear cleaner.

The ability of a carpet to retain a good appearance as long as it lasts is the true measure of its effective life. Appearance-retention qualities are inherent in carpet made from nylon.

Nylon fiber exhibits the following advantages and disadvantages:

Advantages	Disadvantages
Good bulk and cover	High static (some grades)
Crush resistance	
Wearability	
Takes color well	
Good luster range	
Soil resistance	
Good cleaning	
Mildew resistance	

Acrylic fibers are synthetics whose polymer base is composed mostly of acrylonitrile units. The fiber has a high bulk-to-weight ratio; good acid and sunlight resistance; and a bulky, wool-like appearance. It is produced in staple form only to be spun into yarn. High color, life, and resistance to mildew characterize this fiber. Color is added by stock dyeing in the spinning mill while the acrylic is still in fiber form.

Characteristics of acrylic fibers include the following:

Figure 20-1
General Carpet Construction Criteria

Here is a guide to the various carpet terms you should acquaint yourself with before developing your specification.

Magnification of *continuous filament yarn.*

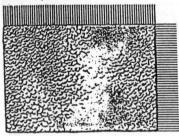

Number of tufts per sq. inch. This is determined by multiplying needles (corresponding to a particular pitch or gauge) by rows or stitches per inch. Example: ⅛ gauge, 8 needles times 8 stitches per inch *equals* 64 tufts per square inch.

Pile Height

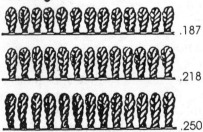

.187
.218
.250

Wire Height

.187   .218   .250

Gauge: (Tufted Fabric) The distance between two needle points, expressed in fractions of an inch.

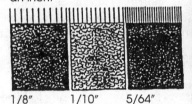

1/8"   1/10"   5/64"

Stitches. The number of lengthwise yarn tufts in one inch of carpet.

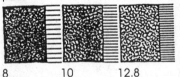

8   10   12.8

Pitch. (Woven Fabric) The number of single ends per 27 inches of width.

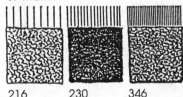

216   230   346

Rows. The number of lengthwise yarn tufts in one inch of carpet.

8   10   12.8

Pitch to Gauge Conversions

Pitch	108	143.9	172.8	180	189	216	243	252	256	270	346
Needles	4	5.3	6.4	6.6	7	8	9	9.3	9.5	10	12.8
Gauge	1/4	3/16	5/32	9/64		1/8				1/10	5/64

Face Fiber. Specify as follows: "The face yarn of the carpet shall be pile of 100% 'Ultron' advanced-generation nylon *or* its equivalent."

Pile Weight per Square Yard. This is the amount of yarn used in the pile of the carpet, excluding the primary backing. Pile weight is measured in ounces per square yard.

— Face Yarn
— Primary Backing
— Latex
— Secondary Backing

Pile weight + Latex + Backing
= *Total Weight*

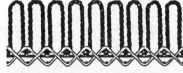

Velvet Weave

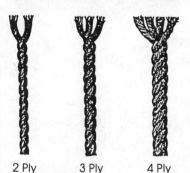

2 Ply   3 Ply   4 Ply

Construction Methods

Wilton Weave

Tufted

Knitted

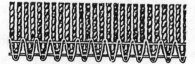

Axminster Weave

Fuse-Bonded

Advantages	Disadvantages
Low static level	Low abrasion resistance
Excellent cover and bulk	Alkali resistance
Wide color range	
Moisture resistance	
Mildew resistance	

Olefin fiber is a synthetic polymer whose base is ethylene, propylene, or other olefin. It is the lightest commercial fiber, has excellent strength, and is resistant to chemicals and abrasion. It is dyed in liquid form prior to being extruded into continuous filament yarns. Thus, the dye process is known as "solution dye." It is highly moisture and stain resistant; however, olefin is a petroleum based product and the oily residue in soil will bind more readily to its surface. If spillage is a problem in an area being considered for carpeting, olefin will provide excellent protection against stains. Proportionally more soiling will occur, however, with a resulting increase in maintenance costs. The following characterize olefin:

Advantages	Disadvantages
Colors solution dyed	Low resilience
Good cover and bulk	Limited color
Abrasion resistance	
Stain resistance	
Low static level	
Mildew resistance	
Initial cost	

The following describe and diagram the major manufacturing processes for carpeting.

Carpet Backing

Carpet specifications must also include the type of backing used or they will seriously affect the quality of the installation. Justifiable arguments exist for specifying both jute and synthetic carpet backings. A choice must be made based on the most appropriate product for the particular installation.

Jute is a natural cellulosic fiber made from certain plants of the linden family that grow in India and Bangladesh. Jute yarns are used for woven carpet backing, yarns, and twine. Woven jute fabrics are used in tufted carpet as primary and secondary carpet backing.

Jute absorbs adhesives well and forms tight mechanical bonds, preventing delamination between carpet and backing. Installers frequently prefer jute backing because it stretches better than synthetics, goes around corners easier, and accommodates irregularities better. It also absorbs moisture, however, and can mold and rot when wet. When wet, jute tends to shrink as it dries.

Synthetics

Synthetics are highly resistant to mold and mildew. They are not damaged by moisture, will not rot, will not contribute to face yarn stain if the carpet is wet, and remain odor-free. Synthetic carpet backings reduce static buildup in computer areas. The addition of carbon to the primary backing combined with face yarn treatment reduces static by about 80 percent. Together, they eliminate essentially all noticeable and computer-damaging static.

Attached cushion backings are a special type of carpet backing. Made of urethane foam, this backing forms a built-in carpet pad that is glued directly to the floor. One disadvantage is that at replacement time, most of the pad remains glued to the floor.

Tufts of carpet yarns punched into primary backing will pull out unless a "glue" is applied to the back of the carpet. Sometimes, this coat is the final step in backing the carpet; in this case the carpet has a unitary back. The coatings, made of latex or polymer, are spread on at room temperature and then baked dry or spread on hot and allowed to cool. Both methods lock in each yarn bundle while forming a back ready to be glued down.

Carpeting with unitary backing is made for glue-down installations. Office areas with heavy traffic are ideal locations for glue-down unitary-backed carpet. Premium adhesive is essential. Installation of latex unitary tends to be more complicated and therefore more expensive because installers must follow precise instructions.

Latex unitary is nonporous and will resist evaporation. Therefore, it is necessary to let the adhesive tack before the carpet is committed to the adhesive. It is less flexible than conventional backs of jute. It must never be folded, creased, bent, or stretched as it is difficult to flatten.

Carpets with unitary backings are extremely durable and provide an exceptionally strong tuft bind. However, the other properties of this thermoplastic backing must be evaluated in relation to the requirements of the specific installation. Just as important, a crew experienced with this type of backing should install it.

Carpet Life Cycle Costing

Low cost is an important consideration, but initial low expense is only one aspect. While the initial purchase price for carpeting may be higher than for conventional floor coverings such as vinyl tile, long-term cost is demonstrably less, with substantial overall savings from extended wear life at high retention levels for appearance. Total use cost is the best basis for comparison. The use-cost concept evaluates the three basic elements of value in relation to cost.

- How much does it cost to buy and install?
- How long will it last?
- What will it cost to maintain?

The installed cost of carpet is on the average greater than noncarpeted floors. However, its combined maintenance costs are so much lower that its total use-cost varies from 45 to 52 percent less than noncarpeted floors.

Flammability Testing
It is important to be familiar with potential fire hazards and apply this knowledge in specifying materials and systems. Interior finishes and furnishings have caused many deadly fires in the past. Often it takes these tragedies to prompt federal or state governments to enact legislation to protect the public.

In the first critical moments of a fire, ignited materials will either contribute to or prevent the fire's spread. Factors to consider when evaluating particular materials for safe use include the amount of heat, smoke, and toxic gases released and interaction with the other materials.

Although flammability connotes ease of ignition or flame spread rate, in actual practice it concerns performance of a product subjected to a specified test. When determining flammability of carpeting, many tests may apply.

Methenamine Pill Test: DOC FF-1-70.   DOC FF-1-70 applies to carpet, DOC FF-2-70 applies to rugs. The National Bureau of Standards developed this test and the Department of Commerce adopted it in 1970. Since 1971 this test has been required by law for all carpet offered for sale in the United States. It is the Federal Trade Commission standard.

Eight 9 in. by 9 in. carpet samples are first placed in a drying oven for two hours and then in an air- and moisture-tight desiccator. A 9-in. square metal plate with an 8-in. diameter hole in the center is placed over a carpet sample. A timed methenamine pill is placed in the center of the sample and ignited. If the charred area does not extend to within 1 in. of the edge of the hole in the plate—on at least seven of the eight samples—the carpet passes the test. The rating system is pass/fail.

Steiner Tunnel Test: ASTM E-84, NFPA 255, UL 723.   The Steiner Tunnel Test is required by the Public Health Service and Life Safety Code for contract carpeting installed in health care units participating in Hill-Burton and Medicare programs (developed by Underwriters Laboratories). This test subjects carpet specimens to a heavy flame source and uses flame spread as a comparative measure. Carpet samples 25 ft. long by 1 ft. 8 in. wide, mounted pile down on the ceiling of a test tunnel, are subjected to heat and flame in a temperature range of 1,600°F to 1,800°F under standard draft conditions. Test duration is ten minutes or until sample has burned out completely, whichever comes first. Progress of flame along length of test sample is observed every fifteen seconds and the greatest distance of flame spread is then used to calculate a flame-spread rating. A flame-spread rating of 75 or less is necessary to meet Hill-Burton programs. Other flame-spread classifications defined by the National Fire Protection Association (NFPA) Life Safety Codes for its rating system are 0-25 = A, 26-75 = B, 76-200 = C, 201-500 = D.

Flooring Radiant Panel Test: ASTM E648; NFPA 253; NBS IR 75-950, NFPA 101. This test has been approved as a replacement for the E-84 Steiner Tunnel Test and is used by many regulatory agencies; however, some may still require the Steiner Tunnel Test. The panel test measures the heat required to sustain combustion in carpets exposed to radiant energy and flame. Samples are tested in the normal end-use configuration. A carpet specimen is exposed to a radiant heat flux that decreases along the length of the specimen. The specimen is ignited at the highest heat flux end and allowed to burn until it will not support combustion. The heat flux at the point the flame extinguishes is the critical heat flux and is expressed in watts per cm sq. A pass-fail heat flux level of 0.5 watts/cm sq. or higher is generally recommended for corridors and exit ways in hospitals and other such institutions; 0.25 watts/cm sq. is recommended for corridors and exit ways in schools, offices, and other buildings.

When the Flooring Radiant Panel Test is used to measure flammability, the National Bureau of Standards (NBS) Smoke Chamber Test is sometimes used to measure smoke density. Most government regulatory agencies approve the Flooring Radiant Panel Test for nonsprinkled corridors and primary exit ways. The Methenamine Pill Test would then be used for room carpet and sprinkled corridors. The rating system is as follows:

- Class 1 = Minimum 0.45 watts/cm sq.
- Class 2 = Minimum 0.22 watts/ cm sq.

Smoke Density Chamber Test: ASTM E662 and NFPA 258. The Smoke Density Chamber Test is the same as the NFPA 258. It measures solely the smoke density characteristics of carpet under controlled laboratory conditions to determine the specific optical density of smoke within a closed chamber. The chamber is a closed cabinet 2 ft. by 3 ft. by 3 ft. A

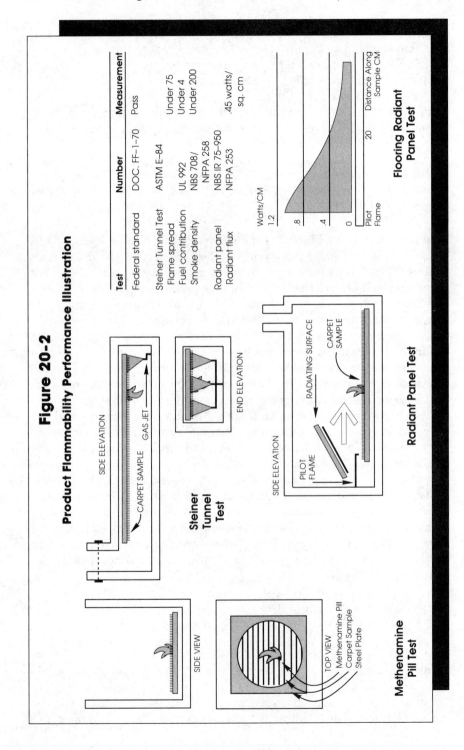

Figure 20-2

Product Flammability Performance Illustration

Test	Number	Measurement
Federal standard	DOC. FF-1-70	Pass
Steiner Tunnel Test	ASTM E-84	
Flame spread		Under 75
Fuel contribution	UL 992	Under 4
Smoke density	NBS 708/	Under 200
	NFPA 258	
Radiant panel	NBS IR 75-950	
Radiant flux	NFPA 253	.45 watts/
		sq. cm

Steiner Tunnel Test

SIDE ELEVATION

CARPET SAMPLE   GAS JET

END ELEVATION

Methenamine Pill Test

SIDE VIEW

TOP VIEW
Methenamine Pill
Carpet Sample
Steel Plate

Radiant Panel Test

SIDE ELEVATION

RADIATING SURFACE

CARPET SAMPLE

PILOT FLAME

Flooring Radiant Panel Test

Watts/CM

1.2
.8
.4
0

Pilot Flame

20   Distance Along Sample CM

sample 3-in. square is supported vertically in a holder while exposed to heat under two conditions: flaming and smoldering. A photometric meter with a vertical light path measures the varying light transmittance as smoke accumulates. These measurements are then used to calculate the specific optical density. The results are averaged for three samples tested and reported as average specific optical density.

The rating system includes an index range from 0-800 units. Most federal agencies require a smoke density of a maximum of 450 average of the flaming and nonflaming results.

Carpet Estimating
For planning purposes, a quick estimate of the square yardage required can be figured by calculating the square footage from the floor plan, then dividing by the number of square feet in a square yard (9) and adding 20 percent for waste. This will generally be excessive, but will provide a budgetary figure.

If floor plans do not exist for a particular area, it should be measured and a drawing prepared. Begin by measuring and sketching on graph paper the length of walls in the area. In addition to the overall measurement, measure the short walls; these are called "broken measurements." To ensure that none of the walls is angled, total the broken measurements to make certain the sum equals the overall measurement of the wall. Rooms commonly have angled walls, and this can be detected if the lengths of the parallel walls are not identical.

Measure and mark the distance carpet is to go into the doorways. Check the floor clearance of doors. If installation will include carpet and padding, allow for this thickness, or doors must be removed and trimmed. Mark the swing of doors on the sketch, as this may be needed later in the planning process to determine the direction of the pile.

Stairs present a special problem. Measure the width of the stairs in several places to detect size variations. Two methods exist for installing carpet on stairs: the "waterfall" method, which uses one continuous piece of carpet; and the "cap and band" method, which covers the stairs in separate pieces. Begin the waterfall method by measuring the length of one tread and its riser and multiply that figure by the number of steps for the total length. In addition, take an overall measurement of the entire length and compare the two. With the cap and band method, first measure each tread (cap) from the crotch to underneath the lip where it meets the top of the riser. Measure each riser. Check for variations by making random measurements of several stairs. Mark the details of the stair measurements on the sketch.

Include information about special details such as type and condition of floors, or whether shoe mold is to be removed. Note existing carpet to be removed, whether it is glued down or over a pad, and the condition of the flooring beneath the existing carpet.

Although small pieces of waste padding can be effectively used on stairs and fill areas, it is a relatively minor matter compared to the waste of carpet. Therefore, most estimators compute padding yardage to equal the amount of carpet required.

Most carpet experts use the rule of thumb formula of 2-1/2 linear feet of tackless strip for each square yard of carpet. When drawings or measurements of the areas are available, a closer estimate can be obtained by computing the total linear feet and adding 10 percent for waste.

The most common width of carpet used commercially is manufactured in twelve-foot widths. Each width of carpet must lie with its pile going in the same direction. Finding the best layout for the carpet will depend on the most economical use of yardage, maximum performance of the carpet, and desired appearance. When planning layout, factors to consider include placement of seams away from high-traffic areas, no right angle seams through doorways, and a minimum of one-foot-wide fill pieces.

To simplify the layout of the carpet, use a scale-size template. By moving the template around the drawing, potential arrangements can be determined easily.

Carpet Installation

The following should be used in determining whether an installation should be stretched in or glued down.

1. Size of Job. Generally speaking, jobs with a long run between anchor points will be difficult to properly stretch. This can be aided where separate offices are involved, permitting a 4 x 4 or 2 x 8 board to be used as a base for the power stretches; otherwise, a 25-foot run would be the maximum.

2. Layout of Job. Large open areas with furniture or partitions which interfere with proper original stretching (and hinder restretching) should not be stretched in. Likewise, irregularly shaped or angular areas should be avoided. Multiple office space connected by a maze of corridors also presents a distinct stretch and/or restretch problem.

3. Underlayment. Underlays that are too soft can cause problems.

4. Use. Heavily trafficked areas or areas in which wheeled equipment is routinely used are to be avoided with stretch-in. Padding accentuates traffic patterns and impedes the movement of wheeled equipment.

5. Style Innovations. If the designer specifies bias cuts, inserts, or other innovations, proper stretch-in is often impossible.

6. Flammability. Flame-spread performance of any carpet is dramatically and negatively affected by underlayment due to the insulative effect of the pad which prevents heat dissipation through the carpet. Where regulations do not specify that the flame spread test must be made over a pad but it is known they cannot be met in such a system, the stretch-in method should not be used.

When stretch-in is appropriate, the following considerations are important:

1. Amount of Stretch. Each product should be stretched slightly past its stabilization point to avoid growth and buckling as it relaxes. Most installers take responsibility for the first restretch if difficulty in properly stretching occurs initially.
2. Layout and Carpet Care. Proper stretch-in requires proper fastening around the entire perimeter and at all seams. The carpet must be laid in one direction, and the back must not be abused (dragging heavy furniture, exposure to wheeled traffic) prior to or subsequent to installation. Diagonal cuts are to be avoided.
3. Mechanical Requirements. Power stretchers are recommended in all sizes of contract installations but are essential in larger ones. Large installations also require commercial tackless strips with three rows of pins.

Carpet Wear
Several factors determine the life expectancy of carpeting: abrasion resistance, appearance retention, and maintenance. Abrasion resistance relates directly to wearability, while appearance retention relates to such characteristics as crushing, fading, soiling, and matting. Improper maintenance can accelerate wear as gritty abrasive dirt accumulates, dulling the color and reducing resilience.

Whether a carpet is functionally acceptable is still a subjective matter. Laboratory methods for measuring abrasion resistance employ the Taber Abraser and Rollstuhl tests, among others. These tests are based on the number of cycles required to abrade the pile fiber completely to the primary backing.

The multilobal structure in various deniers of nylon fibers provides exceptional bulk and gives excellent resistance to crushing and matting, even in high-traffic areas. This high degree of resilience minimizes the traffic lanes and deep indentations from heavy furniture.

Tuft bind is also a measure of how well the carpet will wear. The ASTM Test D1335 determines the pounds of force required to pull the tuft out of the back of the carpet. Tuft bind is obtained by proper application of the back coating. A single tuft in a loop pile carpet should withstand a minimum of eight pounds of pull force for most end use applications; four to five pounds is generally adequate for cut pile carpet. A higher tuft bind is recommended when the possibility of deliberate raveling exists, such as in grade school installations.

Wear is defined as appearance loss, not as fiber loss. The ability of a carpet to retain a good appearance as long as it lasts is the true measure of its effective life. Appearance retention qualities are inherent in properly constructed carpet, installed with an appropriate end use in mind.

Atmospheric contaminants such as ozone and other gases contribute to color fading. The advanced generation nylons have less open physical structure that provides resistance to gaseous penetration and thus aids in color stability.

Solution dyed yarn discourages fading because the color is permanently locked into the fiber. Proper dye selection and fixation will assure color clarity through resistance to fading, crocking, and repeated cleanings.

Industry test procedures accepted by the American Association of Textile Chemists and Colorists (AATCC) to determine colorfastness include:

- Atmospheric Fading (AATCC 129). This test determines the color change of the carpet when exposed to ozone gas in the atmosphere under high humidities. The International Gray Scale Ratings are: 5—no change; 4—slightly changed; 3—noticeably changed; 2—considerably changed; and 1—much changed. A shade change rating of at least 3 after three cycles of exposure is desired.
- Lightfastness (AATCC 16E). This method determines the colorfastness of textile materials to light in a xenon arc fade-ometer after material is exposed to sixty "AATCC fading units" and judged visually for change. A Gray Scale rating of at least 4 is desired.
- Crocking (AATCC 8). This is the degree of color transfer from the carpet to a white cloth rubbed in a standard fashion across the carpet's face. After twenty friction cycles, the color transference is rated visually on the AATCC Chromatic Transference Scale. Results should be 4 or above.
- Shampooing (AATCC 138). This measures the color change caused by severe shampooing. Test specimens are rated visually on the Gray Scale Standard. Results should be below 4.

Pile density is important for the carpet to retain its appearance with wear. Dirt tends to remain on the surface of dense pile and can be vacuumed away. Permanent crushing is less likely with dense pile. A dense surface will feel hard underfoot, but comfort underfoot can be improved with a high-density commercial pad. A cushion can also significantly reduce pile compaction. However, in areas of heavy traffic, especially wheeled traffic including carts and wheelchairs, carpet should be glued directly to the floor.

Preventive maintenance is important. Entry points must have walk-off areas—grids, carpet tile, or other removable and cleanable surfaces. Outside entrances should be covered with outdoor carpet and swept daily. Parking lots should also be swept periodically to prevent foot traffic from carrying dirt into the building.

Multicolored or all-over patterns hide soil better than light or dark solids. Loop-pile carpets are most effective in hiding textural change. Cut-pile fibers become compressed with wear, whereas loop-pile fibers flex and bounce back.

The maintenance required and the cost of materials is closely related. Nylon, which costs more than olefin, will require less maintenance. On the other hand, olefin is a good choice for areas with less traffic.

Because of heavy traffic in school buildings, even the most durable carpets wear at a rapid rate, especially at the seams. Several manufacturers have developed bonding processes for carpets guaranteed against edge or seam ravel, at less than 10 percent weight loss of pile face fiber, and with static resistance effective for the life of the carpet.

An antimicrobial treatment also offered deters bacteria growth, a problem in health care facilities, cafeterias, and some classrooms. In offices and classrooms static can cause problems with computers. Total electric compatibility (TEC) carpets feature a special conductive backing that manufacturers guarantee will not cause disruption or malfunction of electronic equipment.

Static Buildup
Topically applied static treatments are not permanent. With use, these coatings will wear off. The most effective static dissipator for nylon, olefin, or wool is a carbonized fiber added in the construction of the carpet to absorb and discharge excessive static. With a conductive element added to the yarn bundle, carpets will effectively keep static buildup below the sensitivity level. (For cut pile constructions a conductive back may be required.) An effective test method to determine the static propensity of carpets is the AATCC-134, step test with Neolite soles. This test induces and measures static buildup on carpets by simulating conditions under which the static electricity may become objectionable. Peak charge generation (at 70°F and 20 percent relative humidity), developed by walking or shuffling traffic, is monitored under carefully

regulated conditions and related to the threshold of charge above which objectionable shock may be experienced. For areas with delicate electronic equipment, the equipment manufacturer should be consulted for maximum static control levels that can be tolerated.

Modular Carpet   Many factors have influenced the popularity of modular carpet or carpet tile. It is cost-effective, has good quality control, performs well, is easily maintained, and can be used to create unique custom designs. Advantages also include less office disruption during installation, increased flexibility, extended life, and easier access to the subfloor.

The flexibility afforded by carpet modules enables rearrangement in offices without patching the carpeting where power and telephone lines were installed. When workstations are moved in an open plan furniture system, damaged tiles can simply be picked up and replaced.

The life cycle of carpet modules can be extended from two to five years by selectively replacing and rotating tiles subjected to heavy traffic, excessive soiling, or abnormal abuse. In-house employees can easily perform this task.

Carpet tiles are particularly appropriate in installations using flat cable or raised access floors. With other systems, such as trench ducts, carpet tiles are the most practical floor covering.

Unique design capabilities are possible with carpet tiles because of the variety of colors, patterns, and textures. Contrasting colors can be used as borders, to indicate departmental separation or efficient traffic flow. Many carpet modules are available in coordinating broadloom so that it is possible to denote a hierarchy of areas with a cut pile broadloom in one area and a coordinating looped pile carpet module in another.

Resilient Flooring   A wide selection of resilient flooring materials exists; the price ranges from inexpensive linoleum to the more costly vinyls. Installation is simple and inexpensive; however, some of these materials cannot be installed on floors that are either on-grade or below grade. The resilient flooring materials on the market include linoleum, asphalt tile, cork, vinyl composition tile, vinyl, and rubber.

Linoleum is a synthetic material manufactured mostly in sheet form. Linoleum has limited resistance to acetone, and is unstable to strong alkaline solutions. It was the first synthetic flooring available and has been widely used for heavy duty installations, including flooring for battleships.

Asphalt tile, though still available, has generally been phased out in favor of newer synthetic tiles. It was widely used simply because it was the least expensive. Asphalt tile was used in factories, housing projects, and many other facilities where durability and economy are important. It is brittle and hard underfoot, but practical.

Cork is the only natural material used in resilient flooring. It is resilient and acoustical but not appropriate for heavy duty use. Cork must be kept waxed to preserve the surface. It can become more attractive with age, developing a rich warm patina from many applications of wax.

Vinyl composition tile (VCT), previously vinyl asbestos tile (VAT), reflects the current concern over products containing asbestos, which has been eliminated from many commonly used products. This type of tile is only slightly more expensive than asphalt, but has many advantages as it is softer underfoot, grease resistant, easily maintained, and available in many colors and patterns. Solid vinyls are the most durable, and many designers prefer their natural appearance rather than the imitations of other materials. A solid color floor will show heel marks and other dirt more readily than a patterned or textured floor. In high-traffic areas, a marbleized appearance or a textured surface is more appropriate.

A trend in flooring today is 100 percent rubber flooring in a studded tile. These tiles have raised circular or rounded square patterns which are attractive, resilient, long wearing, and nonslip; they have excellent acoustical properties, resist burns and most chemicals, and minimize breakage. The manufacturer has resolved the problem of dirt accumulation around the raised studs by sloping the sides of each raised stud.

An accessory item used in commercial installations to trim off many resilient floors is vinyl wall base, which is available in cove or toeless base. In finishing resilient flooring, a cove style base is generally preferred, as it hides the uneven cut edge of the flooring. This is available in the following heights: 1-1/2 in., 2-1/2 in., 3 in., 4 in., 6 in., and 7 in., with 2-1/2 in., 4 in., and 6 in. being the most commonly used. It comes in 4-foot pieces or 100-foot rolls and molds to form inside and outside corners. Preformed corners are available. Vinyl wall base is unbreakable, easily cleaned, and never needs painting.

Ceramic/Quarry Tile   Tiles are one of the most attractive, durable and versatile surfacing materials for indoor and outdoor use. They offer tremendous design potential as borders and in patterns. Ceramic tiles come in many colors from bold shades to subdued hues. For a look demanding warm colors and earth tones in numerous shapes, textures, shades, and sizes, quarry tile provides a rich, natural look. This tile exhibits the strength and durability needed in educational environments. In addition, some quarry products are finished with abrasive grain surfaces to improve slip resistance.

Though tiles provide a durable surface in hard-wear areas, they cannot tolerate direct blows, as in the dropping of heavy objects. Cart traffic can crack and break them, especially along unprotected edges. In work areas where people must stand for long periods, rubber mats can cushion the surface and help reduce fatigue.

Trim pieces for tiles come in all colors, with flat or roll-top. Outside corners are precast, and the straight base will not shrink or pull away if properly installed. When selecting tiles, be aware that some imported tiles do not come with a full line of trim pieces.

Wall Covering

Every wall is a material in itself and ideally no material need be covered. Designers today prefer honesty of materials; for example, the desirability of brick walls. Designers will remove many surface layers of old paint and plaster to reach these structural walls in old buildings.

Wallpaper is the material commonly associated with wall coverings for interiors. Today, many patterns and solids exist in every imaginable color. If the intent is to achieve a particular effect, and if a strong pattern or color is desired, a well-designed wallpaper can be a meaningful asset. Often a strong paper works better on one wall, instead of surrounding the whole space with a dominating pattern.

Most designers note that a well-planned interior, conceived as a total design, does not need the superficial decoration of printed paper; the superfluous pattern and color might actually detract. Plain walls, walls of solid colors or textures, or walls of natural materials are usually more acceptable, especially in the institutional environment.

Attractive wallpapers, however, can serve a specific purpose and have some intrinsic qualities of their own. These include textured papers, often made from natural materials such as silk and grass cloth. Advantages include improved acoustical properties and an atmosphere of interest and warmth. The lamination of linen, burlap, or other textures onto paper backing provides an attractive background in areas where an elegant image is desired. These natural fibers should, however, be treated with a protective sealant to prevent excessive soiling.

Plastic-coated or vinyl wallpapers are useful wall coverings in kitchens and bathrooms. Washable, they stand up better than painted surfaces to steam or grease. The best of these wall coverings are vinyl-coated fabrics, rather than coated papers, which are appropriate in all high-traffic areas. Vinyl-coated fabrics come in different weights; the heavier the anticipated wear, the heavier the material should be. The cost of some of the heavy vinyls is quite high but is justifiable in that the material can withstand countless scrubbings.

One special-purpose wall covering provides advance warning in case of fire before there is actually smoke or open flames in the room. Early warning effect (EWE) wall coverings, when heated to 300°F, emit a colorless, odorless, and harmless vapor that will activate ionization-type smoke detectors, which represent 85 percent of those installed. The 300°F trigger point for these wall coverings is well below the ignition temperatures of most common room materials, including paper, cotton, polyethylene, and polyurethane foam. The EWE may be triggered by electrical outlet overloads that heat wall surfaces, electrical fires in walls, fires started in other rooms or in core service areas, and other situations where smoke and fire danger may not be readily detected by smoke alarms.

Depending on the project budget and the designer's imagination, there is almost no limit to the materials that might be used for wall coverings: fabric, leather, wood veneers, wall carpet, or metallic materials. Cork is frequently used for practical purposes, such as tack space or sound-absorbing properties, as well as for its appearance.

Textiles

In judging a fabric for durability, the weave should be examined—the tighter the weave, the longer the fabric will wear. In fabrics where the colors and pattern are tightly woven in with colored threads, the fabric will wear better than a printed fabric. To check a fabric, hold it up to the light. The less light showing through, the tighter the weave.

The blending of fibers combines the unique properties of each and can produce a more attractive and durable fabric than that of one fiber. For example, a fiber which takes color well and is lustrous, but not particularly sturdy, can be woven with one which is duller, but durable, to produce a vivid and heavy-duty fabric. The appearance of a fiber can be altered by its construction or by blending. Textiles can be divided into natural or man-made fibers.

Natural Fibers   Those of animal origin include wool, silk, mohair, felt, and leather. Silk and wool, the luxurious and costly natural fibers, offer durability, resilience, and beauty. To clean silk, professionally dry clean. Wool can be spot dry cleaned or washed in a cool, sudsy water solution.

Natural fibers of vegetable origin include cotton, linen, and jute. Cotton has fair resistance to wear and sunlight and a soft feel; it dyes well but must be treated to avoid excessive soiling. Its care involves dry cleaning or washing, depending on the other fibers with which it is blended.

Man-Made Fibers   The following man-made fibers are all of chemical origin:

- Acrylic (Orlon, Creslan, Acrilan, Zefran). This has a soft woolly feeling with fair resistance to sunlight. It has good cleanability characteristics and takes vivid color well. Acrylic is normally used to create plush velvet looks. It wears well and will not bag or stretch after continued seating. Clean acrylic with mild, water-free solvents.
- Nylon (Antron, Enka, Chemstrand, Caprolan). Exceptionally rugged and durable, nylon resists signs of wear and tear. A man-made fiber offering the best resistance to soil, it dyes well and will not fade. Professional dry cleaning is recommended.
- Olefin or Polypropylene (Herculon, Vectra). This fabric offers high resistance to abrasion and stains. It has a softer feel than nylon, good resistance to fading when solution dyed, and is very sensitive to heat. In humid climates where mildew can be a problem, it is a good choice. Use only water-based cleaning solutions for its care.
- Polyester (Dacron, Fortrel, Kodel). Polyester is crisp and strong and fairly resistant to wear and sunlight. It is most like natural cotton in its appearance and physical properties. Its resistance to heat is low. This fabric accepts color well and is easy to clean using mild water-free solvents.
- Rayon (Avril, Enica, Fortisan). This is composed of regenerated cellulose (a wood by-product). It dyes well, is soft to the touch, and has fair resistance to wear and sunlight. Rayon can be constructed to look like cotton, silk, or wool. To care for it, dry clean or wash, depending on other fiber blends.

There are also fibers of metallic origin. These fibers are made of aluminum, silver, or gold threads, usually in combination with natural or man-made fibers.

Woven Fabrics   When any fiber or blend of fibers is woven together, the visual texture and pattern of the fabric is created. Two basic methods of weaving upholstered fabrics exist: flat and pile. Flat weaves include tweeds, twills, and satins. They have no pile although they may be coarse and nubby because of the uneven size of the yarns. Woven-pile fabrics are those in which an extra set of warp or filling yarns is interlaced with the ground warp and filling. In this way loops or cut ends are produced on the surface of the fabric. The base or ground fabric may be either plain or twill weave.

Nonwoven Fabrics   These fabrics are knitted, flocked, or tufted. Knitting is a method of construction in which yarns are looped and interlocked instead of woven. Flocking involves creating a velvet effect using cut fibers applied electrostatically. Tufting is another method of locking yarns on the surface. These loops can then be cut to create a velvet surface. Another classification of nonwoven fabrics includes those fabrics created through a process of pressing or bonding fibers together with an adhesive.

Window Treatments

Window treatments include many decorative or functional methods for finishing a room. Aside from aesthetics, they have great practical value. They can insulate against winter heat loss and summer heat gain, control glare, provide privacy, absorb noise, and lower maintenance costs. The total environment should be considered when determining whether blinds, shades, draperies, or any other treatment is used. Cost-effectiveness is always an important aspect of window treatments in an institutional environment.

The following items are components of cost-effectiveness. They should be considered when making a decision regarding the least costly window treatment that will satisfy requirements.

- Initial Cost. Materials, fabrication, and installation costs vary. For example, drapery costs would be considerably higher than those for roller shades.
- Energy Conservation. This depends on window orientation and could amount to a sizable reduction in air conditioning and heating capacity.
- Expected Service Life. The amount of use and type of maintenance determines service life. Blinds have a service life of approximately ten years; shades, three to five years; and draperies, five years.
- Maintenance. Vacuuming and periodic professional cleaning should be included in regular maintenance costs.

Blinds   Flexibility is the key to their popularity. Many options address every type of window requirement. Blinds that are one color inside and another color outside ensure a unified building exterior appearance while maintaining inside design flexibility. Blinds can be custom-made to almost any shape opening: A-frame, bay window, inclined, tapered, cutouts, circular, or arched. Two blinds on one headrail enable one to be raised while the other is lowered.

Blinds are available with heat-absorbing or -reflecting finishes to help cut energy costs. If heat buildup between the blind and glass is a concern, as it may be with thermal glass, special drop-down brackets allow an additional 1/4-in. gap at the top of the blind. This permits the heat buildup in the airspace to be vented. Another alternative involves eliminating the top slat from the blind to increase the air gap. Additional air gaps at the sides and bottom of the blind can also be specified.

Vertical blinds combine the flexibility of blinds with the luxury of draperies. They give a dramatic, contemporary look to a room, while controlling light and privacy. Vertical blinds are available in many colors and materials, including fabrics, plastics, and aluminum. Replacement fabric vanes allow easy repair; fire retardant vanes are also available.

When specifying blinds, it is best to require that the contractor be responsible for inspection of the site, approval of mounting surface, installation conditions, and field measurements, rather than simply furnishing measurements to a vendor. Costly mistakes can occur if measurements are not exact.

Types of blinds include: painted aluminum, 1/2-in., 1-in., 1-3/8-in., and 2-in. slats; natural wood, 1-in. or 2-in. slats;, audiovisual, 2-in. slats; sun controller for the exterior and interior, 1-in., 2-in., and 3-1/2-in. slats; and vertical, 2-in. and 3-1/2-in. vanes in aluminum, fabric, and plastic.

Shades   Shades control light and privacy, maintain interior temperature levels, and accent windows. There are shades for exterior use, pleated shades, and blackout shades for those areas where complete blackout of light is necessary. Shades are available in fiberglass-coated polyester or can be fabricated in the designer's own fabric to coordinate with an interior decorating scheme. Shades present many creative options; provide superior light control; save energy; and are convenient to install, adjust and, remove.

Pleated shades come in many weights: sheer fabrics to filter light, semi-opaque fabrics to provide more privacy, and thicker fabrics to keep out the sun. Various types of shades include blackout shades, solar screens, and pleated shades.

Curtains and Draperies   Some commonly held misconceptions exist regarding the terminology associated with window treatments. The following definitions will clarify interpretations of these words, which are often used as synonyms.

- Curtains. Window coverings fabricated from sheer or lightweight material such as cotton, polyester, rayon, or blends of these fibers are called curtains. They are used in less formal interiors. Curtains may be used alone or in combination with overdraperies. They may be lined or unlined and are generally shirred on a rod but may also be pinch pleated. Hung inside a window casing, they should reach to the window sill. Hung on an outside casing, they should hang to the bottom of the apron or to the floor.

- Draperies. These are also commonly called "drapes." They create a more formal mood and are generally of heavier fabrics. They are usually lined, of pleated construction, and weighted at the bottom. Draperies are generally hung on traverse rods that allow them to open and shut. They may be hung to the bottom of the apron or to the floor.
- Valance. A separate top or horizontal portion of the drapery treatment is called a valance. Valances were originally used to hide the drapery hardware, but have survived for decorative reasons. Valances are generally four to six inches deep and made of softly draped, gathered, or pleated fabric.
- Cornice. A three-sided box-like top for a window treatment, with the open side of the box facing the wall, is a cornice. This overhanging box is sometimes used, as is a valance, to hide drapery hardware. A cornice is generally from four to seven inches deep and fabricated of wood, plaster, or metal. It can be upholstered to match the draperies or in another coordinating fabric. A properly designed cornice can add height to short windows.

Though there are no hard and fast rules, the following generalizations will generally apply.

Valances should not be used in rooms with extremely low ceilings. A valance with curved lines makes the window appear wider; one with square lines makes it seem narrower. Straight draperies without a valance or cornice make windows seem taller.

Draperies that are tied back soften a room's severity. A pair of looped-back curtains makes a window seem narrower than a single curtain tied back.

Tiebacks should be located either above or below the center line of the window. Usually, the higher the tieback, the taller the window appears. Straight, plain draperies, as a rule, are not looped back.

French doors should be treated as windows. If between rooms, they should not be draped. For privacy, they can be fitted with sheer curtains gathered on small rods at the top and bottom.

Bay windows or two adjacent windows should be treated as one, with a single drapery at the outer edge of each. This gives the effect of one large window and makes them appear much wider. If a valance is used, it should run across the windows.

Casement windows require special treatment. Those that swing inward are generally fitted with shirred curtains fastened to the top and bottom. Those that swing out are usually fitted with straight-hanging curtains or draperies.

Draperies and curtains should present a uniform appearance from the street. All windows, at least those on the same level, should have the same kind of curtains, or draperies with white linings.

Maintenance, obstruction of view when closed, and possible breakage when used with heat-absorbing glass are some of disadvantages of draperies.

Four major types of drapery construction are used in commercial installations: pinch pleat systems, stack pleat systems, roll pleat systems, and accordion-type pleating systems. Pinch pleat systems are probably the most commonly used. They are constructed with pleater tape and are generally attached to the slide carriers of a standard traverse rod.

Installation specifications should include a drawing of the window and wall with bracket locations clearly marked. The drapery workroom will need specific instructions and a sample of the drapery fabric. To avoid delays caused by flaws in the fabric, order extra yardage.

Drapery Flammability Regulations   Many codes recognize drapery covering more than 10 percent of the wall area an interior finish. The most frequently quoted flammability codes are those of the City of New York, the City of Boston, and the State of California.

1. The City of New York requires all flame-retardant chemicals be approved by a board of standards and appeals. After receiving approval from the Board, a number is issued. This number is used on a certificate stating that the fabric has been treated with the approved flame retardant.
2. The City of Boston requires that a sample of the treated fabric be tested by the Boston Fire Department. A certificate of flame retardancy and statement of intended use must be furnished with the sample to the fire department.
3. The State of California requires that the State Fire Marshal approve all flame-retardant chemicals. California law also requires that the flame-retardant treatment be applied in an approved manner, by a licensed finishing company.

Fabrics such as fiberglass, wool, and some modacrylics are considered inherently flame resistant. These fabrics do not require flame-retardant treatment. Fabrics containing a blend of saran, verel-mod-acrylic, and rayon are mildew-, rot-, and vermin-proof and will melt rather than support flame. Even though these fabrics are inherently flame-retardant, designers should have materials tested to determine if fabrication or finishing has impaired their natural properties.

Cabinetry

One indication of quality in cabinetry and case goods is drawer construction. The drawers should have concealed dovetail construction at the front, and in better quality cabinetry, also at the back. The drawer bottom should be substantial and grooved into the sides. For added strength, small glue blocks are used. Better grades of cabinets have side and back panels of five-ply veneer. The sides and usually the back should be grooved into the posts.

If a project includes custom-built cabinetry, it is sometimes preferable to separate it from the general contract. This permits careful selection of a cabinetmaker. Drawings should be prepared covering type and grade of materials, finishes, hardware, and special equipment. Cabinet details are usually drawn at a large scale—1 in. to 0 in. or even full-scale. If the designer is not familiar with detailing, he or she may prepare small-scale drawings and require shop drawings from the cabinetmaker for approval.

Furniture

Furniture Styles   Designers should know the history of furniture and be able to recognize the more important periods. The strongest influence on the current interpretation of traditional furnishings originates from the seventeenth century.

In general, period furniture can be divided into two major categories: formal and informal styles. Formal describes furniture originally designed for the royal courts and spacious homes of the wealthy. The informal style included simpler pieces made by local craftspeople, using crude tools and local woods. Provincial styles and Early American furniture are examples of the informal category.

Modern describes a new design form that breaks away from previous forms. An expression of the twentieth century, it uses new materials in new ways. Functionalism is the key and determines form with emphasis on line, proportion, color, texture, and finish.

Both traditional and contemporary furniture are used in institutional settings. The most appropriate selection would consider the total environment, rather than personal stylistic preferences.

Well-designed furniture exists in either contemporary or period styles. In planning furniture requirements, consider the image you want to create—one of solid, conservative values, or one of progressive, efficient simplicity.

Seating   The selection of seating is important. Workers spend many hours each day at a desk, and the right chair promotes efficiency, relaxation, and production. A determination must first be made of the functions the seating must perform. Then it should be evaluated for durability, cost, comfort, ergonomics, appearance, space savings, safety, and availability.

Durability ensures your investment. Test the seating under actual conditions and ask for references of others using the product under similar conditions.

In addition to the initial cost, consider the handling and maintenance costs. The cost of arranging and moving furniture to and from storage or rearranging or moving seating for cleaning purposes can become greater than the initial cost.

Seating comfort is important as it can affect the degree of learning in a classroom situation, the acceptance of waiting in a lounge area, and the pleasure of a banquet event. Comfort in office seating increases efficiency and job satisfaction.

Ergonomics relates to all elements in the person's work environment, including sound and lighting, layout, carpeting, desks, files, and seating. The following factors should be taken into consideration when evaluating seating: seat height, appearance, space savings, safety, and availability.

Upholstered Furniture   Purchasing upholstered furniture can be deceptive. Unlike case goods, quality construction in upholstered goods can be difficult to detect. An attractive fabric can hide inferior products and workmanship. Items to be considered when evaluating upholstered furniture are: frame construction, springs, padding material, and fillings.

Upholstery Flammability Regulations   The designer must be aware of particular flammability hazards in certain types of installations, i.e., areas where smoking is permitted; places where people sit for extended periods, such as transportation seating; and lounge areas in public buildings. Areas where the lighting level is low, and where live-in accommodations include bedding, such as dormitories, are also hazardous.

When planning upholstery for these areas, the fabric should be inherently flame resistant, or protected by a flame-retardant treatment.

Upholstery fabrics that do not meet the Class 1 requirements of the U.S. Department of Commerce Commercial Standard 191-53 should not be used on upholstered furniture.

Surface treatments such as tufting and seams on seat areas should be avoided. Tufting should be limited to vertical surfaces. Cigarettes rank high among ignition sources and each tuft in a seat cushion provides an area where a cigarette can burn unnoticed. Seams in seats tend to split, exposing the filling to possible ignition. If possible, specify seating with at least a 1-in. gap between the seat and the back.

Office Landscaping   Office landscape designates an informal, open, flexible system of furniture arrangement based on the interrelationships among groups to allow more efficient communication. Partitions and components required to support the work of each area compose the landscape. The partitions are available in various heights to provide different levels of privacy. Generally, they do not reach the ceiling; however, some manufacturers, in an effort to make them more appealing, have provided a complementary line of partitions that reach the ceiling, forming private offices where required.

Because these systems are open, provisions for noise control must be carefully planned. Ceilings should be of acoustical materials, and floors carpeted. Acoustical panels should be placed where noise is generated to absorb as much of it as possible. Sound masking systems can be very helpful in lowering the noise level. Draperies and plants are also effective.

Although some form of flexible office furniture system has been available since the late 1940s, this type furniture became popular during the 1970s and seemed to be the answer to all office layout problems. However, in the late 1970s this trend began to change as management and staff complained about the lack of privacy and the problem with noise. Full-height partitions (called by various names—movable, demountable, or relocatable) became popular. Their popularity seems to be continuing, as these partitions are compatible with and offer the flexibility of the lower-height systems, but provide greater privacy and sound control. The open office of today uses both types of systems. More consideration is now given to the employee's need for privacy as well as the need for accessibility.

Many important factors should be considered before purchasing a system: flexibility and ease of reconfiguration, simplicity of installation, capability for handling electrical requirements for power, and communication and data processing equipment as needed. It should provide design options such as a variety of panel sizes, components, and finishes.

Furniture Standards   The objectives of a standards program are:

- Volume purchasing savings. Vendors will often offer advantageous terms above and beyond the usual quantity discounts when the line is made "standard."
- Management time savings. Streamlining the selection and acquisition process eliminates catalog skimming.
- Reduced competitive behavior among employees. Consistently applied standards reduce competitive behavior among employees, while helping eliminate jealousy and resentment over office size and furniture quantity.
- Aesthetic consistency. Furniture standards programs often deal with visual design and attractiveness of office environments.
- Improved environmental function. Problems of using furniture and space to the best functional advantage are often addressed through standards, rather than leaving each employee to use trial and error to find the best arrangement for a particular job function.
- Multiple workstation question. Function problems involving the arrangement of many employees and such overall considerations as the Occupational Safety and Health Administration's (OSHA) fire and safety regulations are more easily and consistently dealt with on a standards level than case by case.

Lighting

Three general categories of light sources are available: natural daylight, incandescent electric light, and electric discharge lighting.

Daylight is constantly changing throughout the day in position, intensity, diffusion, and color. In any design using natural daylight, three conditions should be considered: light directly from the sun combined with reflected light from a clear sky, light from a clear sky only, and light from an overcast sky. Various indirect variables also affect daylight, including local terrain, landscaping, water, fenestration, daylight control systems (shades and louvers), decor, and artificial light.

A light-producing wire (filament), which burns to incandescence in a vacuum or atmosphere of gases, produces light in an incandescent lamp. Hundreds of this type are available, and each is designed for a particular practical or aesthetic purpose. Four classes are most important.

- General service lamps are the most common. They come in a wide range of intensities and sizes and produce light in all directions.

- Tungsten-halogen (often called quartz or iodine) lamps are small and of comparatively long life.
- Reflectorized lamps are actually fully enclosed lighting instruments. They feature a light source, reflector, and lens within a single glass enclosure that can be screwed into any socket.
- Decorative lamps are designed to be seen "as is"; their bulb shapes are globular, conical, tubular, chimney-like, and flame-shaped.

Electric discharge lamps are available in two types:

- Low-intensity discharge lamps, common in office installations, are usually fluorescent are tubular in shape.
- High-intensity discharge (HID) is a compact light source including mercury vapor, multivapor, and high-pressure sodium. HID sources have traditionally been used in industrial or street-lighting applications, although they are now in all forms of architecture.

Both types have one aspect in common—they must be used with a special device called a ballast. The ballast regulates the amount of electricity used.

Ceiling Lighting Systems   Ceiling lighting systems are the most popular type of lighting. The ease with which plastic parabolic louvers can be adapted for retrofitting existing fluorescent fixtures with prismatic lenses contributes to their popularity. By doing this, glare on video display terminal (VDT) screens and other surfaces can be eliminated. Lighting designed using new energy-saving products and techniques costs little more than the ordinary fluorescent troffer with a prismatic lens.

Indirect Lighting   Indirect lighting is somewhat more costly because fixtures have to be more attractive as they are not hidden in the plenum.
Ceiling maintenance is an important factor in indirect lighting. A clean, new light-colored ceiling has 80 percent reflectance. After three years, it loses about 30 percent of that reflectance. Other disadvantages include hot spots on the ceiling when lights are placed too close it; a "cloudy day" environment with a high ceiling; and, if placed too low, direct glare.
With conventional troffered ceiling light, partitions can create dark shadowed areas in work spaces. Task lighting can illuminate dark areas, but changes in the workstation configuration also change the lighting

pattern. The new integrated lighting systems are more flexible, moving with the workstation.

Workers report eye strain related to VDT use. In tests using comparisons between direct or indirect lighting, workers gave the highest ratings to indirect lighting, citing relative freedom from glare on the computer screen, from lights, and from other reflective surfaces. They also reported feeling more productive and preferred the overall subtle light distribution rather than the glaring intensity of direct overhead lighting.

Fluorescent is the most popular in classrooms and in hallways. Energy-efficient fluorescents operate on reduced wattage, which saves on energy consumption.

For outdoor applications, incandescent or high-intensity discharge sources—mercury vapor, metal halide, or high-pressure sodium—are the most prevalent. High-pressure sodium has a 24,000-hour life expectancy, thus it lasts longer than the incandescent. Incandescents have about a 1,000-hour life expectancy. Incandescent and high-pressure sodium light sources are not affected by extremes in temperature. Fluorescents are not recommended for outdoor use.

High-pressure sodium lighting offers the advantage of low maintenance over incandescents because of the longer life. Operating costs are also lower because high-pressure sodium uses less energy. In spite of the high cost, paybacks on energy efficient lighting come quickly. In short, significant energy savings, improved security, and additional savings through lower maintenance costs can be achieved by the proper selection of lighting type.

Acoustics

Masking sound is one effective way to increase sound privacy. By slightly increasing the ambient sound level, masking sound covers distracting noises. Masking sound is adjusted and fine-tuned to give exactly the right level of acoustical privacy without becoming a nuisance. Masking systems must be programmed to their most desired level in each particular case.

In an open office environment, masking sound is critical. For the closed office, masking sound can result in confidential privacy. Masking can provide sound privacy without resorting to more expensive conventional construction techniques, such as insulating the drywalls or extending the walls through the suspended ceiling to the structural ceiling above. The masking system can also accommodate other audio functions, such as paging and music, utilizing the same speaker system.

20.5 FURNITURE ARRANGEMENT AND SPACE PLANNING

Furniture Arrangement

Standardized furniture arrangements are almost useless, since each client's needs are unique. To provide a furniture arrangement which will be both aesthetically and functionally successful, the designer must analyze the space, determining the flow of traffic and activities. Relationships of scale, mass of furniture to the area, and contrast of elements all must be considered.

Analysis of Space   The designer should first make a thorough analysis of the space. On the first visit to the area the designer should note dimensions and indicate all architectural features, existing lighting, HVAC supply, electrical outlets, and existing finishes in the area. Photographs are particularly helpful.

Flow of Traffic   A scale drawing of the floor plan should be prepared if none is available. On this preliminary plan, the traffic paths should be indicated by arrows from the entry to all points of interest within the space—exits to other rooms, closets, storage, and windows. This effectively divides the room into zones of activity. The designer must know the intended use, then he or she can determine furniture requirements and assign activities to zones based on the square footage required for each activity.

Scale and Mass of Furnishings   Scale and mass in an interior is based on their relative proportion to persons, other objects, and the space they occupy. An interior should appear neither crowded nor underfurnished. If an object were removed, the space should appear incomplete.

Large areas allow large-scaled furnishings. Small-scaled objects generally look insignificant in large spaces. Distribution of mass should be balanced throughout the space. The specific location as well as the overall space must be considered. For example, a piece of furniture should relate in proportion to the wall against which it is placed.

Contrast of Elements   To avoid monotony, the lines of furnishings and architectural features should vary. A room whose focus is high windows and doors needs horizontal balance. Conversely, a space with strong horizontal architectural accents needs the balance of high pieces of furniture to heighten the vertical line of the space.

Balance in the space and between objects gives a harmonious composition. Too much similarity or lack of contrast causes a space and the objects in it to appear dull and uninteresting. The success or failure of the design depends on how well the space functions and how well it serves the needs of the client.

Basic Guidelines

The following general guidelines offer suggestions for planning the arrangement of furniture.

1. Plan each room with a purpose. Decide what the room will be used for and by whom.
2. Use furniture in keeping with the scale of the room.
3. Provide space for traffic. Doorways should be free. Major traffic lanes must be unobstructed. It is sometimes necessary to redirect traffic. This can be accomplished by turning a sofa, a desk, or chairs toward the room and at right angles to the door with a passageway left for traffic.
4. Arrange furnishings to give the room a sense of equilibrium.
5. Achieve a good balance of high and low, angular and rounded furniture. Where furniture is all or predominantly low, the feeling of height may be created by incorporating shelves, mirrors, and pictures in a grouping.
6. Consider architectural and mechanical features. There should be no interference with the opening of windows, swinging of doors, or heating or air-conditioning devices. Lamps should be placed near electrical outlets.
7. Do not overcrowd a room. It is always better to be underfurnished than overfurnished.
8. Generally, large pieces of furniture should be placed parallel to the walls.
9. Avoid pushing large pieces tightly into a corner, or close against floor-to-ceiling windows where a passageway should be allowed.
10. Arrange the heaviest furniture grouping along the highest wall in rooms with slanted ceilings.
11. Provide adequate lighting for all activities.

In planning office layout the following may be helpful. (See Figure 20-3.)

1. Office floor space must be conserved, but not at the expense of appearance, production, or comfort.
2. Place related departments near each other.

3. Each employee, including his or her desk, chair space, and share of the aisle, requires 50 to 75 square feet of working space.
4. A general conference room where confidential meetings may be held will eliminate the need for many private offices.
5. A minimum of 9 feet by 12 feet is a standard size for small private offices.
6. Standard widths for main circulating aisles vary from 5 feet to 8 feet. Less important aisles vary from 3 feet to 5 feet.

Space Planning

Programming   Programming is the determination of the parts and their interrelationships. Precise information is vital to the effective planning and layout of office environments. Considerations to address include the amount, kind, and configuration of space and the relative closeness or relationships of each unit.

Space determination should begin early in the planning process. Decisions must be made as to which location is appropriate for each function. This preliminary figure is, however, only an estimate, determined without detailed analysis. Functional relationship should be established before the division of space gets too involved. Later, particular pieces of equipment may necessitate detailed planning.

A flowchart, sometimes called a "bubble chart" or space relationship diagram, should be prepared to indicate all related activities and groups, without concern for actual space required by each. Next, through careful programming, the designer establishes the space required for each activity. Then the area is fitted into the relationship diagram. This preliminary layout, once refined, becomes the final floor plan.

Several ways of establishing space requirements are: calculation, conversion, space standards, and rough layout.

The calculation method involves a physical inventory prepared for each area. Inventory control lists are usually available for this purpose. Each activity or area is broken down into subareas. An assessment of space required for each subarea is made. This is then multiplied by the number of elements required to do the job, with extra space added for storage and service.

The conversion method establishes the space presently occupied and converts it to the proposed amount. Before making the conversion to the new plan, the designer must decide if the occupied space is less than the amount actually needed.

Another method, established space standards, is a practical way to determine space requirements any time a given situation arises. Stan-

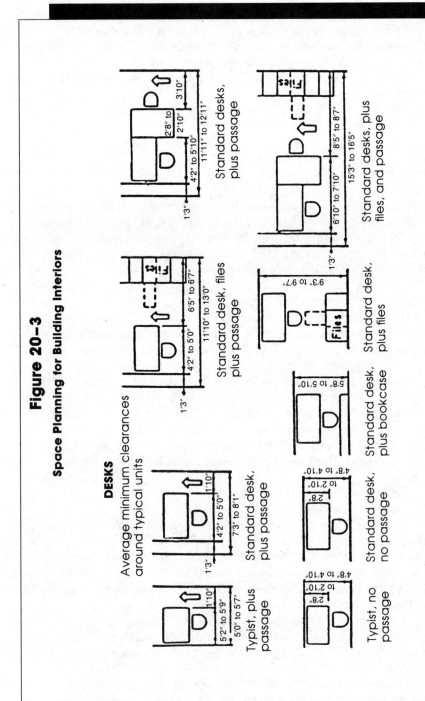

Figure 20-3
Space Planning for Building Interiors

DESKS

Average minimum clearances around typical units

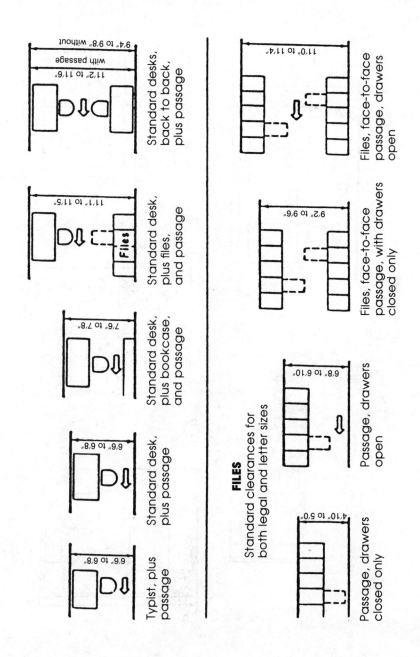

9'4" to 9'8" without
with passage
11'2" to 11'6"

Standard desks,
back to back,
plus passage

11'0" to 11'4"

Files, face-to-face
passage, drawers
open

11'1" to 11'5"

Standard desk,
plus files,
and passage

9'2" to 9'6"

Files, face-to-face
passage, with drawers
closed only

7'6" to 7'8"

Standard desk,
plus bookcase,
and passage

6'8" to 6'10"

Passage, drawers
open

6'6" to 6'8"

Standard desk,
plus passage

FILES

Standard clearances for
both legal and letter sizes

4'10" to 5'0"

Passage, drawers
closed only

6'6" to 6'8"

Typist, plus
passage

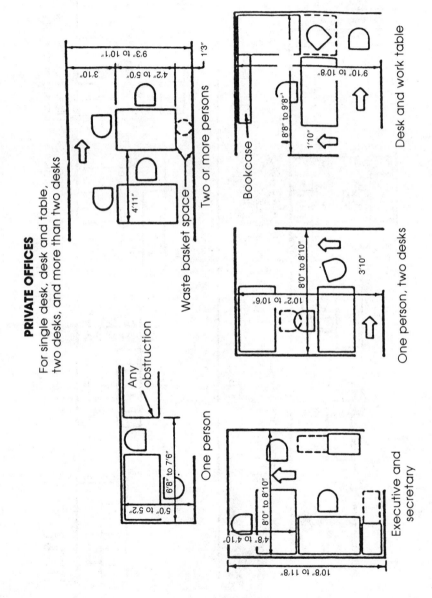

PRIVATE OFFICES

For single desk, desk and table,
two desks, and more than two desks

One person

Any obstruction
5'0" to 5'2"
6'8" to 7'6"

Two or more persons
9'3" to 10'1"
3'10"
4'2" to 5'0"
4'11"
1'3"

Waste basket space

Bookcase
Desk and work table
9'10" to 10'8"
8'8" to 9'8"
1'10"

One person, two desks
10'2" to 10'6"
8'0" to 8'10"
3'10"

Executive and secretary
10'8" to 11'8"
8'0" to 8'10"
4'8" to 4'10"

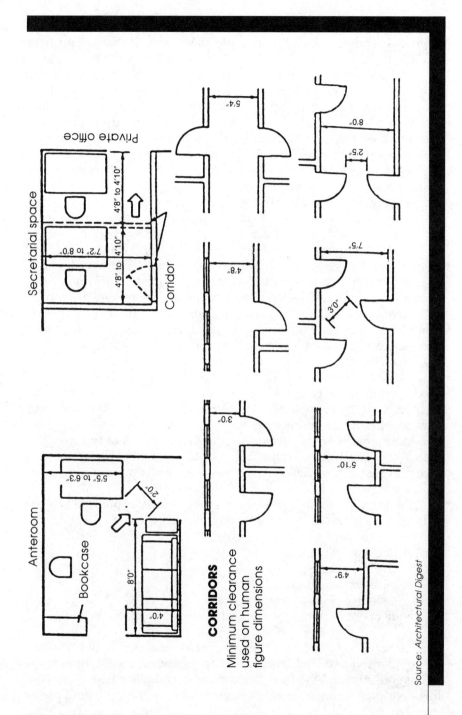

Private office

Secretarial space

4'8" to 4'10"

7'2" to 8'0"

4'8" to 4'10"

Corridor

Anteroom

Bookcase

5'5" to 6'3"

2'0"

8'0"

4'0"

CORRIDORS

Minimum clearance
used on human
figure dimensions

5'4"

8'0"

2'5"

4'8"

7'5"

3'0"

3'0"

5'10"

4'9"

Source: *Architectural Digest*

dards must be applied consistently. It is important to record how the standards were established and apply them fairly if they are to have credibility.

The planner or designer should meet first with management and establish goals. An organizational chart should be obtained. Meetings should be scheduled with personnel in various departments. Questions that should be asked are, How many people are in the group? What are their jobs? What are the furniture and equipment requirements to support the work performed there? Are there any plans for expansion?

After the planner obtains this information, it must be evaluated for actual needs versus wants of the client. The planner will prepare a written program, listing personnel, furniture, equipment, and services. He or she will then compute the square footage required for these functions. Finally, approval must be obtained on the program.

During this phase a furniture, furnishings, and equipment (F&E) inventory should be prepared. Three categories of F&E must be listed: 1) as is—items that can be moved without any attention; 2) refinish—items that must be refinished or reupholstered before they are acceptable; and 3) new—items that must be purchased. In purchasing F&E, count back from the planned moving date to determine the lead time necessary and always allow extra time for unexpected delays.

The most precise method of determining space requirements is the rough layout method. It is advisable in certain critical areas involving fixed equipment, large machinery, or multiple workstations. With this method, scale floor plans and templates are used to determine exact location of furniture and equipment.

Most projects are restricted by space limitations. As a rule, they are more restrictive than any other factor—except funding. If requirements exceed availability, reductions must be made. Lower priority area reductions are preferable to across-the-board cuts.

Solving the problem of limited space can be approached in the following ways:

1. Authorize overtime.
2. Improve procedures.
3. Organize wasted space.
4. Move storage areas to leased spaces.
5. Divide operations into groups and spread to available buildings.

Preliminary Design   At this point, a cost analysis should be made for comparison and justification. During this phase the analysis of the written program and the flow diagram are turned into a floor plan. With this floor plan a construction estimate can be prepared by multiplying the floor area required by the square foot construction cost. The furniture and equipment budget should be prepared at this point, then the total preliminary budget can be quoted. This phase of design is sometimes called a feasibility study.

Final Design   The floor plans are prepared during this phase. The space should be accurately measured, including size and location of structural elements. Furniture and equipment layouts are drawn, architectural materials chosen, and finishes specified. Mechanical engineers will be retained and air-handling equipment located and sized. This plan and an outline specification of materials and equipment permit refinement of the initial estimate.

Presentations   Presentation to the client is generally in graphic form, arranging floor plans and elevations, rendered perspectives, samples of fabrics and floor coverings, and photographs of furniture on display boards. Computer graphics can aid in the client's understanding. With information on plans and elevations, many computers can create perspective drawings. Some even "walk through" the space, simulating reality for the client, who is usually not as able to visualize the space from a two-dimensional drawing.

Working Drawings and Specifications   The general contractor uses the final drawings and specifications to properly estimate the job. They should contain all the information necessary to complete the project. Any item not accounted for in these documents may necessitate a change order, with an almost certain increase in costs.

All necessary approvals should be in writing. The specifications should be designed to protect and provide the quantity and quality of work expected. After bids are received and approved, the drawings and specifications, approvals, and costs are incorporated into the contract and actual work begins.

Supervision   The last phase of a project involves supervision. If the job is a large one, a representative should be on-site at all times. At this stage a designer's job involves, at the least, interpretation of the documents, approval of shop drawings, decisions regarding alternate submittals, preparation of change orders, expediting purchases, coordinating contractors' installations of new furniture and equipment, the physical move into a new space, punch-lists, and pay estimates.

Installation   In most institutions, the designer supervises furniture and equipment installations. Preparation for installation is most important and includes preparing installation plans and drawings; arranging for any maintenance work needed; scheduling the moves; and notifying everyone involved. Drawings and written instructions are the best way to communicate. Every drawing should show the north arrow, scale being used, identification of the building, sheet number, project identification, date, and the name of the person preparing the drawing.

Three basic phases to an installation should occur: planning, actual installation, and follow-up.

In the first phase, planning and scheduling begin, inventories are prepared, disposition of any existing equipment and furnishings are determined, communications are set up among in-house personnel and contractors, work orders are prepared, departmental personnel are notified, and decisions are made regarding furniture or equipment to be relocated. In coordinating the installation, the designer should use checklists of items likely to be overlooked. These lists should establish what is to be done, when it is needed, and who is to do it.

In the second phase, the actual installation, the designer must be on hand for layout interpretation. As the installation proceeds, the designer makes periodic checks on the status of the work and keeps work crews informed and coordinated.

The third phase, follow-up, requires the designer to inspect the installation to verify that all items are delivered undamaged and layout conforms to the drawings. If not, the designer must have any discrepancies corrected.

20.6 BARRIER-FREE ACCESSIBILITY

Barrier-free does not merely imply ramps and adequate door widths for the handciapped. The APPA publication *Modifying the Existing Campus Building for Accessibility: Construction Guidelines and Specifications* provides technical data and illustrations of standards. Aside from the obvious architectural barriers, psychological barriers exist. When handicapped persons must enter by a service entrance or ask assistance in opening doors, they feel humiliated and helpless.

The major federal act guaranteeing rights of equal access for the disabled is the Rehabilitation Act of 1973, Section 504, which states that "no otherwise qualified handicapped individual in the United States . . . shall, solely by reason of handicap, be excluded from participation in, be denied the benefits of, or be subjected to discrimination under any program or activity receiving Federal financial assistance."

Colleges and universities are required to make "reasonable adjustments" to enable disabled students to fulfill academic requirements and to assure that these students are not excluded from programs because of the absence of necessary modifications. Depending on the nature of the disability, modifications may include changes in the length of time required for completion of degree requirements, substitution of specific courses required, and changes in the way which specific courses are conducted.

Most colleges and universities take the position that all common space should be accessible to the handicapped. Other areas are made accessible on an "as needed basis."

On a campus-wide basis, curb cuts, ramps, and less hazardous signage and landscaping are necessary. On an individual building basis, restroom modifications; lowered telephones and water fountains; widened doors; ramps; and where feasible, elevators are needed.

Mobility-impaired individuals are commonly provided housing on the ground level of dormitory buildings. This policy is not well received by many proponents of rights for the handicapped as they believe this is discriminatory and isolates the person from the mainstream of activity.

There are exceptions to the rules and regulations to eliminate architectural barriers. The following exceptions are currently allowed by the federal government in accordance with Public Law 90-480, Subpart 101-19.604 "Exceptions," paragraphs a through d, as amended 1968:

1. The design, construction, or alteration of any portion which need not, because of its intended use, be made accessible to, or usable by, the public or physically disabled people.
2. The alteration of an existing building if the alteration does not involve the installation of, or work on, existing stairs, doors, elevators, toilets, entrances, drinking fountains, floors, telephone locations, curbs, parking areas, or other facilities susceptible to installation or improvements to accommodate physically disabled people.
3. The alteration of an existing building, or of such portions thereof, to which application is not structurally possible.
4. The construction or alteration of a building for which plans and specifications were completed or substantially completed on or before September 2, 1969. However, any building constructed under the National Transportation Act of 1960, the National Capital Transportation Act of 1965, or Title III of the Washington Metropolitan Area Transit Regulation Compact shall be designed, constructed, or altered in accordance with ANSI standards regardless of design status or bid solicitation as of September 2, 1969.

In many states, a state governmental agency, such as the Texas State Purchasing and General Services Commission's Architectural Barriers Department, will review for compliance and approve plans and specifications submitted prior to bidding and award of contract. In other states another agency reviews only college and university construction plans. In still others the college or university is governed by its own board of regents.

Whatever the governing body, after review it will decide to what extent the project shall be made to comply. Plans and specifications will be approved only when the documents reflect compliance with the appropriate accessibility standards and specifications, generally those of the American National Standards Institute, Providing Accessibility and Usability for Physically Handicapped People (ANSI A117.1-1986).

Upon completion of projects, on-site inspectors determine whether the appropriate standards have been met during construction. All complaints received by the commission or board must be investigated and resolved or referred to the proper authority with possible legal recourse.

20.7 SUMMARY

This chapter is intended to provide an understanding of the critical issues of building interior design. It serves to assist the facilities manager in developing guidelines for routine in-house decisions as well as in communicating better with consultants.

ADDITIONAL RESOURCES

Antes, Victor. "Some Viewpoints on Office and Task Lighting: A Recent Seminar." *Architectural Lighting*, Vol. 1, No. 7, July/August 1987.

Bell, Doreen. "Efficient, Effective Lighting." *School and College Product News*, September 1987.

Coons, Maggie and Margaret Milner, eds. *Creating an Accessible Campus.* Washington: APPA, 1979.

Cotler, Stephen R. *Modifying the Existing Campus Building for Accessibility: Consruction Guidelines and Specifications.* Washington: APPA, 1981.

Friedman, Arnold, John Pile, and Forrest Wilson. *Interior Design—An Introduction to Architectural Interiors.* New York: American Elsevier Publishing Co., 1976.

McMillan, Lorel. "Carpet Backs: The Underside View of Your Carpet Selection." *Facilities Design & Management*, Vol. 5, No. 7, July/August, 1986.

Reznikoff, S. C. *Specifications for Commercial Interiors—Professional Liabilities Regulations and Performance Criteria.* New York: Whitney Library Design, 1979.

Whiton, Sherrill. *Interior Design and Decoration.* New York: J. B. Lippincott Company, 1974.

CHAPTER 21

Building Heating, Cooling,

and Ventilating Systems

Raymond G. Alvine
President
Alvine and Associates, Inc.

21.1 INTRODUCTION

The goal of building heating, ventilating, and air conditioning systems is to provide an appropriate environment for the occupants and activities within the building spaces. These systems are among the most vital components of a building; without them, buildings cannot function well. The systems should be as simple as possible to achieve the desired results. Simple systems are generally low in first cost, easily understood and maintained, and most often will result in economical operation. Conversely, sophisticated systems often are not easily understood and are more difficult to operate and maintain, which contributes to higher operating costs, thereby defeating the goal of many sophisticated systems—energy conservation.

Unfortunately, energy conservation measures often require added controls and sophisticated system design and operation. The same is true for systems serving certain activities within buildings such as data processing, medical procedures, and research. Building requirements should be examined carefully and realistically to provide only what is necessary in the mechanical systems while allowing for an appropriate degree of flexibility for the future.

This chapter describes the typical heating, ventilating, and air conditioning systems found in existing buildings, and those that are being incorporated in new and renovation projects. The descriptions allow for a basic understanding of the systems while providing an appreciation of their characteristics on the part of those decision makers who own, operate, and maintain them. This chapter is not intended for system design purposes but does contain material that will assist physical plant personnel in making appropriate decisions when involved in the development of new, renovated, or modified systems. Advantages and disadvantages are also discussed. The term "mechanical system" is used interchangeably for air conditioning, heating, and ventilating systems.

21.2 DESIGN CONSIDERATIONS

Building Functions

The mechanical systems should "fit" the building functional use patterns or "program" as they are often referred to during the architectural design phase of the building. Systems, or parts thereof, should only operate as needed. When a space is unoccupied, the system should maintain minimum conditions required to protect the equipment or materials located therein and permit optimum energy expenditure in returning the space to occupancy conditions.

Perhaps the best building mechanical system arrangement is to have separate systems for separate building functions. A common building type is one that contains offices, classrooms, auditoriums, and, occasionally, food service. These functions can have different hours of operation, including nighttime, weekends, and vacation periods. If separate systems are provided, only those required need to operate and the others can be shut down. Maximum energy conservation is usually achieved when the energy-consuming device does not operate except when each space is occupied.

It is not unusual in poor system design to find a 200-horsepower fan and pump system operating to provide night or weekend cooling to a small area that would require only a few horsepower if a separate system had been provided. Large central systems can be designed to operate at low load to provide environmental control for a few small areas at off-hours, but usually not as economically as separate systems.

Budget

Unfortunately, budget restrictions often dictate the selection of mechanical systems. Those decisions often are short-term and bottom-line oriented, to the detriment of future operational and maintenance costs. Early budget planning must incorporate planning for appropriate mechanical systems; therefore, an understanding of the numerous options that may be available and appropriate is vital. When the budget will not allow for the desired number of separate systems, a larger system that can be divided into subsystems or zones in the future, and thus offer economical part-load operation, may be possible. Designing for future enhancements can often be done at little or no extra cost when funds are not available for the desired system. When faced with critical choices between what is desired and the budget restriction, life-cycle cost analysis can often prove that the desired system will have a short payback period, thereby justifying reevaluation of the budget based on the savings over the life of the building.

Budget planning should never compromise the design of critical medical, research, or similar facilities for which appropriate environmental control is essential.

System Zoning

Zoning of building mechanical systems can be defined as providing for specific areas (zones) that will have individual control of the space environment. This control can be accomplished by having a separate system for each zone, or a large system capable of providing specific areas with separate control. A building can have several separate systems that are able to provide additional zoning to specific areas within the gross area served by each separate system. This is probably the most common arrangement.

While basic minimum zoning is mandatory, excessive zoning is costly to build and can add unnecessary maintenance expense. A balance must be achieved.

Basic Zones   The basic building zones are determined by the impact of weather on the building. The primary factor, of course, is the solar effect on each exposure as the sun moves around the building each day and changes elevation with the season. It is possible to find, in some parts of the United States, the peak cooling demand for the south exposure to occur in the fall of the year when north exposures require heating. Appropriate design can accommodate off-season cooling. The interior zones are not affected by the weather except for the roof, and therefore must also be separate.

The typical building has a perimeter zone on each of the four sides, and an interior zone. If it is a classroom or dormitory building with a single double-loaded corridor, the zones can be reduced from eight to two zones. If the building is multistory, the upper floor contains a separate set of zones due to the roof exposure. It is common for interior zones to have no heat because they are surrounded by spaces at the same temperature. They typically need year-round cooling.

Functional Zones   Most building functions require system zoning beyond that dictated by the weather. These zones are created to serve such diverse areas as offices, classrooms, auditoriums, common areas, and computer rooms. If individual spaces have the same exterior exposure or interior zone function, they can be combined into a larger functional zone. Often offices are zoned based on hierarchy of individual zones for managerial or department heads and multi-office zones for staff personnel. If several rooms are placed in a common functional zone and some of the rooms do not have typical heat loss and gain, the controls cannot be located to provide a suitable environment for all the rooms.

Individual spaces that are included in a zone cannot have temperature, humidity, air purity, or hours of operation requirements that are significantly different from the remainder of the zone unless the whole zone is upgraded to that level. However, it may be economical to include a few spaces with simple demands as a part of a larger sophisticated zone. An example would be support rooms such as offices for a research operation, or small spaces adjacent to a surgical suite.

Space for Mechanical Systems

One of the least understood and most often neglected aspects of building design is the need for adequate space for installation, maintenance, and future modifications of the mechanical systems. Restricted mechanical space results in extra costs to the architect, engineer, and the contractor during the construction process, and to the occupants during the life of the building. This situation is most often created by efforts to provide maximum "usable" space, and aesthetics considerations. Successful building design does not lose sight of the long-term goal—to serve its purpose during its useful lifetime without imposing unnecessary hardships on the occupants. If a mechanical system provides the required environment, is accessible for routine maintenance, and the space occupants are unaware of its existence, it is most successful.

A mechanical system must "fit" the building functionally. Similarly, a building must fit the mechanical system it dictates. There must be ample space for the installation of ducts, pipes, and terminal units, in addition to the other systems involving ceiling space and shafts. There must be space for future modifications that are certain to occur, and for maintenance access to equipment and controls. Mechanical systems operate for many years, and components will fail and must be replaced. This can include fan shafts, chillers, or heat exchanger tubes. It is not unusual to find that a new chiller cannot be installed in the space occupied by the old chiller due to inadequate access for removal and replacement. Mechanical space can sometimes be reduced in large systems if the air-handling unit is field built instead of factory built. This is because factory built equipment is generally short and wide due to manufacturing economics.

Heating-Cooling Source

The source of the heating and cooling media can be within the building or supplied by a central plant. Occasionally, the choice of mechanical system will dictate the source. The following systems generally dictate that the source be at the building:

* Evaporative cooling.
* Packaged heat pumps—water, air, or earth source.
* Packaged unitary equipment such as rooftop and through-wall types.

Others can generally operate from any source.

Noise and Vibration

Noise and vibration from mechanical systems can make an otherwise successful system unacceptable. Noise and vibration control must be a team effort involving the occupying department, architect, structural engineer, and the mechanical engineer. The occupying department is involved in the location of the mechanical spaces, which should be away from critical spaces. Otherwise, the construction costs will increase due to the type of floor or walls required to attenuate the noise and vibration. The architect must be aware of limits of the equipment available to attenuate the noise generated by the equipment. Beyond those limits, the noise and vibration must be contained or reduced via mass, concrete foundations or slabs, or massive walls and ceilings. The design must be reviewed with regard to noise interference with functional use.

21.3 AIR CONDITIONING SYSTEMS

The following discussion covers the basic types of air conditioning systems used in buildings. The entire mechanical system for a building may include several of the systems outlined below, creating an infinite variety of combinations within a building. These variations are often dictated by the differences in requirements for temperature and humidity control for the different functions housed.

All-Air Systems

All-air systems are those having the heating and cooling equipment, including coils, fans, and filters, located in a central point such as a mechanical room, and the conditioned air transported to the spaces by a ductwork system. The heating and cooling media required are connected to the central air unit and are not distributed throughout the spaces. Some of the advantages of all-air systems are as follows:

- Centralized location of equipment consolidates maintenance and operations.
- The ability to cool with outside air by incorporation of a fresh air or economizer cycle provides free cooling to all spaces during mild weather, and to interior spaces in the winter.
- It permits a wide choice of zones.
- Air systems provide a convenient means of humidity control.
- Return air or exhaust fans are often incorporated into air systems to provide improved control of air circulation and building pressurization. On large systems, return air fans are a distinct advantage in preventing doors being blown open or being hard to open. They can also help control "stack effect" in high-rise buildings.

Single Zone System

The single zone system is the most fundamental type of air conditioning system. It operates successfully only if all the spaces included in the zone have similar exposures to the exterior weather conditions and similar space occupancies and operations. A single zone system contains all the elements necessary to provide the environmental conditions for the space, including cooling and heating coils, filters, fans, and controls. Figure 21-1 shows the basic elements of a single zone system. The fan draws air through the coils and, therefore, is called a "draw-thru" system.

A building may have multiple single zone systems. One of the advantages of this type arrangement is that, if one system fails, the other zones are unaffected. A single zone system also has the advantage of being designed specifically for the zone served without compromising environmental conditions in other areas of the building. The systems are usually quite simple and easily maintained. They are generally limited to relatively small areas, except in cases of unusually large interior zones. This limitation can necessitate an excessive number of systems in a large building, thereby increasing costs, maintenance, and the requirements for mechanical space. The cooling medium can be chilled water or direct expansion refrigeration from a compressor located within the unit or exterior to it. The compressor/refrigeration cycle can either be water cooled or air cooled. The heating media can be steam, hot water, recovered heat, gas, oil, or electric. The choice of cooling media results in

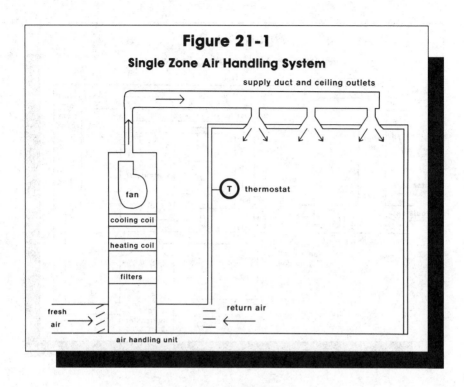

Figure 21-1

Single Zone Air Handling System

supply duct and ceiling outlets

fan

thermostat

cooling coil

heating coil

filters

fresh
air

return air

air handling unit

varying degrees of operation and maintenance difficulties. A single zone unit can be arranged to cool with outside air.

Multizone Systems   In the air conditioning industry, the phrase "multizone system" refers to an air-handling unit that is specifically designed to provide multiple areas throughout a building with individual space temperature control simultaneously. The basic unit has the usual air conditioning components found in a single zone system including the heating and cooling coils, filters, fresh and return air dampers, and controls. Figure 21-2 illustrates a typical multizone unit.

The multizone unit differs from the single zone unit in that it is a blow-thru unit, meaning that it blows rather than draws the air through the coils. The reason for this arrangement is the way the unit operates. The unit has a cooling coil and a heating coil, stacked one on top of the other. The air blown through the coil then can enter what is referred to as a "cold deck" if it goes through the cooling coil or the "hot deck" if it goes through the heating coil. The "deck" is actually a plenum or discharge space downstream of the coils. This can be thought of as a reservoir of hot or cold air. The hot or cold air can be mixed through a set of dampers into a single duct that is extended to each zone.

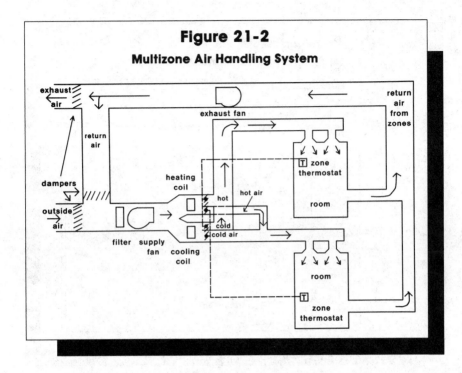

Figure 21-2
Multizone Air Handling System

A thermostat in the zone controls the hot and cold deck dampers to mix the air to the right temperature to meet the space needs, whether it is heating or cooling. In the continuous cooling season, no heat is applied to the heating coil, which becomes a bypass section. Room air that has been returned to the unit is thus passed around the cooling coil and mixed with the cold air that has passed through the cooling coil to maintain the required delivery temperature. At full-load conditions in a zone, the bypass or hot deck damper would be closed, with the cooling damper full open. As the load drops off due to a change in solar conditions or space activities, the cooling damper modulates towards the closed position and the bypass damper opens to raise the delivery temperature to avoid overcooling the space. In the winter the operation is reversed. A multizone system is also capable of cooling with outside air during mild seasons of the year.

A multizone unit has the advantage of being able to serve many zones at a relatively low first cost. A disadvantage is that the zone ducts are fixed and, if there is to be a remodeling of spaces or loads are increased within the zone, major ductwork changes would be required.

A multizone unit has certain inherent inefficiencies, particularly in the heating season. Due to the fact that the unit is serving many zones, some of which may require year-round cooling, there must always be a supply of cold air. The cooling air temperature source is achieved by mixing cold outside air with warmer return air; all the air is then blown through the coils at the colder temperature required for winter cooling. Typically this would be 55°F. While this air from the cold deck is able to cool the rooms needing it, the air entering the heating coil is below the temperature of the rooms needing heating. Heating the air to match the room temperature is wasted energy, unless the heating coil itself is using waste heat from possibly another cycle in the building, such as the heat pump. One method of minimizing this disadvantage is the use of controls to detect exactly how cool the air needs to be at any given time and thereby keep the mixed air temperature as warm as possible.

In summary, a multizone unit is an air-handling system that can mix warm and cold air to appropriate simultaneous temperatures for different zones, and deliver it through separate ducts to maintain required temperatures. The unit is traditionally a low-velocity, low-pressure system requiring a moderate amount of horsepower for the fan.

Dual Duct Systems   Dual duct air conditioning systems found great favor in the period between World War II and the change in design philosophy resulting from the oil embargo in 1973. A dual duct, constant volume system is flexible in accommodating building modifications, and easily achieves balanced air flow and maintains desired temperatures in the individual zones. Historically, double duct systems have been high velocity, high pressure, requiring unusually high fan horsepower, contributing to their inefficiency. In recent years, dual duct systems have been medium pressure or low pressure, thereby greatly reducing the horsepower.

A dual duct system is basically arranged in the same manner as a multizone system. The major difference is that instead of single ducts being extended from the air-handling unit to individual zones, the hot deck and the cold deck are each connected to separate ducts, and the two ducts are extended to each zone. The temperatures in the individual ducts are controlled similarly to that of a multizone unit. In some configurations, there can be separate fans for the hot deck and the cold deck. The double duct system has the same inherent inefficiency as the multizone system in the mixed air cycle during the winter relative to the heating of the mixed air from approximately 55°F back up to room temperature.

Figure 21-3 shows a typical double duct system. Mixing of the air for the space takes place in mixing boxes at the entrance to the zones. The mixing box has dampers controlled by a room thermostat. An automatic device within the dampering system maintains a constant volume of supply air. The box is self-balancing, provided the duct system is capable of delivering air to the box at the required inlet pressure. The mixed air is discharged from the box and enters a low-velocity duct system with diffusers to introduce air into the zone spaces. Large zones may require several mixing boxes.

Figure 21-4 shows a modified double duct air-handling unit wherein the return air delivered to the hot deck through the coil will not be mixed with outside air, thus eliminating the inefficiency of the standard double duct or multizone systems. This arrangement can be very energy efficient in the heating season since it has the capability of transferring heated air from interior spaces to other portions of the building.

A double duct system has the disadvantage of requiring an extra duct that claims space above the ceiling and, as evidenced from the drawing, requires extra depth for hot and cold ducts to pass over the main trunk ducts. This can be minimized with careful planning by using a structural system's voids.

A double duct system cooling source can be chilled water from a remote chiller or direct expansion from a compressor located near the unit. Heating can be furnished by steam, hot water, reclaimed energy, or electricity.

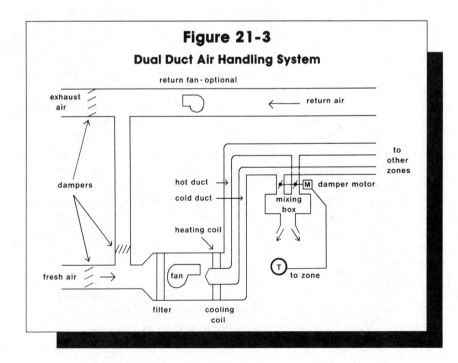

Figure 21-3
Dual Duct Air Handling System

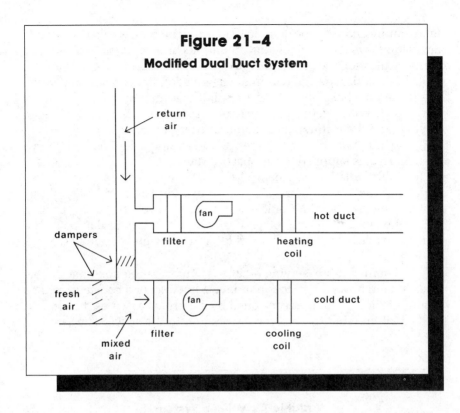

Figure 21-4
Modified Dual Duct System

To provide greater economies of operation, double duct systems can be modified to provide variable volume to the spaces served, rather than constant volume. This method of operation allows the fan to operate only as required for the sum of the individual loads, whereas a constant volume system always delivers the total air that is required by each room at its peak load condition. The sum of the peak loads for each space can be 20 to 30 percent higher than the peak load on the system, thereby wasting fan horsepower by circulating more air than needed. Eliminating the hot duct distribution system to the interior zone boxes can lower first and operating costs. The box then is simply a variable volume box. A double duct system is relatively high in first cost compared to a single zone or multizone system. However, it is a flexible system with regard to modifications and generally provides good space conditions.

Variable Air Volume Systems   There are two ways to control the temperature of a space. One is to deliver a constant volume of air and vary the air temperature. The second is to deliver air at a constant temperature and vary the quantity. This latter method is called a variable air volume system. Variable air volume technology was available for many years prior to the oil embargo of 1973, but was of little use because of its more critical design requirements for successful operation and the availability of cheap energy. As a result, the technology was not highly developed. With energy cost increases, the system has become more popular and the technology has improved significantly.

The basic variable air volume system is a single duct "cooling only" system. Heat is supplied to the space at the zone level. This can consist of fin tube radiation on the walls or a heating coil in the air duct supplying the zone. Figure 21-5 illustrates the basic variable volume system. The air-handling unit is a draw-thru type with a fan, cooling coil, optional heating coil, filters, fresh air, and return air dampers. The unit is capable of cooling with outside air in the winter and mild seasons of the year.

The terminal box serving a zone is similar to the box on a double duct system; however, it does not have a hot duct or a constant volume control device. A damper controlled by a thermostat varies the amount of cold air entering the box for distribution to the space. The terminal

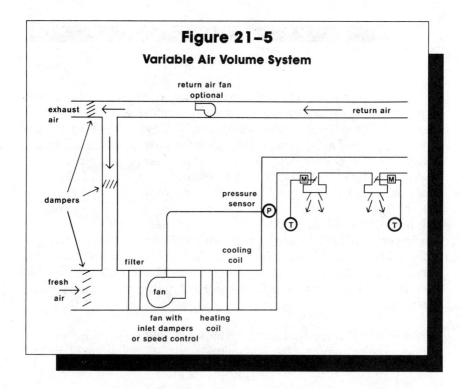

Figure 21-5

Variable Air Volume System

unit can be one of many types, ranging from a simple damper in a duct to a sophisticated box with sound attenuation lining and adjustable minimum and maximum volumes. It can also be an induction type if the air supply is at a high enough pressure. An induction type induces air from the ceiling plenum to mix with the cold air, providing a larger air supply to the space while varying the amount of air that is delivered by the fan system.

A major objection to the variable volume system is that at low loads the air quantities are often greatly reduced, causing a lack of air circulation. In addition, the reduced air flow dictates a critical selection of air outlets. Under low air flow, typical air outlets simply "dump" air into the room. Variable air volume systems also tend to have acoustical problems due to the variation in air volume.

Fan powered terminals can overcome variable air volume flow within the space. This unit is similar to the variable air volume box as it also has a thermostatically controlled inlet damper that varies the amount of cold air coming into the box from the central system in proportion to the room requirements. However, there is a fan within the box that mixes return air, either directly from the room or from the ceiling plenum, and circulates air at a constant rate to the space.

Control techniques are also available to maintain minimum air flow without overcooling the space. The controls can vary the supply air temperature, requiring more air for cooling as the temperature of the supply air is raised or by the installation of a reheat coil. Zoning of the supply air ducts can also offer greater energy savings by separation of zones on the basis of the weather's impact.

In cold climates, the air-handling unit should have a heating coil and reverse acting space thermostats to provide for rapid warm-up after a period of setback to cooler temperatures.

While a variable volume system is fundamentally a cooling-only system, heating coils can be placed at the terminals to form a reheat system which is, in effect, a variation of a multizone system.

Variable air volume systems can be designed for a set minimum air flow or to terminate all air flow to a room upon a call for no cooling. The variable air flow characteristic of the system requires careful design to maintain proper ventilation as required by code and the needs of the occupants.

A variable volume system is flexible relative to future space changes. Generally, its costs are similar to or less than a double duct system, depending upon the method of providing heat.

Air-Water Systems

Air-water systems are those in which both air and water for heating or cooling are distributed to the spaces throughout the building. In all-air systems, air is the primary means for temperature control at the space level. In an air-water system, both air and water are available at the space level to provide temperature control.

Fan Coil Systems   Fan coil systems are one of the earliest air-water systems to be used to provide temperature control and air circulation for individual spaces. The unit consists of a cabinet containing an air circulation fan, a coil to be used for either heating or cooling, water connections, and a control valve with a thermostatic control device that is remotely mounted or self-contained in the cabinet (see Figure 21-6). The fan coil unit can be floor-mounted against the wall, generally below windows, and surface-mounted on the ceiling or above the ceiling, concealed and connected to ducts and air outlets. Ventilation air can be supplied to the fan coil unit through the exterior wall in the case of a floor-mounted unit, through a separate ventilation air duct system directly connected to the floor-mounted unit, or to the concealed units above a ceiling. In cold climates, the wall opening is a source of problems such as freezing of the coil, dirt, and insects.

Fan coil units, when properly selected, are quiet, easily maintained, and simple to operate. They cannot cool with outside air, but when installed around the perimeter of a building with operable windows, cooling with outside air is not needed. While fan coil units provide individual temperature control to a given space, the water supplied to them has to be zoned relative to the impact of the weather on the building (north versus south, for example) and the functional zone requirements. The piping system can be a two-pipe system with the pipe dedicated to heating or cooling, which would not permit simultaneous heating and cooling to different areas unless zoned. A four-pipe system can be installed providing hot and cold water to each fan coil unit at all required times.

Fan coil units are not satisfactory in areas where clean air is important. The condensation on the cooling coil forms a breeding ground for bacteria. Fan coil units and similar equipment using cooling coils should not be used in such areas because of the inability to filter the supply air.

Fan coil systems are relatively energy efficient. They are usually equipped with a three-speed motor. Selecting the units based on the middle fan speed, hence volume, is desirable because it provides for quieter operation and a cushion for future load increases (for a small added cost). They are generally limited to use on the perimeter of the building.

Unit Ventilators   Unit ventilators were introduced before World War II and are a variation of the fan coil system. The major differences are that unit ventilators generally are larger and can circulate more air and,

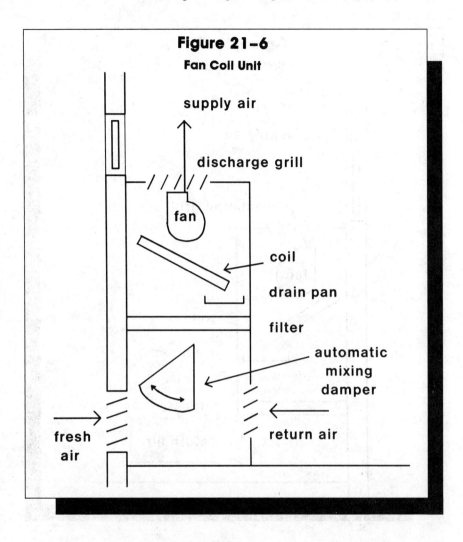

Figure 21-6

Fan Coil Unit

supply air

discharge grill

fan

coil

drain pan

filter

automatic mixing damper

return air

fresh air

therefore, heat and cool larger spaces. They can also cool with outside air. Figure 21-7 illustrates a typical unit ventilator. The space temperature controls are typically designed to automatically go from heating with no fresh air until the space is warm, to minimum fresh air as required by code when the room temperature has been achieved, and to modulation of the heating valve to the "off" position as the space temperature becomes satisfied. As the space temperature continues to rise, the fresh air damper opens and provides a cooling effect until the damper is 100 percent open.

Unit ventilators are often installed with fin tube radiation or auxiliary air ducts (connected to the unit air supply) under the windows that

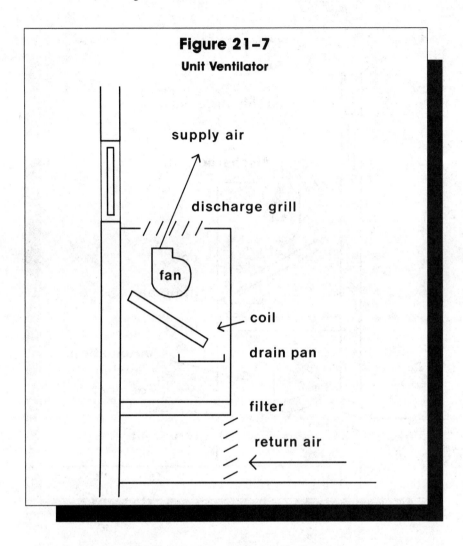

Figure 21-7
Unit Ventilator

supply air

discharge grill

fan

coil

drain pan

filter

return air

provide an air curtain of warm air over the windows. The fin tube can keep the space warm during the unoccupied hours without the fan. The original units functioned for heating only. They subsequently were designed to provide cooling using the same coil but with a combination heating-cooling thermostat. A drain pan is required to collect the condensate from the coil.

The fans of unit ventilators are designed for quiet operation, making them ideal for libraries and classrooms. The fan horsepower required is quite small, and, as in the case of the fan coil system, the overall horsepower required for air circulation for either cooling or heating is often substantially less than that of an all-air system. Unit ventilators also have the advantage of relatively simple maintenance of the fans, valves, and coils. When the economizer cycle is used, the controls are more sophisticated and require more maintenance for satisfactory operation.

Due to their size, unit ventilators occupy more floor space than fan coil units. The louvers on the exterior of the building can also have a negative effect on the architectural design. The units are generally limited to use at the perimeter of the building. They can also be installed on or above the ceiling. The wall openings can create problems similar to those experienced by fan coil units if the damper and filters are not well maintained.

Reheat Systems   A reheat system is a variation of an all-air system. A heating coil is installed directly in the duct serving each zone. The central fan system supplies air to all of the zones at a constant temperature, adequate for cooling any space in the zone. Those spaces not requiring the low-temperature air have a space thermostat that will actuate the heating coil to raise the air temperature to the point required to prevent over-cooling. The heating coil can be steam, hot water, recovered heat, or electric. In addition to controlling space temperature, reheat systems are used where close humidity control of the space is required. A space humidity controller cools the air to the point where condensation occurs and the air is sufficiently dried. The air is then reheated to the appropriate delivery temperature. Sophisticated reheat systems for humidity control are generally one-zone systems serving such areas as computer rooms.

Reheat has the advantage of providing excellent space temperature and humidity control. The major disadvantage is its relatively high energy costs. All of the air has to be cooled to satisfy the warmest space within the building while the remainder of the air must be reheated to an acceptable delivery temperature. Reheat systems generally require careful maintenance and calibration of controls, and monitoring to avoid even greater energy consumption. Installation of the coils and controls above ceilings can lead to problems where space is at a premium. Figure 21-8 shows a typical reheat system.

Operating economies can be achieved by designing a reheat system with the air supply zoned into spaces with similar cooling loads and functional uses, thereby minimizing the amount of reheat. A reheat system generally is undesirable except when the heating is with recovered energy. Most energy codes limit the amount of reheat that can be applied to a building, except for requirements such as computer rooms, hospital operating rooms, and similar applications. The reheat system is relatively inflexible since coils, pipes, and ducts all have to be modified for building modifications.

Figure 21-8
Terminal Reheat Air Handling System

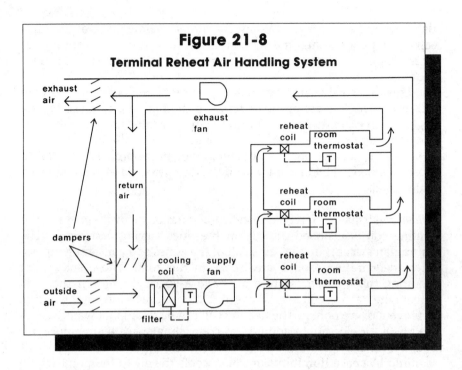

Induction System   Induction systems were introduced shortly after World War II and achieved great popularity as a solution for quality air conditioning for existing high-rise office buildings. Traditionally it is a high-velocity system using small round ducts to each unit, with the units placed around the perimeter below windows. Generally, the ducts are installed vertically, parallel to the exterior columns of the building. Figure 21-9 shows the typical unit.

The induction unit has a plenum to which the high-pressure air duct is connected. Discharge nozzles on the outlet of the plenum provide high-velocity jets of system air, inducing room air to provide a total air discharge quantity approximately equal to four times the amount of high-pressure air introduced. This is similar to the process in which a high-pressure jet of water in a pool can circulate large quantities of water. The unit has a coil that can be used for heating and cooling. The induction process draws the room air through the coil and mixes it with the high-pressure air jets. In the cooling mode, when chilled water is circulated through the coil, the room air drawn through the coil is cooled and mixed with the high-pressure air supplied to the unit. In the heating season, hot water is circulated through the coil and heat is provided in much the same manner. The temperature of the primary air is centrally controlled on an outside air temperature schedule.

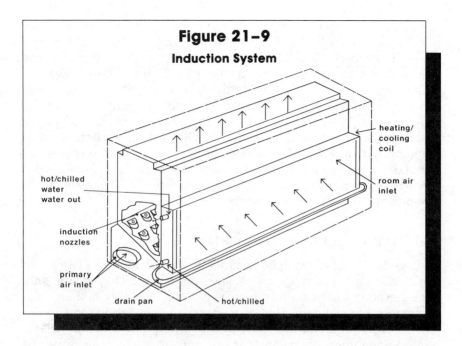

Figure 21-9

Induction System

During the unoccupied hours in the heating season, hot water can be circulated through the coils with the high-pressure primary air fan turned off, in which case the unit acts as a convector. Under extreme cold conditions, the fan may have to be operated periodically. This cycle provides significant energy savings.

The minimum amount of primary air is normally determined by ventilation requirements. The air supplied to the induction unit is from a central air-handling unit with cooling coils, heating coils, filters, and controls similar to that in a typical all-air system. The main air-handling unit can operate with up to 100 percent fresh air. However, due to the small ratio of primary compared to total air, typically one-fourth, induction systems cannot cool individual spaces with outside air alone.

In most systems, the primary air is sufficiently dehumidified at the main air-handling unit to avoid condensation on the cooling coils in individual units. However, a drain system for condensate in the induction units is advisable. The temperature of the water to the induction unit coil is critical if drainage is not provided. Induction units have the advantage of being able to circulate the total space air requirements without a fan installed within the unit. The horsepower required for moving the air in the room comes from the main fan system.

Induction units have the advantage of providing individual space control, little or no cross-contamination among rooms (depending upon design), relatively quiet operation, and minimum maintenance. If the nozzles are too small, they will clog with dirt and a major maintenance problem will occur. The units have filters that require attention. The induction system has the disadvantage of a high fan horsepower requirement. The system is not highly flexible, but the multiple units generally provide enough space rearrangement flexibility to cover most contingencies. Air-water induction units generally are limited to the spaces around the perimeter of the building with a separate air conditioning system serving the interior. They are widely used in offices and dormitories, with an induction unit in each room and a separate system serving common use areas. The units have recently been available in low-pressure designs to save energy.

Multiple Package Unit/Unitary Systems

Package type unitary equipment provides the advantages of low cost and a wide variety of types, styles, and applications. They require only the extension of basic utilities such as gas and electricity and are relatively simple to maintain. They also offer the advantage, in some installations, of no failure of the entire system when only one unit fails. A disadvantage involves maintenance of numerous pieces of dispersed equipment. The life expectancy of package equipment is less than that of high-quality standard air conditioning components such as centrifugal chillers, pumps, and central fans.

The major objection to package equipment is the effect of equipment location on maintenance. The equipment is generally compact and can be difficult to maintain above ceilings, in tight closets, or outside in inclement weather. Despite these disadvantages, appropriate situations exist in which this equipment can be used effectively. One application is in remote or rural areas where the maintenance staff and factory service required for more sophisticated equipment are not available.

The heating capacity of many package types of unitary equipment has little relationship to the cooling capacity. This should be carefully checked to adjust the capacity to the proper size.

Window Units   Window air conditioning units are the most common and easily recognized type of package unitary air conditioning equipment. They offer the advantage of low first cost, portability, adaptability to existing wiring systems, individual space control, low maintenance due to hermetic design, and simple controls. Often a simple solution for cooling a limited area, this spot cooling can be for human comfort or for another functional need.

Window units have numerous disadvantages including on-off control with no modulation, high noise level, localized drafts, unsightly appearance, and relatively high operating costs. Despite these disadvantages, they provide effective air conditioning for such spaces as isolated small security buildings, maintenance shops, and offices. Window units are available with electric heating coils.

Through-the-Wall Units   A through-the-wall unit is actually a variation of a window unit that was developed as the need for air conditioning expanded rapidly throughout the country. They are, in effect, fan coil units with individual compressors and heating elements. The units are available in attractive cabinets that can blend in with the architectural design of the space. They have many of the same disadvantages as a window unit; however, they are generally of higher quality resulting in a lower noise level, improved operating economies, variable fan speeds, improved controls, and better access for maintenance.

Through-the-wall units are often used in offices that are occupied throughout the week when the remainder of the building, such as a church, is shut down. They offer individual room control and the loss of a unit does not affect other spaces. Through-the-wall units cannot provide cooling with outside air.

Through-the-wall units are similar to window units in that the condensing portion is located outside the exterior wall and uses the air as a heat rejection medium. Ventilation air in nominal amounts can be obtained through the exterior louver or by ducting the air to each space from a central unit.

Heat Pumps, Air Source   All air conditioning refrigeration cycles are, in effect, heat pumps. Heat available from room air, products, and objects is extracted by the refrigeration cycle and transported to a point of discharge through the condenser. A heat pump is able to reverse the cycle and discharge heat to the space in the heating season. To do this, the heat pump must have a source of heat. In the air source heat pump, the outside air is the heat source or "heat sink." The unit, during the heating cycle, cools the outside air from the ambient to a lower temperature prior to discharging it back to the outside. The heat extracted from the outside air is then discharged into the space via the compression cycle with the cooling coil being used as the condenser. If a window unit was simply removed from the window and mounted in reverse, it could function as a heat pump. Air source heat pumps can be found in such forms as window units, through-the-wall units, or residential furnace-cooling combinations, and larger commercial package type units including rooftop units.

Heat pumps have the advantage of requiring only one utility source. They can provide individual space control or serve larger areas depending upon the type of equipment in which they are incorporated.

The air source heat pump's ability to heat with outside air declines dramatically as the outside air temperature drops to a point where it is ineffective as a heating unit. This occurs at 0°F to approximately 10°F. To overcome this, the units are provided with supplementary electric heating coils. These coils can be multiple staged, or single elements. The heat pump's primary advantage, relative to energy costs, is the ability to provide heat from the electrically operated refrigeration cycle, thereby greatly reducing the heating costs when compared to straight resistance electric heating units. Depending upon utility rates, air source heat pumps can be competitive in a properly designed system. Figure 21-10 shows the typical air source heat pump cycle.

All heat pumps operate at relatively low room supply air temperatures during heating, requiring careful design of air distribution to avoid drafts.

Heat Pumps, Water Source   Some of the disadvantages of air source heat pumps are overcome by the use of water as a heat sink. The water can come from a closed circuit condenser water system connected to a heat source, such as a boiler in the winter, and a heat rejection point such as a closed circuit cooling tower system in the summer. Other sources can include looping of pipes in the earth to provide a heat sink, the installation of pipes in small low-volume vertical wells, standard well water, lakes, and condenser water from the refrigeration cycle of a unit used to provide cooling year-round. The water source generally operates at a relatively constant water temperature. In the case of ground and well water, the temperature ranges from 55°F to 65°F. In the case of mechanical systems, the water temperature can vary from approximately 85°F to 105°F. Generally, water source heat pumps do not require supplemental resistance heating and offer a lower electric heating cost throughout the entire heating season. Water source heat pumps can also be a form of energy conservation and operate very efficiently in a well-designed system in which heat removed from a process or an interior space is used to heat perimeter spaces or processes at the same time.

A unitary closed-circuit, water source heat pump can, in appearance, be very similar to an air source through-the-wall system or a fan coil unit. The units can also be located in closets and above ceilings. One of the advantages of a closed loop system is the ability to heat and cool simultaneously throughout the building. Spaces requiring cooling reject the heat into the closed loop water circuit which then becomes available for extraction in spaces that require heating, such as occurs in the spring and fall when the south zones of a building need cooling and the north zones need heating. Water source heat pump systems of the small indi-

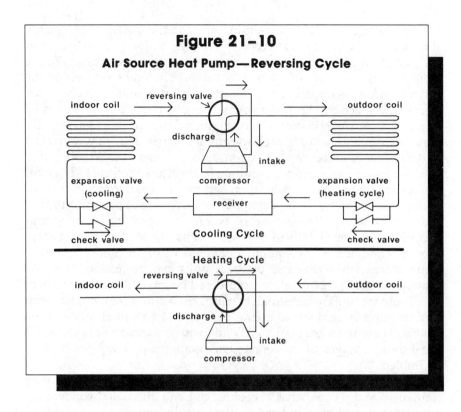

Figure 21-10

Air Source Heat Pump—Reversing Cycle

Cooling Cycle

indoor coil — reversing valve — outdoor coil

discharge — intake

expansion valve (cooling) — compressor — expansion valve (heating cycle)

receiver

check valve — check valve

Heating Cycle

indoor coil — reversing valve — outdoor coil

discharge — intake

compressor

vidual type cannot provide cooling with outside air directly. Depending upon the quality of the equipment, noise may be a problem. Ventilation air can be provided by a ducted system to each space or to the intake of each unit.

Outdoor Unitary Equipment   As the name implies, this type of equipment is generally located outside of the building, usually on the roof. The equipment is complete within itself and is connected to the ductwork within the building. This equipment can vary from small systems of approximately 5 tons for individual spaces, up to large systems well over 100-ton capacity. Depending upon the size and sophistication, outdoor unitary equipment has the ability to provide cooling with outside air, can have return fans for positive control of ventilation and building air pressure, and can be equipped with sophisticated controls and air filtration systems making it suitable for providing environmental control for critical operations. Outdoor unitary equipment can be single zone, multizone, or connected to double duct and variable volume systems.

The location of exterior rooftop units and the questionable quality of construction often found in rooftop units are major objections to their use on buildings considered permanent with long life expectancy. To use rooftop units to avoid providing adequate mechanical space within the building is false economy. The cabinet of a rooftop unit is, in effect, the mechanical space building or envelope. It is often fragile and can present major maintenance problems and significant reduction in energy efficiency. The maintenance of rooftop equipment in inclement weather can be difficult and, under certain circumstances, dangerous. When rooftop units are used in applications requiring sophisticated control of environmental conditions, the very location becomes a negative factor. It is not uncommon for first-time users to go through a cycle of pleasant surprise over the low first cost, mild concern over higher operating costs, realization of maintenance difficulties, and ultimately total disillusionment over the condition of the equipment after years of operation. There are many places where the use of these units can be justified, but the consequences must be carefully considered before making the decision.

There are rooftop units that, in effect, are penthouses complete with corridors and large doors allowing personnel access to all parts of the system. These units are of unusually high quality and do not exhibit the usual disadvantages of outdoor unitary equipment. They can be field assembled.

Outdoor unitary equipment can be completely self-contained with compressors, direct expansion cooling coil and air cooled condensers, gas furnaces, and electric heat, or they can be connected to a remote source of chilled water for cooling, steam, and hot water for heating. Heat can also be reclaimed heat available from another operation.

Indoor Unitary Equipment   Indoor unitary equipment generally has the complete package located within the building and is connected only to an exterior source of utilities and condensing media source for the refrigeration cycle. Utilities can be electric or gas, and the condensing media can be a remote air-cooled condenser or water from an appropriate source, such as a cooling tower or well. Indoor unitary equipment can be installations such as a typical residential furnace with air conditioning to larger sophisticated systems capable of handling double duct and variable volume systems. Their size generally ranges from 1 to 2 tons to over 50 tons. The typical installation has an air-cooled condenser. Small units are available for location above ceilings and can be connected to a ductwork system serving several rooms. The air-cooled condenser would be located outside on the ground or on the roof near the unit. These are generally referred to as "split systems." Units can be arranged to provide cooling only or heating and cooling, and to provide cooling with outside air in larger systems. Unitary equipment has the same advantages and disadvantages of other systems described herein. They generally have a low first cost as compared to conventional systems utilizing air-handling units and chilled water/hot water heating and cooling media.

Computer Room Air Conditioners   Sophisticated unitary package equipment has been developed for computer applications requiring close control of the space environment. These units are generally of high quality and provide complete and accurate control of temperature, humidity, and, where required, air filtration. They are designed to be totally independent of other portions of the building air conditioning system and are designed to operate year-round. While they can be connected to a central plant, the most common installation is the individual package type. The condensing source can be a remote air-cooled condenser or a closed circuit loop with an antifreeze solution and an outside radiator where required.

Humidification is usually provided by evaporation of water via electric resistance heating elements. The evaporation of water introduces maintenance problems due to the collection of scale and flushing of the system. Steam from a remote source can also be used for humidification.

Of necessity, a computer room unit incorporates a reheat cycle for maintenance of precise humidity levels during the cooling operation. Computer room units are often tied into emergency power sources that serve the computer system complex. In the sizing of computer room units, it is appropriate to include redundancy. Most units are of the multiple compressor, refrigerant circuit style in each package unit. Selection of enough redundancy to permit one or more failures of a refrigeration circuit will protect the operation of the computers.

Radiant Cooling

Radiant cooling is not widely used but can be effective in certain applications. It requires no space in the occupied areas. Metal cooling panels mounted in the ceiling can be used in hospital rooms for burn patients who cannot be covered and should not be subjected to air motion. Radiant panels cannot be permitted to become sufficiently cold to cause condensation; the water must be kept warmer than the dew point of the room air. Dehumidification of the space is provided by introducing a relatively small amount of air that has been dehydrated in a cooling coil. This air also provides the required ventilation for the space. Radiant cooling panels are expensive to install when compared to other systems and require careful operation monitoring.

Radiant cooling coils that can be concealed behind valances provide relatively good comfort from the radiant cooling and the conductive effect of the air circulation over the valance. Radiant cooling systems generally are high in first cost.

Humidification/Dehumidification

Specific levels of humidity may have to be maintained for comfort or process environments. Since the maintenance of humidity levels can have a major impact on energy consumption, the need for specific control must be carefully considered. Achieving acceptable levels with low first costs and acceptable operating costs requires careful planning and design.

Humidification is relatively simple with most air conditioning systems. All-air and many air-water systems can have the humidity introduced directly into the air stream going to the spaces. It can be provided by the introduction of steam or by vaporizing or misting moisture into the air stream. Steam can come from a central steam plant, an in-house steam boiler, or from package-type electrically heated steam generators. The package-type steam generators have the maintenance problem of scaling and mineral deposits.

In certain environments, chemicals used in water treatment in steam generating plants are unacceptable. This includes areas involving biological, pharmaceutical, and organic work; artwork; and historical document storage, where chemical deposits may have an undesirable effect. Under these conditions, a pure steam generator is required, either a package-type electric generator or a generator using steam from a central source to boil water containing no boiler compounds to form the pure steam.

Humidification lends itself easily to zoning by the introduction of the humidity into the air stream serving a specific zone. Humidifiers can also be located within the space independent of any air stream. These are generally wall-mounted and can be provided in multiple units.

Dehumidification in most buildings is achieved by the condensation of the moisture in the air on the cooling coil during the cooling cycle. In most climates, this moisture removal during the air conditioning cycle operation provides the supply air with acceptable humidity levels.

Under light load conditions, or when a cooling system is oversized, the cooling does not cycle on long enough for the appropriate amount of moisture to be removed. The space dry bulb temperature might be satisfied, but high moisture results. In a space where the moisture gain is relatively high compared to the typical heat gain, special measures must be taken to remove the moisture. This can be accomplished with a reheat system where the cooling coil is kept on long enough and cold enough to remove the moisture. The air may then be too cold to introduce into the space without reheating. This method provides an accurate means of controlling the humidity within the space, but requires higher operating costs.

Dehumidification can also be achieved with desiccants, both liquid and dry. Silica gel, the material often packed with valuable photographic and electronic equipment in shipping containers, is the most common type of dry desiccant. Large rotary wheel mechanical dry desiccant systems are available that circulate space air through the desiccant. As the desiccant absorbs the moisture, it is rotated through a hot air stream that drys and regenerates it. This type of operation requires heat for the drying process. The equipment is often used in areas where air conditioning is not required, as the warm desiccant introduced in the main air stream has a heating effect. There are package systems that provide heating, cooling, and desiccant dehumidification.

Liquid-type desiccants consist of a desiccant spray chamber with a piping system and spray nozzles, a basin containing liquid desiccant, and pumps to recirculate the desiccant throughout the system. A separate regenerator section warms the liquid desiccant to boil off the moisture picked up from the air stream passing through the spray chamber. Lithium bromide is a typical absorbent-type salt used for this application. Liquid-type dehumidifiers can be used in areas where air conditioning is not required, or in conjunction with air conditioning systems. The application provides accurate control of space conditions, and can remove large amounts of moisture. The air stream must be provided with good filtration to minimize dirt deposits in the spray system.

Water Spray Chamber

When moisture in the air comes in contact with a surface colder than its dew point, moisture will condense and be removed from the air. This principle applies not only to the metal surface of the coil but to any surface, including glass, masonry, plant life, and water. If a water spray is chilled to a point below the dew point of an air stream passing through the spray, the moisture in the air stream will condense on the water droplets and the moisture will be removed from the air stream. This method of humidity control should only be considered in special applications and requires careful design. Air streams contain dust and dirt, and sprays used for either dehumidification or humidification provide a filter action that introduces dirt and foreign matter into the liquid system. Care must be taken to prevent fouling of the spray nozzles and eventual deterioriation of the system. This problem can be minimized by appropriate air filtration prior to introduction of the air stream into the spray chambers.

21.4 HEATING SYSTEMS

Since heat is one of the most fundamental requirements of human survival, the development of heating systems has a long history and has resulted in a wide variety of options for today's buildings. Many of the systems are common and readily understood by the layperson. However, sometimes the reasons for the choice of a specific piece of equipment or system by engineers may not be so readily understood.

Radiation

Radiation generally can be considered as a heat source located directly within the space. The word "radiator" is a common term applied to the old cast iron radiation found in buildings built before World War II. Cast iron radiation has little use in today's modern building. There are, however, various other types available.

Fin Tube   Fin tube radiation, perhaps the most common type in buildings today, consists of a copper or a steel pipe with fins along the heating portion of the element. These fins can be copper, steel, or aluminum and the pipe size, fin size, and spacing determines the heating capacity. Fin tubes can be provided singly or stacked in multiple lengths. Radiator-type units provide heat via radiation and convective transfer of heat by the air flow over the unit.

Fin tube can be built into the perimeter finish of the building by providing air space at the floor and an outlet above the fins for circulation. Generally, this process is convective only since the cover acts as an insulator. Fin tube can also be provided with a variety of metal covers designed to meet the economic and aesthetic considerations of the installation. Metal covers tend to become warm and provide some radiant heat.

Fin tube control is achieved by the operation of a manual valve, an automatic valve under the control of a space thermostat, or by control of the water temperature supplied to the unit. Damper control of fin tube is not recommended, as the cover will act as a hot radiator when the damper is closed. Fin tube radiation is often used in conjunction with cooling-only variable volume systems. Fin tube radiation has the virtue of providing a blanket of warm air at the perimeter of the building, greatly increasing human comfort. Steam or hot water can be the heat source.

Convectors   A convector is similar to fin tube radiation, although the heating element can consist of a small coil similar to that in a fan coil unit. A convector coil can be built into the perimeter of the building in much the same fashion as a fin tube or can be contained in metal cabinets. Styles of metal cabinets are generally determined by economics and aesthetic considerations. Convectors are often used where space will not permit the installation of long sections of fin tube. They are used in stairways, entryways, and relatively small spaces. Convectors can use steam or hot water as a heat source.

Electric Radiation   Electric radiation generally takes on the same form as convectors or fin tube. It is most commonly baseboard or individual cabinet electric heaters mounted in walls, or in ceilings in certain applications. Electric baseboard provides individual space temperature control. The controls can be incorporated in the unit or consist of a wall-mounted thermostat.

Forced Air Heating

The circulation of air to provide heating offers certain advantages in most applications. Forced air circulation provides for rapid heat transfer, the use of small compact heaters for relatively large heating requirements, and the ability to heat relatively large spaces from a single source and to distribute the heat as needed.

Unit Heaters   Unit heaters are most commonly used in industrial areas such as warehouse facilities, storage facilities, shops, and other areas that are not air-conditioned. The unit heater consists of a fan and a heating coil mounted in a cabinet, with discharge louvers or, in certain cases, duct collars for connection to a ductwork system. Unit heaters are controlled by a space thermostat that cycles the fan and the heat source control valve. The heat source for unit heaters can be steam, hot water, natural gas, or electricity. Because the fan can throw the air stream a relatively long distance, the units are generally used for heating large areas. Unit heaters have the advantage of requiring no floor space. Their use is limited to areas where aesthetics is not a major concern.

Cabinet Unit Heaters   Cabinet unit heaters, generally speaking, are floor or ceiling mounted, surface mounted, or recessed. They are similar to fan coil units. They generally use steam or hot water for heating media, although electrical applications are common. Their main function is to provide heat in a space where their aesthetic appearance makes them far more acceptable than the typical unit heater. They are used in vestibules, stairways, and other areas that need a high-capacity heat source in a relatively compact unit. Generally, the controls cycle the fan and the coil heat source valve. If a valve is not provided on the heat source, the cabinet can become a convector and cause overheating of the space.

Air-Handling Units   Air-handling unit operation has been described in various systems such as multizone and single zone units. Introduction of heat via the air-handling units offers the advantage of lower first cost, simplicity of operation, and no loss of space throughout the building for piping and heating equipment.

Furnaces   Furnaces often serve as a heat source for a building that does not require cooling or can be used in an installation where cooling will be provided at a later date. They can be mounted vertically on the floor or horizontally in a space above ceilings. Furnaces have the advantages of low first cost, relatively high air circulation rates, and, depending upon the fuel, economies of operation. They can be gas fired, oil fired, or contain electric heating elements.

Make-Up Air Units   Certain operations and functions within a building require replacement of air. This can be air exhausted from a cooking operation, maintenance operations, painting, chemical processes, or where special air cleanliness is required. Make-up air units can use steam, hot water, gas, oil, or electricity as a heat source. The most efficient type is a direct-fired gas unit in which the combustion process takes place in the air stream supplied to the space, providing 100 percent efficiency of energy use. Units of this type are designed and approved in accordance with appropriate code authorities with an acceptable ratio of combustion products and air. Make-up air units should be installed to operate only when required by the exhaust cycle. While low first costs can be a temptation to use the make-up unit to provide heat during the off-hour periods, this results in high operating costs due to the use of all outside air. A separate supplemental heat source should be provided to maintain minimum temperatures during off-hour periods.

Electricity   Electricity is an available source of heating in a forced air system. Its use should carefully consider the cost impact of electric demand charges. Where electricity is used, consideration should be given to multiple heating elements providing stepped control of heat as well as demand limiting. Electric heating elements are very simple to maintain, generally low in first cost, and can provide for as many individual zones as desired. Electric heating can be the most desirable form of heat where the costs are acceptable.

Radiant Heating

Radiant heat from the sun is the earth's fundamental energy source and provides the necessary heat for human survival. Radiant heat operates by virtue of the temperature difference between the hot surface and the cold surface, and is independent of the intervening atmosphere. The radiant heat transfer varies as the difference of the fourth powers of the temperatures of the surfaces involved. This is more easily understood when one compares the effect of radiant heating under a direct and extremely hot source such as a lamp or radiant coil, and the effect of a surface at a moderate temperature such as a convector. Generally, it requires little or no space within the occupied area and is easily controlled. Radiant heat can be used for spot heating purposes or throughout an entire area.

Ceiling Panels   Ceiling panels are one of the most common forms of radiant heat in modern buildings. They can be integrated into the ceiling system to match the textures and support system. Electric radiant heat panels are flexible and can be relocated easily. Radiant heating can also consist of metal ceiling pans connected to copper pipes circulating hot water. A space thermostat modulates the water valve or the electric circuit to maintain space temperature. Ceiling panels have the advantage of quick recovery of surface temperature to provide radiant heat to the space occupants in a relatively short period of time. The low mass of a ceiling panel also prevents overheating of the space due to excessive heat retention when cycled off.

Floor Panels   Floor panels generally consist of hot water pipe circuits buried in a concrete slab. They are expensive to install, slow to respond to load changes, and can cause overheating due to the mass involved. They are inflexible with regard to space rearrangements and changes in zone control. Their use is limited to such areas as warehousing and maintenance facilities. They offer greater comfort to personnel working in a building where the air temperature is kept relatively low.

Gas-Fired Radiant Heat   There are two forms of gas-fired radiant heat. One is high intensity with a radiant element exposed to the space occupants and made incandescent by the combustion process operating directly against the ceramic radiant element. These units are simple to install, easily relocated, and provide quick high-intensity spot heating.

The products of combustion are introduced into the space and, therefore, a ventilation system is required. Maintenance is required to keep the surfaces free of foreign matter that will reduce the radiant characteristics of the ceramic materials. The ceramic material is often fragile and easily damaged during maintenance operations.

Low-intensity gas-fired radiant heat generally consists of a tubular combustion chamber and long horizontal flue gas pipe used to conduct the flue gases from the combustion chamber to the exterior of the building. The system operates in the lower radiant temperature as opposed to the incandescent range. It is extremely efficient; products of combustion can be cooled to temperatures as low as 100°F or less prior to discharge to the atmosphere. Most radiant systems are proprietary with regard to the design and installation techniques. At present, the American Society of Heating, Refrigerating and Air Conditioning Engineers (ASHRAE) has no specific standards for calculating capacity requirements for radiant heating equipment other than the standard heating load calculations available for other heating systems. Materials of construction are extremely important in the installation, particularly where flue gas temperatures are low enough to permit moisture condensation that can result in corrosion from the formation of sulphuric acid. The heaters can be mounted in many configurations and are adaptable for warehouses, maintenance shops, industrial arts classrooms, and certain multipurpose activity areas. In building areas where the atmosphere is contaminated, combustion air should be drawn directly to the burners from the outside. Typical installations range from 60,000 to 120,000 Btus per hour for each burner with multiple burners being installed.

Electric Radiant Heating   Electric radiant heating has been available for many years and can consist of incandescent heating elements directly exposed to the space with an appropriate wire protective guard. Other electric panels have glass or metal heating surfaces that offer a more attractive appearance, ease of cleaning, and greater safety. Controls are either integral or a space thermostat. Electric heating panels are versatile as to location and relocation. They are useful for spot heating where the remainder of a building temperature can be lowered. Radiant-type heaters with an easily cleanable glass surface are used in hospital operating rooms to provide heat when the main air conditioning system is off.

Steam Heating

Building steam heating system pressures rarely exceed 125 pounds. Low-pressure steam heating systems offer the advantage of moderate steam temperatures when compared to higher pressure steam and low-pressure boilers; they require less stringent monitoring than high-pressure boilers do under most codes. While steam heating systems using radiators directly within the space are not common in modern buildings today, they are found quite frequently in older buildings. Objections to steam include excessively hot radiation temperatures, difficulty of pipe installation due to the need to drain condensate, excessively large supply pipe sizes, and the tendency of return lines to corrode. An additional disadvantage is that the entire system, including piping, is at excessively high temperatures most of the time.

Systems exist that can operate under subatmospheric and vacuum conditions and can have steam at lower temperatures. These systems require good maintenance to maintain the vacuum. Orifices are installed in the inlet to the radiation which restrict the flow of steam, creating subatmospheric conditions within the radiation unit itself due to the vacuum maintained at the radiator outlet. In effect, the steam temperature can be "reset" down by varying the pressure within the radiator. This can be effective in a properly maintained system but is not in common use today. In many early heating systems, the main steam riser is extended from the basement or boiler room level up into the attic space. There the steam piping system is divided into branches and the steam is downfed to the radiation around the perimeter of the building. The main reason for one or more large risers is the economics of pipe sizing resulting from a single riser. When steam is supplied vertically, the condensate, by its very nature, flows down against the steam. This requires oversized steam pipes to prevent water hammer. A single oversized riser is much cheaper than multiple risers.

Figure 21-11 shows an upfeed system, common in buildings today. A horizontal main runs around the perimeter of the building connecting to the vertical risers. Steam can be zoned in much the same manner as in air systems. Typically, it would be zoned by weather exposure because its primary function occurs only during the heating season. Separate mains are provided for each exposure of the building with a motorized valve controlling the flow of steam to that particular exposure. An outdoor thermostat with solar compensation or a thermostat located in a "typical" room provides control for the zone. Additional control for the spaces within the zone can be provided at the radiation with manual valves, self-contained thermostatic valves, or wall-mounted thermostats. Existing steam systems with perimeter radiation can provide the heat necessary for the installation of a variable volume system or air conditioning system in a remodeled building. Low-pressure steam can furnish the heat necessary for coils found in air-handling units that provide heat to the zones via the air temperature supplied.

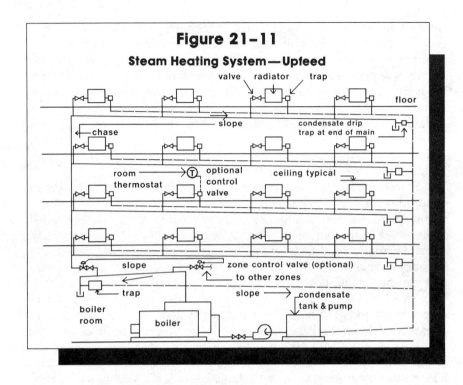

Figure 21-11
Steam Heating System—Upfeed

A major disadvantage of a steam heating system is the space required by horizontal runs. The pipe should be pitched uniformly approximately one inch in fifty feet. Every time the horizontal steam main encounters an obstruction, the gravity flow of liquid condensate within the pipe presents complications that have to be accommodated.

Steam systems require careful maintenance of the steam traps. Typically, radiation found in spaces has a thermostatic trap. Large coils often have a float and thermostatic trap in the case of a low-pressure steam coil, and a bucket trap for high-pressure steam coils. One of the operating characteristics of low-pressure steam heating systems is the air trapped within the radiation that must be eliminated. Traps are typically designed to provide for the removal of air. Standing cast iron radiation can be provided with a separate air vent due to the large volume of the steam chamber.

When steam traps leak, the entire heating system supply and return operates at essentially the steam supply temperature, creating excessive fuel use. It is not unusual for this type of loss to amount to 20 to 25 percent of the energy consumption of a building. With modern electronic temperature-sensing devices, it is relatively easy to determine whether or not a steam trap is functioning properly.

Steam used in heating coils has a tendency to freeze up rapidly when used for heating fresh air. In a multizone unit, or any air-handling unit with a long steam coil, the end of the coil located farthest from the steam inlet tends to be colder. In the case of a multizone air-handling unit, if a small zone is attached to the hot deck on the far end of the coil, it will often have insufficient heating capacity due to a lower air temperature provided by the colder end of the coil. Double feed coils are available where long coils are used. This eliminates most of the problems of cold spots in the coil.

One of the major advantages of steam is that, unlike hot water heating systems, it can be distributed without pumps. As a result, steam heating systems have very low energy transportation costs. Typically, the only energy required, other than that for the boiler burner, is the pump required to return the condensate back into the boiler. In the case of a gravity system, pumps are not required.

Hot Water Heating

Hot water heating systems have many advantages including relatively small pipe sizes, flexibility relative to routing throughout a building, the ability to vary the water temperature through a wide range, ease of zoning, and quiet operation. Their greatest advantage, of course, is the ability to be combined with a chilled water system, providing heating and air conditioning from the same piping system and often the same air conditioning and heating device, such as the fan coil unit and air-handling unit.

Hot water heating systems experience little or no corrosion if properly operated and maintained. Entrained air in a hot water heating system causes corrosion and circulation problems. The initial water introduced into the system can attack the pipe for a brief period of time; however, that action soon stabilizes itself. If the water is not replaced, drained off, or lost through leakage, corrosion essentially stops. A mistaken notion on the part of many heating system operators is that chemical treatment should be added periodically to a hot water heating system. This should only be true if that judgment is based on careful analysis. Even the introduction of a small amount of new water will only cause a mild amount of corrosion. It is not unusual to open up gravity hot water heating systems that have been operating for sixty-five years in residences and find essentially no corrosion of the piping. Excessive chemical treatment of hot water heating sytems can destroy radiation and zone valves. Physical plant personnel should question regular chemical treatment for a closed water system, be it chilled water or hot water.

Hot water heating systems can be zoned in much the same fashion as a steam system; however, they have the additional advantage of being able to have the temperature varied within each zone. In a high-rise dormitory building with individual room radiators, it is entirely possible to zone the entire face of the building based on exposure and vary the water temperature to maintain uniform temperatures in all spaces in the zone. Rooms with manual radiation control can provide uniform space temperatures throughout the day as the sun strikes the face of the building in the morning and the far side in the afternoon. Uniform temperatures are also maintained throughout the night. The manual radiation valves within each space permit the occupant to select his or her own specific temperature adjustment within the range of the radiator capacity and the water supply temperature provided.

Hot water heating systems, due to the reset capability, have lower heat losses and greater energy economies. Typically, hot water heating systems are designed for a 20°F temperature differential between the temperature leaving the heating source and the return. This differential is seldom achieved because it is based on peak heating conditions. Systems can be designed for large temperature differentials if they are for heating only. Differentials of 40°F and 60°F can be used, which reduce the pipe size and pumping costs considerably. This approach requires careful sizing of the radiation devices due to the large temperature drop experienced. In long pieces of fin tube radiation, the far end can become excessively cold. Where a hot water heating distribution system also serves as a chilled water system, in most cases the pipe sizing is determined by the chilled water flow and temperature drop in most cases.

Figure 21-12 shows the layout of a typical hot water heating system with perimeter radiation. The system is shown with zones for the various exposures of the building, individual zone pumps, and mixing valves. Hot water heating systems should be balanced when they are started up and the balancing valves should be of a type that can be closed and reopened to the balance point, either by a marking or a mechanical stop device. Balancing of systems can be achieved with a reverse return piping system return shown in Figure 21-13. With this type of installation, the actual distance through any circuit is equal to the distance through any other circuit. The system then is essentially self-balancing. While this may take more pipe, it is an easily maintained system relative to flows throughout the various parts of the building.

A properly sized hot water heating system will operate with relatively low pumping costs. They can be provided with multiple pumps or one large individual pump with a standby pump and one or more zone water temperature control valves.

Figure 21–12
Hot Water Heating System—Direct Return

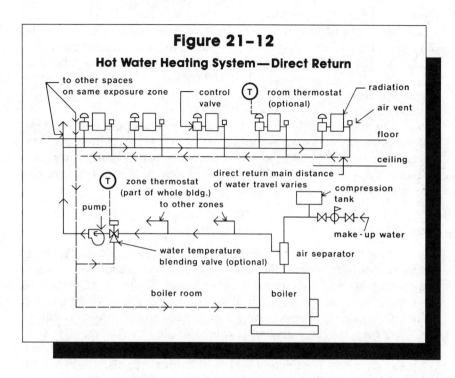

Figure 21–13
Hot Water Heating System—Reverse Return

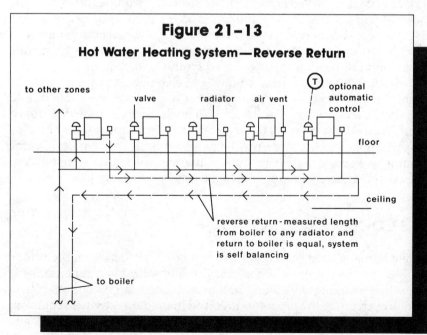

A hot water heating system should be designed so that air can be eliminated from all high points as well as from radiation and coils. The system is often used with all-air air conditioning systems and particularly with variable volume systems. The control of the radiation can be integrated with the air conditioning control for each zone to avoid simultaneous heating and cooling of the space.

Hot water heating systems are particularly adaptable to resetting temperatures lower for unoccupied hours of operation, and for heat reclaim purposes. The heat can be condenser water from an air conditioning cycle or heat pump cycle, or it can be waste heat from a separate operation in the facility.

Electric Heating

Electric heating is the most versatile heating system available, being flexible, requiring little building space, and having a relatively moderate first cost when compared to steam or hot water. Electric heating devices are available in all the configurations found for steam or hot water. Individual control is relatively simple. In the cases of high-quality equipment, temperature controls can provide multiple steps for varied supply temperatures similar to those found in hot water heating systems. Where electric heat is provided within individual spaces, it is generally 110 or 120 volts, in some cases 230 volts, all single phase. Where electric heating coils are installed within air-handling units, they can be 230 to 440 volts and connected to a three-phase system. In the typical coil installation, the heating elements are subdivided into steps to provide modulation of heating capacity based on the load.

Some of the major disadvantages of electric resistance heat are its higher operating cost, and its impact on our natural resources due to generation and transmission losses. When electricity is provided from a local hydropower system or from another operation such as cogeneration, electric heat can be practical and appropriate. Electric heating systems have relatively low maintenance costs. Properly designed and selected equipment should have a relatively long life.

21.5 COOLING SOURCE

While humans have survived the evolutionary process from prehistoric to relatively recent times without air conditioning, most Americans expect their working and living accommodations to be comfortable. In addition, many of the processes involved in modern activities require air conditioning for successful operation, including computer rooms and research and medical facilities. Most of us are familiar with old-fashioned methods of cooling but one that should be noted here was the use of ice. A ton of air conditioning is the energy equivalent of melting one ton of ice in a twenty-four-hour period, equivalent to 12,000 Btus per hour. This has become a convenient method of measuring air conditioning. The sources of cooling today involve mechanical devices of varying degrees of simplicity or complexity of design, operation and maintenance, and varied energy sources.

While low first cost of a system is still an important consideration, energy costs have become a major factor in the selection of air conditioning primary equipment. Larger electrically driven mechanical cooling equipment should be provided with a combination demand and watt-hour meter as well as an elapsed time meter. In the case of heat source machines, condensate or fuel supply can be metered. The following is a discussion of the more common types of equipment that provide a source of cooling for air conditioning systems in colleges, universities, and institutional facilities.

Evaporative Coolers

In arid climates it is possible to accomplish acceptable cooling for many operations through the evaporation of water. In a typical evaporative cooler used for a single zone application, water is sprayed into a chamber with air passing through it, or water flows through an absorbent pad placed in an air stream. As the moisture evaporates, the evaporation process extracts the latent heat of vaporization from the air, thus cooling the air. This process also raises the relative humidity. In a dry climate the resultant humidity is still at an acceptable level for human comfort.

Evaporative coolers have been incorporated into more sophisticated air conditioning systems where mechanical refrigeration and evaporative cooling are combined. The evaporative cooler can be used for the cooling of fresh air or through a heat transfer process to supplement the mechanical refrigeration.

Evaporative cooling offers a significantly low first cost when used as the only source of cooling. When used with mechanical refrigeration, it reduces the capital investment and lowers energy requirements. Whether it is by water introduced over an evaporative media similar to a filter or an air spray, evaporative cooling provides a degree of air cleaning. Evaporative cooling presents major maintenance problems due to the buildup of mineral deposits and mildew within the evaporative cooler.

Compressor/Direct Expansion Cycle

The compressor/direct expansion combination is one of the oldest and most popular refrigeration systems. Figure 21-14 illustrates a typical compressor/direct expansion refrigeration cycle. The refrigeration effect in a compression cycle is caused by the expansion of the liquid refrigerant into the gaseous state.

The liquid refrigerant is vaporized through an expansion value to a lower pressure into a cooling coil, causing cooling. The compressor draws the refrigerant gas out of the coil and raises it to a high pressure which also raises the temperature. The high-pressure gas is cooled in a condenser and becomes liquid that is stored in a receiver tank to repeat the process.

Reciprocating Compressors

Reciprocating compressors are piston-type machines and typically are sold as package components complete with all necessary operating and safety controls. They can be connected to a remote air-cooled condenser or be provided with a water-cooled condenser with water being supplied from a cooling tower or other source. Reciprocating compressors are available in sizes up to approximately 200 tons. The larger sizes of package-type units are often equipped with multiple compressors. Most

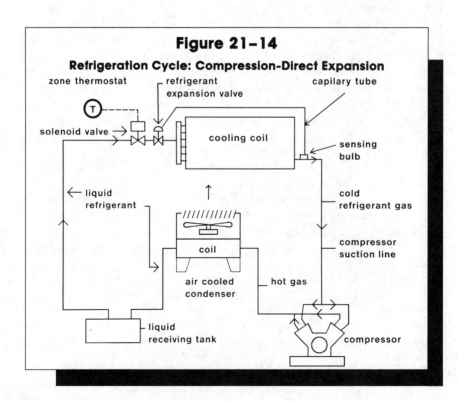

Figure 21-14

Refrigeration Cycle: Compression-Direct Expansion

are electrically driven. The units can be furnished in hermetic, semihermetic, or open type. Capacity modulation for reciprocating compressors is provided by using multiple compressors or a combination of multiple compressors and step unloading of compressor cylinders.

Reciprocating compressors tend to be noisy and their location should be carefully chosen. They have a higher energy consumption than centrifugal compressors for a net cooling effect, although improved design has significantly reduced the energy consumption of the reciprocating type. All compression-type equipment can be modified for use as a heat pump. Reciprocating compressors can be connected to a direct expansion system serving one or more cooling coils. They can also be provided with an evaporator shell to provide chilled water for an air conditioning system. Well-designed and -maintained reciprocating equipment can have a life expectancy of twenty to twenty-five years.

The dimensions of modern equipment are such that they will pass through a normal door. Solid-state controls are available with today's reciprocating equipment, monitoring operating conditions and providing safety protection and diagnostics of abnormal conditions. The controls can also be designed to be interconnected with energy management/monitoring systems. These types of controls should be seriously considered on any 20-ton or larger unit. Typically, an air-cooled compressor could require 1.2 to 1.4 kW per ton as compared to 0.9 to 1.1 kW per ton for a water-cooled type.

Reciprocating chillers can be driven by gas engines fueled with natural gas. With the potential for gas engine exhaust heat reclaim, the operation of a gas engine drive can be economical.

Centrifugal Chillers

The centrifugal unit is also a compression cycle chiller, using the compression effect of the centrifugal force of an impeller rotating at high speed. The tip speed of the impeller determines the compression of the refrigerant gas expelled. The design of the impeller provides the low-suction pressure necessary to evacuate the refrigeration chamber and the higher discharge pressure required for the cycle. Centrifugal chillers are of a higher first cost than reciprocating chillers and are available in sizes from one hundred up to several thousand tons. They generally are water cooled, although air-cooled centrifugal chillers are available.

Centrifugal chillers are designed with single, dual, or multiple stage compressor units. They are hermetic, semihermetic, and open drive. Centrifugal chillers provide chilled water to an air conditioning system; they are rarely used to provide direct expansion refrigeration. A centrifugal chiller typically has a long life and is easily maintained. The water-cooled condenser can receive water from a cooling tower, a process source, a well, or a heating system in which the chiller can function as a heat source (heat pump).

Centrifugal chillers are relatively quiet in operation and are available in low energy requirements per ton capacity. A reading of 0.64 kW per ton at full load is not unusual. Capacity control of a centrifugal chiller is achieved by controlling suction inlet vanes or by varying the speed of the impeller.

Electric Drives   The majority of centrifugal chillers used today are driven by electric motors. The electric motors can be either hermetically sealed within the refrigeration cycle or externally (open) mounted. The choice is usually based on personal preference. Some manufacturers do not offer the externally mounted motors.

Gas Engines   Gas engines have been used successfully to drive centrifugal compressors. A gas engine is adaptable to a combination system where a standby generator can be placed on the opposite end of the drive shaft of the gas engine. Under this arrangement, the gas engine offers standby power at a relatively nominal cost. The engine cooling system can provide heat for reclaim, including steam for heating or absorption cooling. The gas engine increases the maintenance cost over that of a centrifugal chiller with an electric drive.

Turbine Drives   A steam turbine drive on a centrifugal chiller can be quite economical, particularly if the steam is from a waste heat source or if the turbine exhaust is used as the steam supply for low-pressure absorption-type chillers. With an inlet pressure of approximately 200 pounds and with an exhaust pressure of approximately 12 pounds to the absorption machine, which then condenses the steam, a steam rate of 9 to 10 pounds of steam per ton of refrigeration can be achieved. In plants with a heavy investment in existing absorption machines and the availability of high-pressure steam, this can be a retrofit option. Steam turbine installations of this type are called "piggyback" operations, and the combined chilled water system can operate down to 10 to 15 percent of the total capacity. The drawback is that, under light loads with the absorption machines providing the only cooling, the steam rate would return to the typical 19 to 20 pounds per ton. Steam turbine installations of this type have been provided in capacities of several thousand tons in a single unit.

Absorption Chillers

Single Effect Chillers   The absorption chiller became popular during the period of low energy costs. The coefficient of performance, a measure of the ability to convert energy into cooling, is approximately 1 for a low-pressure-type absorption machine. This compares to a much better coefficient of performance of 3 or better for an electric-driven refrigeration cycle. At a coefficient of 1, it takes approximately the same amount of energy input to produce the same cooling effect output. With a coefficient of 3, for every Btu energy input the net cooling effect is 3 Btus.

The low-pressure absorption machines have fallen into disfavor because of the high operating cost, but are making a comeback through combining the chillers with energy reclaim cycles such as cogeneration, or where waste heat is available for operation of the chillers. Absorption refrigeration is available in a wide range of capacities, from household refrigerators to machines of 1,800-ton capacity.

Absorption machines have sensitive operation conditions. They use lithium bromide salts in liquid form for the refrigeration cycle. The salts are corrosive in the presence of air. The cycle requires a high vacuum, making it difficult to prevent air leakage into the system.

Water, the refrigerant, is sprayed into the high-vacuum chamber. Under these high-vacuum conditions, water boils at a temperature of approximately 32°F. The evaporation of the water in the chiller chamber cools the tubes containing the circulating chilled water.

The lithium bromide salts form the "pumping" part of the cycle, absorbing the moisture that is evaporated. The moisture-laden salt liquid collects in the bottom of the container and is pumped to a section where heat is introduced to boil off the moisture. The moisture is recondensed into water ready to repeat the cycle. High energy costs have led to the development of two-stage high-pressure absorption machines that have energy consumption requirements of approximately one-half that of the low-pressure-type unit. They can be competitive against electric drive chillers under certain utility rate schedules. Absorption machines are relatively quiet in operation. They can use gas, steam, or hot water as an energy source, and generally require water for condensing. A low-pressure absorption machine is sometimes referred to as a "single effect" unit due to the nature of its cycle as compared to a high-pressure machine.

Double Effect Chillers   Double effect absorption machines were developed to improve operating efficiency. These machines typically have a "double effect" cycle and today's modern design can either use high-pressure steam, high-temperature hot water, or be direct fired. Due to modifications of cycle design and improved efficiency, the units can operate at an energy rate of 9 to 10 pounds of steam per ton or 11 to 12 cubic feet of gas per ton. These efficiencies reduce the energy requirements by 50 percent when compared with a single effect absorption type chiller. Double effect absorption chillers operate in much the same fashion relative to the use of lithium bromide and water for the refrigeration cycle as the single effect units. Double effect absorption chillers are air and water cooled and available in sizes from 5 to 1,500 tons. Generally, the chillers are water cooled, but air-cooled units are available in smaller sizes.

Screw-Type Chillers

Screw-type chillers are another type of compressor chiller. Rotary helical screws, as illustrated in Figure 21-15, provide the compression. Capacity control is obtained by varying the distance between the helical screws or the portion of the helical screw that is exposed to the refrigeration circuit. They can operate with either direct expansion or chilled water systems and be air or water cooled. They can be exceptionally quiet in operation and have fewer moving parts than found in the reciprocating or rotary type compressors. Screw-type machines are available in capacities from 40 to approximately 800 tons. In recent times more major manufacturers are offering screw-type chillers that can be very competitive against reciprocating and centrifugal chillers in the 80- to 150-ton range.

Well Water Cooling

The use of well water for cooling has a long history in the United States. Early uses consisted of cooling for movie theaters, department stores, and places of assembly. Many of the early applications were unsatisfactory because the well water temperature, normally between 55°F and 60°F, was too high to remove moisture from the air in the cooling coils. It is possible to use well water for cooling a building for the major portion of the cooling hours per year in climates with design conditions as high as 95°F dry bulb and 78°F wet bulb, which would be typical for many areas of the United States. When used in combination with mechanical refrigeration, it has been found in certain instances that the mechanical refrigeration was used only twenty to forty hours per year.

Well water cooling can be used without adverse impact on the water quality and availability from the source. It has been used successfully where the water contained iron in the order of 15 to 20 parts per million. If the circuit is completely enclosed, the mineral precipitation is usually minor and easily cleaned. It is not unusual for well water systems to be in use for twenty years with little evidence of deposits in the coils and pipes. The well water coils should have removable heads for inspection and cleaning of the tubes.

The water can be returned to the ground uncontaminated and at a slightly elevated temperature, on the order of 5°F or less. Well water

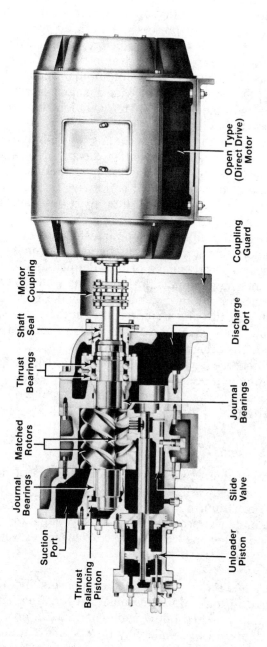

Open Type
(Direct Drive)
Motor

Coupling
Guard

Motor
Coupling

Shaft
Seal

Discharge
Port

Thrust
Bearings

Journal
Bearings

Matched
Rotors

Journal
Bearings

Slide
Valve

Suction
Port

Thrust
Balancing
Piston

Unloader
Piston

Figure 21-15
Screw-Type Compressor

cooling can be achieved at one-third to one-fifth the energy requirements of a typical electric installation. In addition to use with a mechanical system, well water can precool the fresh air for places of public
assembly or food service operations before being used as condenser
water. After use as condenser water, it can be used for lawn irrigation or
similar purposes, or make-up water for another operation. Well water
can be used in precooling coils to provide a major portion of the cooling
of the return air with the mechanical refrigeration being brought on for
dehumidification or additional cooling.

A well can be used to replace a cooling tower. In many portions of
the country, a well water system is far cheaper than a conventional
cooling tower system and avoids the use of chemicals. A well is available at any time of the year, which is not always possible with open
cooling tower systems. Wells require little space and have exceptionally
low maintenance requirements.

Wells have been used for heat pump installations as a heat sink. In
certain applications, the supply and discharge wells can have their functions reversed to take advantage of the thermal conditions available.
This also provides an automatic flushing of the well screen. The use of
well water for air conditioning, when properly designed, has been approved by public health and water resource authorities in a number of
states. The same wells have been approved as a source of water for fire
protection when the design meets the necessary requirements. The supply well and discharge (recharge) wells must have significant separation
or short-circuiting will occur and the water temperature will drastically
increase. A separation of 300 feet minimum is common, with greater
distance preferred.

Condensing Systems

All mechanical refrigeration systems need a means of heat rejection.
This heat rejection generally takes place in a condenser. The condenser
transfers the heat from the refrigeration cycle to the heat sink, either
water or air. Condensing can be provided by cooling towers, air-cooled
refrigerant condensers, the evaporative condensers, or water from wells
or bodies of water.

Air-Cooled Condensers   Air-cooled condensers find applications in
systems up to 150 tons. Many reasons exist for using air-cooled condensers: initial low first cost, low maintenance cost, no chemical treatment required, and ready availability for operation at any time of the
year. Air-cooled condensers can be an integral part of the package of the
equipment, such as in unitary equipment, or can be located remote from
the compressor. During times of high outdoor temperatures, air-cooled

condensers cause the refrigerant cycle to operate at higher pressures with resultant increases in energy consumption. The remainder of the year, at lower ambient temperatures, the condenser provides sufficient cooling surfaces for more economical operating costs.

Cooling Towers   Most large refrigeration systems use water as the cooling media. A cooling tower provides the point of heat rejection into the atmosphere by evaporation of the water. Cooling towers offer the advantage of lower energy costs in the refrigeration cycle, the ability to be located quite remote from the refrigeration equipment, and the ability to closely control the condensing pressure and temperature of the refrigeration circuit.

Cooling towers have a disadvantage of requiring water for make-up, blowdown for removal of solids resulting from the evaporation process, and chemical treatment. Cooling tower condensing systems require more maintenance than air-cooled condensers due to the water impact on the tower components, the condenser water piping, and the condenser water tubes. The refrigeration condenser tubes require periodic cleaning to maintain system capacity and efficiency. Cooling towers are available in factory-assembled packages in sizes from 10 to 700 tons, and in field built models from 200 tons and above. Towers are available in induced draft, forced draft, single flow, and double flow configurations. The choice of the type of tower is based primarily on economics and the application.

Corrosion and deterioration of the components can severely limit the life of a cooling tower. Towers should be specified to meet the appropriate Cooling Tower Institute and federal standards. A cooling tower system requires pumps to circulate the water from the tower to the refrigerant equipment.

One of the disadvantages of a cooling tower system is that, in cold climates, the water may freeze. With appropriate design, cooling tower systems can be made to operate year-round using bypasses that direct the warm water from the chiller directly into the cooling tower basin. Any well-designed condenser water system in a climate where freezing can occur should include a cooling tower basin or sump where the water can be stored without danger of freeze-up. Vertical turbine pumps can be used in an installation of this type. The system would be readily available for cooling at any sudden onset of warm temperatures in the winter. This would be particularly vital in installations such as hospitals or research centers.

Evaporative Condensers   Evaporative condensers can be used on closed refrigeration circuits and for cooling condenser water in heat pump circuits where exposure of the heat pump condenser water to the atmosphere is undesirable. The evaporative condenser circulates water through spray nozzles in a circulating air stream. The net effect is to cool the refrigerant tube bundle in the evaporative condenser. These condensers are easily adaptable to year-round operation by connecting the discharge and the intake openings with a return or bypass duct. Dampers can be installed that modulate the proportions of fresh air and return air to maintain the desired temperature within the condenser section. In cold weather, they can be operated dry without circulation of the water for the spray system.

Well Water   Well water, as previously discussed, is an appropriate source of condenser water. All of the advantages and auxiliary uses of the water listed previously apply. A well water system can be considerably lower in first cost than a condenser water system and eliminates the problem posed by the unsightly appearance or size and weight of the typical piece of condensing equipment, and the need for chemical treatment.

Atmospheric Cooling

Today's modern buildings and the functions therein often create the need for carefully controlled year-round air conditioning. Computer operations are the most common examples of this condition. In northern climates, outside air temperatures during a great portion of the year are sufficiently cold to provide the immediate cooling for such spaces. This is often referred to as "free cooling," similar in many respects to cooling with outside air on an economizer cycle. The typical computer room operation cannot use outside air directly for cooling due to the stringent moisture control requirements.

Figure 21-16 illustrates a method of obtaining free cooling in cold weather by the use of a cooling tower, a water circulation circuit with or without antifreeze depending upon the weather, and plate-type heat exchangers. Plate-type heat exchangers have the advantages of being efficient, subject to little or no damage due to freeze-up, and increased capacity at a relatively moderate cost (by simply adding more plates). In a typical northern midwest climate, these systems can provide cooling whenever the outside air temperature is 45°F or lower. In such applications, they can be designed with sufficient capacity to provide up to 100 percent of the cooling requirements as the temperature drops. This can occur for a number of hours of the year in the case of facilities such as computer rooms, which often operate twenty-four hours a day. The plate-type heat exchanger transfers the cooling from the cooling tower circuit to the chilled water circuit for the air conditioning system. Freeze-

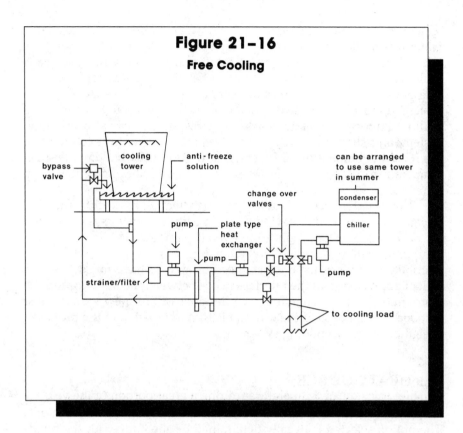

Figure 21-16

Free Cooling

up protection must be provided for the chilled water since the antifreeze solution can be below freezing.

Shell-and-tube heat exchangers are subject to severe damage in the event of a freeze-up. Their use is not normally recommended.

In more moderate climates, the antifreeze can be eliminated and the condenser water can be circulated either directly through the chilled water circuit after appropriate filtration or through a plate-type heat exchanger. In all cases, it is recommended that duplex basket-type filters be provided in the circuit ahead of the plate-type cooler where the liquid has been exposed to the atmosphere. This type of filter can be cleaned while the system remains in operation.

Central Plant

All buildings can be served by a central chiller plant, discussed in Chapter 27. It is emphasized here that the interface of a building chilled water system to a central plant system must be appropriate if the chilled water distribution system is to be successful. Systems can be designed with all the pumps in the central plant. In most systems, however, each building has its own pump and herein lies the potential for problems. The pump, in effect, becomes a secondary pump for the chilled water system. It must be capable of circulating the water through the building without imposing excessive back pressures on the central distribution system, and should be provided with valves and controls to maintain the required temperature differential flow within the building. A small temperature differential indicates excessive flow that can potentially rob other buildings on the system.

The maintenance of a relatively high temperature difference between the entering and leaving water in a chilled water system design for new buildings can reduce the overall pumping requirements for a campus system or for an individual building. Many central chilled water distribution systems have experienced trouble or have failed due to a lack of appreciation of the interface needs between the building and the distribution system. Therefore, the designer of any new system must respond to the needs of the central distribution system in the proposed design of the new building system.

21.6 HEAT SOURCE

The heat source for a building can be derived from numerous options. The option selected is usually determined by the budget for the building, energy costs, history of previous success, and the institution's preferences. If a facility has no need for steam, hot water might be the obvious choice. In a facility housing medical operations, food service, or laboratories where steam is required, the source of heat could most economically be steam.

Boilers

The following is intended to supplement Chapter 26, Heating and Power Plants, and is oriented to building boilers.

Steam Boilers   Steam boilers require careful monitoring of the condition of the water and generally require water treatment. Water treatment is particularly required if there is any loss of water due to leaks or steam consumption for humidification. Water treatment is also required to provide protection for the condensate return system that is subject to corrosion due to the presence of air. Chemicals that provide a film inside the condensate return pipes are generally added to the boiler water for this purpose. Steam boiler systems must be "blown down" periodically to remove the mineral deposits left by the evaporative process.

Fire tube boilers are most commonly used in steam heating systems for average buildings. Cast iron sectional boilers are also used, though not as often. They are often subjected to thermal shock by the introduction of the hot water heating system's relatively cool return water against the end plates of the boiler. This temperature stress can cause distortion of the boiler shell and significant damage to the boiler. Careful design can avoid this problem. A steam boiler operates at a relatively constant temperature throughout all its internal flow circuits and usually never experiences thermal shock. The steam from the boiler can be used in a heat exchanger (converter) to heat the water required for a hot water heating system.

Hot Water Boilers   Hot water boilers are found in all the same models and configurations as steam boilers. They are completely filled with water and fired in the conventional manner with water temperature being the controlling factor. The controls on the boiler are also very similar except for the need for a water level control on the steam boiler. Both types of boilers need low water cutoffs and an automatic means of providing make-up water for safety. Hot water boilers are popular in this country because, in many cases, codes require that a boiler operator be in constant attendance for a steam boiler but not for hot water boilers.

In many hot water heating systems, it is desirable to vary the temperature of the hot water to meet the actual load in the building. This increases the occupant comfort and energy efficiency. It is not advisable, however, to vary the water temperature by varying the temperature of the water in the boiler. Most boiler manufacturers caution against operating the boiler at too low a water temperature which causes condensation of the products of combustion in the boiler and the flue and subsequent corrosion. It is recommended that the water temperature variation be accomplished by blending valves with the boiler operating at a constant temperature. The blending valves mix cooler return water with hot boiler water to provide the desired supply temperature.

The advent of pulse-type combustion burners has led to the development of high-efficiency hot water boilers. The reduction of flue gas temperatures by extracting heat is one of the main sources of added heat in a high efficiency boiler. This reduction of flue gas temperatures leads to limitations of the temperature of the hot water generated, in effect requiring a low-temperature hot water system. Obtaining equally high efficiencies with a steam boiler is impossible because of the need for higher temperatures to boil the water to form steam.

Cast Iron Sectional Boilers   An older form of boiler is a cast iron sectional type. The design consists of a number of cast iron sections bolted together and connected by openings in both the top and the bottom of each section. Steel sleeves form a watertight seal between sections, allowing free circulation of water or steam throughout the boiler. Cast iron sectional boilers can be used for steam or hot water. They are highly resistant to corrosion but susceptible to cracking under thermal shock. The boilers require a relatively small amount of floor space, and first costs are comparable to a fire tube boiler. Cast iron sectional boilers have been successfully used for many years. They are often used to replace boilers in relatively inaccessible boiler rooms as they can be field assembled for a relatively moderate additional cost.

Modular Boilers   Many boiler systems within buildings were grossly oversized prior to the energy crisis. Typically, the heat loss calculations were made and 25 percent was added for pickup, 10 to 15 percent for piping losses, then two boilers were installed, each capable of providing 75 percent of the inflated figure. Often, only one boiler was ever required under the most severe weather conditions. The net result was a typical seasonal operating fuel efficiency of 30 to 40 percent.

Heating equipment efficiency is rated at full-load conditions. At part-load conditions, the efficiency generally is significantly reduced. The use of numerous small boilers, each operating at full-load conditions in a sequential fashion, offers a vastly improved seasonal operating efficiency. Although these systems were available prior to the energy crisis, in many cases their higher first cost could not be justified in view of cheap energy prices. Today, however, they are finding wide application in both steam and hot water systems. Proprietary and nonproprietary designs are available.

Some systems give the appearance of a series of domestic hot water heaters connected to pipe manifolds and individual heater pumps. Typically, on a call for heating, one boiler is placed in operation and functions until the load increases beyond its capacity. At that point, subsequent boilers are brought into operation, maintaining essentially a full-load operation on each.

Where oversized boilers have been taken out and replaced with a series of modular boilers, energy consumption reductions of up to 30 percent have been obtained. Multiple boilers of relatively small capacity are used with individual pumps. Fewer, larger boilers are used in much the same manner. The larger boilers, however, tend to be the typical fire tube boiler used for steam or hot water heating systems but of the smaller sizes.

Modular boiler systems can also provide domestic hot water efficiently. This is particularly important in installations where domestic hot water consumption is relatively high.

Often a number of the boilers in the modular boiler installation never come into operation. In effect, the package is oversized. This is not necessarily undesirable, in that the extra boilers provide standby capacity and the ability to add to the load in the future as the building heating requirements expand, and it does not affect the operating efficiency. The extra boilers indicate that a true heating load is difficult to predict due to diversity and other factors. In a new building, the tight fit of the building components reduces the load that the designer anticipates will develop as the building ages.

It is interesting to note that most central heating plants with multiple boilers operate on a modular basis. The plants often have a summer boiler sized to match the summer load.

Electric Boilers   As previously discussed, electricity has a number of highly desirable features for use as a source of heating energy. Its undesirable features are its cost and its impact on nonrenewable energy sources. In many buildings, it can be considered wise to use electric boilers for the heating source rather than electric heating units distributed throughout the building. This facilitates switching the types of boilers as energy source economics and availabilities change.

A typical air conditioning and heating system for a building using forced water flow is essentially independent of the fuel source for heating the water. Under certain applications, such as cogeneration, it is possible to install a supplemental electric boiler to improve the overall energy efficiency of the plant. Electric boilers are typically 200-480 volt, three phase. Capacity control is obtained by modulation of the number of heating elements made active to match the load. The heating elements in an electric boiler are also subject to deterioration as a result of mineral deposits. This can be avoided by selection of appropriately enclosed or sheathed heating elements. Electric boilers are available for steam or hot water.

Heat Pumps   As mentioned previously, the heat source for a building can be from one or more heat pumps. In many applications, this can provide an extremely flexible system. Small modular heat pumps can be relatively economical and are low in first cost.

21.7 VENTILATION—AIR QUALITY CONTROL

In the past, ventilation addressed primarily odor control, fume removal, and, in some instances, moisture control. Tightly built modern buildings necessitate more careful consideration of ventilation to protect the health, well-being, and productivity of individuals. Much research is being done to determine acceptable levels and the best means of monitoring and controlling contaminants within the space. Dilution appears still to be one of the most easily controlled options available. Dilution ventilation with outdoor air, of course, impacts the energy consumption of the building to the point, in some instances, where it can be a major portion of the building energy requirements.

Some research indicates that monitoring certain easily detected space contaminants such as carbon dioxide, and limiting the amount within the space, will, in effect, keep other potential contaminants at or below acceptable levels. Detectors are available for a number of potential contaminants. Their future successful application can be a significant factor in indoor quality control and conservation of energy.

Code Requirements

In the design of any facility used for human occupancy, ventilation must conform to the applicable codes. Most local codes are based on nationally recognized standards with local considerations included as modifications to that standard.

The major ventilation standard used today is ASHRAE Standard 63 that sets forth the ventilation requirements for buildings based on occupancies and functions within the building. In addition, there are other standards that must be met, depending upon the nature of the facility. Medical facilities must comply with U.S. Public Health Standards. In the case of contaminants that adversely affect human health, the organization must meet Public Health Service industrial hygiene standards.

Toilets and Locker Rooms

The buildup of objectionable odors is one of the major motivating factors for adequate ventilation of these spaces. Often the odors themselves are not harmful but merely objectionable. The nature of the odor source should be considered regarding the method of removal and operation of the ventilation system. Some odors are generated only during a specific function and are short-lived. Others are pervasive and continue beyond the function involved. Locker rooms and other athletic faciliities are examples of the latter.

Moisture generation, an additional contaminant, usually ceases when the use of the space terminates. These factors may recommend different operating levels of ventilation at different times. The design of a ventilation system for a locker room should consider the moisture problem, and suitable corrosion-resistant materials should be used for ductwork, air grilles and diffusers, and interior space finishes.

Food Service

Food service ventilation involves applicable health and safety codes, including fire protection. Range hood exhaust systems can require large volumes of exhaust air, imposing the need for make-up air and the consequent high operating costs. Careful design of kitchen range hoods by knowledgeable people can greatly reduce the ventilation exhaust and make-up air requirement. The specific location of cooking equipment below the hood can also reduce ventilation requirements by grouping similar items in a smaller area.

High-temperature cooking operations involving open flames, frying, and similar grease-related operations should be grouped together if at all possible. These sources of contamination require relatively high rates of ventilation compared to ovens or vegetable steamers. The latter require moisture and heat ventilation, but do not require ventilation for contamination.

The removal of fumes from grease-related operations involves a potential fire hazard. As a result, range hoods must meet applicable fire codes and include an automatic fire suppression system. The construction of the range hood and the exhaust ductwork must meet health and fire codes that require the internal cleaning of the ductwork and the ability of the ductwork to withstand the higher temperatures generated by a grease fire. Filters are not 100 percent efficient and grease will migrate throughout the system and can contaminate the surfaces of the building near the point of discharge. Generally this is an unsightly condition and not particularly hazardous, but it increases maintenance. Roof-mounted upblast fans are to be preferred for exhaust of grease-laden air. Building food service exhaust systems that are properly designed in accordance with codes will result in a more easily maintained and safer exhaust system. The exhaust of air over dishwashers, for example, is primarily to reduce the moisture. The ductwork for this operation should be noncorrosive and the points of pickup should be as close as possible to the source to reduce the amount of ventilation required.

Make-up air can be provided through a variety of types of equipment depending upon the season of the year and the climate. In arid climates, it can be provided by evaporative coolers to furnish make-up air that is conditioned. In other climates, direct mechanical refrigeration is usually required. In the winter, direct-fired gas make-up heaters are the most energy efficient means available if this equipment is compatible with the physical plant operations. Make-up air can be introduced directly at the hood with or without tempering. Under certain conditions, no tempering of the make-up air is required if the hood and make-up air ductwork system are properly designed.

Maintenance Operations

The types of ventilation required for maintenance operations vary greatly. Some maintenance operations are quite simple, consisting mostly of using power-driven bench tools, soldering, light welding, and occasional manual painting. These types of operations need general room ventilation of the type that is ordinarily found in maintenance buildings with operable windows and doors and the typical wall exhaust fan. Ventilation for maintenance operations, however, should be designed to conform to code and, in cases of hazardous operations, should be specifically designed to meet the standards set forth in the *American Conference of Governmental Industrial Hygienists Manual of Recommended Practice*, "Industrial Ventilation," and the applicable NFPA standard.

Shops   Maintenance shops on the typical college campus are usually fairly large and have diverse operations. The ventilation should consist of specific local ventilation for individual tasks and general ventilation for the entire area for removal of fumes that escape from localized systems or that are generated from operations conducted in inappropriate locations in the shops. The use of solvents and cleaning fluids presents a health and an explosion hazard that is often not recognized. These operations, if they are extensive or highly concentrated, cannot be handled by general ventilation and should be performed in a location designed for the use of the fluids.

Painting   Painting is one of the most common yet most critical types of operation found in maintenance that requires ventilation. Maintenance workers paint repeatedly throughout their years of employment and, as a result, are subject to the cumulative effect of different hazardous components. Paint exhaust systems should be designed for the size of the objects to be painted and the type of paints used. Small bench-top booths are appropriate for minor spray-painting operations. Such exhaust systems can be relatively simple with a fan discharging the air captured by the hood directly outside.

As the operation becomes larger, such as where furniture or even vehicles are painted, the exhaust system arrangement should provide an individual room for the operations. The exhaust air path through the paint room should be directed toward one end at an appropriate velocity, usually 100 feet per minute, and, where required, the exhaust air should be filtered prior to discharge. Filtration can consist of dry filters or water-wash filters or a combination. The fresh uncontaminated air should pass over the operator first, then to the paint operation.

Some painting operations also involve paint-drying areas. These areas should also receive appropriate ventilation, or the time spent in the space should be limited, with the room flushed with air between operations. Appropriate design of the electrical system in the painting and drying areas is required to avoid explosion hazards.

Maintenance Garages   Garages for vehicle maintenance should be provided with two types of ventilation:

1. General ventilation should be provided throughout the entire area to dilute the contaminants to an acceptable threshold level for the space occupants.
2. In cases where internal combustion engines are being operated for maintenance and testing purposes, tailpipe exhaust systems should be mandatory.

Woodworking Operations   The ventilation for many woodworking operations can be quite simple, such as a portable vacuum unit at the power tool. For larger operations such as a carpenter shop, a central exhaust system can be installed. Such a system should be designed in conformance with the Industrial Ventilation Manual and should have a central dust collector for separating the wood chips and sawdust from the exhaust air before discharge. The exhaust from the collector can be filtered with an appropriate grade of filter and a major portion of the air recirculated back to the space to provide significant energy saving in make-up air heating.

Grinding Operations   The ventilation of grinding operations can be relatively simple by having small ducts with flexible connections and appropriate hoods attached to the power grinding operation if it is bench-mounted. Hand grinding of large objects should be done in an appropriate exhaust booth. It is possible to recirculate air from a grinding operation if it is filtered. However, the filters become contaminated and loaded quite readily, so it is not normally cost-effective.

Ventilation System Maintenance and Safety   Exhaust systems for maintenance operations are important because the very nature of the maintenance operation presents a hazard to the occupants of the space and those performing the operation. In many cases, the exhaust product is not only hazardous but presents a fire or explosion hazard, and the system design should account for both of these. However, the best exhaust system will be ineffective with inappropriate maintenance and operation. Filters must be changed; all electrical wiring and devices should be maintained in an explosion-proof manner where required.

The location of the exhaust discharge must be carefully selected relative to the surrounding structures and building openings to avoid introducing the contaminants into an occupied space.

Parking Garages

Parking garages present a special problem due to the widely varying rate of contamination within the space. Parking garages that are used throughout the day in facilities with large numbers of visitors have a relatively constant rate of contamination. Facilities for office workers and staff have peak contamination on arrival and departure, with far less between those times.

Many garage ventilation codes require a specific and continuous rate of ventilation on the order of one cubic foot per square foot of enclosed parking garage throughout the period of occupancy. This rate is generally unnecessary for many hours of the day and has a major impact on energy requirements. It is preferable to design garage ventilation systems based on carbon monoxide monitoring devices located throughout the facility. These devices can vary the rate of ventilation depending upon the concentration of contaminants. In general, enclosed parking garages should have a relatively small ventilation fan that runs continuously, and larger fans for the primary ventilation. The detection of contaminants can sequence additional fans to increase the ventilation. Carbon monoxide sensors do not necessarily respond to diesel fumes. Depending on the climate, tempering of the make-up air may be required if there is potential for freeze-up of piping within the garage.

Make-Up Air and Energy Conservation

A variety of methods provides make-up air to ventilation requirements. These include the simple introduction of unconditioned air to the space for dilution. Direct-fired gas heaters are the most efficient to use in the winter. Evaporative coolers operate most efficiently in summer and in arid climates.

Careful planning and appropriate strategies can greatly reduce the investment in first cost and fuel for make-up air systems. Wherever air must be conditioned, energy conservation measures should be introduced. Generally, they are cost-effective on a life-cycle basis if the air quantities are large. In many cases, make-up air for exhaust operations can be supplied from adjacent spaces or systems, thereby avoiding excessive energy costs.

Moisture Control

Ventilation systems are used for the control of moisture at swimming pools and other facilities involving high rates of moisture generation. It is a mistake, however, to rely solely on ventilation for the protection of the envelope of the building. An enclosed swimming pool area or similar facility must be designed with adequate vapor barriers or constructed of materials not subject to deterioration by moisture. These include concrete and various types of metals, either noncorrosive or appropriately clad. A building in a cold climate that has paths with a high rate of heat transfer directly to the outside should be monitored carefully for potential building damage. It is not unusual to see the entire veneer of a building enclosing a swimming pool become detached from the basic envelope structure because of moisture migration. Ice can form within walls to the point where the pressure of the ice expansion will cause the wall components to separate.

Moisture can be kept at reasonable levels at the swimming pool with ventilation and in many cases with the appropriate application of heat pump systems. The ventilation can range from simple dilution in mild climates to energy-intensive systems that mandate serious consideration of energy recovery.

Operating Considerations

While ventilation is necessary, it is a constant source of potential energy consumption. Heat recovery systems are desirable, but are not 100 percent efficient and the loss is continuous during system operation. Monitoring of ventilation systems and education of responsible parties constitute a difficult and ongoing process. If a facility can be metered, the parties involved can be made aware of and possibly held responsible for the impact they have on the overall operating costs of a building. Metering of individual utilities at points of use is a desirable arrangement. Ventilation operation success or failure can be pinpointed by such metering in buildings with high ventilation requirements.

21.8 HEAT RECOVERY

The art of heat recovery is not new and has been practiced in major power plants and industrial operations for many years. In subarctic climates, the practice has even involved residential ventilation systems for many years. Heat recovery is not 100 percent efficient, although some systems can achieve energy recovery levels as high as 80 percent. For many building systems designed prior to the energy crises, heat recovery may be the only means for reducing high energy costs. This is particularly true in buildings that require 100 percent ventilation air, such as medical and research facilities.

Air-to-Air Heat Recovery

Figure 21-17 illustrates a typical air-to-air heat recovery system. These can achieve efficiencies up to 65 percent. They require that the exhaust and supply air streams be adjacent to each other at the point of heat recovery. These systems have limited use in highly contaminated air streams due to the danger of cross-contamination, although there are good prefiltering, purge units available, and seals eliminate this danger in most cases. Effectively designed and maintained filtration systems are required for optimum performance. Air-to-air systems are relatively easy to clean. Properly designed and installed, they can be very successful.

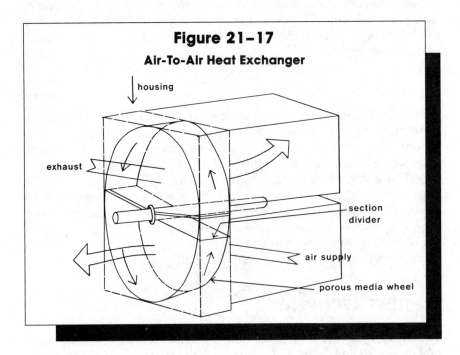

Figure 21-17

Air-To-Air Heat Exchanger

Heat Pipe/Coil Equipment

Figure 21-18 illustrates a heat pipe type of air-to-air recovery. The design is based on a refrigeration cycle. The tubes in the finned coil contain a refrigerant and a secondary internal tube with a wick. The opposite ends of the coil are exposed to make-up air and exhaust air. The high-temperature air causes the refrigerant to vaporize and flow to the cooler end, where it condenses and gives up the heat. The liquid refrigerant migrates back to the warm end of the coil via the wick, where it exits the tube and the process is repeated. Tilting of the coil can control its capacity. Heat recovery devices of this sort can achieve recovery efficiencies as high as 80 percent. These are generally easily maintained systems. They also require that the make-up air and exhaust air stream be adjacent.

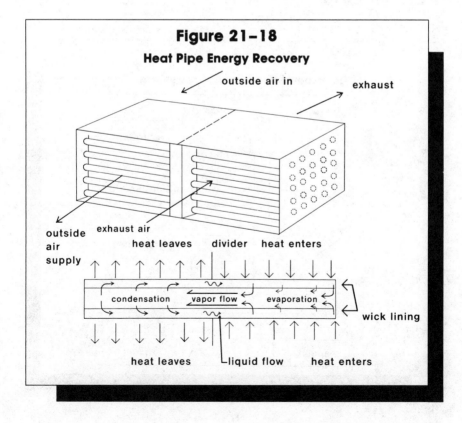

Figure 21-18

Heat Pipe Energy Recovery

Runaround Systems

Figure 21-19 illustrates a runaround system for heat recovery. These systems are applicable where the make-up air and the exhaust air streams are not adjacent. They are particularly applicable in retrofit applications in existing buildings. The system simply consists of two coils, one in the exhaust air stream and the other in the make-up air stream. A piping system, complete with pumps, circulates a heat transfer media between the two coils. Control can be achieved by varying the media flow or simply cycling the pumps. In cold climates, antifreeze must be added to the system, although it reduces the efficiency and increases pumping costs. Such systems can achieve efficiencies as high as 45 percent. Runaround systems have been applied to energy transfer within buildings involving other than exhaust and make-up air systems.

A simple method of energy recovery involving a typical water type coil used for air conditioning can be applied to a laundry or similar operation requiring a large amount of domestic hot water. The coil is placed in the hot exhaust air stream from the dryers or irons.

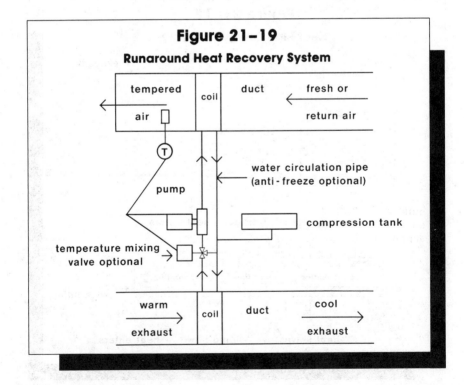

Figure 21-19

Runaround Heat Recovery System

Plate-Type Heat Exchangers

In some operations, it is necessary to transfer heat from one water or air system to the other while keeping the streams separate. Plate-type heat exchangers meet this requirement. They are efficient, easily installed, and easily maintained systems. However, large sizes are required to avoid high pressure drops. They can achieve heat transfer efficiencies as high as 70 percent.

Filters

Filters can be one of the most effective and most economical heat recovery devices by permitting recirculation of cleaned air. Recent changes in medical facility ventilation requirements and improved filters have permitted the recycling of air in surgical suites and similar operations, resulting in increased air quality control and greatly reduced energy requirements. Recirculated air brings with it energy that would have been lost; consideration of energy recovery should start at the level of air filtration and purification to limit ventilation via outside air.

21.9 FILTERS

The choice of filters available for buildings is almost endless. They come under two general classifications of disposable and permanent. Within each type, there are varying degrees of filtration efficiency available. A filter should only be as efficient as required, since the cost of filter installation and maintenance increases with efficiency. A 25 percent efficient filter means that 75 percent of the dirt passes through the filter. All high-efficiency filters should be downstream from lower cost roughing filters whose prefiltering action will greatly extend the life of the high-efficiency filter.

Disposable Filters

Disposable filters are available in rectangular form and in blanket form that can be cut to size and spread over a suitable mounting surface. There is a variety of thickness and media available. The media can be fiberglass or a proprietary-type plastic material, treated or untreated. Treated ones generally contain viscous material for impingement-type filtration. Roll-type filters with disposable blanket media can be operated by advancing the filter media manually, or automatically based on lapsed time or pressure differential across the filter.

A bag-type filter provides a relatively high level of efficiency. Such filters are gaining in popularity and have relatively low air resistance and greatly extended periods of time between filter changes.

HEPA Filters

A high-efficiency particulate air (HEPA) filter must be used in certain medical and research operations. These filters generally require special airtight mounting frames, roughing filters, and careful monitoring of the maintenance. This is generally true of all high-efficiency filters but is most critical for HEPA filters.

Chemical Type Filters

Chemical-type filters use citrus derivatives or similar compounds to absorb the odors contained in the air stream. They are available in many different sizes and types and are energy efficient in that the exhaust air can be recirculated.

Carbon Filters

Carbon filters have a long history of use for odor removal. They have been used on submarines for many years. In the past, the low cost of energy made their use uneconomical. With today's energy prices, carbon filters can often be used effectively for the removal of odors and permit the recirculation of air. Carbon filters require periodic regeneration of the carbon and eventual replacement.

Electrostatic Filters

Electrostatic-type filters work on the principle of electrically charging particles as they pass through the filter, and attracting the charged particles to an oppositely charged dust collector plate. Electrostatic filters can achieve efficiencies above 95 percent.

21.10 PIPING SYSTEMS

The design of piping systems for heating and cooling of buildings has evolved into five or six major systems, a few minor and little-used systems, and combinations of the various sytems depending upon the type of building and the HVAC systems installed. Prior to the development of air conditioning, piping systems were used for heat only and were limited to hot water heating or steam heating. Many times the choice of piping systems was dictated strictly by economics. On other occasions the actual physical construction of the building determined whether or not water or steam was used for heating.

Steam tends to be more restrictive relative to placement of the pipes in the building because those pipes must be pitched to drain condensate that accumulates in the supply line and is discharged in the return line from the heating equipment. This water must be continuously drained. Water piping, on the other hand, has the unique ability to pass over or under obstructions and to be placed horizontally without it adversely affecting the operation of the system.

The choice of piping systems applicable to heating and cooling systems within buildings covers a wide variety of options. The final selection generally is a function of whether or not the system is heating or cooling or a combination and the construction budget for the facility. Excessively elaborate piping systems are not necessarily the best choice as they offer more opportunities for improper operation which results in higher energy consumption and the very discomfort that they are purported to avoid. This is particularly true where interconnections exist between heating and cooling systems.

Hot and Chilled Water Piping

The choice of the type of piping system can greatly affect the energy required for pumping and the volumes of water to be pumped for system operation. A well-designed system recognizes the impact of the design on the pumping and is able to take advantage of the best features of each system without imposing undue energy requirements for pumping. The type of control valve can also influence the pumping requirements. When three-way valves are used so water bypasses the coil when full flow is not required, constant volume of pumping is required. The pumping system must always pump a quantity of water equal to the sum of the peak loads in the entire system. With a two-way valve that throttles the flow of water, the pump will only pump the amount of water required for the load.

One-Pipe System   The success of a single pipe system depends upon the use of "monoflow" fittings, specially designed tees to divert the water from the main into the radiation and then back into the same main. As the water passes through the radiation, it is cooled and reintroduced into the main, which lowers the supply water temperature to the following radiation. Each successive radiation must have its size increased because of the lower supply water temperature. One-pipe systems are not recommended for cooling.

Two-Pipe System   A two-pipe system is the most common for heating and cooling. It has a supply main and a return main with pipe sizes varying based upon the water flow within each portion of the system. Two-pipe systems can be divided into two categories; one is the direct return, the other the reverse return (see Figures 21-12 and 21-13). In the direct return system, the first connection to the supply main is the last connection to the return and, therefore, has the shortest travel. The water could short-circuit through the first heating or cooling device, affecting the flow through the other devices unless the system is carefully balanced, and the balance can be lost if the balancing valve is closed and not opened to the previous setting. The system can also be affected by a change in the heating and cooling device which would have a pressure loss different than the previous device when it was balanced. Direct return systems are used quite often due to the economics of installation, but are not recommended if a reverse return arrangement can be installed. A balancing valve installed in such a system should have a permanent marking for its setting if it has to be closed for maintenance.

Reverse return systems result in equal water travel for all the heating or cooling devices. The first connection to the supply main is also the first connection to the return main. The water travelling through any device essentially has an equal length path; therefore, all have an equal path and the system tends to be self-balancing.

It is not unusual to have combinations of reverse and direct return. In some high-rise buildings, the horizontal main around the perimeter of the building can be installed in reverse return, and the vertical risers to spaces can be direct return. This is not particularly desirable, but the building construction may not permit a reverse return to be installed economically or practically for the riser portion of the system.

Three-Pipe System   Three-pipe systems were developed in the 1950s when energy was cheap. They have a chilled water supply main, a hot water supply main, and a common return. Both the heating and the cooling devices discharge the water into the common return main, mixing hot and cool water. Through a complicated system of controls, the system proportions the flow of water back to either supply main. The system can provide heating and cooling simultaneously; however, the control of water temperature is not accurate and energy is wasted. This system should not be used.

Four-Pipe System   A four-pipe system is simply the use of two two-pipe systems, one for heating and one for cooling. The need for such a system is based on the need to have cooling and heating available simultaneously. Each heating and cooling device has four pipes connected, a supply and return for both the hot and chilled water. The equipment can have a heating coil and a cooling coil, or a single coil with an arrangement of valves that permit either cooling or heating water to the coil.

A problem with this system is that often valves do not seat properly, causing leakage; significant amounts of energy can be wasted if the four pipes are connected to a common coil wherein the heating and cooling water become mixed. It is advisable to have additional control valves in four-pipe systems to isolate a heating or cooling zone. Leaking coil valves would not have as much impact since the zone supply is cut off.

A good compromise in many buildings is to have a combination of four-pipe and two-pipe systems.

A four-pipe system is more costly and should be investigated carefully. Some buildings require chilled water year-round due to computer operations or similar functions. This would dictate that the chilled water system be separate from the hot water heating system.

Primary/Secondary Systems

Piping systems in themselves generally are operated with a single pumping source. The pumping source may be one or more pumps operating in parallel. They are referred to as primary pumping systems. Under certain conditions, it is advantageous to have what is called "primary/secondary" pumping systems. The main advantage of this system can be found in the ability to provide better control over the flow of water and the pressures required in the various sections of the system. The primary system essentially becomes a reservoir of either cold or hot water, circulating the water throughout a loop to which is connected all of the secondary systems. The secondary pumping system can serve a single air-handling unit, a group of air-handling units, or an entire building. Primary and secondary pumping systems can be used to great advantage in a central chilled water plant. Some, however, would not choose a primary/secondary distribution system because of the imbalance that can be caused by the individual pump pressure added to the secondary system. In an improperly designed or operated primary/ secondary system, it is possible for the return water pressure in the primary return main to become higher than the supply water pressure and actually reverse the flow of water through a building and back into the primary supply main, or restrict its ability to have adequate flow.

Steam Piping Systems

Steam is rarely used for heating modern buildings. Water systems can be designed to handle both chilled and hot water, and a water piping system is easier to install. Steam systems can be divided into low-pressure and high-pressure systems, which are very similar in their operation. Low-pressure systems can be further divided into gravity return, pumped return, and vacuum return.

One-Pipe Gravity Return   In a one-pipe gravity return system, the supply main also functions as a return. The supply main rises from the boiler to the point of entry into the heating system and from there pitched downward back to the boiler. The radiators are connected by a single pipe to the main. The steam flow is upward in the connection to the radiation; the condensate flows out the bottom of the radiator opening, down into the same pipe and back into the main. One-pipe systems exist in some older homes that have been acquired by universities and other institutions.

Two-Pipe Gravity System   A two-pipe gravity system is similar to the one-pipe system. It is more flexible in that the return and the supply are separate, so less water hammer noise potential exists in the supply main. The supply main can be run in a different location than the return.

Two-Pipe Pumped Return System   A two-pipe pumped condensate return system is similar to the two-pipe gravity system except that the water is returned to the boiler by a pump. The radiation devices can be below the water level of the boiler or in any location. The condensate is always drained to a condensate receiver connected to a pump. This receiver is placed at the low point in the system, which can be well below the location of the boiler and quite remote. This is the most common type of steam heating system in buildings today.

Vacuum Return System   In the vacuum return system the condensate return has a specially designed pump capable of creating a vacuum on the return line. By varying the pressure in the system, it is possible to have steam at temperatures considerably below the traditional 212°F. The steam pressure can be modulated; this is turn modulates the temperature in much the same manner as the water temperature of a heating system.

A vacuum system requires a tight piping system. If the system has leaks, the pumping becomes excessive and the energy costs increase.

Piping Materials

The most widely used materials for piping systems are copper and steel. Steel pipe is generally threaded up to 2 inches and welded beyond. Copper pipe is fabricated with soldered systems throughout except at valves and connections to equipment. Generally, the selection of materials is based on the first cost of the installation. It is not unusual to find copper used to 2 inches with steel beyond. Whenever dissimilar metals such as copper and steel are connected, they require proper isolation connections to avoid electrolytic corrosion between different materials in piping systems or between the piping system and connected equipment.

Plastic piping systems are widely used in the renovation of buildings due to the ease of handling and fabrication. Standards have been established for all types of plastic piping to ensure appropriate strength and quality for the intended use. Plastic systems offer the advantage of relatively low fabrication costs. If hot water is to be involved, selection of material and the support are extremely important. Problems will develop if the plastic pipe is not supported in strict accordance with the manufacturer's recommendations for the operating temperature.

Valves

Valves are needed for isolation of a system for maintenance or for emergencies. They must be placed at every piece of equipment. Selection of valve types is also important. Gate valves can be used for isolation because their first cost is low and they perform acceptably. Gate valves should not be used for throttling due to poor control and rapid deterioration. Globe similar valves are used for throttling, but not for isolation because of their high cost.

Butterfly valves are an acceptable alternative to gate valves and, in certain circumstances, can be used for modulating control. Ball valves in the smaller sizes are gaining wide acceptance for isolation and balancing. Plug valves have been used for shut-off and balancing for many years. All hydronic systems require balancing for proper operation. Balancing valves should be designed for the intended purpose and should be capable of permanent marking or stopping at the point of balance. Valves used for balancing flow should have a mechanical stop open position so that the valve can be closed for maintenance work and reopened to the balanced condition.

21.11 DUCT SYSTEMS

Duct systems are simple in appearance yet can have a significant impact on the first cost and the operating costs of a facility. High-quality ductwork generally costs more, but is a good investment. Poor-quality ductwork generally results in high operating costs due to leakage. Ductwork systems are divided into high-pressure/high-velocity and low-pressure/low-velocity systems.

The generally accepted standards for ductwork construction have been established by SMACNA (Sheet Metal and Air Conditioning Contractors National Association) and ASHRAE. Currently, the SMACNA standards have more than one classification based upon the system air pressure. Duct construction standards do not specifically address the subject of air distribution design. They set standards for the quality of construction of the duct system relative to structural integrity and potential leakage. The lower the air velocity and pressure, the more economically the air distribution system will operate. A low-velocity system requires more space for installation and possibly higher first cost, but due to lower operating costs is the most econmical on a life-cycle cost basis. The traditional high-velocity system is generally unacceptable by today's energy conservation standards.

High-Velocity/High-Pressure Systems

The velocity and pressures involved in a high-velocity/high-pressure system can be as high as 5,000 feet per minute and 8-10 inches of water pressure, compared to 1,000 to 2,000 feet per minute and 3-4 inches for a low-velocity/low-pressure system. The horsepower requirements for a high-pressure system are on the order of 300 percent greater than for the low-velocity system. The duct system requires relatively high-quality construction to eliminate air leakage and to limit noise levels. A majority of the ductwork is spiral, machine fabricated, and essentially airtight. Fittings are of relatively high quality and are welded or stamped and formed. Connection between duct and fittings involves the use of high-quality tapes and sealants. A high-velocity ductwork system can reduce the cross-sectional area of the required duct by as much as 60 percent.

Low-Velocity/Low-Pressure Systems

These systems generally consist of rectangular ductwork. Round ductwork is increasing in popularity due to low cost, air-tightness, ease of installation, and efficiency. The structural requirements for a low-velocity/low-pressure system are far less than those of a high-velocity system, and it tends to have far greater leakage if improperly constructed. All low-velocity ductwork specifications should be written specifically regarding leakage. Leakage as high as 25 percent is not uncommon in poorly built systems, but low-pressure proprietary duct construction systems are available that limit leakage to as little as 1 percent. Low-velocity systems generate less noise than high-velocity systems. However, improper fittings, construction, and design can result in unacceptable noise levels.

Duct Material

The most widely used material for ductwork today is galvanized sheet metal. The gauges and construction methods for galvanized sheet metal have been well-established by ASHRAE and SMACNA.

Fiber Glass Ductwork   Proprietary systems involving fiber glass boards can be formed into acceptable ductwork systems. These systems should be limited to areas where the duct is not exposed to damage from impact. The system must be carefully designed relative to the air pressures involved.

Some of the early fiber glass duct systems experienced failure of the materials and adhesives used to form connection between duct sections and fittings. This problem has been recognized by the industry and apparently solved, although the history of success of the materials used in a fiber glass system should be checked. A fiber glass system offers relatively moderate first cost, low fan horsepower requirements, and quiet operation.

Flexible Ductwork   Flexible ductwork, insulated or uninsulated, has been available for many years. Although it offers lower first cost, its main advantage is that it can be fitted into tight spaces. The potential for increasing fan horsepower due to high resistance or improper installation must be recognized. A sharp turn in a flexible duct can result in excessive pressure loss and reduced flow to the space. Flexible ducts should be limited to no more than four feet, and should be installed in a relatively straight route.

Flexible Connectors   Flexible ductwork must meet the requirements of NFPA standards for ductwork. A flexible connector does not meet the ductwork standard but meets the NFPA requirements for the final connection between an air distribution system and an air outlet device or piece of equipment. The length of these connectors is strictly limited by code. An attempt to use this material for ductwork can result in rejection of the system and expensive changes, besides reducing the life safety of the installation.

Lined Ductwork   Ductwork has been lined for many years to reduce noise levels and to provide insulation. Generally, lined ductwork is cheaper than ductwork with insulation applied to the outer surface. Lined ductwork imposes a modest fan horsepower penalty. This can be overcome by increasing the duct size, although this increases first cost. Lined ductwork is particularly applicable in mechanical spaces and other areas where exposed insulation would be subject to damage. It cannot be used in facilities or operations where the liner fibers can be entrained in the air delivered to the space, such as in critical medical facilities.

Special Ductwork   Many systems require special ductwork due to the nature of the material conveyed. This can include moisture, corrosive fumes, and air laden with grease, dirt, and dust. Corrosion-resistant ductwork is used in removal of moisture or chemical fumes from laboratory hoods and maintenance cleaning operations. Stainless steel solves many problems, but it can fail rapidly in certain atmospheres. PVC and similar materials are used for laboratories. Aluminum can be used in systems where moisture is removed and chlorine content is not excessive. Any system involving the transportation of fumes and dirty or corrosive atmospheres should have the material specifications carefully verified against codes and industry standards. Food service exhaust ducts must comply with NFPA recommendations and local codes.

Return Air Plenums

Return air ductwork is frequently eliminated and the ceiling space used for return air. Life safety codes have specified the required materials of construction for the plenum. Ceiling return air plenums and return air shafts operate successfully and greatly reduce the cost of ductwork. A return air plenum that is not appropriately constructed can greatly increase energy costs due to infiltration of outside air or air from noncooled or heated spaces. It must be recognized that the plenum is under a slight negative pressure and, therefore, must meet the construction standard for air tightness of a ductwork system. All too often the exterior facia of a building serves as the outer boundary of the plenum and is poorly constructed for such a service. These designs should be carefully checked and the construction monitored.

21.12 CONTROLS

General

A successful HVAC system design must correlate the complex interrelationships of the building functions, system options, equipment options and capabilities, capabilities of operating personnel, acceptable operating costs, and the budget. Any of the above factors can dominate, but the final design incorporates the most acceptable balance.

The control system is an integral part of the design process. It is not "added on" to a design. A sound understanding of controls, their functions, and capabilities is vital to the HVAC system design process, from earliest stages through the actual use of the system. For satisfactory operation, controls must be properly designed and understood by operating personnel. Controls can waste energy yet produce the desired space conditions and, therefore, not be suspected. Simplicity of design is characteristic of most successful systems.

Earlier discussions covered HVAC system selection including primary systems, subsystems, and zoning. Time of day, use of space or load occurrence demands that control systems be able to recognize differences and variations and control the HVAC components to produce the desired results.

Control technology has evolved into three major types of systems, each capable of a wide range of applications and variations of control sequencing, monitoring, and action. In recent years, there has been an explosive development in the electronic/computer-based area that has opened many new options.

The following material is a general discussion of controls. For a more in-depth examination of the subject, the reader is referred to ASHRAE's "HVAC Systems and Applications."

Types of Control Systems

Control systems are divided into three basic groups based on their main source of power.

Pneumatic   Pneumatic control systems are powered by compressed air (15 to 35 psig) that is distributed through a piping system to controllers that vary the air pressure supplied to damper motors, valve motors, and various switches and relays as required to maintain appropriate HVAC system function and space conditions. Compressed air is supplied by an air compressor.

Pneumatic systems are easily installed, economical, relatively simple to maintain, and offer a wide range of compatibility between manufacturers. Until the development of solid-state electronic controls, they were the most popular large systems.

Electric/Electronic   Electric/electronic control systems use electricity as the power source. The electricity is used at either line voltage or reduced low voltage, and supplied to a control device through the action of a sensor controller such as a thermostat. In some cases, the electric signal will operate a mechanical switch to provide pneumatic control of a valve or damper operator.

Electric controls are relatively simple to install and operate. Their cost is not excessive and they can be readily modified in the field. They are most common on small or simple systems.

Electronic controls operate at low voltage and their operation includes signal conditioning and amplification. The electronic equipment is capable of sensing status, comparing it to a desired condition, and causing electromechanical devices to act as required. The development of solid-state circuitry has greatly expanded this type of control. Direct digital controls (DDCs) are becoming the choice in most new designs due to accuracy of control and the variety of operations available. For more information, see Chapter 25, Central Monitoring and Control Systems.

Self-Powered Systems   A self-powered system derives its energy from the process it controls, and can also use other auxiliary sources. An example is the control of a gas valve on a kitchen oven. As the oven warms up, the pressure increases within the sensor and causes the valve to modulate through a linkage. Air pressure in a duct can be used in a similar manner to control a damper.

Two-Position Control

In the simplest control concept, the space thermostat starts or stops the operation of a system component such as a fan, pump, compressor, valve, damper, or heat source. The result is a two-position control system that provides a result that is often acceptable but subject to temperature variations between the on and off cycles. This simple control can be upgraded by the addition of a time clock to activate and deactivate the system for predetermined periods. Further sophistication can be added by a second thermostat that provides an alternate temperature setting during unoccupied periods.

Modulating Control

To improve the operation of the system and the resulting space conditions, the next level of control generally involves the continuous operation of the system while the space thermostat varies the rate of heating or cooling effect by varying the flow and/or temperature of the air serving the space. Time-of-day controls via clocks and unoccupied temperature settings are also available with these controls.

Reset Control

The above control arrangements provide temperature control for individual spaces or zones based on the HVAC system design but do not recognize the next opportunity to control the system as a whole for improved operation of the space controls and system efficiency. By varying (resetting) the temperature of the hot water heating or chilled water system, the temperature of the air delivered to the system, or in some cases the steam state, the entire system can be made to respond in general to the load while the space or zone controls can provide the easier final control action required. Reset controls vary the heating or cooling media temperatures inversely with the outside conditions or the maximum load on the system. Heating hot water would be hottest (180°F to 220°F) in extremely cold weather and then be cooler as the outside temperature rises, until the system would be shut down at some predetermined outside temperature, usually 65°F. The system reset can also be determined or arranged to be influenced by the solar gain, wind, space with the largest demand, demand limits on energy, and system media temperature change such as drop or rise in temperature of water returning from the coils or air returning from the space.

Except for the simplest HVAC systems, the cooling or heating media is always available during system operation. Pumps and fans run continuously while the chiller or hot water operation is cycled by the controls to maintain or reset a desired water temperature. The existence of continuous media supply at the appropriate temperature permits the numerous zones in a system to respond appropriately and efficiently to a wide range of space demands.

Reset of system media temperature can be at the zone level. In a hot water heating system, the relatively cool return water temperature from the zone would be blended with hot water from the boiler or converter through a thermostatically controlled mixing valve to produce the appropriate zone supply temperature. A reset system would be provided for each exterior zone.

Valves and dampers generally operate more quietly and smoothly and provide better control at the middle range of operation than near the open or closed positions. Resetting the media temperature helps avoid the extremes.

Central Control

Centralized control of the HVAC system is preferable to local control, and generally exists in larger facilities. Central control can vary from a single point start-stop station to a central computer performing complex operations based on the analysis of data monitored by the system. The advantages of centralized controls include the following:

- Reduced labor cost due to remote monitoring and adjustment.
- Reduced energy cost due to time-of-day, reset, and other functions that are adjusted for peak efficiency.

- Reduced maintenance through early detection of problems.
- Early detection of system stoppage or malfunction that can adversely affect operations within buildings.
- Improved life safety through shutdown of systems, modifying system operation, and other monitoring of conditions within the building during an emergency.

The problem of compatibility among various manufacturers' products can be very serious in central control systems that utilize DDCs. This problem has resulted from the lack of standards for component manufacture and protocols for writing software. The problem can result in the loss of all options for price competition or system change. The purchase of a system should include unit price guarantees for parts, for future expansion, and for annual maintenance for up to five years. Annual maintenance costs can amount to more than 25 percent of the original installation cost once the first-year guarantee period has expired. Bidding on long-term guarantees has resulted in significant cost reductions. For an in-depth analysis of this problem and related concerns, reference is made to the report of the Committee on HVAC Controls, *Controls for Heating, Ventilating and Air Conditioning Systems*, published by the National Research Council, National Academy Press.

DDCs are a significant advance in control technology, and are often very appropriate. They provide greater system accuracy, reliability, and more control strategies for optimum operation and energy conservation.

Even a poorly conceived HVAC system can achieve significant savings with a computer-operated central system for data gathering and system function control in accordance with a predetermined program. The program can be from a simple start-stop up to a very complex system with distributed programmable solid-state control panels linked to a central computer. The distributed panels are typically located at the controlled equipment, and are capable of stand-alone operation, responding only to the signals from the central computer for time-of-day modifications and similar functions. The choice of systems options is almost limitless. Herein lies the conflict between the desire for maximum optimization through multiple features and the important need to avoid undue complexity. A review of successful installations is a good guide for selection.

Life Safety

The development of life safety codes has dictated that the HVAC systems in a building must respond appropriately to a potential fire situation. The response can range from the simple shutdown of a fan and closing of smoke dampers, to a sophisticated sequence of controlling the fans and dampers to reduce or limit smoke migration by creating a negative pressure in the fire zone. Special ventilation systems for fire exit stair towers, atriums, corridors, and elevator shafts would also be activated by the control system. The control system would monitor the operation and report the required status data for all required functions.

Life safety fire alarm and evacuation systems, security systems, and central control systems for HVAC systems are available as a package. The decision as to whether the systems should be combined or separate must be evaluated in each case.

Quality

The failure of many control systems can be traced to the quality of the installation and to the quality of the installed devices. Often thermostats and other sensing devices require weekly maintenance to stay calibrated. It is also common to find that the system is malfunctioning due to the placement of control devices in locations where they are difficult to service, are exposed to excessive heat or moisture, or in some cases are overlooked by operating personnel.

The cost difference between a high-quality sensing device and a poor one may be significant in terms of percentage; however, a malfunctioning control can cause significant energy waste in a very short time. In one case, a control malfunction mixed chilled water with hot water for a month before the failure was discovered when the utility bill arrived for the chilled water and steam—$64,000 in 1983.

Industrial-grade sensing devices and controls are recommended where the operation is critical. Where the entire system operation is not critical, a mixture of industrial and commercial grade controls can be used. Humidity control for operating rooms, research areas, and similar places should have industrial-grade controls.

Maintenance

Maintenance of controls is an ongoing task that requires knowledge consistent with complexity of the installed system. Often, the operating staff does not have the level of knowledge required. The maintenance can be done all in-house, shared with outside contractors, or all contracted. In cases where the systems are complex and can cause significant economic loss if malfunctions occur, in-house personnel should be given formal training. Care should be taken to ensure effective maintenance in order to understand and keep abreast of new developments and techniques, and to fully understand systems and their components. On-the-job training is generally not adequate for controls maintenance personnel.

ADDITIONAL RESOURCES

American Society of Heating, Refrigerating and Air Conditioning Engineers. "HVAC Systems and Applications," "Refrigeration," "Fundamentals," and "Equipment." In *ASHRAE Handbook*. Atlanta, Georgia: ASHRAE, 1987.

Hittle, Douglas C., William H. Dolan, Donald J. Leverenz, et al. "Theory Meets Practice in a Full-Scale Heating, Ventilating and Air-Conditioning Laboratory." *ASHRAE Journal*, November 1982.

Hittle, Douglas C., and David L. Johnson. "Energy Efficiency through Standard Air Conditioning Control Systems." *Heating/Piping/Air Conditioning Magazine*, April 1986.

CHAPTER 22

Building Electrical Systems

Mohammad H. Qayoumi
Associate Executive Vice President
Facilities Development and Operations
San Jose State University

22.1 INTRODUCTION

The electrical distribution system to most college and university buildings is 13.2 kV, 4,160 V, or 2,400 V, three-phase AC. The voltage is transformed to 480/277 V or 208/120 V for distribution within the building. This chapter covers building systems using low voltage transformers.

Two principal types of transformer connections are used. The grounded delta system, shown in Figure 22-1(a) is somewhat obsolete but can be found in some older buildings. It supplies 240 V three-phase, 240 V, 120 V, or 360 V single-phase. The more preferred type of transformer connection is the grounded wye secondary, shown in Figure 22-1(b).

Usually, one transformer is used that has 480 V three-phase secondary for motor control centers and 277 V single-phase for fluorescent lights. A second transformer is used that has 208 V three-phase for the three-phase 208 V loads and 120 V single-phase for general purpose power outlets.

From the transformer, the power goes to the main distribution panels—an assemblage of circuit breakers (see Figure 22-2). Standard distribution panels have four, six, eight, twelve, sixteen, eighteen, or twenty-four circuits, each equipped with circuit breakers or fuses. A main circuit breaker is required for the main distribution panels. The power from the main panel is distributed to secondary panels and eventually to the loads.

A good design allows at least 25 percent system growth in distribution panels and includes a directory of the circuits and the levels served. If panels are in public areas, they should be locked to all but authorized persons.

Figure 22-1
Transformer Connections

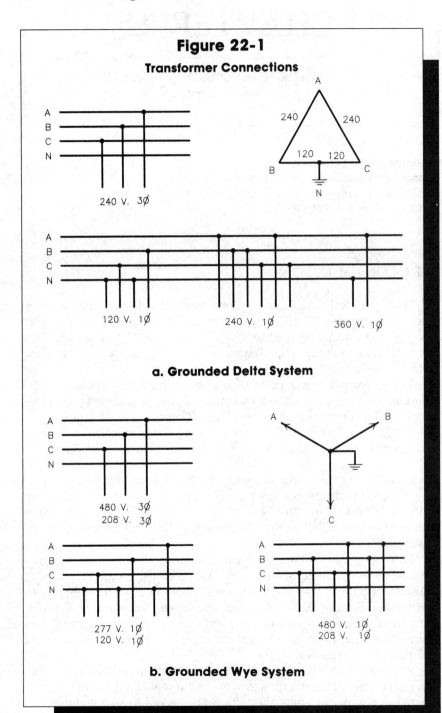

a. Grounded Delta System

b. Grounded Wye System

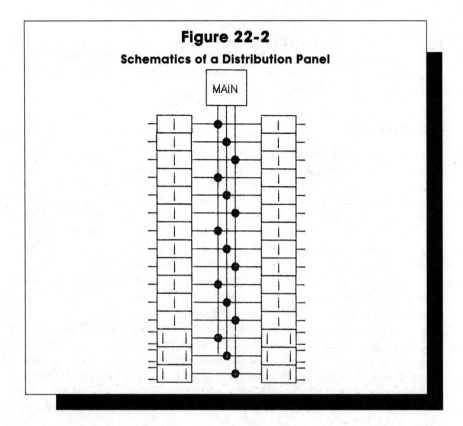

Figure 22-2
Schematics of a Distribution Panel

22.2 ELECTRIC WIRE

A conductor is a material that easily conducts electricity, requiring little electrical stimulation to induce an electric current. Copper and aluminum are common conductors. The current-carrying capacity of a conductor is determined by its physical size and the ambient temperatures. Therefore, in the design of a circuit it is important to ensure that the rate at which heat is rejected in the conductor is equal to or greater than the rate which heat is generated in the conductor.

Although a conductor's resistance is very small, it is measured as a positive number. When the current passes through the conductor, heat is generated. The amount of heat generated varies directly with the square of the current, and the amount of heat rejected is a function of the circumference of the wire and the ambient conditions. To ensure a proper heat rejection rate, wire size must be increased at a higher rate than wire capacity.

For example, to maintain a higher heat rejection rate than heat generation rate, doubling the conductor size means the current-carrying capacity is less than doubled. Doubling the wire cross-section area increases the circumference by 41.4 percent. However, doubling the current increases the amount of heat generated by four times. Moreover, lower heat rejection at higher temperatures will require derating the current capacity of the wire.

Wire Sizes

Wire size is measured in circular mils (CM). A mil is one thousandth of an inch. A circular mil is the area of a one mil diameter circle. The American Wire Gauge (AWG) is the most commonly used measure in the United States. However, AWG should not be confused with the gauge used to measure steel wire for non-electrical applications. The AWG scale consists of wire numbers, which are even, starting with the number 40 representing a wire diameter of 0.003 inches. The smaller the wire number, the larger the cross-sectional area.

Building wiring applications commonly use wire sizes of 14, 12, 10, 8, 6, 4, and 2. Wires larger than 2 are called 1/0 (one-naught), 2/0, 3/0, and 4/0. A wire larger than 4/0 is not designated by a numerical size, but rather by its cross-sectional area in mil circular mil (MCM). One MCM is equal to 1,000 CM such as 250 MCM, 500 MCM, or 750 MCM. These size designations are used for building wiring. Odd number size designations are commonly used for magnetic wires such as those used for motors and transformers. Number 8 or smaller wire can be solid or stranded, but number 6 and larger wire must be stranded to achieve the desired flexibility.

Wire Colors

Grounded wires are designated only by white or gray insulation. The grounding wire is identified by green or green with yellow striped insulation, or, in some cases, will be uninsulated. Hot wires have blue or yellow insulation, in that order, depending upon the number of hot conductors.

Wire Insulation

Indoor building wire is suitable for voltages up to 600 V. The most common wire insulation, thermoplastic, comes in many different types. Types TW and THW are the most common and can be used in wet or dry applications. When type TW is used, wire temperatures should not exceed 140°F; when type THW is used, temperatures should not exceed 167°F. RHH and THHN types are used only in dry locations, and the wire temperature should not exceed 194°F. THHN and THWH types have an oil resistant final insulation layer that adds strength and greater insulating capacity. XHHW type has a cross-linked synthetic polymer, which also adds strength and even higher quality insulation.

Wire Size Selection

In addition to ampacity, an important factor in the wire-size selection is the voltage drop. The voltage drop on branch circuits should be kept below 2 percent, and on the feeder and branch circuit, below 3 percent. It is important to keep the voltage drop to a minimum because in addition to the energy loss, voltage drop has a negative effect on electrical appliances. For instance, a 5 percent voltage drop on an electric motor means a 10 percent drop in output power. Similarly, for incandescent lamps, a 5 percent voltage drop means a 16 percent drop in light output; for fluorescent lamps, a 10 percent voltage drop means a 3 percent drop in light output.

Use the following formula to determine the appropriate wire size in circular mils:

$$CM = \frac{(\text{One way distance in feet}) (\text{Amperes}) \times (22)}{\text{Desired voltage drop}}$$

Note: 22 is the ohms per CM foot value of copper wire.

For three-phase applications, multiply the above formula by 0.866. Higher voltages are preferred for larger loads because they limit the voltage drop. For example, 277 V is preferred over 120 V for fluorescent lamps and 480 V is preferred over 208 V for larger motors.

Wires in Parallel

In some instances, two or more wires can be used in parallel instead of using single wire. The National Electric Code (NEC) specifies that parallel wires must be larger than number 1/0, be of the same material, have the same length and cross-sectional area, and terminate in the same manner.

Wire Splices and Terminations

The weak links in building wiring systems are usually wire splices and terminations. It is important to ensure that splices and terminations are electrically and mechanically correct. Screw-type terminals should have more than two-thirds wrap in the clockwise direction, with no overlap. Copper wires or copper-clad aluminum wires commonly require solderless connections since aluminum rapidly forms aluminum oxide—a poor conductor—when exposed to air. The aluminum connectors should be able to bite through the oxide layer. Today's soldering connections are seldom used for building wiring.

22.3 CONDUIT SYSTEMS

A conduit wiring system provides a high level of mechanical protection for the electrical circuits. This system reduces the probability of fire due to overloaded or short-circuited conductors. With a conduit system, the circuit wires are easily replaced, easily removed, or new circuits are easily pulled if there is space. Conduits may be buried in walls or surface mounted. The ambient conditions determine the type of conduit, the type of coating, and the type of fitting. Dust tight, vapor tight, or water tight conduits are available in ten foot lengths. The size is determined by the internal diameter in inches. The standard sizes are 1/2 inch, 3/4 inch, 1 inch, 1-1/2 inch, 2 inch, 3-1/2 inch, 4 inch, 4-1/2 inch, 5 inch, and 6 inch. The most common types of conduits are rigid galvanized conduit, intermediate metal conduit, electric conduit, rigid PVC conduit, and flexible conduit.

Rigid Galvanized Conduit

Rigid Galvanized Conduit (RGC) provides the highest level of mechanical protection. RGC is made of heavy-wall steel that is either hot-dipped galvanized or electro-galvanized to reduce the damaging effects of corrosive chemicals found in insulations. RGC differs from wafer-type conduits in that the interior surfaces are prepared so that wires can be easily pulled. The wall is approximately 0.109 inch thick. The disadvantages of RGC are its high cost, its heavy weight, and its difficulty of installation, (i.e., cutting and bending).

Intermediate Metal Conduit

Intermediate Metal Conduit (IMC) is similar to RGC but the wall thickness is about 70 percent less, making it lighter, less expensive, and easier to install. Check local ordinances before installing IMC.

Electric Metal Tubing

Electric Metal Tubing (EMC) has a wall thickness about 40 percent less than RGC, making it lighter and less expensive. EMT is used mostly for branch circuits above suspended ceilings. Unlike RGC and IMC, EMT is not threaded into a fitting or box. EMT mostly uses compression or set-screw fitting joints. EMT can be jacketed with polyvinyl chloride (PVC) to make it resistant to corrosive chemicals. Take proper care to prevent damage to the PVC jacket during cutting or bending.

Rigid Aluminum Conduit

Rigid Aluminum Conduit (RAC) is lightweight, rustproof, and provides a better grounding system than RGC. Since aluminum is a nonsparking metal, it is safe when used near explosive gases. Due to RAC's relatively fragile nature, it should not be installed in concrete slabs. Rigid steel elbows usually are used with RAC.

Rigid PVC Conduit

PVC conduit is lightweight and works well even in highly corrosive areas or places where moisture and condensation are a problem. Two advantages of PVC conduit are that it has no voltage limitation, and it resists aging from ozone and sunlight exposure. Since PVC is not conductive a grounding conductor may also be required.

Flexible Conduit

Use flexible conduit when a connection is needed with vibrating or moving parts, such as motors, or when rigid conduit cannot be formed to a required contour. Flexible conduit normally is used for short distances of no more than sixty feet. PVC-jacketed, liquid-tight, flexible conduit is used for damp locations.

22.4 ELECTRIC MOTORS

Electric motors are rotating machines that convert electrical energy into mechanical energy. The two main elements in motors are the stationary elements (the starter, brushers, yoke, armature winding, and motor housing) and the rotating elements (the field winding rotor and the slip rings). Most motors can be classified as either synchronous-type or induction-type motors.

Synchronous Motors

Synchronous motors, rarely found in modern building systems, have been in use since 1890 and are almost identical to synchronous generators, the only difference is the direction of flow of electrical and mechan-

Figure 22-3

Schematic Diagram of Three-Phase Synchronous Machine

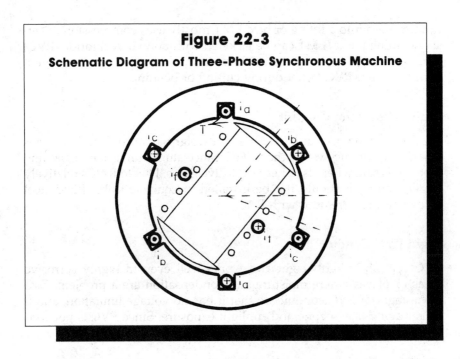

ical energy. A schematic appears as Figure 22-3. A synchronous motor has two types of rotor, the salient pole for slow speeds, and the round rotor for faster machines. Synchronous motors require AC power for the starter and DC power for the rotor.

Synchronous motor speed is directly related to the power line frequency and to the number of poles. The number of revolutions per minute equals 120 F ÷ P (F = line frequency, and P = number of poles). A unique characteristic of a synchronous motor is that it has an average non-zero torque only at synchronous speed. At steady conditions, it runs only at one speed, making synchronous motors ideal when constant speed is required.

Synchronous motors can have leading, unity, or lagging power depending on the field current and motor output.

Despite the favorable characteristics, synchronous motors are viewed as special purpose motors because they are more expensive than induction motors and require both AC and DC power.

Three-Phase Induction Motors

In an induction motor, the stator uses alternating current. The rotor power is supplied by the stator through transformer action. Induction motors have two types of rotors, wound and squirrel-cage. A wound rotor has a poly-phase winding with the same number of poles as the stator. A squirrel-cage rotor has conducting bars in the rotor cove which is shorted in both ends by conducting rings.

Unlike the synchronous motor, an induction motor runs slower than the synchronous speed. The per unit difference between the actual speed and the synchronous speed is called the slip, which equals

$$S = \frac{n - n_1}{n}$$

(n = synchronous speed, n_1 = motor speed)

In a synchronous machine, the stator and rotor fields are stationary compared to each other, while in an induction machine, the stator field rotates at a slip frequency (SF). Since the slip is normally 3 percent to 10 percent, for a 60 Hz line frequency, the slip frequency is between 2 and 6 Hz. Because of the low slip frequency, the rotor impedance is mostly resistive, implying that the rotor current will be in phase with and proportional to rotor voltage. The torque characteristics of the motor are shown in Figure 22-4.

An important note: at synchronous speed, the machine torque equals zero, implying that an induction machine will never run at synchronous speed and will always run at a slower speed. This concept is called the motoring region of the torque curve. Further, if the mechanical torque is applied from an outside source the motor will operate as an asynchronous generator. This concept is called the motoring region.

If the motor is running in a particular direction and two of the phases are switched across that direction, the motor will produce a torque in the opposite direction of the motor's rotation. This action will slow down the motor, which, if it is still energized, will start rotating in the opposite direction. This is the braking region of the torque curve and is a technique for slowing down large three-phase induction motors (see Figure 22-5).

The torque characteristic curve of induction motors is a function of the rotor resistance. The higher the rotor resistance, the higher the slip the motor will be running. Also, as shown in Figure 22-6, the maximum breakdown torque is achieved at a slower speed. Therefore, varying the resistance of the rotor changes the starting and running torque.

Motor designs are divided into four classifications: A, B, C, and D.

Class A.   Motors designed for normal starting and torque applications. Class A rotor resistance is the lowest of all four classifications. These motors have low slip. The starting torque is about twice as high as the full-load torque and the maximum torque is even higher than that. The full-voltage starting current can be as high as five to eight times the

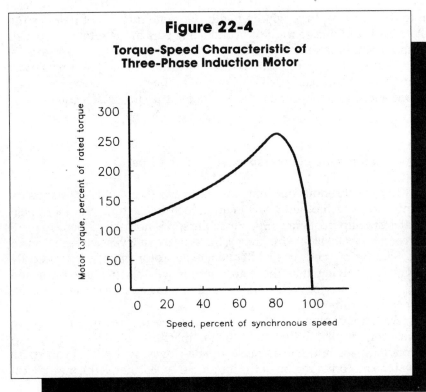

Figure 22-4

**Torque-Speed Characteristic of
Three-Phase Induction Motor**

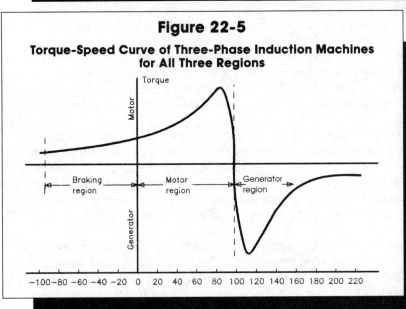

Figure 22-5

**Torque-Speed Curve of Three-Phase Induction Machines
for All Three Regions**

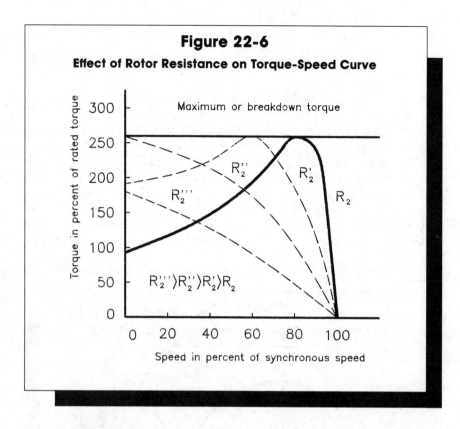

Figure 22-6

Effect of Rotor Resistance on Torque-Speed Curve

rated current, a disadvantage of class A motors. If a high starting torque is not necessary, a reduced-voltage start is achieved using an auto-transformer. Another disadvantage of class A motors is that, after starting, the torque makes a small dip before beginning to increase. Under high load, the motor might not speed up beyond the dip in the torque curve. This phenomenon is called cogging. Cogging creates high losses in motor power and sustained operation will heat up the motor and eventually will burn up the windings.

Class B.   Motors designed for normal starting and running torque and low slip. Class B rotors have higher reactance than class A, but the maximum torque is lower than class A. The starting torque is the same, but with 25 percent less starting current. Full-load efficiency and slip are good, but, because of high reactance, the efficiency and power factor will be a little lower than class A.

Class C.   Motors designed for high starting torque with low starting current. Class C rotor resistance is higher than class B, and the running efficiency is lower than class A and class B. These motors are usually used for high starting-torque applications like compressors and conveyors.

Class D.   Motors designed with the highest torque. Class D rotor resistance is higher than class C and the full-load slip is about 10 percent. Class D motors are mainly used for intermittent loads with high starting torques like punch presses, shears, and centrifuges.

The most desirable motors have high starting torque and high running efficiency (see Figure 22-7). At startup, rotor resistance is high and, as the motor approaches running condition, rotor resistance drops to a minimum value. To accomplish this, wound rotors add external resistance to the rotor circuit between the slip rings during startup and short the slip rings when the motor approaches full speed. Wound rotors

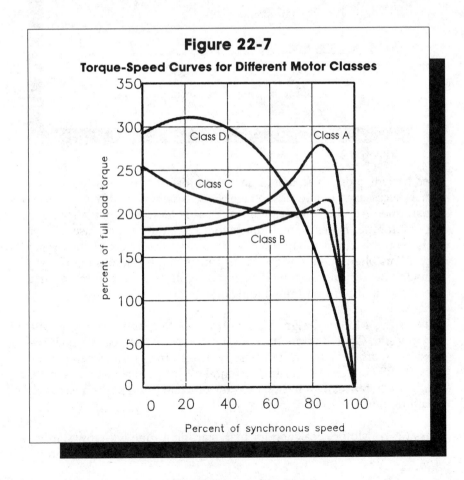

Figure 22-7

Torque-Speed Curves for Different Motor Classes

also can be used for adjustable speed drives. The main disadvantage of wound rotors is their cost.

Squirrel-cage rotors, as discussed so far, have only one rotor resistance value, implying a compromise between high startup torque and high running efficiency. To overcome this problem, double squirrel-cage rotors with an inner and an outer cage are used. The inner cage is deep in the rotor core and has lower resistance and higher reactance. The outer cage is at the face of the rotor and has a higher resistance and lower reactance. During startup, since the rotor current frequency is close to line frequency and the outer cage has the lowest reactance, the outer cage's impedance is much lower than the inner cage and most of the current flows through the outer cage. Therefore, the rotor exhibits high resistance. As the rotor approaches running speed, rotor current frequency is low, which means that reactances will have very little effect on the impedance of the total circuit. Since the two cages are parallel, the effective rotor resistance is equal to the parallel resistance combination of the inner and outer cages. Therefore, the rotor exhibits low resistance at running condition.

Electric Motors and Energy Management

The total electrical energy consumed in the United States is about 20 trillion kilowatt-hours each year. Electric motors consume more than 13 trillion kilowatt-hours each year. About 60 percent of the electric motor energy consumption occurs in commercial and industrial applications. If the efficiency of all commercial and industrial motors was improved by an average of 3 percent, the energy savings would be 23.4 billion kilowatt-hours. An average of 6 cents per kilowatt-hour results in an annual savings of $1.4 billion. For example, a 30-horsepower motor with an efficiency improvement of 3 percent that works ten hours a day for 250 days a year, means a savings of $167 per year or a total of $3,340 over the average twenty-year life of the motor.

Since motors consume such large amounts of electrical energy, and in view of escalating energy costs, the energy efficiency of motors must be considered.

Motor losses eventually convert into heat and lower efficiencies increase the winding temperatures thus reducing the useful life of a motor. Motor energy losses come from three sources.

1. Copper losses due to the windings resistance—a function of the motor load.
2. Iron losses due to the laminated core of the starter and the rotor, and the magnetic field. These losses are independent of the motor load

and are the summation of hysteresis losses, eddy current losses, and magnetic flux leakage losses.
3. Mechanical losses independent of the motor load and due to the losses in bearings, fans, and brushes.

In addition, the electrical system conditions can cause more motor energy losses. A motor operated outside its rated frequency and voltage has greater losses and its power decreases. Voltage unbalance also increases motor energy losses. A 3.5 percent voltage unbalance means an additional 20 percent motor energy loss, as well as additional motor vibration that increases the wear and tear to the motor. Oversizing motors also increases the motor energy losses, because the motor's rated efficiency will not be achieved; it will always be lightly loaded. Oversizing motors also means higher operating costs and higher capital outlay to acquire the motor and its associated equipment, such as transformers, switchgears, wire sizes, and conduits.

Size motors properly for a given load. Oversizing motors means lower power factors for induction motors and a power factor correction is necessary. If this correction were not made, the electric utility would charge a penalty for a low power factor because the utility must supply a higher current for the same real power. To the utility this translates into larger generators, transformers, switchgears and distribution systems, and higher line losses.

Efficiency

Efficiency is a measure of a motor's effectiveness in converting electrical energy to mechanical energy. A motor's efficiency is expressed as the ratio of the motor's output to its input. Efficiency is also expressed as the ratio of a motor's output power to its output power plus losses. The lower the losses, the higher the motor's efficiency. Also, the higher the output load, the higher the motor's efficiency, which means the highest motor efficiency is achieved at a rated load, and the efficiency is lower for partial loads. Generally speaking, large motors have higher efficiency than small motors. Also, high-speed motors have greater efficiency than low-speed motors. Therefore, a higher speed motor with a reducing gear system might be more energy efficient than a lower speed motor, despite the mechanical energy losses created by the reducing gear.

In induction motors, efficiency is also a function of the motor slip. The higher the slip, the higher the motor energy losses which cause heating of the windings, reducing the useful life of the motors. Multi-speed motors have a lower efficiency than single speed motors. Single-winding multispeed motors are more efficient than two-winding multispeed motors.

A small percentage increase in motor efficiency greatly reduces motor losses. For instance, a motor efficiency increase from 85 percent to 88 percent translates into a 20 percent reduction in losses, and a longer operating life for the motor.

Proper care increases the useful life of motors and ensures maintaining good motor efficiency. A basic maintenance program includes periodic inspections and correction of unsatisfactory conditions. Inspection includes checking lubrication, alignment of motor and load, belts, sheaves, couplings, tightness of the belts, ventilation, presence of dirt, input voltage, percentage of unbalance, and any changes in load conditions. Dust build-up on fans, misalignment of gears and belts, and insufficient lubrication increases motor friction, thus reducing the efficiency and the life of the motor.

Motor Control Centers

There are two types of motor control switches, manual and magnetic. The manual switch is used for fractional horsepower motors and is a toggle switch that turns the motor on or off. The manual switch is simple and inexpensive. The magnetic switch has three advantages. First, it has a low voltage protection feature that disengages the electromagnetic unit if the line voltage drops below a certain level, preventing the motor from over-heating. The unit remains disengaged even if the voltage level goes up again. Second, the magnetic switch is operated by a variety of methods. Third, for larger motors and higher voltages, the magnetic switch allows low voltage for the control voltage.

Starting a motor is accomplished by full-line voltage or reduced voltage. For larger motors, if initial torque is not a problem, reduced start-up voltage is used, especially if system capacity is limited.

Full Voltage Magnetic Starters

A schematic of the simplest full-voltage magnetic starter is shown in Figure 22-12. The main circuit consists of three contactors—one per phase—in series with overload relays. The control circuit consists of a normally closed "on" pushbutton, a normally open "off" pushbutton, a relay coil, and a normally closed overload relay contactor. When the magnetic start button is pressed, the coil is energized and the contactor is closed. Since the auxiliary contact across the pushbutton also closes, the circuit still remains closed after the "on" pushbutton is released. But if the "off" pushbutton is pressed, the coil circuit is interrupted, deenergizing the coil which opens the contactor.

Figure 22-8

Typical Effect of Power Factor on Percent Rated Load for Squirrel Cage Induction Motors

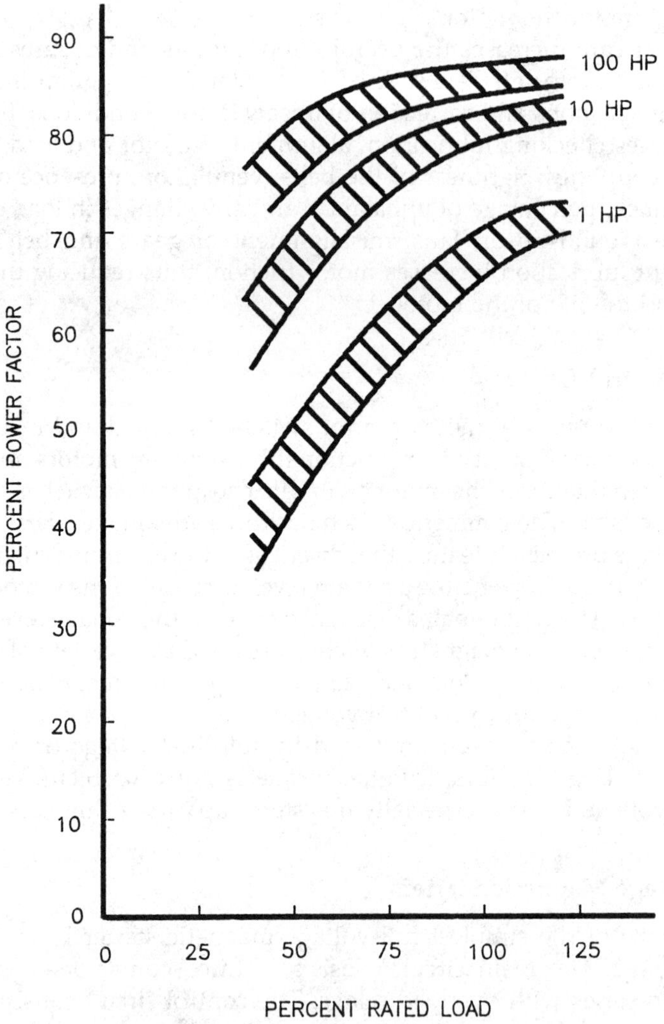

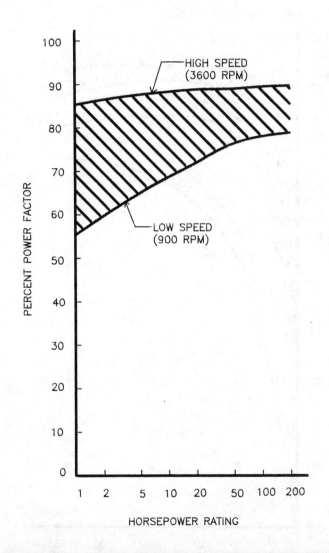

Figure 22-9

**Typical Effect of Power Factor on Horsepower Rating
for Different Motor Speeds**

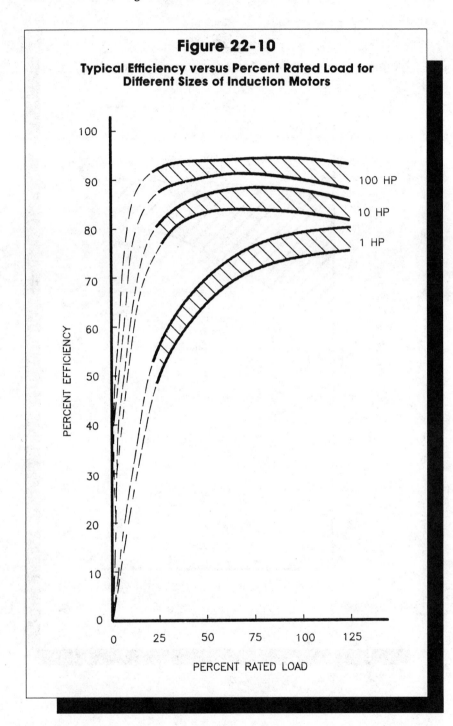

Figure 22-10

Typical Efficiency versus Percent Rated Load for Different Sizes of Induction Motors

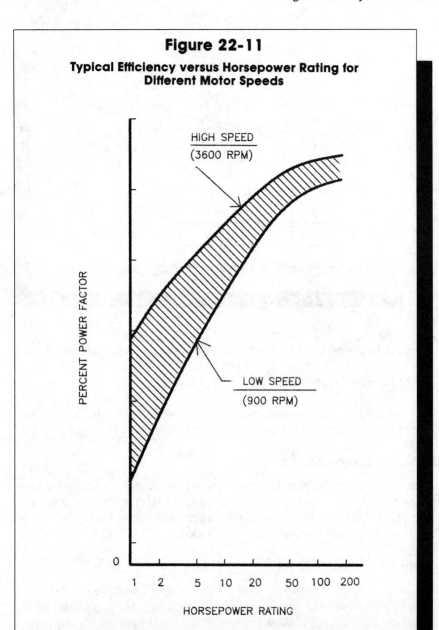

Figure 22-11

**Typical Efficiency versus Horsepower Rating for
Different Motor Speeds**

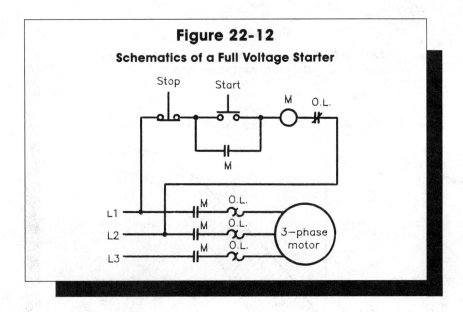

Figure 22-12

Schematics of a Full Voltage Starter

If it is necessary to start or stop the motor from more than one location, start buttons can be added in parallel, or stop buttons can be added in series as shown in Figure 22-13.

Sometimes the desired control-circuit voltage can be lower than line to line voltage. In that case a transformer is used (see Figure 22-14).

Forward/Reverse Starter

A motor might be required to run forward or reverse. To make a three-phase motor run in the opposite direction, interchange two of the leads (see Figure 22-15). Two sets of contactors are needed and should be electrically and/or mechanically interlocked.

Reduced Voltage Starters

The full voltage start-up current can be three to six times the rated current. To lower the start-up current, the three main techniques for reducing the starting voltage applied to the motor are: series resistance, using an autotransformer, and using a wye-delta starter. In series resistance, when the motor is started, resistance occurs in series with the motor (see Figure 22-16).

As the motor speeds up, contractors 1A, 2A, 3A (in that order), and the resistance are shunted. The relays, 1A, 2A, and 3A, are energized by the timer circuit or the centrifugal switch. A second method for reducing

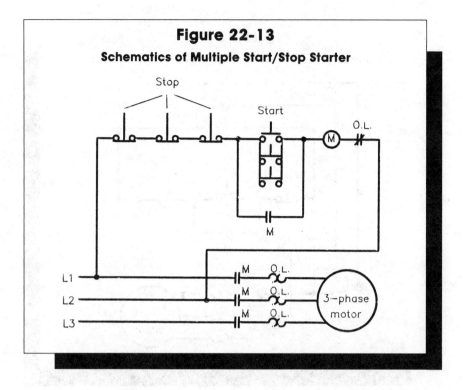

Figure 22-13

Schematics of Multiple Start/Stop Starter

starting voltage, using an autotransformer, shunts the autotransformer when the motor approaches full speed.

To reduce starting voltage using a wye-delta starter, the motor winding is connected in wye when the motor is started and connected in delta a short time after starting (see Figure 22-18). The wye-delta transition is an open or a closed transition. A wye-delta starter reduces the start-up current by two-thirds. Reduced voltage starters limit the starting current at the cost of reduced start-up torque.

Variable Frequency Drives

Most industrial processes require variable speed motors. The speed of an AC motor is determined by the line frequency of 60 Hz. To effectively vary motor speed, use a variable frequency drive (VFD). A VFD consists of a DC rectifier, a filter circuit, and an invertor (see Figure 22-19). Sixty Hz line voltage is converted to DC voltage and then is converted to AC voltage. The control circuit determines the output frequency and, thus, the speed of the motor.

The invertor circuit changes DC voltage into three-phase variable-voltage/variable-frequency AC output. The invertor consists of at least

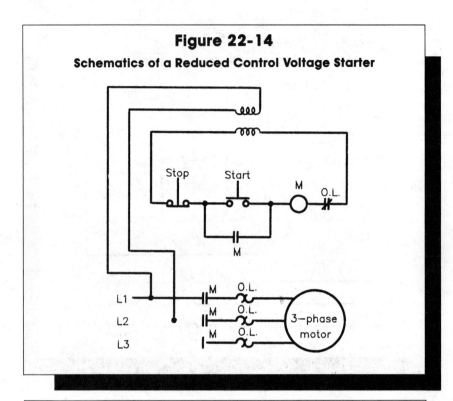

Figure 22-14

Schematics of a Reduced Control Voltage Starter

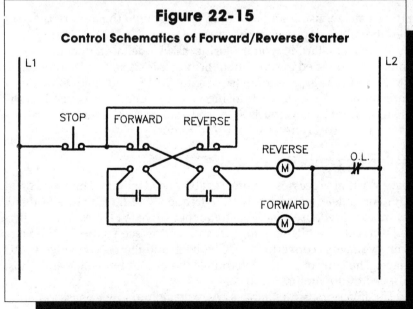

Figure 22-15

Control Schematics of Forward/Reverse Starter

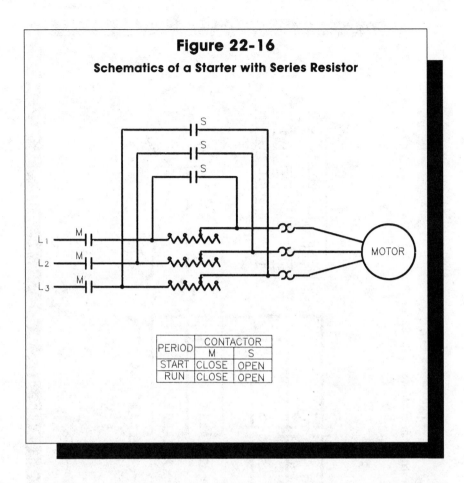

Figure 22-16

Schematics of a Starter with Series Resistor

PERIOD	CONTACTOR	
	M	S
START	CLOSE	OPEN
RUN	CLOSE	OPEN

six thyristors, each conducting 180 degrees per cycle. The switching sequence produces a three-phase output voltage. The output frequency is determined by control circuitry.

The three common types of variable frequency drives are: adjustable voltage input (AVI), current source invertors (CSI), and pulse width modulation (PWM). The voltage in AVI is controlled by the DC input to the invertor and means using either a silicone controlled rectifier (SCR) to carry input voltage, or diode rectifiers in conjunction with a chopper. AVI has the simplest of the three invertor types for control circuitry and also has regeneration capability (see Figure 22-20).

CSI receives DC input voltage from an SCR-bridge in series with a large inductor, creating the current source (see Figure 22-21). In a PWM invertor, the output voltage wave form has a constant amplitude with periodically reversing polarity that provides the output frequency. The output voltage also is varied by changing the pulse width. PWM has the

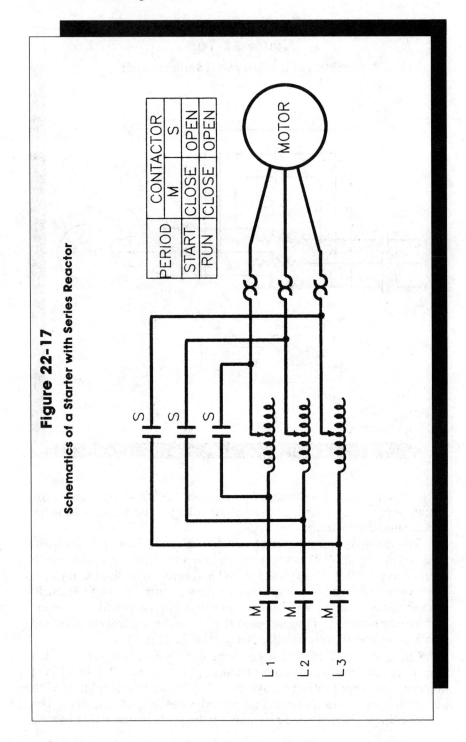

Figure 22-17

Schematics of a Starter with Series Reactor

PERIOD	CONTACTOR	
	M	S
START	CLOSE	OPEN
RUN	CLOSE	OPEN

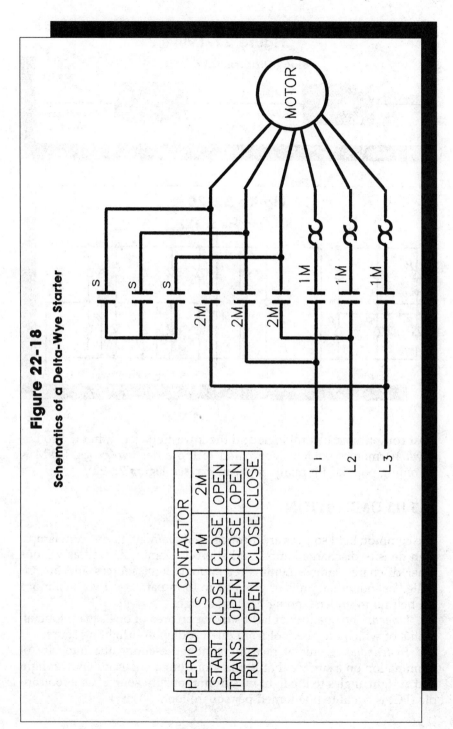

Figure 22-18

Schematics of a Delta-Wye Starter

PERIOD	CONTACTOR		
	S	1M	2M
START	CLOSE	CLOSE	OPEN
TRANS.	OPEN	CLOSE	OPEN
RUN	OPEN	CLOSE	CLOSE

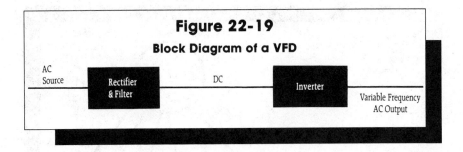

Figure 22-19

Block Diagram of a VFD

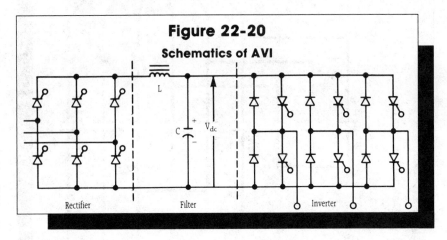

Figure 22-20

Schematics of AVI

most complicated control logic and the lowest efficiency, but it also has fewer harmonic problems compared to the other two types. PWM is becoming popular for many applications (see Figure 22-22).

22.5 ILLUMINATION

The common light sources are incandescent filament, fluorescent lamps, high density discharge lamps, and short-arc lamps, as well as various other discharge lamps. Luminaires support light sources and are installed as individual units or grouped to form patterns. Two definitions are helpful in understanding lighting design.

Lumen: The quantity of light striking an area of one square foot, all points of which are one foot from one-candlepower lighting source.

Footcandle: A unit of measurement representing the intensity of illumination on a surface that is one foot from a one-candlepower light and at right angles to the light rays from that light source. One footcandle (FC) is equal to one lumen per square foot.

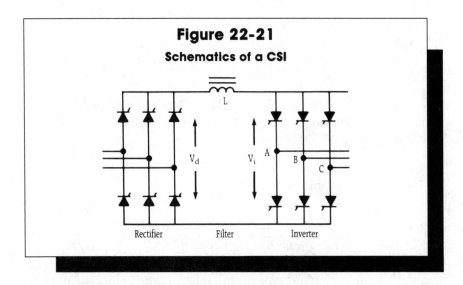

Figure 22-21

Schematics of a CSI

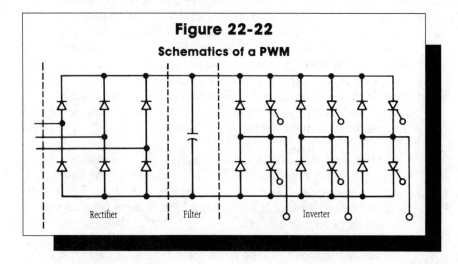

Figure 22-22

Schematics of a PWM

Lighting Calculation

The lighting levels recommended by the Federal Energy Administration are 75 FC for prolonged office work that is visually difficult; 50 to 80 FC for classrooms, libraries, and offices; and 5 to 15 FC for hallways and corridors. For comparison, the illumination levels of some natural light sources are:

- Starlight   0.0002 FC
- Moonlight   0.02 FC
- Daylight   100-1,000 FC
- Direct sunlight   500-1,000 FC

Several methods exist for calculating the number of fixtures required for a particular area. One of these methods—the Lumen Method—is summarized as follows:

1. Determine the required lighting level.
2. Calculate the room cavity ration (CR):

$$CR = \frac{5 \times \text{room height} \times (\text{room length} + \text{room width})}{\text{room length} \times \text{room width}}$$

Using the lighting tables, the cavity ratio combined with wall reflectance and ceiling cavity reflectance gives the coefficient of utilization (CU). CU is a function of the ceiling and wall reflectance as well as room geometry; it is the measure of ratio of the lumens reaching the working surface to the total lumens generated by the lamp. The higher and narrower a room, the larger the percentage of light absorbed by the walls and the lower the CU value.
3. Determine the illumination loss factors. From the time a luminaire is installed and energized a number of factors contribute to loss of illumination. The major factors contributing to loss are:

- Lamp lumen depreciation due to age.
- Luminaire dirt depreciation. This is a function of the ambient conditions. A clean area has a depreciation of about 0.9; a dirty environment, around 0.5. Cleaning light fixtures on a regular schedule is recommended.
- Voltage to luminaire variation. This is a bigger problem for incandescent lamps than for fluorescent lamps. For an incandescent lamp a 1 percent change in line voltage causes a 3 percent change in lumen output. For a fluorescent lamp, a 2.5 percent change in line voltage causes a 1 percent change in lumen output.

4. Calculate the number of fixtures required:

$$\text{Number of fixtures} = \frac{\text{FC} \times \text{Area}}{\text{Lumens per lamp} \times \text{CU} \times \text{Light loss factor}}$$

5. Determine the location of lights based on the general architecture, task, and furniture arrangement.

In addition to the *quantity* of light, the *quality* of light is equally important. Quality of light concerns proper light color, proper light distribution, and lack of glare. A relatively bright area within a relatively dark or poorly lighted area causes glare.

Lighting Control

A simple pole switch is the simplest form of light control. A dimmer switch supplies illumination control and can be surface mounted, flush mounted, or controlled by a pull chain. For safety, mount the control switch on the hot wire rather than the neutral wire. If light control is needed from two locations, then use three-way switches as shown in Figure 22-23. If additional controlling points are required, use two three-way and four-way switches (see Figure 22-24). The "on/off" designation is not found on three-way and four-way switches because the lights can be on or off depending on the position of all switches.

For controlling large banks of light, use a lighting contactor. The circuitry is similar to direct start motor control center. Here the control voltage can be different from lighting voltage, and the lights can be controlled remotely. Lighting is an involved discipline and a short discussion cannot cover the topic. A more comprehensive treatment of this topic is listed in the references at the end of the chapter.

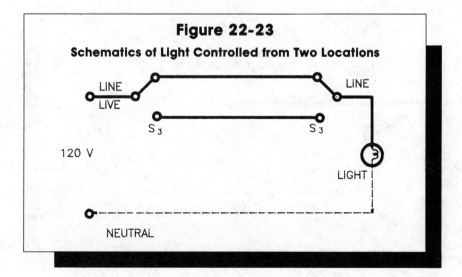

Figure 22-23
Schematics of Light Controlled from Two Locations

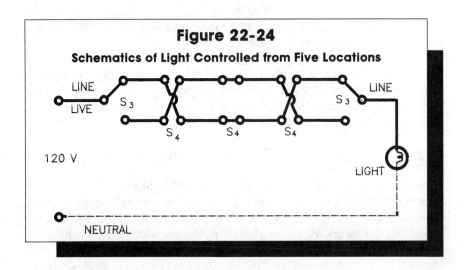

Figure 22-24

Schematics of Light Controlled from Five Locations

22.6 POWER FACTOR

Power factor is the ratio of real power (watts) to apparent power (volt amperes). It is determined vectorially as the cosine of the angle between the line voltage and current (see Figure 22-25). With alternating current and the presence of nonresistive loads (motors and transformers), the real power will be less than apparent power, so power factor will be less than unity.

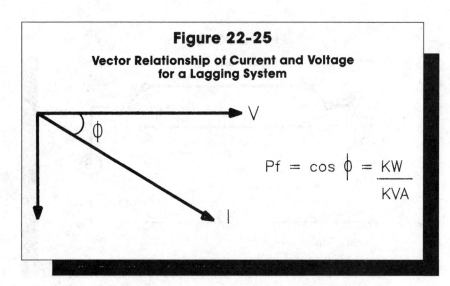

Figure 22-25

Vector Relationship of Current and Voltage for a Lagging System

$$Pf = \cos \phi = \frac{KW}{KVA}$$

Looking at power factor differently, line voltage multiplied by line current results in apparent power or VA. Apparent power can be graphically broken into two components: real power (watts) and reactive power (or VARs) (see Figure 22-26).

Notice that, for the same apparent power, real power varies inversely with the size of the angle. Moreover if the angle is positive, it is call a leading power factor; and, if the angle is negative, it is called a lagging power factor. In most power systems the current lags relative to the voltage due principally to motor load but also to some extent, to other loads. Therefore, more current is required to provide a given amount of real power if the power factor is less than unity.

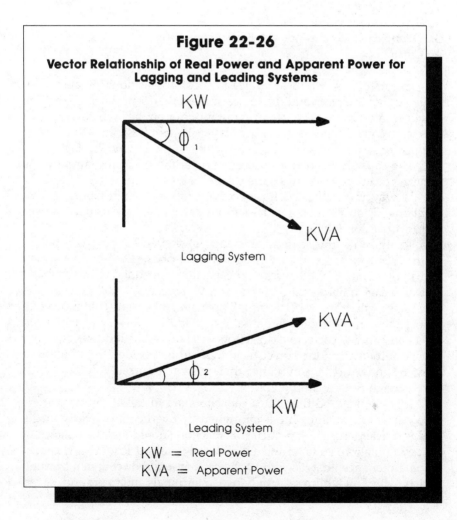

Figure 22-26

Vector Relationship of Real Power and Apparent Power for Lagging and Leading Systems

KW

ϕ_1

KVA

Lagging System

KVA

ϕ_2

KW

Leading System

KW = Real Power

KVA = Apparent Power

A low power factor implies lower system efficiency. Most electrical utilities include a power factor penalty in their rate structure to discourage customers with low power factors. In addition, a close to unity power factor is important to reduce system loss, transformer size, cable size, and power cost and to help stabilize the system voltage.

Power factor improvement is accomplished in two ways: by operating equipment at unity power factor and by using auxiliary devices to supply the magnetizing power or kilovars needed by the load. Equipment that operates at unity power factor are incandescent lamps, resistance heaters and unity power factor synchronous motors.

Auxilliary devices for power factor improvement are:

1. Overexcited synchronous motors.
2. Synchronous condensers.
3. Overexcited synchronous or rotary convertors.
4. Capacitors.

Capacitors are the best choice in most applications because they have no moving parts and the losses are less than 1 percent. Capacitors can be located at the loads, in the substations or on the line. Power factor correction on the lines is generally less costly, but it is better to position the power factor correction capacitor close to the low power factor.

The capacity needed to improve power factor is calculated by the general formula shown in Figure 22-27.

However, usually it is not necessary to go through laborious calculations. Multiplication factors can be determined by using a power factor correction table.

To illustrate the system efficiency improvement through power factor improvement, consider a 100 HP, three-phase, 208 V motor which has a power factor of 80 percent. If capacitors are added to improve the power factor to 85 percent, 90 percent, 95 percent, or 100 percent, the line losses will drop by 12 percent, 21 percent, 30 percent, or 35 percent, respectively. If the motor is partially loaded, the power factor is even lower and adding corrective capacitors will reduce line losses even more. Over-compensating for power factor should be avoided. In addition to wasted funds, it results in higher-than-system localized voltages which can damage certain equipment.

It is emphasized that, after capacitors are installed, proper care is needed. The capacitor's life is shortened by overheating, over-voltage, and physical damage. A capacitor inspection should include a check of fuses, ventilation, voltage, and ambient temperature. Prior to any capacitor maintenance, first disconnect the capacitor and discharge it through a heavy duty, 50 K ohm resistor between terminals and to ground. Avoid

Figure 22-27
Derivation of the Capacitor Table Formula

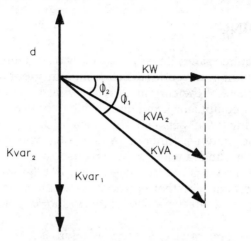

$Pf_1 = \cos \phi_1 = \dfrac{KW}{KVA_1}$

$Pf_2 = \cos \phi_2 = \dfrac{KW}{KVA_2}$

Pf_1 = Existing Power Factor

Pf_2 = Desired Power Factor

$Kvar_1$ = Existing Reactive Power

$Kvar_2$ = Desired Reactive Power

$\tan \phi_1 = \dfrac{Kvar_1}{KW}$ $KW \tan \phi_1 = Kvar_1$

$\tan \phi_2 = \dfrac{Kvar_2}{KW}$ $KW \tan \phi_2 = Kvar_2$

Required Capacitance = d = $Kvar_1 - Kvar_2$

$\qquad\qquad\qquad = Kw (\tan \phi_1 - \tan \phi_2)$

discharge by short circuiting large capacitators, because the sudden release of a large discharge can injure the operator.

22.7 GROUNDING

Grounding is a required safety item for secondary distribution. There are two distinct grounding categories. First is system grounding, which means grounding one of the current-carrying wires to avoid a floating system. Second is equipment grounding, which consists of placing a non-current-carrying wire between the metallic frame of electrical equipment and the conduits, armor or armored of a ground rod. Therefore, reference to "grounded wire" usually refers to a system ground, in which case, if the circuit is on, the wire is hot. But "grounding wire" refers to the equipment wire that has no current under normal conditions. Grounding eliminates the possibility of shocks and minimizes lighting damages.

Whenever the topic of electric shock is discussed, the question of danger normally arises. Shock danger is not due to the high voltage of the equipment, but to the current flowing through the human body. A current of one milliampere (MA) is not perceptible. Between one to eight MA causes mild to strong sensations. Eight to fifteen MA is unpleasant but the shock victim can release the object producing the electrical current. A current above fifteen MA causes a muscular freeze, and above seventy-five MA is fatal.

Ground Fault Protection

The National Electric Code (NEC) requires ground fault equipment protection. Ground fault interrupters (GFIs) protect equipment from low grade faults that are not large enough to be interrupted by conventional overcurrent protection devices, such as fuses or circuit breakers. The function of GFIs is often misunderstood. It is easier to state what a GFI is not. GFIs do not protect people or prevent shocks. They neither prevent ground faults nor protect the equipment from a high grade fault. GFIs only protect equipment from low grade faults. The principle behind GFIs is simple: using a current transformer surrounding the live wires, the current remains within the wires and the net current is zero. However, if leakage occurs, the net current is not zero and the GFI will trip the circuit breaker.

A GFI is required if the line-to-ground voltage in a grounded wye service is between 150 V and 600 V and service disconnect is rated at 1,000 amperes or more. For health care facilities, provide at least an additional layer of ground fault protection downstream towards the load. Like conventional current protection systems, coordinate GFIs to assure selectivity. As mentioned earlier, a GFI does not prevent ground fault and, to eliminate the possible causes of ground fault, required maintenance is recommended including cleaning insulators, replacing cracked insulators, and tightening loose connections.

ADDITIONAL RESOURCES

Clidero, Robert K. *Applied Electrical Systems for Construction.* New York: Van Nostrand Reinhold Co., 1982.

Earl, John T. *Electrical Wiring Design and Application.* Englewood Cliffs, New Jersey: Prentice-Hall, 1986.

Lighting Handbook. Bloomfield, New Jersey: North American Philips Lighting Corporation, 1984.

Richter, Herbert P. and W. Creighton Schwan. *Practical Electrical Wiring.* New York: McGraw-Hill, 1987.

CHAPTER 23

Fire Protection

George E. Godward
Fire Marshal
The University of Texas at Austin

23.1 INTRODUCTION

Fire is a particular kind of oxidation known as combustion. When oxygen is released rapidly in a fire, energy in the form of heat, light, and visible gases is released. Fuel, high temperature, and oxygen must exist for combustion to occur. These requirements influence fire safety in building design. The choice of building structural and finishing materials controls the available fuel. Sprinkler systems deprive the fire of the necessary high temperature. Suppression systems that cover the fuel with foam or dry chemicals or displace the oxygen with another gas such as carbon dioxide, deprive the fire of oxygen.

The three objectives of building fire systems are to protect life, to protect property, and to provide continuity of operation.

Because fire protection influences virtually every aspect of building design and could not be covered in a single chapter, this chapter simply provides an introduction to the applicable codes and standards, describes building fire protection equipment, and presents a general approach to fire protection.

23.2 BUILDING FIRE PREVENTION CODES

National Codes

In general, all construction requirements are a part of the building code including fire safety requirements such as provision of exits, requirements for flame spread of interior finish, and enclosure of vertical openings and fire suppression systems. These codes usually are administered by the building department; but their maintenance is covered in a fire prevention code.

The following is a listing of building and fire prevention codes currently applicable in the United States:

Building Codes
1. AIA (American Insurance Association).
2. ICBO (International Conference of Building Officials).
3. BOCA (Building Officials and Code Administrators).
4. SBC (Standard Building Code, originally called Southern Building Code Congress International).

Fire Codes
1. NFPA (National Fire Protection Association)—twelve volumes.
2. UFC (Uniform Fire Code), published by ICBO.
3. BOCA (Basic Fire Prevention Code).
4. Southern Standard Fire Prevention Code.
5. Fire Prevention Code, published by the AIA.

Each organization and its codes are discussed in the appendix of *Fire Chief's Handbook*, 15th edition; or in Section 7, Chapter 15 of the 16th edition.

State and Local Government Codes

State governments regulate building construction for the safety and health of the public. This power is usually delegated to local governments.

Building code requirements usually apply to construction or for major alterations to existing buildings; they are rarely retroactive.

The building official's authority and responsibility generally ends and the fire official's begins once an occupancy permit is issued. However, many communities require that both the building and the fire officials work together.

The methods by which states establish building regulations vary. In some states, the state code establishes the minimum below which local regulations cannot go, or requires the local government to adopt the state code. In some cases adoption is optional. This results in a wide variety of local codes. Some local governments draft their own code; some simply adopt one of the model building codes; and others modify one of the model building codes.

23.3 BUILDING CLASSIFICATIONS - UNITED STATES

Fire protection and fire safety requirements are classified by type of construction, based upon the fire resistance of the materials used for the structural elements.

Ten construction types are identified in NFPA 220 and in B/NBC model building code. Nine construction types are identified in the UBC and SBC model building codes.

For uniformity in building codes and standards, the Model Codes Standardization Council (MCSC) recommends dividing classifications into two groups: non-combustible and combustible. According to the MCSC, to rationally compare the various types of construction, a notational system was needed to identify the fire resistance required for three basic elements of a building: the exterior wall, the primary structural frame, and the floor construction. The three-digit notation that was developed is as follows:

First digit   The hourly requirement for exterior bearing-wall fronting on a street or lot line.

Second digit   The hourly requirement for the structural frame, or columns and girders supporting a load from more than one floor.

Third digit   The hourly requirement for floor construction. In addition, for heavy timber, the notation "H" was used.

Figure 23-1 shows the MCSC recommended types of construction, and Figure 23-2 shows the NFPA 220 fire resistive requirements by types of construction.

23.4 OCCUPANCY CLASSIFICATIONS

Most building codes do not treat colleges and universities as educational occupancies because they are combinations of other occupancies. Codes apply occupancy requirements based on the actual use of the space. Classrooms for fewer than fifty occupants are treated as business occupancies, and classrooms with an occupant load of fifty and more are considered assembly occupancies. Thus, a college or university's educational mission does not imply special fire or life-safety treatment.

To comply with the NFPA, apply the provisions in Life Safety Code 101 regarding construction, interior finish, fire suppression and detection systems. If a building has mixed occupancy type, apply the requirement providing the highest level of life safety.

Figure 23-1

Model Codes Standardization Council
Recommended Types of Construction

Noncombustible
Type I (433)   Type II (222)
Type I (332)   Type II (111)
                      Type II (000)

Type III (211)
Type III (200)

Combustible
Type IV (2HH)

Type V (777)
Type V (000)

A Comparison Between the Model Codes and NFPA 220 Based on the MCSC National System

NFPA 220	I(443)	I(332)	II(222)	II(111)	II(000)	III(211)	III(200)	IV(2HH)	V(111)	V(000)
UBC	—	I FR	II FR	II 1-hr	II N	III 1-hr	III N	IV HT	V 1-hr	V N
B-NBC	1A	1B	2A	2B	2C	3A	3B	4	5A	5B
SBC	–	II	—	IV 1-hr	IV unp	V 1-hr	V unp	III	VI 1-hr	VI unp
B-NBC	1A	1B	2A	2B	2C	3B	3C	3C	4A	4B

Figure 23-2

Fire Resistive Requirements for Type I through Type V Construction

	Type I		Type II			Type III		Type IV		Type V	
	443	332	222	111	000	211	000	200	2HH	111	000
EXTERIOR BEARING WALLS—											
Supporting more than one floor, columns or other bearing walls	4	3	2	1	0¹	2	0¹	2	2	1	0¹
Supporting one floor only	4	3	2	1	0¹	2	0¹	2	2	1	0¹
Supporting a roof only	4	3	1	1	0¹	2	0¹	2	2	1	0¹
INTERIOR BEARING WALLS—											
Supporting more than one floor, columns or other bearing walls	4	3	2	1	0	1	0	0	2	1	0
Supporting one floor only	3	2	2	1	0	1	0	0	1	1	0
Supporting a roof only	3	2	1	1	0	1	0	0	1	1	0
COLUMNS—											
Supporting more than one floor, bearing walls or other columns	4	3	2	1	0	1	0	0	H²	1	0
Supporting one floor only	3	2	2	1	0	1	0	0	H²	1	0
Supporting a roof only	3	2	1	1	0	1	0	0	H²	1	0
BEAMS, GIRDERS, TRUSSES & ARCHES—											
Supporting more than one floor, bearing walls or columns	4	3	2	1	0	1	0	0	H²	1	0
Supporting one floor only	3	2	2	1	0	1	0	0	H²	1	0
Supporting a roof only	3	2	1	1	0	1	0	0	H²	1	0
FLOOR CONSTRUCTION	3	2	2	1	0	1	0	0	H²	1	0
ROOF CONSTRUCTION	2	1½	1	1	0	1	0	0	H²	1	0
EXTERIOR NONBEARING WALLS	0¹	0¹	0¹	0¹	0¹	0¹	0¹	0¹	0¹	0¹	0¹

¹ Requirements for fire resistance of exterior walls, the provision of spandrel wall sections, and the limitation or protection of wall openings are not related to construction type. They need to be specified in other standards and codes, where appropriate, and may be required in addition to the requirements of this Standard for the construction type.

² "H" indicates heavy timber members.

23.5 FIRE DETECTION AND SUPPRESSION SYSTEMS

Fire Detection Systems

Various devices are available for the early detection of fires. These devices can automatically initiate several critical functions, such as sound an alarm, notify a central station or fire department, open automatic sprinklers, close fire doors, and shut down ventilating fans. They can be grouped into three categories: 1) heat detectors, 2) smoke detectors, and 3) flame detectors.

Heat Detectors   *Fixed temperature type* heat detectors are actuated when the sensing element reaches a specific temperature. Most operate by closing an electric circuit when the set temperature is reached. There may be a delay between the time ambient temperature rises and the time it is sensed by the detector. The *rate of temperature rise type* heat detectors function on the principle of rate of temperature increase at the detector (in degrees per minute). These heat detectors are effective over a wide range of temperatures, and can be set to respond quickly to flash fires. They may fail to respond to a fire that propagates slowly.

Smoke Detectors   *Photoelectric detectors* are actuated when visibility is decreased by smoke. Smoke entering a light beam either obscures the beam's path or reflects light into a photocell. These detectors are effective where the type of fire anticipated generates a large amount of smoke before temperature changes are sufficient to activate a heat detection system. *Combustion products detectors* work on the principle of detection of products of combustion, and are available in ionization or resistance-bridge types. The ionization type employs ionized gasses to detect a change in air. The resistance-bridge type operates when combustion products change the electric impedance of an electric bridge grid circuit. These detectors are useful for giving early warning of a fire. They will function when combustion products are still invisible.

Flame Detectors   Flame detectors respond to radiant energy from glowing embers, coals, or actual flames that radiate energy. The four basic types are infrared, ultraviolet, photoelectric, and flame-flicker. These devices are sensitive to invisible radiant energy.

Fire Suppression Systems

Several types of building fire extinguishing systems are described in Figure 23-3.

Figure 23-3
Types of Sprinkler Systems

Type	Description	Comments
1. Wet pipe automatic sprinkler system.	A permanently piped water system under pressure, using heat-actuated sprinklers. When a fire occurs the sprinklers exposed to the high heat open and discharge water individually to control or extinguish the fire.	Automatically detects and controls fire. Process structure. May cause water damage to protected books, manuscripts, records, paintings, specimens, or other valuable objects. Not to be used in spaces subject to freezing. On-off types may limit water damage. See NFPA 13, Standard for the Installation of Sprinkler Systems and NFPA 22, Standard for Water Tanks for Private Fire Protection.
2. Pre-action automatic sprinkler system.	A system employing automatic sprinklers attached to a piping system containing air that may or may not be under pressure, with a supplemental fire detection system installed in the same area as the sprinklers. Actuation of the fire detection system by a fire opens a valve which permits water to flow into the sprinkler system piping and to be discharged from any sprinklers that are opened by the heat from the fire.	Automatically detects and controls fire. May be installed in areas subject to freezing. Minimizes the accidental discharge of water due to mechanical damage to sprinkler heads or piping, and thus is useful for the protection of paintings, drawings, fabrics, manuscripts, specimens and other valuable or irreplaceable articles that are susceptible to damage or destruction by water. See NFPA 13, Standard for the Installation of Sprinkler Systems and NFPA 22, Standard for Water Tanks for Private Fire Protection.

3. On-off automatic sprinkler system.	A system similar to the pre-action system, except that the fire detector operation acts as an electrical interlock causing the control valve to open at a predetermined temperature and close when normal temperature is restored. Should the fire rekindle after its initial control, the valve will reopen and water will again flow from the opened heads. The valve will continue to open and close in accordance with the temperature sensed by the fire detectors. Another type of on-off system is a standard wet pipe system with on-off sprinkler heads. Here each individual head has incorporated in it a temperature sensitive device which causes the head to open at a predetermined temperature and close automatically when the temperature at the head is restored to normal.	In addition to the favorable feature of the automatic wet-pipe system, these systems have the ability to automatically stop the flow of water when no longer needed, thus eliminating unnecessary water damage. See NFPA 13, Standard for the Installation of Sprinkler Systems and NFPA 22, Standard for Water Tanks for Private Fire Protection.
4. Dry pipe automatic sprinkler system.	Has heat operated sprinklers attached to a piping system containing air under pressure. When a sprinkler operates, the air pressure is reduced, a "dry-pipe" valve is opened by water pressure, and water flows to any opened sprinklers.	See No. 1. Can protect areas subject to freezing. Water supply must be in a heated area. See NFPA 13, Standard for the Installation of Sprinkler Systems and NFPA 22, Standard for Water Tanks for Private Fire Protection.
5. Standpipe and hose system.	A piping system in a building to which hoses are connected for emergency use by building occupants or by the fire department.	A desirable complement to an automatic sprinkler system. Staff requires training to use hoses effectively. See NFPA 14, Standpipe and Hose Systems.

6. Halon automatic system.	A permanently piped system using a limited stored supply of a Halon gas under pressure, and discharge nozzles to totally flood an enclosed area. Released automatically, by a suitable detection system. Extinguishes fires by inhibiting the chemical reaction of fuel and oxygen.	No agent damage to protected books, manuscripts, records, paintings, or other irreplaceable valuable objects. No agent residue. Halon 1301 can be used with safeguards in normally occupied areas. Halons may not extinguish deep-seated fires in ordinary solid combustibles such as paper, fabrics, etc.; but are effective on surface fires in these materials. These systems require special precautions to avoid damage effects caused by their extremely rapid release. The high velocity discharge from nozzles may be sufficient to dislodge substantial objects directly in the path. See NFPA 12A, Standard on Halon 1301 Fire Extinguishing Systems and NFPA 12B, Standard on Halon 1211 Fire Extinguishing Systems.
7. Carbon dioxide automatic system.	Same as No. 6, except uses carbon dioxide gas. Extinguishes fires by reducing oxygen content of air below combustion support point.	Same as No. 6. Appropriate for service and utility areas. Personnel must evacuate before agent discharge to avoid suffocation. May not extinguish deep-seated fires in ordinary solid combustibles such as paper, fabrics, etc.; but effective on surface fires in these materials. See NFPA 12, Carbon Dioxide Extinguishing Systems.

8. Dry chemical automatic system.

Same as No. 6, except uses a dry chemical power. Usually released by mechanical thermal linkage. Effective for surface protection.

Should not be used in personnel-occupied areas. Leaves powdery deposit on all exposed surfaces. Requires cleanup. Excellent for service facilities having kitchen range hoods and ducts. May not extinguish deep-seated fires in ordinary solid combustibles such as paper, fabrics, etc., but effective on surface fires in these materials. See NFPA 17, Dry Chemical Extinguishing Systems.

9. High expansion foam system.

A fixed extinguishing system which generates a foam agent for total flooding of confined spaces, and for volumetric displacement of vapor, heat, and smoke. Acts on the fire by:
a. Preventing free movement of air.
b. Reducing the oxygen concentration at the fire.
c. Cooling.

Should not be used in occupied areas. The discharge of large amounts of high expansion foam may inundate personnel, blocking vision, making hearing difficult, and creating some discomfort in breathing. Leaves residue and requires cleanup. High expansion foam when used in conjunction with water sprinklers will provide more positive control and extinguishment than either extinguishment system used independently, when properly designed. See NFPA 11A, Standard for Medium and High Expansion Foam Systems.

23.6 FIRE SUPPRESSION REQUIREMENTS BASED ON BUILDING/OCCUPANCY CLASSIFICATIONS

Fire suppression requirements vary depending on which model code is used for the construction guide.

For example, the NFPA Life Safety Code 101 establishes the following criteria:

Assembly   Every Class A and B assembly occupancy shall be protected throughout by an approved automatic sprinkler system (See exceptions).

Laboratories (Research)   Every high-hazard industrial occupancy operation or process shall have automatic extinguishing systems or other such protection.

Business Occupancies   Although there are no specific requirements for automatic sprinkler protection, it should be noted that high-rise buildings are required to be protected by automatic sprinklers.

Residence Halls   According to the Life Safety Code 101, residence halls come under the headings of hotels and dormitories. No specific sprinkler protection is required for residence halls, with the exception of those for high-rise buildings.

It should be noted, however, that certain incentives and economic advantages exist when sprinkler systems are installed, for instance, reduced insurance premiums, ability to build larger and higher buildings, and reduced degree of fire resistivity—dead ends, travel distance, exit discharge, delay release hardware, restricted opening protection, interior finish, corridors, operable windows, and detection systems. The Life-Safety Basic Uniform and Standard Codes make concessions in many areas if sprinkler systems are installed.

Another economic consideration involves business interruption; a major fire loss seriously impairs an institution's ability to maintain its daily operation and level of excellence.

23.7 LIFE SAFETY CODE 101

As stated previously, most codes no longer treat colleges and universities as educational occupancies (as defined by the Life Safety Code 101) because college and university buildings are combinations of other occupancies. Codes now consider the actual use of the space and apply the proper occupancy requirement.

NFPA Life Safety Code 101 contains a specific classification of college and university facility use as follows:

- Instructional building—business occupancy.
- Classrooms under 50 persons—business occupancy.
- Classrooms, 50 persons and over—assembly occupancy.
- Laboratories, instructional—business occupancy.
- Laboratories, non-instructional (research)—industrial.

Other types of occupancies that may be found on a campus are specifically outlined in the Life Safety Code as follows:

- Health care occupancies.
- Hotels and dormitories (residence halls).
- Apartment buildings (married student housing).
- Lodging or rooming houses (co-ops).
- Storage occupancies.
- Occupancies in unusual structures (underground and window-less facilities).
- One- and two-family dwellings.
- High-rise buildings (seventy-five feet or higher).

Once occupancy type has been established for a facility, apply the provisions in Life Safety Code 101 regarding the features of fire protection and building service and fire protection equipment, including any specific criteria as outlined in the chapter on occupancy.

If a building has mixed occupancy type, apply the requirement providing the highest level of life safety.

The Life Safety Code Handbook, which is highly recommended, provides background information on the reasons for certain code provisions and gives some suggestions through text and illustrations on how code requirements can be implemented.

23.8 COMPUTER FACILITIES

Electronic computer and data processing equipment is common on college and university campuses and, in many cases, little or no protection from fire is provided for this extremely expensive equipment or the information it contains.

The following factors should be considered prior to installing computer equipment when determining the need for protection of the environmental function, programming, records, and supplies:

- Life safety aspects of the function.
- Fire threat of the installation to occupants or exposed property.
- Economic loss from loss of function or loss of records.
- Economic loss from value of equipment.

Additional information regarding the requirements for installation of electronic computer and data processing equipment—special building construction, rooms, areas, or operating environment, or fire protection for the equipment—is in NFPA 75, Standard for the Protection of Electronic Computer/Data Processing Equipment.

23.9 LABORATORIES USING CHEMICALS

Laboratories fall into one of two categories:

1. *Laboratories, Instructional:* These are constructed and protected in accordance with the Standards for a Business Occupancy.
2. *Laboratories, Non-Instructional (Research):* These buildings are constructed and protected in accordance with the Standards for an Industrial Occupancy.

The Life Safety Code 101 establishes basic construction and fire protection criteria for both the types of laboratories. However, more stringent requirements may exist in local or state codes. Use the National Fire Protection Association, Standard 45, Fire Protection for Laboratories Using Chemicals (1986) for guidance in this area.

Basically, laboratory units are classified A, B, or C, according to the quantities of flammable and combustible liquids contained in the unit, both in storage and in use (see Figure 23-4).

Laboratory-unit design and construction depends on the laboratory-unit fire hazard classification, the area of the laboratory and the protection to be provided (see Figure 23-5).

Hazardous chemicals shall not be brought into a laboratory work area unless design, construction and fire protection are commensurate with the quantities involved (see Figure 23-6).

Also safe storage areas must be provided for materials with unique physical or hazardous properties, such as temperature sensitivity, water reactivity, or potential for explosion.

The quantity and size of cylinders in laboratory work areas that contain oxygen, flammable gas, liquified flammable, and gas with a health hazard of three or four shall comply with the requirements shown in Figure 23-7.

Figure 23-4

Maximum Quantities of Flammable and Combustible Liquids in Laboratory Units Outside of Flammable Liquid Storage Rooms[7] (All Quantities in Gallons)

Laboratory Unit Class	Flammable or Combustible Liquid Class	Excluding Quantities in Storage Cabinets[7] and Safety Cans — Maximum Quantity[3] Per 100 Square Feet of Laboratory Unit	Excluding — Maximum Quantity[3,4] Per Laboratory Unit — Unsprinklered	Excluding — Sprinklered[6]	Including Quantities in Storage Cabinets and Safety Cans — Maximum Quantity[3] Per 100 Square Feet of Laboratory Unit	Including — Maximum Quantity[3,4] Per Laboratory Unit — Unsprinklered	Including — Sprinklered[6]
A[1] (High Hazard)	I, II and IIIA[5]	10 / 20	300 / 400	600 / 800	20 / 40	600 / 800	1200 / 1600
B[2] (Intermediate Hazard)	I, II and IIIA[5]	5 / 10	150 / 200	300 / 400	10 / 20	300 / 400	600 / 800
C[2] (Low Hazard)	I, II and IIIA[5]	2 / 4	75 / 100	150 / 200	4 / 8	150 / 200	300 / 400

[1] Class A laboratory units shall not be used as instructional laboratory units.

[2] Maximum quantities of flammable and combustible liquids in Class B and Class C instructional laboratory units shall be 50 percent of those listed in the table.

[3] For maximum container sizes see Figure 23-6.

[4] Regardless of the maximum allowable quantity, the maximum amount in a laboratory unit shall never exceed an amount calculated by using the maximum quantity per 100 square feet of laboratory unit. The area of offices, lavatories, and other contiguous areas of a laboratory unit are to be included when making this calculation.

[5] The maximum quantities of Class I liquids shall not exceed the quantities specified for Class I liquids alone.

[6] Where water may create a serious fire or personnel hazard, a nonwater extinguishing system may be used instead of sprinklers.

[7] See description of Flammable Liquid Storage Room in Section 4-4 of NFPA 30. Flammable and Combustible Liquids Code. See description of Storage Cabinet in Section 4-2 of NFPA 30.

For SI Units: 1 gal = 3.785 L; 100 sq ft = 9.3m².

Figure 23-5

Construction and Fire Protection Requirements for Laboratory Units

Laboratory Unit Fire Hazard Class	Area of Laboratory Unit Square Feet	Nonsprinklered Laboratory Units Construction Types I and II		Nonsprinklered Laboratory Units Construction Types III, IV and V		Sprinklered Laboratory Units[2] Any Construction Type	
		Separation From Non-Laboratory Areas	Separation From Lab. Units of Equal or Lower Hazard Classification	Separation From Non-Laboratory Areas	Separation From Lab. Units of Equal or Lower Hazard Classification	Separation From Non-Laboratory Areas	Separation From Lab. Units of Equal of Lower Hazard Classification
A	Under 1000	1 Hour	1 Hour	2 Hours	1 Hour	1 Hour	NC/LC[3]
	1001-2000	1 Hour	1 Hour	N/A[3]	N/A	1 Hour	NC/LC
	2001-5000	2 Hours	1 Hour	N/A	N/A	1 Hour	NC/LC
	5001-10,000	N/A[3]	N/A	N/A	N/A	1 Hour	NC/LC
	10,001 or more	N/A	N/A	N/A	N/A	N/A[3]	N/A
B	Under 20,000	1 Hour	NC/LC[3]	1 Hour	NC/LC	NC/LC	
	20,000 or more	N/A	N/A	N/A	N/A	N/A	
C	Under 10,000	1 Hour	NC/LC[4,6]	1 Hour	NC/LC[4,6]	NC/LC[4,6]	NC/LC[4,5]
	10,000 or more	1 Hour	NC/LC	1 Hour	NC/LC	NC/LC[4,6]	

[1] Where a laboratory work area or unit contains an explosion hazard, appropriate protection shall be provided for adjoining laboratory units and nonlaboratory areas.

[2] In laboratory units where water may create a serious fire or personnel hazard, a nonwater extinguishing system may be substituted for sprinklers.

[3] N/A = Not Allowed; NC/LC = Noncombustible/Limited-Combustible Construction.

[4] May be ½ hour fire rated combustible construction.

[5] Existing combustible construction is acceptable.

[6] Laboratory units in educational occupancies shall be separated from nonlaboratory areas by 1-hour construction.

For SI Units: 1 sq ft = 0.093 m².

Figure 23-6

Maximum Allowable Container Capacity[1]

Container Type	Flammable Liquids[2]			Combustible Liquids[2]	
	IA	IB	IC	II	IIIA
Glass	1 pt[3]	1 qt.[3]	1 gal	1 gal	5 gal
Metal (other than DOT Drums) or Approved Plastic	1 gal	5 gal[3]	5 gal[4]	5 gal[4]	5 gal
Safety Cans	2 gal	5 gal[4]	5 gal[4]	5 gal[4]	5 gal
Metal Drums (DOT)	N/A[5]	5 gal[4]	5 gal[4]	60 gal[4]	60 gal

[1] This table is taken from NFPA 30, Flammable and Combustible Liquids Code, except for allowable quantities of flammable liquids in metal DOT drums.
[2] See B-1 for definitions of the various classes of flammable and combustible liquids.
[3] See Exception No. 1 of 7.2.3.2 and A-7.2.3.2.
[4] In instructional laboratory work areas, no container for Class I or II liquids shall exceed a capacity of 1 gallon, except that safety cans may be of 2 gallon capacity.
[5] N/A = Not Allowed. See Exception No. 2 of 7.2.3.2.
  For SI Units: 1 gal = 3.785 liters. 1 qt = 0.95 liter. 1 pt = 0.48 liter.

NFPA Standard 45 provides additional information including fire protection, explosion hazard protection, ventilating systems and hood requirements.

23.10 MICROELECTRONICS TEACHING FACILITIES

Until recently, very little guidance existed in the development of microelectronic facilities. The Uniform Building Code and its companion publication, the Uniform Fire Code, provide the most updated information. A microelectronic facility is classified as Group H occupancy, Division 6 in accordance with the UBC.

Strict compliance with construction and fire protection criteria is highly recommended due to the highly unstable, flammable, toxic and poisonous gases used in the production of microchips.

A code review prepared by the architects or consulting engineers simplifies the process of determining the occupancy classification and the specific construction/fire protection criteria. Further information is

Figure 23-7

Maximum Quantity and Size Limitations for Compressed or Liquefied Gas Cylinders in Laboratory Work Areas[1]

	Flammable Gases and/or Oxygen		Liquefied Flammable Gases		Gases With Health Hazard Rating of 3 or 4
	Sprinklered Space	Nonsprinklered Space	Sprinklered Space	Nonsprinklered Space	
Max. No. of Cylinders per 500 sq. ft. or less	6	3	3	2	3
Max Cylinder Size (in.)	10 × 50	10 × 50	9 × 30	9 × 30	4 × 15
Approx. Water Volume (ft.)	2.0	2.0	0.6	0.1	

[1] In instructional laboratory work areas the total number of cylinders shall be reduced to three maximum size cylinders or ten 2 in. × 13 in. cylinders (or equivalent volume); in all other cases twenty-five 2 in. × 13 in. cylinders (or equivalent volume) shall be permitted.

in the Uniform Building Code, Chapter 9 and the Uniform Fire Code, Article 51.

To further simplify the process of determining the occupancy and construction classifications, architects or consulting engineers should provide a fire protection summary and standardized code documentation based on the governing codes. Cross reference these documents to ensure that all areas are properly classified based on their use, and to determine special fire suppression needs based on a known process or from past experience with a using agency.

Classifications must be correct. Improper classification adds costs through excessive protection of structural members, vertical shafts, and exit ways.

ADDITIONAL RESOURCES

NFPA Codes, Standards, Recommended Practices and Manuals. (See latest NFPA Codes and Standards Catalog for availability of current editions of the following documents.)

NFPA 10—*Portable Fire Extinguishers*, 1984.

NFPA 11—*Low Expansion Foam and Combined Agent Systems*, 1983.

NFPA 11A—*Medium and High Expansion Foam Systems*, 1983.

NFPA 12—*Carbon Dioxide Extinguishing Systems*, 1985.

NFPA 12A—*Halon 1301 Fire Extinguishing System*, 1987.

NFPA 12B—*Halon 1211 Fire Extinguishing Systems*, 1985.

NFPA 13—*Installation of Sprinkler Systems*, 1987.

NFPA 13A—*Inspection, Testing and Maintenance of Sprinkler Systems*, 1987.

NFPA 14—*Installation of Standpipe and Hose Systems*, 1986.

NFPA 17—*Dry Chemical Extinguishing Systems*, 1985.

NFPA 17A—*Wet Chemical Extinguishing Systems*, 1986.

NFPA 18—*Wetting Agents*.

NFPA 30—*Flammable and Combustible Liquids Code*, 1987.

NFPA 45—*Fire Protection for Laboratories Using Chemicals*, 1986.

NFPA 70—*National Electric Code*, 1987.

NFPA 71—*Installation, Maintenance and Use of Signaling Systems for Central Station Service*, 1987.

NFPA 72A—*Installation, Maintenance, and Use of Local Protective Systems for Guard Tour, Fire Alarm, and Supervising Service*, 1987.

NFPA 72B—*Installation, Maintenance, and Use of Auxiliary Protective Signaling Systems for Fire Alarm Service*, 1986.

NFPA 72C—*Installation, Maintenance, and Use of Remote Station Protective Signaling Systems*, 1986.

NFPA 72D—*Installation, Maintenance, and Use of Proprietary Protective Signaling Systems*, 1986.

NFPA 72E—*Automatic Fire Detectors*, 1987.

NFPA 72F—*Installation and Use of Emergency Voice/Alarm Communication Systems*, 1985.

NFPA 72G—*Installation, Maintenance, and Use of Notification Appliances for Protective Signaling Systems*, 1985.

NFPA H—*Test Procedures for Local, Auxiliary Remote Station, and Proprietary Protective Signaling Systems*, 1984.

NFPA 75—*Protection of Electronic Computer/Data Processing Equipment*, 1987.

NFPA 96—*Installation of Equipment for the Removal of Smoke and Grease-Laden Vapors from Commercial Cooking Equipment*, 1987.

NFPA 99—*Health Care Facilities*, 1987.

NFPA 101—*Safety to Life From Fire in Buildings and Structures*, 1985.

NFPA 220—*Types of Building Construction*, 1985.

NFPA 325M—*Fire Hazard Properties of Flammable Liquids, Gases, and Volatile Solids*, 1984.

NFPA. *Fire Journal.*

NFPA. *Fire Protection Handbook*, 16 editions.

CHAPTER 24

Laboratory Fume Hoods

Fred Manas
Mechanical Planner
University of California, Davis

James D. Wilson
Assistant Physical Plant
Administrator
University of California, Davis

24.1 INTRODUCTION

This chapter addresses the selection, application, and maintenance of laboratory fume hoods. Currently, the codes and technical standards governing the design and installation of fume hoods are being revised to reflect increased awareness of safety in the laboratory. Fume hoods should be considered a specialized part of the total ventilation system designed to protect the laboratory user, people who work on or near laboratories, and the environment.

24.2 DEFINITION

Chemical and biological laboratories are the main users of fume hoods. They are used to exhaust toxics, contaminants, and noxious odors to the outdoors and to avoid aspiration into the building's HVAC system.

The Scientific Apparatus Makers Association (SAMA) defines a laboratory fume hood as a "ventilated enclosed work space intended to capture, contain and exhaust fumes, vapors and particulate matter generated inside the enclosure. It consists basically of side, back, and top enclosure panels, a work surface or counter-top, an access opening called the face, a sash and an exhaust plenum equipped with a baffle system for the regulation of air flow distribution."

Fume Hood Location

The volume of air exhausted by fume hoods affects building HVAC systems by increasing heating and cooling loads, changing air balances, and introducing noise and drafts. The design of the HVAC system and the location of the fume hood within the laboratory are important to the success of an installation. Stable and consistent air flow into the face of a fume hood may not be possible if the fume hood is too near a doorway or window, in a high traffic area, or near HVAC grilles or diffusers. Actual airflow into the face may be observed by using a smoke bomb, however, any HEPA filters in the exhaust system should first be removed to avoid plugging them with smoke particles.

Face Velocity

The velocity of air entering the fume hood face is the key factor in its safe performance. The volume of air is adjusted to maintain the required velocity. What face velocity should a fume hood actually have? Opinions range from about 100 to 150 linear feet per minute (FPM). SAMA standard LF 10-1980 lists hoods from Type A to Type C and suggests 125-150 FPM for certain critical operations. ASHRAE research project 70, Caplan and Knutson, found 60-100 FPM to be adequate. Some OSHA regulations require 150 FPM. The old philosophy "more is better" does not apply to fume hood face velocities. On the contrary, there is data that face velocities around 100 FPM may be more effective in providing safety than higher velocities. There is a growing consensus among safety experts that 100-125 FPM is the safest range for even the most demanding materials such as carcinogens, acids, and radioisotopes.

Velocity readings should be taken with the sash in the normal operating position or at maximum opening.

Measurement of the FPM can be accomplished by dividing the face opening into a grid of approximately 12-inch squares and measuring the air velocities at the center of each square using an accurate anemometer (see Figure 24-1). The readings should not vary by more than 10 percent within the desired range. A minimum six point traverse is necessary for a four-foot face opening, eight for a six-foot hood.

Fume hoods should be tested on a predetermined schedule, SAMA standard LF-10-1980. Face velocities should be checked at least once a year and after blower or duct changes, repairs, or HVAC modifications. For quick reference, the date and FPM can be posted on the hood. New installations should be tested before use, but equally important, and most often overlooked, is testing after remodel work.

Fume Hood Construction

There is a large variety of hoods available from various manufacturers. The materials used and the method of construction should be carefully

Figure 24-1

Walk-In Hood

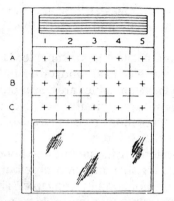

Walk-in hoods are tested with one sash closed. Repeat measurements with bottom open, top closed.

Bench Mounted Hood with Horizontal Sliding Sashes

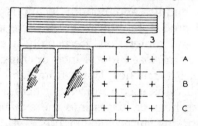

Open face to maximum. Repeat measurements with open area at left, right, and center. Take readings at the center of each sq. ft. of area.

Bench Mounted Hood
Combination Hood (Tested with lower door closed)
Auxiliary Air Hood (Tested with auxiliary air off)

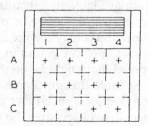

Divide hood face into grid. Readings should be taken at the center of each sq. ft. of area.

tailored to the intended use. The materials with which the fume hood is made should be resistant to the chemicals to be used, lined with impervious surfaces to prevent contamination, and assembled to form a smooth continuity that encourages airflow and prevents accumulation of chemical residuals in cracks and corners that will be difficult to decontaminate.

There are many optional features available. Hoods may be provided with gas, air, steam, electrical, and other utility outlets. Sinks, drains, cup sinks, and even steam tables are commonly included. Explosion proof or external lights are typically provided. Special accessories might include air bypass openings (see Figure 24-2), air-flow alarms, and special linings and exhaust filters.

There are several options available in fume hood sash design. The sash is an operable glass for shielding and observation purposes. The sash may be vertically or horizontally movable. The sash should be positioned to provide the user maximum protection, but can be moved to enlarge the opening while setting up apparatus in the hood.

Baffles in the rear plane of the hood arrange the airflow for removal of vapors and particulates by the exhaust system. The three-slot baffle is standard with top, middle, and bottom locations (see Figure 24-3). ASHRAE 110-1985 procedure indicates that there is an optimum slot sizing. The bottom and center slots are usually fixed in size. The top baffle is adjustable from closed to a 2-inch opening. The center baffle has a slot opening of 1-1½ inches. The bottom baffle has a slot opening of 2-3 inches. An airfoil is used to direct air across the bottom of the fume hood to sweep heavier fumes into the exhaust and prevent air turbulence at the working surface (see Figure 24-4).

Exhaust System

The fume hood exhaust system may be a single exhaust blower for each hood or it may be several hoods together on one exhaust blower. Materials used for the duct and blower are determined by the use of the fume hood. Blowers and ducts are available in galvanized or stainless steel, coated with special materials such as epoxy or plastic, or made completely of PVC. Resin or plastic ducts may require a metal sheath to meet fire code requirements. Transit ducts are found in many installations.

For the safety of personnel that might be on the roof, and to assure that exhausted air is dispersed into the atmosphere, the blower exhaust should be vertical and extend at least seven feet above the roof or any windbreak, wall, or parapet. To avoid reentry the exhaust must be well away from and downwind of air intakes for the building's HVAC system.

Blowers should be mounted at roof level. Auxiliary or in-line fans should not be installed in the hood or duct to assure a negative pressure in the duct in the event of blower or duct failure.

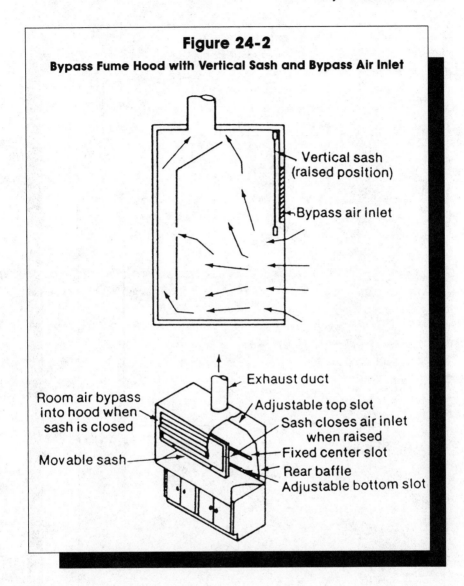

Figure 24-2

Bypass Fume Hood with Vertical Sash and Bypass Air Inlet

Vertical sash
(raised position)

Bypass air inlet

Exhaust duct

Room air bypass
into hood when
sash is closed

Adjustable top slot

Sash closes air inlet
when raised

Movable sash

Fixed center slot

Rear baffle

Adjustable bottom slot

Maintenance

Procedures for both routine maintenance and emergency repairs should be written, and maintenance and lab personnel should be trained in safety procedures.

Maintenance workers should not attempt repairs or filter changes with the exhaust system running. Protective clothing and respiratory protection should be used when working on fume hoods or exhaust

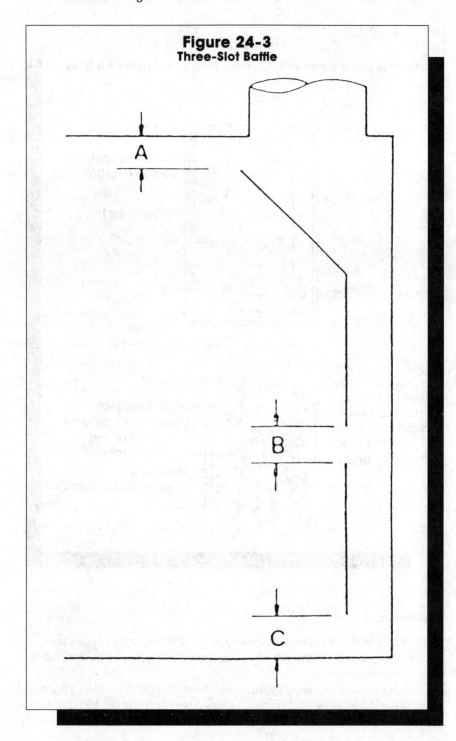

Figure 24-3
Three-Slot Baffle

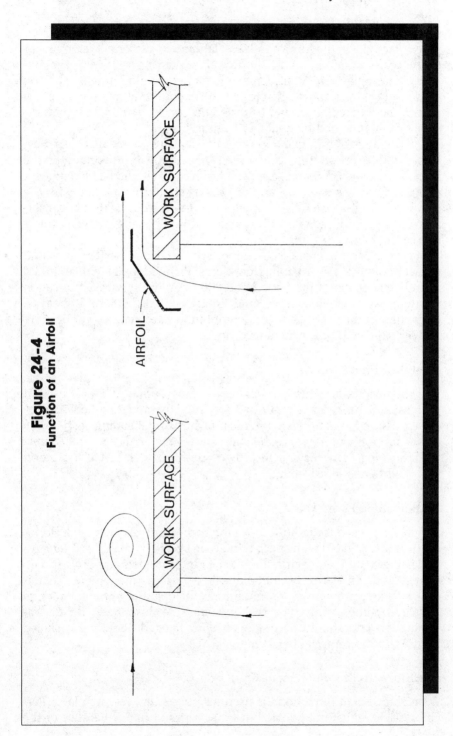

Figure 24-4
Function of an Airfoil

systems, even when shut down. A good safety procedure includes stopping all activity in the fume hood, and laboratory personnel removing or capping all containers in the hood before starting repairs or maintenance. During a system failure, lab personnel should immediately stop work and cap or remove chemicals before requesting maintenance. All parts to be worked on should be tested for contamination and, if necessary, decontaminated by qualified technicians.

In the case of multiple hoods on an exhaust system, all hoods must be secured before shutting down the exhaust blower or working on the system. To avoid confusion, each exhaust blower should be marked with all hood locations it serves, and the hoods should be marked with the blower. During repairs, each hood should be posted with an "out-of-service" sign. Additionally, all users should be given advance notification of maintenance shutdowns.

Preventive maintenance is important to reliable performance and reduces potential safety liability problems. Planned maintenance should include inspection of the fume hood and its utility services, lubrication of motor and fan, inspection and adjustment of belts and sheaves, inspection of ducts and fans for deterioration, face velocity verification, and air balancing between ganged hoods.

Chemical Fume Hoods

The chemical fume hood is probably the most common, and is used in process and research laboratories for low- to moderate-hazard processes. This type may have a vertical or horizontal sliding sash and is most commonly used where there are known materials and procedures. An indicating manometer will provide the user with visual indication that the hood is functioning.

Radioisotope Fume Hoods

Fume hoods used for radioisotopes in process and research laboratories are usually provided with special shielding and HEPA exhaust filters. An indicating manometer across the filter to indicate pressure drop should be installed. An alarm should be installed with the manometer to indicate excessive pressure drops and inform the operator of the hood of an unsafe condition. This type of hood must be dismantled for decontamination and should be equipped with flanged neoprene gasketed joints with disconnectable fasteners.

Perchloric Acid Fume Hoods

A perchloric acid fume hood is used in process and research labs. Perchloric acids must not be used in other types of hoods because of the explosive characteristics of perchloric salts that may accumulate on inner hood, duct and blower surfaces, and joints. These salts are water soluble and require a wash down of the complete exhausting system from the stack down to the baffles in the rear of the fume hood. A trough and drain system is provided in the hood to collect the wash-down water. To prevent build-up of the unstable salts, wash downs must be regularly scheduled according to the amount of perchloric acid in use. Explosion may result if the salts are subjected to impact or heat. A thorough wash down is essential before performing any maintenance.

This kind of hood requires ducts of smooth, impervious, and cleanable materials resistant to acid attack. Non-metallic material, PVC, or stainless steel with high chromium and nickel content, not less than #316, are recommended. Because perchloric acid is an extremely active oxidizing agent, organic materials cannot be used in the exhaust system in such places as joint gaskets or coatings. Perchloric acid hoods are not usually installed in an exhaust system shared with other hoods because of the potential for organic materials to be mixed with the acid in the air stream. All joints should be glued or welded and finished smooth. Sprinkler heads should be installed inside the exhaust system at all changes of direction and connected to a water supply to provide the necessary wash down. HEPA filters should not be installed in perchloric hood exhaust systems.

Canopy Hoods

Canopy or range hoods are not fume hoods and, while useful for exhausting heat and smoke from specific areas, are not appropriate for chemical and research purposes.

Biological Safety Cabinets

Biological safety cabinets are also referred to as safety cabinets or ventilated safety cabinets. There are four classes of cabinets and two sizes, four feet and six feet.

Class I is a partial containment cabinet. The front opening is fixed, allowing room air to pass, preventing microbial aerosols from escaping into the laboratory. The 10 percent exhaust system is suitable for flammable substance, animal autopsy, and low biological agents. Its main function is to protect people, not materials. It may be filtered by a HEPA filter on the exhaust system.

Class II-A has a fixed opening. This design provides for recirculation of about 70 percent of its total air. Flammables, toxic agents, or radioactive material should not be used in this cabinet. The exhaust and supply is filtered by HEPA filters. Exhaust may be expelled into the laboratory, but it is best to hook it up to building exhaust systems. The cabinet protects people and research materials.

Class II-B has a sliding vertical sash and maintains an inward air flow. It is designed to exhaust 70 percent through the work area and recirculated 30 percent. Use this cabinet with low-level volatile materials and trace levels of chemical carcinogens in tissue cultures. Exhaust and supply is filtered by HEPA filters, which is exhausted from the building.

Class III is a specially designed unit for use of high-risk biological and chemical materials. This unit has a gas tight, negative pressure containment system, so laboratory workers and agents have a complete physical barrier between them. This cabinet has the highest protection factor for the laboratory worker. Highly infectious and radioactive materials are used in this cabinet. A sealed front with rubber arm holes is where all work is performed. HEPA filters are used on the supply and exhaust system, with 100 percent of the air exhausted from the building.

Laminar Flow

Laminar flow hoods are for product protection, not for lab worker safety.

Effect on HVAC System

Today's increased concern for laboratory safety has caused the HVAC system to become more sophisticated. Air flows are balanced to maintain minimum room air changes and static pressures relative to adjacent spaces. The air exhausted by fume hoods becomes an integral part of the balanced equation. At one time it was common practice to equip fume hoods with a switch to shut down the exhaust fan during periods of unuse. However, shutdowns or changes in the volume of air exhausted will disrupt the room's air balance, unless the hood utilizes a separate air source or the HVAC system is a variable air volume type that is designed to compensate automatically. The use of multiple fume hoods on a common exhaust system also precludes the use of local switches for user safety.

Energy Conservation

Fume hoods equipped with auxiliary air supply systems are offered by most manufacturers and are designed to introduce a curtain of air at the face opening instead of exhausting conditioned room air. If unconditioned outside air is used, the user and the research materials in the hood will be subjected to prevailing outside temperatures. The use of heated or cooled air in an auxiliary supply system may still result in energy conservation because the hood and its supply system may be shut down without affecting the room. This type of system is useful in retrofit installations when supply air to a room is not adequate to support the demand of an added fume hood exhaust.

Another way to reduce the unnecessary venting of conditioned air is to reduce the exhaust fan speed to a lower rate and close the sash at night or when the hood is unused. A switch operated when the sash is in the closed position can control the fan speed. Periodic checks of the laboratory air balance will help assure efficient energy use and reduce complaints about room environments.

24.3 CODES AND STANDARDS

Occupational Safety and Health Administration:

- User Safety (Federal) Reg. 29 CFR 1910.1003-0.1016.

Scientific Apparatus Makers Association:

- Laboratory Fume Hoods Standard: LF 10-1980.

American Conference of Governmental Industrial Hygienists:

- Industrial Ventilation Recommended Practice, 1976, P.A.
- STEL and TLV-C short-term exposure limit and threshold limit ceiling valve.

ASHRAE:

- Method of Testing Laboratory Fume Hoods Standard: 110-1985.
- The Rating of Laboratory Hood Performance: *ASHRAE Journal*, October 1979, pages 49-53.
- Laboratory Fume Hoods, A Performance Test: RP70 ASHRAE Transactions, 84 (I) 1978.
- Fume Hood Diversity for Reduced Energy Consumption: ASHRAE Transaction 1983, V. 89, Pt 2A and 2B.

National Safety Council, Research and Development Section:

- Survey Report on Lab Hoods: Circa 1984.

Geneva Research (Saunders, G.T.):

- Updating Older Fume Hoods: *Journal of Chem. Ed.*, V. 62, page A178, June 1985.
- A No-cost Method of Improving Fume Hood Performance: American Lab., page 102, June 1984.

CHAPTER 25

Central Monitoring and Control Systems

Jeffrey Cosiol, P.E.
Managing Principal
The Kling-Lindquist Partnership,
Inc.

John C. Miller Sr., P.E.
Industrial Systems Specialist
The Kling-Lindquist Partnership,
Inc.

25.1 INTRODUCTION

Central monitoring and control systems (CMCS) can integrate the monitoring and control of the service systems in various facilities, such as the fire, security, HVAC, and utilities systems, and have been used in the physical plant environment for many years. These systems have the ability to monitor data from various systems, and to perform control functions based on these data. A definition of modern CMCS is "a centrally located system that receives data from the service systems in various facilities for the purpose of monitoring and controlling a group of facilities and systems."

All CMCS connect input and output (I/O) devices from various systems to a central location for monitoring and control. Typical input and output signals might include an on-off contact closure from a smoke detector, or a continuous 4- to 20-milliampere analog signal from a pressure transmitter.

Over several decades, three types of CMCS have evolved: the hardwired system, the hardwired/multiplex system, and the distributed intelligent system. They differ primarily in the method used to connect the I/O devices to the central location. The hardwired/multiplex and distributed intelligent systems are built for use either where there are long distances between I/O devices and the central monitoring and control location, or where there are high I/O device concentrations in various remote areas.

Current state-of-the-art CMCS use new advances in technology to enhance the speed of data communications and improve the operator interface. These systems use artificial intelligence techniques to improve ease of use, by providing the operator with context-sensitive menu screens that directly pertain to the functions being used.

Just as in recent years in the commercial building controls industry, there is a growing emphasis on central monitoring and control systems for colleges and universities as they streamline physical plant operations and reporting functions. Increases in labor costs and the need for increased security are other incentives. Recent developments in electronic hardware and computer software have decreased the cost of CMCS implementation. CMCS are becoming more user-friendly and no longer require operation and maintenance by computer programmers. It is now possible to change monitoring and control functions without costly and complicated reprogramming. This flexibility allows operators to easily fine-tune the operation of facility service systems.

25.2 SYSTEM DESCRIPTIONS

Hardwired Systems

Hardwired CMCS were the first systems used at central locations. These systems connected monitoring and control devices to one central location, using individual wires or pneumatic tubes for each I/O device. As systems became larger, covered greater distances, and included more I/O devices, the hardwiring of these systems became costly and impractical.

Analog signals for measuring various process variables, such as pressure, temperature, flow, and level, were transmitted as low-energy, low-voltage direct current (DC) signals, or as pneumatic (air pressure) signals. With both long signal wiring and pneumatic tubing, line losses are important and must be accounted for by individual signal loop calibration or compensation. Since pneumatic lines are susceptible to signal transmission lag, leakage, and potential volume problems, limitations are placed on how far pneumatic signals should be transmitted. Generally, to maintain acceptable accuracy, the distance limitation for pneumatic monitoring and control systems is only 200 to 600 feet, and for pneumatic indication 600 to 1,000 feet. For low-level electrical signals (e.g., 0 to 10 volts DC, 1 to 5 volts DC), distance affects accuracy due to line losses. This problem was partially solved by using low-energy signals that were based on variable current levels at a higher, constant voltage (e.g., 4 to 20 milliamperes at 24 volts DC).

However, longer distances still required more calibration, and the costs of running wires over long distances were sometimes prohibitive. These inherent limitations led to the development of the second form of central monitoring and control system, the hardwired/multiplex system.

Hardwired/Multiplex Systems

The earliest hardwired/multiplex systems performed switching functions at remote locations. They used low-voltage pickup relays at the ends of the control circuits to multiply contacts and minimize wiring costs between the I/O devices and the central control location. These relays were also less susceptible to line losses over long distances. They were only used for discrete on-off or open-close control requirements, and not for analog circuits. However, as systems again grew in size and complexity, this type of hardwired/multiplex system became costly and required much maintenance.

Developments in electronics soon produced a more advanced type of hardwired/multiplex system. Instead of running multiconductor cables containing individual circuits from I/O devices to the central monitoring and control location, the I/O devices are individually wired to local multiplexers, which in turn communicate with multiplexers at the central monitoring and control location over either two-wire or four-wire cables. Rather than pickup relays, a central computer is usually used to provide improved control and monitoring capabilities. Both discrete on-off and analog control and monitoring functions are supported.

This system is identical to the hardwired system at both ends, but vast amounts of wiring were eliminated between the two locations. This system can also reduce construction installation time, since less wiring is required. The disadvantage of the more advanced hardwired/multiplex system is that the scan time for each input or output increases as the number of I/O devices increases, and in some cases this causes unacceptable delays. Figure 25-1 shows the first two types of systems.

Distributed Intelligent Systems

These systems are similar to the advanced type of hardwired/multiplex system. However, instead of local multiplexers, the I/O devices are wired to intelligent field panels which are connected to the central monitoring and control system. This system can provide monitoring and control of local I/O devices, record keeping, historical trend analysis, and maintenance and operations scheduling at each intelligent panel, without continuous data transmission to the central control station.

In the distributed intelligent system, should either the central computer system or communications system fail, the intelligent field panels will continue to operate. This arrangement improves reliability over the

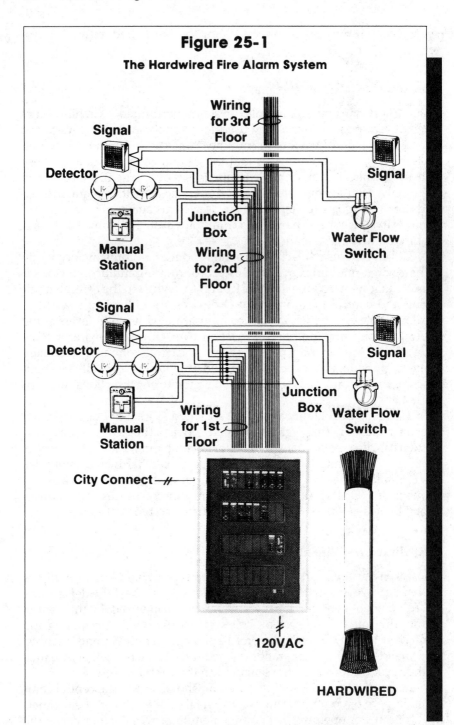

Figure 25-1

The Hardwired Fire Alarm System

Wiring for 3rd Floor

Signal

Detector

Manual Station

Junction Box

Wiring for 2nd Floor

Signal

Water Flow Switch

Signal

Detector

Manual Station

Junction Box

Wiring for 1st Floor

Signal

Water Flow Switch

City Connect

120VAC

HARDWIRED

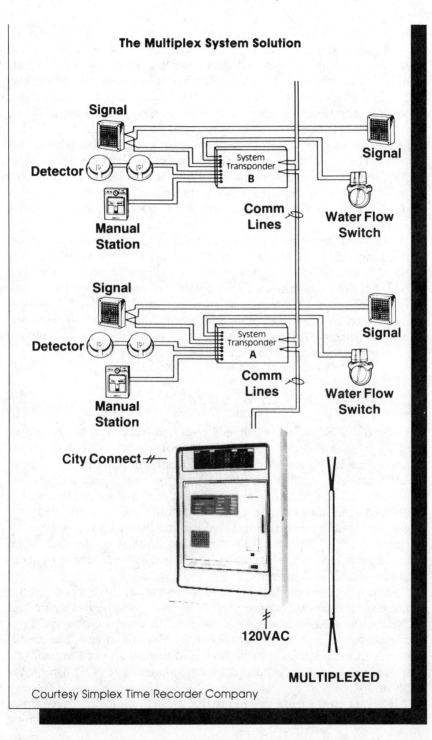

The Multiplex System Solution

Signal

Detector

Manual
Station

System
Transponder
B

Signal

Comm
Lines

Water Flow
Switch

Signal

Detector

Manual
Station

System
Transponder
A

Signal

Comm
Lines

Water Flow
Switch

City Connect

120VAC

MULTIPLEXED

Courtesy Simplex Time Recorder Company

hardwired/multiplex system, in which all monitoring and control functions originate at the central location. In addition, if duplicate sensors are used and one fails, the system can automatically operate from a functional sensor without a shutdown. The system will "alarm" the failure and indicate its location for repair. Some systems can also be configured to have standby backup operation when an intelligent panel fails.

Reporting functions may be accomplished on a programmed interval basis, on an event occurrence basis, or on a request from the central location. Historical data may then be analyzed for potential areas of facility operations improvement. The distributed intelligent system can transmit data to the central station and to other intelligent panels in a local area network (LAN), using fiber optic cable or twisted, shielded pairs.

One variation on the distributed intelligent system uses I/O devices that are individually addressable from the intelligent field panels. These "smart" I/O devices need not be individually hardwired to the field panels, but are interconnected by a single two-wire, bidirectional communications cable. This system is generally feasible if many I/O devices are clustered in one area; otherwise, many cables may be required, increasing the cost. An example of this type of system is the "intelligent fire protection system" shown in Figure 25-2.

25.3 COMPARISON OF SYSTEMS

The use of a distributed intelligent system instead of a hardwired or hardwired/multiplex system requires careful consideration of the functional and performance requirements for central monitoring and control at the particular facility. While a distributed intelligent system has greater flexibility than a hardwired system and is more reliable than a hardwired/multiplex system, it is usually more costly. In some cases, the distributed intelligent system can be justified based on future industry trends and the ability to obtain product support over the long term, which is usually lost to older, less technologically advanced systems as market demand decreases.

Figure 25-3 summarizes in broad terms the various types of central monitoring and control systems. It lists the various attributes desired for a CMCS, and is based on a system designed to serve multiple buildings and locations with different applications. The advantages and disadvantages of each system can be reviewed against the operational and cost requirements to determine the most suitable type of CMCS for the application.

It is easy to see from this figure that as technology improved, most system attributes also improved. Only in the degree of standardization

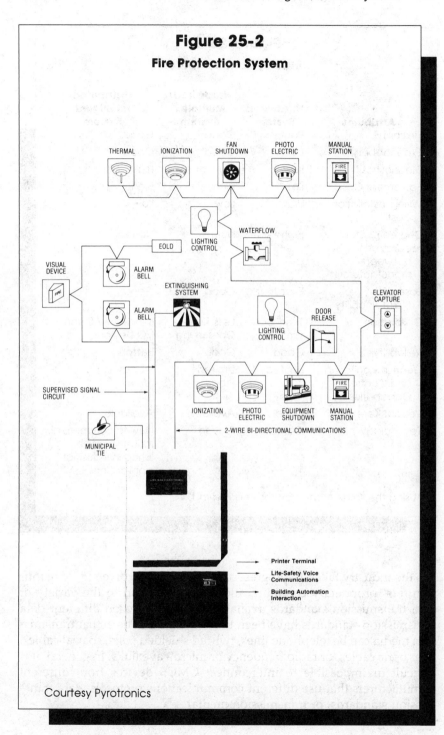

Figure 25-2
Fire Protection System

Courtesy Pyrotronics

Figure 25-3

CMCS System Attributes

Attributes	Hardwired System	Hardwired/ Multiplex System	Distributed Intelligent System
Flexibility	Poor	Good	Good
Expandability	Poor	Good*	Good*
Diagnostics	Low	High	High
Equipment Costs	Low	High	High
Wiring Installation Cost	High	Low	Low
Degree of Standardization between manufacturers	High	None	None
Ease of Maintainability	Excellent	Good	Good
Calibration	Time-Consuming	Less Time-Consuming	Minimal w/ Smart I/O Devices
Reliability	Good	Good	Better
Central Monitoring and Control Capabilities	Limited	Limited Programming	Programmable
Record Keeping	None	Available	Available
Technology	Outdated	Proven	New to commercial industry (established in industrial applications)

*Using the same manufacturer's equipment.

has the industry failed to progress, due in part to the diversity of manufacturers' proprietary communications protocols and to the variety of data transmission standards available. At least a dozen different data transmission standards have been used in CMCS. The actual transmission media can be telephone lines, twisted shielded pairs, coaxial cables, fiber optic cables, or radio frequency or microwave links. In general, it is difficult or impossible to interconnect CMCS devices from different manufacturers that use different communications protocols, data transmission standards, or transmission media.

Some of the newer multiplex and intelligent CMCS now offer centralized monitoring and control using personal computers at the operator's console for smaller systems. These systems are generally less expensive than non-PC-based systems, and they usually do not need to be operated by specially trained computer programmers. In most facilities, personnel trained to use PCs are readily available, which allows existing staff to operate the CMCS. Since the size and functionality of PC-based systems are limited, larger systems generally use minicomputers.

25.4 SYSTEM APPLICATIONS

General

Modern CMCS can include a wide variety of monitoring and control applications that only a few years ago were generally purchased as separate systems, even from the same supplier. These monitoring and control applications include heating, ventilating, and air conditioning; lighting; fire safety; communications; security; elevator control; and various utilities. In colleges and universities, where special laboratories and research and development facilities exist, special environmental monitoring and control requirements are also prevalent.

In some cases, having a modern CMCS attracts grant money for unique experiments and research not feasible without accurate, reliable central-station environmental control and monitoring capabilities. It is therefore important that physical plant administrators consider both present and future needs when installing or upgrading CMCS. Some CMCS applications are discussed below on an individual basis. Four other pertinent chapters in this manual should also be consulted: Chapter 21, Building Heating, Cooling, and Ventilating Systems; Chapter 44, Energy Management; Chapter 45, Central Energy Systems; and Chapter 46, Building Energy Systems.

Fire Alarm and Fire Protection Systems

The monitoring and control of fire safety systems to minimize the impact of fire-related conditions on people and facilities is perhaps the most important function of a CMCS. However, CMCS coordination of the lighting, HVAC, security, utilities, and elevator control systems is important for proper implementation of life safety functions.

Both active and passive fire and smoke control systems are involved in fire protection, detection, and suppression. CMCS are used to coordinate the active control systems, which include the automatic and manual detection, alarm, public address (PA), smoke control, and fire suppression (e.g., sprinklers, Halon) systems. The operation of these systems must be coordinated with the HVAC, elevator control, and access control (exit door) systems. There may also be connections to the security, lighting, and utilities systems.

Even in small fires, the effects of heat, smoke, and gases must be dealt with quickly. Coordinating the operation of air-handling systems and smoke barriers to effectively remove smoke from the fire area and prevent migration of smoke to adjacent areas is very important because smoke is more dangerous than fire. People need to be alerted by alarms and directed by a PA system, or possibly by an automatic voice message digitizer system.

In most campus facilities a central fire command station exists, which shows the fire detection and alarm status and supervises the various active fire and smoke control systems' I/O devices. A two-way firefighter's communications system interface is also usually provided. Having all this information centralized is often essential to controlling a fire and minimizing loss of life and damage to property.

Security

Security systems are used to ensure the safety of personnel and property, and to provide controlled access to many types of facilities. In some cases, the location of the facility determines the need for security systems. If the facility is in a safe community, only minimal perimeter or intrusion detection may be required. In high crime areas, extensive perimeter security monitoring may be necessary. The contents of a facility may also dictate the scope of security systems. Where valuable equipment or records are stored, isolation of the facility is needed. Limited access may be required where experiments are conducted or highly dangerous chemicals or equipment are kept. All these specific requirements must be identified as design criteria in the earliest phase of the project.

Many different types of security systems exist. Some examples are card access systems; closed-circuit television (CCTV), which may include special cameras that operate in low light for outdoor use; paging and intercom systems; interior and perimeter intrusion detection systems; and watchtower observation systems. CMCS can, where needed, provide coordination between these systems and lighting or warning systems.

In most facilities, it is important to monitor and control security systems for remote locations at a central station. This allows immediate, appropriate action to be taken when a problem occurs. There may also be local control panels at individual buildings which operate independently of the CMCS, but are connected to the CMCS for monitoring or reporting and logging of events.

Utilities

Energy monitoring and control systems (EMCS) are often employed to optimize the energy use of mechanical, electrical, and other utility systems. However, CMCS can also provide monitoring of fuel, electrical, water, sewer, and other utility systems for historical trend data and alarm functions. Low fuel tank levels, low water tank levels, or excessive energy consumption or demand are examples of conditions that could be monitored and alarmed by CMCS to prevent future problems or unnecessary expense. Although not always the most important application of CMCS, utilities are commodities that are often taken for granted.

Data Transmission

As discussed earlier, several types of data transmission systems exist. It is important to note where each can best be applied in order to use them effectively. The primary data transmission media used for CMCS are twisted shielded pair cable, coaxial cable, fiber optic cable, radio transmission, and microwave. Not all of these are applicable to colleges and universities.

The multiplexers used in hardwired/multiplex and distributed intelligent CMCS typically use twisted shielded pair or coaxial cables for data transmission. The coaxial cable is more expensive, but is capable of higher data transmission rates and is used in systems with a large number of I/O devices. These cables generally work well unless they pick up electromagnetic or radio frequency interference (EMI/RFI, also known as "noise") that the CMCS was not designed to tolerate.

Where even higher data transmission rates are required or EMI/RFI is a concern, fiber optic cable is the preferred solution. Fiber optic cable is immune to lightning damage and other electrical grounding and noise problems. At present, fiber optic and coaxial cable are comparable in cost. Radio or microwave data transmission is used where data must be transmitted over long line-of-sight distances and cable installation is impractical or too expensive.

In actual practice, the CMCS supplier will limit or select the use of a particular data transmission system. As an example, in heavy electrical equipment rooms where switchgear or large motors or generators are installed, fiber optic cables would be preferred because of immunity to electrical noise. However, if the CMCS supplier does not have equipment with a fiber optic interface, twisted pair or coaxial cable would have to be used.

Central Monitoring and Control System Combinations

Although not all the possible monitoring and control applications are discussed in this chapter, it is possible to note which monitoring and control functions are most frequently provided. A combination matrix, Figure 25-4, shows the various potential system combinations for a CMCS or EMCS. For instance, fire detection systems often interface with HVAC systems for smoke damper control, with elevator controls to minimize loss of life, and with telecommunications systems to alert the campus and local fire departments. Similarly, security systems interact with lighting controls and with telecommunications systems to alert security staff or local police departments. CMCS can provide a maintenance management function to keep track of equipment operation and help in scheduling normal and preventive maintenance.

The centrally located CMCS station serves as a focal point within the campus where critical areas and equipment within each building may be remotely monitored and controlled. The central station allows supervisory, maintenance, fire department, and other emergency personnel to gather during critical times. Centralization of data allows such personnel to quickly assess conditions and make informed decisions that might not otherwise be possible.

Nonetheless, care must be taken when selecting the I/O devices and system conditions to be monitored at the central monitoring point.

Figure 25-4
System Applications Combination Matrix

Applications	CMCS	EMCS
Fire	Yes	*
Security	Yes	*
HVAC Control	*	Yes
Lighting Control	*	Yes
Elevator Control	Yes	*
Critical Spaces Monitoring	Yes	Yes
Maintenance Management	Yes	Yes

*Typically for monitoring purposes only.

If an emergency systems operator is required to monitor non-emergency conditions or equipment functions, he or she may be overwhelmed with non-emergency signals and status reports, and emergency indications may go unnoticed. EMCS used for the monitoring and control of building environmental equipment, such as boilers, chillers, and air handlers, may not normally be monitored or controlled by the same personnel responsible for the campus emergency systems. It may be advisable to have separate CMCS and EMCS central stations.

The following is a checklist of concerns for the combining of functions within a single CMCS:

1. If HVAC, fire alarm, security, and other campus functions are monitored by one system, all monitoring and control may be lost if the system fails. Proper consideration of backup local control or redundancy in the system for critical loops may prevent this problem.
2. The combining of several system applications into one package requires that the entire package meet the most stringent code requirements applicable to any individual part of the complete system.
3. If all systems are supplied and installed by one supplier, certificates of occupancy may be difficult to obtain on time if problems in one area of the system cause delays in completing other areas.
4. Many suppliers do not manufacture combined EMCS and CMCS, which may limit competitive bidding.
5. The supplier's technical personnel may not be properly trained in all disciplines being combined; for example, HVAC technical personnel may not understand fire or security concepts.
6. Extensions of central systems manufactured by one supplier are usually extremely proprietary. Compatible equipment can usually be obtained only from the original supplier.
7. If portions of a combined system become obsolete, the entire system may require replacement.

These points are important when considering how the CMCS functions are to be segregated. Even when CMCS equipment is provided by different suppliers, it should be centrally located, where possible, to enhance operational coordination among the responsible groups.

The following is a description of the CMCS support room of the command center shown in Figure 25-5, top, for the Alfred I. duPont Institute of the Nemours Foundation. In the background are the audio fire message system amplifiers and voice message digitizers for programmed communications to respective building areas. The two panels in the right foreground house the computers which operate this system. The third panel from the right is the CMCS minicomputer. The CRT and keyboard next to the minicomputer are the programmer's console for programming system software or changing the configuration. The larger CRT and keyboard to the left are a color graphic operator's terminal, which can be used to operate the CMCS as is normally done from the command center. On the far left are dual disk drives for system data storage.

Figure 25-5, bottom, is the CMCS command center. It employs one full-time operator on each of the three shifts to provide continuous attended operation. At the top of the vertical board to the left are four large and eight smaller CCTV security monitors. To the right are two zone annunciators for the service and occupied levels of the facility's four floors. These zone panels monitor zone exhaust, air pressure, and general alarms for the automatic paging fire evacuation system. At the consoles from right to left are the fire phone console; the fire and smoke management system CRT; two building automation CRTs; a color printer; the security console with CRT and camera control module; and at the far left, the CCTV CRT and videocassette recorder. Behind the operator are four printers.

Applications in Campus Environments

CMCS in today's college or university campus environment must address many concerns. Physical plant administrators must first set specific campus-wide goals for CMCS, such as centralization of all HVAC, lighting, fire alarm, and security data; single point historical data collection of critical environmental conditions; distributed control in individual buildings; and centralized utilities control. Once specific goals have been identified, the more detailed aspects of CMCS design may be considered.

The location of the central monitoring and control station should be based on operational requirements. Those who operate the system and respond to alarm information should have easy access. Therefore, if powerhouse operators and security personnel need immediate access to the CMCS to perform monitoring and corrective action, then both user groups may require the CMCS operator's CRT terminals and printers. The CMCS computer hardware could be located at either user's location, depending on space availability, environmental conditions, power requirements, and physical security.

In campus applications, physical plant administrators must consider the existing on-site communications systems when deciding on the data transmission medium. Microwave signals and other radio frequency devices can interfere with each other. Fiber optic cable has great promise for campus CMCS due to its inherent immunity to lightning,

COURTESY ALFRED I. DUPONT INSTITUTE

Figure 25-5
CMCS Support Room (top)
Command Center (bottom)

grounding problems, and electrical interference, and its small size and weight. Fiber optic cable can be pulled through existing conduit and manholes serving power distribution or other utilities functions.

Many different types of twisted pair and coaxial cable exist to suit almost any application. Coaxial cable and twisted shielded pair cable can also be installed in existing conduit and manholes. Care must be taken in placing these cables adjacent to existing wiring to avoid potential problems caused by electrical interference (EMI/RFI). Grounding is also a major concern in wireline communications. Building grounds (which always vary) must be isolated from the communications media.

Special Environmental Control Applications

Special environmental monitoring and control of laboratory chambers, clean rooms, and research and development (R&D) facilities housing long-term studies are an important campus CMCS application. Standards laboratories, for example, require tolerances of only plus or minus 1°F and plus or minus 2 percent relative humidity (RH). General laboratories usually require tolerances of plus or minus 2°F to 3°F and plus or minus 3 to 5 percent RH.

In clean rooms, the particulate limit varies as much as the environmental conditions, depending upon the required use. Some clean environments may be as clean as Class 10,000 (parts per million), or as superclean as Class 10. The environmental control tolerances may range from plus or minus 3°F and plus or minus 10 percent RH to plus or minus less than 1°F and plus or minus 1 to 2 percent RH. To maintain humidity, as the high end of the range (e.g., 30 to 50 percent RH) is reached, air cooling is required to lower the humidity, with reheat for temperature control. At the lower end of the range, humidity is generally added to maintain a setpoint in the middle of the desired range (e.g., 40 percent RH).

In computer rooms, it is important to keep temperatures down and humidity up. By maintaining relatively high humidity, static electricity is minimized and potential electronic component failures are reduced. Electronic components also show an increased failure rate as the ambient temperature rises (especially above 120°F).

Fume hood control for laboratories is a specialty area today with many regulations pending. A continuous flow of air through the fume hoods to the central exhaust system is necessary. On larger hoods, it is also important to have a good exhaust system design not affected by partial fume hood use (at one end), which may allow fumes to blow back through the end not in use.

25.5 SYSTEM IMPLEMENTATION

General

Central monitoring and control systems can be developed as a major capital project comprising a central panel and many control and monitoring points, or by an incremental approach as a series of smaller projects. These smaller projects can eventually be networked together as the systems come on-line. Either approach can be utilized for larger or smaller campuses. Implementation of CMCS requires careful short- and long-term planning, as discussed in the following sections.

Developing Site Needs

The needs of a particular CMCS site depend in part on whether it is an existing facility or a new facility. If it is an existing facility, the need for compatibility with existing equipment must be determined. For a completely new facility without connections to other existing systems or buildings, a different approach can be taken. Compatibility is not as pertinent a question and the benefits of newer technology may be much easier to achieve. The facilities managers must determine the immediate needs and the direction they wish to take with regard to plans for future development.

To select the most suitable system type, system applications need to be reviewed for potential use and analyzed for the particular mix of I/O devices involved, as well as the physical concentration levels of inputs and outputs to the system. The type of monitoring and control to be done at the CMCS is also important. The amount of historical data to be collected for later retrieval needs to be estimated. Report formats should be determined, and graphic display requirements should be established. The number of I/O devices can be estimated from the type of systems being considered for interface to the CMCS.

Cost Implications

The degree of sophistication and flexibility desired in a CMCS will determine the overall cost. Higher levels of flexibility require more system programming and higher purchase, maintenance, operating, and expansion costs. The types of suppliers considered to supply a CMCS will also determine whether the system will be a standard product with standard application programs. When CMCS functions are combined with EMCS and HVAC functions, the system costs can be higher than if these systems are purchased separately, due to the limited number of suppliers and the imposition of strict code requirements on subsystems.

If the proposed system is larger than the supplier's standard product or has special requirements, the modified system may be a "one-of-a-kind" for which support may be limited in the future. Careful selection of system requirements will determine whether a system can be supplied at a reasonable price. Larger systems generally will require the integration of equipment from several manufacturers, necessitating specialized software that will have a cost impact. Smaller systems can be furnished by both smaller and larger system suppliers, maximizing competition.

Future expansion plans may warrant purchasing a larger system than is immediately required, to obtain equipment with sufficient capacity for economical expansion. This sometimes will cause a higher first cost, but will yield a lower long-term cost. To minimize costs, unit price expansion costs can be requested from the system supplier at the time of purchase.

Ease of operation and maintenance has a direct impact on the number of required staff. Systems which self-diagnose by indicating the location of a problem can assist in trouble-shooting, reducing staffing, and reducing overtime. In summary, the initial cost of the system is an important factor, but the operating, modification, and expansion costs of the system must also be considered when selecting a CMCS.

Equipment Criteria and Functional Requirements

The following is a list of typical equipment criteria that must be considered when configuring a CMCS:

1. Central and local (remote) control and monitoring capabilities.
2. Computer memory capacity.
3. Number and location of alarm and logging printers.
4. Type of operator interface.
5. Number and location of operator consoles.
6. Type of field panels, intelligent or multiplex.
7. Field panel spare I/O device capacity.
8. Data transmission medium and configuration.
9. Sensor and control requirements.
10. Grounding requirements.
11. Hardware redundancy requirements.
12. Speed of response to monitoring and control functions.
13. Intrinsic safety requirements.
14. Noise (EMI/RFI) immunity requirements.
15. Surge protection requirements.
16. Future expansion requirements.

The equipment requirements may be influenced by applicable codes and by insurance carrier requirements.

The following is a list of typical functional requirements that must be considered when configuring a CMCS:

1. Control functions (analog and digital).
2. Monitoring functions.
3. Historical data storage requirements (volume and duration).
4. Trend analysis requirements (which are to be analyzed, and at what intervals).
5. Applications software programs.
6. Types of systems interfaced (e.g., fire, security, lighting, elevator control, maintenance management, HVAC, EMCS, and critical environmental monitoring).
7. List of inputs and outputs.
8. Diagnostic requirements.

System Design

Specifications and drawings generally represent the system design requirements. The system design should be prepared after present and future needs have been carefully analyzed, system design criteria have been set, and the project program and budget have been developed. When these documents have been completed, the owner and end user should review them to ensure that the system meets their needs. The end user must be involved with the design, since the best equipment is of little use if it does not suit the user's needs. All the areas covered under Section 25.5, System Implementation, should be included in the specifications and associated drawings.

System Procurement

Once the system design has been completed, the procurement cycle can begin. There are several ways to approach the procurement of a CMCS. It can be obtained from general contractors through a subcontract with a supplier-installer; it can be a turnkey, stand-alone purchase from the system supplier-installer; or it can be a hardware and software purchase with the owner installing the system. Most systems can be obtained with a service contract covering maintenance and repair, although the decision to purchase this contract is the owner's, as is the extent of the service agreement. Costs of spare parts for the first year of operation and subsequent years are often part of the procurement pricing request at the time of initial bidding. These costs can be added to the purchase and installation costs to determine the overall system cost, including operation and maintenance. The preferred procurement method is the turn-key method with a maintenance and service contract, to avoid division of responsibilities if problems occur during the warranty period.

Documentation

It is important with any system purchase to obtain adequate documentation. This documentation generally falls into two categories. The first is shop drawings which indicate how the supplier plans to install the system in response to the contract drawings and specifications. The second category is the detailed hardware and software descriptions needed to troubleshoot and modify the system, including, but not limited to, the user and maintenance manuals. These documents generally consist of various equipment catalogs and software documentation, which include magnetic storage media containing the system program and configuration. In some cases, if documents or drawings have been produced by computer-aided design (CAD) methods, tapes or floppy disks may also be made available for the owner's use. At the end of the installation phase of the project, "as-built" drawings are also required to properly document the system as it is actually installed. The system program or configuration tapes should also be obtained for the facility engineer.

System Installation

Installation of central monitoring and control systems requires careful consideration of two important aspects. First, the equipment layout at the various locations requires an understanding of the system features and limitations. Placement of some components of the system may be limited by the maximum permissible length of sensor and communications cables. The arrangement of other components may be limited by how many I/O or interface devices may be connected to each field panel. Second, certain types of equipment must be located in environmentally controlled environments to prevent malfunctions from high or low temperatures or humidity levels (low humidity may cause static electricity problems). It is also important that environmentally sensitive components be stored under controlled conditions during the installation period to prevent damage.

System Testing, Checkout, and Warranty

Factory testing of CMCS hardware and software is vital to the successful start-up and continued operation of a CMCS, and can facilitate the field checkout, assuming proper installation. A factory-tested system usually requires less start-up time. The system should undergo field checkout after installation to verify the specified performance, and to locate and resolve any unforeseen problems. A thorough field checkout is insurance against later shutdowns caused by oversights during the construction and installation process.

Owners and users of CMCS usually are involved with the testing of their system to become familiar with its operation. This leads to a better understanding of the system's performance and can make the owner's acceptance of the system more meaningful. To protect the owner a contract clause should require "acceptance by the owner" in CMCS specifications. A warranty that covers all needed parts and labor for a reasonable period of time (one or two years is customary) is generally very beneficial.

Personnel Training

Having well-trained personnel to operate and maintain the CMCS is very important and can make the difference between a successful or unsuccessful operation. Personnel should receive operational hardware familiarity training and system software training during the installation, checkout, and acceptance of the CMCS.

Maintenance

There are two different approaches to maintenance of CMCS. The owner can either use in-house staff to maintain the system, or enter into a service contract with the system supplier. Where systems are simple and sufficient trained personnel exist within the owner's organization, the owner may decide to maintain the system with parts supplied from the equipment manufacturer. If the system is complex and if the owner has to rely on the system supplier to maintain the system properly, a maintenance and service contract may be justified. Rarely do CMCS warranties cover normal maintenance.

System Upgrade or Expansion

It may become necessary to modify an existing CMCS. The need may arise from a change in facilities use or an expansion which must be tied into the system. Often, newer hardware and software is available, and this may require a decision as to whether an equipment upgrade is desirable. If newer equipment is considered, its compatibility with existing equipment from an interface and communications standpoint must be properly analyzed to prevent replacing equipment unnecessarily. In many cases, the spare I/O device capacity of the existing system may be sufficient to deal with minor changes. System software may also be updated to provide better performance.

25.6 CONCLUSION

Central monitoring and control systems provide physical plant administrators with the ability to coordinate the operation of multiple facilities and systems. Recent technological developments in CMCS include the use of fiber optic cable, which is immune to lightning strikes and electrical interference; intelligent field panels, which enhance reliability by performing monitoring and control at the local level independent of the central computer; and "smart" I/O devices, which reduce wiring requirements between I/O devices and field panels. The purchase of a CMCS from a single source supplier, who may integrate equipment from other suppliers, is the preferred procurement approach. In this way, the supplier, not the owner, will be responsible for the integration of all system equipment and software.

There is no substitute for a well-coordinated and well-specified CMCS planned to meet both short- and long-term goals. The system's capabilities and functions must be properly defined to meet present and future needs within a reasonable budget. CMCS should play a major role at colleges and universities in the future, as better coordination of increasingly complicated facilities systems becomes more important.

ADDITIONAL RESOURCES

American Society of Heating, Refrigerating, and Air Conditioning Engineers. *ASHRAE Technical Data Bulletin: Intelligent Buildings*. Atlanta: ASHRAE, 1988.

Haines, Roger W. *Control Systems for Heating, Ventilating, and Air Conditioning*, fourth edition. New York: Van Nostrand Reinhold, 1987.

Johnson Controls, Inc. *The Intelligent Building Sourcebook*. Lilburn, Georgia: The Fairmont Press, 1988.

CHAPTER 26

Heating and Power Plants

David J. Miller, P.E.
Director for Utilities
Iowa State University

26.1 INTRODUCTION

The basic power plant cycle includes three energy conversion stages: fuel to heat, heat to mechanical energy, and mechanical energy to electricity. Although the applications and processes involved in a plant are complex, the basic cycle has not changed significantly since the middle of this century. However, increased fuel and energy costs have greatly increased the importance of heating and power plant efficiencies, leading to the development of new technologies for improved efficiencies. Additionally, it is advisable to continually review the cost-effectiveness of the various power plant components and auxiliaries. Many technologies that were not cost-effective in plants built before the 1970s require periodic reevaluation in the light of increased energy costs.

Today's physical plant professional must evaluate alternatives to meet energy requirements, and make decisions regarding large capital expenditures for heating and power plant additions and alterations. This necessitates an understanding of the basic heating and power plant cycles and equipment.

This chapter discusses the fuels, processes, and equipment of central heating and power plants. The discussion of fuels and firings, boiler control, and emission control, applies generally to all sizes and types of boilers.

Reference is made to attainable efficiencies in this chapter. However, the purpose is to describe the components and functioning of heating and power plants. Their operation, including cogeneration, is discussed further in Section VII, Physical Plant Operations.

26.2 CENTRAL PLANT SYSTEMS

Boilers are the basic building block of any utility system for the generation of hot water or steam. They are used by virtually every college and university, whether fueled by gas, oil, coal, or refuse. They may be located in a central heating plant or distributed among various campus buildings as package boilers. The energy derived from these boilers is in the form of steam. This steam is used to 1) generate electricity through turbine generators; 2) heat buildings with direct steam or hot water; and 3) cool buildings with steam-driven centrifugal or absorption chilled water systems. (See Figure 26-1.)

These three uses comprise the basic power plant cycle. To increase the efficiency of this basic cycle, a variety of auxiliary equipment is available, including economizers, air preheaters, feedwater heaters, superheaters, and various heat exchangers that maximize the use of the heat generated in the burning of fuels. In addition, other equipment such as mechanical collectors, dust collectors, electrostatic precipitators, baghouses, scrubbers, and waste water treatment systems are required to satisfy emission standards.

26.3 BOILER TYPES

There are two basic types of boilers in use: fire tube and water tube. Boilers may be further classified as either package or field-erected units, based on the manufacturing method and installation. A package unit is built, tested before shipment, and delivered as a one-piece unit, requiring little field erection other than connection of auxiliaries. Field-erected units require field assembly of the various components of the boiler.

Fire Tube Boilers

Fire tube boilers, developed in the early nineteenth century, are made of a shell that holds the water. Fire tubes run the length of the unit. Flames and hot gases from the burner pass through the tubes, from which heat is transferred to the water. Fire tube boilers are primarily used in heating systems. They are usually large and have thick shells. The boilers are manufactured in ratings that allow as much as 20,000 pounds of steam to flow from the boiler in one hour at a maximum practical operating pressure of around 250 pounds per square inch (psi). The rating of these boilers is often given in terms of boiler horsepower, such as 600 boiler horsepower for a 20,000-pound-per-hour unit.

Fire tube boilers feature simple, rugged construction and relatively low initial cost. Their large water capacity makes them relatively slug-

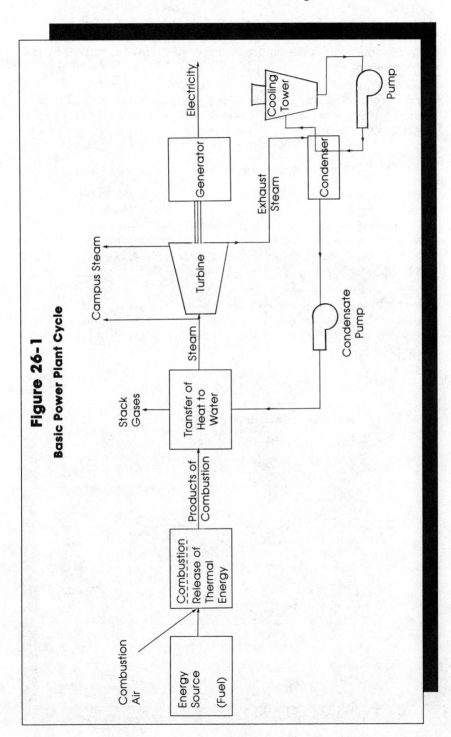

Figure 26-1
Basic Power Plant Cycle

gish in operation and slow to achieve operating pressure from a cold start. Several operational configurations can be used depending upon the number of times the hot gases are routed through the shell. Two-pass, three-pass, and four-pass designs are available. Additional passes increase the initial cost as well as the unit efficiency. Forced draft is normally used with multiple passes of the combustion gasses. (See Figure 26-2.)

Water Tube Boilers

There exists a wide variety of water tube boilers, complicated by the numerous methods of classification: straight tube or bent tube; horizontal, vertical, or inclined tube; longitudinal or cross drum; and so on. But their distinguishing characteristic is that the water is contained in tubes, which are located in the combustion chamber. The tubes are connected to a header, which connects to a steam drum. As heat is transferred to the water in the tubes, steam is generated and flows to the steam drum.

The initial cost of a water tube boiler is higher than that of an equivalent fire tube boiler, but efficiency is significantly higher. Package-type water tube boilers are available in sizes up to 100,000 pounds of steam per hour.

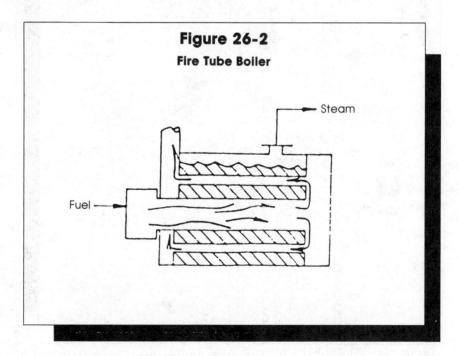

Figure 26-2
Fire Tube Boiler

26.4 FUELS

A wide variety of fuels are now used in central plant steam-generating units. Primary fuels such as natural gas, fuel oil, and coal are often augmented with alternate fuels such as refuse derived fuel (RDF), bark or other wood products, petroleum coke, anthracite culm, and various manufacturing by-products.

Each fuel must be evaluated on the basis of its availability and price delivered to the point of use. Transportation charges often can exceed the actual cost of the raw fuel. In evaluating fuels, consideration must be given to impurities in the fuel that may affect combustion performance or environmental emissions, as well as the variability in the higher heating value (HHV) of the fuel measured in units of Btu per pound. The higher heating value of the fuels varies from 23,500 Btu/pound for natural gas to 4,000 Btus/pound for anthracite culm. Ash and moisture content also must be monitored. In fluidized bed combustion, a limestone source must be secured that has adequate reactivity to remove sulfur from the flue gas efficiently.

The normal range of heating values for various fossil fuels are as follows:

Natural gas	20,000-23,500 Btu/lb (1,000 Btu/ft)*
No. 1 fuel oil	19,670-19,860 Btu/lb
No. 2 fuel oil	19,170-19,750 Btu/lb
No. 4 fuel oil	18,280-19,400 Btu/lb
No. 5 fuel oil	18,100-19,020 Btu/lb
No. 6 fuel oil	17,410-18,990 Btu/lb
Bituminous coal	11,500-14,500 Btu/lb
Sub-bituminous coal	8,500-11,500 Btu/lb
Lignites	6,300- 8,300 Btu/lb
Anthracite culm	4,000- 5,000 Btu/lb

*Btu is defined as one British thermal unit equal to the amount of energy required to raise the temperature of one pound of water 1°F.

26.5 PRINCIPLES OF COMBUSTION

Combustion of all fossil fuels is the mixture of oxygen with carbon and hydrogen (oxidation) to release heat, carbon dioxide, and water. If there is a lack of oxygen, some of the carbon will not be completely oxidized and carbon monoxide will be formed. Carbon monoxide is itself a fuel with a heating value of about 4,300 Btus/pound, so its formation indicates incomplete combustion of the fuel. The products of combustion may also include nitrogen and sulfur oxides, which are regulated pollutants that can cause chemical fouling and corrosion of boiler equipment. (See Figure 26-3.)

Three conditions must be met for combustion to occur:

1. The fuel must be gasified.
2. The oxygen-fuel mixture must be within the flammable range.
3. The mixture must be above its ignition temperature.

Once the combustion process is started, the quality of combustion is determined by time, temperature, and turbulence. Good combustion is rapid, has a high flame temperature, and is turbulent. Turbulence is the key factor in boiler furnace combustion. If turbulence is high, mixing of the oxygen and fuel will be good and combustion will be rapid and result in a high temperature.

The specific amount of air required to complete combustion is known as "theoretical air." In actual combustion, excess air is required because the mixing of fuel and air is never perfect. The amount of excess air depends upon the boiler type, fuel properties, and burner or stoker characteristics. Since excess air is supplied to the combustion process, all the available oxygen in the air will not be used. Excess air requirements are stated as a percentage, as is the excess oxygen in the flue gas.

To measure the percent of excess oxygen in combustion products, an oxygen analyzer is used. From the measured excess oxygen and known chemical composition of the fuel, the excess air can be determined. Measuring oxygen is generally preferred to measuring carbon dioxide; the instrumentation is simpler and cheaper, and the oxygen-to-excess air relationship is less variable than carbon dioxide-to-air.

Figure 26-3

Basic Combustion Equation

$$CxHX \quad + \quad O_s \; + \; N_2 \quad + \quad S \qquad CO_2 \; + \; N_2 \; + \; SO_2 \; + \; HEAT$$

Fuel   Air   Impurity   Products of Combustion
                         (Sulfur)

26.6 FIRING SYSTEMS

Natural Gas

Natural gas contains 25 percent hydrogen and 75 percent carbon by weight. It is the cleanest burning and easiest to handle of all fuels. Products of combustion include water, carbon dioxide, hydrogen, oxygen, and nitrogen oxides. Many designs of gas burners exist, differing primarily in the orientation of burner orifices and their location in the burner housing.

Oils

The use of oil is more complicated than natural gas because of the preparation required. Solid foreign matter is removed by straining. The oil is heated by tank and flow line heaters for lower viscosity and is atomized before mixing with combustion air. A gun introduces oil into the burner in a fine spray. The carbon-to-hydrogen ratio is about 88 percent to 12 percent, with traces of nitrogen and sulfur. Products of combustion include water, carbon dioxide, nitrogen, oxygen, nitrogen oxides, sulfur, and particulate matter. The particulate matter sticks to tubes and boiler surfaces and leads to boiler fouling if these are not cleaned regularly. Sulfur oxides combine with water to form sulfuric acid, which is a major cause of boiler corrosion. (See Figure 26-4.)

Coal

Coal Combustion—General   In a coal-burning system using stoker/ grate firing, air is supplied to the combustion process in two parts. Primary air is first admitted under the fuel bed and overfire air, or secondary air, is later added above the bed. The primary air rising through the fuel bed first comes into the oxidizing zone where most of the oxygen is consumed to form carbon dioxide. The carbon dioxide then rises through the reducing zone, which extends to the surface of the fuel bed, and a portion of the carbon dioxide is converted to carbon monoxide by reacting with the carbon. This combustible gas then passes into the combustion space above the bed where overfire air is admitted and the combustion process is completed. As a general guide, about half the air by weight is supplied below the bed and half above the bed. The rate of burning is controlled by the primary air, and the completeness of combustion by the overfire air. The products of combustion vary with the grade of coal, but include carbon, hydrogen, nitrogen, oxygen, sulfur, moisture, incombustible materials, and nitric and sulfur oxides.

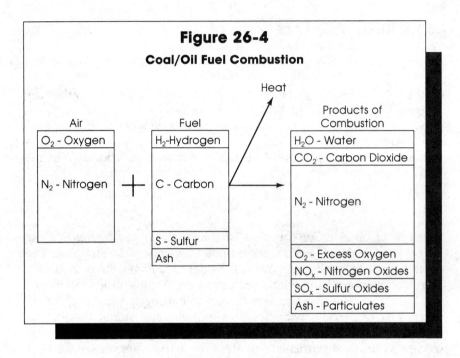

Figure 26-4

Coal/Oil Fuel Combustion

With a coal-burning system using pulverized coal, the primary air transports the pulverized coal into the furnace. Secondary air is then admitted to provide more oxygen for combustion and to stabilize the flame. Tertiary air may be introduced at some point remote from the main combustion zone in order to complete the combustion process. The principal advantages of using pulverized coal over other types of coal are:

- Capability for better mixing of the fuel and air, which permits the use of less excess air.
- Ability to burn the fuel at high rates.
- Flexibility of control, which permits quick response to changing requirements.
- Minimization of fuel waste in starting, banking, and other steps.
- Ability to maintain high rates of combustion without forced draft due to the absence of a thick fuel bed.

Stokers   Mechanical stoker-fired boilers were developed early in this century. They evolved from hand-fired boilers, which became prevalent as coal became a popular fuel and demand increased for higher rates of combustion. In all types of stoker boilers, coal is the primary fuel burned on a moving mechanical grate. These grates are available in several configurations including stationary or dump grate, chain grate, travelling grate, vibrating grate, and spreader stoker. Each type of grate has been developed to burn best with specific fuels, such as coal, wood products, or municipal waste. Chain-grate or spreader-stoker boilers are the most common for coal-burning units rated 200,000 pounds per hour steam flow or less. In the case of a spreader stoker, coal is routed into the furnace where it is partially burned in suspension before reaching the grate. Mechanical stoker boilers can handle a wide variety of fuels. Response to load changes is moderate, since there is a large supply of fuel in the bed at any time. Overall unit efficiencies of 80 percent can be expected. (See Figure 26-5.)

Pulverized Coal   In a pulverized coal boiler, grinders (pulverizers) are used to turn the coal into a fine powder. Coal supplied to the pulverizer can be in various sizes ranging up to two inches. The pulverized coal is then dried and classified before being conveyed into the boiler by a combustion air stream. Three of the most widely used pulverizers are the ball and tube type, the ball and race type, and the roll and ring type.

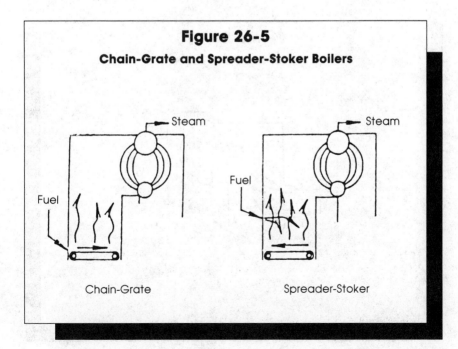

Figure 26-5

Chain-Grate and Spreader-Stoker Boilers

Chain-Grate   Spreader-Stoker

Pulverized coal burners are similar in design to oil-fired burners and combustion is similar to that of gas. Combustion temperatures can reach 2,000°F, at which temperature many coals form ash deposits and slag that can build up in steam-generating sections of the boiler. Response to load change is rapid and overall unit efficiencies are high. Overall unit efficiency is high, approaching 86 percent. (See Figure 26-6.)

Fluidized Bed   Use of fluidized bed boiler technology is rapidly growing in the United States. This method of combustion burns the fuel in a turbulent atmosphere, generated by entering the combustion air at the bottom of the furnace, in the presence of limestone which absorbs the sulfur. The fuel may either be contained in an agitated bed or completely suspended by air, depending on the unit design. Two advantages of using this method of combustion are the removal of sulfur (and thus compliance with environmental standards without additional equipment such as scrubbers), and the ability to use many kinds of fuel. The disadvantage is that the limestone can be used only once. Three primary types of fluidized bed boilers are available: bubbling bed, dense bed, and circulating type.

Bubbling bed boilers are considered to be the original fluidized bed boilers. They have a relatively low velocity of combustion air moving

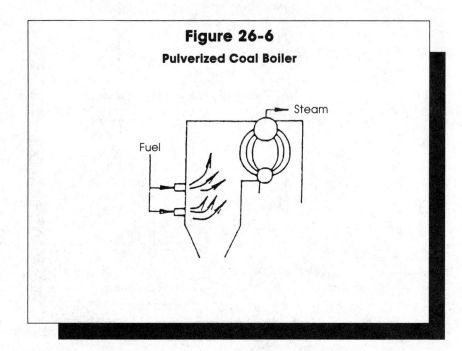

Figure 26-6
Pulverized Coal Boiler

through the bed. This produces a bubbling phenomenon characteristic of this type of combustion. Most bubbling bed boilers have heat exchange tubes inside the fuel bed to absorb the heat of combustion from the fuel. An inert material, such as sand, often is added to the fuel bed with limestone to achieve the desired interaction between the fuel and inert materials. The fuel bed material is typically 6 feet in depth in a bubbling bed design.

Dense Bed boilers are similar to bubbling bed boilers except that the inert material is typically river rock. Bed depths on these units may reach 9 to 10 feet. The violent action of this bed allows dense bed boilers to accept different types of fuels as well as a larger fuel size due to the bed capability to fragment and abrade the fuel.

In the *circulating type* boiler, combustion air velocities are increased such that a definable bed is not experienced. Rather, the fuel is completely suspended by air or air-entrained. As the bed is dispersed, the fuel is more evenly distributed throughout the volume of the combustion chamber. Better fuel utilization and increased heat absorption in the combustion chamber walls means that in-bed tubes are not required. These boilers typically are smaller in size and have a higher combustion efficiency.

All fluidized bed boilers have the capability of handling a wide variety of fuels. They can handle feedstocks such as coal, refuse-derived fuels (RDF), wood waste, agriculture product waste, anthracite culm, petroleum coke, or any combination of these fuels. Response to changing load demands is rapid, approaching that of the pulverized coal boilers. Overall unit efficiencies are in the 86 percent range. (See Figure 26-7.)

Waste Heat Boilers   Waste heat boilers are used in many cogeneration facilities. This type of combustion uses the hot gases from another process, such as exhaust gases from a gas turbine, to transfer heat to steam generation banks. The gas stream may or may not have a fuel content. The steam generating sections of these boilers are typical of any of the boiler types previously mentioned. Usually a supplementary fuel, such as oil or gas, is required to maintain a constant furnace temperature.

Cyclone Boilers   Cyclone boilers use one or more small combustion chambers attached to a conventional furnace and steam-generating section (convection pass). These small combustion chambers are operated with a turbulent atmosphere at high temperatures. Slag is intentionally formed in the combustion chamber and drained out of the cyclone area. This boiler design results in reduced furnace size and the capability to burn a large variety of fuels due to the turbulent combustion chamber.

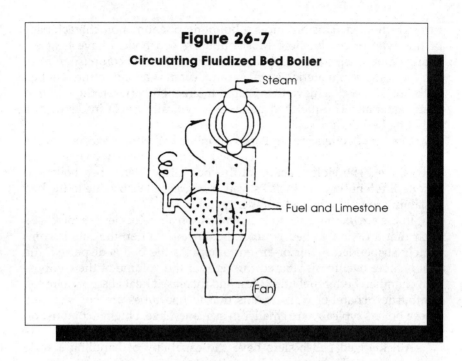

Figure 26-7

Circulating Fluidized Bed Boiler

These boilers produce high levels of nitrogen oxides (NOX) because of the higher combustion temperatures.

26.7 BOILER EFFICIENCIES

Three factors can inhibit the transfer of energy from the combustion zone to the steam and water contained in the boiler, resulting in lost energy: combustion factors, heat transfer factors, and steam loss factors.

Combustion Factors

The sources of heat loss in steam generators fall into three categories: flue gas waste heat, combustible losses, and radiation losses.

Flue Gas Waste Heat   Flue gas waste heat, that which goes into the exhaust stacks, exists in two forms: dry gas loss and moisture loss. Dry gas loss is the unrecovered sensible heat energy contained in the hot flue gases, excluding water vapor. Moisture loss consists of both latent and sensible heat of the water vapor resulting from the combustion of hydrogen, and any moisture present in the fuel or combustion air.

Two methods are used to reduce flue gas losses. One method is to reduce excess air to a minimum. Reduction of excess air reduces the amount of air in the flue gas that can absorb heat, which reduces the flue gas velocity and thereby increases the heat transfer to the water or steam. Excess air can be reduced by modifications to the type of fuel, the burner, or the stoker. It is normally achieved by better mixing of the fuel and air.

An alternate method is to reduce flue gas losses is to increase heat recovery from the flue gases. Care must be exercised, however, in reducing stack temperatures in boilers that have economizers, air preheaters, and other auxiliary equipment because reduced stack temperatures may lead to condensation of the water vapor. The water vapor, in turn, can combine with sulfur to form a corrosive acid in the equipment or the stack.

Combustible Losses   Combustible losses are those which result from incomplete combustion of the fuel. They are evidenced by combustibles in the ash or other signs of incomplete combustion such as solid combustibles in the ash, carbon carry-over in the fly ash, carbon monoxide, and unburned fuel. Corrections are made primarily by reinjecting ash into the combustion zone or by introducing combustion additives. The corrections of this condition for each fuel type follow.

Natural Gas—Carbon monoxide is the only combustible product normally formed in the combustion of natural gas. It results from too little or too much excess air, from insufficient fuel-air mixing, or from flame impingement on cold water walls. Care should be taken to ensure that the burner is operating in the acceptable excess air range, that diffusers and other mixing equipment are operating properly, and that the flame shape prevents impingement.

Fuel Oil—Carbon monoxide is formed during the combustion of fuel oil as it is for natural gas, and the corrections are the same. In addition, the formation of carbon monoxide may result from improper oil viscosity and inadequate atomization. These conditions can be corrected by checking and adjusting the oil temperature and the operation of the diffuser and atomizer.

Pulverized Coal—Carbon monoxide and carbon carry-over may be formed by the same factors affecting combustible formation in natural gas, and can be corrected in the same way. Incomplete combustion can result from variations in coal sizing. Generally the coal must be pulverized so that 70 percent will pass through a 200-mesh screen.

Stoker-Fired Coal—Without careful monitoring, carbon monoxide and smoke may be formed by too much or too little excess air or when loads are low in the combustion of stoker-fired coal. Correcting the supply of excess air, increasing overfire air velocity, and shifting loads from other boilers may overcome the problem.

With stoker-fired coal, solid combustibles are always present in the fly ash, but the amount of unburned material can be reduced. Cutting down on solid combustibles in the fly ash can be accomplished by reducing the excess air, which will decrease the particulate and carbon carry-over. Carbon carry-over also can be diminished by fly ash reinjection, but reinjection will normally increase the particulate loading at the stack.

Carbon monoxide, carbon carry-over, and clinkering (solidified slag) may result from too many fines (undersized coal), wet fines, insufficient bed thickness, improper undergrate air distribution, or improper feeder adjustments on spreader stokers. Plant engineers should check for proper combustion conditions.

Radiation Losses   Radiation loss results from heat that escapes through the boiler shell. This loss constitutes a higher percentage loss in low-load conditions and with smaller boilers because of the increased surface-to-volume ratio. Radiation losses can be cut by ensuring that both the boiler jacket and duct work are in good condition.

Heat Transfer Factors

Deposits inside and outside the heat transfer tubes act as insulators that impede heat transfer. When deposits accumulate, less heat is able to be absorbed by the water or steam. The condition normally can be detected by monitoring flue gas temperatures; rising temperatures indicate that less heat is being transferred in the boiler and more is lost to the stack. Improper combustion can speed soot deposits on boiler tube surfaces. Several steps must be taken to counteract buildup. For example, water tube boilers should be subjected to frequent soot blowing, sometimes as often as three times a day. Water side deposits can be controlled by effective water treatment and by mechanical or chemical cleaning.

Steam Heat Loss Factors

Steam heat losses can result from faulty steam traps, leaks to the environment from steam distribution lines, and inadequate insulation of steam lines. Of the three, malfunctioning steam traps may be the most important. A variety of tools exists for detecting faulty traps, such as temperature-indicating crayon, temperature-actuated color-changing tape, surface temperature gauges, and ultrasonic detectors. Loss from distribution pipes should be checked and the cost-effectiveness of added insulation recomputed periodically as energy costs rise. The amount of insulation is determined when steam lines are installed, based on cost-effectiveness. However, increases in energy costs change the incremental cost-versus-benefit relationship, and at some point it may be cost-effective to add insulation.

Figure 26-8 identifies a variety of boiler problems and their common causes.

26.8 POWER PLANT AUXILIARY EQUIPMENT

A variety of auxiliary equipment may be added to the basic boiler system to recover heat and increase overall unit efficiencies. The most common auxiliary equipment, heat exchangers, increase the temperature of either the water or air supplied to the boiler. An explanation of various heat exchangers and other types of auxiliary equipment follows. (See Figure 26-9.)

Since each installation is unique, no attempt has been made to quantify the potential savings realized by increased efficiencies when auxiliary equipment is added. Any analysis of potential savings must take into account equipment configuration, steam characteristics (pressure and temperature), purchased power costs, and fuel costs. A study must be made of each power plant by qualified engineers to determine efficiency improvements through the addition of auxiliaries.

Economizers

The most commonly used auxiliary to increase unit efficiency is the economizer, which transfers heat from the flue gases to the boiler feedwater. Flue gases are passed through a heat exchanger (economizer) as they leave the steam generating section of the boiler. Most economizers operate at a relatively low temperature, thus requiring a large amount of surface area. Economizers must be operated above the gas dew point to avoid the condensation of flue gas on the economizer tubes and to prevent external corrosion. To prevent internal corrosion caused by dissolved oxygen, water to economizers generally is deaerated.

Air Heaters

Air heaters recover heat from the flue gas by warming combustion air before it enters the boiler. Air heaters can be either recuperative (tube type) or regenerative (rotary type). In older plants without air heaters, a chimney of sufficient height will produce enough draft to maintain negative pressure in the furnace. When air heaters are added to these structures, an induced draft fan must be used to overcome the air flow restriction introduced by the air heater. Air heaters typically are placed

Figure 26-8

Boiler Performance Trouble-Shooting

System	Problem	Possible Cause
Heat Transfer Related	High Exit Gas Temperature	1. Buildup of gas- or water-side deposits
		2. Improper water treatment procedures
		3. Improper sootblower operation
Combustion Related	High Excess Air	1. Improper control system operation
		2. Low fuel supply pressure
		3. Change in fuel heating value
		4. Change in oil fuel viscosity
	Low Excess Air	1. Improper control system operation
		2. Fan limitations
		3. Increased ambient air temperature
	High CO and Combustible Emissions	1. Plugged gas burners
		2. Unbalanced fuel/air distribution in multiburner furnace
		3. Improper air register settings
		4. Deterioration of burner throat refractor
		5. Stoker grate condition
		6. Stoker fuel distribution orientation
		7. Improper overfire air systems
		8. Low fineness on pulverized systems

Figure 26-9

Boiler Efficiency Improvement Equipment

Air Preheaters	Transfer energy from stack gases to incoming combustion air.	2.5% for each 100° decrease in stack gas temperature
Economizers	Transfer energy from stack gases to incoming feed-water.	2.5% for each 100° decrease in stack gas temperature, 1% for each 10° increase in feed-water temperature
Firetube Turbulators	Increase turbulence in the secondary passes of firetube units.	2.5% for each 100° decrease in stack gas temperature
Combustion Control System	Regulate quantity of fuel and airflow.	0.25% for each 1% decrease in O_2
Sootblowers	Remove boiler tube deposits that restrict heat transfer.	Dependent on gas temperature
Blowdown System	Transfer energy from expelled blowdown liquids to incoming feed-water.	1-3% depending upon blowdown quantities and operating pressures

after the economizers in the flue gas flow. An ideal air heater design would reduce the gas temperature to near but not below its dew point, the temperature at which moisture begins to condense out of the gas. Operation below the dew point will cause excessive corrosion from acids formed from sulfur products in the flue gas.

Superheaters and Desuperheaters

Boilers used for heat systems can operate at or near the saturation temperature of the steam, the temperature at which the water is vaporized and the water and vapor are in equilibrium. However, steam supplied to turbines must be well above the vaporization temperature, both for efficiency and to prevent damage to the turbine blading from condensation. The temperature of the steam is raised above its saturation point in a method called superheating. Superheat sections in the boiler remove steam from the drum and raise the temperature further to the desired superheat temperature.

Superheat temperature will vary according to load, and the characteristics of radiant versus convection superheaters are distinctly different. Radiant superheaters absorb heat by direct radiation from the flame, but will exhibit a drop in steam temperature as load increases. Convection superheaters outside of the radiant portion of the boiler will exhibit a steam temperature rise as load increases due to the increased mass flow of gases within the boiler. To control these temperatures and deliver consistent steam quality to the turbines, desuperheaters must be applied. Desuperheating is accomplished by spraying pure water into the steam so that the steam temperature is lowered to the desired point. Proper application of a desuperheater can control the overall steam temperature and quality. Desuperheaters may be applied at the exit of the boiler or between boiler superheater sections.

Feedwater Heaters

The water supplied to the boiler is termed the feedwater. Feedwater heaters may be used with boiler systems that supply extraction-type turbines to increase the overall plant cycle efficiency. Feedwater heaters are heat exchangers that heat the feedwater with steam extracted from the turbine, or with the turbine exhaust. The two basic types of feedwater heaters include the closed feedwater heater, in which the heat is transferred by means of a shell and tube type exchanger, and the open feedwater heater, in which the water and steam are mixed to accomplish feedwater heating. Deaerators are most commonly the open type. Typically, a rise of 10°F in feedwater temperature will result in approximately a 1 percent savings in fuel consumption.

Blowdown Heat Recovery

The concentration of impurities in the boiler increases with operation because of system leakages and impurities in the boiler make-up water. To keep impurities at an acceptable level, it is necessary to remove water concentrated with impurities from the boiler, a process called "blowing down" the boiler. This blowdown is accomplished by a combination of periodic and/or continuous removal of water from the boiler system. Removal is typically done from the steam drum or drums and the downcomer areas of the boiler. The amount of heat lost during blowdown tends to be high, so some sort of blowdown heat recovery system is often used and easily justified. Heat from boiler blowdown water is recovered by routing to a heat exchanger through which feedwater is flowing, extracting the heat from the hot boiler blowdown water which would otherwise be wasted. Additionally, low-pressure steam from the flash tank may be used to supplement extraction steam and other steam requirements of the plant.

Ash Reinjection

Complete, or 100 percent, combustion is not possible. There will be a certain amount of unburned carbons in the fly ash entrained in the flue gas exiting the boilers. Carbon content of the fly ash varies from 1 to 20 percent. This carbon loss can dramatically affect the overall efficiency of the boiler system. Ash reinjection involves capture of this fly ash and the corresponding unburned carbons for reintroduction into the combustion zone. Two common points of ash collection for reinjection are at the bottom of the economizer section, or at the discharge of the mechanical collector.

Combustion Additives

Previous discussions have centered on auxiliary equipment that may be added to the basic boiler system to increase overall system efficiencies. A fireside approach also may be used to increase efficiency, particularly when fuel oil and coal are used. Because these fuels are not homogeneous in nature, variations in combustion characteristics can be anticipated due to impurities and physical characteristics. Combustion additives help oxygen react with the combustible elements of carbon and hydrogen in the fuel. Combustion catalysts increase the reaction rate between the carbon and oxygen and lower the reaction temperature, resulting in more carbon being burned at a given excess air level. This increased carbon utilization directly increases overall boiler efficiency. When fuel oil is burned, oil additives may be used to dissolve and disperse complex hydrocarbons that can interfere with the combustion process, thus increasing carbon utilization and creating higher system efficiencies. An additional benefit of combustion additives is that particulate emissions may actually be reduced, since unburned carbons often comprise a significant portion of the particulate emission from a unit. In particular, stoker-fired boilers often experience decreased particulate emissions with the use of combustion additives.

26.9 POLLUTION CONTROL EQUIPMENT

An expanding variety of federal, state, and local environmental regulations and restrictions govern power plant emissions. Jurisdictions vary from state to state, but any major plant addition or modification is likely to require oversight and approval from any or all of the regulating agencies.

Mechanical Collectors

Mechanical collectors are used to control particulate emissions. These collectors change the velocity and direction of the gas stream sufficiently to allow the heavier particulates to fall into a hopper below. Mechanical collectors can be used to collect large amounts of particulate matter often in series with other pollution control devices. Many mechanical collectors use a tube design whereby each tube is an individual centrifugal dust collector. Particulate matter is collected through cyclonic action created by turning vanes on one end of the tube. Collector tubes range in diameter from 6 to 24 inches. Mechanical collectors have no moving parts, and are characterized by low-pressure drop across the unit. They do, however, require maintenance because they must be kept clean to operate correctly. Their collection efficiency depends upon size and weight of the particles; they are more efficient in removing heavier particles. Mechanical collectors can remove up to 90 percent of all particulates.

Electrostatic Precipitators

Electrostatic precipitators often are used when collection efficiencies of 99 percent or less are needed. Electrostatic precipitators give an electrical charge to the particles in the gas stream and then attract those charged particles to a collecting electrode. The electrostatic precipitator's electrical field operates at a high DC voltage level (typically 50,000 to 75,000 volts), imparted to a framework of weighted wires. The charged particles are collected on electrically grounded suspended plates. These plates are rapped or vibrated mechanically to remove the fly ash to a storage hopper. Performance is a function of the chemical constituents of the coal and the electrical characteristics of the fly ash. Efficiencies will be notably higher when burning higher sulfur coals. A properly designed precipitator requires full definition of the fuels to be burned.

Bag Houses

One of the most efficient methods of particulate removal is the bag house. Bag houses can remove up to 99 percent of all particulate matter, and are smaller and less expensive than a comparable precipitator. A bag house removes the fly ash from the boiler exit gases by passing the exhaust through fabric filters. Collection is allowed to continue until the pressure drop across the bag house reaches a predetermined level, at which time the bags are cleaned. The ash cake formed on the fabric also acts as a filter, so that maximum collection efficiency occurs immediately prior to cleaning the fabric filters.

There are two basic designs, differing in the method by which the bags are cleaned. A reverse air bag house collects the fly ash on the inside of the bags and cleans them by reversing the air flow through the bags. A pulse-jet bag house collects the fly ash on the outside of the bags, and the bags are cleaned by pulsing with a jet of compressed air.

A variety of bag materials, weights, and mesh design is available to meet collection needs. Bag design depends on the characteristics of the flue gas, not on sulfur content of the fuel or on the type of fuel being burned. Their use may be limited by high temperature or humidity conditions, because of the fabric used.

Scrubbers

Federal, state, and local environmental regulations require most new boilers to have gaseous emissions limitations. Gaseous pollutants are more difficult to manage than particulate matter. The most common restrictions apply to sulfur and nitrogen emissions, but many installations are also regulated for trace elements, heavy metals, organic compounds, and other toxic emissions. The most prevalent pollutant is sulfur dioxide. The sulfur oxides can be controlled by removing sulfur prior to or during combustion, as with fluidized bed combustion. The primary method of removing sulfur from the exit gases after combustion is with scrubbers.

Wet Scrubbers   A wet scrubber system removes sulfur dioxide from the flue gas by introducing a limestone slurry into the flue gas stream in a spray type chamber. The atmosphere within a wet scrubber is much like that of a wet cooling tower. A wet scrubber system is characterized by large water usage, large quantities of waste materials, and high operating costs. If sulfur recovery is desired, a magnesia solution is substituted for the limestone slurry to recover a sulfur product. Nearly 90 percent of all sulfur oxides can be removed with wet scrubbers.

Dry Scrubbers   One type of dry scrubbing, the spray dryer system, uses lime reagent that is atomized and mixed with the incoming flue gas. The lime droplets react with the sulfur dioxides in the flue gas and are simultaneously dried. The spent solids are collected in the bottom of the absorption chamber. The dry scrubber system is advantageous because water usage is minimized, waste drying is unnecessary, and a dry fly ash conveying system can be used to handle wastes generated. Another type of dry scrubber removes sulfur dioxide from the flue gas stream by passing the flue gas through a fixed absorbent bed material, such as char. The absorbent bed material is regenerated once the material becomes saturated.

Compliance Equipment

In order to demonstrate compliance with state, federal, and local emission restrictions, it may be necessary to add gas analyzing equipment to the boiler. The complexity of the equipment and the reporting requirements will vary depending upon the regulating agency. Equipment costs range from $25,000 to $200,000 per boiler installation.

Opacity Monitors   Opacity monitors measure particulate emissions from a specified source. While the boiler exit gas would certainly be one source, other points may require monitoring to establish compliance of other equipment, such as coal-handling dust collectors, ash blower exhausts, or any other dust-laden particle stream.

Continuous Emission Monitors   The regulating agency often requires continuous emission monitors (CEMs) after any significant plant modification or addition. These monitors provide extensive analysis of the flue gas stream for sulfur dioxide, nitrogen oxide, dilutive gases, or other regulated gaseous emissions. A typical CEM system consists of a gas sample point, gas analyzers, and data reduction computers with output devices. The three basic types of continuous emission monitors are *in situ*, extractive, and dilutive extractive. The *in situ* device is mounted at the point of collection on the gas ductwork or at the chimney, with the analyzers mounted at the sample point and the data reduction hardware at some remote location. The extractive system extracts a flue gas sample and transports it to a remotely located analyzer cabinet, where the data reduction equipment is also located. The dilutive extractive system suctions the flue gas through a metered orifice to provide a diluted gas sample to the gas analyzers and data reduction equipment.

26.10 TURBINES

Operation—General

Steam turbines receive high-pressure, high-temperature steam from the boiler and convert the thermal energy to mechanical (shaft) energy, which can then drive a generator or a chiller. The steam passes through nozzles, giving it a high velocity, then impinges on the turbine blading to rotate the turbine shaft. The conversion process involves pressure and temperature reductions as thermal energy is converted to mechanical energy. The steam expansion process can be in several turbines connected to a common shaft, referred to as high-, intermediate-, and low-pressure turbines.

Turbine Efficiency

The efficiency of any heat engine relates to temperature, which in turn relates to pressure. The basic formula for heat engine efficiency is:

$$\text{Efficiency} = \frac{T_1 - T_2}{T_1} \times 100$$

Where:
T_1 = Inlet temperature
T_2 = Outlet temperature
(Temperatures in absolute -°F + 460)

From the formula it can be seen that the larger the ΔT (T_1 - T_2), the more efficient the engine.

ΔT can be increased in two ways: increasing the inlet temperature and pressure, and lowering the exhaust temperature and pressure. Raising the inlet temperature and pressure requires alloy steels to withstand the higher temperatures and pressures, and more elaborate piping arrangements, insulation, pump capacities, and feedwater heating to avoid boiler stresses. Lowering the exhaust temperature and pressure is generally more feasible. However, steam should not be allowed to condense in the turbine.

At 15 psi, one pound of water produces 26 cubic feet of steam or 7,776 square inches. The 15 psi pressure would therefore exert 58 tons of pressure on each pound of steam being exhausted from a turbine at atmospheric pressure. This pressure must be overcome. For example, by reducing the pressure from atmospheric (approximately 15 psi) to 5 psi, efficiency would be improved by almost 6 percent.

The foregoing is the principle involved in a condensing turbine, discussed below.

Types of Turbines

Back-Pressure Turbine   Technically, a back-pressure turbine exhausts at or above atmospheric pressure. The inlet temperature and pressure are relatively high, although they operate over a wide range of conditions. A typical use is in cogeneration, where the turbines exhaust into a steam distribution system that supplies the campus thermal requirements.

Condensing Turbine   In a condensing turbine, the exhaust is condensed, lowering the pressure to 2 to 5 PSI and thus lowering the ΔT. Additionally, the treated feedwater is retained, collected in a hot-well, and pumped back to the boiler. With condensing turbines, steam generally is extracted after one of the turbine stages to meet the campus thermal loads.

Gas Turbines   Combustion turbines are popular as prime movers of electrical generators. They have the benefit of short lead times and low capital cost. Gas turbines come on-line quickly (less than ten minutes) and can offer an excellent solution to backup power requirements or for peak shaving to limit electrical demand charges. Natural gas and fuel oil are typical turbine fuels. Gas turbines range in size from several hundred kilowatts to several hundred megawatts.

The basic gas turbine has three main sections: compressor, combustor, and turbine. The compressor draws air in from the atmosphere, pressurizes it, and introduces it to the combustor. Fuel is added and burned in the combustor and the hot gases are allowed to expand through the turbine section. Increased efficiency can be developed by adding a regeneration (air heater) section, an intercooler (split compressor and cooler) section, or a reheat (split turbine and second combustor) section. Another method used to improve gas turbine system efficiency is the combined cycle plant, which routes the hot turbine exhaust gases to a boiler section to extract additional thermal energy and generate steam. Typically, an auxiliary fuel is used in the boiler to promote complete combustion and to control steam temperature.

The only pollutant of concern with gas turbines is NOX. Gas turbines can be high NOX generators, and some method of control usually is required. Control methods include water or steam injection into the combustor to keep flame temperature low, and use of selective catalytic reduction (SCR). Steam injection also will increase power from the turbine by boosting the mass flow through the turbine. Selective catalytic reduction consists of ammonia injection into the exhaust stream.

Condensers   Condensers are heat exchangers that transfer heat from the turbine exhaust directly to the atmosphere or to a cooling water from which it is released to the atmosphere. They generally handle large quantities of heat, and differ in the method of ultimate transmission of heat to the atmosphere. The following are major types:

1. Once-through cooling. The water is pumped from a source such as a lake or river, through the heat exchanger, and back to the source. The discharge must be sufficiently removed from the source to avoid heating it.
2. Cooling pond. Water from the condenser is discharged into a pond, from which heat is transferred to the atmosphere by evaporation, convection, and radiation.
3. Spray pond. In a spray pond, the water is sprayed five to ten feet in the air. They require only about 5 percent of the area of a cooling pond for the same heat transmission. Spray ponds sometimes are used to supplement cooling ponds during hot weather.
4. Natural draft evaporative cooling. This method employs a cooling tower with water sprayed counter to the air flow. Natural draft cooling requires large structures and therefore high construction costs.
5. Mechanical draft evaporative cooling tower. These can be either forced or induced draft. They have a lower construction cost than natural draft cooling towers, but require large quantities of water which causes high operating costs.
6. Dry cooling towers. These can be either direct, in which the steam from the turbine condenses in finned tubes in the cooling tower, or indirect, in which the heat from the turbine exhaust is transferred to a second fluid that is then pumped to the cooling tower.

26.11 CHEMICAL TREATMENT

A sound chemical treatment program is essential in the power plant cycle to protect the large capital investment associated with a centralized heating plant. Boiler water must be treated to lessen scale formation, corrosion of metal, and carry-over of solids. Scale will lower the thermal efficiency of the unit, and corrosion will decrease its life while increasing outages due to tube failures. In addition, solids carry-over will damage equipment, particularly steam turbines when the contaminated steam enters the turbine blading. The cooling water must be treated to protect against scale, corrosion, microbiological contamination, and fouling, the effects of which are increased maintenance costs, reduced heat transfer efficiency, and production cutbacks or shutdowns.

Boiler Water Treatment

Pure water is an active solvent that will pick up or dissolve part of everything with which it comes in contact. The average level of impurities in midwestern U.S. water is about 500 parts per million (ppm) or about one-half pound of residue for every 1,000 pounds of water which has been evaporated. These impurities can cause scale, corrosion, and carry-over within the boiler itself. In the past, most boiler feedwater was treated with phosphates until the development of chelate and polymer-type chemicals. These chemicals condition the calcium and magnesium in the feedwater so that these impurities will remain in suspension to prevent the formation of scale on boiler surfaces. Most boiler feed-water systems also contain a deaerating feedwater heater which removes oxygen and dissolves gases from the feedwater. If additional oxygen scavenging is desired, chemicals such as sodium sulfite and hydrazine are added. A good boiler internal treatment program includes the addition of hardness-controlling and degasing chemicals, with a blowdown system to discharge concentrated solids from the lower regions of the boiler.

Cooling Water Treatment

Cooling water systems provide an environment where corrosion, scale, and microbiological contamination and fouling can become problems. Corrosion is an electrochemical phenomenon that must be controlled by adding corrosion inhibitors to the cooling water. Corrosion inhibitors establish a protective film on either the anode or cathode elements of the cooling water system. Chemicals such as chromates, nitrites, orthophosphates, bicarbonates, and polyphosphates typically are used. The primary protection in the prevention of scale is control of phosphate levels (or pH) in the cooling water, and system blowdown to eliminate impurities. Typically, pH is controlled by an acid feed system and microbiological contamination is controlled by adding biocides to the cooling water. The most common chemical used as a biocide in cooling water systems is chlorine.

26.12 WATER TREATMENT

Centralized heating and cooling plants with associated boiler supply water, condenser cooling water, and chilled water systems consume large amounts of water. Many municipal water systems cannot cope with this large water demand so heating plants must operate their own water treatment plant. This provides the heating plant with a source of potable water for use in the boiler, cooling tower, chilled water system, and other uses. Depending upon the raw water source, a wide variety of equipment and systems may be used to develop potable water. This potable water is used directly in chilled water and cooling tower systems; but additional processing equipment, such as condensate polishers, zeolite softeners, or demineralizers are needed to further purify the water for use in the boiler.

Water Plants

A variety of equipment is used to produce a potable water supply from raw water sources such as wells, lakes, and rivers. Although the system equipment and configurations may vary dramatically, the principles of operation are the same. The primary processes are clarification and sterilization.

Clarification is the removal of suspended matter and color from the water supply. The suspended particles may be removed with settling basins, filters, or coagulating chemicals. Many systems involve several or all of these. Water plant design is dependent upon the raw water source, the desired potable water quality, the design and emergency flow rates, and the available equipment space. Water treatment plants may include such equipment as aerators, flash mixers, flock tanks, settling basins, clarifiers, lamella filters, gravity filters, pressure filters, and a variety of chlorinators and chemical feed equipment.

Sterilization is the process of controlling the level of microorganisms in the potable water to a point lower than the applicable standards in a particular jurisdiction. Sterilization is generally accomplished with chlorine. Both maximum and minimum chlorine residual levels will apply to most potable water systems.

Condensate Polisher

Large power generation plants often use condensate polishers to further remove impurities from the condensate flow from the turbine generators. University systems employing extraction steam export systems must cope with the return of condensate from remote building systems and significant lengths of distribution piping, which all add to the impurities of the returning condensate. For these systems, condensate polishers are generally used in the campus condensate return system before the reintroduction of this flow into the boiler. Most condensate polisher systems incorporate a mixed bed design with ion-exchanging cationic and anionic resins in a deep bed configuration. Bed depths vary from two to six feet. Condensate polishers can effectively control contaminants such as iron, copper, sodium, chloride, silica, calcium, and magnesium to significantly improve the quality of water in the heating plant cycle.

Zeolite Softener

Potable water does not provide a satisfactory water for use in the boiler itself because of the solids dissolved in the water. Zeolite softeners may be used to soften the water source by removing scale-forming solids. A sodium zeolite system softens hard water by exchanging the calcium and magnesium salts for various soluble sodium salts. This softener consists of a vessel containing a bed of zeolite resin which attracts the hardness from the water as the water percolates downward. When the electrolytic charge is exhausted in the bed, the bed is regenerated. This is accomplished by rinsing the resin bed with a solution of ordinary salt, which is rinsed out, rendering the softener ready for another cycle of operation. This system of softening is relatively simple and economical to operate since ordinary salt is used as the regenerate material. One drawback is that this method of softening does produce water with a high alkaline content that must be corrected chemically.

Demineralizer

Demineralizers also may be used to soften water for the boiler. In the demineralizing process, the water is passed through both cation and anion exchange resins to remove the scale-forming impurities. These positive- and negative-charged ion beds trap the impurities, allowing only pure water to leave the system. When regeneration of the resin bed is required, the cationic resin is regenerated by washing with an acid solution and the anionic resin is washed with a caustic solution. Demineralizers are available in two configurations, mixed bed and dual train. In the mixed bed system, the anion and cation exchange resins are contained in one unit. In the dual train system, separate beds exist for the anion and cation resins. The main advantage of demineralization is its ability to produce better quality water than can be obtained by any other method. The initial capital cost is significantly higher than for other methods.

Reverse Osmosis

Reverse osmosis is another method available to pretreat boiler water and remove impurities. This process utilizes a membrane which is selectively semipermeable (open to the passage of fluids). This membrane allows only the desired ions to pass between two chambers. High internal operating pressures of 300 to 900 psi overcome osmotic pressure and concentrate dissolved solids on one side of the membrane, thus filtering out impurities. This type of system generally is more costly to operate and install than a comparable demineralizer. However, chemicals are not required and the generation of waste products is lessened using reverse osmosis as compared to demineralizers.

26.13 CONTROL SYSTEMS

Combustion controls have two purposes: to adjust the fuel supply in order to maintain the required steam flow or pressure under varying loads, and to maintain the optimum ratio of combustion air to fuel. There are three basic control systems, each with variations: on-off, positioning, and metering.

On-Off Control System

On-off control is regulated by a steam pressure-actuated switch. When the pressure drops to a preset level, fuel flow is increased and operation continues at a constant firing rate until the pressure rises to a preset level. This type of control generally is used only for fire tube and very small water tube boilers.

Positioning System

Positioning controls also respond to steam pressure. In this system, however, the controller responds to changes in the steam drum or header pressure by positioning fuel supply valves and forced draft dampers. This type of control is used on single burner boilers and is restricted to systems that burn one fuel at a time. There are three types of positioning controls:

- Fixed positioning. A single actuator moves both the fuel and air controls to preset positions through mechanical linkages. This system cannot compensate for changes in fuel or air density, or fuel supply pressure, so controls are normally set for high excess air to guard against dropping below the minimum excess air requirements.
- Parallel positioning with operator trim. Pneumatic or electronic positioning of the fuel and air supply controls are actuated by a single pressure controller. A combustion guide is required to enable the operator to position the excess air flow. This is the most widely used type of combustion control for units below 100,000 pounds per hour.
- Pressure ratio. A parallel pneumatic or electronic system is used with the wind-box-to-furnace/burner pressure ratio to trim the fuel flow and airflow. Manual controls to change both

the ratio of pressure and excess airflow are normally provided, with a combustion guide.

Metering System

In a metering system, the fuel flow and airflow are metered and the fuel supply and air supply controls are modulated in accordance with measured flows. This kind of combustion control is restricted to fuels that can be accurately metered. A refinement of this system is cross-limited metering, which limits the change in fuel flow through control logic to available airflow at all items. The airflow also is tied to fuel flow. The system can be further refined by using a continuously monitored flue gas analysis and by trimming the fuel-to-air ratio based on the oxygen content. This compensates for variations in fuel heating values and combustion air conditions.

Most boilers at this time are controlled by microprocessors. Software-based systems offer controls that are flexible, responsive, dynamic, and easily tuned to match the system requirements. However, there also is a tendency to incorporate more complex control strategies requiring technical personnel on-site for design and maintenance of the system. The rewards often are seen in higher system efficiencies and fewer forced outages. Even an older boiler often can be made 1 or 2 percent more efficient by retrofitting a microprocessor-type control system for the pneumatic or analog-type controls already in place. Cost recovery can occur quickly when facility fuel budgets range in the millions of dollars.

ADDITIONAL RESOURCES

Combustion-Fossil Power Systems, Combustion Engineering, third edition. Rand McNally, 1981.

NALCO Chemical Company. *The NALCO Water Handbook*. New York: McGraw-Hill, 1979).

Resource, Inc. *Power Plant Steam and Mechanical Fundamentals*. Commonwealth Edison Company, 1976.

Steam/Its Generation and Use, 38th edition. Babcock & Wilcox, 1972.

"Steam Generation, a Power Special Report." *Power Magazine*.

CHAPTER 27

Central Chiller Plants

Thomas G. Atlee
Program Manager
Lockwood, Andrews, & Newnam, Inc.

27.1 ADVANTAGES OF CENTRAL PLANTS

The merits of a central chilling plant over independent air conditioning systems at each building are fairly well established and accepted. Factors favoring the central system include: 1) operating economies associated with high efficiency equipment, 2) localized operation with fewer operating personnel, 3) quality and timely maintenance due to concentration of major equipment and convenience to shop area and parts storage, and 4) centralized location of cooling towers to reduce objections to noise and drift. The central chiller plant can be a separate facility; however, it is usually located with the central heating plant, especially if some of the chillers are steam driven. A central plant consolidates a major portion of the utility consumption in one area where it can be monitored for the most efficient utilization.

Central chiller plants can take advantage of the diversity factor in the sizing of equipment and operation of the plant. The diversity factor is defined as the demand in tons upon the central plant divided by the total load of the connected buildings. The diversity exists because the peak demand for all buildings does not occur at the same time. Factors that affect diversity include solar loads, which change each hour of the day; thermal storage, which is related to the materials of construction; and building usage, which causes the peak cooling demand to occur at different times. For example, dormitories may have reduced loads during the day and peak loads in the evening; libraries and laboratories can have substantial loads during the day and may extend into the evening hours; classrooms and administrative areas usually have peak demands during the day, but auditoriums and athletic facilities have peak demands associated with usage. The diversity factor will vary from campus to campus, and ranges from 0.60 to 0.80.

Central Plant System Criteria

The central chilling plant system criteria is a set of requirements that provide guidelines for the design and operation of the plant equipment and the thermal systems. The central chilling plant represents only part of the overall chilled water system and the system criteria should not be limited to this facility alone. Other equally important parts include the primary distribution system and the secondary distribution system associated with each connected load. A single philosophy must exist for the design and operation of the entire chilled water system if the individual parts are to function correctly and economically. Many central plant operating problems and difficulties can be traced to a common cause; the primary chilled water system is not compatible with the secondary chilled water system.

The system criteria is a tool to be used in the selection of equipment, and to develop operating procedures. The criteria must be established when the design of the central chilling plant is started and it must create a compatible design between the plant, distribution system, and the buildings served. The requirements established by the system criteria must be considered each time the plant is expanded or a new building or facility is added. The combined characteristics of all the building air-side systems is one of the major factors in developing the system criteria. These same characteristics will be a determinant of plant economics. Air side systems must not be operated far from their design conditions if economical and quality air conditioning is to be provided.

Primary Distribution Systems

A central chilling plant system requires supply and return piping to deliver chilled water to the various buildings. This is the primary distribution system and it may be an intricate network of pipes with hydraulic loops and cross connections serving many buildings or loads. A large network distribution system can also be served by several plants simultaneously. The piping system may be direct-buried in the earth, located in a shallow trench, or it may be routed in a utility tunnel. The materials of construction will depend to a large degree on the environment in which the piping will be located. These and other factors concerning the distribution system are discussed in more detail in Chapter 29, Heating and Cooling Media Distribution.

The primary distribution system must be designed as carefully as any part of the chilled water system. Size and location of the pipes should be determined from a thermal utility master plan. Pipes should be sized and located to accommodate future buildings, if applicable. Pumping cost must also be considered. The pipe cost is a one time item, while pumping costs are continuing, so there must be an optimum balance between the two in design.

Total, Firm, and Reserve Capacity

Central chilling plants usually have multiple water chilling units, cooling towers, pumps, boilers, and associated equipment. From time to time each item of equipment will be out of service for cleaning, maintenance, or repairs. Cleaning and maintenance usually require a scheduled outage for a relatively short period of time. On the other hand, repairs to a major item of equipment may not be scheduled. Planned outages are normally scheduled during periods of minimum cooling loads.

The total capacity of a central plant is the sum of the capacities for all units installed. But the "firm" capacity is the sum of all units installed less the capacity of the largest unit. This assumes that all units are operational and can produce their rated capacity; otherwise only the units actually operational at the time should be used to determine plant capacity.

The firm capacity is the maximum capacity that the plant can be expected to produce on a continuous basis. As buildings and new loads are added to the system, reserve capacity is used and expansion of the plant will eventually be required. Reserve capacity is any plant tonnage above the maximum system demand up to the firm capacity.

Flow Versus ΔT

A common term used to express the flow of chilled water in a system is gallons per minute per ton (GPM/TON), and this value is related to the differential temperature (ΔT) between the supply and the return. The relationship is given by the formula GPM/TON = 24/ΔT. For example: A central chiller plant designed for a 16 degree ΔT will have a flow rate of 1.5 GPM/TON. [24/16 = 1.5 GPM/TON]

In systems having a large number of three-way valves and if the secondary bypass is not controlling the return water temperature, the chilled water temperature is allowed to run wild. As the load drops off and the three-way valves bypass more primary water, the return temperature will drop. It is possible for the ΔT to drop to 8°F or less. An eight degree ΔT has a circulation rate of 3 GPM/TON, which is twice the value for which the chiller was designed. For this reason it is sometimes necessary to put two or more chillers on line during the cooler months, not to satisfy the cooling load but to meet the high campus flow demand.

27.2 SYSTEM COMPONENTS

Water Chilling Equipment

The three types of chillers most commonly used in central chiller plants today are centrifugal, reciprocating, and absorption.

Centrifugal Chillers

Centrifugal chillers are by far the most widely used. They are available in a wide range of sizes—from about 90 through 10,000 tons. They are simple to operate, reliable, compact, relatively quiet, low vibration, and designed for long life with low maintenance. Centrifugal chillers can be selected for hermetic or open type drives. Hermetic units use a hermetic compressor with an electric motor totally enclosed in a refrigerant atmosphere. The refrigerant provides the cooling for the motor, which can be smaller and less expensive than the open type. However, they consume slightly more power than an identical capacity open drive unit, and in the event of a motor failure the repairs are considerably higher. Open type centrifugal chillers use a compressor driven by a steam turbine, reciprocating engine, or an electric motor. The drive type is discussed in more detail in the section on prime movers.

Reciprocating Chillers

Reciprocating chillers have been included in some central chiller plants, but they are normally too small for this type service. They are available in sizes from 10 tons to 200 tons, so several units must be used together to meet large cooling loads. Reciprocating chillers are generally lower in cost per ton capacity than other types, but they have a shorter life expectancy and maintenance costs are higher. Due to the nature of the design, they tend to vibrate and are noisy.

Absorption Chillers

Absorption chillers are used in many central plant applications. They are available in sizes from 100 through 1,500 tons and are usually operated by low-pressure steam or hot water. Absorbers can be single-effect type, which use about 18 pounds of steam per ton-hr, or they may be double-effect type which use about 12 pounds of steam per ton-hr. The lower shell of an absorption chiller contains the evaporator and absorber and operates under a relatively high vacuum (6 mm of mercury). The low operating pressure within an absorption chiller makes the unit sensitive to condenser water temperature variations. These variations must be limited to about 5°F of design temperature, which requires a control and a bypass valve in the condensing water piping. The higher operating and maintenance costs associated with these chillers, as compared with those of compressor-type units, usually make them uneconomical to use except where electric power is expensive, where fuel costs are low, or in balancing electrical and thermal loads in the case of cogeneration.

The cost of electricity and fuel, and balancing electrical and thermal loads, are the most important factors in selecting the energy source for a water chilling unit or for an entire plant. The relative cost of electricity and fuel can be used to determine which will be the most economical.

There is no assurance that the selections today will be the most economical selections in the future as energy prices change.

Prime Movers

Several different types of prime movers are used to drive centrifugal chillers. Electric motors and steam turbines are the most common, but reciprocating engines and gas turbines have also been used with varying degrees of success. The steam turbine drive is excellent for larger tonnage chillers because it is a smooth rotating power source, available in all horsepower ranges, and can usually match the compressor's design speed without using a speed-increasing gear. Steam turbine drives are sometimes selected to make use of existing boilers in a central heating plant. Using the existing boilers saves on the capital cost, improves the year-round load factor on the steam generating equipment, and takes advantage of possible reductions in off-season fuel rates.

Electric motors are the most common drives on centrifugal chillers, especially with hermetics. But hermetics are available only up to about 1,850 tons, so conventional type motors are used on open drive centrifugal chillers in the larger sizes. Electric motor drives offer several advantages but also have limitations. Synchronous electric motors run at exact speeds—3,600 rpm, 1,800 rpm, 1,200 rpm, 900 rpm, and so on. Induction type motors run at slightly less than synchronous speeds depending on the slip. However, centrifugal compressors operate most efficiently at speeds much higher than the available motor speeds, so it is necessary to provide a speed increasing gear between the motor and the compressor. The speed-increasing gear imposes additional frictional losses and additional equipment that must be maintained. Gear losses may amount to 1 1/2 to 2 percent of the required compressor brake horsepower. It is sometimes possible to eliminate the speed-increasing gear by selecting a two-stage compressor that operates at 3,600 rpm. This speed may be less than optimum for the compressor, but will not result in as much loss as a gear. Also, 3,600 rpm motors in 2,000 and above horsepower sizes are not off-the shelf items; each is custom designed and manufactured to meet the requirements of the application. Another factor to consider is the number of motors in each speed range that are manufactured, because experience plays a large part in reliability. There are considerably more 1,800 rpm motors manufactured than 3,600 rpm motors.

Motors in the large horsepower sizes can be manufactured to operate at practically any voltage. However economics will be a key factor in the selection of the voltage. The voltage is usually related to the horsepower—the higher the horsepower the higher the voltage. Normal voltage ranges are as follows:

Horsepower Range	Voltage
100-500 HP	480-2,400 V
500-5,000 HP	2,400-5,000 V
5,000-10,000 HP	5,000-12,000 V

Existing electrical service must be considered when selecting the voltage for a new large tonnage chiller. It may be necessary to bring in a new feeder or change transformers. In many cases the central chiller plant will be the largest electrical load on campus, and the plant may become the focal point for the incoming utilities.

Chillers can be operated at constant speed by using the inlet guide vanes and hot gas bypass at part load conditions, both of which waste energy. A compressor with a variable speed drive can be operated at its optimum speed for various part-load conditions. Steam turbines can be operated at variable speed by adjusting the governor and the hand wheels on the nozzles. Electric motors can provide variable speeds outputs if equipped with adjustable frequency control. Various designs for this type equipment may exist. One type rectifies commercial three-phase power to DC that is then inverted with a silicon controlled rectifier (SCR) to an adjustable-frequency power supply with a quasi sine wave which can be used to drive induction and synchronous motors over a wide speed range. A similar device uses a combination of a variable frequency thyristor converter and a synchronous motor. This device takes advantage of the reverse voltage (counter EMF) generated by the synchronous motor to switch off the thyristors. The resulting controller requires fewer components than a conventional inverter and is capable of operation at much higher power ratings and voltages. They are available in sizes up to 15,000 horsepower.

Variable speed drives are also possible if the plant has a source of variable frequency power, such as on-site power generation that can be isolated and operated independent of the serving electric utility company. Several large central chiller plants have successfully incorporated this type of variable drive with their cogeneration facility. In one subplant, all power from the 5 mW cogeneration unit is used to drive two 2,500 ton chillers and the associated cooling tower fans, condensing water pumps, and chilled water pumps. There is no connection between the cogeneration unit and the serving utility company so the unit is not limited to operating at synchronous speeds. During the cooler months, when the chillers normally operate at part load, instead of throttling the inlet guide vanes, the speed of the cogeneration unit is reduced and the resulting power frequency power causes the chiller and the associated motor drives to slow down. Chilled water from this plant in winter months has been produced using only 0.41 kW per ton total including all auxiliary equipment.

Heating Equipment

Although heating and steam generating equipment are covered in other chapters, certain aspects are related to the central chiller plant. A central heating plant can serve the campus heating requirements with relatively low temperature/pressure steam or hot water. However, higher temperatures and pressures are required for steam turbines for the chilling units. On the other hand, the lower temperature and pressure may be suitable if single stage absorption chillers are used. Double effect absorption chillers will require steam pressures of 125 psig minimum. Steam turbines can be condensing or non-condensing types and can be selected to operate on saturated steam at a few hundred pounds of pressure or on superheated steam at several thousand pounds of pressure. The most common and economical type for central chiller plants is from 250 psig saturated to about 400 psig with 100 degrees of superheat. Many factors must be evaluated in order to determine the best combination of temperature and pressure for a given installation.

Other options to consider include high temperature, high pressure hot water systems (250°F to 400°F) as well as direct fired absorption chillers. Steam or hot water from heat recovery boilers associated with cogeneration units can have a dramatic impact on both the heating and cooling systems. The campus heating load in the warmer months of the year may be considerably less than the heat recovered from the cogeneration unit, but it may be possible to balance the load by installing absorption chillers or steam turbines to utilize the recovered energy. However, the Federal Energy Regulatory Commission (FERC) has ruled that in order to have a "qualifying facility" the energy recovered from a cogeneration unit must be used in a process or to heat buildings. Therefore heat used in an absorption unit to make chilled water can be counted, but steam used in a steam turbine driving a centrifugal chiller cannot be counted. Having a "qualifying facility" gives the owner certain rights that can be enforced through the FERC, such as standby power and the option to sell excess power to the utility company.

Electric System

The electrical system is discussed here only as it affects the central chiller plant or vice versa. The chiller plant will have a substantial electrical load even with turbine drives or absorption chillers. This is in large part due to all the pumps, fans, and auxiliary equipment of the system.

Dual feeders from the serving electric utility company are common on many campuses. If these feeders are from different utility transmission systems it will provide more flexibility and reliability of the electrical service and therefore improve the overall reliability of the central cooling system. The central plant will require a considerable amount of space for the electrical switchgear due to the number and size of motors served. Transformers will also be required at the plant to serve the lower voltage equipment. Due to the amount of electrical equipment normally associated with the central cooling plant this may be the logical place to locate the incoming feeders, substations, buses, and switchgear to serve the entire campus.

The central chiller plant can also have an impact on the electrical system, depending on the type of equipment selected for the larger horsepower drives. Motors for chillers can be synchronous or induction type. The synchronous motors can be specified with equipment to provide power factor correction.

The electrical system is a critical element of the central chiller plant, requiring comprehensive engineering design. It should be incorporated in the electrical utility master plan with projections for future expansion of the distribution system and the central plant. It should also address on-site power generation (cogeneration and/or emergency power generation).

The central plant provides a convenient place for the electrical switchgear of the plant equipment and the campus distribution switchgear. It is also a good location for metering equipment associated with the monitoring and control of this important utility. Having the primary electrical switchgear in or near the central plant can be even more advantageous if cogeneration equipment is installed. See Chapter 47, Cogeneration.

Cooling Towers

Cooling towers come in many different types and configurations—packaged, field erected, counterflow, crossflow, induced draft, and forced draft. They are a part of every central chiller plant from a few hundred tons to several thousand tons, except where air cooled condensers are used for smaller plants. Another type chiller that does not require a cooling tower is the packaged air cooled water chilling units, which are available in sizes up to about 240 tons. Cooling towers are the most economical method for rejecting heat.

Although available in various types and configurations, the main difference in the larger towers is the materials of construction; metal, wood, ceramic, fiberglass, and plastic.

Metal Towers   Metal towers are assembled at the factory and shipped to the job site, complete and ready for installation. As the name implies, all the major components are constructed of galvanized metal including the enclosure, basin, fill, deck, stack, and fans. This tower is limited to a few hundred tons because of shipping limitations.

Wood Towers   Wood towers are the most common of all towers, because they are economical and easy to fabricate. Wood towers have been the choice for many years. The shortcomings of wood towers have been identified and either corrected or eliminated as much as practical and economical. Redwood was the choice material for many years for the structure, fill, decks, casing, and basin. Other pressure-treated woods have proved to be economical substitutes in some cases. Asbestos cement siding was used for the outer casing material and the louvers on wood towers for many years, but corrugated fiberglass panels are now used. Fiberglass stacks have become standard on most wood towers because they are durable, lightweight, and can be fabricated into a smooth venturi shape. A properly designed stack can reduce the fan horsepower if it has a venturi shape and is tall enough (12 to 16 feet). The basin of wood towers can be constructed of wood or concrete. If a tower is to be located on the roof of a building, the basin may need be wood if there are weight limitations. If the tower is located on the ground, a concrete basin and sump may be the best choice since the concrete is practically maintenance free. Also, the basin depth and therefore the volume of water is unlimited with a concrete basin, whereas there are practical limitations on the size and volume of a wood basin.

Ceramic Towers   Ceramic refers to the material used for the fill, which is a refractory clay tile with multiple openings. The tiles are stacked several layers deep with the openings of the tile in the vertical direction so that water can fall down through the opening and air can be drawn up through them. This gives good contact between the water and air, a primary objective in any cooling tower. The tile fill is supported on concrete columns and beams and the enclosure, deck, and basin are all constructed of concrete. The stacks may be concrete or fiberglass. Except for the mechanical and electrical equipment (fans, gears, motors, and distribution nozzles), there is little that can fail or deteriorate on a ceramic cooling tower. The advantages of a ceramic cooling tower are its long life, no loss of capacity due to fill sagging or failure, it is fireproof, and it can be made aesthetically pleasing. The main disadvantage is the high initial cost. Hybrid designs have evolved that try to take advantage of each type. One design uses the ceramic tile fill in a factory fabricated fiberglass enclosure. This greatly improves the first cost of the ceramic type cooling tower, but there is not enough history on these units to predict the possible maintenance costs. Another hybrid is a tower with concrete basin, enclosure, and fan deck with PVC film fill and fiberglass stacks. Compared with the wood tower this design improves the life and the looks while decreasing the fire hazard all at a reasonable increase in first cost. PVC will burn or melt only if it is held in contact with a flame. It does not support combustion and will extinguish itself when the flame is removed.

Cooling Tower Capacity   Deciding on the design of a cooling tower for performance is based on the amount of heat to be rejected, the flow of water, the temperature in, and the desired temperature out. The tower must be guaranteed to satisfy these requirements under the worst atmospheric conditions normally expected (the design conditions). The tower is also expected to operate satisfactorily during winter, rain storms, temperature inversions, high winds regardless of wind direction, walls or buildings that block the flow of air, regardless of the water treatment or lack thereof, and any other adverse condition including little or no maintenance. Towers are also expected to operate efficiently without causing any problems such as drift. If the central chiller plant is to operate year round, the cooling towers must be equipped with equipment to facilitate operation at part load conditions. This includes two speed motors or variable speed for the fans plus a bypass with modulating value so that all or part of the return condensing water can be bypassed directly to the basin in order to control the temperature of the supply water.

Cooling Tower Piping   The cooling tower piping consists of condensing water return piping that will distribute water to the hot water basins near the fan deck level (crossflow type tower) or to a distribution spray header located inside the tower above the fill (counterflow type tower). Balancing valves are required to adjust the distribution of the water over the fill. The condensing water supply piping starts on the suction side of the condensing water pumps and may be a pipe connection through the wall of the sump preferably with a suction bell located near the floor of the sump. If the pump is a vertical turbine type the suction bell will be mounted directly to the bottom of the pump. Other piping associated with the cooling tower is the water make-up line with a float operate valve and the overflow pipe which limits the maximum elevation of the water in the tower. The overflow line ties directly into the drain system and each tower cell should have a drain valve so that each can be drained and cleaned independent of the other cells. Other lines would possibly include chemical feed lines, sample lines, and fire protection piping. Any small diameter lines or lines with stagnant water should be protected from freezing by heat tracing or draining during winter months.

Cooling Tower Screens   Cooling tower screens are required to keep paper, leaves, feathers, rags, and other debris out of the condensing water system. On a wooden basin the screen is located over the sump, which is mounted on the bottom of the basin. Access to the screen is through a door in the tower casing. Towers with concrete basins may have dual screens located between the tower basin and the sump. Most of the debris will collect on the first screen, which is the first to pull when cleaning. The second screen remains in place to catch any debris in the water while the first screen is out. Screens with small openings require more cleaning but they keep the water cleaner. Screens with larger openings may let too much solid matter pass into the circulating system. The opening should always be smaller than the diameter of the tubes in the chiller condenser. If the chiller has 3/4-inch tubes then use 1/2-inch or smaller openings for the screens. The overall size of the screens will determine the velocity through them. The recommendations of the Hydraulic Institute call for a velocity of one foot per minute (1 ft/min) or less through the screen.

Pumps

The major pumps associated with the central chiller plant are the chilled water and condensing water pumps. Other pumps that may be required include condensate return pumps, in the event that steam turbine drives are used. Booster pumps will be required for the chilled water system if the plant water pressure is below the system pressure. Chilled water pumps may be an end section type, horizontal double section type, or vertical turbine type. The type selected will be influenced by the flow, head, efficiency, and space availability.

Variable speed motors should be considered for the chilled water system. They allow the flow through the plant to be adjusted to the flow to the system, and improve the overall operating economics. This could be accomplished with variable frequency type drives or eddy current type couplings.

Maintenance must be considered in designing pump insulation. It will be necessary to remove the insulation to work on the pump. The insulation should be in two or more pieces that can be removed and reinstalled without damage.

Pump seals are mechanical or packing gland type. Mechanical seals are good provided the water is clean and the water treatment is compatible with the seal material. Replacing a mechanical seal is more difficult and time consuming than repacking the gland type seal. The packing gland seals depend on friction between the shaft and the packing material to prevent leakage. To prevent damage to the shaft, the packing should not be too tight. It should allow one or two drops of water to leak each minute which will provide cooling and lubrication to the shaft at this point.

Condensing water pumps can be end suction, horizontal double suction, or vertical turbine type. If horizontal double suction type or end section pumps are used, the cooling tower basin must be at an elevation sufficient to provide a positive head on the suction side of the pumps. Vertical turbine pumps tend to be the preferred type for the larger tonnage cooling towers. The vertical turbine type pumps allow most of the basin to be located below grade, which in turn improves accessibility to the pump motors and cooling tower screens. The sump pits associated with the vertical turbine pumps should be designed in strict accordance with the recommendations of the Hydraulic Institute. If end suction or horizontal double suction pumps are selected for the condensing water system it will be mandatory to elevate the cooling tower basin or locate the pumps in a pit in order to provide sufficient head to the suction of the pumps. Since the head is so critical it is not advisable to use Y-type strainers on the suction of these pumps. It is best to use a rough screen inside the tower basin and then pump through a Y-type strainer to remove the small debris.

Controls and Instrumentation

Operating and safety controls are furnished as part of the chiller package. Instrumentation such as pressure gauges, thermometers, and flow measuring devices must be specified where they are required or desired. Pressure gauges should be provided on the inlet and outlet of all vessels, pumps, and strainers. Thermometers with wells should be provided at the inlet and outlet of all equipment where a change in temperature will take place. Flow measuring devices should be installed in chilled water, condensing water, steam lines, and in the make up water line to the cooling tower. The flow meters must have sufficient straight runs of pipe upstream and downstream of the meters to ensure meter accuracy.

Chillers with electric drives must have sufficient instrumentation for measuring the amount of electricity consumed by the unit. This will be necessary in order to check the performance of the chiller and to monitor its efficiency. Consideration should also be given for any additional points that may be required for existing or future data processing systems.

Pumpout and Storage Units

The pumpout unit is used to transfer refrigerant between the chiller and the storage tank. It can be skid or tank mounted. It is usually furnished by the chiller manufacturer as part of the chiller package. A large plant usually has one pumpout and storage unit system to serve all chillers that have the same refrigerant. The storage tank is sized for 200 or 300 percent of the capacity of the largest chiller. This gives volume to keep some refrigerant on hand yet have space to put a charge in when it is necessary to remove the refrigerant from the chiller. The tank has an additional space to accommodate expansion of the stored refrigerant. Otherwise, an overfilled tank may vent excess refrigerant to the atmosphere through its relief valves. All relief valves and rupture disks on a pumpout and storage system must be vented to the outside.

Auxiliary Equipment

In addition to the major items of equipment, central chiller plants include other items that are classified as auxiliary equipment. Plants have two water systems that require conditioning and treatment. Condensing water systems have equipment to monitor the quality of the water, add chemicals, maintain desired levels of dissolved solids, and add makeup water to offset evaporation, leakage, and blowdown. Additional equipment may include sidestream filters or separators. The chilled water system will have pot feeders for adding corrosion inhibitors to the system, a coupon station for measuring the effectiveness of the inhibitor, and possibly a filtering systems to remove solids such as dirt, rust, and debris from the water. These items of auxiliary equipment are discussed in more detail in the energy conservation section.

A feature that may be included in the chiller plant is thermal storage. Several types have been developed—one uses one or more tanks to store large volumes of chilled water, and another type stores ice which is blended with the chilled water as it is needed.

Expansion tanks on the chilled water system are required to accommodate the expansion and contraction associated with any thermal liquid system and to provide a point of constant pressure in the system. This is also the place to maintain static pressure on the system and introduce makeup to the system. A source of compressed air or nitrogen is required if the tank is to maintain a high static pressure. The tank should be equipped with automated controls to maintain water makeup and air pressure in the correct proportions. Some expansion tanks are built with bladders to isolate the air from the liquid. If the system is designed to operate at a constant pressure, the makeup booster pumps should be provided with a small hydropneumatic tank to allow the pump to cycle. Otherwise the pump must run continuously and provision must be made to prevent the pumps overheating. This can be accomplished with a small bleed valve or a drain with a small fixed orifice. On-line tube cleaning systems for chillers may also be considered auxiliary equipment.

27.3 DESIGN

Discussion of the design of the chiller plant refers to the total plant facility, its operations, and its interface with other buildings on campus. The term "design" is also used to describe the layout of equipment, the construction features of the plant building, thermal/hydraulic piping systems, electrical systems, control systems, manufacturing details on items of equipment, the HVAC system, plumbing system and several other auxiliary and support systems.

The design of the central plant, or any thermal utility facility, should be the final product of much thought and planning. This normally includes conceptional ideas, evaluation of many scenarios, visualizing the entire facility, sketches, modeling, and perhaps some trial and error effort to work out the conflicts. The design must incorporate requirements, recommendations, and appropriate provisions of various codes, ordinances, and standards such as the National Electric Code, OSHA, ASME, EPA, FERC, fire and health codes, water quality, air quality, safety, building codes, industry standards, and requirements of the serving utility companies. The design requires an investigation of all details and coordination of the many ideas and requirements into an optimum end product or facility. A good design will make provisions for future expansion and anticipate the need to be flexible in order to take advantage of new ideas, equipment, and technology. A design that considers only present needs and technologies probably will not be a cost-effective facility in the future.

During the development of the design for a central chiller plant the primary concern is the process, equipment layout, access for maintenance, and future expansions. A plant building should not be designed until the layout of the equipment and all support systems are well established. The building is an enclosure to protect the water chilling equipment and should be a functional part of the overall cooling facility, not the dominant factor. The process should not be changed to accommodate the size or restrictions imposed by the building. The site or location for the plant is a similar situation. If major equipment layout changes are required to site-adapt a plant to a particular location, then perhaps it is the wrong site.

Equipment Criteria and Specifications

Major items of equipment such as chillers, pumps, and cooling towers should not be purchased without a set of detailed specifications on the items being purchased. These specifications establish the minimum quality and the maximum energy consumption that will be acceptable for each item. The equipment should not be accepted until it is tested to prove compliance for capacity and performance. Sample chiller test requirements of purchase specifications are shown in Appendix 27-A. The cooling tower and pumps should also be tested as a condition for acceptance. The specifications should require a CTI (Cooling Tower Institute) test and certification of capacity after the tower is installed and made operational. The pumps can be tested by an independent hydraulic lab for compliance with the design requirements.

Piping Systems

The major considerations in the design of the piping systems are pressure and temperature within the system, velocities in the pipes, pipe materials and its compatibility with the contents, expansion and contraction, supports, and insulation. The most common piping material and method of fabrication for central chiller is standard weight, black steel pipe with welded fittings. Methods used to join the pipe include welding and grooved pipe with bolted couplings. The method selected is usually a personal preference by the owner, the engineer, or perhaps the contractor if both methods are allowed. Smaller size piping systems, 20 inch and under, use forged steel welding fittings. Forged or prefabricated fittings are not available in the larger sizes, but must be designed for fabrication in accordance with the ASME codes.

The velocity of the fluid in the pipe is directly related to the pressure loss in the system; the higher the velocity, the higher the losses. It is therefore inversely proportional to the pipe size—the smaller the pipe the higher the velocity for a given flow. Smaller pipes equate to lower first cost but the higher losses mean higher pumping cost in perpetuity.

Expansion and contraction does not present much of a problem in chilled water systems because the ΔTs are relatively low, but it cannot be ignored. Pressure relief valves should be provided in sections of chilled water lines that can be completely isolated by tight seating valves.

Insulation

Thermal insulation with vapor barrier are required on chiller evaporators, refrigerant suction lines, compressors, expansion tanks, chilled water supply and return lines in the plant, and any other equipment connected to the chilled water system that is subject to sweating. The vapor barrier should be sealed at regular intervals along the pipe so that in case of a leak or damaged vapor seal, the travel of the moisture will be limited.

Chillers, heat exchangers, and tanks should be insulated with material such as fiberglass or closed-cell foam rubber sheet insulation. Aluminum jacketing is the preferred finish for all low temperature insulated surfaces in the plant. Removable heads on chillers and heat exchangers should be insulated with covers that are easily removed to allow access for inspection, cleaning, and dismantling.

All low temperature insulated piping systems should have insulation at each hanger, support, and anchor. The insulation should also be protected with shields of galvanized metal extending not less than four inches on either side of the support bearing area and it should cover at least half of the pipe circumference. Preinsulated steel pipe is a popular material and minimizes field insulation labor.

Acoustical insulation is used to reduce the noise level on certain items in the central plant, such as chiller condensers and compressor discharge piping. Alternate layers of insulation and sheet lead, each sealed air tight, is used as a sound barrier on noise producing equipment. An aluminum jacket is a recommended finish and will protect the acoustical insulation.

Plant Cooling/Dehumidification

Air conditioning in a central chiller plant has been largely limited to the office, control room, and perhaps the electrical switchgear area, with the balance of the plant cooled by ventilation.

Cooling and dehumidifying of the central chiller plant should be considered for plants located in areas of high humidity or with electric motor driven chillers. Air conditioned plants are easy to keep clean, have better security, reduce maintenance on electrical gear, extend equipment life, and create better working conditions. Although it is generally not practical to air condition plants that have chillers and boilers in the same space, spot cooling may be an option.

Vibration

Practically every machine with rotating parts is susceptible to vibration. An unbalanced rotor is the most common cause of vibration and can result in noise, gear and bearing wear, mechanical fatigue, power loss, and possibly machine failure. Vibration can be either a cause of trouble, the result of trouble, a symptom of trouble, or any combination. Monitoring the vibration levels helps determine the time to overhaul a machine. This allows for scheduling the repairs into the regular maintenance program.

A problem with vibration monitoring is selecting the parameter to use for the vibration measurements: displacement, velocity, or acceleration. Vibration can be measured in terms of any one of these three, but each has a unique feature and application. Displacement measurements can be used on low-speed equipment such as cooling tower fans, but is inadequate for a variable-speed gas turbine. Acceleration may be the best choice to monitor antifriction bearings, but would not be satisfactory for a heavy-cased compressor with sleeve bearings. The selection of the proper analytical equipment requires technical expertise. It is important to realize its potential and include it in the preventive maintenance program.

27.4 OPERATIONS AND MAINTENANCE

General

A central chiller plant represents high capital costs and continuous high operating costs. Maintaining the equipment in good working order, and with proper controls and adjustments for optimum energy efficiency, takes on great importance. In the following paragraphs, certain operations and maintenance considerations unique to central chiller plants are discussed.

Maintenance

Performance Checks   All equipment in the plant should be checked from time to time to be sure that it is operating efficiently. This is vitally important on the larger items of equipment, such as chillers that use the largest portion of energy. A unit that has scaled-up heat exchangers, improper refrigerant charge, bad seals, worn parts, or that is dirty will consume more energy than a similar unit that is well maintained. The energy input divided by the output (kW/ton or lbs steam/ton) is a convenient yardstick on performance. This should be calculated continuously. If the values begin to change the cause should be determined and corrected. A heat balance should periodically be made on all major equipment.

Data Logging   The importance of keeping records on equipment is well accepted. For many years the history of the performance of equipment was limited to logs that were filled out by the operators plus utility receipts. Many plants now have computer based data logging systems. They can log all data monitored on any time interval, and can provide operating profiles on an hourly, daily, weekly, monthly, or yearly basis. They can monitor performance continuously and sound an alarm if allowable limits are exceeded. Computer systems can also include a preventive maintenance program that can provide a complete history on the past and present condition of each item of equipment.

Water Conditioning and Treatment   Chilled water and condensing water systems are subject to solids build-up, which reduce the efficiency of the heat exchange equipment. The chilled water system is contaminated to some degree each time a new building is added to the system or the distribution piping is modified. The degree of contamination depends upon the condition of the new pipe installed and the thoroughness of the flushing and cleaning prior to connecting the system. The condensing water system is contaminated continually because it is an open system. The condensing water system picks up dust, leaves, paper, feathers, and similar items that must be removed from the water. Cooling towers are usually equipped with screens ahead of the pumps to remove the large items, but the smaller particles pass through and may settle out in areas of low velocity in the system. The most effective cleaning systems use either filters, fine screens, or separators. These cleaning systems tend to have relatively high pressure drops so a side stream operation will be more economical and should provide satisfactory results.

Chemical treatment of the chilled water system usually includes the addition of a corrosion inhibitor. The system is equipped with a feeder for introducing the chemicals, plus monitoring of its effectiveness. The corrosion inhibitor protects the piping from rusting and pitting and prevents the general deterioration of the piping system. This conserves energy by preserving the integrity of the heat exchange surfaces, and prevents an increase in pumping head due to system deterioration.

The condensing water system is an open circulating system and is subject to problems of scale, corrosion, slime, and algae. As water is evaporated in the cooling tower the dissolved solids will be concentrated in the remaining water. If the concentration is allowed to build up, the solubility of various salts will be exceeded and scale will form on the hotter surfaces, such as condenser tubes. This can be controlled by blowdown or bleed-off in some cases, but it may be necessary to feed sulfuric acid for pH control in addition to the blowdown if the water is extremely hard and high in alkalinity.

Water that is recirculated through a cooling tower is saturated with oxygen and therefore corrosive. Chromate-based corrosion inhibitors are the most effective chemical treatment available but are being phased out due to environmental considerations. Where chromates cannot be used, nitrite, polyphosphate, zinc, silicate, or an organic-based treatment may be used.

Open recirculating cooling water systems provide optimum conditions for microbial growth and these microorganisms can adversely affect the efficiencies of the operation by sheer numbers, metabolic waste products generated, or deposits created. Microbiological treatment programs use oxidizing and non-oxidizing biocides including chlorine, hypochlorites, organic chlorine donors, or bromine compounds. Chlorine gas is very effective but must be used carefully because excessive chlorine will increase corrosion and adversely affect tower wood.

The water treatment program for any central chiller plant should be formulated by water treatment professionals. Consulting services are generally necessary to supervise the treatment program and to monitor its efficiencies through laboratory analysis.

Some plants have tried to reduce their expenses by cutting back or eliminating the chemical for water treatment, and have caused irreversible damage to their systems. Occasionally a new nonchemical device appears on the market with claims for scale and corrosion control in cooling and boiler systems. These nonchemical devices may be based on mechanical, electrical, magnetic, electrostatic, or ultrasonic principles. If a nonchemical water conditioning device is being considered, it should be thoroughly investigated. Several successful applications on similar facilities should be inspected and evaluated.

Energy Conservation

Conversion and Modifications   There may be enough change in the prices of electricity and fuel to make it economical to change the driver on an existing chiller—for example, to replace a steam turbine on a centrifugal chiller with an electric motor. This is also the time to review the efficiency of the chiller to see if it can be improved. A chiller can be derated, from 4,000 tons to 3,000 tons or perhaps even to 2,000 tons, which will lower the horsepower requirement and result in a good kW/ton operating factor. Changing the drive line and derating the unit requires assistance from the original manufacturer to determine the best speed, revised capacity, and other modifications that will result in an optimum power requirement. This method of energy conservation is viable only if the plant can afford to give up some of the installed capacity.

Trying to maintain a good plant efficiency when the ΔT begins to drop is usually a losing battle. A low ΔT may require two or more chillers be on the line, each operating at 50 percent load or less, just to satisfy the flow requirements in the system. Again this is because the plant has no control over the return water temperature. Plants that regularly experience this problem should consider a chiller piping modification that will convert the chiller evaporator from a two-pass arrangement to a single-pass. This will allow the chiller to process twice the amount of water when the ΔT is half the design ΔT. For example, a 2,000 ton chiller, 12 degree ΔT, 4,000 GPM with a two-pass evaporator, can process 8,000 GPM when the ΔT is down to 6 degrees by changing over to single-pass. This will save energy because it is more efficient to have one chiller operating near full load than two chiller operating at less than half load. The valves should be equipped with pneumatic operators so they all can be repositioned at the same time.

Tube Cleaning Systems   Automatic on-line tube cleaning systems for chiller condensers are proven energy conservation methods. They are designed to keep the inside (water side) surface of the tubes free of any deposits that would interfere with the heat transfer process. Two types of on-line tube cleaners are available: a brush system and a sponge rubber ball system. In the first type, the flow of water through the condenser is reversed and causes a small brush to be pushed through each tube. A plastic cage at the end of each tube holds the brush until the next cleaning cycle. The second type injects sponge rubber balls into the water entering the condenser. They pass through the tubes and are then collected by a screen located in the leaving water. From the collection screen the balls are routed to a circulating pump that reinjects them into the entering water.

Refrigerant Charge   Each chiller has a recommended charge of refrigerant based on information from the chiller manufacturer. These recommendations are based on maximum summertime cooling. The theoretical charge for other operating conditions will be different. Operating personnel from various parts of the country have reported significant energy savings by reducing the charge during periods of low-load operation.

Thermal Storage   Thermal storage can be an effective means for conserving energy under the right circumstances and conditions. The equipment associated with a thermal storage system, large enough to serve a central chiller plant, is expensive. Therefore, it is necessary to evaluate the economics of this option carefully. Some utility companies are participating in the funding of thermal storage projects and offer reduced rates for night or off-peak consumption. It usually takes both of these factors to make the project viable. Thermal storage systems tend to be large, especially if storing chilled water. An ice storage system requires less space for the storage, but it requires additional cooling capacity to produce the ice.

27.5 SUMMARY

Central chiller plants offer several advantages over building air conditioning systems including operating economies, fewer operating personnel, quality maintenance, consolidation of cooling towers, and improved aesthetics. Central plants can take advantage of the diversity factor.

A central chiller plant is only a single part of the overall chilled water system, which includes the distribution system and the connected loads. Each part of the system has unique features or requirements that must be taken into consideration. These factors are governed by a set of rules or standards known as the system criteria. The criteria establishes the design requirements for the system and it is used to develop the operating procedures. The flow of chilled water is the one item that is common to the chiller plant, the distribution system, and the connected loads. Also the flow rate per ton of cooling is related to the ΔT between the chilled water supply and the chilled water return.

Water chilling units may be centrifugal, reciprocating or absorption types. Centrifugals are the most common type units used in central chiller plants, followed by absorption type. Centrifugal chillers can be hermetic or open-drive type. The open-drive units can be driven by an electric motor or a steam turbine. These units are available in sizes from 90 tons through 10,000 tons. Absorption units are available up to 1,500 tons and operate on low- and medium-pressure steam, plus a direct fired unit that operates on oil or natural gas. Reciprocating chillers are too small for most central plant applications. The cost of electricity or fuel (gas, oil, or coal) at the time of evaluation will be the most important factor to consider when selecting the energy source for a new chilling unit. The relative cost of these energy sources will indicate if steam drive or electric drive is more economical.

It is common for the central chiller plant to be located in or adjacent to the central heating plant. This is even more important if absorption chillers or steam turbine drive chillers are used because it will keep most of the steam generation equipment and steam use equipment in the same area. The electrical system will be similarly affected if the central plant chillers are electric driven. The electrical system should be designed in accordance with an electrical utility master plan that makes provisions for future expansion of the distribution system as well as the central plant.

ADDITIONAL RESOURCES

Leitner, Gordon F. "Some Tube Fouling Investigations and the Effect of Fouling on Chiller Performance." Central Chilled Water and Heating Plant Conference, Syracuse University, 1979.

Lowrance, Randy M. and Billy M. Nichols. "Optimum Chiller Performance Through On-Site Power Generation and Energy Recovery." Central Chilled Water and Heating Plant Conference, Syracuse University, 1979.

Nichols, Billy M. and Stephen M. Redding. "Conversion of Chiller Drives" in *Proceedings of the 67th Annual Meeting of the Association of Physical Plant Administrators of Universities and Colleges.* Washington: APPA, 1980.

Temple, Stuart. Testimony Before the House Appropriations Committee, February 4, 1987, on DOE Funding for DHC Research in FY 88. *District Heating and Cooling,* First Quarter 1987, pp. 10-11.

Westcott, Ralph M. "The Role of Water in Central Plant Chilled Water Systems." Central Chilled Water Conference, Pasadena, November 1973.

Appendix 27-A

Test Requirements of
Chiller Purchase Specifications

a. General: The following tests shall be conducted as a condition of final acceptance of the equipment. All factory and field tests shall be certified by the equipment manufacturer.

b. Leak Tests: The compressor, chiller, and condenser shall be leak tested at the factory in accordance with applicable pressure vessel codes and manufacturer's test standards which shall be submitted for record purposes. The tubes and water boxes shall be hydrostatically tested. Prior to charging the unit, the manufacturer shall evacuate the system as follows. Connect a vacuum pump to the high and low side of system with a wet bulb vacuum indicator. Open all valves in the system and start vacuum pump. Continue to run pump until wet bulb indicator reads 35°F or corresponding pressure of 0.204 absolute pressure inches of mercury. At this point, with pump still running, open the system at point furthest from the pump and admit refrigerant vapor through a drier to break vacuum back to 0 pounds. Then close system and continue to run pump until 32°F reading of wet bulb indicator or corresponding pressure inches of mercury. Wet bulb indicator shall be valved out of system, open only when taking reading. At time of dehydration the ambient temperature should be 60°F or higher.

c. Capacity Tests: All capacity tests shall be performed by a factory based engineer. A representative of the owner will be present during capacity tests. All test instrumentation, excluding flow tubes, shall be furnished by the manufacturer. A complete list of all instruments with record of accuracy and calibration shall be submitted to the engineer for approval prior to testing.

(1) Full Load: Full load test shall be conducted using the method prescribed in Appendix A of the latest revision of ARI Standard 550, with the exception that flow-through vessels will be measured by the use of ventures installed under this contract which have been calibrated at an independent hydraulic testing

lab. Water side of cooler and condenser may be cleaned by the manufacturer at his option, prior to testing. The water side fouling factor during the test will then be assumed to be 0.00025. To correct for fouling, the machine will be operated at a leaving chilled water temperature Y°F lower in the evaporator and X°F higher in condenser than design where X and Y are calculated as follows:

$$X \text{ or } Y = \frac{R}{e^k - 1} - \frac{R}{e^L - 1}$$

$$\text{Where } K \doteq \frac{RA}{(r_{oc} + r_o)Q} \quad \text{and} \quad L = \frac{RA}{r_o Q}$$

Y   = Correction to be subtracted from leaving chilled water temperature, degree F.

X   = Correction to be added to entering condensing water temperature, degree F.

R   = Water temperature range, degree F.

E   = Heat exchange outside surface ft.

Q   = Full load heat rate, Btu/hr.

r_o = Overall heat transfer resistance = $\frac{A}{Q}$ (LMTD).

e   = Natural log.

r_{oc} = Fouling correction (rated fouling - 0.00025) (A_o/A_i)

LMTD = Log mean temperature difference.

A_o/A_i = Ratio of external tube surface to internal surface.

The system when performance tested as above for a one hour period shall produce not less than 95 percent rated capacity and the power input per ton of not more than 105 percent of rated power input per ton when operating at designed conditions. The chilled water flow rate will be adjusted to compensate for a water temperature rise less than design rise to provide design load to the chiller. Anticipated rise is 10°F. Tube velocity shall not exceed 10 FPS during tests.

(2) Part Load: In addition to the full-load test, for information purposes only, one hour part-load tests shall be

conducted in a similar manner for part loads fixed as nearly as possible at 80 percent, 60 percent, and 40 percent full load by manipulation of entering chilled water temperature. The unit shall also be operated at 25 percent of the design capacity to demonstrate that surging does not occur.

(3) Report and Data: At the conclusion of all field tests, the manufacturer will provide two copies of a formal test report to the owner, showing observed data, corrections to conform data to the specified fouling factors in chiller and condensers. The specification should also include a penalty requirement in case the equipment fails to perform as quoted by the manufacturers. The following is a sample clause.

Non-Performance Penalty

In the event the performance tests indicate a deficiency in tonnage or an excess in power requirements, the manufacturer shall make revisions necessary within 60 days after initial tests are complete to bring the unit up to design requirements. The manufacturer shall perform all subsequent retesting. In the event the deficiency cannot be corrected by field modifications, then the following payment for inadequate performance will be imposed:

(1) For each ton below 95 percent design tonnage required by the field test, a sum of one thousand dollars ($1,000) will be deducted from the manufacturer's final payment. If the unit is 10 percent or more below the design tonnage, the entire unit shall be replaced.

(2) For each kilowatt input or fraction thereof above 105 percent of base kilowatt input, a sum of one thousand dollars ($1,000) will be deducted from the manufacturer's final payment. If the unit is 10 percent or more above base kilowatt input, the entire unit will be replaced. Base kilowatt input will be calculated by multiplying test tons by the approval performance data power input ratio (kW/ton at design conditions).

CHAPTER 28

Electrical Distribution Systems

Mohammad H. Qayoumi
Associate Executive Vice President
Facilities Development and Operations
San Jose State University

28.1 INTRODUCTION

Electricity is a unique power source in that it must be used at the instant it is generated—it cannot be stored or stockpiled to meet future requirements. Generating capacities must be able to meet instantaneous peak load requirements. From the time that the first system to sell lighting to New York City was installed in 1882, this has created two problems: how to deal with the voltage drop during transmission over long distances and how to meet widely varying voltage requirements. High-voltage alternating current and the development of the transformer resolved these problems and made possible efficient distribution systems that would meet wide-ranging customer requirements. It also led to the phenomenal growth of the electric industry.

Electric systems in use at the turn of the century were direct current systems. The generation systems were small, the distribution network was limited, and the voltage levels were low. Alternating current distribution systems became operational around 1910, when it was recognized that interconnecting generation sites produced economic benefits. The need for higher voltages became apparent as the size of the electric networks increased in size and power-carrying capability.

Although simple in concept, today's electric distribution equipment and systems are characterized by highly sophisticated technologies that continue to develop rapidly. Since electricity is invisible and its effects are not readily discernible, a mathematical approach is needed to achieve a full understanding of the design and operation of modern distribution systems. This requires highly technical training and is beyond the scope of this manual; the intent here is to describe the physical devices, their purposes, and their relationships in order to provide a more general understanding of the systems.

Presently, the transmission line voltages in the United States are 345,000, 500,000, and 765,000 volts. For distribution systems, utilities use 13,200, 69,000, and 138,000 volts. The primary voltages for medium to large customers are 13,200, 4,160, and 2,400 volts. Three main research projects dealing with higher transmission line voltages:

- 1,000 kV line by Bonneville Power Administration
- 1,000 kV line by EPRI (Electric Power Research Institute) and General Electric Company
- 2,000 kV line by AEP (American Electric Power) and Swedish ASEA (Allamanna Svenska Electriska Atievalaget)

The introduction of high-voltage direct current (HVDC) transmission lines have opened new horizons. The advantage of HVDC over AC for long distances is its lower cost. Presently, the break-even point is 500 miles. For transmission lines longer than 500 miles, HVDC is cheaper than AC, and vice versa. Using HVDC, as the voltage of a cable is doubled the power-carrying capability of the cable is quadrupled. However, as the network voltages increase, so does the cost of design, installation, and maintenance.

The electric distribution systems described here are typical of university-owned facilities at which electricity (whether generated on campus, purchased, or both) is received and further distributed to points on campus. Not covered are situations in which a municipally or commercially owned electric utility furnishes electricity in utilization voltages to individual buildings.

College and university electric distribution systems generally consist of the following: 1) a switching station for receiving the electricity into the university system, 2) switching substations, 3) high-voltage conductor circuits, 4) transformers, and 5) system protection.

28.2 SWITCHING STATIONS

Switching stations perform a number of essential functions. They switch electric power from a larger transmitting system to the college or university system, and switch the electric that is generated on campus into the system. A switching station normally will have more than one feed, or there will be more than one station serving the college or university system, each with a separate feed. The station provides for switching between feeds as necessary.

For greater reliability of service, a two-feed system is recommended. During normal operation each feeder carries about half of the campus load, in which case the tie switch connecting the two feeders remains open. Should a feeder be lost, the feeder switch will open and the tie switch will close, thus minimizing power interruptions. This switching can be manual or automatic. For life-sustaining applications such as medical facilities, a triple feed system is advisable, if economically feasible.

The switching station reduces high-voltage electricity from the incoming system to the voltage that is required by the college or university distribution system. For safety and economy in equipment costs, and due to limited transmission distance, university systems usually operate at lower voltages. The transformers in the switching station reduce incoming voltages to levels at which a university or college system is designed to operate. Normally, the incoming voltage to a university campus is 4,160 V, 13.2 V, or 138 kV depending on the campus size. The campus distribution voltages are 13.2 kV, 4,160 V, and 480 V.

Finally, the switching station houses fault detection and circuit interruption facilities to protect the institution's system from exterior faults and overcurrents.

28.3 SWITCHING SUBSTATIONS

Substations in the distribution system perform functions similar to switching stations. They switch the electric service of the supply mains from the switching station, usually located on the campus periphery, to feeders that supply campus areas. Substations contain sectionalized assemblies of switches, circuit breakers, and metering equipment that control and monitor electrical service to the feeders, which in turn supply individual buildings or groups of buildings. Substations may house transformers for stepping down the power to utilization voltages or to an intermediate voltage. The elements of a substation are discussed next.

28.4 SWITCHES, FUSES, AND CIRCUIT BREAKERS

Switches are circuit-interrupting devices that can make, break, or modify the connection in an electrical network, typically only under normal circuit conditions. Fuses are overcurrent protective devices that interrupt the circuit under fault (abnormal) conditions and usually are employed in combination with switches. Circuit breakers are switching devices that can make, carry, and interrupt the circuit under normal conditions and under special abnormal conditions. Therefore, switches are used only during normal operations, fuses operate only when abnormal conditions occur, and circuit-breakers can perform during either condition. Switches, fuses, and circuit breakers are rated based on the system voltage, continuous current capacity, and short-circuit current interrupting capacity. Figure 28-1 diagrams a switchgear assembly.

Circuit Interruption

Assume that a purely resistive load is connected to a system. The switch is closed, the system is energized. At the time the switch begins to open and the contacts are separated, an arc is drawn between the two contacts, thus generating high temperatures. The high temperatures ionize the medium between the contacts and sustain the arc. As the current waves go through zero, arcing ceases and the voltage across the contacts increases. As the voltage builds up, a restrike occurs due to high electric field and the hot plasma still available from the initial arc. The above process will continue and additional restrikes will occur until the contacts have opened wide enough and the plasma has cooled enough that a restrike cannot occur. This is the time the circuit is interrupted.

Since in a resistive circuit no energy is stored in the system, current and voltage are in-phase. If the contacts can withstand the arcing, the circuit will be eventually interrupted in a few cycles at most. But if there are reactive elements in the system (particularly if there is a capacitor) arc quenching can be a problem.

Two parameters need to be considered when opening a circuit-interrupting device: transient recovery voltage (TRV), and the rate or rise of recovery voltage (RRRV). If a device has higher RRRV than the system, then the dielectric value between the two contacts grows faster than the system and therefore no restrikes can occur. Similarly, if a device has a higher TRV than the system, then the dielectric value between the contacts can withstand the peak system transient voltages and no reignition can occur. Therefore, quenching the arc and avoiding restrikes are key elements in the operation of circuit interrupting devices, and different technologies have been developed to address this problem.

Interrupter Switches

Interrupter switches employ unique techniques for extinguishing the arc by lengthening it, squeezing it, and cooling it. On opening, the switch blade separates from a set of contacts in the arcing chamber and draws an arc, which increases in length as the blade moves. Within the arcing

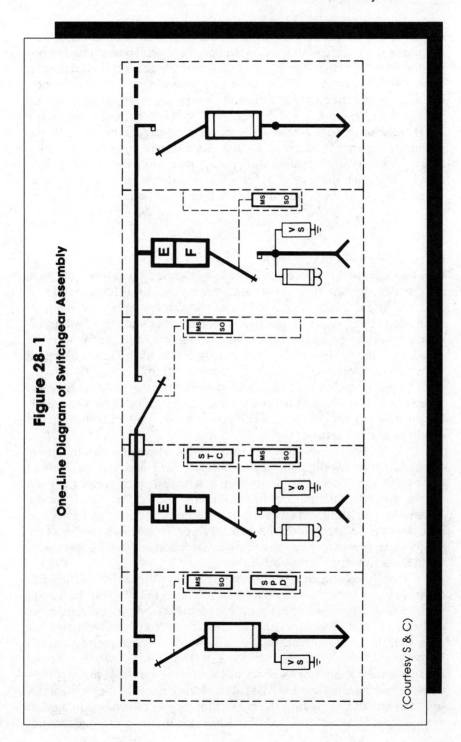

Figure 28-1

One-Line Diagram of Switchgear Assembly

(Courtesy S & C)

chamber, the arc is squeezed by a mechanism that compresses it. Furthermore, the hot arc is allowed to play on the special quenching materials that line the arcing chamber and that generate gases that cool the arc. Ultimately, through the processes of elongation, constriction, and cooling, the arc is extinguished. Interrupter switches typically are used on systems rated from 4.16 kV through 34.5 kV with current-interrupting capabilities of up to 1,200 amps, and with the capability to withstand momentary currents of up to 61,000 amps. Interrupter switches may also have a duty-cycle fault-closing rating, permitting them to close into a fault a specified number of times while remaining operable and capable of carrying and interrupting their rated continuous current.

Fuses

Fuses are overcurrent protective devices designed to interrupt the circuit when a fault condition occurs. There are essentially two types of fuses: solid-material fuses and current-limiting fuses. These fuses employ a fusible element in air surrounded by a solid-material medium that generates deionizing gas from the heat of the arc. Fast, positive fault interruption is achieved by the high-speed elongation of the arc within the fuse tube, and by the efficient deionizing action of the gases liberated from the solid-material arc-extinguishing medium. The arc is lengthened by a spring-charged mechanism within the fuse, which is released when the fusible element melts due to an overcurrent, thereby separating the contacts at high speed. With power fuses, the arc extinguishes at a natural current zero.

Current-limiting fuses employ a fusible element surrounded by sand. An overcurrent melts the fusible element and the arc formed causes the surrounding sand to vitrify, which in turn creates a glass tunnel that confines the arc. Rapid cooling and restriction of the arc increases its resistance. As a result, the current is reduced and forced to an early current zero before its natural zero. This causes high-voltage surges on the system, much like those occurring in any device that uses a vacuum as the interrupting medium.

Power fuses and current-limiting fuses have other significantly different performance characteristics that affect their suitability for circuit protection. Power fuses contain fusible elements that are indestructible and do not age. The time-current characteristics of power fuses are permanently accurate; neither age, vibration, nor extreme heat caused by surges will affect the characteristics of these fuses. There is no need for any "safety zones" or "setback allowance." Because of these performance characteristics, power fuses allow fusing closer to the transformer full-load current, providing the maximum degree of protection against secondary-side faults. This attribute also facilitates coordination with upstream protective devices by allowing the use of lower ampere ratings or settings for these devices, resulting in faster response.

The construction of current-limiting fuses, on the other hand, makes them susceptible to element damage caused by in-rush currents approaching the fuse's minimum melting time-current characteristic curve. Because of this potential for damage, and because of the effects of loading and manufacturing tolerances on the time-current characteristic curve, a safety zone or setback allowance typically is required. This safety zone or setback allowance, combined with the shape of the time-current characteristic curve, results in the selection of a current-limiting fuse ampere rating substantially greater than the transformer full-load current. However, the use of such a high ampere rating is undesirable, since the degree of transformer protection will be reduced, and thus coordination with the upstream protective device may be jeopardized. Also, since high-ampere-rated current-limiting fuses typically require the use of two or three lower-ampere fuses connected in parallel, increased cost and space requirements may result.

Selection of the various types of protective devices and their ratings and settings is a complex matter. However, publications are available that provide complete, simplified procedures for selecting the optimal fuse, taking into consideration all factors associated with the application. Fuses typically are used on systems rated from 4.16 kV through 34.5 kV and are available with continuous current ratings of up to 720 amps and with short-circuit interrupting ratings through 50,000 amps symmetrical.

Air Circuit Breakers

Air breakers use the simplest technique for extinguishing the arc—they lengthen it, and in this way can interrupt up to thirty times their full rated current. Air circuit breakers are of different types. A horn-gap type uses V-shaped arc-interrupting devices. As the contact is opened, the arc is drawn at the bottom of the horn. But due to higher temperatures and electromagnetic forces, it will move up the horn. As the arc becomes larger, it is cooled by convection. Another style is the molded-case circuited breaker, in which the arc is cooled by forcing it to go through narrow insulated fins called arc chutes. Air circuit breakers are used for low-voltage systems (up to 600 V) with current-interrupting capabilities of up to 100,000 amps.

Air-Magnetic Breakers

In an air-magnetic breaker, the magnetic field is applied on the arc, forcing it along a number of insulating fins. As the arc lengthens, it cools down and extinguishes. Two sets of contacts operate in air-magnetic breakers: main and arcing contracts. The arcing contacts carry the current when the main contacts open, so arcing contacts are first-make, last-break contacts.

The arc chute where the arc is extinguished consists of a number of insulated fins. The arcing contacts initiate the arc above the bottom of the slot, which establishes a magnetic field before the arc is drawn. The arc runner configuration moves the arc up the chute. In the meantim the air puffer blows a jet of air across the contact to help move the arc up the arc chute. Air-magnetic breakers are used for up to 4 kV and 15 kV systems with interrupting ratings as high as 1,000 mVA.

Oil Circuit Breakers

In an oil breaker, the arc is drawn under oil. As the arc is established, oil around the contact is vaporized and a large bubble surrounds the arc. Hydrogen comprises roughly two-thirds of this bubble, and since hydrogen is an unfavorable gas for ion-pair production, the arc is cooled and interrupted.

Oil breakers are used outdoors for up to 345 kV. At 34 kV they are capable of interrupting as high as 57,000 amps. Environmental requirements for oil circuit breakers are not as stringent as those for a magnetic air circuit breaker, but oil breakers are prone to fire and explosion.

Vacuum Circuit Breakers

A vacuum is an ideal environment in which to open switch contacts. As the contacts open in a vacuum, an arc is initiated, but due to the high dielectric value of the vacuum, the arcing plasma cannot maintain itself and is extinguished in less than twenty microseconds. The arc is interrupted at first current zero and usually does not reignite. A one-quarter-inch gap is sufficient to interrupt 100 kV. Vacuum breakers do not require a supply of gas or liquid, so they are not fire or explosion hazards. Unlike oil breakers, they can be installed in any environment. They are compact and lightweight, and switch operation is silent and requires relatively small amounts of energy to operate. They can be used outdoors, in manholes, or in metal-clad switchgear for indoor operation (see Figure 28-2).

Sulfur Hexafluoride Circuit Breakers

Sulfur hexafluoride (SF_6) circuit breakers have been in use for the past thirty years (see Figure 28-3). Here, the arc-extinguishing medium is a

Vacuum Interrupter

Vacuum Interrupter Pole Unit

COURTESY WESTINGHOUSE

Figure 28-2
Typical Vacuum Switch

colorless, odorless, nontoxic, noncorrosive, nonflammable, inert gas with an excellent dielectric value. These breakers are available for voltage loads ranging from 13 kV to 765 kV. The remarkable performance of SF_6 as an arcing medium is due to its ability to recover quickly; it is almost 100 times more effective than air in extinguishing the arc.

Sulfur hexafluoride breakers have many advantages. They are lightweight, self-quenching, compact, present no fire hazards, and can be installed in any position. The ambient environment for SF_6 breakers are less restrictive than for other types. The disadvantage in using SF_6 breakers is their high cost. But as the technology improves, they will become more cost-competitive with oil and air-magnetic breakers.

COURTESY G & W

Figure 28-3

SF₆ Switchgear

Metal-Clad and Metal-Enclosed Switchgear

This is a particular type of electrical equipment in which the circuit breakers, disconnecting devices, relays, metering, potential transformers, and current transformers are in separate metal compartments (see Figure 28-4). When the switch assembly is removable, it is called metal-clad; when it is not removable, it is called metal-enclosed. This type of switchgear normally is used for voltages between 13.2 kV and 34.5 kV.

28.5 TRANSFORMERS

Different generation, transmission, and utilization requirements dictate different voltage and current combinations, hence the need for a component capable of changing, or transforming, voltage and current at high power levels in a reliable and effective way. This is the function of the power transformer, an extremely important link between the transmission and usage of electric power. Transformers make it possible to generate energy at any suitable voltage, change it to a much higher voltage for transmission over long distances, and then deliver it to a college or university system at still another voltage.

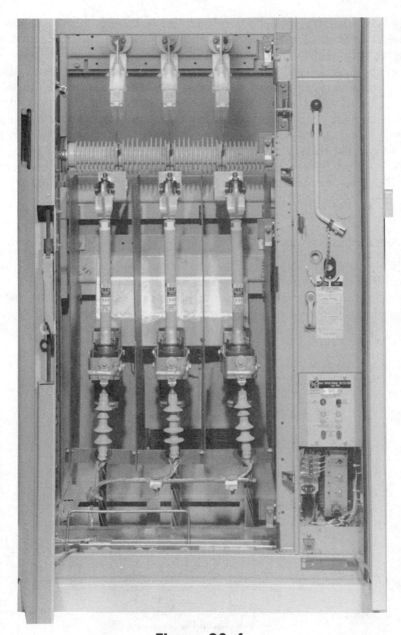

Figure 28-4
Metal-Enclosed Interrupter Switch

All transformers have two basic elements: two or more windings insulated from each other and from the core, and a core that usually is made of thin, insulated, laminated sheet steel. Power transformers used for stepping down the voltages in a distribution system are classified according to type of core construction and type of cooling employed.

Two types of core construction are core and shell. In the core type, the magnetic circuit comes in the form of a single ring with the primary and secondary windings encircling the two legs of the core (see Figure 28-5). In the shell type, the relative positions of the coils and the magnetic circuit are reversed. Here the winding forms a common ring in which two or more magnetic circuits are interlocked (see Figure 28-6). Figure 28-7 is a schematic drawing of a transformer.

Transformer Ratings

Like most other electrical equipment, transformer limitations are thermal in nature. The nameplate data indicates the permissible winding temperature when the transformer is loaded up to its rating. If the windings are subjected to sustained high temperatures, the insulation life will shorten tremendously and could cause a failure.

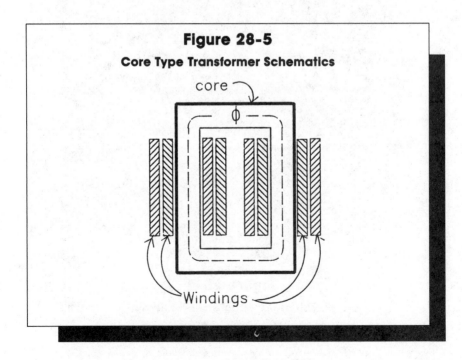

Figure 28-5

Core Type Transformer Schematics

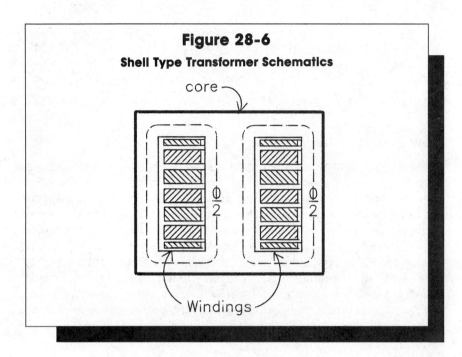

Figure 28-6

Shell Type Transformer Schematics

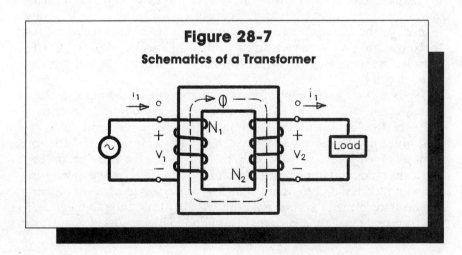

Figure 28-7

Schematics of a Transformer

It is important to note that the temperature rise in a transformer, or any other electrical equipment, is a function of kVA and not the kW. Moreover, the nameplate data is based on 40°C of ambient temperature; if the ambient is higher, the nameplate rating should be derated according to the manufacturer's relevant data.

Transformer Insulation Classes

There are currently four insulation classes with their related NEMA specification and temperature limits. In Class A transformers, provided they are operated at a maximum ambient temperature of 40°C, the temperature rise on the winding will not exceed 55°C. Class B transformers use a higher-temperature insulating material, so at an ambient temperature of 40°C or lower, the temperature rise on the winding will not exceed 80°C. For Class F transformers, at an ambient temperature of up to 40°C, the winding temperature rise will not exceed 115°C. Class H transformers use insulation that can withstand high temperatures and are the most compact transformers. At an ambient temperature of up to 40°C, the winding temperature rise will not exceed 115°C.

Transformers in Parallel

When the load increases so much that one transformer cannot meet the power demand, an additional transformer can be connected in parallel. If two transformers are connected for parallel operation, the turns ratio and the impedance of both units must be examined to ensure proper load-sharing between the two with little or no circulating current. Otherwise one transformer might be overloaded while the other is lightly loaded, or the circulation current between the two units may be such that one unit will be overloading with a relatively small load. This situation will result in high losses without ever utilizing the full capacity of both units.

When two transformers are installed in parallel, the units must be a matched set. This means that, in addition to primary and secondary voltages, the line frequency, the transformer connection, the turns ratios, and impedances are such that they will share the load based on their relative kVA ratings. If both transformers are the same ratio, then the turns ratios and impedances are almost identical. For two transformers with identical 3 percent impedances (which is typical of most distribution transformers) a 1 percent difference in turns ratio can mean a 15 to 20 percent circulating current. In addition to higher losses, circulating currents reduce the total capacity of the transformers.

Transformer Types

There are three common types of transformers: dry, mineral oil, and PCB.

Dry Transformers   Dry transformers use air as coolant. Air circulation is achieved either by natural convection or a forced air system. Dry transformers usually are larger than oil or PCB transformers of equivalent rating. They are explosion-free and self-extinguishing, less expensive, and usually are used for relatively small loads. The ambient condition is important for dry transformers, since a source of clean filtered air is needed.

Oil Transformers   Oil transformers are the workhorses of power distribution systems. They can be self-cooled using natural circulation of the oil, or air-cooled using blower fans. The transformer's core and winding are surrounded by an insulated mineral oil, which protects the insulation and provides cooling and dielectric strength to the transformer. Since the oil must be able to withstand voltage surges and thermal and mechanical stresses, as well as act as a good coolant during the entire useful life of the transformer, the oil should be supplied or approved by the transformer manufacturer, and adequate care exercised to guard against its deterioration.

The major cause of oil deterioration are water and oxidation. Moisture contamination can result from condensation, especially when the transformer is down, drastically reducing the oil's dielectric strength. An increase of water by 10 to 50 parts per million reduces the dielectric strength by half. Oxidation causes oil deterioration, which results in sludging.

Oil transformers are used both outdoors and indoors. Since they are fire hazards, they must be installed in a vault indoors to conform to fire codes.

PCB Transformers   Polychlorinated biphenyl (PCB) is a dielectric fluid that has been used in transformers and power capacitors since about 1960. It is a stable compound that has good fire-resistant characteristics. Manufacturers of transformers have preferred PCB over mineral oil since PCB transformers do not require a vault. PCB liquid is known under the generic name of Askeral. Some of its common trade names in the United States are Aroclor, Asbestal, Chlorextol, No-Flamol, Pyronal, Elemex, Dykanol, and Interteen.

In 1976 Congress enacted the Toxic Substance Control Act, which required the Environmental Protection Agency to establish rules governing the disposal and marketing of PCBs. The final marketing and disposal rules appeared in the *Federal Register* on February 17, 1978 and the proposed PCB ban rule appeared in the *Federal Register* on May 31, 1979 and took effect on July 2, 1984. Based on these laws, civil penalties of up to $25,000 per day can be imposed by the EPA for each violation of the regulations; penalties of up to $25,000 per day additional and imprisonment of up to one year may be imposed for willful or knowing violations. It is important to note that in addition to the violating companies, officials and employees are subject to the same penalties.

Based on these regulations, liquid-filled transformers were divided into the following three categories according to PCB concentration.

Below 50 ppm. If the PCB concentration is below 50 ppm, the transformer can be rebuilt. The transformer oil can be reclaimed, used as fuel or used for production of oils and lubricants. The transformer can be sold for salvage or disposed of in a municipal landfill. There is no requirement to keep records or display the PCB concentration on the transformer.

50 to 500 ppm. If the PCB concentration is between 50 and 500 ppm, the transformer is called PCB-contaminated. The transformer can be rebuilt or sold for salvage with proof of concentration level, and the transformer fluid can be disposed of in a chemical landfill or an EPA-approved boiler. There is no requirement to keep records or test the transformer; however, the transformer oil must not be diluted to lower the PCB concentration level.

Above 500 ppm. For concentrations level over 500 ppm, the transformer is classified as PCB. An up-to-date record of PCB transformers including the transformer rating and the volume of the liquid must always be on hand, including all maintenance records. An EPA-approved label must be installed on the front of the transformer. Other requirements include:

- Transformers must be stored in an EPA-approved facility.
- The oil can only be incinerated in an EPA-approved incinerator.
- Periodic inspections are mandatory.
- Spills and cleanups must be reported.
- Curbs and dikes must be built around the transformer to contain a spill.
- The transformer cannot be sold or rebuilt.
- The oil must not be diluted to lower the concentration level.

On October 30, 1980, the courts ruled that there was a lack of evidence to support EPA's classification of transformers as totally enclosed and asked EPA to remandate the rules. On August 25, 1982, the

Federal Register's proposed "PCB Electrical Use Rule" was published. This amended the May 1979 rules by allowing the continuation of PCB transformers around food- and feed-handling facilities until October 1, 1985, after which date they would be banned.

Until this time, EPA had not directly considered the probabilities of fires that involved PCB and the associated environmental risks. Fire incidents involving polychlorinated dibenzofurans (PCDFs) and polychlorinated dibenzodioxins (PCDDs) prompted EPA to reassess fire-related PCB incidents, and the following regulatory measures were passed on July 17, 1985 for transformers having greater than 500 ppm concentrations:

- The use of 480/277 in or near commercial buildings is prohibited as of October 1, 1990.
- The installation of PCB equipment in storage is prohibited.
- Registration of PCB transformers with local fire departments and removal of all combustible materials is required as of December 1, 1985.
- Exterior walls and gates where PCB transformers are housed must be marked as of December 1, 1985.
- Enhanced electrical protection must be installed on 480/277 as of October 1, 1990.
- The national response center must be notified immediately during an emergency.

It is safe to assume that PCB-related accidents can have significant environmental impacts. Insurance costs of PCB transformers are increasing rapidly. It is perhaps only a matter of time until their use will be banned, so it is prudent to periodically to follow developments in the electrical trade journals and the *Federal Register*.

28.6 HIGH-VOLTAGE CONDUCTORS AND CIRCUITS

There are two basic circuit systems for feeding from the substations to building systems: the radial system and the network system. In the radial system, separate feeders radiate out from the substation, each supplying an area. From these feeders, subfeeders or branches split off to transformers serving individual buildings or a cluster of buildings. The radial circuits are equipped with tie switches so that, in the event of a fault, the circuit can be supplied by another feeder. Radial feeders with loop or throw-over switching are most commonly employed.

In the network system, the secondaries of two or more transformers are tied together. Adjacent transformers may be supplied from the same or different feeders. Distribution, therefore, is normally at utilization voltages.

Three principal factors determine the distribution voltages: 1) energy loss in transmission versus cost of equipment, 2) strength of the conductor, and 3) overhead versus underground installation. There is a trade-off between the cost of energy loss in transmission and the cost of transmitting equipment. For a given percentage energy loss in transmission, the cross section and consequently the weight of the conductor required to transmit a block of power vary inversely as the square of the voltage.

The strength of conductors also must be considered. Overhead transmission lines must be strong enough to carry any load that may be reasonably expected. The most severe loads are experienced during winter ice and wind. Underground conductors must be able to withstand allowable stress to which the cable is subjected during installation. The need for adequate physical strength of a cable will help determine its electrical conductive capacity.

When comparing costs on overhead or underground transmission lines, it should be noted that the cost of underground construction is much higher. Overhead lines, however, are unsightly and detract from an attractive educational environment. They also create problems of routing to building transformer vaults, since these often are located in basements. As a consequence, underground transmission lines are most commonly used in new installations.

The power cables are critical elements of the high-voltage network because they are the arteries of the system. Traditionally, they are the system component that receives the least attention, perhaps since "out of sight is out of mind." Cables usually are located in duct banks and insulation that weakens prior to failure cannot be seen, often resulting in inadequate maintenance. It is important to realize that the reliability of the electrical network can be greatly improved, and costly downtime avoided, by relatively little attention to the cables (see Figure 28-8).

Cable Insulation

Paper-inpregnated lead cable (PILC) and varnished cloth (VC) have been the insulation workhorses of the industry since 1910. PILC has compound migration problems if used on vertical risers, and termination and splicing also are more difficult. VC cables are relatively more expensive for the quality of the dielectric, but they do not have the compound migration problems. The combination of VC cables for vertical risers and PILC for horizontal runs has been used successfully.

During the past two decades the petrochemical industry has introduced a variety of polyethylene compounds as insulation materials that

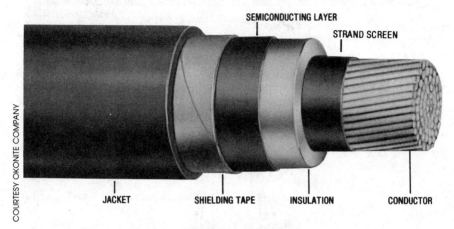

SEMICONDUCTING LAYER

STRAND SCREEN

COURTESY OKONITE COMPANY

JACKET   SHIELDING TAPE   INSULATION   CONDUCTOR

Figure 28-8
Typical Section of High-Voltage Cable

have good insulating characteristics, such as high moisture resistance, low temperature characteristics, high ozone resistance, and greater abrasion resistance. These cables are lighter in weight compared to PILC, and terminations and splicing are relatively easier.

Termination and Splicing

There are different splicing kits available, and manufacturers have a wide variety of techniques for splicing. Therefore, it is important to first make sure that the proper size and type of splice is used for every situation, that the manufacturer's recommendations are followed, and the work is performed by skilled personnel. Cable splices and terminations are usually the weakest points in a cable system, so adequate attention has to be devoted during installation and subsequent maintenance. A typical section of cable splice is shown in Figure 28-9.

Cable Maintenance

Insulation Resistance Test   This test determines the insulation resistance between the conductor and ground. A megohmmeter is used to measure the resistance (see Figure 28-10). It is basically a high-voltage ohmmeter consisting of a small DC generator and a milliampere meter. The generator is hand-cranked or driven by an electric motor, the latter being preferred for consistency of rotor speed. Megohmmeters generally have ranges from 100 V to 5,000 V.

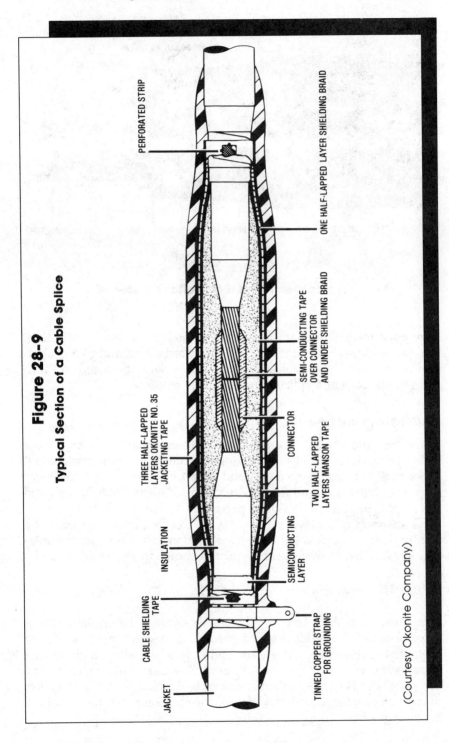

Figure 28-9

Typical Section of a Cable Splice

PERFORATED STRIP

ONE HALF-LAPPED LAYER SHIELDING BRAID

THREE HALF-LAPPED LAYERS OKONITE NO. 35 JACKETING TAPE

SEMI-CONDUCTING TAPE OVER CONNECTOR AND UNDER SHIELDING BRAID

CONNECTOR

TWO HALF-LAPPED LAYERS MANSON TAPE

INSULATION

SEMICONDUCTING LAYER

CABLE SHIELDING TAPE

TINNED COPPER STRAP FOR GROUNDING

JACKET

(Courtesy Okonite Company)

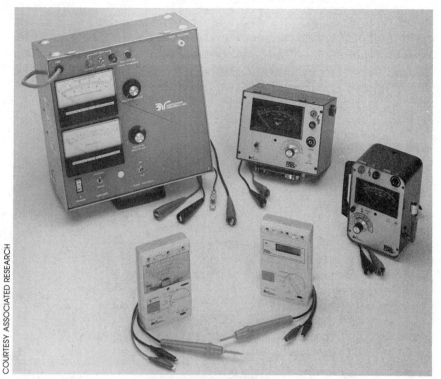

Figure 28-10

Various Types of Megohmmeters

Good insulation is indicated by an initial dip of the milliampere meter pointer toward zero, followed by a steady rise; the initial dip is due to the capacitive effect of the cable. If the pointer makes slight twitches down scale, however, this implies current leakage along the surface of dirty insulation. In order to compare the insulation with historical record, a spot test is performed. The megohmmeter is applied for sixty seconds and the reading is recorded at the end of this time.

Dielectric Absorption Test   This test provides better information than the spot test and takes considerably longer than the insulation resistance test. Since the current is inversely related to time, insulation resistance will rise gradually if the cable is good, and flatten rapidly if the insulation is faulty. The insulation resistance is plotted against time.

High Potential Test   The above two tests cannot determine the dielectric strength of cable insulation under high-voltage stress. A high potential test, or hypot test, applies stress beyond what a cable encounters under normal use. It is the only way to obtain positive proof that the cable insulation has the strength to withstand overvoltages caused by normal system surges. There are two types of hypot tests, AC and DC. The AC hypot is used almost exclusively for insulation breakdown. If applied properly, DC hypot is a nondestructive test, so it is commonly used for maintenance (see Figure 28-11).

Surge Arrestors

Surge arrestors protect electrical apparatus against overvoltages from lightning, switching surges, and other disturbances. Without arrestors, flashover and equipment damage can result.

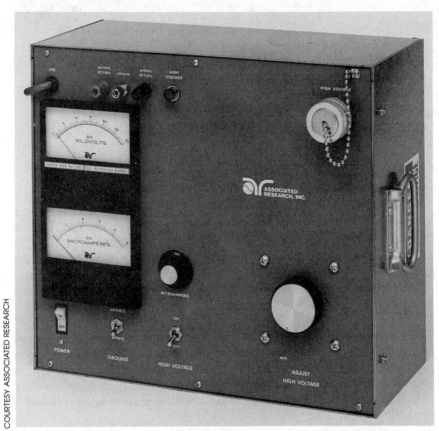

Figure 28-11
Typical DC Hypot

During normal system voltages, arrestors are dormant. When a high-voltage impulse is imposed on the system, regardless of source, the arrestor will ground it, thus preventing it from going through the equipment. There are three classes of surge arrestors:

- Station class arrestors, the best type of arrestor since it is capable of discharging the most energy.
- Intermediate arrestors, which have lower energy discharge capability than station class arresters.
- Distribution arrestors, which have the lowest energy discharge capability and the least desirable protective level.

28.7 ELECTRIC POWER GENERATION

Generators

Generators are electromechanical devices that convert mechanical energy into electrical energy. The theory behind how a generator operates is based on Faraday's, law which states that a voltage will be induced on a conductor if it moves through a magnetic field. The induced voltage is directly proportional to the number of turns in the conductor, the strength of the magnetic field and the speed at which it moves through the field. In addition, the closer the magnetic field is crossed at 90° the higher the voltage. There are three types of generators: DC, AC synchronous, and asynchronous. Most of the generators used in the industry today are synchronous.

A synchronous generator is structurally identical to a synchronous motor. The magnetic field is produced by a direct current in the rotor circuit. The rotor, also called the exciter, is powered by brushes and slip rings. The armature circuit located in the stator produces the electricity. There are a number of different ways to power the exciter field. One is to supply it from a separate DC generator, but in most cases the exciter is fed from the armature through a diode and a silicone-controlled rectifier (SCR). The diode converts the AC power to pulsating DC, and the SCR provides voltage regulation. Here the generator is initially excited by residual magnetism.

A third way to power the exciter field is to have two rotors—one main, one auxiliary—on the same shaft. The small auxiliary winding is excited initially by residual magnetism. The AC voltage generated in the winding goes through a set of diodes and supplies the main rotor. In addition, a stationary exciter field regulates the voltage output of the generator. Since the entire exciter circuit is on one shaft, there is no need for brushes and slip rings. These units are called brushless generators and require less maintenance than other generators.

Asynchronous Generators   If an induction motor is driven faster than synchronous speed by a prime mover, it will become a generator. Since the generator speed is different from synchronous speed, it is called an asynchronous generator. The generated power frequency varies and is always more than 60 Hz. Asynchronous generators are simpler in construction and cost less than synchronous generators. This is why most small cogeneration units use asynchronous units. Also, if the prime mover energy is not controllable, such as in wind-powered generators, asynchronous units are the most appropriate. The power output of an asynchronous generator usually is not used directly; instead it passes through a rectifier bridge to convert it to pulsating DC power. The DC power feeds an inverter which converts the power to constant 60 Hz AC power before it supplies the load. Harmonics can be a problem in these units, so they are limited to less than 150 kW in size.

Emergency Generators   In using emergency generators, both the normal power source and the emergency generator are connected to a transfer switch. If the normal power source fails, the emergency generator is started. In about six seconds the generator attains its rated voltage and frequency and a transfer switch sends the load over to the emergency generator. When the normal power source is restored, there is usually a six- to ten-minute delay before the load is transferred back to normal power. This transfer can be done manually as well as automatically, depending on the configuration of the transfer switch.

When the normal power goes out and then is restored, the power to the load is interrupted twice, presenting a potential problem for computers, digital PBXs, and life-sustaining equipment. In such applications, an uninterruptible power supply (UPS) is used. In a UPS, AC power is obtained by connecting battery power with the use of inverters. The transfer switch and the generator are connected to the battery charger which supplies power to the batteries. The load does not sense any normal power interruptions unless both the normal power and emergency generator are out of operation and the battery charge drops below a certain point.

Cogeneration

Cogeneration is the production of more than one form of energy simultaneously; it usually refers to producing electricity and heat energy. Cogeneration is discussed in detail in Chapter 47 of this manual. The electrical concerns regarding the interconnection of cogeneration to the utility power grid are examined here.

When allowing interconnection of cogeneration, utilities are mainly concerned that the systems do not jeopardize the safety of utility personnel and the quality of service. During normal conditions, the utility needs to know if the power produced by the cogeneration site will be used entirely by the customer and, if not, how much of the power will be sold to the utility. Moreover, it wants to ensure that the harmonic voltage and frequency tolerances of the dispersed generation site meet the grid tolerances. During emergency conditions, network faults must be detected by the cogeneration device and isolated from the grid.

The utility electric distribution network is radial, so that isolation of an area requires opening and locking a main circuit breaker. With cogeneration, the power network is no longer radial but becomes a loop distribution system. Therefore, it is crucial for the utility to record the location of all cogeneration units and have access to a manual load-break disconnect at all times. The interconnection requirements of a cogeneration system depend on interconnection voltage, transformer configuration, protection scheme, and on-site load and generation capacity.

Electrical Protection for Cogeneration   In a utility distribution network, the overcurrent equipment is arranged in a series of overlapping zones to clear a fault on a prearranged sequence of primary devices and backups. This is achieved by coordinating the time-current characteristics of fuses, circuit breaker reclosers, sectionalizers, and relays from a substation. In a faulted condition, the available current drops as it moves from the substation to the customer site because of an increase in systems impedance. Therefore, coordination is relatively simple. With cogeneration interconnection, a bidirectional power flow on the distribution system can continue to energize the part of the network separated from the utility system reference source. Moreover, a cogeneration site can contribute additional overcurrent during faults, which may cause the protection services to operate prematurely.

This high current level from the cogeneration site is over and above the available fault current from the utility, thus shortening the average melting time of the line fuses. On a 15 kV system, a small synchronous cogeneration unit of a few megawatts can reduce the fuse melting time by more than 30 percent; in an induction generator, the reduction in melting time is about one-third of the synchronous generator.

Another problem lies with the utility's autoreclosures. The faults that occur with an overhead transmission system are usually momentary and self-clearing. After a fault, the autoreclosure closes the circuit a few cycles after the circuit was interrupted, and the customer downtime for such momentary faults is minimal. With cogeneration in the system, although the utility breaker has interrupted the circuit, the fault is fed by this unit and does not get a chance to clear. Therefore, when the circuit is closed by the autoreclosure, the fault has not cleared and this increases downtime. The presence of cogeneration changes the available fault and the system coordination for in-house systems as well as the utility grid.

Another concern utilities have with cogeneration is the problem of islanding. Islanding means that the cogeneration site is operating independently of the reference voltage and frequency of the utility power grid and is no longer in synchronism with it. Islanding can cause several problems. Utility personnel might assume that by opening the line breaker the circuit is de-energized. The generator voltage and frequency variations might cause costly damage to the load. If the utility breaker is closed without synchronizing the cogeneration unit, serious damage can also be incurred by the generator and the breaker.

The harmonics generation from cogeneration sources must also be studied. Since for economic reasons the magnetic core of in-house generators is not made of the same high-quality materials as the utility grade units, the core nonlinearities of cogeneration units will produce harmonics that cause problems with computers and other sensitive electronic equipment.

Minimum Protection Requirements   If an internal electrical fault occurs within the cogeneration unit, the available fault from the utility grid will cause major damage. Therefore the electrical protection needs of a cogeneration system should not be taken lightly. The required protection depends on unit size, generator type, in-house load, and interconnection voltage. For small units where power is totally used in-house, overcurrent, over/under-voltage and current directional relays are required. If power will also be provided to the utility grid, then in addition to the first two relays, over/under-frequency and negative sequence relays will be needed. For larger units the following additional protection relays are recommended:

- Differential protection
- Loss and excitation
- Overspeed
- Motoring protection
- Stator and rotor protection
- Overheating.

For induction units, surge overspeed and internal short protection are recommended. It should be kept in mind that the protection levels suggested here are only guidelines; local utility requirements and the site conditions must be taken into account.

To summarize, before the advent of cogeneration, facilities were only receivers of power; today they are a partner in the power grid with the utility. It is the responsibility of both sides to ensure that the reliability and safety standards of the network are not compromised when connecting cogeneration systems.

28.8 SYSTEM PROTECTION

Short-Circuit Faults

Electric current always follows the path of least resistance. What confines electricity in a conductor is the dielectric around the conductor. If the insulation between two conductors or a conductor and ground drops to zero, a large current is going to flow in the circuit. This is called short-circuit current because the current has found a shorter path than going through the load.

The short-circuit current can be as high as 10,000 times the rated current. Fault current can be destructive and cause equipment damage, fire, and personal injury. The short-circuit current magnitude is not a function of the load, but of the capacity of the power source and the length and size of the conductor. A water dam can serve as an analogy for potential short-circuit current. Normally, the water flow in a dam is dependent on the pipe size. But if the dam breaks, the water flow will depend only on the total water available in the dam, independent of the pipe size.

For an electrical system the available short-circuit current is explained in the following example. Consider a circuit in which a 500 V, 10 kVA load is connected to the utility through two possible transformers to the utility system. The transformer choices are a 10 kVA unit with an impedance of .2 ohms and a 10,000 kVA unit with .02 ohms impedance. The load impedance is 25 ohms. So for both transformers the normal-load current is 20 amps.

If there is a short-circuit at any point on the cable, the available current in each transformer will be different. Available fault current in the first transformer will be 2,500 amps, while in the second transformer it will be 25,000 amps. In the first case, the fuse must only be able to interrupt 2,500 amps, but in the second case the fuse must be able to interrupt 25,000 amps, since its available fault is higher.

There are four sources for short-circuit currents: the utility system, in-house synchronous generators, induction motors, and synchronous motors. The available fault from the utility is directly related to the size of the utility transformer. For a synchronous motor, the available fault current is four to five times its full-load current, and for an induction motor it is two to four times its full-load current.

There are two types of faults, symmetrical and asymmetrical. A symmetrical fault is a three-phase fault, sometimes referred to as a bolted fault (see Figure 28-12). Here it is assumed that all three-phase conductors are brought together simultaneously. About 5 percent of short-circuit failures are due to symmetrical faults. All other faults— such as line-to-ground, line-to-line, or line-to-line-to-ground faults, are referred to as asymmetrical faults (see Figure 28-13).

When the system is in a faulted condition, it can disrupt the transmission network in one or more of the following ways:

- Allowing large currents to flow, which can damage equipment.
- Causing electrical arcing, which can start fires or damage equipment.
- Raising or lowering system voltage outside acceptable ranges.
- Causing a three-phase system to become unbalanced, which in turn causes three-phase equipment to operate improperly.
- Interrupting the flow of power.

The protection of a high-voltage system is designed to safeguard against these disruptions. It works to detect and isolate faults, it keeps as much of the system in operation as possible, it restores the system as soon as possible, and it discriminates between normal and abnormal system conditions so that protective devices will not operate unnecessarily.

There are three types of components of a protection system: fuses, relays, and circuit breakers. A fuse is a device that opens a circuit if an overload or short-circuit occurs. It consists of a short fusible link held under tension. When the current is increased beyond a certain point, the link will melt and the spring will pull the contacts further apart, thus interrupting the current in the circuit. The main selection criteria for fuses are voltage rating, ampacity, and interrupting rating, to which the following guidelines apply.

- The voltage rating of a fuse should always be equal to or greater than the system voltage.
- The ampacity of the fuse should be equal to the rating of the load.
- The interrupting capacity of the fuse should be equal to or greater than the available fault current.
- The time-current characteristics of the fuse should be such that system selectivity is assured.

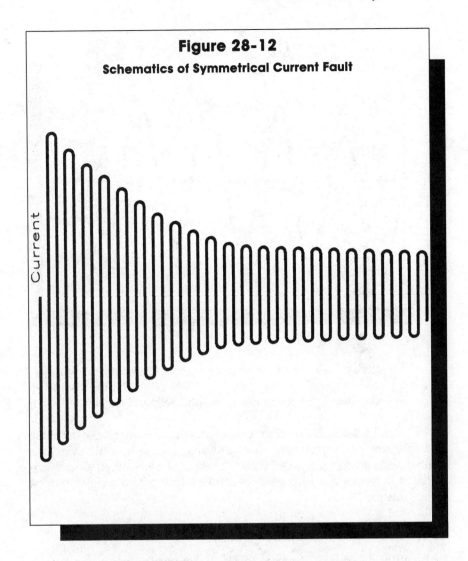

Figure 28-12

Schematics of Symmetrical Current Fault

Protective relays are used to minimize the damage to electrical equipment by interrupting the power circuit during a fault. There are four types of protective relays: electromagnetic attraction, electromagnetic induction, thermal induction, and electronic. Protective relays must have the following characteristics:

- Reliability. They may be idle for several years then suddenly be required to operate quickly.
- Selectivity. They must not respond to abnormal but harmless system conditions, such as sudden changes in load.

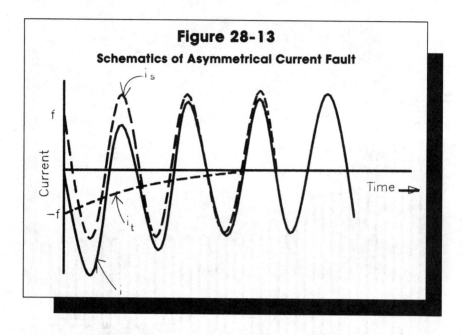

Figure 28-13

Schematics of Asymmetrical Current Fault

- Sensitivity. They must be responsive enough to perform in every case required.
- Speed. They must make decisions and respond quickly.

Circuit breakers are mechanical devices that are capable of breaking and reclosing a circuit under all conditions, even when the system is faulted and currents are great. Circuit breaking occurs when a mechanical latch is released, which enables a coiled spring or a weight to open the contacts.

Selection of System Protective Devices

In institutional power systems, such as university campuses, circuit breakers have been used for applications requiring complex relaying schemes or high continuous currents. However, for most applications a choice of either circuit breakers or power fuses is available. Fuses have achieved widespread use in most such applications because of their simplicity, economy, fast response characteristics, and freedom from maintenance (see Figure 28-14).

Circuit breakers and their associated relays are commonly used where the reclosing capability of the circuit breaker is an advantage, such as applications involving overhead lines which have a relatively high incidence of transient or temporary faults. This reclosing feature is neither useful nor desirable in institutional power systems where the conductors are arranged in cable trays, enclosed in conduits or bus ducts, or underground. The incidence of faults on these systems is low, and the rare faults that do occur are not transient and result in significant damage that would only be exacerbated by an automatic reclosing operation.

The relaying associated with circuit breakers is available in varying degrees of sophistication and complexity (see Figure 28-15). Systems requiring differential protection, reverse-power relaying, or non-current

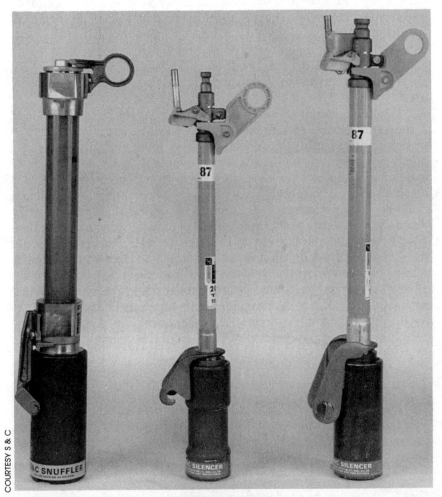

Figure 28-14

Power Fuses

magnitude tripping of the protective device typically require circuit breakers. However, the size of transformers normally associated with institutional power systems generally do not warrant such sophisticated protection. Indeed, many users find that the complexity of such protective relaying, with its requirement for periodic testing and recalibration, is a distinct disadvantage.

Circuit breakers also are used in applications requiring a very high (above 720 amps) continuous current-carrying capability. While they may be an advantage in some cases, a higher degree of service continuity can be achieved with less expensive power fuses by subdividing the system into a number of discrete segments, with the result that a fault on one segment of the system will affect fewer loads. This high degree of segmentation also allows the use of smaller transformers located strategically throughout the university's electrical distribution system, eliminating the need for the long, high-ampacity secondary conductors that are required where fewer, larger, and widely separated transformers are used.

Where high continuous current-carrying capability is not required and where reclosing or sophisticated relaying is not justified, such as in medium-voltage and institutional power systems, power fuses offer a number of advantages. Power fuses are simple to install and require no maintenance of any kind; even after years of neglect, power fuses will operate properly. Recalibration is neither required nor possible; hence, elaborate testing procedures are not needed, eliminating the possibility that a carefully engineered coordination plan will be disturbed accidentally. Power fuses, unlike circuit breakers, provide fault protection for the system without depending on a source of control power, such as storage batteries and their chargers. Such batteries may be found completely discharged and thus incapable of tripping the circuit breaker should a fault occur. In addition, for high-magnitude faults, power fuses have inherently faster response characteristics than circuit breakers, permitting more rapid removal of faults from the system.

Types and Symptoms of Failures

The major cause of electrical failures is the breakdown of insulation, although some failures are caused by the absorption of moisture, oil, grease, and dust into the cores and by excessive heat, vibration, overvoltage, and aging.

Dirt   Moisture or condensation of airborne chemicals causes electrical leakage, which in turn causes tracking and eventual flashover.

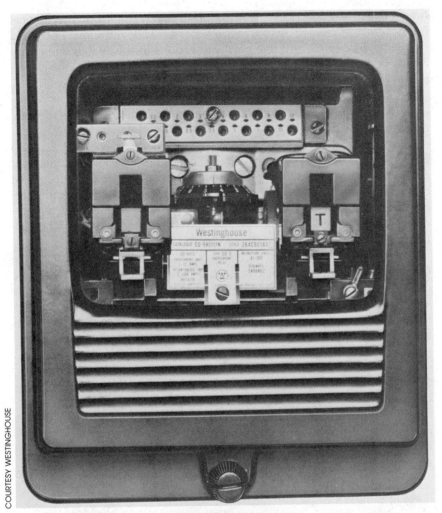

Figure 28-15
Typical Overcurrent Relay

High Ambient Temperature   A 10° to 15° overheat above the rated temperature will cause insulation to embrittle, deteriorate, and shorten the useful life of equipment by half.

Oil Leakage   Excessive loss of oil or compound will result in equipment loss. Once the insulation material is lost, a void is created and dielectric values will be drastically reduced.

Internal Failure   Loose connections may result from mechanical forces that are created by surges, overloads, and vibration. Loosened terminals, fuse clips, and live part connections in the switch will create excessive heat, and thereby accelerate further deterioration of the system.

Overload   Overload produces excessive heat that decreases the useful life of the equipment.

High-Voltage Surge   High-voltage surges are a serious problem for most utility companies. Surges create flexing and physical displacement of component parts, which in turn leads to loose connections and overheating. Surges also produce stability problems that may lead to resonant failures. Surges also can cascade into the secondary side and create failures.

Corona   Corona is a discharge due to electric stresses. It can be caused by high electric fields, dirt, moisture, sharp bends in cable, severe weather conditions and faulty design. It can be detected by its secondary symptoms: ozone odor, radio and television interference, visible pulsating of blue or green color, crackling noises, and the production of a gray powder on the unshielded cable.

Ferroresonance   Ferroresonance is usually caused by a single-phase opening where no secondary load exists on the transformer. The inductance of the transformer and the capacitance of the cable can form a series-resonant circuit and create instantaneous voltage up to fifty times the normal rating, which can give rise to a violent explosion in cables and transformers. Indications of ferroresonance are:

- Loud humming and vibration of a transformer.
- Spark-over of arrestors on open phases yet to be closed.
- Overvoltage breakdown failure of cables, transformers, and arrestors.
- Motors running backwards.

Ferroresonance can be prevented by:

- Grounding neutral on all transformer wye windings.
- Energizing transformers with the same load.
- Energizing cables first, then the transformer.
- Installing fuses both at the cable entrance and at the transformer.
- Energizing all three phases simultaneously.

Flashover   All of the failures mentioned so far will eventually result in flashover if corrective action is not taken. The usual trigger for flashover is dirt and moisture over the insulation. As an arc is established, heat is generated and starts a cascade effect.

28.9 INSTRUMENTS

Test Instruments

Electrical test instruments are the tools used to perform maintenance on power systems. For low voltages, the multimeter and amprobe are used. With a multimeter, voltage and resistance can be measured, while the current is measured with an amprobe. For high-voltage systems, the following instruments are used.

Infrared Detector   The use of infrared units can greatly enhance visual inspection because problems such as overloads, imbalances, loose connections, and dirty cores in a dry transformer can be readily located.

Megger   A megger, hand- or motor-driven, will give a quick analysis of the integrity of the insulation on a cable or in a transformer. The 2,500 volt megger is effective for troubleshooting cables, motors, and transformers.

Hypot Tester   A hypot tester normally is used when the condition of cable cannot be determined with a megger. Although the hypot tester has the capability to test up to 80 kV, tests are usually preferred up to two and a half times the operational voltage. Great care must be taken with this instrument to avoid damaging the cable by imposing excessively high stress voltages.

Phase Meter   A phase meter is used to test fuses or to phase two feeds to one another. It is also used for draining capacitance from a system during a shutdown, and for proving that the system is de-energized prior to the attachment of ground connections.

Glow Stick   A glow stick is an excellent way to test for fault potential on an unshielded cable. It is of no value for testing a blown fuse or for discharging a system.

Dielectric Tester   A dielectric tester gives a quick analysis of the dielectric value of oil. Moisture, pH, and other tests also should be considered when using this tester. A two-year test program on all liquid-filled apparatus is recommended.

Metering

The need to accurately measure electrical energy became critical after the energy crisis of the 1970s. The instrument for measuring electrical energy is the kilowatt hour (kWH) meter. It measures the cumulative energy consumption over a period of time. Another useful measurement is electrical demand (kWD). It is measured in kilowatts and signifies the maximum power demand within a time period. Utilities use demand costs as part of the total electric charge, so by measuring power demand the institution can analyze consumption patterns for possible reductions. Additionally, the difference between peak demand and the substation rating indicates the available spare capacity, which is useful information when considering future distribution expansion.

For low-voltage systems of less than 150 amps, a kWH meter is connected directly to the service. For high-voltage systems and larger currents, potential transformers (PTs) and current transformers (CTs) are utilized. Potential transformers have the same primary voltage as the system but have a secondary voltage of 120 V. Current transformers are shaped like doughnuts and placed around the power conductor. Since CTs are constant current sources, if the CT circuit is opened when energized an explosion can result due to high voltages.

Electric meters are subject to drift, so they should be periodically tested and calibrated. The magnitude of service and the critical importance of the data will determine how often they should be calibrated.

Use of Capacitors for Power Factor Correction

Power factor is an important value in load consideration and measurement. Alternating current was adopted principally to take advantage of transformers that do not operate with direct current, and also helped simplify motor design. At the same time, problems were introduced by the presence of inductive reactance in the circuit and reactive power required by motor loads. Because of the reactive power, principally in motors but to some extent in other loads, the current lags in time relative to the voltage. Therefore, more current is required to provide a given amount of power. The power factor is the quantity by which the apparent power must be multiplied to obtain the active power of the circuit. There is no way to eliminate this component of current, but it can be neutralized by adding another load to the circuit in the form of capacitors. Capacitors can be located at the loads, in the substations, or on the lines. Power factor correction on the lines generally is less costly.

Obtaining Clean Power

Alternating current electricity is a pure sinusoidal wave of one single frequency. More specifically, in the United States this frequency is 60 Hz.

Ideally this is the shape of AC power at all times. In a real system, as long as the circuits have linear elements (resistors, capacitors, and unsaturated inductors) the wave shape will remain the same during steady-state conditions. But as soon as nonlinear elements are introduced in the circuit (rectifiers, thyristors, and saturated inductors) the wave shape will become distorted. Therefore, some of the harmonic sources in a power system are saturated transformers, arc welders, voltage rectifiers, inverters, uninterruptible power sources, variable frequency drives, and self- and line-commutated converters. In addition to harmonics, electrical surges also introduce power glitches with values much higher than system voltages.

These harmonics and glitches can be a major nuisance for many types of sensitive electronic equipment, including personal computers. Usually the greatest challenge is finding the source of noise in the power system. Some common techniques for protecting devices from these problems are the use of isolation transformers, reactors, harmonic filters, uninterruptible power sources, and surge suppressors.

ADDITIONAL RESOURCES

Electrical Utility Engineering Referrence Book—Distribution Systems. Pittsburgh, Pennsylvania: Westinghouse, 1965.

Fink, Donald G. and John M. Carroll. *Standard Handbook for Electrical Engineers,* tenth edition. New York: McGraw-Hill, 1968.

Glenn, D. J. and C. J. Cook. "A New Fault Interrupting Device for Improved Medium Voltage System and Equipment Protection." *Proceedings of the IEEE/IAS Annual Meeting,* October 1984.

Mason, C. R. *The Art and Science of Protective Relaying.* New York: John Wiley & Sons, 1967.

Miller, H. N. "DC Hypot Testing of Cables, Transformers, and Rotating Machinery." Associated Research, Inc., Manual 16086.

Qayoumi, Mohammad H. *Electrical Distribution and Maintenance.* Alexandria, Virginia: APPA, 1989.

Turley, S. Q. "Ferro-Resonance Oversimplified." *Transmission & Distribution,* October 1966.

Underground Systems Reference Book. New York: Edison Electric Institute, 1957.

Viermerster, P. *The Lightning Book.* New York: Doubleday, 1961.

CHAPTER 29

Heating and Cooling Media Distribution

John R. Swistock
Director, Physical Plant Operations
University of Virginia

29.1 INTRODUCTION

There has been a growth in central heating, cooling, and electric power generation plants in colleges and universities since the early 1970s. Much of this growth has been to achieve the greater energy efficiencies and economies of large central plants, including the better coordination of electric and thermal loads that they make possible.

Heating and cooling media distribution systems provide an essential link between the central plants, or other heating and cooling media sources, and campus buildings. Their function is to convey a given quantity of the media, liquid or vapor, from the central plants to the buildings without undue heat loss or gain.

Surface traffic, aesthetics, and efficient heat transfer usually require that the heat transfer media be piped underground. An underground system, however, has many negative aspects. It is costly to install, difficult to maintain in a hostile environment where ground water promotes corrosion and destroys the insulating quality of materials, and soils, especially where disturbed in installation, can shift and settle to put additional structural loads on the system. Malfunctions in the distribution systems are more frequently the cause of service interruptions than the central plants themselves.

Underground heating and cooling media distribution systems are assemblies of fluid carrying pipes, in enclosures to provide insulation, accommodate the thermal movement of the piping, and provide protection from the underground environment. To minimize energy losses and service interruptions, they must be professionally planned, designed, operated, and maintained.

29.2 HEAT TRANSFER FLUIDS

Steam

Steam has been the principal medium for heat distribution from central plants to buildings since the early 1900s. Steam distribution systems are generally classified as high or low pressure. There is no standardized pressure dividing the two; low pressure systems usually distribute and deliver steam at the pressure utilized in the buildings. They are generally associated with heating plants that are designed to produce steam at the desired utilization pressures.

High pressure systems distribute the steam at much higher pressures than can be utilized, necessitating pressure reduction at entry to buildings. These systems often receive the steam from the electric power generation process either by extraction or the turbine exhaust.

Heat losses in steam distribution systems increase with higher pressures, since higher pressures mean higher temperatures. Therefore, higher pressure lines are more heavily insulated than are low pressure lines. Distribution systems are generally operated at the lowest pressure that will provide adequate service to the most distant customer on the system under the most demanding circumstances. While it is possible to continuously vary steam pressure with load conditions, as with outside temperature, this is usually not practical. However, system pressures can be reset with long-term changes in load, such as from summer to winter operation.

Heat losses in steam systems occur not only through transmission from the lines to surroundings, but through condensate losses. Most of the usable energy in steam is the latent heat of vaporization, released as the steam condenses to water. Heat transmission losses can cause condensation in the steam lines. This condensation is extracted from the steam line, collected, and returned to the boiler. Steam traps are used to avoid the loss of steam in removing the condensate; they permit the drainage of condensate (water), but not of steam. On properly insulated steam systems, service problems and energy losses are perhaps related to steam traps more than to any other element in the system. Steam traps are discussed later in this chapter.

Because steam is a gas and its pressure is determined at the central plant, no pumps are required in the steam lines. This contributes to economical delivery over relatively long distances.

Since modern boilers use chemically treated water, returning condensate to the boiler feed-water represents significant savings in steam generation costs. Condensate is collected from buildings, and from transmission lines, at as low a pressure as possible and returned to the central plant through a combination of pump and gravity systems, depending on local situations. Condensate lines are usually installed parallel to the steam distribution lines for ease of construction, collection, and return of drip water condensate. Since the volume of the condensate, a liquid, is much less than the volume of the same weight of steam, the condensate lines are much smaller than the steam lines.

In most buildings, condensate collection piping returns condensate to a sump where it is pumped into the condensate return piping system, then to the central plant. Condensate from steam lines is forced by steam pressure through steam traps into the condensate piping. If a trap fails, the result is steam loss into the condensate lines, where it condenses and raises the temperature and pressure of the condensate system. If such steam loss becomes excessive, the pressure in the steam line is reduced, lowering the dew point and thus forming more condensate and further reducing the efficiency.

Since almost all steam distribution systems operate at relatively high pressures and temperatures, steam leaks can create significant safety hazards. High pressure steam can easily erode steel as it escapes. Leaking joints rapidly worsen and can lead to explosive failures in piping systems.

Figure 29-1 is a schematic diagram of a section of a typical campus steam distribution system.

Hot Water

Transmission energy losses and maintenance requirements with hot water systems are generally less than with steam. Hot water can be pumped over longer distances than is practical with steam. In general, hot water is the more economical media for distribution to heating systems. However, its use is limited because many college and university buildings require steam for laboratories, medical facilities, and other uses. It would not be economical to operate a water distribution system for heating and a steam distribution system for other uses.

Hot water systems with temperatures in excess of 220°F must be pressurized to prevent the water vaporizing into steam. This requires working pressures from 50 to more than 250 psig, depending upon the water temperature. System pressure is generally provided by air pressure at the expansion tanks. Because of the high cost of constructing and operating systems with pressures over 250 psig, hot water distribution systems are generally not designed to operate at temperatures over 400°F.

Higher temperature systems are more energy efficient, in that more thermal energy is moved per pound of media. Since the system is closed from the hot water generator through the supply piping to the heat exchanger and returned to the hot water generator, very little media is

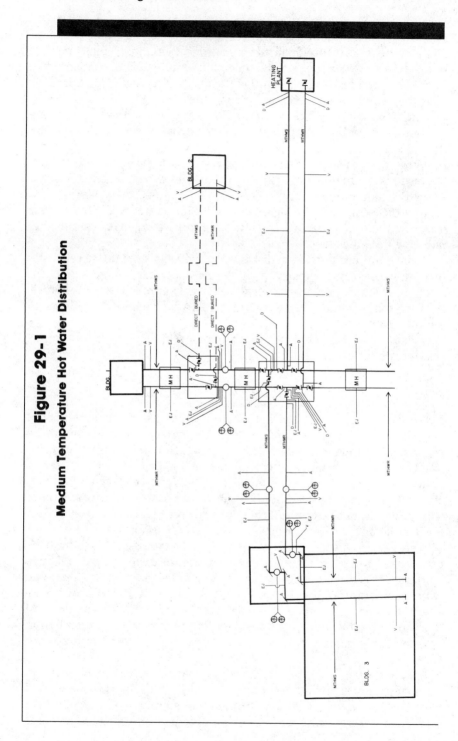

Figure 29-1

Medium Temperature Hot Water Distribution

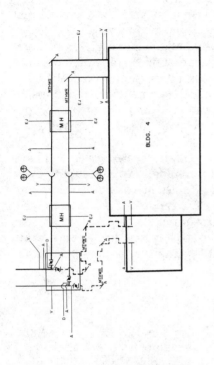

LEGEND

MANHOLE
A   ANCHOR
V   VENT
EJ   EXPANSION JOINT
D   DRAIN
⋈   BUTTERFLY VALVE
O   RISE IN ELEVATION

⌣   LOWERING OF ELEVATION
MTHWS   MEDIUM TEMPERATURE HOT WATER SUPPLY
MTHWR   MEDIUM TEMPERATURE HOT WATER RETURN
------- DIRECT BURIED LINE
        MEDIUM TEMPERATURE HOT WATER LINE IN TUNNEL
⊕   BALL JOINT

lost. With effective insulation, heat losses are less than with higher pressure steam. Hot water systems require energy for pumping and maintaining system pressures.

Because high temperature systems operate at high pressures, safety is a continuous important consideration. If pressure is lost, there is a sudden explosive conversion from water to steam. It is essential that system pressure integrity be maintained.

Pumping systems must be specially designed for high temperature water. While the hydraulic requirements are similar to any high pressure water system, pumps seals and other components must be designed to withstand the high temperatures. In high temperature and pressure systems, pump seals are extremely important. High temperature mechanical seals are available that minimize water losses and are relatively maintenance free.

It has long been common practice with hot water systems to have two or more pumps to allow several pumping rates, depending upon demand. However, the development of efficient variable speed pump motors makes it possible to provide a full range of flow rates to meet varying loads with a minimum number of pumps.

Figure 29-2 is a schematic diagram of a typical hot water heating distribution system, showing the relative simplicity of the system compared to a steam distribution system.

Chilled Water

Building cooling systems are often already in place, utilizing various types of cooling units designed for specific temperature differentials and flow rates, when central chiller plants and chilled water distribution systems are designed and installed. In the design of the central system, three interdependent factors must be matched: 1) water flow rate, 2) water temperatures including temperature rise through cooling coils, and 3) operating pressures. The supply water temperature must meet the design requirements of the building cooling system, while the return water temperature must meet design considerations of the central plant.

Design flow rates are determined on the basis of the temperature rise in the system. A high temperature rise requires a low flow rate and reduced cost of piping, pumps, and pumping. A low temperature rise requires a high flow rate with higher pumping costs. A low temperature rise usually means a low supply temperature, which may reduce the chiller efficiency. It is generally more economical to utilize maximum temperature rise with minimum water circulation. The relatively low temperature rise of chilled water systems necessitates a larger volume of water than with hot water systems, and therefore greater system capacity.

Because line temperatures are closer to ambient temperatures, expansion and contraction of piping is much less than with a heating system and insulation requirements. Most conventional chilled water distribution systems provide chilled water directly to cooling coils in the buildings being served, without a heat exchanger and separate building piping loop. Building systems are thus an extension of the distribution supply and return lines. This is similar to the connections in low-temperature hot water systems.

Flow rates to cooling coils are controlled by various types of valving systems. In larger buildings, circulation pumps will be used to circulate water in the building, rather than relying on the pressure difference between supply and return lines in the distribution system.

Since the cooling systems for smaller buildings may be designed to use the pressure difference between the supply and return lines for proper flows, this pressure difference must be maintained for all load conditions. In addition to adequate pumping capacity in the central chiller plant, pressure control valves and cross connection lines in the distribution system maintain the pressure difference between supply and return lines and ensure adequate, even flows to buildings as required.

Insulation for chilled water distribution lines is necessary to minimize heat gain from the environment, and to control condensation on the piping and equipment. Since ground moisture migration is from hot to cold, vapor barriers are provided on the exterior of the conduits housing the piping and insulation. As temperature differences between the distribution piping and environment are generally much less with chilled water lines than with heating lines, insulation designs are usually determined by condensation control requirements.

29.3 THE DISTRIBUTION SYSTEM

Surface versus Underground Installation

Heating and cooling media distribution systems can be installed above ground or underground. Above-ground systems are less expensive to install and maintain. They are exposed to more severe weather conditions, and are susceptible to damage from wind, hail, vandalism, and other causes. Underground systems are protected from the weather, but are exposed to ground water, structural loads of shifting soils and surface loads, and are difficult to maintain. Surface traffic and aesthetic considerations usually dictate that distribution systems be installed underground.

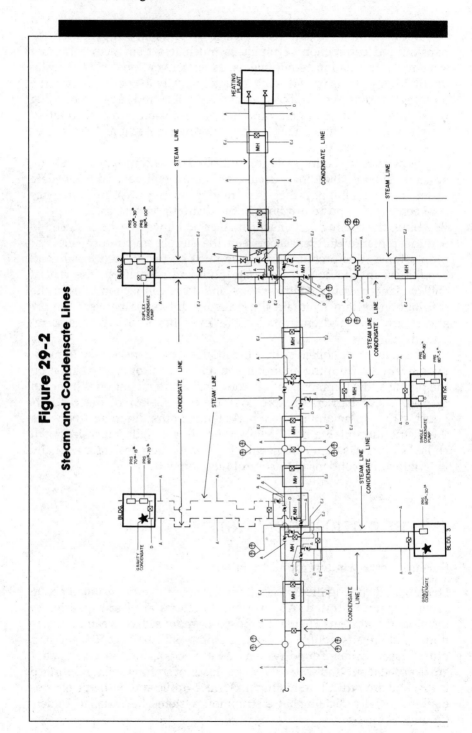

Figure 29-2
Steam and Condensate Lines

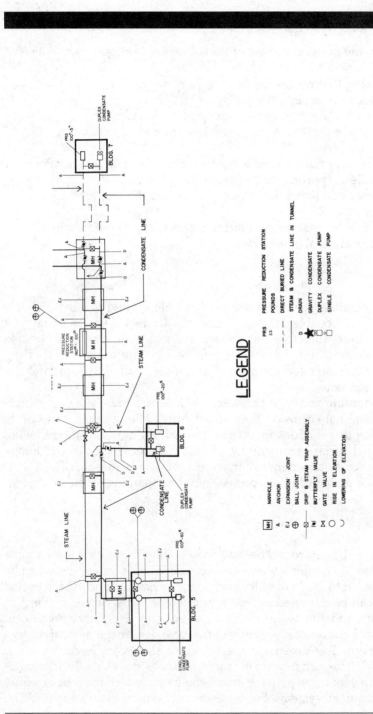

LEGEND

MH	MANHOLE	
A	ANCHOR	
EJ	EXPANSION JOINT	
⊕	BALL JOINT	
⊠	DRIP & STEAM TRAP ASSEMBLY	
⋈	BUTTERFLY VALVE	
✕	GATE VALVE	
◯	RISE IN ELEVATION	
◡	LOWERING OF ELEVATION	
PRS	PRESSURE REDUCTION STATION	
#	POUNDS	
— — —	DIRECT BURIED LINE	
	STEAM & CONDENSATE LINE IN TUNNEL	
D	DRAIN	
	GRAVITY CONDENSATE PUMP	
	DUPLEX CONDENSATE PUMP	
	SINGLE CONDENSATE PUMP	

Underground Systems - General

Underground systems consist of the following principal components:

- Piping that carries the fluid.
- Insulation around the piping.
- Conduit that houses the piping and insulation.
- Anchors that divide the lines into individual expanding sections.
- Pipe supports and guides, which permit coaxial movement while supporting the weight of the pipe without sagging.
- Expansion joints that accommodate the thermal expansion of the pipe.
- Manholes that provide direct access to the underground systems at suitable intervals.

Piping

A major consideration in the selection of underground piping is that it is not readily accessible for repair and replacement. The material and thickness must therefore be selected for long-term use and possible changes in pressures. Joining sections of pipe are most critical. They transmit expansion and contraction and must be able to withstand the resultant stresses.

Condensate and high pressure drip lines are more subject to internal and external corrosion than steam lines. The internal corrosion is largely due to variations in oxygen and carbon dioxide content, while the external surface temperature of 120°F to 160°F creates conditions favorable for electrochemical attack if moisture is present. The life of condensate piping can be expected to be less than that of steam piping.

Conduits

General   Underground heating and cooling distribution systems can be installed in conduit systems or direct burial. Conduit systems can be subdivided into box conduits and tunnel systems, and direct buried systems can be classified as field fabricated or prefabricated systems.

Steam and hot water distribution systems experience significant expansion because of the temperature changes in the system and its environment. The expansion may produce significant forces which, if not provided for, can rupture the piping. Expansion is usually accommodated with expansion joints or expansion loops, which must be carefully engineered in all systems, but are especially critical in direct burial. The expansion considerations with chilled water are much less because the temperature variations are much less. The temperature differential between the earth and the piping system also determines the insulation requirements for the system. While steam and hot water systems must be well insulated, direct buried chilled water systems require less insulation, none in some cases.

Direct Buried Systems   Most field-fabricated direct buried steam and hot water systems are placed in a trench surrounded by a hydrocarbon or chemically treated powdered chalk material that provides insulation and good protection from ground water. Most problems and failures with these systems are caused by water penetrating the fill material at pipe supports and hangers, or where the material was improperly installed. It is important that manufacturers recommendations be carefully followed when applying the mineral powder to avoid creating a moisture path to the pipe. Expansion in these systems is provided by placing a loosely fitted mineral wool at direction changes or expansion loops in the mineral powder, or encasing certain types of expansion joints in mineral wool. Manholes are required in these systems for access to pressure reduction valves and for mechanical expansion joints that require periodic inspection and maintenance.

Pre-engineered direct buried systems are manufactured by several companies. In these systems the carrier pipe for the water or steam is surrounded by insulation and an outer jacket that holds and protects the carrier pipe and insulation. These sections are available in twenty- to thirty-foot lengths. The systems have uniquely designed joints and many incorporate expansion into the system of joints between sections, eliminating the need for separate expansion joints or loops. Most problems with pre-engineered, prefabricated systems are caused by faulty field installation, especially in joining sections of piping. Good quality control during installation is essential to ensure proper operation of the system after it is in service. Direct buried systems are less expensive to install than tunnels or separate conduits. Pre-engineered, prefabricated direct buried systems have come into wide use in recent years.

Conduits and Tunnels   Conduit systems range from large walkthrough tunnels to small box conduits. They are field constructed, consist of a concrete trench with removable concrete covers, and insulated piping suspended with pipe supports are inside the trench. Once installed, access to the piping is by excavation and removal of the concrete trench covers. These systems may not be covered with soil, but, instead they can be left exposed and sometimes used as sidewalks. Where distribution systems must be relatively deep in the ground, small box conduits are seldom used because of the problem of access. These systems require manholes at all equipment that requires servicing, including expansion joints, valves, and steam traps.

Tunnels and box conduits can be economically constructed of prefabricated sections, which are placed in trenches, water proofed, and back filled. Cast-in-place concrete trenches and tunnels are in some cases more economical than precast. This is particularly true where long sections of tunnels or conduits permit slip-form construction.

For maintenance and operations, distribution systems installed in tunnels are the most desirable. Tunnels allow ready access to all components for inspection, maintenance, and repair. And perhaps most importantly, systems installed in tunnels are more protected from ground water. The added construction cost of tunnels may be offset by long-term lower maintenance and repair costs.

Tunnels must be provided with adequate ventilation and lighting to provide a safe environment for physical plant personnel.

Because most tunnels provide direct access to central plants and building mechanical spaces, access must be controlled. Valves and other equipment located in tunnels present a potential for very damaging vandalism. Of even greater concern, however, is the safety hazards of steam and hot water lines and exposure to friable asbestos insulation in the confined spaces.

In tunnel systems, manholes are required for access to long sections where reasonable access from buildings cannot be provided. In direct buried system, manholes are required for valves and other equipment. Most modern manholes are made from precast concrete or steel sections.

Anchors and Expansion Joints

Thermal expansion can exceed three inches per one hundred feet of pipe length in steam and hot water systems. Some pre-engineered direct buried systems provide for this expansion in the system joints. In all other systems, provision for expansion must be included in the design. Failure of expansion systems to function properly is a common cause of system leaks and failures.

There are many types of expansion joints, bending, corrugated or bellows, sliding, ball or swivel, and couplings. Bellows and sliding types are the most prevalent in underground systems. Bellows are easier to install and require less maintenance. Sliding expansion joints require accurate installation, close alignment, and frequent inspection. They are used where frequent cycling occurs.

Insulation

The thermal performance of insulation in an underground system is dependent upon several factors, including thermal efficiency and stability after being exposed to water. Thermal insulation retards heat flow at the published rate only when the cellular structure contains a dry gas, usually air. A small increase in moisture greatly increases the conductivity. It is normally assumed that insulation will be wetted sometime, so provision must be made for its rehabilitation and consideration given to its performance after rehabilitation. Draining and drying of insulation are best accomplished by an annular air space between the outer surface of the insulation and the inside surface of the conduit.

Before the late 1960s, asbestos was widely used for piping systems insulation. Today, calcium silicate and glass foam are more commonly used for high temperature applications. Fiberglass and plastic foam insulations are used in lower temperature applications. Hydrocarbons, other mineral powders, and insulating concrete are used in direct buried applications. Each of these materials have advantages and limitations, and the temperature as well as exposure to moisture must be considered in selecting insulation.

Calcium silicate has a better insulation value than foam glass, but will break down when it becomes saturated with water. Foam glass is extremely resistant to water damage, but it has a poor mechanical strength and is more expensive than calcium silicate.

Plastic foam insulations will break down and burn at high temperatures, as will the binders used in manufacturing fiberglass batts and sections. Field applied foams require careful application to assure that voids are not created and that the material components are accurately mixed during application. Hydrophobic mineral powder must be properly placed to assure proper protection and insulation of piping.

Steam Traps

Steam traps are an important part of all steam distribution systems. Their function is to discharge condensate and air from steam piping without allowing steam to escape. There are five basic operating types of steam traps, with variations of each.

1. Float traps operate by the rise and fall of a float created by a change of condensate level in the trap. The discharge from the flow trap is generally continuous since the opening at the valve is proportioned to the flow of condensate through the trap.
2. Bucket traps discharge intermittently as condensate fills the trap. There are two types: the inverted and the upright bucket trap.

3. Impulse traps depend on the property of condensate at high pressure and temperature to flash into steam at lower pressure. This flashing action is utilized to govern the movement of a valve by causing changes in pressure in the control chamber above the valve. The discharge of an impulse trap is pulsating or intermittent, but not so infrequent as with the bucket type trap.
4. Thermodynamic traps have only one moving part, a valve disk, which is operated by using the kinetic energy of steam.
5. The thermostatic trap has a temperature sensitive bellows that opens and closes the valve that discharges the condensate. This trap is usually quick acting and, therefore, more efficient in minimizing the amount of steam loss while allowing rapid and total release of condensate. This is generally the choice for higher pressure steam distribution systems.

All steam traps have intricate mechanisms and require frequent inspection to ensure that they are functioning properly and not permitting steam loss. Energy losses through malfunctioning, improperly sized, or applied steam traps may exceed all other energy losses.

29.4 CORROSION CONTROL

Steam and condensate lines are subject to both internal and external corrosion. Internal corrosion is due primarily to variations in oxygen and carbon dioxide content, while external is due to a combination of moisture and high temperature. Condensate piping is more susceptible to corrosion than steam piping.

The coating of piping systems to protect from ground moisture and provide cathodic protection is the principal method of preventing external corrosion. The criteria for selecting coating include:

1. Capability to withstand temperature of the piping.
2. Resistance to ground stresses.
3. Dielectric qualities.
4. Resistance to water penetration.
5. Mechanical strength to withstand scuffing.
6. Flexibility.

The principal coatings used are asphalt, coal tar, and epoxy. Dissimilar piping should not be used when there is a possibility of electrolyte between the two. This results in an electrochemical reaction that erodes metal from one of the pipes.

29.5 METERS

Historically, steam, hot water, and chilled water distribution systems on campuses have not been metered except for cost determination for purchased utilities. However, since the mid-1970s, meters have become an essential part of energy management programs.

Steam service can be measured by metering the steam flow or condensate return. The preferred system depends on the nature of the steam loads and the condition of the condensate return system. Condensate return metering is preferred if all condensate is returned to this system and is collected at a convenient point for metering. Condensate meters are accurate, dependable, and relatively trouble-free.

Steam flow meters must be used to measure use when all condensate is not returned to the system. This occurs when steam is used in processes from which the condensate is not returned, such as in food service operations, hospital sterilizing equipment, and laboratories. Steam meters are not as accurate as condensate meters.

There are three basic types of steam flow meters. The first uses differential pressure devices such as orifice plates, Pitot tubes, or flow nozzles. The second type is the turbine meter, either full profile or sampling. Vortex shedding meters operate on the principle of analyzing the changed characteristics of vortexes caused by an obstruction inserted in the steam flow.

Metering chilled water and hot water requires simultaneous measuring of water flows and temperature changes. British Thermal Units (Btu) meters, widely available from several manufacturers, do this and integrate the data through a computer to give direct Btus consumed as a readout.

29.6 SYSTEM MAINTENANCE AND OPERATION

To assure dependable service and the most cost effective operation of distribution systems, a comprehensive preventive maintenance program is required. There should be detailed inspections of the entire system at least annually, and testing of those components such as steam traps, valves, and expansion joints for which the functional integrity cannot be verified by inspection. Malfunctioning components of an underground system can result in major energy losses, yet can be detected only be careful inspection and testing.

29.7 NEW TECHNOLOGIES

The increase in energy costs since the mid-1970s has spurred studies for greater efficiencies in the production and distribution of heating and cooling media. One of the technologies being developed is thermal storage. This involves generating heating or cooling media prior to its required use.

A promising application of this is the production of chilled water or ice at night, and during off-peak electrical demand hours, and using it to provide chilled water during high electrical demand times. Producing chilled water for air conditioning consumes large amounts of electricity. Most electric power companies offer rate schedules that have significant incentives to use electricity at low demand times, such as late night, rather than high demand times such as afternoons of working days. There are chilled water storage systems that manufacture chilled water at night, store it in insulated tanks, and use it to minimize chilled water production during the day. This also allows the total system to produce more peak cooling (measured in tons or Btus per hour) than the installed chillers could normally produce.

A further refinement of this technology involves the production and storage of ice. The ice is then used to make chilled water for distribution. This permits chilled water systems to be operated at temperatures as low as 35°F. This allows a greater temperature rise across coiling coils, permitting smaller piping systems. These evolving technologies can be used not only for new installations, but some can be adapted to existing conventional chilled water systems.

Computer based energy management systems have made it possible to centrally manage steam, hot and chilled water generation, and distribution systems to provide cost-effective and dependable services. This makes possible management of electrical demand charges and, in some cases, allows management of natural gas use, making possible the purchase of natural gas at reduced rates.

29.8 SUMMARY

Efficient and dependable heating and cooling media distribution systems are essential to achieving the advantages of central heating and cooling plants. The distribution systems are costly, and have a life expectancy of at least twenty years. They present many problems, most due to ground moisture and difficulty of access for maintenance. To be energy efficient, they must be carefully designed, constructed, and maintained.

ADDITIONAL RESOURCES

American Society of Heating, Refrigeration and Air Conditioning Engineers, Inc. *HVAC Systems and Applications*, 1987 ASHRAE Handbook. Atlanta, Georgia: ASHRAE, 1987.

Committee on District Heating and Cooling, Energy Enginering Board, National Research Board, and National Research Council. "District Heating and Cooling in the United States." *Strategic Planning and Energy Management*, Volume 7 Number 2, 1987.

King, Reno C. *Piping Handbook*, fifth edition. New York: McGraw-Hill Book Company, 1967.

SECTION V

FACILITIES

PLANNING, DESIGN, AND CONSTRUCTION

Section Leader:
William D. Middleton, P.E.
Assistant Vice President, Physical Plant
University of Virginia

CHAPTER 30

The American Campus as a

Work of Art and Utility

Werner K. Sensbach
Director of Facilities Planning
University of Virginia

It has been said, first we shape our buildings, then our buildings shape us. Where would this old adage apply more aptly than at American university campuses, where the mission of the institution is education, where young, open minds absorb indelible impressions that last for a lifetime, and where money and skills are constantly at work to create and maintain a physical environment of utility and beauty.

From the start, Americans have taken particular pride and an abiding interest in the accomplishments, as well as in the appearance, of their colleges and universities. But today our society has assigned many roles to its university campuses: to provide a useful and inspirational environment of higher education for its youth; to serve as a paradigm of communal life, reflecting man's ordering hand at work; and to portray the image of a place, to which people may retreat in memory from time-to-time. Today, in a rapidly changing physical world, American college campuses also present the double image of innovation and preservation, of progress and repose, of change and continuity.

30.1 IN THE SHADOW OF A LONG BUILDING TRADITION

Like a history book opened up and come to life, American campuses can give a vivid account of 350 years of changing styles in architecture, landscaping, and the use of building materials. The deeper influences reach back into the Renaissance and medieval centuries.

Eight hundred years ago the first universities grew in the shadow of Notre Dame Cathedral in Paris and in the narrow streets of Bologna. Located far away from urban centers, Oxford and Cambridge adapted the enclosed court of the medieval cloister, and thus furnished the collegiate prototype in the Anglo-Saxon realm.

Since many Puritans of the Massachusetts Colony were graduates of Emanuel College of Cambridge, they recreated a familiar image when they founded Harvard College in 1636. While the prototypical English college is enclosed on all four sides and accessible only through a defensible heavy gate, the American colleges, from the beginning, preferred an open arrangement in which three individual college halls formed an academic U-shape, leaving the fourth side free to the community and the unobstructed view of the horizon.

This reflection of man's unshackled position in society and an enlightened relationship with nature carried forward into Thomas Jefferson's plans of 1817 for the University of Virginia. A shaft of space, formed by a parallel row of colonnaded buildings, directs the view from the Rotunda, the central library, into the distant Virginia mountains as a symbol of harmony between the man-made world, a beneficent nature, and the heavens above.

30.2 FORM AND FUNCTION OF THE EARLIEST UNIVERSITY BUILDINGS

If we look for images of the earliest American colleges, buildings such as Massachusetts Hall at Harvard, Connecticut Hall at Yale, and Nassau Hall at Princeton quickly come to mind as prototypical structures. With a height of three or four stories frequently the largest buildings in the whole community, academic halls usually housed all manner of college activities: dormitories for up to fifty students, recitation halls, library, kitchen, dining hall, and single rooms for unmarried teachers.

When the need for enlarging the college arose, it usually required the sustained effort of the already strained energies of the whole community. For the "Doubling of the College" at Yale in the 1750s the whole New Haven populace was enlisted in felling timber, digging clay, and making brick in an effort that extended over several years. In order to avoid such exhaustion of community resources and energy, Thomas Jefferson later proposed an open plan that permitted the addition of smaller, more economical building units, which could be fitted comfortably into the fabric of his "academical village."

At Charlottesville, Thomas Jefferson designed the University of Virginia grounds with its open lawn, pavilions, gardens, colonnades, hotels, serpentine walls, and its Rotunda in neoclassical architecture to serve as an "example of chaste architecture" and to exert a lifelong influence on the aesthetic sensibilities of the young students.

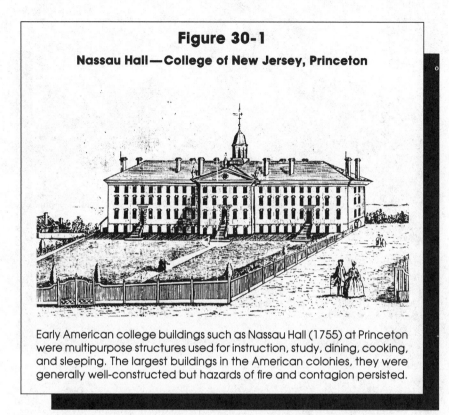

Figure 30-1

Nassau Hall—College of New Jersey, Princeton

Early American college buildings such as Nassau Hall (1755) at Princeton were multipurpose structures used for instruction, study, dining, cooking, and sleeping. The largest buildings in the American colonies, they were generally well-constructed but hazards of fire and contagion persisted.

30.3 FROM PASTORAL TO URBAN CAMPUS

With Oxford and Cambridge as guides, the founders of American colleges traditionally chose campus sites away from existing settlements and population concentrations. Lest the diversions of the city of Boston proved too tempting for the youthful Puritan scholars, Harvard's founders chose a site at Cambridge, two hours away from the harbor bars and other seaport temptations.

The state charter for the University of North Carolina stipulated a location for the campus twenty miles away from any existing city or town of the state. The campus master plan of 1795 called for the layout of "ye adjacent village," Chapel Hill. At that time, only the campus of William and Mary College assumed urban importance in the shaping of the baroque city plan of Williamsburg, Virginia. It came to occupy a pivotal location as the terminus of the mile-long Duke of Gloucester Street, opposite the House of Burgesses.

Colonial colleges saw their purpose in bringing up young men "to

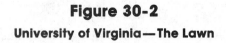

Figure 30-2
University of Virginia—The Lawn

With the design of the University of Virginia, Thomas Jefferson placed a regular pattern of Cartesian clarity on the virginal landscape of a frontier society. Espousing Palladian artistic principles, the neo-classical buildings of Virginia combine utility with an architecture of symmetry, perspective, and proportion.

teach and to preach." When the independent American states created state universities, they hoped to generate a cadre of capable loyal public servants, lawyers, and judges to whom the administration of the New Republic could be entrusted. But not until Thomas Jefferson developed a plan for "an useful American Education" did the idea of a "comprehensive" university first appear in American educational annals.

It was quite a different environment that spawned the urban universities in the latter part of the 19th century. Urban universities, some of which were exclusively graduate schools, emerged at the fringes of older cities, sometimes in the warehouse districts or residential neighborhoods, as did Johns Hopkins in Baltimore, MIT in Cambridge, Northeastern in Boston, Temple in Philadelphia, and the University of Chicago, which settled along the midway of the 1893 World Columbian Exposition.

Sometimes dubbed "street car universities," they initially had no need for student dormitories but saw their role in providing intensive advanced education in the newly developing fields of engineering, science, and social research for an increasingly urbanizing society. In the process, they also changed the image of the traditional university campus from a pastoral setting to a place of turbulent urban energy. Over the years, urban universities paradoxically strove to carve out academic quadrangles and open spaces from their dense urban fabric, both as symbolic gestures as well as useful design elements. Expansion into adjacent city neighborhoods has been the cause of much town-gown friction within the last decades.

30.4 THE NEED FOR A DESIGN PHILOSOPHY

Through the many years of their existence, American universities and colleges have lavished much care, thought, and financial resources in the development and maintenance of their campuses. The logic of an efficient utilities and services system may have the power to convince a skeptical state legislature to provide adequate funding. However, the elusive, aesthetic qualities that account for the ambiance and the architectural excellence that distinguishes one university campus from another are hard to pin down and difficult to subject to engineering measurement.

Thomas Jefferson, again, was the first to argue an aesthetic philosophy of design when he explained the use of ornate neoclassical elements in his architecture. The scale and style of the university buildings were to be "proportionate to the respectability, the means and the wants of our country . . . not what was to perish with ourselves, but what would remain, be respected and preserved thro' other ages." Fortified by this philosophy, he established an artistic palette of architectural opportunities never imagined before and not achieved since the completion of his masterpiece, the Grounds of the University of Virginia.

Methods of Design Analysis

If a campus architect wants to discern the aesthetic qualities and design opportunities inherent on the campus, he or she may benefit from the use-analysis methods common in urban design as established by such urbanists as Gordon Cullen, Kevin Lynch, and Lawrence Halprin. With the aid of a careful analysis of the architectural image of the campus, the university may incorporate a philosophy of design into its master plan. The plan is made up of three parts: *program*—an examination and identification of goals, design objectives, and needs; *performance*—a prescription of standards and criteria for design; and *perception*—an elaboration of the perceptual dimensions of design (spatial, visual, and chronological).

In order to record the findings of a design analysis, a campus architect, short of devising his or her own shorthand method, would benefit from using the design vocabulary of five elements: paths, edges, nodes, precincts, and architectural landmarks. This information may be amplified by recording changes of use and density in the campus landscape as they occur in the course of a day in a temporal sequence. The usefulness of the master plan will be greatly enhanced if it is informed by the insights of a sensitive spatial, aesthetic analysis.

Scale as Design Determinant

While the aesthetic appeal of a campus space may be traced to the skills and influence of a single, solitary, form-giving genius, campus design, as an ongoing process, will require agreement on artistic conventions to facilitate the dialogue between architects, engineers, and clients.

What, for example, is our understanding of "human scale," the term so frequently used in urban design as well as in campus planning? The term derives from our sense of visual perception and our ability to move about effortlessly and pleasurably within architectural or landscaped spaces. It is based on one fixed, immutable scale, the human body.

The forward-focused human eyes perceive the visible world in an irregular conical shape of 130° horizontal and a 75° vertical coverage. Within this "general field of view" is embedded a detailed field covering a narrow cone of sharp focus. These visual capabilities determine our sensory perceptions and affect our responses.

Within the categories of design scale, several dimensional qualities may be detected. If we stand within a range of three to ten feet from other people, we can clearly understand normal voices, discern subtleties of speech, and observe facial emotions. We can distinguish facial expressions up to forty feet and recognize a familiar person up to about eighty feet. Therefore, "intimate" spaces rarely exceed eighty feet in their minor dimension.

Bodily motions and gestures, however, can usually still be recognized up to 450 feet away, which is also the distance at which we can distinguish a man from a woman or observe athletic action, making it the ideal maximum viewing distance for a sports stadium. Urban spaces not exceeding 450 feet can therefore be considered "communal" spaces in which large crowds can participate in common events.

As we proceed to larger dimensions, we lose our ability to see objects smaller than six feet high—e.g. people—when they are further than 4,000 feet away. Within these "monumental" spaces people cease to play a significant part in the functioning of a man-made enclosure. The vast vistas of the Versailles Gardens and the Washington Mall serve useful ceremonial functions and achieve monumentality, but have transcended the "human scale."

30.5 THE ARCHITECTURE OF UNIVERSITY CAMPUSES

In the course of its long history, architecture absorbed many artistic subtleties which derived from an amalgam of structural capabilities, visual perceptions, and aesthetic theories. The builders of classical Greece, having observed how the bright Mediterranean light "eats away" from the substance of the fluted marble columns, compensated for this visual loss by adding a "swelling" (entasis) to the middle portion of the column.

Thomas Jefferson, in designing the University of Virginia, gradually increased the distance between the pavilions starting from the Rotunda, in order to emphasize the equidistant regularity of the structures facing the Lawn. Through the centuries, architects from Vitruvius to Palladio to Le Corbusier have developed aesthetic theories that explain the past and prescribe for the future.

Figure 30-3

University of Virginia, 1819

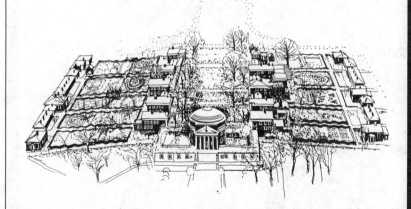

In the layout of the University of Virginia grounds, Thomas Jefferson dematerialized the bulkiness of the typical college building by distributing college functions in smaller "pavilions" the size of country houses. In this "academical village" individual student rooms are wedged between the larger structures which hold professors' residences, classrooms, and dining halls. The whole ensemble is crowned by the "Rotunda," a library building at the top of a large "lawn."

In the second half of the 19th century, John Ruskin's architectural theories, expressed in his *Seven Lamps of Architecture,* exerted a powerful influence on American campus planning. As a consequence, Yale University, deprecating its simple spartan structures as "brick barracks" and "muse's factories," tore down its colonial brick buildings to replace them in the Gothic style. Today only Connecticut Hall is left to tell of Yale's venerable early years as a colonial college.

After 1945, when postwar generations swelled the enrollments of almost every college and university, modern, unadorned, form-follows-function architecture easily invaded American campuses. Large, squat, air conditioned research and classroom structures succeeded the tradi-

Figure 30-4
University of California-Santa Cruz, Kresge College

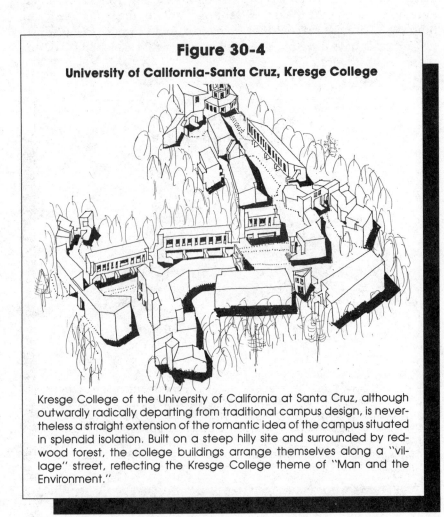

Kresge College of the University of California at Santa Cruz, although outwardly radically departing from traditional campus design, is nevertheless a straight extension of the romantic idea of the campus situated in splendid isolation. Built on a steep hilly site and surrounded by redwood forest, the college buildings arrange themselves along a "village" street, reflecting the Kresge College theme of "Man and the Environment."

Figure 30-5

University of Virginia—Colonnades

In the architecture of the University of Virginia, Thomas Jefferson introduced the neo-classical style as a reflection of the ideals of democratic
Athens and republican Rome. This architectural model to the New
American nation is rich in architectural symbolism, vistas, covered walks,
play of sunlight, trees and lawn, as a mirror of man's ordering hand.

tional, single corridor, cross-ventilated college buildings. In the process,
they all but abandoned the ambiance, the intimate spaces, and the
careful landscaping inherent in the older campus core.

In contrast, today's "post-modern" architects are trying to reintro-
duce traditional symbolic elements in their design. They have discovered, for example, the inviting effect of an arched entrance way, the
sense of shelter projected by a pitched roof, and the sensual play of light
and shadow in a carefully sculpted building facade.

In a world of discontinuities and conflicting theories, it appears that
those campuses have fared best which permitted variety in unity, yet
maintained regular building heights, continued using vernacular building material traditional to their area, and considered the spaces between
the buildings as important as the buildings themselves. With the aid of a
thoughtfully developed, flexible master plan and the interest of an alert,

intelligent university community, an institution should be capable of integrating all kinds of architectural styles into the fabric of its grounds and survive any past and future architectural theories—so long as these are friendly to people and consider technical progress only subservient to the well-being of the community.

30.6 CAMPUS LANDSCAPING—VARIETY IN UNITY

American campuses derive their distinction through the fine balance between aesthetically pleasing buildings and a carefully landscaped environment. In his plan for the University of Virginia, Thomas Jefferson called for a "lawn of trees and grass," bordered on three sides by academic buildings and residences. In this tradition, the "academic

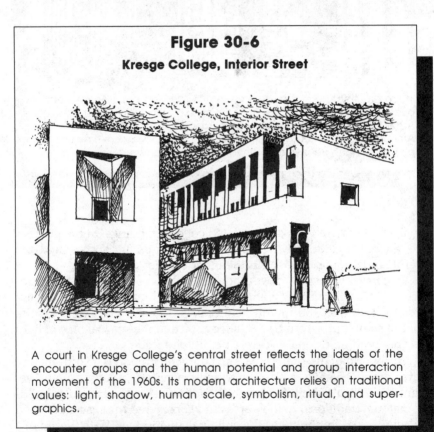

Figure 30-6

Kresge College, Interior Street

A court in Kresge College's central street reflects the ideals of the encounter groups and the human potential and group interaction movement of the 1960s. Its modern architecture relies on traditional values: light, shadow, human scale, symbolism, ritual, and super-graphics.

quadrangle" derives its quality from the harmonious relationship between buildings and open spaces.

Urban universities, existing in dense urban environments have problematic conditions of a different nature. But even they, as shown by Boston University, Temple University in Philadelphia, or Virginia Commonwealth University in Richmond, have managed to carve out intown academic quadrangles and park-like open spaces.

Traditionally, landscape architects have lent their skills to the development of campus landscape. Frederick Law Olmsted, with more than two dozen campus plans to his credit, is probably the most influential landscape architect and planner of American campuses. Wherever a university has followed a policy of employing many different landscape architects for individual design tasks, the campus tends to gain variety but loses uniformity.

Unity is an essential in landscape, as it is in architecture, and its continuity can only be assured by a landscape philosophy supported by the university community and by a competent staff. In an age of affluence, when residential landscaping has become the hobby of the urban gardener, the tendency of overplanting with flowering and ornamental shrub has affected campus landscaping across the continent. If ornamental campus landscaping is not carefully kept within bounds, it will quickly turn into an expensive maintenance liability. Thomas Jefferson's advise to plant "trees and grass" on the university grounds is as appropriate and useful today as it was in the early nineteenth century.

Pedestrian walkways are the sinews of a university campus. Their convenient locations and choice of surface material can affect the quality of the university grounds far beyond the cost of their construction. When selecting the appropriate surface material, one may keep in mind the surprising survey result Kevin Lynch received when he asked his students at MIT how they remembered paving materials they had experienced in their youth. The preferred surface material turned out to be neither brick paving, cobblestone, concrete, gravel, nor sand, but asphalt pavement. Although the walks across Harvard Yard are indeed of asphalt macadam, other universities have opted for more traditional material such as brick, irregular flagstones, rectangular-cut natural stone, granite, limestone, or simply concrete, all depending on availability, cost, ease of maintenance, and comfort and safety of the pedestrian.

Each campus also appears to have its special landscape problem spots, green spaces pounded into dust, which no amount of landscaping seems to be able to remedy. Problem areas however may uncover special opportunities, especially if the area acts as interim space and pedestrian "Venturi" channel between two larger academic areas. Such a spot may beg to be converted into a lively community space inviting passersthrough to spend some time. But, only a sensitive designer can release a

Figure 30-7

University of Pennsylvania — Walkways

Visitors, alumni, and students alike use and enjoy campus walks. The quality of old narrow walkways may be substantially improved by widening with compatible paving material, as on the University of Pennsylvania campus.

problem space from its bondage and turn an abomination into an attraction.

Street Furniture

The institution that builds classrooms, laboratories, libraries and dormitories, also has to provide for loading docks, trash dumpsters, rubbish bins, bicycle racks, street lights, emergency telephones, parking and street signs, newspaper vending boxes, kiosks, benches, and bus stops. Intended to make daily life of campus easier and more convenient, this "street furniture" also has the potential of creating visual havoc in a campus environment. Placed haphazardly and without coordination it will give the impression of visual confusion and may turn the campus into an obstacle course.

However, street furniture of carefully chosen design, unobtrusively placed, can greatly reinforce the feeling of safety and convenience conveyed to students and visitors to the campus. There are many excellent commercial products of varying designs and materials available. When no satisfactory commercial design can be found, campus designers may

Figure 30-8
University of Virginia—Thornton Hall

Present

Future

Campus grounds abound with unexplored aesthetic opportunities. Frequently, improvements can be simple and inexpensive: completing a disjointed system of walkways, opening up vistas by limbing up trees, relocating shrubbery, and introducing interesting patterns of sidewalk surfaces.

need to devise their own solution. Campus architects at the University of Virginia, for example, despairing over the inadequacy of commercially available emergency telephone standards, resorted to their own design which was built in the university shops at considerable savings.

30.7 THE CAMPUS AFTER DARK

At night, when darkness envelops the university grounds, a different campus reveals itself along its lighted pathways, below illuminated windows of dormitories and research labs, and around spotlighted towers and building facades. After women students entered the universities in greater numbers, security lighting increased dramatically, yet not always in a manner that would enhance the aesthetic integrity of the nighttime campus.

Lights placed too low, i.e., less than eight feet above ground level, have the capacity of blinding the viewer and cause the opposite of the intended effect. Most unshielded light sources placed below eye level, though well intended, merely annoy and irritate, inviting students to destroy them.

Nighttime lighting of university campuses presents one of the most important, yet unused, opportunities available to the campus engineer. Like a skillful stage designer, he or she may select from an extensive arsenal of lighting devices, well designed street lamps along pedestrian walkways, spotlights reflecting from building walls, and up-lighting of major trees and shrubbery areas to create a tracery of light, providing not only security, but also extending the hours of use and the visual integrity of the campus.

When we realize that university and college campuses are more than brick and mortar, or tree-lined alleys and academic quadrangles, we will discover that they touch us at our emotions, respond to our need for shelter and satisfy our sense of beauty. If the caretakers of American campuses are also sensitive to their responsibility as guardians of a rich cultural heritage, they will find satisfaction in knowing that through their work they will preserve and pass on a national treasure that will enrich the lives of future generations.

Whether for an "academical village" or a "multi-university," American college campuses will endure as long as they respect their traditions and uphold Aristotle's definition of the human community as a "place where common people can live a simple life for a noble end."

ADDITIONAL RESOURCES

Blumenfeld, Hans. "Scale in Civic Design," in *The Modern Metropolis: Essays by Hans Blumenfeld*, ed. P.D. Spreiregen. Cambridge, Massachusetts: The MIT Press, 1967.

Lynch, Kevin. *Site Planning*. Cambridge, Massachusetts: The MIT Press, 1962.

Turner, Paul Venable. *Campus*. Cambridge, Massachusetts: The MIT Press, 1984.

CHAPTER 31

Facilities Planning and Space Management

Clinton N. Hewitt
Associate Professor and
Associate Vice President, Physical Planning
University of Minnesota

31.1 INTRODUCTION

Facilities planning and space management is a decision-making process that gives direction to a continuing search for ways to improve existing conditions, and promotes change to accommodate new requirements. During periods when all requirements cannot be fully met, effective facilities planning and space management is critical in maximizing the use of available resources. The planning process can help evaluate and assign priority to needs and utilization policies both campus-wide and, in the case of public institutions, statewide.

This chapter presents guidelines and techniques to plan campus facilities and effectively manage campus spaces. Each institution must modify and adapt the procedures to fit the campus organizational structure and unique characteristics. The fundamental purpose of the processes presented is to promote examination, discussion, and cooperation in the search for solutions to facilities and space management problems.

31.2 INSTITUTIONAL PLANNING

Institutional planning is a process that requires the integration of academic, financial, and physical planning. Such planning is cyclical in nature and requires the development of procedures and schedules to ensure that the various activities occur in the proper sequence. This is important to not only maximize the financial commitment that an institution must make to the process, but to, in fact, preserve the process.

On many campuses, "crisis" planning has replaced the more formal and organized process. This results in sporadic responses to campus needs and, frequently, prevents campus-wide support for planning decisions. It also will often subject campus administrators to criticism for failing to maximize the allocation of campus resources. Institutional planning or comprehensive planning is a continuous and collaborative process and the proper allocation of people and funds must be provided on a consistent basis.

Another important characteristic of the institutional planning process is its ability to respond to changing needs. In other words, it must be easy to amend so that directions based on future projections can be adjusted to reflect the realities of the present. This suggests that the process is more important than the product (the long-range planning document). The process is dynamic while the product is static; the process invites participation while the product limits it.

Many campus plans are product-oriented and simply fill a spot on the shelves of campus administrators and planners. Because they are highly static, they do not provide the flexibility to deal with changing needs and an unpredictable future. In many instances, colleges and universities must struggle to change direction because of the inability of such plans to accommodate new circumstances. This has resulted in many campuses missing opportunities to develop the type of physical environment that enhances the educational experiences of its faculty, staff, students, and visitors. During periods of abundant resources, mistakes can be corrected. Unfortunately, most campuses today must operate within an environment of limited resources, making the institutional planning process more critical than ever before.

There is no standard formula that will guarantee a successful plan or planning effort. The planning process for any organization or institution is comprised of a unique set of circumstances that demands continuous, careful assessment. The result of such an assessment should allow the institution to assemble the appropriate combination of methods and resources to carry out the planning process.[1] There are, however, certain basic steps that will ensure that the planning process is responsive to the campus needs and accommodate reassessment and refinement.[2] A typical institutional planning cycle involves:

1. Review existing plans; if none exist, begin with the determination of the mission (goals and objectives of the institution).
2. Prepare basic planning assumptions.
3. Request and review academic and support department plans.
4. Determine institutional needs.
5. Evaluate existing resources (financial, facilities, and land).
6. Prepare alternatives (action strategies).
7. Review plans and strategies with departments.
8. Prepare final plans, budgets, and strategies.

9. Seek approval by governing boards.
10. Implement final plan (action strateties).
11. Evaluate the process and outcomes.
12. Initiate next planning cycle.

As one of the components of a comprehensive institutional plan, it is important to establish the proper relationship of facilities planning to the comprehensive planning process. (See Figure 31-1.) Physical planning, in its broadest concept, relates to the total campus environment. Its basic focus is to support and encourage the goals and objectives of the institution through the management of its physical environment.

Designed to facilitate the teaching, research, and service mission of an institution, the primary objective of physical planning is to achieve timely development of facilities needed for academic and service programs in an efficient, cost-effective manner.

Physical development directly affects the financial realities of an institution and the delivery of academic programs. Therefore, a planning framework should be established to identify essential actions and strategies to ensure interaction between the three elements of institutional planning. Integrated academic, financial, and physical planning can be an effective force in implementing the goals and objectives of an institution.

The precise definition of planning objectives and the establishment of a specific methodology for project planning and development can minimize the cost of replacement, renovation, and relocation of facilities necessitated by changes in academic priorities. Physical planning is a vehicle to achieve an enriched academic environment that links multidisciplinary research, technological innovation, and visionary instruction.

Physical planning is a process structured to promote cost-effective development decisions that best serve academic and administrative goals and objectives. This process operates on the premise that the development of facilities and their ongoing management can best serve specific program needs if university standards of space planning, facility programming, design, and construction management are closely linked.

Physical planning, in its most technical definition, must be practiced by those within the institution as an integral component of the organizational structure. Despite campus planning documents (long-range planning studies, space analyses, academic planning studies, and site plans), if planning is not practiced by the decision-makers, it simply does not exist. Much of the rapid development that occurred after World War II and during the 1960s came as a response to rising enrollment levels throughout college and university systems. Enrollments leveled off at the end of the 1970s and have declined slightly during the 1980s.

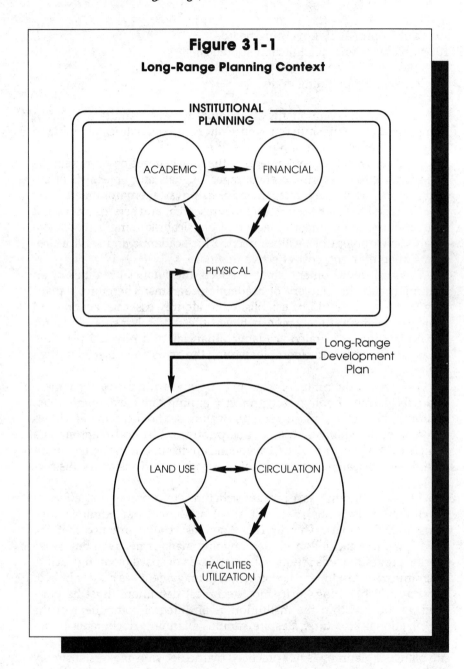

Figure 31-1

Long-Range Planning Context

This gave rise to the term "steady-state," which planners use to describe a phase of development where the emphasis is placed on maintenance and improvement of existing facilities, while new construction activities are confined to only the highest priorities of academic and support needs.

It should be emphasized that steady-state does not mean that facilities will be used until they wear out; rather, during this period, maintenance and improvement increasingly becomes more important. The term steady-state has confused some to believe that it is not so important for comprehensive facilities planning to take place. On the contrary, facilities planning becomes easier to justify because improvement in the physical environment is quite clear to both the campus user and the general public. The physical appearance of the campus can more clearly give rise to the need for comprehensive facilities planning than overall comprehensive institutional planning. On the other hand, good facilities planning can ensure that physical resources are appropriately allocated in support of the mission of the institution and make clearer the need for overall comprehensive planning.

With the tools available to planners and administrators today, there is no excuse for failure to use the physical environment to enhance the learning experience. Decision-makers must assure that facilities serve the purposes of the institution through thoughtful and effective planning and management. Policies and guidelines must be developed that promote a dynamic relationship among all three planning components.[3]

31.3 LONG-RANGE DEVELOPMENT PLAN

A long-range development plan (LRDP) brings together existing resources and projected needs, serves as an effective instrument for organizing needs and resources, and establishes the process through which the resolution of planning issues can be maximized. Planning goals and objectives can be determined and strategies developed to achieve them. Recommendations more easily evolve when needs and resources are matched with goals and strategies in an ongoing planning process. Following the examination of several alternatives, the option that best meets the resources and goals of the institution can be recommended as the course of action to follow.

Planning recommendations should include suggestions for immediate and long-term actions, and written and graphic illustration of concepts and policies. The immediate problems of the campus can be addressed by short-term actions; however, conceptual suggestions and policy recommendations should respond to projected future needs. A specific, fixed physical plan is not recommended because such a plan is bound to be superficial and grow obsolete quickly. Development guidelines that provide overall direction yet recognize the inflexibility of bricks and mortar should be documented. Ideally, these guidelines allow for the creative input of the people being served, the staff-assigned monitoring responsibility, and subsequent professional consultants retained to carry out the implementation of the plan.

Needs and resources change over the years, so specific recommendations may have to be adjusted. But the goals, objectives, and strategies to achieve them should remain consistent with the institution's mission to give direction to the implementation process. Accordingly, it is important to evaluate the needs, resources, and list of goals and strategies periodically to ensure that they remain consistent with reality. An LRDP will become ineffective if a process to review and change it in response to new information, ideas, and conditions is not established.

The development of an LRDP involves a sequence of steps and planning studies. (See Figure 31-2.) The steps described in the following paragraphs are based upon an approach developed in the Office of Physical Planning at the University of Minnesota with planning consultants and used to prepare LRDPs for the campuses in the system. The initial document, *Tactical Report*, outlines the major planning issues, many administrative in nature, and establishes the overall procedures for conducting the planning process.

The planning base inventory catalogues existing resources and projected needs of the institution. Information gathered pertains to natural systems data (geology, soils, hydrology, shadows, and weather) physical facilities data, space utilization data, and so forth.

More detailed planning issues and the goals and objectives those issues generate, are usually outlined in other supportive reports.

The final report, the LRDP, describes: 1) a review of the overall process, 2) a summary of the existing situation (resources), 3) a summary of needs, 4) recommendation including a description of planning goals and strategies, and 5) a procedure for implementing the development plan. A planning advisory committee comprised of representatives from the faculty, staff and students and, in some cases, city planning agencies and residents of surrounding neighborhoods should be appointed to oversee the process. Such a group can provide major input from the campus population relative to issues and resulting recommendations. *The planning staff, however, should take the leadership in executing the study.* During the course of the long-range planning study, additional studies (such as parking and facility utilization) may be conducted. The conclusions in these studies will impact final recommendations.

The primary resources that are pertinent to physical planning are the land, existing physical plant, faculty and staff, and enrollments present and future. The land and its assets should be evaluated through

Figure 31-2
Campus Planning Process

1 Outlining the process
1. Identify scope & context of planning project.
2. Identify interest groups.
3. Identify general issues.
4. Develop time/task framework.
5. Establish management procedures.
6. Initiate planning base for inventory work.

2 Assemble academic and administrative planning data
1. Develop enrollment projections.
2. Develop space utilization data.
3. Develop space need projections.
4. Develop financial projections.
5. Predict future academic and administrative structure.
6. Identify future departmental and program relationships.

3 Assemble utilization data
1. Inventory existing space.
2. Develop computer program for data analysis.

4 Assemble planning base data
1. Conduct issue analysis.
2. Inventory natural and ecological systems.
3. Inventory support systems.
4. Inventory movement systems.
5. Inventory existing academic relationships.
6. Conduct character analysis of existing campus environment.
7. Develop format for presentation of data base information.
8. Prepare planning base inventory document.

5 Facilities utilization study
1. Determine efficiency of facilities utilization on campus.
2. Develop methodology for ongoing space management.

6 Formulate planning framework of land use and circulation
1. Briefing and study organization by consultants.
2. Assemble and analyze base information, issues, and existing goals and policies.
3. Develop and test alternative planning guidelines.
4. Coordinate planning guidelines.
5. Develop and test land use and circulation plan alternatives.
6. Coordinate planning framework.
7. Print draft report.
8. Present draft plan to state legislature or other body.

7 Refine planning policies and framework
1. Reevaluate planning goals, policies, & framework plans.
2. Finalize recommended policies & framework plans.
3. Establish procedures for implementation & monitoring of plan.
4. Prepare final LRDP document.
5. Present LRDP to all appropriate interest groups.

8 Decisions on implementation
1. Adopt or revise recommended plans.
2. Implement policies and plans.

9 Monitoring and implementation of plans
1. Evaluate effectiveness of policies and plans.
2. Revise goals if major changes occur.
3. Revise policies if major changes occur.

a site analysis process and quantified as much as possible to facilitate planning decision-making. The amount and types of space available in existing structures should be described in a building space inventory or a facility utilization study.

The future growth of a campus is not only dependent upon the number of students, faculty and staff, their needs and desires, but also upon the amount and potential of available land to support growth. The characteristics of different areas vary greatly in their ability to support various types of functions and intensities of use. Some areas will readily support major structures or development, while conditions in other areas would make construction economically infeasible. In addition, areas have varying topographies, vegetation, microclimates, and visual appeal, all of which affect the value and potential use of the land.

Planning for the future use of available land must be based on thorough investigations and analyses of all areas of the campus. To aid in determining the best use of the land, the entire campus could be divided into sites that are considered to be homogeneous in their characteristics and which would be treated as units for future use and development.

In defining homogeneous sites, three basic factors are considered: 1) ecological/physical land characteristics, 2) current land usage, and 3) visual characteristics. Homogeneous sites are established through visual inspection. The boundaries of some sites are well-defined by existing development, while others are defined only by a change in topography, vegetation, or variations in natural habitat. Each site should be evaluated according to specific requirements for each land use category.[4]

Enrollment Projections

Enrollment projections cannot be relied on as hard, fixed facts. Analysts can, at best, look at the numbers of elementary students coming up through the educational system, recent education trends, and changes in social conditions and apply known formulas to estimate future enrollment levels.

When enrollments are tied to space needs and academic plans, a set of planning horizons can be established. These horizons are:

- Short-range planning (two to four years)—Enrollment predictions for this range must be specific and accurate. Planning within this time frame typically involves facilities that are in the programming or building request stage. Projections should include numbers of people using the facility, related space requirements, teaching methods, functional relationships, and operational needs.

- Mid-range planning (up to ten years)—Projections within this time frame indicate basic societal, educational, and cultural trends that may affect enrollments, programs, teaching methods, and utimately, space needs. Such projection data allows physical planners to locate facilities and functions within the planning framework in general terms.
- Long-range planning (up to fifteen years)—Projections for this time horizon define enrollment ceilings, educational goals, and basic trends. Within this context, the planning framework functions as a statement of the ultimate physical goals of the institution.

To add even greater flexibility to long-range planning, future needs of the institution should become a direct function of current enrollment levels rather than the anticipated enrollment levels of future years. This approach can provide a more meaningful and realistic method for pacing future requests for additional facilities.

Academic and Support Space

To ascertain the kinds and amounts of academic and support space available, a comprehensive facilities inventory should be completed to reflect the functional uses of the space at the initiation of the LRDP study. The process and procedures used to determine the kinds and amounts of available space should reflect the quality and intensity of use.

It is necessary to determine the amount of space necessary for an institution to conduct its educational activities. A space model using nationwide averages can be employed to determine the total amount of space for various types of institutional space (such as classrooms, offices, library). The purpose of this type of analysis is to determine the total space needs of an institution. Although a model can be used to analyze activities, space standards and guidelines must be changed from an institutional average to a figure that is representative of the specific activity being analyzed.

Using this type of analysis, it is possible to determine the quantity and kind of additional space needed to conduct educational activities or the amount and kind of space that is available for conversion to other uses.

Care must be taken in interpreting the quantity of space that is over or under the quantity suggested by a specific space guideline/standard. A variance of plus or minus 10 percent from the space guideline/standard for a particular kind of space is normally considered within reason for this type of institutional space analysis. If a particular space classification has a variance of more than plus or minus 10 percent, the need for further, more detailed analysis is required.

Campus/Community Issues

To encourage participation in the planning process and to identify campus/community issues, issue analysis sheets could be distributed to students, faculty, staff, and affected neighborhoods in the surrounding community. (See Figure 31-3.) Meetings should also be held with individuals, committees, organizations, city officials, and other interest groups to identify areas of concern during the course of the study.

The issues generated by the issue sheets and related meetings should be organized according to the general planning areas outlined in the planning base inventory (natural systems; program relationships, or academic issues; housing, social, recreational, and commercial facilities; utilities and service; and transportation). All issue sheets submitted should be kept on file for future reference.

The goals and strategies of the institution generally determine the reconciliation of needs and resources, and specific recommendations for implementation. As emphasized in an earlier section, a "fixed" physical plan is not produced because it will become obsolete quickly. The more ideal approach, a framework plan, allows for the creative input of the institution as responses to changing conditions are required.

Land Use

Land use considerations address the large-scale overview and general physical organization of the campus. The following are guidelines intended as a foundation for a generalized concept for campus development that promotes a sensitivity between activities and the physical demands on land resources.

- The highest and best use should be made of all land.
- Land use conflicts with neighboring residential and commercial areas should be avoided.
- Campus activity areas should complement each other. Development should promote visual interest and functionally fit the rest of the campus.
- Facilities should only be constructed on sites that best meet programmatic and environmental objectives. Consider a "don't build" policy to preserve historic or open space objectives.

The final plan should provide adequate areas for all major land use components including academic expansion, housing, open space, recreation, parking and circulation.

Figure 31-3

Long Range Development Plan
Issue Analysis

From: ☐ student   ☐ staff   ☐ male   Date: _____
       ☐ faculty   ☐ non-university   ☐ female

Issue

Source of information

Current situation

Comments

Recommendations

| F/S | D5 | Issue no. _____ |

Transportation

The transportation goals and objectives of an institution should cover five broad categories: 1) general access to campus, 2) vehicular circulation, 3) parking, 4) pedestrian and bicycle circulation, and 5) transit. Following are some general guidelines.

- Transportation modes should be coordinated to ensure maximum efficiency and service, convenient parking, and the various modes of transportation should be listed as a single system. The system should be coordinated with local transportation facilities.
- Access to the campus should be sensitive to community concerns (social and environmental quality, property values, open spaces, cultural and historic facilities).
- Campus users should be able to reach their destinations directly and without confusion. To minimize confusion and to direct campus-oriented traffic to routes designed to accommodate them, a comprehensive directional signage system should be developed.
- Long- and short-term parking required for the normal functioning of the campus should be accommodated on the campus.
- Parking facilities should complement the campus character, natural amenities, and pedestrian activities. The transition from vehicular circulation to parking and pedestrian circulation should be orderly and logical.

Physical Facilities

Physical facilities generally refers to all permanent improvements including academic, administrative, housing and commons functions. The expansion of academic facilities should occur only after careful and thorough evaluation of projected needs and capabilities of existing facilities. Once needs are established, the following (listed in priority order) is a general approach to best determine the most logical method of meeting the program requirements: 1) higher utilization of existing space, 2) renovating existing structures, 3) infill (adding vertically or horizontally to existing structures), and 4) expansion of facilities in areas of the campus where buildings currently do not exist.

Housing

It is important that an institution establish a housing policy that reflects students' needs and overall institutional goals and objectives. It is desirable to provide a variety of housing types to allow students a choice of living styles. Housing should be easily accessible from academic and support areas and the institution must be sensitive to, and avoid conflicts with, adjacent residential areas.

Nonacademic Facilities

Indoor and outdoor nonacademic facilities play an important role in the development of faculty, staff, and students' institutional experience. Careful thought should be given to the development of those areas to promote active use throughout the day and higher use of facilities year-round. Commons facilities should be an integral part of the pedestrian circulation system and provide for a variety of activities. Subcenters at strategic locations extend the services provided at the main campus center. The development of passive and active outdoor recreation facilities should preserve any unique characteristics of the campus.

Utilities and Services

Frequently, the utilities and service elements of the general campus system are overlooked as minor issues and, unfortunately, such neglect leads to unnecessary expense and conflict. A consolidated utility system should be developed, consistent with the projected needs of the campus. Such a system will simplify maintenance and future needs for extension or expansion of the utility network, and will be less costly.

Campus Landscape

The institution should address, in a specific way, the goals for the campus landscape by establishing policies and principles that will bring unity and beauty to the campus environment. Organizing the many campus elements into a unified pattern will achieve a visually coherent and attractive image and preserve its distinctive characteristics. The establishment of policies and principles to guide and discipline development on the campus will not only preserve, but enhance environmental qualities vital to the mission of most institutions. A primary landscape goal for the campus should be to present an image with a high degree of continuity and quality.

For the LRDP to be an effective tool, it is essential that it be continually reviewed and updated. Ideally, this should occur every two years, but not more than four. The process for updating a master plan is similar to the development of the initial campus plan. Consultants may be used for certain components such as transportation or analysis of utility systems, but for the most part, members of the planning staff and a campus planning advisory committee should be able to accomplish this work. Figure 31-4 illustrates the organization of an updating effort that is consistent and supportive of an existing campus LRDP. The management of this effort can be modified to suit the staffing or organizational pattern of the campus or office responsible for planning. The important principle is the need to periodically review and update the plan.

31.4 FACILITIES PLANNING PROCESS

Master Planning for Facilities

It is important to establish procedures for the development of facilities consistent with the completed LRDP. There are nine basic steps to achieve an orderly development of facilities. (See Figure 31-5.)

Organization of the Planning Effort   When an institution decides that new or improved facilities are needed to support its general mission and, more particularly, the academic plan, it is necessary to organize the planning effort to develop specifics. This first step involves appointing persons to participate directly in the planning effort, the establishment of time frames and a determination of resources available to prepare plans. The committee is typically given the title planning (or building) advisory committee and usually is appointed by the chief financial officer of the institution. The committee normally coordinates the planning efforts that analyze programs and facilities that constitute the framework for the facilities planning study. The membership of the committee should include the director of the physical planning staff (usually the chairperson or co-chairperson), representation from the physical plant staff (ideally the director), students, faculty, and other staff. The ideal size for the committee is five to seven members.

Define Purpose and Objective   The committee's initial step is to define its goals and objectives on the basis of the charge given by the appointing authority. In addition to establishing a schedule to complete the study, special assignments of individual members of the committee and a determination of the need for assistance from outside consultants must be accomplished during this step.

Development of Data   This step involves the collection of pertinent data that requires examination, evaluation, and analysis to determine the needs of a particular department or unit that is engaged in planning facilities. The space programming and management office can provide information on the current inventory and utilitization of facilities. The

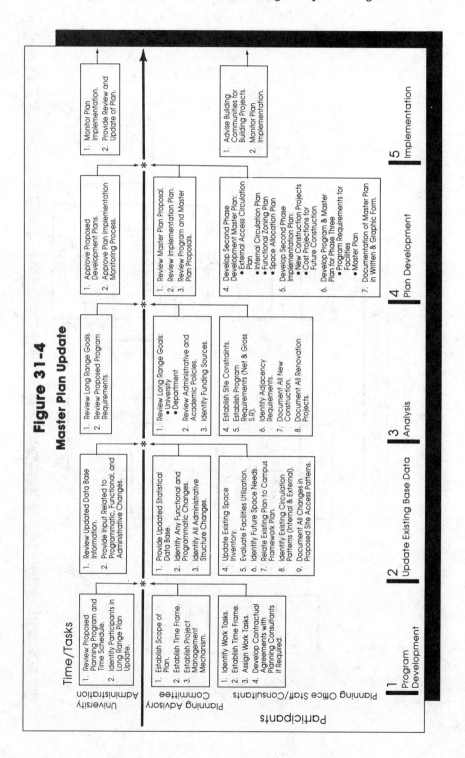

Figure 31-4
Master Plan Update

Time/Tasks

Participants

University Administration

1. Review Proposed Planning Program and Time Schedule.
2. Identify Participants in Long Range Plan Update.

1. Review Updated Data Base Information.
2. Provide Input Related to Programmatic, Functional, and Administrative Changes.

1. Review Long Range Goals.
2. Review Proposed Program Requirements.

1. Approve Proposed Development Plans.
2. Approve Plan Implementation Monitoring Process.

1. Monitor Plan Implementation.
2. Provide Review and Update of Plan.

Planning Advisory Committee

1. Establish Scope of Plan.
2. Establish Time Frame.
3. Establish Project Management Mechanism.

1. Provide Updated Statistical Data Base.
2. Identify Any Functional and Programmatic Changes.
3. Identify All Administrative Structure Changes.

1. Review Long Range Goals:
   • University
   • Department
2. Review Administrative and Academic Policies.
3. Identify Funding Sources.

1. Review Master Plan Proposal.
2. Review Implementation Plan.
3. Review Program and Master Plan Proposals.

Planning Office Staff/Consultants

1. Identify Work Tasks.
2. Establish Time Frame.
3. Assign Work Tasks.
4. Develop Contractual Agreements with Planning Consultants if Required.

1. Update Existing Space Inventory.
2. Identify Future Space Needs.
3. Relate Existing Plan to Campus Framework Plan.
4. Identify Existing Circulation Patterns (Internal & External).
5. Document All Changes in Proposed Site Access Patterns.

4. Establish Site Constraints.
5. Establish Program Requirements (Net & Gross S.R).
6. Identify Adjacency Requirements.
7. Document All New Construction.
8. Document All Renovation Projects.

4. Develop Second Phase Development Master Plan:
   • External Access Circulation Plan
   • Internal Circulation Plan
   • Functional Zoning Plan
   • Space Allocation Plan
5. Develop Second Phase Implementation Plan:
   • New Construction Projects
   • Cost Projections for Future Construction
6. Develop Program & Master Plan for Phase Three
   • Program Requirements for Facilities
   • Master Plan
7. Documentation of Master Plan in Written & Graphic Form.

1. Advise Building Communities for Building Projects.
2. Monitor Plan Implementation.

1	2	3	4	5
Program Development	Update Existing Base Data	Analysis	Plan Development	Implementation

Figure 31-5

Comprehensive Master Planning for Facilities Process

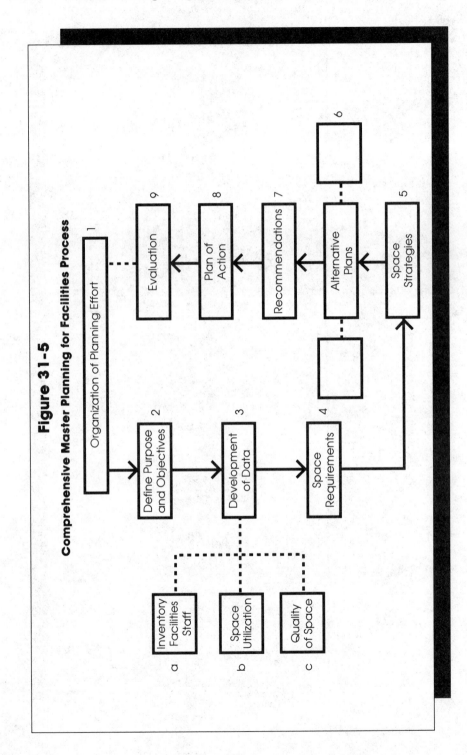

investigation and evaluation of existing conditions, including physical condition of structures, mechanical and electrical systems, exterior and interior utilities, expansion potential, handicapped access, building codes, and fire and life safety can either be carried out by staff or special consultants. *Critical to the work of the committee is the review of the approved academic plan.* Academic plans are the foundation of any master planning for facilities, and it should include a statement of objectives, funding resources, course and project data, and faculty/staff requirements. The academic plan must be consistent with the goals, objectives, and policies of the institution.

Space Requirements   It is necessary to determine the amount of space required to accommodate academic programs. Space standards or a facilities model can be used to determine, numerically, the amount of square feet required. The development of this information provides a basis for examination of the facilities needs and the comparison with existing conditions. In this step, it is also necessary to evaluate the qualitative needs of programs, including a listing of the facilities required to house programs, identification of the kinds of spaces required, and the relationship of facilities to the overall institutional inventory.

Space Strategies   Program needs of institutions can be met in several ways: construction of new facilities, renovation and upgrading of existing facilities, leasing space off-campus for the duration of a need, and utilizing university space in a more systematic and cooperative way. A conservative approach to expansion is recommended, with the decision based on the most cost-effective alternative that will meet the academic and administrative goals of the institution. The following sequence is recommended to provide for additional space in a productive and creative way.

1. Increase the efficiency of assigned space without sacrificing program quality.
2. Lease space off-campus, especially for programs that have short termination periods.
3. Renovate space to achieve more productive use.
4. Expand buildings onto existing facilities.
5. Build new facilities.

The fifth option listed should only be considered when it is determined that current facilities cannot be renovated and added to accommodate long-range academic plans. If the recommendation is new construction, it should be supported by the following factors.

- The activity to be housed is important to the mission of the institution.
- Expanded facilities are necessary.
- Costs can be justified on the basis of demonstrable benefits to the institution (and the state in the case of public institutions).
- Current facilities are not available or cannot be suitably renovated to achieve the desired results.

Alternative Plans   It is important to develop alternative plans for consideration by decision-makers. There is no straightforward method to determine the precise plan that will meet all of the needs of academic programs. The solution to a problem has many paths and it is necessary to consider the various paths before a decision is made. This is especially important in the public setting, where decisions are frequently challenged. Alternative plans are also necessary to review and draw conclusions about the various space strategies developed. It is clearly better to consider alternatives at this stage in the planning process than to be challenged after the master facility plan has been completed. It also must be recognized that it is impossible to consider all of the possible alternatives. Therefore, at some point a decision must be made on the alternatives that have receive the most detailed analysis. Although this could result in a particular alternative being missed, the planning process is dynamic and it should be possible for the planning committee to evaluate an alternative suggested by a colleague, administrator, or citizen.

Recommendation   Probably the most challenging step in the procedure is the development of recommendations for consideration by the campus administration. Careful evaluation of the solutions that will support and accommodate academic programs and plans must be observed. It requires detailed planning on the part of the facilities planners on the team, the academic planners, and the consultants. This is also the most difficult step in the process, because it requires compromise and cooperation on the part of the committee members. The committee must review the pros and cons of the various alternative plans and evaluate the strengths and weaknesses of each. At this stage it is possible that additional details are necessary to reduce the number of alternative plans and to zero in on the plan or plans that will best meet the institution's objectives and goals. Some type of matrix system should be developed at the first stage of evaluation to systematically reduce the number of alternatives. It should also be recognized that there will probably be no perfect alternative, so consideration should be given to extracting from the various alternatives ideal components to recommend in the final plan.

Plan of Action   After the committee has developed its recommendations, it is necessary to prepare a plan to implement them. The plan of
action includes space strategies, funding alternatives, and a mapping of
steps that the institution should take to reach the completion phase.

Evaluation   Since planning is a continuing and dynamic process, it
is important that evaluation become part of the facilities planning cycle.
The process is improved by continuous evaluation and refinement of the
data analysis and the steps in the process. The planning advisory committee is in the best possible position to evaluate the process, having
experienced its use over a period of months. The final report to the
administration should include the committee's evaluation of the process
and recommendations that would improve the next planning cycle.
Another approach would be to evaluate each of the steps outlined
during the execution of the study so that adjustments can be made and
hopefully, subsequent steps may be carried out in a more effective way.

31.5 SPACE MANAGEMENT

There is an increasing demand for more effective allocation and utilization of university facilities by institutional officers, governing boards,
and state legislatures who provide a major portion of capital funds for
public institutions. Procedures are necessary to provide explicit justification when additional space or new construction is requested, and such
procedures should be applied routinely to all programmatic space needs.
In addition to the usual technique of evaluating capacity and project
needs, space management procedures must address the quality of space
and provide incentives for better utilization.

A space management plan represents an objective means of systematically assessing space requirements and utilization. (See Figure 31-
6.) In addition, it will extend the traditional methods of evaluating the
capacity of university facilities and projecting future facilities requirements by including qualitative analysis, as well as management incentives. An office of space programming and management or similar organizational unit should serve as the locus of activities in the collection,
assembly, and analysis of space data.

The space office serves as an invaluable aid to decision-makers and
campus planners in identifying problem areas and providing alternative
options to facilitate objective and rational space assignment decisions.
The general responsibilities of the office are:

- Maintaining a campus-wide space inventory.
- Conducting an annual audit of all rooms in university-owned

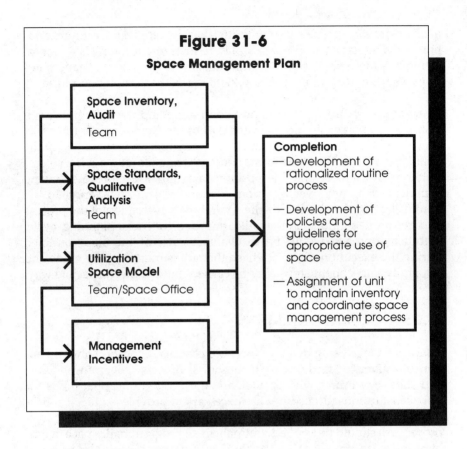

Figure 31-6

Space Management Plan

or leased space (on larger campuses, the objective might be an audit of all rooms every two to three years).

- Continuously auditing all space in which changes are due to allocation or renovation.
- Preparing an annual utilization report of all instructional space, which involves an assessment of the level of utilization for classrooms and instructional laboratories for each quarter or semester.
- Maintaining or developing space standards to determine appropriate levels of space assignment and utilization.
- Employing qualitative guidelines to assess the suitability and adequacy of space programs.
- Providing support to academic and administrative units in responding to programmatic needs through objective and well-documented space analyses and recommendations.

Successful implementation of the space management plan will require the cooperation and active support of the administration, space users, and numerous support units.

31.6 SPACE INVENTORY/AUDIT

One of the most crucial and essential elements of space management is the inventory. An accurate space inventory provides the administration (space manager) with information on the current assignment and usage of all university facilities. Such information can vary from the sketchy to the detailed. Unfortunately, the degree of inventory accuracy is usually inversely proportional to the number of descriptive data elements collected and maintained.

The minimum information on each discreet space would be an identifying room number, area, user department, and programmatic use. Additional useful information can be collected for each room, but collecting unnecessary details can easily make the process cumbersome. The terminology and descriptions used in the inventory should be consistent with the classification outlines provided in the *HEW Facilities Inventory and Classification Manual* or other systems that are used uniformly throughout the institution.

The space inventory/audit is useful and effective only if it is reasonably accurate and up to date. An essential principle of inventorying space is that the amount of data should be limited to that which is necessary and relates to the resources the university can allocate to support the management of the system. For this reason, the scope of data collected and reports generated should be carefully evaluated to achieve the optimum balance between the quantity and accuracy of data collected.

A well-developed and comprehensive space inventory provides a broad range of information extending across campuses, including such physical characteristics as fixed equipment and laboratory services. In situations where this level of detail is provided, the information can be used for such other purposes as the recovery of space-use overhead from grants and contracts to the development of maintenance schedules within physical plant.

The space inventory/audit process proposed in the plan can be implemented by the space office staff, assisted when necessary by students or other temporary clerical help. The staff should initiate a department-by-department audit of space, beginning with the larger, more stable departments so as to minimize some of the disruptions and maximize the validity of the inventory. Thereafter, an ongoing audit will assure that each space is checked annually or at least every two years.

The following is a general approach to an ongoing inventory/audit process.

1. The space staff obtains the departmental (or building) listings for a given department from the facility analyst or the person responsible for keeping such records.
2. The space staff upgrades listings before the on-site visit.
3. The director of the space office notifies department chairpersons (dean or director) before the actual on-site audit starts.
4. The director of the space office and space staff meet with the department chairperson to obtain additional information on programs, and personnel for departmental listings before walking the space.
5. The space staff walks the space, noting any changes in space configurations (room numbers or area) or in space classification (HEGIS program or use).
6. The space staff requests updated building change notices (BCNs) from the facilities office to make changes in space configuration.
7. The space staff reports changes to the facility analyst and the inventory is updated.
8. The space staff prepares a "clean" departmental listing and sends a copy to the department chairperson.
9. When all departments in a building have been audited, the facility analyst checks the inventory against the latest BCNs to ensure that no room is missed.
10. Utilizing the campus space standards, the space staff obtains departmental information so that projected space needs can be compared with current space. This information is utilized in the preparation of capital needs reports.

31.7 SPACE STANDARDS/QUALITATIVE GUIDELINES

The second step in planning for space use is to evaluate the amount of space required for a specific program. Such evaluation is pragmatic at best, since no absolute standards exist.

The plan proposes that the space programming and management staff, augmented by members of the academic community, will develop standards or guidelines for the university which, using unique parameters for a given program or department, would provide the "total envelope" of space needed. This team might also establish recommended sizes for offices or other specific facilities. After standards have been adopted, projected space needs can be compared to actual space being used so as to determine whether a given department (program) has enough space, needs more space, or perhaps should relinquish some space.

Space standards, as applied in the decision-making process of space allocation and building program planning, can be beneficial tools. The objectives of implementing space standards are twofold: to provide guidelines that would accurately express the space requirements of the institution, and to shape the guidelines into tools most appropriate for assessing the utilization of institutional facilities.

A critical component that has typically been missing from space analysis is adequacy—the quality and suitability of existing space for present and future programs. If this factor has not been previously considered, space in temporary buildings or obsolete facilities is assumed to be just as valuable to a department as space in a newly constructed building. It is simply improper to compare, for example, laboratory space in a temporary building with laboratory facilities in a new structure. Any comprehensive investigation of university facilities must take into account the issue of space adequacy. Crucial to an improvement in the effectiveness of space management is the adoption of a complete set of institutional standards relating space to programs.

Colleges and universities have utilized a combination of standards described by Bareither and Schillinger and varying adaptations of other models. This approach frequently raises questions, either by departments when an analysis suggests that there is an abundance of space or, in the case of public institutions, the legislature, when campuses report that their utilization is more the norm or even higher than those of their peers.

Standards may be defined as the average assignable square feet of a given type of space considered adequate for each kind of activity at an institution. As indicated earlier, because each department's resources and programs vary considerably, space standards cannot be uniformly applied across departments or colleges. This is especially true in developing standards for research space or for clinical space in the health sciences.

Research space is difficult to evaluate as it involves space requirements for types of activities that are not readily predictable. When attempts are made to translate this portion of an educational program into square feet, accusations are usually made about stifling research development or creating mediocrity through a space-leveling formula. The space management plan will respond to these concerns by focusing on the assessment of actual levels of research productivity rather than forcing arbitrary numeric standards.

The plan proposes that a space management staff, augmented by members of the academic community, explore the development of space standards for the university that also take into account the factor of quality. Ideally, a matrix of architectural/environmental factors should be developed that would provide a vehicle for bringing the numeric space standards into the real world of a complex and dynamic university. A possible approach would include the rating of space by quality. In this method a new building could be given an "A" rating and its appropriate utilization rate, whereas an older building could be given a "B" or "C" rating (depending upon age and quality of the space) and a different set of utilization criteria determined. An investigation of the quality of the space should take into account:

- Location.
- Noise level.
- Ventilation or air conditioning.
- Shape.
- Efficiency of space (including energy efficiency).
- Aesthetic quality.
- Historical value (it might be desirable to maintain a space at a lower utilization rate due to its historical value).
- Health and safety standards (building and handicapped codes).

31.8 UTILIZATION—SPACE MODEL

After the space standards have been established, the next step in the plan involves the development of a space model and the execution of space utilization studies. As previously indicated, there are two principal methods to carry out such a utilization analysis: a comparison of the allocation of space with similar institutions, and a comparison of campus guidelines with theoretical allowances generated by other systems.

It is more effective to establish a university space model—one especially constructed to reflect the teaching, research, and service mission of the institution—and conduct a campus utilization study on the basis of the model. The plan proposes that the space office, assisted by the academic community, develop such a space model. With respect to the actual utilization studies, it would simply require the accumulation of program data by the academic member of the team and the application of the data by the space programming and management staff to the space model to provide utilization reports.

It is worth repeating that since space standards do not normally take into account the physical constraints of building areas (inappropriate size, shapes of rooms, obsolescence, ventilation system), nor the specific characteristic of individual activity taking place in such spaces (often this will decrease the efficiency of utilization of the space), such an application may not reveal the true utilization picture. With this in mind, it is essential that persons carrying out the utilization studies be thoroughly knowledgeable about program requirements and that the evaluation criteria should be carefully developed and accepted by the users of the spaces being surveyed.

In summary, the utilization of existing facilities is primarily concerned with two issues: are optimum numbers of persons occupying a space?, and is optimum use being made of the space?

Facility utilization should not be judged solely in terms of the number of students or faculty per square feet area, or the frequency of room use. One should take into consideration the quality of the space, as well as any special requirements of the program that must be carried out in the space.

31.9 MANAGEMENT INCENTIVES

In the final analysis, the heart of a space management system is the method of allocating space. How and by whom such decisions are made varies from campus to campus. In some situations, space is controlled by the chief administrative officer staffed by a space management office that allocates space and gives the authority to manage such space for programs. Another approach places the authority and responsibility for the management of space on the shoulders of a "space czar." Although the management of space can be allocated to a dean or department head, under such a scheme there is no incentive for a dean to become serious about the management of such space. A department that has abundant space essentially pays little attention to how effectively it is being used.

On the other hand, departments that have a shortage of space continually work with space officials to find additional space or to better utilize the space that has been allocated. To successfully implement the concept of "deans as managers," a process must be developed to encourage the deans to more effectively manage their space. A method employed by some U.S. institutions focuses on a concept of space costing or space renting.[5]

Essentially, in the face of increasingly stringent budgets, it is felt that department heads should become more aware of the costs involved in space resources, both in terms of original construction, remodeling, and in the operation and maintenance of the facilities. The intent is to encourage administrators to think in terms of the tradeoffs that may become a fact of life in budget planning (such as determining what portion of the departmental budget would be needed to support space versus equipment and staff).

A potential financial model entails the "purchase" by the central administration of excess space from departments that allows the departments to use such funds for other program needs. It is felt that under such an option, departments that want to expand or explore new programs but lack the funds to do so would exercise the option to carefully inspect the space they are assigned and determine whether such space could be "sold" to the administration. Irrespective of the management incentives developed, it is generally found that the space allocation process is more acceptable to the faculty and administrators when the policies and procedures are developed with the participation and concurrence of the faculty and staff and that such policies are clearly communicated to all and are fairly implemented.

Figure 31-7 is a graphic illustration of guideline components used in the application of a facilities model. The purpose of the guideline components is to specify space standards, allowances, and utilization goals to be used in defining space or an academic or support program. The application of these various space guidelines will produce a building "envelope" that will support a department's program. It is necessary to determine the design and size of specific rooms within the building envelope on an individual basis.

It is apparent that the execution of a space management plan requires an institution to embark on a major project and demands a significant commitment of time and resources. It is nonetheless important that a plan and office be established and sufficiently funded for the future maintenance of adequate and efficient spaces for university programs.

31.10 SPACE PLANNING PROCESS

To successfully implement a space planning effort on the campus requires the establishment of a process related to the daily request for changes in facilities that is coherent, consistent, and coordinated in a fair manner to all of the campus community constitutents. Such a process will also provide facilities that meet functional requirements at the least cost and allow the space planner to effectively respond to questions of needs, timing, and costs. A campus space planning process developed and refined over several years consists of seven primary steps:

1. Need
2. Request
3. Utilization analysis/application of space model
4. Problem definition

Figure 31-7

Guideline Components—Facilities Model

Classroom
.89 ASF for each weekly contact hour between instructor and student based on 16 ASF station size scheduled 30 hours per week with 60% of stations occupied.

Office
150 ASF for each full time employee requiring office space based on 120 ASF for primary office and 30 ASF pooled for conference, reception, etc. (Up to 40 ASF of individual research space can be transferred into office category.)

Research Lab
Depending on discipline 20 ASF—450 ASF for each research faculty and advanced grad student.

Instructional Lab
Depending on discipline 1.0 to 8.0 ASF for each weekly contact hour between instructor and student based on 16 ASF to 244 ASF station size. Room scheduled 20 hours per week with 80% of stations occupied.

Library
Stack = 1 ASF for each 20 volumes
Study = 30 ASF times 20% of students and 10% of faculty
Service = 20% of stack and study space

Student Unions
9 ASF for each FYE student

Athletics
68.000 ASF for first 5,000 students
9 ASF for each student over 5,000
35 ASF for each PE major
20 ASF for each PE minor

Commons
1 ASF for each instructional station and employee

> **Non-Guideline Facilities**
> (Armories, field buildings, animal quarters, greenhouses, assembly, exhibition, computer, shops, warehouses, vehicle storage)—requirement based on existing allocation and level of use.

5. Recommendation
6. Decision
7. Implementation.

Figure 31-8 depicts the sequence of the steps in this process. The center box illustrates the three major components of space management: utilization, inventory, and audit. Space on the campus is constantly being used—sometimes well, other times poorly—during each day.

It is necessary to conduct utilization studies to determine how well space is being used and whether it is the appropriate space for a program and its users. The foundation for conducting such utilization studies is the inventory and the audit. As emphasized earlier, an important principle of inventorying is that it is absolutely essential that an accurate record of space is kept and that the record is up to date.

These three space management components continually interact and require that 1) the inventory is constantly updated, 2) an auditing of the assignment and use of space on the campus is carried out frequently, and 3) utilization is monitored on a consistent basis.

The first step in the space planning process requires the identification of a need for an additional office, laboratory, or research space. It is important that the individual or the department making the request put its need in writing. The action required on such a request involves a number of persons on the campus, and a written statement allows for a more effective and efficient response. Verbal requests can be misunderstood and even forgotten. This step also provides a record for the files if, at some point, the response is challenged or an inquiry is made about why a certain renovation is or is not taking place. Another advantage of committing space needs to writing is that it forces the requester to think about the request and, in some cases, will cause modifications or, in an unjustifiable case, a decision to not make the request after all.

The second step in the process is the development of the specifics of the request. Each request must be carefully evaluated and special requirements documented. It may require visiting with the requestor for

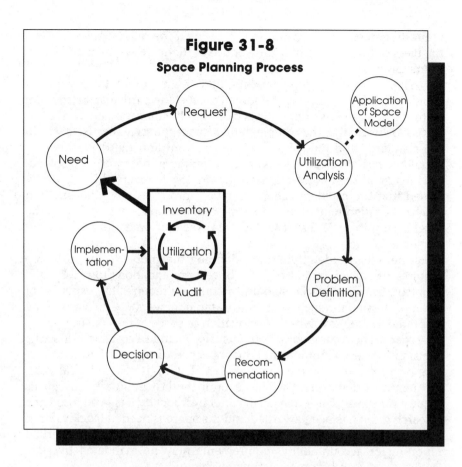

Figure 31-8

Space Planning Process

further clarification and site investigation. At this stage, it is possible to convince an unjustifiable space request to be cancelled. It also involves confirming "ownership" of the space in question. Frequently, a request is submitted for the renovation of a space that has not been officially assigned to the requestor, but the space was obtained through a temporary agreement with the department whose space it is.

The third step requires a utilization or allocation analysis of the space assigned to the department or unit making the request. Space models that evaluate, allocate, and predict space needs will provide for an adequate and acceptable examination and avoid the controversy and the frequent comment, "Why don't you contact my peers and identify the allocation of space in their programs and use that as a measure of how much space I need?" If the campus does not have a space model, existing campus standards and guidelines should be applied to the requesting department or unit to determine if the request is justified on the basis of the number of faculty and staff in the department and credit hours taught.

The fourth step is problem definition. It is important to fully understand the problem that must be solved to meet the particular space need. With the department's request clarified and the utilization analysis completed to ensure that the complement of space that is requested is within the standards and guidelines for the program and the department, it should be easy to clearly document the problem that must be resolved. Frequently, at the end of this step the process is reversed if it is determined that the problem can be resolved through some other method (such as reassignment of the department or unit space or rental), or if the need is so miniscule that it would be a waste of time and resources to pursue a solution.

After clearly identifying and defining the problem, the fifth step requires the development of a set of recommendations to resolve the problem. This is a crucial step and frequently requires the expertise of other professionals (such as architects and engineers), particularly if the recommendation involves the renovation of space or the construction of new space. The recommendation must also include a cost analysis so the decision-maker will understand the impact on campus resources to execute or implement the recommendation. Timing is also a critical item. Frequently, a department will wait until the last minute to submit its request for space. This often occurs after new faculty has been hired or a research grant has been awarded and the space is needed quickly. Since other professionals on the staff must become involved, and since certain reporting or accountability requirements may be mandated by state agencies, this can become a serious problem.

Following the development of a recommendation, the decision to proceed or not to proceed (step six) must be made. If the steps in this process have been carefully followed, it should allow the decision-maker to render that decision quickly, because the facts will be available to support the recommendation and budgetary implications can be placed into the context of the institution's overall resources.

The seventh step is implementation. After the decision has been made it simply becomes a matter of execution. The resolution of the space issue is reflected in the center box of Figure 31-8 where the inventory is modified to include the new space data, the utilization of space continues, and the auditing process is periodically applied.

It must be emphasized that many other activities occur between these seven primary steps and these activities could cause a reversal of the process. For example, if at the end of the utilization analysis it is recommended that the department should set some priorities before determining its need for space or space modification, the process is reversed, either to the request stage or the center box. Another important outcome of establishing a space planning process is that it allows space management to assume an effective role within the overall planning cycle at an institution.

Frequently, only lip service is given to incorporating space management into the campus system and the institutional planning cycle frequently makes no mention of facilities management. It is not acceptable to ignore or pay only minimal attention to campus facilities and the real impact that facilities have on the institution's budget. The maintenance and use of campus facilities must be given careful attention during the annual budgetary process, not only at times when reductions in the budget must be accommodated in order to protect faculty or academic programs. The development of a space planning process will place important emphasis on the need to include facility planning and management as part of the cycle of institution-wide planning. It will bring to the attention of the decision makers the problem of space, its cost implications, and its impact on the programs of the various collegiate units, and it will require that these factors be examined each year during the planning cycle.

An important benefit of this seven-step process lies in future planning. Justifiable needs can be met more effectively and efficiently with the prospect of fewer errors, which translates into savings in terms of both dollars and time. The campus community should be well informed of the space planning process. There is a general and expected dislike of surprises on space matters and a preference for an organized, routine method to deal with requests. With a well-organized, well-publicized, fairly executed process, fewer decisions will be challenged and implementation will be easier.

31.11 CONCLUSION

A well-organized facilities planning and space management process is vitally important to the general operation of a campus and essential to the achievement of the institution's primary mission. In addition to appropriate funding and organizational status for this component of the institutional planning process, clear documentation of the roles of the various participants, what input is expected, and how the report will be used is important in maintaining an effective process.

Finally, the techniques and procedures in this chapter should not be construed as the one answer to facilities planning and space management problems on the campus. Depending upon the unique characteristics or organizational structure of the campus, some of these procedures may be inappropriate. Campus planners should use the methodologies and procedures as guidelines and modify them to fit institutional needs.

NOTES

1. Clinton Hewitt, Kenneth Stebbins, and Eric Wheeler, "Campus Planning: The Process Is the Product," *Architecture Minnesota* (February 1978).
2. Kenneth Brooks, Marlon Conrad, and William Griffith, *From Program to Educational Facilities* (Center for Professional Development, College of Education, University of Kentucky, 1980).
3. Office of Physical Planning, University of Minnesota, "On Planning and Management—A Guidebook to Facilities Improvements," an unpublished office document, September 1985.
4. University of Minnesota, *St. Paul Campus, Long-Range Development Plan* (John Andrews Architects, 1972).
5. Educational Facilities Laboratories, *Space Costing: Who Should Pay for the Use of College Space?* (New York, July 1977)

ADDITIONAL RESOURCES

Association of American Medical Colleges Group on Institutional Planning. *Current Space Allocation Mechanisms and Space Standards Utilized in Medical Schools and Health Centers of the United States and Canada.* June 1981.

Bareither, Harlan D. and Jerry L. Schillinger. *University Space Planning.* Urbana, Illinois: The University of Illinois Press, 1968.

Braver, Roger L. *Facilities Planning.* American Management Association, 1986.

Brevard, Joseph H. *Capital Facilities Planning.* Washington: American Planning Association, 1985.

Cavanaugh, R.B. *How to Manage Space.* Winchester, Massachusetts: R.B. Cavanaugh Publications, 1984.

Dahnke, Harold L., Dennis P. Jones, Thomas R. Mason, and Leonard C. Romney. *Higher Education Facilities Planning and Management Manuals.* Boulder, Colorado: Western Interstate Commission for Higher Education, 1970.

DeChiara, Joseph and Lee E. Koppelman. *Site Planning Standards.* New York: McGraw-Hill, 1978.

Dober, Richard P. *Campus Planning.* Cambridge, Massachusetts: Reinhold Publishing Corporation, 1963.

Fink, Ira. "Campus Dispersal: Planning for the Location and Relocation of University Facilities." In *Planning for Higher Education.* The Society for College and University Planning, Vol. 13, No. 1, Fall 1984.

——. "University-Community Relationships." *Planning for Higher Education.* The Society for College and University Planning, Vol. 14, No. 1, 1986.

Hales, H. Lee. *Computer-Aided Facilities Planning.* New York: Marcel Dekker, 1984.

Hewitt, Clinton. "Campus Renewal in the 1980s: The New Voyage of the Beagle." In *Responses to Fiscal Stress in Higher Education,* Robert A. Wilson, ed. Center for the Study of Higher Education, University of Arizona, 1982.

——, Kenneth Stebbins, and Eric Wheeler. "Campus Planning: The Process is the Product." *Architecture Minnesota,* February 1978.

Lewis, James Jr. *Long-Range and Short-Range Planning for Educational Administrators.* Boston: Allyn and Bacon, 1983.

Lynch, Kevin. *Site Planning.* Cambridge, Massachusetts: M.I.T. Press, 1981.

Nesmith, James N., ed. *More for Less, Academic Planning with Faculty Without New Dollars.* Itasca, Illinois: Nordic Hills, 1974.

Parekh, Satish B. *Long-Range Planning, An Institution-Wide Approach to Increasing Academic Vitality.* New Rochelle, New York: Change Magazine Press, 1977.

Probasco, Jack. *Space Planning Guidelines for the Public Two-Year Campuses* and *Space Planning Guidelines for the Public Universities.* Columbus, Ohio: Ohio Board of Regents, 1974.

CHAPTER 32

Project Programming and Design

Waller S. Hunt Jr., AIA, AUA
University Architect
University of Virginia

32.1 INTRODUCTION

As discussed in Chapter 31, Facilities Planning and Space Management, the facilities master plan is the chief document with which a college or university can project facility requirements. With an established academic program, a well-thought-out and well-defined master plan, and an accurate accounting or inventory of existing space, the institution can identify the facilities required to meet planned growth. Once space needs and a time frame for meeting the needs are established, projections can be developed for the size and cost of proposed facilities. This initial program development can guide facilities acquisition through the design and construction stages.

The planning process is lengthy, costly, and often difficult to explain to the potential user. Customary institutional facilities planning involves six major elements of a conventional planning and construction process:

1. Programming of space.
2. Schematic drawing stage.
3. Preliminary drawing stage.
4. Working drawing stage.
5. Bidding stage.
6. Construction stage.

Most institutions of higher education use this conventional process because it provides relative ease in managing the planning and because it fits the authority designated by the control agency, be it state government or a board of trustees. Other options may be available for the design and construction of facilities, such as fast-track, design-build, turnkey, and construction management (CM). All offer certain advantages to an institution, and each will be discussed later.

Most institutions use the conventional procedure; they often commission an architect or engineer to prepare drawings and specifications and provide contract administration during construction. Members of the American Institute of Architects (AIA) as well as other professional architects can provide all required services for all of these stages.

The process involves the following stages for a typical architectural contract, as defined by the AIA: 1) preparation of schematic drawings, pre-outline specifications, and statement of probable cost, representing 15 percent of the total contract; 2) the preparation of preliminary drawings, outline specifications, and another statement of probable cost, sometimes referred to as the design development stage, 20 percent; 3) preparation of the working drawings and technical specifications, known as the contract documents, 40 percent; 4) review of bids and advice on low bidder, known as the bidding stage, 5 percent; and 5) contract administration, 20 percent. Preparation of as-built drawings can be obtained as additional services.

In addition to these procedures, other options are available for the planning and construction process in the private sector beyond those available to public institutions. State laws and regulations typically govern procedures for the planning and construction of capital programs and may limit the options available to public institutions. State procedures generally establish strict guidelines governing the conduct of planning and construction; selection of architects, landscape architects, or engineers; and, in many states, format of standard state construction documents.

Regardless of the method selected, proper management of the planning and construction process is essential. The facilities management or physical plant unit is generally the administrative division responsible for the buildings and the grounds of the institution. Physical plant usually controls the design and construction of facilities as well as maintains and improves the facilities throughout their life cycles.

Many of these services require the expertise of architects and engineers to prepare the necessary drawings and specifications to enable the constructors, whether physical plant personnel or outside contractors, to perform the necessary work in a correct, orderly, and timely manner. It is then necessary to exercise proper management for these many, diverse responsibilities.

32.2 CLASSIFICATION OF FACILITIES PROJECTS

The above services can be broadly classified and defined.

Maintenance   This is the recurrent, day-to-day, periodic, or scheduled work required to preserve or restore a facility immediately to such condition that it can be effectively used for its designed purpose. For example, an old hot water storage tank ruptures and must be replaced. Replacement will restore service.

Repair   Repair is the restoration of a facility to such condition that it may be effectively utilized for its designated purpose. Repair is done by overhaul or replacement of major constituent parts that have deteriorated by action of the elements or usage. Such deterioration has not been corrected through maintenance. An example would be replacing roofs or air-conditioning compressors. Normal improvements such as new insulation for the roofs or new refrigeration lines can be considered repair when such replacement appears imminent at greater expense.

Renovation   This service is the total or partial upgrading of a facility to higher standards of quality or efficiency. Under certain conditions a renovation may also be classified as an improvement. Examples are new installation of air conditioning and installation of grid ceilings to facilitate replacement of incandescent lighting with more efficient fluorescent lighting.

Alteration   Alteration is the changing of internal arrangement or other physical characteristics of an existing facility so that it may be effectively used for its designated purpose. Interior partitions can be rearranged to provide a specific space for a certain function, or space can be converted to a different use by the installation of new equipment. For example, a classroom can be changed into a computer lab.

New Construction   This category is the erection of a new facility or the addition or expansion of the exterior of an existing facility that adds to the building's overall dimensions. New construction can involve support facilities for the buildings including outside utilities, parking, roads, walks, and landscaping. Improvements are closely related to renovations; they are often confused with each other.

Improvement   This is the addition of quality features to existing space by upgrading mechanical or electrical systems or architectural finishes. Examples are installation of carpet on floors that are not worn or otherwise unsatisfactory, the addition of air conditioning, or installation of incandescent lighting to create an aesthetic condition.

32.3 PROJECT DEFINITION AND DESCRIPTION

General definitions and descriptions dealing with the planning and construction process follow. Many institutions may not necessarily follow these specific steps under their procedures. The descriptions are arranged in sequence.

Project Justification

Each project must be justified, whether by a simple form or by a detailed analysis, as is often the case with many public institutions. The justifications address the present conditions and their effect on the function of existing space; obvious need for new, renovated, or improved space; advantages of a new facility or improvement; alternatives considered; impact on existing space; utilization of any space vacated; standards of comparison and final recommendation based on the quantity of space; cost of operation and maintenance; cost of the facility or improvement; financing; and the time element necessary for planning, construction, and move-in. (The cost estimate preparation and breakdown will be discussed later.) Basically, there must be a demonstrated need for the facility including a proposal for its financing, operation, and maintenance.

Project Investigation

The purpose of the project investigation is fourfold:

1. To make an assessment of the existing facility in terms of current function and the physical aspects of the facility, including a complete inventory of architectural, structural, mechanical, and electrical features.
2. To analyze the manner of operation of the user to determine exact functions in the everyday operation and to conceptualize improvement to the existing physical arrangement or explore ideas for replacement facilities. These studies may require the services of architects or engineers. Replacement facilities should fulfill the need for improved arrangements and provide accurate projections of the space needs to accomplish the arrangements.
3. To prepare a formal statement on the program of spaces, if alterations or additional space are indicated, or a description of the service to be recommended. Program should include architectural, structural, electrical and communications, mechanical and plumbing, maintenance, energy conservation, and fire and safety code implications.
4. To prepare a general statement of anticipated total estimated cost.

Program Statements

A careful analysis and understanding of the operation or function of the space to be altered, improved, or constructed is the first order of the process toward a workable and successful project. The user can best describe the failure of the existing space and desired features. But often the user tends to downplay some aspects of the project and may overlook the need to consider certain other elements, or the user may concentrate on important areas without consideration of the total space. For example, users consistently are surprised to find that a janitor's closet is needed on every floor or that a janitor's supply space is needed somewhere in a building. They are quick to react to the idea that mechanical equipment should be placed where maintenance crews can have quick and adequate access and the equipment will be protected from damaging ambient conditions of dust and weather.

Other misconceptions involve the total area of the building or its net-to-gross ratio. For example, researchers spend the majority of their lives in labs or associated offices. Their career may depend upon how they can demonstrate positive results from their research. They are not concerned with what makes the building serve the user well until some feature is missed or does not work. They are not concerned with the number of toilets in the building, the width of the corridors, or the capacity of the facility to serve the handicapped. When square footage is added for these necessities, the user thinks of the cost for nonproductive space. It is often difficult to convince users that a prerequisite for a successful building is good planning for all features.

Standards established for other successful projects must be demonstrated to those who lack experience with the total requirements for a facility. Many standards or references are available for determining the size of a classroom, conference room, or office.[1] There are also standards for the estimation of additional space to provide circulation, mechanical, electrical, structural, and support spaces. These standards, however, are not readily available since every building differs in some manner. Architects differ as well in their design approach, and the initial programming must take this into consideration. Building types vary in the net-to-gross area ratio depending upon campus and administrative limitations. A large, spreadout, unrestricted campus may encourage a low net area ratio while a crowded urban campus encourages compact buildings and perhaps the use of multistoried buildings.

Space is a resource in the campus inventory. It forms the environment of the operation to be housed and helps to attract competent academic and research personnel. Like all resources, space must be utilized in a most effective and efficient manner. The planning for such space is no less important.

Basically the program of spaces to be developed for a facilities alteration or new construction of a building encompasses the following outline. List all spaces to be used directly by the organization by types and number of spaces, including the number of seats in such facilities as classrooms, teaching labs, computer labs, and auditoriums. To each type of space add a net assignable square footage derived from the space standards used by the institution and based on the type of space. To the total of this area apply a modifier to estimate the additional space necessary to cover such non assignable spaces as stairs, corridors, public toilets, elevators, escalators, mechanical spaces, electrical closets and enclosures, telephone and computer terminal rooms, janitor closets and storage spaces, and other nonusable space such as that occupied by interior partitions, chases, structural elements, exterior walls, and over-hangs. The total of these produces the gross square footage of the facility. Depending upon the type of building, the net-to-gross ratio varies. (See Figure 32-1.)

The net areas shown in Figure 32-1 for labs, classrooms, library stack space, and faculty office areas are representative areas derived from standards presented in *Space Planning Guidelines* by the Council of Educational Facility Planners International (1985). Housing and dining net areas and percentages to obtain all gross areas are based on recommendations of the *1987 Dodge Assemblies Cost Data*.

Preschematic or Preplanning Studies

The preschematic or preplanning study, as the process is known to some institutions, is the initial step through architectural or engineering services in confirming the program of spaces; the study of basic siting considerations, architectural configuration, and materials to be used in the facility; the construction cost implications; and ultimately the total project cost. Often included are the environmental impact statement, fixed and movable equipment lists, and studies of energy conservation.

Figure 32-1
Net-to-Gross Space Ratios

Type of Building	Net Area	Gross Area	Ratio
Lab, research 50 sf/station	50	83	60% gross
Classroom, teaching 16 sf/ student	16	27	60% gross
Dining, 33.5 net sf/seat	33.5	48	70% gross
Single student housing, 160/bed	160	215	75% gross
Library, stack 10 nsf/volume	.1	.16	60% gross
Office facility	140	215	65% gross

This process is intended to demonstrate better the need of a facility by reporting the conclusions of the study of the various aspects peculiar to the project.

The process produces schematic architectural or engineering drawings and outline specifications of sufficient detail to identify the site relationships, the massing of the proposed building, and an expression of exterior treatment as far as materials, openings, and shape are concerned. Floor plans may be only single line diagrams representing the general layout of the spaces but clearly relating the functional aspects of the design. Mechanical equipment may be identified only in block form. The cost of professional services for the preplanning study varies from about 15 to 20 percent of the total estimated fee. Often the firm that completes the preplanning study allows some credit for this work should that firm be selected to continue with planning beyond the preplanning study.

Cost Estimates

Five types of cost estimates are commonly used in the design process: 1) the square foot method; 2) the cubic method (a derivation of the first); 3) the unit type; 4) the "in-place" type; and 5) the materials and labor type. There are variations of each, but basically they are used as follows:

1. The square foot estimate uses the cost per gross square foot for other similar facilities as a basis for estimating the cost per gross square foot for a proposed facility. Of limited accuracy, the estimate must be adjusted for inflation, elasped time, site conditions, and geographic location. Good historical or other data are essential for improved accuracy.
2. The cubic method uses as its foundation the square foot method described above but goes into more detail by comparing the altitude, or third dimension, of the example with that of the proposed facility in terms of cost per cubic foot.
3. The unit type estimate deals in broad comparisons, is not accurate, and should be used only for a rule of thumb comparison estimate. This approach compares, for example, the cost per bed of a dormitory or hospital with a given number of beds in the proposed facility, dining seats in a dining facility, or volumes in a library.
4. The in-place estimate is more detailed than above methods and is more accurate. A more detailed set of drawings and outline specifications contributes greatly to the accuracy. This type uses the actual quantity to take off assemblies such as square feet of brick wall or plastered walls, acoustic ceilings, and concrete structure, multiplied by known unit costs for similar systems. This system is also based on

historic data of systems costs including labor, overhead, markup, and profit and is not essentially as accurate as the materials and labor takeoff method.

5. The time and materials type is the most accurate and is used by all contractors and most professional estimators. It depends upon good, complete drawings and specifications and complete detail. Each material system is computed based on a common quantity, with the labor for installation applied to the material cost. Upon completion of estimating all components, general conditions, contingency, time for construction, weather and labor considerations, the inflation to the midpoint of construction, overhead, and profit are added for the complete estimate.

In all estimates except the latter, a bidding contingency of about 5 percent should be added because all of the first four types are dependent upon past history of prices based on some low bidder's price in the past. The estimate for the new facility should then be set to the approximate middle of the anticipated bid range.

Once the construction cost is estimated for a project, a line item total project estimate can be developed with consideration of the estimated cost of architectural-engineering fees, printing drawings, landscaping materials, movable furnishing, construction contingency and inflation, and finally a schedule reflecting the necessary times for development and construction.

32.4 THE PROJECT DESIGN TEAM

Depending upon the complexity of the project, the designer may be one person or a whole team of professionals, an independent architect or engineer or a staff designer. The complexity of the problem and the ability of the designer to handle difficult design problems are the key questions in selecting the design team. If proper design qualifications are met, a staff designer is usually involved with routine renovations on a limited scale. For more extensive work it may be to the advantage of the institution to seek the services of an experienced nonstaff professional who can devote full time to the problem. In some cases the complexity or the size of the project may dictate that a large professional firm or one with specific qualifications be commissioned.

As mentioned, several options are open for design services. The most common is the commission of an architect or engineer for preparation of schematic, preliminary, and working drawings, plus construction contract administration. This is the standard arrangement for professional services contracts. Other design options include the use of design-build or turnkey procedures.

Selection of Architectural and Engineering Consultants

The process for the selection of architects and engineers for normal services varies from state to state or among institutions. In some cases, particularly with private institutions, a direct selection process is followed. In general however, public agencies use a comparative method, which requires that all qualified professionals or those expressing an interest in a project be considered. Those considered best qualified are short-listed for interview and ranked before fee negotiations. This ranking should be based upon each professional firm's relevant qualifications and experience, quality of design work, and availability and capacity for the planned project.

Under almost all selection procedures the prospective fee is not a consideration in this ranking process. Fee negotiations are conducted with firms only after ranking, and in the order of ranking. If a satisfactory fee arrangement cannot be established, negotiations with the firm are halted and begun with the next ranked firm, and so on until an appropriate fee arrangement is made or the process is restarted by a new advertisement. An important element of a successful negotiation is the institution's good understanding of an appropriate fee basis for the project.

In emergencies, almost all procedures allow direct selection of the most qualified and experienced firm available. Fee negotiations are generally concluded quickly, based on some established scale or other known quantity such as hourly or per diem rates. The professional can begin work on a problem without delay under this procedure.

Another method of selection, although not often used by public agencies, is the design competition process. In this case the project is described in a so-called program. The program provides the rules of the competition, all design requirements, size, total budget, site parameters, and the like, together with the conditions of the competition. An architectural review committee is established; a prize or reward, usually a contract to continue planning and construction, is agreed upon; and the competition is advertised. Architectural and engineering teams or other qualified individuals can usually compete. Within the established time limits the professionals design a facility and complete schematic drawings, outline specifications, and a statement of probable cost. Detailed site study is also essential.

The review committee, usually composed of at least three qualified architects, then reviews and ranks the proposals according to aesthetic consideration, ability to meet the requirements, uniqueness of design, and cost restraints. Other qualities may also be judged, depending on the intent and rules. The winning firm is usually awarded the contract for continued planning plus a suitable monetary reward for the effort. There can be second and third prizes for other firms as well. The system's advantage is a view of the design before the architect is selected. This can be most important when attempting to achieve a specific design quality.

Fee Negotiations

Fee negotiations must be based upon a clear understanding of the scope of the project and the services to be furnished, both as basic and as additive services. While the rules and antitrust laws do not allow the AIA or any architectural or engineering professional group to set fees in advance by the use of a standard fee, many institutions have their own fee guidelines based on a percentage of construction cost. While this is the most common approach, there are other methods of contracting for professional services, including

- Professional fee plus reimbursement of expenses.
- Multiple of direct personnel expense.
- Hourly, per diem, or salary.
- Varieties, including set fee based on hourly rates and set fees based on percentage of estimated cost at preliminary stage.

Design fees are difficult to predict or establish. On the one hand an institution may project prospective fees in terms of its own experience or the experience of other institutions, based upon cost for design services for a specific project. However, projects vary in complexity, scope, time available to perform the services, and cost to the professional. Therefore while an institution may consider a percentage of the construction cost, the professionals may think of fees in terms of their cost of doing business, including a reasonable profit. Both parties should find a mutual basis for negotiations.

Recently a number of institutions compared fees based on a percentage of the construction cost. That comparison of average fees in 1981 by geographic location is illustrated in Figure 32-2. The sample fee rates are based on 1981 information compiled by a southeastern university system.

For new construction smaller projects receive higher fee consideration. A similar curve representing a higher fee rate would represent the fees related to remodeling, renovations, and improvements. Engineering fees follow similar curves but, like fees for improvements, the scale is

Figure 32-2

Geographic Identification of Fees Paid for Design of New Construction

A   A large western state system of universities and colleges
B   A southeastern state university system
C   A midwestern Great Lakes area state university system
D   A northeastern state university system
E   Virginia State Division of Engineering and Buildings guidelines—
     Colleges
F   A northwestern university

Constr. Cost (thousands)	Percentage by System					
	A	B	C	D	E	F
$ 1	8.8	9.1	7.5	11.8	8.8	9.0
50	8.3	8.4	7.5	9.3	8.6	9.0
100	7.7	7.8	7.5	8.3	7.7	9.0
200	7.3	7.5	7.5	8.0	7.2	8.5
300	6.8	7.3	7.2	7.6	6.9	8.2
400	6.7	7.2	6.9	7.4	6.7	8.0
500	6.5	7.1	6.8	7.2	6.6	7.9
750	6.2	6.8	6.7	6.8	6.2	7.7
1,000	6.1	6.7	6.4	6.5	6.1	7.5
1,500	5.9	6.5	6.2	6.4	5.9	7.4
2,000	5.8	6.4	6.0	6.3	5.7	7.0
3,000	5.5	6.0	5.8	6.2	5.5	6.7
4,000	5.2	5.9	5.7	6.0	5.3	6.3
5,000	5.1	5.8	5.5	5.8	5.0	6.0
7,500	5.1	5.7	5.4	5.7	5.0	5.8
$10,000	5.1	5.4	5.3	5.7	5.0	5.5

generally higher since engineering work is often more complex. When projects involve renovations, a factor is often applied to increase the fee due to the unknown quantities of the concealed work and involvement with existing systems. A typical modifier ranges from 1.2 to about 1.5, depending upon the cost of the work, with the higher factor applied to the low end of the fee schedule. The complication of air conditioning may also create the need to increase the fee. Typically architects charge an additional 10 to 15 percent of the fee for including air conditioning, solar heating, or similar complex mechanical systems. Since engineers are hired specifically for these types of complex projects, the factor is not normally applied to engineering fees. The AIA fully recognizes the above direct, comparative, and design competition methods; any member is prepared to deal with contracts of those types.

Evaluation of Architectural and Engineering Performance

Often small colleges have no opportunity to become knowledgeable of the many professionals who constantly apply for commissions. These institutions must select the professional with utmost care. With those professionals who are applying for the first time, the institution should make every effort to determine previous clients, types of work involved, and relative size of the current work load. A quick check with clients, contractors who have worked with the candidates, the Better Business Bureau, and a credit agency may prove beneficial.

The institution should also evaluate the performance of the professionals who provide services. The criteria for such evaluation may involve:

- Ability to meet deadlines and schedules for production and delivery of documents.
- Ability to understand the program or needs of the owner.
- Degree of accuracy and completeness in the documents.
- Number of errors and omission and type of change orders required.
- Willingness to accept responsibility for errors or omissions.
- Willingness to work out conflicts in documents or with contractors in a timely fashion.
- Degree of effort toward acting on behalf of the owner in dealing with contractors.
- Apparent frequency of litigation involving error and omissions.

This evaluation should be recorded and used in the final analysis and closeout discussion of the project with the architect.

32.5 SERVICES OF THE ARCHITECT AND ENGINEER

The architects, engineers, and their consultants provide many services. The American Institute of Architects lists the following services: analysis, promotional planning, design and construction, contract administration, and related areas of services. APPA lists those services under the following headings: predesign services, site analysis, schematic design, preliminary and final design, and construction phase services. Certainly only the largest firms could undertake many of these services with available staff. However, most firms are fully acquainted with consultants who can accomplish the necessary service in concert with the principal firm. The classification as additional services under a standard contract or independent services does not influence the professional in the overall scope of work. Fees for the work, depending upon its complexity, availability of staff or consultants, and the schedule of requirements, can be negotiated as a fixed fee, hourly, or plus reimbursement of expenses.

The services usually required by colleges and universities involve the following:

A. Predesign services
1. Preliminary investigative reports involve evaluation of existing conditions, a minor scope of work, and a statement of probable cost for the total project.
2. Financial analysis includes revenue bond financing when dealing with operational and amortization financing on revenue-producing projects, land value and availability studies, and interim and long-term financing.

B. Site analysis
1. Survey of potential buildable areas on the main site.
2. Study and report on the capacity of the site to support the intended function including the building, exterior areas, service facilities, walks, covered areas, drives, lawn areas, landscaping, utilities, grading, and drainage.
3. Preparation of independent environmental studies addressing expressed or identified concerns.
4. Study of land use concepts for potential expansion.
5. Study of development of neighboring political subdivisions in terms of potential restrictions on development of the owner's property.
6. Relationship of site to transportation.
7. Climatological considerations.
8. Development of operational programming including detailed functional layout, space requirements, equipment and furnishings, and maintenance requirements.
9. Special site analysis involving seismic and soil conditions.
10. Special code, site restriction, and zoning studies.
11. Design and construction scheduling.
12. Feasibility cost studies.
13. Promotional services including preparation of renderings and drawings for promotional or development purposes, public relations briefings, and special communication studies.

C. Schematic design
1. Preplanning studies including justification for the facility, addition, or improvement; a method of accomplishment; a program of spaces to be developed considering the inventory of existing like space; the economics of locating, building, financing, operating, and maintain-

ing the facility; location requirements; personnel requirements; evaluation of energy conservation potential; list of legal concerns; site studies, schematic drawings, and outline specifications; a statement of probable cost; and an environmental impact study.
2. Operational design and planning including operational procedures, systems and processes, functional requirements, layout, and relationships; equipment and furnishings specifications and drawings; installation diagrams; testing and checking procedures plus maintenance and upkeep procedures.
3. Completion of schematic drawings as an extension of the preplanning study or preparation of complete schematic drawings, outline specifications, and statement of probable cost.

D. Preliminary and final design
1. Completion of preliminary design stage as a continuation of the schematic drawings, involving the further development of elevations, floor plans, mechanical, plumbing and electrical plans, site planning, and details plus the continued development of outline specifications and statement of probable cost.
2. Preparation of contract documents or working drawings and detailed specifications for bidding or price proposal purposes based on approved preliminary drawings. This stage converts the design into the language of the constructor through detailed drawings and notes.

E. Construction stage services
Depending upon the organization of the college or university, contract administration responsibilities may be divided between the professional and the institution's construction management team, or the entire package may be included as part of the professional's basic services. If the institution is staffed for construction management, these services can be divided as indicated below with the institution performing any or all of the tasks listed. It is not recommended that the professional's responsibilities be reduced beyond that shown below, nor is it necessary to reduce the professional's responsibility. Careful attention should be given before removing construction administration from the professional's services due to liability concerns.

Contract Administration as the College or University's Responsibility—Option

- Attend prebid conference and advise prospective bidders as necessary.

- Advertise for bids, conduct prebid conference, receive bids, and open bids.
- Review contract for intent and completeness.
- Review performance and payment bonds.
- Review subcontractor's list of materials and examples.
- Award contract, prepare contract, and transmit notice to proceed.
- Review progress schedule and approve or reject, including bar charts and critical path methods of scheduling.
- Review schedule of values and approve or reject.
- Review samples and obtain necessary college or university approvals.
- Establish standards of acceptability for workmanship.
- Review test reports.
- Judge performance of contractor; that is, degree of conformity with contract and progress of the project as constructed.
- Approve requests for payment for work accomplished and materials placed on the job.
- Make inspections for determination of degree of completeness.
- Conduct inspections with fire marshal and report on inspection results.
- Reject work not in compliance with contract documents.
- Report on above items to the college or university and professionals.
- Reject unsafe or unsatisfactory work.
- Issue field reports.
- Collect and review all guarantees, instructions, and schedules from contractor.
- Conduct final inspection with professionals and fire marshal.
- Inspect for completion of punch list items.
- Issue completion statement and approve final payment.
- Issue approval of occupancy statement.
- Conduct warrantee inspections.

Additional Services as the Professional's Responsibility

- Review contract for intent and completeness.
- Answer questions and render decisions on conformity of materials and samples.
- Review and approve or reject shop drawings including required resubmitted shop drawings. Furnish copy to owner.
- Reject unsafe or unsatisfactory work whether by review of submission or actual site visits.

- Interpret contract documents including any changes.
- Prepare necessary change orders; review and advise owner on cost proposals. On those required change orders involving correction of errors or omissions on behalf of the professionals, there should be no reimbursement for those design services.
- Review test reports as requested.
- Review field reports as requested.
- Conduct final inspection as requested and prepare punch list.

The usual AIA contracts for professional construction and administrative services include most of the above responsibilities as noted; however, architects and engineers are prepared to deal with modifications to those responsibilities in order to respond to varying needs and types of contracts. The college or university would do well to discuss any modification of responsibilities with legal advisors. In particular, liability insurance coverage is essential, and the institution must be careful to avoid the loss of any coverage through oversight.

32.6 ARCHITECTURAL AND ENGINEERING CONTRACTS

A clear understanding between the institution and the professional is essential for a successful project. That understanding must define the mutual relationships and obligations of each party to the other. In order to have a legal contract, six test conditions must be met:

1. There must be a meeting of the minds as to the intent of the agreement. Attention is invited to the use of a checklist and a memorandum of understanding.
2. Each party must be capable. The parties must have the authority to contract and be of legal age.
3. Parties must be of sound mind.
4. The purpose must be legal.
5. There must be an offer and an acceptance.
6. There must be consideration. Consideration normally takes the form of money.

The intent of the contract is one of the most important elements to the college or university administration; without a clear understanding of goals and costs, there may be areas of disagreement. A standard checklist can be an important tool in preparing a contract. The checklist can actually become a part of the contract known as the *memorandum of understanding*.

Most state institutions use standard forms of agreement that can incorporate all the conditions of the contract in one document; others refer to recognized documents. The AIA and most professionals use a standard form that has been prepared with the professional's benefit in mind. A state agency, however, usually must use a standard document prepared by the state. Regardless, the intent is always to have a document with standard conditions and without unexplored areas that could lead to mistakes or misunderstandings. The standard conditions, known as *general conditions of the contract,* provide explanation or description of the rights an responsibilities of each party as noted in the following example:

A. *Architect's services*
  * Basic services statement.

1. Schematic design stage
  * Preliminary evaluation of program and budget requirements.
  * Alternative approaches to design and construction.
  * Schematic drawings, outline specifications, and statement of probable cost.

2. Design development stage
  * Drawings and other documents to fix and describe size and character of project based on approved schematics, including statement of probable cost.

3. Construction documents stage
  * Preparation of bidding documents based on approved documents

4. Bidding or negotiation stage
  * Assistance to owner in advertising and receiving bids.
  * Assistance to owner in deciding on contractor and award of contract.

5. Construction stage—administration of construction contract
  * Definition.
  * Explanation as to owner's representative.
  * Site visits (not required to be exhaustive in number).
  * Updating owner.
  * Guard against defects and deficiencies in work but not responsibility for construction means or acts of the contractor.
  * Access to work at all times
  * Determination of monthly amount owed to contractor.
  * Issuance of certificates of payment.

- Interpretation of the requirements of contract documents.
- Decisions on claims and interpretations.
- Final artistic decisions.
- Authority to reject work.
- Review and approval of shop drawings.
- Preparation of change orders.
- Inspections.
- Duties and responsibilities unchanged without written consent.
- Additional services as listed.

B. *Owner's responsibilities*
1. Provision of full information and budget.
2. Designation of representative.
3. Furnishing of legal description of land and survey, which designers may assume is correct.
4. Furnishing soils engineering and other standard testing.
5. Furnishing all legal services.
6. Provision of written notice to designers concerning any known faults.
7. Approvals and decisions as expeditiously as necessary.

C. *Construction cost*
1. Definition.
2. Items named to be included in design and identification of equipment designed.
3. Evaluation of owner's budget including fixed or nonfixed limits of construction cost.
4. Responsibility for construction cost and determination of cost.

D. *Direct personnel expense—definition*

E. *Reimbursable expenses—listing*

F. *Payments to professional*
1. Based on type of contract initial and periods or statement schedules for balance schedule of payments as established by the AIA:
   Schematic stage—15 percent
   Design development stage—35 percent
   Construction documents stage—75 percent
   Bidding or negotiation stage—80 percent
   Construction administration—100 percent
2. Exceeding initially agreed-upon contract time through no fault of the professional.
3. Method used for determining fee (type of contract).
4. Additional services payments.

5. Withholding of payments.
6. Project suspension or termination of contract.

G. *Accounting records*
1. Definition and owner's designated representative.

H. *Ownership and use of documents*

I. *Arbitration*
1. Rules or arbitration.
2. Notice of demand for arbitration.
3. Award by arbitration.

J. *Termination of agreement*
1. Written notice period.
2. Compensation and termination expenses.
3. Appeals.

K. *Governing law*
1. Miscellaneous provisions.
2. Principal place of delivery of service.
3. Statute of limitations and substantial completion.
4. Waiver of rights.

L. *Successors and assigns*

M. *Extent of agreement*

N. *Other conditions or services*

O. *Basis of compensation*

The above conditions, rights, and responsibilities vary with the type of contract but usually apply to most projects conducted under AIA documents—except the areas involving payment.

Basic Types of Contracts

The AIA recommends the following types of contracts for professional services.

Fixed Fee   All agreed-upon work is done for one basic fee regardless of the cost of construction, extent of normal involvement, or complication. This type of contract provides for fees for additional services should scope or other changes require such additional services and a listing of reimbursable items. The advantages to the owner vary and primarily involve knowing the basic cost of fees in advance and acquiring full services without concern that the professional will slant the design toward more expensive results. Changes with this type of fee are difficult to negotiate. There is usually a provision for delays, under which the fee may be adjusted or renegotiated should the project exceed a certain time frame.

Percentage of the Construction Cost   This has been more or less the standard type of professional services contract for most colleges and universities. It simply provides a set or variable percentage rate based on an initial estimate of construction cost. The percentage is applied to the final construction cost upon completion of the work and includes change orders. Variations involve a percentage for a single stipulated-sum construction contract cost, separate stipulated-sum construction contracts, single cost-plus-fee onstruction contract, and separate cost-plus construction contracts.

While a sliding scale percentage is not emphasized, it is often considered. It recognizes that the professional's efforts are not in direct proportion to the cost of the construction but diminish somewhat from low-cost projects to higher-cost ones. The advantages accrue from the fees being generally based on historical data that provide a profit to the professional and yet accomplish the work for a reasonable sum as far as the owner is concerned. Owners, however, fear that the professionals will not control cost because they earn higher fees if the cost increases. This should not be a concern; the properly written professional services contract contains a method of controlling the construction cost. A common method is to require a complete rework of the plans if the cost exceeds the initial and agreed-upon estimate.

This type of contract or agreement also provides for additional services and reimbursement for certain items. Again, a common provision causes the fee to be adjusted or renegotiated should the project exceed a certain time frame. This fee arrangement is best suited when scope and cost are definite.

Professional Fee plus Expenses   This type of professional services contract is based upon an estimated number of hours required for the job times the standard hourly rates charged by the firm's principals and a multiple times the number of hours estimated for nonprincipals, plus expenses. It also provides a rate for any agreed upon consultants. There are provisions for additional services, again based on hourly rates times a multiple.

Reimbursables are extra. Normally a provision concerning delays causes the fee to be adjusted or renegotiated should the project exceed a certain time frame.

The obvious disadvantage of this type of agreement is the inability of the college or university administration to determine what is reasonable in terms of the professional's time. There is difficulty in gauging the cost of the expenses as well. This type of fee arrangement is well suited for special-purpose projects that require close attention by the professional.

Multiple of Direct Personnel Expense   This type of fee arrangement is well suited for providing service when indefinite scope, unusual procedures, or partial services are required. The fee is based on regular pay rates for the personnel involved times a multiple between 2.5 and 4.0. The multiple is computed on the basis of the firm's overhead, fixed costs, and profit. This arrangement is well suited to covering the design fees for change orders when the scope is unknown. However, fees add up quickly when using a multiple.

Salary, Per Diem, or Hourly Rate   This arrangement is not used as often as others for professional services, but it is excellent for investigative work or work that is of short duration. It is thought to be the most fair arrangement for the professional since every hour spent can be reimbursed.

32.7 CODES AND STANDARDS

All colleges and universities in the United States are now placed under the jurisdiction of a building code for the purpose of protecting the buildings and persons from heavy loss as the result of fire. Primarily there are four major codes that serve institutions, whether under state or local authority: Building Officials and Code Administrators (BOCA); International Conference of Building Administrators (ICBA); Southern Building Code Conference International (SBCCI); and Life Safety Code by National Fire Protection Association (NFPA). There are other codes in use as well, including some industrial codes, all dependent upon enforcement by building and fire inspectors. Usually enforcement at state administered institutions is by a state fire marshal, while the non-state facilities are regulated by the local building inspector.

For the college or university administrator responsible for seeing that new space is developed while maintaining the existing, it is necessary to recognize the fact that as time passes, the complexity of the codes increases as well as the degree of interpretation by the code administrator. The field of the code material involves a multitude of information covering zoning, seismic, solar and energy considerations, architectural techniques, structural, mechanical, plumbing, electrical, alarm and fire suppression systems, elevators, escalators, and barrier free access, and the proper application of such information toward a safe environment for the students and staff. Building safety is no accident; a conscious effort on behalf of all involved must be dedicated to the task.

Classification of College and University Buildings

Most codes classify higher-education buildings (other types are high-hazard, residential, mercantile, and industrial facilities) as "assembly." Depending upon use, some office space, such as faculty and student office space associated with a classroom building, may be classified as assembly. Other office space such as personnel or administrative space, may be classified as office space. The intent is to make as much educational and associated space fall under one classification as possible so as to limit the various differences in single buildings. Where a use such as high-hazard is involved (a laboratory, for instance) within a classroom building, the more restrictive classification rules.

Adequate planning for fire separation of walls and floors, creative planning of separation of functions, and provision of adequate numbers of exits may help to offset the high cost of such mixed-group classifications.

Construction Classification

Because of intended long-term use, most college and university construction involves more permanent materials than those used in ordinary construction. The use of such materials leads to more fire-resistant construction. BOCA has identified four basic types of construction that can be used by the college or university:

- Type I.   Noncombustible—Protected, 1A and 1B.
- Type II.   Noncombustible—Unprotected, 2A and 2B.
- Type III.   Noncombustible/combustible—Heavy timber, protected, unprotected.
- Type IV.   Combustible—Protected, unprotected.

Under these classifications most college and university construction is Type I, noncombustible, protected, 1A and 1B, or Type II, noncombustible, unprotected, 2A and 2B, except housing that is not classified as assembly space. Type I deals with buildings constructed with approved noncombustible materials in corridors, halls, partitions, structural elements, floors, ceilings, and roofs. Similar materials are required for protection of egress routes. Other type code classifications may be used in college work but limitations as to number of floors, area of floors, and special egress or fire suppression systems may be imposed. Type I is the category most often selected because of the intended life and use of the structure. Many exceptions are based on agricultural or other non-habitable uses, which enable the college to be less restrictive in its needs.

Colleges and universities normally rely on the architect and engineer to select the fire code classification that meets the code requirements while providing the facility within the budget, program, and time constraints. However, under proper management the institution should initially investigate, as fully as practical, the code constraints and requirements that will be placed on the project—in terms of the code itself and the site and utilities. If planning for utility services is delayed until the designers have actually designed the layout of the facility, delays may result in developing funding for the necessary utility expansion.

While college buildings are better protected from fire damage than they were twenty years ago, with the modern fire and smoke detection systems, required fire suppression systems, and fire-rated assemblies, broader restrictions appear on the horizon. Urban institutions may face competition for adequate water supplies and fire department services. Zoning regulations requiring more restrictive building setback lines and the ever-increasing demand for vehicle routes and parking affect the manner in which the institution can deliver a reasonably priced facility.

Provisions for the handicapped or barrier-free access also affects design considerations that require, by code, adequate provisions to allow access to various programs for all students and faculty. Because many institutions did not provide such facilities prior to 1970, they are today playing catch-up—at considerable cost.

One additional code that has an impact on medical or institutional space in particular, and some colleges specifically, is the life safety code. This code, as the name implies, is dedicated to the protection of life, not just property. Used in hospitals, medically associated projects, and most federally funded projects, this code is more restrictive and requires more egress stairs, shorter corridors where practical and fire alarm and suppression systems. Additionally the code regulates the use of the certain "outgassing" characteristic materials and restricts some materials through flame-spread requirements.

Codes today regulate more and more building techniques, materials, and provisions used in construction for lighting; ventilation; sound transmission; structural considerations; soil mechanics; mechanical, plumbing, and electrical systems; and asbestos containment. The codes are complex and difficult to analyze; the physical plant administrator and the project manager must know these building codes.

32.8 DESIGN GUIDANCE

The complexity of the planning and construction process makes it appear difficult for the college or university to obtain good value for the dollar spent toward the construction program. In the case of student accommodations, housing must be adequate, durable, safe, and yet not so costly as to be impractical to build and finance. Research is a major factor of the modern university and requires space that is economically constructed, adequate in its support environment, flexible enough to be modified quickly and inexpensively, and able to shelter the research reliably for long periods.

Academic space as well must adequately meet the needs for long-term utilization. To assure that these conditions and demand goals are met, the physical plant organization must support and promote good sound planning and construction techniques. To accomplish these goals and objectives, certain advanced steps must be taken to shape the events and promote the final outcome.

Architectural design is a difficult process to control or influence. On the one hand the architect is hired for design and technical expertise. On the other hand the application of that expertise is not always beneficial to the college or university. Typically, an inexperienced architect may design something of a monument to the profession without complete consideration of the financial impact on the owner. The institution, through its committees and management teams, must monitor closely the planning process and consistently refine the goals, objectives, and established procedures of the particular project. Should this happen, however, the project schedule will be in jeopardy.

Project Documentation

The best method to control and guide the project is adequate documentation. From the first document concerning the project a complete, uncomplicated statement of the intent is necessary. This statement should address also the size, special features, special relationships, possible locations or sites, and the cost implications both from the construction standpoint and the operational standpoint. It should identify possible sources of funding.

Sometimes referred to as the project criteria, the statement must be concise and prepared in a professional manner. It is usually prepared from input by the requestor and physical plant representatives. The document will set the tone for the duration of the design stage and will be used for reference throughout the course of the project construction. As a guideline the following checklist is offered:

- Recognize existing conditions.
- Consider the existing site conditions (for new construction).
- Identify space requirements and specific functional aspects.

- Specify the unique requirements for lighting, temperature, humidity, acoustics, and communications.
- Note any known unique code requirements and codes to be used.
- List special materials and equipment required.
- Describe known and available utility support.
- Identify grounds requirements including landscaping, walks, roads, parking, outside lighting, watering systems, fire protection features, trash removal, zoning regulations, and environmental concerns.
- List or document the institution's administrative procedures regarding design and construction.
- Point out solutions to problems that have worked well on previous projects.

Additional documentation involves state or institutional guidelines for quality of construction and the minimum standards acceptable, the professional services contract, and the project budget and schedule.

Institutional Design and Construction Guidelines

The institutional guidelines provide an important element in the instructions to the designers, serve as a listing of standards for use of materials and techniques, provide a direct means of controlling future maintenance and operating problems, and aid the project manager as a management tool and the construction administrator in administering the contract and performing inspection—all toward achieving quality of design coupled with economy of construction and operation.

The data used in the guidelines are usually based on experience of the staff, with information from all elements of the institution and its physical plant administration concerning construction, management, safety, health, fire control, quality and availability of materials, dependability, energy conservation and simplification, and operational and maintenance efforts.

Typically the guidelines are prepared in accordance with the standard uniform construction index used in architectural specifications. This system is used by most architects for a materials and manufacturers' file index system and most manufacturers of architectural materials use it in their promotional work. The system places all construction matters into sixteen basic divisions, with Division 17 as a special information section.

Of particular interest is Division 1 of the guidelines, which provides information concerning the following:

Administrative Procedures
- Intent of standards.
- Design and construction objectives.
- Communications and routing.
- Architect or engineer definitions and services.
- Codes, standards, and reference material.
- Review authorities and procedures.

Presentation Criteria and Procedures
- Preplanning study and schematic stage.
- Design development stage.
- Contract documents stage.
- Construction administration stage.
- As-built drawing stage.

General Administrative and Technical Information
- Continuity of institutional operation.
- Utility shutdowns and connections.
- Noise, dust, mud, and construction debris.
- Temporary toilets.
- Safety, health, and fire protection.
- Site information and existing material.
- Insurance requirements.
- Finishes in general or specific requirements.
- Operations and maintenance manuals.
- Surveys and test borings.
- Materials testing and inspection.
- Archaeological sites.
- Salvage and demolition.
- Renovation project procedure.
- Balancing of HVAC systems.
- Barrier-free access.
- Full-time project representative and project construction inspector.
- Design errors and omissions.
- Faulty construction.
- Project closeout procedures.

Postconstruction Procedures
- Punch list procedure and closeout.
- As-built drawings and specifications.
- Certificate of occupancy.
- Warranty inspection.

Appended Information
- Standard details that the institution has found to be economical, long in life, simple to maintain, and workable and satisfactory.

Reference Codes and Standards

Architects and engineers are responsible to the owner to provide a design that meets the applicable codes and building regulations. That responsibility cannot be overstressed and must be recognized by the designer. Reviews by trained individuals of the institution's planning staff will reveal many of the potential faults of the documents or some of the failures to meet the codes as well as determine if the standards as outlined are being met.

Known noncompliance code issues must be corrected prior to issuing the documents to the constructors. An up-to-date listing of applicable codes is beneficial, but the designers must be put on notice to investigate in detail which specific codes apply to the project. The owner must not accept responsibility for how the codes are applied. As discussed, codes and building regulations, including zoning ordinances, benefit the owner and those who will utilize or occupy the facility. Every effort must be made to build a facility that is as much in compliance with those codes and regulations as is possible.

Building Committee and Other Internal or External Review Groups

The function of the building committee is to make decisions affecting the design and construction of the new or renovation project. These decisions are limited to the latitude given to the building committee by the institution and are not necessarily all-encompassing. In some institutions the committee acts in an advisory capacity to the administrative office responsible for new construction and renovations; this is usually the department of physical plant but in some cases is the budget office. The makeup of the committee is typically composed of voting members of the requestor's organization, budget representatives, administrative units, and physical plant personnel.

The project manager assigned to the project functions as the liaison between the committee, designers, and reviewers or controlling agencies and looks to the committee as the project's focal point or predominant intellect, if not the final authority. In some cases, project reviews may dictate a change in course from committee recommendations and must be sanctioned by the administrative office in charge.

Reviews of projects take on many aspects and involve the committee, project manager, users, physical plant operation and maintenance organizations, security, and fire protection within the institution and, when the institution is a public facility, such external agencies as state review offices and is responsible to the state. State approvals may involve actual plans reviews by a central construction authority, budget reviews by the central state budget division, space reviews by the state education agency, health departments, agencies responsible for environmental controls, state fire and insurance offices, and, when aesthetics are the concern of the state, the state art review agency.

Additionally, some states exercise control over historic facilities for protection of their historical significance. Some control semi-industrial schools or research facilities for protection of the public. In some cases a state may extend its authority to the institution, local political subdivision, or some building authority. In the case of non-state controlled or private institutions the external reviews are normally required and assisted by the zoning office or building inspector of the local city or county including the fire department, fire code review, and police, sanitation, and utility offices.

The documents of the various phases of project development—master plans, site plans, schematic, design development, and contract documents—usually must be reviewed and approved as consistent with the intent of state regulations, fire codes, and zoning ordinances. Financial reviews, particularly revenue bond issues, are also involved when dealing with state agencies or when funding is through a local authority or bank.

32.9 PROJECT MANAGEMENT

The success or failure of a project in terms of cost, schedule, ability to fulfill requirements of program, and economy of operation depends heavily upon effective management of the project. The goal of adequate and successful project management directly involves the project manager and the administrative and staff support dedicated to the project. The project manager must have the proper resources and time to carry out the necessary functions and responsibilities. An excessive number of projects will result in a breakdown of the management concept itself and may render the process useless.

The chief functions of a project manager involve being the institutional technical representative for a given project, dealing with procedures, acting in an advisory capacity to the committee on new construction and renovation techniques and organization of the planning of the project for selection of the professional designers, submitting documents and reports in a timely fashion, maintaining records, initiating and maintaining cost estimates, scheduling, and handling communications. The project manager's general responsibilities include:

- Assists and coordinates with the requestor the development of the program, justification, and projected cost data.
- Sets the pace for the project building committee by establishing realistic schedules and encouraging committee action as necessary.
- Assists in selecting professionals for the services required, arranges for interviews and fee negotiations, and prepares various memoranda and contract forms pertaining to professional services.
- Maintains a network of informational contacts and maintains communication with parties involved.
- Proposes methods to accomplish necessary tasks, guides the professionals in their relationship with the institution, encourages good management practice and action by proper and established procedures, and suggests goals and objectives for the project.
- Attends all meeting pertaining to the project and serves as the center for communications between the committee and the professionals by producing appropriate records of transactions and decisions.
- Understands the organization and environment of the requestor.
- Reviews and approves requests for payment by the professionals.
- Reviews and makes recommendations on all proposals by professionals and checks drawings for compliance with program requirements, including engineering reviews of mechanical, plumbing, electrical, utility, and site designs.
- Prepares status reports of project and finances, coordinates these with committee and budget officers, and monitors the budget to assure financial requirements can be met.
- Schedules drawing and other document reviews, including code reviews, and obtains written approvals.
- Coordinates the necessary action to specify and purchase furnishings at the appropriate time.
- Assures effective design solutions through coordination with the institution's design guidelines.
- Provides follow-up services at close of project including assistance in final inspection, financial closeout, and debriefing from

requestor, design professionals, and construction managers or administrators.

The authority of the project manager is limited to that as established by the physical plant administration through the job description, depending upon the qualifications of the individual manager, and is usually limited in the decision-making role but quite broad in terms of communication. The qualifications include professional training and experience in architecture, landscape architecture, or engineering, or experience in project management to the degree that educational requirements are offset. A familiarity with architectural and engineering terminology, code issues, and cost estimating are desirable qualifications.

32.10 DESIGN REVIEW AND APPROVAL

As discussed, a complete review of the drawings and specifications prior to construction is important. The project should undergo several different reviews: 1) a *program review*, which compares the areas depicted by the plans with those of the required program and compliance with space utilization guidelines, 2) a *technical review*, which covers the architectural, structural, site, mechanical, plumbing, and electrical plans and the various related sections of the specifications, including general and special conditions, and compliance with fire safety and handicapped access code provisions, 3) *cost or budget review* through the process of estimate checks and a professional estimate and schedule review and coordination, and 4) a *general review* for compliance with zoning regulations, site utilization, sufficiency of site development and landscaping, and conformance with environmental regulations.

A review of all building plans by the physical plant organization itself is particularly important since the building will be in physical plant hands for maintenance, repair, and operation throughout its entire life.

32.11 PROJECT COST CONTROL

Cost control for the construction of a college or university building is a continuing process from the initial estimate to the final closeout statement, involving the finance or budget office, the building committee, the project manager, and most important of all the designer. It can often be difficult to maintain a budget for a project because of initial mistakes or estimating budget, an insufficiently developed basis for the initial estimate, pressure to include items not in the original program, pressure from designers for changes in the design to improve the aesthetic quality, or unanticipated inflation.

Establishing Project Budgets

The development of an initial project budget can be critical. Frequently an initial budget can be challenged by the project advocate as too high, and the estimator must assure that the project is jeopardized neither by an excessively conservative budget nor by an overly optimistic one. Therefore, the best available estimating data for comparable projects must be used.

Studies have demonstrated that college and university buildings generally cost more than most commercial structures because of a generally greater complexity, dictated by cost considerations as multistory constructions, longer spans required for flexibility in utilizations heavier floor loadings, multipurpose utilization, more extensive functional equipment, and more complex and critical HVAC and other mechanical and electrical system requirements. These considerations are particularly demanding for research facilities. For all college and university buildings, planning for the lowest life-cycle costs for owning, maintaining and operating a building over a long life dictates the use of higher-quality materials and institutional-grade equipment and systems rather than lower cost (and shorter life) commercial grades.

Following is a step-by-step summary of the preparation of an initial project estimate:

- First establish the size, type of use, and general density of the building. Required net assignable area must be converted to gross area by an appropriate ratio. Large classroom buildings used as school centers or with a large influx of students have a lower net-to-gross ratio. A simple administrative office building does not require internal space for large crowds and has a higher ratio. *Time Savers Standards* has excellent examples of net-to-gross figures for college buildings that can be used for area projections.
- Establish the floor-to-floor height of the facility so as to compare the cubic cost and include any abnormal roof structures such as mechanical equipment enclosures.
- Determine the predominant use by floor. A laboratory building with a few offices is a lab building, while a classroom building with chiefly offices is predominantly an office building, but the code rates the floor classification as an assembly facility.
- Collect comparable building cost data on similar types of buildings note their location and month and year bid plus the Engi-

neering News Record (ENR) Building Cost Index for that date. Select as many examples as practical (at least three) for comparison. Using a cost-per-square-foot figure, convert each building cost example to the local location at an identical point in past time for which there is a common ENR Building Cost Index; add an adequate inflationary figure for the period of time to the bidding date. Average all figures on the cost-per-square-foot basis and the cubic basis. The calculated average represents the average low-bid cost for the project at bid time. Because the projects used in the comparison may have had large change orders, and because these costs must be adjusted to attempt to place the figure in any imaginary midrange of the bidders, a factor must be added. Based on the experience that bidders are within a 5 percent spread of each other, add 5 percent to the average figure. Use this cost to project a building construction cost; to it add utility and other site development costs for a complete construction cost. Site costs are usually unit prices applied to direct quantity takeoffs. If a range of costs is desired, then assume a low cost at 5 percent below the adjusted average and a high at 5 percent above the adjusted figure.

Once the adjusted cost figures are decided upon, the balance of the line items may be computed and added in preparation of the total project estimate. APPA's standard project estimate can be used as a checklist and as a basis for the total project estimate (see Figure 32-3).

To add to the flexibility of the format, it may be desirable to add a few line items, depending upon how detailed one wishes to make the estimate. As an example, the following items might be considered for additional detail and greater overall accuracy:

- 604. Programming and preplanning studies.
- 606. Feasibility and special studies.
- 613-1. Archaeological excavations and studies.
- 628. Site work instead of nonstructural improvement.
- 630. Inflation.
- 655. Structural investigation.
- 664. Project management.
- 669. Other costs, interest, and insurance during construction and work by owner.

With the project budget in place there must be a method of tracking the system throughout the life of the planning and construction process.

Figure 32-3

Project Cost Estimate

Project: _____ Date _____
Account Code: _____ By _____

Project Development
   603. Relocation & Renovation $_____
   604. Programming $_____
   605. Cost Control $_____
        Subtotal $_____

Site Preparation
   610. Alterations $_____
   611. Surveys $_____
   612. Demolition $_____
   613. Test Borings $_____
        Subtotal $_____

Construction (New Building or Renovation)
   614. Utilities to Site $_____
   620. Construction Cost $_____
   621. Nonstructural Improvement $_____
   622. Landscaping $_____
   623. Fixed Equipment $_____
   624. Special Fixed Equipment $_____
   625. Parking Area $_____
   626. Street and Sidewalk Repair $_____
   627. Other (Specify) $_____
        Subtotal $_____

Construction Contingency
   629. Percent of 620 thru 628 $_____

Fees
   650. Architects, X% of 620 thru 628 $_____
   651. Architect's Cont. Percent of 629 $_____
   652. Engineer $_____
   653. Landscape Architect $_____
   654. Interior Design $_____
        Subtotal $_____

Legal and Administrative
   661. Interest $_____
   662. Legal Costs $_____
   663. Construction Administration $_____
        Subtotal $_____

Miscellaneous
   666. Moving $_____

667. Government Field Expense $_____
668. Other Cost (Specify) $_____
      Subtotal $_____

General Contingency
669. @_____ percent $_____

Movable Equipment and Furnishings
670. Movable Technical and Scientific $_____
671.-689. $_____
      Subtotal $_____

TOTAL ESTIMATED CAPITAL COST $_____

When scope or funding changes, the budget must be reordered. When there is a change in a line item, the budget is no longer accurate without a total adjustment, or when the sum of the line items exceeds the past total, the entire budget must be recomputed.

A budget spread sheet can eliminate much of the confusion about such budget adjustments. Budgets can be maintained on a computer disk; after updating or adjusting the program can cause the arithmetic between line items can be done automatically. This relieves the project manager in most cases of the task of running through the budget to find the correct balance. The change in a construction line can be programmed into the computer to cause a reordering of the entire column of figures.

Additionally, the budget form can show the original budget for comparison with the corrected column. Further refinements allow the accumulation of expenses and obligations to date and to be recognized. The spread sheet budget then not only saves project manager time but enables others to review the history of the budget quickly and accurately.

Independent Cost Estimates

The usual professional service contract requires the delivery of a statement of probable cost at least twice during planning. These cost statements, however, may need verification that the project remains within budget. For this purpose it is advisable to have an independent estimator review the preliminary drawings and outline specifications to develop a comparative estimate, using the quantity and unit cost takeoff method. This estimate should be updated at the contract document phase to provide a final check just before bidding.

Additionally, some contracts for professional services provide that the independent estimate prepared at the completion of the design development phase is the basis for fees throughout the remainder of the services. The independent estimate then becomes essential and must be as accurate as possible.

Use of the Project and Construction Contingencies

Every project budget should have a line item for contingencies to cover unforeseen budget items and to provide a reserve to cover potential increased costs of inflation. Generally a project contingency should range between 5 and 10 percent for new work, depending upon the complexity of the project; 10 to 15 percent for renovation projects, again depending upon complexity; and an annual inflation rate, all based on the projected construction cost.

Cost Reduction and Value Engineering

Project cost control must be maintained by continuing evaluation and estimating throughout the design development process. As a valuable part of this process, an independent review for cost reduction or value engineering savings can identify costs for elements of work that are not essential to the project or alternate construction methods or materials that can achieve the same purpose at a lower cost.

This is not a basic service of an architect or an engineer but a service offered by cost consultants who may be trained architects, engineers, or contractors who specialize in examining systems, finishes, techniques, and details; they can recommend substitutions to lower costs without necessarily lowering overall quality. While the architect or engineer might obtain these services as consulting services, it may be more advantageous to the owner to hire the consultant directly so that the consultant can be more responsive to the task and less concerned about pleasing the architect or engineer.

32.12 BIDDING DOCUMENTS

Most institutions utilize a competitively bid, lump sum approach to construction procurement. This procedure typically assures competitive pricing, but successful contracting on this basis requires a complete and effective set of contract documents for bidding purposes.

These contract documents include the contract, general conditions, supplementary general conditions, special conditions, technical specifications, contract drawings and any addenda issued in reference to them. All of them, except the drawings, form the project manual that refers to the drawings and thereby incorporates them as part of the contract. Since the specifications are a major part of the contract documents, it is essential that they be clear, as simple as possible, and specific to the project. Unfortunately, architects and engineers often try to reuse specifications by simply changing the names of the projects and fashioning necessary modifications to adapt the old specifications. This can lead to serious mistakes when the text is not carefully checked against the specific requirements of the project.

To avoid this problem, a good specification model or standard can be used. A computerized model facilitates updating and access, but care must be taken to assure that it fits the requirements of special or specific items of work.

One such program is arranged by the standard uniform index:

- Division 1—General data.
- Division 2—Site work.
- Division 3—Concrete.
- Division 4—Masonry.
- Division 5—Metals.
- Division 6—Wood and plastics.
- Division 7—Thermal and moisture protection.
- Division 8—Doors and windows.
- Division 9—Finishes.
- Division 10—Specifications.
- Division 11—Equipment.
- Division 12—Furnishings.
- Division 13—Special construction.
- Division 14—Conveying systems.
- Division 15—Mechanical.
- Division 16—Electrical.

Specifications

In some offices the technical specifications are written by the principal who is designing the project and preparing or supervising the drawings. In a large office specialists in specification writing or a specification consultant usually are used. In any case, the specification writer must be qualified with technical materials, understand the cost of materials methods and systems, and be able to present the material in a logical and systematic manner without repetition, omissions, and conflicting statements.

The document is read by contractors, subcontractors, workers, suppliers, engineers, and insurance agents—as well as lawyers in the event of litigation. The specification writer must at all times be aware of specifying material that can be obtained and installed at least expense and yet does not delay the project.

Technical specifications should use basic principles of grammar and composition and should avoid legal phraseology. Sentences should be short, simple, and concise. Words with more than one meaning should be avoided. Hyphens, commas, and semicolons should be used sparingly: misplaced or omitted punctuation may change the intended meaning of a sentence completely; it is advisable to separate compound sentences into separate elements utilizing independent subjects and verbs.

The telegraphic style of writing specifications, which substitutes punctuation for verbs, is often misread and can confuse a reader unused to the system. Likewise, the careless use of certain words can lead to a misinterpretation of the meaning. Specifications are intended to amplify and clarify information detailed on the drawings. In conveying this information the wording should be direct, not suggestive or recommendatory, but require good workmanship at all times.

The written information must be accurate, brief, and fair to the involved parties as well. Every effort must be made to avoid conflicting information and conflicting drawings and specifications. Courts have ruled that when a conflict exists between specifications and drawings, the written word of the specifications takes precedence over the drawings. Because of the potential problems of unclear specifications or conflicts between drawings and specifications, a careful review and comparison can be valuable in avoiding disputes during construction.

Although there are several different methods of writing specifications, the two basic types are the performance and the procedural specifications. With the performance specification method, the intended final result is specified step by step, rather than by identifying various methods, materials, and systems. The written material provides the minimum acceptable performance. For example, a college needs to repair fire damage to equipment without delay. A statement as to what the equipment must do, what characteristics it must have, and when it is to be installed is required.

The following examples are in the procedural category.

Descriptive Specifications   As the name implies, a complete description of the product, characteristics, and quality required is necessary. The result should achieve the level or performance desired. For example, the equipment to be replaced has an aesthetic consideration; therefore the finish, shape, and material can be specified for clarification.

Brand-Name Specifications   The specifying of brand names and model numbers is common in private work where the professional identifies a product that is preferable in terms of quality and aesthetics. However, most public procurement procedures will not permit this type of specification unless at least three acceptable brands are listed. Additionally, should contractors find a different brand that meets the criteria, they may request acceptance of that brand.

Closed Specifications   The closed specification is a refinement of the brand-name type in which a brand is named, with no substitutions accepted. This sole-source procedure usually is justified by colleges and universities by the statement that spare parts are on hand for the unit and several other units of the same brand are in service at the same location. To use another brand would not be cost effective and may jeopardize existing maintenance agreements.

Multiproduct Specifications   This is essentially the same as the closed specification except the owner may desire to achieve more competitive prices on a limited basis.

Open Specifications   The opposite of the brand-name specification, this allows any brand to be proposed as long as it meets the minimum specification. An or-equal statement in a brand-name specification essentially opens the specifications to any products unknown to the specification writer that meet the requirements.

Reference Specifications   Typically the item desired is referred to by a standard specification. The brand is not mentioned. Federal specifications are an example of this method.

Combination Specifications   As the name implies, this involves the use of a combination of the above types, but one must be aware of potential problems resulting from the mixing of various parts, equipment or systems. Some may not work.

Construction Documents

Construction documents or working drawings have as their primary purpose a graphic representation of the physical aspects of the project: what is to be built, where, what size, how high, etc. Drawings must be complete, intelligible, convenient to handle and use, and economical to produce. They should present only the essential information with as little written description as possible.

The standard layout for the working drawings involves the following:

- *General.*
  Title sheet, table of contents, schedule of material indications, schedule of material notations and symbols, and list of abbreviations.
- *Architectural.*
  Site plan, area location, demolition, excavation, utilities, grading, erosion control, and landscaping plans.
  Floor plans: sub-basement, basement, first floor (including adjacent site work), upper floor plans, and roof enclosures.
  Schedules for room finishes, doors, windows, hardware, and special equipment.
  Roof plan with parapet walls and structures.
  Elevations, exterior and interior.
  Sections.
  Details.
- *Structural.*
  Foundation plan including spread footings, pilings, or caissons.
  Floor plans.
  Roof plan.
  Structural sections.
  Schedules including footings, beams, joists, columns, and lintels.
- *Mechanical.*
  Mechanical site plan with mechanical and plumbing utilities.
  Plumbing plans.
  Plumbing details.
  Plumbing schedules including fixtures, large valves, and special equipment.
  Stack and riser diagrams including hot and cold water.
  Heating, ventilating, and air-conditioning floor plans.
  HVAC details, riser diagrams, etc.
  HVAC schedules.
- *Electrical.*
  Electrical site plan, including outside lighting and electrical distribution, feeder lines, transformers, and signal and communication systems.
  Electrical floor plans for power and for lighting.
  Electrical details and riser diagrams.
  Electrical, communication and signal schedules including light fixtures, and panel boards.

Topographic and soil test boring data may also be attached to the working drawings as a part of the contract documents or as information only. Often when made a part of the contract documents, the contractor takes this to mean exact information; if exact conditions found on the site do not coincide with that information, an extra may be requested. If the information is given as information only, then the contractor may make whatever additional investigation is necessary to determine more exact subsurface data.

Checking the Documents

While the professionals use various check lists for specifications and drawings, plus the experience of the job capital and the partner in charge, there is still the possibility of omitting essential information. The institution's project manager should then review the documents, using a checklist as a follow-up check. This action may save many hours of work at the end of the job and will certainly enhance the possibility of getting the ever elusive set of perfect documents.

General Conditions

The general conditions of the contract state the rights and responsibilities of the parties to the contract, including their agents, and set forth the procedures pertaining to the implementation of the contract. The conditions are intended to regulate and govern the obligations of the parties under the contract, not the internal workings of either party; the standards of acceptability of work and materials; the conditions under which the contract is to be executed; the materials or systems to be used; and the required schedule of completion.

Historically, binding contract documents have had general conditions, written or implied. As the construction industry developed in the nineteenth century, various builders and engineers used their own versions of the general conditions. As more builders went into business, more versions of general conditions developed, each tailored to fit the individual needs of the contractor or writer. In 1888 the first uniform general conditions were established; they have been revised and rewritten continually since. They are available through the American Institute of Architects or the Associated General Contractors of America.

Currently three forms of the general conditions are promoted by the AIA: the standard form, A201; the standard form modified for inclusion of federal requirements through supplementary conditions, A201 and A201/SC; and the construction management edition, A201/CM. All three forms are composed of fourteen articles, except A201/SC, which adds two additional articles. Each form begins, "This document has important legal consequences; consultation with an attorney is encouraged."

Typically most general conditions identify or provide for the following:

- Article 1: Contract Documents—defines the documents, contract, work, and project; execution, correlation, intent and interpretations; and copies of documents furnished and ownership of same.
- Article 2: Architect—defines administration of contract duties and authority.
- Article 3: Owner—defines information by owner and owner's right to stop work and right to carry out work.
- Article 4: Contractor—defines review of contract documents, supervision and construction procedures, labor and material, warranty, and taxes; permits, fees and notices; cash allowances, superintendent, responsibility for those performing work, progress schedule, drawings and specifications at the site, shop drawings and samples, use of site, cutting and patching of work, cleaning up, communications, and indemnification (of owner and architect).
- Article 5: Subcontractors—defines award of subcontracts and other contracts for portions of the work, subcontractual relations, and payments to subcontractor.
- Article 6: Separate contracts—owner's right to award sixty-six separate contracts, mutual responsibility of contractors, cutting and patching under separate contracts, and owner's right to clean up.
- Article 7: Miscellaneous provisions—governing law, successors and assigns, written notice, claims for damages, performance bonds and labor and material payment bond, rights and remedies, royalties and patents, tests, interest, and arbitration.
- Article 8: Time—defines progress and completion, days and extensions of time.
- Article 9: Payments and completion—contract sum, schedule of values, progress payments, certificates for payment, payments withheld, failure for payment, substantial completion, and final payment.
- Article 10: Protection of persons and property—includes safety precautions and programs, safety of persons and property, and emergencies.
- Article 11: Insurance—defines contractor's liability insurance, Owner's liability insurance, property insurance and loss of use insurance.
- Article 12: Changes in the work—includes change orders, claims for additional cost, and minor changes in the work and field orders.

- Article 13: Uncovering and correction of work—includes uncovering of work, correction of work, and acceptance of defective or nonconforming work.
- Article 14: Termination of contract—prescribes methods of termination by the contractor and termination by the owner.

For those institutions that may have federal funding for their construction projects, some federal agencies require of certain additional general conditions. In the case of AIA A201 the following additional articles are required:

- Article 15: Modifications of the general conditions—includes definitions, modifications, and substitutions dealing with cash allowances; subcontractors, concerning disqualified subcontractors; award of subcontracts, listing of approved subcontractors; performance bond and labor and material payment bond, requiring 100 percent coverage of contract amount; contractor's liability insurance, requiring coverage in specific amounts; and property insurance, requiring coverage at the site until work is completed.
- Article 16: Additional conditions—includes substitution of materials and equipment, federal inspection, lands and rights-of-way, equal opportunity, certification of nonsegregated facilities, prevailing wages, contract work hours and safety standards act, apprentices and trainee, criteria for measuring diligent effort, determination of ratios of apprentices or trainees to journeymen; variations, tolerances and exemptions; enforcement, payrolls and basic records, compliance with Copeland regulations, withholding of funds, subcontracts, contract termination-disbarment, use and occupancy of project prior to acceptance by the owner and enumeration of the drawings, the specifications and addenda.

Often incorporation of the Federal Supplementary General Conditions requires inclusion of the Life Safety Code as a governing code in design of the project. Additionally a federal agency may require the review of the contract documents at any stage of development.

Bid Forms

There are many ways of presenting the offer or proposal for the work to be performed, but the two most common are stipulated sum, also known as the lump-sum fixed price, and cost of the work plus a fee, also known as cost plus fee. Each has variations but basically all proposals fall under a competitive or a negotiated basis. Some examples are:

Competitive	Negotiable
Lump-sum fixed price	Cost plus fixed fee
Unit price	Cost plus percentage-of-cost
Hourly	Reimbursable
	Guaranteed maximum
	Incentive

Each has advantages and disadvantages for any one project. Often the authority under which the institution operates determines which method is used. Institutions typically use the competitive method of lump-sum fixed price. The unit price method is also used when known quantities cannot be predetermined. A good example of the unit method is a contract that requires the furnishing and installation of pilings, using a unit of length measure. The cost plus fixed fee methods or percentage of cost may be used for specific projects involving many unknowns, such as a building to be constructed within a certain time frame but initially without full development of the scope of the equipment or equipment support systems.

The typical bid proposal for a lump-sum contract proposal includes the following documentation: form of proposal, signed by the officers of the company or corporation; bid bond, in the appropriate amount, usually 5 percent of the base bid; and a statement, if necessary, concerning the ability of the firm to contract. In some bidding procedures the contractor is allowed to submit so called "work papers" in case there is an error in the arithmetic of the low bidder and that firm wishes to withdraw. The work papers can establish proof of the error so that the contractor may withdraw without penalty.

Timely completion is a recurring problem in construction. Three basic methods encourage completion on schedule: the essential condition method, the liquidated damages method, and the progress of the work method. Contractors usually cannot be held responsible for conditions beyond their control such as fire, wind, flood, and strikes. The essential condition method makes failure to complete work on an agreed-upon schedule a breach of the contract. In the event of delayed completion the owner may attempt to recover actual damages incurred.

The liquidated damages method establishes a daily monetary value for delayed completion in lieu of the actual loss. In private work, a corresponding incentive clause may provide a bonus for every day the contractor finishes early. This is a much more workable liquidated damages clause, although it is usually not permitted in public sector work.

The progress of the work clause may be a more workable arrangement for schedule adherence, although it has no enforcement clause other than actual or liquidated damages. This approval uses a critical path method or other tracking schedule to alert the owner, designers, and contractor to potential schedule problems at an early stage. With an established completion date, by stipulation in the specifications, by acceptance of the contractor's stated time of completion, or through a negotiated completion date, the contractor can initially be encouraged to finish by that date, or to correct any problems before they create an unresolvable time issue.

32.13 DESIGN ALTERNATIVES

Aside from the standard design by one party and competitive bidding by another, several alternatives are available to institutions for accelerating the design and construction process, depending upon the governing authority under which the institution is operating and the type of project. Design-build, turnkey, fast-track, and construction management are all systems that can save time in the design construction stages.

In the design-build process architects and engineers may be in the employ of a contractor or may join the contractor to form a team for purposes of designing and building a specific project. The advantages of this method include both cost and time savings.

Successful use of the design-build method requires a significant involvement by the owner. Detailed requirements must be set forth in the request for proposal, and the architectural, engineering, and financial proposals associated with the selection process must be carefully reviewed. The design-build process can be used to great advantage on a specific project requiring little deviation from the standard facility, simple mechanical and electrical requirements, and limited aesthetic control.

In the turnkey alternative typically, the owner can negotiate or accept bids for full design and construction services for the rapid and full development of a project. When the construction is finished, the owner has only to turn the key for a complete and workable facility. Variations allow the owner to furnish the land and to contract for architectural and engineering services separately, or the constructor may select the design team. Additionally financing can be a part of the constructor's service, or the owner can arrange for separate funding. This process works well for institutions that might want to duplicate a facility or are interested in a complete student housing complex, for example.

Fast-track construction is gaining interest because of its time-saving features. The procedure involves design and construction as an overlapping process. As an example, the structure of the building may be completed before interior design is finished. The process is not totally effective without the full cooperation of the designers and the constructors. The process works well for large buildings and can significantly reduce the time of combined design and construction.

Construction management contracts are a variation of the fast-track method. The main difference lies in the hiring of a construction management firm or consultant to work with the designers for cost and material quality and schedule control during the design stage and in the hiring of contractors for the various trades and/or systems during the construction stage. The CM may participate as a member of the design team during the project planning stage and then assume a role similar to a general contractor during the construction stage.

Two different responsibility tracks are established for the role of the CM under the construction manager procedure. The CM may be hired as an agent of the owner, with limited authority, or may be hired as a separate contractor acting independently and fully responsible as any contractor is to an owner. Regardless of the CM's position, the construction management procedure can best be utilized on large, complex projects.

32.14 MANAGING THE DESIGN PROCESS

Effective management of capital projects, especially in the design process, is essential to any institution of higher education. Costs for these major investments must be carefully controlled; the institution must assure that the completed facilities effectively serve their intended purposes and can be economically maintained and operated. New space must be acquired in an orderly, economical, and timely fashion to allow the institution to reach its goals and objectives and to support fully the needs of the academic and research functions.

Without proper facilities whole programs may be delayed or not established. Poor or inadequate facilities may drain financial resources, act as a constraint to the staffing of important academic or research positions, and discourage gifts, grants, and other support by negative impact upon the institution's public and academic image. Effective project management during the design stage of new construction or renovations and improvements can promote a successful project by involving personnel with technical knowledge of buildings and their systems, training in management, and a basic understanding of the needs, goals, and objectives of the institution.

Project Management

Project management involves technical support to a building committee or administration concerning the project; advice on matters pertaining to new construction, renovations, and appropriate design and construction guidelines and standards; organization of the project; assistance in the selection of design professionals; and maintenance of communications with all responsible parties during the planning process.

An important function of project management is facilitating the establishment of goals and objectives for the project. Those may involve the following:

1. Final cost within budget.
2. Completion on schedule of each segment of planning and construction.
3. Achievement of functional and efficient use of space.
4. Use of long-life, serviceable materials at the least cost.
5. Exposure of all materials and equipment to life-cycle cost analysis.
6. Promotion of code compliance, barrier-free access, and efficient energy use.
7. Development of attainable staffing requirements.

While project management may not require decisions by the project manager, these decisions often result from the project manager's effort through a committee. The manager must identify the decision needed, develop alternatives for discussion, establish the limits, and create the atmosphere in which the committee can be guided. To accomplish this the manager must avoid surprises; fully involve the requestors, committee and designers; promote payoff expectations rather than penalties, and always set the stage for the needed action.

In summary, William B. Foxhall defines the project manager in his book *Professional Construction Management and Project Administration* as:

> the client's voice, agent and purse string. He rings the
> starting bell when a project exists as a serious intent.
> He expedites the owner's decisions at key points as
> the project develops. He may be one man or a depart-
> ment or staff. He may be a consulting firm or a devel-
> oper. He may be, in fact, a special kind of architect.
> He is the rim and the spokes of our project wheel. He
> may or may not have detailed, technical construction
> expertise among his own resources. If he has, he

should ideally use that knowledge only for communications. . . .

The project manager may be a member of the institution's staff, an outside consultant, or a third party to perform the required duties.

Project Tracking and Reporting Procedures

An essential management tool for the project manager is the process of tracking and reporting the progress of the project. This may be the simple circulation of letters reflecting progress, publication of a status report, or the advanced tracking procedure of the critical path schedule. A typical project report format might include the following elements:

- Project title and identification.
- Project requestor or originator.
- Using unit or department.
- Locations.
- Original budget.
- Current budget.
- Architect/engineer.
- Construction contractor.
- Project manager.
- Contact telephone numbers.
- Project schedules based upon events in the project cycle, with dates for original schedule, current schedule, and actual attainment dates.
- Current status summary.

These reports should be updated and circulated on a regular basis to all by offices or individuals involved or concerned with the project. The use of personal computers affords a convenient and expeditious means for readily maintaining and updating project status reports.

Project Checklist

For any major facilities project dozens of checks, reviews, approvals, or other procedural actions may be required to carry out the project in accordance with all applicable laws, regulations, policies, and procedures. Unless these requirements are approached in an organized way by the project manager, it can be easy to overlook a required action at the proper time. The use of a detailed project checklist, set up in accordance with the normal schedule of events in the life cycle of a project, is an excellent way to assure that all requirements are met in a timely manner. The project manager must then refer to the checklist on a regular basis to initiate required actions, to note their completion, or to note that a particular action is not applicable. As with project-reporting procedures, the use of a computer on facilitating employment of a checklist procedure.

NOTES

1. *Handbook of Professional Practice*, Vols. I-III (Washington: American Institute of Architects, updated monthly).

ADDITIONAL RESOURCES

Abbett, Robert W. *Engineering Contracts and Specifications*. New York: John Wiley & Sons, 1963.

Ayers, Chesley. *Specifications: For Architecture, Engineering and Construction*. New York: McGraw-Hill, 1975.

BOCA Basic Building Code/1981. Homewood, Illinois: Building Officials and Code Administrators International, 1981.

BOCA Basic Energy Conservation Code. Homewood, Illinois: Building Officials and Code Administrators, 1981.

BOCA Basic Fire Prevention Code/1981. Homewood, Illinois: Building Officials and Code Administrators, 1981.

Branningan, Francis. *Building Construction for the Fire Service*, second edition. Quincy, Massachusetts: National Fire Protection Association, 1983.

Building Codes and Public Safety, slide presentation, National Conference of States on Building Codes and Manuals.

Building Construction Cost Data. Duxbury, Massachusetts: R.S. Means, 1987.

Callender, John. *Time-Saver Standards*, fifth edition. New York: McGraw-Hill, 1974.

Dodge Cost Systems. New York: McGraw-Hill, 1987.

Facilities Design and Construction Guidelines. Charlottesville, Virginia: University of Virginia, Department of Physical Plant, 1988.

Foxhall, William B. *Professional Construction Management and Project Administration*. New York: AIA and Architectural Record Books, 1972.

Glough, Richmond H. *Construction Contracting*, second edition. New York: Wiley-Interscience, 1975.

Guidelines for Development of Architect/Engineer Quality Control Manual. New York: National Society for Professional Engineers, 1979.

Hauf, Harold D. *Building Contracts for Design and Construction*. New York: John Wiley & Sons, 1981.

International Conference of Building Officials Code. Whittier, California: ICBO.

Kobert, Norman. *Aggressive Management Style*. Englewood Cliffs, New Jersey: Prentice-Hall, 1981.

Lathrop, James. *Life Safety Code Handbook*, second edition. Quincy, Massachusetts: National Fire Protection Association, 1981.

National Building Code. New York: National Board of Fire Underwriters.

Sanderson, Richard L., ed. *Readings in Code Administration*. Vol. I, *History/Philosophy/Law*; Vol. II, *Fire Protection Technology*; Vol. III, *Building Materials/Systems/Standards*. Chicago: Building Officials and Code Administrators International, 1975.

Southern Building Code. Birmingham, Alabama: Southern Building Code Congress International.

Space Planning Guidelines. Columbus, Ohio: Council of Educational Facility Planners, 1985.

Uniform Construction Index, second edition. Washington: AIA-CSI-CEC NSPE, Producer's Council, Specifications Writers, 1983.

CHAPTER 33

Use of Computer Aided Design and

Drafting in Facilities Management

Dale C. Norton
Architect II
The University of Texas at Austin

33.1 INTRODUCTION

Facilities management is largely a matter of allocation of resources. Management can be more effective through a better understanding of what resources are required and where and when these resources should be allocated. The advancement of the profession includes a never-ending search for tools that assist in this endeavor.

For years the practice of facilities management, like other professions, changed little. Copiers made life easier and, at the same time, increased the amount of paper to be handled and stored. Then came typewriters that were able to make corrections, followed by word processors that showed even the skeptical how computers could serve as a tool. Computer aided design and drafting (CADD) is perhaps the most significant tool now available to facilities managers; it is part of a system that is promoting change in the whole approach to facilities management.

CADD is a marriage of hardware and software yielding the synergistic result of a useful tool. Basically a graphic data base, CADD is a tool that uses the power of the computer for both words and numbers. As a tool for designers and drafters, CADD is both fast and flexible. Like word processing, it allows for quick "cut and paste" and provides the opportunity to quickly explore a number of options. Through predrawn details and notes, replicating repetitive tasks, and automatic dimensioning, CADD significantly reduces the time required to produce design drawings and construction documents. This is especially true when modifying documents that are already in the system memory. Vendors claim speed increases of four to ten times that of manual drafting. While this may not be realistic, clearly a drafter trained on a fully implemented CADD system can produce a drawing faster than by working with traditional tools.

Furthermore, a CADD system can provide consistent accuracy well beyond that attained by manual methods. Because most CADD systems work in full-sized dimensions, they can provide more accuracy than can be accomplished by the construction craftsperson. Since dimensioning is automatic, much of the mathematical errors and omissions of the drafter are eliminated by CADD.

Many physical plant departments have installed CADD workstations. They attest to the usefulness of CADD in creating drawings, cost estimates, and other drawing-related information. Individual CADD workstations (see Figure 33-1) are limited, however, in that each serves only one person at a time, provides limited information, and distribution is little different than conventional drafting production.

While superior to manual drafting, this arrangement fails to take full advantage of the power of the computer. Each stand-alone workstation must have its own copy of all the data that may be required by the

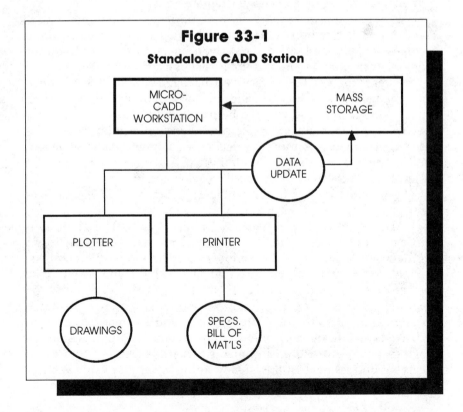

Figure 33-1
Standalone CADD Station

designer or drafter. This means time lost in duplication of disks or transferring data from one storage medium to another. There is always the possibility that a current work update will be overridden by an inadvertent update.

By networking workstations together (see Figure 33-2), the same information can be used by any number of designers and drafters. Most importantly, everyone is assured of using the most current data in the system, since there is no longer a need for multiple copies of the data to be located at each workstation. This has the effect of enhancing the productivity and usefulness of the system. This network is still limited to the designers and drafters.

Employees in other departments have to translate the information on the drawing to a form that is appropriate for their needs. Even if they computerize their work, the same data is being repeatedly entered into computers. This redundancy is what computers are meant to eliminate. Additionally, one or more input errors can cause conflicting information among departments, again leading to the same conflicts and confusion that the computers were intended to prevent.

What is needed is a system that fully integrates drawings and all other related data (Figure 33-3). This would put information at the fingertips of those who need it, and all information would be consistent because it is updated at the source. Everyone in all departments would have access to the same data.

To realize this type of system requires the networking of the CADD systems with data bases, spreadsheets, graphics packages, and word processors. This amounts to a network of networks, and the approach is already being accomplished by some facilities organizations.

While these systems are large and complex, the resulting ease of access to information has proved worthwhile. Smaller, limited versions of these comprehensive systems are appearing on the market for existing micro- and mini-CADD systems. Already this type of system is affordable to medium and large organizations, and smaller groups are expected to soon find them within reach.

33.2 HISTORY OF CADD

It is unlikely that anyone could have imagined systems such as micro-CADD when the computer age exploded in the 1960s. In those days computers were huge machines that required the most delicate treatment. Drawing with a computer was an afterthought. The calculating power of computers was first directed toward producing hyperbolic parabolas and other interesting geometric patterns. These applications

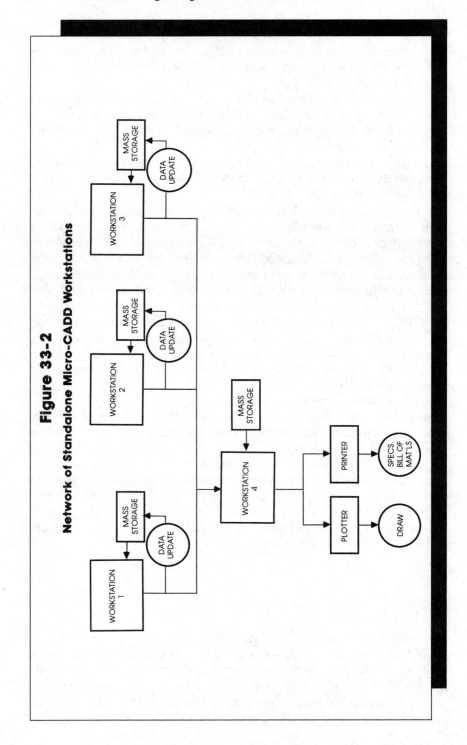

Figure 33-2

Network of Standalone Micro-CADD Workstations

Figure 33-3

Network of CADD Terminals to Minicomputer

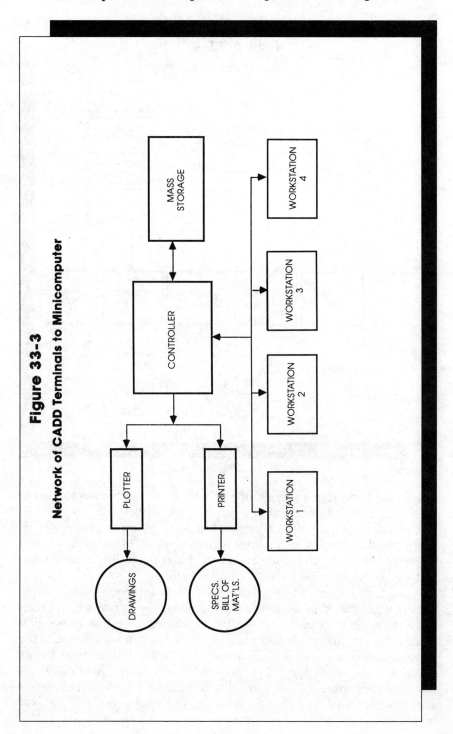

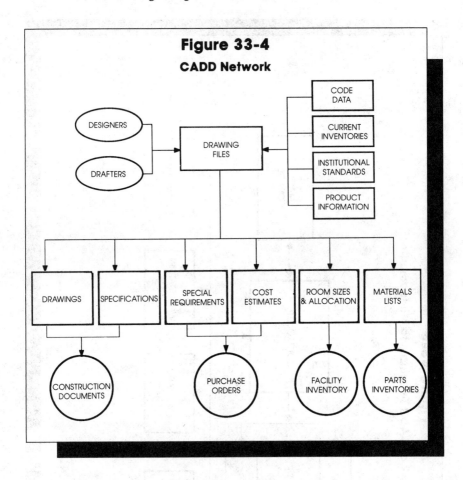

Figure 33-4

CADD Network

caught the interest of college students who used their access to the big machines to experiment with the graphic possibilities.

It was not long before attention turned to trying to produce engineering and architectural drawings with computers. Many of these early attempts failed, and the best were far from successful. But it was a start, and led to the first true computer aided drafting.

Originally intended for use by electronics engineers and drafters, CADD was limited in flexibility. Furthermore, the hardware and software requirements for a CADD system limited access to those who could afford to buy and house a large mainframe computer. Some of the large architecture/engineering firms who had purchased or leased mainframes attempted to adapt them for construction. These early systems required input in the form of punch cards, a slow and laborious process to produce even a simple drawing. The results were crude at best by today's standards.

In the mid-1960s the video display terminal began to replace keypunch machines. This was a major advance for those who worked with computers. Although it slowed the system down when a number of people used the machine at once, the net effect was to speed data entry, and data entry operators began to replace key punchers.

Large firms could now afford to develop their own CADD systems that would produce acceptable two- and three-dimensional drawings. However, because they were still so cumbersome to use, these systems often were found to be more effective as marketing tools than as production machines. Construction documents continued to be produced manually, even in firms with sophisticated CADD systems.

In the late 1970s, the development of reasonably powerful minicomputers, known as super-minis, allowed faster data entry. More complex and powerful CADD systems quickly followed, and the industry began to take off. Mini-computers had existed for some time, but they lacked the speed and power of the mainframes and were not useful as CADD machines. The super-mini was another story; technological advances made them as fast and as powerful as some mainframes had been just ten years earlier.

These were the first true CADD machines. Their appearance coincided with other advances in technology in output hardware. Color output and other features became affordable to the those who could afford these computers.

At about the same time, the micro-computer appeared, displaying many of the capabilities of mini-computers of the late-1960s and early-1970s. Although slower, they were cheaper and more portable than the minis and they quickly found their niche with small businesses and individuals. However, they lacked the horsepower required to handle the complexity of CADD.

The IBM-AT was the first successful micro with the necessary power for CADD. A number of clones followed quickly in the early-1980s. Today, there are a number of manufacturers who produce micros that make excellent CADD machines. Apple's Macintosh II is rapidly establishing itself as a leader in the CADD field. IBM, in an attempt to free itself from the limitations of its DOS operating system, has followed Apple's lead by producing the PS-2. This is a promising machine that, as yet, lacks the software to compete in the CADD market.

In a reversal of the normal flow of computer development, microcomputers have moved into the large offices. Out of necessity, links were developed to connect micros with minis as terminals. This ability to switch the function from terminal to stand-alone made the micro even more useful in the office.

As both hardware and software have become more efficient, the size and cost of CADD has continued to plummet. The last ten years have seen continuous advances in the field. This has led to mass distribution which in turn has lowered costs, leading to further developments. Today $10,000 will buy a satisfactory micro-CADD workstation. The future no doubt will bring faster, cheaper, and more powerful CADD systems for use in all areas where drawings are the main means of communication.

As CADD systems have proliferated, the issue of compatibility has grown. Construction, like facilities management, is not an isolated endeavor. Firms work together; architects, engineers, contractors, and various consultants, suppliers, and subcontractors all contribute to construct or renovate facilities. As more computers and CADD systems are in use, the transfer of data becomes more critical. The economy with any computer application is realized after the data is inside the machine. When each firm involved in a project must enter the same data that already resides in the memories of the other team members' computers, much of the savings in time and labor is lost.

Obviously, if facilities managers could receive all data for new facilities from consultants already in electronic data form, little further input would be necessary to prepare the data for manipulation. In the past this has often been all but impossible. Unfortunately, few systems have been designed to communicate with each other, and much data is lost in the transfer from one system to another. One university physical plant department ran into this problem. Their CADD package of Hewlett-Packard hardware with software from a third party could only pass about 40 percent of a drawing back and forth with the utilities department that had an existing CADD package of hardware and software from Hewlett-Packard. This was the case despite the vendor's claims of complete compatibility.

In the past, little was done to improve the translation between systems, but recent strides have been made to overcome this problem. At first each manufacturer and software developer struggled without any common standards. This led to customers who were "locked in" to the system they chose. It guaranteed repeat customers, but it also made them unhappy customers. As the number of installed systems grew, more users discovered that more data would be available to them if their system would just communicate with the system that held that data.

Finally, systems suppliers could not ignore the clamor for compatibility. A tentative effort produced the Integrated Graphics Exchange System (IGES). Due to the reticence of suppliers to share information about their systems with competitors, it took a tremendous effort to produce even this limited standard for the transfer of CADD data between systems.

Although IGES was promoted as a panacea for compatibility, it proved to be more of a placebo; it was really nothing more than a filter that strained data that passed through it. For instance, it provided for only four types of lines. A utility drawing which used ten indicators for the different kinds of piping on a project would suffer terribly in the translation. Some lines would simply not transfer with the drawing, and others would change from one type to another. Text faired no better; it might transfer or it might not, depending on the typeface or whether it was upper- or lower-case. The situation was becoming desperate for CADD users and threatened to choke the industry.

Only with the emergence of AutoCAD by Autodesk, the undisputed leader in the field of microcomputer CADD, has this situation changed. With enough systems installed, the interest of third party vendors was drawn to this system. As with IBM-AT hardware, this software has become the standard of the industry. From several sources, interfaces have begun to appear to make AutoCAD compatible with most, if not all, other systems on the market. Many systems can now talk to each other using AutoCAD as an interpreter.

As the importance of compatibility for the user has become clear, translators are being developed for direct communication between many different systems. The near future appears to hold the promise of true compatibility among virtually all systems. This will make it possible for consultants to send to the facilities manager completed (as-built) drawings on a media that can be fed directly into the facilities manager's CADD system.

33.3 CONCERNS WITH CADD

The problems with CADD are the same as with any other computer system. They are mainly data entry and security, two issues that dominate the implementation of any sophisticated computer system. There are other problems, of course. Staff anxiety about working so intimately with computers, space requirements, training, and cost all must be considered with the installation of a system.

Data Entry

When the only way to enter written data onto a computer was to transfer it from written form to number code or keypunch cards, only the largest organizations with tremendous volumes of data could justify hiring specially trained technicians to input the data. Today, even small organizations can input large volumes of written or numerical data relatively inexpensively. Moderately trained data entry operators can quickly transfer information from standard forms onto computer memory in order to create an alphanumeric data base.

A similar solution to the problem of creating a large CADD data base has not been found. For many facilities this can be a formidable task. Consider all the drawings in the files of a physical plant organization. To become part of the data base, each drawing of every existing structure and utility must be input into the computer's memory. This is in addition, of course, to all the information about renovations of existing facilities and construction of new facilities that must be input as they occur.

Currently, the entry of CADD data is an expensive proposition requiring highly trained operators. Usually these operators are drafters who must be trained in-house to use the specific CADD system involved. As soon as they are well-trained on the system, they find themselves in demand and are often induced to change jobs by offers of higher salaries. This tends to create a never-ending cycle of training for some organizations, which restricts them from getting up to speed on their systems.

Even with well-trained operators, it can take a commitment of months or even years to input all the necessary data in a meaningful way. There are shortcuts, but they have often been unsatisfactory. A digitizer can scan a drawing and add it to the data base quickly, but it results only in a simple copy of the drawing or print. A scan does not provide a separation of information into layers. All information on the sheet would be no more than a jumble of lines. Walls, pipes, and text would have equal status on the sheet to the same extent that they do on the original, except, of course, that some or all of the text could be lost in the translation to electronic data. Considerable time is required to convert the lines into entities, to move entities onto separate layers, and to clean up the text. The result is hardly faster than drafting, and considering the required purchase of costly equipment, may not lead to significant savings.

Some consultants will perform this service. Obviously they require specific direction in order to provide with a truly useful product. Being experienced with the hardware and software, they can often be much faster than newly trained drafters; however, this is still quite expensive and is justified only in special cases.

Security

Security may be an even greater concern than data entry. Security involves keeping out the hackers and the disgruntled employees. It also means preventing accidental deletions of data and the maintaining the confidentiality of personnel and other records.

A security system should allow users to access only the data that is necessary to perform their duties. System users fall into two categories of data access. The first group needs only to view certain data and the second group needs to view and modify the data. Many departments might need to look at, or even print/plot copies of construction drawings, but only the design/drafting department should be able to modify those drawings. Likewise, other departments may maintain data that design/drafting needs to view but not change.

It is important to note that the real issue is not whether a drawing is changed, but whether it can be saved back to the central memory. Some departments or personnel within departments might need access to some, but not all, data that is available in the system. Controls should prevent unauthorized viewing of data, as well as unauthorized modification of the data.

An additional security concern is the inadvertent deletion of data. If two drafters are working on the same document making different revisions, it would be possible for one to delete the changes made by the other. If both operators save their work, the last to save will delete the work of the first. The system will require the establishment of an office policy to enable a person or mechanism to be responsible for merging the data of both before it is saved.

Included in this controller's responsibilities would be regular backups to the data. Considering the cost of entering and organizing the data, duplicating lost work would prove costly and be demoralizing to the staff. At least two backups are recommended, with one close at hand at all times and the other locked away in a safe, fireproof environment. The need for backups cannot be emphasized too strongly.

Some security measures are necessary to protect the investment in the system. This includes both the hardware and software, but it need not be too rigorous. A lockable area for the equipment is in order, with access limited to need. An obvious rule-of-thumb is that the more valuable the equipment, the better the lock that needs to be provided.

Data protection is more subtle, and perhaps more important. Although much of the data will not be sensitive, some will. A password would probably provide enough security to block a casual intruder, but a serious, knowledgeable hacker will be able to penetrate most any security device, given enough time. There is not much point in trying to stop them, since the occurrence of such vandalism is still rare. Regular backups can replace altered data.

There is a new security concern sweeping the nation due to media exposure—computer viruses. These are programs that worm their way onto a system and then begin to change themselves, thereby damaging the system. While this is a real problem, the amount of contamination has probably been exaggerated. Systems that are accessible to outsiders through a network or modem are in the most danger from this type of sabotage. Again, reloading backed-up data can minimize the damage.

Computer Anxiety

It is likely that some or all staff will have some concerns about the implementation of a CADD system. Many people have some anxiety about dealing directly with a computer; others question the aesthetic quality of computer drawings as compared to manual drawings; still others worry that they will be replaced by a machine.

Computer anxiety is common and the myth of computer infallibility scares many people. Dealing with a computer can sometimes be frustrating even to the most dedicated believers in computer technology. This anxiety can be diminished somewhat by the manager through gradually including even the most reticent staffers in the selection of the system and allowing concerned staffers to view demonstrations and ask questions about the system's operation. Adequate training will help when the system is selected. Finally, maintaining a delicate balance between pressure to learn the system quickly and emphasis on the enjoyment of the experience will aid the staff in the conversion. This means allowing the staff some time to become comfortable with the system before placing tight deadlines on a system project.

Another tactic is to encourage experimentation outside of normal hours. Offering some incentive to employees to invest their time and energy in becoming more proficient with the system is one way to speed the process of making full use of the CADD. Keep in mind, however, that once any employee is fully qualified to operate the CADD their value rises with their productivity.

Concerns About Quality

Many employees will express concerns about the quality of the computer-generated output. This is especially true of architectural designers and drafters. It is true that a good manual drawing is capable of more nuance than a computer drawing; this can be a disadvantage at times, since some information may not be transmitted as clearly in a machine-produced document. However, it is also true that most manual drawings are not up to these high standards either.

What is really at issue is a fear of the loss of personal identity. Many designers and drafters have spent years developing their lettering, line weight, details, and other signatures of their work. Theirs is genuine concern that they are being relegated to button-pushing on a machine that will spit out mechanical drawings of a mechanical environment. This is a real issue, since they will be losing some direct control of the output to established standards. For these people, it is important that they see that the CADD will allow them some flexibility in the way they use it. They will have difficulties adapting to a system that is rigidly different in its approach to inputting lines than their manual drafting style.

All possibilities of data input should be fully demonstrated in advance. There are major differences in approaches to inputting data with different systems. Beware of any demonstration limited to fast production of ellipses, circles, and rectangles. Although a room may be rectangular, the drafter should be able to think of drawing walls, not shapes. Finding the right system can make all the difference in allaying employee fears.

Job Security

Job security is often an employee concern. The idea of automation within an industry always makes some people nervous about their positions. While this fear is real, it is not well-placed. CADD systems, and computers in general, will not threaten those people who realize that these machines are nothing more than tools, like their pencils and scales. These people will find that using the tools effectively will make them better at their jobs, and consequently, more valuable to the organization. Not only will the quantity of their work improve but so will the quality.

Planners will find that they have more correct data to make better plans. Since that data can be assembled more quickly, and since the data can be more easily manipulated, they can explore more options than ever before. Refinements will be possible that would have been too time-consuming in the past.

As the organization becomes more efficient, it can do more with its resources. There is never a point at which no maintenance needs to be performed and no requests are made for new or renovated space. There will still be a need for skilled operators to organize the data and make use of it.

This tool is no replacement for people. It can make their work better, faster, and more effective, but beware of thinking that the purchase of a workstation will equal an employee. A tool will only be as good as the use that is made of it.

33.4 IMPLEMENTING CADD

Space requirements for workstations must be considered when purchasing a CADD system. Consider how many workstations will be required for the functions planned. What kinds of output devices are anticipated? What kind of mass storage devices will have to be accommodated? All of these will require space. This should be premium space with adequate lighting and ventilation. Trying to crowd the equipment into some inaccessible corner, with poor lighting and ventilation, is self-defeating; it will result in fatigued employees who will not reach the level of productivity that is a major goal of the implementation.

Training is also required in order to get the most out of any CADD. The more intuitive the operating system, the less training is required for the operators to become familiar with the functioning of the system.

Even the simplest systems will require some training for full utilization. While it is easy to watch a demonstration of how a system operates, it takes practice and direction to master it. When the system is set up in the drafting room, all those sales demonstrations seem to fade from everyone's memory.

A careful approach to staff access to this training is essential. Too many organizations delegate the training to one or two people, usually the head drafter and an assistant. Dependence on only one or two people to fully understand the system can lead to problems. Most likely, their productivity will drop as they find their time is spent working with others. If these people are out of the office at the same time, productivity will suffer. It may not take long for these people to feel indispensable, and act accordingly.

The manager of the drafting department should receive full training. In addition, several people who will use the CADD daily should be trained by the vendor. One of these should be a person who has the time, patience, interest, and understanding to train the rest of the staff.

Among those who should receive secondary training is anyone who will be setting schedules for the operators. These people will need a firm understanding of the process and effort required to produce drawings on the system.

If the CADD is used only as a drafting package, it will lose much of its value. Designers will also need to learn to use the system. They will find that by using the CADD, concepts will take shape more rapidly and become more refined. Then, when the drafter takes the original file to embellish it with necessary detail, mistakes and confusion are avoided.

Hardware requirements will vary depending on the system selected and specific needs. It is important that the hardware meet the requirements of the software selection. Other considerations are the type of output required, input devices with which the staff is comfortable, and the type of mass storage that is appropriate for the organization's needs.

Generally the considerations for selecting a make and model of any piece of hardware are as follows:

- Compatibility with the system
- Speed
- Cost
- Maintenance and support record
- Quality of output

The relative priorities of these criteria will necessarily vary from one organization to the next.

Various kinds of output devices are available. Both plotters and printers can produce color output and a quality range of major proportions. Plotters can be single-pen, multi-pen, or electrostatic. Printers can be dot matrix, letter quality, or laserwriter and each has its own assets. Input devices are, if anything, even more varied than output devices. The choices are light pens, mice (mechanical and optical), scanners, and, of course, keyboards. It is likely that there will need to be some combinations of input and of output devices required for any networked or even multi-workstation CADD system.

Monitors also should be investigated thoroughly before acquisition, since they come in all sizes and shapes. The question of color versus monochrome is an issue that is often handled by purchasing both. A large color monitor is usual for viewing the drawing, while a smaller monochrome displays necessary text. Another consideration is pixels per inch (usually expressed as numbers such as 640 x 860), especially for color monitors. This denotes the resolution of the screen. Generally, the higher these numbers are the easier it will be to read the screen. Also, the closer the two numbers are to each other the more accurate a shape will appear on the screen.

33.5 MAKING USE OF CADD

There are a number of applications for a CADD system in the management of facilities. These range from the barest planning, to detailed documents for construction, to maintenance control.

Planning documents can include long-range campus plans, design proposals for construction projects, and cost estimates and materials lists for evaluation of proposed projects.

Long-range campus plans have proved their usefulness over the years. It is becoming clearer that, as universities find the need to stretch their budgets to cover more costly projects, it is more necessary than ever to know well in advance the amount and kind of resources projects are likely to consume. This information, along with issues such as source of funding and user demand, can lead to better, more cost-effective decision-making regarding resource allocation.

Design drawings have always been a requirement for planning a construction project. Applying CADD to this process is obvious, but many designers hesitate to move into CADD because of a fear that it will inhibit the design process. Although some CADD systems approach design in a more appropriate manner than others, often designers do not approach the CADD with the attitude that it will work. Like any tool, it works only as well as it is applied to the problem.

The proper system can make the design process faster, easier, and more thorough. As the process progresses, the designer will be able to keep an eye on the effects that changes will have on inventories, budgets, and schedules. The relationship of these three dimensions can be quickly reviewed and updated, and since alternates are so easy to generate, the designer will be able to explore choices that might not have been considered in the past. For presentation to the user, the computer can generate presentation drawings. If it is the preference of the designer, the computer can produce two- and three-dimensional drawings that can be used as the basis for overlays of more traditional presentation drawings.

Under no circumstances should this tool be relegated to the use of drafters only; the benefits of the increase in productivity must not be limited to those lowest on the salary scale. The full benefit of CADD can only be derived from the application to all appropriate documents.

Cost estimation is a valuable attribute of CADD software. A spreadsheet linked to the data base will produce an estimate for the specific design. Estimates can be updated automatically as the design and construction documents progress. The result is that those who need to know can be apprised of any budgetary effects throughout the process. The ability to see the results of any proposed change is useful to all team members.

Perhaps the most obvious application for CADD is in the production of construction documents. This is where libraries of standard construction details can cut the time necessary to turn a design concept into finished drawings. Libraries can consist of standard details such as roof penetrations, wall sections, and furniture. If these libraries are linked to standard product data on a spreadsheet, the software will be able to produce an outline specification and a materials list for the project. If a word processor with a comprehensive specification is linked to this attribute, a complete set of specifications can be quickly assembled. The automation of the tedious but crucial task of producing specifications is one of the strongest arguments for acquiring a CADD system.

Other kinds of libraries include drawing conventions such as north arrows, door schedules, title blocks, and other repetitive items. Additional libraries of user-defined details and diagrams of standard assemblies and systems can be maintained for inclusion on the documents. All of these can be included in the documents by a few clicks of a mouse or strokes on the keyboard. The reduction of document development time can be enormous.

Most institutions hire consultants to produce some or all of their planning and construction documents. The acquisition of a CADD system can allow some of this work to be shifted to in-house staff. The extent to which this shift occurs will vary among institutions, so a thorough cost-benefit analysis will be necessary to determine the optimum balance of internal to external production.

Even if it is determined that full reliance on consultants should be maintained, there is much to be gained through the installation of a CADD system. If compatibility is achieved, the consultants' work on CADD can be downloaded into the CADD system. This will form a data base of information for future projects, so that the next consultant will receive data that is as accurate as possible. Additionally, this data can still be manipulated for in-house planning and design studies, inventory requirements, and maintenance schedules. The value of this kind of information will be significant.

The purchase of a system will require some consideration. Foremost will be the intended uses of the system. It should have been designed from the ground up to do whatever the user is intending to do. There is a difference in the way a delineator approaches a schematic drawing and a construction drawing. Have the demonstration include the production of some of the kinds of documents intended for production on the system. Salespeople who are not forthcoming may indicate the treatment you can expect after the purchase.

Beware of trying to adapt a system that was designed for electronics or some other field that is not directly related to planning and construction of facilities. The salesperson is not likely to mention this situation, but one clue is if the dimension lines can only be displayed and printed with arrows for terminators. If the system is not designed to display both tics and dots as terminators in addition to arrows, no one experienced in production of construction documents was involved in its development.

There is a great variety of CADD software available, and hardware manufacturers are almost as varied. A few systems have emerged as leaders and as such will prove to be better supported by third parties, but a lesser known system may prove to be more appropriate for a particular organization. As a starting place, software by Autodesk, Intergraph, Holguin, and VersaCADD should be investigated. Hardware by IBM, Apple, Compac, Hewlett-Packard, and VAX are all good machines and well-supported. Other vendors certainly should be investigated as well.

Whatever system is selected, it will require setup and arrangement. Look to the vendor to answer any questions about the installation of the equipment and initial testing to verify its function. This may be as simple as hooking up a few wires or as complicated as inserting circuit boards, adjusting the equipment, and checking the diagnostics of the software.

All of these issues are important in identifying the most useful system. How much time will operators spend waiting for the screen to refresh itself? Thirty seconds can be a long time to wait for the results of some small addition to a drawing. Are there limitations to the number of workstations on a system? How far apart can they be? What kind of hardware will the system accommodate? These factors can have long-range effects on the productivity of the production of both planning and construction documents.

33.6 INTEGRATION OF COMPUTER SYSTEMS

Drawings provide only a part of the information with which facilities managers deal. Knowing that there is a door in a particular wall is helpful, but a facilities manager needs to know much more information about it. What kind of door is it? What paint was used to finish it? When was the last time it was painted? What lock is in the door? Who has been assigned a key to it?

There are also many people who never produce drawings but who work with the information that drawings provide. Much of this information may be maintained in different departments that may or may not communicate with each other on changes that take place over time. The department responsible for scheduled maintenance might not be notified, for instance, that a room was painted as part of a renovation. Therefore, a crew shows up the next day for regularly scheduled painting only to find that it no longer needs to be painted.

Drawings alone cannot solve these issues of communication. There has to be a linking of drawings with alphanumeric data that can encompass the diverse information that the different departments require to perform their duties.

Integration of data has come through attributes that add to the capabilities of the system. Spreadsheets and word processors have been added to these systems to handle the necessary data. Some systems even interface with third party software that are more versatile and powerful than many of the system attributes.

The ability to link to internal or external information and data repositories will allow for automatic updates to all linked data. This means that making changes to the drawing of a building could automatically update the listing of key numbers, maintenance schedules, personnel assignments, equipment lists, net assignable area, supply availability, building use schedules, and virtually any other type of data that would be affected by alterations or additions to the facilities.

Critical to this automated system is a central repository for information, a place that holds all the information or, at least, a controller that will provide only necessary access to data. The person responsible for the operation of the system must be aware of who is accessing what data at all times. That person should also see to the maintenance of the hardware and regularly back up the data in order to protect it from loss. These are all important duties and may require full-time dedication to perform adequately on medium and large systems. Assurance that all data on the system is as current and correct as possible is essential.

The critical factor is that the system must be bidirectional. Of course the various departments must be able to view the current data that they require. Access to the CADD data base will make this possible. Many departments will need to be able to modify the data as well. This process of modification should be as automated as possible and can include the use of equipment such as bar code readers to maintain inventories of supplies and equipment. This will allow the designers and operators to expedite the process by making use of available materials. Combining this with a strong preventive maintenance program will allow the identification of unsatisfactory equipment. This information can lead to an ability to refine the design process.

33.7 CONCLUSION

Looking into the future, the next great accomplishment for CADD will probably come in the area of direct data input. By applying other advanced technologies, faster and more accurate input of data will be possible. Connecting laser measuring devices, sonar and infrared devices, and perhaps x-ray devices to the system, fast, accurate area calculations could be made. Even conditions inside walls and under slabs could be accurately depicted on drawings that would be formatted and layered from the start. These will allow surveys of existing facilities to be completed quickly by a relatively small crew.

This advance will prove to be a boon for large physical plant organizations that have a high percentage of existing facilities to new facilities. It will allow them to convert themselves to CADD more completely, since all the facilities will be on-line so quickly. Transition time will be minimal, and confusion will be reduced.

With these advances, facilities managers can look forward to being better informed with up-to-date information. Departments will know more about the activities of other departments, and everyone will be able to accomplish their duties with less uncertainty about the information they are sharing. All this should lead to the ability of the facilities team to identify problems and apply the available resources to a solution more efficiently than ever before.

ADDITIONAL RESOURCES

Association of Physical Plant Administrators of Universities and Colleges. *Computer Applications*. Alexandria, Virginia: APPA, 1988.

Crosley, Mark Lauden. "Adjusting to the Expanding Uses of Computers." *Architecture*, January 1989.

Lumpkin, Davis B. "Getting Started in CAD." *Patterns for Progress*. Alexandria, Virginia: APPA, 1987.

Molnar, John. *Facilities Management Handbook*. New York: 1983.

"Hot New Market Lures A-E Players to Cutting Edge." *Engineering News Record*, April 1985.

Rowe, Thomas. "Young Pioneers CIFM at Cost-Conscious Merrill-Lynch." *Facilities Management and Design*, September 1988.

"Which Facility Management Software Systems Fit Your Operations?" *Buildings*, September 1988.

CHAPTER 34

The Construction Process

David G. Reed, P.E.
Director, Facilities Management
University of Missouri-St. Louis

With additional contributions by Charlie Hindeleh.

34.1 INTRODUCTION

This chapter deals with the construction process and the challenges that are associated with that process. Construction has been called a dispute-prone activity, and there exists a likelihood that such disputes may be taken to court. In order to minimize such disputes and to see a successful outcome, it is necessary for all participants to:

1. Create fair, realistic and effective performance requirements.
2. Communicate these requirements to all concerned parties.
3. Devise and comply with communication systems which inform all participants of relevant events and intended courses of action.
4. Devise and follow methods for resolving disputes fairly and effectively.[1]

The owner can take several steps to improve the chances for success throughout the construction process. The first and perhaps most important is to employ qualified design professionals to prepare the construction documents. The owner should take an active role in the review of the construction documents before advertisement and resist the temptation to proceed with bidding before the documents are complete. The contract language should be tailored to the owner's needs rather than using a convenient, standard contract. Last, the owner should develop and implement contract administration and construction management procedures to ensure consistent and effective management of construction projects.

This chapter discusses some suggested procedures for the administration and management of construction projects. The discussion includes types of construction contracts, contractor selection, contract administration, management procedures for construction, and legal issues and considerations.

34.2 TYPES OF CONSTRUCTION CONTRACTS

Owners of construction projects have a myriad of contract types available today to accomplish their construction needs. Each contract should specify the duties to be performed by the party under contract. The scope of these duties can be tailored to include almost anything the owner needs, including design and management as well as construction responsibilities. However, the selection of the appropriate contract is limited by state law for many public institutions to include only those types of contracts that are determined by competitive bid.

The decision by the owner regarding construction contract type is an important one and should be based on the ability of the owner's organization to administer the contract. Some types require much coordination during the construction process, such as construction management, multiple-prime, and fast-track contracts. Simpler methods, such as conventional lump sum contracts, are administratively less complex and require the coordination of only one contractor on the project.

Although consultants are often used by owners for project management and construction inspection, it is best for owners to have in-house design and construction professionals for these functions. Ultimately the owner must live with and maintain ill-conceived and poorly constructed facilities and therefore should take an active role whenever possible during the design and construction process.

In the following sections the different types of construction contracts are presented, together with the advantages and disadvantages of each.

Conventional Lump-Sum Contract

The conventional lump-sum or fixed-price contract is the most common of the traditional forms of construction contracts. It employs a linear sequence of events that requires plans and specifications to be completed before bidding the entire project. The contract is typically awarded to one contractor who subcontracts with other firms to complete all work identified in the contract. (See Figure 34-1.)

Design plans and specifications may be prepared by the owner's professional design staff or by an architect/engineer (A/E) retained by

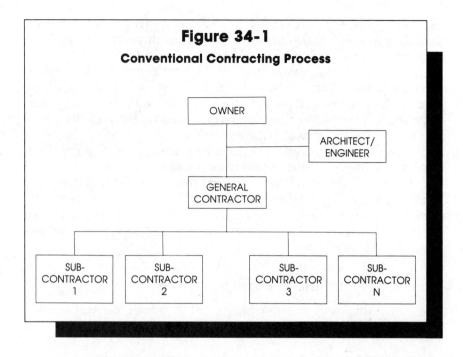

Figure 34-1

Conventional Contracting Process

the owner. These documents must be precise, definite, and complete in all detail to enable the owner to seek lump-sum bids. The bid process usually solicits competitive proposals from all interested and qualified bidders. However, a private owner may elect to negotiate with a particular contractor for reasons of the latter's experience and reputation. Public institutions often put negotiation clauses in the specifications to allow them to negotiate with the low bidder to award a contract within the available funds.

Under this type of contract the contractor is under an obligation to complete the work as originally shown and specified regardless of the difficulties (except certain legal exceptions and those provided for in the contract) experienced during construction.

A variation of the lump-sum contract is the unit price contract where, although the units may change, the price per unit is fixed when the contract is executed. The owner normally estimates the quantities associated with each unit; the bidder is then required to quote unit prices and extend those unit prices based on the estimated quantities for each bid item. The total prices of all bid items are added to establish the total bid amount.

The unit price method can be competitively bid and can be useful for work of unknown quantities or certainty, such as asbestos removal, excavation, asphalt repair and replacement, or concrete repair and replacement. The unit price contract can specify the length of the contract period if the owner desires a means to make repetitive types of repairs as required without a bid for each project.

The principal advantage of the lump-sum contract is the relative certainty to the owner, for both design and cost considerations, before commencing construction.[2] The scope of work and the construction costs are well-defined and the contractual relations between the owner and the contractor are established before construction starts. In fact, if the construction documents are accurately and completely prepared, this form of contract is the easiest to administer.[3]

The disadvantage of the lump-sum contract is the length of time required to complete the design process and all construction documents before bidding the work. For this reason the owner must carefully plan the initiation of the project design so that actual project construction will occur at the proper time.

Construction Management Contracts

The American Institute of Architects (AIA) defines the construction management process as

> managing the design and construction of a stated project to achieve an architectural and construction program at the lowest beneficial cost to the Owner within a reasonable profit framework for the partici-pants. . . . The management function is an agency of the Owner, may be performed by the Owner, dele-gated to the contractor, the architect or an indepen-dent party, or some combination thereof.[4]

In the typical arrangement the owner hires a construction manager (CM) as an agent to coordinate the entire design and construction pro-cess. Concurrently the owner normally retains an architect/engineer for design services. The objective is for the owner, CM, and A/E to work together as a project team, treating the project design, planning, and construction as integrated tasks from project inception to completion. (See Figure 34-2.)

During project development and design the CM advises and makes recommendations concerning construction activities and bid packaging, prepares and controls budgets and scheduling, coordinates the procure-ment of long lead items, and assumes duties related to bidding and contract award activities.

The CM should package bids in such a manner as to enhance the overall project schedule and to take advantage where possible of local

Figure 34-2
Construction Management Process

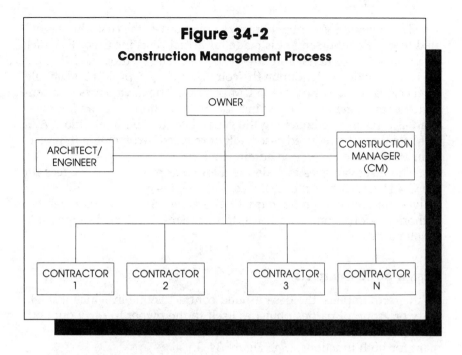

contractor expertise. The bid packaging is an important consideration for the owner as well since a construction contract is awarded for each bid package.

During construction the CM performs management, administrative, and supervisory functions related to construction through project completion. The CM is responsible for inspection, monitoring, time and cost control, contract administration, payments, shop drawings, project reports and records, and change orders.

Many variations of the CM approach exist, including arrangements for the CM to assume any combination of duties usually carried out by the A/E and a general contractor. The basic variations are

- The CM represents the owner with the A/E consultants and contractor, usually for larger and more complex projects.
- The CM assumes the A/E duties. This is sometimes known as design-manage.
- The owner acts as its own CM. This assumes the existence of in-house capability to carry out the respective duties.
- The CM plays a more active role in construction and acts as a general contractor.

The type of CM contract preferred by many is the cost-plus negotiated form.[5] Reimbursement is made for actual costs incurred plus a fee for profit, contingencies, and other expenses. The method of setting the fee is usually dependent upon the complexity of the project and should be specifically addressed in the CM contract. The advantages of a construction management process include the reduction of contractor overhead as a result of eliminating the general contractor. In addition, A/E fees often may be reduced as a result of reduced involvement in project estimating and construction administration.

The disadvantages include the additional project expense fees for the CM in addition to the A/E fees. If the CM is given responsibility to deliver the project on time and within budget without being given the authority to force contractors to perform, the result can be disappointing for all parties.

Design-Build Contracts

As the term implies, the design-build contract is one in which a single party or group of parties obligates itself to the owner to carry out both the design and the construction of a project. The owner has one agreement for both functions. (See Figure 34-3.)

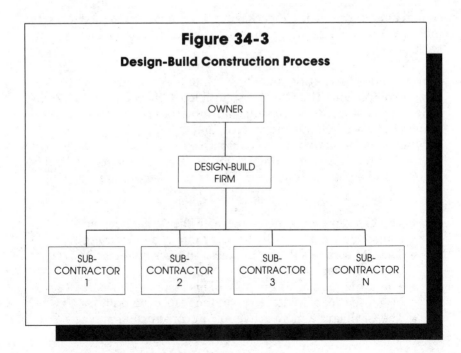

Figure 34-3

Design-Build Construction Process

OWNER

DESIGN-BUILD FIRM

SUB-CONTRACTOR 1   SUB-CONTRACTOR 2   SUB-CONTRACTOR 3   SUB-CONTRACTOR N

Although there are many variations, the two basic approaches to this type of contract are the joint venture team and the sole contractor approach.[6] Under the former the A/E joint ventures with a contractor to form a design-build team. This team either negotiates directly with the owner or enters into competitive bidding for the design and construction of a particular project.

Under the latter either full-service engineering companies or contractors with in-house design capabilities undertake the responsibility for the design and the management of construction, including procurement of materials.

For most institutions the design-build process should probably be limited to reasonably simple projects, such as parking structures and warehouse facilities. Although other types of projects have been constructed with the design-build approach, the need to develop detailed program information precludes most complex projects from consideration. Also the evaluation of prospective design-build firms is difficult for even simple projects and should take into consideration aesthetics, function, and other design-related issues as well as cost.

A single agreement for design and construction is an advantage to the owner in that the time between inception and completion is minimized, uncertainties of cost are reduced, and responsibilities of design and construction lie with one party. However, additional demands are placed with the owner to have pre-established and definite design criteria available to identify the project requirements.

This could be accomplished through the owner's staff or through outside professional help who would also monitor the different aspects of the work for adherence to these requirements. Also, the owner must be capable of closely coordinating the work since there is an overlap of the design and construction activities.

Turnkey Construction Contracts

The turnkey contract, an abbreviation for turn the key, comprises all functions required to allow the owner to start operating a newly constructed facility.[7] As with the design-build contract, a single party is under agreement with the owner to perform both project design and construction, as well as other functions necessary to the project implementation such as site selection, land acquisition, and financing. (See Figure 34-4.)

Whereas design-build contracts are normally carried out by a joint venture or a single company, turnkey contracts are almost always a single-company function.[8] In addition to their technical capabilities, turnkey companies have financial resources that enable them to assume short- or even long-term financial services.

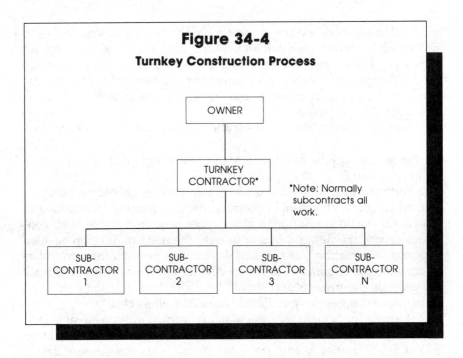

Figure 34-4

Turnkey Construction Process

OWNER

TURNKEY CONTRACTOR*

*Note: Normally subcontracts all work.

SUB-CONTRACTOR 1

SUB-CONTRACTOR 2

SUB-CONTRACTOR 3

SUB-CONTRACTOR N

The turnkey process should be considered for projects to be located off the university-owned premises, such as a warehouse facility. The process might also be useful if the institution does not wish to use available funds or secure interim financing for the project. In the case of the latter, the turnkey contractor would hold a mortgage on the property until the institution completed all payments to the turnkey firm.

Multiple-Prime Contracts

Under the multiple-prime contract the project is constructed by several prime contractors, each having a separate agreement with the owner to carry out a certain portion of the project independently of the others (see Figure 34-5). This is in comparison to single-prime contracts, where the entire project is constructed under one agreement between the owner and the general contractor.

The principal advantage of this type of contract is the cost savings to the owner realized by the elimination of markup on work that would otherwise be subcontracted and by better prices through increased competition. It also enables the owner to obtain highly skilled specialty contractors and gives considerable flexibility in letting out the work.

However, unless the work is rigorously planned, coordinated, and controlled, and contract documents carefully prepared, this type of contract can prove troublesome.[9] Interface responsibility, coordination between contractors, and allocation of liability for job delay are a few examples that cause extra construction expense and possible litigation.

Fast-Track Construction Contracts

The main objective of fast-track contracts is to reduce the time a project takes from conception to completion by overlapping the activities of design and construction. Preliminary or incomplete plans and specifications prepared by the A/E are used for bidding and selection of the general contractor.

Usually, the owner receives preliminary proposals from several contractors and selects one with whom further negotiations are carried out. Such negotiations result in a cost-plus agreement with a fixed or percentage fee; a cost-plus agreement that is converted to a lump sum or guaranteed maximum after plans and specifications are completed; or a lump sum or guaranteed maximum cost based upon the A/E's preliminary plans with supplemental design detail criteria submitted by the contractor.[10]

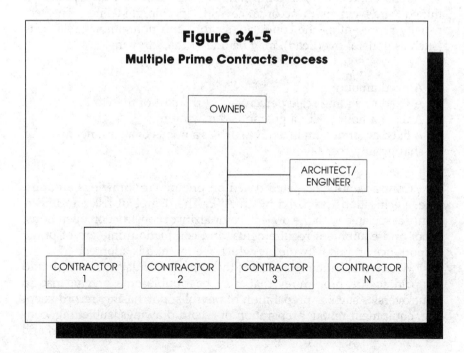

Figure 34-5
Multiple Prime Contracts Process

During construction the A/E continues to prepare detail drawings in packages commensurate with planned construction activities. Such preparation is done in coordination with the owner and the contractor to avoid delays in the progress of work and in some cases to utilize suggestions from the contractor to effect cost savings.

The advantage of fast-track contract can be realized by reducing the time required to construct the project. The main disadvantage to the owner is committing to the project before the preparation of complete construction documents, therefore without development of a firm cost for construction.

Cost-Plus Contract

The cost-plus contract is generally recommended when design plans and specifications cannot be completed before construction begins; many changes are anticipated during construction; or in case there is emergency work. The contract is awarded through negotiation between the owner and the contractor with reimbursement being the costs of performing the work plus a certain fee. Since this contract requires negotiation, it is not often used by public institutions.

Costs are reimbursed to the contractor as incurred within predetermined yardsticks or in accordance with specific guidelines. The fee, usually representing the contractor's profit and nonreimbursable costs (such as general overhead), may be one of the following:

1. A fixed amount.
2. A fixed or sliding scale percentage of the cost of the work.
3. A fixed amount with a guaranteed maximum.
4. A fixed amount with incentive such as a bonus or an arrangement for sharing any cost savings.

Contracts are negotiated based on preliminary drawings and outline specifications prepared by an A/E. The degree of risk and uncertainty associated with the project, complexity of construction operations, labor and equipment requirements, and completion time are of prime importance and usually dictate which fee method is adopted.

When negotiating contracts of this type, particular attention should be paid to the procedures that may be troublesome or give rise to controversies such as preparation of payrolls, purchasing, record keeping, equipment rental, preparation of record drawings, subletting, considerations of overhead, reimbursable and nonreimbursable items, and accounting and payment procedures. Common understanding and mutually agreeable procedures regarding the above at the beginning of the contract better serve the interest of the owner and check the incentives for running up costs by the contractor.

The advantage of a cost-plus contract is that construction can begin before the completion of design, and thus save time. The disadvantages include the lack of incentive for the contractor to reduce or hold down project costs, requiring the owner to be more involved in construction inspection and administration. In general, contractors prefer cost-plus contracts and owners do not since this method of contracting shifts all responsibility for construction risks to the owner.

34.3 CONTRACTOR SELECTION

The means by which the contractor is selected can vary depending on the requirements and preferences of the owner. The contractor may be selected on the basis of competitive bidding, negotiation with a selected contractor, or a combination of both. Competitive bidding is usually required by law on public projects; however, private owners are at liberty to choose their selection method.

Competitive bidding could be of the open or closed type with the former being the predominant one. Under open bidding, prospective bidders use the same bidding documents provided by the owner, with bids being opened and read publicly. In closed bidding there is no prescribed bid form, and there is no public opening. In either case, however, the bid price is final, and there are no subsequent changes or negotiations.

Negotiated bidding is normally limited to privately financed work. Here the owner foregoes the competitive bid process and selects particular contractors with whom negotiations are conducted. Such selection is based on the contractors' reputation, qualifications, and experience. Negotiation can end with any of the mentioned contract types. However, many of the negotiated contracts end with the cost-plus type.

The following sections amplify the bidding procedures carried out normally in open competitive bidding. These procedures have inherently been used for what is known traditionally as linear construction. Linear construction refers to the phases of design, bidding, and construction following each other in a consecutive manner.

The bidding process starts with the advertisement for bids, is followed by a prebid meeting, bid opening, and evaluation of bids, and ultimately culminate in the contract award.

Advertisement for Bids

The advertisement describes the nature, extent, and location of the work and the originating authority together with the time, manner, and place in which the bids are received and opened. It also indicates where bidding documents, plans, and specifications can be obtained and the deposit required.

The advertisement for bids is a most important step in the design and construction process. For competitive bids the advertisement must be seen by many contractors in order to assure the owner of the best possible price. One method to help in this regard is to establish a list of contractors desiring to bid the institution's construction work. This list can be developed through the use of a contractor questionnaire sent to all interested contractors, which asks for pertinent information such as company name and address, company contact and phone number, type of construction work accomplished by the contractor's personnel, and bonding capacity.

If the contractor list is computerized, it is a relatively simple task to send all contractors in the file a copy of advertisements for work that meets the contractor's size and type requirements. This notice to the contractors is in addition to the normally required public notice for public institutions, which requires advertisements to be placed in newspapers or other publications for a specified time.

The use of newspapers can be useful in advertising projects, but if a list of interested contractors is developed as indicated, the response from the newspaper advertisement becomes minimal. Therefore, the institution should consider the use of an abbreviated advertisement to be placed in newspapers or other publications, providing the bare minimum of information such as project name and location, room number and building name for receipt of bids, bid date and time, and name and phone number of the institution's contact for information.

A more descriptive advertisement could be sent to all contractors on file as well as included in the bid documents. Particularly for small projects, the above procedure can represent significant cost savings for the project.

Prebid Meeting

Prebid meetings are initiated and conducted by the owner, usually for large and complex projects or for remote sites. A preset agenda for prebid meetings is useful. After advertisement and at least two weeks before the bid opening, the owner and A/E should meet with prospective bidders and subcontractors at the job site. There are a number of reasons to conduct a prebid meeting, such as:

1. To give the owner an opportunity to introduce the project A/E and the owner's construction representative.
2. To review project details and requirements.
3. To review the institutions contract documents and construction procedures.
4. To emphasize certain aspects of work and explain unusual requirements to the bidders.
5. To answer questions.
6. To inspect the site.

The A/E should be required to describe the project in detail, conduct the question-and-answer session, and lead a tour of the job site. If necessary, the A/E should later issue an addendum to clarify or modify ambiguous contract items questioned at the prebid meeting.

Addenda

During the bidding period, corrections, changes, or revisions to the contract documents may be needed. Notice of such modification is transmitted to all prospective bidders through addenda issued by the A/E or the owner. These addenda should be of a standard format as specified by the owner, must be in writing, and become part of the contract documents.

It is the responsibility of the A/E or the owner to see that copies of all addenda reach all prospective bidders in time to enable them to incorporate the addenda items into their bids. For this reason it is advisable for all addenda to be issued at least seven calendar days before the bid opening date. Bidders must acknowledge on their bid proposal form receipt of all addenda, otherwise their bids may be ruled nonresponsive by the owner, particularly if the unacknowledged addendum represents a substantial cost change to the project.

Bid Openings

A public bid opening is usually conducted by the owner at the time and place specified in the advertisement for bids or as revised by subsequent addendum. The bid opening is normally attended by the owner and construction representative, the A/E, and interested bidders and should be conducted in strict accordance with guidelines adopted by the owner, such as those outlined below.

Bids should be received at a specified location (and only that location) until the bid closing time. The owner must know the exact time since no bid should be accepted after the bid closing time. The owner should have a clock that serves as the official time. Each bid proposal should be stamped or marked with the date and time received. Immediately after the bid closing time, the owner should take all bids to the place of the public bid opening.

Upon arrival at the bid opening room, the owner should make any appropriate introductions and remarks, such as the anticipated contract award date, the institution's contract approval process, the A/E's estimate of cost, and the date of the next meeting for the institution's governing board (if the project must be approved by the board).

At the opening time the owner's representative announces the beginning of the opening and recording of bids. Bids are usually opened in the order they were received. They should be read by the owner and recorded by the A/E, or vice versa. For each proposal the following is called out or announced:

- Bidder's name and address.
- Enclosure of bid security, type, and amount or percentage.
- Enclosure of bidder's statement of qualifications.
- Addenda acknowledgment and any other enclosure material.
- Name and title of person signing proposal and how the bid was made: corporation, partnership, joint venture, or individual.
- The bid amount with the recorder echoing the amount as recorded.

At the conclusion of each bid any irregularities or qualifications are announced and recorded. Contract documents should discourage contractors from qualifying their bids by stating that the qualification of a bid may disqualify the bid from consideration. Although the owner may wish to consider cost saving methods after the award, it is critical that all bids be based on the specified materials and methods; time is also an important aspect to consider.

After the last proposal is read and recorded, the bid-opening session is pronounced concluded. The schedule and procedure for determining and announcing the successful bidder should again be reviewed. Questions and comments regarding the bid opening may be taken after that.

Some possible irregularities in the bid submittals may invalidate the bid as determined by the institution's legal staff. Possible examples include bid bond not signed, proposal form not signed, bidder's statement of qualification not enclosed, addenda not acknowledged, and unit cost or bid alternates not quoted or qualification of the proposal. If a bid is determined to be invalid or nonresponsive during the bid opening, the bid should be immediately returned to the bidder without reading or recording the bid amount. The owner usually reserves the right to waive informalities in bids, such as items that do not affect the cost or schedule, and to reject any and all bids.

Evaluation of Proposals

Following the close of the bid opening session, the bids must be evaluated, analyzed, and compared to determine their completeness and conformance to the project requirement and estimated budget.

The bid review is normally carried out by the A/E in coordination with the owner, and should include checking the completeness of the price data, assessment of the bidder's statement of qualification and examination of unit prices, if such prices were requested.

The bids are tabulated to include each alternate requested in the proposal and then compared to the owner's budget to determine the lowest bid within the budget. This process can be made much simpler by listing the alternates on the bid proposal form in the order of the owner's priority. Also it is easier if all alternates are additive rather than a mix of additive and deductive alternates.

Once the low bid is determined, the contractor's ability to perform the work at the bid price must be evaluated. If the low bidder is considerably lower than the next low bidder, then it is probably appropriate to ask the bidder to review the bid for completeness.

In this case it is good practice to require the low bidder to meet with the owner and A/E to review the bid and project requirements in detail before determining whether the contract should be awarded to the bidder. If the bidder discovers a bid error or omission, the owner must then decide the disposition of the contractor's bid security and consider the award to the next low bidder.

Where prequalifications or invitation is not practiced or allowed, the bidder's capability to carry out the contractual duties is normally evaluated by reviewing the contractor's qualifications, which should be submitted with the bid. The evaluation process, once completed, leads to a recommendation regarding the successful bidder and consequently the award of the contract.

Contract Award

On selection of the contractor the owner normally prepares a notice of award and forwards it by certified mail together with the contract, performance bond, and insurance requirements to the contractor. This notice sets forth the conditions pertaining to the award.

However, it does not authorize the start of construction, which is contingent on the parties' executing the agreement and the owner's issuing a notice to proceed. In some instances it may be necessary to authorize the contractor to begin the purchase of materials before issuance of the notice to proceed. If necessary, the notice of award letter should give that authorization as well as submit the contract documents to the contractor for execution.

Usually, the contract period is specified to begin on the date of the contractor's receipt of the notice to proceed. The owner may be faced with a potential problem unless the contract documents limit the amount of time available to the contractor for the execution of the contract documents.

One solution is to revise the definition of the contract period to begin on the date the contractor actually receives the contract documents for execution. An appropriate time must be added to the contract period to allow for both the contractor's time required to execute the contract documents (probably fifteen calendar days) and the owner's time required to review and execute the contract documents and issue a notice to proceed (perhaps seven calendar days).[11]

This method forces the contractor either to promptly execute the documents within the fifteen calendar days provided in the contract period or be faced with a corresponding reduction of time available to complete construction. The owner should be aware that this method also requires the owner to be prompt in the issuance of a notice to proceed after the receipt of all contract documents from the contractor.

34.4 CONTRACT ADMINISTRATION

The administration of construction contracts can be a difficult and challenging task. The contract administrator is often faced with decisions for which no clear answer seems to exist. It is within this context that the contact administrator normally must function since the more clearly defined problems are usually resolved in the field by the owner's representative. This section addresses the contract administrator's responsibilities and concerns during the construction process, whereas the following section deals more directly with the actual procedures as implemented by the owner's representative.

For the purpose of this and subsequent sections, the owner's key personnel who are involved with the construction process are defined as follows:

- Contract administrator—the institution's duly authorized representative, having the primary responsibility for the execution and administration of the construction contract.
- Owner's representative—the contract administrator's autho-

rized representative, having the primary responsibility for the coordination, documentation and inspection of the construction work (duties may vary depending upon the institution's needs).

- Architect/engineer (A/E)—the professional responsible for the preparation of the project plans and specifications, with the ultimate responsibility for the proper function and performance of the completed project.

In some institutions the lines of responsibility are not as clearly defined as indicated above. For instance, the contract administrator may also be the owner's representative on the site. In other cases the A/E may act as the owner's representative and take an active role on-site during the construction process. Regardless of the specific assignment of responsibilities, there are several keys to the successful administration of contracts:

1. The owner's representative must be given the authority to make decisions on the job, within established limits. Otherwise the owner's representative does not have the power necessary to enforce the contract requirements.
2. There should be one central contact for all parties involved in the construction process—normally the owner's representative. It is of prime importance that all communications for the A/E, contractor, and owner go through the owner's representative. In this manner the owner's representative can be fully informed and responsive to all matters relating to the project, such as potential changes and conflicts. In addition all decisions should be made through the owner's representative in order to keep the lines of authority and communication clear to all parties.
3. The contract administrator, as well as the owner's representative and the A/E, should strive throughout the construction process to be fair and reasonable, to be consistent with established policies and practices, and to make decisions in a responsive and timely manner.

Consistent with these suggestions, it is desirable to have an experienced and knowledgeable professional as a contract administrator. Clearly the contract administrator faces many difficult decisions that can impact the operation of the institution and therefore must be fully qualified by education and experience to make those decisions.

This section addresses items of concern and interest to the contract administrator. The items discussed typically require direct involvement by the contract administrator, such as contract initiation and project closeout procedures, payment process, project coordination, project schedules, change orders, and dispute resolution.

Preconstruction Meeting

A preconstruction meeting, with all the principal parties involved in the construction of the project, takes place before actual construction. The meeting is normally arranged and conducted by the owner, and a preset agenda helps to focus on the items that need to be discussed. It should provide a forum for the discussion of general administrative procedures pertaining to the project as well as review details of the project. It is essential that all key members of the project team be represented. Preconstruction meetings typically include the owner, the owner's representative, the A/E, the contractor and superintendent, and, if possible, the subcontractors and their assigned representatives.

The optimum time to conduct the preconstruction meeting is after all subcontracts have been awarded.[12] This allows all key members of the project team to be introduced and to get a clear understanding of the procedures involved in the administration and management of the project.

The preconstruction meeting should specifically cover the following items:

1. Introduction and role of all project team members.
2. Procedures for communications.
3. Procedures for contractor submittals.
4. Use of the owner's premises.
5. Special project requirements.
6. Construction schedule.
7. Potential change orders.
8. Review of the general conditions.
9. Payment procedures.
10. Review of all questions regarding the contract requirements, clarifications, and general concerns.

The preconstruction meeting is a good opportunity for the contract administrator to meet the project team members, as well as express the administration's concerns and desires. In fact, it would probably be beneficial in most cases for the contract administrator to conduct the meeting. However, after the meeting, the contract administrator should be less active, although still involved, in order not to usurp the authority of the owner representative and diminish his effectiveness in the field in dealing with the contractor and A/E.

Notice to Proceed

The beginning of the construction period is normally established by a written notice to proceed that the contract administrator sends by certified mail to the contractor. The notice to proceed is sent after the contractor submits all required items, such as the signed contract, insurance certificates, performance bond, and list of subcontractors.

This notice allows the contractor to commence operations. No work should be permitted on the site until the notice to proceed is issued because the bonding and insurance are not in effect until the contract is officially approved and the contractor authorized to proceed. Contracts usually require the contractor to commence work on the date the notice is received or within a specified period, such as ten days after its receipt.

Payment Process

There are a number of concerns for the contract administrator regarding the payment process during construction, including the requirements for the contractor's schedule of values, procedures for submission of progress payments, procedures for the review and approval of pay requests, requirements for retainage, and the process for final payment.

Schedule of Values   For most contracts it is good practice to require the contractor to prepare a schedule of values or breakdown of costs. The schedule should be prepared before the first pay request and should detail the costs associated with each construction activity. The detail for each work activity should typically include the following:

- Description of the work activity.
- Quantity of work and the unit of measure.
- Estimated material costs including shipping and taxes.
- Total estimated costs including labor and material, plus application of the contractor's overhead and profit.
- Planned start and completion dates.

From the contract administrator's point of view, it is important to require actual quantities of work to be identified by the contractor on the schedule of values. In case of dispute during a pay request regarding work in place for any work activity, it can be clearly resolved by measuring units installed rather than by simply guessing the percentage complete. Although there may not be time for the owner's representative to check all units installed for each pay request, it is recommended that periodic spot checks be made to assure the owner of proper disbursement of the institution's funds.

It is also important to have the contractor separate the material costs on the schedule of values for each work activity, particularly if the owner reimburses the contractor during construction for materials stored on site. If a question arises regarding the value of the material stored on site, the owner can refer to the original value given by the contractor and the most recent pay request to determine the quantity of units installed. The difference between the original value and the current value for installed units establishes the maximum allowable value for materials stored on site at any given time.

The schedule of values can be used to establish not only pertinent cost data but important schedule information as well. This is particularly useful if the owner uses a computerized system to process contractor payments and analyze construction progress. In addition to the schedule information requested on the schedule of values, it is probably wise to require the contractor to prepare a construction schedule, at least in bar graph form, detailing each work activity and the associated time frame for construction. Although there might appear to be some duplication of effort, in most cases the progress schedule must be prepared first in order to establish the proper sequence of work. Then the dates can be entered on the schedule of values. The preparation of a progress schedule by the contractor requires some thought be given to the proper planning and sequencing of the work rather than conveniently pulling the dates from the air.

Progress Payments   It is customary for projects of more than a limited duration to require partial payments as the work progresses, normally on a monthly basis. Depending upon the contract provisions, the pay requests may be prepared by the owner, the A/E, or the contractor. However, the contractor typically prepares the progress payment request and then submits it to the owner or A/E for checking, approval, and payment. Progress payments usually compile the cost of the work accomplished to date. The process for checking and approving pay requests can be enhanced by requiring the contractor to prepare all requests with the assistance of the owner's representative.

The contractor's request for payment should be made in the format required by the owner. The form, if not a standard AIA or NSPE (National Society of Professional Engineers) document, should require the contractor to list all work activities and report units installed for each work activity. The value of the work in-place is determined by multiplying the units installed by the unit costs identified in the contractor's schedule of values. This method of measurement is called an earned-value method; it is much more reliable in determining the value of work in-place than could be derived by guessing at the percentage complete for each activity or the project.

In addition to the measurement and identification of units installed, the owner's form should contain spaces to record actual start and finish dates for each activity. This is of particular interest to owners with computerized payment systems, since the actual construction dates can be compared to the planned dates to establish useful progress information.

The pay request form should contain a statement above the contractor's signature certifying the following:

- All items and amounts shown in the pay request are correct.
- All work has been performed and materials supplied in accordance with the contract requirements.
- The contractor and all subcontractors have complied with the labor provisions of the contract.
- The payment does not constitute acceptance of the work by the owner.
- The payment does not constitute a waiver for the contractor for defective work or deviations from the contract requirements.

The actual wording of the certification statement should be reviewed by the institution's legal staff.

Review and Approval of Pay Requests   Also of prime interest to the contract administrator is the process by which pay requests are reviewed and approved. The expeditious processing of a contractor's pay request strengthens the owner's ability to foster and maintain a good working relationship with the contractor. On the other hand the inability to process a contractor's pay request quickly has been the cause of many trials and disputes.

The first step in minimizing the review and approval time required for pay requests is to examine thoroughly the number of signatures required and the need for each. For instance, if the owner has a representative on-site to inspect and manage the project, what purpose is served by requiring the architect/engineer to review and approve the pay requests? This is not to suggest the A/E should not review and approve work in place, but if the owner's representative is on the job more regularly than the A/E, then requiring the A/E's signature on a pay request only slows down the process. The A/E could be given a copy of the pay request for review and information without requiring a signature. Any discrepancies found by the A/E could be resolved either by adjustment of future requests or, if a substantial error is discovered, by having the contractor revise and resubmit the request. Some institutions may also require administrators other than the contract administrator to sign pay requests, even though they may not be familiar with the details and progress of the project. Ideally the only signature needed on the contractor's pay request should be the on-site representative who is most familiar with the project and progress to date, in most cases the owner's representative. If the owner's representative works with the contractor during the preparation of the pay requests as suggested, the requests can be approved immediately upon submission for payment without disputes regarding work in place.

The next step in speeding the review and approval process is to examine the process for the preparation and approval of vouchers or other accounting documents as required to make payment to the contractor. The ideal situation would be to have the accounting document prepared immediately upon receipt of the pay request by the owner representative's or contract administrator's office staff, requiring only the signature of the contract administrator. The goal should be to process the contractor's pay requests in a timely manner: within two weeks from receipt is reasonable, but certainly no longer than a month if good working relations are to be maintained with the contractor.

The value of each pay request for lump sum contracts should be determined by measuring units installed, or work in place, for each work activity. As indicated, it may not be possible for the owner's representative to measure all units installed, so some quantities may be estimated in terms of percentage complete. Once the quantity of work in-place is determined for each work activity, the value of the completed work is calculated based on unit costs as provided in the contractor's schedule of values. Then the values for all work activities can be summed to establish the value for all work in place.

In addition contractors are often reimbursed for materials stored on site, so a value must be established for all materials thus stored. Contractors are normally reimbursed for only a portion of the total reported value of the materials stored on site, such as 90 percent, to protect the owner from possible errors in reporting.

The contractor's pay request should also include approved change orders, either completed or in progress. Therefore, the contractor's total pay request should include the value for all completed work, plus the allowable value for materials stored on site, plus the value of all approved change orders, less an established amount to be retained by the owner until the project completion. This amount is called *retainage.*

Most of this discussion relates to the administration of lump-sum contracts. However, many of the principles apply to other types of contracts. The major differences between lump sum and other types of contracts develop in the format and timing of the request, and not the review and approval process. For instance, negotiated contracts of the cost-plus types usually provide for the contractor to submit payment requests at specified intervals during the contract time. A common provision is a weekly reimbursement of payrolls and monthly reimbursement of all other costs, including a pro-rata share of the contractor's fee.[13]

Retainage   The contract administrator is often involved in the determination of the proper amount of retainage to be held for projects. In accordance with the terms of the contract, a prescribed percentage of each progress payment is usually retained by the owner. A retainage of 10 percent is typical although reduced percentages and other retainage arrangements are used. The retainage is kept by the owner until the project closeout requirements are met. Final payment is then made to the contractor, including the accumulated retainage.

Retainage is considered by some to have an undesirable effect upon the contractors and their subcontractors, especially on large projects. The owner has custody of the contractor's money for prolonged periods of time; the contractor may experience cash flow problems and be forced to borrow at high rates.[14] This in turn may reflect in higher cost of construction for owners as contractors might raise their bids to accommodate for retainage requirements. Likewise, subcontractors are affected since the general contractor normally applies the same retainage on the subcontractor's payments.

To offset these undesirable effects, changes have been introduced recently to retainage requirements. To an increasing extent, construction contracts provide for a 10 percent retainage only during the first half of the project (until the work is 50 percent complete). Subsequent payments are either paid in full or the retainage is reduced to 5 percent for the remainder of the project. However, if the contractor falls behind schedule after the project is more than 50 percent complete, the owner should reserve the right to increase retainage back to 10 percent.

While retainage is commonly used on lump sum contracts, full reimbursement is normally made on cost-plus contracts. However, as the project reaches a certain percentage completion (80 percent is sometimes used), additional payments are withheld until a prescribed amount has been retained by the owner.[15] This amount is then kept until the project closeout and final payment.

Owners consider retainage a protection against possible problems such as the contractor's failure to remedy defective work or payment of damages. Some may question why contract bonds are not normally used against these eventualities? It should be recognized that contract bonds that are provided by the contractor are only affected upon the default of the contractor and consequently the breach of the contract. Therefore, retainage is much more readily available to the owner in the case of problems since it is under the owner's control.

Final Payment   The contract administrator normally takes an active role in closing out projects. Final payment to the contractor should be made only after the contractor fulfills all requirements of project closeout. The final payment request is processed in the same way as monthly payments. The owner may require the contractor, before processing the final payment request, to furnish written acknowledgments by all subcontractors and material suppliers that they have been paid in full by the contractor for all work done or materials supplied by them.

The contract administrator should request the contractor to submit with the final payment request a notarized letter certifying that all subcontractors and material suppliers for the project have been paid in full; that all labor cost, fringe benefits and material costs have been paid; and that the project has been completed in accordance with specifications and drawings. Many institutions require the submission of lien waivers in lieu of the above. The exact language and certification requirements should be reviewed by the institution's legal staff.

The acceptance of final payment by the contractor is often construed as a release of all claims against the owner but should not release the contractor from claims for defective work or work completed not in accordance with the project plans and specifications.

Project Schedules and Budget

The use of effective control techniques by the contract administrator is a basic element in the efficient management of construction projects. Control of project time and cost during the construction period is reflected through the use of schedules and budgets. Before field operations begin, a detailed time schedule and a project budget should be prepared.

A common contract provision requires the contractor to provide the owner with a construction schedule before the start of construction activities. Depending upon the extent and complexity of the project, the construction schedule could be any of the basic scheduling methods: bar charts, velocity charts (S-curves), or computerized network diagrams (generally critical path method, CPM).

Bar charts are often required since they are easy to understand by all levels of management. As a scheduling tool, bar charts convey the relative timing and duration of the respective project activities (broken down to major elements) and allow the monitoring of actual progress versus the planned progress.

S-curves show the relationship between time and output (in percentage of completion or dollar amount) in a straightforward manner. They permit comparison of the cumulative actual progress versus the cumulative planned progress.

Computerized network diagrams, especially critical path methods, are often used on large and complex projects. They display the various work activities, the time-versus-activity relationship, the interrelationships of activities, the dependencies of activities on one another, the critical activities that control the project duration, and the sequence in which the work is to be accomplished.

CPMs may be time framed. This allows the complex CPM networking to be analyzed almost as easily as a bar chart.

These scheduling methods can provide an invaluable tool for construction progress analysis and monitoring, but only a few institutions can afford to implement the computerized CPM networks since they require considerable time and effort to update. Unless all schedule responsibility is delegated to the contractor, including timely updates, most institutions will probably control and monitor construction progress with the use of bar graph schedules.

The project schedules described above for construction activities are applicable to design services. They are of utmost importance to contracts utilizing design-build, turnkey, or multiple prime contracts. Under design-build or turnkey projects, the project schedules allow the thorough integration of both activities (design and construction) into a single plan of action. Network diagrams (CPM) are singularly suited to accomplish this. Under multiple prime contract, project schedules allow the identification of interface activities of the multiple contracts in addition to the individual activities of these contracts.

Construction schedules are usually checked by the owner to ascertain the accuracy and practicality of the various activities. This is done early in the construction period after the contractor submits a schedule. In checking, attention should be given to the various critical paths included and the critical items that might later lead to claims. Construction schedules would, if necessary, then be modified through mutual negotiations and agreement with the contractor.

During construction, schedules should be regularly updated as needed. No project plan is perfect; deviations from the original program are unavoidable. Updating involves revising the schedule of the unaccomplished work to reflect the effect of the changes that have taken place. The original schedule, however, should be kept for reference in case of schedule disputes. Construction schedules are effective in analyzing delay claims. The effect of a given delay on a given activity, group of activities or the whole project can be ascertained with accuracy, especially when the CPM method is used.

A project budget is normally developed at the time of project conception, and then revised periodically during schematic design and design development to reflect changes in the scope of work. The final budget should be prepared before the contract award since construction normally accounts for the major cost item in the budget. Budget allocations relate also to other items necessary for the project realization. Design fees before and during construction, change order costs, costs of owner procured equipment and material, costs of the owner's supervisory and administrative personnel, land acquisition, and other direct and overhead costs are all expenditures that have to be taken into consideration in preparing a project budget. Of particular interest to the contract administrator is an estimated schedule of monthly payments for construction. This information can be developed from construction schedules. It can be used by the contract administrator to estimate periodic expenditures.

Project Coordination

The contract administrator should usually delegate the responsibility for project coordination to the owner's representative since it is important all directions and communications for the project be through the owner's representative. The contract administrator's desire for good project coordination can be enhanced through the establishment of written procedures. Typical sections in the procedures manual regarding project coordination should cover guidelines for written communications, phone conversations, construction coordination meetings and other special meetings.

In addition, the contract administrator probably reviews the status of all construction projects regularly. This can be accomplished by requiring monthly construction review meetings, where the owner's representatives review each project in detail. All change orders and potential problems should also be reviewed at these meetings. The contract administrator can use this opportunity to discuss pertinent topics with the on-site representatives. The monthly meetings can be a positive step toward consistency on the campus in interpreting and administering contracts.

Change Orders

After the award of a construction contract, it often is necessary to issue change orders to modify the requirements of the project plans and specifications. There can be many reasons for the change, but regardless of the reason most projects must have change orders to produce the originally intended project. This section deals with the contract administrator's concerns regarding change orders; the more detailed change order procedure are discussed in 34.5, Management Procedures for Construction.

The contract language normally allows the owner to make a change without obtaining consent by the contractor to the change. However, an unwilling contractor may price the change order to reflect dissatisfaction with the change. The most effective way to avoid claims and disputes is to agree upon the scope and cost of the change before the start of work.

The contractor should not start any change order work prior to the receipt of a written authorization from the owner. Although these rules must sometimes be broken in the case of emergency work, the contract administrator is better served by delaying the project to reach agreement with the contractor on the change order price rather than resolving the issue later in court.

Depending upon the specific language of the contract, changes may stem from additions to or deletions from the work, concealed conditions, changes in owner requirements, or changes to the contract time requirements. Changes are often requested by the contractor, the A/E, or other sources like outside public agencies or private individuals. However, the owner's power to order changes is limited to the original scope of the project. This subject is discussed in more detail in the section entitled "Legal Issues and Considerations."

Contractors often claim they have performed extra work and request a change order to be issued when they disagree with the A/E's interpretation of the specification and drawing requirements. The best safeguard for the owner in these cases is to require the contractor to submit a written claim before the commencement of the work in question. Failure of the contractor to submit the required protest would preclude compensation for the work.

To eliminate a potential point of contention in the administration of change orders, the construction contract documents should establish limits for the contractor's overhead and profit percentages. In addition the contract language should clearly define those items to be included in the contractor's overhead and profit allowances. For example, the contract might contain a statement similar to the following: "The overhead and profit charged by the contractor shall be considered to include, but not limited to, performance bond, builder's risk and public liability insurance, job site office expense, incidental job supervision, field supervision, company benefits, general office overhead, and costs associated with preparation of design documents, layout drawings, or shop drawings."[16]

Another consideration for the contract administrator is the request for time extensions by the contractor. The request may be associated with a change order or due to an unrelated event or act. In general, time extensions should be given when the change or event outside the contractor's control results in a delay to the project completion. If a CPM network is used on the project, the effect of a change can be readily determined. Otherwise the owner should require the contractor to explain the cause and extent of the project delay thoroughly. The contract administrator should be aware that indiscriminate denial of time extensions may open the institution to claims stemming from the contractor's efforts to accelerate the work to meet the contract completion date.

Therefore, as in all aspects of contract administration, reason must be judiciously applied in reviewing time extension requests.

Dispute Resolution

During the implementation of the contract, disputes may arise between the owner and the contractor regarding the latter's claims for payment of extra costs or time extensions. Claims can stem from a variety of conditions such as owner-caused delays, changes in work, interpretation of the contract document requirements, changed or concealed conditions, and suspension of work. Since disputes are almost unavoidable during the construction process, the contract administrator needs to develop a procedure to settle claims and disputes.

Construction contracts should include provisions for settling claims and disputes. The language used should stipulate when and how the contractor should advise the owner concerning any situation that could lead to a claim. The contract documents should also require the contractor to continue with the disputed work (unless the work involved is beyond the scope of the contract), relying on remedies in the contract for settlement. However, the contractor should be required to file a claim with the owner before commencing disputed work.

The process for the review of claims should be detailed, indicating each step for the review. The initial review is normally performed by the A/E who prepared the plans and specifications and therefore is responsible for their interpretation. The review by the A/E should be done in conjunction with the owner's representative, who should be cognizant of all details of the request. Normally the A/E either recommends approval of the claim, rejects the claim, suggests a compromise, or requests additional supporting data. If the contractor is not satisfied by the A/E's response, then the contract documents should provide guidance for further review.

The next logical step is for the owner's representative to make a decision. The decision should be based upon the owner representative's knowledge of the situation and should represent an independent evaluation, not predetermined by the A/E's decision. The owner representative's decision should be given to the contractor in writing. If the contractor is not satisfied, some contracts provide for an administrative review or for arbitration.

The administrative review process provides the contract administrator an opportunity to issue a judgment regarding the contractor's claim. The contract administrator should also review the claim with the purpose of reaching an independent, reasonable position. Additional reviews are available if the institution requires them; however, the decision reached during the administrative review should in most cases be final. Additional reviews at this point probably prolong the process and cause the institution needless expense. Any options available to the contractor after the contract administrator reaches a decision are normally outside the contract provisions, as would be the case if the contractor decides to take the claim to court.

For some institutions, arbitration procedures may be employed in the resolution of disputes in accordance with the construction industry arbitration rules of the American Arbitration Association. The award rendered by the arbitrators is final. The process is not available to many public institutions, but they may have their own mediation process that often helps. Although unavoidable in some cases, disputes can be minimized by the owner's team if all involved in the review process use common judgment and reason to reach decisions.

Project Closeout

The contract administrator's last involvement with the project should be associated with the project close-out procedures. The institution's closeout procedures should include activities pertaining to the final inspection, contractor submittals and certifications, and acceptance of work and final payment by the owner. For many institutions, the owner's representative may be responsible for coordinating the completion of these items.

Project closeouts typically begin with the contractor's request for a final inspection. The final inspection should be attended by the owner's representative, the A/E, and the contractor's superintendent. The final inspection culminates with a punch list that shows all items still requiring completion or correction before the work can be accepted. The punch list is important since it lists all patent defects (those defects that can be readily discovered by inspection or observation).[17] Care should be taken in the preparation of the punch list, since the owner may lose any claim for defective work (patent defects) after the final payment is made. In addition to defects in the work, the punch list can and should include contractor submittal items such as as-built drawings, operating instructions and service manuals, warranties, and certifications. This procedure encourages the contractor to submit all required drawings, manuals, warranties, and certifications in a timely manner since final payment should not be processed until completion of all punch list items.

An important consideration for the contract administrator is the form of certification required by the contractor at the time of project closeout. Many institutions require the contractor to submit lien waivers for all subcontractors and suppliers. This is to protect the owner from claims by unpaid subcontractors and material suppliers. In some states potential liens can be avoided by the use of no-lien contracts that preclude the assertion of liens by subcontractors and suppliers. Another form of protection for the owner is the requirement that the contractor furnish a payment bond at the start of construction. In addition, it is probably wise to require the contractor to submit an affidavit that all labor and material costs have been paid, all subcontractors have been paid, and all work completed in accordance with the contract requirements. Since state laws and institutional policies and prodedures vary, it is advisable to check with the institution's legal staff to determine local requirements.

Upon completion of all punch list items, including the above contractor submittals and certifications, the final payment can be processed. The final pay request should be reviewed and approved by both the the owner's representative and the contract administrator. Also, since this is the final payment, the A/E should be required to approve the pay request and further certify the project to be complete in accordance with the contract requirements. The date when all punch list items were completed is significant, since it can be used as the beginning of all warranty periods. After the A/E certifies the project as complete, the contractor's final pay request can be processed.

Sometimes the owner must occupy and use a completed or partially completed portion of the project before the entire work is completed. This is generally termed *partial occupancy*. Procedures followed in accepting the intended portions are the same as those mentioned. However, the warranty period for the portions occupied by the owner should start on the date that portion is finally accepted by the owner.

Soon after the contractor's final payment is made, the contract administrator's final administrative tasks begin. The primary ones often include

- Financial accounting for the entire project including a compilation of all direct costs, such as A/E fees, survey and testing fees, movable equipment, and furniture expenses, telephone installation costs, landscaping expenses, moving expenses, advertising costs, and other project-related expenses.
- Preparation of the final project report to the owner, including an evaluation of contractor and A/E performance.
- Organization and filing of complete project records. Some of the project documents may be required to operate the completed facility while others may be needed later in case of claims or other legal requirements.

The preparation of the above documentation is the final step in closing out a project—and an important one. It is all too easy to move on to the next project without documenting the difficulties and successes experienced on completed projects. Project evaluation sheets on file can aid the owner in appraising both architect/engineers and contractors when new projects are being considered for design and construction. Without evaluating the project immediately upon completion, many details that should be considered in future contract awards can be lost or forgotten.

34.5 MANAGEMENT PROCEDURES FOR CONSTRUCTION

This section deals with the procedures required to assure effective management of construction projects, particularly by the owner's on-site representative. This section refers to the on-site representative as the owner's representative. Although some of the topics are the same as in the preceding section, the information here reflects the responsibilities and concerns of the owner's representative. The topics discussed in this section include project reporting and documentation, project communications, project scheduling, payment process, change orders, shop drawings and project closeout.

Project Reporting and Documentation

The owner's representative should follow established reporting and documentation procedures for every construction project. The objective is to produce a comprehensive historical record of information and events during the construction process. The purposes for requiring project documentation are numerous, such as providing reference material for future projects, furnishing details for progress evaluation studies and, perhaps most important, providing information for potential litigation or investigations. All projects should be documented, regardless of their size and complexity.

As indicated, all communications should go through the owner's representative. This ensures that the owner's representative is cognizant of all project activities, as well as allows the timely communication of important project directives or changes. The owner's representative should keep project files during construction for correspondence, minutes of meetings, job records, progress payments, test reports, change orders, shop drawings, surveys, manpower records, progress photographs, and other project-related information.

Although not specifically mentioned, it is implied that the owner's representative is responsible for inspection of the work. The reports and documentation discussed in this section are in most cases a result of the inspecting activity. Poor attention to details on the site can result only in less than desirable project documentation; therefore, on-site inspection must be done thoroughly and regularly. The following are suggestions for the reporting and documentation activities in detail.

Daily Job Log   The daily job log is one of the most important job records used by the owner's representative (see Figure 34-6). It is intended to document project progress in as much detail as possible. A daily job log is prepared every working day for each project. Every problem, irregularity, and noteworthy occurrence on the project must be included. By giving time and careful attention to completing job logs, the owner's representative makes an invaluable contribution to documenting the total project. This documentation serves as a central source of information about project progress and as justification in the event of a major conflict or delay on the project.

Daily Phone Log   Every phone call that relates to significant activity or decision is recorded on a separate phone memo. Calls regarding clarification, potential problems, and directives to the A/E or contractor are documented. Phone memos for each day can be attached to the daily job log. Phone calls are an efficient and inexpensive means of exchanging information, especially when there is an immediate problem. However, documentation of phone calls is vital especially if they are to serve as justification for actions taken on the project.

Photographic Reporting   Photographic reporting of project progress provides a complement to the daily job log. Photographs of significant occurrences, objects, or activities during construction are of definite value to those who plan and supervise construction. Regular photo reporting also portrays an accurate, coherent record of project progress.

For major construction or renovation, the owner's representative should take a general picture of each identifiable step in the construction process. The final goal is a photo essay of the project, beginning with a picture of the site immediately before construction and ending with a picture of the completed project. Problems or conflicts on any project should be documented with photographs. In general any deviation from the plans and specifications or any evidence of unacceptable workmanship should be documented with a photograph. After development the owner's representative should organize the photographs, with notes as necessary on the photos or in the daily job log.

Worker Report Form   Some institutions require the completion of worker report forms to record the number of workers employed on site

Figure 34-6
Daily Job Log

Page _____ of _____

1. Project Number: _____

2. Project Title: _____

3. CPM Signature_____4. Date:_____

5. Contractor: _____

6. Weather Conditions: _____

7. Comments:_____

_____

_____

_____

each day, including minority workers, for each trade listed. If required, the contractor should give the completed forms to the owner's representative to attach to the respective daily job logs. (See Figure 34-7.)

Minutes of Meetings   Minutes of meetings are usually prepared after the owner's representative or anyone else conducts a meeting related to the project. The minutes should include the time, date, and location of meetings; the name and address of attendees; the time the meeting ended; and all important topics discussed during the meeting. The minutes can be prepared by either the A/E or the owner's representative and then sent to all attendees.

Figure 34-7
Worker Report Form

1. Project #: _____ Contract #: _____ 2. Campus: _____

3. Project Title: _____

4. Contractor: _____

5. Superintendent Signature: _____ Date: _____

	Total Number of Workers	Total Number of Minority Workers
Asbestos Workers	_____	_____
Boilermakers	_____	_____
Bricklayers	_____	_____
Carpenters	_____	_____
Cement Masons	_____	_____
Communications Workers	_____	_____
Electricians	_____	_____
Elevator Constructors	_____	_____
Engineers - Portable & Hoisting	_____	_____
Pipe Fitters	_____	_____
Glaziers	_____	_____
Laborers (Building - General)	_____	_____
Lathers	_____	_____
Linoleum Layers & Cutters	_____	_____
Marble Masons	_____	_____
Millwrights	_____	_____
Iron Workers	_____	_____
Painters	_____	_____
Plasterers	_____	_____
Plumbers	_____	_____
Pile Drivers	_____	_____
Roofers - Comp., Slate, Tile	_____	_____
Sewer Tile Layers	_____	_____
Sheet Metal Workers	_____	_____
Stone Masons	_____	_____
Sprinkler Fitters	_____	_____
Terrazzo Workers	_____	_____
Tile Setters, Floors & Walls	_____	_____
Tile Layer Helpers	_____	_____
Truck Drivers, Teamsters	_____	_____
Tuck Pointers	_____	_____
Waterproofers, Spray	_____	_____
Welders, Acetylene & Electric	_____	_____
Other _____	_____	_____
_____	_____	_____
_____	_____	_____

A/E Site Visit Report   Every visit to the site should be recorded by the A/E on special forms (see Figure 34-8). The form should include spaces to record the date, time, and purpose of the visit. Also there should be space to record site observations and comments, as well as instructions, resolutions, or directives to the Contractor. It is advisable that the A/E prepare the site visit report at the conclusion of the visit. Copies of the report can be distributed to the contractor if deemed necessary.

The owner's representative should review and approve all site visit forms to provide a basis for claims for additional compensation by the A/E. Often the A/E agreement with the owner stipulates that the A/E be reimbursed for site visits over and above the number specified to be included in the A/E's basic scope of services. There should be no additional compensation for site visits as a result of design errors or omissions.

Materials and Workmanship Test Reports   These reports are usually conducted and prepared by authorized persons as stipulated in the contract documents. Such reports include factory test reports on materials supplied, laboratory reports on materials and workmanship (i.e., concrete, asphalt, gravel, cylinder tests, and compaction tests) as well as other reports pertaining to testing and commissioning of the installed work. Copies of test reports are sent to all parties concerned, with a copy to the central project file.

Special Reports   Special reports include injury, property damage, accidents, safety violations, and hazardous issues reports. Information pertaining to these events, actions taken, and outcomes should be recorded in detail by the owner's representative, based on any official reports prepared and personal observations and actions.

Feedback Reports   These include in-house reports prepared to reflect updated information for each project in progress. They can include all project particulars, revised contract amounts, percentage of funds expended and work completed, comments, and any special notes. Reports of this type can provide project information for the owner's representative for the periodic construction coordination meetings. Such reports provide a valuable information for discussing the status and progress of each project.

All reports and documentation should be kept in a central file that is available to the contract administrator as well as the owner's representative. However, it is often convenient to keep a copy at the job site, particularly if the site is remote from the owner's home office. Those

Figure 34-8
Consultant Site Visit Report

1. Project Number: _____ 2. Project Title: _____

3. Consultant: _____

4. Consultant Representative: _____

5. Contractor: _____

6. Construction Project Manager: _____

7. Date of Visit: _____ 8. Site Visit #: _____

9. Time Visit Began: _____ 10. Time Visit Ended: _____

11. Visit in Contract? (✔) _____   _____
                          Yes   No

12. Purpose of Visit: _____

_____

_____

13. Site Observations & Comments: _____

_____

_____

_____

_____

_____

_____

_____

_____

_____

_____

14. _____ 15. _____
    Consultant Rep. Signature   CPM Signature

documents most often needed at the job site include copies of correspondence, job drawings, submittals, payments, and test reports.

Some of the filing headaches can be alleviated through the use of computerized project information systems. A substantial amount of project information can be stored, generated, and transmitted by computer, such as cost accounting data, schedules, progress payments, and time status reports. Many options and configurations are available in regard to computer equipment and software. The effective use of computers in connection with construction projects can result in substantial time savings and increased productivity, as well as provide accurate and timely project information.

Project Communications

Probably the single most important issue that needs to be resolved at the beginning of a construction project is the establishment of proper lines of communication for the efficient resolution of job-related questions and problems. The logical central contact for most institutions is the owner's representative. All communications should go through the owner's representative, including memos, letters, directives, reports, and verbal directives and statements. This includes communications from the A/E, contractor, contract administrator and any other interested parties. It is generally preferable to establish the owner's representative as the only direct link between the contractor and the A/E, and to require all project matters to be communicated to pass through that person.[18] Regardless of the type of communication used, the major goal is that the right information reaches the right people at the right time.

An exception may occur in the processing of shop drawings. Since it is standard practice for the A/E to review and approve shop drawings and other contractor submittal items, the contractor may send such materials directly to the A/E with only a copy of the transmittal letter sent to the owner's representative. The return of reviewed shop drawings to the contractor should be handled similarly; however, in the case of approved or approved-as-noted drawings, the owner should be sent an appropriate number of shop drawings for reference.

Similarly subcontractors and material suppliers should submit and receive communications and shop drawings through the general contractor (for lump-sum contracts). The prime or general contractor should receive and approve all such submittals before submittal for acceptance by the A/E or the owner.

The owner's representative uses several forms of communications throughout the life of the project. Following is a brief discussion of the different forms:

1. Formal communications. These include written memos, letters, and reports. Memos and letters are probably the best form of communication. The act of writing forces the writer to organize clearly the material to be communicated. Reports are necessary for transmitting or summarizing information.
2. Verbal communications. These include telephone calls, job-site conversations, and meetings. Telephone calls are used for their ease and expendiency in transmitting information. However, in matters relating to decisions or important actions, they need additional written backup or confirmation, especially if required to serve as documentation or justifications for actions taken.

The documentation of important job-site conservations with the contractor and A/E has been discussed in regard to daily job logs and A/E site visit forms. The difficult task for the owner's representative is to determine which conversations should be recorded. The goal should be to include all questions or statements regarding contract requirements or interpretations, as well as those that may result in a claim.

The importance of meetings in disseminating information was also discussed. Although meetings are included under the heading of verbal communications, all meetings should be documented by the owner's representative and minutes of the meetings should be distributed to all concerned.

Project Scheduling

After project schedules have been prepared by the contractor, the owner's representative should review and approve them. The review by the owner's representative should be complete and detailed since the contractor's progress will be compared to this schedule. Therefore, it should be as realistic as possible.

However, the original schedule is often disrupted because of unforeseen situations. Consequently, after the construction operations commence, continuous evaluation of the actual progress must be made against the established schedule.

As a result of systemmatic monitoring of the contractor's progress, the owner's representative should take appropriate actions when required to return the work on schedule. The project schedule should be changed only in the case of drastic modifications to the scope of work or requirements for the work. Otherwise the contractor should be notified in writing that the project is behind schedule and be required to submit a written response outlining corrective measures to be implemented.

Changing the contractor's schedule should not be confused with updating activities. Whereas changing the schedule revises the baseline for progress measurement, updating simply adds to the original data so current status of work activities can be compared with the original baseline. Updating of the actual schedule information should be done at least monthly concurrent with the processing of the contractor's pay request, or more often if possible.

The actual schedule analysis is easier if the institution uses a computerized project information system and the contractor submits schedule data with the schedule of values as discussed. The schedule data can be used to produce graphs or networks that depict actual progress as compared to planned progress. Since work is seldom completed in the exact order as planned, it can be difficult to determine the actual status of the work. However, the process can be made easier if the critical activities are identified. The critical activities are those that, if delayed, will result in a corresponding delay to the overall project completion. Once the critical activities are identified, the owner's representative can more easily evaluate the status of the project.

If the institution does not use a computer for project management purposes, other means should be employed to provide updated schedule information. One method is to require the contractor to submit an updated bar chart schedule along with each pay request. Although the bar chart is not highly sophisticated, it does a good job of representing the time required for each activity and can be easily updated. The bar chart provides a reasonable alternative to the more detailed CPM networks, which probably only the larger contractors can provide.

The maintenance and monitoring of the contractor's schedule is an important task not to be taken lightly. If the owner's representative takes the initiative, there are many opportunities during a construction project when schedule concerns and suggestions can be presented to the contractor. By actively reviewing the contractor's work schedule, the owner's representative can often save valuable time and avoid delays.

Payment Process

As mentioned, the contractor commonly prepares pay requests and submits them to the owner's representative. The basis for all pay requests is established by the contractor's schedule of values, which is submitted at the beginning of the project. No payment can be processed until the schedule of values is reviewed and approved by the owner's representative.

During the review of the contractor's schedule of values, the owner's representative should generally reject any item that will not be incorporated into the project, such as contractor mobilization or demobilization. An exception is normally made for the payment of the contractor's performance and payment bond. Otherwise all activities that do not result in work in place should be included in the contractor's overhead. The overhead should be distributed to all activities on a pro rata basis or some other agreed upon basis.

Another concern to the owner's representative while examining the contractor's schedule of values is the review of the contractor's unit costs. Since work in place should be measured rather than guessed at, it is important to review the unit costs for fairness. If the unit costs seem unreasonably high or low, the contractor should be asked to verify or modify them as required. It is possible for contractors to negate the effect of retention by skillfully adjusting unit costs. After the review and approval of the contractor's schedule of values, the payment process can begin.

The actual pay request normally contains four parts:

1. An evaluation of work in place based upon the original costs supplied in the contractor's schedule of values.
2. A schedule of approved change orders either in progress or complete.
3. A form to claim materials stored on site.
4. A summary to determine the payment amount due, based upon the values for each of the components above.

If the institution uses computers in processing contractor payments, the schedule of values information can be input to produce a pay request form. If the payment process is done manually, the information required is still the same.

Part 1 of the pay request form should list all work activities shown on the schedule of values along with the associated quantities and unit costs, and provide spaces to indicate the quantities installed during the pay period. Also space should be provided to calculate the value of work in place for each work activity. If the process is computerized, actual construction start and finish dates should also be recorded. If the owner's representative works with the contractor to measure work in place, the approval process can be greatly reduced. As indicated, it may not be practical to measure all work in place; however, it is wise to at least spot check quantities installed. After agreement between the contractor and owner's representative is reached regarding units installed, the value for all work in place can easily be determined by using the unit costs provided in the contractor's schedule of values. The addition of the value of work in place for all work activities determines the total earned amount for Part 1.

Part 2 of the pay request is the tabulation of approved change orders, which amend the contract amount. Generally, payment should be made for any authorized change order either in process or complete. The owner's representative should be careful not to overestimate the value of completed change order work. On the other hand, contractors should not be penalized for doing change order work by having to wait for payment until all work is complete.

The third part of the pay request covers materials or equipment stored on site. Some contracts do not allow payment for materials stored on site and indicate that no payment shall be made until the materials and equipment are actually incorporated into the work. If the owner allows payment for materials stored, then several guidelines must be established. First, the contractor needs to know what type of material can be stored, who will determine whether the material qualifies for payment, and where the material can be stored. Without answers to these and other questions, the owner's representative is in for a difficult situation in dealing with the contractor.

Although not as definitive as might be preferred by the owner's representative, some contracts state that payment is made for only those items considered to be major items of considerable magnitude. Furthermore, the materials must be suitably stored in a bonded warehouse or on the site, and the determination of acceptable items shall be made by the owner's representative. Providing the materials and equipment claimed are acceptable to the owner's representative, the contractor must simply submit invoices for materials received to storage and subtract those materials taken from storage and incorporated into the work for each pay period.

The last part of the pay request is the summary that simply tabulates the payment due based upon the values determined for each component. A method used by some owners to determine the contractor's payment is first to add the amount of the original contract work earned to date (from Part 1) to the value of all change order work performed to date (from Part 2) to establish the total earned value to date. It is typical to retain a portion of the contractor's earned amount as retainage as discussed previously. The retainage percentage is normally applied to the total earned value to date (the sum of Parts 1 and 2) and then subtracted to yield a net earned value to date. A percentage is then applied to the material storage total from Part 3 (such as 90 percent) and the resulting amount added to the net earned value to date. Finally, previous payments should be subtracted to determine the amount due this payment.

Although difficult to explain in a simple, straightforward manner, if the process is computerized, it is truly a straightforward task. Once the contractor and owner's representative have both signed the pay request, it can be submitted for further processing. As suggested, in many cases the only signature truly required on the pay request is the owner's representative's. Other signatures normally serve only to slow the processing of the payment. Many institutions have a separate accounting document that must be prepared after receipt of the pay request, and this accounting document probably should be signed by the contract administrator rather than the owner's representative. If there is a separate accounting document, additional signatures on the pay request are redundant and not required. Although this process eliminates the A/E from the approval of pay requests, the A/E should still be involved in the review process. In most cases any serious problems identified by the A/E after the owner's representative has given approval can be taken care of before the contract administrator's approval of the accounting document for payment.

Change Orders

One of the most important and time-consuming tasks for the owner's representative is the management of change orders. To be effective in managing change orders, all requests and directions must go through the owner's representative. If the A/E, contract administrator, or any other party is allowed to deal directly with the contractor without going through the owner's representative, the authority of the owner's representative can be undermined and control of the project can quickly be lost.

Changes may stem from a variety of sources as mentioned. They may be the result of design errors or omissions, natural events or unknown circumstances during construction, budgetary considerations, material availability or delivery problems, or any number of other conditions for change. Change orders are written to authorize a change in the work, contract amount, or contract time. Change orders usually originate with a reqest for a change order issued to the contractor and culminate with a formal change order signed by both the contractor and the owner.

The initial step in the change order process is to determine the validity of a change order request. Usually, unless the work is clearly outside the intent of the contract documents, the A/E is asked to make an interpretation or judgment. The A/E's interpretation or judgment should be reviewed by the owner's representative and perhaps the contract administrator if the position seems unreasonable. After the A/E and owner's representative reach agreement as to the validity and scope of the change order, the owner's representative should issue a change order request to the contractor.

The institution should use a standard change order form to document all requested changes (see Figure 34-9). As soon as the work is identified as a potential change order, a change order request form should be completed. The form should include spaces to record important project and accounting data, as well as a detailed description of the

Figure 34-9
Change Order Request Form

	Number	
	Date	
Contractor	**Requested By (Name)**	
Project Name Campus	**Project Number**	
Architect/Engineer	**Estimated Cost of Change**	
University Authorization (Name) Date	**Type of Change**	
Description of Change (include reference drawings if pertinent)	☐ A: Construction	
	☐ B: Design	
	____ Proj. Coord. Initials	
	☐ C: Emergency	
	Method of Costing	
	☐ Lump Sum	
	☐ Time & Material	
	☐ Time & Material with Fixed Maximum Cost	
	☐ Unit Price	
Reason for Change (Scope Change, Design Error, Site Condition Change, etc.)	**Accounting Data**	
	Change Order Number	
	Source of Funds	
	Time Extension	
Change Order Approvals	Contract Date	
Construction Project Manager Date	Actual Cost of Change	
Consultant (if required) Date	Architect/Engineer Fee	
Associate Director of Facilities Management—Construction Date	Other Charges/Fees	
Associate Director of Facilities Management Date	Construction Project Manager Fee	
Director of Facilities Management Date	Administration Fee	
Campus Representative/Coordinator (if required) Date	Total Cost of Change Order	

change order work and reason for the change. The owner's representative is normally responsible for the completion of the change order request form, as well as all associated correspondence and documentation. The change order request form should have spaces for additional approvals upon completion by the owner's representative, after all documentation is complete.

For budget purposes it is important to identify the cost impact of each change order as quickly as possible. The owner's representative can help in this regard by estimating the cost of the change order at the time of conception. Although this estimate may only be a rough figure and not very accurate at the time of conception, at least the contingency budget is affected by the estimated value. If there are a number of change order requests in process, the errors can be somewhat offsetting with the resulting contingency balance reasonably close to correct. It is better to reduce the available contingency with bad cost estimates than not to reduce it until actual costs are accumulated. The initial or conceptual cost estimates should be replaced as soon as more reliable cost information is available so the contingency balance is also more accurate.

The change order request form should identify the type of change requested, according to the following definitions:[19]

1. Construction-related change orders that do not alter the original design intent and do not require a change in the design of the project.
2. Design-related change orders that alter the original design and possibly the original intent of the project.
3. Emergency field orders that are issued by the owner's representative to perform emergency work involving life safety or to prevent an immediate major delay in project progress.

Also, there are four generally accepted methods to detemine the cost associated with change orders:[20]

1. Lump-sum method for which supporting data from the contractor is submitted, evaluated, negotiated, and approved before writing the change order.
2. Unit cost method in which an authorization to proceed is based on the unit costs negotiated and agreed upon in the original contract.
3. Time and material method for which the contractor provides detailed and actual time and material cost information to be signed daily by the owner's representative and submitted with the payment request after completion of the work.
4. Time and material with a fixed maximum cost, which is similar to type 3, except that a cost limit is negotiated before starting the work.

After the owner's representative has recorded all pertinent information on the change order request form, additional information must be obtained from the A/E and contractor. Depending on the type and nature of the change order, the supporting data requested from the A/E could include the following:[21]

- All design documents required by the contractor for the implementation of the change order request.
- Detailed cost estimate.
- Recommendation regarding any associated time extensions.
- Approval of the change order request.

At the same time, or after receipt of all required design documents, the owner's representative should ask the contractor for supporting data as follows:[22]

- Itemized breakdown of all labor and material costs including quantities and unit costs.
- Markup of overhead and profit consistent with the contract documents.
- Time extensions, if applicable.

The above data from both the A/E and the contractor is for a normal, construction, or design-related change order priced on a lump sum or unit cost basis. For obvious reasons emergency field orders must often proceed before the receipt of all supporting data. In the case of emergency work, the owner's representative should issue a letter to the contractor authorizing the work to proceed and establishing the method of costing, such as using a time and material basis. In order to verify the contractor's actual time and material costs, the owner's representative should require the contractor to submit time cards and material invoices daily for approval. If the owner's representative does not approve the contractor's costs daily, it is not uncommon for a dispute to occur after the completion of the work regarding the total actual time and material costs.

For nonemergency changes the owner's representative reviews all requested supporting documentation from the A/E and contractor before either approving or disapproving the change order. This process can be tedious if the initial documentation from either the A/E or the contractor is incomplete or incorrect, but with the proper instructions and directions the owner's representative should be able to reach a conclusion within two weeks of the initial requests for documentation. If the institution's normal approval time for change orders greatly exceeds two weeks, the change order process should be reviewed to eliminate unnecessary delays. Approval culminates with the owner, often the contract administrator, issuing a formal change order stating the compensation amount and the adjustment in the contract time if applicable. In the event of disapproval and disagreement the owner may require the contractor to perform the change order work by force account. In this case, the cost of the change is determined by the contractor's actual cost of material and labor to execute the change, plus applicable overhead and profit. The owner's representative should approve the contractor's time and material for the work involved daily as previously indicated.

Shop Drawings

It has been suggested that all communications and directions go through the owner's representative. An exception to that general rule must be made in the case of shop drawings to speed the review process. All shop drawings should be submitted by the contractor directly to the A/E for review, with only a copy of the contractor's transmittal letter sent to the owner's representative at the time of submittal. After review for general conformance to the specification requirements by the A/E, the A/E should send the owner's representative a copy of approved shop drawings at the same time they are returned to the contractor. This process allows for a quick turnaround of shop drawings and reduces the possibility for disputes regarding the time required for A/E review of shop drawings.

Although working drawings and specifications prepared by the A/E are adequate for bid pricing and general construction purposes, they do not include all details required for the fabrication, manufacture, and erection of many project components. Shop drawings include fabrication and erection drawings, manufacturer's drawings and catalogue cuts, test and performance data, schedules, wiring diagrams and descriptive data pertaining to machinery, equipment and methods of construction and all that is necessary to carry out the intent of the contract documents.

Shop drawings are usually prepared by the manufacturers or vendors, or their assigned agents, and should be submitted to the general contractor or subcontractors. Subcontractors should then submit all shop drawings to the general contractor for review and approval before submission to the A/E.

Shop drawings should then be submitted to the A/E for review in the form and quantity stipulated in the contract documents. Such review is the responsibility of the A/E since shop drawings are basically an amplification of the A/E's design. The review and approval given by the A/E is qualified. Such approval relates to the general conformance to the contract documents and does not constitute a complete check by the

A/E nor relieve the contractor of responsibility for errors in shop drawings or for failure to perform the contract requirements. The word *approval* is used but many A/Es no longer write that, but instead simply stamp and initial drawings as having been reviewed. The A/E's failure to note errors in the contractor's shop drawing submittals has been the basis for many disputes and therefore for the owner's sake demands more than a cursory review by both the contractor and A/E of all shop drawings. After the A/E's review, the shop drawings should be returned to the contractor for distribution if approved or for resubmittal if rejected.

It is the contractor's responsibility to schedule the submittal of shop drawings to the A/E to ensure the timely delivery of materials and equipment to the project. To assure the owner of the timely review of shop drawings, the owner's agreement with the A/E should specify the maximum review time allowed—normally within two weeks of receipt is reasonable. In addition, the construction contract documents should specify a minimum period (usually two weeks) for the approval process. In order to encourage the early submission of shop drawings, the owner should consider using language in their construction documents requiring the submittal of all shop drawings before the processing of the contractor's third pay request (or within ninety days of notice to proceed). If similar language is used in both the A/E and construction contracts, the owner's representative can better manage the time required for shop drawing review.

Project Closeout

One of the owner representative's most important and often most frustrating responsibilities is in association with project closeouts. At this time the new tenant is making demands to move into the new or renovated space before completion of all work, and the contractor is beginning to make plans for the next project. Good procedures for project closeouts can help the owner's representative deal effectively with this situation.

Upon completion of all requirements of drawings, specifications, and change orders, the contractor should notify the owner's representative by letter of readiness for final inspection of the project. A copy of this letter should be sent to the A/E and the contract administrator.

In order to assure the owner of proper documentation, the contractor should be required to furnish the following for approval before the final inspection:[23]

- Complete set of as-built drawings sent to the A/E in accordance with requirements of the contract documents.

- Operating instructions, parts lists, and service manuals sent to the A/E in accordance with requirements of the documents.
- As-built wiring diagrams, piping riser diagrams, and required manuals for elevators sent to the A/E in accordance with requirements of the documents.
- Warranties sent directly to the owner's representative.

After receipt of all required documentation, the owner's representative should then arrange for a final inspection wth the contractor and the A/E. Representatives of the A/E, the contractor and the owner's representative should then inspect the project item by item making a record of any deficiencies or corrections required to comply with drawings, specifications and change orders. Care should be taken in the preparation of a punch list since claims for patent defects in the work may be lost after final payment is made to the contractor.

The A/E representative is normally responsible for the preparation of a detailed punch list, organized by system or work component. The punch list should have provisions to record the name of the person making the correction, date the correction was made, and date of the owner's representative's inspection and remarks.

The contractor should notify the owner's representative when all items on the punch list have been completed. The owner's representative in turn should verify the completion and inform the A/E accordingly. The A/E should then be satisfied that all items have been completed and issue a certification of completion in writing to the owner's representative designating the project complete in accordance with the plans and specifications as modified by change orders and establishing the date of final completion.

In case the owner wishes to take partial occupancy before completion of all work, the same procedures for final acceptance may be followed. The punch list for the portion of work to be occupied must be performed before partial occupancy. Partial Occupancies can be used to operate a piece of equipment or a system, as well as an area. The owner's representative should send a letter to the contractor detailing the system, equipment or area to be accepted for use by the owner. Upon completion of all punch list items for the equipment, system, or area accepted for partial occupancy, the A/E should submit certification of completion for that portion and establish the date of final completion.

The owner should require some type of certification from the contractor regarding the payment of subcontractors and material suppliers. This can be accomplished several ways, such as requiring lien waivers for all subontractors and material suppliers. Another method is to require the contractor to submit a notarized letter certifying that all labor, material costs, subcontractors, and manufacturers furnishing material and labor for the project have been paid in full and that the project has been completed in accordance with contract documents.[24]

After the owner's representative has received all required documentation and certifications, the contractor's final payment can be processed. The owner's representative should then evaluate both the performance of the A/E and the contractor for reference and document all project difficulties. Without the immediate recording of this information, important details that might prove helpful on future projects can be quickly forgotten.

34.6 LEGAL ISSUES AND CONSIDERATIONS

As indicated in the introduction to this chapter, the construction process is a dispute-prone activity. These disagreements can stem from a variety of job circumstances, such as changes in work, contract interpretation, and delayed payments. Since the construction process is complex, it is important for all participants to:

1. Create fair and realistic performance requirements.
2. Communicate these requirements to all participants.
3. Employ communication systems that inform all participants of relevant events and directives.
4. Devise and follow methods for resolving disputes fairly and effectively.[25]

The first item indicates the need for fair construction contract documents. The contract documents include the actual contract plus the bid proposal, plans or drawings, specifications, general and special conditions, soil and site test reports, any addenda or modifications made before signing of the contract, and any other applicable documents. Although this subject is broad and could demand a separate chapter or book to discuss in detail, the owner should be aware that the documents generally not only set forth the scope of work, contract amount, and time of commencement and completion but also establish the guidelines for sharing project risks.

The general conditions normally specify how risks are to be shared by the owner and the contractor in articles covering concealed or subsurface conditions, liquidated or actual damages for completion delays, and no-damage-for-delay clauses. The owner should recognize the need for fair and reasonable sharing of construction risks with the contractor. Although it may appear to some to be better to have the contractor assume all risks, the use of one-sided language in the contract documents results in dramatically higher bid prices that ultimately cost the owner much more than necessary.

The second and third items deal with communications during the construction process. Effective lines of communication must be established for the proper management of construction projects. The owner's representative normally should be the central contact, with all communications and directions going through that person.

The final item deals with the resolution of claims. The general conditions should specify how claims and disputes should be resolved on the site. Claims are usually resolved through mutual agreement between the owner and the contractor, based on the recommendation of the A/E in many cases. If claims and disputes cannot be resolved on site, the resulting dispute should then be submitted to various levels of administrative appeal and ultimately arbitration appeal boards or courts.[26]

This section discusses some of the potential problems associated with construction projects. Although this section does deal with legal considerations, no attempt is made to discuss legal issues in their entirety. This information is intended merely to give the owner an awareness of potential problems, such as those associated with changes in work, constructive changes, differing site conditions, suspension in work, possession before completion, time extensions, acceleration of work, and contract interpretation, as well as review the insurance requirements for construction projects.

Changes in Work

All construction contracts should allow for changes in work to be made by the owner during construction. These changes might include additions, deletions, modifications, changes in the manner of work performance, kind of materials, or contract time. They may stem from errors in the specifications or drawings, differing site conditions, changes in the owner's requirements after the contract award, or even suggestions by the contractor.

Construction contracts typically give the owner the right to order changes to be made at any time. This is accomplished through the use of change orders that specify the scope of work and adjustment in contract price and time as discussed in previous sections. It is important that all changes be authorized in writing, before the start of the change order work if possible.

Changes should be within the general scope of the contract. Otherwise a contract modification may be required. One author states that "on all public construction contracts, there is the further problem with respect to changes that are clearly and obviously outside the scope of the changes clause of the contract. In such instances a contractor may be ineligible to be paid for such work because it is subject to competitive bidding before the required work can be lawfully performed."[27] This rule is sometimes bent by the owner to complete expeditiously work outside the original scope of work. The owner should resist such temptation and use the required bidding process to award contracts for work outside the intent and scope of the project.

Constructive Changes

Constructive changes are those that result from the actions of the owner that can be construed as a change to the original contract without the issuance of a formal change order.[28] The action has the same effect as a formal change to the contract under the change clause. Consequently, when the contractor is requested to carry out work in addition to or in a different way from that stipulated by the contract, a constructive change has taken place and the owner should reimburse the contractor for any additional expenses or grant an extension of time, or both as applicable.

Differing Site Conditions

Differing site conditions, also known as *changed conditions*, are defined in many contracts as "subsurface or otherwise concealed physical conditions that differ materially from those indicated in the contract documents, or to unknown physical conditions of an unusual nature that differ materially from those ordinarily found to exist and generally recognized as inherent in construction activities provided in the contract documents."[29]

These physical conditions usually pertain to subsurface or concealed situations, unknown at the time of bidding by either the owner or contractor. It is common practice that during bidding all information concerning the site is made available by the owner. The contractor should use this information to become familiar with the existing conditions and correlate observations with the requirements of the contract.

Who pays for the differing conditions depends on the provisions in the contract. Most contracts provide for an equitable adjustment in the contract sum and time if actual conditions were found to differ materially from those indicated in the contract documents. "The advantage to the owner of including such a clause in his contract is that the contractor need not include a 'contingency factor' in his bid price, thereby presumably resulting in a lower price to the owner for the work."[30]

In considering whether contractor claims qualify under the contract clauses for changed conditions, the essential questions are:

1. Are the conditions materially different from those indicated in the contract documents?
2. Are the conditions materially different from those ordinarily found to exist and generally recognized as inherent in construction activities of the character provided for in the contract documents?

If the answer to either question is *yes*, the contractor is entitled to additional compensation or a time extension.

A common disclaimer clause used in construction contracts states that neither the owner nor the A/E is responsible for the accuracy of subsurface data provided. Such a disclaimer clause, even though it may provide some protection for the owner and A/E from misrepresentation claims, does not prohibit the contractor from additional compensation for a changed or differing site condition.

If a differing site condition is encountered, the contractor should notify the owner in writing within a specified amount of time. Many disputes can be avoided if agreement can be reached between the owner and contractor in regard to changed or differing site conditions before the start of the work in question. In most cases the A/E is required to investigate the condition and make a recommendation to the owner. In a disagreement between the owner and the contractor, the owner should closely monitor and document the disputed work. Failure of the contractor to keep detailed records of all associated costs may jeopardize a claim for reimbursement, although an equitable adjustment should be made to the contractor when warranted.

Suspension of Work

Suspension of work normally refers to the owner's action of ceasing work on all or part of the project without actual contract termination. Suspension of work generally falls under two main categories.

The first relates to the contractor's failure to carry out orders or to perform satisfactorily any of the contract provisions. The owner, by a written order, can direct the contractor to cease work on the affected part of the work. Such an order should include reference to the applicable sections of the contract and the conditions under which work may be resumed. However, the suspension of work represents a risky move by the owner and should be done only after careful consideration and after attempts with all other methods to get the contractor to perform.

The second category relates to suspension of work due to unsuitable weather or unfavorable conditions, generally associated with conditions beyond the reasonable control of the contractor. In most cases it is advisable to obtain the contractor's concurrence to suspend the entire project. For this type of suspension the contractor is normally reimbursed for all additional costs associated with the delay and granted an extension of time.

To avoid or at least limit possible claims, the process of suspension and resumption of work should be well documented and recorded by the owner.

Possession Before Completion

Possession before completion, also known as *partial occupancy*, refers to the act by the owner to occupy and use a portion of the project before the final completion of the total project. Partial occupancies can be issued to cover the owner's use of an individual piece of equipment or system as well as an area. The issuance of partial occupancies usually results from either the contractor being behind schedule or the owner changing the schedule requirements.

If the owner finds it necessary to occupy partially completed areas of the project, such occupancy shall commence at a time mutually agreed upon by the owner and the contractor. The contractor's surety company must also consent to the partial occupancy. Construction contracts typically provide that the consent of the contractor and the surety company not be unreasonably withheld. To avoid potential contractor claims for interference with his remaining work, the owner should carefully consider the need for a partial occupancy and resist taking over partially completed areas if possible.

Before the issuance of a partial occupancy, the A/E should conduct an inspection along with the contractor and owner's representative. Upon completion of all punch list items, the A/E should prepare a letter to the owner's representative establishing the date of final completion and certifying the completion of all work associated with the partial occupancy. The warranty period for the occupied part of the project should begin at the time established by the A/E.

Construction contracts typically specify that the issuance of a partial occupancy does not constitute the acceptance of any work not in accordance with the requirements of the contract documents. In addition, if the owner revised the contract schedule, the contractor shall be compensated for additional costs associated with delays or extra work as a result of the owner taking partial occupancy. However, if the owner issues a partial occupancy because the contractor failed to complete the project on time, the contract documents should not entitle the contractor additional compensation.

Time Extension

During the implementation of a contract, circumstances often cause delay and consequently necessitate the addition of time to the original contract completion period. For this to occur the contract documents must first stipulate the completion period as well as state that time is of the essence. Without these provisions time is not considered part of the basic agreement between the contractor and the owner.

Generally there are two types of delays: excusable and inexcusable. Excusable delays are normally associated with those events beyond the reasonable control of the contractor, such as delays caused by the owner, the A/E, or by *force majeure* or acts of nature. Examples of *force majeure* include wars, revolutions, strikes, fires, floods, earthquakes, hurricanes, epidemics, and similar disasters. The remedy for most excusable delays is an extension of time equal to the actual delay. Since most excusable delays are not attributable to either the contractor or the owner, generally the contractor is not entitled to additional compensation.

Inexcusable delays are those usually associated with conditions that existed at the time of bidding and of which the contractor had knowledge, or those caused by the contractor's negligence. Other delays determined to be within the contractor's reasonable control are considered to be inexcusable and do not constitute grounds for claims for extra time.

The owner must be responsive to the contractor's needs throughout the construction process to avoid delaying the contractor. Some possible hindrances or interferences by the owner that might delay the contractor's ability to perform are as follow:

1. Delay in issuing change orders.
2. Delay due to defective owner specifications.
3. Delay in the issuance of a notice to proceed.
4. Delay in making the site available to the contractor.
5. Interference with the contractor's work, either by the owner's employees or by other contractors.
6. Delay in the approval of submittals.
7. Delay in investigating differing site conditions.

Some owners try to skirt the delay issue by using no-damage-for-delay clauses in the contract documents. In effect the use of such clauses places all risk and responsibility for owner delays with the contractor. Since no-damage-for-delay clauses allow the owner to interfere unfairly with the contractor's performance, most clauses of this sort are not favorably viewed by the courts.

Contracts should specify the time period within which the contractor must forward the claim for an extension of time, such as within twenty days of commencement of the delay as indicated in the AIA contract documents. In order for the owner and the A/E to assess the validity of the claim, the contractor's claim should include all supporting data of the delay as well as the probable effect of such delay on the progress of the project.

One last provision for time extensions needs to be mentioned, and that is in association with change orders. As mentioned, change orders should specify not only the change in the contract amount but also the change in the completion period. In evaluating requests for time extensions, the contractor should be able to support the claim for additional time. The time extension granted by the owner should equal the actual delay to the completion of the project and not neccessarily equal the amount of time required to do the change order work. In other words, the time extension should equal the impact of the change order on the critical path of the project.

The owner should also ensure that a change order time extension is not concurrent with another change order. In other words, a change order may have already extended the project a sufficient amount such that the proposed change order has no impact on the critical path, even though the contractor has claimed additional time.

Changes frequently have an impact upon subsequential work that is not in itself changed. The term *impact* is used and refers to the interference that the change in one part of the work creates upon another. Costs of such interference should be recognized and the consequential cost or time delay should be considered in reimbursing the contractor. For instance, a significant change in the concrete foundation work on a project may cause masonry work to be performed in winter rather than fall, thereby resulting in considerably higher costs to the contractor. The contractor, however, must keep detailed records to recover the consequential costs from the owner.

Acceleration of Work

Acceleration of work refers to the owner's direction to the contractor to speed the work in order to complete the project in less time than the current rate of work permits. Acceleration of work can result from either the owner's interest to complete the project before the official completion date or the owner's concern that the project is lagging behind schedule as a result of the contractor's fault.

Under the former the owner's request to accelerate is treated as a change order with the contractor usually entitled to compensation reflecting relevant incremental costs plus applicable overhead and profit. However, under the latter, the owner can order the contractor to make up for the lag period without incurring any liability for extra costs.

The owner should be reasonable in granting time extensions to the contractor when requested. If the owner has not allowed time extensions when entitled, the owner may be liable for any acceleration costs by the contractor. The unreasonable denial of time requests by the owner leaves the contractor with the option of accelerating work to meet the contract completion date. If the contractor takes the dispute to court, it is probable the contractor will be awarded compensation for the acceleration costs. Had the owner granted the time extensions when requested, the contractor's only compensation would have been an adjustment to the contract period. Therefore, when the project completion date is not critical, the unreasonable owner might pay dearly for unneccesary acceleration costs.

Contract Interpretation

Construction contracts often assign the A/E as an interpreter of the contract documents and the judge of the performance of both the owner and the contractor. However, they may differ in the broadness of authority bestowed upon the A/E and the finalty of those decisions. Some contracts assign the A/E as the arbiter of disputes between the owner and the contractor. Others provide that those decisions are not final and either party can exercise their rights to appeal provided the A/E has made a first-level decision.

However, most construction contracts agree that the A/E will render interpretations of the contract documents as necessary for the proper execution and progress of the work, and that claims and disputes arising therefrom be referred initially to the A/E for a decision.

Decisions and interpretations made by the A/E shall be consistent with the intent of, and reasonably inferable from, the tender documents. When the A/E is given final and binding authority, it is limited to matters of fact rather than law. In disputed matters pertaining to the latter, the A/E has no jurisdiction and either party has the right to exercise litigation or in some cases arbitration. Contract documents are normally explicit about the procedures to be followed in these circumstances.

In cases where contradictions or conflicts exist in the contract documents, the question of precedence is usually addressed clearly in the contract. Specific conditions prevail over general conditions, words over respective figures, specifications over drawings, and handwritten provisions over typed or printed provisions. In addition contract documents are considered complementary and what is required by any shall be as binding as if required by all.

It is helpful to use a systematic approach to contract interpretation. The use of a systematic approach can reduce contractor risk and owner and A/E liability. The results of this approach can yield more consistent and timely resolution of disputes and ultimately reduce owner costs and liabilities.

The quick and reasonable resolution of contract interpretation disputes can result in continued good working relationships between the contractor and the owner. However, that relationship can quickly be strained to the limits by unreasonable interpretations. As one author puts it, "Unreasonably harsh interpretation of the specifications, always against the contractor, results in excessive costs, effectively robbing him of the already thin margin of profit he is trying desperately to preserve."[31]

Insurance Requirements

While implementing their projects, owners must have assurances that protect their interests against possible misfortunes. These pertain to the risks associated with contractual relationships and the possibility of serious accidents. Owners' interests lie in the smooth and successful completion of the projects in accordance with the contract documents and in preventing financial losses resulting from serious accidents.

To accomplish this, many insurance policies can be tailored to suit the owner's needs. However, some of the common policies used in typical construction projects are the bid bond and the performance bond; these are used as a guarantee of contractual obligations to complete the project, the builder's risk, the worker's compensation, and the comprehensive general liability bonds provide protection for the project and third parties against loss or damage.

Construction contracts typically make the contractor responsible for obtaining coverages of these insurance policies. To assure this coverage, the contractor is required to secure either copies of the policies, or certificates of insurance to the owner before commencing construction.

Worker's Compensation   The worker's compensation insurance protects the employer against loss due to statutory liability as a result of job-related injury, sickness, or death of an employee during employment on a particular job. Benefits are prescribed by state law and include medical, hospital, and recuperative expenses; income allowances; disability payments; and in the event of death, maintenance payments for the dependants of the deceased. This type of insurance is written by private surety companies except in some states that have either monopolistic or competitive state funds.

The prime contractor can either include all workers on the project in worker's compensation insurance or require that subcontractors have their own. Construction contracts commonly include this provision as part of the contractor's liability insurance.

If the prime contractor were not insured, the worker's compensation liability may lie with the owner (or jointly with the prime contractor); however, the owner would have legal recourse against the prime contractor for failure to carry the required insurance.

In construction contracts where the owner exercises direct supervision and management, the owner must carry the insurance as the prime contractor. The owner may also require that contractors provide their own certificate of worker's compensation insurance to protect their own employees.

Builder's Risk   Builder's risk insurance provides coverage for the structure during the course of construction. There are two main types of builder's risk policies: the all-risk form, which is most commonly used, and the named-peril form, which is seldom utilized. The all-risk is a broad form policy to insure against all direct physical loss or damage, from any external cause except for the stated exclusions. However, many of the exclusions can be removed for additional premiums.

At a minimum the builder's risk policy provides for protection of the project proper. In addition, coverage can be provided for items pertaining to the project. For example, the all-risk policy may also cover materials and supplies at the job site or while in transit, tools and equipment, temporary structures, and others. The all-risk policy is extremely flexible and can be varied substantially to give the insured the coverage that suits particular needs.

Typical language in the contract documents of the AIA documents stipulate that unless otherwise provided owners shall purchase and maintain the builder's risk policy. However, most contractors would rather provide their own to suit their needs. Particular construction contracts should therefore address this subject clearly.

Builder's risk policies normally specify that the project should not be occupied by the owner during the construction period without the prior consent of the insurer. The contractor remains responsible for the project until the owner has made formal acceptance.

Comprehensive General Liability   Comprehensive general liability insurance comprises at least two or three forms of contractor liability insurances covering losses that could occur during construction operations and after. It includes basically the contractor's public liability insurance and completed operations liability insurance.

The contractor's liability insurance protects the contractor against the legal liability for bodily injuries to persons (not employees) or damage to property of others not under contractor's control or custody, when such injuries or damage arise from the contractor's own operation.

Contractor's contingent or protective liability insurance protects the contractor for the legal liability arising out of acts or omissions of subcontractors for bodily injuries to persons (not his employees) or damage to property of others not under the contractor's control or custody.

Completed operations liability insurance protects the contractor for the legal liability for bodily injuries or damage to property of others arising out of projects that have been completed. Whereas the liability insurance described above affords protection while the contractor is executing the project, this insurance affords protection after the project has been completed by the contractor and accepted by the owner.

Because the contractor's responsibility does not end with the completion of the project, liability extends for the full period of the applicable statute of limitations. Statutory periods vary from four to twenty years in the various states, with the average being about seven years.[32] It starts with the substantial completion of the work or acceptance of the work by the owner.

The comprehensive general liability is not an all-inclusive policy and thus has some exclusions such as personal injury, injury to the contractor's own employees, automobile liability, and damage to property under the contractor's care and custody. However, these can be insured at additional costs through an endorsement to the basic comprehensive general liability policy or separately.

The growing incidence of third-party claims against the owner or the A/E has resulted in the inclusion of hold-harmless clauses in construction contracts. These clauses provide that the contractor assumes the legal liability of the owner, the A/E, or a material dealer as the contractual agreement stipulates. This is called the *contractual liability insurance* and can be covered by specific endorsement to the general liability policy.

Bid Bond   Bidding documents routinely require bidders to submit with their bid proposals proper bid security that guarantees that the bidder, if declared successful, will enter into a written contract with the owner and furnish contract bonds as specified in the contract documents. Bid securities may be in the form of bid bonds, cashier's checks, bank drafts, money orders, or other forms of negotiable securities.

A bid bond is executed by both a bidder and a qualified surety company for an amount stated in the bidding documents. This amount is usually a percentage of the bidder's proposal (including additive alternates) and varies between 5 and 20 percent with 5 percent being a common requirement.

The bid security of the successful bidder is normally retained by the owner, possibly with those of the next two best bidders, until a contract has been executed and satisfactory contract bonds furnished. Bid bonds of the remaining unsuccessful bidders are usually returned shortly after the bid opening.

Should the successful bidder decline to execute a contract with the owner or fail to deliver contract bonds as required in the contract documents, the bid security can be realized by the owner in lieu of resulting damages. In this respect, two forms of bid bonds exist. These are the liquidated damages bond, in which the entire bond amount is paid to the owner as damages for default, and the difference in price bond, in which the owner is reimbursed the difference between the bids of the defaulted bidder and the next best bidder, up to the face value of the bid bond. The latter form of bid bond is the one more commonly used.

Performance Bond   The successful bidder should be required to deliver a performance bond at the time of execution of the contract with the owner. It guarantees to the owner that the work will be performed and completed in accordance with the contract documents. It is executed between the selected contractor and the contractor's qualified surety and, once delivered, cannot be canceled by either party without proper approval and notice.

If the contractor were declared to be in default under the contract, the surety would be under obligation to remedy the default. It may either assume the responsibility of completing the contract within a prescribed period or obtain jointly with the owner a bid for completing the contract in accordance with its terms and conditions and make available such funds to pay the cost of completion less the balance of the contract price.

Customarily performance bonds cover warranty periods prescribed in the contract and have a face value that denotes the maximum amount the surety will pay for completing the project.

34.7 SUMMARY

Construction is not an easy process to administer or manage, as this chapter attests. However, methods are available to the owner to help make the process more successful. These include the develpment and implementation of effective administrative and construction management procedures. Also, the development of contract documents that reflect the owner's interests and requirements will help. And, in dealing with both A/E's and contractors, the owner should strive to:

- Be fair and reasonable.
- Be consistent.
- Be responsive in making decisions.
- Be clear and precise in giving directions.
- Be timely with payments.
- Establish clear lines of communications.
- Be familiar with the contract requirements.
- Be knowledgeable of construction law.
- Limit work to the original project scope.
- Listen to both sides of issues before making a final judgment.

If these suggestions are followed, the owner's probability for a successful construction program is greatly enhanced.

NOTES

1. Justin Sweet, *Legal Aspects of Architecture, Engineering and the Construction Process* (St. Paul, Minnesota: West Publishing, 1977), p. 235.
2. Robert F. Cushman and William J. Palmer, *Businessman's Guide to Construction* (Dow-Jones Books, 1980), p. 181.
3. *Ibid*, p. 182.
4. Robert A. DeGoff and Howard A. Friedman, *Construction Management: Basic Principles for Architects, Engineers and Owners* (New York: John Wiley & Sons, 1985), p. 3.
5. Thomas C. Kavanagh, Frank Muller, and James J. O'Brien, *Construction Management* (New York: McGraw-Hill, 1978), p. 136.
6. Cushman and Palmer, *Guide to Construction*, pp. 227, 232.
7. University of Missouri, *General Conditions of the Contract for Construction* (Columbia, Missouri: University of Missouri, 1987), p. 134.
8. *Ibid*.
9. Richard H. Clough, *Construction Contracting*, fifth edition. (New York: John Wiley & Sons, 1986), p. 15.
10. Cushman and Palmer, *Guide to Construction*, p. 220.
11. University of Missouri, *Construction Project Management Procedures Manual* (Columbia, Missouri: University of Missouri, 1986), p. III/6.
12. Edward R. Fisk, *Construction Project Administration*, second edition. (New York: John Wiley & Sons, 1978), p. 154.
13. Clough, *Construction Project Management* (New York: John Wiley & Sons, 1972), pp. 230-31.

14. Clough, *Construction Project Management*, p. 153.
15. Clough, *Construction Project Management*, p. 230.
16. University of Missouri, *General Contract Conditions*, article 7.
17. Sweet, *Legal Aspects*, p. 433.
18. Fisk, *Construction Project Administration*, p. 38.
19. University of Missouri, *Project Management Manual*, p. III/15.
20. *Ibid.*, pp. III/15, III/16.
21. *Ibid.*, p. III/16.
22. *Ibid.*, p. III/16.
23. *Ibid.*, p. III/143.
24. *Ibid.*, p. III/144.
25. Clough, *Construction Contracting*, p. 235.
26. *Ibid.*, p. 167.
27. J. B. Bonny, ed., and Joseph P. Frein, assoc. ed. *Handbook of Construction Management and Organization* (New York: Van Nostrand Reinhold, 1973), p. 47.
28. Clough, *Construction Contracting*, p. 161.
29. University of Missouri, *General Contract Conditions*, p. GC/11.
30. Clough, *Construction Contracting*.
31. Bonny, *Management and Organization*, p. 2.
32. Clough, *Construction Contracting*.

SECTION VI

WORK

MANAGEMENT

AND CONTROL

Section Leader:
Paul F. Tabolt
Director of Physical Plant
University of California at Berkeley

CHAPTER 35

Overview of Work Management and Control

David R. Howard, P.E.
Executive Director
Facilities Planning and Operations
San Francisco State University

35.1 GENERAL

The five essential management functions are planning, organizing, staffing, controlling, and directing.[1] The discussion of work management and control in the following chapters will be concerned with the application of these five elements to physical plant maintenance and operations—a necessary and extremely important component in all institutional activities, including higher education.

Work management and control, or maintenance management, in colleges and universities has evolved rapidly over the past two decades, reflecting a change in attitude toward the maintenance task by top level administrators and managers. The maintenance function had little importance at many institutions because of the newness of facilities constructed during the post-World War II expansion period (the 1950s and 1960s). It now has become increasingly apparent that the physical plant must be maintained if it is to continue to provide the kind of service and environment necessary for quality education programs in a safe and healthy setting.

Plant expense is also a source of growing concern to educators, legislators, taxpayer groups, and others. Maintenance and operating costs were exacerbated by the rapidly escalating cost of energy in the early 1970s, which focused attention on the heavy impact facilities have on monies available for educational programs. With the cost of utilities for educational institutions tripling since 1965-66, physical plant budgets now represent an estimated 11 to 13 percent of the total general and educational expenses of colleges and universities throughout the United

States.[2] This level of expense warranted priority attention, and as a consequence, the discipline of maintenance management, pioneered in industry and embraced by federal agencies, is finally receiving the emphasis in higher education that it has long deserved.

Equally important to this changed attitude toward maintenance is the increasing awareness that the cost of deferred maintenance—required repair and modernization work on the plant that has been delayed by inadequate budgets, especially during the past twenty-five years—has now exceeded $20 billion for urgent needs, and an estimated total need of $60 to $70 billion.[3]

Expenses and potential expenses of this magnitude demand the ultimate in good management techniques to control their growth and eliminate waste.

Objectives and Scope

The basic objectives of maintenance management are to provide the climate, organization, leadership, training, procedures, resources, and judgment that will allow the maintenance function to provide necessary maintenance and repair services to the campus facilities. These services ensure the plant's continued use and protection; afford a safe, secure, healthful, and enriching environment for students, faculty, and staff; and enhance the appearance of and service to the community in which the institution is located, while being as cost effective as possible.

Essential elements of these objectives are:

- Reduction of facility depreciation.
- A reduced rate of equipment and structural failures.
- Lower maintenance costs.
- An effective and efficient organizational structure.
- An experienced, well-trained, and motivated staff.
- Improved planning and scheduling of work.
- Management of resources to eliminate waste while providing needed materials, parts, tools, and equipment.
- A control system that regulates, accomplishes, and accommodates the measurement of maintenance activity.

Benefits

An effective work management and control program can provide meaningful benefits to an education institution, in spite of the difficulties in assessing the value of such efforts in dollars and cents. Plant maintenance in learning and research institutions does not lend itself to the profit/loss analysis of industry (particularly production line industry).

There the manufacture of tangible goods precisely determines the actual worth of the maintenance activity.

The intangible benefits of an improved environment, student and faculty morale, user comfort and convenience, personnel safety and security, and community pride that are generated by well-maintained, aesthetically pleasing campus facilities should not be minimized simply because they cannot be quantified. They all contribute significantly to the effectiveness of any education program. Well-maintained facilities allow the institution to satisfy its teaching and research objectives to a greater extent than would be possible in a rundown, hazardous, insecure, and unattractive facility of which no one could be proud.

As for more tangible results or expectations from the application of modern maintenance management techniques, a conservative estimate of time lost in an average maintenance organization due to coordination is approximately one-third of the net working day, of which 40 or 50 percent can be saved by the use of good management.[4] Another authority suggests that 20 percent savings have been demonstrated in industry and government installations by applications of planning, scheduling, and work measurement.[5] And another rule of thumb is that for every dollar expended in good planning, at least five dollars will be saved in maintenance expense.[6] Yet APPA's deferred maintenance study, *The Decaying American Campus: A Ticking Time Bomb*, reports that of every dollar spent on maintenance, four dollars are being deferred.

A good maintenance management program can improve productivity, reduce the number of personnel required to perform a given workload, and improve the level of maintenance. The higher level of maintenance will in turn reduce the frequency of equipment and system failures and the required overtime to repair, as well as reduce waste in material, equipment, and tool purchases. A well-maintained physical plant will use less energy, require less effort to keep clean, and experience a slower rate of deterioration. This affords a greater degree of protection to the capital investment. Effective maintenance management is good business.

35.2 RESPONSIBILITIES FOR WORK MANAGEMENT AND CONTROL

Generally the responsibility for upkeep of the physical plant in colleges and universities rests with the senior administrative officer, who may carry a title such as vice president for administration, administrative vice chancellor, business manager, or vice president for business affairs, among others.

The more direct responsibility for maintenance management most frequently resides with a physical plant administrator bearing a title such as director of facilities management, director of physical plant, director or superintendent of buildings and grounds, director of plant operations and maintenance, or director of maintenance, among others.

General Responsibilities

Maintenance management in a physical plant organization most frequently encompasses the following general responsibilities:

- Planning and scheduling of as much of the maintenance load as practicable.
- Establishing an efficient communication system for effective coordination and direction.
- Designing an organizational structure with clear lines of authority and grouping of related skills and equipment.
- Developing an effective training program for upgrading personnel.
- Developing a practical set of controls and procedures that allow the orderly, timely, and efficient accomplishment of required facilities work.
- Establishing a meaningful performance measurement system and a quality control function.
- Developing an annual budget that identifies required operating funds as well as adequate allowances for special repair requirements and deferred maintenance work.
- Actively recruiting a qualified and energetic work force.
- Maintaining a safe, secure, and accessible environment for all students, faculty, staff, and visitors to the campus.

Management Policies and Principles

The character and style of a maintenance organization are reflected in how it gets the job done. This is influenced in large part by the policies and principles adopted and adhered to by the facilities management department.

Certainly a work approval system should be adopted, and published, that provides fair treatment to all clients with facilities requirements on the campus. A well-defined list of descending priority categories of work, combined with a formal definition of the differing classifications of work, is necessary. Sometimes the classifications will include levels determined by monetary limits.

A typical priority definition system is outlined below:

Priority 1—*Hazards to Life, Health, and Property*
Work required to provide or restore adequate security to facility, to eliminate hazards to life or health (safety), or to protect valuable property.

Priority 2—*Essential Support*
Work needed to accomplish the institution's primary objectives (teaching and research), to prevent a breakdown of essential operation or housekeeping functions, or to improve the operating performance of a necessary system.

Priority 3—*New Programs*
Alterations or additions required to accommodate experimental programs, revised teaching approaches, added functions, or reorganizations.

Priority 4—*Desirable*
Convenience and environmental improvement items not qualifying for higher priority.

A typical work classification system consists of the following:

Class	Abbreviation	Examples
Maintenance	Maint.	Checking, inspecting, servicing, adjusting, minor repairs, hardware replacement, repainting, patching, sealing, random tile replacement, cleaning, cleanup, pruning, trimming, treating, applying, fertilizing, scarifying, mowing.
Repair	Rep.	Repair or replacement of obsolete, worn, broken, failed, or inoperative systems or components; restoration, rehabilitation, reglazing.
Alteration	Alt.	Modification, expansion, change in configuration or capacity, modernization.
Minor Construction	MC	New work, addition, extension, erection.

Installation	Inst.	New equipment or systems in or on an existing structure, facility, or property.
Fabrication	Fab.	Assembly or manufacture of furniture, shelving, bulletin boards, pinboard, signs, sash, picture frames; includes installation when appropriate.
Delivery/Pickup	Deliv.	Movable items such as plants, shrubs, bleachers, carnival booths, platforms, furniture, books, equipment.
Loading/Unloading	Load	Material, furniture, equipment.
Demolition	Demo.	Disconnect, strip, cannibalize, salvage, remove, destroy, raze, tear down; includes hauling to appropriate disposal point.

A policy on level of effort or maintenance standards should also be adopted that specifies the frequency of maintenance or repair. A standard on the quality of materials to be used sometimes helps define the expectations of clients.

One of the guiding precepts of maintenance work is to do it as effectively and as cheaply as possible while maintaining a consistently high level of quality. If costs of certain kinds of work by the maintenance force or materials, utilities, and equipment controlled by the maintenance organization are to be charged back to any clients, a clear and concise policy on chargeback must be published and carefully followed.

These are only a few of the more important policies and principles that a well-managed plant function should cultivate. There are many of lesser importance or with only limited application because of campus peculiarities.

Maintenance Engineering

A number of tasks in maintenance management benefit from the technical knowledge and analytical skills normally associated with an engineering discipline. Only larger organizations can afford a full-time employee for these tasks. But even part-time application of maintenance engineering by an overseer can be valuable to the modern maintenance activity.

The following elements of a good maintenance management program are the maintenance engineer's responsibilities:

- Complete a facilities inventory and condition survey. (For assistance, see APPA's *Facilities Audit Workbook*, written by Harvey H. Kaiser, as well as APPA's criteria for self-evaluation used for the Award for Excellence in Facilities Management program.)
- Compile an equipment inventory.
- Develop maintenance standards that define a level of effort showing expected frequency of key actions.
- Develop a five-year plan for special repairs incorporating all deferred maintenance and those repairs projected as requirements in future years.
- Create an equipment standardization program for greater redundancy in maintenance actions and reduced parts inventories.
- Develop materials standards and standardization to reduce stock inventories maintained and promote specialization of techniques used for maintaining, restoring, and improving the quality of facilities while reducing failure frequencies.
- Perform maintainability assessment on all new construction designs and equipment proposals.
- Evaluate new ideas concerning materials, equipment, procedures.
- Develop or select appropriate time standards for a work measurement program.
- Develop or promote adequate training programs for equipment or building features that exist or are planned for installation on campus.
- Develop and conduct a performance analysis program including periodic reporting.
- Establish failure analysis for installed electromechanical equipment, vehicles, and construction equipment.
- Evaluate planned equipment overhauls for unforeseen problems.
- Implement warranty analysis and exercise when appropriate.
- Establish work methods analysis and productivity improvement.
- Evaluate preventive maintenance actions and frequency of application.

As this listing indicates, the discipline of maintenance engineering draws heavily on what could be construed as industrial, mechanical, electrical, or other specific fields of engineering. In reality, it is the application of engineering techniques to the maintenance function with its own diverse and unique problems and concerns. See Chapter 41, Principles of Industrial Engineering in Facilities Management, for a fuller discussion of this topic.

Planning and Scheduling

Probably no other function characterizes the modern approach to maintenance better, or has had a greater impact on the improved efficiency and effectiveness of maintenance activity, than that of work planning and scheduling—work control. A maintenance organization makes a significant change for the better when it starts planning jobs and scheduling from a central office by specialists, and stops relying on the shop foreman or supervisor to decide what work to do today and to chase materials and equipment.

The work management and control function is generally responsible for the following tasks:

- Receipt of work requests following a formal procedure for work definition, priority setting, and approval.
- Compliance with a maintenance plan and a preventive maintenance program in its scheduling activities.
- Operation of a service call or minor emergency response system.
- Planning all work involving more than a determined number of workhours, and excluding that work which can be categorized as routine maintenance, such as preventive maintenance, service calls, or periodic servicing.
- Preparation of advance work schedules, usually on a weekly basis, and maintenance of a master schedule.
- Requisition of necessary materials and parts, and inventory control.
- Providing pertinent shop drawings, sketches, and work authorization documents to shop foremen.
- Maintaining progress status and cost data on all individual work requests and orders.
- Follow-up on jobs with elements (materials, workhours, equipment, access) that cause a variance from allotted schedule or that are predicted to do so.
- Maintaining an awareness of backlogs by shop or specialty.
- Evaluating work measurement and performance.

- Periodic reporting system of accomplishments by the work force.
- Maintaining vehicle and construction equipment status and scheduling maintenance and repair for this equipment.
- Maintenance of construction status and warranty information.

The primary objective of the modern maintenance organization is to induce the involvement of first-line maintenance supervisors in the planning and scheduling process, thus allowing them to spend their time in the field overseeing the work actually being done. Shop or craft supervisors should spend 15 percent or less of actual work time on nonsupervisory tasks.[7] Organizing the maintenance function to provide central planning and scheduling can allow for the achievement of this goal.

Building Maintenance

Supervisors or managers of the building maintenance function maintain physical structures and their installed service systems and equipment such as plumbing, heating, ventilation, air conditioning, and electrical. These managers still have a sizable number of responsibilities that could be categorized as maintenance management, even though central planning and scheduling may relieve first-line supervisors or shop foremen of those management tasks.

In smaller organizations building maintenance managers may be assigned many of the responsibilities of maintenance engineering. These managers are responsible for helping develop an adequate budget and ensuring that funds are expended as wisely as possible. This requires the continuing assessment of work routines, techniques, material applications, and facility conditions before and after maintenance or repair is performed.

Other management tasks of building maintenance involve establishing seven important activities:

1. An adequate work inspection system.
2. A viable preventive maintenance program that is adhered to religiously.
3. Adequate stock levels of critical or much-used parts, materials, subassemblies, and tools.
4. Effective emergency response plans.
5. Good employee relations.
6. Worthwhile training programs.
7. A system that identifies safety hazards, security compromises, and property damage and ensures their correction at an early date.

The manager or supervisor is also involved in make-or-buy decisions for new parts or components, whether to contract work, or to use the in-house work force. He or she also has a strong voice in fitting jobs to the capabilities of specific individuals in the work assignment process. Finally, this leader has a responsibility to participate actively in the scheduling process, explaining to work control or the scheduling function when something planned is impractical because of factors not apparent to the planner or scheduler.

Utilities

The maintenance management responsibilities of the supervisor of utilities correspond closely to those of the managers of building maintenance. Certain other peculiar management responsibilities may apply, and they are usually determined by where the institution obtains its utilities. If purchased from an off-campus producer such as a public or private utility company, maintenance responsibilities are not as great as when utilities are generated on campus using in-house labor and owned facilities.

The unique management responsibilities of the utilities function include:

- Maintaining a current awareness of safety codes, operating requirements and licensing regulations, and ensuring compliance.
- Designing and promoting campus-wide energy conservation practices.
- Establishing utility consumption patterns and altering operations and usage to coincide with less expensive rate structures.
- Studying and developing more favorable utility contracts for the institution.
- Adhering to and accomplishing timely compliance with regulations of the Occupational Safety and Health Administration, Environmental Protection Agency, and other regulatory agencies.

Grounds Maintenance

Grounds maintenance on campus is carried out in a public, fishbowl-like atmosphere. Every mistake or lack of adequate maintenance is seen by many people. This open environment and the influence campus appearance has on student morale and community pride, coupled with the necessity to assign grounds maintenance personnel to widely scattered areas of the campus on a given day, requires astute field supervision and good management practices.

Traditionally, grounds maintenance has been conducted as a relatively independent function within the physical plant organization. It is often considered last when establishing a work control system featuring centralized planning and scheduling of work. This happens even though grounds maintenance can benefit as much from improved coordination, advance planning, and resource management as any other function. The grounds maintenance supervisor should be included in all periodic scheduling meetings and the work control section should expect input from grounds maintenance on a regular basis. The management tasks discussed for building maintenance apply to the grounds function as well.

Grounds maintenance is relatively labor intensive and requires supervisors to be alert to labor saving ideas in material, tool, and equipment applications. Seasonal changes and field usage are most important to grounds management. A detailed master schedule of maintenance activities must be developed, kept current, and adhered to.

Compliance with a wide variety of federal, state, and local health and safety regulations is characteristic of grounds maintenance. A control system that outlines requirements and ensures compliance is especially helpful in the storage and application of pesticides and other controlled chemicals. Grounds maintenance workers are exposed to more hazards than other workers in physical plant and usually have a higher incidence of injury accidents. This reason alone makes an effective safety program most important. A periodic certification program that stresses safe use of the equipment is also instrumental in reducing accidents.

The grounds maintenance supervisor should review landscape plans for new construction projects and campus renovation jobs to assure reasonable maintainability. Also, he or she must use good judgment in purchasing large lots of bagged and bulk materials and ensuring that they are stored and controlled properly.

Custodial Services

The nature of the custodial function is such that managers must have good people-handling skills above all else. The most labor intensive of all maintenance responsibilities, custodial service requires the repeated accomplishments of a limited number of cleaning tasks. The skills required are readily found; thus, the pay scale is traditionally lower than any other maintenance discipline.

Some people find completing a simple task repeatedly, knowing it will have to be done again soon, frustrating and unsatisfying. This dissatisfaction frequently precipitates a higher degree of personnel problems that can manifest themselves in higher absenteeism, more discipline problems, increased number of grievances, shoddy or marginal work, chronic tardiness, insubordination, quarreling among employees, rumor mongering, and high turnover rates. Motivating a work force with these kinds of occupational characteristics can become the primary management concern.

Much custodial work must be done when a room or building is unoccupied (even though there is an increasing trend toward daytime shifts and better scheduling). This adds to the problem of good supervision, because the custodial force is widely dispersed during routine operations. Continuous field supervision is a necessity for the custodial force that meets its cleaning objectives. Central planning and scheduling and other maintenance management tasks, described in the maintenance engineering and building maintenance are required in the custodial function as well.

The need for improved management techniques in this area has been documented repeatedly, as well as the significant monetary savings available to education institutions.[8] Any function that costs from 20 to 40 percent of the physical plant budget—of which personnel expense comprises some 95 percent of that cost—is certainly a fertile area for applying good management principles.

Some proven techniques include:

- Developing a level of effort or cleanliness standards. (APPA has developed a set of custodial staffing and service guidelines.)
- Conducting a facility inventory from a custodial viewpoint, to define the job required.
- Using time standards to determine the resources required to do the job.
- Maintaining a current schedule of room/area usage.
- Organizing the custodial force so that field operations can be completed efficiently under adequate supervision.
- Developing and conducting an effective training program.
- Developing a master schedule in coordination with the work control center.
- Establishing a periodic maintenance program (and adhering to it) for those tasks not required on a daily basis.

These and many other techniques will be discussed in detail in Chapter 50, Custodial Services.

35.3 ORGANIZATION AND PERSONNEL

Basic to maintenance managers' needs in doing their jobs is an organizational structure that allows for accomplishment of plant maintenance requirements in an efficient and effective manner. Of course, the finest organizational design in the world will not satisfy this requirement by itself. The organization must employ workers who demonstrate a sufficient level of skill, experience, energy, and conscience, and in numbers and total capability consistent with the characteristic workload of the plant.

Following is a description of various organizational structures used in maintenance work and a discussion of the more important factors to consider when developing an organization scheme. Also included are criteria for determining what constitutes an appropriate work force in numbers, skill levels, and supervisory ratios. (For further information on this subject, see Chapter 1, The Facilities Organization, and Chapter 2, Staffing for Physical Plant.)

Types of Maintenance Organizations

Facility maintenance activities have found their way, by design or chance, into a more or less structured discipline of responding/directing relationships. These relationships can be categorized as centralized organizations, decentralized or area organizations, functional organizations, or a variation of these. The three schemes are defined as follows:

- *Centralized or Shop.* This organizational type relies on one central location, such as a corporation yard or shop compound, from which crews are dispatched to conduct maintenance of a facility. Usually this structure segregates the various craft disciplines into specific shops with their own supervisor or foreman. This has been the most popular organizational scheme for conducting facility maintenance on college and university campuses.
- *Decentralized or Area.* The campus is divided into geographical zones and all, or a significant amount, of the facility maintenance responsibilities in that area are assigned to a supervisor and a smaller team of craftspeople. These teams are usually made up of mechanics with various skills or specialties or in some cases with multiskilled individuals who accomplish a particular level of maintenance such as preventive, corrective, or renovation tasks. Many times the area or zone teams are provided specialty work or heavy equipment help from a centralized cadre that supports all such organizational elements.

- *Functional or Operational.* This form tends to group responsibilities by type of major activity such as preventive maintenance, alterations and minor construction, equipment overhaul, installation work, window washing, renovation.

Most physical plant organizational structures are not pure forms of any one the basic categories, relying on some aspects of the other categories to satisfy a peculiar requirement in a more cost-effective manner.

In determining what constitutes the most practical organizational structure for a maintenance activity at a given physical plant department, a number of factors should be considered:

- Physical layout of the campus.
- Condition of buildings, structures, and systems.
- Complexity of systems.
- Level of effort required to maintain plant adequately.
- Craft specialties that physical plant demands.
- Skill levels of available personnel.
- Existing organization structure of administrative and academic branches of institution.
- Location of shops and storage areas.
- Location of most critical campus systems or special problems.
- Travel time requirements.
- Communication systems available, their location, quality, and capability.
- Analysis of local craft union organizations, rules, contracts, and natural affiliations.
- Assessment of best time of day to perform specific tasks (determines work shifts).
- Availability and location of special-use equipment and personnel skilled in its operation.
- One building trade or skill's relation to another; their common reliance on the same skills, techniques, equipment, tools, or materials.
- Talent and skills of incumbent managers and supervisors.

The advantages of a centralized organization include:

- Consolidation of more capable supervision.
- Greater source of talent and experience to draw on in making work assignments.
- Easier dispatching of correct skill level and appropriate equipment and materials.

- More efficient pieces of equipment and numbers of skilled operators upon which to draw.
- Lesser impact of personnel absences (more flexibility in employee assignments and work load for a given day).
- More efficient use of emergency response personnel.
- Better training facilities and higher quality trainers.
- Greater demand for specialists, thus attracting more expertise.
- More efficient administration.
- Easier planning, scheduling, and coordination of effort.
- More convenient vehicle and shop equipment maintenance.
- Easier to determine job performance and status of projects.
- Easier to provide common direction and ensure its use.
- Improved security of resources.

The major disadvantages of a centralized organization are the increases in time required to transport personnel, materials, tools, and equipment to and from the job site, and a lesser degree of craftsperson familiarity with the buildings/systems requiring work. This translates into:

- Increased response time on most emergencies.
- Possible lower productivity and quality of work.
- Less "pride of ownership" and familiarity with facility details.
- Increased transportation/communication expense.
- Less effective field inspection of jobs.
- Lower awareness level of maintenance requirements.
- More time required for adequate job assessment.

The decentralized or area concept of organization has not found widespread application in education institutions except at some of the large universities or those with geographically separated campuses, large dormitory complexes, or married student housing areas. The idea has merit in special situations to supplement a centralized or functional organization structure—in spite of the decided movement toward central planning, work control, and computerization—in the physical plant functions of colleges and universities or those with geographically separated campuses, large dormitory complexes, or married student housing areas.

Advantages of the decentralized maintenance organization include:

- Reduced time loss due to travel.
- Faster response time on minor emergencies.
- Higher quality of work due to "pride of ownership" generated

in workers familiar with buildings and systems and knowledge of their clients.
- Opportunity for greater worker productivity.
- Closer supervision and inspection of completed work.
- Greater sense of team effort by workers, inspiring closer cooperation.

Disadvantages of the decentralized organization include:

- Lowered management awareness of level of maintenance in plant.
- Diverse levels of maintenance between areas or zones.
- Poor supervision less obvious to management on a daily basis.
- Costly duplication of equipment, tools, and materials.
- Less efficient utilization of equipment.
- Lowered levels of expertise in personnel.
- Personnel absences have greater impact on work schedule.
- Greater tendency to improvise, thus introducing safety hazards.
- Greater frequency of slack periods in service call operations.
- More administrative tasks levied on supervisor.
- Communications between field and office more difficult.
- Greater exposure to theft, vandalism, and misplacement of resources.

Variations of the functional organization concept have been used for years to apply specialized talent and emphasis to problem situations on college and university campuses. The rather limited geographical scope of most campuses favors a centralized organizational structure as the basic vehicle from which to work. John Heintzelman suggests that the purely functional organization would have distinct groups for inspection, maintenance, repair, overhaul, construction, housekeeping, and salvage.[9] Plant organizations in postsecondary education have made some use of this concept to augment, temporarily or even permanently, what usually is a predominantly centralized organization. The concept applies to heavy industry and a production line environment much more readily than it does to the average campus.

In a climate where appreciation of the need for maintenance of existing facilities is growing, such as in higher education, the monies for capital improvements and enrollments are shrinking. Emphasis on major remodeling and construction by in-house maintenance forces is declining, thus making the utilization of functional teams with these specialties less appropriate than in the past. One area may see a growing application of functional groups to augment a centralized organization. This is in the assignment of preventive maintenance and "find and fix" tasks to a multiskilled team of mechanics. The team continuously rotates through major campus buildings on a fixed schedule. Their efforts augment, and partially encompass, a computerized preventive maintenance program.

Equipment overhaul teams and renovation teams may become more popular in campus organizations as well, as emphasis on maintenance and repair increases in an era of diminishing budgets.

The following are advantages of a functional or operational organization:

- Efficient use of highly skilled specialists.
- Improved use of expensive tools and equipment.
- Efficient solutions to problems of life, health, and property hazards that may exist in campus buildings.
- Prompt correction or compliance with mandates from federal and state agencies.
- Needed alterations for new programs provided or support of reorganization within the institution.
- Money saved using in-house staff on a project rather than contracting the work.
- Increased efficiency and faster job completions through work repetition.

The disadvantages of a functional organization structure include:

- Decline in maintenance on physical plant unless used for preventive maintenance only.
- Possible development of some jealousy and resentment between functional teams and other plant employees.
- Possible segregation of equipment in locations removed from needed areas.
- Draw-down of materials, equipment, tools, and vehicle levels on which the rest of the organization depends.
- Tendency toward isolationism and independent operations; ignoring of rules, regulations, and central policy.
- Weakened team spirit in whole organization as the functional team becomes more independent.
- Complications in logistics of communications.
- Less talent available for routine operations.
- Little time for training because of demands on functional team work.

These are some of the more pertinent arguments for and against the selection of a specific organizational structure. The inclination to focus on one pure form of organization invariably changes with time. Then it becomes evident that for improved effectiveness and productivity the average plant organization must be ever-changing in order to cope with new requirements of the plant, improving technologies, lower purchasing power, and changing capabilities of the work force. A pure form of any of the three organizational schemes discussed here will quickly be outdated in practice.

Basic Factors for Development of the Maintenance Organization

Most people have a desire to be productive and to spend their work time doing something worthwhile. To make this effort as valuable and efficient as possible, activities must be organized so that individual workers receive necessary direction, instruction, assistance, material resources, and training in a timely manner with as little duplication and wasted effort as possible.

In establishing the appropriate organizational structure for satisfying these requirements, consider the following basic factors:

- Operational objectives of the maintenance activity.
- Cost considerations.
- Kind of personnel required to manage, supervise, and perform actual maintenance.
- Site or campus peculiarities with regard to locale, climate, geographical spread, prevailing architecture, size, physical condition, or usage patterns.
- Procedures required to accomplish characteristic activities.
- Physical limitations set by law, policy, labor contract, or tradition.
- Skills and experience of personnel available for hire.

Management is responsible for designing an organizational structure and administering that organization in such a manner that every worker can be productive.

There are many organization principles that apply to virtually any structured activity taking place on a sustained basis. Maintenance organizations are no exception. Following are some of the more important principles to consider when developing an organizational scheme.

- Lines of authority (and reporting) should be clear and distinct.
- Vertical lines of authority should be as short as possible.
- Like functions should be grouped together.
- Number of managers/supervisors are determined by the distinct sections identified.

- One position in every organization should be responsible for performance of an entire activity.
- Responsibilities of each unit should be defined in writing.
- Assigned responsibility must be accompanied by an appropriate degree of authority and should be levied at the lowest possible level.
- There is a practical limit on span of control or number of persons one individual can supervise. Under normal circumstances this should be limited to about five with up to twelve when work is repetitive and problems are few.
- Coordination between functions is a must and should be encouraged.
- Physical arrangement of facilities and limitations on use can affect organizational patterns.
- Staffing is decided by the volume of work to be done.
- Lines of communication should be simple and direct.
- In any successful maintenance activity no simple function can stand on its own. All units must rely on other units—at least part of the time—if the maintenance objectives are to be satisfied. Management should encourage these interactions as much as possible by designing an organizational scheme that makes coordination easy and fosters an attitude of teamwork.

These principles can be used to ensure that a critical consideration is not overlooked in formulating a new organizational structure. To flesh out the organization's skeleton, however, a number of other factors should be acknowledged as well:

- Policies the maintenance organization is expected to follow.
- Relationship of maintenance organization to institution.
- Controls on amount and type of work to be done by maintenance activity.
- Desirable skills, experience, and characteristics of people to employ.
- Coordination and communication scheme.
- Procedure manual for maintenance activity.
- Basic work rules required by institution, labor contracts.
- Categorization of work by priority, workhours, response time, kind of work, dollar limits.
- Approval levels.
- Safety and security requirements.
- Campus activity schedules (to determine required shifts and operations).

- Availability of transportation and access to areas to be maintained.
- Peculiar aspects of plant that require special recognition in the maintenance organization.

When the foregoing factors are considered in the development of a new—or the revitalization of an old—physical plant organization and sufficient time has elapsed to allow practical application, the chances of satisfying campus maintenance requirements increase significantly.

Staffing the Maintenance Functions

The modern maintenance organization increasingly relies on sophisticated management tools and techniques and advanced technology in materials, tools, and equipment applications. This dependence, which is an effort to counter the effects of fewer personnel, expanding responsibilities, more complex systems, and aging plants, requires greater selectivity in the people hired to perform plant maintenance. Gone are the days when specialists could be used on a narrow range of tasks, often waiting for an emergency to develop or new construction or alteration to be initiated, so they could "do their thing." Maintenance is an ongoing process that rewards lapses with accelerated deterioration, increased failures of critical components, and lowered environmental quality.

Above all else, employees of a maintenance-oriented activity must be conscientious and honest. The nature of much of the work requires that the individual mechanic or service person work independently, without benefit of close supervision. Neglecting to perform prescribed tasks on the recommended frequencies or in the accepted manner, while reporting the work as complete, can precipitate situations even worse than if a planned maintenance program had never been started. Plant maintenance employees must be reasonably intelligent, trainable, preferably experienced, flexible, proud of the job they do, people-oriented, and immune to the distractions of a busy campus.

Maintenance managers and supervisors must be enlightened. The broad scope of the responsibilities of the plant maintenance function, the significant portion of the campus budget administered, and the complex elements used by the work force and management to obtain more cost-effective maintenance and operations make it imperative that maintenance leaders be highly trained, experienced, and business-oriented. Administrators and supervisors must be completely open to new ideas, able to analyze without bias, and less tradition-bound than their predecessors. Maintenance managers of institutions are relying more on management techniques and control methods developed in business and industry. Leaders must be aware of that changing technology. This highlights the need for regular training and exposure to new ideas for the maintenance function to remain cost-effective and successful.

Knowing what kind of people are needed and then hiring them are two different matters. Recruiting should be conducted with as much exposure as possible. Administrators should take time to fill vacancies, even doing without needed services, when the quality of applications does not meet the organization's needs. The idea of promoting only from within is a dangerous and outmoded philosophy. It is only effective in the maintenance organization that is certain it is the best and cannot improve.

Admittedly, institutional plant maintenance does not usually have pay scales as high as business or industry. Job security, continuity, and fringe benefits must be emphasized to attract good employees. On college and university campuses the general atmosphere, as well as cultural and educational opportunities, are positive selling points. Being part of the educational process that provides an important and necessary service for the future welfare of the country, the world, and its citizenry is a worthwhile and satisfying endeavor.

Flexibility-Adaptability of the Organization

The physical plant maintenance function must be flexible and adaptable to succeed in the modern era of reduced budgets, shifting emphasis on energy consumption, expanded technology, lower personnel strength, and increasing scope of responsibilities.

Flexibility and adaptability both denote an ability to change. For the purposes of this discussion they will be differentiated by assuming flexibility is the ability to change directions rather quickly, once a course of action has been decided. While adaptability suggests the capacity to take on new or added responsibilities with only a minimum of lost motion.

Establishing flexibility in an organization ensures that the people who actually turn the wrench, operate the equipment, and push the broom are not overly concerned or restricted by the notion of crossing jurisdictional lines between trades, crafts, skills, or classifications. The maintenance worker functions in an isolated environment more than most other occupations, frequently finding minor problems not previously identified that require correction immediately to eliminate a safety, security, health hazard, or danger to property. It is much more efficient to have the person who finds the problem to fix it before leaving the site, rather than causing additional trips by someone carrying another title. The only concern should be whether the correction can be made safely and properly without worsening the condition that already exists. The employees who exhibit this spirit of self-reliance generally are highly motivated, proud of their abilities, and not under any unusual pressures from their peers or local labor unions to adhere to a strict hands-off policy.

The kind of person who does this best is one with broad experience, talents, a clear and logical mind, and who follows appropriate safety practices. He or she normally displays an inquiring nature and accepts changes in original direction with ease, not hesitating to voice a concern management or supervision may not be aware of.

Organizational flexibility is enhanced by:

- Maintaining centralized tool cribs where spares in good condition are always available.
- Employing capable operators in central equipment pools.
- Maintaining a number of ready back-up jobs for weekly schedules (or overscheduling by 10 percent) to keep the workers busy when unforeseen cancellations occur.
- Maintaining current files of design drawings, utility maps, condition survey files.
- Being aware of current class schedules, planned events, contract status, existing warranties.

The adaptability of an organization is characterized by its performance when a new requirement is identified unexpectedly. It is the wherewithal to get on with the usual work load while coping with, or quickly marshaling the required resources to undertake, added demands of the institution.

In the adaptable organization a sizable portion of the work force and management must be open to new ideas, training oriented, and willing to experiment to find a better mousetrap. The capability an organization to be adaptable is enhanced by developing and implementing the following:

- Emergency response procedures for specific scenarios.
- Recall rosters for emergencies after normal work hours.
- Blanket purchase orders with local suppliers for rapid acquisition of needed parts, materials, tools on a hurry-up basis.
- A strong spirit of cooperation with institution personnel services and purchasing functions.
- Reference library of leading technical and professional periodicals, books, manufacturer's brochures for maintaining knowledge of current developments.
- Effective and pertinent training programs.

- Good long-range planning related to the master plan of the college or university.
- A capable emergency response or service call force composed of outstanding tradespeople, linked by radio communication to a control center.

The most obvious means of attaining flexibility and adaptability is through hiring temporary personnel when the work load surges or special skills are required beyond the capability of the permanent work force. On-call purchased labor (contract), temporary hires, casual labor are terms applied to these kinds of workers. Their employment can effectively satisfy physical plant requirements. Besides the acquisition of added capability, temporary workers can be laid off when the workload or budget recedes with no continuing obligation, or the option not to call for service. Problems can arise in the permanent work force if the wages for the temporary employees are higher or if they are assigned to work normally done by permanent employees.

Most institutions operate with personnel regulations or policies that set a limit on the term of employment for a temporary worker (not obtained through a fixed-end contract), beyond which the worker automatically attains probationary status as a permanent employee. This can have serious budgetary consequences if not managed properly, but the concept is too valuable to ignore for the added flexibility and adaptability it affords.

The flexible and adaptable physical plant maintenance function operates with confidence that it can cope with any situation.

NOTES

1. John E. Heintzelman, *The Complete Handbook of Maintenance Management* (Englewood Cliffs, New Jersey: Prentice-Hall Inc., 1976) p. 5.
2. Robert L. Jacobson, "Colleges May Pay Dearly for Delaying Maintenance," *The Chronicle of Higher Education* (November 14, 1977) p. 7. (Credit William W. Bowman, University of California at Berkeley.)
3. Sean C. Rush and Sandra L. Johnson, *The Decaying American Campus: A Ticking Time Bomb* (Alexandria, Virginia: APPA, 1989).
4. Thomas B. Foster, "Can You Measure Maintenance Performance?" *Petroleum Refiner* (January 1961) pp. 123-128.
5. Bernard T. Lewis, *Controlling Maintenance Costs* (Englewood Cliffs, New Jersey: Prentice-Hall Inc., 1966) p. 75.
6. Heintzelman, *The Complete Handbook of Maintenance Management*, p. 21.

7. Robert R. Ruhlin, "Maintenance Control Function," *Management Handbook for Plant Engineers*, ed. Bernard T. Lewis, P.E. (New York: McGraw-Hill Book Company, Inc., 1977) pp. 1-47.
8. *A Basic Manual For Physical Plant Administration*, ed. George O. Weber (Washington: APPA, 1974) p. 131.
9. Heintzelman, *The Complete Handbook of Maintenance Management*, p. 101.

CHAPTER 36

Maintenance Management Systems

David J. Gojdics
Director of Physical Plant
Emory University

Edward B. Phillips
Fiscal Officer
University of North Carolina at
Chapel Hill

With additional contributions by David R. Howard, P.E.

36.1 INTRODUCTION

This chapter describes maintenance management systems that can be used in the management of both small and large plant departments. The best system for a particular operation can probably be developed from those described. Plant administrators and their staffs can provide the best maintenance management system for their particular institution's facility.

Excessive reliance upon past practices, outdated procedures, and the resistance to change in the maintenance management field result in lower productivity and higher costs. New maintenance management systems and techniques make it possible to increase the productivity of people and reduce costs. Progressive maintenance management has advanced far beyond breakdown maintenance and "fighting fires." It now includes management systems for requesting and authorizing work; planning, estimating, and scheduling work; performance measures and controls such as work sampling techniques; and cost accounting systems designed especially for controlling maintenance costs.

Objectives

The basic objectives of a maintenance management system are as follows:

1. Reduce overall maintenance costs by achieving the most from each maintenance dollar spent.

2. Minimize equipment and system breakdowns.
3. Optimize use of maintenance staffing, equipment, and materials.
4. Achieve better management control of planning, scheduling, quality of work, labor productivity, and costs.
5. Improve facilities and equipment maintenance in the broadest sense, including both the technical aspects and methodology.

36.2 WORK REQUEST SYSTEM

The work request system is the basis for establishing sound, accurate information upon which estimates, work orders, and follow-up can be based. Work requests can be generated from any element of the campus community, and thus they may be varied in style and detail, as well as their influence on physical plant.

Any work request system should be as simple as possible while still providing the comprehensive information needed to get the job done by the proper service area. This would include the building name and number, room number, person making the request, and the type of service needed. Since these requests come from different parts of the institution, the request system must be flexible enough to meet all the needs of those who use it.

Requests for service from the plant department may come in the form of telephone calls, memorandums, preprinted forms, inspection forms, verbal requests, or by electronic mail. It is management's decision to determine how these different types of request formats will be handled by the work control program.

Requests from Within the Plant Department

Work requests that are generated from within the physical plant department come from several sources. These can include maintenance repair reports from housekeeping personnel, landscape personnel, building inspection reports, repair requests generated from the preventive maintenance system, or project requests. Generally, these requests come into the work control center in written form. However, some minor maintenance tasks and requests for urgent (emergency) service are usually accepted by telephone.

Whatever the source of the request from within the department, it is essential that as much information as possible be obtained from the requestor. The information will help work control center staff issue the appropriate work order to a service unit capable of accomplishing the designated task. At a minimum, the information supplied should include the following:

- Building name.
- Exact location where the work is to occur.
- Detailed description of work needed.
- Person making the request.
- Date.

This information might be all that is needed to generate a work order in a small institution. But in larger institutions, where detailed financial records are kept, a request with the following categories of information would be appropriate:

- Building/area name.
- Building/area number.
- Date of the request.
- Date by which the work must be completed.
- Urgency of the request. (Is essential service interrupted? Are there special deadlines to be met?)
- Exact location of job.
- Approval by appropriate administrator.
- Work classification (financial account for the type of job to be done).
- Detailed description.
- Specific machine number.
- Preventive maintenance or inspection report number generating the request.
- Special scheduling instructions.

Requests from Other Departments

The basic difference between work requests that evolve from within the plant department and those that come from other departments or administrative units is that often the area making this request will be billed for the services provided. Therefore, the information contained in the in-house request would also be needed on the request from an outside department or customer. The only additional piece of data needed would be the budget line or financial code to be used to fund the project.

The facilities manager should design a format most appropriate for the particular campus. Many departments use preprinted forms, while others prefer to have memorandums sent in for each request. Some organizations find that a combination of preprinted forms and letter requests works best for the operation.

Another essential element of the request system from outside departments is the designation of authorized individuals to make requests for plant services. To avoid unauthorized or duplicate application for service or project work, a liaison system should be established. A designated individual makes requests for each building on the campus. The building liaison official should be appointed through administrative channels so they will have the proper authority to complete their assignment. Building liaisons can help establish the priority of the request, schedule work within critical use areas, and assist in getting the proper detailed information to allow for timely service.

Flow Chart of Work Request System

Figure 36-1 illustrates the flow pattern for all requests including written, oral, or emergency.

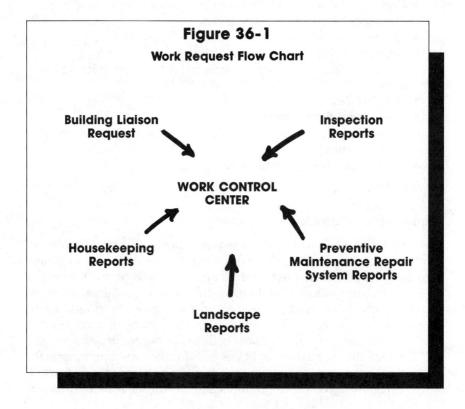

Figure 36-1
Work Request Flow Chart

Building Liaison Request

Inspection Reports

WORK CONTROL CENTER

Housekeeping Reports

Preventive Maintenance Repair System Reports

Landscape Reports

36.3 WORK ORDER SYSTEM

The primary mission of a facilities organization is to provide services to the institution. The quality of this service and the response time to a request for service often are primary indicators of the image that the campus community has of the service organization.

In order to maintain a good service image the facilities department must have a well-defined procedure for completing a work request by the appropriate service unit. The common document that accomplishes this task is the work order. The purpose of a work order system is to provide management control of a task from the time it is first reported until it is completed and billed through appropriate accounting procedures.

A basic requirement for a functioning work order system is a work control center. This should be the only area within the department that accepts service requests and issues these tasks to the individual service units. Normally, the work control center is also equipped with communications equipment such as radios, keys, and other support data to assist in the completion of work projects.

The size of a work control unit will vary with the size and organizational composition of the institution. At a small college the work control function may be handled by the director's secretary, whereas in a large institution the work control unit may include several clerks, a scheduler, a preventive maintenance coordinator, or a material expediter.

Whatever the size of the work control center there are some basic elements that should be addressed in developing this function:

- Control of work flow—administration of the work order system, estimating job costs, setting job priorities, scheduling, and work order coordination.
- Performance evaluation—constant evaluation of shop performance against estimate.
- Long-range planning—development of long-range scheduling to anticipate the needs of the building and service units.
- Documentation—supplying management with the proper information on job performance, backlog, materials flow, and staffing utilization.

As a general rule, if facilities managers must document the costs in labor and material for specific tasks performed by the department, then they should operate a system that requires individual work orders to be issued for every task performed.

Work Generation

Following the receipt of a specific task that requires action by the maintenance staff, the work control center creates an instrument that alerts the proper service unit and establishes the proper information channels to allow for an accounting of this work. This instrument is the work order.

The work order is the most important document in the total work control system. It alerts a shop that there is a task to be completed, defines the location of the work, details the work to be done, allocates resources (estimates time and material to be used), authorizes the work, and certifies completion of the job. The format of a work order may vary, depending on the needs of the department. They may be computer generated, typewritten, or handwritten. Work orders should be consistent in the conveyance of information, and they usually contain the following information:

- Sequential work order number.
- Date of the request for service.
- Date of issue to the service area.
- Building/area where the work is to be done.
- Building number.
- Department making the request (physical plant is a department like any other).
- Budget code to be charged for the work.
- Name of person making the request.
- Coordinator assigned to the project, if applicable.
- Approval of appropriate administrator.
- Work classification number.
- Detailed description of the project.
- Scheduling details and assignment of priority (emergency, routine, renovation project).
- Assignment of appropriate shop or trade crew.
- Estimates of labor and materials to be expended on the job.
- Certification of completion by the appropriate supervisor.
- Date of completion.

Much of the information needed for the issuance of the work order can be obtained from the work request form. This relieves the work control center of the task of gathering this necessary information.

Once the work order has been created, sufficient copies should be produced so that there is one for the work control center, the cost accounting section, the scheduler, the shop supervisor, and the worker assigned to complete the job. Also, some type of form should be generated to inform the person making the request of the work order number and the schedule for the completion of that task.

Costs accrued against the work order number are captured by the accounting section. When the work order has been completed, it should be signed by the appropriate supervisor and submitted to accounting. This notifies management that the job can be billed as appropriate and is ready for inspection.

Work Authorization

Plant management establishes the appropriate level of approval needed to authorize a work order since the work order generates an expenditure of funds. This would include those requests from other departments and from within the plant department. Again, the building liaison system can define those people authorized to have a work order issued for each department.

Within the plant, minor repairs or routine maintenance items could be authorized by a shop supervisor. Other types of routine maintenance should be approved by the work control supervisor or the scheduler. Any project work should be approved by the appropriate superintendent, assistant director, or director. All capital improvement projects undertaken by the facilities department should be approved by the director or other appropriate senior manager.

System Reports

The work order system should be structured to produce management reports that help the administrator monitor all aspects of the system. Basic reports include:

- Jobs in progress—reports all work orders that are active in the system with their accumulated costs.
- Backlog report—indicates the jobs that have not been started that are in the system. A report of this nature should be kept by shop in chronological order.
- Completed work order summary—all projects that have been completed over a designated period of time with performance by shop and efficiencies for management analysis.

Computerized systems enable plant administrators to create almost any type of report needed to better complete their assigned task, if the necessary data for the report are contained within the existing work order information.

Flow Chart of Work Order System

Figure 36-2 illustrates the flow pattern for all work orders.

36.4 PLANNING SYSTEM

Planning is the process of deciding how organizational objectives will be met. It involves examining overall goals, establishing intermediate goals

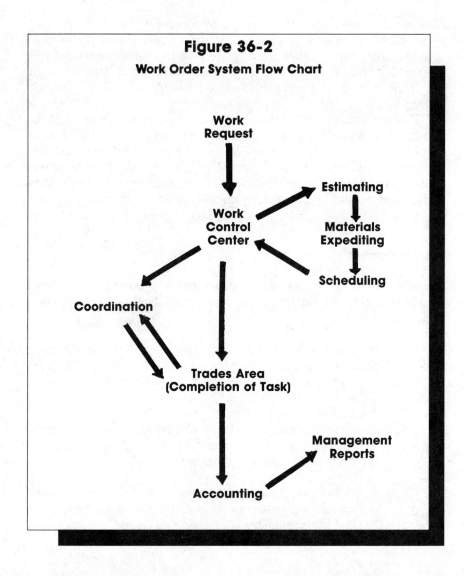

Figure 36-2
Work Order System Flow Chart

and objectives, defining alternate ways of attaining the objectives, and deciding which method to use. It is a process of thinking about a desired outcome and trying to anticipate what steps are necessary to produce it. In simplest terms, planning is decision making.

These familiar activities are all part of planning: setting goals, policies, and procedures; budgeting; estimating; designing facilities; and scheduling.

Scope of Planning

Everyone in the organization must plan—from the custodian deciding what cleaner to use for a certain stain, to the director trying to decide how to reduce campus-wide energy use. One of the main differences among planners is the time frame with which they are dealing. Managers have to be concerned with both long- and short-range plans, while other employees can usually limit their concerns to immediate tasks.

Long-range plans normally project three to ten years forward. A determining factor in facilities planning is the life of the buildings and equipment. Buildings are designed for a life of about fifty years, roofs fifteen to thirty years, and equipment three to fifteen years.

Short-range plans normally cover from one to three years, while operating plans are for weekly, monthly, or quarterly time periods. There is considerable variation in these time spans among institutions. Those given here illustrate typical planning cycles.

Long-Range Planning

Long-range plans are closely tied to the needs and goals of the academic and student communities, so close coordination is needed between facilities managers and these groups.

Normally, long-range plans include such items as:

- Painting of buildings.
- Roof replacement or repair.
- Replacement or rehabilitation of basic building systems such as hot water heaters, boilers, air conditioning systems, and power distribution equipment.
- Major renovations.
- Replacement of motor vehicles.
- Replacement of physical plant shop equipment.
- Replacement of retiring employees.
- Replacement or major changes in landscape plant materials.
- Conversion from one energy source to another.

Ideally, long-range plans should evolve into short-range plans that translate into operating plans. When a plan is set and then constantly evaluated and changed over a long period of time, it has a much greater chance of success than does a plan that is hastily fashioned. Of course, not all plans can follow this evolution, but major ones with high financial consequences should proceed this way as often as possible.

Short-Range Planning

Short-range plans should contain much less uncertainty than long-range plans. Factors such as student enrollment, equipment needing replacement, economic conditions, and funding are usually more predictable in the period of one to three years.

Typically, the first year is planned in considerable detail while the last two years are more general. Often, the first year is planned and stated in terms of budget categories and accounts.

One- to three-year plans are generally stated in dollar terms. Key goals or activities are enumerated with the dollars needed to attain or support them. Non-dollar measures such as labor hours, planned work orders, staffing additions or deletions, target dates, and schedules are usually covered in operating plans for the current year.

Individual Job Planning

Physical plant activities can be broadly grouped into two types.

1. Activities that are predictable, continuous, and ongoing on a daily basis. Examples are routine housekeeping and grounds maintenance; preventive maintenance; operation of systems such as heating plants, recycling plants, and motor pools; and administrative and supervisory functions. Because of their repetitive nature, these activities are difficult to separate into projects or jobs that have a definite beginning, end, and purpose.
2. Activities defined on a job-by-job basis. In fact, most workhours that do not fall into one of the above categories are spent on specific jobs or projects that can be described and planned fairly accurately. Methods for doing this are the subject of this section.

Elements of Job Planning   Jobs differ in many ways—by priority, labor hours required, material content, degree of planning possible, whether the purpose is preventive or corrective, urgency, and time available for accomplishment. The differences are so significant, in fact, that managers establish different systems for handling the different types of jobs encountered.

Typically, two systems are used for job planning. The criterion used for deciding under which system a job will be handled is usually its labor content. A cutoff point is selected and jobs on one side are handled one way, and on the other side another way. The cutoff point varies with the organization but is usually in the eight- to thirty-two-workhour range.

The reason a cutoff point is chosen in this range relates to the distribution of jobs, by size, usually found in plant departments. Analysis of the labor content of all jobs completed last year in an organization would show roughly the following characteristics: 80 percent of the jobs consume the time of only 20 percent of the work force, and conversely, 20 percent of the jobs consume 80 percent of the work force's time. The 80/20 relationship may vary 5 or 10 percentage points either way in a department, but the basic ratio remains.[1] The cutoff point for any organization is that labor content below which about 80 percent of the jobs fall.

Many managers, either intuitively or through actual studies, recognize that jobs exhibit these characteristics and design job planning systems accordingly. Their systems reflect detailed attention to the 20 percent of the jobs accounting for 80 percent of the workhours, while the large number of small jobs receive much less detailed attention.

Small Job Planning   Small jobs—those of less than eight to thirty-two workhours, depending upon the cutoff point chosen—are the most difficult to plan. Most emergency, routine service, and minor repair tasks fall into this category. By their nature, and sometimes by their urgency, it is not practical to attempt to plan this kind of repair or service. More often than not, the exact nature of the job and the work required are not known until a mechanic arrives at the job site and makes a diagnosis. Usually the mechanic handles the job from beginning to end with little or no assistance.

Management planning for these jobs looks at them in aggregate rather than on a job-by-job basis. Systems such as the following are established to provide for effective performance:

- Separate crews, even separate shops, are established to respond to all small job requests.
- Attempts are made to stock material frequently used, and material planning and ordering is based on historical analysis of usage and on automatic reordering procedures.
- Versatile tools that are applicable to most minor jobs are stocked and supplied.
- Record keeping on work performed is often general in nature.
- Rapid means of dispatching workers are established with extensive use of radio and paging equipment.

- Often jobs are not estimated at all, or simple ballpark estimates are made.
- Except for emergencies, work is done on a first-in/first-out basis, but with appropriate consideration to priority.
- Feedback and status reporting are usually done on an exception basis—only when unusual problems arise.
- Scheduling is done by the shop foreman rather than a central staff scheduler.
- The mechanic is often the only plant employee who communicates with the user or customer.
- Minimal status checkpoints are established, and all that may be known by anyone other than the mechanic is simply whether the job has been assigned or completed.

Compared to the systems established for larger jobs, the above methods result in relatively loose control of small jobs. However, the cost versus the benefit of tighter planning and control in this area is usually judged to be a poor exchange. In trying to get the most from limited resources, most managers choose to concentrate on large job planning.

The remainder of this section deals with planning large jobs, those above the thirty-two-workhour cutoff point.

Estimating   Effective management of the physical plant operation depends heavily on estimates. They are one of the basic foundations for planning and controlling construction and maintenance work. A complete discussion on estimating can be found in Chapter 13, Cost Control, under the subheading "Labor Productivity Improvement."

Method of Accomplishment   Large job planning requires defining, step-by-step, how a job will be accomplished. All events necessary are listed in their proper sequence, labor workhour estimates including crew sizes are applied to each event, and the material and equipment needed for each event are defined. Once all this information has been documented, basic job planning has been done.

If time is of the absolute essence, or the job is unusually large or complex, additional planning techniques may be used. Bar graphs (Gantt Charts), PERT, and critical path method (CPM) are techniques for detailed planning that assure the minimum loss of calendar time. While these techniques are useful for planning individual projects, they are of little help in effectively managing many projects simultaneously. Still, for certain projects these techniques are necessary and beneficial.

The level of detail needed in describing and documenting each step or event depends upon how the job plan will be used. In organizations with refined systems, the writeup for each step is so complete that few decisions are left to the mechanic. For each step the writeup includes the shop involved, the trade within that shop, and a detailed method for accomplishing the task. In addition, bills of material, equipment lists, and drawings are also provided.

Managers using detailed planning such as this want to leave nothing to chance and want to minimize the number of decisions made by the shops and the mechanics. If supporting systems of equal refinement are in place, a high level of effectiveness and productivity results.

Most plant managers must settle for more general job plans that give a brief description of the event, the workhours required including crew size, the shop responsible for the event, and possibly the trade within that shop. Major items of material are also frequently specified, but not usually the equipment or tools needed.

The advantages of defining and documenting how a job will be accomplished include the following:

- It is absolutely necessary if any kind of effective scheduling is expected.
- Shop personnel are freed to concentrate on their prime responsibilities. Mechanics lose less time at job sites. Foremen have more time available for direct supervision.
- Those concerned with supplying material and equipment are better able to coordinate their efforts with the shops.
- Potential problems are recognized and solved before the job starts, not after.
- It provides a means of stating quantitatively the amount of work completed and remaining. This is valuable for progress reporting purposes.

36.5 SCHEDULING SYSTEM

Scheduling is an extension of planning. It defines, preferably in writing, what the plans are in terms of labor and—in sophisticated systems— material and equipment. It seeks to level the workload and it provides the basis for measurement of performance and control. Scheduling defines how resources will be used over a period of time and provides the basis for evaluating actual use versus planned use. Also, when work is being done for a customer, it is the means of determining milestones and completion dates.

Scheduling can be divided into three types: master scheduling, weekly scheduling, and daily scheduling.

Master Scheduling

Master scheduling is the broadest, longest range type of scheduling. It looks forward to a horizon that is at least three months, but can be years, in the future. A typical master schedule has the following characteristics:

- It has a three- to six-month horizon. This will depend mostly upon material delivery and the department's ability to adjust staffing up or down. If material deliveries are long and staffing levels are difficult to adjust, the master scheduling horizon will be extended farther out.
- Only large jobs or projects are scheduled. Typically, large means anything with more than twenty-four to thirty-two workhours of labor. No attempt is made to schedule emergency or minor repair work.
- The period of time covered by the schedule is divided into bi-weekly or monthly increments, or a combination of these. For example, if a six-month horizon is used, it might be practical to divide the first two months into four periods of two weeks each, and the remaining four months into four monthly periods. It is usually not practical to use shorter periods of time for master scheduling because too many uncertainties exist and too many changes will be made.
- A separate master schedule should be maintained for each shop so that individual skill or trade bottlenecks can be seen.
- Jobs are slotted into the time periods based upon shop capacity, material delivery expectations, customers' needs, and seasonal requirements. Any one of these factors, or all of them together, can influence how the job is scheduled.
- Care is taken to avoid exceeding the capacity of each shop. To do this, the capacity of each shop must be calculated and updated regularly. For master scheduling purposes, simple calculations are best. For example, if the carpenter shop has five people, its capacity is 200 workhours per week (5 workers X 40 hours/week/person).
- All available capacity is not scheduled. Typically only 50 to 80 percent of available workhours are scheduled. The remaining 20 to 50 percent are reserved for absenteeism, nonproductive work, and emergency and routine repair jobs. Figure 36-3 is an example of a typical master schedule.
- Master schedules are usually reviewed and approved at a high level in the organization. The projects scheduled are sizable, deadlines are important, and funds expended will be significant. In addition, good institutional relations can be greatly in-

Figure 36-3
Typical Master Schedule

Shop: __Carpenter__   Date: __3-14__

Time Period	1st Half April	2nd Half April	May	June	July	Aug	Sep	Oct
Capacity (workhours/work day)	24	24	24	24	32	32	32	32
No. of work days in period	10	9	20	21	21	22	20	22
Planned workhours available	240	216	480	504	672	704	640	704
Total load (workhours)	200	220	470	450	370	340	340	240
Net workhours available	40	-4	10	54	302	364	300	464

Scheduled Workhours

Jobs or Projects	1st Half April	2nd Half April	May	June	July	Aug	Sep	Oct
# 6387 ABC Hall	180	10						
# 8522 XYZ Dorm		150						
# 3701 Bldg. #8			160	160				
# 2232 Bldg. #10 - Room 201	20	20						
# 6757 Bldg. #11 - Room 20		40						
# 8700 DEF hall								
New addition - XYZ Hall			100	50	50	120		
Dean Dokes office			180	80				
Alumni Bldg. roof						180	180	
Admin. Bldg. renovation			30	160	160			
Stairway West Parking					160			
Bldg # 8 - Rms. 101, 102, 103						40	160	
Bldg # 12								240

fluenced by the plant department's performance on these projects.

- In well-run master scheduling systems, the schedule becomes frozen one to two months out; changes are only allowed in the third month and beyond. This greatly stabilizes the planning and scheduling process and contributes to high productivity and schedule reliability.

Weekly Scheduling

The master schedule feeds the weekly schedule with jobs or projects that have been anticipated and planned well in advance. The weekly schedule also contains large unplanned jobs that arise unexpectedly or result from a shift in priorities. Examples would be emergency repairs, new projects with a high priority in which material delivery is not a problem, or routine work that goes on continuously but cannot be defined too far in advance.

Weekly schedules have the following characteristics:

- While master schedules cover only 50 to 80 percent of shop capacity, weekly schedules attempt to cover 80 to 90 percent of shop capacity.
- Jobs under twenty-four to thirty-two workhours duration are not included on the weekly schedule.
- Weekly schedules, which are issued for each shop, reflect known absenteeism (vacations or sick leave) in the shop capacity figure for a given week.
- The weekly schedule does not define the individual mechanics' daily work, which is done under daily scheduling. The weekly schedule shows simply the number of workhours that should be spent by each shop on each job for every day of the work week; Figure 36-4 is an example of a typical weekly schedule form.
- Jobs are not scheduled until major items of material have been checked for availability.
- Weekly meetings are held between the scheduler and shop supervisors to communicate actual versus scheduled performance.
- The scheduler is in constant contact with the shops to stay informed on staffing availability and changes, which is necessary to assure that the shops are not under- or over-loaded due to unknown situations.

Daily Scheduling

Daily scheduling is the process of converting the weekly schedule into individual mechanics' daily assignments. This is best done by the shop

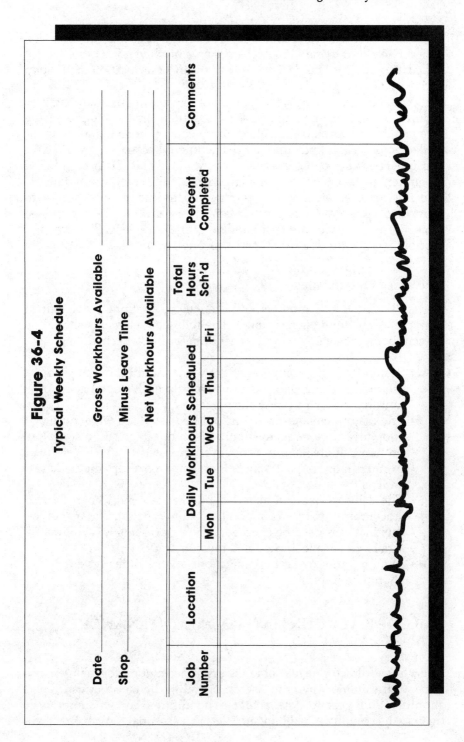

Figure 36-4

Typical Weekly Schedule

foreman. Foremen typically do this by simply posting the daily job assignments next to individuals' names on a blackboard or other type of visual display. This board is placed in a conspicuous location in the shop and is updated regularly (at least daily).

Not surprisingly, organizations that have no other scheduling procedures do have rudimentary daily scheduling at the shop level by foremen. When master scheduling and weekly scheduling are also installed, supervision finds that daily scheduling becomes more effective because it becomes part of an overall coordinated plan. Daily scheduling by a foreman covers not only the large jobs on the weekly schedule but also the small emergency and routine repairs (under twenty-four to thirty-two workhours duration). Except in the most sophisticated systems, these small jobs are best handled at the shop level on a first-in/first-out basis, with due regard for their priority, of course.

Necessary Prerequisites

Certain basic systems must be in place, before anything more refined than daily scheduling is attempted. The following elements should be present before installing weekly scheduling or master scheduling:

- A step-by-step description of the work should show the shop required and the labor hours needed for each step; it is important that the steps reflect the actual sequence of the job.
- The major items of material should be listed if a warehouse or shop inventory exists to supply the minor items; if no stock is on hand, all items of material must be listed.
- In multitrade shops it may be necessary to specify the trade as well as the shop.
- The delivery status of materials not on hand must be tracked. If stockrooms exist for common items, only material unique to individual jobs need be checked; if no stockrooms exist, all materials for each job scheduled must be tracked.
- In all but the smallest organizations a work order system should be in place.

36.6 COST ACCOUNTING FOR MAINTENANCE MANAGEMENT

Every plant director needs some means of accounting for maintenance expenditures. One way is to use an operating budget that can report monthly and year-to-date actual expenditures and encumbrances against the overall annual budget. This is an essential tool for the director and represents the real world of actual expenditures against budgeted funds. However, most operating budgets tend to summarize cost items and have no allowances for the kind of detail a director needs to manage efficiently.

To meet this need for detailed cost information concerning such expenses as annual repair charges in a given residence hall or the specific charges on a given job order, the director needs some type of cost accounting system. The type of system depends on the size and type of institution, the budget available to support a cost accounting staff, and the manager's personal emphasis on the need for this type of detailed reporting.

Whatever type of system, it is important to remember that cost accounting systems are, for the most part, based on standard and average cost information. This information approximates actual expenditures but does not always equal the actual cost as reported against the operating budget.

Although an average or standard cost system may not tie exactly to the actual costs incurred on a particular job, it does give the manager an excellent approximation of that cost. And it is often a fairer cost, especially if a self-supporting facility is paying for the service. When a shop charge rate is based on an overall average or composite of the individual salaries within the shop, problem situations are avoided whereby one department might receive a larger bill because the highest paid mechanic happened to handle that particular service call.

Establishing a Standard Cost System

The first matter to address in establishing a cost accounting system is to determine what type of labor rates will be utilized. One system might use broad overall rates based on certain segments of the organization's salary grades, with rates designated for laborers, trades helpers, and mechanics. Another system might base its rates on job classifications, with different rates for a Carpenter I or a Carpenter II.

A third approach, and the one that will be addressed in detail here, involves establishing a standard labor charge rate for all employees within a particular shop or work unit. This composite rate is used to account for all labor charged out by the shop during the fiscal year.

To establish a shop rate, pertinent data on shop personnel must first be summarized. See Figure 36-5. In this simplified example all employees in the shop and their current salaries have been included. Next, the cost of employee benefits paid by the employer are added, as well as the individual shop's share of direct supervision and support costs allocated on the basis of employee count.

Figure 36-5

Salary and Staff Benefit Summary

Position Title	Position No.	Salary Grade	Salary Step	Actual Salary
General Utility Worker	73489	53	1	$ 8,500
Trades Helper	73458	57	3	11,000
Carpenter I	73484	57	2	10,500
Carpenter I	73492	57	4	11,500
Carpenter II	73464	61	2	12,500
Carpenter II	73520	61	7	15,500
Cabinetmaker	73564	61	5A	14,000
Carpenter Supervisor II	73551	65	4	16,500

Position Count 8		Subtotal		$100,000
	FICA	6.70%		6,700
	Retirement	9.90%		9,900
	Health Benefits	$425 @ 8		3,400
		Total		$120,000
Direct Supervision and Support (See Figure 2-6)				$ 12,200
		Total		$132,200
Average cost per position		$16,525		
Cost per hour		$7.94		

Figure 36-5 reflects a total annual cost of $132,200 for salary related items. This figure is divided by 8, the number of positions in the shop, to get an average cost of $16,525 per position. This average cost is then divided by 2,080 hours (40 hours/week X 52 weeks/year) to get an hourly shop rate of $7.94.

This shop rate of $7.94 per hour is called the cost accounting rate and will be used to calculate labor charges for maintenance and repairs funded in the physical plant budget and to assign dollar values to annual leave, sick leave, and holidays.

Leave Factor   When billing a self-supporting facility for work not provided for in the plant budget, the cost accounting rate, in this example $7.94, will be indexed by a leave factor of 1.1429 to absorb the cost of holidays, annual leave, and sick leave. This indexing is justified for the following reason: If the self-supporting facility were to employ its own carpenter, it too would only have the carpenter's services available for approximately 1,820 hours per year, rather than the 2,080 hours for which the carpenter is paid.

The annual salaries for direct labor employees are based on fifty-two weeks a year at forty hours each week for a total of 2,080 hours a year. However, an individual worker will not be available to actually work 2,080 hours a year due to holidays, annual leave, and sick leave.

Studies at one university show that the average number of weeks taken per employee per year is as follows:

	Weeks Taken
Holidays	2.0
Annual Leave	2.6
Sick Leave	1.9
Total	6.5

These 6.5 weeks represent a leave index factor of 14.29 percent.

$$\text{Total Annual Hours } 52 \times 40 = 2,080$$
$$\text{Leave and Holidays } 6.5 \times 40 = \underline{(260)}$$
$$\text{Available Hours} \quad 1,820$$

260 Leave Hours ÷ 1,820 Available Hours = 14.29 percent
2,080 Total Hours ÷ 1,820 Available Hours = 1.1429

Therefore, to absorb the cost of this nonproductive time the carpenter shop's cost accounting rate of $7.94 per hour is indexed up by the factor of 1.1429 to a billing rate of $9.08.

Figure 36-5 showed only a small portion of overhead costs being absorbed in the labor rate. Obviously in some organizations there will be a considerable amount of administrative overhead. Whether all or part of this overhead is absorbed depends on the specific institution's overall budget structure and the organization's need to recover those costs from self-supporting facilities on campus.

Material Costs   In addition to labor, the other major component of a cost accounting system will be material or supply costs. Here, as with labor rates, there are limitless variations that can be used to charge out materials. Some organizations charge materials at current cost, others at average cost. Some index these costs to cover overhead expenses, and still others only index materials that are charged to self-supporting facilities. Again, the type of system used depends on the individual institution's budget and billing philosophy.

Figure 36-6

Schedule of Direct Supervision and Support

Direct Supervision and Support	Shop Direct	Carpenter	HVAC	Plumbing	Total
	Employees	8	10	14	32
	Percentage	25%	31%	44%	100%

Position	Gross Salary			
Trade Services Superintendent	$22,000	$ 5,500	$ 6,820	$ 9,680
Secretary IV	9,800	2,450	3,038	4,312
Area Coordinator	17,000	4,250	5,270	7,480
	Totals	$12,200	$15,128	$21,472

Computerized Cost Accounting

Once the method of deriving labor and material charge rates is established, management needs some type of system (preferably a computerized one) to track, record, and invoice these charges. Again, there are an infinite number of systems available; for this discussion, we will examine only one.

This job order system starts with the premise that all labor and material costs will be charged to individual job order numbers with the exception of leave, holidays, and training sessions. Job orders contain the following information (data elements) directly related to the cost accounting system:

1. Department Responsible for the Charges—physical plant or self-supporting facility.
2. Building/Area/Vehicle Number—"ledger" number used to record charges made throughout the month and fiscal year from the various individual job orders.
3. Work Classification Code—a numeric code with a descriptive alpha statement used to distribute charges within a particular building, area, or vehicle, for example, 2220 Floor Tile Repairs. This information is used to give some detail to the charges made in a building during a month or fiscal year. Following is a partial listing of work classification codes:

21XX Building Shell
   2110 Door Closers
   2120 Door Numbers
22XX Floors
   2210 Floor Refinishing
   2220 Floor Tile Repairs
   2230 Ceramic Tile Floors
23XX Foundations and Footings
   2310 Waterproofing
24XX Roofs
   2410 Waterproofing
25XX Walls
   2510 Masonry
   2520 Painting
   2530 Plaster
   2540 Millwork
   2550 Sheetrock Installation
   2560 Sheetrock Patching and Repairs
   2570 Window Screens
26XX Windows
   2610 Blind Repairs
2620 Glazing
   2630 Window Repairs
   2640 Window Shades
   2650 Security Screens
   2660 Storm Windows
   2670 Window Screens
27XX Hardware
   2710 Key Cutting
   2720 Lock Combination
   2730 Lock Installation
   2740 Lock Repairs

4. Coordinator—responsible for seeing that all shops phase their work properly and that the job is complete before a final billing is made.
5. Work Category—used to indicate type of billing to be made (a regular invoice or transfer voucher).
6. Description/Instructions—detailed information on the particular task to be performed.
7. Estimate—projected costs for the work broken down by labor hours and dollars, material dollars, and total labor and material dollars.
8. Shops Involved—listing of the shops authorized to perform work and charge against a particular job; gives an estimated completion

date by shop and the individual estimate of labor and material costs by shop.

Daily Time Sheets   Shop employees complete a daily time sheet, listing the individual job orders they worked on and the time spent on each job. These time sheets are preprinted by the computer system with the employee's name, social security number, and assigned shop. See Figure 36-7.

The time sheet information is entered on a CRT terminal by a cost accounting clerk. The system edits this data on-line and, if correct, stores it on a disc for overnight updating.

Material Tickets   Daily issues from the physical plant warehouse are, in most cases, charged directly to individual job order numbers. Those items that are not charged directly are transferred to the shop's stock and charged out as they are used on individual jobs. These material tickets are accumulated in the cost accounting office and entered via CRT terminals in a manner similar to time sheet entry.

On-Line Information   Once the time sheet and material charges have been updated to the system, direct on-line inquiry can be made into the system through the same CRT terminals used to enter the data.

This on-line inquiry gives the supervisor or manager virtually instant access to the individual status on any job order. Elements on the inquiry screen include:

Job order number
Priority
Work category
Purchase order/reference number
Work classification code and short alpha description
Coordinator's name
Building/area/vehicle number and name
Who requested the work
Who approved the job order issue
Description of work requested
Responsible department
Dates:
>   Requested by customer
>   Passed to scheduler's file
>   Issued to first shop involved
>   Estimated completion
>   Last transaction
>   Completed

Figure 36-7

Physical Plant Daily Time Sheet

Name: _____   Shop: _____   SSN: _____   Date: _____

Overtime ☐   (Enter your work activity row by row, from left to right as numbered.)

Job Order	Hours	Job Order	Hours	Job Order	Hours
1.		2.		3.	
4.		5.		6.	
7.		8.		9.	
10.		11.		12.	
13.		14.		15.	
16.		17.		18.	
19.		20.		21.	
22.		23.		24.	
25.		26.		27.	
28.		29.		30.	

TOTAL HOURS _____

Employee's Initials _____   Foreman's Initials _____

Financial code information
Summary of estimated and actual charges based on
labor hours/dollars and material dollars
Efficiency percentages
Amount invoiced to date

Also available on a separate inquiry screen, accessed through the one described above, is detailed information for each shop involved in the job. This screen shows the following information for each shop involved in the job:

Dates
       Estimated completion
       Issue
       First transaction
       Last transaction
       Completion
Estimated charges
Actual charges
Efficiency percentages

With the above on-line information and hard copy reports of jobs in progress, the job order coordinators, shop foremen, and plant managers have ample access to the information they need to manage the organization efficiently.

This information, and a special billing report that highlights those jobs ready to be billed, is used by the cost accounting staff to invoice self-supporting facilities for work they request.

Monthly Reporting   As a part of the computerized cost accounting system, several management information reports can be produced on a monthly or more frequent basis. These reports should show both current period (usually current month) and fiscal year-to-date information. Labor and material charges are reported by shop unit with grand totals for the entire operation.

Figure 36-8 shows an example of a cost accounting system report for departmental services. It displays the current month and year-to-date labor and materials expended on services to self-supporting facilities. Note that the labor figures by individual shops are reported in the cost accounting rate, and only the grand total is indexed up to the billing rate.

Preventive Maintenance

Time and materials spent doing preventive maintenance are an important element of any cost accounting system and should be reported separately from regular maintenance work. In a computerized system job orders for preventive maintenance can be assigned a special code or work category and the computer programmed to report this as a separate item.

Cost Accounting/Equipment Number System

Cost accounting systems benefit from logical numbering schemes as much as do general purpose accounting systems. Use alpha codes rather than numeric codes wherever possible. Computers can easily handle both alpha and numeric codes, and it is much easier for managers to remember an alpha code such as CR for carpenter shop, than a numeric code such as 2310.

When it is more efficient to use numeric schemes, care should be exercised that they help the employees use the information the numbering system represents. The scheme should be planned in a logical and systematic manner as in Figure 36-9, which will help identify the vehicle type by its number.

Federal regulations require colleges and universities to depreciate their property, facilities, and equipment as a part of figuring overhead rates for federal contracts and grants. To comply with these regulations, institutions have established comprehensive asset management systems. Usually these systems require that any piece of movable equipment with a value of $200 or more be tagged and inventoried at least once a year.

If possible, incorporate these fixed asset numbers into the cost accounting system. However, with the volume of items to be inventoried from the entire campus community, these numbers may not be suitable if the department is responsible for physical plant property and equipment only.

36.7 PERFORMANCE MEASURES/WORK SAMPLING

Performance measurement is an ingredient of control. It tells management how its operation compares with accepted standards. These standards may be generated internally or they may come from outside sources. Both are needed.

Figure 36-8
Departmental Services Report

DEPARTMENTAL SERVICES	Current Month				Year To Date			
Operations	Labor Hours	Labor $	Material $	Total Labor & Material $	Labor Hours	Labor $	Material $	Total Labor & Material $
I. Building Serv.								
Coliseum Crew	—	$ —	$ —	$ —	—	$ —	$ —	$ —
Floor Crew	11	71	—	71	47	321	1	322
Housekeeping	131	747	38	785	202	1153	38	1191
Pest Control	101	888	179	1067	215	1907	321	2228
Radiation Crew	16	88	—	88	38	213	—	213
Sub Total Build. Serv.	259	$ 1794	$ 217	$ 2011	502	$ 3594	$ 360	$ 3954
II. Landscape Serv.	1067	$ 6741	$ 360	$ 7101	1179	$ 11228	$ 374	$ 11602
III. Trade Services								
Carpenter	2126	$ 19213	$ 13659	$ - 32872	3626	$ 31809	$ 16039	$ 47848
Electric	1043	9314	9506	18820	1933	16998	11598	28596
General	1190	9282	2303	11585	1786	13933	2723	16656
Hardware	363	3570	4212	7782	600	5838	5166	11004
Paint	758	6517	915	7432	1161	9979	1722	11701
Plumbing	991	8532	2674	11206	1556	13263	4074	17337
Refrigeration	662	6436	2260	8696	1247	12374	4832	17206
Sub Total Trade Serv.	7133	$ 62864	$ 35529	$ 98393	11909	$ 104194	$ 46154	$ 150348
Sub Total Operations	8459	$ 71399	$ 36106	$ 107505	14190	$ 119016	$ 46888	$ 165904

Word Processor	—	$ —	—	$ —	—	$ —	—	$ —
Vet Services	—	$ —	—	$ —	—	$ —	—	$ —
General Services								
Automotive Garage	178	$ 2307	3243	$ 5550	347	$ 4522	4931	$ 9453
Heavy Equipment	389	3763	300	4063	707	6686	480	7166
Mail Crew	—	—	—	—	—	—	—	—
Motor Pool	—	—	—	—	—	—	—	—
Warehouse	—	—	—	—	2	14	—	14
Waste Disposal	8	78	—	78	16	156	—	156
Sub Total Gen. Serv.	575	$ 6148	3543	$ 9691	1072	$ 11378	5411	$ 16789
Engineering								
Design Services	42	$ 777	—	$ 777	53	$ 1000	—	$ 1000
Steam Plant	—	—	—	—	—	—	—	—
Sub Total Engineering	42	$ 777	—	$ 777	53	$ 1000	—	$ 1000
Grand Total DPS	9076	$ 78324	39649	$ 117973	15315	$ 131394	52299	$ 183693
Grand Total @ Billing Rate		$ 89516	39,649	$ 129165		$ 150170	52299	$ 202469

Figure 36-9

Motor Pool Numbering System

Number Series	Vehicle Type
1000 - 1999	Subcompact sedans
2000 - 2999	Compact/mid-size sedans
3000 - 3999	Full-size sedans
4000 - 4999	Compact/mid-size station wagons
5000 - 5999	Full-size station wagons
6000 - 6999	Cargo vans
7000 - 7999	Passenger vans
8000 - 8999	Buses
9000 - 9999	Trucks

Sooner or later, most managers begin to wonder how their operations compare to other physical plants at other schools, or to the typical school. They seek performance measures common to all physical plants. They even wonder whether absolute measures of performance are available rather than measures that are relative to someone else.

Another aspect of the facilities manager's efforts to control labor costs have focused on that part of an individual's day when he or she is doing productive work—sawing, measuring, drilling, sweeping, pruning. Labor standards for these activities have been established time and again, and systems have been used to measure how productive this effort is. This approach was used because productive time is the largest part of an individual's day.

In recent years, however, increasing interest has been shown in trying to determine how the nonproductive portion of an individual's day is spent. Even when sophisticated work measurement and control systems are in place, only about 70 percent of an individual's day is spent on productive work.

Management is now becoming more concerned with how the balance of a worker's time is used. Work sampling is a relatively inexpensive and effective way to gather this factual information.

See Chapter 13, Cost Control, for a complete discussion of performance measures. Work sampling is discussed in detail in Chapter 41, Principles of Industrial Engineering in Facilities Management.

36.8 MANAGEMENT CONTROLS

Managerial control is the process of comparing actual results with planned or expected results and taking corrective action if the deviation is judged unacceptable. The corrective action frequently takes the form of additional planning, organizing, and directing. In many ways the need for control drives the other management processes.

Detailed written procedures and reports may not ensure good control. Extensive paperwork can be found in both excellently and poorly managed facilities. Effective control starts with managerial observation and evaluation, it is enhanced by proper organization of activities, and it is aided through feedback and reporting.

Observation and Evaluation

Effective control should not start with reports. They help, but it is difficult to design them to tell the whole story. The first and most important form of control is exercised when managers walk their campuses, objectively observing and evaluating the condition of the buildings, equipment, and grounds. When they observe personnel at work and evaluate their productivity, when managers listen to and analyze the complaints received from the campus community, when they see and question how much emergency versus planned and routine work is done, and when they see the wise or indulgent use of energy, managers learn much about the organization's performance.

Observation and evaluation set the overall level of expectation against which actual results can be compared. If this is not done first and continuously, other control measures can lose their relevancy. Some may argue that management expectation is part of goal-setting, which is in turn a part of planning—not control. While this may be true in theory, in practice many plans are not fully understood until they are interpreted. The communication of management expectation is a way of interpreting plans, and this frequently occurs after the plans have been put into effect.

Organizing for Control

Effective control can be enhanced by the way the plant department is organized. Certain basic elements should exist in any department that is under good control, regardless of its size. Some of the most important elements are:

- Building and equipment inventory provides factual information on what is to be maintained and replaced when needed.
- Maintenance standards define the level of maintenance expected. Certain facilities, because of their age, use, or budget restrictions, may be deliberately maintained at a minimum level. Other facilities may require the highest level possible with no

compromise. Whatever the level, it should be defined in writing to avoid false expectations.
- Work classifications indicate how work will be handled. The types of work done by physical plant are so varied that one system for organizing all work is not usually adequate. For example, a different approach is needed for emergency equipment repairs than for routine housekeeping. The following eight work classifications developed by the Department of the Navy are useful:

> Emergency work.
> Service work.
> Minor work.
> Specific jobs.
> Standing jobs.
> Supplements to authorized work.
> Amendments to authorized work.
> Rework.[2]

Small institutions do not need this many classifications. Perhaps four would be enough: emergency, routine, standing, and nonproductive. The number of classifications and what they are called is a matter of individual choice.
- Numerical identification marks each item in the inventory. This makes it much easier to collect historical information on work done for each item. In well-developed systems, all work done is also slotted and collected in various categories, each with a numerical identity. For example, any kind of heating, air conditioning, or control system repairs might be collected in a category called HVAC repairs. This allows for gathering data such as Building Number 13 had $8,000 worth of HVAC repairs in the last two years; or 2,000 workhours were required last year for pruning all plants on campus.
- Work order systems were discussed earlier in this chapter. A good work order system is one of the basic elements of control.
- Material coordination is vital to control and difficult to establish. (See Chapter 15, Procurement and Materials Management.)
- Shop scheduling is helpful to small plants that need a system of daily scheduling of individual workers. In larger organizations weekly scheduling and master scheduling are mandatory.

Many organizations, from the smallest to the largest, create a separate department whose primary responsibility is to install and administer the above control elements. These departments are frequently given the name Work Control Center. These control centers are often assigned the following duties:

- Administration of the work request system.
- Job planning and scheduling.
- Material coordination.
- Estimating, including establishment of labor and material standards.
- Developing, monitoring, and analyzing the preventive maintenance program.
- Performance measurement, including management reports.

Once management's expectations have been communicated and the basic organizational elements are in place, meaningful reports can be designed and generated. Some of the most useful types of reports will discussed.

Cost Control Reports

Cost control reporting usually takes two forms. The first are accounting-oriented reports. These cover budget versus actual costs for the total physical plant, or its major subdivisions, on such items as salaries, materials, supplies, utilities, equipment, fringe benefits, and other such accounts. Top administrative managers are the main users of this information.

The second type of cost reports are job cost reports that show all actual material and labor charges made to individual jobs. Superintendents, supervisors, and foremen usually find these more useful. Job cost reports often show the estimated material and labor so that an actual versus estimated appraisal can be made. See Chapter 13, Cost Control, for further information on cost control reports.

Equipment Failure Reports

Equipment failure reports are generated from records produced by the basic system. The work order system and the job cost system collect historical information on work done to the items in the building and equipment inventory. This is accomplished by classifying the work into categories and keeping records of work done using building and equipment identification numbers. In small institutions it may be perfectly adequate to keep a simple data card on each item and simply write down any significant work done to the item.

Equipment failure reports are the result of manual or computer-assisted analysis of the costs resulting from maintaining the inventory items. Ideally, the highest cost items can be easily identified each time the report is prepared. If this is done, the equipment failure report serves its purpose to management. Use of the information produced by this report can be extensive. Two basic questions the report raises are: Why is failure occurring—inherent design weakness, abuse, poor maintenance workmanship, or lack of preventive maintenance? and, When is it time to stop repairing the item and seek replacement? Reports do not directly answer these questions, but reports do enable conscientious managers to ask more insightful questions (evaluate) and generate action (plan) to obtain the answers.

Labor Productivity Reports

Any measures of productivity attempt to relate output to the effort required to obtain that output. In labor productivity reports, output is usually stated in terms of planned or estimated workhours. The effort required to produce this output is simply the actual workhours spent. Productivity is usually defined as the ratio of planned or estimated workhours to actual workhours.

If a basic work order system is in place and estimating of at least large jobs is done, labor productivity can be easily measured on a job-by-job basis. For example, if a job was estimated to take 56 workhours and it actually took 60 workhours, the productivity is $56 \div 60$, or 0.93. If the job only took 54 workhours, the productivity would be 1.04 ($56 \div 54$).

Since the report on completed jobs contains the data needed for a productivity calculation, productivity indexes are often included as a part of this report. Using this report allows not only the calculation of productivity on each job, but also the calculation of a total productivity figure that includes all jobs completed in a given month.

In the strictest terms, it is not sufficient to include only the mechanic's, custodian's, or laborer's time in the actual time spent on a job. This does not give a true picture of labor productivity, because it fails to recognize other labor inputs required to complete the job. What about the efforts of the foreman, the materials manager, and the engineer who designed the job? What about the time spent for training, rework, planning, and other indirect activities? A true productivity measure for the total department must include all these indirect, yet important, efforts that support the employee working directly on the job.

While the completed jobs report, showing actual versus estimated performance, is one of the best productivity reports, other types of labor measurement are also useful. Other reports often used include backlog, labor utilization, overtime, and absenteeism reports.

Backlog Report   Backlog reports try to measure how much known work remains undone at any point in time. The amount of known work remaining is stated in terms of total workhours.

While it is important to be able to track the total workhour backlog, managers usually find it more meaningful to think of backlog in terms of the number of days, weeks, or months worth of work represented by the total workhour backlog figure. To do this they relate the workhour backlog to their workhour capacity.

Labor Utilization Report   This is one of the most basic and most useful labor reports. It is simply a breakdown of how physical plant's total hours are spent. The report divides total payroll hours (or dollars) into various predetermined classifications such as productive work, rework, lost time, vacation, paid sick leave, training, meetings, and breaks. In the best systems there is complete reconciliation between this data and the payroll.

This report is prepared from the daily time sheets filled out by each employee. The labor utilization report does not show productivity per se. It simply shows how employees are spending their time without trying to relate this to work output. The report is nevertheless useful for determining:

- Proportion of total hours spent on work orders. (This can be compared to the planned proportion.)
- Amount of lost time occurring.
- Actual workhour capacity for productive work—for use in scheduling.

Overtime Report   These reports show the number of hours spent for which a wage premium, or other type of penalty, is paid. Overtime reports often express overtime hours as a percentage of total workhours, which can be a more meaningful control index.

The existence of some overtime should not necessarily be considered a sign of poor control. Overtime within a range of 5 percent of all regular hours worked is usually acceptable. More overtime than this starts to reflect on the organization's ability to plan and schedule work. Less than this could indicate a staffing excess.

Absenteeism Report   The level of absenteeism is an important indicator of how employees view the personnel policies, as well as how tightly or loosely the policies are administered by supervisors and managers. Monitoring absenteeism for this purpose is basic to personnel management.

Absenteeism reports should also be used by planners and schedulers for helping determine workhour capacity and staffing requirements. If a certain task, such as preventive maintenance, requires 3,850 workhours per year to perform, absenteeism figures help determine the number of employees required.

Gross hours available from each worker each year	
(40 hours/week/person x 52 weeks/year)	2,080
Less: Absenteeism and nonwork time	
Vacation (10 days)	(80)
Sick (assume 5 days or use past records)	(40)
Holidays (10 days)	(80)
Nonwork time (meetings, training, lost	
time—25 days)*	(200)
Net available hours per person per year	1,680

Number of employees required: 3,850 ÷ 1,680 = 2.3 employees

*This figure can be obtained from the labor utilization report.

36.9 CONCLUSION

This chapter has introduced and explained several methods of managing the maintenance task of a large or small plant department. The use of these techniques should enable the plant administrator to know his or her organization better, and provide a solid foundation for the reduction of costs while increasing productivity.

Tightening budgets, funding competition, and aging facilities make it essential that the facilities department of any college or university be operated in the most efficient manner possible to get the greatest return for every dollar invested. Good maintenance planning, scheduling, and management will help accomplish this task.

NOTES

1. *Maintenance Management of Shore Facilities*, November 1977. Publication Number NAVFAC MO-321. Naval Publications and Forms Center, Philadelphia, Pennsylvania.
2. See note 1.

ADDITIONAL RESOURCES

A Guide to Improved Maintenance Management. Engineering Management Division. New York: Syska and Hennessy, Inc., Engineers.

Buffa, Elwood S. *Basic Production Management*, second edition. New York: John Wiley & Sons, 1975.

Comparative Costs and Staffing Report for College and University Facilities. Alexandria, Virginia: APPA, biennial.

Heintzelman, John E. *The Complete Handbook of Maintenance Management.* Englewood Cliffs, New Jersey: Prentice-Hall Inc., 1976.

Lewis, Bernard T. *Developing Maintenance Time Standards.* Boston: Farnsworth Publishing, 1967.

Loopo, L. Paul. "Work Sampling—What, Why, and, Especially, How." Presentation at APPA Institute for Facilities Management, 1982.

"Maintenance and Operations Cost Study." *American School and University*, annual.

Management Handbook for Plant Engineers, ed. Bernard T. Lewis, P.E. New York: McGraw-Hill Book Company, Inc., 1977.

Newbrough, E.T. *Effective Maintenance Management* (New York: McGraw-Hill Book Company, Inc., 1967).

"Operating Cost Survey Report," *Cleaning Management*, annual.

Planner and Estimator's Workbook, March 1980. Publication Number NAVFAC P-700.2. Naval Publications and Forms Center, Philadelphia, Pennsylvania.

Suber, L. Terry. "Work Sampling: What, Why, and How," *1981 APPA Annual Meeting Proceedings*. Washington: APPA, 1981.

CHAPTER 37

Use of Computers in Work Management

Clyde H. Gordon
Owner/Principal
Clyde H. Gordon & Associates

Gerry M. Smith
Administrator,
Plant Operations Services
California State University
System

With additional contributions by Dennis P. Cesari.

37.1 WHY COMPUTERIZATION?

No one could be unaware of the revolution in data processing and automation in facilities management. Today's maintenance managers fall into two groups: computer users and those about to become computer users. If you do not fall into the first group, this chapter may help to ease your inevitable transition.

Still, legitimate questions remain—Why? Does it make sense to go through the time and expense of converting present operations to computer systems? Managers can use the following simple test to measure their readiness for using computers for maintenance management (check one or more boxes):

☐ I need to save money this year on my budget.
☐ I can get a good deal on the hardware.
☐ I'm taking a course—Introduction to Data Processing.
☐ Most of my professional associates use a computer in their operations.
☐ When I hired a new plumber last month, my carpentry supervisor complained that he had the bigger backlog. I need more timely, detailed, or accurate information in order to better manage my plant.
☐ My warehouse could supply the parts to build two complete 1949 Studebaker pickups, but a water pump for one of my late model Fords takes an emergency purchase order. I need tigher control over warehouse stocks.

☐ The paint shop was told to start work on the engineering department remodel job last week, but the carpenters were not done. The functions I manage need to improve communication/coordination among themselves.

☐ My president called yesterday wondering when I would get around to painting his office. Of course I said we would start immediately, but to tell the truth, I did not even know he wanted it painted! I need a way to keep work requests from "falling through the cracks."

If you checked any of the first four boxes, you will be in for disappointment and grief. If your checked any of the last four, you should be thinking of the switch to a computerized maintenance management system. This chapter will explain exactly why.

In the long run many computer applications for maintenance management will pay back handsomely. But for the first year, or more, costs are likely to exceed benefits by a wide margin. Computer system start-up costs, for even modest applications, can run beyond expectation. It is not unusual to exceed budgets for hardware by 20 to 30 percent and software by as much as 100 percent. These cost overruns have five basic reasons:

- Underestimating the size to which your system will eventually grow. Our experience with large and small schools has shown that within two years of installation, most of them either expanded, or needed to expand their system.
- Failing to consider other applications that suddenly become compelling once the system is operating. Adding an inventory control module after the fact to a system not initially designed with that in mind will blow your automation budget.
- Everything taking more time than was estimated.
- Discovering that problems were operator errors caused by a lack of training and understanding. Adequate training for your staff and extensive documentation for your system are as important as the computer hardware itself.
- Finding that the limited software package selected inadequately met actual management needs. Begin your automation project with an absolutely bulletproof, written statement of your needs and expectations.

Managers should consider computer applications for maintenance management because manual and semi-automated solutions cannot handle the complexities of effective facilities management. With the many uncertainties surrounding both revenue (will enrollments flatten or decline?) and costs (what will happen to energy costs this year?), maintenance managers of education facilities need the best decision-making tools available in order to use resources most effectively.

It is certainly possible to establish and operate a manual preventive maintenance system. Several companies produce systems that use specially designed cards in racks or trays with color-coded tabs to indicate schedule due dates. Entering information onto the cards takes no longer than entering the same data into a computer terminal. If there is an error on the card, however, it has to be thrown away or, at best, erased and retyped. On a computer terminal, a few keystrokes correct the error while saving the remaining accurate data. Similarly, retrieving information from a single card may take only a minute or two—not much longer than calling up a single item from the maintenance inventory on the computer. But sorting and compiling records for reports is another story altogether. The computer does chores in seconds that require hours, or even days, for a clerk to complete.

There is a particular difficulty in comparing costs of operating a computer system with a manual or semi-automatic system. With a computer system managers would never be satisfied with the crude, aggregated information available to them from manual systems. Labor cost reports provide an example of this principle. Without a computer system (or even with one that is not programmed to generate the proper reports), labor costs are probably analyzed only as far as the following:

Total payroll costs, week ending 2/13/88	**$27,506.30**
Physical plant administration	1,753.40
Carpenter shop	2,369.75
Plumbing shop	1,650.00
Metal shop	1,308.00
Electric shop	3,215.60
Central plant	4,692.10
Custodial	4,800.60
Grounds	1,408.60
Laborers	1,208.25

With an especially hard-working staff, further distribution might include:

Trades and mechanical	
Preventive maintenance and central plant operation	$ 6,516.70
Alteration and modification projects	4,561.69
Repairs and emergencies	1,955.00
Annual and sick leave	906.06
	$13,939.45

However, no matter how hard your staff works, this limited analysis only becomes available two weeks to a month after the week being analyzed, too late for you to spot a problem and take corrective action.

With a properly designed computer system, a manager could expect all of the above data plus the following:

- Detailed work order costing, current week and year-to-date.
- Work order budget versus actual labor, current week and year-to-date.
- Absentees by shop, name, or badge number; hours in current week and year-to-date.
- Percent of all allowable labor cost by building, current week and year-to-date.
- Lost-time report by craft and type of delay, current week and year-to-date, percentage of total time.

In addition, this detailed information is available immediately, with items outside of your preset parameters already flagged for review.

There is only one reason to convert maintenance management systems to the computer. Computerization enables one to manage better, so much better it is hard to imagine how we operated before. A well-designed computer system allows maintenance managers to make decisions that put them in control of situations that they only reacted to previously.

37.2 ORGANIZING AND SELECTING THE SYSTEM

Start with Applications

Managers sometimes mistakenly establish a staff, negotiate for hardware and software, and then design applications. This is exactly backwards. The kind of system, including the number and caliber of people to operate it, is a function of what you want to accomplish. There are dozens of possible applications for computer systems in maintenance management. Some are stand-alone or single-purpose applications. Others are integrated into an interactive system where transactions flow from program to program, file to file, interrogating and updating records on a continuous basis. The following list illustrates a few of the applications.

Single-purpose application	*Interactive with*
Key control	Intrusion detection/security

Alarm circuit testing	Security monitoring or building management system
Space management	Space and facilities data base
Space inventory	Space and facilities data base
Personnel management	Payroll and labor cost
Work requests	Work control system
Work order estimating	Work control system
Work order scheduling	Work control system
Work order monitoring	Work control system
Work order costing	Work control system
Preventive maintenance scheduling	Planned maintenance and work control system
Deferred maintenance backlog	Programmed maintenance system
Cyclic maintenance work order/projects	Programmed maintenance system
Budget/financial management	Work control system
Stores inventory	Work control system
Bench stock inventory	Work control system

Energy Management Systems

Supervisory controls	Building management system
Load shedding start-stop	Building management system
Flow rate optimization	Building management system

Building Management Systems

Fire alarms and recording	Energy management system
Security detection alarm	Energy management system
Equipment operation control	Energy management system

Since system designs vary, the functions listed above will often be combined or integrated into various modules to make up a system, or they can stand alone as single purpose applications. Beware of the latter. So-called systems made up of a conglomeration of stand-alone applications mean duplication of effort, incompatible methods of storage and analysis, and sometimes contradictory management information. If your needs analysis points to an integrated system combining a number of these functions, incorporate this as a goal in all future planning. Everything need not be implemented at once, in fact most users of these systems would recommend a gradual process. The goal of an integrated system needs to be firmly fixed.

Because the last two major categories, Energy Management and Building Management Systems, are functions of data points and circuitry rather than management information, they have been dominated by large manufacturers of alarms and thermostats. Until recently, the packaging and costs for these systems obscured the primitive logic and decision-making capability of the systems. There are now several cost-effective systems on the market with varying reputations for reliability, product support, operator training, and service. An engineering study by a firm specializing in design and selection of building management and/or energy systems could be the best possible investment before inviting vendors to submit proposals.

Remember a few simple rules when considering computer applications for maintenance management.

- Start with the area most likely to pay back rapidly.
- Don't try to begin with a grand scale, integrated system. Do plan to join logical modules or subsystems later on. In order to do this planning effectively, you will likely need the help and advice of a qualified systems analyst.
- Time spent in the planning process will prove invaluable as you progress through the installation and implementation of your system. Waste a little time now in over planning, rather than a lot of time later trying to correct early errors.
- In all but the simplest single purpose application, the help and advice of a qualified systems analyst will be needed, preferably one with experience in maintenance management.
- No system will do everything you and your staff want. Even a system developed in-house will miss this mark since your wants increase along with your sophistication, much faster than a programmer's ability to write the system.

Managers approach choosing the application with the best payback the same way they make any other management change. Treat it as a problem in work simplification or value analysis. Ask these questions:

- What made me mad today?
- What took too long?
- What was the cause of a complaint?
- What was misunderstood?
- What did we waste?
- What job took too many people?
- What cost too much?
- What was too complicated?
- What job involved too many motions?

The answers should provide a long list of needs. Then have staff, key supervisors, and managers answer the same questions. Their contribution is needed before making a choice. Also quiz a few workers for ideas and suggestions. Ask them to visualize a genie offering them three wishes to change anything about their work environment that would benefit the organization as well. They often come forward with valuable observations and insight.

Software Options

After choosing an application for investigation (and you may start with a dozen), you must choose between purchasing commercially available software, or developing the software in-house.

Commercially Available Software   You may want to search for already-developed software. Some programmers disparagingly refer to it as "canned" software. The term should not bother you. It may be much better to eat canned food than to go hungry or pay too much for fast food. You should look for commercially available software because custom-developed software may cost ten to fifty times as much. Be realistic. The first year, whatever you spend on hardware, you are likely to spend an equal amount for software. If you insist on custom development, the cost can be much greater. In examining existing software, there will probably be desirable features that are not available. This reflects the trade-offs made whenever we shop for a house, an automobile, or select a vendor for cleaning materials.

There are several ways to analyze canned software. One is to have the vendor demonstrate it. This is usually slick and impressive—as long as you stay with the demonstration setup. In simulating your situation you may be able to "crash" the system. If so, you have made an important discovery. Look further. You may be able to envision how the application could be changed to fit the department's requirements and circumstances and the difficulties that might be encountered. But in most cases it is not realistic to modify commercially available software. Depending upon the system and on your budget, some changes are realistic if the software is "modifiable"; but be aware that custom modifications are expensive and may not be supported in future releases of the software.[1]

Another way to analyze a commercial software package is to compare it with a list of required and desirable capabilities or features developed from your needs analysis. Be careful of defining required features. Be sure they really are *required*. You do not want to unnecessarily eliminate an otherwise acceptable system because of an ill-perceived "requirement."

Documentation

The ideal software package would be designed by geniuses to be run by idiots. After looking at the documentation—written instructions for using the program—you might think it is the other way around. Examining documentation is an inexpensive way to estimate the level of difficulty a software package might present. "Brochures will not do; you need the manual that describes the program's capabilities and operating procedures in detail. Reading the manual is important on two counts: it gives you a good idea of the program's true capabilities, and it tells you what level of documentation your operators will have to cope with, should they be called on to use these programs."[2]

Writing for a special computers section of the May 1982 *AirCal Magazine*, Umberto Tosi and Dina Moro Sanchez offered the following advice: A once-over of a computer product's documentation will shed light on three main considerations crucial to deciding if that product is right for you.

- It can tell you specifically just what the equipment or program can and cannot do.
- It can give you an idea of how easy or difficult it is to perform the machine's or program's operation.
- The quality of the documentation itself, especially its accessibility, will tell you if you will be able to rely on it to solve problems as they arise, refer to it on a variety of operations, and/or use it to train employees and coworkers.

Good documentation has the following characteristics:

- A concise, two- or three-page overview of what the system can do.
- A set of instructions, written in plain English, that show the user how to set up and operate the machine or program in a step-by-step manner and begin with the simple and move to the complex.
- A reference section for routines and functions, rather than a list of technical specifications, and good documentation including separate 'cheat sheets' or laminated cards for quick reference to the most commonly used commands and functions.
- A telephone number for technical assistance, toll-free in the best cases.[3]

In-House Development of Software

If none of the commercially available software packages you examine meet your needs, you may want to develop the software in-house. As compared to canned software, "homegrown" software may be better because the software meets more needs; there is a high level of satisfaction with the software because you are allowed input into the development; the development process will help to streamline or combine operations and make them more efficient; and it is possible to grow into an application and build as you go. However, the cost of homegrown software is far greater than that of purchased software, and getting started takes longer.

When considering developing software in-house, you must be able to devote money, people, and hardware to the effort. You must give the computer programming staff your full support. You must plan for the extended time-frame the development will take. Since you developed the software in-house because the available commercially-developed software did not meet expectations, the homegrown system must meet more user expectations, otherwise it will be viewed as a failure. You must be prepared to manage the system and update as necessary.

37.3 PRELIMINARIES TO SYSTEM SELECTION

Only after developing a list of available software packages that appear to meet the requirements of the highest priority applications, should you consider hardware. Ideally, defining the application would lead to selection of available software. Optimum software selection would dictate the range of possible hardware.

In practical terms, however, there are other considerations. Some institutions have central data processing departments and dedicated systems with certain availability criteria. Further, institutional policy may give the data processing department veto power over all new computer applications. Fundamental differences exist between operating as a remote terminal or batch-process user from a central mainframe versus using a stand-alone or dedicated small computer.

Note the working definitions that follow. Understanding the jargon, lingo, or terminology is vital to the chapter's remaining discussion.

A Short Glossary

Batch Processing—This method of processing accumulates data entry in groups or batches (such as decks of punch cards or a disk file) and processing is done at a later, scheduled time.

Central Processing Unit (CPU)—A CPU contains the electronic logic that actually receives individual instructions and causes the events specified by the instructions to occur.[4] The CPU is connected to the memory and an external interface.

Computer or Computer System—The computer is "a box containing a lot of electronics; on its own it is useless. The computer without a computer system is equivalent to an engine without an automobile. And the power of the computer determines the amount of computing a system can do."[5] A computer system contains a central processing unit (CPU); an information storage unit (tape or disk); and Input/Output (I/O) devices such as a keyboard, a CRT display screen or monitor, and a printer.

CPU Memory—Memory is information stored in an electronically coded fashion. Two types of memory are found in computers: read/write memory or random access memory (RAM), which is lost when power is turned off; and read only memory (ROM), which is not lost when power is turned off. In some personal computers, ROM contains a few important programs that bring the computer to life when the power is switched on. The most important one is called the bootstrap program, because the computer "pulls itself up by its own bootstraps." Computer experts say the program "boots" the operating system.

CRT Terminal—A CRT monitor and keyboard are combined in one unit.

Data Base—A data base is a repository of stored information organized in such a way that data is easily retrieved. The term is generally associated with an organized base of data that is stored within a computer and usable by multiple applications. An everyday example of a non-computer data base is the telephone directory.[6]

Field—In a data base management system (DBMS), a field contains an item of information. It corresponds to the column of a paper data base. A field description consists of three parts: the field name or title; the field type (whether character, numeric, or logical), which tells the kind of data that may be stored in a field; and the field width (number of spaces needed in the field to contain the data).

File—A file is a collection of information or records such as a data base or a command file organized and stored for a specific purpose.

Keyboard—A keyboard is "similar to a typewriter keyboard. It is used to 'talk' to a computer."[7] For data entry, a numeric (ten-key) pad is a desirable feature in addition to the typewriter keyboard. Other special keys peculiar to computer applications such as control, function keys, and cursor control/directional keys are generally part of the keyboard.

Mainframe—A mainframe is a large data processing system operated at a central location for many users who submit jobs for batch-processing or enter data and control programs on-line from remote terminals. "In general, mainframe computers are the largest and most powerful machines, minicomputers are intermediate, and microcomputers are the smallest. In reality there is a lot of overlap among products."[8]

Mass Storage Memory—Peripheral storage devices such as disk drives and tape drives provide a place to store programs or data created in the random access memory.[9] This way information is not lost when the power is off and more than the internal memory capability may be used. Without mass storage memory, a computer is little more than a toy, since this is where files and records that are routinely accessed and updated reside.

Microprocessor—The microprocessor is the CPU of a microcomputer or computer-on-a-chip. It uses Large Scale Integrated (LSI) circuits or Very Large Scale Integrated (VLSI) circuits. A single 64K chip may be no larger than your thumbnail, although the most common ones are about two inches (fifty-one millimeters) long.

Minicomputer—This term is rapidly losing its significance. Minicomputers were once scaled-down mainframes designed for smaller applications, not as powerful or fast as mainframes but useful for multi-terminal, multi-task use. The average minicomputer system costs $25,000 to $100,000, contrasted with microcomputer systems that cost $1,500 to $20,000. "There are some minicomputer manufacturers whose products cost two or three times as much as a microcomputer without being any better. They still manage to sell, based on slick advertising and a history of satisfied customers. But the successful and growing minicomputer manufacturers charge more because they offer more."[10]

Multi-user and Multi-tasking—"Multi-tasking computer systems perform a number of chores concurrently. Other names that refer to this capability include multi-user, time-sharing, time-slicing, multi-programming and multi-terminal." Multi-tasking, in its simplest form, requires the CPU to perform a second job while it waits to continue processing a first job. This is the time in which the operator, keyboard, and input/output device are creating and capturing another character for the CPU to process. "The computer appears to perform two things simultaneously since the tasks outlined above are measured in thousandths or millionths of a second."[11]

Networking—Hardware and software are designed to connect individual computers to a common data base, such as TELENET, the SOURCE, and others, or to one another, as in a Local Area Network (LAN).

On-Line Processing—To process information on-line, a system senses and responds to changes as they occur, generally from a keyboard or terminal. The term applies to systems in which information is introduced and processed immediately.[12]

Operating System—An operating system is an "integrated collection of service routines for supervising the sequencing of programs by a computer. Operating systems may perform debugging, input/output, accounting, compilation, and storage assignment tasks."[13] Many operating systems are "dedicated," which means they work only on one manufacturer's computer, while others are designed to fit any computer using the same or similar CPU. There are almost always differences from one manufacturer to another that require modifications to applications programs.

Peripherals—Peripherals are devices used with the computer such as a printer and disk drives. Computers lacking these devices can do little more than calculate or play simple games.[14]

Programming Language—The programming language is a set of conventions by which programmers tell the computer how to make programs work. Examples of commonly used languages include COBOL, FORTRAN, BASIC, and 'C.'

Record—A group of one or more words containing related information about a common subject creates a record. One or more records create a file.[15]

Report—A report consists of logically arranged and formatted information useful to managers. A report may be as simple as a list or as complex as a general ledger.

Software—Computer programs, or the instructions to the machines, are called software as contrasted with the components of a computer system, referred to as hardware. Software is broadly divided into two classes: system software and applications programs. System software generally includes programs that make the components of the computer system act as a system. Applications programs make the computer, acting as a system, perform a particular function for you.[16]

Institutional Policies and Considerations

In a perfect world, the user department (physical plant in this case) would choose the maintenance management software best suited to its need, budget, and expertise; they would then install and operate it on the computer that best fit it. In this world all software will operate properly on all hardware and the user selects each on its own merit. In our would, however, there are trade-offs that we must consider. Using a data processing department's mainframe computer may limit you to a narrow selection of software. However, more and more software companies are learning to offer their product in versions to operate on a variety of computer hardware.

In the decision-making process, managers should examine the trade-offs between using a central data processing department's mainframe versus operating a stand-alone system. Institutional policy may already dictate the method used.

Data Processing Department Mainframe

Pros

1. Should have powerful, fast equipment.

2. Staff is available to manage the facility, set priorities, deal with hardware and software maintenance people, handle system upgrades, and so on.

3. DP programming staff should be available to custom fit software to your needs, support your usage by debugging, and make changes as needed.

4. DP manager has to make all the tough decisions about allocating scarce resources of time, storage capacity, and programming support.

Cons

1. Equipment may be fast, but not readily available to administrative departments. You may be relegated to batch operation only, or, if using a terminal on-line, you may find instructional and other uses occupy the equipment all day. Fast internal processing means nothing if you do not have access to it for your work.

2. DP staff may see physical plant jobs as a nuisance and give your work low priority.

3. DP staff may choose not to support your software usage.

4. DP manager is responsible to the entire institution, not just facilities. Priorities may not suit your needs.

Facilities Department Stand-Alone System

Pros

1. No question exists about resource allocation—all goes to physical plant.

Cons

1. Several potential applications in maintenance may compete for time, disk storage space, software purchase, or development budget. Now the manager must become his or her own DP manager and make tough decisions about resource allocation.

2. The department will be able to use bright student assistants to do lots of programming inexpensively.

2. Bright student assistants graduate or leave for greener pastures. Unless they document extremely well as they program, the department may be stuck with software that cannot be used or modified, or is unreliable due to lack of testing.

3. Facilities managers can add to, upgrade, or change hardware and software when budget justification exists.

3. This may or may not be true, depending upon the institution's procurement and control regulations. New hardware or software procurement may require feasibility studies and various levels of approvals.

Stand-alone systems are usually not going to be supported by the institution's central data processing department. They simply cannot afford it. This means that physical plant must have a data processing person of its own or use only well-written and well-documented, user-friendly software. Someone must be responsible for managing the in-house computer and its resources: CPU time, disk storage space, software and peripherals budget, maintenance agreements, and warranties. Managers need sound advice on prospective applications in order to evaluate the costs and benefits and then set priorities.

There are drawbacks to investing heavily in one specialist. This person may soon learn enough to be able to sell his or her capabilities to the highest bidder. An alternative may be to have on retainer a systems analyst. He or she would be available on fairly short notice, and would be knowledgeable of the department's hardware, system capabilities, software (both system and applications), and maintenance needs.

General Purpose Software

Before choosing a particular computer system, investigate what general purpose software runs on the vendor's system. Adam Osborne calls it intermediate software. General purpose software may be more important than the special applications such as preventive maintenance or inventory control, which may be your highest priorities. There are three major innovations, developed in recent years, that fit into this group: word processing software, data base management systems, and electronic spreadsheets.

These programs are invaluable. Once mastered, they open the door for many applications that individuals—non-data-processing managers—can tailor to suit exact needs. There are many variations of each of these innovations.

Word Processing   First, consider the merits of word processing. If budget restrictions allow for only one software package, this is it. We have experienced the change a good word processing software package makes in an office. In an engineering firm where two secretaries could not keep up with correspondence, proposals, and reports, one operator who has mastered word processing was able to more than equal the previous work output. There are many word processing packages on the market. For personal or single-user small computers, the most popular are designed to run on the DOS operating systems. MultiMate, Word Perfect, Xywrite, and Word Star are four examples. In his book *Introduction to Word Star*, Arthur Naiman explains what word processing can do for the user:

> Basically, a word processor does what a typewriter does, only better. The main difference between them is that on a word processor, what you write is stored as electronic (or magnetic) impulses, instead of as marks on paper. Word processors can do this because they're computers that have been programmed to let you type in text, edit it, and have it printed out.
>
> You type on a word processor just like on a typewriter, but instead of the text appearing on a piece of paper, you see it on a screen—a CRT or cathode ray tube similar to the one on your television set. The text only shows up on paper when you order a printout (also called a hard copy). It doesn't matter when, or how often, you make a printout of the text. This gives you the freedom to make whatever changes are necessary, without having to worry about all the retyping that such changes would normally involve.
>
> A word processor also lets you:
>
> — Change a word (or an entire phrase) everywhere it occurs in a manuscript, in a matter of seconds;
> — Move whole sections of text around from one place to another (and then move them back again if you want);
> — Find the next (or last) occurrence of any word or phrase; and
> — Store blocks of text and print them out in various combinations.

> When you go to print out your text, you have available several effects you can't get (or can't get easily) with a typewriter. Some examples are boldface, automatically centered lines, justified right margins, automatic page numbering, automatically indented blocks of text, and automatic paging.[17]

Applications of word processing to maintenance management include specifications for projects especially where standard language, or boiler plates, must be merged with special conditions; personnel lists and rosters; and correspondence of all kinds. Word processing is particularly useful in drafting agreements where many changes must be made before the final text is approved—as in labor negotiations.

If word processing will be used in a multi-terminal environment, select a word processor that works on the operating systems available. A recent development in word processing is desktop publishing. Desktop publishing software runs on microcomputers and was made popular by Apple, Inc. Its popularity was also spurred by the introduction of inexpensive laser printers. These packages allow the user to mix text and graphics on the same page and are used to design forms, newsletters, and advertisements.

Data Base Management System   The second type of generative software to research is a data base management system (DBMS). Just as there are many word processing systems, there are many data base managers. Availability for different operating systems, languages, and hardware vary, but several run on the ubiquitous DOS. Non-computerized data base management systems include the telephone directory, an auto parts store, and the college or university library. The telephone directory provides a great deal of information (address, phone number) accessed by only one key—NAME. A more sophisticated directory is the city criss-cross directory in which residents can be found by address as well as by name. The telephone company can also search their data base by telephone number and find the name of the subscriber.

In an auto parts store, a customer tells the clerk that he needs a master cylinder for a 1973 Volkswagen Beetle. The clerk looks up the part in the set of catalogs that provide an identifying part number, a bin location for the part in stock, and a price. The clerk, catalogs, price lists, and storage bins correspond to a data base management system. The actual parts on hand correspond to each item of information in the data base.

In some specialized libraries one is not allowed access to the stacks where the books are kept. Instead users must search through the card catalog and various indexes for the information they want. The user then writes the code numbers of materials on a slip of paper and gives it to the librarian who in turn sends a "gnome" to the stacks. The gnome retrieves the book or periodical. In this case the book is the data item and the card catalogs, indexes, librarian, gnome, and stacks correspond to the data base management system.

The above illustrations fall short of describing the power of a well-designed DBMS. Far from retrieving single items of information, the DBMS can be sorted and manipulated to produce reports of all types. In an inventory system, for example, the reports might include:

- A catalog of all line items including quantity available, average unit price, and descriptive information.
- A list of inventory that has not moved (0 issues) in the past six months.
- A list in descending order of fastest-moving inventory items.
- Calculation of total inventory value and the number of "turns" for past year.
- A buy-list for items reaching minimum quantity level, with economic order quantity of each.

Small businesses use data base management systems for such operational areas as payroll and accounting, standard tax reporting, inventory management, flooring charges, mailing lists, daily cash register tally, and transaction recording. Maintenance and plant engineering organizations use DBMS software for tracking all kinds of information including emission logs, health and safety records, vendor performance records, and hazardous waste manifests.[18]

Electronic Spreadsheet   The third category of generative or intermediate software worth investigating is the electronic spreadsheet. An electronic spreadsheet is nothing more than an array or matrix of rows and columns for repetitive calculations. Its name implies its primary use: as an electronic version of the accountant's columnar pad. The beauty of its use is in asking "what if" questions for simulation purposes.

For example, a pro-forma statement projecting profit/loss for a period of time can be created for a given set of conditions. Any number of variables or relationships may be changed and the program recalculates the results instantly. The entire spreadsheet may be stored in memory, printed out on hard copy, or only variables without values may be saved for future use. The applications for an electronic spreadsheet are limited only by the user's imagination.

Applications in maintenance include calculation of staffing requirements for custodial, grounds, or equipment maintenance. Once operational tasks are identified and time standards established, quantities and frequencies may be manipulated to determine effects on staffing requirements. Budget planning may be the most used application in maintenance. A spreadsheet can be used to see the consequences of budget reductions or unfunded replacement reserves.

System Requirements/Specifications

Whether the hardware purchased is a packaged system or components and whether the software is canned or custom designed, someone must prepare a set of specifications in order to know what is needed and how to buy it. When computer hardware cost $100,000 to $500,000 and more, almost all software was custom designed. Paying a consultant $10,000 to $30,000 for a specification was easily justified. When an entire system—hardware and software—costs $25,000 to $100,000, such a specification is not justifiable; but there must be one. The answer is to write your own specification.

A specification is a description of the functions the system should perform. In writing a function definition, rely heavily on the previously written needs analysis. Later you may decide to have some tasks performed manually as they are now. A function definition should include these four parts:

- An operations summary.
- A description of information the computer is to store (files).
- A description of hardware size, power, and storage requirements.
- A description of information that managers want the computer to generate (reports).

The Operations Summary   Define all the functions you expect the computer to handle. The definition should be complete in scope, but not in detail. The detail, if needed, can follow later. Complex functions should be represented by using block diagrams that show the interaction (if any) between different operations.

The next step is to determine what information you want the system to keep for each function, e.g., detailed data on work orders kept readily accessible for two years. Estimate the size of that block of information in records. The following sample would be appropriate to a medium size facilities organization. It could expand or contract radically for larger or smaller organizations.

Operation 1: Work Order Tracking	*No. of Records*
Open work orders	1,000
Closed work order (two-year history)	20,000

Employees	150
Shops	25

Operation 2: Stores Inventory

Inventory line items	10,000
Open requisitions	100
Closed requisitions (two-year history)	2,000

Operation 3: Preventive Maintenance Scheduling

Equipment inventory	3,000
Open work orders	(See above)

Now specify what data each record is to maintain. Again, this should be driven by your needs analysis. Do you want a detailed record of corrective work performed? How about recording the name of the person submitting a work request? These considerations will help a prospective vendor or your data processing staff decide how much data storage you will require.

Data Input   For complex functions describe the information that must be input to each function. Write a short description of each input operation. Estimate total characters input for each operation and divide by average typing speed to estimate the minimum time required to input information for each entry time. Some items may require input monthly (accounts receivable), some weekly (such as payroll), and some semi-monthly (such as accounts payable) if bills are paid twice each month. How many individuals will perform your data input operations? Could they realistically share a CRT terminal without disrupting their work? (Probably not.) From these estimates, you can construct a calendar of input time required.

Data Output   Write a brief, narrative description of each report you want the computer to generate. Estimate the number of printed pages each report represents and how often you want the report generated. List all reports to be printed, the number of pages per report, and the frequency to be printed. Summarize the output demands to be made of the computer. This will be helpful in selecting the system. How many individuals need access to the informaiton that will be stored on your coputer system? Remember that the biggest advantages of computerizing your department will flow from the system's ability to quickly and widely disseminate accurate information. Will these individuals need a terminal of their own? A terminal shared with others? Or will copies of reports suffice for them?

General Steps for Computerization

The steps to follow in selecting a computer system today do not differ from those described in 1970 by Edmund J. Wells, management advisory services manager for Haskins & Sells. Wells outlined these steps in the process of mechanizing the small office:

1. Determination of objectives and advantages.
2. Definition of requirements.
3. System design, evaluation of alternatives.
4. Design implementation.
5. Conversion.
6. Continuing operations.

According to Wells, participants in this process should include top management (represented by a results-oriented project head), middle management (represented by a project coordinator), office staff, a consultant, and the manufacturer's representative.

The consultant, or systems analyst, would produce much of the work needed for steps two and three. This includes help writing the entire function definition described above. Few managers are able to develop this information without professional guidance. In describing step three Wells wrote:

> A preliminary evaluation will normally allow the system approach to be determined and the vendor list to be narrowed to four or less—preferably less. The proposal request should encourage creative system design by the vendors. Where adequate, proven package systems should be selected in preference to custom systems.[19]

37.4 SPECIFIC MAINTENANCE MANAGEMENT APPLICATIONS

Labor Reports

One of the real tragedies of the past twenty years has been the selection of payroll as one of the first uses of the computer. Because of the highly repetitive transactions and fairly simple logic, it seemed a natural. Unfortunately, many of these early systems were designed to produce little more than payroll and the mandatory reports required by the Internal Revenue Service. Thought was not given to the other uses of the same data, such as personnel information and labor cost (a component of job or work order costing). Consequently, we remain plagued by payroll systems that furnish no real management reports.

Payroll, personnel, and labor cost reporting systems share many of the same data elements. This has led to the popularity of using data base management systems for these functions:

Payroll System	Personnel System	Labor Cost System
Employee name	Employee name	
Employee number	Employee number	Employee number
Employee rate gross pay	Employee rate gross pay	Employee rate gross pay
Employee dependents	Employee dependents	
Withholding data		
Employee net pay		
Employee hours worked	Employee hours worked	Employee hours worked
Leave hours earned	Leave hours earned	
Leave hours taken	Leave hours taken	Leave hours taken
		Hours worked on job

While this list is not complete, it illustrates the point that, with planning, a system can provide one data base that satisfies the needs of several different systems serving different management functions.

Definition and Design

In order to calculate and establish the proper data base requirements, we must begin with the desired reports. From report format and content, we can establish the data element listing, which—when defined—becomes the data element dictionary.

Before designing report layouts, think about the uses of the reports for managers. What we might want to know includes:

- Personnel complement—how many people by classification do we have on the payroll?

- Active or inactive status—for a specified period were any employees on disability, medical workers compensation leave, military leave, or any other leave of absence of a long-term nature?
- Short-term paid leave or unpaid absence—how many people of which classification and pay rate were on annual leave, sick leave, personal holiday, or other short-term nonworking time, paid or unpaid?
- Net work time to be accounted for. By classification, how many hours were charged to actual work time?
- Does absenteeism plus actual work time account for all hours represented by total personnel complement in the pay period? If not, what is required to reconcile the difference?
- Where were actual work hours used? Progress and cost monitoring required detail showing distribution of hours and cost compared to work orders (by number), zone or building, craft or shop, type of work (preventive maintenance, repair, operation, project), and if any hours charged to accounts for which reimbursement is forthcoming.

The first three items might be combined in a single listing or generated in separate summary reports. The format should be determined by the use for the information. Similarly, the last three items could be presented as individual, detailed listings or arranged as portions of a management summary. The best way to develop layouts is to take previously developed information and arrange it in various ways. Then use the configuration that presents the information managers need in the most readable form. Do not accept a report format that is unwieldly, hard to understand, and does not summarize data in a concise manner. If a manager has to read through pages of printouts with a calculator in hand to summarize the real data, valuable management time is lost.

Once the format and data elements are agreed upon, the data elements list and data element dictionary should be constructed. The length and quantity of records are a matter of arithmetic, but true file size and storage requirements are a function of the operating system. Your systems analyst will determine the storage space required in consultation with the data processing staff or prospective vendors.

Inventory Control

As in preventive maintenance, the capabilities and complexities of inventory systems vary. At the most basic, an inventory system classifies stock and allows for perpetual updating of quantity on hand by a simple formula:

Beginning Inventory
+ Acquisitions
− Issues
+ Turn-ins (items returned unused to stock)
= Ending Inventory

If a dollar value, as well as description and quantity, is assigned to each class of item, then inventory valuation may be kept current as well. LIFO (last in/first out), FIFO (first in/first out), and moving average are popular costing methods.

It is important to know what is on hand, and how it is moving (inventory "turns"). How close to a predetermined optimum level present quantities are also becomes significant. A more comprehensive system can calculate economic order quantities, allow you to "reserve" stock on hand for an upcoming job, list vendor sources for stock needing replenishment, write purchase orders (even issue sight drafts), and cost out issued quantities to work orders.

Work Order Control

Computerized lists of active work orders are great time savers even in their simplest form. Because work orders are written to be performed (completed), the very nature of the record keeping is dynamic. This is especially true when multiple crafts are involved and material must be processed before scheduling work. Large work orders may remain active or open for many weeks or months. Updating the status alone requires a great deal of retyping of lists. Therefore, a simple system should contain at least the following data:

- A log of when a work request was received, the order number assigned, date approved, and date sent to shop(s) for completion.
- Estimated value in labor and materials, by craft.
- List of work orders completed during a given period.
- List of work orders not completed or open.
- Completed labor cost data, by craft and materials.
  A more comprehensive system interacts with payroll and inventory stems to produce these reports:
- Available staffing by shop for future weeks.
- Sequencing of operations among crafts on larger jobs.
- Backlog of work orders not in process, reported by craft.
- Priorities currently assigned each work order.
- Outage data for each work order.

- Procurement status on materials not in stock of each work order.
- Cost data in variety of ways for management purposes.

The task is large, but manageable. The rewards are great, but not without cost. You can successfully computerize your department with careful planning, limited outside help, realistic expectations, and a reasonable budget.

NOTES

1. Jack Colby, Chris Sparks, and Tom Droege, "Purchasing Software versus In-House Development," Panel Discussion, APPA Information Management Workshop (Duke University, October 1988).
2. Adam Osborne with Steven Cook, *Business System Buyer's Guide* (Berkeley, California: Osborne/McGraw-Hill, 1981), p. 80.
3. *Ibid.*, p. 38.
4. *Ibid.*, p. 40.
5. *Ibid.*, p. 38.
6. Robert A. Byers, *Everyman's Database Primer* (Culver City, California: Osborne/McGraw-Hill, 1981), p. 272.
7. *Ibid.*, p. 278.
8. Osborne with Cook, *Business System Buyer's Guide*, p. 45.
9. Byers, *Everyman's Database Primer*, p. 278.
10. Osborne with Cook, *Business System Buyer's Guide*, pp. 90-91.
11. Thom Hogan, *Osborne CP/M User Guide* (Berkeley, California: Osborne/McGraw-Hill, 1981), p. 190.
12. Harold Sackman, *Computers, System Science and Evolving Society* (New York: John Wiley & Sons, 1967), p. 614.
13. *Ibid.*
14. Byers, *Everyman's Database Primer*, p. 279.
15. North Carolina State University/Center for Urban Affairs and Community Services, *Computer Technology for Physical Plant Operations* (Raleigh, North Carolina: Center for Urban Affairs, 1983), p. 53.
16. Osborne with Cook, *Business System Buyer's Guide*, p. 42.
17. Arthur Naiman, *Introduction to WordStar* (Berkeley, California: SYBEX, 1982), pp. 1-3.
18. "Computers: Extending the Boundaries of Plant Engineering," *Plant Engineering*, Vol. 37, February 3, 1983, p. 49.
19. Edmund J. Wells, "Mechanizing the Small Office," *Management Services*, September-October 1970, pp. 17-21.

ADDITIONAL RESOURCES

A Practical Guide to Word Processing and Office Management Systems. Maynard, Massachusetts: Digital Equipment Corporation, 1982.

Hawkey, Earl W. and Joseph Kleinpeter. *Computerized Management of Physical Plant Services.* Washington: APPA, 1983.

Hildebrand, James K. *Maintenance Turns to the Computer.* York, Pennsylvania: Maple Press Co., 1972.

Software Dictionary. Minneapolis, Minnesota: Honeywell Corporation, 1980.

CHAPTER 38

Preventive Maintenance

Michael J. Dwyer Jr.
Executive Director of Campus Operations
University of Arkansas for Medical Sciences

38.1 INTRODUCTION

The words preventive maintenance are being used by engineers and plant directors across the United States. Preventive maintenance in itself is not a new concept and it has been around in manufacturing plants for years. The United States Air Force became an early champion of a rigorous preventive maintenance program when it started placing intercontinental ballistic missiles in silos around the countryside. Many of these silos were well over 100 miles from their support base over rugged terrain that was sometimes impassable during periods of adverse weather. It became apparent to the planners that the old maintenance concept—fixing something when it broke—could not keep the missiles force on alert. Only with a preventive maintenance program, coupled with a mandatory time change or replacement program, could the necessary requirements be met.

As work forces become smaller and costs continue to increase, each department must operate in the most efficient and economical manner possible. Waiting for something to break and attempting to fix it— sometimes in a makeshift manner—is certainly not an acceptable means of operation. Although a certain amount of breakdowns cannot be avoided, a preventive maintenance program will reduce these breakdowns to a minimum.

Some believe that only larger institutions need, or can afford, a preventive maintenance program. Regardless of the square footage or budget, a preventive maintenance program can be a definite benefit to any type or size educational facility. The key is to fit the program to the needs of the institution.

Definition

The term preventive maintenance is not new, although it may be to some college and university administrators. General agreement can usually be reached on what constitutes the elements of a preventive maintenance program; however, there are many definitions of what the program is. Preventive maintenance is defined here as a program in which wear, tear, and change are anticipated and continuous corrective actions are taken to ensure peak efficiency and minimize deterioration. It involves a planned and controlled program of systematic inspection, adjustment, lubrication, replacement of components, as well as performance testing and analysis.

In some cases, the term planned maintenance is synonymous with preventive maintenance, but it may also include such repetitious work as general lamp replacement and overhaul procedures. A worker scheduled to do planned maintenance knows the specific maintenance function to be performed upon leaving the shop, whereas a preventive maintenance worker only performs an inspection and does not actually do any maintenance work unless minor repairs are indicated or are part of the preventive maintenance tasks. Preventive maintenance includes cleaning, adjustments, lubrication, minor repairs, and parts replacement. All are performed on scheduled frequencies (weekly, monthly, quarterly, semiannually, or annually) in accordance with written maintenance instructions.

Philosophy and Role of Preventive Maintenance

Preventive maintenance (PM) is a state of mind. For a preventive maintenance program to be effective, it must be fully understood and wholeheartedly supported from top management on down through the work force. If the individuals performing the work do not understand and believe in the program, it will not be successful. Historically, when workloads become heavy, it is the preventive maintenance program that is first cut back. Over time this treatment will lead to the elimination of any effective program.

When considering a PM program, questions often asked are: What percentage of the labor force should be used in the preventive maintenance program? How many workhours will it take? How many dollars should be spent in carrying out a preventive maintenance program? The best answer is: whatever is enough. Once managers determine what equipment to place in the program and the type of inspection to perform, the cost in dollars and workhours can be calculated. Although at first glance the requirements may seem excessive, the plant director must balance program requirements with available resources in order to implement the desired program.

Benefits and Objectives

A successful preventive maintenance program produces many benefits, almost all of which are some type of cost savings. One of the primary objectives of a PM program is the reduction in downtime of critical systems and equipment. Obviously, some downtime is unavoidable, even in the performance of preventive maintenance tasks themselves. It is the unscheduled downtime that causes major problems, and which can be reduced to a bare minimum. A good preventive maintenance program extends the life of the facilities and equipment. It also improves equipment reliability. Preventive maintenance will ensure that equipment is operating properly (at the right speed and temperature), which will reduce energy consumption and, in some cases, improve safety by identifying and quickly correcting unsafe conditions. Building preventive maintenance will also improve the overall appearance of the facilities, thus improving the image of the institution and the physical plant department, since unscheduled breakdowns are held to a minimum.

Economics of PM

The cost of scheduled repairs is significantly less than the cost associated with major breakdowns. As illustrated in Figure 38-1, the initial cost to implement a preventive maintenance program will be more than current maintenance costs. Over time, as the effects of the preventive maintenance program are realized, there will be a cost savings. Because more work is performed on a scheduled basis, there will be less overtime and greater maintenance labor productivity. This means a reduction in staff can be realized even though the preventive maintenance program is an addition to current workloads. Depending on the size of the facility and the type of maintenance performed, outside contract maintenance and repairs should also decline as a result of the preventive maintenance program.

The improved system reliability will extend equipment life, thus protecting the capital assets of the college or university. This, in turn, will reduce capital outlays since equipment will be replaced less frequently. Reduced energy consumption will also affect overall costs. Finally, better management control of operating costs will be achieved since the majority of work will be performed on a scheduled basis and panic budgeting will be eliminated. The objectives of a preventive maintenance program

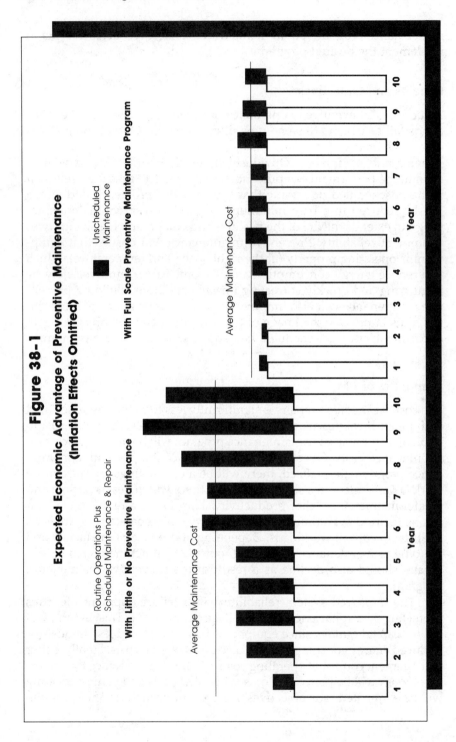

Figure 38-1

Expected Economic Advantage of Preventive Maintenance
(Inflation Effects Omitted)

will minimize equipment and system breakdowns and reduce total maintenance cost.

Basic Criteria for a PM Program

All preventive maintenance programs contain the same basic elements and develop in three basic phases: planning, implementation, and operational. The planning phase is by far the most important phase and extremely time consuming. If individuals are available on a part-time basis, it may take as long as a year to complete the planning phase. Even if someone is assigned full-time, it will take several months to complete all the steps required. During this phase a complete equipment inventory is established, the type and frequency of inspections are determined, a yearly schedule is developed, and the personnel are selected to perform the tasks.

The shorter implementation phase consists primarily of preparing and distributing work orders and the associated daily and weekly scheduling of work. The full magnitude of the preventive maintenance program as determined during planning should not be implemented at one time. This will be discussed in greater detail below.

The third phase is a continuing phase of preventive maintenance tasks. Important elements within this operational phase that must be closely monitored include an assessment of appropriate PM tasks, as well as proper frequency. Equipment grows old, uses change, and techniques vary. An effective preventive maintenance program is not static, but needs regular review and updating in order to remain viable and effective.

38.2 BASIC ELEMENTS OF A PM PROGRAM

The fundamental elements of a preventive maintenance program are preventive maintenance instructions, historical equipment records, feedback data, scheduling, and control.

Preventive Maintenance Instructions

Preventive maintenance instructions (PMIs) are those instructions or directions indicating specific tasks for the mechanic to perform on a given piece of equipment. These instructions must be specific enough to indicate what the mechanic should do or look for, and simple enough to be placed on a 5 x 8 inch card that the mechanic can carry to the job site (Figure 38-2). The frequency of inspections must be included in the instructions so the mechanic will know which particular tasks to perform on any given inspection.

Historical Equipment Master File

The historical equipment master file should be the central reference for all equipment for which physical plant is responsible. Not only should it contain identifying data for each major piece of equipment and auxiliary items, but it should also include desired operating characteristics (Figure 38-3). The master file indicated when preventive maintenance was performed, any malfunction discovered, and the corrective action taken. Parts replacement must also be recorded in the master file in order to maintain a complete history of each item. This history helps determine costs and establish supply inventory levels.

Feedback Data

A preventive maintenance program is incomplete without a positive method for evaluating the results of the program. The feedback includes workhour and material requirements to maintain the program, as well as an evaluation of the program's effect on emergency calls, equipment breakdowns and replacement, and overall improved maintenance scheduling and productivity.

There will always be equipment deterioration with subsequent breakdown or failure, as well as a certain number of breakdowns due to equipment defects. Since a preventive maintenance program will never eliminate this type of failure, there must be a distinction drawn between preventable and nonpreventable breakdowns. Analysis of the cause of equipment failure will reveal whether it was unavoidable or not. Some 40 percent of all equipment failure is due to weak components that probably could not be identified prior to the failure. The PM program is aimed at the other 60 percent that can be controlled.

Feedback may be useful in developing design requirements for new equipment. Design criteria may require the equipment to be more accessible for preventive maintenance tasks, or eliminate and/or improve parts that require excessive maintenance or have a high rate of failure. In addition, management will always ask what savings have been realized as a result of the preventive maintenance program. With feedback data these questions can be answered easily.

Scheduling

Implementing a preventive maintenance schedule into an already existing work schedule may require major adjustments in thinking and

Figure 38-2

Preventive Maintenance Instructions

Equipment Name: _____ **Card No:** ____

Frequency of Inspection_____

Shops & number of personnel required _____

STEPS	M	Q	S	Y	TIME

Tools/Materials required:

Figure 38-3

Maintenance Record—Historical File

MAINTENANCE RECORD

ITEM:

SHOP: LOCATION:

EQUIPMENT		ELECTRICAL EQUIPMENT	
Name		Equipment	
Serial No.		Make	
Machine No.		Serial No.	
Date Installed		Model No.	
Bearing No.		Type Frame	
Bearing No.		Voltage	
Seals No.		Phase	
Model		Amperes	
Machine Cost		KW	
Filter No.		Horse Power	
Belt Type		Watts	
Shaft Size		R.P.M.	
		Shaft Size	
		Drive	
		Circuit	
		Panel No.	
		Date Installed	
		Total Cost	

scheduling techniques. Prior to scheduling work orders, the entire work force must be thoroughly briefed on the intent and methods of implementation of the preventive maintenance program. To be successful a total preventive maintenance program must receive the support of everyone in the maintenance area, including those in the purchasing function. The purchasing staff is key because they normally prepare the purchase requests or bid documents that must include parts lists and the manufacturer's suggested PM program. Everyone's cooperation is especially vital if there is a union involved. Additional details for scheduling a preventive maintenance program are discussed later in this chapter.

Control

The overall management of the preventive maintenance program should be under the control of one individual at a fairly high level within the plant department. The level of this individual is important for two reasons: to emphasize to everyone within the maintenance organization that the preventive maintenance program is important and will receive the director's attention, and to ensure that the individual has the authority—as well as the responsibility—to manage the preventive maintenance program and supervise journeymen, mechanics, apprentices, and helpers from a number of different crafts.

38.3 EQUIPMENT AND FACILITIES TO INCLUDE IN A PM PROGRAM

What should I include in the preventive maintenance program? The actual items that are included in the initial implementation of the PM program will be the result of an evaluation of needs and resources available. In all likelihood, items will be added and deleted from the program on a continuing basis as needs and resources change from month to month and year to year. However, the initial list of equipment and facilities should be as broad as possible regardless of the resources available. Once the magnitude of the program is determined, equipment can easily be deleted. Be innovative in selecting items for inclusion in the program.

Inventory of Equipment and Facilities

Many administrators find that an accurate master equipment list does not exist within physical plant. A master list may be found in the accounting department, but it will probably not be current. Now is the time to establish an equipment file that will be a single source of data, both static and dynamic, for each piece of equipment and/or facility the plant department maintains. To determine the accuracy of the equipment, list someone must walk through all the facilities and look at the items.

After all the items are listed, an equipment numbering system must be established. In most facilities, a numbering system was initially used, but new equipment and buildings have been added and an update is sorely needed. The numbering system used should help a preventive maintenance worker locate a particular item. It will prove beneficial if a combination of letters and numbers identify the equipment location by building, floor, or equipment room. Remember to build in the ability to expand the system if more equipment is added in a particular location.

An equipment numbering system is shown in Appendix 38-A. This system not only identifies equipment, but also is used in the maintenance cost accounting system to segregate costs by maintenance classification and equipment item, subsystem, basic system, and building. With this system the maintenance manager can continuously review and analyze preventive, planned, and corrective maintenance; repair costs; and the relationships among them.

In addition to identifying location, the inventory should include a record of maintenance activities describing the work done; parts used and their cost; characteristics of the equipment such as operating speeds, electrical requirements, and so on; manufacturer's name, location, and manuals; suppliers of major components and parts; and some indication of preventive maintenance tasks required, either a list of the tasks or reference to a separate document containing these tasks. Printed forms are available for maintaining these records, or they may be developed in-house to meet specific user requirements (see Figure 38-4).

It may be difficult to find some of the data necessary for the master equipment file. Data sources include equipment name plates, purchasing records, manufacturers' manuals and brochures, and workers' memories. It may be necessary to write the original manufacturer for much of the data needed or to call other facilities using the same type of equipment for that information. When new equipment is purchased, obtain the requisite information from the manufacturer at the time of installation, along with operating manuals and spare parts lists.

Analysis and Selection Process

In developing a preventive maintenance program, a manager may select items for inclusion in the program based on the number of breakdowns a particular piece of equipment has. Remember, some breakdowns and defects are unavoidable and would not necessarily change with preventive maintenance. But if one agrees that a preventive maintenance pro-

Figure 38-4

Maintenance Record

Equipment No.			Location		P.M.I. Card No.	
Type Insp.	Date Comp.	Worker No.	Type Insp.	Date Comp.	Worker No.

Equipment Description	Jan	Feb	Mar	Apr	May	Jun	Jul	Aug	Sep	Oct	Nov	Dec

Reverse Page

Date	Worker No.	Replaced Components of Unit

gram is useful and necessary, then it follows that all equipment should be included. Three factors help determine which equipment to include: 1) the importance of the equipment to the functioning of the facilities, 2) the direct cost of equipment failure, and 3) the indirect cost of equipment failure. Ratings of importance for each factor range from five to one. A priority score is obtained by multiplying the ratings of the three factors (see Figure 38-5).

For example, a small air conditioner serving a computer area and having an estimated repair cost of $400 plus an indirect cost of $500 for unused labor and machine time loss might be scored as follows:

Factor 1   3
Factor 2   2
Factor 3   3
Priority score = 3 x 2 x 3 = 18

A consensate pump might be scored:
Factor 1   2
Factor 2   2
Factor 3   3
Priority score = 2 x 2 x 3 = 12

Equipment with a priority score of less than a preset number probably cannot economically be included in a formal maintenance program. The preset number is determined by the available staffing plus funds and usually ranges from seven to nine. However, equipment with low priority scores should be maintained informally. For example, condensers should be cleaned, operation of water coolers checked, or small fans lubricated once a year. It may be most appropriate to send a repairperson around to check all such equipment items once a year during the summer, for example.

38.4 WRITING PM INSTRUCTIONS

One of the most difficult tasks in planning a preventive maintenance program is determining which PM tasks the technician should actually perform and with what frequency. Too many tasks or too frequent performance will overload a preventive maintenance program and make its implementation impossible. Eliminating or overlooking critical tasks could create a false sense of security and lead to a series of maintenance failures. Extremely complex tasks are probably out of the realm of a preventive maintenance program and may require highly trained individuals who are not readily available in the plant department. Whenever possible, preventive maintenance tasks should be standardized for

Figure 38-5

Guide to Setting Priorities for Preventive Maintenance

Factor 1	Factor 2*	Factor 3 +
(5) Major basic facilities equipment critical to safety and functioning of entire institution. Boilers, electrical switchgear and distribution, emergency generator, water supply, fire alarms or fire fighting equipment.	(5) Over $1,000	(5) over $1,000 or serious injury.
(4) Equipment with direct relation to individual safety.	(4) $500 to $999	(4) $500 to $999
(3) Equipment essential to operation of department or major area. Air conditioning and ventilation systems, key laundry equipment, walk-in refrigerators, dishwashers, key laboratory equipment.	(3) $250 to $499	(3) $100 to $499
(2) Equipment essential to smaller operations, for individual comfort or savings. Floor machines, machine tools, condensate pumps, business machines, conveyors, automatic doors.	(2) $100 to $249	(2) Less than $100
(1) Equipment not essential to operations but for comfort or convenience, for which many spares are available and individual replacement cost is low. Water coolers, small fans or ventilating equipment, small air conditioning units, carts, most furniture, television sets.	(1) Less than $100	(1) Essentially no cost

Score equipment by multiplying priority numbers of the three columns. Example: 2 × 4 × 2 = 16

*In using this column, estimate the magnitude of the cost of major repair or replacement, whichever is the case.
+ In using this column, estimate the costs involved to the institution as a whole if the unit in question fails. This includes such things as overtime, lost time by employees, cost of alternative temporary solutions to the problems.

Source: *Hospital Engineering Handbook*. Third Edition. American Hospital Association.

each type or class of equipment. This will simplify training and reduce preventive maintenance time.

Reference Documents

Most operating manuals or manufacturer's brochures will recommend some type of preventive maintenance schedule, which may be overly cautious and recommend an excessive oil or lubrication schedule. If manuals are not on hand, obtain them from the manufacturer or contact other institutions that have already implemented a preventive maintenance program and have the same type of equipment. One of the best sources of information is located within the plant department. The foreman or technicians who have been maintaining the equipment over a long period know the tasks they perform when the equipment fails and usually have a good idea what causes a failure or, better yet, what might prevent it.

General maintenance manuals published by such agencies as State Building Services, General Services Administration, and Department of Navy Civil Engineering provide excellent references in determining preventive maintenance tasks on most items of equipment found on college and university campuses today.

Contents of PMIs

Preventive maintenance instructions should be standard to common components when possible and should be developed according to like items or groups of items. These instructions should emphasize preventive maintenance actions or checks and investigative actions such as checking for noise, vibrations, excessive weakness, overheating, and overall operation. Actual work might include alignments, adjustments, lubrication, cleanliness, and minor parts replacement such as belts.

To write the instructions it may be useful to observe the equipment in question to identify all required tasks. The tasks to be performed must be written on some type of checklist or card and contain as few words as possible. At the same time, the instructions must ensure that each task description is specific, accurate, and easily understood. Keep in mind the educational and training level of the mechanics who will be reading, interpreting, and performing the inspections (see Figures 38-6 and 38-7).

Determining PMI Performance Frequencies

One of the main goals of a preventive maintenance program is to reduce failures and major breakdowns. A major factor in determining the inter-

Figure 38-6

Preventive Maintenance Procedure

Equipment No._____ Equipment name:_____

Inspection Frequency ____(Monthly)_____

1. Change filters, 12 required, 24 by 24 by 8.
2. Check all bearings for noise or excessive temperature.
3. Check belt tension and condition.
4. Operation of traps, steam pressure, 5 lbs.
5. Check for leaks in unit around pipes and correct.
6. Clean area.

Inspection Frequency ____(Annually)_____

1. Shut down, open up for inspection and cleaning.
2. Remove guard on belt.
3. Take tension off belts.
4. Check bearing condition.
5. Replace belts and take up proper tension.
6. Check sheave alignment with yardstick, correct.
7. Replace guard.
8. If new belts are required, return in 24 hours to take up stretch.

Inspection Frequency (Semiannually)_____

1. Grease fan at two fittings.
2. Wipe up excess grease.
3. Remove plugs from electric motor, insert special fitting on fill.
4. With motor running force grease into bearing until grease appears at drain hole.
5. Remove special fitting and replace fill plug.
6. Run 20 minutes and replace drain plug.
7. Wipe up excess grease.

Repair Record

Date	Work Accomplished	Cost

Source: *Energy Management Series*, Volume 7, Syska & Hennessy, Inc.

Figure 38-7

Physical Plant Preventive Maintenance Instructions

PMI Number   05VEF1   Exhaust Fan Maintenance Instructions

	Weekly	Monthly	Quarterly	Semi-annual	Annual
Workhours		0.40	0.40		
Crew Size		1.00	1.00		

FREQ	CRFT	Task Descriptions
M	M	Check extent of corrosion and condition of paint, including motor
M	M	Tighten loose bolts, nuts, fasteners, and mounting support, including motor
M	M	Report/replace worn/damaged malfunctioning components, including motor
M	M	Repair/report causes of overheating, excessive vibration and unusual noises, including motor
M	M	Lubricate bearings/rollers/sleeve bearings, including motor
M	M	Clean screens and louvers, including motor
M	M	Tighten fan hub/sheave set screws (if applicable)
M	M	Check belt for wear, tension and alignment. Adjust as necessary or report if replacement is needed (if applicable)
M	M	Check sheave alignment. Report excessively worn sheaves, including motor (if applicable)
M	M	Check flexible connector (if applicable)
M	M	Clean the area
M	M	Complete maintenance record

val of preventive maintenance inspections is the frequency of breakdowns or defects and the consequences of such conditions. The seriousness of a breakdown is a function of the cost of operating or not operating the equipment (whether or not it is critical to instructional activities), and/or involves safety of personnel and property. Other factors that might be considered are the type of equipment and its usage. Some tasks may be based on operating hours rather than on a calendar.

Environmental conditions also play a part in determining inspection frequency. Such things as dust, water, and heat must be considered.

Task frequencies will vary according to the age of the equipment and may be performed as often as daily, but are usually scheduled on a weekly, monthly, quarterly, semiannual, or annual basis. Tasks should also be categorized into equipment that is operational or nonoperational, and may require a test run for proper performance evaluation. Tasks established for one piece of equipment can easily be modified for all other similar items in order to reduce writing time.

Estimating Staffing to Perform the PMIs

Another difficult task in the development of a preventive maintenance program is the establishment of total staffing/workhours required for the program. As stated earlier, the program at this stage is not staff-limited. It is only after total workhours have been determined that the program should be modified in order to meet available resources. In the establishment of staffing requirements only estimate basic time—the time needed to perform the task at the equipment location. What if the technician determines that maintenance tasks, other than those specifically required for the inspection should be performed? Generally, the technician will perform an additional task if it does not require a return to the shop for spare parts. Remember that task length is only estimated. It will vary with the mechanic performing the task and the condition of the equipment at the time of inspection.

Now the plant director must evaluate the workhours available. Some authorities say the cost of the preventive maintenance workhours should equal 4 percent of the capital value or ensured value of the equipment being maintained. This sounds good on paper but to actually determine 4 percent of investment may prove difficult, if not impossible. There will likely be more workhours required than available. But remember, all items under consideration were placed in the initial program with the realization that they might be removed later.

It is now necessary to review the equipment included in the program and eliminate those items whose breakdowns result in the least cost both in time and operation to the institution. Next, the frequency of tasks should be reviewed and changed as appropriate to reduce workhours. The next items for review are the actual tasks. A limited preventive maintenance program is better than none at all. Therefore, it is generally better to change frequencies or tasks rather than drop the item from the program completely.

38.5 SCHEDULING PREVENTIVE MAINTENANCE

The key to implementing a preventive maintenance program is in its schedule, and the key to a good schedule is balance. Preventive maintenance tasks should not be grouped during any particular period but should present an even work flow over a given period of time.

Developing a Master Schedule

The master preventive maintenance schedule should span a full year and cover all tasks that fall within this period. Tasks should be distributed on a monthly basis keeping required workhours balanced from month to month. Generally, equipment downtime should be spread throughout the year, although there are items that can only be taken out of service when they are not needed (Christmas vacation or spring break). Lengthy inspections on some equipment should be scheduled seasonally. Heating equipment should receive yearly checks in the summer, while air conditioning should receive major checks in the winter.

Another good method of master scheduling preventive maintenance is to establish the schedule on a fifty-two-week basis. Figure 38-8 is a form specifically designed for this type of master scheduling. Using this form the master schedule is developed as follows:

1. For a building, list the equipment number, description, and PMI number for each equipment item selected for the PM program.
2. Refer to the PMI for each equipment item for the frequencies at which each task is to be performed—weekly (W), monthly (M), quarterly (Q), semiannually (SA), or annually (A). Indicate the week of the year during which each frequency will be performed by placing a W, M, Q, SA, or A in the top half of the weekly square. In the bottom half of the square enter the estimated workhours required to perform the PM tasks at that frequency.

1	2	3	4	5	6	7	8	9	10	11	12	13
W	W	W	W M	W	W	W	W M	W	W	W	W M	W Q
.5	.5	.5	1.0	.5	.5	.5	1.0	.5	.5	.5	1.0	1.5

3. After the frequencies and workhours have been entered for all equipment items, total the workhours required annually for each equipment item and the workhours required weekly to perform the PM as scheduled.
4. If necessary, the weekly workhour requirements can be balanced between weeks by sliding the M, Q, SA, and A inspections one way or the other.
5. If the total workhour requirement is excessive in light of available workhours, it can be reduced by extending the frequencies where feasible.

Figure 38-8

Preventive Maintenance Master Schedule

BUILDING/FACILITY _____

Equip No.	Description (Noun)	PMI No.	Week 1	2	3	4	5	6	→	49	50	51	52	EST. MH.
TOTAL WORKHOURS													

This type of PM master scheduling is easily programmed on a computer. The computer schedules by each week of the year as indicated on the master schedule.

Staffing availability will fluctuate due to special events such as holidays, summer vacation periods, and so on. Knowing the workhours associated with each preventive maintenance task, it is possible to balance the workhours to meet the availability of personnel. Equipment downtime or inactivity is kept to a minimum with the least disruption to the campus and its educational activities.

Developing Weekly Schedules

Monthly schedules are broken down into weekly schedules in much the same manner as the yearly schedule was broken down into a monthly schedule. However, there should be some spare or unscheduled time planned into the overall preventive maintenance schedule, either the last day of each week or the last week of the month. There will always be missed schedules due to sickness, unprogrammed emergencies that may require the services of the preventive maintenance team, or equipment that cannot be taken out of service as originally scheduled.

The preventive maintenance program should be transferred from the master schedule (i.e., for one year) into some type of readily available weekly/monthly schedule. If the system is to be a manual system, it can be done using a marked calendar, a cardex system filed by the day of the month, visual files that are color coded to identify a particular month, or any other suspense file that serves the same purpose. The visual files appear to be the most economical and simplest to use. A quick scan of each drawer will indicate items that must be scheduled during the forthcoming month. If a permanent color code is not desirable, a color tab may also be used. The movable tab has the advantage of lending flexibility to scheduling since the month can easily be changed without redoing the whole card. For large preventive maintenance programs monthly scheduling boards may be useful. These boards indicate the preventive maintenance tasks scheduled for the month broken down by a particular craft or shop. Even more effective is a computerized preventive maintenance schedule that prints out the task to be scheduled on either a monthly or weekly basis.

A computer scheduled PM work order is shown in Figure 38-9. Based on the annual PM master schedule, the computer was programmed to schedule the quarterly (Q) preventive maintenance instructions for the exhaust fan the ninth week of the year by shop number 05. The bottom of the work order is used by the mechanic performing the work to enter applicable feedback data. This work order with all others

Figure 38-9

Computer-Scheduled Preventive Maintenance Work Order

PREVENTIVE MAINTENANCE SYSTEM
SCHEDULED PM INSTRUCTIONS

EQUIPMENT NO. ECJ-V-EF-012
FAN EXHAUST
11TH FLOOR ELEVATOR RM
MANFACTURER BARRY BLOWER
SERIAL NUMBER 32389

EXHAUST FAN MAINTENANCE INSTRUCTIONS	OK	INC	NEEDS MAINT.
1. Check extent of corrosion and condition of paint, including motor	___	___	___
2. Tighten loose bolts, nuts, fasteners, and mounting support, including motor	___	___	___
3. Repair/replace worn/damaged malfunctioning components, including motor	___	___	___
4. Repair/report causes of overheating, excessive vibration and unusual noises, including motor	___	___	___
5. Lubricate bearings/rollers/sleeve bearings, including motor	___	___	___
6. Clean screens and louvers, including motor	___	___	___
7. Tighten fan hub/sheave set screws (if applicable)	___	___	___
8. Check belt for wear, tension and alignment. Adjust as necessary or report if replacement is needed (if applicable)	___	___	___
9. Check sheave alignment. Report excessively worn sheaves, including motor (if applicable)	___	___	___
10. Check flexible connector (if applicable)	___	___	___
11. Clean area	___	___	___
12. Complete maintenance record	___	___	___

FEEDBACK DATA

STEP	WHAT WAS WRONG	MATERIAL

LABOR DATA

NAME	TIME	NAME	TIME

Figure 38-10

PMI Transmittal Report

**PREVENTIVE MAINTENANCE SYSTEM
TRANSMITTAL REPORT**

Equipment No.	Equipment Description	PMI	F	Crew Size	Est. Work-hours
	Total estimated workhours for building EAH				0.70
ECJ-A-FR-001	FAN RETURN A/R	05AFR1	M	1	0.75
ECJ-A-FR-002	FAN RETURN A/R	05AFR1	M	1	0.75
ECJ-A-FS-001	FAN SUPPLY A/R	05AFS1	M	1	0.50
ECJ-A-FS-002	FAN SUPPLY A/R	05AFS1	M	1	0.50
ECJ-A-FS-003	FAN SUPPLY A/R	05AFS1	M	1	0.50
ECJ-V-EF-001	FAN EXHAUST	05VEF1	M	1	0.40
ECJ-V-EF-003	FAN EXHAUST	05VEF1	M	1	0.40
ECJ-V-EF-006	FAN EXHAUST	05VEF1	M	1	0.40
ECJ-V-EF-008	FAN EXHAUST	05VEF1	M	1	0.40
ECJ-V-EF-012	FAN EXHAUST	05VEF1	Q	1	0.40
ECJ-V-EF-013	EXHAUST FAN	05VEF1	Q	1	0.40
	Total PM work orders requiring	1 WKR		11	5.40

scheduled for the ninth week of the year is sent to the responsible shop with a PMI transmittal report (see Figure 38-10).

Scheduling Controls

In order to assure that the required tasks are performed there must be a strong commitment by management to the preventive maintenance program. Individuals assigned to preventive maintenance work must not be pulled from their schedule except in extreme emergencies. There will always be some preventive maintenance tasks each month that are not completed for one reason or another. The system developed must monitor these tasks to reschedule or cancel them. If similar problems continue month after month, the overall preventive maintenance program must be reduced in scope.

There are two basic methods of controlling the preventive maintenance schedule once it is established. One method is to fix the time when each inspection is to be performed—the annual inspection will always be performed in January, the semiannual inspection in July, and quarterly inspections in April and October. If one of these inspections is delayed, it will either be performed the following month or be canceled and the rest of the inspections will be performed during the same month. The other method of scheduling is to slide each inspection according to when the last inspection was performed. If the yearly inspection is delayed one month, all future inspections are delayed one month. This second method is the most practical but much harder to control. It causes a lot more administrative work if the preventive maintenance program is not computerized.

There must also be some follow-up method to ensure that the given tasks are performed as required. This follow-up should be performed by a preventive maintenance foreman or quality control inspector at regular intervals. Analysis of equipment breakdowns may also indicate a lack of proper preventive maintenance inspections.

38.6 PM MANAGEMENT CONTROLS

The control described above concerns scheduling and lower-level supervision (foremen and below). There should be additional controls and management tools that are used by the facilities director.

Performance and Effectiveness Indexes

A control that is important to management involves some type of cost accounting. The preventive maintenance program, like all maintenance activities, should have some interface with the general accounting system. This may be through a computerized transfer of cost figures or a manual entry of maintenance data into the accounting system. In order to provide a true picture of the preventive maintenance program, costs (labor and material) should be segregated from other maintenance activities such as corrective maintenance, repairs, and construction. PM costs should also be segregated by buildings and system type (HVAC systems, electrical systems, plumbing systems). There should be a relatively simple way of comparing estimated time to perform a given task versus the actual time. This comparison must be made of a number of repetitions of the task in order to average out idiosyncrasies caused by different mechanics performing the tasks, different conditions, and so on. The plant director should receive cost information about the preventive maintenance program in terms of workhours, material, and total dollars.

The preventive maintenance program should be compared to the overall maintenance effort by determining percentage of preventive maintenance work orders performed versus total work orders, workhours spent on repair versus total workhours available, and direct costs of repairs versus total maintenance costs. The full effects of a preventive maintenance program in labor and dollar savings will not be realized for at least twelve to eighteen months after implementation. Therefore, the initial implementation of a preventive maintenance program will require an increased expenditure in spare parts and possible additional staffing, if the original maintenance effort is to remain at the same level.

Equipment Failure Reports

PM activities are recorded in a historical data file for each piece of equipment. This information, coupled with equipment failure rates, is another way to evaluate the effectiveness of a preventive maintenance program. Certain items should be flagged as critical and brought to the attention of the plant director. Critical items include equipment with three or more of the same type failures in any one year, the ten items of equipment down the most number of times during a month, and the ten items of equipment that cost the most to maintain. An equipment failure report identifying these items will change rapidly after the first two or three months of a preventive maintenance program and can be used as a major indicator of the success of the program itself.

38.7 ORGANIZATION AND STAFFING

As with any labor intensive program, the individuals selected to schedule, monitor, and perform the tasks are vital to the success of the preventive maintenance program. The idea of a preventive maintenance program will probably be a new concept to many members of the plant department. Their understanding and acceptance of the program is paramount to its success.

Organization

The type of organization formed to implement a preventive maintenance program will vary according to the size of the institution, the classification of employees within the plant department, and the desires of the director. During the task-selection procedure, attention should have been given to the types of employees required to perform the tasks (electrician, plumber, general maintenance worker). Preventive maintenance work may be performed by individuals from various shops, by a preventive maintenance shop itself, or by a preventive maintenance team under the management of a preventive maintenance foreman. The means chosen is usually determined by the size of the facility and/or the classification of the maintenance workers themselves. If a union exists within the maintenance department, it may also play a role in deciding what types of employees perform the preventive maintenance tasks.

The most efficient classification of worker to perform a preventive maintenance task is that of a general maintenance mechanic—one who can check electric motor, a pump, and an air-handling unit all at the same time—rather than requiring three separate journeymen to check each major piece of equipment. Within the scheduling office the same individual should schedule all preventive maintenance tasks. This ensures consistency, and the scheduler develops a thorough knowledge of the overall program.

Staffing

There is no question that the implementation of a preventive maintenance program will require additional personnel to perform the administrative tasks. Usually, the preventive maintenance scheduler can also maintain and keep current the equipment history records, as well as adjusting the schedules to reflect inspections. In large institutions adjusting schedules may require the services of a clerk and a preventive maintenance scheduler, especially if the scheduler is responsible for scheduling other maintenance activities. In the long run a preventive maintenance program will reduce the overall maintenance man-hours required, so additional staffing on a temporary basis is not recommended. It is more practical to reduce other activities during the implementation phase of the preventive maintenance program.

Personnel Qualifications and Skills

A successful program rests on the selection of individuals to perform the actual preventive maintenance tasks. These mechanics must have technical skills including knowledge of the equipment and its operation, troubleshooting abilities, and familiarity with the plant's overall design and function. They must have personality traits that lend themselves to performing repetitive tasks and completing paperwork. Over time, complacency can do more to undermine the overall preventive maintenance program than any other single factor. It is not uncommon for some preventive maintenance workers to develop the attitude that they "checked a certain piece of equipment last month, so why bother to look at it again this month." Other individuals performing preventive maintenance work may take great pride in their work and feel personally responsible for the equipment they inspect.

Studies have been conducted to determine whether individuals should perform only preventive maintenance tasks or a mixture of regular maintenance activities and preventive maintenance work. The advantage of the latter, of course, is that an increased variety of jobs tends to alleviate boredom. When this type of scheduling is used, individuals tend to perform the preventive maintenance tasks in a more professional manner in order to preclude failure and a subsequent repair job. On the other hand, if workers perform only preventive maintenance tasks, they get to know the equipment much better, recognize changes from inspection to inspection, and in some instances, can even identify a change in sound from one inspection to another.

38.8 IMPLEMENTATION OF THE PM PROGRAM

After completing the planning phase in a satisfactory manner, the implementation phase of the preventive maintenance program should proceed smoothly. There is really nothing more to do than perform the inspections required. Some details need to be finalized at the beginning of the implementation phase.

Policies and Procedures

So that all staff can fully understand the importance and significance of the program, the director should publish an operating policy concerning the preventive maintenance program. Along with the policy, written procedures that direct the actual operation of the program should be provided. These procedures should describe the purpose of the program, responsibilities of each section of the department, the actions required by these sections, procedures to be followed by the mechanics involved in performing the tasks, details concerning issuance of work orders, time and material reports, maintenance of the equipment historical cards, and so on.

The procedures should present an outline of the organization established to implement the preventive maintenance program and the proper channels to follow when problems arise. These procedures should be distributed to the individuals directly involved in the PM program and to all supervisors within the department. This way they will better understand the importance and workings of the preventive maintenance program (see Figure 38-11). A sample administrative procedure for a computerized PM program is found in Appendix 38-B.

Training Personnel

Although the individuals assigned to perform preventive maintenance tasks were selected for that purpose, there will be some additional

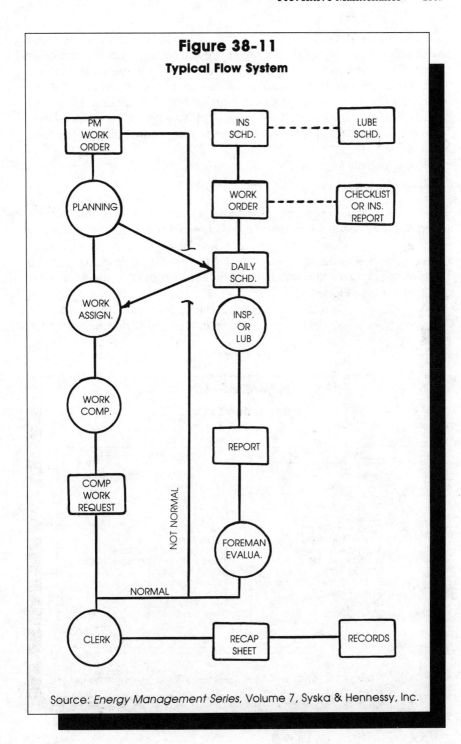

Figure 38-11

Typical Flow System

Source: *Energy Management Series*, Volume 7, Syska & Hennessy, Inc.

training required especially in the areas of proper documentation and work accountability. If the mechanics are unfamiliar with the particular piece of equipment, they will need time to review the operating manuals and perform the initial preventive maintenance tasks under supervision. Once the preventive maintenance program is in full operation, replacement personnel may be trained by accompanying an experienced mechanic who is selected for his or her communications skills and teaching ability.

Special Tools and Supplies

The preventive maintenance task cards should identify any special tools or equipment needed to perform preventive maintenance inspections. It may even be necessary to purchase special tools to perform certain preventive maintenance tasks. After the mechanics become familiar with the equipment and tasks, they will automatically know what tools are needed (see Figure 38-12).

As stated earlier, stock levels for certain spare parts may need to be increased as a result of the preventive maintenance program. Items such

Figure 38-12

Inspection Tools

Tools	Inspection Uses
Stethoscope	Valve, Gear, Bearing Defects
X-Ray Equipment	Material Flaws
Dye Penetrant	Material Flaws
Ultraviolet Light	Material Flaws
Magnetic Particles	Material Flaws
Ultrasonic Testers	Subsurface Defects
Vibration Meters	Rotating Machine Defects
Recording Ammeters	Electric Equipment Performance
Recording Voltmeters	Electric Equipment Performance
Recording Temp. Gages	Bearings, Hydraulic,
Recording Press. Gages	Pneumatic Systems
Surface Pyrometers	Temperatures
Megger	Electric Motor Insulation
Infrared Sources	Temperature Gradients
Nuclear Sources	Moisture Detection

Source: *Energy Mangement Series,* Volume 7. Syska & Hennessy, Inc.

as belts, gaskets, and filters will probably be used quickly as a result of the program. Although use of additional material will initially increase the cost of the preventive maintenance program, the savings as a result of reduced downtime and failures will far exceed the additional cost of material.

Implementation

A preventive maintenance program should be implemented in phases with no more than 40 percent of the program implemented in the initial phase. Phases may be determined by area, building, relative importance of equipment, or ease of tasks. Work orders for preventive maintenance should include equipment identification, location, and type of preventive maintenance check—weekly, monthly, quarterly, semiannual, annual.

Information provided by the mechanic performing the task should include workhours required, material used, individual identification, and any major problems discovered but not corrected. The equipment historical files must then be updated indicating the preventive maintenance tasks performed, any excessive materials used, and any work performed or needed other than preventive maintenance. Accident prevention and proper safety habits must be emphasized during the implementation phase of the program.

Common Problems and How to Avoid Them

During the early stages of a preventive maintenance program, the maintenance repair backlog will greatly increase. This happens because equipment is being looked at on a scheduled basis and major defects identified. The backlog will return to normal after the preventive maintenance program has been operating a number of months.

Problems can develop rapidly if the employees assigned to the program do not fully understand the basic philosophy of preventive maintenance. It cannot be repeated enough—the program's success depends on the attitudes of the workers. Many programs have been started but not given a high enough priority. They were soon dropped for lack of effectiveness. Other programs run into difficulties because management did not develop the proper controls or personnel were not properly trained. Improvements in equipment operation will be noticeable after about six months, while overall cost savings will not be identified until almost twelve months.

38.9 CORRECTIVE MAINTENANCE

Corrective maintenance is the study of historical records (repetitive failures) to determine the actions needed to prevent reoccurrence and then taking proper corrective actions. Corrective maintenance results from a good preventive maintenance program.

A preventive maintenance program needs regular review and updating. Some of the initial frequencies selected for performing preventive maintenance tasks will have to be changed (either increased or decreased). In addition, the time required to perform the tasks will also change, especially as mechanics become more proficient.

Maintenance Analysis

As a result of the preventive maintenance program and the documentation associated with it, failures and breakdowns will be identified easily. A maintenance analysis program will identify the cause of these failures (faulty design, faulty manufacture, incorrect operation, lack of proper preventive maintenance). Maintenance analysis can also identify mean times between failures of components and overall expected life of a piece of equipment (see Figure 38-13).

Corrective Action

After maintenance analysis is complete, it may be necessary to revise preventive maintenance tasks and/or frequencies, and establish a schedule for changing equipment component parts based on estimates of the mean time between failures. It may even be necessary to replace the item itself or perform major modifications in order to improve operating characteristics. An analysis of the preventive maintenance program may indicate that improved supervision is all that is necessary to improve the program.

A financial analysis of the program should also be made on a periodic basis in order to determine not only the cost of the program but its effect on overall maintenance costs. Generally, the distribution of total maintenance costs with a formal preventive maintenance program should be as indicated:

	Labor Percentage	Material Percentage
PM	15	5
Planned	75	75
Repairs	10	20

As used above, preventive maintenance indicates work done in the preventive maintenance program itself. Planned maintenance is work

Figure 38-13

The Economics of Preventive Maintenance
Maintenance Analysis Curves

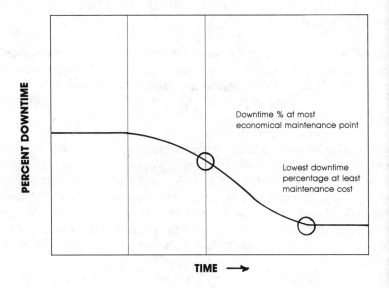

PERCENT DOWNTIME

Downtime % at most
economical maintenance point

Lowest downtime
percentage at least
maintenance cost

TIME ⟶

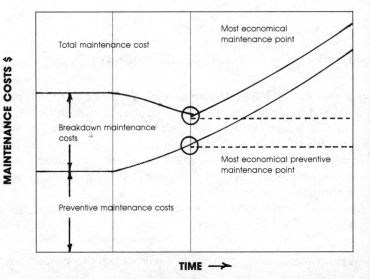

MAINTENANCE COSTS $

Total maintenance cost

Most economical
maintenance point

Breakdown maintenance
costs

Most economical preventive
maintenance point

Preventive maintenance costs

TIME ⟶

identified through the PM program or by other means and performed on a scheduled basis. Repairs identifies work done when equipment actually breaks down and must be fixed immediately.

38.10 COMPUTERIZATION OF PREVENTIVE MAINTENANCE

To invest in a computerized system for preventive maintenance only would be a major mistake. A preventive maintenance program should be one part of an overall maintenance management system, a system that is built on a data base that includes such items as equipment inventory, personnel identification, salaries, and a stockroom and/or material inventory. This type of computerized system can also be expanded into areas such as work order monitoring, scheduling, and identifying deferred maintenance backlogs.

There are great variations in complexity among preventive maintenance systems. The simplest systems store an inventory list of items to be maintained and work orders. The work orders are arranged in some schedule (in code or full text) that tells workers which task is to be performed. The minimum data input to a preventive maintenance program is:

- The types of equipment (or other items such as roofs or drains) to be maintained.
- The number of items there are.
- The location of each item.
- The task to be performed and its frequency.

It is also preferable to determine which craft or shop will perform each task, and the length of time the task should require.

With this information, it is possible to build a schedule of total staffing requirements by craft. With this schedule, managers can balance the workload over the year and maintain relative frequency intervals between performance of each type of task (monthly, quarterly, semiannual, or annual).

After work is performed, it is desirable to capture certain information from completed work orders:

- List of work orders completed each period, those still open, or uncompleted.
- The time charged to each work order; compare actual time to the standard established for the task.

- Repairs needed beyond the scope of the preventive maintenance mechanic.
- Report of work orders written for such repairs.
- Any outages required to schedule the work on a given system. List of people to contact before outage.
- Equipment maintained only during the heating season, or only during the cooling season.

With all the above information built into the original data base, the system can be designed to capture historical information, print out age requirements in advance, give management current and year-to-date cost data, develop trend information on percentage completion or preventive maintenance tasks by craft, and compare standard times versus actual times for types of equipment and crafts.

Data storage requirements will range from about 300 characters for each inventory item in a single system to as many as 2,500 characters for each item in a comprehensive system. On a large campus even a simple system would be hard to accommodate with a floppy disk computer system.

Use of Bar Coding in Preventive Maintenance

The data necessary for maintaining a computerized maintenance management system is managed by data input operators, office managers, or workers themselves, all member of the physical plant department.

Reflection quickly leads to the realization that most of the data input is a manual transcription from some resource document or record. In the case of preventive maintenance, even though we may start with a computer generated work statement, the response to the computer is hand-written by a mechanic, and this must be transcribed to the computer. Parts disbursement to mechanics are hand recorded and transcribed to the computer, as are time cards.

There are two major problems with this process. First, a lot of labor time is used in originally recording and redundantly transcribing the information. Second, a large amount of error is introduced. Writing skill is not an essential qualification or characteristic of a good mechanic. Their hand-written information has potential for the introduction of substantial error. Zeros, nines, and sixes are often difficult to distinguish. The data entry person will not only transcribe mistakes due to incorrect interpretation, but they too can be expected to make errors. The nonproductive time consumed in recording and transcribing incorrect data, then researching and correcting the errors and fielding telephone calls, becomes overwhelming. And it does little for relationships with over-billed clients.

The next important step would seem to be to bypass the people input process as much as possible. Bar coding seems to be the answer at present. Supermarket check-outs are automated to read and record the bar code on product labels, thus speeding up the charging process and providing for a high degree of accuracy. Industry uses bar coding to identify and manage components on assembly lines and in stock. Modern warehousing is becoming more and more dependent upon bar coding. Many physical plants are capitalizing on the benefits of the system.

In general, a bar coding system for the input of preventive maintenance data consists of the following:

1. Each item of equipment on a preventive maintenance schedule has a bar coded identification number. The coded numbering system can identify the building, floor, and function of the equipment, such as "refrigeration" or "heating."
2. Each job order has a bar coded identification number, which includes the equipment identification number.
3. Each worker has a bar coded identification number.
4. Time is bar coded by fifteen-minute increments in each shop.
5. Each spare part used in preventive maintenance is bar coded.

In operation, when a worker completes a preventive maintenance task, a bar code reader is used to read the job order number, worker identification number, and time expended to the nearest fifteen minutes. As repair parts are drawn, their bar code numbers are read in conjunction with the job order number.

At the end of each day, the bar code readers are picked up and the data down-loaded directly into the computer. The computer automatically cost accounts all time and material against the project, and simultaneously records all work activity to each worker's personal time record and adjusts the parts inventory.

Implementation of such a system requires two to three bar code label makers for physical plant, and one or two bar code scanners (readers) for each shop.

Once established, a bar coding system permits the input of computer data by quickly passing a hand held scanner over numbers rather than writing the numbers on a time card. For hundreds of workers, each working on ten or more items of equipment each day, the cumulative time saving is tremendous. And errors in the introduction of the data into the computer system are virtually eliminated.

38.11 CONCLUSION

Although guidelines have already been provided, for many the question remains. How many workhours and how much material should I commit to a preventive maintenance program? There should be no doubt that a well-run preventive maintenance program will result in significant savings in both workhours and material over the long term. But, equally important, an effective PM program will improve the overall operation of the plant equipment, reduce breakdowns and interruptions of service to the educational facilities, enhance the professionalism of the plant department, and greatly ease the strain on its director.

ADDITIONAL RESOURCES

Comprehensive Maintenance and Repair Program, second edition. State of Maryland, Department of General Services, 1983.

Computer Applications. Critical Issues in Facilities Management #1. Alexandria, Virginia: APPA, 1987.

Controlling Maintenance Costs. National Foreman's Institute, Bureau of Business Practices, 1976.

Hospital Engineering Handbook. American Hospital Association, 1974.

Preventive Maintenance Guidelines. Plant Engineering Library, Technical Publication 55-12.

Work Control. Critical Issues in Facilities Management #2. Alexandria, Virginia: APPA, 1988.

Appendix 38-A

"Dual-control" Numbering System

ADVANTAGES

- One Number Serves Two Purposes
  - ☐ Equipment Identification
  - ☐ Cost Accounting
- Segregates Costs (Labor & Material) by Maintenance Category
  - ☐ PM
  - ☐ Planned Maintenance
  - ☐ Corrective Maintenance
  - ☐ Repairs
- Segregates Costs (Labor & Material) by Maintenance Category
  - ☐ Building
  - ☐ Basic System
  - ☐ Sub-system
  - ☐ Equipment Item
- Very Adaptable to ADP
- Simple System for Personnel to Use

FORMAT

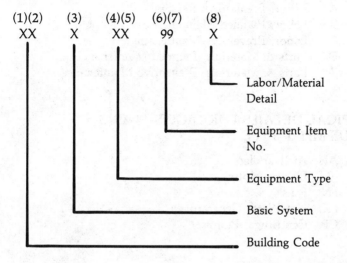

(1)(2) XX	Building Code
(3) X	Basic System
(4)(5) XX	Equipment Type
(6)(7) 99	Equipment Item No.
(8) X	Labor/Material Detail

EXAMPLE

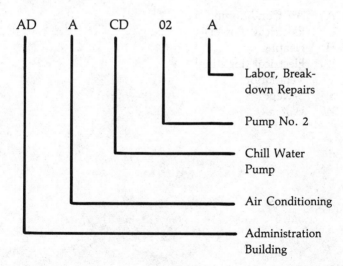

AD	Administration Building
A	Air Conditioning
CD	Chill Water Pump
02	Pump No. 2
A	Labor, Breakdown Repairs

TYPICAL DETAILS FOR DIGIT #8

A   Labor, Breakdown Repairs
B   Labor, Planned Maintenance
C   Labor, Preventive Maintenance
D   Parts & Materials, Planned Maintenance
E   Parts & Materials, Preventive Maintenance

TYPICAL DETAILS FOR DIGITS #4 & #5— EQUIPMENT TYPE

AH Air Handlers
EM Electric Motors
FN Fans
HG Hot Water Generators
CP Centrifugal Pumps

TYPICAL DETAILS FOR DIGIT #3—BASIC SYSTEM

A   Air Conditioning
E   Electrical (Power)
H   Heating
L   Electrical (Lighting)
V   Ventilation
S   Sewage
W   Water

EXAMPLE OF PHYSICAL SEGREGATION OF EQUIPMENT

AD-0-00-00-0	**Administration Building**
AD-A-00-00-0	**Air Conditioning System**
AD-A-AH-01-0	Air Handler #1
AD-A-EM-01-0	Electric Motor #1
AD-A-AH-02-0	Air Handler #2
AD-A-EM-02-0	Electric Motor #2
AD-A-CP-01-0	Chilled Water Pump #1
AD-A-EM-03-0	Electric Motor #3
AD-A-PP-01-0	Piping/valves
AD-H-00-00-0	**Heating System**
AD-H-BR-01-0	Boiler #1
AD-H-BR-01-0	Boiler #2
AD-H-CP-02-0	Condensate Pump #2
AD-H-EM-04-0	Electric Motor #4
AD-H-PP-01-0	Piping/Valves
AD-E-00-00-0	**Electrical Power**
AD-E-SG-01-0	Switchgear #1
AD-E-TF-01-0	Transformer #1
AD-E-PN-01-0	Power Panel #1
AD-E-WN-01-0	Wiring

Appendix 38-B

Administrative Procedures

SUBJECT: Preventive Maintenance Program

I. Purpose

To establish a procedure for scheduling, accomplishing, and controlling the Preventive Maintenance (PM) Program, and to assign the specific responsibilities of each action organization.

II. Action Organizations
Technical Services and Construction and Maintenance

III. General

Preventive maintenance is the utilization of planned services, inspections, adjustments, and replacements designed to ensure maximum utilization of equipment at minimum cost. The preventive maintenance program consists of the development, implementation, and evaluation of Preventive Maintenance Instructions (PMIs), and procedures and evaluations of repetitive problems of all maintenance performed. Specifically, PM includes cleaning, adjustments, lubrication, minor repairs, and parts replacement that are performed on scheduled frequencies in accordance with written Preventive Maintenance Instructions. Major repair jobs identified by the PM process are performed as planned maintenance projects through the normal work order system.

IV. Definitions

A. *Departmental Services* Those services rendered by the Physical Plant as requested by departments or other comparable agencies within the university. Such services are normally for the exclusive benefit of the requesting department. Included in departmental services are fabrication or installation of departmental equipment; operation, maintenance, and repair of departmental equipment; supply of materials for departmental use; rendering of moving and hauling services; extension of utilities to accommodate departmental equipment, etc. Departmental services are paid for by the department making the request.

B. *Institutional Services* Those services performed by the Physical Plant for which funds have been appropriated through the normal budget process for operating and maintaining the general institutional facilities, buildings, and grounds. Such services include lighting, heating and air conditioning, utilities, care of restroom facilities, cleaning of buildings, trash disposal, care of grounds, and maintenance and repair of buildings, etc. Such services are rendered without charge to any department.

C. *Preventive Maintenance Instructions (PMIs)* Detailed task instructions delineating the specific work to be accomplished on a recurring basis of Weekly (W), Monthly (M), Quarterly (Q), Semiannually (S), or Annually (A) to ensure maximum utilization of the equipment/facilities for a minimum cost.

D. *Planned Maintenance Work Order (PWO)* The scheduled replacement of major components or repairs that have been identified by the PM program or other sources as necessary to prevent a failure of the equipment in the near future.

E. *Corrective Maintenance Work Order (CWO)* The analysis of repetitive failures and the determination of corrective action, such as the replacement of equipment or major components.

F. *Cyclic Maintenance (CM)* Planned Maintenance that has a frequency greater than one year.

G. *Emergency Work Order (EWO)* Unplanned repairs to restore a failed system to its designed function.

V. Responsibilities

A. Department of Technical Services (TS) is reponsible for weekly scheduling, analyzing, updating, and managing the Preventive Maintenance Program.

B. Department of Construction and Maintenance (C & M) is responsible for daily scheduling, completion, analysis, and cost accounting of the Preventive Maintenance Program.

C. Academic and Support/Service Departments approve/ disapprove all Departmental Maintenance Programs recommended by Physical Plant and include appropriate fund citation.

VI. Procedures

A. *Scheduling of PM Programs*

1 . Maintenance Engineering Branch of TS will provide the data entry of the master schedule developed by Maintenance Engineering and provide input for any changes that may develop as the program progresses—frequency change, addition/ deletion of equipment, etc.

2. Planning and Scheduling (P & S) section of TS will *reserve* the workhours by shop as scheduled by the automated program in each weekly schedule. P & S will forward 2 copies of the weekly Transmittal Report and the copies of the PMIs to the appropriate Construction and Maintenance shop scheduler one week prior to scheduled work accomplishment. Central Scheduling will coordinate with the appropriate departments any equipment shutdown that may be required to accomplish the scheduled PM.

3. C & M shop schedulers will include the PM work in the daily schedule to ensure that the PM is accomplished each week. One copy of the Transmittal Report will be forwarded to the appropriate shop supervisor with the PMIs for each piece of equipment.

4 . C & M shop supervisors will assign the PM work to the craftsmen in accordance with the daily schedule to accomplish the maintenance tasks as outlined on each PMI.

B. *Completion of Scheduled Work*

1. C & M shop supervisors will issue the appropriate PMI to the craftsmen when assigning the scheduled maintenance.

2. The craftsmen will complete the PMI Feedback Data for each piece of equipment *at* the job site as the maintenance is performed. The craftsmen *must* indicate by checking one of the three status blocks as to whether: (1) maintenance is complete; (2) maintenance is incomplete; (3) equipment needs maintenance. If status (2) or (3) is checked, an explanation is required in comments section. The craftsman will always enter his or her name and time spent performing the work on each PMI.

C. *Cost Accounting*

1. The computer programs will generate a preventive maintenance work order for each equipment number scheduled.

2. Each craftsman will complete the PMI Labor Data by listing his or her name and time spent in performing scheduled maintenance on each PMI. Bench stock items (oil, grease, nuts, bolts, etc.) will not be charged on each PMI. Materials (belts, bearings, couplings, etc.) will be charged against work order number when issued by Central Stores issue clerk.

3. C & M shop supervisors will review each PMI for completeness of performance and time charges, then forward to C & M clerical staff for data entry.

4. C & M clerical staff will enter workhours and craftsman's social security number for each PMI completed by work order.

D. *Program Analysis and Generation of Planned Maintenance Projects*

1. The C & M shop supervisor will review each completed PMI to determine if additional maintenance is required. The supervisor will initiate a work request with Planning and Scheduling if additional maintenance is required.

2. P & S will process an individual work order requested by the work center supervisor for cost purposes and scheduling. They will also forward copies of each PWO and EWO to maintenance engineering for further study and evaluation.

3. Maintenance Engineering will review *all* planned maintenance work orders and emergency work orders and coordinate with C & M superintendents on possible changes needed to prevent excessive PWOs or EWOs on any equipment. Change of frequency and tasks will be coordinated between C & M superintendents, shop supervisors, and Technical Services engineers prior to any corrective maintenance work order being procesed or any changes to the scheduled PM. The Maintenance Engineer will also initiate work requests to P & S for Corrective Maintenance Projects.

4. Special, exception reports will be generated by the computer program. Examples of these reports are:

   a. PMIs scheduled, not completed (monthly)
   b. Ten items of equipment with highest maintenance dollar (monthly, semiannually, and annually)
   c. Facility Subsystem with greatest maintenance expenditure (annually)

Additional reports will be generated as program progresses and in accordance with management needs.

E. *Updating Equipment Inventory and Schedule Changes*

1. P & S will initiate an Equipment Data Sheet each time a piece of equipment is replaced by shop work order or contract. This Equipment Data Sheet will be forwarded from P & S to the responsible shop supervisor for completion. The completed Equipment Data Sheets will be forwarded to Architecture & Engineering Services for action by the Maintenance Engineer. The same procedure shall be followed for all additional equipment installed and for all equipment removed from service.

2. Maintenance Engineering will review forms for completeness and assign an equipment number to additional inventory. Additional PMIs, if needed, will be developed and coordinated with C & M personnel.

3. Clerical staff in A & E Services will provide the data entry to the PM Data Files for additions or deletions of equipment.

4. Changes to the schedule for added/deleted equipment will be coordinated by Maintenance Engineering and C & M to ensure balanced manpower requirements.
5. Clerical staff in A & E Services will provide data entry of new PMIs and schedule changes.

VIII. Approvals

_____   _____
Director of Physical Plant   Director, Plant Management
                                      and General Services

DISTRIBUTION

Physical Plant Assistant Directors, Superintendents, and Supervisors

Academic Deans and Department Chairpersons (Information Copy)

Vice President for Business Affairs (Information Copy)

Director, Office of Planning Services (Information Copy)

Directors, Administrative Offices (Information Copy)

CHAPTER 39

Major Maintenance and Capital Renewal/Replacement Programs

Harvey H. Kaiser
Senior Vice President
Syracuse University

39.1 DEFINITIONS

Facility management responsibilities for work management and control include programs for major maintenance and capital renewal/replacement. Organizational structures for managing these programs vary. Larger institutions may divide the responsibilities between maintenance management and design and construction departments; at smaller institutions a physical plant department will manage both programs. Because the programs emerge from two concepts—accounting and plant operations—there is a built-in confusion about their meanings. The issue of deferred maintenance further complicates clear delineation of terms and operational applications to achieve the basic goal of extending the life of existing facilities.

An institution may be simultaneously conducting programs for major maintenance, capital renewal/replacement, and deferred maintenance. The decision to create three separate programs is not unusual and usually evolves from different sources of funding and/or different components of facilities management to supervise the programs. Major maintenance is recognizable as a routine part of current fund operations and maintenance. A limit for the cost of maintenance work can shift the designation to the category of a capitalized project. Thus, an accounting decision can separate major maintenance from capital renewal. Rules are not fixed on distinctions between the two categories and can lend to confusion in selecting priorities of work.

Replacements in the form of new construction are routinely designated as capitalized and join together with renewals as capital renewal/replacement programs. As a form of capitalized construction, replacements are interchangeable with new construction, whether they are actually replacing an existing facility or an addition to plant. Linking capital renewals with replacements more accurately describes a program for renewal of existing plant assets as distinguished from totally new additions to plant assets.

Deferred maintenance programs result from a campus policy to group deferred major maintenance projects, and sometimes other plant needs, into a program funded separately from major maintenance or capital renewal/replacement.

Defining the three terms as they are generally used aids in selecting work priorities and budgeting practices. The first term, major maintenance, is derived from the Classification of Accounts jointly developed by APPA and NACUBO. (See Appendix 12-A.) Major Repairs and Renovations, Section 6 of the Classification of Accounts for operations and maintenance of plants provided by current funds, includes "expenditures for those major jobs or projects that must be accomplished but are not funded by normal maintenance resources received in the annual operating budget cycle." The distinction between major repairs and minor repairs should be defined by the institution.

Renewal and replacement is an accounting term used to distinguish a subgroup of plant fund assets from capitalized additions and improvements to plant. However, institutional accounting practices vary; decisions are made sometimes to capitalize portions of major maintenance and renewal/ replacement. The scope, complexity, cost, and duration of a project can dictate whether major maintenance should be included in maintenance management or by a separate design and construction department under overall work management and control. As an alternative to using in-house maintenance and design staff, a major maintenance project requiring plans, specifications, and competitive bidding can be designed by consultants and constructed by contractors. Capital renewal and replacement usually requires external assistance in design and construction to avoid dedicating facilities management staff to lengthy, time-consuming projects.

Both major maintenance and capital renewal and replacement require supervision by facilities management staff to coordinate campus conditions: access during construction, interim relocations, utilities, and assure project delivery in conformance with specifications, budgets, and schedules.

Planning budget requirements for major maintenance and capital renewal/replacement derives from principles of capital asset depreciation. Although higher education does not generally record depreciation of plant assets, it is an economic fact of life that facilities have a limited productive or useful life. The concept of life cycle defines useful life of a facility as the aggregate of the life or durability of individual building components and systems. In common terms, a building does not wear out all at once but fails by components or systems. A planned program of major maintenance and renewal by components and systems is necessary to correct deterioration and extend a facility's life.

Before bringing these terms together as operational guides for facility managers, deferred maintenance requires definition. Although origins of "deferred maintenance" as a rallying cry for a problem of major magnitude, rather than simply what managers do when money runs short, are unclear; its usage is confusing. The deferral of maintenance is routine for the most able managers. Under-budgeting regular maintenance accrues into a host of familiar needs: roof repairs, exterior site drainage, repointing of masonry, malfunctioning control systems, and deteriorated building sealants and flashings are familiar examples that accumulate into problems requiring major funding for correction.

The introduction of the term deferred maintenance emerged in the early 1970s as college and university administrators began to recognize the serious nature of plant problems on their campuses. The deteriorated plant conditions produced by ignoring older facilities during higher education's post-World War II expansion were compounded by poor designs for institutional durability, cost cutting that rapidly produced space but with inferior construction techniques, and innovative materials showing early failures. Soaring utility costs, inflation-reduced operations and maintenance budgets, and increased government regulations resulted in further deferral of maintenance.

An early effort in attacking the problem occurred with an action by the Nebraska State Legislature. In 1977, Legislative Bill 309 defined deferred maintenance as:

> any measures taken to correct structural or mechanical defects that would endanger the integrity of a building or its components or allow unwanted penetration of the building by outdoor elements, or measures taken to correct a waste of energy, including minor repairs, alteration and maintenance painting, cost of materials, hiring of building maintenance personnel, and other necessary expenses for the maintenance of roofs, exterior walls, retaining walls, foundations, flooring, ceilings, partitions, doors, building hardware, windows, plaster, structural ironwork, screens, plumbing, heating and air conditioning equipment, or electrical systems, but excluding decorative finish or furnishing, building additions, or installation of additional summer-winter air conditioners.

This definition could also serve for major maintenance and suggests the temptation to bypass the annual budget and fund major maintenance through a deferred maintenance program. The difference is that a deferred maintenance program is a comprehensive, one-time approach to control a massive backlog of work through a separate category of funding. Deferred maintenance can be defined as follows: maintenance work deferred to a future budget cycle or postponed until funds are available.

Major maintenance and deferred maintenance are forms of expenditure to accommodate the deterioration process of facilities; both programs cope with facility renewal. As a strategy to achieve funding to eliminate problems of facility deterioration, deferred maintenance programs can be expanded to include life safety, code compliance requirements, and provisions for handicapped accessibility. In contrast, major maintenance is a planned activity of facility renewal funded by the annual operating budget beyond routine maintenance repairs. The failure to perform needed repair, maintenance, and renewal by normal maintenance management creates deferred maintenance.

39.2 CURRENT ISSUES

The Magnitude of Capital Renewal

The question repeatedly asked by federal and state agencies, governing boards, foundations, and corporate donors is: How large is the problem of facilities deterioration, and how much is needed to remedy conditions?

In managing higher education institutions the concepts of *capital asset management* and *functional improvements* are often mixed to create a confusing picture of the capital needs.[1] Unclear distinctions and priorities between capital asset management and functional improvements blur sharp definitions of overall capital funding requirements.

The first concept, capital asset management, emerges from the need to offset normal facilities deterioration. Buildings, grounds, utilities, and equipment have requirements for renewal over varying life cycles. Capital asset management includes preservation of building enclosures, structural frames, interior finishes, and mechanical and electrical systems. Infrastructure of roads, parking areas, electrical service systems, and campus utilities are additional components of campus capital assets. Meeting life safety standards and compliance with regulatory standards, especially those required for a healthy environment (asbestos and PCB transformer removals, hazardous waste and toxic material control, and adequate building air circulation), are also aspects of extending the life of capital assets. This is a program independent of the intended use or reuse of a facility.

Adequate capital reserves fund projects to ameliorate deterioration and correct deferred maintenance. With approximately 50 percent of higher education's physical plant built between 1950 and 1975, a major infusion of capital was required during the past two decades to protect plant investments. This was not invested, however, as illustrated by the pervasive presence of deferred maintenance.

The second concept, functional improvements, is the provision of adequate facilities to meet the mission of teaching, research, and public service. The construction of a variety of facilities on individual campuses was postponed because of fiscal uncertainty. Choices were made to use operating budgets to fund academic programs, student life, or increase compensation rather than risk unsuccessful fund-raising campaigns for new facilities. One explanation for the recent trend of an increase in capital projects is the decision by campus administrators and governing boards to simply "do it."

Over a decade ago, the problem of campus deferred maintenance was referred to as "a ticking time bomb." The threat on a nationwide basis was then estimated in the range of $40 to $50 billion for deferred maintenance and plant renewal. Trends during the past ten years show a wide range of action. Higher education plant investments nationally in 1986 were $3.9 billion and $4.3 billion in 1987. Projections for 1988-1990 are $11.4 billion. Approximately 62 percent of this total was allocated for new construction, 12 percent for additions, and 26 percent for renovations.

The last comprehensive national survey of facilities conducted by HEGIS (Higher Education Government Information Survey) in 1973 estimated that approximately 20 percent of all higher education space was in an unsatisfactory condition. Results of a recently published APPA/NACUBO/Coopers & Lybrand research report, *The Decaying American Campus: A Ticking Time Bomb*, show little evidence that conditions have improved. The estimates in 1988 were for $20 billion in "urgent" needs and a total renewal/replacement need of $60 to $70 billion. Examples of system-wide and independent campus plant condition surveys confirm that high levels of deferred maintenance persist. Estimates from detailed facilities audits report $30 to $35 per gross square foot is required for deferred maintenance and capital renewal for *all* campus space.

A recurring response to requests for funding capital renewal is that annual expenditures for operating and maintaining facilities and plant additions should have routinely compensated for renewal needs. The logic is reasonable: funds expended on operations and maintenance directly affect conditions of campus facilities and expenditures for plant additions represent capitalized investments to replace obsolete facilities, meet new program requirements, and enhance the quality of campus life.

In reviewing plant operations and maintenance expenditures for the past decade, one might expect increased proportions of total budget expenditures to compensate for larger enrollments and expanded facilities. The additional space, wear and tear on facilities, higher required levels of maintenance for more technologically sophisticated buildings, drastically increased utility costs, and inflationary effects on maintenance costs for personnel, materials, and services exceeding rises in the Consumer Price Index demanded more funds for operations and maintenance. The accumulation of plant improvement needs for the older campus buildings and the large amount of plant added to meet enrollment growth in the 1960s and early 1970s, now reaching an age of increasing maintenance costs, justify additional plant operations and maintenance funding.

Despite these demands, the portion of operations and maintenance funding has remained nearly level through fiscal years 1975 to 1984. Fluctuations have been less than 1 percent, ranging from 10 to 11 percent of total education and general expenditures for operations and maintenance. The conclusion is that unless additional funding to operations and maintenance (O&M) budgets is made for renewal, replacement, or plant additions, the unfunded needs of deferred maintenance will continue to grow.

However, federal and state legislators, campus administrators, and governing boards want more than a general estimate of need. Faculty, staff, students, and alumni will testify to the needs. Prospective students and donors also convey the message by admissions applications and contributions. The importance of facilities appearance to student recruitment is underscored by the study of the Carnegie Foundation for the Advancement of Teaching on how students choose a college. For 62 percent of the students, "appearance of the buildings and grounds was the most influential factor during a campus visit."[2]

Hard data is demanded to justify the claims for campus capital renewal and replacement needs. At the campus level, responses can be prepared by conducting detailed facilities audits. Rigorously prepared and creatively presented, these audits of condition have proven effective in securing funding.

Repair and replacement needs vary by region, building type, the extent of use and abuse, and quality of original construction and maintenance management. Levels of current fund allocation for operations and maintenance and special appropriations for capital renewal and replacement also affect funding needs. But, as sure as death and taxes, building systems and components deteriorate and need replacement. Plumbing wears out, roofing breaks down and leaks, window frames warp, patched-up electrical wiring becomes dangerous, HVAC systems fail to heat or cool, and equipment can no longer be replaced. These are glamorless priorities. In competition with academic program enhancements, acquisition of new technological advances in computing and other equipment, and improvements in campus life facilities, renewal or replacement of deteriorated facilities will remain a low priority unless aggressive action is taken by facilities managers.

Funding Requirements

A campus' awareness that deteriorating facility conditions have reached the point of a significant liability immediately opens the question: How much is needed to correct the problem?

As background, the various budget streams contributing to major maintenance and renewal/replacement should be drawn into perspective. Figure 39-1 illustrates the flow into facilities improvements from the two funding sources (current and plant funds) for preventing building deterioration and renewing or replacing facilities. Current funds routinely provide for major maintenance and capital funds provide for capital improvements. Deferred maintenance is also supported by capital funds. An additional funding source is identified as an annual renewal allowance and is budgeted from current funds.

An important reminder is that annual funding for physical plant operations and maintenance is expected to accommodate major maintenance to compensate for the aging process of facilities and equipment. Major maintenance is typically treated as a residual category after budgeting for administration, building and equipment maintenance, custodial services, utilities, and grounds maintenance. The residual treatment of major maintenance has proven to be inadequate to meet plant needs and is how most campuses reached their current levels of deferred maintenance. The preferred approach is to establish an appropriate level of major maintenance *and* renewal funding in the operating budget to prevent the continuing deterioration and obsolescence of facilities and equipment.

Annual allocations for facility renewal can occur either in the major maintenance component of the operations and maintenance annual budgets or as a special line item with identifying specific projects. The choice is made by the strategy most acceptable to campus budgeting practices. The important principle for campus policy makers to remember is that a one-time elimination of deferred maintenance priorities does not solve the problem. Campus facilities continue to deteriorate and become obsolete. An annual allocation for facilities renewal is required to prevent future accumulation of deferred maintenance. Estab-

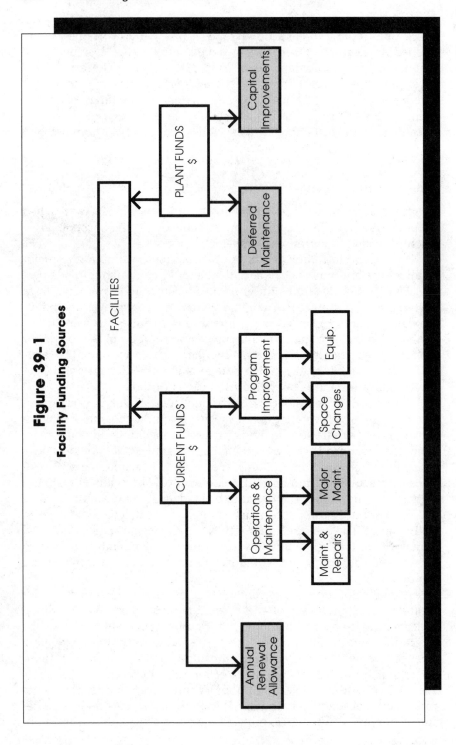

Figure 39-1

Facility Funding Sources

lishing an appropriate level of annual funding at the beginning of a comprehensive facilities program may have to include catch-up costs. As needs are reduced to manageable proportions, the operating budget can accommodate priorities as they are identified. The end result is a program that maintains campus facilities in good repair, functionally adequate for teaching, research, campus life, and public service.

A guideline for an annual renewal allowance uses life-cycle concepts without an audit of conditions of designating specific projects. The use of an allowance provides flexibility in determining which projects will be funded in any given year and gives facilities managers confidence that funds will be available to meet capital renewal needs. Empirical studies for life-cycles of individual building components provide general parameters for annual capital renewal allowances. Acknowledging variances for age and type of facilities, a recommended range for annual capital renewal funding is 1.5 to 3 percent of total replacement value of plant; some recommend even higher amounts. Several formula methods for developing annual renewal allowances are outlined by Sherman and Dergis in "A Funding Model for Building Renewal," Harvey H. Kaiser in *Crumbling Academe*, Cushing Phillips Jr. in "Facilities Renewal: The Formula Approach," Daniel D. Robinson in *Capital Maintenance for Colleges and Universities*, and Hans Jenny in *Hang-Gliding or Looking for an Updraft*. All are cited at the end of this chapter.

A common budget management pitfall is the use of major maintenance and capital renewal funding for program improvements. The first category deals with deteriorated facility conditions and protection of capital assets; the second category addresses renovations for functional inadequacies, obsolescence, new academic or other program requirements. As final budget decisions are reached, pressure is often applied to shift major maintenance and renewal funding to meet program needs. This is an element of "budget politics" that compromises protection of plant assets.

A systematic approach adopted at the University of Washington in the 1980s produced significant results in increasing spending for deferred maintenance projects from $15 million in 1981-83 to $38 million in 1988-89. The multi-part strategy includes building an externally reinforced consensus, internal monitoring, a review and priority-setting system, and a conscious budget strategy that separates deferred maintenance from projects that serve teaching and research directly. Each element of this strategy played an important political as well as technical role in reinforcing the priority to be given to the repair and updating of building systems.

Another such example is the effort of Vanderbilt University, which has taken an aggressive, proactive approach to the funding of its capital renewal and deferred maintenance priorities. Vanderbilt has instituted, among other funding programs, a building component replacement reserve, a utility reserve account, and an asset depreciation reserve.

The central purpose of the academic enterprise is programs, and facilities are viewed as a supporting medium for conducting programs. The facilities manager must remain a staunch advocate to preserve major maintenance and renewal funding while creatively accommodating program requirements whenever and wherever possible.

A Prospectus

Speculation on major maintenance and campus renewal/replacement for the rest of this century offers some insights to facilities managers for long-range budget planning. Backlogs of deferred maintenance will continue to require campuses to offset deteriorated buildings, grounds, utilities, and equipment with deferred maintenance programs. Those campuses that have not yet launched programs will be engaged in surveying conditions, setting priorities, and seeking funding to correct facility conditions. Evolving academic programs and stress placed on "hot" subject areas will require renovations, building renewal, and plant additions.

Some trends now evident indicate the following.

Science and Technology   Facilities constructed for science and technology in the post-Sputnik era of the 1960s are reaching the end of their useful life. Undergraduate and graduate teaching laboratories and research space will require upgrading and facilities created for new technologies and sophisticated equipment.

Multidisciplinary Programs   Shifting emphasis towards multidisciplinary programs will replace some older, traditional academic departments with new organizational and space configurations. Computer innovations affect these changes, along with policies of government, corporate, and foundation funding sources.

Telecommunications   The impact of divestiture by voice communications sources has moved campuses into an era of self-owned telecommunications systems. More and more campuses are becoming private telephone companies. Simultaneously, the dramatic evolution of computing technology has placed computers in administrative offices, faculty offices, classrooms, and student residence halls. The result has been a trend to combine voice and data with integrated switches (computers) for transmission over comprehensive systems for internal campus and external connections. (See Chapter 48, Telecommunications Systems.)

Computer Systems and Spaces   The widespread distribution of access to campus computing requires "wiring the campus." A new inside and outside cable plant will be required to coordinate the task of connecting central computing equipment to local area networks, computer terminal clusters, and individual workstations. The conversion of existing spaces and creation of new facilities will increases in environmentally controlled spaces. A consequence is increased utility costs and more technically sophisticated facilities management staff.

Historic Preservation   Continued interest in preserving older campus facilities and respect for the context of buildings and outdoor spaces are forces that will affect plans for major maintenance and facilities renewal. The pre-World War II campus facilities will reach an age when considerations for national or local designation as historic structures will cause campus constituencies for preservation to develop. Many campuses that saw dramatic growth in the 1950s and 1960s will also face alumni advocates who have a nostalgic feeling for preserving the campus as they knew it and will resist change to older facilities. Adaptive reuse solutions requiring creative approaches will be necessary as an alternative to major alterations or demolition.

Economic and Social Development   The need to expand external funding sources will bring education into closer partnership with government and corporations. A central theme now emerging is the role campuses can play in economic and social development of local communities, regions, and the nation. A further goal is the application of academic research to economic and social problems. Transfer of technology from campus laboratories to industry is an example of this trend. Another is the creation of multidisciplinary institutes dedicated to community service. Campus improvements will be required for increased public access and upgrading of campus space to meet corporate standards, improved overnight accommodations, and auxiliary services for visitors.

Quality of Campus Life   Undergraduate and graduate students, faculty, and staff will demand facilities that respond to contemporary standards of living. This includes residence halls with modernized, more private accommodations, air conditioning, and a reduction in communal shared space. Recreation facilities will require improvements and expansion following patterns of social emphasis on fitness and life-long wellness. More indoor and outdoor recreation facilities will be provided in response to this demand.

Regulatory Standards   Ongoing and expanded programs for environmental health and safety, accessibility for the disabled, and life safety

are additional tasks for facilities managers. As new environmental hazards are discovered and regulations developed, facilities managers will
be required to understand the nature of the problem and acquire knowledge to plan and implement corrective programs.

39.3 MEASURING MAJOR MAINTENANCE AND CAPITAL RENEWAL REQUIREMENTS

Determining funding needs for major maintenance and capital renewal
can be achieved by one of two methods: a formula approach or an audit
of existing conditions.

Formula Approach

The formula approach is driven by capital budgeting requirements and
provides an annual allowance for major maintenance and capital renewal. Using basic information on building age and comparable replacement costs for similar building types, systems and components,
calculations for an individual building can be developed for an annual
renewal allowance by hand or computer spreadsheet. Repetition of the
process for all campus buildings provides an estimated allowance for
annual operating budgets and capital budgets. The renewal allowance
represents a pool of funds for individual projects based upon selection of
priorities. It is well advised that methodology and application should be
thoroughly understood before selecting the formula approach.

The mechanics of formula approaches for a capital renewal allowance were developed by Sherman and Dergis in "A Funding Model for
Building Renewal" and refined for computer application by Cushing
Phillips Jr. in "Facilities Renewal: The Formula Approach." Both references provide background and details that are readily applicable. A
common concept in the formula approach is that buildings can be
viewed as a collection of systems and components that last for different
intervals of time. Guidance for defining a building by systems and
components is available from *Dodge Construction Costs Systems* or *Means
Building Construction Costs Data*. Typical breakdowns are by primary
structure (foundation, frame and exterior walls, floor, and roof systems);
secondary structure (ceilings, interior walls and partitions, windows,
and doors); service systems (heating, cooling, plumbing, electrical, and
conveying systems); and safety systems.

Another concept of the annual renewal allowance compensates for
the fact that buildings with an average fifty-year life cycle do not generate a constant 2 percent of current renewal value each year for fifty years

Figure 39-2

Annual Facility Renewal Allowance

Renewal Allowance (25-Year Systems) = Building Age ×

$$\frac{\text{Replacement Cost of 25-Year Systems}}{325}$$

Renewal Allowance (50-Year Systems) = Building Age ×

$$\frac{\text{Replacement Cost of 50-Year Systems}}{1,275}$$

Total Renewal Allowance = Renewal Allowance (25-Year Systems) + Renewal Allowance (50-Year Systems)

Calculation of Adjusted Age

Adjusted Age = (Renovated Fraction)/(Years Since Renovation) + (Unrenovated Fraction) × (Age of Building)*
*Up to 25 years for 25-year systems, up to 50 years for 50-year systems

(Note: The "sum of the digits" for a maximum age of 25 years is 325 (1 + 2 + 3 . . . .+25=325) and for 50 years is 1,275.

Source: Phillips, Cushing Jr. "Facilities Renewal: The Formula Approach." pp. 112, 114.

as a renewal allowance, but have varying life cycles. A formula that "skews" funding towards older buildings to be consistent with renewal needs recognizes that the effects of aging accumulate greater (and more expensive) funding requirements. Sherman and Dergis accomplish this by a "sum-of-the digits" method representing the fifty-year life of a building. A basic formula divides the age of a system or component by the sum of the years of its maximum age. Phillips refined the concept of maximum age by grouping different systems and components into twenty-five or fifty-year life cycles and the effect of renovations on updating life cycles (see Figure 39-2).

Replacement costs for twenty-five or fifty-year life of systems are average square foot costs derived for typical buildings of similar use, construction types and building area adjusted for required cost differences. A sample of facilities categories and replacement costs for major building systems grouped in fifty and twenty-five year categories is illustrated in Figure 39-3. A sample calculation of an annual renewal allowance is illustrated in Figure 39-4.

An annual renewal allowance for a facility can be calculated by multiplying the current replacement value by the replacement index.

Figure 39-3

Total Replacement Costs—Major Building Systems

Facility Category Number	Facility Category	Notes	50-Year Systems								25-Year Systems		
			Exterior Walls	Partitions	Conveying Systems	Specialties	Fixed Equipment	Plbg & Fire Protection	Electrical	Total 50-Year	Roofing	HVAC	Total 25-Year
1	Classroom/Admin	1	4.86	4.47	0.00	2.07	6.61	5.64	8.62	32.27	0.71	11.66	12.37
2	Laboratory	1	4.41	4.41	0.00	2.17	5.97	7.39	10.24	34.59	1.43	12.55	13.98
3	Vocational Schl	1	6.75	4.32	0.00	2.62	2.86	1.94	6.26	24.76	2.43	3.35	5.78
4	Library	1	5.69	5.12	0.72	2.31	8.07	4.90	8.00	34.80	1.59	10.73	12.32
5	Gymnasium	1	6.85	4.68	0.00	1.05	5.69	5.63	5.27	29.16	1.37	7.16	8.53
6	Swimming Pool	2, 3	11.79	8.19	0.00	0.00	2.64	2.60	3.97	29.19	1.71	9.39	11.10
7	Auditorium	2, 4	10.23	2.92	2.13	0.00	5.24	1.79	8.93	31.24	3.43	8.65	12.08
8	Student Center	1	5.66	2.16	0.00	5.79	9.34	5.66	5.27	33.88	1.53	8.39	9.92
9	Central Util Plt	1	4.21	0.23	0.00	0.41	4.89	3.61	7.96	21.32	1.79	4.17	5.95
10	Shop	1	3.35	0.16	0.00	0.00	1.18	1.56	5.80	12.04	1.29	2.21	3.49
11	Medical Clinic	2, 5	9.19	8.40	4.56	0.00	3.94	3.67	3.28	33.04	1.70	5.51	7.21
12	Med Ctr/Hospital	1	15.78	13.51	6.08	10.09	3.56	14.22	17.20	80.44	0.85	15.78	16.63
13	Residence	1	3.36	3.27	0.00	0.46	1.91	1.36	1.51	11.87	1.51	2.16	3.67
14	Dormitory	1	5.63	4.29	3.23	1.25	2.17	3.65	4.11	24.33	0.28	4.48	4.76
15	Other (Warehouse)	2, 6	3.75	0.35	0.00	0.98	0.00	2.00	1.91	8.98	2.61	2.20	4.81

Notes: 1 - Dodge Construction Systems Costs—1985 (Regional Factor—0.78)
2 - Means Square Foot Costs—1985 (Regional Factor—0.85)
3 - Includes $50,000 For Pool Equipment & Bleachers (20,000 Sq. Ft.)
4 - Includes $70,000 For Elevator & Special Fixtures (7,000 Sq. Ft.)
5 - Includes $100,000 For Fixed Equipment
6 - Sandwich Panel Construction (20,000 Sq. Ft.)

Source: Phillips, Cushing Jr. "Facilities Renewal: The Formula Approach," p. 111

Figure 39-4

Calculation of Renewal Allowance and Renewal Backlog

		A	B
Total Repl Cost		$13.98/GSF	$34.59/GSF
Building Area		50,000 GSF	50,000 GSF
Age		25 Years	40 Years
Years Since Renovation		16 Years	16 Years
Percent Renov		50%	50%
Adjusted Age	=	0.5 × 16 + 0.5 × 25	0.5 × 16 + 0.5 × 40
	=	20 Years	28 Years
Renewal Allowance Factor	=	20/325	28/1,275
	=	0.0615	0.0220
Renewal Allowance Calculation	=	0.0615 × $13.98	+ 0.0220 × $34.59
	=	$42,988	+ $38,049
ANNUAL RENEWAL ALLOWANCE		A + B = $81,037	

Source: Phillips, Cushing Jr. "Facilities Renewal: The Formula Approach." p. 115

An alternate approach to those described above is the Replacement Index Method to calculate an annual renewal allowance. Replacement cycles and the resulting costs for replacing building systems and components produce an index expressed as a percent of the current replacement value of a facility that must be renewed annually. Funds would not necessarily be spent at this rate but are a reserve for projects as they are identified. In practice, the recommended level of funding major maintenance and capital renewal is incorporated into the operating budget for annual expenditures and accumulated as a reserve for future needs.

A replacement index includes the following factors:

- Facility Type. Systems and component costs vary widely across the range of facility types.
- Date of Construction. Original construction and date of additions or major renovations affect renewal scheduling.
- Facility Systems and Components. Quantity and quality of in-

stalled systems and components of a facility will determine replacement requirements.
- System and Component Life Cycles. Predictable life of systems and components affects future requirements.

A replacement index for the purpose of computing an annual renewal allowance for a facility uses the following steps (see Figure 39-5).

1. Building Type (Column 1). Select information for a similar building type from Means or Dodge construction cost reports for the current year. The list of components developed for replacement cost indexes should be consistent for all building types.
2. Costs per Gross Square Foot (Column 2). Obtain component costs per gross square foot from institutional records or published reports. The total for the components should equal the building cost per gross square foot.
3. Percent of Total Construction (Column 3). The percent of total con-

Figure 39-5

Replacement Index for a One- to Four-Story Office Building

Column 1	Column 2	Column 3	Column 4	Column 5
Building Component	Cost per Gross Sq. Ft.	Percent of Total Construction	Average Year Before Replacement	Replacement Index=% per Year of Total Value
1. Foundations				
2. Substructure				
3. Superstructure				
4. Exterior Closure				
5. Roofing				
6. Interior Construction				
7. Conveying				
8. Mechanical				
9. Electrical				
10. Special Construction				
11. Sitework				
12. General Conditions				
13. Design Fees				
TOTALS				

struction is calculated by dividing the cost of each component into total project cost.
4. Average Year Before Replacement (Column 4). The life cycle for each component is also available from published sources and a table of estimated component life should be prepared for use on replacement index calculations for all buildings. An adjustment in the average year before replacement in the prepared table should be made for renovations or other major system renewals.
5. Replacement Index (Column 5). The replacement index for each component is calculated by multiplying the percent of total construction (Column 3) by average year before replacement (Column 4). The result is placed in Column 5 and the total of the component indexes results in a replacement index for the facility.

Manually completing the preparatory work or use of readily available software in developing formula input for a campus or system provides a practical and flexible tool for capital budgeting. The concept of an annual renewal allowance by the formula approach or replacement index method has been applied successfully in developing additional funding and is recommended for capital budget planning.

The effort to develop formula funding procedures continues to evolve. A new funding model, "Financial Planning Guidelines for Facility Renewal and Adaption," has been developed in a joint project of the Society of College and University Planners, APPA, National Association of College and University Business Officers, and Coopers & Lybrand.

The Facilities Audit

The most reliable source for major maintenance and capital renewal/replacement needs is a survey of conditions provided by a facilities audit. The detailed facilities audit evaluates the physical condition and functional adequacy of buildings, grounds, utilities, and equipment. Types of audits vary. Some are comprehensive, recording basic building information, noting specific maintenance deficiencies, describing functional adequacy, and defining priorities for budgeting. Others are more general to determine overall building conditions and maintenance needs.

Guidelines for a facilities audit vary with the purposes for conducting the survey. A comprehensive audit approach is recommended for institutions with poor records on facility conditions and functional adequacy and for campuses setting out on a deferred maintenance program. A more general approach to assessing conditions and identifying major maintenance priorities is appropriate for institutions with ongoing programs and sufficient data bases of existing conditions.

The outline of the self-evaluation process for a comprehensive facilities audit is shown in Figure 39-6. A reference for conducting the audit is *Facilities Audit Workbook* published by APPA.[3] A comprehensive audit provides the following: 1) a description of individual building systems and components; 2) a rating of the systems and components conditions; 3) an overall rating of facility condition and functional adequacy; and 4) records maintenance deficiencies. This approach establishes a data base for a facility with comments on current maintenance needs and can be annually updated.

The audit approach described in *Facilities Audit Workbook*—as well as similar techniques developed by states, colleges, and universities—divide a building into major systems, components, and functional characteristics. A sample rating form summarizing a building audit is shown in Figure 39-7. A facility is assigned a total number of points (100) and each component is assigned a value typical of its portion of a total facility (possible). Using a separate form for each component the auditor inspects conditions, deducts deficiencies, and enters a rating (actual). For example, a foundation system valued at 13 percent of the total structure has some defects and is rated at only 10 percent of "new condition." Adding up all the actual ratings of components produces a total rating for a facility. Cost estimates for correcting observed conditions can be calculated using the building rating and multiplying by replacement value. Individual component costs for corrective projects can also be estimated by this deficiency method. Emergency conditions noted in the audit can be flagged for detailed estimates of labor and materials.

A refinement for the audit form is noting priorities by work category (maintenance work orders, maintenance projects, and capital projects) and costs for correcting deficiencies. Summaries of all campus facilities ratings and maintenance deficiencies provide a comprehensive campus overview and are useful for supporting budget requests, comparisons to other institutions, and meeting state or other governing agency reporting requirements.

The first phase of an audit is designing the overall process. Initial decisions define the scope of buildings, grounds, utilities, and equipment to be audited. The amount of detail to be covered is also determined, based on purposes of the audit, deadlines, staff availability, and projected costs for conducting the survey. Defining prime responsibility and who will conduct the audit has a direct effect on the results.

A senior member of campus facilities administration should have overall responsibility for the audit to ensure consistency and implementation of findings. Facilities evaluations can be conducted by in-house staff, by consultants, or a combination. The scope of the project and amount of detail to be covered will influence this decision. Whichever

Figure 39-6
The Self-Evaluation Process

PHASE ONE — DESIGNING THE AUDIT

STEP I — Determine the Scope of the Audit

A. What to include
   1. Buildings
   2. Grounds
   3. Utilities
B. Depth of audit
   1. Need
   2. Cost
   3. Time
C. Phases
   1. Comprehensive audit
   2. Condensed audit

PHASE TWO — COLLECTING THE DATA

STEP III — Design a Plan of Attack

A. What information to collect
B. Who will collect information
C. Schedule

PHASE THREE — PRESENTING THE FINDINGS

STEP VI — Summarize

A. Building characteristics
B. Building evaluation summary

STEP II — Select Team

A. Prime responsibility
B. Members
   1. Institution
   2. Consultants

STEP IV — Collect the Data

A. Buildings
   1. Physical data
      a. Primary systems
      b. Secondary systems
      c. Service systems
      d. Safety standards
   2. Functional data
B. Grounds
C. Utilities

STEP VII — Prioritize

A. Repair and renovation projects
B. Five-year program

STEP V — Evaluate and Analyze Data

A. Physical evaluation
B. Functional evaluation
C. Priority repairs and renovations
D. Maintenance needs
E. Cost estimates

STEP VIII — Report/Present

A. Define audience
B. Identify data required
C. Design presentation

Figure 39-7

Physical Facilities Evaluation Summary

Building Number & Name _____

Location _____

Survey Date _____

Survey Team _____   _____

_____   _____

	Ratings	
	Possible	Actual
Primary Structure	(40)	( )
1. Foundation System	13	_____
2. Column & Exterior Wall System	13	_____
3. Floor System	7	_____
4. Roof System	7	_____
Secondary Structure	(9)	( )
5. Ceiling System	3	_____
6. Interior Walls & Partitions	3	_____
7. Window System	2	_____
8. Door System	1	_____
Service Systems	(34)	( )
9. Cooling	10	_____
10. Heating	10	_____
11. Plumbing	5	_____
12. Electrical	8	_____
13. Conveying	1	_____
Safety Standards	(5)	( )
14. Safety Standards		_____
Functional Standards	(12)	( )
15. Assignable Space	4	_____
16. Adaptability	4	_____
17. Suitability	4	_____
	TOTAL 100	

BUILDING RATING*		
S. Satisfactory	95–100	_____
2. Remodeling—A	75– 94	_____
3. Remodeling—B	55– 74	_____
4. Remodeling—C	35– 54	_____
U. Demolition	0– 34	_____

staffing pattern is used, staff responsibility and involvement in the survey is necessary.

The second phase of an audit is data collection and evaluation. Preparation for this phase includes assembly of facility plans and specifications, maintenance and operations manuals, maintenance records, energy costs (if available), and other data useful to the audit team. Next, the audit forms should be prepared. Basic formats available are designed for manual entries and tabulation. These can be adapted to software programs and assist in summarizing building rating, preliminary project estimates, and generating management reports.

The collection of data should be designed to establish data bases for future retrieval of information on a specific facilities component, system, or specialized equipment. An integrated data base with each campus building referenced to plans, specifications, operations manuals, routine maintenance logs, and maintenance deficiency reports provides a ready source of information for future investigations. Data collection should also anticipate the design of summary reports for use in presentations of facilities' condition findings. As a collection of building ratings kept on file, the audit will be of little use. When conceived as reports used to identify comparable building conditions and maintenance projects, the audit becomes a useful tool in selecting project priorities and presenting budget requests.

39.4 SELECTION OF PRIORITIES

The facilities audit will furnish two types of information to senior administrators and other decision-makers who need to set facilities priorities. First, those facilities that have the greatest need based on the severity of both physical conditions and functional performance can be selected; second, the audit results will help plan maintenance tasks and capital project budgeting.

Priority selections from the facilities audit can be made for several purposes. Maintenance work orders, maintenance projects, and capital projects can be estimated and scheduled for work assignment. Management decision making on operating and capital budgets is supported by the facilities audit information as a basis for the selection of priorities.

Maintenance deficiencies comments entered on the component inspection forms can be estimated, preferably using quantities of labor and materials, design fees, and other owner's costs. General estimates of costs from similar projects are not specific enough to determine priorities. Reliable sources should be used. Where staff is available, their experience with maintenance and similar projects is vital for estimating projects. Architects, contractors, vendors, and special consultants should be retained for assistance in preparing estimates where necessary.

Priorities by Character of Work

Categorization of priorities requires consistent treatment of audit noted deficiencies and functional improvement requests, since funding decisions are made based on these categories. Typically, categorizing involves separating capital projects from maintenance work orders or maintenance projects, estimating project requests, and then summarizing project requests for a five-year budgeting cycle. Selection of funding priorities is based on a systematic categorization to develop a plan for funding maintenance and capital projects from operating budgets or special funding allocations for capital projects.

A comparison of building ratings will not automatically show the order in which items should be addressed. For example, a facility that rates a 74 is not automatically worse than one that rates a 75. However, it is valid to conclude that those facilities in the 50-74 range will need more immediate attention than those in the 75-100 range. Also, each location has its own priorities—the audit results may not show some qualitative elements that would affect funding.

One suggested outline for ranking priorities by point values is shown in Figure 39-8. Three priority levels are described that can be interpreted from the component rating forms. The audit team manager adds his or her knowledge of overall plant conditions. Careful judgment is necessary in choosing the priorities to fit with strategic planning and other policy considerations.

Another scheme of selecting priorities uses broad descriptive categories grouped to assist in determining priorities. Suggested categories are described below.

1. Liability Proposals—Special matters requiring early attention to remove jeopardy through life safety, property damage, regulatory, or court ordered actions.
2. Program and Operational Purposes—Actions necessary to support an organization's mission and meet operational requirements.
3. Economy and Efficiency Measures—Projects that also support program and operational objectives, but deserve special attention because they will result in immediate or eventual cost savings.

Separate Priority Lists

Separate priority lists can be developed from the deficiency reports entered on the component rating forms to fit budgeting practices of the

Figure 39-8
Project Priority Levels

PRIORITY LEVEL I	Point Value

I-1 Life Safety and Legal Compliance — 10

a. Hazardous life safety building or site conditions that will jeopardize people, programs, equipment; unless corrected will cause suspension of facilities use.

b. Repairs, renovations, and improvements required for immediate compliance with local, state, and federal regulations.

I-2 Facility Damage or Deterioration — 9

Repairs, renovations, and improvements to facilities that, unless corrected, will lead to a loss of a facility.

I-3 Cost-Effective Measures — 8

a. Repairs, renovations, and improvements required to prevent serious facility deterioration and significantly higher labor costs if not immediately corrected.

b. Energy conservation to reduce consumption with a rapid return on investment.

PRIORITY LEVEL II

II-1 Mission Support — 7

Actions required to support functional activities.

II-2 Delayed Priority I — 6

Repairs and renovations less compelling than Priority I.

II-3 Deferred Maintenance — 5

Deferral of repairs or renovations that will lead to major damage to a facility and loss of use, hamper building utilization, or affect economies of operation.

PRIORITY LEVEL III

III-1 Project Completion — 4

Building or site improvements uncompleted because of inadequate funding or other reasons. Improvements are necessary for proper functioning, economic maintenance, and suitable appearance of new construction.

III-2 Delayed Deferred Maintenance — 3

Repairs and renovations that can be postponed.

III-3 Anticipating Actions — 2

Actions carried out in anticipation of longer range development: land acquisition, infrastructure development, and advance planning for capital projects.

III-4 Reduction In Scope   1

Modify scope to a smaller scale or consolidate with other projects.

operations and maintenance department and decisions by the facility manager. This preference is determined by the different funding sources available for maintenance work orders, maintenance projects, and capital projects. The cost ranges of deficiency categories can be adjusted by type of work. In making a review of all projects, opportunities should be analyzed to "package" several projects for economies of scale. For example, roofing repairs and replacements for several buildings are commonly grouped together into a single project to allow for lower unit pricing. Similar operations, such as erecting scaffolding or suspending use of portions of buildings, also lend themselves to cost efficiencies and minimize building use inconveniences.

Intangible Factors

There are other factors that do not readily lend themselves to categories but should be considered when making funding decisions. Staff morale makes a positive contribution to overall productivity and can be influenced by sufficient space and properly functioning, well-furnished and equipped, attractive, and well-maintained facilities. Staff recruitment and retention is affected by physical appearance of facilities and the architectural qualities of buildings and site aesthetics. For this reason, historic preservation is an emerging factor affecting priorities.

Facilities in a marginal condition considered for replacement may be more valuable if they are retained and improved because of their importance to historic continuity or as a focal point for a community. Organizing these categories and intangible factors into a specific set of selection guidelines enables decisions based on technical evaluations and an organization's requirements.

Management Philosophy

Two concepts influencing final priority decisions are need and risk. For example, are projects for improving quality of the environment selected before life safety or operating economy projects?

In the final analysis, selection of priorities by management is the relative weight given to the protection of plant assets, fiscal instability by postponing deferred maintenance or energy conservation measures, visual image of the organization, and the risk of erosion of function and quality of environment. Although these matters may seem relatively intangible, they can be as debilitating as the more obvious physical consequences of deferring high-priority building and site repairs.

Selecting priorities for major maintenance and capital renewal/replacement faces similar temptations that occur in developing annual operating budgets. Established in a political environment of satisfying short-term needs, in contrast with long-term institutional goals, the annual operating budget becomes a compromise between alternatives. Overcoming this traditional approach to distribution of resources requires clear policy guidelines in selecting priority projects. Principles guiding the priority selection process are:

- First, major maintenance in the annual operations and maintenance budget should be reserved only for projects offsetting facility deterioration and extending the life of plant assets.
- Second, major renovations or new construction for program improvements should be funded separately from major maintenance.
- Third, deferred maintenance or renovations should be funded as special appropriations on a project-by-project basis.

An effective means for reviewing the major maintenance and capital renewal/replacement needs together is delegating assembly and analysis of requests to the facilities administrator. Project costs originate from this source and the necessary data in budgets and schedule can be prepared in a uniform manner. Although the review of requests is supervised best in this manner, there are several sources of information: the facilities administrator should be responsible for major maintenance requests based upon facilities conditions; academic program requirements are defined by academic administrators and translated into requests for special allocations or capital funding; and auxiliary managers develop requests similar to academic programs.

Capital Budget Review Committee

Minimizing the vicissitudes of the budget process can be handled by a capital budget review committee represented by the campus chief executive officer, chief academic and business officers, and the facilities administrator. Monitoring of progress on major maintenance, capital renewal/replacement, and special allocations should be done by the committee on a frequent basis, preferably on a quarterly schedule. This permits a routine opportunity for introducing emergencies and new priorities and enhances management of institutional cash flow. Reports provided by the facilities administrator should summarize status of previously authorized and funded projects and lists of proposed projects for the following budget year. An additional report summarizing anticipated projects for a "rolling" five-year period assists in overall campus long-range budgeting.

An annual meeting of the committee provides the formal approvals to be incorporated into the routine budget cycle for the following year. Use of this process integrates major maintenance, capital renewal/replacement, and capital improvements. Where deferred maintenance programs have been established, they should be included in the review committee responsibilities of overall institutional fiscal management.

The process of selecting projects for funding is supported by guidelines for assigning priorities. A preliminary evaluation is made classifying projects by possible funding source. Self-amortizing projects are separated and evaluated on their own merits. Next, capital construction is defined and set aside from the priority selection process under criteria different from major maintenance and program improvements.

Capital construction projects for new structures or major additions are usually self-defined by program scope, complexity, and costs. Distinguishing between maintenance and capitalized construction eases the task of prioritizing major maintenance and program improvements to be funded from annual operating budgets. Classifying a project as capital construction is usually guided by costs. Minimum limits of $10,000 to $100,000 should be based on an institution's budgeting practices of funding facility improvements.

Invariably, major maintenance and program improvements funding needs will exceed available budgets. Special allocations for unfunded projects by operating budgets can be aided by following the guidelines for priority selection. The process of selecting project priorities is a systematic categorizing to arrive at funding decisions. Occasionally, first priorities for available funds are bypassed and lower priorities advanced when improvement projects are selected before repair and renovation projects. For these reasons, it is essential that an institution use the facilities audit as the basis for developing a facilities improvement policy to meet the funding needs of observed conditions.

39.5 EFFECTIVE PRESENTATIONS

A successful presentation for major maintenance, capital renewal, and deferred maintenance funding begins with thorough preparation, a sense of the decision-making environment, and other issues facing an approving body. A thoroughly prepared presentation, well-documented and imaginatively delivered, effectively conveys a message. Although difficult to accept, all of the technical expertise involved in preparing project budget requests can be wasted effort if not effectively presented. Do not overlook groundwork for building personal credibility and campus awareness for improving facilities conditions.

Begin with preparation for the presentation. The documentation must be meticulous in preparation and detail because the sharpest fiscal minds in the institution will usually be present. Any references to costs, financing alternatives, or cost-benefits will undergo thorough scrutiny. Expect the unexpected: "What happens if we *don't* do the work?" or, "Can't our own people do the work as regular maintenance?" Also, be prepared for the rigors of a dissertation defense when facing a committee made up mostly of academicians. Intellectual exploration of proposals is routine. Seeking alternate solutions or requests for further information should be expected for comprehensive projects as well as minor items.

The major difference between presenting facilities project requests in an academic environment and other presentations comes from understanding the audience's orientation. Some requests will be larger than many considered essential to the academic enterprise. A much needed roof replacement could equal the cost of a distinguished professor and operating support for a year or setting up of a new research institute. A year's proposal for deferred maintenance could equal a percentage point increase in faculty salaries or student tuition.

The list of projects and printed documents is the backbone of the presentation and should be attractively designed and informative. Material should have concise summaries and available explanatory documentation. Keeping jargon to a minimum aids in the receptiveness of the audience to the presentation. Do not sacrifice oversimplification for credibility; design the documents for ease of cross referencing. Establishing the importance of the subject is essential. The University of Washington discovered this with its videotape of existing conditions; a slide show by the University of Maryland on the destructive impact on academic programs and campus life caused by deteriorating facilities was persuasive to its Board of Regents. Facilities managers who have provided guided tours for governing board members to personally view life threatening conditions, possible loss of plant assets, and unattractive campus facilities' appearance prior to a presentation on budget requests have found they created valuable allies for their cause.

At quarterly or annual reviews of budget requests for major maintenance and capital renewal/replacement, the facilities manager must play the role of technician, counselor, and politician. Communication to the intended audience is the watchword; graphics, visual aids, and comprehensible reports should provide conclusions and recommendations that stand on their own merits.

The supporting printed material for a budget review session should be submitted in advance to all participants. With clarity, conciseness, and attractive design in mind, a suggested format includes:

1. A brief introduction explaining the organization of the report. Definition of project groupings by funding sources can ease understanding of accompanying technical material.
2. A summary listing of projects that identifies the facilities, short descriptive project titles, and project budgets. A helpful display will present funding sources separating education and general, departmental funding, auxiliary enterprises, and special allocations.
3. Detailed project descriptions presented on individual sheets for each project.

Once the supporting data has been compiled and a presentation approach conceived, how does one gain support for major maintenance and capital renewal/replacement requests? The answer is by thorough preparation and developing an effective presentation; one that gains acceptance for conclusions and recommendations. Consider the following items when presenting budget requests.

Overview   Does the presentation show an understanding of the institution's budgetary process and current fiscal position? Do the conclusions and recommendations fit into long-term institutional policies and goals?

Credibility   The credibility of the physical plant staff is extremely important. Physical plant must be able to defend its current maintenance practices and show that previously allocated funds were well managed. A solid track record of projects delivered within budget and on schedule helps in creating credibility.

Competency   The physical plant staff indicates its competency by the technical accuracy and judgments made in preparing budget requests. This is also reflected by implementation of previously approved projects.

Thoroughness of Preparation   Budget requests must be thoroughly researched, data carefully analyzed and accurate in all ways. A simple mistake in calculation or unsupported conclusions can cast doubt on an entire presentation.

Sympathetic Senior Administrator   An institution's budget is competition for limited financial resources. Without the assistance of a strong advocate, major maintenance and capital renewal/replacement requests may be rejected or, at best, decisions postponed. A senior administrator who understands physical plant needs and can support the presentation's conclusions and recommendations is invaluable in the review process.

Preparation for Implementation   A proposed schedule disciplines the facilities manager in preparing for budget approvals and project implementation. Listing budget requests without determining how and when the work will be done can help to shorten a promising career. Supervisory and trades staff to be involved in project completion should be consulted in budget request preparations. End products are better with their participation and avoid misconceptions about project scope, budgets, and schedules.

And remember: Communicate.

39.6 MANAGING THE MAJOR MAINTENANCE AND CAPITAL RENEWAL/REPLACEMENT PROGRAM

How to Manage

Managing the major maintenance and capital renewal/replacement program is a broader challenge than managing routine maintenance. A subtle difference is that the facilities manager must interact at different organizational levels; not only with directly supervised staff, but also with others at the same level or higher in the organization. *How* to manage a major maintenance and capital renewal/replacement program starts with clear understanding of the following.

View a facility as a collection of components and systems. Facilities are made up of many components forming systems. For example, deterioration in the structural frame can cause breakdowns in other parts of the superstructure or exterior enclosure system. Evaluation of a repeated maintenance problem should consider the effect on other components nd building systems. Major maintenance or capital renewal can be avoided by maintenance management reviewing information on unsatisfactory minor conditions to prevent them from developing into major ones.

Keep track of facilities conditions. The annual facilities audit is an important tool for facilities management. The facilities manager who remains familiar with facilities conditions through regular condition audits can anticipate major problems and avoid budget surprises in overall campus fiscal management. The facilities audit should be performed annually to note current problems and future priorities.

Maintain a multi-year major maintenance and capital renewal/replacement program. A multi-year capital budget plan designed to "roll over" each year covering approximately five years provides senior administrators the opportunity to regularly review campus capital requirements. A long-range capital plan also benefits facilities management by offering flexibility for emergencies or unanticipated special situations. When the magnitude of capital budgets have been reviewed and afforded, there is leeway in adjustments within annual allocations.

Understand differences between maintenance and construction. The categories may be so familiar that important differences go undefined. The issue of how much staff to dedicate to construction projects is routinely facing facilities managers. Proportions of staff time and materials devoted to routine maintenance and to major maintenance is an indicator of balance in allocating resources. Facilities managers can take pride in their staff's construction accomplishments, but they are misdirected if they look at their labor pool primarily as a construction team. Unless located in an area where competition from contractors is unavailable, the wrong emphasis is being placed on work management if the majority of staff labor hours is in major maintenance.

Manage maintenance as opposed to maintaining management. Managing maintenance means having work control and capital budget planning in place. All institutions need a work control process to analyze requests, assign tasks, and control material purchases. These operational features contribute to a responsive service organization. Capital budget planning is part of a multi-year capital budget plan integrating all funding streams with work priorities: routine and major maintenance, capital projects, and deferred maintenance. Failure to bring these basic management programs into routine operations is a sign of a complacent management and a sign of an organization prepared to complain about inadequate funds and a lack of appreciation for management and staff that is dedicated, loyal, hard working, and usually overworked and underpaid.

Remember that facilities management is a support service. The central purpose of an academic enterprise is quality of academic programs. The quality of campus life for all members of the campus community is a close second. In terms of allocation of resources, facilities come in at least third. Overcoming disappointments in funding shortfalls can be found by satisfaction in providing efficient service. Prompt responses to service requests, explanations for delays and postponements, and attention to meeting needs for special campus requirements are traits of the service organization.

The facilities manager who understands this can take a fresh approach by standing back and reviewing plant conditions, including buildings, grounds, utilities, and equipment. Walk through the buildings and keep in mind the operations and maintenance budget; be candid in the self-evaluation of the maintenance management's effectiveness; and have a feel for the previous annual funding for major maintenance and the tempo of plant additions. Is this a quiet period or one of increasing activity? Is there a shift from new construction to renovations? Set aside frustrations over "inadequate" budgets and be self-critical of work control, staff performance, and the presentations of requests for increased base budgets and special capital appropriations.

The facilities administrator walks the grounds and through buildings from basement to roof and records deferred maintenance, especially life safety categories and a building's exterior envelope—roofing, flashings, mortar, or other sealants—and places where deterioration permits moisture penetration; checks the operating records for repeated failures of mechanical systems and complaints about heating and cooling; finally, observes environmental safety conditions such as exits, toxic waste storage, fire sprinklers, smoke detectors, and for any obstacles to the mobility impaired.

This is an informal checklist to set the facilities manager to the task of preparing a strategy for a major maintenance program. Formal aspects of the program begin with senior plant administrators evaluating the institution's overall facilities management program. Later, tasks are defined by the small campus administrator to personally take on with available assistants, or for larger campus administrators to delegate to staff.

Comprehensive Facilities Management Program

A comprehensive facilities management program is a collection of goals and objectives gaining the greatest efficiency and economy from available resources. A comprehensive program includes coordination of work management for routine and major maintenance, capital projects, and deferred maintenance. The four major areas of a comprehensive facilities management program are:

1. Physical Planning Policy: Guidelines for land use, physical development including future site improvements and building locations, util-

ities, and traffic and circulation. Academic goals, enrollment and employment projections, and quality of campus life are essential parts of a physical planning policy.

2. Audit and Analysis: Regular facilities audits of physical conditions and functional adequacy are complemented by management performance reviews to analyze organizational structure, staffing, and work management practices.

3. Facilities Requirements: A multi-year plan revised annually identifying capital needs of all campus facilities includes major maintenance and capital projects. All facilities needs are outlined by priority with preliminary cost estimates and schedules. Space programs and feasibility studies are prepared to accompany funding requests and prepare for project implementation.

4. Capital Budget Planning: Results of annual facilities audits are joined with program improvement needs for academic and campus life for regular reviews by a capital budget review committee. Facilities' needs become part of overall fiscal management through this process.

Each of the major areas of a comprehensive facilities program translate institutional policy into work management. For example, the physical planning policy indicates overall land use with facilities and campus grounds designated for maintaining present use or where change is expected. The audit and analysis can disclose major facilities problems or management issues that will affect near and long-term use of facilities and requirements impacting capital budget planning. Facilities requirements include plans for projects that can modify maintenance programs and affect staffing and technical specialization for plant operations. Facilities management will be required to supervise design and construction of plant additions and deferred maintenance; capital budget planning will demand organization of data on conditions and selection of project priorities, and presentations for funding major maintenance and capital renewal/replacement projects.

Tasks involved in comprehensive facilities management programs are digestible assignments if divided into specific assignments in an organized fashion. Performing them successfully are the earned credentials of a competent manager and a capable staff. Organizational structures designed for comprehensive facilities management provide a balance between the administrator with leadership ability, technical skills and experience, and the supervisory staff. Working for capable leadership, the different aptitudes for maintenance and construction are unified to implement strategies for long range integrity of the campus physical plant.

On the off-chance that the personal tour by the facility adminis-trator was disturbing, a plan of action to manage major maintenance would be the immediate priority. Doing tasks simultaneously rather than sequentially creates forward motion on a plan and prevents awk-ward gaps between promises and delivery of results. Experience some-times unpleasantly acquired justifies the saying that today's credibility expires overnight; yesterday's successes are erased by today's failures.

A Plan of Action

A suggested plan of action for major maintenance and capital renewal/replacement includes:

1. Building a contingency of campus support.
2. Developing a work plan.
3. Inventorying conditions.
4. Selecting priorities.
5. Setting funding requirements.
6. Seeking funding sources.
7. Creating public awareness.

Continue the cycle until results are produced. The actions are nec-essary to prevent further plant deterioration and protect the institution's physical assets.

NOTES

1. Harvey H. Kaiser. "Rebuilding the Campus: A Higher Education Priority for the 21st Century." *Educational Record*, Winter 1989.
2. Ernest L. Boyer. *College: The Undergraduate Experience in America.* (New York: Harper & Row, 1987.)
3. Harvey H. Kaiser. *Facilities Audit Workbook: A Self-Evaluation Process for Higher Education.* (Alexandria, Virginia: APPA, 1987.)

ADDITIONAL RESOURCES

American Council on Education. "Rebuilding the Campus." Focus issue on rebuilding the nation's college campuses. *Educational Record*, Winter 1989.

Association of Physical Plant Administrators of Universities and Col-leges. *Executive Briefing: The Decaying American Campus.* A three-tape video that establishes the deferred maintenance problem, provides several case studies of campus solutions, and offers financing ideas and alternatives. Alexandria, Virginia: APPA, 1989.

Jenny, Hans H., with Geoffrey C. Hughes and Richard D. Devine. *Hang-Gliding or Looking for an Updraft: A Study of College and University Finance in the 1980s—The Capital Margin*. Wooster, Ohio: The College of Wooster, 1981.

Kaiser, Harvey H. *Crumbling Academe: Solving the Capital Renewal and Replacement Dilemma*. Washington: Association of Governing Boards of Universities and Colleges, 1984.

Kaiser, Harvey H., ed. *Planning and Managing Higher Education Facilities*. San Francisco: Jossey-Bass Publishers, Inc., 1989.

National Science Foundation. *Scientific and Engineering Research Facilities at Universities and Colleges: 1988*. Washington: NSF, 1988.

Phillips, Cushing Jr. "Facilities Renewal: The Formula Approach." In *Proceedings of the Seventy-Third Annual Meeting of the Association of Physical Plant Administrators of Universities and Colleges*. Alexandria, Virginia: APPA, 1986.

Robinson, Daniel D. *Capital Maintenance for Colleges and Universities*. Washington: NACUBO, 1986.

Rush, Sean C. and Sandra L. Johnson. *The Decaying American Campus: A Ticking Time Bomb*. Alexandria, Virginia: APPA, 1989.

Sherman, Douglas R. and William A. Dergis. "A Funding Model for Building Renewal." *Business Officer*, February 1981.

CHAPTER 40

Contracting for Services

William D. Middleton, P.E.
Assistant Vice President, Physical Plant
University of Virginia

40.1 INTRODUCTION

Contracting for services is a frequent requirement for physical plant organizations. It is often the preferred and most economic means of doing certain categories of work.

Effective contracting for services requires careful management attention. Through sound contracting procedures we must clearly identify the nature of the goods and services to be provided and the terms and conditions under which they will be furnished by the contractor.

This chapter will discuss some of the reasons why contracting for physical plant services may be necessary or desirable; the principal types of contracts utilized for physical plant services; and some of the principles for developing contractual requirements, obtaining contractor offers, evaluating offers and selecting a contractor, and establishing and managing contracts. Construction contracts are addressed in Chapter 34, The Construction Process.

40.2 THE CONTRACT ALTERNATIVE

A discussion of the contracting alternative for performance of physical plant services should begin with consideration of why or when contracting may be most advantageous, the types of services that may be contracted, and some of the principles of effective service contracting.

Advantages and Disadvantages of Contracting

There are many reasons why it may be necessary or desirable to contract for physical plant services. Following are some of the most common advantages of contracting:

- To obtain specialized services that are infeasible to be provided with in-house staff.
- To obtain infrequently-required services for which it is infeasible to maintain permanent staff.
- To avoid the high capital costs involved in maintaining an in-house capability to provide the service.
- To obtain greater economy and efficiency in the provision of services.
- To meet peak workload requirements.
- To obtain the management resources of a large organization that cannot be developed at the level of an individual institution.

There are potential disadvantages of contracting that must be carefully weighed. Some of the most common ones:

- Contractor employees usually will not have a level of loyalty or dedication to the institution comparable to that of its own permanent employees.
- Contractors, and contractor employees, may often prove less responsive to special needs or changed requirements of the institution than its own staff.
- Profit-motivated contractors will typically provide only the minimum level of service required to satisfy contract requirements.
- Periodic changes in contractors as contracts are renewed results in a lack of continuity in services and poor service during the start-up period for a new contract.

Some of the most common advantages and disadvantages of in-house work performance compared to contracting for services are summarized in Figure 40-1.

Services That Can Be Contracted

There are several basic categories of physical plant services that are often provided on a contractual basis, either wholly or in part.

Professional and consulting services may include:

- Planning and design services.
- Architectural and engineering consulting services.
- Project management.
- Professional studies and investigations.
- Development of management and operating procedures and systems.

Figure 40-1

In-House Performance versus Contracting for Services

IN-HOUSE	CONTRACT
Advantages	
• Continuity.	• Avoid capital costs.
• Staff loyalty and dedication.	• Obtain specialized services.
• Flexibility in staff utilization.	• Obtain services infrequently required.
• Emergency response capability.	• Meet peak work-load needs.
• Lower costs (sometimes).	• Lower costs for specialized services (usually).
• Responsiveness.	• Obtain management resources of a large, specialized organization.
	• Volume purchasing power.
	• Avoid inventory requirements.
	• Eliminate support space requirements.
	• Higher productivity in specialized services.
	• Greater flexibility in adjusting to changing service level needs.
Disadvantages	
• High capital costs.	• Lack of continuity.
• Equipment costs.	• Inflexibility in staff utilization.
• Inventory requirements.	• Minimum performance level.
• Space requirements.	• Higher costs (sometimes).
• Personnel management requirements.	
• Less flexibility in varying staffing levels.	
• Skill limitations for specialized services.	
• Lower productivity (sometimes).	

Construction services may include:

- New construction.
- Renovation, alteration, and improvements.
- Maintenance and repair.

Maintenance and operation services are typically a continuing or long-range requirement and may include:

- Facilities and equipment test and inspection.
- Continuing facilities, equipment preventive maintenance, and maintenance service.
- Operation of facilities plants and systems.
- Refuse collection and disposal.
- Grounds maintenance.
- Snow removal.
- Custodial services.
- Pest control.
- Transportation services.

Management services for the physical plant function are sometimes provided by contract and may include:

- Management of a particular operation or function.
- Management and supervision of the entire physical plant function.

Basic Principles of Contracting

A contract may be defined as an agreement that specifies the promises each party has made to the other.

The National Association of College and University Business Officers, in its publication, *Contracting for Services*, has defined a contract as follows:

A contract is an agreement between two or more competent and authorized parties in which one of the parties, the offeror, promises something of value to the other party, the acceptor, in return for that party's promise to perform or refrain from performing certain activities.

A contract can be either verbal or written; if written, it can be anything from a brief, informal record of understanding to a complex and formal document. Normally, of course, the contracting done for physical plant services will be in the form of formal, written contractual agreements.

Regardless of the contract type or form, it is absolutely essential that there be a true "meeting of the minds" between the parties to the contract if it is going to be a successful agreement.

In developing a contractual agreement, it is important that this contractual documentation clearly establish an understanding concerning:

- The specific goods or services to be provided.
- The required performance and quality standards for the goods or services.
- The delivery requirements and schedule.
- The consideration to be paid to the contractor, and any related terms or conditions.

Failure to clearly establish these basic understandings in a contractual agreement can lead to claims and disputes.

40.3 TYPES AND FORMS OF CONTRACTUAL PROCUREMENTS

Types of Procurement Procedures

There are two basic types of procurement procedures that are normally used:

Competitive Bidding   Under this form of procurement, contractors compete for the work on the basis of price, with the contract normally awarded to the responsive and responsible contractor with the lowest price offer. Responsive means that the bid meets the requirements of the request for bids. Responsible means that the contractor has a capability and a record of performance that indicate that he or she is capable of doing the work.

Negotiation   Under this form of procurement, a contract is established through negotiation with one or more contractors. In a competitive negotiation procedure, contractors typically compete on the basis of a number of selected criteria which may include price. Sometimes, negotiation may be conducted on a non-competitive basis with a single contractor.

Forms of Contractual Procurement

There are several forms of contractual procurement commonly used for physical plant services.

Lump Sum Contracts   This is the typical form for construction contracts. The characteristics of required services for this type of contract include:

- A "one time" requirement.
- Can be fully defined by plans and specifications.
- All offerors can supply an essentially identical product or service.

Lump sum contracts are usually established through competitive bidding, but can be negotiated as well.

Unit Price Contracts   This is the typical contractual form for continuing or repetitive maintenance service requirements. Typical characteristics of the required services include:

- The service is required continuously or intermittently over a period of time.
- The required services can be fully defined by specifications.
- All offerors can provide an essentially identical service.
- The total quantity of each required service may not be known.

Unit price contracts are usually established through competitive bidding, but can be negotiated as well.

Requests for Proposals (RFP)   This is the best form for many types of contractual procurements when:

- Offerors cannot all provide identical services.
- Each offeror is expected to propose a somewhat different way of providing the required service.
- The qualifications and experience of the individuals who will provide the required service from the offeror are important.

An RFP form is a type of competitive negotiation.

40.4 DEVELOPMENT OF CONTRACTUAL PROCUREMENTS

There are four major phases to the process of establishment of a contractual for physical plant services:

1. Definition of requirements—This first step in a contractual procurement process requires determining the scope and nature of the required contractual service and describing it in a way that will establish a clear contractual requirement.
2. Obtaining contractor offers—Having defined what is to be procured by contract, offers must be solicted from contractors for the provision of the required service in a way that permits judging which is the most advantageous offer for provision of the required service.
3. Evaluating offers and selecting a contractor—After offers have been received, they must be evaluated to determine the best offer and a successful contractor selected.
4. Establishing the contract—Having selected the successful contractor, a satisfactory contractual agreement must be formed.

Following are more detailed analyses of the major phases in establishing a contractual procurement.

Defining the Requirement

This first step requires determining the scope and nature of the services required and describing them clearly. This is done by formulating a statement that clearly defines:

- What is wanted.
- How much, when, and what standards of quality and performance are required.

This can be done in several ways:

- Development of plans and/or specifications.
- A statement of performance objectives and standards.
- A general statement of requirements.

It is important that the task of defining requirements be done well. A little research into available specifications and standards, or comparable contract documents developed by others, should prove helpful. It is usually not necessary to "reinvent the wheel"; good standard specifications and contracts have already been developed for almost any type of contractual procurement. Trade associations and government agencies have often developed standard specifications that can be used or referenced. Other institutions have probably already contracted for comparable services, and they might be willing to make their specifications available. Caution should be exercised in the use of specifications or contract forms developed by contractors or suppliers. Typically, these documents are designed to protect the contractor.

Any institution will have a number of standard requirements, terms, or conditions that will apply uniformly to all contractual procurements. In construction contracting, these are usually incorporated into general conditions that are made a part of every contractual procurement. The same idea, however, can be applied to any form of contractual procurement.

Obtaining Contractor Offers

Contractor offers for the performance of physical plant services can be made in several forms, depending upon the basic form of contractual procurement.

Lump Sum Bids   In this form, typically used for construction contracts, the contractor submits a lump sum offer for the performance of the required services. Often a request for bids will require that the lump sum proposal be broken down among several items of work, or that separate prices be provided for alternatives, but the basic concept is that the contractor offers to do the required work for a specific price. Typically, lump sum offers are submitted in the form of sealed bids, which are received and opened under formal, established bid opening procedures.

Unit Price Bids   For repetitive services where the actual quantity required may be indefinite or variable, bids may be requested on a unit-price basis with a separate unit price for any number of separate definable and measurable units of service. In order to arrive at a basis for contract award, these unit prices may be extended on the basis of estimated quantities of each that may be required during the contract period in order to arrive at a total price proposal.

When bids are received in this manner, it is important that estimated quantities be carefully developed. If not, a contractor can maximize his potential earnings under a contract by "unbalancing" his unit price bid for items of work where the estimated quantity may be understated.

"Time and Material" Contracts   A variation of the unit price form of contract that can sometimes be useful is what is sometimes called a "time and material" contract, which establishes a unit price basis for labor and a basis for payment of material and equipment costs incurred by the contractor. Examples of this form of procurement are contracts that provide a basis for the performance of unspecified maintenance, repair, or renovation work. The contract terms establish the basis for payment to the contractor for each specific task assigned under the contract.

When this form of contract is used, it is advisable to include in the terms a means of fixing the price of each task prior to its accomplishment, or at least a means of establishing a "cap" on the price.

Proposals   Where it is desired to consider a number of variables in determining the best offer for the performance of work, proposals should be requested that establish such information as:

- The qualifications and experience of the contractor, as well as key contractor staff who will be assigned to the performance of the required work, for services of the kind being procured.
- A description of the specific service offered by the contractor in response to the requirement.
- The price of the service.
  In requesting proposals, it may be desirable for the owner to establish both mandatory and preferred terms.
- Mandatory terms should be limited to those considered essential to the planned contact. This will permit the maximum possible competition for the work.
- Preferred terms can include any provisions which the owner would like to have. The degree of responsiveness to these preferred terms can be an important part of the evaluation process.

Evaluating Offers and Selecting a Contractor

Contractor Qualifications   There are several methods available to assure that contractors offering to perform services will prove responsible.

Selected bidders list—Under this procedure, only contractors who have been identified as qualified and capable of providing the required service in an acceptable manner are invited to submit proposals or bids.

Pre-qualification—Under this method, prospective contractors for provision of the required service are asked to submit information concerning their qualifications and experience, resources, financial capability, and the like. Through evaluation of these submittals, only those contractors deemed to be fully capable of providing the required services are invited to bid or submit proposals.

Bid bond—Through a bid bond, a bonding company provides an assurance that a contractor, if the lowest bidder, will enter a contract under the terms offered. Typically, the bonding company must pay the difference in cost between the lowest bid and the next lowest, or up to 5 percent of the amount bid, if the contractor fails to enter into a contract.

Evaluation and Selection   Once offers have been received and contractor qualifications are established, offers are evaluated and a contractor selected basically as follows for the various type bids:

Lump sum bids—Contract award is normally made on the basis of the lowest price bid for performance of the required work from a responsible contractor.

Unit price bids—Contract award is made in a similar manner as for lump sum bids. The contractor whose unit price bids provide the lowest estimated total cost for the required services is awarded a contract.

Proposals—Offers received on a proposal basis are typically reviewed and evaluated on the basis of the criteria for evaluation and selection stated in the request for proposals. Following review and evaluation of each proposal, the evaluator typically assigns scores to each proposal for each of the stated criteria, and a numerical evaluation determines the best overall proposal.

In the request for proposal procedure, a "best and final" procedure is often used. This provides a means for requesting changes and refinements to improve proposals so that they will better meet the needs of the requestor. Under this two-step procedure, the evaluator meets with each contractor, following an initial evaluation of proposals, to discuss any specific changes and improvements to the proposal that are desired. Each contractor then has a period of time to revise and improve his or her proposal before submitting a revised "best and final" proposal for final evaluation and selection of the successful contractor.

Negotiation may be required with a contractor to modify a proposal to better meet the needs of the requestor, to establish price, to reach agreement on some specific conditions of the contract, or other considerations.

Negotiated contracts—These are established on the basis of negotiations with a single prospective contractor.

Professional services contracts, for example, are normally established this way in a two-step process:

1. Determine the professional firm considered best qualified for the work.
2. Negotiate a price and other contract terms and conditions. This same approach may be applied to other types of contracts whenever we want only a specific contractor for some reason. Public institutions, however, are typically limited in their ability to do this.

It is just as important with a negotiated contract as it is with other types of contracts that a clear definition of the contract requirements be established.

For successful negotiation of contract price, terms, and conditions, it is important to begin negotiations with a good idea of what the price should be, and what terms and conditions are appropriate.

In the case of professional architectural and engineering services contracts, for example, there are generally-accepted fee schedules that can be used as a guideline and standardized contract forms.

For other types of goods and services similar material may be available, or a determination of what prices, terms, and conditions other agencies have used for similar contracts can be determined.

Establishing the Contract

A contract is formed through formal documentation that establishes the "meeting of the minds" required between the two parties. Typically this formal contract will incorporate any plans or specifications that formed a basis for the contractor's offer, the request for proposal document, the contractor's offer or proposal, any terms or conditions that were negotiated following selection of the contractor, or other contractual requirements.

The successful contractor may be required to provide a performance bond, under which a bonding company guarantees performance of the required services in accordance with the contractual terms and conditions. Labor and material payment bonds may also be required as a means of assuring that subcontractors and suppliers will be paid.

40.5 EFFECTIVE CONTRACT MANAGEMENT

Effective and successful contract administration requires the development of well-defined contract administration procedures. Following are some of the most important elements of effective contract administration.

- A contract administrator should be designated who will be the formal representative of the owner in all contractual matters. It is important that other parties from the institution not attempt to give direction to the contractor, and that the contractor understands that any instructions from the institution must be taken only through the formal contract administrator or his or her designated representative.

- An inspection/evaluation procedure should be established to assure that the quantity, quality, and timeliness of the services provided by the contractor meet the performance standards of the contract. It is important that a formal record be made of all inspection or evaluations of contractor-provided services. This should include a final overall performance evaluation to be considered when future contract awards to the same contractor are contemplated.

- Contract payments should be made promptly in accordance with the contractual agreement. The owner should have an adequate procedure for verifying that all work has been satisfactorily performed as invoiced. This can be a particular problem in many types of maintenance service contracts. A specified basis should be established for reduced payment when service standards required by a contract are not fully met. Unit price contracts will usually prove helpful in dealing with problems of this type. Another effective procedure for dealing with substandard performance is the use of a scoring system, under which a numerical score reflecting the quality of services against the contract requirements is established on a regular frequency. Contract payments are then reduced when the quality of service falls below the required level. This system can work quite well for maintenance services such as custodial or grounds care.

- A claims and disputes procedure should be available to provide a formal basis for resolving any disagreements between the contractor and the owner.

- A contract renewal procedure is often advantageous for continuing maintenance service contracts or other types of continuing service contracts. This permits the continuation of uninterrupted service from a satisfactory contractor for an additional period of time. Typically, terms and conditions for contract renewal should be incorporated into the original request for bids or proposals, with the contractor's terms for price adjustment at renewal submitted as part of the original bid or proposal.

ADDITIONAL RESOURCES

National Association of College and University Business Officers. *Contracting for Communications Services*. Washington: NACUBO, 1984.

————. *Contracting for Services*. Washington: NACUBO, 1982.

CHAPTER 41

Principles of Industrial Engineering in

Facilities Management

H.C. Lott Jr.
Assistant Vice President for
Plant Management and Construction
The University of Texas at Austin

41.1 INTRODUCTION

The roots of industrial engineering were established during the Industrial Revolution beginning in the early eighteenth century in England. During this period there were many new inventions, such as the spinning jenny, spinning frame, power loom, and the steam engine that led to the organization of factories with a relatively large number of workers. With the founding of the factories came new thinking concerning the management of people and machines. This thinking was advanced by several individuals who were closely involved with the inventions of the period and the startup of the first factories.

Sir Richard Arkwright, the inventor of the spinning frame, is credited with developing and administering the first code of factory discipline. In the late 1700s, James Watt Jr. and Matthew Bouton, managers of a foundry, pioneered many manufacturing developments and initiated a remarkable cost accounting and control system. It is interesting to note that all of this early work in management development was carried on independently by these individuals with no attempt to create a formal body of knowledge about management concepts.

At the end of the nineteenth century, the individual efforts in several countries began to emerge as a body of management knowledge. This emergence was led by a number of people from the United States, including Frederick Taylor, Henry Gantt, Frank and Lillian Gilbreth, and Harrison Emerson. Taylor's chief contribution was in the area of methods improvements, while Gantt was active in developing management principles and procedures. The Gilbreths performed initial time and motion studies, and Emerson wrote on improving operational efficiencies.

These management pioneers combined their early contributions to formulate basic principles as a scientific approach to management, and these activities became known as scientific management. Industrial engineering grew out of such areas of scientific thought as organization, methods, and work measurement. Although the profession had existed for many years, it was not until 1955 that a definition of industrial engineering was endorsed by the American Institute of Industrial Engineering. This definition is as follows:

> Industrial Engineering is concerned with the design, improvement, and installation of integrated systems of men, materials, and equipment. It draws upon specialized knowledge and skill in the mathematical, physical, and social sciences, together with the principles and methods of engineering analysis and design, to specify, predict, and evaluate the results to be obtained from such systems.

As industrial engineering began to be recognized as a profession in the 1930s, this branch of engineering was associated almost entirely with the manufacturing industry and, more specifically, in the production area with little, if any, application in the facilities management field. It was after World War II that progressive-thinking plant engineers began to apply industrial engineering principles to assist them with the management of their responsibilities.

41.2 QUANTIFYING PHYSICAL PLANT SERVICES

In order to effectively apply the principles of industrial engineering to the management of physical plant functions, it is important that the manager understands the differences between "production" activities in a manufacturing plant and the maintenance and operation activities of an institutional physical plant organization. Production activities are highly standardized and repetitive, which make them predictable by the use of statistical analysis techniques.

With a few exceptions, physical plant is a service organization, and service functions do not lend themselves readily to quantification. One problem of applying industrial engineering to physical plant services is the problem of quantifying the service output. The problem is resolved by developing a hierarchy of work units. A work unit is defined as any amount of work, or the results of such work, that are convenient to use as an integer when quantifying the work. The work units should have the following criteria:

1. They should provide a clear hierarchy of countable, transformable units of quantification from the "objective" to the "workload"; the resources required for the larger or higher orders of work units should be divided into that needed for the smaller or lower orders of work units; the resources required for the smaller ones should be readily aggregated into the resources needed for the larger work units.
2. They should permit a meaningful forecast of the workload to be made in terms related to the required resources, or convertible to such terms.
3. At one or more levels, a firm relationship of the work unit to required resources should be established; at these levels a work count, the number of times a work unit is to be performed, should be a meaningful number with respect to required resources.

By developing a work unit hierarchy for facilities management tasks, the whole range of industrial engineering concepts can be usefully applied. Of course, as in any industrial engineering problem, cognizance must be taken of: 1) the nature of the tasks and appropriate criteria of success, 2) the underlying service-subject-matter aspects, and 3) the human problems internal to the organization.

Few physical plant organizations in higher education have a professional industrial engineer on their staff who is dedicated to the enhancement of the facilities management functions by the application of industrial engineering principles. This function is normally initiated by the director, or one of his or her associates, and the performance is delegated to a subordinate with the knowledge and interest to perform the work.

The activities of industrial engineering in physical plant organizations center primarily around the construction and management of facilities as they relate to the cost and efficiency of providing service to the building occupants and the maintenance function.

In the discussion that follows, the focus will be on those industrial engineering principles or concepts that are most utilized for improving the facilities management functions.

41.3 METHODS ENGINEERING

One of the major objectives of any successful manager is to increase the efficiency in all the functions for which he or she is responsible. The application of "methods engineering" techniques will greatly enhance the manager's efforts to improve the efficiency of the organization. Methods engineering is a term that describes a collection of analysis techniques that focus attention on improving the effectiveness of people and machines. It enables the manager to subject each of his or her operations to a precise and systematic analysis, with the objective being to eliminate every unnecessary element of an operation and focus on the best method of performing the necessary elements.

Some of the major methods engineering techniques are work sampling, work measurement, value engineering, work simplification, process charting, operation analysis, and time-motion studies. All of these techniques can be effectively applied in physical plant management to increase the efficiency of the organization. The first four of these techniques are the most utilized and are discussed here in more detail.

Work Sampling

Work sampling is an industrial engineering technique used for work measurement and analysis of time utilization of both workers and machines. The technique is less personal than the traditional time-motion studies because it is usually applied to groups of people or machines rather than individuals.

Work sampling is the most economic way to obtain detail information on the delays and productivity of people. Work sampling in itself does not improve operations, but serves as a management tool that provides the facts upon which actions can be taken and decisions made, which result in improved operations.

There are many possibilities for useful applications of work sampling in the management of physical plant activities. All physical plant supervisory personnel should become familiar with this management tool and its application in identifying problem areas.

Work sampling is a statistical approach to data gathering based upon the laws of probability. It assumes that a sufficiently large number of observations, made at random intervals, will provide a reasonably reliable picture of what is actually occurring most of the time. The greater the number of observations made, the more reliable the results will be. The technique simply observes and records an activity at a particular time. It does not concern itself with the duration of the activity or how long it is observed.

A work sampling program will not only measure the productive effort of employee groups, but, more importantly, it will measure the nonproductive efforts. The analysis of the nonproductive time aids management in improving the productivity. Work sampling should not be used to measure the performance or deficiencies of individual workers.

Work sampling can be used to measure the effectiveness of the entire maintenance management program—design, estimating, planning, scheduling, material handling, travel modes, and staffing control. The unit of measure for the effectiveness of a program is the productivity, which is normally referred to as the "P" Factor.

The purpose of a work sampling program is to establish a reliable procedure for measuring the effectiveness of maintenance management in terms of labor productivity. The basic objectives of a program are:

- To establish work sampling as a continuous and ongoing management tool in the physical plant organization.
- To determine the overall work productivity of construction, maintenance and operations shops, custodial, grounds maintenance and transportation crews, and other labor units in terms of percentage of time.
- To promote an ongoing review and revision of management policies, job procedures, and methods with the ultimate objective of increased productivity and job knowledge.
- To accumulate basic workhour utilization data for reconciliation with estimated and actual labor data.

In planning a work sampling program it is essential that the elements of work analyzed are carefully defined. The work effort of physical plant personnel can be classified into three major categories: productive, indirect productive, and non-productive. Each major category is subdivided into its respective elements.

Productive Work   This category includes actual on-the-job work. It excludes the kinds of work and delay time in the elements defined below under indirect productive and nonproductive categories. Examples of productive work are: sawing, nailing, digging, cutting, tightening bolts, measuring, cutting and threading pipe, and machine process time even though the operator may be idle (such as a machinist watching a lathe).

Indirect Productive Work   This category includes the following activities:

1. Job preparation—This element includes work to prepare for a job, exclusive of material handling, travel, and planning. It does not include such nonproductive elements as waiting for transportation, waiting for instructions, and so on. Examples of job preparation are the erection or dismantling of scaffolds and the handling of equipment and tools at the job site.

2. Material handling—This element includes receiving tools and materials at the stores warehouse and loading and unloading materials on the truck.
3. Travel—This element includes walking or riding to and from the job site.
4. Planning—This element includes mechanics talking and reading about the work to be performed. It does not include job preparation or any of the elements under nonproductive. It includes such work as talking to supervisor or coworker about the work, studying blueprints or job order.

Nonproductive   This category includes the following elements:

1. Waiting—This element includes time spent waiting for another person to finish the work, because he or she is in the way; waiting at storeroom; waiting for instructions, materials, or transportation.
2. Personal—This element includes the time required to satisfy normal personal needs, such as cleanup, dressing, and washroom and rest periods.
3. Idle—This element includes the idle time at either the job site or another location. It does not include waiting or personal time.

Unobserved   This element is used for recording workers who are missed because they cannot be located at the scheduled job site or their whereabouts cannot be determined.

A graduate industrial engineer is not required for the design and performance of a work sampling study. The technique and procedure is simple and anyone with normal intelligence and an understanding of mathematical statistics can be trained to perform the studies. Ideally, the most benefit can be obtained by having a continuous program that requires a full-time employee to make the observations and manage the function. This position normally has the title of work analyst.

A small institution that cannot afford a full-time work analyst can take advantage of work sampling by training a person available part time to make the studies periodically. First-line supervisors and clerical personnel are often used for this purpose. The responsibilities of a work analyst performing a work sampling study are as follows:

- Perform the observations.
- Tabulate the results.
- Summarize the results on charts and/or graphs.
- Maintain control charts for each study.
- Analyze the sample results and other observations made during the study.

- Brief responsible supervisors on the results of the study for their respective shops or units.
- Make recommendations for making changes in work procedures and methods that will decrease the delay times and increase the productivity of the workers.

The work analyst designs the specific study to determine the productive, indirect productive, and nonproductive times and their elements for each shop or unit. Normally, the times studied will be the same for all units.

- In most cases the accuracy to be maintained for the study will be an accuracy of $\pm$ 5 percent at the 95 percent confidence level.
- The number of observations required to maintain the above accuracy for each work category or element being studied. The number of observations are calculated as follows:

$$N = 4(1\text{-}P) \div S^2P$$

Where:
N = Number of random observations (sample size)
P = Percent occurrence of the activity being measured
S = Desired accuracy (expressed as a percent)

- The number of trips that required to obtain the necessary number of observations. This is based upon the number of workers being sampled.
- The routes to be followed through the campus in order to observe the workers in accordance with daily work schedule. It is important that the routes are made in a random manner.
- The times that the observations will be made during the work day. To ensure no bias is introduced into the study results, a table of random numbers is utilized for selecting the times of observation.

The work analyst makes the observations of the shop/unit personnel being studied in accordance with the study design. Throughout the work day the observations are recorded on a work sampling observation sheet (Figure 41-1). A work sampling observation is an instantaneous one, that is the work analyst places the worker in the proper category/element the instant he is observed. At the end of each day the work analyst tallies the daily observations for each category/element, accumulates the totals, and calculates the cumulative percents. The cumulated percents are then plotted on a control chart. The work analyst continues the study until the sample size is obtained. The final percentages for each category/element is then calculated and entered on a chart or graph for review, analysis, and discussion with the responsible supervisor.

It is convenient to use a tape recorder for recording the observations. The data analysis can be expedited by inputing the data directly into a personal computer that is programmed for calculating the category/element percentages, plotting the control charts and the final charts of the studies. The MacIntosh PC with the Excel software package is excellent for handling the data output of the studies.

Work Measurement

Work measurement is the development and/or application of time standards for any type or element of work. It is not a substitute for good management, yet without the use of time standards a physical plant department cannot operate efficiently and effectively. The department may have the most skilled craftspeople, up-to-date tools and equipment, and the latest computerized maintenance management system. Yet they may still be operating at only 50 percent of labor capacity due to the lack of a common unit of measurement for each job that is fully understood by supervisors and craftspeople when considering goals, performance, and costs. The results of work measurement are improved scheduling, increased production by the same size work force due to an increase in craftsperson productivity, and closer supervision by foremen.

Generally, there are four methods used in establishing standards for maintenance work measurement:

1. Measurement by foreman—Work orders are sent directly to the foreman responsible for performing the work. It is the foreman's responsibility to determine the scope of work and estimate the time for performance based upon his or her judgment and experience. This is not a good method because it takes the foreman away from the prime responsibility of supervising the craftspeople.
2. Measurement by historical records—This method requires a statistical analysis of historical time data on completed jobs to obtain an average that is considered a suitable standard. It is important that the standards based on averages be updated at least once a year to ensure they are based upon current data.
3. Measurement by work sampling—Daily work sampling studies are performed to determine the productivity of each worker, the average productivity of each shop, and the productivity trend. When devel-

oping work standards utilizing work sampling it is necessary that the personnel being studied are performance rated and some type of unit work count is maintained.

4. Measurement by standard time data—This approach uses basic industrial engineering principles such as methods time measurement, and the use of predetermined time standards to develop elemental standard time data and estimating data. A successful standard time data system was developed by the Department of Navy, Bureau of Yards and Docks, which specifically covers facilities maintenance and remodeling work, including preventive maintenance. The title of the system is *Engineered Performance Standards*. An engineered performance standard represents the average time necessary for a qualified craftsperson working at a normal pace, under capable supervision and experiencing normal delays, to perform a defined amount of work, of a specified quality, while following acceptable trade methods. *Engineered Performance Standards* is a tool used by facilities planners and estimators that results in consistent estimating of work hours.

The first two approaches to work measurement relate current performance to past performance. The third and fourth approach take a major step forward because they determine how long each maintenance or remodeling job "should take" based on standards developed by industrial engineering techniques. Although staff costs are higher because someone must be dedicated to the development, application, and analysis of work measurement techniques, the payback is quickly obtained due to the increase in productivity of the trades personnel. In selecting the approach to be used, it is important to analyze the diminishing-returns effect on savings as the degree of refinement increases.

Value Engineering

Value engineering is an objective, systematic method of optimizing the total cost of a facility or system for a specified number of years. Total costs in this case include the ultimate costs to construct, operate, maintain, and replace a facility or system for a specified life cycle. Figure 41-2 graphically illustrates the approximate breakdown of the total costs of a typical facility over a normal life cycle. These costs will vary based on the type of facility, e.g., a research building or an academic classroom building.

The value engineering methodology optimizes the costs by a systematic development of alternate proposals of isolated high cost areas. There are several factors involved in a VE study:

Figure 41-1
Work Sampling

DEPARTMENT _____ SECTION _____ DATE _____

SHOP _____

CREW SIZE _____ OBSERVER _____

	TIME	SPECIAL CONDITIONS
DIRECT PRODUCTIVE		
CRAFT TIME		
INDIRECT PRODUCTIVE		
JOB PREPARATION		
GETTING MAT'LS/EQUIP		
TRAVEL		
PLANNING		
CLEANING JOB-SITE		

BALANCING DELAY

OTHER

NON PRODUCTIVE

WAITING

PERSONAL

IDLE

BREAKS

OTHER

TOTAL OBSERVATIONS

NOTES:

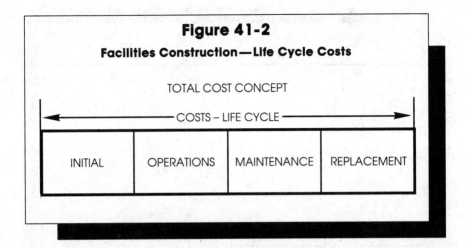

Figure 41-2

Facilities Construction—Life Cycle Costs

TOTAL COST CONCEPT

←――――――― COSTS – LIFE CYCLE ――――――→

| INITIAL | OPERATIONS | MAINTENANCE | REPLACEMENT |

- Availability of required design data.
- Initial construction and installation costs.
- Operational and maintenance requirements.
- Source of required material and availability.
- Prime and/or subcontractors' reaction and experience.
- Conformance to standards.
- If standards are not applicable, existence of sufficient data to develop standards.
- Impact on design to ensure program requirements are obtained.
- Impact on other necessary requirements, i.e. safety, fire protection, and security.

Each of these factors require investigation and evaluation, and input from various sources.

The design for a facility involves principally the architect-engineers' developing plans and specifications, which conform to the design criteria of the institution.

The designers determine which equipment and methods are most suitable from the point of view of economics, function, and maintenance. Generally, the selection is done by the engineer working on the particular aspect of the design. For example, the electrical engineer selects the generators and material for conductors, conduits, and panel boxes. The civil engineer selects the sewage and water systems.

Occasionally economic studies are conducted, e.g., site selection, energy systems selection, and structural system. However, in most instances, any selections or studies are made by an individual, or at best, by a group of individuals within the same discipline. Although normally no formal work plan is followed, in some cases a group is called together, or a full-time employee is available to organize and coordinate activities, or follow through any new ideas generated.

Figure 41-3 represents where the institution's money goes over the life cycle of a typical facility. It is interesting to note that the designers represent the smallest monetary area. This fact warrants some thought especially since these decisions have the greatest impact on total costs. Figure 41-4 is an approximate curve which shows whose decision governs the expenditures of funds. For example, the electrical engineer specified use of certain power equipment that cost $4,500 per unit installed. The construction contractor during this phase can influence the cost of the installation by only a few percent. The maintenance and operations personnel during their phase can influence costs slightly.

Value engineering is often referred to as value analysis and life cycle cost analysis. A more recent term for the function is constructability.

Work Simplification

Work simplification is a method of getting something done, step-by-step, by breaking a job down into simple segments. It is a systematic, common-sense approach to the way a job is done, with a goal of doing it better. The process "stretches the mind" by introducing and confirming the concept of what is useful work.

The heart of a work simplification program in the facilities manage-

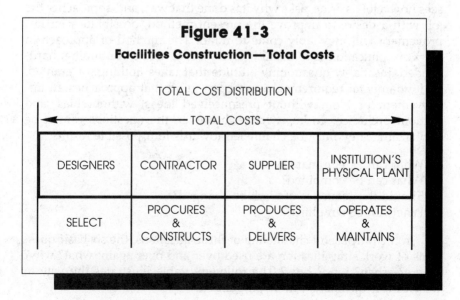

Figure 41-3

Facilities Construction—Total Costs

TOTAL COST DISTRIBUTION

←———————— TOTAL COSTS ————————→

DESIGNERS	CONTRACTOR	SUPPLIER	INSTITUTION'S PHYSICAL PLANT
SELECT	PROCURES & CONSTRUCTS	PRODUCES & DELIVERS	OPERATES & MAINTAINS

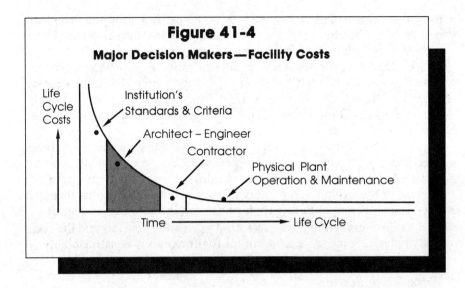

Figure 41-4

Major Decision Makers—Facility Costs

Life Cycle Costs

Institution's Standards & Criteria

Architect – Engineer

Contractor

Physical Plant Operation & Maintenance

Time ⟶ Life Cycle

ment environment is the recognition by the director that his or her supervisors and foremen are a vital part of the physical plant's methods improvement team, and through them tap the enthusiasm of everyone at the working level to perform a better service, at a lower price, and at the right time. Work simplification methods can be used to improve work throughout the physical plant organization.

The basic premise of work simplification is that once a person really sees how a job is done, asks why it is done that way, and approaches the job with a desire to improve the present method, possibilities for improvement will inevitably come to mind. The method of approach in work simplification is to instill in every supervisor a continuing, hard-headed, insatiably questioning attitude that takes nothing for granted. Its fundamental requirement is an open mind that approaches an improvement problem without preconceived ideas, without bias, and without prejudice. To be effective, however, the questions cannot be haphazard. They must be channeled towards four possible results:

1. What can be eliminated?
2. What can be combined?
3. Should the sequence of work be changed?
4. What can be simplified?

In the purposeful channeling of these questions, the six basic questions of work simplification are used over and over again: what? why? where? when? who? how? The following table illustrates the way in which these questions can be pinpointed.

Work Simplification's Six Basic Questions

Key Questions	Idea Kickers	Improvement Possibilities
WHAT is done?	• What is its purpose? • Does it do what it is supposed to do?	Eliminate
WHY is it done?	• Should it be done at all? • Can as good a result be obtained without it? • Is it an absolute must?	Eliminate
WHERE is it done?	• Why is it done there? • Why should it be done there? • Where should it be done? • Can it be done more easily by changing the location of personnel or equipment?	Combine and/or change sequence
WHEN is it done?	• Why is it done then? • Is it done in right sequence? • Can all or part of it be done at some other time?	Combine and/or change sequence
WHO does it?	• Why does this person do it? • Is the right person doing it? • Is it logical to give it to someone else?	Combine and/or change sequence
HOW is it done?	• Why should it be done this way? • Can it be done better with different equipment or different layout? • Is there any other way to do it?	Simplify

The physical plant supervisors who have been properly trained and motivated and who have been given the chance to master the techniques of work simplification will begin to produce time- and money-saving ideas almost immediately. The supervisor in daily contact with the way work is being done can apply the purposeful thought and methods of analysis to specific departmental operations. The supervisor who is properly inspired will carry the spark to the people working for him or her and will draw out their suggestions for improvements.

ADDITIONAL RESOURCES

Barnes, Ralph M. *Work Methods Manual*. New York: John Wiley & Sons, Inc.

————. *Work Sampling*. New York: John Wiley & Sons, Inc.

Engineered Performance Standards. PB 181-120 through PB 181-452, Bureau of Yards and Docks, U.S. Navy.

Karger, D.W. and F.R. Bayba. *Engineered Work Measurement*. New York: The Industrial Press.

Maintenance Management of Public Works, and Public Utilities. Navdocks p.321, Bureau of Yards and Docks, U.S. Navy.

Maynard, R.B., ed. *Industrial Engineering Handbook*. New York: McGraw-Hill Book Company.

CHAPTER 42

Customer Service

Paul F. Tabolt
Director, Physical Plant Operations
University of California at Berkeley

42.1 INTRODUCTION

In the field of facilities management, a customer service philosophy allows and encourages success. Yet in the day-to-day pressures of identifying work, handling requests for service, obtaining materials and supplies, fighting breakdowns and failures, and dealing with personnel and labor relations issues, it is easy to be consumed by thousands of details.

Many physical plant organizations have established a work control section that is responsible for routinely receiving requests, tracking progress, and communicating status information with campus clientele. Despite the centralization of work control management, campus clients continue to feel that after requests are submitted to the facilities organization, their requests fall into a black hole.

The black hole theory surfaces time and again as one ventures from one facilities management organization to another. As the campus feeds information into the facilities organization, it disappears from view, is transformed, passes through several hands, and eventually is acted upon. The campus client asks: Where does it go in the meantime?

The perceived bottomless pit into which the campus pours information and requests for service can be viewed by clients as an incorrigible monster. Pieces of information from the client enter the system and somehow, within the guise of plant management, are transformed into tangible products (designs, specifications, construction, maintenance, renovation, and repairs). How this happens is often viewed as a perplexing and frustrating process by campus users; a process that most prefer to view only from a distance.

Even if the decision is made to centralize some functions of customer service within work management and control sections of the

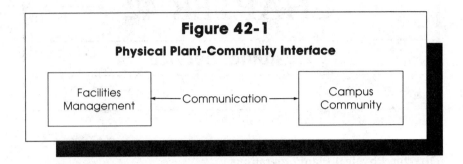

Figure 42-1

Physical Plant-Community Interface

Facilities Management ←—— Communication ——→ Campus Community

organization, this is not a panacea that will resolve the overall dilemma of establishing a universal customer service philosophy and orientation within the facilities management profession. The concept of providing a consistent, continuous, and effective interface between plant management staff and the institutional community is a goal that can be enhanced through work management and control programs designed to improve communication (see Figure 42-1).

The challenge to those in facilities management can be heightened when they face the further challenge of striving for timely and effective communications with the campus community. Work management and control concepts should focus on an interactive approach that records information, sets priorities for requests, creates schedules, and tracks progress while keeping facilities management constituencies informed of ongoing activities. Centralizing customer service or customer responsiveness to work management and control requires a special concentrated focus on key personnel and procedures designed to be interactive with campus users. An ever-present awareness of customer service can help mold customer service advocacy throughout the facilities management organization.

42.2 ESTABLISHING THE COMMUNICATIONS NETWORK

In focusing clearly on the rules of work management and control, the question needs to be asked: In what areas of work do we need to enhance our communication efforts?

- Preventive maintenance
- Maintenance and repairs
- Operations
- Planning and space utilization
- Deferred maintenance/capital renewal and replacement

- Renovations and alterations
- Estimating
- Construction.

There needs to be a starting point that allows information to be channeled more effectively throughout the campus. The development of a formal communications network can assure more effective communication. The facilities management organization typically has the responsibility for the physical activities, but unless there is an established communication link, the information exchange is not likely to be successful.

The first task is to identify and formalize regular communication links, then establish links where none exist. A goal of a high-level, formalized work management program is the identification of individuals from academic, administrative, and research areas who will represent the interests of their constituency to the facilities management organization.

Dependent upon the size of the institution, the number, variety, and complexity of formalized communication links may vary. At a large institution, the general pattern of communications may be as is shown in Figure 42-2.

42.3 THE FACILITIES AS A RESOURCE

Although no two institutions are likely to establish the same pattern for communications, the establishment of a regular pattern that encourages regular, consistent, and continuous exchanges can improve the coordinated facilities management interactions. The facilities management organization may need to establish this pattern. Creating a situation that the institutional administration can accept requires initiating the process at an opportune time and implementing it in a way that the users can accept. The political situation at any given institution requires sensitive, timely, and alert judgment if the communication network is to be successful.

The structuring of networked communication layers within the institutional framework can improve the understanding and knowledge of all involved parties for maintenance, repair, and service tasks through new construction and major capital improvements. In other words, firmly establishing an interactive approach to institutional problems that require strategic involvement for facilities issues can bridge the gap between the facilities management organization and the institutional community.

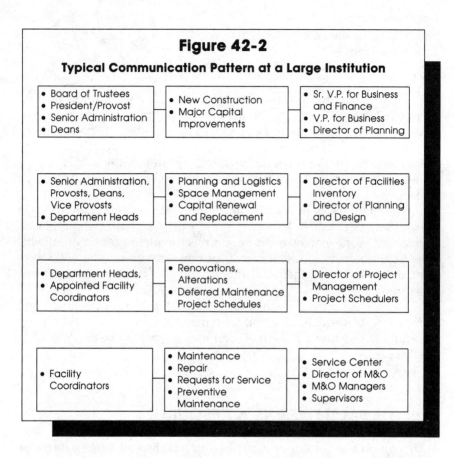

Figure 42-2

Typical Communication Pattern at a Large Institution

• Board of Trustees • President/Provost • Senior Administration • Deans	• New Construction • Major Capital Improvements	• Sr. V.P. for Business and Finance • V.P. for Business • Director of Planning
• Senior Administration, Provosts, Deans, Vice Provosts • Department Heads	• Planning and Logistics • Space Management • Capital Renewal and Replacement	• Director of Facilities Inventory • Director of Planning and Design
• Department Heads, • Appointed Facility Coordinators	• Renovations, Alterations • Deferred Maintenance Project Schedules	• Director of Project Management • Project Schedulers
• Facility Coordinators	• Maintenance • Repair • Requests for Service • Preventive Maintenance	• Service Center • Director of M&O • M&O Managers • Supervisors

A series of communication networks that parallel the academic, administrative, and research communities can aid the process (see Figure 42-3). As an example, those with the highest organizational responsibilities in facilities management must join with those parallel to them in the remainder of the institution for major capital improvements. At lower organizational levels, department heads may join with project managers from the facilities management organization while academic administrative assistants may focus on issues involving maintenance and repair.

If the facilities management executive team can convince the institutional leadership to structure the process in such a fashion, opportunities will open to thereafter define and assign management roles throughout the institutional environment.

The highest levels of this networked process should concentrate on master planning, space planning, priorities, and complications that will be caused by major new construction and major capital improvements.

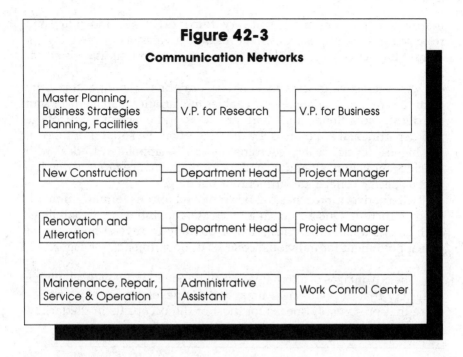

Figure 42-3

Communication Networks

Master Planning, Business Strategies Planning, Facilities	—	V.P. for Research	—	V.P. for Business
New Construction	—	Department Head	—	Project Manager
Renovation and Alteration	—	Department Head	—	Project Manager
Maintenance, Repair, Service & Operation	—	Administrative Assistant	—	Work Control Center

Policies that restrict or limit the cost of construction and decisions that impact design criteria and that help keep projects in line with construction budgets can be addressed at the highest interactive level. This group should collectively discuss staging problems and assign priorities for all new construction and major capital improvement projects. By doing so, the institution will begin to view the facilities as a vital resource, one that should be coopted into strategic planning processes. The role of the facilities will then be integral to obtaining institutional missions.

42.4 FACILITIES COORDINATOR

Typically, new construction or major capital improvements create a host of related relocations, renovations, and alterations. Yet while all of the demands for designs and estimates for renovations and alterations are pouring into the facilities management organization, so are the pressures to care for capital renewal in the form of deferred and major maintenance projects. The community will be interested in major maintenance projects they can see or feel, while the facilities management staff silently cares for the hidden enemies that are waiting for an opportunity to disrupt the smooth operation of the plant. Deciding what information to communicate will vary from individual to individual and from campus to campus, but whenever the activities of one organization disrupt the activities of another, some form of communication is advisable.

An interactive process that enables projects of the highest priority to surface for appropriate review enables the facilities management staff to educate, coordinate, and share problems and concerns with college and departmental appointees. By drawing upon the support of those at the highest levels, facility coordinators can be appointed to deal with specific renovation, alteration, and major maintenance projects that impact a specific college, department, or building.

Alternative approaches can be employed for this formal communication structure. One approach is to create appointments by buildings, such as one appointment for a major building or several buildings, or one appointment for individual colleges or departments (see Figure 42-4).

The advantages of alternative 1 include a familiarity with a building or facility that develops over time, and the development of a primary voice that presumably speaks for most of the occupants in the facility.

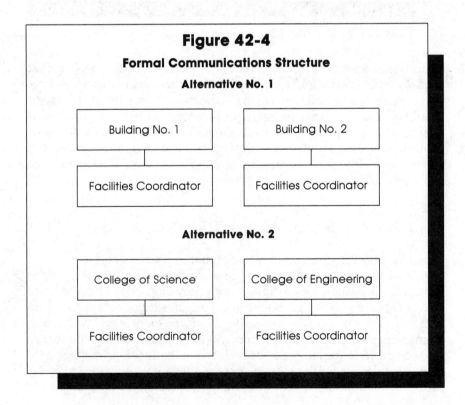

Figure 42-4

Formal Communications Structure

Alternative No. 1

Building No. 1	Building No. 2
Facilities Coordinator	Facilities Coordinator

Alternative No. 2

College of Science	College of Engineering
Facilities Coordinator	Facilities Coordinator

Because many of those in higher education proclaim a primary focus on their academic discipline and, further, do not recognize a formal business hierarchy, it is doubtful that one voice will ever be able to synergize and communicate for the occupants of an entire building.

A drawback to alternative 1 appears when multiple colleges or units share a facility and therefore feel little dependency or allegiance to the appointed facilities coordinator.

Alternative 2 works well when a college or unit is located within one facility, but suffers when two, three, or more colleges or units share the same facility. In such cases, the facilities management organization is faced with multiple contacts whenever there is facility disruption. Also, the sense of ownership of public spaces is somewhat restricted. This lack of ownership can cause confusion among building occupants as maintenance and repair problems are often left unreported. In line with a customer service philosophy, the facilities management organization should elect whichever alternative best fits its environment. The custodial organization should also be enlisted to report maintenance problems that may otherwise be neglected.

The appointment of facility coordinators should correspond to a set of duties for which they will be responsible. Typical duties include:

- Serving as a liaison between the facilities management organization and the building occupants.
- Initiating renovation and alteration requests.
- Placing requests for renovation and alteration into priority order.
- Reviewing project design, estimate, and construction progress.
- Overseeing project budgets and authorizing change orders or budget deviations.

In choosing facilities coordinators, the college or building occupants should look for those individuals who have

- Familiarity with facilities management organization, policies, and procedures.
- Knowledge of institutional policies and procedures that relate to facilities.
- An interest in the facilities they occupy.

If that familiarity or knowledge does not readily exist, then the facilities management organization must provide the training to raise the facility coordinator's understanding of his or her operation.

Because facility coordinators are not usually recognized with financial compensation and are normally established based upon a college's or department's recognized need to centrally process information, the performance of the individual facility coordinator will be based upon traits of commitment, involvement, and initiative. Obviously, some facility coordinators will perform exceptionally well while others will accept or reject their duties and responsibilities as an annoying addition to their normal assignments. Finding ways to recognize and reinforce the facilities coordinators as a vital part of the department communications network is a challenge to all physical plant administrators.

Various methods can be used to stimulate facility coordinator involvement.

Meetings with Other Facility Coordinators   Facility coordinators tend to enjoy exchanging their frustrations, woes, and successes with their counterparts. Organized exchanges can help teach facility coordinators how to work within and outside of the formal organizational system. Their success is best recognized by their collegial associates when they can successfully deliver prompt and effective service. Their failure to deliver physical plant services places them in the miserable role of liaison between user demands and physical plant as the supplier of service.

Special Sessions in their Honor   Get-togethers, luncheons, and coffee-and-donut sessions can serve as small tokens of appreciation for those who assume this sometimes difficult liaison role. Providing facility coordinators with an opportunity to vent their frustrations enables key physical plant personnel to better understand the strengths and weaknesses of their organizations. An informal one-on-one meeting can help to clarify any misunderstandings or problems that develop.

Educational Systems   The development of facilities coordinators as a part of a communication network will not work without the leaders in the facilities management organization providing education to all facilities coordinators on the operation, policies, and procedures utilized within the organization. It is helpful to host informative sessions related to the multitude of opportunities and constraints that impact the facilities management organization. These sessions need not take the form of defensive posturing, but should present the operational framework within which the work can and must be accomplished.

Newsletters   Newsletters announcing changes in physical plant policies and procedures or changes in the physical environment can apprise facility coordinators of what is happening. This extra effort will more solidly establish the relationship between the entities.

42.5 THE FACILITY COORDINATOR'S ROLE IN THE PAPER TRAIL

Once facility coordinators have been identified, their identity must be publicized. Listings of facility coordinators need to be shared with the entire physical plant organization. Those facility coordinators who elect to have a strong involvement with facility issues should be the first to complain when they are not included in facility communications. Professional courtesies on the part of the physical plant organization will be extended to facility coordinators if employees are trained to involve the facilities coordinators in correspondence, communication, and discussions regarding their area of responsibility.

Dependent upon the level of formalization that exists within the organization, requests for new construction, design, estimates, maintenance, and services may be handled in whole or in part through formal paper transactions. If such is the case, the facilities coordinator should receive a copy of all requests that initiate a form or paper trail. The receipt of those requests will enable the facility coordinator to monitor and track progress. A completion notification process to the facilities coordinators needs to be in place so they can follow up on the completed project to verify their satisfaction.

42.6 ESTABLISHING PRIORITIES

Everyone knows the story of the boy who cried wolf. Some campus clients will always fit into that category, but the number may be significantly reduced by inviting facility coordinators to help establish criteria for priority response to service requests. Structuring a facilities coordinator committee to share in the development of priorities can achieve dramatic results—results typically close to what the physical plant organization would develop if they were to act independently. A cooperative approach to priority establishment enables the facility coordinators to better understand the multiple demands for service placed upon the physical plant organization.

Another method that has been employed to determine priorities, particularly in the design and estimation of renovation and remodeling, is to force facility coordinators to place their unit's requests for service in priority order. This can be particularly helpful whenever a large backlog of work is awaiting completion. Placing requests for service will only be successful if the facilities coordinator has the ear of his or her administration and then only if the unit's administration is willing to make what are sometimes difficult decisions. Without requiring an up-front commitment of funds for design or estimating services, some institutions are caught in the dilemma of having artificial requests for service flooding their backlog of work to be performed, such as requests colleges or departments never plan to implement. It may be easier to submit a request for renovation or alteration to the physical plant organization in order to buy time, rather than to say no to a colleague within an academic unit. Forcing the unit to place requests in priority order can flush out the unrealistic requests that only add to the backlog.

Facilities coordinators should also be asked to contribute to the process of identifying major maintenance needs. Their input can help establish major maintenance priorities, but the ultimate decision for major maintenance priorities must lie with the experts within the physical plant organization.

42.7 COORDINATING WORK

Discussions regarding facility availability, utility disruption, dirt, debris, noise, and work schedules should be held with facilities coordinators before work begins. An upfront discussion can help to communicate the unpleasantness of the task before reactions begin to form. Those unprepared for physical plant services often feel the work should be performed without inconveniencing building occupants. It is up to the design, construction, remodeling, and maintenance professionals to forewarn occupants when they will be inconvenienced. This communication process works if all of the players do their part and allow enough time for this communication to filter throughout the affected area.

Unscheduled disruptions or those that permit only a short announcement can be communicated more effectively if a facilities coordinator program is well in place. A work control center that has a facilities coordinator network needs to contact only a handful of individuals in the case of an unscheduled utility interruption and can do so far more effectively than an organization that lacks a consolidated communication network.

42.8 SOLICITING FEEDBACK

By asking the facilities coordinator how the organization performed on a completed task, physical plant administration can more clearly define where to target their efforts for organizational improvement. For instance, when maintenance or renovation projects are completed, the work control center may want to develop and distribute a standard set of questions in a survey format that might include:

- Was this task completed in a timely fashion?
- Were the costs appropriate considering the work performed?
- Were physical plant personnel courteous?
- Were you satisfied with the quality of the work performed?
- Were you satisfied with the productivity of physical plant employees?
- Was all of the work completed?

The practice of soliciting feedback will enable physical plant administrators to obtain a customer's perception of the services rendered. (See Figure 3-5 in Chapter 3, Communication.) Timely questionnaires can generate a listing of problems that warrant corrective action. Timely follow-up on those problems can convert a potentially dissatisfied customer into a satisfied client.

42.9 SUMMARY

Formalization of communications for all physical plant activities can facilitate customer satisfaction. Identifying communication networks can more readily assure the cooperative exchange of information between the facilities organization and the campus community. Facility coordinators must be oriented to physical plant policies and procedures and can provide an invaluable service by contributing to the establishment of priorities. Feedback for those in the formal communication process can help the physical plant administrator recognize strengths while focusing on and correcting weaknesses.

SECTION VII

PHYSICAL PLANT

OPERATIONS

Section Leader:
James T. Mergner, P.E.
Associate Director for Utilities Operations
University of North Carolina at Chapel Hill

CHAPTER 43

Overview of Plant Operations

James T. Mergner, P.E.
Associate Director for Utilities Operations
University of North Carolina at Chapel Hill

43.1 INTRODUCTION

Physical plant operations encompass a wide variety of activities, many of which directly relate to the operation and maintenance of campus buildings, grounds, or utility systems. Other functions not directly related to facilities are organizationally included within the physical plant function.

Energy-related functions such as the operation of central energy systems and building energy systems are important responsibilities of the physical plant department. They must be performed so that they provide for the needs of the campus community in a reliable and safe manner. Since a significant portion of the annual operating budget is dedicated to purchase, production, and distribution of energy, it is essential that this function be performed as cost effectively as possible. Particular attention must be given to sophisticated energy management to be able to minimize overall cost and optimize system reliability.

Custodial services and grounds maintenance both continually influence the overall appearance of the campus. Normally, more than one-half of physical plant employees are dedicated to these two functions; they are the most visible employees in the department's work force and typically have considerably more contact with the campus community than the rest of the department's employees.

The distribution of campus mail is often accomplished by physical plant employees. Other continuing responsibilities include the operation of the campus telecommunication system, the provision of transportation services, trash collection and disposal, and support services for special events.

The safety and well-being of the campus residents is an immediate and continuing concern of the physical plant director. The campus security function is often organizationally assigned to the physical plant department. This function can include both building security and key issue and control.

Additional safety-related responsibilities include the proper operation of building fire protection and suppression systems. Also, elevators must be maintained and periodically inspected and certified as safe to operate. Special purpose ventilation systems including fume hoods must reliably protect building occupants who often use hazardous substances in their work. Close cooperation with the environmental health and safety office is essential to be able to give adequate attention to safeguarding the health of the campus population.

Unusual events such as fires, floods, and storms have a major impact on the physical plant department. Proper planning and training in preparation to respond when an emergency occurs is essential. This enhances the department's ability to be responsive in an actual emergency.

43.2 IMPORTANCE TO THE COLLEGE OR UNIVERSITY

A review of these many functions reveals that the physical plant department interacts with many aspects of life on the campus on a daily basis. Continuing attention and effort are required to ensure that the physical condition of the many campus facilities is sufficient to fully support the diverse activities that take place.

The physical plant director is responsible for providing a safe and comfortable environment for the faculty, students, and staff as they carry out their academic pursuits and research efforts. Also, efficient and timely support services are a prerequisite for the success of these endeavors.

An equally important aspect of the physical plant function is to ensure that the campus provides a positive visual image through proper building maintenance, grounds care, and custodial services. Often, the only impression one might have of the school is one based upon appearance alone.

The provision of physical plant services is expensive and consumes a significant portion of the college or university's annual budget. The physical plant director must efficiently utilize assigned resources to provide for the needs of the campus. Careful control of costs is required to satisfy all the demands placed upon the department, while staying within the funds budgeted for the function.

43.3 ORGANIZATIONAL CONSIDERATIONS

The diverse functions of the facilities department demand a broad spectrum of skills from the work force. This places additional demands on the department's managers, because they need to be familiar with so many different functions. There is considerable interrelationship between many of the functions on a daily basis. Since a college campus rarely closes, many of the physical plant functions demand attention twenty-four hours per day throughout the year. Emergencies can be expected to occur without warning. This necessitates a quick response regardless of time of day or day of the week.

To be properly prepared to carry out the department's responsibilities, the organization must be carefully structured and staffed with the proper number of employees possessing the skills needed. A well-qualified group of managers and supervisors must also be in place to coordinate and direct the efforts of the department's annual budget. In addition, good communications are required because of the many interfaces between the various aspects of the department's operations.

The physical plant function has become increasingly complex. The demands of ever-changing technology and more sophisticated building systems require extensive technical knowledge and expertise to understand and properly operate and maintain them.

CHAPTER 44

Energy Management

Martin J. Altschul, P.E.
Utilities Engineer
University of Virginia

44.1 INTRODUCTION

The high cost and threat of interruption of the supply of fuels and energy, and vastly increased energy consumption in modern college and university buildings, have combined to make energy management a major function in physical plant operations. Energy efficiency considerations permeate virtually all facilities operations. However, the potential for greatest improvements in energy efficiency are in the central plants that convert fuels and utilities to utilization forms, the building mechanical and electrical systems where virtually all energy finds its ultimate end use, and in the coordination of electrical and thermal requirements.

The following three chapters—Central Energy Systems, Building Energy Systems, and Cogeneration for Universities and Colleges—address these three operations. This chapter provides an overview of the goals, potential, organizational considerations, and general procedures and methods in the formulation and execution of an energy management program.

The following chapters in Section IV, Facilities of Higher Education, describe the technical facilities and equipment, and include discussions of energy efficiency: Chapter 21, Building Heating, Cooling, and Ventilating Systems; Chapter 22, Building Electrical Systems; Chapter 25, Central Monitoring and Control Systems; Chapter 26, Heating and Power Plants; Chapter 27, Central Chiller Plants; Chapter 28, Electrical Distribution Systems; and Chapter 29, Heating and Cooling Media Distribution.

44.2 ENERGY MANAGEMENT AS AN INSTITUTIONAL GOAL

Goals of an Energy Management Program

For the first seven decades of the twentieth century, the availability of cheap energy was one of the principal forces in raising the standard of living in western nations to unprecedented levels. Shortages occurred in times of war when oil wells, refineries, and distribution systems became strategic objectives. The post–World War II boom was fueled largely by cheap oil and natural gas that seemed to be available in unlimited quantities. It was anticipated that nuclear fission power plants would supply limitless electrical power for the future.

These attitudes still persist in varying degrees, despite the experiences of the 1970s and 1980s. Energy conservation frequently receives major emphasis only when driven by the economic forces of supply and cost. Plans for restricting campus activities or shutting down buidlings to reduce energy consumption are generally implemented only during energy crises.

However, the oil shortages, coal and transportation strikes, and electrical brownouts of the past fifteen years have brought the realization that energy is a finite resource. Contingency plans for energy shortages have been developed by most institutions, and building codes and institutional policies have been rewritten to incorporate energy efficiency in the design of new buildings.

Environmental problems such as acid rain, the greenhouse effect, and loss of the ozone layer from the use of halogenated refrigerants are under study and will affect the production and use of energy. Environmental concerns about landfills and protection of ground water from contamination, in combination with recoverable energy, have led to the development of solid waste incineration with heat recovery.

Perhaps the most immediate concern is the realiation that effective energy management can produce large cost savings. The purchase of energy in the form of fuels and utilities is a major item in every institution's budget. Even a small percentage reduction in energy consumption can reduce energy expenditures substantially and make these funds available for other purposes.

Energy concerns must be considered an integral part of institutional planning and operation. The successful energy program will allow the institution to meet the challenges listed above with as little impact on its primary goals as possible both in the short and long term. In designing the energy program it is important to remember that energy management is a tool to be used to improve the climate for excellence in education, research, or health care. It is a tool that can be used to reduce costs while providing the proper environment for effectively carrying out the missions of the institution.

As an institution develops its energy management program, it becomes increasingly evident that energy systems are highly interdependent. Changes in lighting affect heating and air conditioning and the function of windows and shades. An operational decision to shut down heating systems in the summer will affect temperature and humidity in buildings that are designed to use heating for control of air conditioning. Because of this interdependency, it is necessary to take an integrated approach to energy management.

Elements of the Energy Management Program

A complete energy management program is more than a series of quick fixes to meet a temporary crisis. A successful energy program requires involvement by the various members of the institutional community on many different levels. There are three mutually complementary elements to such a program.

The first is a system to deliver energy reliably and at minimum cost. Consideration must be given to meeting this goal in both short- and long-range energy requirements. Planning for disruptions of normal energy supplies should be part of an institution's emergency plans, which should include the following:

1. *Alternate delivery systems.* Depending on the application, consideration should be given to multiple electrical feeders into buildings, rail and truck delivery of fuels and contracts with more than one vendor.
2. *Alternate energy sources.* Boilers and furnaces that can fire more than one fuel and emergency generators can provide insurance against disruptions and offer potential for cost savings in many situations.
3. *Curtailment planning.* Interruptions to energy supplies are sure to occur in any system. Curtailment planning involves deciding who gets curtailed and a means to localize that curtailment. Switches and valves in distribution systems must be laid out so as to isolate lower priority areas.

Developing and achieving specific energy conservation objectives is the second element of an energy management program. It cannot be overemphasized that saving energy must always be a secondary goal to ensuring the continuity of operations. The key to identifying successful energy conservation measures is achieving a proper balance between cost savings and operational requirements. The best energy conservation measures not only save energy but also improve working conditions. A program to achieve energy conservation objectives should include the following steps:

1. *Develop energy conservation initiatives.* There needs to be an ongoing process of examining the institution for energy initiatives. Technology and institutions change. Therefore, buildings and systems should be reexamined periodically for energy use and energy conservation opportunities.
2. *Determine the cost effectiveness of initiatives.* First cost, energy savings, changes in maintenance costs, and effect on other aspects of institutional life must go into the evaluation of any energy conservation initiative.
3. *Monitor the effect of energy initiatives.* The decision to embark on any energy conservation action is based on many assumptions, some of which may turn out to be invalid. It is important to monitor initiatives after they have been implemented to avoid repeating mistakes and to refine future actions.

The third element of an energy management program is often the one most difficult for physical plant. It is the integration of overall energy management program into the institutional structure. This involves educating the community as to the program's goals and progress. It involves selling the program, not only to top level administration, but also to the community at large. Money spent on energy costs may be money not spent on faculty salaries or research equipment. It is important for the community to be aware of energy goals and success or failure in achieving these goals through the use of regularly issued reports.

The Roles of Energy Managers and Energy Conservation Officers

Unless an institution is small enough for a single manager to directly oversee the budgeting, operation, planning, and construction of all building systems, there will necessarily be some division of responsibility in the management of energy systems. Energy management will mean different things to the budget officer, the mechanical and electrical superintendent, the institutional planner, and the construction manager. Other, more immediate concerns can easily take precedence over energy if the importance of energy management is not constantly reinforced. There is no natural constituency that has energy management as a primary concern. It is therefore useful to establish a separate energy management function to coordinate the institution's efforts in this area and to serve as spokesperson for energy concerns.

There are different approaches in placing the energy management role within the organizational structure. The institution must decide whether it is large enough to warrant a full-time position, whether the position is to be staff or supervisory, and where the position is to be within the physical plant organization. In larger institutions, consideration may be given to dedicated energy management functions at several levels within the organization.

The Energy Manager   The physical plant organization is the logical location for an energy manager, who is concerned with the operation of manageable energy loads such as:

- Building heating and air conditioning systems.
- Building electrical systems.
- Central heating and chiller plants and associated distribution systems.
- Electrical generation and distribution systems.
- Automotive and bus fleet maintenance and operations.

The energy manager must be in a position to manage fuel use and fuel inventories on a short-term basis, and to supervise shedding of electrical loads for demand management. The energy manager can serve as scheduler for determining hours of operation for heating and air conditioning systems. If the institution has a computerized energy management and control system, the energy manager should monitor and control on a day-to-day or even minute-to-minute basis how energy is used within the institution.

The Energy Conservation Officer   The energy manager is involved in the daily functioning of the institution and is therefore not in the best position to provide oversight of the total energy conservation program of the institution. This oversight can best be provided by a separate individual functioning as the institution's energy conservation officer. The energy conservation position is strictly a staff function, and assumes the role of advocate for energy conservation and planning for the institution.

The energy conservation officer handles publicity for energy conservation programs. Communications with the institutional community can be through employee newsletters, posters, slogans, brochures, and any other marketing tools used to sell programs and ideas (see Chapter 3, Communication).

If the institution has established an energy conservation committee, the energy conservation officer provides staff support for that committee. The establishment of such a committee can be invaluable in developing institutional support for an energy program. The committee should contain a broad cross section of the institutional community, rather than limiting membership to people with technical expertise in energy matters. Because of this, the committee should not be relied upon to resolve technical matters, but rather should provide guidance on broad institutional policies.

An example of a decision best left to the energy conservation committee might be maximum and minimum temperature standards. The committee will need to rely on the energy conservation officer for information on building code and other legal requirements, comfort standards, energy savings, and technical problems with maintaining given temperature levels. Given this information in easily understandable form, the energy conservation committee, representing the entire community, can determine and establish temperature limits that can be accepted by the institutional community and implemented by physical plant.

The energy conservation officer needs to work closely with other institutional organizations that may have significant impact on energy use. Actions taken in the name of safety and security or grounds beautification can affect outside lighting costs and building heating and air conditioning loads. Transportation departments can realize major savings through the purchase of more energy efficient vehicles. Pooling fuel contracts can often result in significant cost savings.

It is also important to establish close relationships with academic departments and others who develop class schedules. Changing times and locations for scheduled activities can result in major reductions in energy use through shutting down building systems. If electricity demand billing is in effect, even greater payoffs are possible if high-demand research activities can be rescheduled to off-peak hours.

The energy conservation officer must lead efforts to develop institutional energy policies. Long- and short-term goals for energy savings can provide both motivation and a measurement of success of energy conservation programs. To be realistic these goals need to accurately reflect other institutional policies. Goals cannot be static, but must consider the planned scope of future programs.

The energy conservation officer needs to be involved in all major construction and renovation projects from conception through design to ensure that energy concerns are addressed properly. If design is done by an outside firm, the energy conservation officer can provide valuable input during the selection of the design team. Just as all people have different strengths and interests, architects and engineers may place varying degrees of emphasis and show more or less sensitivity and creativity in the effective use of energy in their designs. A designer's portfolio will provide many clues as to how energy efficient their future designs will be. Such clues are likely to go undetected given the myriad other concerns associated with selection unless one member of the selection team is trained and has an overriding interest in energy use.

Even the most energy conscious design team will be unaware of special design considerations unique to a given institution or building site. Availability and capacity of centralized electrical, cooling and heating distribution systems, the precise nature of load profiles in nearby facilities, and unique institutional requirements are likely to be unknown to a designer not having an intimate and longstanding knowledge of the institution.

Another area that is even more of an unknown to the outside designer is the capability and configuration of an institution's computerized energy management system (EMS). Such systems represent a fairly new technology. There is wide variability in the capabilities of such systems among manufacturers and even between installations of the same manufacturer's products. The energy manager and energy conservation officer, combined with the EMS support staff, will need to provide the designer with information concerning capabilities and requirements for an EMS installation.

The energy conservation officer should follow projects through design to ensure that energy initiatives incorporated in the schematic design remain in the project as it progresses. Again, as advocate for energy conservation, the energy manager must ensure that the long-range view is maintained as the inevitable competition for construction funds becomes more intense.

A third important function that will probably be handled by the energy conservation officer involves the maintenance and publication of statistics regarding energy use. The raw data for such information is likely to be kept by several sources such as accounting departments and heating/chiller plant operations. Often, however, the requirements of an accounting department in tracking the flow of dollars, or an operational department in projecting inventory and maintaining annual budgets will not be the same as those needed for either historical analysis of energy use or projections of future energy requirements. The energy conservation officer needs to work with these diverse groups to ensure that information on electrical demand, kilowatt-hour use, and power factor is not lost, nor is information on boiler/chiller availability, system efficiency, or the availability of various energy sources.

The energy data base maintained by the energy conservation officer will need to contain more detail than is generally provided by an accounting-based metering system. Energy analysis requires that energy be accounted for by both source and end use. Knowing that a given building costs so many dollars per square foot per year for energy can highlight potential problems. However, useful analysis can only begin when the end use of that energy within the building is known. The most common means of identifying these end uses is by survey and calculation. However, during construction or renovation, the energy conservation officer should be alert to the possibility of configuring meters in such a way as to permit the recording of actual energy use by function.

At appropriate intervals, the energy conservation officer should review this energy data base with the community. Such review might be structured as follows:

- Quarterly publish energy use and cost data on an institution-wide basis accompanied by some discussion of overall trends in energy use.
- Annually compile, analyze, and publish energy data on a building by building basis. This will serve to identify buildings that warrant closer study.
- On a four- or five-year cycle, perform a more detailed analysis of energy use for each building. This analysis should identify energy use by function (heating, lighting, air conditioning, or process use), by area within the building if it is used for multiple purposes, and by time of day and time of year. This analysis should be reviewed with building occupants. It can serve as a preliminary energy audit of the building and can serve as a basis for operational as well as physical changes to the building to better utilize energy.

Organizational Structure for Energy Management

The actual placement of the energy management team within the institution will vary widely. In small institutions, both energy manager and energy conservation officer may be part-time positions, while in large institutions both may require considerable support staff. Personal strengths and weaknesses of the individuals selected for these positions will also play a role in optimizing the structure of the energy management team.

The energy manager must be involved in the day-to-day operations of the institution's physical plant department. Where the work management section is an integral part of the physical plant operational division, this section is a good location for the energy manager. From such a vantage point, the energy manager has a view of all aspects of physical plant activity and can intercede and assist as needed to ensure that actions taken are in accordance with good energy management practices and institutional policies and goals.

An organization that provides more autonomy and responsibility to individual work centers is more problematic. The work management section is more remote from the day-to-day operational decision-making process. Scheduling of operating hours for individual air conditioning systems; selection of fuels for boiler plants, selection of replacement motors, HVAC equipment and lights and ballasts; repairs to building envelope components—all these require input from and feedback to the energy manager, and they are likely to take place without significant interaction with the work management section in a less centrally controlled organization.

The energy manager must be selected and placed in the organization in a way that allows constant communication with each work center and that encourages the cooperation of its manager and personnel. Wherever positioned within the structure, the energy manager must have free access to and a strong influence with electrical and mechanical shop managers and central heating/chiller plant superintendents. If given responsibility for an energy management system, the energy manager should also manage the personnel who directly operate and maintain this system.

The placement of the energy conservation officer within the institution can vary more than that of the energy manager. Given the broad span of contacts needed to adequately monitor and control energy, institutions may elect to make the energy conservation officer a staff position reporting directly to the president/chancellor/chief executive officer of the institution, a strategy common in industry during the late 1970s when energy costs and availability were dominant forces in determining the success or failure of a company. Such placement has the advantage of making energy concerns highly visible to the entire institution. It also provides the energy conservation officer with a means of directly interacting with the institutional decision-making process, not only to provide input but to gain a wider perspective of the role of energy decisions. However, such a structure will tend to isolate the energy conservation officer from both the major energy consuming activities taking place within physical plant and the general institutional community.

The energy conservation officer's primary relationships are with the physical plant operating divisions, the planning and design group responsible for new construction and renovations, and the accounting and budgeting group responsible for managing utility costs. The best place for the energy conservation officer is within the organization encompassing these groups, generally the department of physical plant. Depending upon the structure and dynamics of the institution, the energy conservation officer may be placed within the organization in any of the following locations:

- A position reporting directly to the manager of all physical plant activities.
- A position within the institutional planning group.
- A position within the architectural and engineering design services group.
- A member of the physical plant operations or work management group. In such a structure, the energy manager and energy conservation officer functions can generally be merged within one office.

44.3 ENERGY CONSERVATION MEASURES

Identifying Possible Energy Conservation Measures

The first step in any comprehensive energy management program is to understand where and how energy is being used. Such an analysis can, and eventually should, be made in great detail for all buildings and facilities. Such an understanding of the dynamics of energy use is essential to making major changes in building design and system operation. The idea of developing such a comprehensive understanding for an entire institution can be overwhelming and lead to paralysis.

A practical approach is to conduct this analysis in stages. These stages can be approximated as follows:

1. *Preliminary energy audit.* Classify each building by principal function and calculate energy cost and use on a per-square-foot basis. Using this data and published standards by the American Institute of Architects (AIA) and Department of Energy (DOE), identify buildings that appear to have higher than normal energy consumption.
2. *Energy audit.* Perform a walk-through inspection of each building to identify simple energy-saving opportunities. It is best if the energy auditor is accompanied by workers from mechanical, electrical, and building trades who are familiar with the building, and by someone who occupies the building on a regular basis. Develop a good understanding of the details of building operation and HVAC equipment schedules and parameters and lighting levels can be developed. Identify and correct maintenance deficiencies that result in increased energy costs, such as broken doors and windows, dirty air conditioning filters, and poorly operating furnaces and boilers.
3. *Technical energy analysis.* A professional engineering and architectural team should be assigned the task of reviewing all aspects of building operation, maintenance, and design. The team will examine a number of options for changing energy use patterns that may or

may not require large financial expenditures. All the findings of the energy audit should be reviewed in detail and updated as needed. The team should perform both a cost-benefit analysis and a sensitivity analysis of each option to ensure that savings in one area of building operation will not be offset by additional costs in other areas.

A "model" of energy flows is implied in any action taken to save energy. Energy models and calculations can vary in complexity and sophistication, from the use of common sense through complex solutions of partial differential equations. Energy flows in a building cannot possibly be modeled exactly using any mathematical methods or tools available today. Estimates and simplifications are always needed; the only relevant question is what level of complexity is appropriate for a particular building/energy conservation combination. Choosing a more complex analysis method is no guarantee of more accurate results in absolute terms. However, the additional complexity may allow the model to be sensitive to changes that more closely resemble those of the building.

The most common energy analysis models used in current engineering practice calculate energy flows during worst-case conditions. An assumption is then made that flows during non-peak periods are some fixed fraction of these maximum rates. The simplicity achieved by this type of model makes hand calculations practical and permits almost instantaneous estimates of energy use using even the smallest personal computer. This type of approach is the basis of such calculation approaches as the degree-day and "simplified ASHRAE" methods.

A significant increase in the complexity of the model occurs when the nonlinear relations between energy use and such factors as the position of the sun and air infiltration as a function of wind velocity and temperature difference become important. The response of energy systems such as fans and pumps also is nonlinear with respect to flow. In situations where such effects are important, energy flow calculations need to be calculated for many different conditions. If dynamic response is important because the building can store significant amounts of energy, it is necessary to take into account not only present conditions but also the rate at which these conditions are changing. This is generally done by tracking the energy state of the building on a periodic basis, such as hourly, and including the difference between the current state and past conditions in the calculations.

Such refinements in the analysis require the speed and storage capabilities of high-speed computers. The programming required to perform these calculations is also a major undertaking and few programs have been developed for this purpose. The amount of information related to building size and shape, characteristics of building mechanical and electrical systems, and miscellaneous other data is sizable in such an analysis. In addition, the number of computations performed for a full year's simulation are enormous, so computer costs can also be significant.

The calculation of changes in energy use is only part of the energy analysis. Other factors that have an impact on the viability of any project must be considered. The initial cost of the work, impact on the operation of the building, changes in maintenance practices and costs, the availability and cost of capital, and future changes in energy and other costs all must be examined. A number of different analytical techniques have been developed to compute the relative worth of a project. These are all based on the assumed ability to accurately predict the future, a hazardous undertaking at best. The most common methodologies used for this type of analysis are simple payback and life cycle costing.

A simple payback calculation in made by dividing first cost of a project by projected annual savings. It is important to include all operating and maintenance costs when computing annual savings and to include all project costs in the first cost figure. A project that pays for itself within a short time is more attractive than one with a longer payback period. Implicit in this method but frequently overlooked is the assumption that the cost of capital—and the rates of inflation for energy, operation, and maintenance costs—are all the same and will change at the same rate at all times. Given the uncertainty of money supplies, energy costs, and inflation rates, these assumptions might well be as good as any others for analyzing the worth of a project. It is also necessary to somehow annualize replacement and maintenance costs that may not occur on an annual basis.

A life cycle analysis tracks the various costs associated with a project separately over a predetermined number of years that is arbitrarily chosen to be the life cycle of the project. Adjustments need to be made to convert the value of money in the future to its value now. Calculations may be performed to analyze the merits of a project in terms of net present worth, rate of return, or annual cost (see Chapter 10, Plant Finance). It is important to realize that the different calculation methods can result in different results when evaluating competing projects. In addition, the analysis will be strongly affected by the projections used concerning the various future inflation rates involved.

44.4 ENERGY LOAD MANAGEMENT

The cost of providing needed energy to building occupants is not just the cost of the fuel or utility service. Building capital and maintenance costs need to be factored in. Sophisticated control schemes that can respond to a wide range of demands are more costly to install than simpler, less flexible systems.

There is a similar cost to energy suppliers if the delivery system must match a wide range of delivery rates. Fuel suppliers must keep larger inventories and delivery fleets, and utility companies must build larger generating and distribution facilities to respond instantaneously to peak demands.

The cost of providing for this diversity is handled in different ways. In situations where fuel and delivery contracts vary seasonally, they will rise during periods of peak demand and fall as demand decreases. Annual contracts will include the price for this fluctuation built into the basic fuel rate, which will be higher for a fluctuating demand than for a steady one.

But the system in which the penalty for widely varying loads is most visible is the electric utility system. Electricity rates for almost all large customers, and some smaller ones as well, are calculated based on:

1. The fixed cost of maintaining a service account.
2. The average cost of the fuel used to produce the electricity.
3. A "fuel adjustment factor" to account for short-term variation in the price of fuel and the cost of purchasing electricity from other utility companies during peak demand periods.
4. A "demand charge" based on the peak usage by the service account. Despite the fact that demand charges are based on kilowatts, in most cases it they are not based on an instantaneous peak electric use, but rather on the average use over a short "window" in time, typically fifteen or thirty minutes. Because demand charges are implemented to recapture long-term capital costs, driven by historical peak use, some type of "ratchet" is included. As its name graphically implies, this ratchet allows the demand charge to rise freely but prevents it from falling below some fixed percentage (often 100 percent!) of historical demand. Most common is the twelve-month ratchet that sets demand charges based on the highest demand recorded over the previous year. Thus, an institution may well be paying a demand charge in April based on usage during a single fifteen-minute interval occurring the previous July when peak demand was several times greater.
5. A "power factor penalty" if voltage and current loads for an account are out of phase beyond a predetermined limit. The power delivered, as measured in watts, is based on the amperage times the voltage times the power factor, defined as the cosine of the angle between them. If this phase angle is large, its cosine will be small and it will take more current to provide for a given power requirement. Motors

and other inductive loads cause the current demand to lag behind the voltage demand. Fluorescent lights and other capacitive devices will cause current demand to lead voltage demand.

Additional factors may be included in the rate to account for the time of day or season to reflect overall utility system demand.

These costs are never absorbed by the utility company; they are somehow passed along to the customer. Residential accounts will generally have the charges for demand and power factor included in a much higher basic rate. Thus, inclusion of a demand charge should never be considered a burden on the institution. Rather, it should be seen as a further opportunity to manage and contain energy costs.

Energy systems that can meet building requirements while limiting demand will also reduce both capital and transport energy expenses for the institution. The capital costs for internal generating systems such as boilers and chillers as well as distribution systems are a direct function of peak demand. Smaller systems obviously reduce this expense and minimize pumping costs and electric distribution system losses.

44.5 ENERGY MANAGEMENT SYSTEMS

Almost all energy savings techniques complicate the operation of an institution's energy systems. Managing energy usually calls for an understanding the interdependencies of building systems and the environment and using these relationships to meet the requirements of the occupants. The complexity and ever-changing nature of these relationships require constant adjustment and compensation. In theory, such adjustments could be handled by a team of mechanics, constantly roving throughout the institution detecting changes and adjusting systems to match these changes. A more automated approach would provide automatic adjustment based on the feedback from some type of sensor. Limits are quickly reached as to the number of inputs that can be realistically handled by a standard control system.

Consider, for example, the operation of a damper used to introduce fresh air into building. Some of the factors that need to be considered for the intelligent operation of that damper might be:

1. Fan status.
2. Outdoor air temperature.
3. Outdoor air humidity.
4. Required room temperature.
5. Required room humidity.
6. Internal heat loads in the space.

7. Solar loads into the space.
8. Wind speed and direction.
9. Status of chilled water or DX systems providing cooling.
10. Status of heating system.
11. Number of occupants in the space.
12. The physical activity of those occupants.
13. Pressure relationships within the ductwork to ensure proper air flow.
14. Fuel and electricity costs.
15. Demand on the electric service to the building.

These factors and more are needed if the damper is to operate in an optimal manner, providing exactly the right amount of air to the space at the minimum energy cost. The cost of providing all this information on a continual basis and equating this information into the desired position of the damper would obviously be huge. Therefore, many of these factors are assumed to be at some level when the system is designed and built. Other relationships are factored in on a continual basis using common simplifying assumptions.

Energy management systems are generally presented as a means of achieving certain standard energy conservation techniques. In fact, the ultimate reason for adding such a system is to provide an intelligent means of continually compensating for changes in the parameters and demands placed on a building system. No system to date controls damper operation based on even half of the factors listed above. Indeed, such a system would be prohibitively expensive to install and operate, even if one could find "occupant physical activity" sensors and the like. However, an intelligently designed, installed, and operated energy management system can achieve a significant degree of optimization.

A complete discussion of the control of building systems using computer-based systems is included in Chapter 25, Central Monitoring and Control Systems. In this chapter, however, several features of most commercially available systems directly related to energy management will be discussed. Again, it is important to reiterate that a successful energy management system operation will not be based on the inclusion of a particular software function, but rather on whether the total system installation will allow building systems to operate together to optimally meet the requirements of the institution.

Energy Management Control Functions

Direct Digital and Proportional, Integral, and Derivative Control Methods   Earlier sections of this chapter discussed the importance of minimizing transport, heating, and cooling energy use. As loads change, systems must adjust to accommodate those changes. The response of any system to change cannot be instantaneous. Control systems that undercorrect for changes will never be able to meet space requirements. However, control systems can also overcorrect for change, and such overcorrection or "hunting" of control systems can waste large amounts of energy while yielding unsatisfactory environmental control. The appropriate response of systems to a deviation from its desired state is, in general, based on:

- How far the system is currently away from its desired setpoint. This is known as the proportional term of the control equation. Sensitivity to such error is referred to as the proportional band or throttling range.
- How fast, at any instant in time, the system is correcting itself toward the set point. Velocity is the first derivative of position (error) with respect to time so this term is referred to a the "derivative" part of the control equation.
- How long and to what degree the system has been away from its setpoint. This cumulative error is the integral of the error over time. This term is therefore known as the "integral" part of the control equation.

Control systems that utilize all of these terms are known as proportional, integral, and derivative (PID) controls. Standard building control systems generally incorporate only the proportional portion of the control equation resulting in some error at all times, known as offset. Attempts to overcompensate for the other terms will lead to overcontrolling and hunting, with resultant energy waste. Pneumatic and electronic controls are available that can compensate for the other terms but these add significantly to their complexity and cost.

Controls that receive their correction information from digital computers (including microprocessors) are known as direct digital control (DDC) systems. The basic cost of translating information from the real, analog world to the digital world of the computer and back again is significant. However, added complexity of incorporating the integral and derivative terms is handled by software and does not add to the cost of control. Thus, most systems that incorporate PID control tend to be digital, while those that can ignore the errors inherent in straight proportional control tend to use strictly analog controls.

The use of PID controls is no guarantee of accurate or stable control. Sensors and actuators need to be reliable and the values selected for the terms of the control equation are critically important. Added complexity is the price one must pay for more accurate and stable control. The incorporation of such control can result in more accurate, flexible, and economical control of building systems.

Control at the individual control point level must be absolutely and continuously reliable. Systems that have attempted to implement direct digital control globally from a central location have almost universally been failures. Computer shutdowns and communication link interruptions seem to be unavoidable and are disastrous to direct digital type control. Therefore, DDC almost always involves the use of microprocessor-based controls at the building.

Time-of-Day Functions   A simple means of matching system availability to the requirements of building occupants is by providing service based on time of day. If building occupants do not arrive until 8:00 a.m. and leave by 5:00 p.m., HVAC, lighting, and other systems can be scheduled to provide service between those hours. Systems will generally require some period to warm up or cool down spaces to acceptable levels after being off for a number of hours. The EMS can include some provision for "optimum runtime," starting systems just early enough to achieve acceptable conditions when the occupants arrive. Sensors and algorithms to account for weather conditions, building characteristics, and other factors can be used to continually adjust appropriate startup times.

In the institutional setting, schedules may change on a daily basis to match class hours, lecture schedules, and work demands. To be cost effective, energy management systems must permit easy and rapid changes to system operating schedules. Software that is difficult or awkward to use will tend to be set up to match worst-case conditions, which many times means twenty-four-hour-per-day operation. User interface to this function is therefore critically important for it to be an effective energy management tool.

Duty Cycling of Equipment   Turning HVAC equipment off during the course of the day has been mentioned previously as a possible method for reducing transport energy use. An energy management system interface to such a scheme makes it easy to factor in such variables as space temperature and humidity, system demand, and possibly lighting controls or occupancy sensors as a measure of occupant requirements. Duty cycling software must be integrated thoroughly with time-of-day and demand-limiting functions if conflicts are to be avoided.

Equipment Optimization Functions   The ability of energy management systems to gather data from a wide variety of devices over a large area make them ideal tools for managing optimization functions such as hot deck and cold deck supply air reset for air handlers, and chilled water and condenser water reset for chillers. There is generally a cascading and interrelated effect among all of these functions. For example, an abnormally high room temperature reading should trigger a reduction in cold deck supply air temperature. This in turn will signal the chilled water control algorithm that additional cooling is needed. If the original signal was incorrect because of a faulty sensor, the cost could be enormous. A well-designed optimization algorithm should therefore provide some means of filtering out anomalies in the data it uses from the field.

Optimization routines can also be affected by equipment operating schedules and building occupancy schedules as well as load management schemes. Again, total system integration is needed if optimization routines are to respond correctly to changes implemented by other software functions.

Load Shedding to Limit Electric Demand   The concept of load shedding was discussed previously. The immediacy of the requirement to shed loads within the utility company's demand window and the broad span of control needed to manage loads effectively make an energy management system the only practical means of shedding loads. Again, coordination with other software functions is necessary for a load shedding program to work properly. Another imperative for this system to be effective is the absolute reliability of the energy management system. A failure of the EMS to shed load during one peak fifteen-minute period in the summer can have a devastating financial impact for the next eleven months if loads are calculated with a demand ratchet.

Staffing Requirements

Properly used, an institution's EMS is the glue that binds together the systems affecting energy use. Well-designed software can make the seamless integration of energy systems a possibility under normal conditions. Today and at least in the near future there will be gaps between the ideal and the real capabilities in all but the simplest systems. Often a software developer's vision of how a system should operate does not match real building operations. In addition, mechanical electrical and electronic systems can and do fail.

Therefore, an energy management system cannot just be plugged in and left alone; it requires oversight and supervision. The type of supervision provided will depend upon the nature of the system and the requirements placed upon it. In some cases, energy management tasks are just a portion of the tasks expected of a large, multifunction system. Computers used to monitor and control energy systems may be used for other roles. Such building automation or facilities management systems may incorporate fire alarm, security, and work management functions in addition to those related to energy management. Full-time staffing may be necessary to interface with these other jobs. The institution may find itself in a position in which various contractors have installed a number of small energy management systems, each incompatible with the others and each at its own remote location. These situations will affect staffing decisions.

The concept of the interrelationship among energy systems has been stressed repeatedly throughout this chapter. It is imperative that the overall operation of the energy management system be performed by someone with an overall concept of the institution's energy systems. That is why it was recommended that the energy manager maintain the closest possible relationship with the operation of the EMS.

Wherever possible, large, unified energy management systems should be monitored by technically competent personnel with broad experience with electrical and mechanical equipment. The decisions that the EMS operator will be called upon to make require a thorough, almost intuitive knowledge of building systems. These operators must also have a clear understanding of digital control technology and the particulars of the systems hardware and software interfaces. Marginally competent operators, untrained to do anything other than acknowledge alarms from the system and pass them on to others, cannot effectively use the power of an EMS to its maximum advantage.

In some situations it may be appropriate to maintain a dedicated energy management staff during normal business hours. Police, work reception personnel, or switchboard operators may provide some low-level support for energy functions. Nighttime work crews may also be used to periodically monitor the system. Such arrangements may be cost effective if energy savings cannot justify around-the-clock staffing. However, institutional officers must realize that the energy management system will not be used to its full potential with this type of support.

In smaller institutions, there may be only one knowledgeable person capable of interacting with the building systems through the EMS. In such situations, that person's capabilities may be enhanced by providing him or her with a modem and remote terminal so that problems can be handled off-site. Often, vendors also can provide support for systems in this way

Vendor support is an important but limited tool. In most situations, the vendor will be intimately familiar with his own equipment. However, it is the rare contractor who has a thorough understanding of the equipment the system is controlling and has mastered the political relationships that determine how an EMS can best serve the institution. Such knowledge must be resident within the institution.

44.6 SUMMARY

Energy management is not a discipline, nor is it a set of rules or techniques; rather it is an integral part of all aspects of institutional life. The suggestions and techniques described in this chapter have worked in some institutions and failed in others. The important concept is that both energy use and energy control have costs and benefits associated with them. The successful energy management program will be one in which these costs and benefits best match the realities of institutional, national, and global requirements.

CHAPTER 45

Central Energy Systems

Warren W. Weeks, P.E.
Energy Consultant
Woodside, California

45.1 INTRODUCTION

The continuous, reliable operation and maintenance of an institution's central energy system, heating, cooling, and electrical supply are essential to performing its educational, research, and public service missions. Not only is the reliable performance of the system critical to institutional operations, the efficient delivery of energy services is necessary to control operational cost. It is not uncommon for utility operating expenses to approach one half of the physical plant budget; they are often exceeded only by personnel salaries. For these reasons of reliability and cost it is necessary for the responsible facilities administrator to devote considerable management time to assure reliable utility service at the least possible cost. This chapter will cover the fundamental operation and maintenance procedures that the facilities administrator may use to maximize the inherent advantages of a central energy system in achieving cost-effective and reliable service.

It will first be useful to review the economic and operational advantages of a central energy system, both for the facilities administrator responsible for overseeing such an operation as well as for the manager responsible for a distributed system of individual building heating and cooling systems.

Advantages

- Less capital is required for equipment than the sum for individual buildings in a large system. The total system load will be lower because all connected buildings will not peak simultaneously. This relationship between the sum of the peak loads for individual buildings and the actual aggregate central system peak load is known as diversity factor.

- Campus electrical distribution capital cost is as much as 30 percent lower than with electrical driven chillers located in individual buildings.
- The installation of standby equipment is economically feasible.
- Allows the shifting of system loads between electrical and thermal energy sources to minimize service costs.
- Net assignable square feet for buildings are increased due to the reduction of in-building machinery space requirements.
- Twenty-four-hour supervision by skilled operators is economically feasible.
- Aesthetically undesirable cooling tower plumes, driftloss, and noise are concentrated in a single location instead of at each building.
- Operating and maintenance staffing costs are minimized due to the centralized equipment location.
- Increased efficiencies are possible with large heating and cooling equipment, which reduces operating cost per unit of energy output.
- Part-load performance efficiencies are substantially improved by the ability to meet the system load with the most efficient equipment.
- Continuous, accurate monitoring of operating efficiencies is practical.
- Single point of delivery for purchased utilities allows for favorable rates as a large-volume customer.
- Multiple fuel sources are a practical alternative.

Disadvantages

- High initial construction cost requires a large capital investment.
- Thermal and hydraulic losses occur in a large distribution network; they do not occur in a distributed system where thermal utility services are generated at the point of use.

While the advantages will allow the facilities administrator of an existing system to minimize operating cost, they can also assist the manager of a distributed system in evaluating the potential economics of replacing individual building heating and cooling equipment with a central energy system.

45.2 CENTRAL STEAM/HOT WATER PRODUCTION AND DISTRIBUTION

System Configuration

While variations in the configuration of central heating systems are almost infinite, Figure 45-1 represents the basic arrangement for a steam heating system and Figure 45-2 represents the basic arrangement for hot water heating systems. Common variations in the arrangement of central steam heating systems are as follows:

- Economizers and air heaters fitted to the boiler uptake.
- A mixture of steam and electric driven auxiliary equipment.
- A back pressure or auto extraction/condensing steam turbine for the generation of electrical power.
- Superheaters that add additional energy to the steam before it is fed to steam turbines.
- A variety of fuel handling systems to burn gas, coal, oil, or waste material.
- A full range of combustion controls that range from the simplest single element parallel control to complex multi-element full metering control systems.
- Additional heat exchangers to recover waste heat from boiler blowdown or from deaerating feed water heater vent steam.
- Incorporation of the central production of normal or emergency power, domestic hot water, compressed air, distilled or deionized water, and other specialty services.

Common variations in the arrangement of central hot water heating systems not listed under central steam systems are as follows:

- System pressurization through the use of a nitrogen blanket.
- Air removal accomplished in various manners at the central plant and within individual buildings.
- Numerous variations in the arrangement of pumping systems and internal plant loop arrangements.

Boiler Efficiencies

Boiler operating efficiencies are affected primarily by combustion efficiency, heat transfer efficiency, and steam heat loss. Combustion efficiencies are a function of the completeness of fuel combustion and the amount of excess air delivered to achieve complete combustion. If inadequate air is delivered to the combustion process, it will cause the forma-

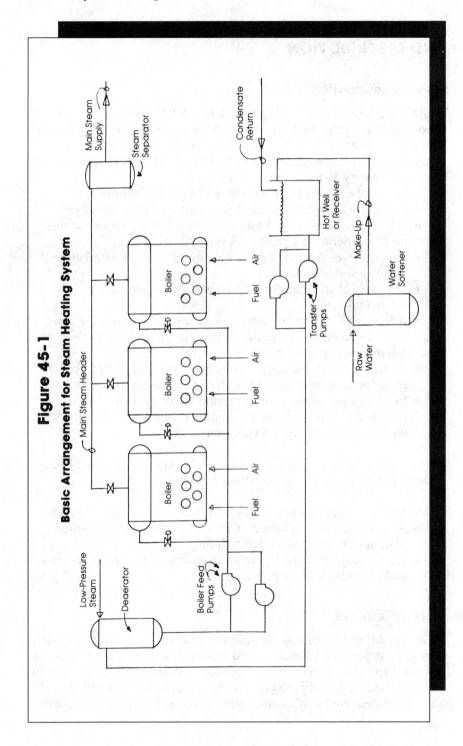

Figure 45-1

Basic Arrangement for Steam Heating System

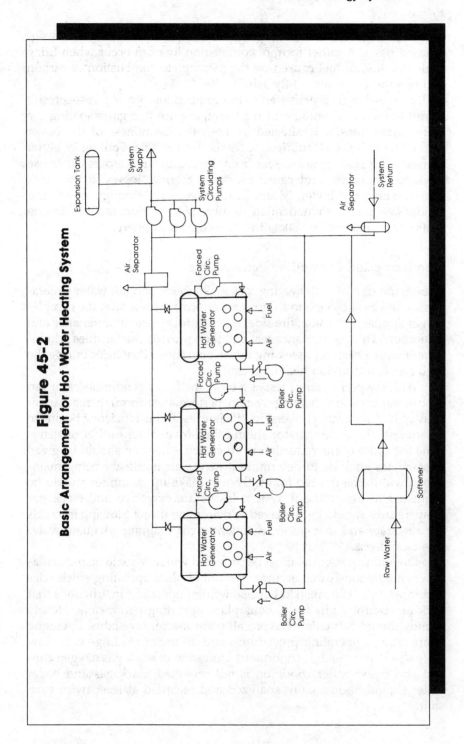

Figure 45-2

Basic Arrangement for Hot Water Heating System

tion of carbon monoxide, resulting in incomplete combustion and significant losses. Another form of combustion loss can occur when firing coal—the loss of fuel caused by the incomplete combustion of carbon and its subsequent loss in fly ash.

If excessive air is delivered to the combustion process, losses result from the increased volume of high-temperature flue gases exiting the boiler. Heat transfer is affected by both the cleanliness of the boiler water side and the cleanliness of the boiler gas side. Fouling of either surface will reduce heat transfer from the combustion process, increase stack temperatures, and cause excessive thermal losses in the stack gasses exiting the boiler. Steam heat losses occur through steam and condensate lines with inadequate or missing insulation, malfunctioning steam traps, and steam leaks directly to the atmosphere.

Monitoring and Controlling Performance

Prior to the start of each heating season, all steam and hot water generators should be subjected to a rigorous performance test after the completion of annual water side, fire side, and control system maintenance and inspection. This performance test will then provide the facilities administrator with a basis for assessing future operating efficiencies during the high fuel consumption heating season.

With the performance test as a base, the facilities administrator can best monitor central heating system performance through regular review of fuel-to-steam conversion efficiencies. If this efficiency begins to deteriorate, the administrator should then investigate further to determine the cause of the reduction in efficiency. Attention should be given to stack gas analysis to determine if excess air levels are being maintained within the desired limits. System make-up quantities should be evaluated to determine if system losses are excessive and stack gas temperatures should be reviewed to determine if soot blowing intervals are adequate and that water treatment is maintaining adequate water side cleanliness.

Operating personnel must be provided with adequate instrumentation to continuously and accurately monitor plant operating efficiencies and must also be furnished concise written operating instructions that indicate control limits for various plant operating parameters. Hourly rounds should be made to record all plant machinery status, operating temperatures, operating procedures, and all meter readings with flow rates where provided. If continuous indication of stack gas oxygen content and boiler water condition is not provided, stack gas and boiler water should be manually analyzed and recorded at least twice each shift.

It is important that plant supervision continually reinforce the necessity of the routine and accurate recording of plant operating parameters as these records will serve a vital role in assisting the facilities administrator in determining the cause of any loss in plant performance efficiencies.

Plant auxiliary equipment should also be subjected to the same annual performance testing made on steam and hot water generators. Pump and drive efficiencies should be tested and compared to manufacturer's data. Deaerating feed water heaters should be tested to assure complete oxygen removal. (If an oxygen scavenger is fed prior to the unit, feed must be discontinued before testing.) All operating instrumentation and controls should be calibrated and adjusted to original specifications. Steam trap function should be verified and valve packing replaced. Valves should be checked to validate their shut-off capability and overhauled when necessary. Make-up water softeners should be tested to determine if mineral removal meets original specifications and resin cleaned or replaced when needed. Auxiliary heat exchangers such as boiler feed water heaters, vent condensers, and boiler blowdown heat exchangers should be cleaned and inspected. Where fitted, stack gas clean-up systems such as electrostatic precipitators, bag houses, and sulfur dioxide removal equipment should be serviced in accordance with the manufacturer's recommendations.

Central heating plant equipment maintenance intervals can be scheduled and tracked through a larger facilities preventive maintenance system or through a smaller system that serves only the central plant. Regardless of the maintenance scheduling system used, a detailed machinery history should be maintained at the central plant on all major equipment. This history should contain all original equipment specifications, parts ordering information, year installed, when services were performed, details on repairs, and parts replaced. This information will be useful in determining service interval requirements and in determining whether a piece of equipment should be repaired or replaced after a major breakdown.

Distribution Systems

The maintenance and operation of steam and hot water distribution are similar in that both types of systems should undergo a rigorous annual maintenance procedure and should be frequently inspected to assure efficient and reliable performance.

The operation of both types of systems is basically limited to start-up and shutdown procedures and their timing. These procedures should be clearly documented and provide for a slow system warm-up process that will minimize stress on expansion joints or pipe anchors and provide adequate air and condensate removal. During the start-up procedure, the entire system should be carefully observed and detected leaks isolated and repaired.

Annual maintenance on central steam distribution systems should include the inspection of all steam traps and the cleaning of steam trap inlet strainers. Major distribution valves should be repacked as should packed-type expansion joints. Pressure-reducing valves should be serviced and calibrated to assure proper pressure control and operating range. The operation of condensate return units should be tested, pumps lubricated in accordance with the manufacturer's recommendations, and pump alternates tested for proper operation. Heat exchangers should be tested to determine cleanliness and serviceability. A simple method of determining heat exchanger performance is to shut down the building steam supply and allow the system to cool, to design return water temperature on the building water side, and then reestablish steam supply and verify that the temperature rise across the heat exchanger closely matches original design specifications. If temperature rise is less than specified, the heat exchanger requires servicing.

Routine maintenance of a steam distribution system should include at least monthly inspection of steam traps with infrared temperature detectors, surface temperature meters, or temperature sensitive indicators. Trap inlet temperature should be approximately 20°F lower than the saturated steam temperature of the system and a 30°F temperature differential should be present across the trap assembly. If inlet temperature is found to be less than 20°F below saturated steam temperature with essentially no differential temperature across the trap, it is "blowing by" and must be repaired. If inlet temperature is substantially below saturated steam temperature and there is no differential temperature across the trap, it is plugged or jammed and must be repaired.

Routine inspections should also include visual location of leaks and deteriorated or missing insulation in the steam supply and condensate return piping. Steam leaks should be repaired as soon as practical to avoid wire drawing of the fittings that will necessitate component replacement or extensive reconditioning. Central plant return condensate should be regularly monitored for hardness to detect leaking system heat exchangers. When hardness is detected at the central plant, an immediate investigation should be undertaken to determine the source of the contamination and repairs made to leaking heat exchanger tube bundles.

In addition to the annual and routine maintenance of valves, expansion joints, and heat exchangers covered under central steam systems, air removal devices in the hot water distribution system will require annual service and monthly routine inspections. These air removal devices should be inspected to ensure they are functioning as designed and shut off once air is removed from the system.

While the facilities administrator responsible for steam and hot water distribution systems installed in a network of tunnels need only institute routine visual inspections and direct measurements to assure reliable efficient performance, the administrator of a direct buried distribution system must resort to innovative indirect measures of system tightness and insulation integrity.

The following is a listing of some indirect measurement techniques that may be employed to assess the performance of direct buried distribution systems:

- Steam losses can be quantified by measuring the condensate discharged from system drip traps. This can be accomplished with a temporary condensate cooler consisting of a long length of coiled tubing immersed in a drum of water. The collected sample is then measured over time to determine losses for the section of the system served by the drip assembly.
- Overall thermal losses in hot water systems can be approximated by measuring the system supply temperature, return temperature, and total flow when all building loads have been shut down and a bypass has been fitted to the ends of all system runs.
- Suspect run of underground piping can be leak tested when out of service by first introducing ether into the pipe followed by compressed air. The pipe is then walked using a combustible gas sensor. As ether is extremely light, it will be detect directly above any leak thus indicating where excavation and repair are needed. (Caution: Ether is explosive, and all sources of ignition, including static charge, must be eliminated prior to its use.)
- Annual aerial overflights while the system is operating and the use of infrared photographs can pinpoint energy losses.

The facilities manager can elect to use the above techniques when system make-up quantities are higher or energy consumption is excessive during low load operation.

Central distribution system annual and periodic maintenance can best be scheduled and tracked through the use of a larger facilities preventive maintenance system. If a larger system does not exist, one must be devised to serve the critical needs of distribution system maintenance.

Metering

For the facilities administrator to effectively manage the performance of a central steam or hot water production system, it is essential that accurate measures of fuel consumption and thermal energy production be available on a regular basis. This measurement is accomplished with a number of strategically placed and accurately calibrated meters. Energy meters fall into three basic types: condensate meters, steam volume meters, and Btu meters.

Condensate meters fall into two categories. One type measures the volume of condensate returned from the system. The second type actually weighs the condensate returned and is more accurate but more costly than simple volume meters. Both types have the disadvantage of not measuring steam losses or consumption in processes such as food preparation, steam sterilization, and humidification.

Steam volume meters also fall into two categories. One type measures the differential across a pressure drop device, such as an orifice or a venturi tube, and through calibration to a specific pressure, measures the volume of steam, and reads out in total pounds. The second type of volume meter incorporates pressure compensation to adjust flow volume based on actual pressures during varying flow conditions to more accurately determine the total mass flow.

Btu meters are the most accurate method of measuring thermal energy consumption or production and are the only practical method for measuring these values in hot water systems. In steam metering applications the volume of steam is metered and compensated for pressure and temperature. The return condensate volume and temperature are also measured. From these measurements, the net energy consumed or produced is calculated through the use of a microprocessor. In hot water metering applications the total system flow, supply temperature, and return temperature are measured. From these measurements, the net energy consumed or produced is calculated with a microprocessor.

A regulator program of annual calibration for all metering devices must be put in place to assure continuous accurate measurement of energy production and consumption. With condensate meters, a known weight of water should be passed through the device and the indicated meter reading should be within 5 percent of the quantity introduced. Steam volume meters are typically calibrated through procedures specified by the manufacturer. Btu meters are calibrated in the same manner as volume meters with the exception that many more sensors must be calibrated to assure accurate performance. Meter calibration records should be maintained in order to quantify variations in measured quantities and actual readings. This information will assist the facilities administrator in determining historical margins of error and evaluating metering data based on historical records.

System Retrofit Opportunities

A wide variety of field retrofit opportunities exist that can substantially improve efficiencies and reduce operating costs. Some options available are listed below:

- Retrofit economizers are available that are compact and designed to replace a section of boiler uptake ducting. This design allows low-cost, easy installation in existing facilities. Care should be exercised in specifying economizers to assure that stack gas temperatures will not be too low during light load operation, resulting in condensation and subsequent corrosion.
- Gas and oil burners are available that will operate at excess air levels as low as 3 percent and have good turndown. Some burners are available as packages complete with burner management systems and forced draft fans. This packaging simplifies the installation in existing facilities and can substantially reduce costs.
- Boiler blowdown heat recovery can be accomplished with the installation of a small heat exchanger to transfer heat from boiler blowdown to boiler water make-up. Another method employs a pressurized flash tank connected to the plant exhaust steam system. In this system boiler blowdown is directed to the receiver where it flashes to steam, thus recovering a portion of the waste heat as low-pressure steam. Automatic blowdown controllers are also available that monitor boiler water conductivity and automatically adjust boiler blowdown, thus minimizing energy loss.
- Modern microprocessor-based controllers are now available that will substantially outperform older control systems. They are also available with economic dispatch that allows the system to automatically adjust loading on combustion equipment to maximize efficiency for any given load where multiple boilers are in service. Oxygen trim control is also available as is multi-element boiler water level control. If oxygen trim control is installed on boilers that operate with negative furnace pressures, care must be taken to ensure that carbon monoxide is not present in the flue gases at low oxygen levels. This is necessary since boiler casing leaks, particularly in floor cooling tiles, will introduce air into the furnace downstream of the combustion process and be detected by the flue gas oxygen sensor, causing air flow to be reduced and, as a result, incomplete combustion. Carbon monoxide control is also available. However, it is extremely complicated and will only be justified on very large boilers.

- Older steam traps that are fitted with needle valve-type non-condensable removal can be retrofitted with thermostatic units. When steam traps are retrofitted, the piping for each size trap should be made consistent so that complete assemblies can be kept on hand. This will facilitate immediate economical replacement if a trap is found to be malfunctioning during routine inspections.
- The addition of insulation to piping may also improve efficiency to the point where it is economically feasible.
- In large distribution systems with low summer loads, the addition of small local steam or hot water boilers may allow the complete shutdown of the central heating system and result in substantial savings. These shutdowns will also allow for comprehensive maintenance to be performed on the entire system in an orderly fashion.

With current stable fuel prices many or all of the above retrofits may not be economically feasible. However, the facilities administrator should thoroughly investigate all retrofit options available so that a timely response can be made should energy prices surge as they did in the mid-1970s.

Staffing

The operational staffing requirements of a central steam or hot water production and distribution system are driven by a number of factors. A major consideration is the complexity of the system and the physical layout of the production facility. In complex systems that encompass central cooling and electrical production as well as central heating, larger operating staffs will be required than for a central heating only facility. In facilities that burn solid fuel, staffing requirements will increase due to the operation of fuel and ash handing systems. Figure 45-3 shows the staffing and organization for a modest central heating facility and should be considered the minimum base in determining staffing requirements. Figure 45-4 shows the staffing and organization for a very large facility and should be considered the most comprehensive staffing arrangement.

Regardless of staffing level or plant complexity, the facilities administrator must arrange the working schedules of operating personnel to assure continuous coverage with a minimum of overtime work. An effective way to achieve continuous coverage is with the rotating shift schedule shown in Figure 45-5. Not only will this schedule limit each operator's work week to forty hours, it will also provide a level of routine maintenance through the use of the relief operator. A variation

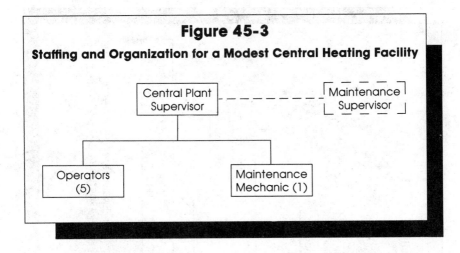

Figure 45-3

Staffing and Organization for a Modest Central Heating Facility

to the schedule shown is to rotate each operator sequentially into the relief position with the charge arranged so that the relief operator moves into the schedule at the beginning of swing shift duty. This variation will allow all operating personnel to share equally in the burden of the relief role.

The maintenance staffing will also be driven by system complexity and the scope of central services provided. However, the facilities administrator has considerable flexibility in determining how these services are provided. On one extreme, all central plant maintenance and repair services can be furnished from central shops not organizationally under central plant management. On the other extreme, all central plant and distribution maintenance and repair can be performed by dedicated staff under the line management function within the central plant organization.

The facilities administrator can best determine which maintenance functions should reside in the central plant organization and which should be provided from central maintenance shops by carefully examining workhour and craft requirements to perform annual maintenance tasks. This examination will clearly identify which maintenance functions can be practically placed within the operating structure of the central plant organization and those tasks that can be more efficiently provided from central maintenance shops. One additional option is the use of contracted maintenance services. This option will be the most efficient for maintenance and repair tasks that require highly trained personnel utilizing specialized equipment and are required on an infrequent or irregular basis. This option may also be of advantage in small facilities without in-house specialty craftspeople.

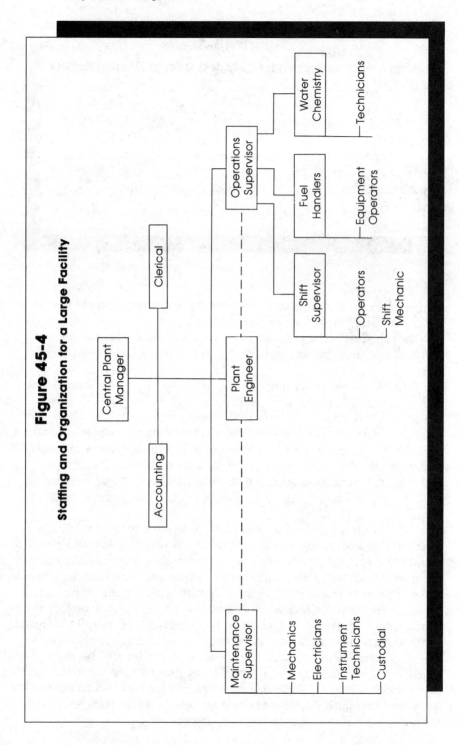

Figure 45-4

Staffing and Organization for a Large Facility

Figure 45-5

Rotating Shift Schedule

	Week 1							Week 2							Week 3							Week 4						
	M	T	W	T	F	S	S	M	T	W	T	F	S	S	M	T	W	T	F	S	S	M	T	W	T	F	S	S
Operator #1	O	O	S	S	S	S	S	S	S	O	O	D	D	D	D	D	D	O	O	G	G	G	G	G	G	G	O	O
Operator #2	D	D	D	O	O	O	G	G	G	G	G	G	O	O	O	O	S	S	S	S	S	S	S	O	O	D	D	D
Operator #3	S	S	O	O	D	D	D	D	D	D	O	O	G	G	G	G	G	G	G	O	O	O	O	S	S	S	S	S
Operator #4	G	G	G	G	G	O	O	O	O	S	S	S	S	S	S	S	O	O	O	O	O	O	O	O	O	O	G	G
Relief Operator	R	R	R	D	R	O	O	R	R	R	D	R	O	O	R	R	R	D	R	O	O	R	R	R	D	R	O	O

D = Day Shift
S = Swing Shift
G = Graveyard Shift
R = Relief and Maintenance Duty
O = Scheduled

Training

The facilities administrator must put in place and maintain an in-house training program to achieve two important objectives. The first is to maintain and improve the skills of existing operating staff. This skills maintenance and improvement program should include regular review of operating procedures, actual exercises in operating the plant in various configurations that would be necessary in the event of equipment failure, changing over to an alternate fuel, review of chemical handling and spill containment, and precise instruction on newly instituted plant operating procures.

The second objective is to train entry level employees in the operation of the central plant to assure a ready resource of replacement operators in the event of staff variances. A similar program should also be implemented to cover the maintenance functions performed by in-house staff. Some maintenance training can be effectively provided with factory representatives from the manufacturers of various plant equipment and can be held on-site to reduce costs.

Regardless of plant size, an effective, regular training program is a cost-effective approach to furnishing reliable and efficient central heating services.

45.3 ELECTRIC PRODUCTION AND DISTRIBUTION

This section will deal primarily with the maintenance procedures for primary distribution systems that are owned by the institution and may include on-site production of electrical power. As electric production facilities located on-site can take a multitude of arrangements, only a basic overview of their operation and maintenance will be given with an emphasis on the evaluation of cogeneration systems for facilities currently without on-site electrical power generation.

System Configuration

While generation system configuration can vary widely, distribution systems will fall in three basic configurations: radial, loop, and primary selective.

Figure 45-6 shows a simplified one-line diagram of a radial feed system where feeders lead from a central substation to serve a number of loads. This type of system is prevalent on older campuses and presents a difficult situation when routine maintenance must be performed as a large number of loads must be interrupted to perform repairs.

Figure 45-7 shows a one-line diagram of a loop feed system where primary circuits are arranged so that feed is possible from either side of the loop arrangement. This type of system allows routine maintenance to be performed on system components with minimized disruption of service.

Figure 45-8 shows a one-line diagram of a primary selective feeder arrangement where two primary feed sources are available to each load. This system provides the most flexibility for operations and reduces outages necessary for routine maintenance and repair to an absolute practical minimum.

Some systems may encompass more than one of the above arrangements and may have more than one voltage for primary distribution with interconnects through transformers from one voltage to another. However, the three basic arrangements will generally describe distribution systems serving most institutions.

Distribution Maintenance Procedures

Annual inspection, maintenance, and periodic testing of all distribution components should be instituted on a routine and regular basis.

Switchgear should be inspected and maintained on an annual interval and should be tested every two years. Routine inspection, maintenance, and testing should include the following procedures.

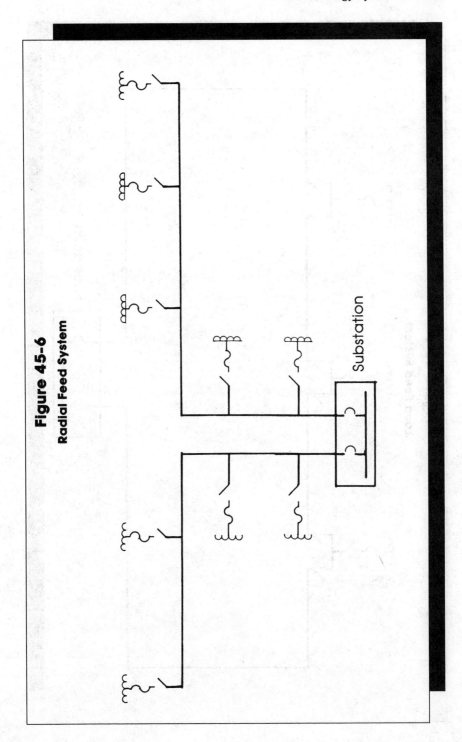

Figure 45-6
Radial Feed System

Substation

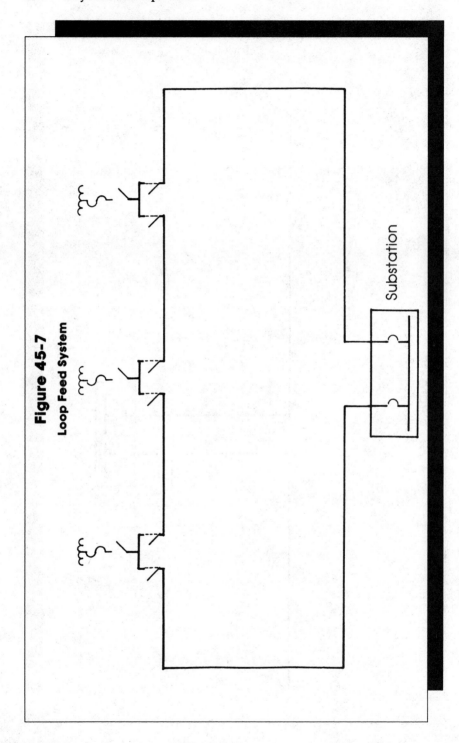

Figure 45-7
Loop Feed System

Substation

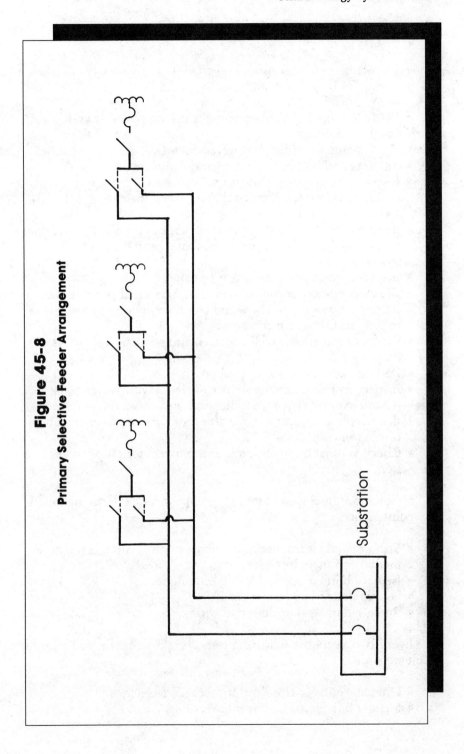

Figure 45-8

Primary Selective Feeder Arrangement

Substation

Annual Inspection:

- Inspect paint for corrosion and condition of protective finishes.
- Check for burned out and missing panel lights and check condition of covers.
- Verify that control knobs and switches are operable and check contact condition.
- Verify nameplate identification of circuits.
- Inspect condition of grounding and connections.
- Inspect bus supports, insulators. Look for evidence of tracking and heated joints. Check condition of bus insulation and tapped connections.
- Inspect cable terminations and potheads and inspect the condition of porcelain on potheads, bushings, and standoff insulators.
- Inspect control and instrument transformers.
- Check condition of control wiring and terminal connections.
- Remove draw-out breakers and check condition of rails, guides, rollers, and shutter mechanism.
- Check cell interlocks, cell contacts, and auxiliary contact assemblies.
- Perform visual breaker inspection.
- Inspect and check instruments associated with switchgear.
- Restore control power to switchgear and check relays for positive tripping and test annunciator for alarm or target operation under test conditions.
- Check ventilation vents, fans, and blowers for proper operation.

Following annual inspection of the switchgear, perform the following maintenance:

- Vacuum and clean interior of cubicles, termination compartments, and main bus bars.
- Replace burned out or missing pilot lights.
- Torque bolted bus connections.
- Replace damaged or defective wiring.

Every two years the following tests should be performed and the results recorded:

- Operate controls; close and trip breakers electrically.
- Megger bus phases and record readings.

- Infrared thermal scan connections and record temperature readings.

Appendix 45-A contains a sample log sheet for recording switchgear inspection, maintenance, and testing.

Liquid-filled transformers should be inspected, maintained, and tested on an annual basis. These procedures should include the following.

Annual Inspection:

- Check finish for rust or corrosion.
- Check oil leaks and inspect cover and hand hole gasket seals.
- Check oil level.
- Check temperature gauge high-temperature indicator and record. (If 75°C or over, contact maintenance supervisor.)
- Check lightning arrestors, where applicable.
- Check external protection, fuses, and cutouts.
- Inspect load break disconnect.
- Check low-voltage circuit breaker (if applicable).
- Check porcelain bushings.
- Check bolted connections on the high-voltage and secondary side.
- Check radiator fins.
- Check ventilation fans (if applicable).
- Check gas pressure on tank where applicable.

Maintenance:

- Repaint or touch up as necessary.
- Clean dust off of radiators.
- Repair leaks (coordinate with risk management deptartment).

Testing

Transformer and oil switch liquid testing procedures can be found in Appendix 45-B of this chapter.

Appendix 45-A contains a sample log sheet for recording liquid filled transformer inspection, maintenance, and testing.

Oil filled switches should be externally inspected and tested on an annual basis and internally inspected and maintained every five years. These procedures should include the following.

Inspection—External:

- Check paint for corrosion or rust spots.
- Check windows for oil leaks and torque nuts on windows.
- Check tank lid and torque fasteners.
- Check operating shaft, inspect oil seals, locks, and stops. Visually inspect linkage (when applicable) and torque fasteners.
- Check oil level.
- Check cableheads for oil or compound leakage and inspect cablehead body and entrances and mounting flanges.

Inspection—Internal (with switch de-energized):

- Check stationary and rotating contacts and wipe area.
- Check rocker arm for loose bolts and rocker arm attachment to mechanism, actuate each way, and check for free operation without binding or interference.
- Check gaskets for cracks and flexibility.
- Check all porcelains for cracks and chips.

Maintenance (at time of internal inspection):

- Clean sludge from insulators, bottom of tank, or other locations.
- Flush and clean the switch interior with new oil and drain.
- Replace all deteriorated lid gaskets with new gaskets where required.

Air circuit breakers should be inspected on an annual basis and tested, maintained, and calibrated every two years. These procedures should include the following.

Inspection:

- Remove and inspect arc boxes for breakage and burning.
- Check thoroughly for loose connections and worn or broken parts.
- Operate breaker mechanism manually to check for friction or binding.
- Check contacts for wear, burning, and alignment.
- Check breaker contacts for "normal" travel and "over-travel."
- Measure voltage drop across contacts and compare to manufacturer's specifications.

- Examine breaker trip mechanism and linkage for friction, interference, binding, rust, and corrosion.
- Check breaker control components and circuits. Look for damaged coils and signs of overtemperature on operating or holding coils.
- Check auxiliary switches for proper mechanical operation. Check linkage, overtravel, and contacts. Contacts should be free of burning, properly aligned and have sufficient spring pressure and overtravel.
- Check closing relay contacts for trip free operation.

Maintenance:

- Disassemble oil dash pots, clean, and fill with new oil.
- Replace broken or burned arc boxes.
- Replace worn or broken parts.
- Remove old oxidized grease and relubricate.
- Clean breaker mechanism by blowing out with dry compressed air and wipe mechanism free of all remaining dust using clean dry cloth.

Testing:

- Megger test with breaker closed and latched. Take megger readings from each pole to the breaker frame and from each pole to the other poles.
- Test shunt trip pickup.
- Test trip out point of undervoltage release.
- Test current overload trip unit, pickup current, time delay for long time trip.

Air Circuit Breaker Calibration Checks

- Pickup: Starting below the expected pickup current value on the longtime delay curve, slowly raise the current through the breaker pole unit until the point is determined at which the plunger or trip bar starts to move to cause eventual tripping of the breaker. Record this current value as "Pickup."
- Long-Time Delay: Next, apply a current of 300 percent of this pickup value. Determine the necessary time to trip the breaker. Record this time as "Long-Time Delay." Allow roughly 10 percent tolerance.

- Resetting Delay: Preset and apply 300 percent of pickup current for a time equal to the lower boundary of the tripping time band on the manufacturer's curves (resettable delay), then quickly reduce the test current to 80 percent of pickup. The breaker should not trip and the plunger, or hinged armature, should return to its normal position. Record the current and elapsed time under the Long-time Delay (LTD) column of the test report.
- Short-Time Delay: Determine the desired setting of instantaneous current from earlier test results or existing setting. Apply 85 percent of this value to the breaker momentarily three distinct times. The breaker should not trip. Record results (tripping current and time) under the "Short-Time Delay" column of test report. Compare results with manufacturer's curve. Some variation may occur. If necessary, adjust trip unit and retest.

Appendix 45-A contains a sample log sheet for recording air circuit breaker inspection, maintenance, testing, and calibration.

High voltage cable should be visually inspected annually and tested every two years. The procedures should include the following.

Inspection:

- Fireproofing, cable insulation, and splices should be inspected for signs of deterioration such as cracks, checking, and for swelling or compound leaks.
- Cable splices and terminations should be inspected for tracking, corona, or signs of overheating.

Testing:

- Insulation resistance of each phase conductor should be tested with a megger and the reading recorded.

Substation batteries should be inspected and maintained on a quarterly basis. The procedures should include the following.

Inspection:

- Check for corrosion at battery terminals and connection.
- Check cases for cracks and signs of leakage.
- Verify battery charger operation and check voltage.
- Check the specific gravity of each cell and check electrolyte level.

Maintenance:

- Add distilled water as necessary.
- Clean off corrosion from terminals; apply Vaseline or No-ox-id grease.
- Tighten all connections.

Appendix 45-A contains sample log sheets for recording battery inspections and tests.

On-site electrical generators and their prime movers should be inspected, maintained, and tested in accordance with the manufacturer's recommendations. Switchgear, protective relaying, and utility interconnect equipment should be maintained in the same manner as described above under switchgear and air circuit breakers. All maintenance performed and test readings taken should be carefully recorded on logs prepared especially for the equipment. Major maintenance or repair of the generator prime mover is best accomplished through contract services from a firm specializing in that type of work.

Almost all of the maintenance procedures described will require service interruptions to one or more building loads. As research activities intensify, resistance to service interruptions by the academic users has grown. It is the responsibility of the facilities administrator to educate the user community about the need and wisdom for regularly scheduled outages in order to minimize the risks of system failures.

Billing, Rate Schedules, and Metering

When utility billings are received, they should be analyzed carefully. Total kW billed and billing demand should be compared with in-plant metering to verify usage. If in-plant demand metering is not available, the utility can usually furnish a computer printout of all demand readings during the billing period. These readings can then be plotted to assist in analyzing the demand and consumption profiles. The billed power factor should be reviewed since capacitors can sometimes fail without indication, and the billing information can serve as an indication to field verify the operating condition of capacitors.

The facilities administrator must maintain frequent communications with the local electric utility to stay current on alternate rates available. It may also be possible to get on the mailing list for rates filed with the local regulatory body and thereby determine, in advance, if new rates proposed will offer savings. As most institutions own and operate off-site facilities, they should also be included in regular rate schedule reviews. This regular contact will also help the administrator learn about changes in the utility system and allow for the assessment of any impact on the institution's system. Frequent communication with the utility will also facilitate coordinating maintenance procedures on both systems and help minimize outages.

Electrical meters are extremely reliable and require little maintenance once accuracy is established. To establish meter accuracy a complete survey of all meter installations should be made and documented. This survey should verify current transformer and potential transformer ratios, current transformer polarity, field wiring, and meter multipliers. It is not uncommon to discover improper meter multipliers or reversed current transformer connections that have existed since installation. Once metering installations have been field verified it will only be necessary to periodically verify meter accuracy with portable metering equipment. This equipment can be rented from equipment suppliers for a modest cost or may be available within the organization to support an aggressive energy conservation program.

Power Factor Correction

Power factor or the relationship between apparent power and actual power is the result of the inductive reactance in loads such as induction motors and lamp ballasts. A low or lagging power factor can create two undesirable conditions. First, most utilities have a penalty for low power factor for large users and second, excessively low power factor in localized portions of the distribution system can cause unacceptably low voltage at the loads. To improve power factor, capacitors can be installed on the system to counteract the inductive reactance of the loads. Capacitors can be installed and switched with loads such as induction motors, connected permanently to the distribution system, or connected to the distribution system and switched.

Permanently connected capacitors are the most economical to install; however, care must be taken to assure that the power factor will not go excessively leading and result in unacceptably high voltage during light load conditions. Switched capacitors can avoid the undesirable leading power factor but will be more costly to install and maintain. Capacitors located at the load are only practical in new construction and should be incorporated in the institution's design standards. In all cases, the installation of capacitors to improve power factor must be compared to the saving offered in the institution's electrical rate. In many instances the most cost-effective measure is to simply pay the penalty assessed by the utility for low power factor. This will not, however, be the case if capacitors' installation are intended to reduce voltage fluctuations or to off-load apparent power from transformer secondaries serving predominantly reactive loads.

Load Limiting

If the institution's electrical demand profile indicates large defluctuations for short durations, the initiation of demand limiting should be considered. Measures to reduce peak demand can be as simple as modifying operating procedures of electrically driven chillers or can be as complex as an automated system that controls all major electrical-consuming equipment. Regardless of the strategy employed to limit peak electrical demand, accurate indication of real time demand is needed. This indication can be derived from in-plant metering or from meter pulses furnished by the electric utility and fed to local readout equipment or an automated load shunting system.

Before demand limiting is initiated, the priority of each load must be established on an institutional basis and endorsed by senior administrators to assure that service curtailments conform to institutional priorities. Even if peak demand control is not undertaken, an institutionally approved priority listing of electrical loads will guide the facilities administrator in managing shortfalls in electrical supply or distribution system capacity, and assure continued service to high-priority loads.

Staffing

Operational and maintenance staffing for an institution-owned electrical distribution system should consist of a minimum of two qualified high-voltage electricians. Staffing requirements may be greater for extensive systems and the actual requirement can be determined by a comprehensive review of workhour requirements for the annual maintenance of system components. The operation and maintenance function should be incorporated into the responsibilities of a central electrical shop to streamline coordination in the maintenance and operation of the entire electrical system and to assure the most efficient service.

Operational and maintenance staffing for on-site electrical generation facilities should be integrated into other central energy systems operations and maintenance. The need for dedicated operating and maintenance personnel will be dictated by the complexity of the system and the amount of maintenance to be performed by in-house personnel.

Training

The facilities administrator must put in place and maintain an in-house training program to achieve two important objectives. The first is to maintain and improve the skills of the existing high-voltage electricians. This skills maintenance and improvement training program should include regular review of circuit switching procedures, proper circuit grounding for maintenance, proper use of flash suits when performing switching operations, proper use and calibration of test equipment, and procedures used when working with PCB or PCB-contained electrical equipment. The program should also include comprehensive training on maintenance procedures for newly installed equipment.

The second objective of the training program is to familiarize other electricians with the procedures associated with the operation and maintenance of high-voltage equipment to assure a continued resource of trained employees. When major equipment is installed or replaced, the needed training should be a part of the purchase specification and should require that on-site training be furnished by the supplier.

To provide training in the operation of the system, a large one-line diagram should be constructed with graphic representations that can be changed to indicate all possible configurations for switching devices. This diagram can be used to simulate switching procedures for training purposes and can also be used in planning and implementing actual system switching.

The training program for on-site generation facilities must also address the same two objectives previously stated for the distribution system and should be integrated with a comprehensive in house program that also encompasses other central utility production facilities.

Cogeneration

Cogeneration or the simultaneous production of electrical power and useful thermal energy has always been an attractive option for large central energy systems. With the passage of the 1978 Energy Act the cogeneration option has become even more attractive as it requires the local utility to allow the interconnection of on-site generators to the utility grid, furnish standby power, and purchase excess power for qualifying facilities. To be considered a qualifying facility the on-site generation system must meet the following:

- The ownership criterion stipulates that the maximum ownership by a utility cannot exceed 50 percent.
- An operating standard stipulates that the system output must be at least 5 percent thermal.
- An efficiency standard stipulates that the system efficiency must conform to the following standard if thermal output exceeds 15 percent: Power output + .5 (thermal output)= 42.5 percent energy output.

If thermal output is less than 15 percent the efficiency must be at least 45 percent in accordance with the above formula.

If an on-site electrical generation system meets the above criteria, it is considered a qualifying facility and the local utility must allow interconnection, furnish standby power, and purchase excess production at the marginal cost of power production for the utility.

In order for the facilities administrator to determine if the installation of a cogeneration system is feasible, the following factors must be carefully evaluated:

- Is there adequate thermal demand to allow the system to be classified as a qualifying facility?
- Can the savings afforded by a cogeneration system offset the capital costs and permanently reduce the institution's base costs for utility services?
- Is there space within or adjacent to the existing central plant to accommodate a cogeneration system?
- Can a long-term fuel supply be secured and at what cost?
- What is the fuel base of the local electric utility? If different from that contemplated for the cogeneration system, what would be the impact of unequal cost increases for the two fuels?
- If excess power would be generated to meet thermal demands, what price would the local utility pay for the excess power?
- Can an operating permit be secured for a cogeneration facility on the institution's campus?
- Will the existing central plant staff be capable of operating a cogeneration system or will additional staff be required?
- Is there senior administrative support for an on-campus cogeneration facility?
- Can the institution secure the necessary capital to construct a cogeneration system or will third-party financing be required and is it available?
- Are grant funds available to finance all or a portion of a cogeneration system?
- Will a cogeneration system be able to utilize existing central plant auxiliary equipment and utility services?
- How would a cogeneration system integrate with planned future facilities development?

If, after a careful review of the above issues, the facilities administrator has not identified any major roadblocks or unacceptable risks, a specialty consultant should be engaged to perform an in-depth analysis of the feasibility of constructing and operating a cogeneration facility.

The consultant's scope of work should require a detailed investigation of all technical, economic, financial, and permitting issues associated with the cogeneration option. The scope of work should also require an in-depth, detailed, "what if" analysis covering such issues as changes in emission standards, fuel price variations, and fluctuations in utility purchase price for excess capacity and forecast the impact on the financial and technical performance of the cogeneration facility.

Before a facilities administrator makes the decision to proceed with the construction of a cogeneration facility, all risks must be clearly identified and quantified as an uninformed decision could commit the institution to considerable long-term financial burdens. Further discussion of cogeneration can be found in Chapter 47.

45.4 CENTRAL CHILLED WATER PRODUCTION AND DISTRIBUTION

System Configuration

Central chilled water plants can have a variety of equipment and combinations of equipment to produce chilled water. Large water chillers are of two basic types, centrifugal and absorption. Centrifugal chillers may be driven by electric motors; condensing steam turbines; back pressure steam turbines; and in limited applications, combustion engines. Centrifugal chillers may be of the open drive type with an external prime mover driving the compressor or of the hermetic type with an electric motor, sealed within the refrigerant circuit, driving the compressor. Absorption chillers may be of the multistage type supplied with high-pressure steam, the single-stage type supplied with low-pressure steam or hot water, and direct fired. A variation of these arrangements, known as piggyback systems, combine a steam turbine driving a centrifugal chiller and exhausting steam into low-pressure absorption water chillers. One or all of these arrangements may be present in a large central chilled water plant with the widest variety represented in plants that have a long history and have undergone multiple phases of expansion.

Pumping arrangements for water circuits within a central chilled water plant normally fall into the following categories:

- Figure 45-9 illustrates a direct primary pumping system where all head loss across the chiller and distribution piping is furnished by a single pumping circuit.

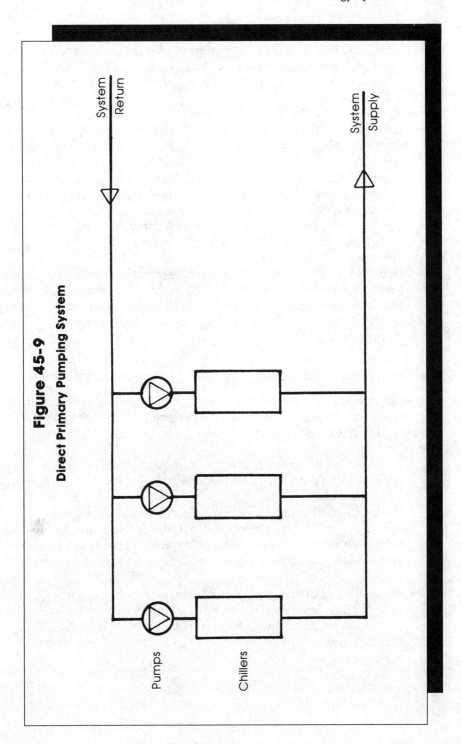

Figure 45-9

Direct Primary Pumping System

- Figure 45-10 illustrates a primary secondary pumping system where the hydraulic head requirements for the chiller and in-plant piping are furnished by one pumping circuit and the distribution system hydraulic head requirements are furnished by a separate, decoupled pump circuit.
- Figure 45-11 illustrates a series pumping arrangement where two chillers are arranged in series. This arrangement may be found in both primary and primary secondary pumping systems.
- Figure 45-12 illustrates a headered arrangement for chilled water pumps where a number of pumps discharge into a common header serving a bank of chillers. This arrangement may be found in both primary and primary secondary pumping systems. This type of arrangement may also be found in condenser water pumping systems.
- Figure 45-13 illustrates a unitary arrangement for chilled water pumps Where a single pump is dedicated to a specific chiller. This arrangement may be found in both primary and primary secondary pumping systems as well as in condenser water pumping systems.

Central System/Building Interface

Hydraulic interfaces between central systems and building systems can vary widely in control strategies but will generally be described by the following hydraulic arrangements:

- Figure 45-14 illustrates a straight primary interface where all necessary building circulating head is supplied by the central system pumps.
- Figure 45-15 illustrates a primary secondary interface where central system pumps deliver water to the building and any residual central system head is throttled away by a control valve and building circulation is provided by building chilled water pumps.
- Figure 45-16 illustrates a hybrid primary/primary secondary building interface where central plant pumps provide building circulation when adequate head is available and building chilled water pumps provide building circulation when central system head is not adequate to meet load requirements.

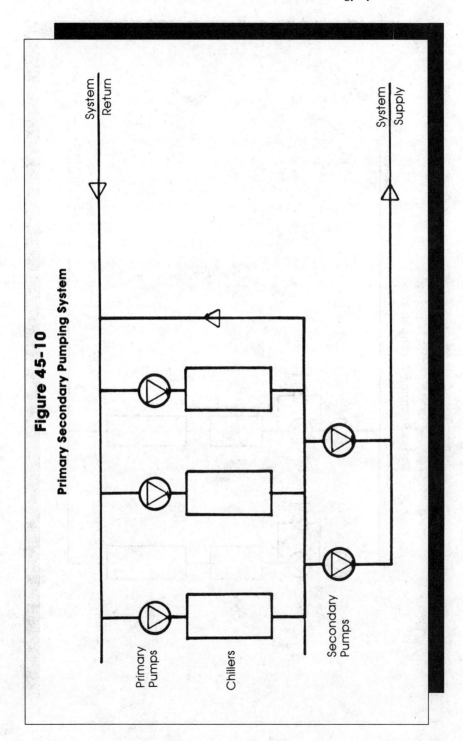

Figure 45-10

Primary Secondary Pumping System

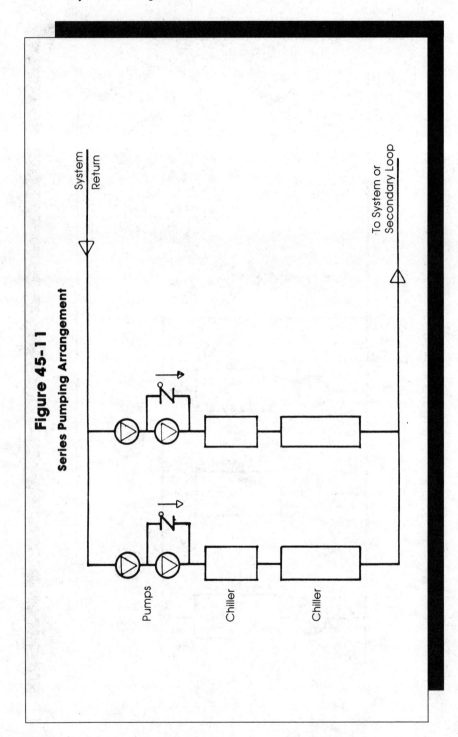

Figure 45-11

Series Pumping Arrangement

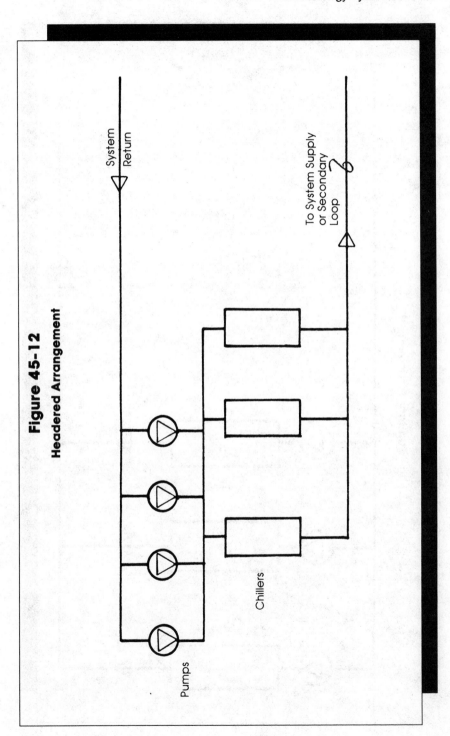

Figure 45-12
Headered Arrangement

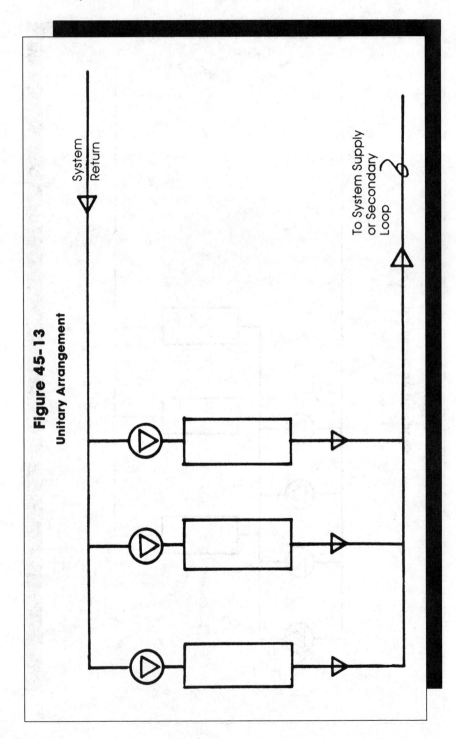

Figure 45-13
Unitary Arrangement

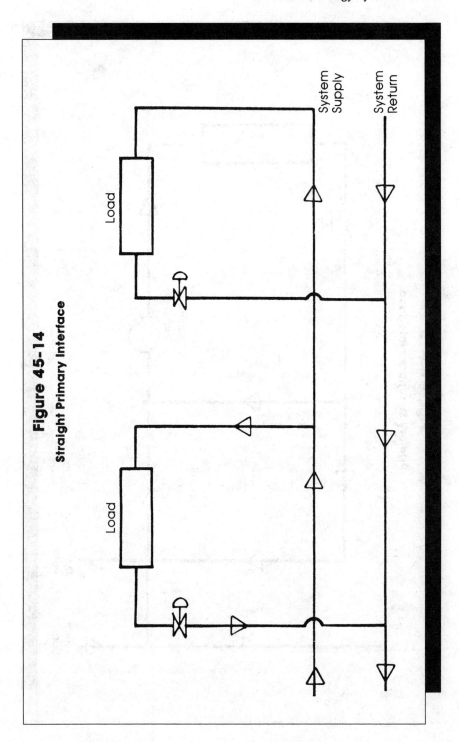

Figure 45-14
Straight Primary Interface

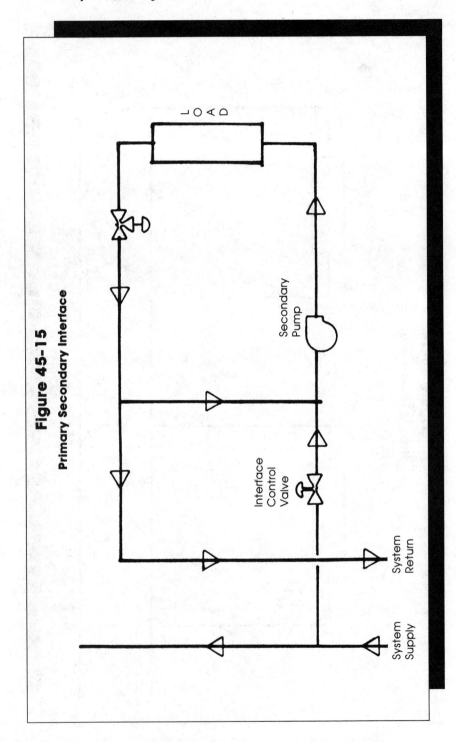

Figure 45-15

Primary Secondary Interface

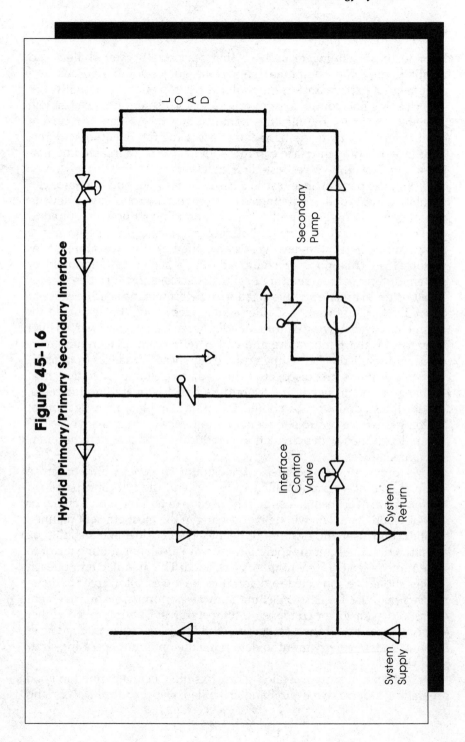

Figure 45-16

Hybrid Primary/Primary Secondary Interface

Monitoring and Controlling Performance

Prior to the beginning of each cooling season, all water chillers and auxiliary pumping equipment should be subjected to rigorous and documented performance testing after the completion of annual water side cleaning and control system calibration. This performance test will serve as a basis for the facilities administrator to evaluate the current condition of cooling equipment and in assessing future equipment performance. Building interface controls should also be calibrated and major system isolation valves tested for tight shut-off.

With the performance test as a base, the facilities administrator can monitor central cooling equipment performance by routinely reviewing the energy required in pounds of steam and kilowatt hours required to generate a ton hour of cooling. Building interface control performance can be monitored by reviewing system differential temperature under various load conditions. If chiller efficiency begins to deteriorate or system differential temperature begins to decrease, the facilities administrator should initiate an investigation to determine the specific cause of the reduction in efficiency. Chiller water sides should be evaluated for cleanliness by reviewing compressor discharge head records versus inlet condenser water temperature and chiller refrigerant temperatures versus leaving chilled water temperature. If significant variances from original specifications are discovered, immediate cleaning of fouled heat exchangers should begin. If system differential temperature decreases, the facilities administrator should initiate a complete investigation of building interface controls to identify and remedy situations where uncontrolled chilled water circulation is reducing overall system differential temperature.

In order for the facilities administrator to control and optimize performance of a central chilled water system, the full- and part-load performance of each chiller should be used to determine which chiller or combination of chillers will deliver cooling in the most efficient manner. Chiller condenser and evaporator heat exchanger cleanliness should be monitored throughout the cooling season by calculating fouling factor to determine when equipment must be cleaned. The manufacturer of each chiller should be contacted to determine the lowest allowable condensing temperature for each machine and the performance improvement measured with lower condensing temperatures. The improved chiller performance should then be compared with the increase in condenser cooling system energy input to determine the optimum operating strategy.

Distribution system/building controls must be maintained in good operating order as well air handler chilled water control valves and control systems. If these systems are allowed to go out of calibration, causing low differential temperature across the central system, the central system efficiency will be penalized in a number of ways. With low differential temperature, the central plant chillers will never achieve full load, and while adequate plant capacity is in place, the load will go unsatisfied. With the excess water pumping requirements caused by low differential temperature, additional heat will be added to the chilled water. This will increase the load on the chillers and the energy requirement for pumping per unit of output actually delivered to the load.

Metering

All chilled water meters are of the Btu type although the calculation of Btu units can be accomplished in a number of ways. Early chilled water meters consisted of a mechanical flow measurement device and two thermal expansion bulbs, one in the supply and one in the return chilled water line. The differential temperature modified the gear ratio of the flow measurement device to read out in Btus. Modern Btu meters consist of a wide variety of flow-sensing elements, several temperature sensing devices, and an electronic processor that receives input from the sensing devices and calculates total Btus.

Flow-sensing elements can be of the ultrasonic type, full-pipe-diameter turbine meters, insertion turbine meters, optically coupled padded wheels, insertion-type differential pressure devices, vortex shedding devices, nutating volume meters, as well as the more traditional orifice plate and venture. Temperature-sensing elements can be of the thermal expansion type, thermocouples, or resistance temperature devices. Electronic devices can range from simple preprogrammed units to fully programmable devices that communicate to even more sophisticated centrally located computer systems.

The accuracy of chilled water meters is a function of the turn down or range of the sensing device, the precision of the flow-measuring element, the accuracy of the temperature-sensing device, and the precision of the unit used to calculate total Btus. When assessing the current or potential accuracy of a chilled water Btu meter, care must be taken to clearly understand the implications of the specifications on the accuracy of the meter's device. For example, a temperature-sensing device with a range of 200°F with an accuracy of 1 percent will be plus or minus 2°F. In a chilled water system with a design differential of 10°F, the accuracy of the system would be plus or minus 20 percent for that application.

For any Btu meter to function within its accuracy range, it must be routinely calibrated and accurate records maintained on the calibration procedure.

Water Treatment

An effective water treatment program is necessary for the continued efficient operation of a central chilled water plant and must prevent fouling of the chiller heat exchangers and reduce system corrosion. Condenser cooling water treatment is the most important facet of any treatment program and must address the prevention of mineral deposits in chiller condensers, control corrosion in the system, prevent the build-up of solids, and control biological growth. Chilled water side treatment requirements are almost nonexistent and should only be considered if system make-up quantities are excessive.

Vendors can provide complete turn key systems that address all aspects of water treatment from the control and feed system to corrosion monitoring and chemical supplies. In large systems the use of bulk chemicals may serve as a cost-saving measure, although this approach will require a staff to handle the water treatment program. The facilities administrator should carefully examine both options to determine the most cost-effective method of furnishing effective water treatment program.

System Retrofit Opportunities

The facilities administrator should consider system retrofits that will substantially improve the operating efficiencies of a central chilled water system and reduce operating costs. Some options available are listed below:

- Cooling coil controls can be modified to return water at a specified temperature by adding temperature control to the coil leaving water temperature. To take advantage of the high water temperature rise of cooling coils during part-load performance, the return water control will only override the leaving air temperature control when return water drops below the set point. A typical arrangement of this control strategy is shown in Figure 45-17.
- Computer control systems are available that will allow automatic dispatch of chillers to assure that the most efficient equipment is in service and appropriately loaded to efficiently serve the system load. These systems can also automatically optimize condensing water temperature and minimize chiller energy requirements.
- Chilled water storage can be added to a system to reduce peak electrical demand as well as serve additional loads without the need for added chiller capacity.

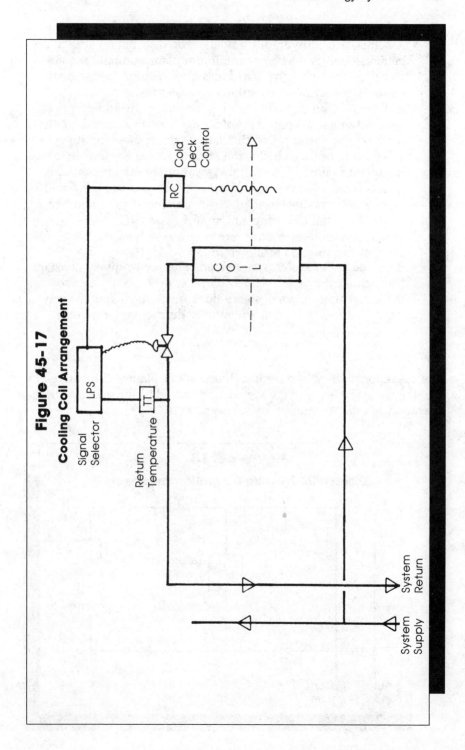

Figure 45-17
Cooling Coil Arrangement

- A computerized hydraulic model of the distribution system can be developed to determine minimum plant pumping requirements to meet any given load and also identify needed distribution system improvement to serve planned growth.
- In systems with primary building interfaces the addition of differential pressure control on buildings near the central plant will prevent uncontrolled circulation within these buildings when air handler chilled water control valves are unable to modulate against high central system differential pressure. A typical arrangement of this approach is shown in Figure 45-18.
- Plate and frame heat exchangers can be installed to take the place of mechanical refrigeration during periods when low condensing water temperatures are possible. A typical arrangement of this method is shown in Figure 45-19.
- If chilled water systems serve loads that are relatively constant throughout the year, such as computer systems or clean rooms, the installation of small stand-alone units may allow the central system to be shut down entirely during winter months.

Staffing

The operation staffing of a central chilled water plant will be driven by the size and complexity of the system and should be integrated with the operation of other central utility services.

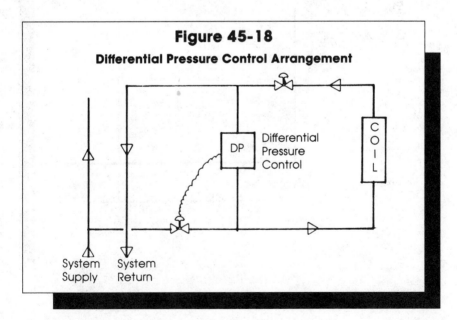

Figure 45-18

Differential Pressure Control Arrangement

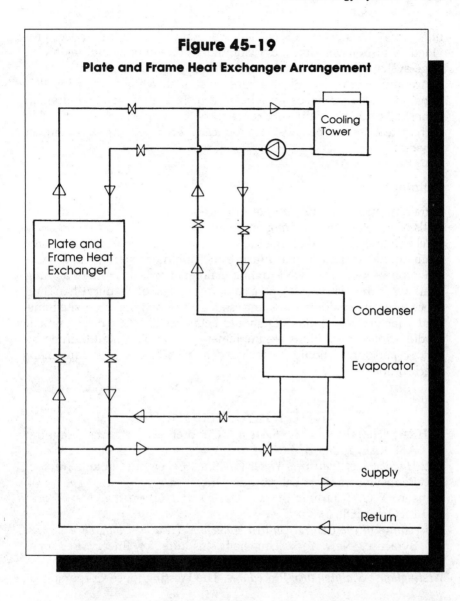

Figure 45-19
Plate and Frame Heat Exchanger Arrangement

The staffing of the maintenance organization for a central chilled water system can have a variety of forms. The maintenance function may be restricted entirely to the central chilled water plant or may encompass the delivery and end use systems as well. Since the total performance of the system not only depends on the efficiency of production but also the efficiency of utilization, an organizational and staffing approach that consolidates both functions under the same line manager may prove the most beneficial. The scope of maintenance services provided by in-house staff is a decision that will require careful review. In large systems it may be more economical to perform annual maintenance and overhauls with in-house personnel, while smaller installations' maintenance needs may be served through contact services. In almost all cases, specialty services such as oil sample analysis and eddy current testing can be most economically provided through contract services.

Training

A training program must be put in place to maintain and improve the skills of the existing operating and maintenance staff and to train entry level employees. The skills maintenance and improvement training program should include actual practice in equipment start-up and shutdown procedures, review of routine maintenance tasks, formal training in all water chemistry tests, and a complete review of chemical-handling procedures. If a major maintenance staff is present, regular on-site training by factory representatives should be arranged. If major equipment modifications or additions are implemented, complete staff training by factory personnel should be included as part of the new equipment specification.

ADDITIONAL RESOURCES

ASHRAE Handbook 1984 Systems. Chapter 13. Atlanta, Georgia: ASHRAE, 1984.

Betz Handbook of Industrial Water Conditioning, eighth edition. Trevose, Pennsylvania: Betz Laboratories, Inc.

Hansen, E.G. *Hydronic System Design and Operation.* New York: McGraw-Hill, 1985.

Proceedings of the Central Chilled Water and Heating Conference - 1979. Syracuse, New York: University Institute for Energy Research, 1979.

Westinghouse Maintenance Procedures. The Westinghouse Corporation.

Appendix 45-A

TEST REPORT

Switchgear

Date: _____

Location: _____

Switchgear Identification:

Mfgr: _____ S.O. _____

Dwgs: _____ Voltage Class: _____ Type: _____

Location: _____

    Cubicle No.: _____

    Application: _____

    _____

Identification: _____

External Condition: ☐ Good   ☐ Fair   ☐ Poor

Consisting of: ___ Total Breakers   ___ Total Instruments

      ___ Total Relays   ___ Molded Case Breakers

A.
1. General inspection of exterior of equipment.   ☐
2. Check panel lights for operation—burned out or   ☐
   missing bulbs and lamp covers.
3. Check control knobs and switches for freedom of   ☐
   movement and contact condition.
4. Inspect for damaged, bent, or twisted doors.   ☐
5. Inspect door handles, locking bars, and mechanisms.   ☐
6. Check door interlocks for positive operation.   ☐
7. Inspect for broken instrument and relay cover glass   ☐
   and burned out phase indicater lights.
8. Inspect for proper grounding of equipment.   ☐
9. Measure resistance to ground.   ☐

10. Dielectric test of bus works and potheads. ☐
11. Inspect bus and support insulators. ☐
12. Torque test bolted bus (exposed connections only). ☐
13. Clean bus insulators—megger test for grounds. ☐
14. Inspect control and metering transformers. ☐
15. Check resistors—grid assemblies and space heaters. ☐
16. Check condition of wiring and terminal connections. ☐
17. Report unsafe conditions. ☐
18. Check bus for support and spacing. ☐
19. Note and report any unmarked circuits. ☐
20. Remove draw out breakers. ☐
21. Check rails, guides, rollers, and shutter mechanism. ☐
22. Lubricate draw out assembly parts. ☐
23. Check cell interlocks and auxiliary contact assemblies. ☐
24. Inspect breaker and cell contacts. ☐
25. Vacuum and clean interior of cubicle. ☐
26. Perform breaker inspection. ☐
27. Inspect and check instruments. ☐
28. Note and record as found relay settings. ☐
29. Restore control power to switchgear. ☐
30. Check relays for positive tripping. ☐
31. Test annunciator—alarm or target operation. ☐
32. Operate controls—close and trip breakers electrically. ☐

B. Bus Megger Test/Infrared Thermal Scan

Phase A _____ Megohm/ _____ Degrees C

Phase B _____ Megohm/ _____ Degrees C

Phase C _____ Megohm/ _____ Degrees C

TEST REPORT

Transformer and Oil Filled Switch

Location: _____ Date: _____

Primary Voltage: _____ Transformer Secondary Voltage: _____

Name Plate ID:_____ Size:____ kVA

Liquid Level: High   ☐
             Low   ☐
             Normal ☐

Transformer Temperature Readings—(from gauges, in degrees Centigrade)

Liquid Temperature: _____

High Spot Temperature: _____

_____

_____

Fluid Color: Normal ☐

Discolored ☐

Highly Discolored Normal ☐

Dielectric Strength: Sample #1 1st Reading_____kV
                             2nd Reading_____kV
               Sample #2 1st Reading_____kV
                             2nd Reading_____kV
               Sample #3 1st Reading_____kV
                             2nd Reading_____kV
               Sample #4 1st Reading_____kV
                             2nd Reading_____kV
               Sample #5 1st Reading_____kV
                             2nd Reading_____kV
                        Tested By: _____

TEST REPORT

Air Circuit Breaker

A. Mechanical Checks

1. Remove from cell (draw out type only)   ☐
2. Remove arc boxes   ☐
3. Inspect and clean arc boxes   ☐
4. Check arc splitter grids and ceramics   ☐

5. Check magnetic "blow-out" coils (if used) ☐
6. Blow-off and clean breaker ☐
7. Inspect breaker for defects or damage ☐
8. Inspect for arc damage and deteriorated insulation ☐
9. Check primary bussings, porcelains, and finger clusters ☐
10. Inspect for burned and poorly mated contacts ☐
11. Replace damaged contacts ☐
12. Replace defective or weak contact springs ☐
13. Check contact alignment overtravel and contact pressure ☐
14. Adjust contacts as necessary ☐
15. Inspect all current-carrying parts for overheating ☐
16. Check shunts and all brazed or soldered connections ☐
17. Check coil terminals and insulation details ☐
18. Check for adequate electrical clearances ☐
19. Check mounting frame and all castings for cracks ☐
20. Check operating mechanism for friction ☐
21. Check for excessive wear and defective parts ☐
22. Check lift rods, latch mechanism, and details ☐
23. Check trip mechanism, latch load, and sneak settings ☐
24. Check manual close, latch, and trip operation ☐
25. Check trip-free operation ☐
26. Remove hardened lubricants ☐
27. Relubricate as required ☐
28. Check auxiliary switches for sequence, good contact alignment, and check operating linkage ☐
29. Check condition of wiring and tighten connections ☐
30. Check terminal blocks and connections ☐
31. Repeat manual close, latch, and trip operation ☐
32. Check mechanical condition of auxiliary devices— shock absorbers, bumpers, position indicators, latch checking switches, key lockout, etc. ☐

B. Electrical Checks

1. Operate breaker electrically ☐
2. Check closing coil connections ☐
3. Megger test closing coil ☐
4. Megger test control wiring ☐
5. High voltage test of breaker (if specified) ☐
6. If Rectox closed, check Rectox output and resistor ☐
7. Check capacitor trip (when used) ☐
8. Measure and record closing coil voltages and current ☐

9. Measure and record minimum closing coil voltage and current ☐
10. Check shunt trip operation at rated voltage and current ☐
11. Check shunt trip operation at minimum voltage ☐
12. Check reverse current trip (if used) ☐
13. Record "as found" overload settings ☐
14. Dismantle and clean oil filled dash pot ☐
15. Install new dash pot oil—reinstall dash pot ☐
16. Calibration check of overloads
    a. Instantaneous trip ☐
    b. Short time delay ☐
    c. Long time delay ☐
17. Make calibration adjustments ☐
18. Recalibrate breaker to higher or lower settings ☐
19. Exchange or repair overload trip units ☐
20. Check electrical close, latch, and trip operation ☐
21. Check trip free operation ☐
22. Check continuity of current-limiting fuses (when used) ☐

C. **Voltage Drop Across Contacts**
    Phase A_____ V
    Phase B _____ V
    Phase C_____ V

Comments: _____

_____

_____

Tested By: _____

TEST REPORT

Air Circuit Breaker—Calibration Checks

Location: _____ Date: _____

Name Plate: _____ Voltage: _____

A. Pick-Up Current   Phase A_____Amps
                      Phase B_____ Amps
                      Phase C_____ Amps

B. Long Time Delay   Phase A_____Sec
                      Phase B_____Sec
                      Phase C_____Sec

C. Resetting Delay
   Phase A   Current_____Time_____Sec
   Phase B   Current_____Time_____Sec
   Phase C   Current_____Time_____Sec

D. Short Time Delay
   Phase A   Tripping Current_____Time_____Sec
   Phase B   Tripping Current_____Time_____Sec
   Phase C   Tripping Current_____Time_____Sec

Tested By: _____

Appendix 45-B

TRANSFORMER AND OIL SWITCH LIQUID TESTS

1. **Testing Insulating Liquids:** Abnormally high or low liquid levels in transformers MUST be investigated for cause.

   a. If fluid level is low, check for leaks. Sight and float gauges are not always accurate.

   b. High liquid level may be due entirely to overfilling, but oil admitted when temperatures are low will expand in hot weather or with normal operating temperatures of equipment, causing oil level to change.

   c. Overtemperature of insulating oils or Inerteen is indicative of several conditions. Overloading of equipment, internal shorts, high resistance connection, or insufficient cooling air due to high ambient of equipment location.

   d. If equipment is not overloaded and ambient temperatures are normal the cause of internal heating MUST be established by internal inspection or test of the equipment. WHEN SUBJECTED TO OPERATING TEMPERATURES ABOVE 90°C, INSULATING OIL WILL OXIDIZE AND RAPIDLY LOSE ITS INSULATING PROPERTIES.

   e. New apparatus containing oil or Inerteen should always have the insulating liquid tested before placing in service. NEW OIL SHOULD TEST 29 kV OR ABOVE. Due to its characteristics, Inerteen when new will show a higher dielectric and should test 30 kV or better.

   f. Oil that has poor dielectric strength when filtered, or highly discolored oil which will not filter clean, should be replaced.

2. **Collecting Samples**

   a. Use only clean, dry bottles or jars and discard them after use. FREE MOISTURE CANNOT BE TOLERATED. To ensure absolute dryness, containers should be heated in an oven for at least one hour at a temperature of 212°F (100°C).

   b. Upon removal from drying oven, sample bottles

should be covered or corked and allowed to cool to ambient temperatures. USE IMMEDIATELY. CAUTION.

c. Oil and Inerteen readily combine. It is practically impossible to separate the two if mixed. Therefore, it is important to avoid contamination of Inerteen with transformer or breaker oil. The presence of oil in Inerteen changes the nonflammable and nonexplosive characteristics of Inerteen.

d. USE SEPARATE TEST CUPS AND FILTERS FOR EACH PRODUCT WHEN TESTING OR RECONDITIONING THESE FLUIDS.

e. ALWAYS use a metal hose or pipe when handling Inerteen. A HOSE MADE OF NATURAL RUBBER SHOULD NOT BE USED. Inerteen can easily become contaminated from the sulfur in the natural rubber and must not be allowed to come in contact with it.

f. Principal causes of deterioration of Inerteen are water, arcing, inorganic foreign matter, acids, alkali, and corrosive sulfur.

g. Oil is similarly affected, particularly by oxidation and carbon by-products of electrical arcing under oil.

Important Note:

When drawing oil samples, always take samples from oil sampling valves at the bottom of break or transformer tanks.

DRAIN OFF AND DISCARD A SMALL AMOUNT OF OIL BEFORE SAVING A TEST SPECIMEN. WATER AND CONDENSATE IN OIL WILL COLLECT IN THE BOTTOM OF TANKS AND IN DRAIN LINES AND WILL DRAIN OFF WITH THE INITIAL OIL WITHDRAWN FROM THE TANKS.

Inerteen samples should be taken from the top of Inerteen filled transformers unless the transformer is in operation, then the sample may be taken from either top or bottom sampling valves. Any moisture present will be mixed due to circulation of the Inerteen.

When drawing samples, waste a small quantity to flush out the sampling connection before taking specimen. USE ONLY CLEAN, DRY BOTTLES OR TIN CONTAINERS WITH SCREW CAPS. Seal immediately and mark samples with the identifying number or serial of the transformer from which sample was taken. AT LEAST A 16-OUNCE SAMPLE OF INERTEEN OR OIL SHOULD BE TAKEN. On transformers, additional samples should be drawn if first quantity of original specimen fails repeatedly on test. WHEN TAKING SAMPLES FOR LABORATORY TESTS, OBTAIN AT LEAST ONE QUART OF OIL OR INERTEEN FOR TEST.

Note: *Oil taken from a PCB transformer, rags, and PCB-contaminated wastes shall be disposed of under the direction of the Risk Management Department.*

3. **Test Procedures**

   a. The standard test cup with which the Portable "Oil-Insulation" Test Set is equipped, should be checked for air gap. The electrodes should be set at 0.100 gap between faces and be clean, dry, and lint free. Clean BEFORE use and AFTER each breakdown test of oil sample. Use new oil or appropriate solvent to clean test cup.

   b. Testing should be performed indoors. The test cup should be at room temperature before use. Ambient temperatures should be between 68°F and 86°F (20 = 30).

   c. Fill test cup with oil to a height of at least 0.79 inches (20mm) above the electrodes. Gently rock the test cup to agitate the liquid and free trapped air bubbles. Place cup in receptacle ready for test. Allow to stand for three to five minutes before testing.

   d. Test voltage should be increased at a rate of approximately 3,000 volts (RMS) per second until breakdown occurs. This is indicated by a steady voltage discharge across the fixed gaps in test cup. Disregard momentary, intermittent arcing across gap. These are transient voltage excursions caused by air or ionization.

   e. Open test circuit immediately upon breakdown, but FIRST note and record the applied voltage at time the breakdown occurs. This will prevent further unnecessary carbonization and contamination of the samples. Repeat the test immediately and compare first and second breakdown values. Applying a breakdown test a third time deteriorates the sample and results will be unreliable.

f. Discard sample, wash test cup with clean oil or solvent. Refill with fresh specimen and repeat test. Five (5) samples tested in this manner, using the average breakdown voltage, will establish the withstand voltage level of the oil being tested.

g. If the initial and second sample from the same specimen satisfactorily meet test requirements for new oil (29 kV or above), further tests may be waived. However if when testing a questionable test value occurs on the first or second sample, five test runs should then be made. The average of five (5) breakdown tests should then be used to establish dielectric strength of the oil sample.

h. Any oil testing 22.5 kV or lower must be filtered until the test value improves to 25 kV or above. If its dielectric strength cannot be improved by this method, it should be discarded.

CHAPTER 46

Building Energy Systems

Richard D. Neidhard
Mechanical Engineer
Motz Consulting Engineers, Inc.

46.1 INTRODUCTION

For any building to be suitable for its designed use, it will consume energy to maintain environmental conditions, provide illumination, and operate the mechanical and electrical equipment. This energy is normally supplied in two forms: electrical or thermal. Whether trying to conserve electrical or thermal (steam, hot water, gas, oil, or coal) energy, it is necessary to understand how it is used and what is required to achieve an optimum operation of the energy-consuming equipment.

This chapter will provide information and guidelines relative to the optimum operation of the energy-consuming systems in a typical college or university building.

Good energy management in the operation of a building is minimizing energy consumption while still maintaining satisfactory living and working conditions for the occupants. Because systems are frequently overdesigned, poorly designed in the first place, not properly maintained, or are in need of replacement because of wear and tear, energy can be overconsumed and therefore wasted. It is this waste that must be reduced or eliminated if good energy efficiency is to be achieved.

46.2 THE INFLUENCE OF BUILDING DESIGN

The physical plant administrator should be deeply involved in all phases of building design. In new buildings or major renovations it is vital that "hands-on" input be given to the design team commissioned to do the work. Every effort should be made to understand what the systems are and how they work and how the design will fit into the overall plan for energy utilization and management.

The interest that a physical plant department shows in the programming and design of a new or renovated building is no reflection on the competence of the designer. But with experience in the operation of mechanical and electrical systems of the institution, the appropriate physical plant representatives should critique the design parameters. If a completed project proves to be a marginal operation, the administrator who did not raise questions during design bears some responsibility for the result.

Perhaps the moral is to seek quality design consultants, but make sure they know that you are keenly interested in and concerned with the progress of their work. Finally, it cannot be emphasized enough the importance for every specification and drawing to be reviewed and checked by physical plant prior to bidding. Once a building or a major renovation is completed, it is too late to complain about the design.

46.3 THE CONSUMPTION OF ELECTRICAL ENERGY

Electricity is the one form of energy that could be described as universal. It can be used to heat, cool, illuminate, and operate all other building mechanical systems. Due to the relatively high cost of electricity compared to other energy forms, it is not normally used for heating. Because so many appliances in a building require electric power, particular attention must be given to the equipment that consumes kilowatts and how that equipment is used and maintained.

Illumination

If good management of electrical consumption in a building is vital to prudent operation, then certainly the power consumed for illumination is important on the manager's list of conservation opportunities. Nationally, about 22 percent of generated electricity is used for illumination. If the removal of heat generated by the lights in use is also considered, efficient lighting systems and the thoughtful use thereof are especially important.

Three items must be considered in the economical use of electricity for lighting:

- Efficiency of the lighting system (lamp and the fixture).
- Level of illumination.
- Economies available in the way lights are used or the length of time the lights are in operation.

Efficiency Efficiency of lighting is the ratio of the number of lumens produced per watt consumed. When Thomas Edison introduced the incandescent lamp in 1879, he revolutionized the world of lighting. Modern incandescents are much more sophisticated than Edison's original version relative to efficiency, durability, convenience, and size. However, as basic as the incandescent lamp is in the field of illumination, it is by far the most inefficient means of electric lighting available today. Mercury vapor, fluorescent, metal halide, and high- and low-pressure sodium lamps have all been developed to obtain more lumens per watt of consumption. Figure 46-1 illustrates lumen output per watt generally available for various types of lamps.

The choice of the type of lamps for each requirement is determined by many factors. Each type listed in Figure 46-1 has its advantages, such as first cost, lighting level desired, aesthetics, weather durability, and vandalism.

Once design, selection, and installation of lamps and lamp fixtures have taken place, the efficiency of a system deteriorates as time passes. Two things occur:

- Lamp lumen output per watt of consumption depreciates over the life of the lamp due to individual lamp characteristics. See Figure 46-2 for a comparison of various lamp types.
- The accumulation of dirt on the reflective surface of the fixture or lens will reduce lumen output. See Figure 46-3.

Lamp Maintenance Lamp lumen depreciation occurs in every type of lamp at a rate that is a characteristic of each type of lighting system. The depreciation rate cannot be stopped, but can be reduced. In addition, there is the problem of dirt accumulation on the fixture and lens. These problems are best handled through a planned maintenance program that includes group relamping, scheduled cleaning of fixtures, replacement of discolored lenses or other defective components, and the cleaning or painting of room surfaces. A program of this sort has a number of advantages:

- The lighting level, over the time cycle of relamping, is maintained close to design level.
- There is a savings in labor costs.
- Projected costs for labor and material are easier to estimate because the program numbers are finite.
- Inventory can be reduced for replacement parts.
- Labor scheduling is easier to control.
- The relamping process can be scheduled to minimize occupant disruption or inconvenience.

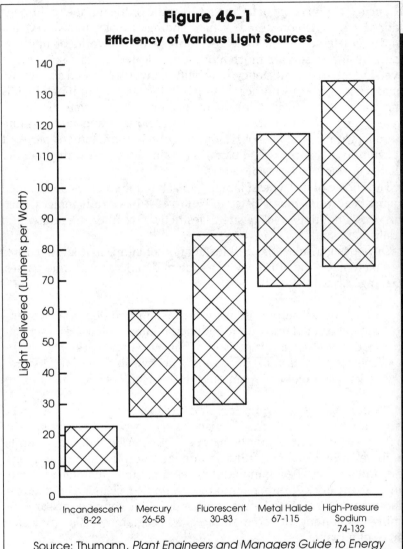

Figure 46-1

Efficiency of Various Light Sources

Source: Thumann, *Plant Engineers and Managers Guide to Energy Conservation* (The Fairmont Press, Inc., 1987).

Figure 46-2

Lamp Lumen Depreciation and Mortality

Lamp Type	Lamp Lumen Depreciation % of Initial Lumens at:		Mortality % of Lamps Operating at:	
	60% Rated Life	80% Rated Life	60% Rated Life	80% Rated Life
Incandescent	95	90	95	85
Fluorescent	85	80	95	80
Mercury	65-75	60-75	95	85
Metal Halide	70-75	68-75	85	70
High-Pressure Sodium	87-90	84-88	85	70

Source: Turner, Wayne C., *Energy Management Handbook* (John Wiley & Sons, Inc., 1982).

- The bottom line benefit is maximized lighting efficiency—lumens per watt.

Levels of Illumination   The correct level of illumination, quite often, is a matter of opinion. Lighting standards have been developed by the Illuminating Engineering Society to assist designers in the determination of layout and fixture numbers. These standards have been reconsidered in recent years to create a better balance between lighting levels and energy consumption. Figure 46-4 is a short summary of recommended lighting levels from the Federal Energy Administration. Note that it emphasizes "on the task only." The design trend in good efficient lighting is to consider the task area rather than an entire room.

Conservation Guidelines for Lighting   Whether one has a new lighting system or a system that has been in use for many years, the opportunities to conserve energy are considerable. The following is a list of some, but certainly not all, of the possible ways a good manager can reduce electrical consumption:

- If the room will be empty for more than thirty minutes, turn the lights off.
- Choose the best lens for the fixtures in the system.
- Install more switches or automatic switches so that unnecessary lighting can be turned off.

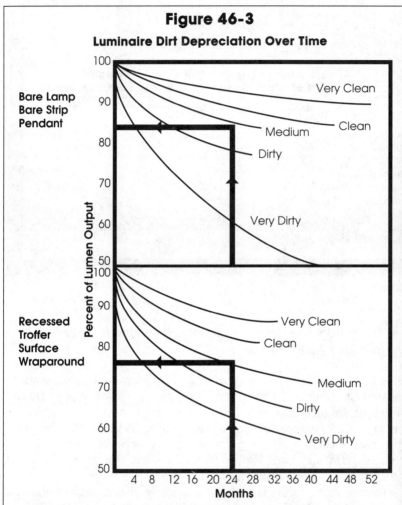

Figure 46-3

Luminaire Dirt Depreciation Over Time

Source: Dubin, Mindel, and Bloome, *How to Save Energy and Cut Costs in Existing Industrial and Commercial Buildings* (Noyes Data Corporation, 1976).

Figure 46-4
Recommended Interior Lighting Levels

Lighting Function	Foot Candles*
Prolonged, visually difficult office work	75 (on task only)
Normal office work, libraries, and classrooms	50-75 (on task only)
Hallways and corridors	5-15 (average)

* Levels are averages and must be adjusted to meet special requirements in individual cases.

- Consider the modification of light fixtures to accommodate more efficient lamps (i.e., high-intensity discharge [H.I.D.] lamps for incandescents).
- If modification is not possible, then consider new high-efficiency fixtures.
- Make sure there is good reflectance (light colors) off the walls and ceilings.
- By lowering the mounting height of ceiling fixtures closer to the task at hand, fewer watts are required to achieve the lighting levels desired.
- Consider the use of furniture-mounted task lighting to reduce the amount of general illumination required.
- Maximize the use of daylight with skylights and windows.

More ideas on how to save electrical energy in lighting are available in the resources listed at the end of this chapter.

Electromechanical Consumption

Electric motors are generally the major power-consuming component to move and compress air, to move water, and to power vertical transportation. The combined use of electricity and thermal energy in a building heating, ventilating, and air conditioning (HVAC) system is the single largest consumer of energy with which management must be concerned. The opportunities to save energy are greatest in the efficient operation of heating and cooling systems. This section will discuss methods to reduce electrical consumption outside of illumination.

Operation of HVAC Systems   The operation of an HVAC system requires the use of electric motors. Through belt drives or couplings, motors will drive pumps, fans, and compressors. Assuming that the motor is sized properly, it consumes electricity at a rate that is related to the resistance it meets in doing its job. Dirty strainers or heat exchangers restrict water flow and dirty filters and coils can restrict air flow. Good maintenance and operating procedures will minimize losses caused by dirty equipment.

Dirty equipment is not the only matter of concern with regard to maintenance and energy conservation for HVAC systems. Proper oiling and greasing prolongs bearing life, whether it be in motors, pumps, or fans. Loose belts and misaligned sheaves are also sources of excessive consumption. Leaky air ducts or piping, and ill-fitting doors or access panels all waste energy and should be the targets for maintenance repairs.

The operation of an HVAC system relative to energy management is a function not only of maintenance but also of how it is operated. Obviously, if a unit is shut down because there is no demand, or if fans are cycled off for brief periods, electrical consumption is reduced. Caution is advised for a program of duty cycling. The operator must be aware of the characteristics of the motors and starters because short cycling with across-the-line starters can severely damage equipment.

Shutting a unit down saves energy immediately, but most of the time it is not possible or practical to do this. Substantial amounts of electrical energy can be saved by slowing down fans or pumps. When heating or cooling loads are reduced, for whatever reason, the quantity of air or chilled and hot water required to meet the load is also lowered. When a fan or pump speed is reduced, its power requirements are also reduced by the power of three. This is represented by the following formula.

$$HP = (RPM\ 1)^3 \div (RPM\ 2)^3$$

Although reducing fan or pump speeds as suggested above can save energy, it must be remembered that motors operated far below their rated output are inefficient and have a poor power factor. It is therefore recommended that thought and care be put into any changes contemplated in this area.

Operation of Vertical Transportation   The use of elevators and escalators in campus facilities has become a way of life. This equipment is not a major consumer of electrical energy in a building, but some activity can be practiced to achieve a measure of conservation. If possible, an automatic control program should be selected for the lowest speed and heaviest loading. This will reduce the number of elevator units traveled per year and subsequently conserve energy. In many installations, a motor generator set will run constantly whether or not the elevator is in operation. In this situation, if there is more than one elevator in the building, consider shutting down one or more units at night and weekends. Special controls, time clocks, or even hand switches can be installed to remove the unit from service.

Conservation Guidelines for Electromechanical Systems
Conservation of energy in the electromechanical area is more than just concern over electrical consumption. Thermal energy is a major portion of the total conservation effort in HVAC and will be covered later in this chapter. It is safe to say, however, that in conserving electricity, thermal energy is also being saved. The following is a set of guidelines earmarked for electrical conservation in building operating systems:

- Shut down ventilation (or exhaust) during unoccupied periods.
- Reduce ventilation rates during occupied periods as long as code requirements are maintained.
- Shut down cooling systems during unoccupied periods.
- Improve chiller and compressor performance by good maintenance procedures and an alert operating program.
- To the extent possible, reduce resistance to air movement throughout an HVAC system so that the amount of air required is reduced.
- Water circulating pumps are also governed by the same basic laws of fan operation. Any reduction to system resistance will save energy provided the flow rate remains constant. With a variable speed pump, energy is conserved because, with lowered resistance, the speed can be reduced to pump the same amount of water. Remember, as the speed is reduced the electricity required reduces by the power of three.
- A well-established and consistent preventive maintenance program on all electromechanical equipment is vital to optimum operation of any system. Lubrication, cleanliness, inspection, and timely repairs or replacements are key factors in good equipment maintenance.

46.4 THE CONSUMPTION OF THERMAL ENERGY

The major consumer of energy in the operation of a building, discounting process or specific research loads, is that which is required to maintain the desired environmental conditions. Heating and humidifying in the winter and cooling and dehumidifying in the summer require both thermal and electrical energy forms. Heat is added in the winter at the rate it is lost and in the summer heat is removed at the rate it is gained.

The building systems and equipment used to heat or cool range from simple hand-operated radiators or package air conditioners to large central systems that heat and cool different areas at the same time under automatic building management control systems.

The various types of HVAC systems will be discussed later in this chapter. The following is a review of what affects heat gain and loss.

Heat Transmission

Each element of the building envelope contributes to heat gain or loss. The walls, roof, floor, doors, and windows will permit heat transfer (in or out) at a rate that is governed by the type and amount of insulation, type of glazing, the fit of doors and windows, wind load, and solar impingement.

Heat loss or gain through a wall is a function of its resistance to heat flow altered by the effect of solar impingement and wind load. Resistance to heat flow is enhanced by the use of insulating materials installed within or on the surface of walls.

Heat transfer through the roof of a building can be considered much the same as that through the walls. There is, however, more concern for conduction and solar gain through roofs when considering heat gain calculations in the cooling season. The absorption value of a roof due to the solar load can be good in the winter with a dark roof, but that same color is poor in the summer.

Transmission through windows and doors can be reduced by the use of double glazing, the installation of storm doors and windows, the use of sun screens, and the use of tinted glass. Tight-fitting fenestration is also important.

Infiltration/Exfiltration

This phenomenon is a major source of heat gain or loss from a building. Infiltration is the cold or hot air that enters through open doors or windows, through loose-fitting doors or windows, or through gaps around doors or windows. Infiltration can be caused by wind loads striking loose fenestration while exfiltration is aggravated by higher pressures within a building than that which is outside.

Solar Impingement

Solar impingement or sun load is good or bad depending upon the season. Obviously, in the summer it is a force that must be dealt with relative to cooling, and during the winter it is a help. Building orientation, window design, shading from trees or other structures, surface coloration, and weather all have an effect on solar impingement. In dealing with solar load, certain items can be adjusted (tinted glass or shading), but other aspects must be accepted and included with the items that cause energy consumption.

Ventilation

Ventilation of a building occurs during heating and cooling. It is required to reduce or eliminate odors and stuffiness and to meet the prevailing code that specifies minimum fresh air requirements in the service for which the building is being used. Fresh air must be heated or cooled, and this consumes a great deal of thermal and electrical energy. Minimizing ventilation air reduces the energy required to heat or cool outside air. When fresh air is -5°F or 100°F, it is easy to see the possibilities for savings.

Types of Building HVAC Systems

After all items affecting the heating and cooling load are considered, the actual work required to maintain the optimum environmental conditions in a building is provided by the HVAC system that is installed. In some cases, the energy manager can help decide what type of system is to be used. In most cases, however, the manager inherits the system and must operate it to the best of his or her ability. The following is a description of the types of systems used in heating and cooling buildings and the steps that can be taken to conserve energy.

Direct Hot Water or Steam Systems   This system uses direct radiation; fin tube convectors, fan coil units, and cabinet or fan-driven heaters with hot water, steam, or electric coils. Radiators and convectors are slow to respond to changes, and occupants often allow them to operate at maximum capacity while regulating room temperature by opening and closing windows.

Conservation guidelines are:

- Clean the air side of all radiators, fin tube convectors, and coils to enhance heat transfer.
- Keep radiators and convectors free from blockage so air can freely circulate around the heating surface.
- Be sure to vent all hot water radiators and convectors to assure water circulation.
- Check radiator steam traps for proper operation.
- Install individual automatic control valves at each radiator to regulate either steam or hot water.

- Consider installing a control valve in the building system supply line that is controlled according to outside temperature. This type of control could be further enhanced with a night setback feature.

Fan Coil System   The fan coil unit is inherently one of the most energy efficient systems available, because all of the energy is delivered to the space through a piping network. It has a small fan, little or no ductwork, and no ventilation capability. It is usually controlled by a thermostat mounted on the unit but can be controlled by a wall thermostat. Fan coil units are efficient in thermally light buildings but not in thermally heavy structures.

Conservation guidelines are:

- Keep air outlets and inlets free.
- Keep filters and coils clean.
- In mild weather shut off fans and let heating coils act as a converter.
- In a building where large numbers of fan coils are used, avoid simultaneous heating and cooling unless humidity control is required in certain areas.

Unit Ventilators   The unit ventilator is closely related to the normal fan coil unit. It is quite often found in classroom situations, because many building codes require ventilation air. By having a fresh air opening and thus an economy cycle, the unit ventilator is relatively efficient for this type of equipment. Like the fan coil, it is an all-piped system with no duct work to require distribution energy to move the air. If installed in a thermally heavy classroom building, the fresh air economy cycle can be used for cooling, thereby eliminating the need for mechanical cooling. A unit ventilator system is classed as very efficient.

Conservation guidelines are:

- Keep air outlets and inlets free.
- Keep filters and coils clean.
- In mild weather shut off fan and let coil act as a convector.
- In a building where large numbers of unit ventilators are used, try to avoid simultaneous heating and cooling.
- Reduce ventilation to that which is required, especially during unoccupied periods.

Single Zone System   A single-zone system provides conditioned air to one zone under control of a zone thermostat. This type of a system is usually installed for large spaces such as auditoriums or large lecture rooms.

Conservation guidelines are:

- Keep filters and coils clean.
- Where humidity control is not essential, consider the modification of piping connections to use the cooling coil for both heating and cooling. Removal of the heating coil reduces air resistance to flow and allows a lower fan speed and subsequent reduction in power. In addition, the larger cooling coil, when used for heating, will permit the use of lower temperature water for a given heat output. Lower water temperatures increase efficiency in the boiler operation.
- Avoid simultaneous cooling and heating unless humidity control is required.

Multizone Systems   In this system a fan discharges air through a heating coil and a cooling coil after which both decks are mixed by a regulating damper that automatically supplies the tempered air through one duct to the zone being served. This system is a form of reheat in which overheating and overcooling of the supply air is an inherent waste of energy.

Conservation guidelines:

- Minimize as much as possible the temperature difference between the hot and cold decks.
- Install an automatic reset that is controlled by outside temperature to adjust coil temperatures and pump operation.
- Inspect for leaky valves and dampers and repair if required.
- Shut off fan and all control valves during unoccupied periods during the cooling season.
- Shut off the cooling valve during unoccupied periods in the heating season.

Dual Duct Systems   In this arrangement both hot and cold air are delivered in separate ducts to each zone. The hot and cold air ducts are attached to a dampered box where the air is mixed in varying proportions according to the needs of the zone. A thermostat in the zone controls the temperature of the mixed air.

Conservation guidelines are:

- Most of the guidelines indicated for a multizone unit also apply here.
- Reduce air flow to the maximum extent possible.

- When cooling is not required, close off the cold air duct and shut down the cooling system, and then operate as a single duct system by rescheduling the warm air temperature according to the heat required. Reverse this procedure when there is no heating load in the cooling season. Each duct is normally designed to handle 80 percent of total air circulated. Converting to single-zone operation will save some fan energy but may produce noise problems that will require some adjustments of dampers or fan speeds.

Variable Air Volume (VAV) System   In this system, air at a constant temperature, either heated or cooled, is delivered to the zones where VAV boxes automatically adjust the quantity needed according to the load requirements. As loads reduce, so too does the air quantity required, and a subsequent saving in fan horsepower is achieved. This system has become popular since the early 1970s.

Conservation guidelines follow:

- Reduce the volume of delivered air to the minimum possible extent.
- Install temperature reset controls to regulate the air temperature according to demand and outside conditions.
- Reschedule the supply air temperature so that the damper serving the zone with the greatest load is fully open.
- Reduce the temperature difference between the hot and chilled water as much as possible.
- Maintain VAV boxes so that they operate as designed to prevent overheating or overcooling.

Terminal Reheat   In a terminal reheat system, dehumidified chilled air is supplied to each zone where it is reheated according to the requirements of the space being served. This system is inefficient and is normally only used now when humidity is an important factor.

Conservation guidelines follow:

- Raise the supply air temperature as high as conditions will permit. This will increase the efficiency of the chiller and reduce the energy expended for reheat.
- Reduce the supply air quantity.
- Operate the system on a demand schedule without reheat if zone control is not critical.
- Allow humidity levels to increase so that the need for low supply air temperatures decreases and the energy requirement for refrigeration also decreases.

Induction Systems   This system is normally found in large buildings. An air handling unit supplies treated primary air at high pressure to individual induction units in the zone being served. The primary air flows through a nozzle system inside the unit, which in turn induces room air to flow over heating or cooling coils. The primary air then mixes with the room air to provide the necessary mix to satisfy room or zone requirements. The typical primary air to induced air ratio is 1:4.

Conservation guidelines follow:

- Reschedule the water temperatures for heating or cooling according to the severity of the load.
- Clean the coils regularly.
- During unoccupied periods in the heating season, shut down the primary air fan and save fan horsepower. During this time, the heating coils in the unit will serve as a gravity convector.
- Check nozzles for enlargement and adjust nozzle pressure accordingly.

46.5 GENERAL CONSERVATION GUIDELINES

This chapter has discussed various types of HVAC systems used in college or university buildings and noted conservation guidelines applicable in each case. Additionally, there are a number of general conservation guidelines that may be of help either in the design of a new system or in the operation of an existing system. It is important to remember that before any kind of an adjustment or alteration is made on heating or cooling equipment to improve energy efficiency, the change should be carefully analyzed and considered. Consider the following general guidelines if planning to establish a new energy management program, or if an energy program is already in existence.

- For one ton of air conditioning the pumping cost of chilled water through piping is about one-tenth the cost of moving cold air through ducts.
- Remember that reducing the resistance to air flow will reduce the power required to move the air. Keep the static duct pressure as low as possible. A good way to achieve this is to increase the size of the duct through which the air flows.
- Enthalpy controls, although difficult to maintain in good working order, are profitable to use on building systems that have at least a 20,000 CFM ventilation rate, where the proper motors and dampers exists to mix the fresh and return air in proper

amounts, and where the climate is conducive to operating conditions.

- A bank of water chillers can be designed to run in series or in parallel. If the cooling load is maximum for only a short number of hours during the day, it is best to run the chillers in series. On the other hand, for prolonged hours of operation at peak load the chillers should be set up to run in parallel.

- The turndown ratio or low-load performance of a chiller is important to consider when purchasing new or replacement equipment. Usually, at low load conditions, the efficiency of a chiller drops off considerably. An engineering analysis should be made regarding the feasibility of installing two smaller chillers instead of one large one. This kind of a move can take advantage of the maximum efficiencies obtained while running at full or near-full loads.

- The use of a hot gas bypass system on a chiller while running at low load is a waste of energy. This is another reason to consider multiple smaller chillers.

- Try to run with the chilled water supply temperature as high as possible. A 2 to 4 percent saving in energy utilization is achieved for each degree the chilled water is raised.

- For each degree the interior temperature is raised or lowered in the winter or summer, it is possible to save as much as 2 to 5 percent of the energy utilization.

- When a high ventilation rate is required, such as in medical or research facilities, it will pay to consider methods of using exhaust air to precondition the fresh air intake. Heat wheels and thermal run-around systems are two methods to achieve heat reclamation.

- In choosing the type of a cooling tower to use, keep in mind that a draw-through forced draft unit uses only 30 to 50 percent of the energy that a blow-through type does. The blow-through type, however, is lower in initial cost and is smaller in size per ton of capacity.

- It is important to keep condenser tubes clean. The rate of heat transfer decreases as scale and dirt build up in tubes. Whether the tube IDs are cleaned mechanically with brushes or by chemicals depends upon the quality of the condenser water and if the water is treated in any way.

- Heat pumps are not as efficient in cooling when compared to a conventional air-conditioning unit of equal capacity. The same is true for heating. They do, however, work best in thermally heavy buildings located in cold climates. It is not good practice to use a heat pump in a thermally light building.

- The need to provide constant heating or cooling for a specific room or area in a building, the rest of which can be shut down at night or over a weekend, may prove to be expensive. In cases of this sort it is wise to consider the installation of supplimental heating or cooling units to only serve the special areas. A computer room is an example of this sort of installation.

ADDITIONAL RESOURCES

Dubin, Fred S., Harold L. Mindell, and Selwyn Bloome. *How to Save Energy and Cut Costs in Existing Industrial and Commercial Buildings.* Park Ridge, New Jersey: Noyes Data Corporation, 1976.

Feldman, Edwin B. *Energy Saving Handbook for Homes, Businesses & Institutions.* New York: Frederick Fell Publishers, 1979.

Smith, Craig B. *Energy Management Principles.* Elmsford, New York: Pergamon Press, 1981.

Thumann, Albert. *Fundamentals of Energy Engineering.* Lilburn, Georgia: The Fairmont Press, 1984.

———. *Plant Engineers and Managers Guide to Energy Conservation.* Lilburn, Georgia: The Fairmont Press, 1987.

Turner, Wayne C. *Energy Management Handbook.* New York: John Wiley & Sons, 1982.

CHAPTER 47

Cogeneration for Universities and Colleges

Billy E. Hiefner
Staff Electrical Engineer
Department of Physical Plant
Rice University

Mohammad H. Qayoumi
Associate Executive Vice
President, Facilities Development
and Operations
San Jose State University

With additional contributions by Carl Romero.

47.1 INTRODUCTION

The utility services required by college and university buildings develop as separate entities over time. The technologies for combining these services for improved fuels and energy economy have always existed, but were not employed because fuels and energy were cheap and readily available. The rapid escalation in costs and threatened shortages of fuels and energy commencing in the early 1970s made the integration of utility systems more cost-effective. Through various education programs, subsidizations, and regulations on the purchase and sale of electric power, the federal government has further promoted the use and development of these technologies.

Colleges and universities have typically provided their own heating and cooling but purchased electric power, water, sewage treatment, and solid waste disposal. Many of these services can be combined to achieve maximum utilization of energy and optimum economies. Supplying the energy necessary for heating and cooling as a by-product of electric power generation is perhaps the most common and cost-effective combination. But others are being employed by colleges and universities, such as the incineration of solid waste for its heat content, and partial reuse of the effluent from sewage treatment for equipment make-up water and irrigation. The objective is to provide the required services with maximum efficiency and minimal overall cost through the utilization of heretofore wasted energy from individual systems.

This chapter is concerned primarily with the integration of electric power generation and heating and cooling. In general, the system that will be most attractive in terms of highest fuel efficiency is one in which electric power generation is combined with heating and cooling, and in which the power generation system is selected on the basis of optimum size to provide the thermal requirements. Any smaller system requires a conventional boiler to provide additional energy for heating and cooling; a large unit requires the electric power generation to compete with large high-efficiency power generation of the utility companies.

Large commercial electric generation stations operate at about 35 percent thermal efficiency. A properly sized electric-thermal cogeneration plant can attain an efficiency of over 70 percent. Such a plant can pay out in as few as three to five years, with continuing savings of 10 to 25 percent per year thereafter.

This chapter defines the cogeneration concept and discusses the criteria to be considered in a feasibility study to evaluate the option in each case. A knowledge of federal, state, and local regulations is further required to determine the type and configuration of the system selected.

Factors to be considered in the design of a cogeneration plant are: cost (capital investment versus operation and maintenance); standby power interface; prime movers (gas turbines versus diesel engines); and type of thermal energy reclaim equipment. Extremely important to an existing institution is the integration of the new system with existing equipment, and avoiding service interruptions during construction.

Finally, consideration must be given to training technicians to operate and maintain the new equipment. This will necessitate planned training sessions with the technical staff, development of operation and maintenance manuals, data acquisition and reports, inspections, and preventive maintenance procedures.

47.2 GOVERNMENTAL REGULATIONS

Definitions

Cogeneration is defined in the rules implementing the Public Utility Regulatory Policies Act (PURPA) as the sequential production of electricity and useful thermal energy from a single energy source.

The PURPA regulations define two cogeneration cycles:

Topping Cycle   This cycle first converts fuel energy into electrical power, with the rejected heat used to provide thermal energy. When some of the useful thermal energy is used to generate additional electrical power, the process is called a combined cycle.

Bottoming Cycle   This cycle first applies input energy to generate thermal energy. The useful thermal energy is then utilized to produce electrical power.

Federal Regulations

For owners of cogeneration systems to receive the full benefits offered by federal regulations relative to parallel interconnection with utility distribution system, standby power service, and sale of excess generated power, the facility must be certified by the Federal Energy Regulatory Commission (FERC) as a qualifying facility (QF). Certification by FERC is on the basis of three qualifying criteria. For a topping cycle, these criteria are:

An Ownership Criterion   A utility cannot own more than 50 percent of the cogeneration facility.

An Operating Standard   A new topping cycle facility must produce at least 5 percent of the total energy output as useful thermal energy.

An Efficiency Standard   When natural gas or liquid fuel is used, the annual power plus one-half the useful thermal energy must be at least 42.5 percent of the total natural gas or liquid fuel energy input. However, if the thermal energy output is less than 15 percent of the total energy output, the requirement increases to 45 percent. (All efficiency calculations are based on the lower heating values of the fuel.) It is important to keep in mind the PURPA defines efficiency as:

Power output + (Useful heat$_2$) ÷ Fuel input (Lower heating value)

which has no scientific significance.

State and Local Regulations

State regulations impose restrictions primarily for environmental requirements. The state air quality control agencies have adopted the federal Environmental Protection Agency (EPA) requirements. Moreover, some states and local governments have set stricter new source regulations than EPA. Air emission requirements for stationary gas and liquid fuel combustion turbines and internal combustion engines are set, and revised periodically, by the EPA.

Electric Utility Interconnection

Cogeneration facilities that are certified by FERC as qualifying facilities are permitted to interconnect with the electric utility distribution system serving the facility. The electric utility has to provide, upon request by the QF cogeneration owner, standby power and must purchase, if requested by owner, the excess electrical power generated. The rate paid by the qualifying facility for standby power from the electric utility is set by the state utility commission. The avoided costs paid by the electric utility to the cogeneration facility for the excess electrical power are also established by the commission. The electric utility serving the college or university installing a cogeneration facility has specific mandatory interconnection requirements.

47.3 FEASIBILITY STUDY

To determine energy cost savings that will result in economical benefits and a realistic payout period, an in-depth feasibility study is required prior to the preliminary design phase of the project. This study includes careful analysis of data and hourly logs from previous seasons to determine electric and thermal requirements. Hourly power usage is usually available from the electrical utility company; hourly logs of heating and cooling usage are usually maintained by plant operators. Previous electric and fuel bills are of limited value since they provide only monthly totals, and therefore do not establish time duration and date of minimum and maximum loads.

47.4 THE COGENERATION CONCEPT

A public utility produces electricity at an overall efficiency of only about 35 percent. Total 65 percent power generation losses are accounted for as follows:

- Condensers, 48 percent.
- Radiation from boilers and other heated surfaces, 2 percent.
- Boiler stack and associated combustion losses, 15 percent.

For a cogeneration system to achieve maximum cost-effectiveness, the system must operate at peak output, and all of the available thermal energy must be used productively. Part-load operation is inefficient, and failure to use the thermal energy obviates realization of the benefits of cogeneration.

Utility power plant and distribution losses result in a heat rate of approximately 11,160 Btus/kWh delivered to the customer's meter. A properly designed cogeneration system, in which all of the available thermal energy is used, can produce 1 kW using less than 4,300 Btus.

47.5 DESIGN CRITERIA—ELECTRICAL SYSTEM SELECTION

Prior to PURPA, electric utilities controlled the electric power distribution grid entirely, and under normal circumstances would not allow any customer to tie in a dispersed generation site to the power grid. This had resulted in a safe and reliable operation of the electric power systems and provided a high quality of service. PURPA started a new chapter in the way the utilities have to deal with dispersed generation sites that not only produce small quantities of power relative to what utilities generate, but also are operated by organizations that are not in the business of producing electricity.

A utility's concern in allowing interconnections is that these systems will jeopardize the safety of utility personnel and the quality of service. During normal conditions the utility needs to know if the power produced by the cogeneration site will be entirely used by the customer or, if not, how much of the power will be sold to the utility. Moreover, it wants to ensure that the harmonic voltage and frequency tolerances of the dispersed generation site meet the grid tolerances. In emergencies, the utility must ensure that network faults are detected by the cogeneration device and are isolated from the grid and that service will be restored. Moreover, it must know that these units do not jeopardize the safety of utility personnel.

The utility electric distribution network is radial, which means that to isolate an area requires opening and locking a main circuit breaker. With cogeneration, the power network is no longer radial but a loop distribution. Therefore, it is crucial for the utility to record the location of all cogeneration units and have access to a manual load-break disconnect at all times. The interconnection requirements of a cogeneration system depend on interconnection voltage, transformer configuration, protection scheme, and on-site load and generation capacity.

There are two types of electric generators, synchronous and induction. A synchronous generator is one type commonly known for AC systems. It produces electricity at 60 Hz and can be connected to the grid by a synchronizing gear. The induction generator produces power at variable frequencies, and an inverter converts the power to synchronized 60 Hz before it is connected to the network. Induction generators are used for small units of up to a few megawatts. Larger units are invariably synchronous generators. Each of the two requires a different protection scheme.

The following are principal considerations involved in installing a cogeneration system and operating an electrical generator in parallel with a utility's electrical distribution system.

1. Type and operation scheme of the protective relay system to be installed.
2. Philosophy of operation and priority to be given to the utility power and cogenerated power in the event of outage of either system.
3. Intent with regard to exporting power to the utility distribution system from the cogeneration system. If power is not to be exported, the generator capacity will be sized to accommodate only the cogeneration on-site facilities base load.

The utility will specify minimum requirements and procedures for safe and effective connection and operation of customer-owned generation equipment on the utility electric distribution system. The customer should discuss the project plans with the utility and receive approvals early in the planning stage.

Utility Interconnection Requirements

In a utility distribution network the overcurrent equipment is arranged in a series of overlapping zones to clear a fault on a prearranged sequence of primary devices and backups. This is achieved with coordination of time-current characteristics of fuses, circuit breaker reclosers, sectionalizers, and relays from a substation. In a faulted condition the available current drops as it moves from the substation to the customer site because of an increase in systems impedance. Therefore, coordination is relatively simple. With a cogeneration interconnection, a bidirectional power flow on the distribution system can continue to energize a part of the network separated from the utility system reference source. Moreover, a cogeneration site can contribute additional overcurrent during faults that may cause the protection services to operate prematurely.

The high current level from the cogeneration site is over and above the available fault current from the utility. This will shorten the average melting time of the line fuses. On a 15-kV system a small synchronous cogeneration unit of a few megawatts can reduce the fuse melting time by better than 30 percent. For an induction generator the reduction in melting time is about one-third of the synchronous generator.

Another problem is with utilities' autoreclosures. The faults that occur with an overhead transmission system are usually momentary faults and are self-clearing. The autoreclosure closes the circuit a few cycles after the circuit was interrupted. In this way the customer downtime for such momentary faults will be minimal. With cogeneration in the system, although the utility breaker has interrupted the circuit, the fault is fed by this unit and does not get a chance to clear. Therefore, when the circuit is closed by the autoreclosure, the fault has not cleared; this means longer downtime for customers. The presence of cogeneration changes the available fault and the system coordination for in-house systems as well as the utility grid.

Utilities are also concerned with the problem of islanding. Islanding means that the cogeneration site is operating independently of the reference voltage and frequency of the utility power grid and is no longer in synchronism with it. Utility personnel might assume that by opening the linebreaker the circuit is de-energized. The generator voltage and frequency variations might cause damage to the load, which can be costly. If the utility breaker is closed without synchronizing the cogeneration unit, serious damage can also be incurred to the generator and breaker.

The harmonics generation from cogeneration sources must also be studied. Since for economic reasons the magnetic core of in-house generators is not made of the high-quality materials from which the utility-grade units are made, the core nonlinearities of cogeneration units will produce harmonics that cause problems with computers and other sensitive electronic equipment.

Most utilities have the following minimum requirements for customer-generated power connected parallel to the utility electrical distribution system:

1. The customer-owned cogeneration facility must be certified as a qualifying facility (small power producer or cogenerator as described in the Public Utility Regulatory Policies Act of 1978) prior to approval for interconnection.
2. The parallel connection of the customer's system to the public utility system must not adversely affect other customers, utilities, equipment, or personnel.
3. Protective devices (e.g., circuit breakers or relays) as specified by the utility must be installed by the customer at the cogenerator's location.
4. The customer must provide an automatic method of disconnecting the generating equipment from the utility system within ten cycles in case of a voltage deviation of plus 5 or minus 10 percent from normal.
5. Voltage flicker caused by the customer must be limited to 2 percent, as measured at the primary point of interconnection.
6. Voltage harmonics introduced by the customer's generating equipment cannot exceed 5 percent of the fundamental 60-Hz frequency for the square root of the sum of the squares of the harmonics and 2 percent of the fundamental 60-Hz frequency for any individual harmonic.

7. The operating frequency of the customer's generating equipment cannot deviate more than 0.2 Hz on a 60-Hz base. The generator shall automatically be disconnected from the utility within ten cycles if the frequency tolerance cannot be maintained.
8. The power factor of the customer's generator must be from 0.90 lagging to 0.90 leading at the generator terminals at all times.
9. The customer will disconnect his generator from the utility within 10 cycles if an outage is caused by a short circuit or ground on the utility system serving the customer's facilities.
10. The customer must provide and be connected to the utility system through a dedicated power transformer.
11. It will be the customer's responsibility to properly synchronize the generator output with the utility.
12 The customer generator shall be separable from the utility by a visible break disconnect device. This device will be accessible and allow padlocking in the open position by utility personnel.

Typical Protective Devices

Commonly used protective devices installed by the customer to satisfy the utility protection requirements are as follows:

Institute of Electrical and Electronics Engineers (IEEE)
Device Numbers and Function

15	Speed or Frequency Matching
25	Synchronizing Device
27	Under-Voltage Relay
32	Directional Power Relay
40	Field Relay
46	Phase—Balance Current Relay
47	Phase—Sequence Voltage Relay
50/51	Phase Over Current Relay
51G	Ground Over Current Relay
59	Over Voltage Relay
62	Time Delay Relay
67	Directional Over Current Relay
81	Over and Under Frequency Relay

Electric Service Outages

During preliminary planning of a cogeneration system, the priority to be assigned to the utility system and the generator system must be established. For short power outages on the utility power system, the circuit breaker that ties the generator output to the utility power system should be automatically opened to isolate the generator. The utility normally has two automatic reclosures of the circuit breaker that feeds the distribution system. The first reclosure is usually within two or three cycles, and the second occurs within ten to fifteen cycles. These two reclosures restore power to the distribution system within a few cycles. The generator system can then be resynchronized with the utility system, either automatically or manually, and the circuit breaker that ties the generator output to the utility system can then be closed to resume parallel operation.

If the utility outage is for a longer period of time and power is not restored to the distribution system after the two automatic reclosures, consideration must be given to power requirements of the cogenerator's on-site facilities. When the generating capacity is insufficient to meet all requirements, some type of load-shedding control is required.

Typically, when utility power fails, a protective relay associated with the utility interconnection circuit breaker operates, disconnecting the utility power system from the generator output. Simultaneously, a signal is sent to the control system, indicating that utility power has failed. At this time, shedding of designated nonessential loads begins to reduce the overall load to within the output capacity of the generator. At this point, the generator system functions as a standard emergency power system. When utility power is restored, the generator is synchronized with the utility power, the two systems are reparalleled, the load-shedding controls are deactivated, and the loads are reconnected to the bus system.

Consideration must also be given to the possibility that, should the cogenerator unit be out of service for any reason, and normal utility power interrupted for an extended period of time, the generator is capable of "black start" conditions, that is, starting without normal utility power. The required electrical components needed to start the cogeneration system under black start conditions will determine the kW size of the required emergency generator set.

47.6 DESIGN CRITERIA—MECHANICAL SYSTEM SELECTION

The most prevalent cogeneration system of colleges and universities is the topping cycle, where fuel energy is first converted to electric power and the rejected heat used as thermal energy. This system offers the following methods for recovering thermal energy:

- Steam generation from heat recovery steam generator.
- Direct use of the exhaust from the combustion engine or gas turbine by a multistage absorption chiller-heater.
- Hot water generation from a heat recovery hot water generator.

The existing cooling and heating systems serving the facility strongly influence the choice of the method to meet the thermal and electric power needs. The type of existing central plant largely determines the most economical method for recovering thermal energy. For example, a steam generation system will normally be most economical when it supplements an existing steam system. This type of system makes the thermal energy available for use in providing all campus utility services. Moreover, existing boilers can provide standby service during periods of scheduled and unscheduled maintenance outages.

Where the steam or hot water demand of the institution during the warm months is less than the thermal energy available from the cogeneration unit, the incorporation of multistage absorption chillers as the primary source of chilled water may be considered. Either an exhaust gas absorption unit or a steam absorption unit can be used. The advantage of using the more efficient direct-fired absorption unit should be weighed against the more flexible steam-fired units. The steam unit flexibility results from the capability to divert steam to other uses when the absorption chiller unit is at reduced loads.

The combined cycle cogeneration system can utilize thermal energy generated by the topping cycle to provide additional electrical power using a steam turbine generator. This type of system offers efficient use of available thermal energy, and is most efficient when large quantities of thermal energy are available. If the combined cycle cogeneration system is interconnected with most utilities, it must comply with the PURPA operation and efficiency standards for a qualifying facility.

Unless a large amount of waste fuel or combustible solid waste is available, the bottoming cycle is normally not a viable system for colleges and universities.

Bottoming cycle cogeneration systems first apply energy to an individual process. The hot exhaust gas is then used to produce steam, which is used to produce electricity. Refuse recovery cogeneration plants are considered to be bottoming cycle systems. If oil or gas is the majority fuel, PURPA's 45 percent operating efficiency standard is applicable.

Ideally, the thermal and electrical needs of a cogeneration system should always match, but in reality they do not often follow the same demand patterns. If this were the case, there would not be any need to buy or sell power to the utility. Therefore, it becomes important to design the system to match one of the two.

In the case of thermal match, steam is generated at substantially higher pressure and temperature than required by the process. The steam may pass through a combination of back pressure and extraction turbines. The electricity generated could be higher or lower than the facility needs, and occasionally it might be the same. This requires a simultaneous buy and sell agreement with the utility.

On the other hand, if the electrical needs are to be matched, it might be economical to maximize generation at one level. Here the necessary agreement with the utility might be for purchase, sale, or a buy and sell agreement depending on the size of the cogeneration unit and the electric demand variation of the facility.

There are basically three different technologies used to power the cogeneration prime mover: steam turbines, gas turbines, and reciprocating engines.

Steam Turbines

A steam turbine is a prime mover that converts the steam energy into rotary motions. The main part of a turbine is a disc mounted on a shaft that has many curved vanes attached to its rim. There is a nozzle out of which the steam comes to the vanes tangentially or at an angle. There are many types of turbines based on the number of step reductions in steam momentum, direction of steam flow, pressure of steam, terminal pressure, or source of the steam. But a common classification is impulse and reaction.

A turbine that utilizes the impulsive force of high-velocity steam is called an impulse turbine. On the other hand, a turbine that makes use of the reaction force—opposite in the flow of steam—produced by the flow of steam nozzle is a reaction turbine. In an impulse turbine the steam directed against the paddle wheel causes the rotation. The pressure drop occurs in the stationary nozzle while the moving paddle absorbs the steam's velocity. To obtain the most economic condition the moving element should be traveling at one-half the steam velocity. This would mean excessive speeds for large turbines. To overcome this problem the pressure staging principal is used. In other words, a limited pressure drop is allowed in every set of nozzles and additional sets of nozzles will exist for every set of rotating elements.

In a reaction turbine the pressure drop takes place in the rotating element. The reaction turbine also has stationary and moving blades. The blades are arranged in such a way that the steam leaves the blades with less pressure than when it entered. This is accomplished by restricting the outlet of the blades that causes the steam velocity to increase. The reaction turbine can be viewed as an expasion nozzle that converts steam pressure to increase steam velocity, which in turn is converted into mechanical energy.

Steam turbines have high overall efficiency and reliability and can use different types of fuel. One of the best uses for the steam turbine is to burn solid fuel such as solid waste, coal, tree bark, and wood chips. Fluidized bed boilers offer greater fuel flexibility, especially in burning high sulphur coals and other solid fuels and waste with sufficient sulphur dioxide (SOx) and nitrogen oxide (NOx) control without any additional flue gas cleanup system. Bubbling bed technology is an older technology that can achieve efficiencies between 70 and 80 percent.

Circulating fluidized bed (CFB) boilers have only been commercially available since 1985 and can achieve efficiencies of 97 percent with fly ash reinjection. There are about half a dozen CFB boilers operating in the United States and more than a dozen under construction, including projects at the University of Missouri, Columbia, the University of Iowa, and Iowa State Universtiy. The appropriate range of the steam turbine is between a few hundred kW and more than one hundred mW. Some of the steam turbine disadvantages are lower electricity-to-steam ratio, higher unit cost, long installation time, longer start-up time, and larger space requirement.

Gas Turbines

A gas turbine consists of a compressor where air is compressed adiabatically, and a combustion chamber where the fuel is burned with air. The combustion product is expanded adiabatically in the turbine that develops the work that will drive the compressor as well as the external equipment, which in the case of the cogeneration will be the electrical generator. The thermal efficiency of a gas turbine increases with increased pressure ratios. The pressure ratio is related to the temperature ratio of the turbine inlet temperature and the compressor inlet temperature. For a fixed atmospheric condition, the higher the turbine inlet temperature, the higher the efficiency. What limits this temperature is the turbine materials.

Gas turbine cogeneration systems have many attractive advantages, namely a high power-to-heat ratio, low capital operating and maintenance costs, shorter construction time, lower required square footage, and high overall thermal efficiency. The main disadvantage is the limited fuel range and relatively shorter service life. That is why large gas turbine cogeneration systems are not economically attractive in areas where the electrical utility generation is coal based. Gas is more expensive than solid fuels for the same quantity of thermal energy.

Reciprocating Machines

The reciprocating cogeneration system has the highest electricity-to-steam ratio. This is due to the thermodynamic difference between reciprocating cycle, where almost two-thirds of the waste heat is rejected in the form of low-temperature energy, and gas turbine, where waste heat is in the form of high-temperature exhaust gas. The other advantages over the gas turbine are high part-load efficiency and lower sensitivity to ambient air temperature. The disadvantages of the reciprocating cycle, however, are higher capital and maintenance costs and possible environmental problems. Reciprocating systems are most suitable for small commercial applications up to a few hundred kW.

Cheng Cycle

The economic factors for running a cogeneration system vary drastically when a more complicated electric rate structure with demand charges, standby charges, energy charges, and time-of-day electric load is optimized with thermal load. One way of overcoming this drawback of the traditional cogeneration system is to use the Cheng Cycle, which has the ability to produce virtually infinite combinations of electricity and steam output. The Cheng Cycle, developed by Dr. Dah Yu Cheng of International Power Technology (IPT), consists of a gas turbine with a matched waste heat recovery steam generator (HRSG). Steam is generated at any temperature and various pressures. When the steam required by the process exceeds the amount produced by recovering gas turbine exhaust gas energy, more fuel can be burned in the duct work between the gas tubine and HRSG. Such a process has a high thermal efficiency for converting supplementary fuel fired for thermal energy.

The operating regime of the Cheng Cycle is shown in Figure 47-1. Normally the system will operate along Lines 1, 2, or 3, or within Region A. Lines 1 and 2 designate electric and thermal output for rated turbines inlet temperature and varying level of steam injection. At Point 2, no steam is injected so the electric and thermal output is equal to the gas turbine. At Point 1, all thermal energy produced from waste heat is injected back to the turbine and a generating efficiency of 39 percent is achieved; while at Point 2, the generating efficiency is 27 percent with a cogeneration efficiency of 86 percent. In Region A the addition of supplemental heat in HRSG allows any combination of thermal and electrical output. Region B represents lower turbine firing temperatures; while in Region C, the electrical output is reduced by turbine derating and absence of steam injection.

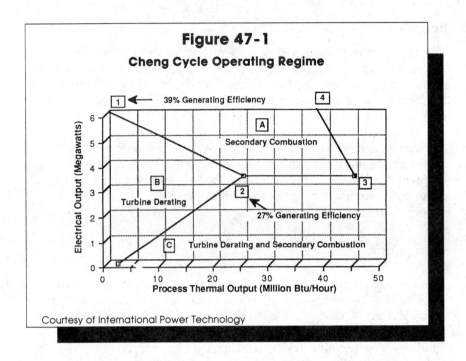

Figure 47-1

Cheng Cycle Operating Regime

Courtesy of International Power Technology

There are three basic modes of operation for a Cheng Cycle. Under normal mode the system works along Lines 1, 2, and 3 where thermal demand is met and the electric output floats. During time intervals where the electric rate is highest, the system operates along Lines 1 to 4 to maximize electrical output. The steam load might or might not be met. On the other hand, when the utility buyback rate is low or the utility interconnection is down, the system will match the thermal and electric needs of the facility. The operating point in this case can be anywhere in Region A, B, or C.

Another advantage of a Cheng Cycle is the low level of NOx emission. Conventional gas turbines have NOx emission rates of 30 to 40 parts per million (ppm) while the Cheng Cycle can achieve an average emission rate below 25 ppm.

47.7 SYSTEM CONFIGURATION

The feasibility study for total energy requirements determines the optimum cogeneration total energy output. The cogeneration system configuration should also be selected at this time, based on the following considerations.

Capital Cost Factors

The initial capital cost must be known to assess the payback period of a prospective system.

Fuel Costs and Electric Power Rates

Escalation rates for fuel and purchased electrical power plus standby electrical charges must be carefully evaluated. Should electric rates escalate faster than the fuel prices, the payout of the system will be sooner than that originally planned. When fuel prices escalate faster, the payout period will be extended. Thorough evaluation, using projections and assumptions where necessary, is required to determine the economic benefits of a prospective cogeneration system.

Operation Cost Factors

Peak Capacity   Output plus maximum on-line operating time require careful evaluation to accurately assess payout periods. All scheduled outages should be included. For planning purposes, an operating on-line performance of 90 to 95 percent is considered achievable. Plant shutdown, variations in steam demand, utility power failures, utility voltage variation, and failures in central plant auxiliary support elements will cause lower operating time for the cogeneration units. As the actual outages decrease below the assumed outages of the study, the payback increases.

Operating Personnel   A properly staffed and trained operating team is essential to achieving the maximum savings available from a well-designed system. The overall operation plant for a new cogeneration system should provide for the stationary operators to be experienced, and properly trained by the manufacturer's operating and start-up engineers.

Maintenance Cost Factors   To assure safe and productive operations, a well-trained maintenance staff is essential. Maintenance personnel and operators perform first-line maintenance tasks. The procurement contract normally provides for three to five years of technical assistance by the manufacturer, plus an operations and maintenance manual prepared by the design engineer. This assistance is extremely important during the first three years of operation. The operations and maintenance manual should include the required major preventive maintenance work to be performed on the prime mover and generator under the guidance of the manufacturer's maintenance engineers. All critical spare parts required for the safe and reliable operation of the system should be specified and stocked. Filters and other consumables must be available on short notice. Plans should be made for utilizing the services of an outside test laboratory for all testing services. The life of system mechanical components is largely dependent on the accuracy of the analysis of oil and water samples.

Plant Overhead During Construction   Added workhours for utility tie-ins, system outages, and additional operations support should be included in the capital cost for the system.

Selection of Prime Mover

Several options are available in configuring the cogeneration system for a college or a university. Many small capacity systems are prepackaged utilizing internal combustion engines. First cost for the larger internal combustion engines is usually higher than for gas turbines due to the cost of equipment foundation, exhaust emissions abatement, heat reclaim systems, and fuel systems. Vibration problems are greater, noise levels are higher, and the cost of multiple-level heat reclaim is higher. Air emissions and maintenance costs are higher than for combustion gas turbines of the same size. Where thermal energy requirements are small and vary over a wide range, the internal combustion engine can be a good choice, especially if the thermal energy pressures and temperature levels do not exceed 15 pounds per square inch (psi) or 250°F, the highest allowable limits in an internal combustion engine water jacket.

Other benefits derived with a gas combustion turbine prime mover are its quiet operation when equipped with acoustic control equipment, lower vibration, lower exhaust emission of NOx, carbon monoxide (CO), and hydrocarbons; lower lubricating oil costs; and longer run time between overhaul and maintenance service.

One natural gas pressure to the facility is important. When sufficient gas pressure is available, the parasitic load of a natural gas compressor is not required.

Combustion gas turbines offer an additional feature not available in the case of internal combustion engines—the efficient supplemental gas burners in the exhaust from the turbine to the heat recovery boiler. This can be used when additional steam generating capacity is needed. On internal combustion engines, a gas burner will not function due to the absence or scarcity of oxygen in the exhaust gas. Electrical heaters are used in lieu of gas heaters to realize higher efficiencies. With gas heaters, operating efficiencies up to 90 percent are possible.

When short periods of part-load operation are planned for the cogeneration unit and a gas turbine is selected, a two-shaft gas turbine can be considered. Two-shaft turbines are designed with separate shafts for the turbine compressor and the power turbine units. This allows the rotating speed of the compressor to be controlled by the load requirements of the power turbine, rather than the speed of the compressor. The two-shaft turbine is capable of maintaining higher exhaust gas temperatures, and thus greater operating efficiencies, at part-load.

Gas combustion turbines' exhaust gas temperatures are in the range of 900°F to 1,000°F, in comparison with 1,000°F to 1,200°F for exhaust gases of internal combustion engines. The weight of exhaust gases from a gas turbine is approximately 3.3 times greater than from an internal combustion engine for the same level of thermal energy (15 to 150 psi steam). The lubrication oil temperature for a gas turbine is about 160°F, while that of the internal combustion engine is about 200°F. Water jacket temperature for internal combustion engines ranges from 180°F to 200°F.

Internal combustion engines offer more efficient operation at part-load with high mechanical efficiency. Exhaust gas temperatures are usually higher than for gas turbines, but the heat generating capacity per brake horsepower output is less than that of the gas turbine. When thermal loads are low and the electrical power requirements are variable, an internal combustion engine may be a good choice, providing the above-stated inherent disadvantage presents fewer problems than a gas turbine.

Thermal Energy—Heat Reclaim Equipment

The cogeneration system's thermal energy can be used effectively for the generation of chilled water, as well as for the heating needs of the university or college. The exhaust heat from the prime mover can be used directly with an exhaust gas lithium-bromide absorption chiller. Simultaneous hot water generation is also possible with the absorption chiller. Where a central steam distribution system exists, the conversion of the exhaust heat to steam using a heat reclaim boiler provides supplemental steam as needed to meet the campus requirements and to generate chilled water, using either absorption chillers or turbine chillers for the central system. In the heating season the campus steam demand would increase while steam for cooling would decrease. In the summer season the opposite would occur.

The thermal energy requirements for lithium-bromide absorption chiller units are as follows:

	Steam Pressure (psi)	Steam Rate (#/hr/ton)	Hot Water (°F)
Single stage	8-15	17.5/18.0	270
Two-stage parallel flow	43-130	9.9/10.6	300-400
Two-stage series flow	15-150	12	300-400

Two-stage lithium-bromide absorption units are manufactured in two concepts, parallel and series. The parallel flow chillers are lower in height and the larger units are smaller in width than the series units.

The parallel chillers can be delivered as an assembled unit, while the larger capacity series units may require, because of height, final assembly at the installation.

At part-load conditions, the per ton-hour steam consumption of two-stage series flow absorber chillers decreases slightly as compared to the constant steam consumption per ton-hour of the parallel flow absorber units. The parallel flow design allows the absorber chiller to operate safely at lower temperatures and lower pressures without causing crystallization of lithium-bromide. The increased efficiency of the parallel flow absorber chiller is partially due to the utilization of the heat of the (refrigerant) water vapor released in the first stage generator to drive off additional refrigerant water vapor in the second stage.

Steam Turbines

Noncondensing turbines used to drive centrifugal chillers are often used in series with steam absorption chillers. The exhaust steam of the turbine is supplied to the absorption chiller, with the condensate returned to the steam generator feed-water heater. The turbine chiller produces one-third of the total load and the absorber chiller produces the remaining two-thirds. To provide sufficient steam energy for the turbine to develop the necessary shaft horsepower and to provide an exhaust steam pressure in the range necessary for efficient absorber-chiller operation, the inlet steam pressure to the turbine is at least 400 psi. The exhaust steam from a noncondensing turbine can be used for other steam services such as heating, cooking, and laboratory services.

47.8 SYSTEM OPERATIONS

To provide for the successful operation of a cogeneration system, the following instructions should be stated:

1. Define the procedures and responsibilities of the operating staff. The qualifications of all operators must be evaluated with regard to responsibilities in the operating or the cogeneration system. Before the system is commissioned, formal training should be conducted for each operator on each major component of the system. This training is usually obtained from the manufacturer. Approximately one month prior to commissioning, the construction contractor should furnish operations and maintenance manuals to the operating staff.

At the time of commissioning of the system, all operators should be instructed by the contractor's start-up engineers and operators on operating procedures.
2. Define data acquisition. All operator logs should be developed and available at the time of system commissioning. The data recorded by operators, or by central energy control, is needed to determine component performance, maintenance needs, information required by equipment manufacturers, information required by the utility company (run time of cogeneration system) for standby service, and to evaluate the cost avoidance achieved by the cogeneration system.

47.9 MAINTENANCE

A successful system requires a well-planned maintenance program incorporating the following:

1. Responsibility for first-line maintenance tasks such as filter changes, oil inspection including laboratory analysis, checking and corrections of any oil leaks, and normal maintenance of water treatment systems. This is normally performed by plant personnel. Oil analysis is performed by a qualified laboratory, with the oil samples obtained by plant personnel.
2. Arrangements for scheduled maintenance, such as a periodic inspection of the gas turbine for engine wear to be performed by the technical staff of the manufacturer. This technical support can be specified in the construction contract specifications. All of the necessary technical information should be contained in the operation and maintenance manuals.
3. The identification and stocking of all expendable supplies.
4. A listing of critical spare parts, price, and availability to be included in all operation and maintenance manuals.
5. Identification of outside services by time period. Services such as instrumentation maintenance for controls, boiler and chiller major maintenance, and vibration and environmental testing should be contracted for if the capability does not exist at the plant.

Cogeneration Impact

Within the 1980s cogeneration has jumped from 4 percent to 7 percent of the nation's electric supply; the Department of Energy (DOE) predicts it will approach 15 percent by the year 2000. Cogeneration has been a means for dodging electric rate increases, but in the meantime, electric utilities in many parts of the country have successfully formulated barriers to cogeneration by adopting tariffs that penalize cogeneration systems.

For instance, special deals are offered to customers to encourage them to stay on the system, or a denial of standby power is threatened if a project is owned and operated by third parties. Standby power became an especially important issue after the ruling that denied Alcon, Inc. (Puerto Rico) standby power; FERC did not find Alcon to be the owner or the operator. In some instances, for long-term contract requirement utilities have established requirements they themselves do not have to meet.

Another problem facing cogenerators is the lack of clearly defined regulations regarding wheeling of power. Wheeling is the selling of electricity to a nonadjacent customer using the utility's power grid or power network.

Although Florida, Indiana, and Texas have required utilities to provide wheeling service to cogenerators, it is still an area of concern. PURPA also has not specifically addressed sale of power by cogenerators to nonutility entities. Public Utility Commissions (PUCs) have encouraged the development of standard contracts that leave little or no room to negotiate for avoided cost methodologies and rates. Nonetheless, California, Connecticut, Florida, and Virginia have done so, and several other states are in the process. In California cogeneration projects have faced two other hurdles: a milestone procedure in which certain goals must be met within specific time frames to preserve the right to sell the power contracted to the utility, standards to limit NOx to 42 ppm, which might cause problems for some gas turbines.

Recently two other external factors helped the cogeneration marketplace. These were the potential tax benefits offered by investment tax credits (ITCs) and depreciation deductions under the accelerated cost recovery system (ACRS); both encouraged third-party financing of projects. But the tax changes of 1986 eliminated ITC and reduced ACRS benefits with immediate tax write-offs. This will sharply reduce cogeneration ventures, which had been justified by large tax benefits.

Does this mean that cogeneration projects will no longer be economically feasible? The answer is no. It means that projects that were originally justified with large tax benefits or large quantities of power sold to the utilities will cease to be attractive. Most cogeneration projects will now be built solely to meet in-house power requirements. A sharp decline will occur in the number of cogeneration projects with 30 mW or more; in contrast there will be a sharp increase in the small package cogeneration market. According to a study by Frost and Sullivan there is a five to seven billion dollar market for small packaged cogeneration units under 5 mW between now and the year 2000. International business information companies predict that cogeneration capacity in the

United States will increase from 17,750 mW to 40,000 mW, and about 7,000 mW will be from facilities below 5 mW.

The potential market for small packaged systems will be shopping centers, apartment complexes, hotels and motels, supermarkets, laundries, and other businesses. The cost range of these systems is between $1,300 to $2,000 per kW. One manufacturer of small package cogeneration has marketed a system rated at 6 to 8 kW electrical with 55,000 Btus/hour of usable heat. This unit is 2.5 by 2.5 by 5 feet in size, weighs about 680 pounds, runs on natural gas, and costs $10,000 to $12,000. The company hopes that this scaled-down model becomes as popular in new homes as air conditioning.

Cogeneration Economics

Ideally with a cogeneration system, a match will exist between the thermal and the electrical needs. In reality such a case will be an exception. Normally, a cogeneration system is sized to match the electrical demand or the thermal demand. In the first case, if there is a shortage of thermal energy, an auxiliary boiler is brought on line. If there is an excess, the steam is sold to a third party or used for running absorbers.

On the other hand, if the thermal demand is matched by the system, any extra electricity produced is sold to the utility. If there is a shortfall, the remaining electricity is bought from the local utility. A feasibility study requires the following data:

1. Determine current and projected electrical hourly demands and thermal needs for a full year.
2. Calculate what is going to be the total energy cost for the full year without cogeneration.
3. Determine a certain cogeneration size based on the earlier discussion on matching the electrical or thermal demand.
4. Using the previously determined load profile, match expected electrical output and in-house demand to determine the increment sold to purchased from the utility. Ensure scheduled and expected unscheduled downtime is accounted for.
5. Determine the standby and emergency power purchases needed from the utility including the cost.
6. Determine the rate schedule for the sale or purchase of the electric power from the utility.
7. Determine the fuel cost for the cogeneration as well as any auxiliary boiler that might be needed. If natural gas is used as the primary fuel, additional effort is needed to determine the optimal rate schedule. This is due to a variety of options, i.e., third-party supplier, interruptible gas, fixed price, or variable price gas.

8. Determine the operation and maintenance costs of the cogeneration system. Also calculate the capital cost of the cogeneration system over its useful life.
9. Use the time value of money (net present value technique) to determine the financial viability of the project.

A number of options for financing cogeneration projects exist. Some of the common ones are:

1. Conventional approach. Here the project will be owned in its entirety by the institution. The source of capital can be internal fund, borrowed capital, or a combination of the two.
2. Joint ventures. The project ownership is shared by more than one institution. To comply with PURPA, a public utility cannot own more than 50 percent of the project.
3. Leasing. In this approach the cogeneration project is built by venture capital and the plant is leased by the institution.
4. Third-party ownership. If the institution wants to remain at a distance from the credit support of the project, including the operation and maintenance problems, a venture capital entity can build and operate the plant. The institution will be entering into a contract for purchase of electricity and steam from the third-party entity.
5. Guaranteed savings. This is more common in smaller-sized package cogeneration systems. Here a developer will offer to install, maintain, and operate the unit, and the host institution will receive a fixed guaranteed savings.

47.10 CONCLUSION

Today the cogeneration market has moved beyond the original intentions of PURPA. The Industrial Fuel Use Act (FUA) of 1978 barred utilities from building new gas- and oil-fired generating plants. This resulted in an increase of availability and a reduction in cost of natural gas, which encouraged more cogeneration and small production systems. As the cost of coal- and nuclear-based electricity grew, larger industrial customers left the system, which further added to the utilities' reliance to increase rather than decrease their dependence on natural gas. This problem will be more obvious when gas supplies drop and prices rise.

Cogeneration has also been responsible for the structural changes that electrical utilities are experiencing. Utilities have had to examine the deregulation of electric utility transmission systems, diversify into non-regulated subsidiaries, and become more competitive in the energy market.

New legislation has emerged at the state level. For instance, cogenerators in California can sell power to adjacent sites. In Connecticut utilities are required to offer thirty-year contracts and provide wheeling to other in-state or out-of-state utilities.

Cogeneration as a means of providing lower costs for electrical and thermal energy to college and university campuses will become more attractive as rate schedules for electrical power continue to escalate.

Substantial economic benefits are possible from a carefully planned, properly designed and constructed, efficiently operated cogeneration system. Careful planning results from an accurate analysis of the energy needs of the facility. A properly designed and constructed system is achieved by carefully evaluating all viable system configurations and major components. Efficient operations result from maximum peak load operating hours, a good preventive maintenance program, and well-qualified operation and maintenance staff. Each of the above factors requires professionalism by all physical plant personnel involved with the project. In conclusion, cogeneration has come a long way, is here to stay, and is going to be a viable option for many institutions.

ADDITIONAL RESOURCES

Bathie, William W. *Fundamentals of Gas Turbines.* New York: John Wiley & Sons, 1984.

Butler, Charles H. *Cogeneration: Engineering, Design, Financing, and Regulatory Compliance.* New York: McGraw-Hill, 1984.

Goble, Robert Lloyd and Wendy Coleman Goble. *Cogeneration: A Campus Option?* Washington: APPA, 1980.

Graham, Frank D. *Power Plant Engineers Guide.* New York: The Bobbs-Merrill Company, Inc., 1983.

Limaye, Dilip R. *Planning Cogeneration Systems.* Lilburn, Georgia: The Fairmont Press, 1985.

Payne, F. William. *Cogeneration Sourcebook.* Lilburn, Georgia: The Fairmont Press, 1985.

Spiewak, Scott A. *Cogeneration & Small Production Manual.* Lilburn, Georgia: The Fairmont Press, 1987.

Woodruff, Everett B. et al. *Steam Plant Operation.* New York: McGraw-Hill, 1984.

CHAPTER 48

Telecommunications Systems

Steve Harward
Director of Telecommunications
University of North Carolina at Chapel Hill

48.1 INTRODUCTION

Today's physical plant administrators at institutions of higher education oversee a wide variety of support services. The diversity of these responsibilities precludes technical competence in each area. This is particularly true in the rapidly changing field of telecommunications.

The traditional role of physical plant as a provider of telecommunications services has evolved rapidly in recent years as colleges and universities have assumed greater responsibility for their telephone systems, and other data and video communications technologies have come into use. This has resulted in the evolution of the physical plant director's role through several stages:

1. Facilitator—responsible for the coordination of basic telephone services. All technical services are typically provided by a third party such as the local exchange carrier, AT&T, or a communications "interconnect" firm. Only basic support services such as centralized operator services and coordination with physical plant trades are provided.
2. Caretaker—assuming additional responsibility for budgeting, cost reallocation, and centralized record keeping.
3. Service provider—providing most or all support for the procurement, installation, and maintenance of telephone system hardware and related services.
4. Systems integrator—responsible for voice, data, and video communications. Uses various technologies to integrate all communications services, including conducting long-range strategic planning.

Following a lengthy antitrust suit against AT&T, first filed by MCI in 1974 over long distance and computer issues, the Department of Justice decided to address the need for competition in the telecommunications industry in a more general sense. In 1982 the Department of Justice, under the leadership of Judge Harold Greene, began to negotiate the operational details of restructuring AT&T and its subsidiaries. In 1984 the Bell operating companies were divested from the parent AT&T, and a new era of competition in the local and long distance telecommunications industry began.

As a result of divestiture, many universities that had depended on the telephone company for equipment and local exchange services faced the dilemma of obtaining required services from different suppliers. Divestiture also triggered speculation that traditional "Centrex" services would migrate to customer-owned, on-premise private branch exchanges (PBXs). These developments caused many universities to initiate plans to acquire their own telephone communications systems, employ technical staffs to install and maintain these systems, and seek greater control of their telecommunications costs.

These events have presented a difficult challenge to the physical plant administrator having responsibility for the telecommunications function. Rapidly changing technological alternatives, organizational issues, service to a wide range of telecommunications needs, new long distance alternatives, and the cost of telecommunications services have displaced the simpler prior concerns of telephone company rate increases.

To deal effectively with these issues and to manage the operation of large institutional telecommunications networks, it has become necessary for most colleges and universities to turn to the professional telecommunications manager. This is best evidenced by the increased membership in professional organizations such as the Association of College and University Telecommunications Administrators (ACUTA).

The remainder of this chapter is devoted to providing the facilities manager with a better understanding of factors that have influenced the role of telecommunications within the university environment today, modern telecommunications technology, and related information—all of which emphasize the need for the telecommunications department to become a communication systems integrator.

48.2 FACTORS AFFECTING THE ROLE OF TELECOMMUNICATIONS

While external factors such as divestiture and legal proceedings have had a dramatic impact on telecommunications, many factors within educational institutions have created a new interest in telecommunications in academia. These factors have caused modern telecommunications systems and networks to be perceived as a university resource rather than a utility. Telecommunications can enhance the ability of colleges and universities to accomplish their primary missions of instruction and research. An understanding of these factors, described below, is important in understanding the telecommunications needs of the college or university.

Computers and Networking

One of the primary influences on the role of telecommunications at universities is the widespread use of microcomputers for administrative and academic applications. The trend toward local, microcomputer-based computing initially took the form of a growing number of stand-alone microcomputers used for basic word processing and spreadsheet applications. This trend was spurred by declining costs for computer hardware and memory, a growing number of applications programs, and increased computer literacy among university administrators, faculty, and students. An outgrowth of this localization of computing was the need to establish communications networks among peer and host systems for the purpose of sharing programs, downloading files, and transmitting mail electronically. Many of these networks were truly local in the extent of their geographic coverage, and decisions regarding the type of network to be used were frequently made without considerations of other campus networks.

Today, however, there are demands to provide communications between these local networks. Additionally, access to large data bases such as library card catalogs and the use of university computers as nodes on regional or nationwide networks have extended the scope of networking requirements. The continuing demand to provide communications connectivity among host computers, remote terminals, stand-alone workstations, and local or regional networks has become a primary focus of many telecommunications planners.

Video Communications

Video communications on university campuses today is required for the following: delivery of interactive instruction to remote classrooms, residence halls, and remote campuses; the transmission of high resolution images for clinical evaluation and research; the delivery of entertainment television programming to residence halls; access to video tape or disc libraries; and teleconferencing.

The requirement for the provision of large amounts of bandwidth to support these video applications has resulted in the implementation of separate broad-band or fiber optic networks. Although the need for data communications networks has been more pervasive, decisions regarding the network medium and topology have frequently been made on the basis of the video requirements.

Voice Communications

The importance of basic voice telecommunications services has often been overshadowed by new demands for data and video communications services. The reliability of the telephone network may have resulted in a lack of realization of its extreme importance as a basic means of communicating. The Centrex or PBX continues to be the communications workhorse for most institutions by processing millions of calls each year. Improvements to voice switching systems that allow the transmission and switching of high-speed data communications channels, the integration of voice and data using the same terminal device and distribution facility, and the use of voice storage and forwarding technology to provide integrated voice-mail systems have brought to university administrators a renewed sense of the importance of the telephone system.

It is conceivable that further technological advances will eventually allow for the total integration of voice, data, and video communications by providing for the establishment of a voice connection, the display of text, and a video image from a single workstation.

Planning

Significant capital investments in new telecommunications systems and associated plant improvements by colleges and universities are another manifestation of the changing role of telecommunications. These investments represent commitments to the use of telecommunications technology by the highest levels of administration. Due to the magnitude of these investments which can be tens of millions of dollars, it is important that planning for telecommunications improvements be closely coordinated with other university planning processes.

The financing of major telecommunications equipment and systems, such as for the installation of a new campus telephone system, often requires special appropriations by state legislatures or private governing boards, the sale of bonds, or third-party financing. The development of a budget proposal for these expenditures, the evaluation of financing alternatives, and the associated approval processes can consume months and involve numerous university administrators. These expenditures must normally compete with other critical university requirements, so the planning must be with the same detail, accuracy, and articulation of need.

It is important that the telecommunications plan be coordinated with other university capital improvement and land use plans. New university buildings or major renovations of existing structures can substantially add to the line requirement and the need for outside plant improvements for new telephone systems. These possible future improvements should be identified in the planning of a new campus telephone system to ensure that sufficient switching capabilities are designed in the system at cutover and that adequate funding is provided for an appropriately sized switch. After cutover of a new system, it is necessary to continually evaluate the impact of new building projects on the configuration and cost of operating the telephone system.

Plans for changes or additions to academic and administrative computer systems can have a significant impact on the utilization of campus telecommunications facilities. The implementation of computer networks may increase the traffic-handling requirements of a digital PBX or require the installation of separate fiber optic, twisted pair copper, or coaxial cable networks in existing underground telecommunications ducts. Because of the dependency of computer networks on telecommunications, it is essential that these planning processes be carefully coordinated. The desired level of coordination may be more difficult to achieve at institutions with separate telecommunications and computing administrative reporting structures. However, the integration of computer and telecommunications planning is necessary to ensure that appropriate services are available for computer networking and data communications support.

Committees

The use of committees in the decision-making process of universities is traditional. It has only been in recent years that committees have played a significant role in the formulation of plans and recommendations for major telecommunications purchases. Today it is common for a university committee to conduct an exhaustive study of an institution's telecommunications needs and make recommendations regarding specific technologies that should be acquired. The composition of these committees should embody the diverse needs of the university as the role of the committee often extends beyond the evaluation of a major system purchase. Committees also establish interface and protocol standards for campus networks and monitor and evaluate the effects of changes in technology on campus telecommunications needs.

Goals and Objectives

APPA has stated that the basic purpose of the plant department is to aid in the creation of a physical environment for education and research, to operate and maintain the physical plant portion of this environment, and to provide services that enhance the use of facilities. This summarizes the role of telecommunications as a supporting service that can be used to help the institution achieve its primary goals and objectives.

A responsibility of the physical plant administrator is communicating institutional goals to telecommunications personnel. It is not necessary that these goals be narrowly defined or limited to those to be accomplished in a short period of time. Rather, each goal should relate to the underlying mission of the institution and provide guidance to the telecommunications manager in setting appropriate objectives. Although all educational institutions share many common goals, there will generally be differing priorities, e.g., improved classroom instruction, research, continuing education, cost containment, and higher student enrollment. Through effective planning, specific objectives can be developed that clearly define how telecommunications can enhance the attainment of these goals.

48.3 TELECOMMUNICATIONS

Voice and Data Switching

Centrex and Private Automatic Branch Exchange (PABX) systems have been the primary voice communications systems of colleges and universities. Centrex is a service provided by the telephone company and the switching function is typically performed by equipment located in the company's central office. Connections to other Centrex users, to the local exchange, and to long distance parties are established by the central office equipment. In conventional Centrex systems, all station lines are connected to the central office by a dedicated pair of wires. PABXs are owned or leased by universities and are located on university property. The PABX performs similar switching functions as the Centrex but with a minimum number of connections to the telephone company's network. Station lines are connected to the PABX rather than the central office. Both Centrex and PABX systems have been used because of their ability to support large numbers of connections and their wide range of features. These systems have also enabled universities to implement centralized management and cost controls. Until recently, most Centrex systems and PABXs were based on analog technology in which voice signals were reproduced based on varying electrical characteristics.

Technological developments that have had a significant impact on Centrex and PABX systems are the use of computer systems to control the switching process (stored program control) and the use of digital switching technology. By improving its ability to rapidly process large numbers of switched connections and to use signaling techniques native to the data communications industry, these developments have made it possible for the "telephone" switch to serve both voice and data communications requirements. The primary benefits realized by the integration of voice and data technology have been the shared use of building wiring for voice and data communications and the use of a single system to provide switched connections for voice and data users.

Wire sharing reduces the cost of new installations, permits new uses of existing telephone wiring, and simplifies the task of managing wiring systems. Despite the advantages of wire sharing, distance limitations of 2,000 to 5,000 feet for the transmission of digital signals over standard telephone wiring impose severe constraints on systems used to support both voice and data communications. Additionally, the maximum data rate supported by standard telephone wiring is 19.2 to 64 thousand bits per second (Kbps). Many data applications require significantly higher data rates.

Techniques used for sharing station wiring range from the use of separate copper conductors that share a common sheath to more complex methods of converting analog voice signals to digital signals and combining the digitized voice and data signals on the same copper pairs.

Systems that deploy the latter method of integration must first digitize the analog voice signals using "codecs." Codecs are microchips placed in the digital sets that code and decode the voice signals. Codecs may use a variety of techniques to accomplish the voice encoding. The most common technique is pulse code modulation (PCM). This technique has been used by the Bell operating companies for years in the toll network. Codecs using PCM sample each analog waveform 8,000 times per second. Each sample is converted to an eight-bit word, thereby producing a standard PCM sampling rate 64 Kbps.

Once the voice signal is digitally encoded, other techniques are used to combine the voice and data signals. Time division multiplexing, time compression multiplexing, and digital echo canceling are three methods used by switch manufacturers to mix, or multiplex, the voice and data signals on shared wiring. Most digital systems operate at transmission speeds that permit the transmission of 64 Kbps of voice, 64 Kbps of data, and an additional 8 Kbps of signaling and control information simultaneously over shared wiring.

Another benefit to the station user from the use of these techniques is the availability of station sets that permit the activation of telephone system features by buttons rather than dial codes. The 8-Kbps control channel between the digital sets and the digital switch is used to communicate signaling information to the switch when these buttons are activated. This form of signaling permits the station user to easily activate and deactivate system features while using the voice or data channels for other functions.

While the ability of digital systems to switch both voice and data is generally considered to be one of the primary benefits of integrated systems, few installed systems take full advantage of this capability. Probably fewer than 5 percent of the total stations served by digital systems are comprised of data terminals. When evaluating the use of digital systems, telecommunications personnel should attempt to anticipate the amount of traffic to be generated by both voice and data terminals to ensure that the system is properly configured.

Voice encoding, multiplexing techniques, and data communications requirements are important technical considerations that must be evaluated prior to the acquisition of a new telephone system. These factors will affect the station wiring requirements, the configuration of the switch, and ultimately the cost of the system.

Local Area Networks

Because of the wide range of data communications needs present on university campuses, evaluations of digital switching systems will be greatly influenced by their data-handling capabilities. However, university administrators should not expect digital switches to be the single solution for all data communications requirements. Local area networks (LANs) provide some unique capabilities within a limited geographical area. The primary advantage of a local area network is its ability to transmit data at high data rates. Many LANs offer considerable economies over digital circuit switching because of the limited geographic area and the small community of interest that they serve. Most LANs operate at transmission speeds of from 1 to 16 million bits per second (Mbps). Most digital switches, on the other hand, support standard data rates of 64 Kbps and may support data rates in excess of 1 Mbps with the use of proprietary interfaces and specific transmission media.

LANs can be categorized by the type of media used, the topology of the network, and the transmission technique employed. Plant administrators should understand the various types of networks because of their impact on building wiring systems and general telecommunications strategies. The media type and the topology of the network are most directly related to wiring issues while the transmission technique can effect the geographical coverage of the network.

LAN Media   The LAN medium is simply the physical facility used to conduct the communications signals between network devices. For the purpose of this chapter, it should be assumed that the LAN devices are within the same building or in buildings on a single campus. Twisted pair copper wiring, coaxial cable, and fiber optic cabling are the most commonly used media. (Microwave transmission links can also be used for networking, but this medium's primary use is between noncontiguous properties.)

1. Twisted pair wiring. Twisted pair wiring is one of the most popular media for LANs. Its primary advantage is its ubiquity. Because many buildings are wired in excess of their actual telephone capacity, spare telephone wiring can often be used for some types of LANs. In addition, twisted pair wiring is easier and less expensive to install than other LAN media. The primary disadvantages of twisted pair wiring are its distance limitations and its susceptibility to lightning. LANs using standard 24/26 gauge telephone wiring are limited to several hundred feet.
2. Coaxial cable. Coaxial cable has a number of advantages over twisted pair. The most significant advantages are its ability to handle a much wider range of frequencies on a single cable and its resistance to noise and lightning. However, coaxial cable is bulkier, rigid, and more difficult to handle that conventional twisted pair. Specialized tools may also be required to complete coaxial cable installations. A detailed design should be completed before the installation of a network using coaxial cable as its medium.
3. Fiber. Fiber optics is a specialized medium used in applications requiring traffic volumes that far exceed twisted pair and coaxial cable capacities. Fiber cables are immune to electromagnetic interference, require little physical space, and are difficult to tap without detection. Unfortunately, the cost of fiber interfaces remains high and splices must be carefully made to avoid transmission loss. Although fiber is widely used in many point-to-point applications, such as in telephone company networks, its use in local area network applications has been more limited.

Topology   The topology of a network is the physical configuration of the network media. Topologies are identified as star, ring, bus (and tree), or hybrid configurations.

The distinguishing feature of a *star* network is that all nodes on the network are joined at a central point. All network media must be wired from each node to the central point in order to establish connections to other points on the network. In most star networks, sophisticated network control functions are performed at the central point in order that network message traffic can be routed to all outlying points on the network. In all star networks, the central node is a single point of failure for the entire network. This vulnerability increases the need for redundancy of central control equipment. A second disadvantage of a star network is that the central node can be a bottleneck under heavy traffic conditions. The central node must have the switching capacity to establish and maintain connections when all nodes are communicating.

In networks having a *ring* topology, the nodes are connected by point-to-point transmission links in an unbroken, circular configuration. Network traffic is transmitted from node to node in a single direction around the ring. Each node must monitor all network traffic, recognize its own address in order to receive messages, and retransmit messages to other nodes. By performing these functions, nodes of a ring network can establish connections to other nodes on the network. Links must be established between new nodes on a ring network and its two adjacent nodes in order to maintain connectivity. For this reason, it is often difficult to prewire buildings for a ring network and anticipate the location of future nodes.

Bus networks connect network devices to a single shared link. In contrast to star and ring networks that have separate point-to-point links between nodes, bus networks use various types of connectors and taps to join nodes to a shared network link. The capability of bus networks to share a common transmission link reduces network media costs, minimizes the need for underground ducts between buildings, and makes this topology an attractive one for implementation on large university campuses. Messages transmitted on a bus network are broadcast to all network nodes. Tree networks are formed by connecting multiple bus networks. In both tree and bus networks, the transmission media is critical to the survivability of the network. Failures or breaks in the tree or bus isolate network connections located beyond the point of failure.

Hybrid networks have no specific configuration. These networks typically form a mesh pattern and are made up of combinations of point-to-point and bus topologies. Hybrid networks are not easily configurable and do not offer the same network efficiencies and cost savings as other network topologies.

For more information on topology, see Chapter 14, Information Management and Computerization.

Transmission Techniques   Descriptions of two transmission techniques follow.

Baseband is a transmission technique that uses the entire bandwidth of the transmission medium to form one communications channel. Baseband signaling can be used in star, ring, and bus topologies and can use twisted pair copper, coaxial cable, or fiber as the transmission medium. Networks using baseband signaling have distance limitations without the use of repeaters to maintain appropriate signal levels. Transmission rates of baseband networks range from 1 to 10 Mbps.

Networks using *broadband* transmission divide the bandwidth of the medium into multiple channels using a technique called frequency division multiplexing. Radio frequency modems are required at each network connection to modulate signals on appropriate radio frequencies. These frequencies may be allocated for a variety of voice, data, and video communications services. Broadband systems obtain their bidirectional characteristics by the use of passive and active system components that allow the radio frequencies to be transmitted and amplified in either a forward or reverse direction. Signals originating from a connected device are transmitted in a reverse direction to a central retransmission location called a headend. At the headend, all reverse signals are converted to forward signals and broadcast over the entire network. Radio frequency modems at the receiving location must be tuned to the appropriate forward frequency in order to receive network transmissions. The transmission rate of a broadband channel is proportionate to its bandwidth. Broadband systems have a greater composite transmission capacity than baseband systems and can be designed to span a greater geographic area. However, broadband systems require careful design to ensure that the transmission requirements of all services can be met without creating interference between channels.

48.4 TRENDS IN TELECOMMUNICATIONS

Clearly the most significant recent trend in telecommunications has been the migration of telephone systems and networks from analog to digital signaling. Digital signaling techniques have been deployed in PABXs on many university campuses for some time. However, it will be necessary for the public switched network to migrate to digital switching before the full benefits of this technology can be realized. The basic concept of using the public network for universal digital switching to establish connections to a wide range of services is commonly referred to as the Integrated Services Digital Network (ISDN). The potential for using the public network to provide end-to-end digital connectivity is currently being explored by a number of national and international committees.

Because a number of digital switching techniques are already used by PBX manufacturers, it is extremely important for standards to be established that define common signaling and interfacing methods to be used in the public network. Much of the work of the various committees involved in planning for ISDN is related to the establishment of such standards. The Consultative Committee for International Telephony and Telegraphy (CCITT) is the primary international organization involved in the standards development.

University telecommunications planners considering the purchase or replacement of a Centrex or PBX must be aware of ISDN developments for several reasons. First, the eventual agreement on ISDN standards will determine the technological life of many of the current PBX products on the market today. Manufacturers of products that do not comply with these standards may eventually be forced to abandon existing products in order to comply with the new standards. Therefore, it is imperative that products be evaluated on the basis of their compliance with established standards. Unfortunately, since not all standards have been adopted, it may be necessary to conduct evaluations on the basis of proposed standards.

Telecommunications planners also need to understand the trend toward ISDN to evaluate the impact of the availability of an integrated digital network on existing campus data networks and voice telephone services. Potential uses of ISDN subscriber loops include simultaneous voice and data transmission, packet switching, and support for two subscriber lines on a single cable pair.

The trend toward the implementation of an integrated digital network is also manifest in the integration of computer and telecommunications technologies. Telephone networks are becoming increasingly dependent upon computer-based technology to handle call processing. Similarly, computer networks depend upon advance signaling techniques of telephone systems to provide high-speed access by network users. It has become the responsibility of telecommunications managers in today's university environment to achieve an appropriate degree of integration of these technologies to meet new demands for telecommunications services and to assist the institution in meeting its goals and objectives.

ADDITIONAL RESOURCES

Business Communications Review. *Integrating Voice and Data: Practical Aspects of Digital Networks.* Hinsdale, Illinois: BCR Enterprises, 1988.

DeNoia, Lynn A. *Data Communication Fundamentals and Applications.* Columbus, Ohio: Merrill Publishing Company, 1987.

Digital Equipment Corporation. *Introduction to Local Area Networks,* 1982.

CHAPTER 49

Grounds Maintenance

Dean A. Ramsey
Assistant Vice President for
Physical Facilities Emeritus
The Ohio State University

With additional contributions by Don Barr, Denise M. Candelari, Michael Dale, James D. Long, John McCoy, and John Nagy.

49.1 INTRODUCTION

Scope

The condition of a campus often influences impressions and attitudes. The grounds sometimes make a first impression that may determine enrollment of students and employment of faculty and staff. As influential as they can be, properly designed and maintained grounds and interior plantings are not necessarily prime areas of concern to administrators. This attitude is changing as more emphasis is being given to the physical condition of the grounds, as well as campus aesthetics.

Unlike most areas of maintenance, grounds are subjected to unpredictable variables. The grounds manager contends with problems of nature and living things, quite unlike a controlled interior environment. Generally, the purpose of grounds maintenance is to provide services that maintain, in an acceptable manner, the exterior portion of the campus, excluding buildings. The mission may be expanded to include maintenance of interior plantings and environments.

49.2 ORGANIZATION

Within the above definition, grounds maintenance organizations exist with varying degrees of success. Success is greatly attributed to leadership. It is important to have trained and enthusiastic supervisors and adequate staffing.

The responsibilities of grounds managers vary from campus to campus, depending on the organization's history and the manager's abilities. Often grounds maintenance divisions are charged with additional responsibilities not directly related to traditional services but which utilize labor more economically. For example, moving crews might be assigned to grounds maintenance because of the availability of heavy equipment, the relationship of special events to outdoor programs, or for additional labor during poor weather conditions.

Another responsibility might be vehicles and equipment maintenance. On most campuses, a high percentage of vehicles and off-road equipment is assigned to grounds maintenance. Because they have the tools and trained personnel, it makes sense that their mission include maintenance of their own and other division's vehicles and equipment. This is especially true in climates that require emergency vehicles to be well maintained at all times.

Grounds maintenance groups generally contain a variety of units or areas of responsibility.

A design/build group may include landscape architects, horticulturists, surveyors, civil engineers, or other grounds specialists. In some cases, this group is aligned under an office of design (university architect or engineer).

The landscape maintenance group is responsible for installing and maintaining plant materials. Groundskeepers, chemical application specialists, arborists, equipment operators, turf specialists, and plant materials specialists are integral to this group.

This group can be organized in several ways. One of the most effective involves the use of zones or areas. Each zone incorporates an area of the campus with the size dependent upon its complexity and the numbers and types of labor and equipment available. If possible, it is an advantage to have an area for each skilled employee. This allows the employee to feel personally responsible for his or her zone and gives the manager the ability to monitor their performance. Area supervisors would schedule equipment and materials to keep each zone supplied. Special tasks such as chemical application, heavy pruning, and planting would be handled by roving speciality crews.

Campus services is a catchall section with various assignments that include maintenance of pavements (walks, streets, parking lots, tennis courts, and other athletic surfaces), masonry repairs, sewers, and heavy equipment services. Moving and special events crews are easily assigned here.

Refuse disposal is an area that ranges from total in-house service to completely contracted services. Building-by-building refuse collection, special disposal, collection of material not included as normal building refuse, litter container services, and in some cases hazardous materials handling is included. Some campuses are responsible for transfer stations and other transportation to landfills or trash-burning power plants.

If this group is responsible for hazardous materials handling, then employees must be trained with special equipment, vehicles, and knowledge to handle these problems. This operation should be part of a safety division or a separate hazardous materials division with environmental health specialists and faculty representatives in charge.

The vehicle and equipment maintenance section is equipped to maintain all vehicles and special equipment used in all campus service operations. Usually, it contains auto mechanics, equipment operators, in some cases laborers, and other equipment maintenance specialists.

An administrative function is responsible for the administrative operations of the entire group. This section keeps records, takes orders, and writes requisitions.

The above responsibilities may be combined in various ways depending on the size of the institution. Larger institutions may separate units under a grounds maintenance division that coordinates the overall effort.

Figure 49-1 shows a typical grounds maintenance organization. This chart identifies separate areas under ideal conditions. From this,

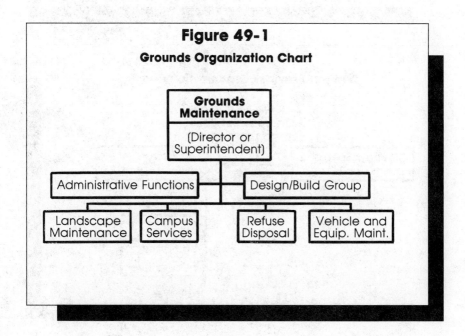

Figure 49-1

Grounds Organization Chart

Grounds Maintenance (Director or Superintendent)

Administrative Functions — Design/Build Group

Landscape Maintenance | Campus Services | Refuse Disposal | Vehicle and Equip. Maint.

various combinations of responsibilities may actually occur depending on campus size. Figures 49-2 through 49-5 show further breakdowns within the grounds maintenance division.

A distinction exists between grounds and custodial responsibilities. It is necessary to have a clear definition of responsibilities for both groups.

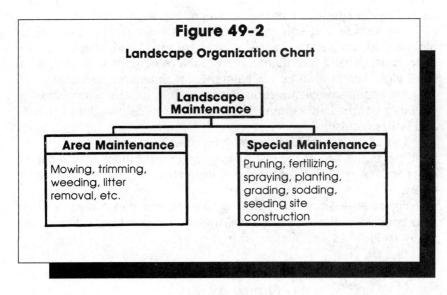

Figure 49-2

Landscape Organization Chart

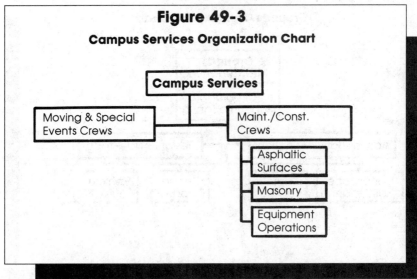

Figure 49-3

Campus Services Organization Chart

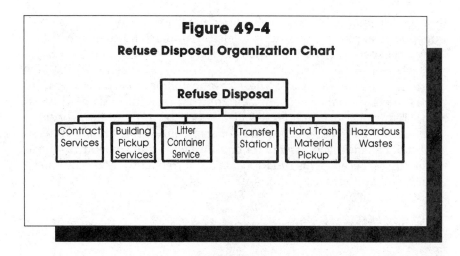

Figure 49-4

Refuse Disposal Organization Chart

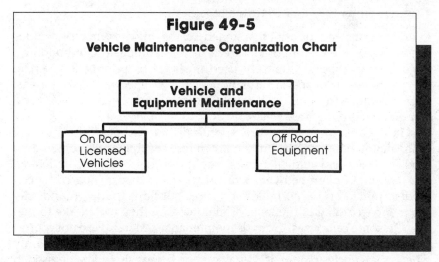

Figure 49-5

Vehicle Maintenance Organization Chart

On large campuses, this dividing line of responsibility can easily be drawn at the entrances to buildings. Jobs inside the building belong to the custodial crew and cleaning or maintenance jobs outside the building belonging to the grounds crew. Sometimes, the entrance, the steps, and sidewalks perpendicular to the building belong to the custodial crew. This avoids confusion over who removes the unauthorized signs posted on the entrance doors or who sweeps the cigarette butts and litter just outside the entrance.

On smaller campuses it is necessary to combine several job functions in one position to effectively utilize the personnel. In this situation it is almost impossible to establish guidelines for the logical division of functions. Employees will need to clearly understand their function if they are expected to perform their duties.

Many functions require good cooperation between the custodial staff and the grounds staff. These responsibilities, or shared jobs, directly affect the other section. One job that falls into this category is snow removal. The grounds crew clearly has the responsibility for snow removal on streets, sidewalks, exterior steps, and parking lots; the custodial staff has the responsibility for entrance ways and sometimes wheelchair ramps. Because this situation can occur frequently, good communication and attitudes are important.

49.3 PLANNING AND SCHEDULING

Grounds Inventory and Maintenance Levels

Every campus has priorities assigned to the maintenance of various spaces. There are the important areas such as administration buildings, major entrances, and intensely used areas. High priority is given to spaces that require special attention—such as special research areas. Priorities range from informal mental notes to completely recorded and computerized programs.

In the area of grounds care, specifically "softscapes," the intensity of the maintenance can be broken down into several levels from high to low. These levels would take into account mowing, weeding, mulching, and amount of plant bed verses turf. Average costs per square foot can be determined and each building or area subsidizing the grounds department according to the level of maintenance they would like to see.

On some campuses, grounds maintenance programs are not coordinated with the general maintenance function; coordination occurs only when emergencies require it. Organized programs should be devised to record priorities of maintenance.

The word priorities has several meanings. In the eyes of a chief administrator, the aesthetic character of the space around a building or on the route he or she travels may be a priority. To a civil engineer a systematic schedule for street and bridge repairs is a priority. However, it is the budgeting process that establishes the order and length of the priority list. Available funds may require retrenchments accompanied by unpopular decisions. In order to continue essential services and actual high-priority maintenance, some priority items may change. When funding levels are restricted, activities with formerly high priorities may become "frills."

The balance of prioritized items should be based on: 1) critical demands, 2) continuing or preventive maintenance, and 3) administrative mandates. Obviously, administrative directives will sometimes be critical and emergency in nature.

Scheduling

Ideally, every item within the boundaries of the campus would be scheduled for maintenance and thus no emergencies would occur. Obviously, this is impossible, but it is not impossible to program items already performed on a set schedule. Many institutions use computer programs that schedule certain types of street maintenance, catch basin cleaning, and plant materials spray programs.

Dozens of separate chemical application schedules exist for treating insects and diseases on lawns, shrubs, and trees. Listing these on a preventive maintenance program reminds the landscape maintenance supervisor to purchase materials, get special equipment ready, and schedule the operation—all at the proper time.

Some types of plant materials maintenance programs, such as mowing and pruning, are difficult to predict due to weather conditions. These items can be scheduled, but are certain to vary. In irrigated areas timing is fairly predictable.

A computerized inventory of all plant materials on campus is especially helpful. Location by grid coordinates, date of planting, complete identification, and special conditions for maintenance are part of this system.

Repetitive Scheduling

Repeated maintenance of specific items varies. Activities repeated daily or weekly, such as litter control, mowing, and street sweeping, may not need a system to remind the operators. Activities that occur less frequently should be marked on a schedule calendar or included in a computerized system. The more often work is repeated, the more accurate time and cost estimates will be.

While fairly accurate time estimates can be made for mowing even extensive grounds, there is still variation due to weather conditions. Growth rates may cause slower mowing and a significant increase in labor hours. This occurs when growth, including weeds, is heavy, which decreases the remaining hours available for other projects. The time required to pick up litter before mowing fluctuates depending on the season, events, academic calendar, and weather.

49.4 TRAINING

Properly training employees has the potential to benefit many aspects of the physical plant department. Training can improve job quality, job knowledge, and safety awareness. In some organizations, training is required by state and federal law. Local, state, and federal governing agencies should be contacted for requirements in your area. Generally, monthly one-hour training meetings comply with most regulations. Training programs will be most effective when they are regular and incorporate realistic situations that may be encountered in the work environment. At training meetings, employees can gain valuable insight into new techniques, new equipment, and safety requirements. Employees should also be solicited for their ideas and feedback.

Documentation of training is essential. Records should indicate the date, topics, and a roster of those in attendance and absent. A copy should be kept on permanent record and other copies sent to the participants both present and absent.

There are several sources for materials that can be purchased, rented, or loaned via public and school libraries, the Occupational Safety and Health Administration (OSHA), professional associations, and some private companies.

Training can reduce injuries and absenteeism by reducing unsafe work habits. Employees that work "smarter" are also more effective in making physical plant more economical.

49.5 EQUIPMENT

With labor costs rising, the proper equipment selection and use are extremely important. Labor reduction for maintenance processes can be dramatic, as well as other operating cost reductions. Supervisors of various maintenance areas should visit institutions with similar problems to compare methods and equipment selection.

In addition to selecting proper equipment, regular maintenance and timely replacement are equally important. Poorly maintained equipment causes delays that may even create emergency conditions. The same problem exists if equipment is worn and undependable.

Budgeting for equipment expenditures is considerably easier if a replacement schedule is followed. This schedule is somewhat variable, but will result in costs being planned. The schedule recognizes the limited life of equipment. At the end of its useful life, equipment is replaced from funds held in reserve. Budget planning administrators see the value of this method, because future funding is predetermined and problem funding is recognized in advance. If possible, replacement schedules and equipment reserves should be entered on a computer program. Items in such a program include department or section account numbers, serial numbers of the equipment, date and cost of original purchase, estimated cost of replacement equipment, amount of dollars set aside each year, amount available in reserve at any given date, and the projected replacement.

Leasing certain types of equipment may be more economical than purchasing. Some companies lease to educational facilities at a rate less than the commercial rate. Considering the cost of capital investment, the outlay of funds is minimal if the lease period is not too long. Equipment is usually leased for a two- or three-year contract, which keeps relatively new equipment in use at all times. This, in turn, reduces the maintenance costs associated with older equipment. Leasing is useful for large or special-use equipment or a series of equipment from one company. Leasing tractors and their allied equipment would include backhoes, snow blades, mowers, and augers.

Certain types of equipment have inherent safety problems that should be noted when purchasing and during operation. Most equipment with safety problems is delivered with shields, dead-man switches, and other devices. Periodically check to see if these devices are in place and working properly. Some of the more obvious ones that are misused are shields around power takeoff shafts, stone guards or mowers, roll bars, and dead-man switches on riding rotary mowers.

As fuel resources change, conversion to diesel engines may be valuable. If this change does occur, extra care must be taken to keep gasoline and diesel fuels separated. Expensive mistakes are easily made. The advantages of diesel equipment include longer hours of operation without refueling and fewer engine problems.

While keeping gasoline and diesel fuels separate, it is also important to designate mixed fuels for two-cycle engines. Two-cycle engines on smaller mowers are particularly useful on steep slopes and for ease of maintenance.

Campus size, geographical location, labor availability, and weather variations influence the selection of equipment. Contract maintenance also causes differences. Some institutions contract all tree work, others perform it in-house. Thus, needs vary for equipment such as chippers, aerial ladders or cherry pickers, special trucks to handle debris, personal climbing equipment, and chain saws.

49.6 GRASS AND TURF

Plant administrators need to remember three principles of turf management.

First, no lawn is stable. It is either improving or declining in quality. Even when a lawn appears to be in good condition, hidden problems may be beginning.

Second, with proper moisture and fertilization a lawn will be established, weeds will be crowded out, and grasses will grow abundantly. This does not preclude invasion by fungi and insects.

Third, grass will not continue to grow in dense shade. Beware of all the miracle advertisements. There are varieties of grasses that tolerate varying degrees of shade, but none can tolerate shade caused by dense trees. Some of the problems of the dry soil and shade combination are caused by trees absorbing much of the water.

Beware also of growth regulators—they are not for every lawn. There are a number of restricted use growth regulators available on the market, and each is effective for different turf situations. Cost factors must be considered to determine the economic feasibility of growth regulator usage. Also, the physiological effects to the turf may cause problems in certain areas.

Non-irrigated lawns usually experience a dormant period from mid to late summer if rainfall falls below levels necessary to sustain growth. This is normal, and the brown-blue grass will turn green with sufficient water.

Seed Selection

Consult a turf specialist or agronomist for seed selection in any given location. As a result of research on turf grass varieties, new selections regularly come on the market. Selection of a combination of grasses suitable for a specific use must be made individually.

Many factors determine selection and include use of the lawn, mowing heights, available water and fertility rates, insect and fungus resistance, shade percentage and intensity, soil factors, and drainage. No common seed mixture is perfect, and no two turf consultants will prescribe the same solution.

Preparation and Planting

Proper preparation for a new lawn assures the desired end result. In new construction, the site is usually in poor condition for the establishment of turf. All kinds of problems have to be corrected. Sheets of plywood are hidden just below the surface, large concrete chunks are imbedded in the soil, buried plaster or lime causes unknown alkalinity problems. Grounds managers must inspect the construction site or unknown problems will occur for years.

During the grading process, the most important problem is drainage. No turf area should slope less than 1 percent—a bare minimum. Pockets of undrained turf will result in a multitude of problems.

Areas compacted by heavy equipment should be loosened or turf establishment will be difficult until the soil loosens naturally, which can take several years. The entire site should be tilled and evenly shaped. It is not necessary to pulverize the soil completely and it is even better if small lumps creating voids of up to one inch remain.

A fertilizer chosen for the specific soil condition should be applied and worked into the surface. Soil analysis is helpful, but an experienced turf manager will know the requirements of a given site based on other lawns in the area.

Several methods of seeding can be used depending on the site. In small areas seed might be distributed by hand-carried rotary seeders. For larger spaces, a slicing seeder or drill might be used, and large areas or steep slopes may require hydra seeding. The latter method can incorporate fertilizer, seed, and mulch in one operation.

Mulch is of utmost importance in the seeding process. It provides protection from erosion, retains moisture, and shades the seed bed. Without mulch, the chances of establishing a lawn are greatly reduced.

Irrigation

Irrigation systems, once deemed frivolous and undependable, have become a viable mainstay for turf and plant maintenance in today's grounds care industry. It not only provides a "cheap insurance policy" for new plant and turf installation, it also serves as a potential source of labor and dollar savings over an extended period of time. Hand watering with hoses and sprinklers is often an inefficient use of water as well as labor intensive (depending on the quality of your work force). Conversely, an irrigation watering source that controls water usage through specific precipitation rates and precise watering times is more effective.

Water use is typically minimized through the use of an "automatic controller" and a rain sensor. These simple devices allow the system to turn itself on and off at a certain time of day and control the length of time each area is watered. In periods of sufficient precipitation the rain sensor will shut the system down until the moisture level is low enough to warrant additional watering. In expansive commercial jobs, irrigation is often managed through a computer. This allows for the control of a system from a central location. Manufacturer-specific programs compute precise watering times and schedules based on regional climate, geography, soil compaction, slope conditions, and specific landscape features to optimize the use of water. In addition, with a change in software, the system controller can also automatically operate fountains, gates, lighting, security systems, and even word processing.

A well or sewer charge meter can yield additional cost savings. A sewage charge meter monitors water used by the irrigation system. This water is not subject to sewage fees (frequently comprising up to 85 percent of the water bill). A typical system will often pay for itself in a few years through the savings on sewage charges. As water management in some communities has become an important issue (sometimes requiring water restrictions), a well will provide a usable source during drought conditions and is acceptable in most communities during restriction periods. It too is exempt from sewage fees.

System selection will depend on:

1. Mechanism desired
2. Mode/method of operation
3. Specific application
4. Size of project
5. Water source/water pressure
6. Climate.

Properly designed and installed irrigation systems require little maintenance. Seasonal watering time periods may be needed to react to severe deviations from regional weather norms and winterization/restart will be required in cold climate areas. Proper operation and an appropriate schedule of watering times will control problems from fungus and thatch when combined with a good spraying and aeration program.

Irrigation systems will benefit any landscape setting and become an asset to physical plant. Once a system is in, it only needs occasional maintenance and in colder climates winterization. Watering amounts are critical. How much water depends on what soil type and turf variety exists and the seasonal changes of the evapotranspiration rate (defined as moisture taken from the soil by plants and air). Several problems occurring with irrigation are increased fungus growth, thatch accumulation, and soil compaction. A good spraying and aeration program will keep these problems in check. Fungus diseases can also be reduced by timing waterings to minimize the length of time, during a twenty-four-hour period, the turf is wet.

Maintenance Problems

As stated earlier, a profusion of disease and insect problems exists in lawns. As the density of a lawn increases, so do problems. The selection of grass for disease resistance is important, and a program of seasonal treatment should be established to cope with standard problems.

One of the common problems of good lawns is the accumulation of thatch. Grass clippings and other miscellaneous particles that build up on the soil surface do not decompose rapidly. This causes a roof effect and reduces the chances of air and water reaching the roots of the grass plants. It also creates an environment conducive to insect and fungus disease growth.

If this layer of thatch gets too thick, it must be removed or a poor turf will result. Chemical dethatchers have been introduced but none have proven successful. Mechanical removal is the only answer, and the lawn must "start over." Aeration and slicing will reduce thatch and extend the time between renovations. Annual aeration of heavy-use areas will reduce compaction and allow moisture to permeate the surface.

Mowing schedules and heights must be regulated. In campus situations, particularly where budgets and human resources are limited, mowing often falls behind schedule. Heavy windrows of clippings can create fungus problems. Delayed mowing will also injure the grass plant by allowing the leaf to be cut severely into the "white" area. The optimum is to cut more often and remove less grass per cutting. As summer passes, the cutting height should be raised to allow more leaf surface to remain. Short cutting heights are harmful to turf health and sometimes cause the plants to die. This also depends on grass variety. Some varieties withstand short cutting better than others.

If properly graded and drained, most lawns can become acceptable if management establishes a systematic program of chemical treatment, fertilization, and irrigation. Each area of the country requires specific programs. If followed, the lawn quality will improve.

Athletic Fields

Quality turf that is required of some athletic fields will require more maintenance.

Irrigation, good drainage, fertilization, aeration, overseeding, top dressing, and chemical application all are necessary to maintain or increase the turf's durability.

Many volumes of literature and university courses detail athletic field installation and maintenance. Of course, no maintenance program exists that assures safe playable turf on overused fields. If such a demand exists for athletic turf, additional areas should be created so that playing fields are not used to the point where the turf is always in a state of decline.

49.7 PLANT MATERIALS

Maintenance problems of plant materials—trees, shrubs, ground covers, and vines—are directly related to the initial selection of the specific plant. If improperly chosen, a plant will be a problem in various ways throughout its life. Many factors must be considered to ensure the proper plant is chosen for a specific location.

The one problem commonly overlooked is space. Many times the plant selected will grow considerably larger than the space allows. This causes continual pruning, and finally, replacement. A common error of designers is to use several plants—causing overcrowding—where one will do the job.

Poor selection may require continuous treatment to condition the soil acidity, or a plant may be chosen that will not withstand wet conditions or areas of poor drainage. Selecting plants that are not hardy enough for a geographical zone or exposing certain plants to sun, snow, or strong winds can be disastrous to certain species.

Soil conditions determine many future maintenance problems. Selection of plants to withstand the various conditions is critical. In urban settings, more and more plants are harmed by air pollutants, and this fairly new problem must be considered.

The person selecting plants for use on campus should be aware of these common problems. Occasionally, a landscape architect or other designer who practices in a different environment and has no firsthand knowledge of special conditions affecting plants on a specific project is selected to create a planting for a given site. The designer will probably use plant lists for the zone intended, but local conditions may be entirely different. Therefore, consultants must be completely familiar with the area and its problems.

Planting

There are several steps in the planting procedure that frequently cause problems. Preparation of the hole is important. In clay soils, the plant will drown if the hole is too deep and the plant cannot drain properly. If the soil is heavy clay and in a low area or confined (as in a parking lot with curbs), a drainage system must be installed. Trees planted in heavy soils with poor drainage die from too much water rather than from a lack of it. When the hole is dug, it should be no deeper than the depth of the ball to plant at the original level. This keeps the plant from settling out of plumb or to a level that will not drain. The hole should be wider than the ball and backfilled with top soil combined with generous amounts of soil conditioner (peat moss, sand, or chips).

The volume of branches and top must be reduced enough to compensate for root loss in digging. The person handling the plant should not lift the plant by the top, which would break or loosen the ball, and the planted tree must be staked properly. Staking reduces losses due to wind, people, and other physical problems. If staked and mulched properly, the base of the tree will also be protected from mower damage. The twine or cord used in securing the ball must be completely loosened and cut away from the trunk. If not, the tree will be girdled and die. This is particularly true when nondegradable twine is used.

Methods of planting should follow the standards set by the American Association of Nurserymen. Their standards also provide guidance for quality and size when purchasing plant material.

Plant Materials Maintenance

All plants require maintenance in varying degrees. There are no plants entirely free of problems. Problems must be dealt with individually since there are thousands of cultivated plants, each with its own requirements.

Maintenance common to all plants includes watering, fertilization, chemical treatment for proliferation of pests and diseases, pruning, and eventual removal.

Determining proper moisture level for the numerous varieties of plants is difficult. Most plants should be thoroughly soaked and allowed to drain to the point of being dry before being watered again. Most plants will drown if overwatered, but drought conditions can also be damaging. Proper balance can only be reached by learning the peculiarities of individual plants.

Most plants used in cultivated conditions require fertilization. Intensity of fertilization varies according to individual plant requirements. Turf grass plants that are irrigated on well-drained soils require fertilization several times each year, but a good shade tree in natural conditions requires fertilization on a limited basis. Related to fertilization is the introduction of various trace elements lacking or trapped in the soil. This again relates to improper plant selection. For example, chlorosis (abnormally yellow color) in several varieties of trees is common, and must be treated. Chlorosis results from a lack of iron in a plant. Iron is either not present in the soil or is not available to the plant because of some other soil condition. One of the most common causes is an alkalinity and iron-deficiency combination. The same plants located properly will not develop chlorosis.

The various chemical treatment procedures are so numerous that only descriptions of common operations are presented.

Target Pest   The insect or other organism must be identified before proper treatment can be selected. Identification includes timing, resistance, and life cycles.

Toxicity   Pesticide application will become a subject of public concern if not properly monitored. Levels of toxicity are indicated by an LD_{50} value. This is the amount of pesticide that is lethal to 50 percent of a test population in a single dose. It is registered in milligrams per kilogram of body weight and is shown both as dermal and oral indicators. This rating does not indicate hazard, rather the killing ability of a chemical. A chemical can be highly toxic but have little hazard potential because of the way it is used (or misused) and the way it is formulated. The lower the number, the higher the risk factor due to less volume of material required to be lethal. LD_{50} is not the only way of determining toxicity, but it is a good indicator.

Phytotoxicity   This describes the effects a selected chemical will have on various, nontargeted plants. Incorrect selection and application methods will result in damage to other plants. An example is 2,4-D injury to shrubs and trees when applied improperly to lawns for broadleaf weeds.

Compatibility   Certain chemicals can be combined to resolve combinations of problems. There are many chemicals that should not be mixed or will not mix for many reasons. Awareness of this condition will avoid many problems.

Other factors to consider when selecting a specific chemical are its effectiveness, residual behavior, method of application, and employees' capabilities to handle application problems.

Shop rules for safety and procedural methods must be established. Reference publications are available suggesting methods of transportation and storage of chemicals, types of protective devices and clothing, and calibration. Information is also available about other use factors of equipment, personal hygiene, and—with today's emphasis on environmental protection—methods of disposal. College and university agencies, such as agriculture schools and health services, state extension services, and manufacturers, are all sources of safety procedures.

The problem of safety due to exposure to agricultural chemicals, and the hazards of absorption into the body, cannot be overemphasized. Health testing procedures are available for use in protecting employees and, in turn, the institution. Chemical absorption can result in absenteeism and serious health problems. A good system of detection can benefit employees, and possibly avoid future legal entanglements if hazards are discovered and treated properly.

Chemical Application

A chemical applicator's license or registration is required by most states for at least one person responsible for chemical application.

Current federal regulations require employers who transport, store, and apply hazardous chemical to have a Hazard Communication Standard Program. This involves obtaining Material Safety Data Sheets (MSDS) from manufacturers for each hazardous chemical on hand. The MSDS must be made available to the employee, and he or she must be trained on how to safely handle each hazardous chemical. For more information regarding the Hazard Communication Standard, contact your local or regional Occupational Safety and Health Administration Office.

Pruning

One of the most misunderstood maintenance procedures is pruning, which should not be confused with shearing. The quickest way to ruin plants and the original intent of a plant selection is to allow them to be sheared into round balls or flat-topped cones, unless a formal garden in intended. The use of the hedge clippers can injure plants and ruin the plants' intended purpose.

Pruning should be done to remove dead or damaged branches, retain original plant shape, control the size of the plant, or for renewal purposes. Trained personnel should perform this function at specific times of the year as needed by the type of plant. On larger campuses, or where labor is a problem, pruning can be done almost any time. Some sacrifices must be made—such as loss of flower or fruit the following season.

Disease control is an important reason for pruning. Some infected plants or groups of plants can be spared the spread of disease if infected branches are removed and destroyed. In some cases, the pruning equipment must be sterilized after each cut to keep from carrying the infection from plant to plant. Dipping tools in alcohol is effective.

Ivy

The maintenance problems associated with ivy-covered walls involve potential damage to masonry and wood moldings.

The two most common ivy plants covering the walls of many buildings are either the deciduous plant, Parthenocissus tricuspidata, commonly called Boston ivy, or the vine that does not lose its leaves, Hedera helix, English ivy. Each has its advantages and disadvantages.

Boston ivy grows rapidly, sometimes as much as ten feet a year. When it loses its leaves each fall, like most deciduous plants it displays fall colors of bright orange, red, and crimson. Boston ivy climbs readily on nearly any surface by using adhesive discs at the tips of its tendrils. These tendrils do not seek cracks or crevices but adhere to the surface. The vine should not be allowed to grow unrestrained behind and between moldings, joints, or on wood surfaces.

English ivy, a dark green-leafed vine, is a much slower growing plant and, in some conditions, not nearly as hardy as Boston ivy. In certain locations, it will freeze back to the ground and must be removed. In the proper location it is an excellent plant as a ground or wall cover. Some smoother surfaces do not have enough texture to support English ivy.

Both vines provide shading of walls and insulation against bright sunshine. Ivy's value as insulation has not been determined but is significant.

The added aesthetic value probably outweighs the negative attitudes, costs to control growth, and potential damage.

49.8 INDOOR AND TROPICAL PLANTS

Interest in indoor plants has risen dramatically in recent years. Although the idea of growing plants inside is not new, it has never been so popular. Now tropical foliaged plants in building interiors have become as necessary as they are fashionable. Plants not only beautify our surroundings, but they create an atmosphere of warmth and life. Most important, office plants provide a comfortable environment that improves worker morale and efficiency.

There are various architectural uses for plants, and architects and designers include interior foliage plants in their plans as a standard practice for several reasons. Plants can be used as a visual screen and to diffuse sound in open-plan space designs; to help soften hard lines or surfaces and add texture to nondescript surfaces; to give people directional clues; and to complement furnishings with color, texture, size, and shape.

Plant Selection

In choosing plants for interior landscaping, or plantscaping, three primary considerations exist: location, type of plant, and size of plant. Location determines which types of plants can be used most satisfactorily and the size suitable for the particular surroundings.

Since indoor conditions are usually not conducive to vigorous plant growth, plants that are already the desired size, or slightly smaller, should be chosen. Indoor plants rarely outgrow their allotted space. Above all, select healthy, insect-free foliage.

Location

Foliaged plants most often found in campus buildings are placed in public areas such as entrances, hallways, lobbies, and lounges. Budgetary limitations often do not allow for plant decoration in private offices. Foliage can be used to personalize a desk, fill the space on top of file cabinets, or create height variation among one-level office furniture.

Light intensity and duration are crucial to plant health. Therefore, it is important to place plants near the light source. The brighter the light provided, the shorter the period of illumination required. Most plants require twelve to sixteen hours of artificial light a day, if that light is between 200 and 500 foot-candles. (A foot-candle is one lumen of light projected on 1 square foot of area.)

Sunlight is the most desirable kind of light, but may be unavailable. If artificial light is the sole source, fluorescent is better than incandescent. Fluorescent light produces darker green foliage and more compact growth. Plants grown in incandescent light have a tendency to become weak and spindly.

Insufficient light results in loss of lower leaves, weak stems, pale coloring, and eventual death of the plant. Too much direct sunlight scorches foliage if adequate ventilation is not provided to reduce heat buildup next to windows.

Temperature and Humidity Control

Foliaged plants require moderation in both temperature and humidity. Generally, what is comfortable for people is appropriate for plants. The specific temperature range in which plants thrive is 55°F to 80°F. Avoid placing plants near drafty doors or windows since these spots may be as much as 20°F colder than the rest of the area.

If the heating, ventilation, and air conditioning system removes too much humidity from the air, there are several ways to increase it around the plants. Set plants on trays of moist pebbles, mist leaves frequently, or install a humidifier. Not enough humidity creates symptoms similar to those of underwatering. Leaf tips turn brown, margins yellow, and growth is stunted. Too much humidity over a long period makes plants susceptible to bacterial and fungal invasions. For this reason, misting leaves is not recommended, but can be done if plants are regularly monitored for disease.

Care and Maintenance

To ensure the success of interior plantings, qualified personnel must be provided. Many grounds maintenance departments have employees with education or work experience in ornamental horticulture or floriculture. Depending on specific departmental policy, the horticulture staff may or may not be required to maintain office and other interior plants. For example, the grounds maintenance horticulture staff may purchase and install foliaged plants, but policy may not allow this staff to maintain them. Office workers where the plants are placed are then responsible for maintenance. In this case, plant care should be assigned to an employee who has an interest in plants.

In large institutions, it is not feasible to have employees care for plants. Hiring a plant leasing firm is an excellent, though expensive way to maintain plants. These firms are experienced at maintaining, as well as selecting and installing, interior foliage. They can provide the skills needed to lengthen a plant's life indoors, and thus reduce replacement costs. In addition to maintaining existing plants, these companies offer purchase only, purchase/maintenance, and lease/maintenance contracts.

Watering

How a plant grows is determined by the controlled environments of building interiors. Light, temperature, humidity, soil moisture, and nutrients are interrelated and affect the strength and health of a plant. Soil moisture is one of the most significant requirements of foliaged plants.

Light, temperature, humidity, and soil type determine moisture needs. Plants use more water when it is hot, and an increase in light or a decrease in humidity increases the need for water.

Watering should not be a routine practice, such as watering the plants every Friday. By testing the soil with a moisture meter or index finger, one can accurately decide if plants need water. Ninety percent of plant losses are due to improper watering, usually overwatering. Most plants need to be watered when the top one or two inches of soil is dry. Some species need more frequent watering, some less.

When it is time to water, add water from above. Subirrigating can cause root rot by saturating the soil airspaces. Use lukewarm water, especially in the winter, since cold water may damage foliage.

Fertilizers and Insecticides

Plants grown in artificial light require only 10 to 30 percent as much fertilization as those grown in natural light. The less light received, the slower the growth rate and a diminished need for nutrients.

A complete fertilizer containing nitrogen, phosphorus, and potassium should be used—preferably one with calcium, magnesium, and iron. Liquid, water soluble, or time-released pellets can be used if they are applied at half-strength. A light feeding every three to six months is appropriate. Too much fertilizer applied too often can result in a salt buildup in the soil. Excess salt causes leaf-tip and margin burn, as well as root deterioration.

Insect problems account for only 5 percent of plant losses, but their control is the most difficult aspect of plant maintenance. Prior to installation, check the plants closely for signs of insects. If insects are found, treat the plant immediately. (One mealy bug can lay up to 600 eggs.) Use recommended pesticides, and follow label instructions carefully. A highly concentrated solution can severely injure foliage, and a weak solution will be ineffective. If a spray is used, treat three times at weekly intervals to kill all of the eggs.

Spraying a plant for bugs in public buildings may be a difficult chore. The Environmental Protection Agency only allows the use of Kelthane, petroleum oils, and natural pyrethrins in public areas. The odor from Kelthane is offensive, and the fumes potentially harmful. Plants should be moved outside, if possible, or to a storage room for spraying.

Cleaning and Pruning

Foliage must be cleaned regularly to keep plants healthy and attractive. A heavy coat of dust clogs the stomata—the cell openings that allow for the exchange of gases and release of moisture. In a greenhouse, plants can be sprayed with one tablespoon of liquid detergent (Dove or Ivory are best) mixed in one gallon water to rinse off dust. To remove chemical residues or heavy dust accumulations, use a sponge or soft cloth and carefully clean each leaf. This method is time-consuming, but does the best job. A feather duster can be used on plants already installed.

Pruning topical foliaged plants can be done to encourage new growth, enhance plant shape, or remove dead or diseased parts. There are two ways to prune—pinching or cutting back.

Pinching of the terminal (end) growing tip is usually done to produce dense, bushy growth. When the growing tip is removed, dormant leaf-producing buds lower down on the stem produce side shoots. This type of pruning is usually done with the thumb nail or scissors. Only a quarter to a half inch is removed, just above the leaf node.

Cutting back is done to thicker or harder steams, and requires pruning shears. The cut should be made flush and at the base of the stem, so as not to leave a stub. Pruning flush with the trunk or stem will ensure clean, quick-healing wounds. Dust large, fleshy wounds, such as those on Dieffenbachia, with a fungicide to prevent stem rot.

4.9 MAINTENANCE OF OTHER GROUND FACILITIES

Maintenance of paved surfaces, storm drainage systems, site furniture, fountains, signage, fences, and retaining walls is an important part of grounds maintenance. Many of the conditions are common, but geographical location causes dissimilar methods of maintenance.

Paved Surfaces

The types of paved surfaces range from loose gravel to fine hand-laid quarry tile or exposed aggregate surfaces. Each material requires its own method of maintenance, but there are some common practices for each.

Before any material is selected, consideration must be given to its intended use, type of traffic, cost to install, cost to maintain, life expectancy, aesthetic conditions, availability of materials, and weather and seasonal factors.

The most common problem of paved surfaces is the lack of drainage. This is particularly true in climates that expose surfaces to continued freeze-thaw cycles. A soft subbase caused by wet, poorly drained conditions results in movement, pumping, and other problems. The importance of good drainage cannot be overemphasized.

Problems with concrete pavements can be attributed to specific causes. As with paved surfaces, drainage is important. However, concrete can be of poor quality for several reasons. First are placement problems. Overworking of surfaces or retempering is common and particularly critical in cold climates. When being poured, concrete can easily begin to harden before the finishers have time to work it.

Improper mix of proportions of materials continues to be a problem. Strength and surface spall problems are directly related to misuse of water, as is the retention of water for proper curing. Concrete that is not immediately sealed or properly protected for curing will have surface and strength problems. Poor selection of aggregate and lack of air entrainment will also cause a variety of failure situations.

Budgets for construction projects are sometimes inadequate and many details are reduced in design. Problems result from reductions in design strengths, or sections of pavements. Surface courses may be omitted, or a less effective surface is installed, with later resurfacing intended. Often breakdown occurs earlier than "scheduled," and money is not available for improvement or repair.

Storm Drainage

Storm drainage problems are frequently caused by undersized lines and backups. Lines that were adequate at one time become inadequate as more hard surfaces are installed, increasing the speed of runoff. Since the greatest cost of installing storm sewers is for labor and catch basins and manholes, always demand oversizing of the pipe. To increase size or add more lines later is expensive, considering site restoration costs.

On many older campuses, combination storm and sanitary sewers were built. At that time, both types of sewage were either treated or dumped directly into nearby streams. Today this causes overloading of both sanitary and storm systems, and is against the law. Enforcement agencies are demanding that these practices be changed.

Total cleaning and inspection of storm sewer inlets and manholes is frequently overlooked until backups or failures occur. This activity should be included in a preventive maintenance schedule.

Site Furniture

A frequently overlooked problem on many campuses is the lack of adequate refuse containers. Even if there are enough containers, sometimes they are inappropriate for a college or university campus.

This may be true of other outdoor furniture as well. Benches, light poles, and planter boxes should harmonize with their surroundings. The disruption of an otherwise pleasant atmosphere occurs if site furnishings are improper. Selection of a standard is wise and should be followed.

Fountains

Fountains are difficult to maintain. The expenditure of dollars and workhours required to keep them in running condition is, at times, questionable. The installation of additional water features should be considered with this in mind.

Ongoing maintenance costs of fountains are usually higher than other installations because of student-related activities. Therefore, the location and design can significantly affect maintenance costs.

The complexity of design and mechanical systems will make a considerable difference in maintenance demands. Varying water movement, lighting, and special spray nozzles contributes to increased cost. Regular treatment in warm climates or during the summer is necessary to control algae growth. Occasional emptying is required for cleaning and to remove objects.

Water attractions are pleasant and usually improve aesthetics. Care must be taken in design to be certain maintenance is possible within realistic budgetary restrictions. In all cases, fountains increase costs.

Signage (Exterior Graphics)

The most significant item that can visually clutter a campus is the proliferation of nonstandardized signage and exterior graphics. Strong institutional rules should regulate all types of signage: visual graphics, posters, traffic control signage, and informational and directional signage. These regulations should stipulate a standard to be followed and place the responsibility and authority for enforcement on one specific division or person.

Bulletin boards and kiosks should be located strategically throughout the campus, and only these should be allowed for posting. Old posters, residue tape, and glue can easily make a campus look shabby.

Building identification and directional and informational signage should all follow a set standard using harmonious colors, locations, sign shapes, and alphabet types. These standards establish an important continuity throughout the campus.

Allowing graffiti to accumulate only encourages more. Materials are available to remove all types of paint and marking materials from various surfaces. As soon as improperly placed posters, signage, and graffiti are discovered, they should be removed. All staff personnel should be trained to participate in this effort.

Fences

Fencing on a campus is sometimes needed to direct traffic. In many cases fencing can be replaced by plants, or pavements can be redesigned to provide proper traffic flow. Extensive use of fencing should be avoided, if possible. Too much fencing may obstruct a view or diminish the aesthetic continuity of space.

The fencing material should be as pleasing and unobtrusive as possible but still do its intended job. A dark plastic coating on chain-link fencing helps it recede visually, or a simple pedestrian fence of heavy timber post and chain creates a park-like atmosphere.

Avoid temporary-looking fences whenever possible. They usually become permanent and detract from the campus setting. If a temporary fence is constructed using a drive post and wire, ribbon or brightly colored tape must be fastened to the wire to make it more visible. Serious accidents can occur with unmarked wire.

Fencing is another of the many items on campus that, if not maintained, will create a less-than-satisfactory appearance.

49.10 SNOW REMOVAL

During the winter months, grounds maintenance crews at institutions in northern climates confront one of the toughest problems in their area of responsibility, and one that has terrible public relations consequences if not satisfactorily handled. This is the removal of snow and ice.

In order to answer questions and serve the institution in a methodical way, priorities must be established and a working system implemented. Snow removal problems vary depending on administrative attitude or demand, location, temperature fluctuation, topography, and availability of funds.

Establishing Priorities

Every person on campus believes that his or her department, parking slot, or building should have first priority for snow removal. However, work can only be accomplished by following priorities that may be unpopular.

At institutions with medical centers that provide twenty-four-hour emergency care, access from major arterial roads and walks to this service is critical. Student health centers that provide similar emergency care would also have a high priority. Second priority is usually assigned to power plant service areas, residence halls, and food services areas. Then the remaining main roads and walks serving classrooms and research buildings are cleared of snow.

Handicap ramps and curb cuts, a high priority for mobility of a limited number of people, are of no value until the surrounding streets and walks are in passable condition. Therefore, ramps and curb cuts should have the same priority as adjacent surfaces.

Employee Notification

A workable system of mobilization is of prime importance. The responsibility of initial notification rests with a department and specific individuals that are on campus during nonworking hours. If snow or ice conditions occur during working hours, the removal process can begin as needed. In the evenings, on weekends, and during nonbusiness hours the responsibility of notification must be clearly established. The job is often assigned to campus security since they are on duty twenty-four hours a day, every day.

Once the person with notification responsibility determines a need—based on established guidelines—he or she should call a supervisor assigned to determine the extent of the emergency. Several people should be on a call list in case the first person is not available. In some cases, this might be a rotating list to allow the responsibility to be distributed.

The supervisor should immediately come to campus, or, if nearby, determine the level of call out needed under the present conditions. At times only a small crew is needed, but if conditions appear to worsen, then varying degrees of callouts—up to an all-out effort—should be activated.

On large campuses where a call-out list is long, the time spent notifying employees can be reduced by forming groups of lists with fewer names to be called by several people. This also frees the primary supervisor to make other decisions and begin the work process.

The decision to call out employees or contractors is difficult and must be based on experience as well as other readily available information. National and local weather forecast information and contacts with local agencies are important.

Supervisors should consider communicating with the institution's top administrators if conditions warrant restricted movement or school closing.

Staffing Requirements

Personnel to form crews for snow emergencies can come from several sources, and duties should be assigned to relate as closely as possible to normal assignments. Custodial employees can remove snow and ice from entrances, steps, and landings. Grounds maintenance people, usually experienced with heavier equipment, should be responsible for snow removal from sidewalks and curb cuts.

Street and parking lot snow removal may be assigned to grounds maintenance crews or to a campus service group that operates heavier equipment and trucks. Equipment maintenance personnel should be on duty to repair breakdowns and install plows. Some institutions supplement their regular maintenance crews with part-time student workers during periods of heavy snowfall.

A strong agreement on participation in emergency call-out procedures should be made with the employees and their labor organizations. Some employees may delay their response to emergency calls, or not respond at all. The established policy should include method of contact, response time expected, payment for overtime or compensatory time granted, and job responsibilities.

In the case of an emergency condition that could last for many hours or days, it is important to phase the working hours of available labor. Repetitive shifts in cold weather should last about twelve hours maximum. Beyond this, efficiency and safety capabilities reduce rapidly.

Just before the first snow or ice conditions are expected, hold a brief meeting of all employees and contractors to explain or review the mission and expectations of the operation and delineate responsibilities of the various crews. It is helpful to ask various agencies on campus to send representatives. Interested groups include security, traffic, custodial, handicapped representatives, and general administration. Problem areas can be discussed and special requests or expectations presented.

Instruction and training in the use of equipment and distribution of salt is invaluable. Damage to the campus can be extreme if care is not taken. Plow damage becomes quite obvious as winter snows melt and grass does not grow.

Attention to details can make snow removal a success. Placing stakes at walk intersections to guide operators when the area is entirely covered or providing coffee and hot chocolate for employees during long hours of overtime improves the operations efforts.

Snow Removal Equipment

Equipment funding, staffing, policy, procedure, local snowfall, and the physical characteristics of the snow removal areas all directly influence the types of snow control equipment best suited for each campus setting. It is important that all of these factors be considered when evaluating equipment since many varieties of equipment and materials are manufactured to clear, remove, and melt snow and ice.

Once policies, procedures, and staffing patterns are established as mentioned in previous sections, other factors can be considered, such as the physical characteristics of the snow removal areas. Characteristics such as street, sidewalk, and parking lot sizes; vehicle weight restrictions; snow emergency zones; street and sidewalk bollards; and bridges all are factors that need to be considered when purchasing or evaluating equipment. Since funding for equipment is generally limited, it is important to select equipment that will be cost-effective. For instance, will the tractors, commercial lawn mowers, and dump trucks be equipped for snow and ice control? To utilize a piece of equipment that might otherwise sit idle in storage will greatly increase the equipment's return on investment. Will the equipment handle the workload during severe weather conditions?

These questions need to be asked in addition to studying manufacturers' recommendations, observing equipment demonstrations, and visiting nearby institutions to observe other snow control programs. Once a program is established, finetuning begins through a trial-and-error process. What works in Cleveland, Ohio may not work in Madison, Wisconsin. As the snow control program is carried out, hold meetings to discuss and review the effectiveness of the snow control program. Implement worthy suggestions from the staff and keep track of what techniques work well.

Be prepared. Organize the snow control program several months in advance. Ensure that supplies are ordered in a timely fashion. Have vehicle maintenance employees winterize equipment to be pulled from storage, and equip the tractor mowers and dump trucks with plows, tire chains, and salt spreaders. Have snow-melting compounds suitable for the local winter conditions ordered and ready in their storage areas.

The *Snowfighter's Handbook*, available from the Salt Institute, contains information pertaining to all phases of snow control.

Snow and Ice Control Plan

As with any emergency procedure, careful advance planning is an essential element of a successful snow and ice control program. If this planning is to be effective, it must be written in a well-organized and comprehensive snow and ice control plan. Among the basic elements of a good plan are these:

- Summary of basic policies and procedures for snow and ice control.
- Establishment of priorities.
- Organization for snow and ice control.
- Control and communications.
- Assignment of responsibilities.
- Personnel assignments.
- Delineation of equipment routes.

To remain effective, a snow and ice removal plan should be reviewed and updated each fall, well in advance of winter weather, and the updated plan should form the basis for refamiliarization and training for all essential snow and ice control personnel.

49.11 CONCLUSION

The importance of a well-maintained campus is beyond measurement in terms of attracting students and faculty. To achieve its goals, an institution needs adequate staffing and funding of grounds maintenance and care. The most important factor is a person of leadership, knowledgeable in this subject, with a sincere interest in the work. Continued care of a campus cannot be guaranteed without the proper equipment and supplies, and as in all maintenance operations, adequate funds are needed to achieve success.

ADDITIONAL RESOURCES

Dirr, Michael A. *Manual of Woody Landscape Plants: Their Identification, Ornamental Characteristics, Culture, Propagation and Uses*, third edition. Champaign, Illinois: Stipes Publishing Company, 1983.

Pirone, Pascal P. *Disease and Pests of Ornamental Plants*, fifth edition. New York: Wiley-Interscience Publication, 1978.

Turgen, Alfred J. *Turfgrass Management*. Reston, Virginia: Reston Publishing Company, Inc., 1985.

The Snow Fighter's Handbook: A Practical Guide for Snow and Ice. Alexandria, Virginia: Salt Institute, 1982.

CHAPTER 50

Custodial Services

Edwin B. Feldman, P.E.
President
Service Engineering Associates, Inc.

50.1 GENERAL

C ustodial services generally represent a great opportunity for cost savings and quality improvement. There are several reasons for this:

1. It has been recognized as a measurable activity.
2. Traditionally, the relatively low wages (typically the lowest in physical plant operations) have minimized the economic impact of overstaffing (today employees receive better compensation and benefits).
3. Custodial work is a low-image, low-status job in the eyes of many people; they would rather deal with something that they feel is more "professional."
4. Time to address the issue has not been available in physical plant management.
5. Some people honestly feel that cleaning work "comes naturally" to people, and that supervisors (often former cleaning workers) have a "feel" for staffing and job assignments. (To test this theory, ask them how long it should take to spray-buff a congested corridor, per thousand square feet, using a high-solids metal interlock copolymer finish, with a 20-inch ultra-high-speed floor machine.)

Building sanitation can be, and should be, approached just as rationally as any other function. As a matter of fact, the steps to be taken would be basically the same as for maintenance or grounds (with some changes in terminology).

Attempts at shortcuts, such as using some national or regional average square footage per worker per day, are doomed to failure. Here are some points to consider:

1. Do you believe your campus is composed of average buildings? Rather, you believe (correctly) that they are all unique.
2. Fiscal restraints may vary greatly from one campus to another.
3. One campus may have a number of high-rise buildings; another may have widely spaced, smaller buildings.
4. Time requirements for work performance depend on such factors as:
   - Quality of supervision.
   - Intensity of supervision.
   - Use of group leaders.
   - Work hours per day.
   - On-campus travel time.
   - Cleaning equipment (size, type, number).
   - Cleaning chemicals and supplies.
   - Physical condition of surfaces.
   - Coloration of surfaces.
   - Types of floors (carpet, resilient, ceramic).
   - Design for maintainability (e.g., wall-hung restroom fixtures).
   - Custodial closets and other facilities.

5. Management's quality objectives may vary greatly from one campus to another.

Any analysis, consultation, or change in the custodial department must be consonant with the administration's objectives and limitations. These, in turn, should be stated in writing. Here are some possibilities:

1. Objectives

   - Save money without disturbing existing quality.
   - Save a greater amount of money, even if some quality reduction is required.
   - Save the greatest amount of money; develop an "austere" program.
   - Save $X per year.
   - Stay within the existing budget.
   - Improve quality, but save the amount of any consulting fee.
   - Improve quality even if additional expense is required.
   - If additional expenditures are required for equipment or supervision no more than $X per year will be considered.

- If additional expenditures for equipment or supervision are necessary, they must be developed through a reduction in staff.
- The benefits of this service should be shared between cost-saving and quality improvement.
- No objective has been set; recommend one as soon as analysis permits.
- Other objectives: _____.

2. Limitations

- Do not consider contract services.
- Currently using contract service; do not recommend its discontinuance.
- Currently have a union agreement (attach copy).
- Do not recommend changes in the union agreement for next negotiations.
- Currently operating under Civil Service regulations (attach copy).
- Do not recommend changes in Civil Service regulations.
- Do not recommend changes in organizational structure.
- Do not recommend changes in supervisory staff.
- Do not recommend changes in work shift.
- Do not recommend changes in supervisor compensation.
- Do not recommend changes in worker compensation.
- Do not recommend changes in titles.
- Do not recommend changes in materials required.
- There are no limitations on this study.
- Other limitations: _____.

50.2 CUSTODIAL AUDIT

A review of custodial operations should be made periodically (e.g., every five years, or related to significant physical and other changes).

The purpose is to improve productivity—to improve cleaning quality and reduce cleaning costs. An audit should not be an expedition in finding fault, assessing blame, or leveling criticism. Rather, it should be a positive exercise.

The basic subjects to be addressed (all to be discussed in this chapter) are:

1. The physical facility
2. Departmental organization

3. Supervision
4. Staffing
5. Job assignment
6. Cleaning equipment
7. Cleaning supplies
8. Cleaning methods
9. Motivation
10. Contract versus in-house cleaning.

The following is a more detailed checklist. Each item listed would have a *negative* effect on custodial performance. Of course, some items are much more important than others.

1. The supervisors are in a union.
2. The supervisors are in a worker's union.
3. The department head does not have a standing appointment with management.
4. No written monthly report is made to management.
5. Workers sometimes run out of supplies.
6. There is no "employee of the month" program.
7. No service pins are awarded.
8. There is no departmental newsletter.
9. No uniforms are provided.
10. Workers are not given individual lockers.
11. Custodial closets are too small.
12. Custodial closets are not properly equipped.
13. The department is not involved in building design and renovation planning.
14. There is no planned orientation for new employees.
15. Classroom training is not given at least once per month.
16. There is no continual supervisory development program.
17. Job assignments are not based on time standards.
18. Relief and project workers are not used.
19. There is no "call list" to replace absences.
20. There is not enough equipment for cleaning.
21. The equipment is not rugged or large enough.
22. The equipment is not maintained properly.
23. There is no scheduled "cleanup" and "put away" time.
24. There is no written procedural manual (methods, frequencies).
25. Some of the chemicals are of poor quality.
26. The floor wax is not high quality.
27. There is no stain removal kit.
28. We are using pine oil disinfectant.
29. We are using steel wool.

30. We are using ammonia.
31. We are using bleach.
32. We are not spray-buffing waxed floors.
33. We do not have enough supervisors.
34. There are not enough walk-off mats and runners.
35. There is no regular program to obtain cooperation from other employees.
36. Our department has no clerical or secretarial help.
37. There is no suggestion box.
38. All workers are rotated in their jobs periodically.
39. An ineffective supervisor may be demoted to a worker position.
40. There is inadequate transportation for supervisors.
41. We do not reimburse unused sick leave.
42. We pay for the first day of absence.
43. Chemicals are not regularly measured.
44. We use scouring powder on a regular basis.
45. Acid bowl cleaner (descaler) is used more often than twice monthly.
46. Group leaders are promoted by seniority.
47. We have not used a consultant in the last five years.
48. Most workers are not assigned by area responsibility.
49. We have an inadequate general storeroom.
50. We use titles such as janitor, maid, or porter.
51. No certificates are awarded for training.
52. We do not have a good mix of men and women in the department.
53. We have four or more supervisors, and all are the same sex.
54. Disciplinary action is not regularly documented.
55. There is no formal quality control program.
56. Management is not regularly involved in ceremonies, awards, tours, or training.
57. We have too much turnover.
58. We have more than 4 percent absenteeism.
59. We do not have a sufficient budget to allow us to attend trade shows or seminars.
60. We do not train our workers on body mechanics.
61. We do not train our workers on safety.
62. We have a pick-up system for supplies, rather than having them delivered to the workers.
63. We do not have a departmental library.
64. Our housekeeping offices are not a model of cleanliness and order.
65. We are not working on the proper shift.
66. We regularly use overtime workers.
67. We have one or more products marked "poison."
68. There are not enough waste receptacles.
69. We do not give special attention to the executive offices.

70. We do not have double tissue dispensers in toilet room stalls.
71. We are not trying to learn more about the contract cleaning industry.
72. Finger and hand marks are not removed as a regular part of the day's work.
73. Graffiti is not removed on a daily basis.
74. Our wax and stripper are not purchased from the same manufacturer.
75. We buy several products in aerosol cans.
76. The budget is operated on a line item basis.
77. Our supervisors are not involved in classroom training.
78. There is no dress code for supervisors.

50.3 MEASURING CUSTODIAL WORK

The Formula

A simple linear equation is necessary to determine workhours needed per year to maintain a given physical plant, and to determine a reasonable day's work for one custodian. From these calculations are derived individual job assignments, equipment and materials requirements, supervisory coverage, and the organization. The formula is:

Work units x Time standard x Frequency = Workhours per year

The work units are the square feet of certain types of areas to be cleaned or, in the case of restrooms and showers, the number of fixtures to be cleaned. This information is obtained from a physical survey of all buildings and areas to be cleaned by the custodial department.

The survey is best conducted using "book-size" plans. Typically, 1/16-inch per foot is an ideal scale for this, since the floor of a building can be represented on an 8-1/2" x 11" page (rarely is a foldout necessary). Thus, the first step involves these book-size plans; an architectural firm, architectural students, or technicians within the physical plant department may develop them. Book-size plans also benefit a similar approach to maintenance staffing, door-numbering systems, location of fire extinguishers, setting up job assignments, and other items.

A separate page should show each floor of each building, and these may all be kept in a three-ring binder, with a divider for each building. A survey is made, and the plan is marked to indicate the use of the area (such as classroom or wet lab), the type of floor surface (such as solid-color carpet or terrazzo), hours of use per day, the days of use per week, and any special problems in that area (such as plaster dust from a fine arts laboratory or ink from a print shop). Those areas the custodial department will not clean (such as a telephone switchgear room) should be deleted.

Time standards for custodial work, as the second factor in the equation, can be obtained from various sources:

1. Historical data. This is not reliable and simply leads to the continuation of inefficiencies.
2. Published data. This has the limitation of being prepared for an "average" facility under average conditions. Each physical plant administrator would justifiably deny having such a facility.
3. Observation. A skilled person who understands time study, and the nature of the work, is needed for this. Do not use a stopwatch for this purpose, as it alienates many people. Rather than timing individual increments of a job, it is best to time the entire job, such as cleaning an entire classroom per thousand square feet. The time study person should be familiar with the mathematics of obtaining reliable information, and the problem with "rating" workers who deliberately slow down or speed up.
4. Consultants. They can also provide the time standards, adjusted to fit a particular campus' requirements, and based on predetermined times that do not require observation. These adjustments are based on many variables (see Appendixes 50-A and 50-B).

The frequency of job performance, that is, how many times per year must this work be done, controls the quality and the cost of doing the work. From a quality standpoint, an office cleaned daily would be at a higher quality level than one cleaned weekly. From a cost standpoint, a less frequent cleaning means a smaller staff.

A good deal of frequency information can be obtained from the knowledgeable personnel in custodial supervision and management, from cleaning manuals, and from consultants. Some of the more knowledgeable suppliers can provide this information as well.

The formula is a "defense mechanism." The custodial department is certainly one of the most frequent targets for budget reduction, as it is not in the academic area and probably because it has not been measured in the past. The administration will often acknowledge measurements and mathematics, having no legitimate counter to this, but will not normally consider guesswork and past history.

When staffing has been worked out as above and management returns with a budget cut, the formula can be used to indicate that the cut requires a reduction in staff, a dependent reduction in frequency, and therefore a dependent reduction in quality. In this case, the custodial manager or physical plant administrator should provide a "shopping list" of items that might be considered in such a budget cut. Some examples might include:

1. Whereas outside windows might have been washed quarterly, a change may be made to annually. The measurement will indicate the potential savings.
2. Furniture may have been dusted daily in offices, for example. If furniture is not dusted by the custodians but by the users of the furniture, a great deal of money would be saved. (At any rate, no custodian should be asked to dust furniture that has not been completely cleared of papers.)
3. Whereas offices and administrative areas might have been cleaned daily, "skip cleaning" can be used in which they are cleaned every other day. Although this would not result in a dramatic budget cut, it might save 15 or 20 percent.

From such a list, the administration can make its determination. Often the decision will be to rescind the budget cut because of the obvious reduction in quality.

A new model for custodial staffing is being developed by APPA's Custodial Staffing Guidelines Committee. Scheduled for publication in mid-1990, this model will include five standard levels of custodial care: an enhanced level for the president's office and specially-funded facilities (such as computer rooms or research labs); an APPA standard, with proper levels of funding and staffing; and three decreasing levels of cleaning based on specific magnitudes of budget cuts to the department.

In the meantime, other ways exist to determine how many custodians are required, and how to assign these individuals. Any of these can lead to a lesser degree of performance, and a limited acceptance of reliability on the administration's part:

- Past operating history.
- Use of published material (experience exchanges).
- Averages determined from polls.
- Determination by the workers themselves.
- Arbitrary change (the pendulum effect).
- Experience, or common sense.

The use of time standards, therefore, is desirable for these reasons:

- Sets a reasonable amount of work for each person to perform.
- Equalizes work load, even if housekeeping-operative employees are assigned different types of work.

- Provides assurance to management that a dollar's worth of housekeeping is being bought for each dollar spent for it.
- Permits measuring the quantity of work performed by groups and by individuals.
- Assists in decision making, including economic decisions, concerning housekeeping.
- Involves steps that increase efficiency.
- Provides accountability to management.
- Justifies staff requirements.
- Allows supervisors to be more effective.

Excuses often heard for not using time standards include:

- We never tried it.
- Is it really good for you?
- It is too messy (requires personal involvement).
- It is impossible to set standards (time-consuming, but not impossible).
- There are too many variables.
- Management will not support it.

Noncleaning Activities

In addition to actual cleaning work, most custodial departments engage in other activities, simply because it is practical or economic. An example of this is relamping light fixtures, as it would be too expensive with licensed electricians.

All noncleaning activities should be cataloged with frequencies estimated, so that the workhours required for this can be added to the actual cleaning workhours required to develop a total. Sometimes this review leads to changes in these activities.

Some of these noncleaning duties might include:

1. Furniture moving
2. Setups for events
3. Grounds policing
4. Snow removal
5. Relamping
6. Mail handling
7. Running errands
8. Chauffeuring
9. Materials handling
10. Locking and unlocking
11. Energy conservation activities

12. Paperwork
13. Cleanup after trades maintenance
14. Maintenance of noncustodial equipment.

Available Hours

Once the actual workhour requirements for cleaning and other responsibilities are determined, it becomes necessary to find out how much
time the custodian is able to devote to this work per year. We must
subtract from the payroll time such items as:

1. Travel time. Most time standards include about 15 percent for travel
   time "within the job"; they do not include travel time between buildings or from the physical plant department to a building.
2. Coffee-break time. In many organizations, this amounts to one hour
   per day.
3. Make-ready and put-away time. (This should actually be built into
   job assignments.)
4. Personal time.
5. Time required for training, union, and Civil Service activities.
6. "Policing" or tending activities. Time may be needed to refill
   restroom dispensers, pick up litter, or mop up spills. There is a tendency, unfortunately, to overlook this important requirement; it becomes even more important when there are evening or weekend
   classes.

Various types of possible work assignments exist for custodial work:

1. In gang cleaning a number of people move through a building,
   perhaps each with a different aspect of the work to perform. This is
   generally nonproductive since a gang normally slows down to the
   speed of the slowest worker. Further, it is difficult to correct poor
   performance or to provide recognition for outstanding work.
2. Team cleaning, using a crew of two or three people, can be beneficial
   for project-type work. Headed by a group leader, such a team could
   shampoo carpets, refinish and restore floors, or seal a gymnasium
   floor. Team cleaning is normally not effective, however, for repetitive
   work.
3. Job specialization entails performing only one type of work, such as
   restroom care or waste disposal. A few justifications exist, such as in
   the case of rapid turnover.
4. Area assignments work best, in general, for custodial work. In this
   case, all repetitive work (more often than monthly) is done by an
   individual within a carefully described geographical area. Thus, the

manager is able to define responsibility, provide recognition for good work, create a competitive atmosphere, and more accurately measure work time.

The use of a relief and projects team is discussed later in this chapter.

Vertical Scheduling

Vertical scheduling is useful in reducing energy costs. In this case, a floor of a building is measured off so that, for example, three different workers are on that floor at the same time, each working in a defined area. They are not working as a team. The lights on the other floors assigned to these workers are not on (assuming an evening or night-shift operation). When the top floor is complete, the workers will turn off the lights and then go to the next floor.

This vertical scheduling has the advantages of minimizing the amount of light (and perhaps air conditioning) that is in use, with the spinoff benefit of better public relations. It also simplifies supervision, because at any time of the work shift, the supervisor knows where to find the people. Finally, the workers like this system, because it puts them in earshot of a fellow employee in case of a problem.

The Impact of Method

There are many different ways to do cleaning work, such as keeping a resilient floor clean and shiny. Although certain methods are discussed below, the point should be made in terms of work measurement that a standard time is meaningless without the determination of the method of work. For example, wet-cleaning a floor using a mop and bucket will take one time and give one quality level; using a two- or three-bucket system will yield another time and a higher quality level; an automatic scrubbing machine still another. Not only does the method control the time, it also requires the determination of equipment (such as the size and type of floor machine) and supplies (such as what type of floor finish).

Custodial operations consist of complex interactions. This hardly represents an insoluble problem; it simply indicates the need for time and the use of caution.

50.4 CUSTODIAL ORGANIZATION

The development of a custodial organization should be from the bottom up, not from the top down as is usually done. Using a long piece of paper (such as from a roll of shelf paper), indicate each building as an individual rectangle in a long row across the bottom. Each rectangle should be identified with the name and number of the building, and the number of custodians needed. Note that this measurement should take into consideration the "indivisibility of labor"; that is, the raw measurement for a given building might show 1.85 people, but it would be natural to put 2 people in such a building, since the remaining time could not actually be used somewhere else (because the make-ready and put-away time as well as the travel time would more than use up the remaining time).

Some buildings might show fractional personnel, which is practical when another nearby building can also use a portion of that person's time, part-time people, or students can be used. It is also possible to provide for fractional measurements through the use of workers who are limited in their performance, such as for medical or handicap reasons. A separate box would be used for policing and tending activities that cut across a number of buildings, or for other personnel whose activities may take place in a number of buildings.

Projects and Relief

Whereas each rectangle would indicate the number of people required each day for each building, these will not always be available. Some workers will be on vacation, some may be on sick leave, and some may simply be absent. If one uses the approach of "doubling up," that is, asking one person to cover the other person's area as well as his or her own, then a great deal of unsatisfactory work results and workers will complain. This is also demoralizing to both the worker who remains on the job and the one who was absent, who must face the results on his or her return to work.

One of the most important recommendations that can be made about a custodial department would be for the provision of a relief and projects team for each supervisor. The number of people for this purpose can easily be measured on the basis of two factors: the number of days per year the average worker misses from the job, and the amount of projects (infrequent work) that must be done.

This is not a suggestion that additional people necessarily be hired for this purpose; it is a suggestion that these people be broken out from the organization and used in this fashion. For example, if the budget authorizes twelve people to maintain a given building, or a cluster of a few buildings, it would not be correct to assign each of these people an area complete job. Obviously, they would not all show up for work every day, and the frequencies that were specified for these buildings would never truly be performed because of the "doubling up." Assign two or three of these people to a relief and projects team. This would require official adjusting of the work frequencies, but they would be performed every day at this new frequency schedule (whereas they were not performed according to the old frequency schedule, where each person had a specific area).

This small team of people would report directly to the supervisor at the beginning of the work shift and would be used to fill vacancies. If any people are left over from this vacancy filling, they would be assigned to project work, on the basis of a calendar that the supervisor keeps for each building under his or her control.

It must be made clear to top administration that the relief and projects team form a key ingredient to the success of this department and to the building of work morale; these people should not be considered supernumeraries, who can be dropped from the payroll when a budget cut is necessary. As a matter of fact, if such a cut is necessary for this example, then people should be dropped from the area assignment (with adjustments in frequency accordingly) without disturbing the relief and projects team.

Some people compensate relief and projects workers at a higher level because they must be available to go to any area and perform any service, using all equipment and supplies. This further provides the advantage of an opportunity for advancement without leaving the worker level.

Group Leaders

That there are numerous benefits in the use of working group leaders, or team leaders, is undeniable. These persons:

1. Can represent a cadre for future possible promotion to supervisor.
2. Provide on-the-job training (if he or she has been trained to do this).
3. Head up a team, such as for floor refinishing and restoration.
4. Lock and unlock buildings and otherwise be involved as a support to security.
5. Make sure that equipment is in working order and that supplies are available.

Note that the group leader is not a supervisor and cannot institute disciplinary action; rather, this person acts as an aide to the supervisor.

In general, the supervisor should be salaried (although he or she may be on wages), whereas the group leader is always on wages. The group leader is part of the work force, and not part of management. For this reason, in a unionized facility, the group leader should be in the union, but the supervisor should not.

Not only are group leaders desirable within a relief and projects team, they can also be used in a building that is somewhat distant (and which cannot be visited by a supervisor as regularly). A research facility located some distance from the campus might be a case in point.

Of great importance is that group leaders should be appointed by merit only and never by seniority. Whereas group leaders are required to be appointed by seniority according to some agreements, such as a union contract, it is recommended that no group leaders ever be so appointed. After all, group leaders named by seniority lead to supervisors named by seniority, a most unsatisfactory situation.

Supervision

How many workers (and group leaders) can a supervisor properly handle in a work force? In general, this type of supervision cannot be accomplished satisfactorily in less than fifteen minutes of contact time with each worker during the day by that supervisor; and that time should be broken into two or more parts. Many supervisors have three hours or less to be in contact with the workers, the balance of it taken up with travel time, personal time, paperwork, meetings, training, contacts with "customers," planning and scheduling, and handling complaints. Obviously, the more of these that can be assigned to someone else, such as clerical help, the more time can be spent with workers, and the more workers can be supervised.

For a supervisor handling peripheral buildings on a campus, such as former residences that have been donated to the institution, a great deal of travel time is required, and a good deal of time is spent simply looking for the custodian. In such a case, it may only be possible to supervise properly ten to twelve of these workers. In contrast, in a high-rise academic building, with high-speed elevators, it may be possible to supervise eighteen to twenty custodians. Between these two extremes lies the more typical situation in which a supervisor oversees fourteen to sixteen custodians. Remember that the provision of group leaders, vehicles, or clerical help increases the number of workers to be supervised properly.

Management

At the top of this department, of course, there must be an individual, one person responsible for all the activities, on whatever days and during whatever shifts the work is done. This person should normally spend most of the time on the day shift, working with physical plant management and other departments.

In the larger organizations, assistant managers are necessary to handle shifts where there are a number of people. For example, there may be an evening shift manager responsible for a few supervisors. In the smaller organizations, some people can report directly to the department head on the day shift, with the basic cleaning work being performed on the evening shift under a supervisor (who might also stand in as assistant manager).

The following involve some special aspects of a custodial organization, some or all of which might fit in to a large university:

1. Relief supervisors may be needed to fill in for absent supervisors. Again, this can be measured just as relief workers can be measured.
2. It may be desirable to have a training officer, supplementing the training by supervisors and group leaders.
3. Quality control might be provided by a staff member, reporting to the department head, just as would the training director.
4. Clerical and secretarial people would be needed, perhaps on more than one shift.
5. Stock control would be required for the larger organization.
6. In a large organization, there may be a specialist to maintain custodial equipment, whereas in smaller operations this is transferred to the maintenance department or performed by suppliers or contractors.
7. There may be a computer operator in a department where the custodial work is computerized; without this, there may be a counterpart for a manual approach to scheduling and record keeping.
8. Contract liaison, such as with pest control operators, contract cleaners, and the like, may be necessary.
9. It is possible that a staff person can handle more than one of the functions above, such as being a combination training and quality assurance person.
10. The maintenance manager may have staff people on a part-time basis or consultants and advisers.

The person to whom the custodial manager should report depends upon the size and nature of the organization. In a smaller organization, he or she should report directly to the physical plant administrator. In a very small organization, the custodial manager may have other functions. In a middle-sized operation, the custodial manager might report to an assistant or associate physical plant director. In a still larger operation, the reporting may be to a buildings and grounds manager or operations manager.

Titles are more important than is normally considered; they have a great impact on the image and morale of the workers and their supervisors, as well as all other parties in contact with the department. By all means, a negative title such as "janitorial," should be avoided, as should the pretentious "sanitation engineering." These days, the title "environmental services" is well-received, as is "custodial" to a slightly lesser degree.

50.5 SPECIAL CONSIDERATIONS

Equipment

Custodial personnel must be properly equipped in order to perform their work. The methods of performing cleaning work, on which time standards are based, require specific tools. The purchase and maintenance of equipment represents a small portion of the custodial budget; thus it would be poor planning to fail to provide this.

Not the least consideration is the "morale impact" of cleaning equipment. The motivation of the worker requires developing the feeling that he or she is an important person doing important work. This cannot be achieved when the department provides the worker with less-than-effective, unattractive equipment. A more measurable impact, however, is on the productivity of the work. Custodial equipment for the educational institution should be rugged and the appropriate size.

It is also desirable to provide sufficient equipment to avoid the sharing during the same shift by two or more workers. For example, two custodians maintaining one floor of an academic building might be required to perform spray-buffing an hour or so per day. It would appear that these two workers could share one machine, but a great deal of time would be wasted in having one worker look for the machine that was being used by the other. The machine would wear out quickly, and contention would develop over who was responsible for its maintenance. To provide individualized equipment, with the worker's name on it for proper identification, would be a small investment compared to the loss of productivity in providing only one machine.

Basic equipment for a custodial department would include many if not all of these items:

- Automatic scrubbing machine (applies solution, scrubs, and wet vacuums in one pass).
- Standard speed floor machine (for scrubbing and spray-buffing in congested areas).
- High-speed buffing machine (for spray-buffing in open areas).
- Wet vacuum (for water removal, such as during floor restoration).

- Dry vacuum (for carpet care; probably more than one size is required).
- Custodial carts (to avoid a great deal of walking from the work area to the custodial closet).
- Mopping outfits (typically double-bucket, with downward pressure squeezer).
- Water extractor (for shampooing carpets).
- Specialized equipment as required (for such tasks as wall washing, window washing, and baseboard care).

Supplies

Just as equipment is fundamentally important to performing cleaning work, so is the provision of chemicals and other cleaning supplies. These supplies must be adequate in amount and should not run out. Running out of supplies indicates to the worker that his job is not important.

Supplies must also be of high enough quality to perform the work without unnecessary repetition. This is especially true of floor wax, the single most important material in custodial operations.

A high-quality floor finish that strips, spray-buffs, and levels properly is not inexpensive. To change a good one to save 50 cents per gallon would be an improper move, since a finish that is adequate in one season might be inadequate in another (and to find out might cost thousands of dollars).

Serious consideration should be given to how supplies are purchased. Normally, an annual purchase commitment, with delivery as required, brings a low price, and saves a great deal of time spent in interviewing sales people. To purchase from too many suppliers would mean that none would be able to devote enough time to be of assistance to the custodial manager. Normally, purchases should be made from two or three major suppliers.

Although the cheapest price per gallon may be obtained by purchasing materials in 55-gallon containers, this would not yield the best value. A great deal of time is spent in pouring materials from large containers to small ones; further, the smaller container might not be properly labeled (which is an OSHA regulation). Much overall economy is achieved when floor waxes and sealers are purchased in 5-gallon containers, with other products in 1-gallon plastic jugs. Thus, a 1-ounce dispensing pump can be put directly into the jug for proper measurement of supplies.

The purchase of supplies in aerosol containers is extremely expensive; such aerosol supplies might be limited to compressed nitrogen (for freezing and removing chewing gum) and insecticides of some types.

Pistol-grip plastic sprayers to dispense chemicals purchased as liquids would be much more practical.

Cleaning supplies can be distributed either on the "pickup" or "delivery" system. Where workers are required to pick up their supplies, a great deal of time is spent in going from the place of work to the supply area; it also provides the worker with a permanent excuse to be absent from his work area. It is much more sensible to have someone deliver these supplies to the custodial closet, such as once every week. This could be done by a supply clerk or a group leader.

Typical chemicals used in a custodial department might include:

- Polymer floor finish, suitable for spray-buffing.
- Floor stripper (purchased from the same manufacturer as the floor finish).
- Water-emulsion floor sealer (for damaged or scratched floors, again from the same source).
- Germicidal detergents (for simultaneous cleaning and disinfecting of restrooms, locker rooms, food service areas, and water fountains).
- General detergent.
- Glass cleaner.
- Hand soap.
- Bowl descaler (for removing mineral buildup in restroom fixtures).
- Carpet shampoo.
- Dust mop treatment (unless this is done on contract).
- Deodorants as required.

Items that should not be in the supply room, and which have been made obsolete by other chemicals and supplies, include:

- Pine oil disinfectant (superseded by the quaternary ammonium chlorides).
- Drip fluid for restroom fixtures.
- Deodorant disks for urinals.
- Steel wool.
- Scouring powder (too abrasive; use scouring lotions).

Finally, the worker must be supplied with expendable items to be able to use the above chemicals, such as wet mops, dust mops, sponges, wiping cloths, and putty knives.

Cleaning Methods

As mentioned earlier, methods must be specified before time standards can be established; and methods rely on a definition of both equipment and expendable materials. Floor care techniques take top priority, since half or more of the custodian's time is involved in floor care. Psychologically, the condition of the floors is a consideration by which more people judge the custodial operation.

Resilient floors, such as vinyl asbestos, should be sealed with a water-emulsion sealer if heavily damaged from sand or other particles, over-abrasive pads, or scouring powder. Sealers are not required for undamaged floors, which would typically be on upper floors. Floors should be finished with three or four thin coats of polymer finish; and this finish should be maintained by spray-buffing, which removes any abraded finish and replaces it. On a more regular basis, the floor should be dust mopped to remove loose, dry soil, and where necessary, wet mopped or auto-scrubbed to remove grosser soils.

Terrazzo floors should be maintained precisely as resilient floors above, except that originally they may require a solvent-penetrating sealer to prevent the concrete grout from dusting, and to avoid the terrazzo's picking up permanent stains. Since terrazzo is a combination of marble chips with a portland cement matrix, marble floors should be maintained the same way.

Concrete floors should be sealed with a solvent sealer, such as polyurethane, to prevent dusting, avoid stains, and simplify regular care. Wood floors should be sealed, again with polyurethane. The great enemy of wood floors is water, and great care should be taken to see that it is used sparingly or not at all.

For carpeted floors, the majority of the soil is removed with regular dry vacuuming, making certain to use a brushing or beater-bar action. A stain removal kit should be kept on hand for carpets and for finished floors. The best carpet cleaning is performed by water-extraction shampooing (which some people, in error, call "steam cleaning"). The time between water-extraction cleaning, which is slow and requires a good deal of drying time, can be extended by surface brightening, such as with a spin-pad underneath a floor machine or with granular cleaning materials. Any type of floor care is simplified through the use of soil-preventing devices, discussed later.

For restrooms, a germicidal detergent is required, so that both cleaning and disinfecting can be accomplished in one step. If the restroom is properly designed, with wall-mounted fixtures and partitions, a proper floor drain, and dispensers protected from the effects of water, then a spray-cleaning system can be used that provides quicker and better cleaning and better odor control. Restroom fixtures require periodic descaling to remove mineral buildup (once per month). It is a frequent mistake to use acid descaler more often, as this can cause a great deal of damage, such as the blackening of fixtures. Scouring powder should be used sparingly or not at all since it is so abrasive and can remove the plating of fixtures. Finally, restroom floor grout should be permanently sealed with solvent sealers (such as moisture-cured polyurethane) to avoid stains and odors, and to simplify cleaning.

Soil Prevention

It is much easier and more economical to keep soil out of a building than it is to clean it up once it has been spread over the floors. Soil prevention is done on a wholesale basis, preventing it from entering the building by the pound; but once inside, soil is removed on a micro-basis, one gram at a time.

Soil prevention is most completely provided for in stages. First, the approach area to the building should be a walkway with a surface that has been "crowned" or tilted so that water (with its soils) will run off. Closer to the building, the approach area should be rough or pebbly to catch soils.

Although exterior matting is helpful, the next item ideally would be a completely grated vestibule; the entire floor area would be covered with a grating, and the soil would fall into a catch pan where it could be removed by the shovelful. The rails of the grating should be no more than 1/10 inch apart, so that narrow heels will not be caught.

Following the grating, a material should be used to catch the finer soils that were not removed previously. This might consist of a carpet runner or carpet squares. This area should be at least 12 feet—preferably 16 feet—in length, so that each foot would fall at least twice on the mat for good soil removal. Of course, it is important to keep the soil removal devices clean, so they do not act as a reservoir for further soil distribution. Carpet squares or matting may be placed on stair landings and in elevators. This will greatly help prevent the spread of soil from the ground floor to the upper floors.

Training

It seems that in an educational institution, where not only the students but the faculty and most administrative staff are undergoing regular training, the custodians often receive none. This is literally because some people feel that custodial work "comes naturally" and does not really require training. A great deal of damage—sometimes irreparable—can be done to surfaces and fixtures because of this. Furthermore, the very act of training people tends to improve their morale while it improves their professionalism.

Three forms of training exist, the first of which is orientation. The welcoming of new employees to the department is a one-time opportunity that should be dealt with positively. There should be a specific orientation program for custodians (and of course for all other employees).

On-the-job training is important for a hands-on feel of the work, especially for the floor machine and wet vacuum work. A group leader can often do this, if this person has been trained. The training that is most often overlooked is classroom training. This should be provided for regular employees, at least once per month for an hour.

Many excellent videotapes are available for custodial training, and the use of slides is also a good training technique. Slides should be personalized to show actual pictures of personnel in their buildings, with the teacher being either a training officer or, better, the first-line supervisor. The supervisor as teacher improves the image of the supervisor in the workers' eyes. It also helps improve the supervisor's self-confidence, especially if he or she has risen through the ranks. Although a slide training program can be completely developed in-house, it is often more economical to buy a basic program and then adjust it to fit one's needs as time and conditions permit.

A special form of training, of course, is supervisory development. This is accomplished by sending supervisors to seminars and workshops, letting them participate in trade shows and conventions, setting up a reading program, and making good use of the role-play technique. Supervisors should also be provided with a library of books for reference purposes and for general reading in their field.

Student Labor

Some organizations have succeeded in using student labor, and some have failed; the difference may well be in how the students were used.

If students are going to work only one or two hours at a time, very little of their time will be productive, because one must provide for make-ready and put-away time, travel time, and personal time. Effective student labor requires that the student work in longer shifts even if on a fewer number of days per week. Probably more productive work would be done in one three-hour shift than in three shifts of ninety minutes each. Students should be properly trained, and properly supervised, by a supervisor who enjoys dealing with students.

Finally, students will perform better when they receive a grade on their performance. A job reference will be forthcoming, if the work performed is proper, that can be used later in seeking employment. Some institutions make provisions for students being absent from their work during exam time; others feel that this is no excuse for being absent from the work, since "cramming" indicates poor planning and improper study habits.

Uniforms

The provision of uniforms for custodians is a controversial issue. It certainly is an avoidable expense, and it is difficult to prove that the investment provides a worthwhile return. However, the cost of purchasing uniforms is far outweighed by the benefits:

- Free work clothing is a benefit for the employee.
- Security is improved (from the standpoint of theft, vandalism, and graffiti) with more people being in uniform, even if it is not a security uniform.
- One can more easily identify an employee from a considerable distance if that person is in uniform. (The desire not to be identified is one reason why some people resent having to wear these uniforms.)
- The worker feels more a part of a team.
- The department has a more professional atmosphere when its personnel are in uniform.

Uniforms are generally more popular when the employees participate in the selection of the style, cut, fabric, and other aspects of the appearance of the uniform; it becomes their uniform rather than management's. Women should have the choice of wearing culottes, pants suits, or skirts. Men should have the choice of wearing square cut or pointed shirts. Most organizations provide four or more sets of uniforms and require the employee to keep them laundered and mended; uniforms should be turned in for replacement when they become unsightly. They should be provided to the worker at the end of the probationary period.

Consultants

Consultants are probably no smarter than the department's own staff, and they may actually end up making a number of the same recommendations that have been made by the staff from time to time. Consultants can, however, bring these benefits:

- Most physical plant departments do not have the staff personnel on hand to make a study of the campus from a custodial management standpoint. Thus, the consultant makes it possible for the department to continue its operation while such a study is being made.
- The consultant is objective and not tied in to past practice or the politics of the institution.

- It is often easier "sell" the consultant's recommendations both to management and to the work force, because of the consultant's experience, reputation, and objectivity.
- The consultant has seen many operations and has pursued many avenues to discover which practices work and how fast they can be implemented. Thus, much trial and error is saved internally.
- The consultant should have predetermined time standards that are adjusted to fit the client's individual situation. These are generally accepted by all levels, including unions and Civil Service Commissions.
- The consultant may also have supervisory development and worker training activities that tie in with the recommendations.

Here are the things to look for if a custodial consultant is to be considered:

1. How does this consulting firm compare with others in the field?
2. Does the company have a considerable reference list of colleges and universities, as well as related institutions, for which it has worked?
3. The consultant's philosophy should indicate that no stopwatches are to be used on the client's premises.
4. The consultant's philosophy should be a noncritical approach, directed toward the optimum activities to be pursued in the future, without reference to past errors.
5. The fee should be stated to include all activities and expenses as a fixed figure. Per diem work might be done for small activities.
6. Sharing the savings is not a good approach to this type of consulting, although it may be to other activities, such as energy management.
7. The consulting firm should provide supervisory development and worker training service to complement its consultation, if requested by the institution.
8. Implementation services should be available, so that the consultant can assist the client in putting the recommendations into practical performance.
9. The consulting firm should be of sufficient size to have back-up personnel, in case any individual becomes ill or changes jobs.
10. The company should have an office and support staff that may be visited by potential clients.

All physical plants are unique, and recommendations made for one might be quite different from those made for another. Some consulting recommendations tend to occur more or less frequently.

Contract Cleaning

Contract cleaning is an alternative for performing custodial operations (as well as other functions) for the physical plant department. It is impossible to make a generalization on the value of contract cleaning for any particular campus. The economic case for contract cleaning is made much stronger for those campuses that pay high wage rates and high fringe benefits, and are paternalistic toward employees. Those custodial managers who use more personnel than necessary will probably be replaced by contract cleaners.

Most contract cleaning specifications are "frequency specs," a listing of how often certain cleaning jobs are performed. Contractors are then asked to bid or propose on such a specification. The price figures usually have a span of 100 percent from the lowest to the highest. An attempt to compare in-house cleaning with contract cleaning on this basis is confusing and misleading.

The proper approach is to develop a specification that might be called "controlled input spec." This is done by measuring the facility, applying time standards and frequencies, and coming up with following inputs:

- Management
- Supervision
- Work force
- Staff (secretarial, stock clerk, truck driver)
- Equipment requirements
- Expendable supplies requirements.

Selected contractors are then asked to bid on the controlled inputs; they are thus required to have on hand each day those things in the list—a specific number of workers, a specified listing of equipment. Since all the contractors will be bidding on the same thing, the "shot pattern" of bids will be much closer—the lowest bid and the highest bid might only be 5 to 10 percent apart. In this case, the lowest bid could be accepted without undue fear, as the job can indeed be done if the contractor uses the proper inputs.

The controlled input specification also provides the considerable advantage of being able to make a direct comparison between in-house and contract cleaning. One prices out the provision of that same management, supervision, or staffing levels that the contractor would require. A special addition to the contractor's price would be the cost of in-house liaison on the campus payroll.

The purpose of this inspector or liaison is to record those items that do not conform to the controlled input specifications, and to make monthly deductions from the payment to the contractor for this failure. Those deductions are made for failure to provide workers and equipment, as well as failure to use those inputs to obtain the correct frequencies.

Where such measurements would indicate a savings of less than 10 percent from in-house costs, it is strongly recommended that the move toward contract custodial work not be made. A good deal of flexibility will be lost through contracting, and it is likely that a number of "extras" will crop up later that will cost more money. There may be greater problems with theft, for example.

If the decision is made to use contract cleaning, these additional steps should be part of the agreement:

1. A three-year contract with options to renew for an additional two years would bring much better results than a one-year contract.
2. A cancellation clause of typically thirty or sixty days should be part of the contract.
3. It may be desirable to have a performance bond, which will eliminate a number of the small and inexperienced firms.
4. Do not fragment the campus into a number of individual contracts. Only the largest campuses might consider two or three contractors.

A special type of contract cleaning is called "contract management," in which the personnel stay on the campus payroll, and the contract company brings in the management and charges a management fee. Sometimes these fees are quite considerable, and when this approach is used, the typical campus only stays with this arrangement for two or three years, then reverts to an in-house operation. In essence, then, for some of these people, contract management is a form. It is, however, a very expensive form of consultation and another approach might be considered.

Quality Assurance

A quality assurance, or inspection, program is needed to optimize custodial performance. This can range from a part-time activity for one person, to one or more full time quality assurance personnel.

The combination of quality assurance and training makes good sense, as provided either by an individual or a group.

The most important aspects of quality control are: 1) that it be based on a series of random inspections (or follow-up inspections for perceived problem areas), 2) that the inspection be based on a form developed for this purpose, and 3) that the program be positive rather than critical.

To assure the random nature of inspections, each job assignment could be indicated on a 3″ x 5″ card, the cards shuffled, and a certain number of assignments selected at random (since obviously not every activity can be checked on every shift). The selected cards would then be placed back in the stack, so that they are available for random sampling on the next occasion. If a worker feels that his or her area has already been inspected and may not be inspected again for a couple of weeks, there may be a tendency to slip.

The inspection form should indicate which areas have not been cleaned satisfactorily. Attempts to reduce these to numbers in terms of quality lead to problems and worker disgruntlement, since trying to quantify quality is a matter of judgment. Different inspectors would make different judgments, in turn differing from those of the workers. The inspection should only determine whether or not the work has been done satisfactorily, but of still greater importance than this is the determination of why the work was not done satisfactorily.

For example, to discover that a terrazzo corridor in a given building was not spray-buffed as it was supposed to have been on the previous shift, is not enough information. One must determine the cause of this, so it can be corrected by the next shift. Some possible causes of that problem would include:

- A broken floor machine
- Improper mixing of spray-buff solution
- Running out of spray-buff product
- A missing sprayer attachment or bottle
- Worker pulled off the job by an emergency
- Improper training
- Inadequate supervision
- Incorrect method
- Worker absence
- Wrong pad
- "Loaded" pad.

Quality assurance should be an exercise in positively influencing future operations, rather than assessing blame for errors.

Part of the quality assurance program should be a system of handling complaints. Each complaint should be recorded, as should the action taken to resolve it (if legitimate). The log would tend to show repetitions and personnel who have a habit of making complaints that are not legitimate.

Another aspect of quality assurance is interviewing "customers" concerning their satisfaction or dissatisfaction with the custodial service that is being provided. This also provides an opportunity to remind them of the limitations placed on this department by budget cuts and the like.

Design for Maintainability

How many times has the custodian or custodial supervisor stated, "I'd like to get my hands on the person who designed this building. It is impossible to maintain!" There is often much justification in such an outburst. Many architects and building designers have little interest or information about the cleaning that will be required.

By all means, the custodial manager, and naturally the physical plant director, should be on any design team or at least have input into the process. The architectural firm should be given guidelines concerning what the institution will and will not accept in the way of design. Such guidelines might be based on a checklist developed from the book *Building Design for Maintainability*.

Here are some particularly pertinent design items to improve the cost or quality of building cleaning operations:

1. Grout for ceramic tiles in restrooms or other areas should never be white; it is almost impossible to keep it white. Rather, it should be a dark color.
2. General flooring, such as vinyl asbestos or terrazzo, should neither be very light (which shows all soil and scuff marks) nor very dark (which shows all dust).
3. Similarly, carpets should be selected to avoid any appearance of a monochrome surface. Rather, the carpet should contain three or four colors in a tweed, floral, or other design pattern.
4. Carpets should be loop-pile, continuous filament nylon, densely packed, and glued down.
5. Restroom fixtures and partitions should be wall-mounted, with partition mountings being made by through-bolts rather than tamp-ins.
6. A properly designed restroom with an adequate floor drain will permit spray cleaning, which is much more efficient than manual wiping.
7. Urinals in restrooms should be of the flooded open-throat (or commode) type, eliminating the need for strainers and avoiding stoppages.
8. Custodial closets should be of adequate size to store supplies, machines, and custodial carts. Although the typical custodial closet is 3 x 5 feet, it should be in the size range of 6 x 9 (or 10) feet. The room should be oblong, rather than square, so it will not be appropriated as an office.

9. Electrical receptacles should be of the spacing and size to avoid long electric wires and extension cords.
10. Each stair landing should contain an electric outlet for cleaning (and other) purposes, as should each elevator.
11. Pivoting windows can provide for inexpensive cleaning from the interior, rather than expensive cleaning from the exterior.
12. "Sandwich" windows with a blind between two panes of glass can eliminate the dusting while also improving energy consumption and reducing exterior noise.
13. All walls should have baseboards, so that the bottom of the wall does not become marked by floor machines and dry mops.
14. A central vacuum is not normally a good investment; the money is typically much better invested in effective vacuum equipment.
15. Provide double tissue dispensers, double towel dispensers, and double waste receptacles in restrooms to avoid complaints and having to police these areas too frequently.
16. Provide entrances to restrooms without doors where possible (such as in airports).
17. Concrete block walls should be coated with epoxy resin to provide easy cleaning and discourage graffiti.
18. Provide soil entrapment or prevention systems, including gratings and recessed matting areas.
19. Flat paints should be avoided because they are easy to mark; semi-gloss enamels are preferred.
20. Waste receptacles and cigarette urns should be wall-mounted, to provide for easier floor cleaning.

Motivation

Motivation for the custodian is a special case, because of the special problems with this type of worker. The worker, and the worker's customers, often perceive cleaning work as a low-image, low-status job. This feeling may be reinforced by the fact that it may be the lowest paying job in the physical plant department.

From this, certainly no one should get the opinion that it is an unimportant job; the campus could not exist without it. Workers need to understand that compensation is determined on the basis of the economic law of supply and demand, not on the basis of whether or not work is important. Millions of people are willing to be custodians (two million of them already are!). Training time is relatively short, but the work is certainly important.

Although much has been written about motivation in general, these comments are particularly important for cleaning workers:

- The essence of motivation is the use of the word "important." A sincere attempt should be made to convince each employee that he or she is an important person, doing important work, and that the institution is an important place to work.
- In the last case, the point could be made that the next student seen walking down a corridor, in the building where the custodian is working, could become a future governor, a future president, a great inventor, or a medical scientist. And the custodian would have helped this person to reach that state by providing an environment for learning.
- Since not everyone is motivated by the same thing, we need a series of motivational activities simultaneously. This is called the "shotgun effect," in which some things will motivate some people, and if many things are being done at the same time, many people will be motivated. This is not to say that everyone is going to be motivated.
- Worker participation is extremely helpful, such as in selecting uniforms or deciding on the best floor machine and which chemical to purchase. This can extend to making contributions to a departmental newsletter.
- It is helpful if top management personnel tour the facilities from a custodial standpoint.

Some of the specific things that can be done in motivation include:

- Purchase of more attractive custodial equipment.
- Purchase of higher quality chemicals.
- Provide the possibility of promotion, such as to group leader.
- Let the worker participate in the selection of uniforms.
- Worker participation in the selection of floor machines.
- A Worker of the Month program.
- Recognition for each month of perfect attendance.
- A monthly newsletter for this department.
- Classroom training programs.

Absenteeism

It is not unusual in a physical plant department for the highest rate of absenteeism to be seen in the custodial staff. A great deal of this problem relates to the morale of the worker.

Actually, many causes of absenteeism exist; but whereas the typical worker is actually out sick only two days a year, the national average indicates that the typical worker stays out and says that he or she is sick fifteen days a year. In some organizations, the figure might be twice that amount and more.

Regardless of the reason, service departments do not function properly unless people are present to do the work. There are three particularly important factors to look into with respect to absenteeism:

1. Most sick leave policies encourage absence. The typical program rewards the worker who stays off the job but punishes the employee who comes to work without fail, because his or her sick leave is later taken away from him or perhaps he is paid 50 percent of it on retirement (the person who took off received 100 percent). Some organizations react to this problem by not allowing sick leave payment for the first one or two days of absence, thus reducing most of the day-at-a-time problems. Other institutions reduce the worker's rate of pay until the problem of absenteeism is improved. Still others use a "leave reimbursement" program so that all unused leave is paid to the worker, even at time of dismissal.
2. Enforcement of the absenteeism rules is a must. Complete records must be kept at all times, and enforcement must be across the board. Especially important is the "pattern of absence" syndrome in which the worker is in the habit of taking off a Monday or a Friday periodically. This can be shown legally to be a disciplinary and even a termination offense, if proper records are kept.
3. Many workers do not want to come to the job because they feel they are being mistreated. Perhaps the foreman is playing favorites or giving newer workers all the dirty jobs. Supervisory development and management's enforcement of proper supervisory action should have a positive effect.

Of course, other actions can be taken. For example, regular training classes, especially in classrooms, and tend to improve the attendance rate, as does recognition for perfect periods of attendance. A "worker of the month" program should have as a fundamental requirement a perfect attendance record for that month.

Graffiti Control

There seems to be in innate desire in many—if not most—people to "make their mark." We see more graffiti (and vandalism) where people are thrown together in highly congested situations, such as in housing projects and overcrowded schools. It is not a recent phenomenon. Some of the ancient pyramids of Egypt contain graffiti.

There are steps that can be taken to minimize this problem (but it may never be solved entirely):

- Provide surfaces that are difficult to write on, such as thermo-plastic laminates and epoxy resins.
- Less graffiti is done in well-lighted areas, so increase the illu-mination, when possible, in restrooms, locker rooms, and stair-wells. This may require as little as keeping the fixtures clean, or using light-reflective paint on the walls.
- Catch graffiti artists whenever possible, and make them pay for the damage. Part of this payment may be working with the custodial staff for a period of time to remove graffiti through-out the campus.
- Rapid removal is important. Graffiti should be considered an emergency cleaning problem because it tends to "grow." Psy-chologists remark that graffiti writers want to be displayed and seen forever; when nothing stays on the walls more than twenty-four hours, most of them will give up.

Some institutions try to localize the graffiti by providing large bulle-tin boards on which people can write, paste, and nail things; this may be cleaned off monthly and repainted. From an exterior basis, a large boulder may be painted and written on by the students.

Computers

The development and use of computers is one of the miracles of our age. They can handle an enormous amount of information quickly but do not, however, do your thinking for you. They will not solve your basic problems, and they will not save you money directly.

A number of software programs developed for custodial operations, however, do an excellent job in these and some other ways:

- Computations (such as multiplying time standards by square footages to develop workhour requirements, which lead to staffing decisions).
- Record keeping (such as absenteeism records).
- Inventory control (such as for chemicals, expendable supplies, and equipment).
- Relief scheduling (such as for weekend or shift coverage).
- On-call lists and phone numbers.
- Physical statistics (such as square footage by floor by building).
- Floor diagrams with shaded areas to indicate job assignments and work frequencies.
- Calendars with "flags" to show such events as the impending end of a probationary period.

All of the above, and a number of other functions, can be handled by computers, but also all of them can be done manually. The principal advantage of a computer is speed.

The application of a computer to a custodial department would be more reasonable for a larger department. It is not reasonable to obtain a computer, and to hire someone to use it, simply because or to justify a previous purchase of a computer.

It is a common misconception that a computer will "straighten out" a custodial department that is not in optimum condition. Actually, the computer should be the last thing that is used—if at all. Decisions and actions concerning many of the other items mentioned herein should be taken first, which will then help determine whether or not the computer would be a good investment. If the computer is obtained too early, incomplete and erroneous information will be fed into it, with the result that inefficient operations are "locked in." Part of the reason for this is that some people think that a computer printout is sacrosanct and free from error, therefore representing the ideal course of action. It may merely have perpetuated poor operating practice.

The Time to Clean

A controversy has always existed concerning the proper time of day to do cleaning on an educational campus. The fact of the matter is, the proper time for one institution would be wrong for another; and more likely, more than one work shift should be used at any given institution, particularly a larger one.

Many factors are interwoven into a work shift determination:

- The availability of public (or other) transportation.
- Personal safety.
- The crime rate in the area.
- The extent of evening classes.
- The arrangement of supervisory coverage.
- Interference with the activities of others, such as faculty and students.
- Imposing safety hazards, such as from wet floors.
- Interruption of custodial work, such as requested to do other tasks.
- Inability to enter a space to be cleaned (e.g., a meeting is being held in the room).
- The need for specially-trained people to be at hand, such as when cleaning a radioactive isotope area.
- The psychology of having "customers" seeing custodians at work.

- Pay differentials for different shifts.
- The effect of "moonlighting," and potential sleeping on the job.
- The organization and size of the custodial department.
- The type of labor market available.
- The use of part-time workers.
- The use of student labor.
- Energy conservation.

In theory, as a general principle, cleaning work should be done when there is the least amount of occupancy of buildings. This would normally be on the third shift, traditionally 11:00 p.m. to 7:00 a.m. This would least interfere with students, staff, and custodians themselves.

When work is done on the day shift, generally, cleaning is effective for the first couple of hours, but relatively little is done thereafter, which results in an overall low productivity rate. In addition, special projects (such as carpet shampooing and floor restoration) have to be done on a later shift.

In general, we recommend evening shift work for a small campus, where all personnel can be supervised by one person (to put three people on one shift, four on another, and four on another, for example, would mean a general lack of supervision). In this case, there may well be the need for one or two people on the day shift to provide policing or tending operations, perhaps under a supervisor—or even group leader—who has other functions.

For the larger campus, it is quite likely that cleaning will be done on all three shifts: policing and tending on the first shift by a relatively small group of people; general cleaning on the evening shift for those areas that do not have evening classes (and it is strongly recommended that evening classes be concentrated in a limited number of buildings); and night shift cleaning for evening-class areas.

Thus it can be seen that the decision concerning work shift, and what proportion of the staff is on each work shift, should be made for the individual campus.

A word of caution: the move from evening shift to day shift cleaning might well see an increase in productivity for a time, and a move from day shift to evening shift cleaning would also show that increase. This may well be the result of the well-known "Hawthorne Effect," wherein workers respond positively to changes that exhibit management interest in their activities.

Job Rotation

Although it would appear to be fair on the surface, it is not desirable to rotate all custodial workers periodically. Take the case of two workers on the second floor of a classroom building. One is performing an excellent job, and the other, substandard. If these two people were rotated the supervision would be rewarding the poor worker, who would be able to "coast" for some time, while punishing the superior worker, who would have a big job ahead in upgrading the new area.

There are occasions, however, when rotation is desirable. The first of these relates to management's desires. For example, management may wish to prepare, or observe, a worker for potential promotion; this can well be done by transferring the worker to a different area. There may be a personality conflict between two workers, or between worker and supervisor, which management may want to try to correct by a transfer. Occasionally, problems with security may be investigated by changing a worker's assignment, to see if the problem goes with the worker.

On the other hand, rotation may be desired by the workers. Some workers, and often the more intelligent ones, become bored with the same repetitive job over. Perhaps such a worker should be placed on the relief and projects team.

There should be qualifications for desired rotation. The job the worker is doing should be acceptable. Also, rotation should not have occurred in the previous twelve months; were it possible for a worker to rotate every month or so, very little work would have to be done by that person to get by. When an employee is doing a good job, likes the work, and the customers are happy, why require an arbitrary rotation?

Operations Manual

It is important for the custodial department to develop, maintain, and regularly update an operations manual. The effect of the manual is multifold. First, it demonstrates a professional, organized approach to the attainment of the department's objectives. Second, it perpetuates the activities of the department, even though some key personnel are lost. (This may, in some cases, eliminate the need to go to contract cleaning.) The manual also avoids much confusion and "reinventing the wheel."

The manual can have dividers for the following sections:

- Organization chart. For the larger organizations, this should be photographic, with pictures of at least the key personnel; some organizations include all personnel who have passed their probationary period.
- Job assignments.
- Job descriptions.
- Work methods.

- Equipment. This would show the size and type of each item of equipment, and its source.
- Chemicals. Again, source would be shown, perhaps as well as equivalent products. Solution or mixture formulas can be shown. This section might also contain "right-to-know" information.
- Safety Information.
- Priority schedule. This would be most useful when short-handed to determine just how far down the priority list the available workhours can take you.
- Information list. Names, addresses, and phone numbers of organizations that might be contacted, such as professional groups, temporary talent agencies, or consultants.
- Work rules. These may be specific to this department, if general rules are included in a personnel manual that would be separate.
- Campus map.
- Emergency procedure.
- "On-call" list. This is a list of personnel (perhaps some of them on partial retirement) who can be called for an emergency or when the department is especially short-handed.

Implementation

When implementing changes, especially of a major or wholesale scale, the following checklist may be useful:

- Preimplementation meetings are needed with management, specific customers, supervisors, the union, and the work force. The basic purpose is reassurance that the changes have been properly researched and are working well. Discussion will be made on what will and will not happen as a result of the implementation. It also provides leaders with information on what to say, and how to answer questions from the workers. Of course, the union should be informed, but their permission need not be sought to make the change if it is within the scope of the contract.
- Preliminary training is necessary, so both the supervisors and the workers will be prepared for the new procedure, job assignment, work shift, and the like.
- Ensure equipment and supplies are on hand before any transition is made to avoid confusion and embarrassment.
- Do not provide too much notice for the change, only what any union contract says, or perhaps, without such an agreement,

two weeks. A longer period provides too much time for concern and general discussion.

- There is always the question, in making changes in assignment and other aspects of the work, as to whether to make these changes piecemeal or wholesale. Piecemeal gives the advantage of making corrections, so the next group of people will have an easier time; but it also indicate that the program is not complete and is on a trial or "guinea pig" basis. The wholesale implementation accomplishes everything quickly. If the proper research were done and if management feels confident with the changes, it is best to make the implementation all at one time.
- Avoid a basis of comparison. When a worker is assigned a larger area to clean (frequencies may be less to make up for this to provide a reasonable day's work) the employee many have the feeling that he or she has been given too much work to do, or at least more than before. In such a case, it is best to transfer that employee to another building, the dimensions of which he cannot compare easily with former assignments.
- The first-line supervisor is the backbone of any custodial (or other) department. During implementation of new activities, the first-line supervisor can make or break such a change, simply by what he or she says to the work force. Supervisors, in a meeting and individually, should be cautioned to be positive, supportive of management's decision, and to display an optimistic viewpoint. Supervisors who do not support management, or are actively engaged in resisting change, should be removed.
- It is important not to criticize past performance when changing procedures or other activities. The emphasis is on "working smarter not harder" (the same emphasis in a training program), with discussion of "tomorrow, not yesterday" being the rule.

ADDITIONAL RESOURCES

Carpet Selection and Care. Irvine, California: Cleaning Management Institute.

Cleaning Management Magazine. Irvine, California: Harris Communications.

Feldman, Edwin B. *Building Design for Maintainability.* Atlanta: Service Engineering Associates, Inc.

———. *Housekeeping Handbook.* Atlanta: Service Engineering Associates, Inc.

———. *Programmed Cleaning Guide.* New York: The Soap and Detergent Association.

————. *Supervisor's Guide to Custodial Maintenance Operations,* Volumes 1 & 2. Irvine, California: Harris Communications.

Floor Care Guide. Irvine, California: Cleaning Management Institute.

Floor Maintenance Manual. Milwaukee: Trade Press Publishing Co.

The How to Handbook of Carpets. Monsey, New York: Carpet Training Institute.

The New Good School Maintenance. Springfield, Illinois: Association of School Boards.

The Professional Housekeeper. Boston: Cahners Book Publishing Co.

─── Appendix 50-A ───

Time Standards (Frequency)

Allowances shown are average times per day required to perform the routine cleaning of the various areas according to the frequencies specified. Unless stated otherwise, the times shown are in minutes per one thousand square feet of floor space. Times are for a typical set of variables, but cannot be considered accurate for a specific condition.

The time standards below are for a minimum quality level; other standards would be required for other levels, such as "moderate" and "high quality."

MINIMUM LEVEL

Area Type: Administrative offices, medical offices, conference rooms, and lounges with resilient or concrete floors.

Task and Frequency	Daily Time Required (Minutes/1,000 sq. ft.)
Daily above-floor cleaning*	4
Dust mop traffic patterns daily	6
Spot mop daily	2
Damp mop monthly	1
Spray-buff monthly	2
TOTAL ALLOWANCE	15

Area Type: Administrative offices, medical offices, conference rooms and lounges with carpeted floors.

Daily above-floor cleaning*	4
Vacuum and spot clean daily	2
Vacuum traffic patterns twice per week	4
Vacuum entire carpet once per week	6
TOTAL ALLOWANCE	16

*"Daily above-floor cleaning" includes the daily removal of all refuse and ashes and occasional spot cleaning and dusting of furniture, glass, walls and other building surfaces, as time permits.

Area Type: Instructor offices, research laboratories and office-laboratory combinations, with resilient, concrete, and terrazzo floors.

Alternate day above-floor cleaning*	2
Alternate day dust mopping	3
Alternate day spot mopping	1
Monthly damp mopping	1
TOTAL ALLOWANCE	7

*Includes removal of refuse and occasional spot cleaning.

Area Type: Medical laboratories, examining rooms, clinics, and locker rooms with resilient, concrete, or terrazzo floors.

Daily above-floor cleaning*	4
Dust mop daily	7
Damp mop with cleaner-disinfectant solution daily	12
Spray-buff once per month	4
TOTAL ALLOWANCE	27

*Includes daily refuse removal and occasional spot cleaning. However, does not include cleaning of sinks or laboratory equipment.

Area Type: Resilient, concrete, terrazzo, and quarry tile ground level hallways.

Daily above-floor cleaning*	1
Dust mop hallways daily	7
Clean entrance mats daily	2
Auto-scrub traffic patterns daily	12
Put down finish in work areas once every two weeks	1
Buff floor once every two weeks	2
TOTAL ALLOWANCE	25

Area Type: Resilient and concrete upper level hallways.

Daily above-floor cleaning*	1
Dust mop daily	5
Damp mop once per week	3
Spray-buff once per week	7
TOTAL ALLOWANCE	16

*Includes daily emptying of ash trays and refuse containers, with spot cleaning of walls and doors as time allows.

Area Type: Regular classrooms, resilient and concrete floors.

Daily above-floor cleaning*	4
Dust mop daily	10
Spot mop daily	3
Apply finish and buff monthly	1
TOTAL ALLOWANCE	18

Area Type: Tiered classroom, lecture halls, and auditoriums with concrete and resilient floors.

Daily above-floor cleaning*	4
Dust mop daily**	13
Spot mop	4
Spray-buff once every two weeks**	3
TOTAL ALLOWANCE	24

*Includes daily refuse removal, chalkboard care, and occasional spot cleaning.
**Vacuum carpeted areas in place of dust mopping and spray-buffing.

Area Type: Prestige book collection rooms, resilient floor.

Daily above-floor cleaning*	2
Dust mop daily	4
Dust mop completely, weekly**	2
Spray-buff monthly**	2
TOTAL ALLOWANCE	10

Area Type: Prestige book collection rooms, wood floors.

Daily above-floor cleaning*	2
Dust mop daily**	4
TOTAL ALLOWANCE	6

*Includes daily refuse removal and occasional spot cleaning and dusting of furniture and walls.
**Vacuum and spot clean carpets in place of dust mopping and spray-buffing.

Area Type: Teaching laboratories with concrete, resilient, or terrazzo floors.

Daily above-floor cleaning	3
Dust mop or sweep daily	7
Spot mop daily	3
Periodically wax and buff	1
TOTAL ALLOWANCE	14

Area Type: Work rooms, book processing areas with concrete or resilient floors.

Above-floor cleaning	5
Daily dust mopping	13
Mop or buff monthly	1
TOTAL ALLOWANCE	19

Area Type: Shops

Trash removal	1
Sweep floors twice a week	5
Spot mop daily	1
TOTAL ALLOWANCE	7

Area Type: Dining areas with concrete or resilient floors.

Above-floor cleaning	5
Move furniture	5
Dust mop or sweep once per day	13
Damp mop once per day	20
Weekly mop, wax, and buff	9
TOTAL ALLOWANCE	52

Area Type: Dining area with carpeted floors.

Daily above-floor cleaning	5
Move furniture	5
Vacuum and spot clean carpets	
daily	<u>29</u>
TOTAL ALLOWANCE	39

Area Type: Kitchens.

Daily above-floor cleaning	3
Dust mop or sweep daily	8
Damp mop daily	<u>12</u>
TOTAL ALLOWANCE	23

Area Type: Computer rooms with pedestal floors.

Daily above-floor cleaning	2
Dust mop daily	8
Light damp mop with kick pad	
weekly	<u>4</u>
TOTAL ALLOWANCE	14

Appendix 50-B

Time Standards (Magnitude)

COMPREHENSIVE JOBS

(These average time estimates include set-up and put-away time, some nonproductive time, and assume reasonable mechanization and training level.)

Washrooms, Locker Rooms, and Related Areas
Work load per 8-hour day

Swing & locker rooms (incl. damp mopping)	15,000–18,000 sq. ft.
Swing & locker rooms (no damp mopping)	17,000–20,000 sq. ft.
Toilet rooms in office areas	120 fixtures (basins, commodes, urinals)
Toilet rooms in plant areas	107 fixtures
Toilet rooms (alternate estimate)	3,000–4,000 sq. ft.

General Cleaning Operations
Work load per 8-hour day

Elevators, freight: no damp mopping	24 elevators
Elevators, passenger: including damp mopping	24 elevators
Overhead office areas: dusting & vacuuming	7,000–10,000 sq. ft.
Stairs: sweep treads, dust handrails	60, 12-ft. flights
Stairs: mop and rinse	45, 12-ft. flights
Storage & supply areas: sweep floors, dust horiz.	40, 60,000 sq. ft.

Unobstructed areas: manual sweeping — 60, 80,000 sq. ft.
Unobstructed areas: power sweeping — 400, 600,000 sq. ft.

Policing Operations
Work load per 8-hour day

Lobbies and corridors	200,000 sq. ft.
Stairs	180 flights
Swing & locker rooms	45,000 sq. ft.
Toilet Rooms in office areas	360 fixtures
Toilet Rooms in plant areas	320 fixtures

General Cleaning Operations
Time per operation

Chair, cafe, wash	36 sec.	Gen'l ofc. dusting 1,000 sq. ft.	12 min.
Classroom (40 desks) dust	5 min.	Partition, wax or polish, 1 ft.	90 sec.
Desk or table, clean & wax	10 min.	Table, cafe, wash	90 sec.
Desk or table, strip & rewax	15 min.	Trash can, wash	4 min.
Desk or table, wash	6 min.	Vacuum & wash drop light	3.3 min.
Desk top, glass, wash	115 sec.	Vacuum & wash floor light	5.9 min.
Dispenser, napkin, refill	90 sec.	Wash receptacle, large, empty	30 sec.
Dispenser, soap, refill	60 sec.	Wash receptacle, small, empty	15 sec.
Dispenser, towel, refill	90 sec.	Windows, washing, typical	40–60 windows
Dust executive office	3 min.		

FLOORS
Minutes per 1,000 square feet

Maintenance Operation	Degree of Obstruction			
	None	Slight	Medium	Heavy
	16–20	18–24		
Auto scrubber-vac, single pass	16–20	18–24	–	–
Buff, 16" single-disc machine	23	32	38	42
Buff, 19" single-disc machine	15	25	30	35
Carpet shampoo, dry foam	65	–	80	–
(Same, but before and after)	110	–	125	–
Carpet shampoo, water extraction	400	–	–	–
Damp mop	14	17	20	28
Dust mop	7	9	11	13
Hose and squeegee	20	25	36	43
Rewax (apply 1 coat wax only)	16	19	22	27
Scrub, manual	75	105	120	135
Scrub, 16" single-disc machine	50	60	85	95
Scrub, 19" single-disc machine	25	30	40	45
Spray-buff, 19" machine	30	40	50	–
Strip once and rewax	110	140	–	–
Sweep, administrative areas	9	11	13	16
Sweep, plant areas	11	14	18	22
Vacuum carpets	20	23	29	35
Vacuum, dry	15	19	23	28
Vacuum, wet	29	33	37	45
Wet mop and rinse	32	36	40	48

FURNISHINGS

Dusting, seconds per item of average size
(Double these figures for damp cleaning)

Item	Sec.	Item	Sec.	Item	Sec.
Air conditioner, unit	90	Desk trays	8	Radiator, enclosed	30
Ash tray	15	Dictator, covered	8	Sand urn	60
Book case, 36″ × 40″	35	Door, flush, dust	25	Spittoon	180
Cabinet, 3′ × 6′	108	Door, glassed, dust	40	Table, large	40
Calculator, covered	8	File cabinet	25	Table, medium	35
Chair, large	43	Fire extinguisher	16	Table, small	22
Chair, medium	35	Glass part. dust sq. ft.	1.2	Telephone	9
Chair, small	22	Lamp, wall fluor.	8	Tel. switchboard	110
Cigarette stand	25	Lamp, desk fluor.	18	Typewriter, covered	7
Clock, desk	8	Lamp, with shade	35	Vending machine	60
Clock, wall	20	Mural, 3′ × 5′	45	Venetian blind	210
Coat tree	15	Pencil sharpener	15	Sofa or divan	150
Desk, large	28	Pictures, framed	15	Waste basket	16
Desk, medium	23	Rack, 6′ coat and hat	90	Wall, dust per sq. ft.	2.1
Desk, small	18	Radiator, open	180	Window ledge per ft.	2

WALLS, CEILING AND GLASS

Cleaning, seconds per item

Item	Sec.	Item	Sec.
Door, wash both sides	150	Wall, marble, wash, per sq. ft.	5.5
Glass part., clear, wash, per sq. ft.	8	Wall, tile, wash, per sq. ft.	9
Glass part., opaque, wash, per sq. ft.	3	Wall, vacuum, per sq. ft.	4.7
Wall, painted, wash, per sq. ft.	9	Windows, wash, per sq. ft.	7.5

REST ROOMS
Cleaning, seconds per item

Basin, incl. soap disp.	120	Receptacle, paper towel	10
Bradley basins, semicircle	180	Shelving, per sq. ft.	12
Bradley basins, circular	300	Toilet, incl. partition	180
Dispenser, napkin	13	Urinal	120
Dispenser, paper towel	7	Wainscot, per 10"	3
Door, spot clean	50		
Drinking fountain	110		
Fixtures, de-stain	180		
Mirror, average	30		
Mirror, large	60		

CHAPTER 51

Transportation

John P. Harrod Jr.
Director of Physical Plant
Northern Illinois University

51.1 INTRODUCTION

As enrollments in institutions of higher education grew through the 1960s and 1970s, campuses expanded in area. Accompanying that growth was an expansion of the services that colleges and universities render to the public, such as extension work. During the same period, off-campus research work proliferated. Vast quantities of general supplies had to be delivered regularly throughout the campus. Physical plant departments were not immune to the demand for more transportation. The personnel and materials that were required to be transported daily to operate and maintain campus facilities increased as well. Transportation requirements have since increased even more extensively than enrollments and facilities.

The function of a college or university transportation service is to provide for the transport needs of the institution with optimum economy. This does not mean that each request must be met. There must be a balance between economy and convenience to users.

Transportation divisions may be required to perform a variety of services, such as the following:

- Automobiles for use by university personnel.
- Bus operations for faculty, staff, and students.
- Taxi pay-by-ride service.
- Maintenance and servicing of all the institution's vehicles.
- Maintenance of heavy equipment such as construction equipment.
- Refuse collection trucks and grounds-care motorized equipment.
- Two-way radio communication with all passenger vehicles.
- Messenger-mail service.

51.2 MISSION OF TRANSPORTATION SERVICES

A goals and mission statement should be developed to provide for the transportation needs of the institution. The evaluation of the transportation needs must consider all factors, including the type of campus (urban or rural), single or multiple campuses, public transportation available, size of campus, and extent of extension service. Following is a typical mission statement:

> Transportation services' mission is to provide safe, economical, and appropriate transportation to faculty and staff to perform their official duties. To fulfill this mission, transportation services will work toward achieving these goals:
>
> 1. To acquire the type and number of vehicles necessary and appropriate to meet the needs of the faculty and staff to perform their duties.
> 2. To rent the vehicles to qualified departments on either short- or long-term arrangements, whichever is most appropriate and economical for their requirements.
> 3. To manage the fleet in a manner that ensures the lowest possible operating cost while maintaining a consistently high mechanical reliability.
> 4. To organize a staff and maintain a facility which provides superior service, repair, reservation, dispatch, and administrative support to the university customer.
> 5. To ensure that the service continues as a financially secure and self-supporting operation as it strives to achieve a nonprofit or break-even status.
> 6. To maintain, repair, and dispose of the vehicles in a manner that brings the highest possible return on money spent.
> 7. To direct our policies and procedures so that they reflect the best way to operate the fleet with the customer in mind.
> 8. To think independently and competitively to obtain the best ratio of dollars spent to miles driven.
>
> We will foster a climate where there is dedication to our central goals while maintaining flexibility for new ideas and participation from faculty and staff.

51.3 FLEET OWNERSHIP OPTIONS

Ownership

Ownership of vehicles and supporting equipment requires high initial expenditures for their purchase. Maintenance requires either extensive facilities, equipment, and staff, or a maintenance contract. The large fiscal outlay may in itself pose a problem for many institutions. An important factor in evaluating outright purchase is that long-term amortization necessitates accurate long-term projections of needs. Another factor is whether there is uniform demand throughout the year. It is difficult to justify ownership of vehicles that may sit idle a substantial portion of the year, such as during summer months when most institutions operate at a greatly reduced level.

Lease or Rental Options

In recent years, leasing motor vehicles has become more popular. This trend stems from the growing number of commercial leasing firms in the market and the wide variety of programs they offer. There are several advantages to leasing. A minimal initial investment is required and the remaining cost is distributed uniformly over the lease period. Maintenance facilities and equipment can be eliminated if full-maintenance lease programs are available. Some lease programs offer an arrangement whereby the customer assumes full ownership of the vehicle at the end of the lease period, while others permit buy-out by the customer at the end of the lease.

In general, leasing or renting is often a viable economic alternative to institutional ownership, if the vehicles are needed only infrequently to meet periodic peak requirements or if only highly specialized vehicles are needed on occasion. The decision to own or lease should be made on the basis of anticipated use, comparison of ownership costs with lease or rental costs, and the availability of vehicles for lease or rent when needed. (See Figures 51-1 and 51-2.)

The following is a brief description of open-end and closed-end leases for purposes of differentiation:

Closed Lease   Sometimes called a "straight" lease, this kind of lease terminates with definite conditions; it is not open for further adjustment. A closed lease does not offer the option to purchase the leased asset or share in the profit or loss on the resale of the vehicle.

Open Lease   The major feature of an open lease is that the lessee shares in the future risk of gain or loss at the time of resale. It can be

Figure 51-1

Typical Transportation Services Long-Term Rental Rates

Vehicle Size & Type	Monthly Rate	Quarterly Rate	Mileage Rate
Passenger Cars:			
Subcompact Sedan	162.00	486.00	.18
Mid-Size Sedan	189.00	567.00	.21
Mid-Size Station Wagon	207.00	621.00	.23
Passenger Vans:			
Mini-van (7 Pass.)	225.00	675.00	.25
Club Wagon (5 Pass.)	252.00	756.00	.28
Suburban (9 Pass.)	270.00	810.00	.30
Maxivan (15 Pass.)	288.00	864.00	.32
Pickups:			
Small Pickup	207.00	621.00	.23
1/2 Ton Pickup	225.00	675.00	.25
3/4 Ton Pickup	243.00	729.00	.27
4 W/D Pickup	279.00	837.00	.31
Vans (Cargo):			
1/2 Ton Van	252.00	756.00	.28
3/4 Ton Van	279.00	837.00	.31
3/4 Ton (P.D. Van)	306.00	918.00	.34
Trucks:			
1 Ton Truck	297.00	891.00	.33
1 1/2 & 2 Ton Truck	342.00	1026.00	.38

1. Monthly Charge: Includes the first 900 miles. Mileage rate will apply for all miles exceeding 900 miles.

2. Quarterly Charge: The quarterly rate will be charged for all vehicles. The mileage rate will apply for all miles exceeding 10,800 per calendar year.

3. Substitutions: The University Car Pool reserves the right to substitute vehicle requested.

Figure 51-2

Typical Transportation Services Short-Term Rental Rates

Vehicle Size & Type	1/2 Day Charge	Minimum Daily Charge	Mileage
Passenger Cars:			
Subcompact Sedan	9.00	13.00	$0.18
Mid-Size Sedan	10.00	15.00	0.21
Mid-Size Station Wagon	11.00	16.00	0.23
Passenger Vans:			
Mini-van (7 Pass.)	12.00	17.00	0.25
Club Wagon (5 Pass.)	13.00	19.00	0.28
Suburban (9 Pass.)	15.00	21.00	0.30
Maxivan (15 Pass.)	16.00	23.00	0.32
Pickups:			
Small Pickup	11.00	16.00	0.23
1/2 Ton Pickup	12.00	18.00	0.25
3/4 Ton Pickup	13.00	19.00	0.27
4 W/D Pickup	15.00	22.00	0.31
Vans (Cargo):			
1/2 Ton Van	13.00	19.00	0.28
3/4 Ton Van	15.00	22.00	0.31
3/4 Ton (P.D. Van)	17.00	24.00	0.34
Trucks:			
1 Ton Truck	16.00	23.00	0.33
1 1/2 & 2 Ton Truck	18.00	26.00	0.38
Trailers:			
U Haul Trailers		10.00	
5 Ton LoBoy with Ramp		5.00	
6 Ton Gooseneck-Beaver Tail		10.00	

1. 1/2-day Charge: Includes the first 35 miles. Mileage rate will apply for miles exceeding 35 miles. Applies only to the hours of 7:30 AM to 12:00 noon or 12:00 noon to 6:00 PM. Vehicle may not be picked up early or returned the following day.

2. Minimum Daily Charge: Includes the first 70 miles. Mileage rate will lapply for all miles exceeding 70 miles.
3. Substitutions: Transportation Services the right to substitute the vehicle requested.

considered as a time payment plan whereby the lessor and lessee agree to sell the vehicle and share in the gain or loss. The advantage to setting up an open lease is the lower monthly rental fee to the lessee.

Special Manufacturer Lease   This type of lease appears to be a cross between the open and closed lease in that neither the dealer nor the lessee have any responsibility for gain or loss in resale value at the end of the lease. The lessee does have the option to purchase the vehicle at market value.

Use of Privately Owned Vehicles

A common practice, particularly at small colleges, is to reimburse individuals for use of privately owned cars driven on official travel. Payment is typically based on a mileage rate. Most state institutions have an established rate that applies to all state agencies. The use of privately owned vehicles is frequently authorized when demand exceeds fleet supply or when an employee wants to combine official and personal business on the same trip, such as taking a vacation trip in conjunction with attending a conference.

51.4 TRANSPORTATION PROGRAM ADMINISTRATION

Vehicle Assignment Policy

Vehicles may be scheduled for use from a central motor pool on the basis of individual requirements, or they may be assigned to units or departments that have major continuous needs. In those cases, equipment may be assigned to the units or departments on a continuing subpool basis. A policy should be developed that defines the conditions under which subpool assignments will be made, and such assignments should then be subject to periodic review on the basis of utilization. Emergency vehicles such as police cars and ambulances, as well as specialized equipment such as four-wheel drive vehicles that must be available on demand, are not subject to the same utilization standards in making assignments.

Utilization Standards

To ensure that the investment in a transportation fleet is held to a minimum consistent with requirements, standards for the utilization of equipment should be established. These standards can be set on the basis of a minimum level of hours of use or miles of operation per month as appropriate to the vehicle type. Utilization standards should address the vehicle's purpose, distances typically traveled in the area in which it is used, and the length of time each month during which the equipment is available. For example, utilization standards would be much higher for a vehicle that is normally assigned to long-distance trips than for one used only for short hauls between campus sites. Similarly, a police vehicle used during multiple shifts seven days a week would be subject to a higher utilization standard than one operated only during a normal forty-hour work week.

Replacement Criteria

Criteria should be developed for replacing vehicles before maintenance and repair costs become excessive. The major factors in determining replacement are age and miles, item repair cost, and cumulative repair cost.

1. Age and Miles. A policy for retiring passenger vehicles may be 75,000 miles or a five-year average disposal. This target mileage and age may be tempered based on specific maintenance information about a particular vehicle or group of vehicles.
2. Item Repair Costs. Normally, no repair should be performed if the cost of repair exceeds 50 percent of the replacement cost.
3. Cumulative Repair Costs. A limit can be set on how much can be spent on repairs throughout the life of a vehicle. The repair limit can be a percentage of the cost of the vehicle. This can be used as a guide with the option to retain the vehicle if its condition, availability, and need so justifies.

Remanufacturing can be a viable alternative for replacing heavy duty, high-value equipment—typically construction equipment, cranes, and transit buses. When considering remanufacturing, specifications must be very specific.

51.5 USER POLICIES AND PROCEDURES

State institutions usually are required to comply with regulations applicable to all state agencies. The institution has the responsibility of informing the institution's vehicle users of any regulations. In addition, policies and some regulations unique to the college or university must be promulgated along with procedures to employees who use the vehicles.

The institution should publish the following information for the college or university community:

- Travel authorization regulations and procedures.
- Driver licensing requirements.
- Authorized passengers or riders.
- Restrictions on personal use.
- Request and prioritization procedures.
- Usage rates.
- Long-term assignment policies.
- Special regulations for student use.

The following policies and regulations are required to be publicized for all users of college and university vehicles:

- Operator care and maintenance.
- Availability and use of institutional credit card.
- Disposition of traffic violation citations.
- Procedure for vehicle pick-up and return.
- Instructions governing accidents and breakdowns.

Insurance

Insurance can be provided by commercial underwriters or by self-insurance. A variety of property damage, public liability, and personal injury coverage programs are available through underwriters. If an institution chooses self-insurance, premiums can be paid into a vehicle-loss reserve account that is drawn on when needed. During a long period of time, self-insurance can be expected to be more economical. Regardless of the method adopted, insurance costs should be determined or estimated. These costs must be included when establishing vehicle rates.

51.6 VEHICLE RATE STRUCTURES

Cost Categories and Rate Computation

Rate structures are based on three categories of costs:

1. Amortization of the cost of vehicles.
2. Fixed costs that include insurance, equipment, salaries, and administration of the transportation system.

3. Variable costs that depend upon the amount of use. These include maintenance and repair; fuels, oils, and other lubricants; tires; and repair parts and supplies.

Various kinds of rate structures are used. The one employed depends largely upon the accounting requirements of an institution. The following example presents a method for computing rates based upon all fixed costs and variable costs. This method can be adapted to virtually any other rate system.

Example Computation of Rate   Before computing rates, certain data need to be determined or estimated. The numbers presented are for example purposes only. The data that need to be gathered are:

- Vehicle replacement cost ($7,500).
- Expected life (five years, i.e., 60 months).
- Residual value ($1,500).
- Estimated mileage (100,000 miles).
- Scheduling efficiency (70 percent).
- Estimated variable costs ($10,000).
- Fixed costs other than replacement ($150 per month).

Daily rates based on fixed costs are determined as follows:

1. Determine net replacement cost by subtracting residual value from actual replacement cost ($7,500 - $1,500 = $6,000).
2. Determine monthly reserve accrual required by dividing the net replacement cost by the vehicle's expected life ($6,000 ÷ 60 months = $100). Group all vehicles of the same category together to obtain an average monthly reserve accrual rate per vehicle type.
3. Add monthly fixed costs to monthly required accrual to determine total monthly fixed costs ($150 + $100 = $250).
4. Determine actual days of use per year by multiplying the number of days per year times scheduling efficiency (365 x 0.70 = 255.5).
5. To determine the daily rate, multiply monthly fixed costs by twelve months and then divide that figure by the actual days of use per year (250 x 12 - 255.5 = $11.74).

To determine mileage rate based on variable costs, divide the total estimated variable costs by the vehicle's estimated total mileage $10,000 ÷ 100,000 miles = $0.10/mile).

The vehicle rate in this example would be $11.74 per day plus $.10 per mile.

Alternate Method of Computing Rate

1. Determine or estimate data:
   Indirect salaries and budget—$185,320
   Quantity of vehicles—246
   Total mileage, all vehicles, one year—2,483,073
   Anticipated insurance rate per vehicle—$245.20
   Original cost—$6,015
   Depreciation rate—0.358
   Retirement mileage—75,000
   Operation cost, average over one year—$0.063
   Uncollected accidents, all vehicles, one year—$14,622
   Maintenance cost, vehicle type, per year—$1,001.86
2. Determine fixed cost:
   - Administrative overhead = salaries budget ÷ total vehicle miles = 185,320 ÷ 2,483,073 or $0.075 per mile.
   - Insurance cost = number of vehicles x insurance cost per vehicle ÷ total miles = 256 x 245.20 ÷ 2,483,073 or $0.024 per mile.
   - Depreciation cost = vehicle cost x depreciation rate ÷ retirement mileage = 6.015 x 0.358 ÷ 75,000 or $0.029 per mile.
   - Total fixed cost = administrative overhead + insurance cost + depreciation cost = 0.075 + 0.024 + 0.029 or $0.128 per mile.
3. Determine variable cost:
   - Operating cost = fuel cost per mile + maintenance cost per mile = 0.0384 + 0.0244 or $0.0628 (averaged by type of vehicle).
   - Accident share cost (repairs to transportation service vehicles not collected from other party or departments, data from records). Uncollected cost ÷ total miles = 14,622 ÷ 2,483,073 or $0.006 per mile.
   - Total variable costs = operating cost + accident share cost = 0.063 + 0.006 or $0.069 per mile.
4. Total cost per mile = total fixed cost + total variable cost = 0.128 + 0.069 or $0.19 per mile.
5. Minimum daily charge = total cost per mile x average miles per trip = 0.19 x 70 or $13.

Thus, the minimum daily charge is $13, which includes the first seventy miles. The mileage rate of $0.19 applies to all miles exceeding seventy.

Van Pool Rates   Many colleges or universities have either established or supported a van pool operation in order to conserve energy, reduce pollution, reduce traffic, or provide a service to their employees. A van pool differs from other motor pool transportation in that it is designed solely to provide transportation between home and the work site. Riders are charged a monthly rate for this service, which is scaled to pay all expenses for acquiring, maintaining, and operating the vans. In some cases funds to establish the operation have been provided by the federal and/or state governments. Rates can be derived by using the systems described above for passenger vehicles. Customarily van pool riders are charged a flat rate per month that includes both fixed and variable costs.

Truck Rental Rates   Rental rates for trucks can be developed by using the same system as outlined for passenger vehicles. The scheduling efficiency for trucks will usually be lower than for passenger vehicles. Their retention period, however, will be longer. When used primarily for maintenance and construction purposes, trucks are normally charged at an hourly rate. For larger trucks, licensing requirements usually stipulate that a driver be provided. The cost of the driver should be added to the truck rental rate.

Bus Rates   Many institutions provide buses for class field trips, athletic team travel, and campus tours. In addition, buses are used to shuttle employees between remote parking lots and campuses or from main campuses to satellite facilities. Due to the high acquisition cost, driver salaries, and operating expenses, bus operations are expensive. High usage rates are therefore required to make bus operations self-supporting. However, other factors such as convenience to students or reduction of campus traffic may be of such importance that bus operations are subsidized. In these cases, break-even rates should be calculated so that the required subsidy can be considered in the decision-making process.

Bus rental rates should include a mileage charge and a time rate such as hourly, half-day, daily, and longer periods. The time rate should incorporate the driver rate, which may include overtime and per diem costs.

Heavy Equipment Rates   Since the amount of travel is a poor indicator of usage for this type of equipment, hourly rates are commonly used. The hourly rate can be determined by using the same factors as passenger vehicles with the exception that variable costs are included in the time rates. Large, expensive pieces of equipment such as cranes, bulldozers, and backhoes are normally retained for many years and therefore require long-term use projections to establish rental rates.

51.7 MAINTENANCE AND REPAIR

Vehicle maintenance and repair can be classified into three categories: driver maintenance, garage preventive maintenance, and repairs. The first two categories are both preventive maintenance, but are separated for description purposes into maintenance performed by drivers and that requiring garage mechanics.

Maintenance by Drivers

A clear policy should be established that directs drivers (operators) of vehicles to periodically check the condition of coolants, lubricating oil, tire pressure, and other routine items that any responsible private owner of a similar vehicle would typically check. The vehicle operator is the first line of defense. Each time a driver signs out a fleet vehicle, he or she should be provided with a checklist of these maintenance items (see Figure 51-3). The checklist should include:

- All fluid levels should be checked: engine oil, radiator coolant, automatic transmission fluid, and power steering fluid.
- Tires should be checked for proper inflation, unusual wear, or penetration by foreign objects.
- Other areas to be checked include, lights, horn, signals, mirrors, windshield washer/wipers, and seat belts.
- Before moving vehicles, brakes should be tested to ensure adequate pedal.
- During operation, the driver should observe operation of instruments, brakes, steering, and engine and power drive components.
- After operation, the driver should inspect the vehicle for fluid leaks or other problems.
- Any problems should be reported to the proper authority.

Preventive Maintenance   Transportation equipment should undergo periodic preventive maintenance inspections and service in accordance with the manufacturer's recommendations. These inspections and servicings, similar to a building preventive maintenance program, can be set up on the basis of hours of operation, mileage, or elapsed time. The preventive maintenance program should include oil change and lubrication, timely check and adjustment of the cooling system's antifreeze, engine tune-ups, repacking of wheel bearings, replacement of cooling system hoses, changing of oil and air filters, replacement of drive belts, checking and adjustment of brakes and transmission fluid, and similar measures. The normal schedule is based upon regular use under normal conditions. The schedule may be accelerated due to harsh use, adverse climatic conditions, or excessive stop-and-go operation. It is the transportation system manager's

Figure 51–3
Car Service Record

Car | Make | Type | Purchase Date | Car No.

Serial Number		Lubrication								Motor			Electrical					Brakes		Steering		Major					Cooling				Misc.		
Date	Mileage	Chassis	Oil Change	Oil Filter	Fr. Wheels	R. Wheels	U. Joints	Muffler	Tail Pipe	Tune-up	Adj. or Grind Valves	Clean Carb.	Battery	Starter	Generator	Distributor	Headlights	Adjust	Reline	Adjust	Alignment	Wheel Balancing	Engine	Clutch	Transmission	Differential	Wreck	Radiator	Water Pump	Hoses	Antifreeze	Tires	Total Price

responsibility to ensure that these measures are carried out, including calling in permanently assigned vehicles when required.

Scheduled maintenance should cover:

1. Oil and filter changes every 3,000 miles for hard service, or every 4,500 to 6,000 miles for normal service.
2. Air filter change at recommended mileage or time interval.
3. Coolant service and inspection, with coolant change every two years.
4. Tune-up depending on severity of vehicle use—some annually, others more often.
5. Hoses and belts checked for softness or wear, and replaced if necessary.
6. Transmission fluid changed depending upon mileage or time, and the fluid's color and level.
7. Exhaust system visual inspection and leak test.
8. Brakes and brake fluid inspection.

A service checklist is included in Figure 51-4.

Vehicle Repairs   Necessary repairs, such as replacement of parts, will normally be identified through preventive maintenance inspections or breakdowns. Where repairs are performed will depend largely upon the garage facilities at the institution and the current workload. Customers can also assist with reporting problems.

When deciding whether to contract maintenance and repair or to establish a college or university garage, the size of the vehicle fleet will usually be the major consideration. Smaller institutions that own a small fleet of vehicles can seldom operate a garage economically because of the large investment in tools and equipment that it entails. Contract maintenance, full maintenance-lease programs, and servicing agreements may be more cost-effective.

At the other extreme, the larger institutions can normally realize greater economies by staffing and equipping a garage. However, even where campus-owned garages exist, few institutions find it cost-effective to provide facilities for body work, replacement of major vehicle components, or overhauls. Since staffing and investment in tools and equipment are so extensive and the work requirements so unpredictable, it is usually more economical to take care of major repairs by contract. A final determination, however, must be made by each institution based upon the size of the vehicle fleet, comparative costs, and availability of local facilities for contracting.

Vehicle Records   A detailed operating and maintenance record should be kept for each motor vehicle. Records should provide a com-

Figure 51-4

Transportation Services Preventive Maintenance Schedule

Vehicle maintenance and energy conservation go hand in hand. A sound preventive maintenance program requires the following procedure to maintain a fleet of vehicles with the fewest dead line units.

I. Maintenance Guides

A. The best start toward good maintenance is to read the owner's manual that came with the vehicle.
B. Post and enter cost of repairs and fuel on CRT daily. (Must be readily available to service personnel.)
C. Service department personnel should be well-informed and dependable.
D. Faculty and staff driving vehicles should cooperate in reporting mechanical problems.

II. Scheduled Maintenance Service A

3,000 miles or every 3 months.

1. Lubricate chassis, door, and hood hinges.
2. Change oil (replacing oil filter if required).
3. Clean or replace air filter.
4. Check all fluids.
5. Visually inspect for fluid leaks.
6. Inspect all safety equipment.
7. Inspect and inflate all tires 2 psi over owner's manual recommendation, but not to exceed 35 lbs on passenger cars (when cold).
8. Road test for performance.

III. Scheduled Maintenance Service B

A. 15,000 miles or 1 year
B. 6,000 miles or 6 months

1. All scheduled maintenance listed in II.
2. Engine performance test (tune-up if required).
3. Inspect exhaust system pipes and hangers.
4. Inspect brake system components.
5. Inspect steering mechanism and suspension.
6. Complete check of electrical system.
7. Inspect body condition (interior, exterior, and glass).

All adjustments and repairs are made to maintain vehicles in a safe, roadworthy condition.

IV. *Example of Cost for Low Gasoline Mileage

If 10 percent of vehicles average 2.4 miles per gallon less than reasonable performance, the average yearly cost per unit throughout fleet goes up $69.44. With 200 vehicles this would be an annual dollar loss of $13,889.

V. Cost-Reduction and Energy Conservation
  A. Driver cooperation—speeding, overloading vehicle, costly ac-
     cidents, and not reporting mechanical problems.
  B. Service department—rigid preventive maintenance program.
  C. Supervision—accurate records and follow through.
  D. Replacement—avoid costly under-the-hood repairs.

plete history of the maintenance and repair performed as well as their costs.

51.8 STAFFING

Staff size for transportation service varies with the size of the vehicle fleet, amount of maintenance and repair handled by the facilities department, and the measure of administrative control that is exercised over use. Small colleges may have only one person to schedule vehicles and maintain requisite records. Larger transportation organizations require mechanics, parts persons, service attendants, fuel attendants, dispatchers, billing and records clerks, and supervisory personnel (see Figure 51-5). Note that leasing vehicles does not eliminate the requirements for dispatching, billing, and other administrative functions. Leased vehicles are in the custody of the college or university, but all functions relative to their use and maintenance—except as otherwise provided for in the lease agreement—are similar to those for owned vehicles.

Equipment Management Information Systems

Management of transportation services can be greatly assisted by the computer. The management end of transportation is a numbers game. Buying the best vehicles for the lowest cost, meeting customer demand, and recording downtime all influence the success of the operation. Computers can record data so you can organize it to generate meaningful reports and make better decisions.

Computerized systems have been developed to assist managers in the following areas:

Figure 51-5

Staffing

Vehicle fleet size determines number of staff.

Small	Service Maintenance Administrative (Typically very few people)
Large	Mechanics Parts personnel Servicepeople Fuel attendant (or automated pumps) Dispatching Clerks Supervisors
Leased	Administrative Fuel Dispatching Billeting Supervision

- Accounting
- Ownership records-registration
- Equipment repair history records
- Cost reports—maintenance and operations
- Performance standards and targets
- Mileage/utilization
- Downtime/shop backlog
- Preventive maintenance scheduling
- Automated fuel dispensing system.

A computer system should provide exception reports as well as scheduled statistical reports, and it should make access simple, with safeguards for privileged information. The system should flag performance that does not meet predetermined standards, and should be designed so that all individual data bases (administrative, maintenance, and operations) are interconnected. A good system will be able to handle a multiplicity of labor-intensive functions according to predetermined schedules and to accommodate updates.

51.9 CONCLUSION

Of all the functions that may be performed by the facilities department, none varies more in scope and methods than meeting the institution's transportation requirements. The rates and availability of vehicles and equipment for lease or rent fluctuate depending upon location. Past practices, however, influence current methods. If purchasing a vehicle fleet and establishing the facilities and organization for its maintenance is not presently cost-effective, continuing an operation where one already exists may be the most economical alternative. Administrators need to remember that a careful evaluation of all factors must be made in each situation to determine the best method for meeting the institution's transportation requirements. This chapter cited the principal considerations for setting up the system and procedures for its operation.

ADDITIONAL RESOURCES

Finucane, William S. and John P. Harrod Jr. "Fleet Management." In *Work Control*. Alexandria, Virginia: APPA, 1988.

CHAPTER 52

Environmental Health and Safety

Ralph O. Allen Jr., Ph.D.
Professor of Chemistry and
Director of Environmental Health and Safety
University of Virginia

52.1 INTRODUCTION

Definition of Risk

The tragic end of the Challenger Space Shuttle mission in 1986 killed seven crew members, halted the U.S. space program, and led to a reevaluation of how NASA conducted its programs. The investigation of this accident has provided valuable insight into safety and risk management. Investigating commission member and Nobel Laureate Richard P. Feynman described the problem as a management attitude that "accepted risks because they got away with it the last time" and noted that this kind of attitude caused decision making to be "a kind of Russian roulette." This illogical attitude is not uncommon because the concept of risk is frequently misunderstood. The Challenger disaster was caused by the failure of an "o" ring. This was not the first time there had been erosion of "o" rings in the booster rockets, but there had never been serious accidents so no corrections were made.

Risk is the product of the probability of something happening times the consequences of the event should it occur. Often, if the consequences of a malfunction, accident, or overexposure are great (loss of life, induction of a fatal cancer), then people consider the activity risky, even if the probability of occurrence is low. This perception often leads to risk management strategies (safety programs) in which a large fraction of available resources are spent trying to avoid the unlikely catastrophe, while at the same time neglecting the common, but less catastrophic, events (e.g. back injuries, slips and falls, crushed/lacerated limbs).

Figure 52-1 illustrates the relationship between the number of incidents that occur randomly and the seriousness of the consequences. If

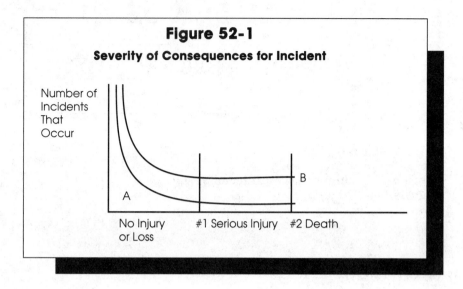

Figure 52-1

Severity of Consequences for Incident

the activity is considered to have greater inherent risk, then the risk curve will be more like that shown as B. Working conditions and employee attitudes both contribute to the number of random incidents that occur. For example, a cluttered work area and high-traffic volume may be contributing causes to such incidents as tripping. Most of the incidents do not have serious consequences, but on random occasions the results are severe. Of the many who trip in a cluttered work area, only rarely will someone fall and break a bone. Managers should not delude themselves into thinking that things are safe when there are no serious injuries. Although the odds are great that an incident will have only minor consequences, there is always some chance of a more severe accident. The risk curve in Figure 52-1 indicates that the catastrophic incident will eventually occur.

The key to managing risks is to design programs to reduce the probability of an event occurring, and reduce the consequences of such an event should it occur. For example, the use of personal protective equipment, machine guards, proper procedures, and mechanical lifting aides all help to reduce the probability that an accident will occur. By providing the proper equipment, facilities, and protocols to make a job safer, a catastrophic risk curve like B can become more like Curve A in Figure 52-1. For example, limiting the quantities of hazardous materials in use at any one time, regular stretching and conditioning exercises (particularly for the back), sprinkler systems in buildings, and emergency exercises (drills) all work to reduce the consequences of an accident.

The purpose of this chapter is to provide information and guidelines to the managers of university and college physical plant departments that will assist in developing and implementing, often in concert with an institutional safety office, programs designed to: 1) reduce losses due to employee injuries, 2) meet the legal requirements of environmental protection legislation, and 3) help to reduce the overall institutional liability.

Responsibility for Risk Management

Risk management is as important to an administrator as fiscal, time, and personnel management. During the 1980s it was apparent that regulatory agencies and the courts considered management and supervisory personnel to have the primary responsibility for safety in the workplace. Only those who have decision-making authority can be ultimately responsible for assuring that the work environment is safe and that employees work in a safe manner.

In addition to the legal responsibility, supervisors have a moral responsibility to help their workers do their job without being exposed to a high risk of disabling injury or occupationally-acquired disease. Safety experts have long emphasized that the direct costs (compensation and medical treatment) of accidents are far less than the indirect costs resulting from lost time and poor morale. Poor morale can result when employees perceive that their welfare is unimportant to management. Of course, the employee bears some responsibility, but they need the knowledge, the proper equipment and facilities, and the motivation that only management can provide. In the final analysis, safety is everyone's job. A formal safety policy or a safety manager can do little unless everyone regards safety as an important part of their job.

In addition to protecting employees, a physical plant administrator also has an obligation to protect the students, faculty, and visitors of the institution. In the past ten to twenty years, societal attitudes towards health, safety, and the protection of the environment have changed drastically. Our society wants a pristine environment and our workers expect to be able to work in an environment where there is little or no risk to their health and safety. To move toward these goals, the body of laws and regulations pertaining to environmental health and safety has grown dramatically in the past two decades and affects all aspects of the U.S. workforce, including those who work for colleges and universities.

Managers must keep up to date on new safety and environmental regulations. This is made difficult because the applicability of new regulations often depends upon the school's location, size, and whether it is a state agency or a private school. Most institutions have a safety office that can keep physical plant advised. However, there is a clear distinction between the operational safety responsibilities of the physical plant management team and the advisory/resource responsibilities of a formalized safety office team. Safety offices are always in a staff position relative to line management and, as such, provide resources and advice to supervisors and upper level management, but are not responsible for the actual implementation of employee and environment protection programs.

Development of Regulatory Programs

Most safety regulations start out as federal initiatives brought about by public pressure or interested lobbying groups (e.g. labor unions, environmental coalitions). After a law is enacted, one or more regulatory agencies must write, publicize, and implement the detailed regulations which are the agencies' interpretations of the law's intent. Although applicable to colleges and universities, new regulations are often written in broad terms for industry rather than for physical plant operations of a college or university.

Once a federal agency finalizes a set of regulations, individual states may agree to implement the federal programs using their own agencies. The state must establish regulations which are "at least as stringent as" those of the federal program. The state regulators may, and often do, adopt more demanding regulations. A common practice is to include the state's own institutions under the regulations even when excluded under the federal program. For example, when the Virginia Occupational Safety and Health Agency adopted the U.S. Occupational Safety and Health Administration's (OSHA) Hazard Communication Standard for chemical manufacturers, all of Virginia's state institutions of higher education and all local school districts were forced to comply with the regulatory program. Private institutions remained exempt until OSHA more recently introduced new standards that covered any facility (not just manufacturers) where hazardous chemicals were used.

The applicability of some regulations depends upon size or magnitude. Under the original EPA hazardous waste regulations, many institutions qualified for less demanding regulatory control as "small quantity generators." Later revisions in the program brought the small quantity generators under more stringent regulatory control. The hazardous wastes produced by physical plant operations must be treated like those from the chemistry laboratories. The total quantity of hazardous waste produced by an institution must be considered in determining the regulations which apply. On the other hand, with the "Emergency Planning and Community Right-to-Know" (SARA Title III) regulations, EPA specifically excluded laboratories and hospitals from reporting requirements. In this case it is probably only chemicals used in physical plant operations that must be reported to a local emergency response committee.

The applicability of health and safety regulations to each program must often be determined by a physical plant administrator who has knowledge of the many aspects of the institution's operations. To make this decision, an administrator must interpret the regulations. However, in the final analysis, it is the regulatory agency, through its inspectors, that will make the official interpretation of the regulations. While an institution can appeal a regulatory agency's interpretation, the decision by the courts will help set the precedents for the interpretation and applicability of regulations for other institutions of higher education.

Understanding and complying with regulations is difficult. However, the consequences of ignoring regulations can be severe in both real costs (fines and liability awards) and in terms of the image of the institution. The objective should be more than simply complying with regulations. The goal should be to protect employees, assure that facilities and programs are as safe as possible, and to minimize the impact of the institution's activities on the environment.

52.2 PROTECTING THE HEALTH AND SAFETY OF PHYSICAL PLANT EMPLOYEES

Regulatory Demands for Occupational Safety

There are two major regulatory programs pertaining to the safety of employees while on the job. The older of the two programs began with the 1902 Workers' Compensation Act, and guarantees employees compensation for on-the-job injuries (including those from chronic exposures to hazardous materials) regardless of fault. An injured employee is paid for any time lost from work and is compensated for all medical expenses. The second major body of regulations began with the 1970 Occupational Safety and Health Act, which established minimum standards of safe working conditions for all employees. Initially the emphasis in safety was upon compliance with the specific OSHA regulations, but the recent trend has been to look more to the overall effectiveness of the safety program with emphasis on educating employees about job safety.

Management Responsibility

The increased emphasis on education is based on the conclusions by safety experts that over 80 percent of all on-the-job accidents are due primarily to the unsafe acts of workers. This may be a simplistic approach, as most accidents have multiple causes, but it is clear that people are a big part of the problem. An unsafe act is a result of not knowing (lack of training), not caring (poor management), or it is intentional. The current concept of workplace safety suggests that accidents are a symptom of problems in management. This suggests that creating a good and effective safety program can help solve other organizational problems. Safety, like any other physical plant program, must be managed effectively and consistently.

Safety and risk management should be treated with the same level of concern as other operational problems (e.g., personnel, finances). Management must establish an organizational safety policy and accept the fact that the cost of safety (in terms of money and employee time) is an investment that will pay off in reduced workers compensation costs, increased productivity, and higher morale.

Lack of procedures assigning accountability within an organization is often described as safety's greatest failing. If a first-line employee or supervisor knows the accident record of their organization will be considered in their performance evaluation, they will surely be more attentive to safety. Pressure to achieve realistic safety goals should be included in the factors used to measure performance, such as productivity, quality, time, and finances. Managers should look for and define operational problems and/or errors that increase the frequency and severity of accidents. The errors that lead to accidents may be the procedures, or lack thereof, or failure to administer effective controls to assure that the procedures are followed. By requiring safe operating procedures to be written and reviewed, managers provide supervisors and employees with the mechanisms to complete a task safely.

Managers not only establish the safety policies, but they must also be certain that a program is carried out. Unsafe conditions and acts must be corrected. Managers should attend safety committee meetings and respond to any requests or proposals from these committees. Timeliness is important. Managers need a good attitude toward safety issues, and should set a good example in order to gain the employees' confidence. In summary, good managers must clearly state their goals with regard to safety by implementing administrative policies and by providing the necessary support to make a safety program work.

Safety Committees

The use of safety committees as part of an overall safety program is traditional. Participation of active safety committees promote safety awareness. Properly constituted and recognized safety committees are conduits for communications in both directions between managers and their employees. The structure of the safety committee may vary depending on the size of the overall physical plant and its organization. Larger organizations may have a system of smaller, grass-roots committees reporting to a senior safety committee, as shown in Figure 52-2. The membership of a safety committee should include first-line workers, supervisors, and high-level management persons.

Committee meetings should be held on a regular basis, be short, and have a formal agenda. Some meetings should have a carefully prepared educational component. Figure 52-3 lists some general topics that can be part of the educational curriculum. Topics covered should include areas of concern raised by committee members or suggested by safety surveys. There should be time for open discussions, reviews of accidents, and reports on the results of safety inspections. Every accident should be reviewed to determine whether the event was foreseeable and preventable. Corrective actions should be considered, and recommendations made to the appropriate administrator for implementation. Administrators should report their actions on all recommendations to the committee. Since the members learn through service on safety committees, it is advantageous to rotate the membership. This also continuously brings new ideas to the committee.

Role of Supervisors

Safety professionals generally agree that the participation of supervisory employees is the single most important factor in making a safety program successful. Supervisors are in the best position to prevent accidents. They see the workers and the workplace every day and are best able to anticipate potential problems. The supervisor is often the most experienced, and therefore can provide the necessary training for the other employees. The supervisor can also communicate the needs and goals of management to the workers.

Safety should be included in the supervisor's job description and formal evaluation. This responsibility must be accompanied by training, motivation, and authority with regard to safety matters. Figure 52-4 outlines some of the things that supervisors can do to enhance safety. To be effective in these activities, supervisors must have the required safety knowledge and motivation.

Supervisors must receive special training, including general principles of safety and management, as well as specific topics related to each supervisor's job. The safety committee meetings can help expand and reinforce the supervisory training. It is the supervisor's responsibility to investigate accidents, determine the causes, and propose changes that will prevent the occurrence of similar accidents. To do this the supervisors must be trained on how to investigate. Figure 52-5 suggests how training objectives should be established and gradually increased.

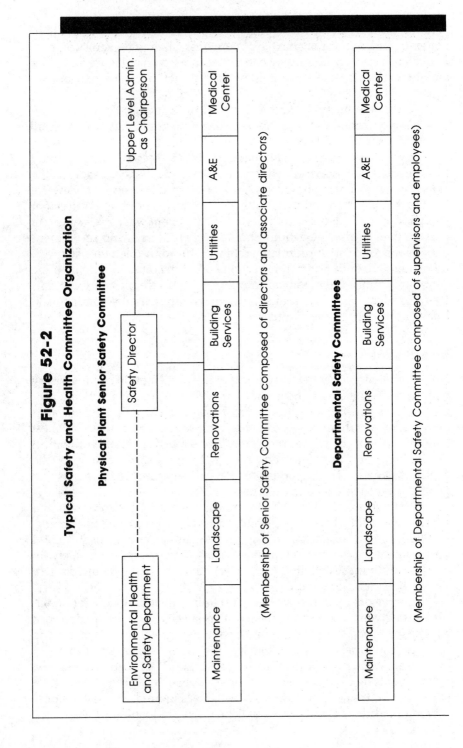

Figure 52-2

Typical Safety and Health Committee Organization

Physical Plant Senior Safety Committee

Upper Level Admin. as Chairperson

Safety Director

Environmental Health and Safety Department

| Maintenance | Landscape | Renovations | Building Services | Utilities | A&E | Medical Center |

(Membership of Senior Safety Committee composed of directors and associate directors)

Departmental Safety Committees

| Maintenance | Landscape | Renovations | Building Services | Utilities | A&E | Medical Center |

(Membership of Departmental Safety Committee composed of supervisors and employees)

Safety Educational/Management Training System
(Safety And Health Organization)

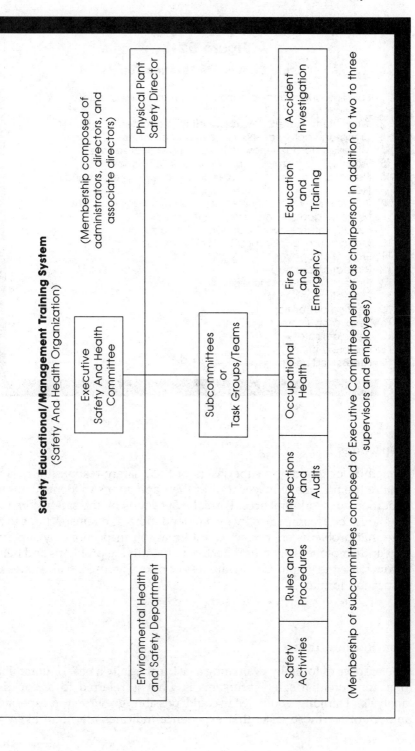

(Membership composed of administrators, directors, and associate directors)

Physical Plant Safety Director

Executive Safety And Health Committee

Environmental Health and Safety Department

Subcommittees or Task Groups/Teams

Safety Activities

Rules and Procedures

Inspections and Audits

Occupational Health

Fire and Emergency

Education and Training

Accident Investigation

(Membership of subcommittees composed of Executive Committee member as chairperson in addition to two to three supervisors and employees)

Figure 52-3
Safety Committee Meeting Topics

1. Spotting and reporting hazards—how to conduct safety inspections
2. What went wrong? How to investigate accidents
3. Lifting and carrying—how to avoid back injuries
4. Materials storage—how to keep your work area safe
5. Working with hazardous materials—Right-to-Know
6. Flammable and combustible liquids—how to prevent and fight fires
7. Portable power tools—electrical and mechanical safety
8. Machine guards—protection in the shops
9. Ladder safety—special dangers of heights
10. Good housekeeping practices and storage
11. Protection of eyes
12. Protection of head
13. Protection of feet and legs
14. Protection of hands
15. Hearing protection
16. Respiratory protection
17. Electrical safety
18. Fire prevention
19. Fitness and health

Inspections

A method of reminding supervisors of their safety responsibility is to require them to make inspections of their operations to identify unsafe conditions or work practices. Formal inspections by the safety committee should be accompanied by recommendations and reinspections to be sure that problems are corrected. Informal self-inspections by supervisors and employees are most effective in identifying problems and helping increase the employee's awareness of risks. Figure 52-6 illustrates an inspection format.

Non-Routine Tasks

The practice of formally evaluating a task, especially a new or unfamiliar one, for potential safety problems is what is referred to as job risk analysis. Thinking about what could possibly go wrong is especially important for those tasks that experience indicates are more likely to

Figure 52-4

Ways To Enhance Employee Safety Awareness

Activity	Examples
Participate in safety training	—Conduct regularly scheduled training of employees by work center/division —Provide specialized training on specific problems
Indoctrinate new employees	—Conduct formal orientation program —Distribute written handouts —Review safety rules/policies —Document training
Enforce safety rules/ policies	—Explain rationale of rules and policies —Provide verbal warnings —Document violations in employee file —Monitor workplace and employee work habits —Use safety as one element in employee evaluation
Encourage employee participation	—Encourage workers to report existing hazards and incidents —Collect information on hazards, near-misses, and unsafe conditions/practices from operationally experienced employees (critical incident technique)
Participate on safety committee	—Investigate safety deficiencies —Review accident reports —Conduct safety inspections —Prepare, review, and present safety training
Conduct internal safety inspections	—Institute formal program with guidelines —Utilize checklist procedure —Conduct frequent (monthly) inspections —Report results to management
Increase supervisor/ employee safety	—Utilize positive reinforcement —Conduct work center/divisional meetings and/or tool box safety sessions —Integrate on-the-job and off-the-job safety programs —Make job safety analysis a team effort
Promote safety climate	—Set the example —Select safety posters (including special purpose reminders) —Distribute folders and brochures —Set up table displays (articles/photos) —Support reward incentive programs —Contact recognition organizations —Conduct safety contests

Figure 52-5

Training Objectives

Objective 1: The final effect of training is defined, and expected behavior is described.

Example: This training will enable you, as a supervisor, to investigate an accident.

Objective 2: The conditions under which the behavior defined in Objective 1 should occur.

Example: As a supervisor, you must investigate any accident involving employees under your supervision and complete an accident report within one working day.

Objective 3: Define the criteria that management will accept in performance or behavior.

Example: The accident report should identify at least three causes that contributed to the accident and at least three corrective actions which the supervisor can take or which can be recommended to management.

produce injuries. Circumstances most likely to produce serious accidents can be categorized as:

1. Contact with high energy sources (e.g., steam, heat, high voltage).
2. Non-routine tasks for which there has been no preparation or training.
3. Construction or maintenance activities involving heights, trenches.
4. Activities in the vicinity of, or involving the use of, flammable or other hazardous materials.

In recognition of the greater severity of accidents involving these factors, OSHA has established rigorous standards for many activities involving high energy sources, noises, temperatures, and workplace exposure to certain chemicals. While many dangerous situations may arise in physical plant operations, they may not be common. In fact, since the more dangerous tasks are usually non-routine, the potential risks become even higher. For non-routine jobs, managers and supervisors may not even be aware of the applicable OSHA standards. The best way to deal with the problem of non-routine tasks is to create a greater general awareness on the part of supervisors and all employees. An ongoing program of training is one way to create greater knowledge and awareness.

Figure 52-6

Supervisor Work Site Safety Checklist

Dept. _____

Building _____

Date _____

A = Acceptable

U = Unacceptable

N/A = Not Applicable

Environmental Conditions:

Work areas (clean, trash removed, sanitary)

_____

Lighting (replace bulbs/switches as needed)

_____

Ventilation/air quality (dust/fumes):
   a. Inspect exhaust fans for cleanliness

_____

   b. Inspect fan blade

_____

   c. Change filters

_____

   d. Check airflow

_____

Door locks/doors open and close properly

_____

Inspect water strainers

_____

Check for leaking pipes

_____

Toxic/Hazardous Materials:

Chemical storage (paints, cleaning supplies, etc.)

_____

Container labels

_____

Cylinder storage

_____

Equipment:

Preventive maintenance:
   a. Equipment properly maintained & serviced

_____

   b. Motors & bearings clean & properly lubricated (grease/oil)

_____

   c. Check all other lubricating points

_____

Lock-out tags available

_____

Motor pump checked for:
   a. Alignment _____
   b. Couplings _____
   c. Leaks _____

Electrical Safety:

Outlets _____

Extension cords/cord fixtures _____
Fuses/circuit breakers _____

Walkways and Structure:
Corridors (clear of obstructions)

_____

Stairwells (rails/treads/risers)

_____

Floors (sagging, warping, cracks, no slippery areas)

_____

Ladders/scaffolds

_____

Machine Safeguards:
Belts, pulleys, chains, gears, rotating parts
   a. Check belt alignment

_____

   b. Replace belts as required

_____

Grinder work rest (within ⅛″ of wheel)

_____

Blades on cutting/sawing machines

_____

Portable hand tools

_____

Fire Protection:
Fire extinguishers
   a. How to use

_____

   b. Regularly inspected

_____

Smoke detectors

_____

Manual pull stations

_____

Fire exits
   a. Signs visible

_____

   b. Know locations

_____

Personal Protective Equipment:
Face

_____

Hearing

_____

Clothing

_____

_____
Supervisor Signature

Personal Protective Equipment

Personal protective equipment is an important part of any safety program. In general, OSHA guidelines and regulations recommend or require engineering controls to prevent the worker from being exposed to a hazardous agent or situation. Engineered solutions are not as readily available for the worker whose job is in the field, and thus personal protective equipment is necessary. Such equipment includes, but is not limited to: safety glasses, hard hats, safety shoes, respirators and dust masks, protective clothing, and machine guards (see 29 CFR 1910.1003-1016). Items such as hard hats and respirators should not be checked out when needed, but rather should be part of the worker's personal equipment. Courts have ruled in many cases that the employer is responsible for providing and paying for the minimum required personal safety equipment. For example, basic safety glasses, including prescription when necessary, must be provided by the employer.

Supervisors play the key role in ensuring that employees use the appropriate personal protective equipment when necessary. Signs on equipment and throughout the shops, such as "Wear Your Safety Glasses," are necessary, but do not fulfill management's responsibility. Supervisors must evaluate employees on the use of personal protective equipment in the same manner as they would evaluate the use of any other tool. The proper use of personal protective equipment is part of an employee's job, and their performance evaluations should reflect this.

Accident Investigation and Analysis

The compilation of accident reports required by OSHA is relatively simple with an effective safety program. By improving the information on the accident reports and by compiling statistics, a manager can have a valuable tool for risk management. Figure 52-7 lists a classification scheme that can be used to summarize the type of accident, nature of injuries, parts of the body injured, the object or physical cause of the accident, and the seriousness. The records can be kept by job classification. Since accidents are random, there may not be enough accidents to provide good statistics. It is, however, useful to look for trends such as incidence by unit and by seriousness.

Accident records are useful in identifying topics for training or other management support of safety activities. The records are also one indicator of the effectiveness of the overall safety program. A detailed analysis of workers compensation accident/injury claims data for a university work force will generally show that most of the injuries are due to employees unsafe acts. For example, injuries from vehicular accidents, many back injuries, and most slip-trip-fall injuries are due to unsafe acts

Figure 52-7

Accident Reporting Classification Scheme

Types of Accidents:

CTRAD	=	Contact—radioactive material/radiation-producing equipment
CT-TP	=	Contact—temperature extreme (hot/cold objects, liquids, weather)
CTTOX	=	Contact—toxic substances (plants, chemicals)
CTNOX	=	Contact—noxious substances (odors, chemicals, dust, blood)
CTCST	=	Contact—caustic substances (detergents, chemicals)
CT-EL	=	Contact—electric current
CTNBT	=	Caught in or between (doors, machinery)
FL-SL	=	Fall at same level (floor, stairs)
FL-HT	=	Fall from heights (ladder, roof)
MAT-H	=	Material handling (heavy objects, patients, furniture)
ST-BY	=	Struck by (objects, liquids, other persons, machine)
ST-AG	=	Struck against (objects, tools, needle sticks)
ST-BT	=	Sting or bite (insects, animals, patients)
OTHER	=	Other miscellaneous types of accidents not included above

Nature of Injuries:

ABRAS	=	Abrasions
BRKBN	=	Broken bones
BRUSE	=	Bruises
BURN	=	Burns
CUT	=	Cuts
DERM	=	Dermatitis, allergic rashes
PUNCT	=	Puncture wounds (e.g., needle sticks)
SPRAN	=	Sprained ligaments
STRAN	=	Strained muscles
BITE	=	Bites or stings
OTHER	=	Other kinds of injuries not included in the groups above

Parts of Body Injured:

FACE	=	Face, except eyes
EYE	=	Eyes
HEAD	=	Top, back, sides of head
NECK	=	Throat, back/sides of neck
CHEST	=	Chest, rib cage, lungs, heart
ABDMN	=	Abdomen, intestines, muscles
BACK	=	All of back, sides of body
BUTT	=	Buttocks including coccyx
ARM	=	Arms including elbows, wrists
LEG	=	Legs including knees
SHLDR	=	Shoulders, back and front
HAND	=	Hands including fingers
FOOT	=	Feet including toes
ANKL	=	Ankles
TOBOD	=	Total body

Causes of Accidents:

CHEM	=	Chemicals, detergents, odors
FLOOR	=	Floors/stairs, slippery, wet, obstacles in way
LADER	=	Ladder
MACH	=	Machines, electric powered only
OBJCT	=	Miscellaneous objects
NEDLE	=	Miscellaneous syringes, needles used in labs and hospitals
PSNPL	=	Poisonous plants
TOOL	=	Tools, hand or electric powered
WETHR	=	Weather, sun, snow, ice
OTHPS	=	Other persons, patients, colleagues
OTHER	=	Miscellaneous other causes of accidents not included above

Severity of Accidents:

NC	=	No cost, minor injury
MC	=	Minor costs, first aid but no disability
OR	=	OSHA recordable, reported to OSHA, employee needs time off beyond day of injury
MAJ	=	Major claim, medical expenses greater than $500 and/ or more than seven days disability

rather than unsafe equipment or conditions. Therefore, an effective loss reduction program must focus on training employees to improve attitudes and work habits. Back injury prevention programs, defensive driver training programs, correct use of ladders and scaffolding, and forklift safety programs are examples of training programs focused on changing human behavior rather than changing the physical condition of the workplace. In order to determine what training programs are needed, and where they are needed, it is necessary to continually review and analyze the workers' compensation data base by the health and safety organization within the institution.

Safety Training

Training provides the knowledge to do a job safely and increases an employee's awareness of on-the-job risks. To be effective, training must not be too complicated. It should provide background to help the employee understand why precautions are taken as well as specific instructions on how to do the job correctly and safely. Frequent, rather than long, training sessions help create an atmosphere where people think more about safety and about how they do their jobs. General safety training may be a function of the safety committee. Many of the training topics given in Figure 52-3 will be of benefit to most physical plant employees. Those employees exposed to greater risks should be given more training that pertains to those specific risks. Subjects or topics that should be stressed during training sessions can be identified by some of the procedures described earlier: 1) accident investigations, 2) trends shown in the compilation of accident statistics (required for OSHA reporting), 3) an inspection program, and 4) employee suggestions.

The development of a specialized training program is useless unless upper level management grants employees time to attend the training courses. Time obviously costs money, but time for safety training must be considered an investment that will pay off in greater productivity and lower insurance premiums. Even though the physical plant organization may not be run as a business-for-profit, employees who are off the job due to work incurred injuries are non-productive and hence increase the cost of completing the required work of the department. Training of new or temporary employees to replace those injured on the job further adds to the cost of work-related injuries. It is far more productive to utilize training time to teach present employees how to do a job safely than to have to use such training time to break in new people.

Hazard Communication—Right-to-Know

In a typical university environment, physical plant employees are potentially exposed to a large number of hazardous materials. In some cases the employee may be directly handling the material as part of the job (e.g. water treatment chemicals or cleaners), and in other cases the work environment, such as a research laboratory, may contain hazardous materials that could expose maintenance workers during routine procedures. The potential for exposure to the materials directly used on the job is usually far greater. The approach that OSHA has used for hazardous chemicals has been to make workers more responsible for their own safety by making them aware of hazards. The Hazard Communication Standard, or as it has come to be called, the Right-to-Know regulations (RTK), establish a mechanism to provide employees with information so that they can protect themselves. Training is an important part of the program as it creates greater awareness of hazardous materials in the work place.

For physical plant employees, one of the greatest problems with hazardous material is that they often do not know when substances are dangerous. OSHA's Hazard Communication Standard contains, among other things, provisions regulating the listing and labeling of hazardous chemicals present in the workplace, the provision of information to employees about these chemicals, and the training of employees in the proper handling of hazardous materials. While the Federal Standard (29

CFR 1910.1200) was promulgated primarily for the manufacturing sector, it is or will be applicable to all hazardous materials present at colleges and universities.

All university employees who may be exposed to or come in contact with hazardous chemicals must be included in the Right-to-Know program. The first of four basic requirements is a written program that describes how the RTK regulations will be implemented. The second requirement is to make material safety data sheets (MSDS) available to all employees. The third requirement is that chemical products have the appropriate labeling. For the most part the labels are the responsibility of the manufacturers, but if the materials are placed in different containers, such as for dispensing bulk liquids, the container must be labeled with the name and hazard associated with the material.

The fourth requirement of the RTK standard is to provide employees with training and information about the overall program and about the specific chemicals encountered in the workplace. This provides employees with information they need to work safely around hazardous substances. General purpose programs aimed at industry often do little to really enhance the knowledge and awareness of employees. It is usually more effective to tailor a program to the specific needs of specific employees.

Figure 52-8 describes a two-part program of initial training for new employees and an ongoing program of more detailed training directed to the needs of the different departments. To aid in this training, it is helpful to enlist the assistance of a knowledgeable health and safety professional, a member of the chemistry faculty, or a RTK consultant. For most employees, the training should be simple and basic. They must learn how to recognize labels and the basic precautions to be taken in response to these labels. Supervisors need to be trained to teach proper handling techniques and to monitor employees to be sure they follow proper work practices.

The requirement to have a Right-to-Know program should be viewed as an opportunity to enhance supervisory participation in the safety program. The supervisor's first task should be to make an inventory of materials being used, and to keep the inventory updated. The inventory process should include observations on how the material is stored and a rough idea of the quantities on hand. Based upon the inventory, management must assign someone with the specific responsibility for obtaining the MSDSs from manufacturers. While these must be kept in the workplace and made accessible to any employee, they may be too complicated to be useful for training employees. Figure 52-9 gives an example of a simplified information sheet that can be useful for giving employees the important safety information about a particular product.

Figure 52-8

Suggested Outline of Employee Information and Training Program

A. New Employee Orientation:

1. An overview of the requirements of the Hazard Communication Standard with an explanation of how it is implemented in the work place at your institution.

2. The location of the chemical product inventory for their work area, the modified MSDS (originals and, if used, any information sheets), and copies of the written hazard communication program.

3. An opportunity for employees to ask questions.

4. On-the-job instruction during the employees' first assignment.

B. Employee Chemical Safety Training:

1. All employees will be reminded regularly by their supervisor about the nature, purpose, proper equipment, and use of any hazardous chemical/product in the work place.

2. An annual formal chemical safety program with emphasis on topics that are department-specific. Topics will include:

    a. Chemicals present in the work place operation
    b. Container labeling
    c. Health hazards
    d. Reduction of exposure through control/work practices and personal protective equipment
    e. Chemical storage and waste management
    f. Physical/chemical characteristics
    g. Reactivity data
    h. Fire/explosion hazards
    i. Observation techniques and methods used to determine the presence or release of hazardous chemicals/vapors in the work area
    j. Emergency procedures in event of exposure and/or spill
    k. Questions and answers

3. Managers will have the responsibility to ensure that all of their employees attend this program, and will maintain accurate employee attendance records (proof to OSHA).

With assistance from the safety office or a member of the chemistry faculty and the MSDS, these forms can be filled out for each substance. While completing these forms, consideration should be given to the suitability of the manner in which the material is stored. If personal protective equipment is recommended, it should be clearly noted on the information sheet. When the proper equipment is not available, recommendations should be made to the safety committee. The completed form helps supervisors train employees by focusing on key items. Whenever a new assignment or procedure calls for the use of a hazardous material, these forms should be given to the employee to review. It is also valuable to have regular programs to review the proper use of safety equipment and procedures for storing and working with hazardous materials. An ongoing educational program on hazardous materials enhances safety awareness for all employees.

52.3 SAFETY OF INSTITUTIONAL FACILITIES

Building Safety and Code Compliance

There are many aspects of facilities management where health and safety codes or regulations are applicable. Compliance with codes helps provide safe facilities for students, faculty, and staff. It is a physical plant manager's responsibility to be aware of the need to maintain safe exits from buildings and to avoid improper storage. Specifically, exits must be kept clear at all times, exit lighting must be installed and kept operational, and any remodeling projects must be carefully reviewed to assure that such work does not eliminate legally required exits or create dead-end corridors. It is often a temptation to use wide building corridors, mechanical equipment rooms, and transformer vaults as storage space. However, such storage is usually illegal and unsafe. Unless management establishes and enforces a firm policy against such storage maintenance workers will frequently store supplies and equipment in these areas as a way to get the job done quickly and easily.

The OSHA regulations cover many other aspects of building safety such as protective railings, roof parapets, fume hood exhausts, machinery guards, emergency showers, eyewash stations, and adequate lighting, but most of these are static building features rather than operational concerns, so they must be addressed during construction and renovation activities. However, it is important that there be someone at an academic institution who is familiar with these code requirements. If there is no formal safety office at an institution, the responsibility is usually assigned to the physical plant department.

Managing Hazardous Materials

One aspect of maintaining safe facilities is to provide for the proper management of hazardous substances. The hazardous materials that are used in physical plant operations include toxic compounds, corrosives,

Figure 52-9

Chemical Product Training Form

Date: _____ Work Center #: _____

Chemical/Product Name: _____

Supervisor Name: _____

1. Discuss with employees the **nature** of the chemical or product they may encounter in the work place.
   _____ FLAMMABLE (flame symbol)
   _____ CORROSIVE (hand dissolving)
   _____ OXIDIZER (ball of flame)
   _____ POISON (skull and crossbones)
   _____ OTHER explain:_____

2. Discuss with employees the **purpose** of the chemical or product they may use in their work area.
   _____ Why they use this particular chemical or product
   _____ What does this chemical or product do

3. Discuss with employees **how to use** this chemical or product **properly**.
   _____ Keep chemical/product away from all sources of fire, sparks, and heat (sun, heaters, engines)
   _____ Adequate ventilation (doors, fans):_____
   _____
   _____ How to properly dispense a chemical or product from a drum or container
   _____ How to properly dilute a concentrated chemical/product
   _____ How to properly dispose of any chemical waste:_____
   _____
   _____ What to do in case of a spill:_____
   _____
   _____ What to do in case of a fire: *Use ABC dry powder extinguisher*

4. Discuss with employees the **proper precautions** to take when using this chemical or product.
   Gloves: _____
   Goggles/safety glasses/shields: _____
   Respirators/masks: _____
   Other: _____

••• ALWAYS WASH HANDS AFTER USE •••

and flammables. Certain academic departments use hazardous materials, to which physical plant employees can be exposed. Management of these substances requires recognition of the potential hazards. The Right-to-Know Standards force manufacturers to provide the necessary information to allow the users to plan for the proper management of any hazardous material. By using the MSDS provided by the manufacturer, decisions can be made on how to store and use the materials. Products can be evaluated to determine whether they can be replaced by something less hazardous. A hazardous substance that is potentially dangerous to personnel and must be managed and disposed of carefully can be replaced with one that is not hazardous. It takes time to compare products using the MSDS and by testing the performance, but it is usually worth the effort.

An important aspect of hazardous materials management is training, and the Right-to-Know program described earlier provides the mechanism to conduct this training. Certain physical plant employees, however, can be exposed to a wide variety of substances being used by others. Building maintenance workers and custodians are concerned about their potential exposure to radiation, radioactive materials, chemicals, and biological materials encountered in the laboratories where they must do their jobs. However, if these agents are all well managed and stored, the small quantities generally used will not represent a significant risk for the casual visitor or worker in a university laboratory.

A uniform system of labeling doors to alert personnel and provide telephone numbers of people who have knowledge of the laboratories and who should be contacted in emergencies can help protect physical plant personnel. Incorporation of the National Fire Protection Association (NFPA) labeling system helps inform physical plant personnel as well as emergency responders (see Figure 52-10). Containers for radioactive, chemical, and infectious wastes should be clearly identified, and custodians need to be trained to recognize the labels.

Good ventilation is important to working safely with chemicals. Protection of laboratory personnel depends upon proper functioning of the HVAC system. When physical plant employees work on the HVAC system, they not only endanger themselves, but those in the laboratory. Both groups can be protected by a formal mechanism to be sure HVAC personnel communicate with laboratory personnel to find out what materials are being used and when is it best to work on the system. There should be procedures to lock out or label the fume hoods when the HVAC system is not operational.

Ventilation systems, including chemical fume hoods, need to be designed carefully to protect personnel from being exposed to chemical vapors. Laboratory design both for new facilities and renovations is a specialized field. Besides ventilation, the design must also include facili-

Figure 52-10

CAUTION

CORROSIVE MATERIALS

HOUSEKEEPERS DO NOT ENTER

ELECTRICAL HAZARD

CHEMICAL HAZARDS

NO SMOKING, EATING OR DRINKING

N.F.P.A.

ADMITTANCE TO AUTHORIZED PERSONNEL ONLY

SPECIAL PROCEDURES OR PRECAUTIONS: _____

CONTACT	NAME	LOCATION	PHONE	HOME PHONE
FOR ENTRY OR ADVICE				
IN EMERGENCY				
IN EMERGENCY				

ties for chemical storage. For further information, see Chapter 24, Laboratory Fume Hoods.

Safety Related Maintenance Programs

Physical plant departments are responsible for the maintenance and upkeep of equipment and mechanical systems installed in the campus buildings. The performance and/or condition of these systems and equipment is specified by various regulatory agencies. Maintaining such equipment within the allowable regulatory limits will usually require that physical plant interface closely with the institution's safety organization. The following list is not meant to be all inclusive, but represents examples of systems and equipment found on almost all campuses that will require careful and continual monitoring.

Fire Alarm and Sprinkler Systems   The condition of such systems must be monitored frequently to assure that alarm systems function properly, all sprinkler valves are open, sprinkler heads are not blocked by bad storage practices, and individual alarm devices have not been silenced or disconnected. Likewise, during construction activities alarm systems may need to be temporarily taken off line.

Emergency Showers and Eyewash Stations   These systems should be checked at least semi-annually to assure that water flows from the device. Since these systems are plumbing fixtures, it is a physical plant responsibility to conduct these routine checks and keep the systems in repair.

Chemical Fume Hoods and General Laboratory Ventilation Systems   Generally, once a laboratory ventilation system is properly balanced it does not require periodic checks unless the laboratory occupants complain of temperatures or odors. On the other hand, fume hoods must be checked at least annually and generally must meet minimum standard of airflow over the working opening of the hood. In many cases, the health and safety office will do the required annual measurement, but there must be a mechanism to be sure that the deficient hoods are properly repaired by physical plant employees.

Cooling Tower Maintenance   A maintenance program must assure that harmful organisms such as legionella bacteria do not become established in high numbers in the cooling tower water system. In the past, chromate compounds have been used to treat cooling tower systems to prevent the growth of such harmful organisms. However, EPA regulations treat discharge of chromium as hazardous waste, so other water treatment chemicals must be used.

Swimming Pool Water Treatment   The maintenance of appropriate bacteriacidal levels of chlorine in pool water is required by local or state health departments. There are hazards associated with the handling of chlorine gas and the quantities may require that the facility have emergency planning under EPA's regulations (SARA).

Domestic versus Industrial Water Supplies—Backflow Prevention Device Testing   Whenever domestic water supply lines are connected to pieces of equipment to provide cooling water or are piped into chemical laboratories, it is necessary to provide some type of device to prevent the reverse flow of water (backflow) into the domestic supply. This is often done by providing a laboratory building with two independent water systems, domestic and industrial isolated from each other by a large backflow prevention device located on the primary water main feeding the building. In some cases, subsystems will be isolated from the domestic water supply by means of smaller, localized backflow devices. In any case, most local codes require that all such devices (other than simple vacuum breakers) be checked annually for proper operation.

Asbestos

A widely publicized hazardous substance that physical plant employees are likely to encounter on the job is asbestos. Because of the widespread use of asbestos as a building material and for pipe insulation, it can be found in most college and university buildings. It was used for fireproofing of structural steel members, soundproofing, insulation on steam and hot water pipes, as an ingredient in floor tiles and certain ceiling materials, and as a major ingredient of transite, which was often used as the base material for constructing fume hoods.

Federal regulation of this material has created great public awareness of the possible health risks due to the inhalation of asbestos fibers. There is often emotional, and in some cases irrational, concern on the part of those who work in the vicinity of asbestos-containing materials. Figure 52-11 outlines the regulations that apply to asbestos. The way in which these regulations pertain to an institution may differ in detail, but the regulatory trends suggest that abatement of the hazard by removal is the only clear way to avoid continuing problems. Abatement is expensive, so careful planning and budgeting are required.

The AHERA (Asbestos Hazard Emergency Response Act) Regulations, enacted by EPA, force local school systems to develop management plans for any asbestos in their buildings. The federal government

Figure 52-11
Current Asbestos Regulations

OSHA:

29 CFR Parts 1910.1001 (General Industry) and 1926.58 (Construction Industry) "Occupational Exposure to Asbestos, Tremolite, Anthophyllite, and Activolite; Final Rules"

29 CFR Part 1910.134 "Respiratory Protection"

29 CFR Part 1910.1200 "Hazard Communication"

29 CFR Part 1910.20 "Medical Surveillance"

EPA:

40 CFR Part 763 (AHERA) "Asbestos-Containing Materials in Schools"

40 CFR Part 61, Subpart M "National Emission Standard for Hazardous Air Pollutants"

40 CFR Part 173, Subpart J "Transportation of Asbestos-Containing Waste"

is giving strong consideration to extending these, or similar, regulations to all public buildings. Many states have already begun to move toward the enactment of similar regulations for their own buildings, including those found at their institutions of higher education.

Facilities managers at colleges and universities would be prudent to understand the AHERA regulations because it is likely that some type of formal management program will be required in the near future. The AHERA regulations require the location of all asbestos in each building be identified and its condition characterized (i.e., loose, friable, or solid). Thus, the first step should be to locate and inventory the friable (crumbly) asbestos in each building. Analyzing suspected asbestos-containing materials requires proper sampling techniques and analytical methods. If these are not available, then qualified contractors and laboratories must be utilized. It is often just as useful to label a material as "suspected asbestos" rather than doing the extensive testing.

Once this inventory is completed, decisions must be made as to whether to leave the asbestos alone, or to encapsulate or remove friable material. Where there is damage to asbestos-containing materials sprayed onto ceilings, immediate remedial action is required to prevent asbestos fibers from being released into the air. Even if the AHERA regulations do not apply to your institution, you must comply with OSHA regulations. No employee can be exposed to airborne asbestos concentrations greater than 0.02 fiber per cubic centimeter without protective equipment (e.g., respirators). Damaged materials and poor work practices can easily create this level of airborne contamination.

In cases where the asbestos is encapsulated by a dropped ceiling, all physical plant personnel should be alerted to avoid disturbing the ceiling. Signs should be placed in mechanical rooms and other places to alert personnel to the potential of asbestos exposure. Pipe lagging, asbestos-containing plaster covered by cloth tape on steam and hot water pipes, is commonly encountered as a part of the heating systems. If the cloth cover is damaged slightly, it can easily be patched with duct tape. No matter where asbestos is used, damage needs to be contained or the fiber concentrations in the air can become dangerously high. If the levels exceed the limits set by OSHA, employees cannot be allowed to work in the area without using respirators.

Everyone should be reminded that being in the vicinity of asbestos-containing materials is not dangerous unless the asbestos is disturbed and the fibers get into the air. If there is concern about asbestos exposure, the only way to know whether there is danger caused by exceeding the levels which OSHA has established is to monitor the air. There are specific procedures that must be used for the air analysis. Laboratories doing this testing should be certified and records of air monitoring should be well documentated.

The complete removal of all asbestos may be so expensive that it is likely that an long-term program will be established to monitor at least some areas containing asbestos. Simple inspections of the material should be performed on a regular basis, with the results recorded along with the results of a periodic air monitoring program. An ongoing monitoring and observation program can: 1) serve to remind everyone that asbestos is present and that precautions must be taken so as to avoid any disturbances, 2) enable the discovery of signs of deterioration or other problems that require immediate attention (abatement or repair), and 3) provide for the documentation of the status of the asbestos. Personnel should be kept informed if there are no problems; if the potential for asbestos exposures exists, the area should be closed off and the asbestos hazard abated.

Asbestos can only be removed by following specified procedures. Failure to properly contain asbestos fibers during abatement can turn a potential problem into a real problem which will be difficult and expensive to solve. Whether an institution hires an asbestos abatement contractor or physical plant personnel are trained to remove asbestos, it is essential that proper procedures be followed. The contractor's activities, or that of the physical plant staff, should be monitored for the protection of the institution. For larger institutions, it is probably more economical to develop an asbestos abatement team within the physical plant department. Since respirators are required for asbestos removal, the OSHA respirator program must also be followed (CFR 20 1910.134).

The fear of asbestos is such an emotionally charged issue that the main problem is perhaps employee/public relations rather than a serious threat to health and safety. During asbestos removal operations someone must ensure that all university or college personnel are protected. In fact, the best form of liability insurance is to monitor and document all abatement activities.

52.4 PROTECTING THE ENVIRONMENT FROM UNIVERSITY ACTIVITIES

Operations of Heating and Utility Systems

The major environmental problems from physical plant operations are related to heating and utility systems and the disposal of wastes. Operation of a heating plant may require discharge permits to limit air and water pollution. If heating oil is used, the underground storage tanks (UST) for heating oil, as well as for gasoline and diesel fuel, are covered by EPA or state regulations. Proper installation of tanks with corrosion protection and mechanisms to detect leaks is required for any new UST. Certain old tanks must be registered and eventually these need to be made corrosion resistant. Some approved method of leak detection is also required for old tanks. Even old tanks that are not in use are covered by these regulations until they are removed form the ground.

Prior to the EPA regulations, it was concluded that a large portion of the underground tanks containing petroleum products had already leaked, although many had not been detected. When the problem is finally discovered, it is often as a result of the penetration of vapors from the badly contaminated soils into building spaces. The clean up of contaminated soils can be expensive. Oil spills from overfilling tanks can cause the same kind of problems. There should then be procedures to prevent, contain, and clean up any spills.

Polychlorinated biphenyls (PCBs) are a class of substances that were utilized as an insulating and cooling medium in electrical transformers and capacitors. EPA has prohibited any further use of PCBs and requires a rigid and well-documented inspection program for all equipment containing PCB liquid still in use (40 CFR 761). Electricians or other maintenance workers must inspect PCB transformers quarterly and document results, and any leaks found must be fixed within 48 hours. The dangers of PCBs must also be covered in the Right-to-Know training for these employees. There are regulations which require that all high-voltage transformers containing PCBs be replaced by 1990. The old transformers or the PCBs must be disposed of as hazardous waste. Disposal is expensive, whether the fluids are removed or whether the entire transformer is taken as waste. Until PCB transformers are replaced, they must be labeled.

Hazardous Waste

PCBs are only one type of hazardous waste. Although physical plant operations are not the only source of chemical waste, they must be included in an institutional program that meets EPA requirements (40 CFR 721). The total quantity of waste generated by the entire institution determines which set of regulations the program must meet. The small quantity generators produce or accumulate between 100 and 1,000 kg of waste in any one month (100 kg is approximately half of a 55-gallon drum). Larger institutions with research programs are likely classified as large quantity generators (more than 1,000 kg of waste per month). If these wastes are not managed properly, the costs can be high. Ignoring the regulations can be even more expensive as there are severe criminal and civil penalties for violations. A report prepared for EPA in late 1987 by consultants ICF, Inc., summarized the problems with educational institutions as follows:

> Budgetary and management constraints frequently do
> not allow educational institutions to develop and fund
> a waste management program. There is often a low
> level of awareness that hazardous waste is generated.
> The 30,000 educational institutions nationwide gener-
> ate about 2,000 to 4,000 metric tons of hazardous
> waste per year. . . . The majority of schools do not
> generate large quantities of waste; however, the waste
> stream is variable and contains a large number of dif-
> ferent constituents. There are many individual genera-
> tors of different types of waste and the population is
> transient, which increases the difficulties in identifying
> the waste stream. Generators include academic lab-
> oratories, art and vocational departments, and mainte-
> nance activities. . . . Current management practices
> range from storage in chemical stockrooms, closets, or
> laboratories and disposal by the drain or dumpster to
> multi-million dollar treatment, storage, and disposal
> facilities. . . . However, the level of awareness may in-
> crease as a result of right-to-know provisions of the
> Occupational Safety and Health Act. The literature in-

dicates that colleges and universities with centralized programs are better able to manage the wastes generated.

There are many reasons to have a centralized waste management program. Physical plant must be a part of this program, and in over 10 percent of the existing programs the physical plant director is responsible for managing these wastes. University and college administrators need to understand that as generators of hazardous waste the institution is responsible for the safe management and ultimate disposal of its hazardous waste. If the hazardous wastes are released into the environment by the transporter or the treatment and disposal facility, the generator can still be held responsible for any harm to the environment and for any clean up costs. This responsibility remains even though the institution has committed no violations and has paid for disposal at a licensed facility. Therefore, it is imperative for colleges and universities to use great care in the selection of reputable and capable disposal companies. The disposal contractor should be investigated to ensure that all applicable regulations are complied with. It is worth the extra costs to be sure wastes are destroyed, as opposed to being buried, as destruction eliminates the long-term liability. EPA regulations are moving toward a complete ban on the burial of chemical wastes.

Most problems that arise in hazardous waste management at educational institutions are due to a lack of awareness and the highly variable nature of the wastes. Lack of awareness can be alleviated by exchanging information between schools. These contacts can lead to cooperation in waste disposal with a single disposal contractor serving several small institutions to reduce costs. The problems caused by the variable multicomponent waste stream must be addressed within the institution itself. The program needs to be formalized with responsibility clearly designated. The best way to eliminate liability (and cost) is to manage hazardous material in such a way as to reduce the amount of waste being generated. Possible methods to reduce the wastes generated include:

1. Recycle unused and unwanted chemicals to different departments or schools.
2. Set up information exchanges so that separate laboratories or schools can coordinate purchases of chemicals.
3. Make sure that everyone understands the false economy of purchasing large quantities to obtain a discount. Purchase only what is required and monitor quantities purchased.
4. Decrease the scale of experiments in teaching laboratories.

5. Reuse solvents.
6. Substitute less hazardous chemicals whenever possible.

Management of wastes is also important. Some of the factors in a centralized waste management program include:

1. Centralize purchasing and inventory of hazardous chemicals.
2. Label materials destined for disposal or for recycling.
3. Institute collection procedures for waste, and train personnel.
4. Keep wastes separated by categories (i.e., do not mix halogenated and flammable solvents).
5. Store waste safely in centralized location.
6. Treat or recover wastes where possible (i.e., neutralize acids and bases in the laboratory, redistill solvents, recover silver from photographic wastes).
7. Be sure wastes taken off site by EPA licensed contractor are destroyed (e.g. incinerated).

Infectious wastes were not included in the original EPA hazardous waste regulations. The standards are not yet uniform, but hospitals, medical schools, and even student health facilities may eventually be required to meet the basic requirements for the disposal of infectious wastes. Disposal will probably require an incinerator or a steam sterilization system. The increased concern about infectious waste is only one part of the general increase in awareness on the part of the public to issues of waste disposal. In many areas even the operation of sanitary landfills is being discouraged or banned.

It is clear that waste, in all its forms, will become more highly regulated and expensive. One needs only to look at the national crisis that developed around the issue of low level radioactive waste to realize how much of a problem waste can be for colleges and universities. The extremely high costs for radioactive waste disposal and the potential loss of disposal facilities threatens to interfere with research and clinical testing that involves radioactive materials.

The liabilities of hazardous waste may also reach into the past. Under the Superfund program, EPA has begun the extremely expensive process of cleaning up some of the worst sites where hazardous materials were used, stored, or disposed of improperly. If the name of your institution can be associated with the contamination of a site due to your past activities, you may have financial liability to pay for all or some portion of the clean up. As noted earlier, even wastes you now ship to a licensed facility will continue to carry liability to your institution unless the wastes are destroyed.

Another aspect of this issue is associated with the land itself. If your institution purchases land that has been contaminated with hazardous materials, through spills or improper disposal practices, you will most likely have the liability for the clean-up costs. Prior testing or specific language in the land contract are ways to help avoid this liability. The concerns about hazardous materials, including asbestos, and the costs associated with the clean-up of these materials has added a new dimension and cost associated with real estate transactions.

Emergency Preparedness and Response

The need for emergency preparedness and response capabilities has often been overlooked or neglected. However, the federal law known as SARA Title III (Superfund Amendments and Reauthorization Act of 1986) and many state and local governmental agencies are now requiring written emergency response plans for any organization using hazardous materials. The extent and complexity of such plans will differ greatly depending on the type and number of potentially hazardous conditions that exist on campus and on the nature of the potential initiating events (earthquake, flood, fire, tornado, riot, or spill of hazardous materials). It is crucial that physical plant becomes heavily involved in developing emergency preparedness and response plans for the campus. Planning efforts must be coordinated with the institution's safety office, the academic departments, and local public service agencies (police, fire, state emergency services).

Responsive personnel will probably be designated from both the physical plant department and the safety office (if one exists), and these people must be trained and periodically retrained to assure that they can not only stabilize any emergency they may be called to handle, but do so in a way that does not endanger their own health and safety. Certain types of emergency response equipment such as emergency generators and lights, radios, light rescue equipment, shovels, sand (to absorb), respirators, and vehicles must be available. This type of equipment must be inventoried, by both type and location, and such information must be made a part of any emergency preparedness and response plan. (See Chapter 54, Emergency Operations.)

Meeting the Challenge

The protection of the environment is important and it is clear that the wide range of regulations which have been applied to the activities of colleges and universities will continue to place financial burdens on the institutions. The problems will not go away and they cannot be ignored just because "you have gotten away with it so far." There are no simple answers on how all these obligations can be met within the institutional constraints. Like the overall safety program, the best results will come from programs that fit each institution. Everyone has struggled with the same problems, so there are benefits in sharing information with others involved in the facilities management of other institutions. It takes time and money to operate an academic institution safely. However, by building upon the experience of others and the information available through organizations such as APPA and the University Risk Management and Insurance Association, it should be possible to make health and safety programs more efficient.

ADDITIONAL RESOURCES

All references in text to CFR are to the Code of Federal Regulations.

Bureau of Business Practice. *Supervisor's Book of Safety Meetings*. Waterford, Connecticut: Bureau of Business Practice, 1981.

Peterson, D. *Safety Management: A Human Approach*. Deer Park, New York: Aloray Publishers, 1975.

"Six Safety and Behavioral Specialists Comment." *National Safety News*, September 1979.

Woodhull, D., N. Crutchfield, and F. James. "Successful Loss Control Programs Require Management's Time, Money." *Occupational Health and Safety*, September 1987.

CHAPTER 53

Building Security

Michael Sheffield
Director, Department of Police
University of Virginia

53.1 INTRODUCTION

F ew facilities functions are more difficult to administer satisfactorily than campus security. College and university buildings require access by large numbers of people during irregular hours. Ongoing research projects often demand attention at specific time intervals that do not necessarily coincide with what are considered regular working hours. In their quest for new knowledge and in preparing for teaching assignments, academicians traditionally set their own hours. In fact, many prefer night work hours and like to use their offices. Moreover, the increasing use of computers and other information-processing equipment in course work necessitates increasingly greater student access to instructional facilities outside regularly scheduled hours. A campus is a place of activity for most of the day's twenty-four hours. Providing personal and facilities security without interfering with the use of facilities is difficult.

Plant departments normally have responsibilities regarding building security, although the specific roles vary widely. At some institutions they have nearly complete responsibility for coordinating all security matters including employing security forces and complete police responsibilities. At the other extreme, they perform only the mechanics of key fabrication, issue, and recovery. Virtually all have some degree of responsibility for key issue and control, and either have responsibility for, or require close coordination with, security forces. This chapter addresses the organization and functioning of security forces, locking and keying systems, and key issue and control.

It is not appropriate or even possible to describe recommended functions and systems in this chapter. Instead, underlying principles and considerations will be discussed in conjunction with the advantages and disadvantages of certain methods that can be used to design or improve systems and procedures to meet the specific needs of each institution.

53.2 CAMPUS POLICE RESPONSIBILITIES

Criminal Investigations

Campus police departments usually have primary responsibility for investigating all criminal incidents that occur at institutions. In doing this, the officers arrest and take to trial criminal perpetrators and develop the evidence necessary to convict them. They also recover lost and stolen property of the institution, faculty, and staff.

As part of the investigative process, it is necessary that the police department maintain a criminal record system. Commonly, a department would maintain criminal records under state and federal guidelines, participate in state and federal computerized files, and maintain other records as needed. They may also prepare uniform crime reports which are sent to state police departments and the Federal Bureau of Investigation (FBI). These reports record the number of serious crimes that occur in an area and are used to compute state and national crime rates.

Maintaining Order

Order maintenance is a major function of all police departments. Campus departments enforce the rules and regulations of the institution as well as laws. Rule violations are usually handled administratively by deans or by a system of student courts.

Special events such as meetings, parties, athletic events, and concerts require extra emphasis on order maintenance. Police officers must maintain order at campus meetings and lectures, especially during demonstrations or strikes. The large crowds at concerts and sporting events require extra concern to ensure the safety of each individual.

Traffic Control and Direction

Officers enforce traffic laws and regulations, which are designed to protect life and property. The extent of enforcement depends on institutional policy, campus location and road design, and the resources available for enforcement.

Traffic direction is a separate component of traffic control. Officers are often assigned to direct traffic on a permanent basis at high traffic areas. They also direct traffic in special situations such as at accidents, construction sites, safety hazards, and at special planned entertainment events such as concerts, sporting events, and parades.

In some cases, the police department will handle parking enforcement even if the college has a separate parking division. When there is a separate parking department, they usually issue parking permits and employ traffic control officers who enforce parking regulations. The police department will ticket and tow vehicles from fire lanes and when the vehicle creates a traffic hazard. They may also ticket and tow vehicles that are in special access zones needed by physical plant or residential life vehicles.

Crime Prevention Programs

Most college police departments provide comprehensive crime prevention programs for the institution. The prevention programs start with reviews and suggestions concerning building plans and site development and continue throughout the building's use.

Each individual department within the institution should be responsible for developing its own crime prevention program, but the crime prevention specialist should help with its development and review the programs on a periodic basis. The crime prevention specialist can also perform the training of personnel involved with the crime prevention program.

Crime prevention specialists also prepare programs for the student population. Some of the common programs concern drug and alcohol abuse, sexual assault prevention, and self-defense classes. Often police departments also sponsor student groups such as student watch, dorm watch, and student escort programs.

Special Services

College police departments usually provide special services for the physical plant and residential life programs. They work as information clearing houses, provide building inspections, and may assist with some personnel matters.

Police departments have evolved into this role because they are open twenty-four hours a day. Late at night, the police department is often the only department that a student or faculty member can reach. The police department then becomes responsible for the disposition of the problem. Even if it is not a normal police problem, the police department will either handle it or contact someone to do so. They also notify residential deans or deans of student life about student emergencies such as deaths, injuries, assaults, and arrests.

Since the police departments provide regular patrols of campus facilities, they can conduct late-night building inspections. They locate unlocked doors and windows, damaged or vandalized property, and hazardous conditions such as fires, gas leaks, and downed power lines. They can also provide maintenance reports on lights that are out and signs that are down or missing.

In some cases, the police department provides background checks on people who are applying for sensitive positions. These background checks are governed by various federal and state regulations and are usually not applicable to all positions. When used for people in sensitive positions, however, background checks may reduce potential liability for the institution.

53.3 POLICE DEPARTMENT ORGANIZATION

Police organizations are normally paramilitary in nature. They are hierarchical, bureaucratic, and wear uniforms.

The hierarchical organization is arranged so there is a recognized chain of command that functions well in emergency situations. Authority within the department runs from the top down with each position on the way indicated by a specified rank. Traditionally the ranks have been chief, captain, lieutenant, sergeant, corporal, and officer. Today some departments use a commander system that runs chief, commander III, commander II, commander I, and officer.

Police departments tend to be highly bureaucratic in nature with written rules, regulations, and procedures. Leeway remains in many procedures, however, because deviations are necessary, due to the nature of the work and the need to protect the safety of the public and the officers.

Uniforms are worn so that officers are easy to identify, which saves time in an emergency. The uniform also serves as a deterrent to criminal activity or to a situation getting out of hand.

Uniforms also make it easier to identify various ranks, including the highest ranking person at the scene. Civilians can easily recognize a supervisor if they wish to make a complaint.

Within the various college organizations, there is no standardization as to where a police department fits into the structure. In some organizations, the police chief reports directly to the college president. In others they report to a vice president or dean.

Many schools have established police advisory committees consisting of representatives of any or all of the following: academic departments, physical plant, administrative personnel, medical departments, and students. The committee benefits the department's representative by providing a forum for voicing concerns, suggesting activities, and reporting problems. The committee benefits the police department by allowing them to handle problems before they become major issues, providing information concerning conditions and problems, and allowing the department to address community concerns. The effect is to create a positive relationship between the police department and the representatives.

53.4 POLICE TRAINING

Most campus police departments receive training equal to or exceeding training requirements of municipal departments.

The first step to professional training is a form of basic training. The amount of training required varies between departments, but in most states there is a basic minimum. Typically, this amounts to ten weeks or more at a state approved academy and results in state certification as a police officer. In many cases, the training is the same as for municipal officers and is performed at the same academies.

After the academy, many officers will receive field training conducted by officers within their own department. This allows the new officer to gain hands-on experience while under an experienced training officer. Usually, new officers must pass the field training program to continue as a campus police officer.

Many states require officers to attend periodic training to remain certified as an officer. This "in-service training" enables the officers to refresh old skills and to be updated on new techniques.

Specialized training may be provided based on the department's needs. The training is provided by law enforcement specialists or other educators. Some of these specialized training programs are in the categories of crime prevention, criminal investigation, computers for law enforcement, and police management. College courses in police science and police management may also be available.

53.5 BUILDING SECURITY RESPONSIBILITIES

Responsibility for building security begins in the planning stages, extends through construction, and continues throughout the building's use.

It is the architect's responsibility to develop a design that promotes the security of the building. For this reason, it is beneficial to choose an architect who understands this responsibility and is familiar with the concepts of Crime Prevention through Environmental Design (C.P.T.E.D.).

The builder also has a responsibility for building security. He must not only closely follow the architect's design, but also must use materials that are crime resistant.

Physical plant has responsibility for maintaining buildings in a safe condition. They must correct any safety problems that come to light as part of their risk management and analysis programs. Physical plant personnel must also keep current on technological changes that affect building security.

If physical plant fails to properly meet its responsibilities, there are several negative outcomes possible. The worst result would be that some harm might come to a student, employee, or visitor. Other consequences may be theft or damage to university property, liability suits from crime victims, and adverse publicity for the institution.

Each academic department that uses the building should be responsible for the security of its own area. They should develop a security plan that outlines how money and property are to be handled and designates specific people to be responsible for keys, locking and unlocking doors, and other security related concerns. It should also outline procedures for bomb and arson threats. The plan should designate the reporting responsibilities of personnel and list who should make police and damage reports.

The department should also perform security training for its personnel, including familiarization with the security plan. Assistance can be provided by the police department's crime prevention specialist.

The academic department must also keep abreast of security problems as they develop. Broken locks and safety hazards should be reported to physical plant for correction on a priority basis. Crimes and suspicious incidents should be reported to the police department. The department also should review its security plan periodically to correct unsafe or outdated procedures.

Campus police departments provide normal police services to campus buildings. They patrol the area looking for suspicious persons or incidents. They also perform building checks, which are sometimes called "checking glass." These checks are performed on a priority basis and rank below calls that require an immediate response.

Police departments usually have crime prevention specialists who can perform professional security surveys and recommend security procedures and hardware. In most cases, police officers can only recommend these changes; they cannot insist that problems be corrected.

It is not unusual for other security personnel to be used for specialized functions. Often, in-house, contract security officers, or watchmen perform security checks and lock doors. They may also control entrances to specialized areas such as hospital visitor entrances or construction areas and loading docks.

53.6 CAMPUS SECURITY PROCEDURES

Implementation of the security program begins with the basic plan and continues throughout the entire process.

When the architect's plans are originally submitted, a crime prevention specialist should review them. In general, the specialist will look for the following conditions and considerations:

1. Lighting location and levels.
2. Entrance locations and controls.
3. The field of view for people within the building.
4. The type and time of building use.
5. What type of natural boundaries are built into the design.

The next step is a review of the building site. The visit ensures that the plans are being followed correctly. It also allows the crime prevention specialist to make recommendations on building materials and building site security.

Prior to moving into the building, there should be a meeting between representatives of physical plant, the police department, and occupying departments. Times and areas of use will be determined, a locking and unlocking schedule will be established, and security responsibilities for each area of the building will be assigned.

Establishing security responsibilities is especially important when there is more than one department in the building. Having clearly designated areas of control helps to develop protective responsibilities among the staff. Each department knows who is responsible for reporting maintenance problems such as locks and lights in each area.

Finally, a contact list for each area should be developed and sent to physical plant and the police department. This permits either department to call out representatives when emergencies occur.

As soon as the building is occupied, the training aspect of the process begins. The staff should be trained in all aspects of the security plan. As time goes on, there should be periodic reviews of the security situation in the building. The department should review departmental policy and revise the contact list. The crime prevention specialist should perform a building survey. Physical plant should also examine the area periodically to determine and repair maintenance problems affecting security.

Although these reviews should be performed according to an established schedule, serious crime activities or safety problems may indicate the need for an unscheduled review.

53.7 ALARMS

Alarm systems are used to supplement other security programs in high risk areas, but do not eliminate the need for other security programs.

There are a variety of alarm types available. They are classified by the type of sensor or type of response. Most alarms may be considered either audible or silent. An audible alarm can be heard at the location. It is designed to scare off the intruder or draw a response from passers-by or the police. If the building is in an isolated area, the effectiveness is considerably lessened.

Silent alarms are not heard at the location, but are transmitted by phone or radio to a monitoring station. They are usually monitored by police or security departments. Since no sound is made at the scene, the alarm does not warn the intruder that he or she has been detected.

There are, of course, combinations of these alarms. In addition, some security systems set off cameras to record the criminal activity. High security areas, such as some government installations, may have alarms systems that actively deter an intruder by locking doors, turning on lights, and activating chemical deterrents.

Alarms may incorporate several different types of sensors. Some of the most common are as follows:

1. *Contact sensors* are attached to doors or windows. When the contacts are separated, the alarm is activated.
2. *Motion detectors* pick up signs of movement within an area.
3. *Heat detectors* pick up heat sources within certain ranges.
4. *Sound detectors* sense sound within certain ranges. In some cases the activated alarm actually allows the monitoring station to hear what is going on within the area. This helps reduce false alarms since the person monitoring the area can confirm the alarm.
5. *Infrared detectors* monitor an invisible light beam. The beams are usually set to cross areas likely to be crossed. If something breaks the beam, the alarm is activated.
6. *Hold-up alarms* are activated manually by a person activating a switch. In some banks, the removal of money from a particular drawer sets off such a manual alarm.
7. *Pressure plates* react to the presence of weight and some react to the absence of weight. They can, therefore, be placed under the flooring to indicate someone walking through, or placed under a valuable object to be activated if it is moved.

Closed Circuit Television (CCTV)

In some systems, closed circuit television is used. It may run continuously or be activated by one of the previously mentioned sensors. Some are monitored continuously; others tape a sequence after being activated. Where CCTV is used, dummy cameras are also sometimes used as a deterrent.

Alarm Responses

There should be preset response procedures established prior to the initial operation of the system. Arrangements need to be made for monitoring and responding to the alarm.

Provision needs to be made to allow the responding agency to correctly identify authorized personnel. The plan should also include a provision for identifying an employee who is operating under duress. This is especially important for banks, credit unions, and other places that handle large amounts of cash.

As with other security programs, periodic review is necessary. A schedule should be maintained to provide for alarm testing and the retraining of personnel. It is also important that the response to an alarm be practiced.

53.8 CAMPUS KEYING SYSTEMS

Most colleges and universities have an integrated campus-wide keying system for all buildings in which all locks are coded and combinated as components of the total system. What follows are the types of keying of locks in an integrated system.

Campus Master or Grand Master Key

The campus master key, sometimes referred to as the grand master, will operate any lock on the system. A campus may have more than one such campus master key, each independent of the others. This arrangement usually stems from a decision to adopt a new keying system without simultaneously converting all buildings to the new system.

Building Master Key

A building master key will operate all locks on the building system, including exterior doors.

Submaster or Area Master Key

Functional areas of a building may be keyed so that each lock is keyed separately but in a way that permits a single submaster or area master key to open all locks on the subsystem.

Interior Door Keys

Two or more locks may be keyed alike and consequently can be operated by the one key. Locks keyed alike are not the same as submaster systems.

Exterior Door Keys

Normally, all exterior doors are keyed alike. There are exceptions such as a building with separate entrances to different functional areas such as academic departments. Typically, all exterior door keys are on the building master system and may be on one or more submasters.

Locks Keyed Separately from the Building Master System

Certain locks in a building may be taken off the building master system. This restricted access is normally due to either safety requirements or to the absence of a need for access by building occupants.

Presented below are the most common separately keyed areas.

Transformer Vaults   Transformers for stepping down high voltages to utilization voltages are installed in vaults keyed separately from the building system. All transformer vaults on the campus can be keyed alike so that maintenance personnel have convenient access to them.

Mechanical Rooms   All mechanical rooms on the campus may be keyed alike, separate from the buildings systems. Only plant personnel, or personnel of contracting firms who are performing work in the building, normally require access to them.

Custodial Rooms   Custodial rooms or closets usually contain a sink and water supply plus storage facilities for custodial equipment and supplies. Like transformer and mechanical rooms, they can be keyed alike throughout the campus though separate from any building system.

Temporary Construction Areas   During alteration projects, additions to buildings, and larger repair projects undertaken by either the plant department or contractor, it is often desirable to secure construction materials, tools, and equipment. Contractors often have their own construction lock cores. The plant department can also set up construction lock cores that are keyed separately from any building system. They can be installed in locks to rooms that have been set aside for the duration of the projects as secure storage areas. Care must be taken not to block building emergency exits.

Special Security Areas   Individual rooms that require high security may be keyed off the building master system. This should be avoided if possible since it requires coding equivalent to that of a new building.

Building Keying System

Whether keying a new building or rekeying an existing one, a building keying plan should be developed. Primary input comes from the building occupants. The plan is used to support the building's functional use. It describes the keying desired for each lock, including those rooms that are to be keyed alike, those rooms that are to be keyed separately from the building master system, and groupings of rooms on submaster systems. Few, if any, colleges or universities have the means for developing codes to meet the keying plan. Consequently, this is normally handled by a single lock company that maintains keying records for the entire campus. All locks are coded to conform with the keying plan and ensure that no code is duplicated. In the event that there are different kinds of locks on the campus, adaptors can be used for conversion to the selected make of lock core. The physical plant department normally holds responsibility for maintaining keying code records for all the locks on campus.

The building keying system pertains only to room door locks of a building. It excludes storage cabinets, lockers, and drawers in individual rooms. In addition, residence halls are not normally included in a campus key issue and control system. The department may furnish residence hall keys upon request or it may perform lock installation, repair, and replacement. However, the responsibility for issuance, control, and return of residence hall keys rests with the facilities manager.

53.9 KEY ISSUE AND CONTROL GUIDELINES

Some guiding principles can be used to set up and maintain a viable key issue and control program on campuses. Presented below are underlying principles for implementing workable and responsive procedures.

Provisions should be made for access, separate from the key issue system, to common-use facilities for scheduled activities. Similarly, a plan should be devised for all doors to be locked beyond regularly scheduled hours. Otherwise it may be necessary to issue keys to everyone who may potentially be the first user of each facility each day.

Locks on doors should be self-locking. That is, they should not require a key to close them. If this policy is not maintained, it becomes necessary to issue keys to each individual who might remain in a building past normal working hours. At that point, responsibility for locking the building cannot be fixed.

The building keying system should not be relied upon for the security of valuable materials and equipment or items that can be pilfered. Vaults, cabinets, lockers, and similar facilities with special locks can be used to meet special security requirements while permitting access for assigned functional use.

Issuing keys to individuals should be based on access needs rather than position. Normally, officials such as deans and department heads are issued keys to all facilities in their charge if they choose, but keys should not be automatically issued without verifying the need. Many officials simply want access to their own offices beyond regular hours.

Keys should be issued permanently only when the need for frequent access outside regular hours can be foreseen. Cutting down on permanent issues can often be done by establishing a system for temporary loan for occasional anticipated situations, for gaining access via the campus police, or other security organization when the need is not anticipated. The same principle should guide the issuance of various levels of keys: building master keys should not be issued for occasional access to areas if normal requirements can be met by the issue of several keys.

Convenience of access to, and security of, the buildings are in direct opposition. Convenience of access, as a result, must be sacrificed in proportion to the degree of security achieved.

No key control system can be effective unless there is compliance and unless the system is the sole source of keys to the institution's buildings. Commercial facilities for duplicating keys are readily available in most parts of the country, and any violation of laws or regulations regarding duplication of keys is committed by the individual requesting the copy rather than the duplicating agency. Employees can often have a college or university key duplicated outside at nominal cost, and more conveniently than can be done through the institution's system. Occasionally, departing faculty and staff members pass their keys along to their replacements. Unless such practices are prevented by the college or university administration, building security will be compromised, regardless of the effort spent on a campus key control system.

Because large numbers of keys are on issue at any one time and rekeying of locks on a campus-wide system calls for recoding to conform with the system, making changes in either the key issue records system or the keying system is time-consuming and costly. Additionally, it inconveniences many people. It is therefore important to protect building keying systems from compromise and to have key issue and recovery systems that are planned, workable, and well-enforced so as to be long-lasting.

Physical plant administrators need to remember that obtaining keys to work spaces is essential to getting work done. Obtaining a key to a work space is not a privilege, such as securing a locker in a recreational facility. Issue systems that require excessive time and effort on the part of the applicant or cause undue delays can interfere with the institution's work.

53.10 ANATOMY OF A KEY CONTROL SYSTEM

There are many kinds of key control systems in use at colleges and universities around the country. Which system to choose will depend upon many factors including the breadth of facilities, size of faculty and staff, building use schedules, value of instructional and research equipment located in campus buildings, size and duties of security forces, and the degree of security desired. However, the administration of any viable system calls for the following actions:

- Assign key issue authority.
- Assign key recovery responsibility.
- Establish procedures for expeditious issue and recovery.
- Maintain up-to-date functional records of issues.
- Assign funding responsibility for building lock and key systems.

Key Issue Authority

Authorization for key issues consists of some combination of a campus policy for issues to individuals and recommendation for issuance from an individual's department or division. If the policy is definitive regarding issuance criteria, little further action is required beyond verifying that the individual meets the criteria. However, if the policy is a general guideline—key issuance will be based on need for access—it is then necessary for a department official, who is familiar with the work requirements of the individuals concerned, to have primary authorization powers.

It is generally accepted policy that no college or university official should authorize the issue of keys to spaces other than those occupied by the organization for which he or she has responsibility. For example, the head of an organization to which a total building is assigned would have issue authority up to and including the building master key. Where two or more departments occupy one building, each may authorize key issues to their assigned areas. However, the issue of master keys to the building could be authorized only by the common superior unless coordination authority was specifically assigned to one party. The issue authority may, of course, be restricted by college or university policy.

Key Recovery Responsibility

The campus policy must prescribe the length of time for which keys may be issued plus the conditions for their return. The return policy is usually set up in the following fashion.

Permanent employees shall return keys:

- Upon termination of employment or transfer to another organization.
- Upon being granted a leave of absence, leave is defined as absence from the campus for a specified period such as thirty days or more.
- Upon request of the issuing authority.

Temporary employees and students shall surrender keys:

- At the end of the semester or period if the student will not need the keys for at least a specified period such as thirty days. The intent is to prevent keys from being kept over summer breaks or during other regular school sessions for which the individual is not enrolled or employed at the institution.
- Upon request of the issuing authority.

Since only the department or administrative heads know the status of individuals in these categories, they usually hold responsibility for the return of keys. If recovery responsibility is assigned in another way, there must be close coordination with the department and administrative heads for the timely recovery of keys.

Key Issue and Recovery Procedures

If undue time and effort are required to obtain a key, it can cause obstacles to compliance. In fact, complicated procedures can cause violations that virtually void the system in a short time.

Unfortunately, the process for obtaining keys often shows bureaucracy at its worst. For instance, it is not unusual for a key requester to be required to complete forms, go to several different offices for approval of the issuance, make a deposit, and then proceed to a key shop located on the outskirts of the campus, only to have to complete the process in reverse to return a key and claim his or her deposit.

The simpler and more convenient these procedures can be for the key requester, the more effective and inviolable the functioning of the issue and recovery system will be.

The minimum functions essential to key issue/recovery and the maintenance of appropriate transaction records are presented below.

Issuances

- Completion of a form by the prospective recipient. The form calls for information on the individual's employment status, department affiliation, and access required.
- Issue approval signature.
- Payment of a key deposit, if required, and verification of the deposit.
- Notification to the campus key shop of the specific access or keys required.
- Fabrication of the keys and marking them with an identification number. This number should be coded so that in case of loss the finder will not readily be able to identify the space to which access can be gained. Recommended coding is a building number and the last one or two digits of the room number.
- Entry of above key information on the issue form.
- Delivery of the key to the recipient and securing of a receipt signature.
- Entry of the issue date and record of transaction into the records system.

Recoveries

- Return of key, ultimately to the key shop.
- Refund of cash deposit if appropriate.
- Removal of issue records from the records system.

As many as possible of these functions should be handled by administrative personnel with minimum inconvenience to key recipients. In fact, routine issues can often be handled almost entirely in the department office. There the requester completes the request form and submits a cash deposit if one is required. The next step takes place via mail or hand delivery. The only other step the requester must take is to pick up and sign for the key at the department office. The same procedure is followed to turn in the key. All business is transacted by the keyholder at the department office. Appendix 53-A describes such a system. In the case of issuance, the requester should have the option of hand carrying the documents through the system to expedite the process.

Record Keeping Principles

Keeping good records of key issues will promote the smooth functioning of the control system. Simply filing a copy of an issue form once a key is issued and then removing it when the key is returned is of little value. To be useful for retaining control and for serving departmental security needs, key issuance records should be kept with the following needs in mind.

A list of all keys that are on issue to persons affiliated with a department or administrative unit should periodically be provided to each department or administrative head for verification of accuracy, for correcting, or for reporting discrepancies.

Prior to the impending key recovery date, a list should be drawn up of all keys that are due to be surrendered. Lists of all keys, temporary or permanent, should routinely be furnished just before the end of the semester.

On request, a list of all keys on issue to a specific person should be furnished.

The name of the individual to whom a key with a specific serial number is charged out is strictly confidential. Only upon request of an institutionally recognized and approved authority should the name be provided.

On request, all individuals to whom keys that grant access to a specific space have been issued should be identified.

These kinds of records may be maintained by each academic department or administrative unit or by the physical plant department. In the past, a centralized system maintained by the department has been used because it could be administered effectively and efficiently. However, as better college and university information systems are developed and become available to all campus entities, the advantages of a centralized records system diminish.

Regardless of where the responsibility for records is assigned, certain information should be recorded for each key issuance. The vital data are:

- Name, institutional status, and organization of the requester.
- Office and name of person authorizing issue.
- Type of key issued (such as master, submaster, room key) and building.
- Key identification number.
- Type of issue. This may be permanent or temporary. If temporary, the date to be recovered should be recorded.
- Date of issue.

No matter where the records are maintained, good practice dictates periodic campus-wide verifications of record accuracy and regular correction or elimination of erroneous or outdated information. Verifications and updates should be undertaken at least annually and, at a minimum, should confirm that the status of persons to whom keys are charged out remains the same as what is shown on the records. This procedure allows for corrective action to be taken in some cases. An example would be the recovery of keys from personnel who have departed from the institution without complying with return requirements. The procedure also helps administrators evaluate the state of building security and may pinpoint areas in the key issue and recovery procedures that need improvement.

Record Keeping Techniques

There are various methods, both manual and computerized, for storing and retrieving information about keys. The volume and variety of information to be recorded and the processes that may be required to retrieve the information in the form that is needed—particularly at large universities—recommends machine storage and processing. If an institution is currently using a good manual system, it is easy to computerize. If, however, an institution is working with a hand-kept system that is not methodical, orderly, or easily understood, starting over with a computerized data base is an option to consider.

One of the capabilities of a computerized system that recommends its use is its capacity for extensive cross-referencing. For example, keys can be searched and identified by building name, room number, key number, employee name, or even authorization. Another advantage is the speed with which information can be retrieved. A third attraction is the ease of updating records on an automated system. The typical hardware for a computerized system consists of a monitor (video screen), a terminal with a typewriter-like keyboard, and a printer. Information can be called up either on the monitor or printed as hard copy. Printing is most useful for reports to other departments.

Funding Responsibilities

The authority over building locking and keying systems and key control is often divided; therefore, campus policies must recognize funding responsibilities. Generally, whichever institutional entity exercises authority over administration of keys bears fiscal responsibility for key control matters. Just how funding responsibilities are divided on campuses according to this principle, however, is described below.

Routine maintenance and repair of locks and lock cores, which includes replacement of malfunctioning parts, is part of comprehensive upkeep of facilities and is, therefore, the funding responsibility of the plant department.

The keying of a new building, which includes purchase and combinating of lock cores, is typically part of the construction cost and is included in the project funding.

Financial responsibility for rekeying of a building, which includes the purchase and the recombinating of lock cores along with complete new key issues, will vary, depending upon the reason for rekeying. If the department that occupies the building holds authority and responsibility for key issue and recovery, and if building security has been compromised by recessive issuances and failure to recover keys, funding responsibility would normally rest with the department. However, if rekeying is brought about by factors beyond the control of the department, such as reassignment of facilities or the need to update an antiquated keying system, funding would normally be assumed by the physical plant department.

The routine issuance of keys, which depends upon faculty and staff turnover, can generally be predicted. However, a department generally has little or no control over it. Consequently, this task is usually best handled by physical plant.

Compliance Strategies

The key control policies and procedures are designed to strike a desired balance between building security and facilities use. Noncompliance with these policies, however, compromises security and may necessitate stringent controls that may create inconveniences, if not actual barriers, to functional use.

The three most prevalent violations by individuals are obtaining keys outside the college or university system, failing to return keys, and losing keys because of a failure to properly safeguard them. What follows are measures that may be taken in order to given emphasis to, or require compliance with, key issuance policies and procedures.

Cash Deposit

Requiring a cash deposit that is refundable upon the return of the key often is helpful in accomplishing key recovery. However, most cash deposits of any kind are based upon intrinsic value. In order to influence recovery significantly, deposit sums would have to be much higher amounts than the cost of fabrication. This may, in turn, cause resentment and lack of cooperation. In addition, deposits sometimes imply that a key has been purchased, and from there the individual can assume he or she has the right to forfeit the deposit. This may lead to resale or passing the key along to a successor for all or part of the deposit. The administration of a key deposit system requires considerable administrative work and complicates the issue and recovery procedures.

Withholding Final Pay or Academic Transcripts

Holding back the final pay of departing employees and transcripts of departing students are strong measures that are certain to achieve a high degree of compliance if they are strictly and uniformly enforced. The legal and public relations aspects, however, should be carefully considered, particularly in cases where enforcement can result in personal loss. An example would be a case where a graduate may be eliminated from consideration for employment because of the withholding of a transcript. Similarly, this policy may cost a departing employee hundreds or even thousands of dollars in withheld salary.

Fines

In lieu of a refundable deposit, fines may be levied for failure to return keys. In order for a policy such as this to work, the fine system must be common knowledge and enforcement must be credible. Enforcement may require additional measures such as those described in the previous paragraph.

The most successful college and university key control systems are those in which personnel are informed of the policies and procedures as well as their purposes, those in which key issues and returns are made as convenient as possible, and those in which an attitude of cooperation by all concerned parties prevails. In short, every effort is made to meet the needs of faculty, staff, and students while maintaining the required level of security.

53.11 KEY FABRICATION AND LOCK TYPES

Key fabrication requirements can be met by a key coding machine that cuts keys to codes or a key duplicating machine. Most colleges and universities have these capabilities. Some possess only the key duplicating machine, which means that one key of each type must be purchased whenever a building, or any portion of a building, is rekeyed. It is, of course, possible to rely entirely on commercial fabrication facilities where available. The method chosen depends upon comparative costs and convenience to personnel, which, in turn, depends largely upon an institution's volume of issues.

Hardware must be matched to special institutional needs. Some fundamentals about locks related directly to unique campus demands are presented below.

The key mechanism of a lock is separate from the lock itself. The part of the mechanism operated by the key contains a tongue that projects into the lock. It contains up to seven pins, each of which can be set for up to ten different positions. The coding sets the position of each pin for unlocking as well as the depth of each notch in the key. The key then raises each pin to the proper height to permit turning the cylinder, the part operated by the key, which activates the lock by means of the tongue that connects with the lock. With a seven-pin set, 78,125 separate key combinations are possible. There are three basic types of locks:

1. *Cylindrical lock,* or key-in knob in which the key mechanism is contained in the knob.
2. *Rim lock,* in which an exterior metal case is mounted on the interior surface of the door.
3. *Mortise lock,* in which the lock is set into a mortise or cavity that is cut into the door.

Mortise and rim locks can be further classified as spring latch or deadbolt. The spring latch can be locked by releasing a thumb latch, while the deadbolt requires a key for locking or unlocking. An advantage to deadbolts is that they cannot be locked inadvertently. Deadbolts are used frequently for residence hall rooms and private offices. However, they cannot be used—except with panic exit devices—on exterior doors or on any door in a building's emergency escape route.

For doors that must afford access to the handicapped, the most satisfactory locks are electrically operated. They are designed so that the electric circuits are deactivated upon locking the door and activated upon unlocking. In entrances that require handicapped access but where electrically operated locks are unavailable, lever handles are preferable. They are especially suited to emergency doors where turning a knob would obstruct a quick exit. For example, lever handles are appropriate for a chemistry laboratory in which the occupant's hands may be burned or covered with a chemical as a result of a fire or chemical spill. Lever handles and foam rubber covers are available for round knobs.

53.12 SPECIAL LOCKING SYSTEMS

Certain areas on a campus require greater security than standard building locking and key control systems can provide. Those are storage areas for flammable or toxic chemicals, areas where radiological materials are kept, and areas that house valuable equipment. Currently there is a variety of high-security locking equipment on the market and periodically new and better equipment is introduced.

The equipment falls into three general categories: locks with specially shaped keys that are difficult to duplicate, combination locks that require knowledge of a code or use of a card reader that is coded for the specific lock, and electrically operated locks that either operate on a time schedule or are actuated from a remote location. All of them work on the principles of being relatively tamper-proof and of strictly safeguarding access to the unlocking information or equipment. These devices usually are independent of the building locking and key control system and are controlled by the director of the facility in which they are used. Physical plant may be assigned responsibility for the secure storage of combinations or duplicate opening devices, but special regulations must be promulgated regarding access.

Presented below are brief descriptions of only three types of the many special locking systems that are available. One variety employs different styles and shapes of keys—such as the triangular key with a dimple—that makes it difficult or impossible for the campus or local locksmith to duplicate. Some of these keys must be ordered directly from the factory. Since they cannot be made by a locksmith, tighter control can be exerted over the keys, but service becomes more difficult.

The second type of device is a pushbutton combination lock. Some are mechanical while others are electronic. They operate by pushing a series of buttons in a given sequence to open a door. They are useful in situations where there is an outside door to a restricted area from which the general public must be barred.

Several types of combination locks are on the market in which a computer can automatically be programmed to change the combination at set times. Some devices have a detection feature that can indicate an alarm condition when someone who does not know the correct combination tries the buttons.

A card reader lock is another form of "nonkey" system that helps restrict entry and exit to an area. The device is really not a lock at all, but rather a method of operating an electric strike. With this system a card is inserted in a machine that reads a special identification code, which then opens up a specified lock. Some systems record who the person is that is opening a particular door and when they gained entry.

53.13 ACCESS FOR PHYSICAL PLANT WORK REQUIREMENTS

One of the most difficult problems to deal with in the realm of key control is how to provide access to buildings for physical plant work.

With many major campuses containing more than 100 buildings, it is not unusual to have between 100 to 200 skilled workers engaged in maintenance and repair work. What the situation demands is numerous simultaneous key issuances and recoveries. It is impossible for one issuing agency to handle all the key issuances and returns that workers require.

Other unique considerations regarding access of plant personnel must be taken into account. They are:

- Access to different parts of the same building may be required by two or more workers engaged in unrelated work.
- Regardless of whether workers are operating on a salaried or charge-back system, the time spent in gaining access is costly. For example, if 100 workers each spend a total of 15 minutes a day to obtain keys or otherwise gain access to work locations throughout the campus, there would be 15 workhours lost time. Therefore, whatever system is used should be efficient and highly responsive to needs.
- Each worker may require access to spaces in several buildings in the course of a day.
- Much of the work of a plant department is decentralized with a minimum of prior planning. For example, a worker sent to correct a problem may not know in advance the specific rooms that will require access.
- It is desirable that individual workers not be charged with, or keep permanently in their possession, keys to all facilities to which access may be required by their work assignments.

Meeting these conditions and requirements is difficult, particularly on a large campus. Three general methods are used.

The first is a system in which each shop has several rings of master keys for the entire campus or for major subdivisions of the campus. These are kept in a locked cabinet in the shop with each ring marked for easy identification. All workers in the shop have easy access to the rings during working hours. The shop supervisor or other assigned person has responsibility for assuring that all key rings are returned at the end of working hours and that the case is locked. Arrangements must be made to gain access to buildings for emergency work that takes place outside regular hours. This can be handled by arranging for a security force to provide access either to the work site or to the key cabinet in the appropriate shop.

A second system uses a sequence lock in each building. A sequence lock is a rim-type lock that contains two interchangeable cores that operate in conjunction with each other. One of the cores is combinated for the building master key, while the other is combinated for the access key. The building master key is trapped in the core. When used to release the master key, the access key is trapped. Workers, therefore, can be issued indexed access keys with which they can obtain master keys to buildings. But to obtain a master key, their access key remains in the lock so that the holder can be identified. The access key cores can be changed when a key is lost or changed periodically to maintain a higher degree of security. To meet maximum work requirements, an adequate number of master keys should be available in each building.

The disadvantages of a sequence lock system are threefold. First, the access keys must either be retained permanently by the individuals to whom they are issued or else another system must be designed for the secure storage of the access keys outside regular working hours. Second, with such a dispersal of master keys, the early detection of a missing master key can be difficult. Third, separate provision must be made for obtaining admittance to the building to gain access to the master keys.

The third method, a variation on the locked-cabinet system, is often used for custodians. A locked box that contains rings of submaster and individual room keys or of individual master keys is located in one of the custodial closets. At the beginning of the work day, the supervisor unlocks the key box and furnishes key rings to custodians for their particular work assignments. At the end of working hours, all key rings are returned and locked in the key box.

53.14 CAMPUS POLICE DEPARTMENTS—GENERAL

Modern campus police departments are far removed from the campus security departments of the past. Although they were called security departments, officers were traditionally watchmen who locked and unlocked doors and watched for fires and safety hazards. The watchmen were not trained to handle problems involving people, and in many cases had no police powers or authority. Minor problems were usually handled by supervisors or deans, and criminal cases were handled by local municipal or state police agencies.

As mentioned earlier, the modern campus police department resembles a municipal department. Campus police officers are career oriented professionals who receive the same or similar training as do municipal officers. Campus police departments perform all normal police activities. These include preventive patrol, investigations, crime prevention, traffic direction and other activities. Most officers are assigned to preventive patrol. These officers have full arrest powers within their jurisdiction. Criminal investigations are conducted, as needed, by trained, experienced investigators.

In many cases, the benefits of the watchmen system were not lost to the colleges. These security departments were often consolidated as separate parts of the police departments. On some campuses, police officers may perform some security functions on a low priority basis.

Since each state and college is different, law enforcement at institutions differ. In many cases, state law defines the duties and responsibilities of campus police officers. In addition, each institution has specialized, unique needs and customs that affect the type of services provided by their police departments.

Although these differences exist, the primary concern of all police departments is protection. A police department's top priority is to protect people from criminal harm. Other responsibilities are to protect property from theft or vandalism, and to protect people and property from accidental harm.

53.15 CONCLUSION

Like most responsibilities involved in the day-to-day functioning of a college or university, building security is not the singular responsibility of any department, but is rather a responsibility shared by all. But in its role of managing the facilities, the physical plant department has the primary concern and responsibility for security. The carrying out of this responsibility varies from administering certain functions to coordinating with and assisting other departments with other functions.

This chapter has aimed to present a comprehensive coverage of the principles and procedures involved in campus security. The long hours of use of teaching and administrative facilities, round-the-clock access to research laboratories, and other access requirements makes it difficult to maintain effective building security. But a sensitive balance must be maintained between access and security to avoid either interfering with the teaching and research functions or compromising security. This balance can be achieved only through the cooperation of all concerned. Physical plant has the key responsibility for achieving this spirit of cooperation.

ADDITIONAL RESOURCES

International Association of Campus Law Enforcement Administrators. *Campus Law Enforcement Journal*. Hartford, Connecticut: Callan Publishing Company.

Peak, Ken. "Campus Policing in America: The State of The Art." *The Police Chief*, June 1987.

Smith, Michael C. *Coping With Crime On Campus*. New York: Macmillan Publishing Company, 1988.

Appendix 53-A

Property and Capital Equipment Policy
Keys to University Buildings

A.   Policy

1. It is the policy of the university that other than during normal working hours, all buildings shall be locked in order to maintain the security of both the buildings and their contents.

2. Staff members and students may be issued keys to university buildings upon the recommendation of the department chair or administrative head and approval of the official in charge of the building, or his/her designee, in accordance with established procedures.
    a) Keys are issued for entry to university buildings for the purpose of conducting university business only.
    b) An authorized individual entering or leaving a locked building shall not permit any individual to enter who would not normally be permitted to enter the building during the hours it is locked. An authorized individual may have guests so long as the guests stay in the proximity of the faculty or staff member having the assigned key and the authorized individual assumes full responsibility for their presence.
    c) An individual entering or leaving a locked building shall be responsible for securing the door and may be held responsible for any loss or damage to university property resulting from failure to do so.

3. Special assignment of keys, where required, (such as to contractors, etc.) may be authorized by the campus business officer (director of physical plant).

4. All keys issued remain the property of the university and shall be returned under the following conditions:
    a) For staff members:
        (1) Upon transfer to another department or building.
        (2) Upon termination of employment.

(3) Upon the request of the department chair or administrative head.

(4) Upon being granted a leave of absence without pay for a period of 30 or more calendar days; however, staff members granted such leaves may retain their key *if* they are authorized to have access to the building and/or office during the leave.

b) For students:

(1) At the end of the academic semester or period after which the keys will not be used for at least 30 calendar days.

(2) Upon the request of the department chairperson or administrative head.

5. Individuals transferring to another department or building may be issued new keys upon the recommendation of the new department chairperson or administrative head and approval as defined in paragraph 2 above.

6. It is the responsibility of the appropriate department chair or administrative head and official in charge of the building or his/her designee, to ensure that all keys are returned under provisions of paragraph 4 above.

7. In no case is a key to be transferred from one individual to another or to be obtained from any source other than from the university. When any transfer or duplication of a key is made or used without university consent, the key shall be recovered and the individual(s) involved reported to the administrative head, dean, or superior officer for appropriate action.

8. Each campus shall be responsible for the establishment and implementation of regulations and procedures necessary for the assignment and control of keys to university buildings. All such regulations and procedures are subject to the review and approval by the Office of the Vice President for Business Management.

B. Regulations

1. Keys to cabinets, lockers, and drawers within buildings or to dormitory rooms are not covered under provisions of this policy. Physical plant will furnish such keys upon request, but the issue, control, and recovery of these keys are the responsibility of the director of the facility.

2. Key issuances are authorized by the department chair, subject to such policy guidance as may be issued by the divisional dean and instructions of the building coordinator.

3. The types and number of keys issued will be limited to the minimum required by regular work assignments.
   a) The permanent issuance of building master keys will be limited to those persons needing frequent access to most of the building, normally department chairs or higher.
   b) Two or more keys may be issued to those requiring access to several rooms throughout the entire building.

4. Procedures for the issuance and return of keys may be altered by the superintendent of physical plant to make keys available to plant personnel as required to meet work requirements throughout the campus.

5. The loss or theft of any key is to be reported immediately to the department chair, who in turn will notify the key shop, physical plant.

6. Lost keys turned in to a department are to be forwarded immediately to physical plant.

7. Applications for keys are made on a *Key Record* (University Form 1).
   a) *Key Record* forms must be typed and must be submitted with all carbons and copies intact.
   b) A separate form is used for each key requested.
   c) *Key Record* forms are available from the storeroom.

8. As standard procedure, physical plant will deliver and pick up keys at the department.

a) Keys may be obtained directly from physical plant by presenting an approved *Key Record* at the key shop, physical plant, general services building between the hours of 8:00-9:00 a.m. and 1:00-2:00 p.m. daily.

b) The department is responsible for contacting physical plant and making the necessary arrangements to have returned keys picked up.

9. Prior to the end of each academic semester, each department will be provided with a list of individuals assigned keys to areas under its jurisdiction.

NOTE: These lists will aid the department in identifying those keys to be returned by students or staff having an ending date of appointment as of the end of the semester.

10. Annually, each department must check and certify the accuracy of an inventory list of keys issued for areas under its jurisdiction.

11. Keys must be presented at the request of any watchman, campus police officer, or other law enforcement official in the performance of his/her duty.

12. Facilities located outside the city limits should contact the physical plant department for any special procedures required by their location.

C.   Procedures: Issuance of Keys

Department   1. Upon request for key, initiate *Key Record* (University Form 1), completing Items No. 1-8.

NOTE: Keys assigned to students (Item No. 3) are temporary assignments (Item No. 4), and *all* temporary assignments (Item No. 4), require entry of a date that key is due to be returned.

2. Approve *Key Record* (Item No. 9).

3. Obtain building coordinator's approval if applicable (Item No. 10) and send form intact to physical plant.

Physical Plant

4. Produce key, and deliver key and copies 1-4 of *Key Record* to department.

Department

5-A. If Applicant Is Available:

a) Obtain applicant's signature on *Key Record* (Item No. 12).

b) Give key and copy 4 to applicant.

c) Give copies 1 and 3 to physical plant representative.

d) Retain second copy and file in alphabetical sequence or in individual's personnel file as reference to whom keys are issued.

5-B. If Applicant Is Not Available:

a) Sign *Key Record* (Item No. 11) and give copy 3 to physical plant representative, retaining copies 1, 2, and 4 intact.

b) When applicant is available, obtain signature on *Key Record* (Item No. 12).

c) Give key and copy 4 to applicant.

d) Send copy 1 to physical plant.

e) Retain second copy and file in alphabetical sequence or in individual's personnel file as reference to whom keys are issued.

D. Procedures: Returning Keys

Department

1. Upon determining that an individual is transferring or terminating employment with the university, review files to see what keys are to be returned.
2. Retrieve key from individual, making certain that key number matches that on copy 2 of *Key Record*.
3. Signify receipt of key by signature on copy 2 of *Key Record* (Item No. 13).
4. Notify physical plant of key to be picked up.
5. Surrender key to physical plant representative and retain receipted copy 2 of *Key Record* until deletion of issue record is verified by next report, after which time copy 2 is destroyed.

E. Procedures: Lost, Stolen, or Recovered Keys

Department

1. Notify physical plant immediately by telephone when a key is reported lost or stolen.
   NOTE: Replacement keys are requested in accordance with above procedures.
2. Pull copy 2 of appropriate *Key Record* from file.
3. Enter "Lost" or "Stolen" in Item No. 13, then sign and date *Key Record*.
4. Forward copy 2 to physical plant.
5. Notify physical plant immediately by telephone when a key is recovered.

Sample Key Record

	PHYSICAL PLANT USE ONLY		
1. APPLICANT'S NAME (LAST, FIRST, MIDDLE INITIAL)	KEY NUMBER	DATE ISSUED	
2. FEDERAL I.D. NUMBER — STATUS OF APPLICANT ☐ FACULTY ☐ STAFF ☐ STUDENT	TYPE KEY	BLDG CODE	DEPT CODE
4. TYPE OF ISSUANCE ☐ PERM. ☐ TEMP. — DATE DUE — 5. TYPE KEY (RM NO.) ENTRANCE—SM NO.	6. BUILDING	7. DEPARTMENT	

8. DEL. KEY TO RM. No.____   BUILDING

9. APPROVED—TYPED OR PRINTED NAME & SIGNATURE OF DEPARTMENT CHAIR

10. TYPED OR PRINTED NAME & SIGNATURE OF ADDITIONAL AUTHORITY (AS REQUIRED)

11. SIGNATURE OF INDIVIDUAL RECEIVING KEY (IF NOT APPLICANT)   DATE

12. SIGNATURE OF APPLICANT (I certify that I have received this key described hereon, and that I have read & agree to the conditions of issuance as stipulated on the reverse side of this form.)   DATE

13. KEY RETURNED (SIGNATURE OF DEPT. CHAIR & DATE)

14. KEY RETURNED (SIGNATURE OF KEY SHOP REP & DATE)

KEY RECORD

1. Physical Plant   3. Physical Plant
2. Department   4. Employee

CHAPTER 54

Emergency Operations

Alan L. Ingle
Assistant Director for Business and Administration
Physical Plant Department
West Virginia University

54.1 INTRODUCTION

There are many emergency conditions that can adversely affect, even interrupt, normal college and university operations. Of even greater consequence, some can harm the lives of students and personnel. Although emergencies are unforeseen situations that cannot be handled routinely, planning for their possible occurrence can lessen their impact. The planning includes anticipating the possible effects, prescribing actions to minimize their damage, and restoring normal operations.

Virtually all components of a college or university have responsibilities for emergency planning, but physical plant departments have the primary responsibility, as well as the technical expertise, for emergency preparedness planning. Most emergencies pertain directly or indirectly to facilities, so physical plant is uniquely organized, staffed, and equipped for handling emergencies.

The types of emergencies that are likely to occur vary. Because emergency preparedness planning must be detailed and oriented to the types of threats that exist at each individual campus, this chapter provides general guidance for such planning.

54.2 OBJECTIVES OF EMERGENCY PREPAREDNESS PLANNING

An emergency preparedness plan provides for meeting emergencies that may, at a minimum, disrupt operations of the college or university. The plan should have as its first priority the protection of lives and property to the maximum extent possible. The second priority is to restore normal operations. The plan should coordinate the efforts of the support activities under the institution's control. Resources outside the institution's control, such as city fire service or utility companies, may be asked for assistance when an emergency occurs, but since they have other responsibilities that preclude their carrying out specific preassigned functions, they should not be directly included in the plan.

The emergency preparedness plan should complement the planning of the college or university safety committee as well as safety programs established by building officials. It should be designed to become operational when an emergency is declared by the administrative head of the institution or other designated authority.

54.3 EMERGENCY IDENTIFICATION

An emergency preparedness plan must be flexible in prescribing actions commensurate with the nature, level, and type of emergency. Appendix 54-A lists eight general emergency conditions, each of which require unique responses. For example, Code 2, civil disaster, requires actions quite different from those of Code 4, utility emergency. Appendix 54-B illustrates classifications of magnitude of emergency conditions, ranging from a watch or alert condition through full mobilization. Appendix 54-C shows a further breakdown of the specific type of emergencies within the eight general conditions.

The three criteria—general nature, magnitude, and type—should be used for planning and can be coded to quickly announce the emergency condition and prescribe the action to be taken. For example, 1B-5 designates a natural element emergency in the warning stage involving flooding; 1D-12 designates a natural element emergency requiring immediate implementation of the snow removal plan.

54.4 PHYSICAL PLANT DEPARTMENT EMERGENCY PLANNING

Following are typical functions of physical plant department units under emergency operations.

General Management

The physical plant director and staff must ensure that policies and procedures are established for emergency operations that are consistent with the institution's plan. During emergencies the director and staff control and direct the functions of the department in support of the institution.

Business Management

The budget should include funding for emergency planning and preparedness, and cost accounting must identify expenditures. Procedures should be established to record expenditures in the execution of emergency operations. Funds expended in both preparation and execution of emergency operations must be separately identified from normal operations for subsequent reimbursement.

Engineering Services

Engineering services has a major role in emergency preparedness and operations. Included are estimating the possible damages to facilities from various contingencies and the resultant impact on university operations, and the development of plans to minimize their effect. During emergencies, engineering services assesses the damages to facilities and determines corrective work required. Campus plats (drawings), especially of utility lines, are critical to emergency planning and operations.

Storeroom Operations

During emergency operations storerooms must be prepared to quickly furnish needed materials and maintain records of the issues in order to assist in determining the special costs of the emergency.

Work Management

The functions of estimating, work order processing, scheduling, and dispatching are essential to effective work management, and especially critical to the control and direction of work in an emergency. Personnel responsible for these functions should be thoroughly cognizant of all emergency plans and carry out their functions to ensure optimum employment of the work force in an emergency.

Crafts Shops

The work of the crafts shops is perhaps the most critical in restoring facilities to a condition so that normal operations can resume. All crafts personnel should be thoroughly familiar with their roles in emergencies.

Grounds and Custodial Maintenance

During and after emergencies, grounds and custodial services may be required for special maintenance and cleaning.

54.5 EMERGENCY OPERATIONS OF A COLLEGE OR UNIVERSITY

During emergencies a college or university may be required to be self-sufficient for a period of time. Outside services may be interrupted, so the resources of the institution must be organized to provide essential services. Each college or university is a unique organization; however, most facilities departments function under the direction of a physical plant or facilities division. Following are typical service units that may be organized and the functions they perform.

Emergency Operations Control Unit

The office of primary responsibility for emergency operations control is the chief facilities manager or designated representative. The purpose is to coordinate and control the functioning of all special services on campus. Its functions are to:

- Establish and maintain contact with outside emergency agencies as required.
- Establish staff, operate a personnel office, and enroll and classify volunteers according to skills both before and after a major disaster or emergency.
- Obtain, through the university legal counsel, legal advisement on matters such as defense of claims, financial settlement of claims, torts, product liability, criminal and civil charges, procedures, and jurisdictions.
- Provide communication to the primary service units as well as other units within the university community. Also provides regular updates on conditions.

Planning, Coordination, and Communication Unit

The office of primary responsibility for this unit is facilities planning and management. The purpose is to provide overall planning and coordination related to emergency situations. Its functions are to:

- In accordance with orders from the emergency operations control officer, take emergency actions as required to maintain continuing coordination and communication.

- Assist the physical plant operations unit in taking all necessary actions to review damages involved in the emergency situation and to advise actions necessary to ensure accuracy of reports regarding the condition of facilities.
- Establish a public assistance center to handle inquiries and provide information on the status of the emergency.
- Establish and operate a communications system linking all service units.
- Identify existing facilities in priority order for use as logistic support areas to provide shelter.

Engineering, Damage Survey, and Demolition Unit

The office of primary responsibility for this unit is physical plant operations. The purpose of this unit is to provide engineering services, damage surveys, emergency repairs, and construction advice or demolition as necessary to minimize the adverse affects of an emergency. Its functions are to:

- Advise fire, police, construction, maintenance suppliers, and others as necessary regarding damage to physical facilities and recommend corrective actions.
- Assist police and fire departments in taking all necessary actions to rescue or protect persons and property.
- Survey campus buildings and infrastructure and report the findings to the emergency operations control center.
- Make surveys to determine the status of buildings for the safety of all concerned. When action must be taken, this unit prepares the necessary documentation to conduct the appropriate function (repair or condemnation).
- Make arrangements with the telephone and utility companies for standby of their service groups.
- Coordinate all utility use and interruption.
- Remove utility service from buildings as necessary.

Housing and Food Service Unit

The office of primary responsibility for this unit is housing and residence life. The purpose of this unit is to operate the university housing and feeding facilities for university personnel and any outside personnel participating in emergency operations. Its functions are to:

- Operate regular food service facilities and establish auxiliary kitchens or mess halls as required.
- Prepare designated buildings for sleeping.
- Make arrangements for feeding and housing external agencies working on campus that do not have their own facilities.
- Cooperate with the department of environmental health and safety and the public safety department in controlling sanitation, safety, and security in the housing and food areas.
- Maintain records of people using emergency housing and feeding facilities.

Law Enforcement Unit

The office of primary responsibility for this unit is the department of security. Its purpose is to perform all functions and duties normally required of a public safety department and be cognizant of procedures to follow in emergency and disaster situations. Its functions are to:

- Coordinate the organization and mobilization of police personnel, equipment, logistics, and auxiliary personnel that might be required to supplement the public safety department personnel. This unit also establishes liaison with private guards or civilian personnel for the purpose of using additional personnel to reinforce sworn police personnel.
- Provide organization, installation, staffing, and operation of all communication facilities to be used for disaster operations under the control of the public safety department.
- Coordinate liaison between the emergency operations officer and the police department, county sheriff's office, state police, and other law enforcement agencies as needed.
- Regular duties include preventive patrols on foot and by car; answering calls related to crimes, fires, collisions, injuries, illnesses, and complaints; conducting investigations; making arrests and related court appearances; custody and disposal of lost and found property; and generally providing for the peace, safety, and security of persons and facilities on university property. The university police are also responsible for preventing and controlling disturbances and demonstrations, and for maintaining security and crime control at public gatherings and similar events.

Health and Safety Unit

The office of primary responsibility for this unit is the environmental health and safety department. Its functions are to:

- Organize and direct or coordinate a university-wide fire prevention and fire control organization.
- Organize, mobilize, and operate facilities for carrying out prevention, detection, and decontamination procedures to combat the harmful effects of radiological, biological, and chemical agents.
- Provide continuous support and consultation to all units and people needing help in order to provide as safe and healthful an environment as possible. Included are:

Fire Service
- Train such volunteer personnel as may be required for auxiliary fire services.
- Maintain necessary up-to-date records of all fire control equipment by location and condition, including maps indicating the location of all fire alarm boxes, telephones, water lines, and fire hydrants.
- By performing systematic inspections, ensure that the fire control equipment in all buildings is maintain in proper working order.
- Survey all facilities to eliminate fire hazards.
- Cooperate with the fire department and coordinate the activities of the university with the county and city to provide efficient operations.

Radiological, Biological, and Chemical Monitoring Service
- Train volunteer personnel for this service as required.
- Provide and maintain an up-to-date inventory of monitoring personnel, apparatus, and equipment.
- Devise methods for the storage, safety, issuance, and use of monitoring apparatus and equipment.
- Provide expertise for procedures assuring both general radiation safety and that of special facilities, such as cobalt storage.

General Environmental Health and Safety
- Survey facilities and environment to determine if they are safe and sanitary.
- Consult and advise all other units whenever necessary on matters related to health and safety.
- Perform hazard monitoring.

The health and safety unit also outlines the procedures for coordinating patient flow and off-campus cooperation between police, emergency rescue services, and the student health office.

Transportation Unit

The office of primary responsibility for this unit is the transportation office. Its purpose is to provide continuous transportation and related automotive services to campus personnel and to utilize serviceable motor vehicles for protecting lives and property as required under emergency conditions. Its functions are to:

- Define the methods to be following in maintaining, establishing, or reestablishing transportation services at the time and place needed and in the volume required by prevailing circumstances.
- Reactivate transportation and related automotive services damaged by a major disaster, and develop an emergency transportation service using vehicles from the motor pool fleet.
- Under the direction of the emergency operations officer, cooperate with local agencies in order to best serve the transportation requirements of the community at large.
- Devise methods for the storage, safety, issuance, use, and repair of vehicles and equipment.
- Prepare and maintain an up-to-date inventory of all forms of vehicles for transporting personnel and equipment and maintaining an adequate fuel reserve.

A roster of emergency action personnel assigned to each unit should be published. "Action sheets" should be developed and maintained for each person assigned specific duties and responsibilities.

54.6 DECLARATION OF EMERGENCY

The administrative head (president or chancellor) should be responsible for the initial declaration of a state of university or college emergency, as well as the end of the emergency. After the emergency is declared, the emergency operations control officer is responsible for directing all emergency operations. The declaration of emergency should therefore be made first to the emergency operations control officer, and then to the campus community and the general public.

Building occupants normally function through a chain of command operation with a building supervisor or other individual in authority. Under this individual's direction, the building committee will develop procedures for identifying and reporting conditions.

When a state of emergency has been declared by the president or designee, the emergency operations control officer shall activate the emergency preparedness plan.

54.7 EQUIPMENT AND RESOURCES

It is extremely important in developing an emergency preparedness plan to identify equipment and resources available in case of need. Each operations unit is individually most capable of identifying the equipment and resources needed in their area of expertise to carry out emergency operations effectively. Their input is necessary to compose and maintain a complete list of available equipment and resources. The location of this equipment and resources is also critical to a successful operation under emergency conditions. The location must be appropriate for prompt access during emergency operations and should be identified in listing the equipment and resources. These lists can be compiled by type of equipment so that any of the operating units can readily identify equipment availability and location. An alternative is to list equipment by operating unit identification criteria, since the equipment normally is stored at that specific facility.

54.8 TRAINING

Training programs should be conducted periodically by the emergency service units to ensure that all personnel are familiar with and competent to execute their emergency assignments.

Each unit head should prepare written instructions for use by personnel in emergencies, copies of which should be supplemental to the emergency preparedness documentation and made available to their alternates for necessary action.

All units involved in emergency preparedness operations should conduct joint mock drills. A campus-wide committee should establish criteria and act as the evaluator of performance in the drills.

54.9 EMERGENCY PREPAREDNESS FUNDING

The actions required in preparing for possible emergencies and the measures taken when emergencies occur are not normally included in the regular annual budgets of institutions. It is necessary, therefore, that special funds be identified for emergency preparedness and that records be maintained of all expenditures in connection with emergencies so that special funding can be requested.

54.10 EMERGENCY PROGRAM ASSISTANCE

Each college or university has certain internal capabilities to develop an emergency preparedness program. This ability will depend in large part on the size of the institution and on the academic and financial resources available. Numerous public organizations also can be used as the need arises. The following is a brief summary of some of these organizations.

National Guard and Armed Services

The state and federal governments, through the National Guard and Armed Services, regularly develop and initiate disaster plan operations that can supplement the university emergency preparedness effort. A typical example of such state planning is shown in the West Virginia National Guard Disaster Plan #011500R dated February 1984. A portion of it reads as follows:

> Disasters may occur anywhere at any time. The primary responsibility for alleviating the effects of such disasters rests with individuals, families, private industry, local and state governments, various volunteer disaster relief agencies and those federal agencies with special statutory responsibilities. In this plan "disaster" means an: "occurrent or imminent threat of widespread or severe damage, injury, or loss of life or property resulting from any natural or manmade cause, including but not limited to fire, flood, earthquakes, storm, epidemic, air contamination, blight, drought, accident, infestation or explosion."[1]

Department of Defense/Defense Civil Preparedness Agency

The federal government through the Department of Defense regularly conducts seminars and publishes planning brochures for various industry and business needs. Brochure Number CPG2-3, dated July 1973, outlines how to hold emergency planning seminars. It includes a handbook on how to plan, organize, and conduct conferences on business and industrial emergency preparedness. The brochure explains how to set up an emergency preparedness seminar that allows the local university emergency preparedness director to bring together key leaders and government officials for an interchange of information.[2]

Law Enforcement/Fire Service Disaster Operations

Local police and fire departments have developed emergency preparedness plans for the community surrounding the campus. Allen Bristow's *Police Disaster Operations* identifies local government's responsibility in emergency preparedness to include: evacuation, post-attack recovery techniques, control of civilian and military traffic, control of ingress and egress from contaminated areas, security, protection of vital facilities, enforcement of special economics, stabilization measures, and explosive ordinants reconnaissance.[3]

This checklist for local police activities may sound ominous, but it makes the point that the local law enforcement agency must be ready to lend assistance when disaster strikes. More importantly, local law enforcement generally is happy to assist in developing plans to control disaster.

Red Cross

The county Red Cross chapter has extensive experience in disaster preparedness planning. The plan usually includes a telephone and personnel directory of the preparedness committee, as well as data on subcommittees concerned with clothing, medical, transportation, warning, supply, shelter, food, and public information. Depending upon the Red Cross unit involved, this information is available through each subcommittee to interested parties.

Federal Emergency Management Agency

The federal government maintains an agency specifically dedicated to emergency management. Among the publications this agency offers is a brochure titled *In Time of Emergency* (#H-14, February 1984) that identifies key emergency conditions that require planning in order to aid in recovery and limit loss. The Federal Emergency Management Agency is prepared to assist local organizations in their efforts to plan for emergencies.[4]

Publications

A wealth of information has been published on the topic of emergency preparedness, and university or community libraries can provide access to much of this planning documentation. Also see Additional Resources at the end of this chapter. Finally, contact other institutions to request a copy of their emergency plans and procedures.

54.11 CONCLUSION

Emergency preparedness planning is and must be unique to each college and university. A great deal of information is available from outside sources and, while this information is transferable to some extent, it must be utilized in light of the unique conditions of the individual institution. Through this analysis, an action plan for emergency operations can be developed that provides for the orderly handling of an emergency and the efficient recovery to normal conditions with minimum cost. The key to successful emergency operations is the extent of physical plant preparation in an orderly, logical way that supports the unique college or university environment involved.

NOTES

1. West Virginia National Guard, *West Virginia National Guard Disaster Plan* (Charleston, West Virginia: West Virginia National Guard, 1984).
2. U.S. Department of Defense/Defense Civil Preparedness Agency, *Industry/Business Emergency Planning Seminars* (Washington: U.S. Department of Defense, 1973).
3. Allen P. Bristow, *Police Disaster Operations* (Springfield, Illinois: Charles C. Thomas, 1972).
4. Federal Emergency Management Agency, *In Time of Emergency* (Washington: Federal Emergency Management Agency, 1984).

ADDITIONAL RESOURCES

American National Red Cross. *Disaster Preparedness Plan*. Morgantown, West Virginia: Monongalia County Chapter of the American Red Cross, 1987.

Bristow, Allen P. *Police Disaster Operations*. Springfield, Illinois: Charles C. Thomas, 1972.

Federal Emergency Management Agency. *In Time of Emergency*. Washington: Federal Emergency Management Agency, 1984.

Foster, Harold D. *Disaster Planning*. New York: Springer-Verlag, 1980.

Healy, Richard J. *Emergency and Disaster Planning*. New York: John Wiley & Sons, 1969.

Indiana University-Purdue University at Indianapolis. *Emergency Handbook*. Indianapolis, Indiana: Indiana/Purdue University, 1977.

Perry, Ronald W. and Alvin H. Mushkatel. *Disaster Management*. Westport, Connecticut: Quorum Books, 1984.

Plant, Fred. "Emergency Operations." Unpublished paper, Saint Joseph College, 1988.

Raphael, Beverly. *When Disaster Strikes*. New York: Basic Books, 1986.

San Jose State University. *Emergency Procedures*. San Jose, California: San Jose State University, 1989.

University of Northern Colorado Emergency Response Plan for U of C in Cooperation With U.S Government. *Federal Emergency Management Agency and Colorado State Department of Disaster and Emergency Service*. Greeley, Colorado: University of Northern Colorado, 1983.

U.S. Department of Defense/Defense Civil Preparedness Agency. *Industry/Business Emergency Planning Seminars*. Washington: U.S. Department of Defense, 1973.

West Virginia Department of Civil Defense and Monongalia County Civil Defense Office. *Monongalia County Resources Inventory for Emergency Operation Simulation Training*. Morgantown, West Virginia: West Virginia University and Monongalia County, 1983.

West Virginia National Guard. *West Virginia National Guard Disaster Plan*. Charleston, West Virginia: West Virginia National Guard, 1984.

―――. *Civil Disturbance Plan*. Charleston, West Virginia: West Virginia National Guard, 1985.

West Virginia State College. *Emergency Response Plan*. Institute, West Virginia: West Virginia State College, 1987.

West Virginia University Safety Committee. *The WVU Emergency Action Plan*. Morgantown, West Virginia: West Virginia University, 1988.

Appendix 54-A

GENERAL EMERGENCY CONDITIONS

Code ID	Nature of Emergency	Description
1.	Natural element emergency	Any unusual natural occurrence that has the potential to cause disruption of normal activities
2.	Civil disorder emergency	Any actions by a person or persons that have the potential to cause bodily harm
3.	Structural emergency	Any emergency related to building or facility problems
4.	Utility emergency	Any problems associated with utilities such as natural gas, electricity, water, communication failure, or erratic operation
5.	Transportation emergency	Any unplanned activities related to equipment and vehicles that have the potential of causing human injury
6.	Chemical emergency	Any abnormal conditions related to chemical utilization
7.	Underground emergency	Any subsidence or disturbance in underground locations

8. Off-campus support
   emergency

Any conditions whatsoever that occur outside the university community where it is deemed necessary to utilize university support.

Appendix 54-B

MAGNITUDE OF EMERGENCY CONDITION

Code ID	Level of Emergency	Description
A.	Watch	Signs of impending problem
B.	Warning	Problem is imminent—get ready
C.	Mobilize	Begin to operate according to appropriate plan
D.	Action	Execute under full-scale emergency operation
E.	Operation	Continue execution
F.	Hold	Stop execution pending further instruction
G.	Demobilize	Revert to normal operation

Appendix 54-C

TYPES OF EMERGENCY CONDITIONS

NATURAL ELEMENT EMERGENCY

Code ID	Type of Emergency	Description
1	Disease	Disease that is widely contagious or has potential to cause plague.
2	Drought	Lack of water for drink.
3	Earthquake	Having a life safety impact on the university community or destruction to property.
4	Evacuation	Any time personnel must be evacuated from a building.
5	Flooding	Natural water level is surpassed causing damage or endangerment to life or property.
6	Forest fire	Natural element emergency in wooded area.
7	Hail storm	Having a life safety impact on the university community or destruction to property.
8	High winds	High winds as identified by National Weather Service.
9	Insects	A large-scale infestation.
10	Land fire	Any fire on campus that involves roads and grounds areas.
11	Landslide	Ground movement.
12	Snow	Having a life safety impact on the university community or destruction to property.
13	Tornado	A tornado condition as identified by the National Weather Service reports.
14	Uncontrolled animal	Depending on its path or area, university personnel are needed

to hold or subdue the animal to protect the university community.

CIVIL DISORDER EMERGENCY

Code ID	Type of Emergency	Description
15	Arson	Intentional setting of a fire whether it's a building or land.
16	Demonstration	Any type of demonstration of a large scale.
17	Domestic disturbance	Any type of problems where one person may cause injury to another due to anger or an out-of-control condition.
18	Evacuation	Any time personnel must be evacuated from a building.
19	Explosion	Any type of explosion that causes danger to personnel, equipment, or structures.
20	Explosives	Any type of material that can explode, will explode, or has the potential to explode and cause destruction to property or personnel.
21	Hostage	A hostile taking of a prisoner for some gain.
22	Looting	Uncontrolled theft of university property on a large scale.
23	Riot	Uncontrolled crowd causing possible danger to life or property.
24	Sniper	Any individual who is endangering life by shooting at others.
25	Suicide	A person attempting to take his or her life.

STRUCTURAL EMERGENCY

Code ID	Type of Emergency	Description
26	Bomb threat	Report of explosives emergency.
27	Building collapse, floor collapse, or any type of structure collapse	Any permanent support failure causing endangerment to personnel or equipment.
28	Building fire	A structural emergency caused by fire.
29	Evacuation	Any time personnel must be evacuated from a building.
30	Explosion	Any type of explosion that causes danger to personnel, equipment, or structures.
31	Jammed elevator	Any time an elevator is jammed while people are on board.
32	PRT collapse	The falling of PRT roadway.
33	Structural damage	Any structural damage that may cause endangerment to life or property.

UTILITY EMERGENCY

Code ID	Type of Emergency	Description
34	Evacuation	Any time personnel must be evacuated from a building.
35	Loss of communication	Cutoff of any type of communication.
36	Loss of gas supply	Utility emergency.
37	Loss of electrical supply	Utility emergency.
38	Loss of water supply	Utility emergency.
39	Major computer failure	Critical computer failure.
40	Mass blackout	Utility emergency.
41	Natural gas leak	Utility emergency.

42	Power lines down	A utility line down on campus.
43	Water contamination	Utility emergency.
44	Airplane crash	Vehicular emergency.
45	Bus crash	Vehicular emergency.
46	Evacuation	Any time personnel must be evacuated from a building.
47	Helicopter crash	Either on campus or near campus.
48	Large vehicle crash	Vehicular emergency.
49	Personnel injury	A need for medical treatment.
50	PRT collapse	The falling of PRT roadway.
51	Train derailment	Off-campus train accident.

CHEMICAL EMERGENCY

Code ID	Type of Emergency	Description
52	Chemical spill	Any type of chemical spilled that may be a life and safety problem.
53	Evacuation	Any time personnel must be evacuated from a building.
54	Food contamination	Any life-threatening emergency relating to food.
55	Nuclear attack	A civil defense emergency.
56	Poison	Any condition that involves poisonous materials accessible to personnel on campus.
57	Radiation release	Any radioactive release either into the air, land, or water.
58	Toxic material	Any kind of toxic material that may be dangerous to personnel or equipment.

UNDERGROUND EMERGENCY

Code ID	Type of Emergency	Description
59	Steam tunnel fire	Underground emergency.

| 60 | Subsidence | A large, sudden subsidence that requires support service. |

OFF-CAMPUS SUPPORT EMERGENCY

Code ID	Type of Emergency	Description
61	Bomb threat	Report of explosives emergency.
62	Demonstration	Any type of demonstration of a large scale.
63	Disease	Disease that is widely contagious or has potential to cause plague.
64	Drought	Lack of water for drink.
65	Earthquake	Having a life safety impact on the university community or destruction to property.
66	Evacuation	Any time personnel must be evacuated from a building.
67	Explosion	Any type of explosion that causes danger to personnel, equipment, or structures.
68	Explosives	Any type of material that can explode, will explode, or has the potential to explode and cause destruction to property or personnel.
69	Food contamination	Any life-threatening emergency relating to food.
70	Forest fire	Natural element emergency in wooded area.
71	Hostage	A hostile taking of a prisoner for some gain.
72	Insects	A large-scale infestation.
73	Landslide	Ground movement.
74	Looting	Uncontrolled theft of university property on a large scale.
75	Loss of water supply	Utility emergency.
76	Mass blackout	Utility emergency.

77	Mine tunnel cave-in	A large cave-in that requires support service.
78	Multi-vehicle accident	Transportation emergency.
79	Nuclear attack	A civil defense emergency.
80	Radiation release	Any radioactive release either into the air, land, or water.
81	Riot	Uncontrolled crowd causing possible danger to life or property.
82	Sniper	Any individual who is endangering life by shooting at others.
83	Uncontrolled animal	Depending on its path or area, university personnel are needed to hold or subdue the animal to protect the university community.
84	Water contamination	Utility emergency.

Appendix 54-D

Emergency Response Organizations

Ambulance (EMS)	Office of Emergency Services
American Red Cross	Poison Control Center
City Managers	Police Departments
County Health Department	Sanitary Boards
County Sheriff	Sanitation Departments
Fire Departments	State Department of Public Safety
Hospitals	State Fire Marshal
National Response Center	State Response Center
(toxic chemicals and oil spills)	Water Commission

Appendix 54-E

Typical Emergency Equipment

Camera
- 35 mm cameras
- VCRs with one camera

Communication
- Area hazards computerized
- Band analyzer
- Communications center
- Communications equipment
- Emergency operations center
- Field telephone/switch-limited AM/SSB
- Limited radio
- Limited radio/wire
- Portable two-way radios
- Public address systems, scanners
- Two-way radios, scanners

Equipment
- Generator power
- Heating equipment (portable)
- Class 60 bridging
- Dozers
- Flares
- Frontloaders
- Fuel transport, field storage, hand pumps
- Heavy-duty bridge craft
- Lifting equipment for bracing
- Marking tape (cloth, white, 2 in.)
- Outboard motors
- Overgarments
- Pole climbing equipment
- Portable maintenance shelters
- Portable mess halls
- Power generation equipment
- Sampling pumps, DuPont P-4000
- Sand bags, empty
- Scuba equipment
- Sleeping bags/blankets/cots
- Tentage

Food
- Alternate water supply

- Emergency feeding
- Emergency rations
- Supply

Housekeeping
- Supplies
- Linens
- Beds
- Paper products

Information
- Hostage negotiation book

Light
- Light engineer equipment packs
- Lightsets—interior/flood
- Maglights (rechargeable flash)
- Steam lights

Meters
- Draeger detector tubes
- Miran 1-A infrared analyzer
- Velometer
- Airflow meters
- Combustible gas meter
- Gas leak detector
- Heat stress monitor
- Hydrogen sulfide monitor
- Mercury vapor sniffer
- Noise dosimeter
- Oxygen monitor
- pH meter
- Sizing sampler
- Sound level meter/octave

Office Supplies
- Calculator
- Computers
- Copy machine
- Record information center
- Safe

Personnel
- Chemical crisis personnel
- Trained assistance personnel
- Crowd control personnel

Protective Equipment
- Containment equipment
- Cartridge respirators
- Chemical containment equipment

- Chemical protective equipment
- Chemical spill cart
- Civil disturbance equipment
- Coveralls
- Crisis personnel equipment
- Decompression chamber
- Ear muffs
- Facepiece
- Fire fighting equipment
- Fresh air ventilation
- Gas/gas disbursing equipment
- Hard hats
- Holding center
- Leather restraints
- Life preservers
- Masks
- Protective chemical goggles
- Riot batons
- Self-contained breathing equipment
- Shields
- Vests
- Water purification equipment

Transport
- Aircraft
- Boats
- Trucks

Vehicles
- Five/ten-ton wreckers with cutting
- M-113 personnel carrier
- M-577 command post with power
- M-578 recovery vehicle
- S&P and lowboy trailers
- Cruisers
- Ladder trucks, heavy equipment
- Light armored vehicles
- Rough terrain cranes
- Rough terrain forklifts
- Ten-ton tractors with dropside
- Ten-ton rough terrain cargo
- Water trailers (250 gal.)

Appendix 54-F

Emergency Operation Functions

Executive Director	— Direct and control the university emergency management organization
	— Establish priorities and allocations for the distribution and utilization of available university resources
	— Ensure that authenticated information is released to the public
	— Ensure that contact and coordination is maintained with local, state, and federal agencies involved
Public Information	— Public and university information
	— Media relations
	— Casualty and inquiry
	— Rumor control center
	— Public information center
Legal Officer	— Advise executive director concerning emergency powers and responsibilities
	— Determine legality of decisions/actions
	— Coordinate legal matters with local, state and/or federal authorities or officials
Military Liaison Officer	— Military affairs advisor
	— Military material support
	— Liaison/coordinator with military units and/or activities (e.g. National Guard)
	— Facilitate transition to martial law
Materials, Maintenance, and Resources	— In charge in absence of executive director
	— Advisor relating to material and personnel requirements
	— Coordinate request for emergency material assistance
	— Assigns priorities to material request IAW policies established
	— Procures material and personnel,

	both public and private, from all available sources
	— Maintenance and repair of facilities
	— Transportation and equipment
	— Construction
	— Shelter upgrading
Emergency Response Coordinator	— Implement emergency response plan
	— Coordinate activities of the emergency management center
	— Brief the executive group
	— Monitor operation activity and keep EMC staff appraised
	— Activate the EMC
	— Personnel alert, recall, staff accounting
	— Coordinate/facilitate EMC staff
	— Documentation of EMC activities
	— Coordinate with police and fire departments and ambulance
Communications Director	— Supervise communications and records functions of EMC
	— Supervise personnel alert, recall efforts
	— Coordinate communications with outside agencies
	— Coordinate all university internal communications
Damage Assessment and Recovery	— Organize and implement damage assessment capability
	— Define severity of damage and loss
	— Prepare damage reports
	— Plan and coordinate recovery operations
	— Plan or reconstitution of the university
	— Prepare after action, damage and loss reports and other records as necessary to document loss and expenses incurred
Medical Health Officer	— Medical training
	— Medical care
	— Mortuary services
	— Notification of coroner

Shelter, Facilities Officer	— Relocation
	— Feeding, lodging, clothing
	— Normal welfare and social services (clergy, psychological)
	— University shelter plan
	— Sustenance support (except feeding)
	— Provide shelters as required by city and county emergency plans
Environmental Safety Officer	— Monitor radiological hazards
	— Advise in all hazardous material matters
	— Environmental health (water purity, waste storage, food contamination)
	— Safety hazards
	— Radiological defense planning and training
	— Law enforcement
	— Traffic direction and control
	— Installation and shelter security
	— Patrol
	— Intelligence
Emergency Services and Public Safety	— Assist in dissemination of warnings and information to campus relocations
	— Fatality identification and field morgue
	— Emergency medical response and coordination
	— Initial fire response and coordination
	— Field command post

Appendix 54-G

Sample Summary of Unique Requirements Due to Time

Daytime

During normal daytime hours (7:30 a.m.-4:00 p.m.), a small college has approximately 1,500-1,600 students, 266 staff and faculty, plus 5-20 visitors within its campus at any given time. While it is true that an emergency during daytime hours could require evacuation of a large number of personnel, also true is that those having specific duties and assignments in implementing the evacuation are available and ready to respond immediately.

Participating Section/ Department	No. of Persons Available
Top Level Administrators	14
Faculty	90
Security Department	2
Utilities	3
Custodial Personnel	7
Other Physical Plant Facilities Personnel	50
Other Staff Personnel	100
TOTAL	266

Evening

During the evening (4:00 p.m.-11:00 p.m.), there are normally as many students and faculty as there are during the day (especially during September-May). However, the number of staff and administrators is only one-third that of a normal day. It follows that almost as many personnel may have to be evacuated during the evening by far fewer staff members.

Participating Section/ Department	No. of Persons Available
Security	2
Utilities	1
Custodial	8
Faculty	90
Resident Directors/ Other Staff	10
TOTAL	111

Late Night and Weekends

During late night hours and on weekends there are normally 280 resident students, approximately 50 persons in resident/ faculty/staff and family, and 5-20 visitors. Consideration must also be given to personnel in library during weekend operating hours.

Participating Section/ Department	No. of Persons Available
Security	1
Resident Directors	3
TOTAL	4

Appendix 54-H

Typical Stages of Emergency Warning

First Stage Warning Alert
1. This stage indicates the possibility of a toxic gas or other emission and will be signaled by a continuous high tone signal from one or more local sirens. In the unlikely event that there is a sudden unexpected release without warning and personnel detect or have unusual physical reactions to toxic materials, they should *immediately* proceed inside the nearest assembly area and begin to execute the first stage of the warning alert.
2. People are to go inside, close windows and doors, shut down air conditioners and other ventilation equipment. No smoking will be allowed inside buildings. Tune radios to local radio and television stations.
3. Students in classrooms or dormitories will move to assembly areas in each of the main campus buildings. Designated supervisors will issue further instructions.
   NOTE: If the alert is sounded during sleeping hours, physical facilities and security personnel will awaken people in dormitory and housing areas.

Second Stage—Shelter in Place
1. In the event that evacuation is not necessary or feasible, personnel will be directed to remain indoors in the designated assembly areas until the hazardous condition has been eliminated.
2. Supervisory personnel at all levels will assist in informing and directing people to seek shelter inside and remain there.

Third Stage—Prepare to Evacuate
1. The third stage warning alert will be broadcast by radio and television and indicates that preparations for evacuation are to be made.
2. People must remain calm, gather any needed items such as medications and clothing, and await further instructions.

Fourth Stage—Evacuation
1. The evacuation order will be issued by radio and television. Supervisory personnel will provide further instructions.

2. People will be directed to proceed to automobiles in preparation for evacuation. Cars will be loaded to seating capacity.
3. People needing transportation should proceed to the bus stop near the student union where vehicles will be loaded.
4. Emergency personnel such as state police and sheriff's department will be at key points to direct traffic.
5. Traffic will be directed away from hazardous areas. Auto radios should be tuned to the designated station for further information.

Appendix 54-I

Factors Influencing Response to Warning

Warning Content
- Clear, direct, simple, practical, relevant
- Specific as to threat and appropriate sanctions
- Amount of information "given"

Individual Perception
- Past experience
- Inner psychological world
- Social and cultural factors

Warning Confirmation
- Source of warning (media, unofficial, family)
- Higher certainty
- Previous disaster experience
- Geographic proximity to disaster

Warning belief

Response/Individual or Group Action
- Official sources
- Accurate and consistent content
- Personal communication rather than impersonal medium of warning
- Perceived certainty and likelihood
- Previous disaster experience
- Increased numbers of warnings
- Observable changes in physical environment
- Perceived behaviors of others (their response, or lack of response)
- Group process (if with peers less likely to believe, while persons with family more likely to believe)
- Informal group interaction may reinforce disbelief
- Closer to threatened area less likely to overestimate magnitude of threat

Appendix 54-J

Model of the Decision-Making Process

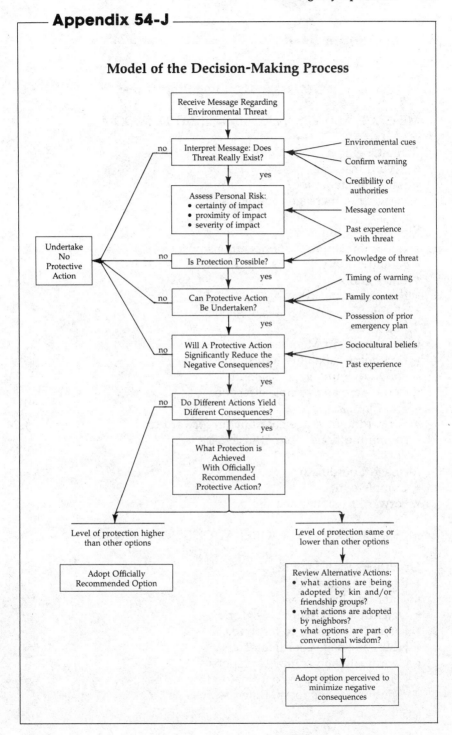

Appendix 54-K

Message-Handling Procedures

MESSAGE ARRIVES IN COMMUNICATION ROOM

Radio Operator
- Record message.
- Enter into radio log.
- Forward to message coordinator.

Message Coordinator
- Determine appropriate operations position.
- Assign priority.
- Enter into log.
- Forward to position.
- Notify plotter of significant events.

Operations Staff Member
- Determine capability to respond.
- Forward, if unable to respond.
- Coordinate and complete response.
- Enter into log.
- Forward to message coordinator; forward to communications room, if necessary.

Message Coordinator
- Complete log.
- Forward to plotter and file.

MESSAGE ARRIVES AT OPERATIONS POSITION

Operations Staff Member
- Record message.
- Enter into log.
- Determine capability to respond.
- Forward, if unable to respond.
- Notify message coordinator.
- Coordinate and complete response.
- Forward to message coordinator; forward to communications room, if necessary.

Message Coordinator
- Complete log.
- Forward to plotter and file.

Message Form

DATE_____ TIME_____

_____ INTERNAL
_____ EXTERNAL
_____ COMMUNICATIONS

NAME:_____ TEL:_____

POSITION:_____ A.C.:_____   _____ URGENT

ORGANIZATION:_____   _____ ROUTINE

FROM:

NAME:_____ TEL:_____   IN RESPONSE

POSITION:_____ A.C.:_____   TO MESSAGE

ORGANIZATION:_____   NUMBER:

MESSAGE:_____
_____
_____
_____

ACTION

INFO

***********************FOR OPERATIONS/MESSAGE CENTER USE ONLY***********************

_____ TELEPHONE   _____ RADIO   _____ TELECOPIER   _____ FLASH REP

_____ NAWAS   _____ CONATS   _____ MESSENGER   _____ MESSAGE
                                                                    NUMBER

OPERATIONS   COMMUNICATIONS
INITIALS: _____   INITIALS: _____   DATE:_____ TIME:_____

Appendix 54-L

Damage Assessment Report

Date _____

_____
County, city, town or special district
1. Casualties: Dead _____ Injured _____ Missing _____
2. Damage to private property:

	Mobile Homes	Homes	Business	Other	Dollar Value	Average % Insurance Coverage/ Unit
	a	a	a	a	b	c
Destroyed						
Major Damage						
Minor Damage						

3. Agriculture damage:
   A. Farm buildings   d. $_____
   B. Machinery and equipment   d. $_____
   C. Crop losses   d. $_____
   D. Livestock   e. $_____
4. Public property damage:
   A. Debris clearance   e. $_____
   B. Protective measures   e. $_____
   C. Road systems   e. $_____
   D. Water control facilities   e. $_____
   E. Public building and related
      equipment   e. $_____
   F. Public utilities   e. $_____
   G. Facilities under construction e. $_____
   H. Private nonprofit facilities   e. $_____
   I. Other (not in above categories) e. $_____
5. Total Damage   f. $_____
6. Remarks:
   NOTE: Append maps, photographs, and any other supple-
          mental material desired.

INSTRUCTIONS FOR COMPLETING DAMAGE
ASSESSMENT REPORT

CASUALTIES: Self-explanatory.

DAMAGE TO PRIVATE PROPERTY:

  a. Report number of units in each category that are destroyed or damaged.

  Destroyed: Self-explanatory.

  Major Damage: Extensive repairs required; structure cannot be used for its intended purpose.

  Minor Damage: Repairs required; structure can be used for its intended purpose.

  b. Report the total dollar value of damage in each category.

  c. Report the average percent of insurance coverage per unit.

AGRICULTURAL DAMAGE:

  d. Agricultural damage assessment should be obtained from the county emergency board (USDA). Attach copy of natural disaster damage assessment report, if available.

DAMAGE TO PUBLIC PROPERTY:

  e. Report dollar value of damage to public property in each category. Categories are explained below:

  Debris Clearance—Removal of trees, limbs, building rubble, etc., from roads and streets to permit orderly flow of traffic; from drainage ditches to allow adequate runoff or flow; from reservoirs to prevent clogging of intakes or damage to structures; from private property within 50 feet of a house; and from any area when considered in the public interest for health and safety.

  Protective Measures—Measures taken to protect public health and safety and to prevent damage to public or private property. Includes construction of emergency levees, pumping and sandbagging, warning signs and barricades, extra police for the emergency, overtime for regular employees.

  Road Systems—Damage includes but is not limited to bridges, drainage structures, traveled ways, shoulders and safety features.

  Water Control Facilities—Damage to dikes, levees, drainage channels, irrigation channels, and debris catch basins.

  Public Buildings and Related Equipment—Damages to public buildings to the extent not covered by insurance, include the physical plan and equipment in hospitals, libraries, penal and welfare institutions, police and fire stations, public office buildings and recreational buildings. Includes vehicles damaged or destroyed by the disaster (not as a result of operations).

Public Utilities—Damage to publicly owned facilities, including water, electric, gas, and sewerage facilities to the extent not covered by insurance.

Facilities Under Construction—Damage to facilities that were under construction at the time of the disaster to the extent not covered by insurance.

Private, Nonprofit Facilities—Damages to private, nonprofit educational, utility, emergency medical, and custodial care facilities.

Other—Includes damages to parks and recreational facilities.

CHAPTER 55

Other Physical Plant Services

Francis R. Bowen
Superintendent of Automotive
Services
North Carolina State University

Gary Yates Coates
Assistant Director for General
Services
North Carolina State University

Barbara R. Blackburn
Manager of Central Services
University of Texas at Dallas

Ray James
Manager, Parking and Traffic
Administration
University of Texas at Austin

This chapter describes five separate services that institutions need to consider in order for a campus to run smoothly: campus mail systems, campus trash collection and disposal, and moving and special events operations, text contributed by Randy Bowen and Gary Coates; office copy machines, text contributed by Barbara Blackburn; and parking and traffic administration, text contributed by Ray James. Each of these topics is discussed in sequence.

55.1 CAMPUS MAIL SYSTEMS

The purpose of a campus mail system is to deliver incoming mail and to route outgoing mail. How this takes place is dependent on such variables as the volume of mail, the size of the institution, the level of service desired, the size of the work space, and the funds available.

The first step in either starting a campus mail system, or improving an existing system, is a thorough analysis of the present operation. The next step would be to establish capabilities that would provide the required services or improve upon what is presently being done. This can be accomplished in many ways. Visiting other campuses and observing their operation will present ideas. The U.S. Postal Service is an excellent source of information. The service has representatives who can provide information regarding rates, delivery and pickup schedules, and other information and ideas for improving the service. In many areas the

U.S. Postal Service sponsors Postal Users Associations. These associations have diverse memeberships consisting of private and public mailers who come together to share information regarding their mail operations. The U.S. Postal Service benefits from the associations because it can use them as a vehicle to measure its effectiveness in the community.

Mail Service Facilities

Ideally the campus mail service facility should be centrally located in order to provide for easy pickup and delivery of the mail. The use of walking routes obviates the need for expensive delivery vehicles.

The size of the facility needed varies with the size of the operation. Systems in small institutions may occupy one small room while those of larger institutions resemble, and in many cases are, branch post offices. Since central campus space is usually at a premium, it often takes a great deal of innovation to fit the operation into the available space.

Depending upon the size of the operation, the space requirements should include the following.

Incoming Mail Holding Area   Whether the mail is picked up from the post office or delivered, an area should be set aside for holding incoming mail until it can be sorted. In order to prevent pilferage, this area should never be in a hallway or other area open to other than mail room personnel. If the mail comes to the mail room in hampers, a dock will be needed to facilitate unloading.

Sorting Area   The sorting racks or bins should be located so as to create a logical flow from the incoming mail holding area to the outgoing mail holding area. Since it is one of the most detailed duties in the mail room, care should be taken to ensure this area is properly lighted. If the sorters stand, fatigue mats should be provided to ease the burden on the sorters legs and feet.

Outgoing Mail Hold Area   This area should be adjacent to the exit and provide adequate space to stage the campus mail and the metered or stamped U.S. mail prior to delivery. If a presort or international mail service is provided, separate space should be provided.

Metering Area   The metering area should be located so that the mail, after it is metered, will be adjacent to the outgoing mail holding area. The metering area requires good lighting, adequate work surface, and enough electrical outlets to handle the scales and postage machines. Since personnel in this area are usually on their feet and standing in one area, fatigue mats should be provided.

Administrative Area   This area should be centrally located with at least one window to allow the supervisor of the mail room to see all activities. In large operations this area is important to provide a quiet area for planning, accounting, record keeping, and employee counseling duties.

Employee Lounge Area   The sorting and handling of mail is a tedious process that requires continuous concentration. Employee fatigue can greatly affect the accuracy and productivity of the mail operation. It is important to have a lounge separate from the work area for employees to take a break from the work routine.

Service Area   This area includes a mail pickup point, stamp sales window, post office boxes in the units with full service or contract stations, and a loading dock or ramp. A well lighted and clearly identified area should be provided for customer access. A safe and adequate area for parking and unloading of delivery vehicles should be provided separate from customer access.

Handling Campus Mail

Campus Addresses   Developing a campus mailing address is the first step in handling the campus mail. The assignment of a unique campus zip code will make the job of receiving mail much easier. The U.S. Postal Service will issue unique zip codes to large users. This simplifies their sorting process and will also decrease the chance of campus mail being misdirected to local addresses.

Campus addresses often pose a problem, especially on large campuses. Large universities have a large number of departments, with frequent departmental relocations. It is often difficult for the mail service sorting staff to keep up with the locations of departments.

One solution to the problem of changing locations is to issue unique box numbers of the departments. The box number always remains the same, regardless of the department location. This makes sorting much simpler, since it is by box number only. Changes would be required only when a department relocation necessitates use of a different delivery route. The routes can be denoted by color coding the box numbers on the sorting bin.

Some systems sort by building name or number. A further sorting is often required after the mail arrives in the building and is usually done by clerical employees in the building. A simple system that avoids this is to have locked departmental mail boxes located in a central point in the building. The mail service employee can pick up and deliver mail to these boxes. To work effectively, the mail should be sorted to the building box numbers before it leaves the mail room.

Delivery Routes   After the mail is sorted, there should be an effective method of delivering it throughout the campus. Routes should be developed for speed and efficiency. Pickup of outgoing mail should always accompany the delivery of incoming mail. Over time the mail service should try to make its pickups and deliveries within a certain time frame. This will help the customers to know approximately when to have their mail ready.

The method for delivery should be by foot with the use of a cart whenever possible. Vans, cars, scooters, and even golf carts can be used for delivery. It should be noted that some of the small specialty vehicles are expensive and often require more maintenance than standard vehicles. Slow speeds coupled with stop-and-go driving are hard on vehicles.

Interdepartmental Mail   Interdepartmental mail constitutes a large portion of the mail on most campuses. Departments should be instructed to bundle this mail separately in order to keep it from being mixed with outgoing U.S. mail. This eliminates an additional sorting step. When the departmental mail arrives in the mail room it should be sorted with the same priority as incoming posted mail. Many campuses use a campus mail envelope for the transmittal of interdepartment mail. The form most used is a reusable envelope with a series of blank address lines on both the front and back of the envelope. The user marks through the last lines used and enters the new address. Some of these envelopes can be used as many as fifty times. This system makes sorting easier and it saves money on envelopes. The address used on the envelope should be simple and easy for the sorter to read. It should be limited to the addressee name, department name, and campus box number.

Speed letters are an effective means of campus communication. Many campuses use an 8-1/2″ x 11″ formatted letter that can be bifolded, addressed, and sent as an interdepartmental letter.

Some institutions place boxes for campus mail at strategic points on the campus. This service provides a convenient drop and pickup point for campus mail. These boxes may be located in conjunction with U.S. Postal Service boxes, but they should be clearly identified as being for campus mail only.

Mail sorting is one of the most time consuming and tedious duties in the mail room. At times the work load created by incoming mail may be greater than the available staffing level can handle. It is important to have established sorting priorities. This ensures timely delivery of the most important mail. A good guide to priorities is the U.S. Postal Service's class system, and sort in the following order:

1. First class and campus mail
2. Second class
3. Third class (single piece)
4. Fourth class (parcel)
5. Third class (bulk).

Permits and Outside Mail Services

Permits can save a great deal of postage expense. They guarantee a reduced rate for catalogs and advertisements that are regularly mailed for colleges and universities. Efforts should be made to reduce the number of these permits to give better control and to reduce expenses. Incoming reply permits can also save money and ensure a higher percentage of replies on advertisements and surveys, by saving the expense of enclosing a stamped return envelope.

In recent years there has been a proliferation of outside mail services. These range from carrier services to presort and special handling services. Courier services are extremely helpful for the overnight delivery of mail between isolated campuses and intracity. Private institutions may contract with private couriers, while public institutions often have local or state governmentally operated services available.

Presort services will take all of an institution's first class mail and presort it by zip code so that the mail can be posted at a reduced presorted rate. The savings between the regular first class rate and the presort rate, usually about $.4, is split between the presort service and the institution. Many institutions save thousands of dollars each year using these services.

A more recent service is the international mail service, which will negotiate to pick up and handle an institution's overseas mail for a reduced rate. The service flies the mail overseas where it is handled by a service similar to the presort service. The mail is posted at a rate far below U.S. Postal Service rates and mailed from the overseas point.

Accounting System

Aside from personnel and equipment costs, the basic cost in a mail system is the cost of postage. It is imperative that the mail service institute an accounting system to monitor this expense. This is especially important on campuses where each department is responsible for its own postage expense. In decentralized operations, the mail is posted in individual departments which have their own postage machine, and it is then picked up and disbursed by the campus mail service.

In centralized operations the mail is separated, bundled, and tagged in the department and is then picked up by the campus mail service for posting and disbursal. In the centralized operations, the tag identifying the department and its account number is used by the postage machine operator as the bill or record for charges for that particular bundle of mail. The postage machine operator will post the postage cost and verify the piece count to the tag. The tag, which is usually carbonized, is used to post the charge to the proper account in the ledger. One copy is usually kept in the mail service accounting office files and the other copy is sent to the department with the postage expense bill.

Mechanized mail room accounting systems are beginning to appear on the market. Most are designed to operate with microcomputers and can improve the speed in which reports are processed. Some of these systems are designed to work directly from the postage scales, which will greatly automate the accounting operation. It would be wise to look at more than one "live" system before a decision is made to purchase any system. The software and hardware can be quite costly. Together with repair service and providing for unforseen down time, a poorly selected system can be quite expensive.

Contract Post Offices

Many campuses operate full-service post offices. These operations are convenient for students, especially in isolated areas. The U.S. Postal Service will pay some campuses or individuals, either through a bid process or by agreement, to operate contract post offices. The service is usually offered because it would be too costly for the U.S. Postal Service to operate a station in the area. The contract stations are subject to audit by the U.S. Postal Service, since all of the stamps and money orders are furnished by the U.S. Postal Service. Usually the operations are for convenience rather than profit. However, a contract post office located adjacent to the campus book store or student center will create traffic and business for these operations.

Student Mail

The problem of handling student mail can be approached in many ways. Some institutions provide boxes in residence halls and the mail is sorted and placed in the boxes by mail service employees or student workers. Other campuses have central campus post offices that provide rental boxes for the students. Still others rely on U.S. Post Offices located in the community to rent boxes to the students. While this last system may not be more convenient for the students, it saves the institution additional handling expenses.

Mail Service Staffing

The selection of personnel is one of the most important aspects of mail service. The success of the operation depends on reliable employees. Small operations will require the most versatile employees, since each person will share the burden of the various jobs in the mail room. Larger operations, on the other hand, tend to be more specialized with some employees engaged primarily in sorting, others in delivery, and still others in posting outgoing mail. Even in centralized operations it is important to cross-train employees so they can handle more than one job, thereby making the operation more flexible. Some operations test applicants for incoming positions to ensure that the prospective employee has the mathematics and reading skills to be a productive member of the team. Because stamps cost money, a person without good mathematics skills would take only a few hours to create havoc for mail room accounting.

Uniforms are used by some mail operations to identify their employees. This is especially important on large campuses where the mail service employees go into areas not generally open to the public. Other systems require their employee to wear name badges identifying them as university employees.

The schedule of the mail service will vary depending upon the size of the campus and the volume of mail. Part-time employees can reduce the payroll costs, since they can be brought in during peak periods to sort or deliver the mail. Students represent a good source of available part-time help. If the volume is heavy, skeleton or part-time crews can be used to sort the mail during peak periods or on weekends. This is especially helpful during holidays when the mail room will fill up with incoming mail.

55.2 CAMPUS TRASH COLLECTION AND DISPOSAL

Developing a Collection and Disposal System

Solid waste management on college and university campuses is a vital activity. The overall purpose is to remove the campus refuse in an efficient and cost effective manner. Failure to provide these services in a timely manner results in an unsightly and unsanitary environment and inconvenience to faculty, staff, and students.

In developing these services to meet the need of each individual campus, a thorough waste flow analysis is essential, and must be conducted on a continuing basis. For recycling, a waste composition analysis is necessary. The seasonal nature of the higher education process, and the types of wastes generated due to institutional makeup, must be prime considerations in developing a waste management system.

There are substantial resources available in the public and private sectors to aid waste managers in best determining their institution's needs. City and county governments are normally the managers of suitable sanitary landfills as well as a waste handling and transportation system. A few areas are served by privately owned landfills. Local regulations on both landfilling and municipal service availability must be known. These regulations explain the types of wastes accepted for landfill and the parameters for operation.

Some items may be unacceptable in the local sanitary landfill, such as radioactive, chemical, yard wastes, and white goods, and must be disposed of by alternative methods. The local municipality should be able to guide the waste manager in developing a suitable program to best meet the institution's needs in accordance with local services available.

In determining the institutional approach to waste management, local private sector haulers can be an invaluable resource. It may be most satisfactory and/or economical to contract all waste handling services with a local private hauler, especially if the college or university lacks sufficient equipment, maintenance, and human resources. Another alternative is for the local private hauler to provide consulting services. A comprehensive survey should be made of waste management services and facilities available, and a disposal system then developed to meet the institution's needs with optimum utilization of the services.

A variety of trade publications and international organizations can help in developing waste management systems. *Waste Age* magazine provides articles, technical features, and system management information. This magazine is free to members of the National Solid Waste Management Association (NSWMA), an international group of private haulers that also provides a range of information services relative to waste management.

World Wastes is another publication that provides a wealth of information relative to the management of solid waste. These magazines not only provide management with information, but also provide technical specifications and updated advertising on all types of equipment and services. Other publications that might prove helpful are *Commercial Carrier Journal* and *Fleet Owner*.

The public-sector counterpart to the NSWMA is the Governmental Refuse Collection and Disposal Association (GRCDA), a group of public sector haulers. Their annual and chapter meetings bring together thousands of public waste management professionals for the discussion of problems and potential solutions.

Contracting Refuse Collection and Disposal

After evaluating the institutional needs, it may be preferable to contract with either a private firm or a municipal hauler for the services. If contracting is desirable, certain actions should be taken.

Identify Requirements   Determine the frequency and timing of the service, and the types of wastes generated at each site. For instance, an agricultural, engineering, medical, or research-oriented institution may have sizable quantities of hazardous and biological wastes that require special handling.

Weekly and Seasonal Services   After determining the service needs, prepare the contract, specifying on a weekly and seasonal basis the exact services to be performed. Due to planned or prospective new construction or special needs, special arrangements should be included as potential add-ons. Bids for these services on a per container basis should be requested. This special aspect of waste services may be more difficult for a municipality to accommodate than a private hauler. Lead time notification for these services should be specified in the contract. Private haulers may be willing to provide management services and advice as to the most effective applications for each container siting or for the type of system to be used. In addition, make the contract flexible enough to accommodate changes in need.

Once a contractual agreement is established, institutional waste managers must be thoroughly cognizant of the quality and timeliness of the services contracted. Regular checks are a necessity. A single manager should be given the responsibility for managing the contract, and making the relevant decisions. This function could be handled well as an adjunct responsibility to housekeeping, landscaping, or automotive managers in physical plant.

In-House Refuse Disposal

If it is more desirable to handle waste disposal in-house, the same system analyses must be undertaken to determine need. Except for the few new colleges or universities, waste is already being managed to some degree. A reevaluation may be appropriate, especially with changes in waste quantities, increased tipping fees, or obvious shortcomings in the existing system. Hazardous and biological wastes do not belong in normal building wastes. The special handling and management requirements for these wastes may be more suited to contractors that have the equipment and resources to provide these services to more than one user. This is an area of waste management in which institutional needs require careful evaluation.

After identifying requirements by sites, the decision can be made on the best waste handling system. The following commercial waste handling systems are available.

Front Loaders   Front loaders can handle four- to ten-cubic-yard steel waste containers. The truck consists of a cab and chassis mounted compactor box and lifting forks. The trucks are long wheelbase vehicles and require space for maneuvering. They cost up to $120,000 per unit. Containers for this system can be purchased for $500 to $900. Each manufacturer should be evaluated and local availability of parts determined. Diesel-powered trucks with automatic transmissions have generally been most satisfactory. Overhead clearance is severely limited with this system.

Rear and Side Loading Systems   There is more than one type of rear loading system. The original Dempster Dumpster drop-bottom system utilizes four- to twelve-cubic-yard waste containers and open skip containers. Complete trucks for this system cost around $45,000. Containers run about $4,000, but this equipment often is available through salvage outlets. These boxes are sited near a building. When filled they are hauled to a compaction trailer, which holds sixty-five to seventy-five cubic yards of compacted waste and, when full, is pulled to the landfill by truck tractor. This system works well in constricted spaces, as short wheelbased vehicles can be utilized to pick up loaded containers at the site, hauled to the transfer trailer where its load is dropped, and the box returned to its site. This system has low maintenance and low operating costs, but is not suitable for long hauls. It can be very effective on a highly congested, urban type application. The containers can be easily cleaned when the waste load is dumped.

Manually loadable compaction trucks, which load from the rear, are available for $40,000 to $60,000. These vehicles are normally used in municipal household collection. They are not suitable for collection of dining hall or industrial waste. However, this system could be effective on a small campus.

There are also rear and side loading vehicles that sell for around $60,000 per unit, which pick up and dump automatically the newer plastic rollout containers that hold less than two cubic yards of waste. These systems could be utilized effectively on small campuses with low-quantity waste generators, or for campuses with well-developed recycling programs.

Again, these rear and side loaders have their own compaction and ejection systems. When full the truck must be driven to a landfill and dumped. Any vehicle accessing a landfill has higher than normal maintenance costs and downtime.

Transfer Stations   Waste is normally dumped into a waste compaction trailer through a top mounted hopper system and compacted. The waste can be delivered using some of the aforementioned systems, or waste can be gathered using pickup trucks and dumped into the trailer. Again, system quantities, container siting, and campus layout would determine the efficiency of a transfer trailer type system. This system can also be utilized to haul the leftover wastes from a recycling operation since a conveyor can dump directly into the trailer. When loaded these trailers are pulled to a landfill by truck-tractor. The total cost for a transfer trailer/truck-tractor is $80,000 to $100,000.

System Maintenance

The best system from a maintenance standpoint is one that can be easily serviced by operators on a daily basis, has locally available parts, and has a lengthy serviceable life. Any equipment purchased should either be serviced by a local or nearby dealer, or shop facilities capable of heavy equipment and hydraulic maintenance should be available. If equipment is to be maintained in college or university shops, care should be taken to ensure the shop has the capacity to service the types of vehicles and waste equipment purchased. Container maintenance is also important. Not only should containers be cleaned and deodorized on a regular basis, but steel containers should be serviced and repaired on a preventive maintenance basis. At least every four years, or fewer as required, containers should be derusted and painted.

Waste Recycling

In the future, the recycling of waste may be effective in reducing the overall costs of waste management. Landfilling (tipping) fees and marketability of recycled products are of prime concern. Currently landfill fees vary widely throughout the United States. In the northern, northeastern, and western United States, landfill fees of $35 per ton are typical. As areas in the country grow in population and industry, such as the mid-Atlantic and southern states, the costs of landfilling can be expected to rise. It is important for a waste manager to know the status and outlook of local landfills. Their capabilities, tipping fees, and expected service life—as well as long-range planning by state, city, and county governments—affect college and university waste planning.

On university campuses, there is a large quantity and variety of paper wastes, cans, scrap metals, and bottles. If local landfill fees are high, landfill hauls are long, and if there are viable local markets for recycled products, recycling may be a long-term option for disposal of 50 to 80 percent of a university's waste generation. Leaf and limbs from grounds maintenance can be mulched and reused in campus landscaping. On some campuses this can constitute up to 25 percent of campus waste generation. Construction rubble, except wood, can be used as fill materials at remote campus sites. Other materials such as paper, cardboard, glass, cans, and metals can be collected using source separation, in which materials are saved by office or housekeeping staff for scheduled drop off at the campus waste recycling center, or can be removed from the waste stream manually from some form of conveyor system or tipping floor.

Waste Incineration

Another method of waste reduction is disposal by incineration. This option is currently being studied for numerous municipalities in the United States and is widely used in Europe. Most of the facilities being constructed use the heat generated in incineration to produce steam and/or electricity, and the resultant ash and hard products are landfilled or sold. For institutions that generate large quantities of paper waste, the production of refuse derived fuel can be consolidated with some form of recycling effort and can be used as a supplement to wood or coal fired boiler systems. There are commercially available systems that can be purchased to produce this fuel. Depending on the constituency of the waste flow, up to 75 percent of paper waste can be recycled using this method, reducing the need to utilize landfills and reducing the need for capital investment in transportation assets. Again, it is important to know the direction that community and state planners are taking in managing their waste flow, as this will affect college and university operations.

Summary

In scheduling waste disposal operations, timely service is the prime consideration. It is essential to haul a container when it gets full, not before or after. The waste manager must therefore maintain communication with customers to insure optimum planning. Haul scheduling at some times of day may be inefficient. It might be better to make pickups early in the morning or during the night. Again, this depends on campus traffic patterns, the system utilized, and patterns of waste generation. There are computer programs available that can be effective in aiding the scheduling process. As each university system has differences, so do the waste disposal systems. It is necessary to know what the trash is, where it is, when it is most accessible, and then plan the hauling schedule to meet the need.

The most effective work force for any type of waste disposal system will consist of people who can operate independently, and who have a dedication to responsibility.

Supervisors in waste handling, recycling, and hauling operations must have an abiding concern for safety and proper training. Waste disposal trucks are large and visibility is limited. Equipment operators should be patient, especially in highly congested areas, and they should be well qualified. Operator training should be thorough and include the basics of mechanical operation for their assigned vehicle. Currently drivers of heavy trucks must meet the health and licensing standards set by the Commercial Motor Vehicle Act of 1986. They should be trained and required to maintain logs and perform all daily preventive maintenance checks on their equipment to detect any serious mechanical defects.

A first-rate waste management system is determined by its personnel and their dedication to the job. Equipment mechanics must be well versed in hydraulic systems, their operation and repair. They need to understand that waste equipment downtime can have devastating effects on the health and well-being of every person on campus.

A viable waste management operation will be thoroughly thought out and attended to on a continual basis. It must be adaptable for additional needs or seasonal adjustments. It must be safety oriented, and personnel must be properly managed to protect sizable capital investments. Last, waste management must have eyes to the future. New laws affecting landfills and waste generators will require fiscal attentiveness and long-range plans.

55.3 MOVING AND SPECIAL EVENTS OPERATIONS

There are continuing requirements for physical plant's personnel to move equipment and organizations and to make physical preparations for special events. These operations can range in size from moving a desk from one office to another to setting up and decorating a stage and seating for thousands for commencement exercises. Most of the projects are relatively simple and require only personnel and few tools. However, there are occasional complex projects, such as the installation of valuable and sensitive laboratory equipment or moving valuable paintings or statuary, that require special skills and equipment.

Much of the work requires careful timing. Preparations for graduation exercises and other special events must be completed by a specific time, yet cannot be accomplished far in advance because the spaces involved lack security or are regularly used for other purposes.

Size and Organization of Moving/Special Events Crew

The size of the work crew to handle the moving and special events presents a dilemma; it is necessary to keep the crew small enough so there will be continuous work, yet large enough to meet the timing requirements. From a purely economic standpoint, it is normally more cost-effective to contract intermittent operations. However, there are advantages to having a university work crew that is knowledgeable of the facilities and specially trained for unique tasks to handle many of the projects.

The most common strategy for handling the moving and special events requirements is a combination of the following:

- Size and train the crew to handle the routine moving and special events, such as small scale moving of office or laboratory equipment and setting up for registration or graduation.
- Include the crew in another organization with non-routine functions they can be trained to handle, totally or in part, with special training. Perhaps the most common practice is to include the moving/special events crew in the custodial organization and use it for such non-routine tasks as window and wall washing, cleaning of lamps and light fixtures, and moving of furniture for floor waxing or carpet shampooing.
- Contract for the major moving operations such as occupying of a new building or relocation of departments.

In employing this strategy, it is important that the moving/special events crew maintain its separate identity and is carefully scheduled and supervised to perform the work as planned. Such an arrangement can easily evolve into poor control and a conflict of interest in which the crew neglects either the custodial or moving/special events work. The crew should not become intermixed with the custodial crew, as this will result in custodians being used for moving/special event work at the expense of their routine custodial work.

Training

The work of a moving/special events crew involves heavy manual labor and the use of heavy lifting and moving equipment such as cranes, forklifts, moving vans, and special rigging equipment for lifting. It also involves the use of smaller moving equipment such as hand trucks, jacks, slings, and dollies, as well as hand tools for the disassembly and assembly of furniture and equipment. For the expeditious accomplishment of tasks without damage to the materials and equipment being moved, and to avoid injury to the workers, it is important that crew members be carefully trained in both the equipment used and the techniques involved.

Funding for Moves/Special Events

Due to the difficulty of determining project costs, especially if the crew divides time with custodial work, the moving/special events crew is generally salaried. If operating on a charge-back system, the physical plant generally funds the work required by the university administration, such as relocation of departments, occupancy of new buildings, and set-up for special university events. The departments are generally required to fund work initiated by the department, such as moving furniture or equipment within the department.

55.4 PROVISION AND MAINTENANCE OF OFFICE COPY MACHINES

With the introduction of high-tech office machines, there has been an increasing need for an expeditious, cost-effective maintenance service for the equipment. In the future, costs for necessary service and preventive maintenance of this equipment will only increase. In a university environment, one solution would be to have well-trained in-house service technicians to service typewriters, dictators, transcribers, calculators, copy machines, personal computers, printers, and laser printers.

Scope and Responsibility

Supplying and maintaining a service department for office machines should consist of the rental, parts and service of typewriters, dictators, transcribers, calculators, and copy machines. Personal computers and printers are not cost-effective items to stock for rental because of the many different configurations available in the marketplace.

Standardization is probably one of the most important factors to any in-house service department. When a machine cannot be repaired on-site, similar equipment should available to be used as a loaner. Standard parts can be kept in stock so the customer does not have any significant downtime. If using an outside vendor for service, the repairperson often will not have the necessary part at the time, and a loaner machine may not be available; therefore, the customer may be without a machine.

Cost-effectiveness plays an important role. The cost of in-house maintenance is about half that of an outside vendor. The training and cross-training of technicians is also important. There are several ways to keep the technicians updated, such as participating in outside professional organizations, attending seminars, training school, trade shows, reading technical magazines, and contacting vendors.

Organization and Staffing

When organizing and staffing an office machine service department, an inventory must be taken of the equipment already on campus and a survey performed of the campus community to get a feel for their attitude about an in-house service. Some of the questions that should included in the survey follow:

1. How many typewriters, calculators, dictators, transcribers, copy machines, personal computers, printers, and laser printers do you have?
2. What is the manufacturer and model number?
3. What is the age of each machine?
4. Is the equipment currently covered by a maintenance agreement and, if so, how much does the agreement cost?
5. How would you feel about an office machine service department?

After analyzing the results of the survey, a fairly accurate estimate of the needed type and number of machines can be made.

Revenue, Typical Charges, and Turnover of Machines

The main source of revenue for an operation of this nature is the rental and maintenance cost. An additional source can be a typewriter rental program for students. Most office and copy machines should be amortized over a five-year period. However, some equipment such as low-use copy machines can be kept in use longer than five years. This trend will also hold true for most typewriters, since computers are used more than typewriters. When machines become obsolete, they either can be traded in or sold at an auction or surplus sale.

When calculating the monthly charge for in-house service, include the cost of the equipment, replacement cost, maintenance cost, and technician's salary. If amortized over a five-year period, determine the percentage that parts and salaries will increase during the time frame.

Following are typical monthly rates, including rental, service, and parts:

- Typewriters, $21 to $35
- Calculators, $3.30
- Dictators, $5.30
- Transcribers, $13.50
- Copy machines, $120 to $300.

55.5 PARKING AND TRAFFIC ADMINISTRATION

The management of a campus motor vehicle parking program is a major responsibility of all facilities administrators, particularly in today's mobile environment. Most colleges and universities are attended by large numbers of commuting students. Add to this the many faculty and staff who desire close-in parking at any hour of the day or night, and the administration of parking becomes a major challenge.

Few colleges and universities enjoy sufficient convenient parking for all campus users, and the situation is constantly changing. The most convenient parking lots often are planned sites for further campus development: a new academic building, a laboratory, or a gymnasium. Few colleges and universities will ever have the amount of parking that consumers expect and demand when going to a shopping mall.

Scope and Functions

The scope and responsibility of a campus parking office ranges from a simple single-purpose function to one with multiple complex relationships. Each institution must make basic decisions concerning parking on campus. Is parking on campus a privilege or an inherent right? How will parking be regulated and controlled? What sanctions will be used to ensure compliance with the rules and regulations?

Many campuses have set up a system of payroll deduction for permit fees; the demand for such a system increases as permit fees increase. An administrative check system is needed to ensure that people do not leave employment without returning their permits or cancel their payroll deduction while keeping their permit privileges.

Because parking spaces are generally in short supply, some form of enforcement system is required. This can range from the local municipal police citing and towing vehicles, down to a campus courtesy patrol. Many large colleges and universities have a full-scale campus police department that can issue citations (see Chapter 53, Building Security). In many universities, parking and traffic administration is under the auspices of the director of physical plant, while the campus police may be a separate entity. In other institutions, parking is part of the campus police department. It is important that parking enforcement be directly under the administrator or manager of parking. This ensures that parking enforcement receives the proper attention and is not in competition with security and law enforcement.

Enforcement of the rules and regulations must be swift and consistent; lax enforcement can lead to chaos in the parking lots. Campus constituents generally respond best to a reasoned approach as opposed to arbitrary rule enforcement. When people understand the purpose of policies and rules, most are cooperative.

Many colleges and universities collect charges from parking citations issued on campus. All charges and the infractions to which they relate must be shown in the enabling regulations, which are approved by the appropriate authority (such as the Board of Regents or Trustees). Usually it is easier to handle if the charges are administrative in nature and not a part of the legal system. At many large universities, these charges are collected by the parking and traffic administration office. Even when the citing of violators and the collection of charges are administered by the same organization, it is important to keep the two functions separate to avoid any indication of collusion or a citation quota system. As an alternative to collecting charges directly, some schools, principally in California, have an arrangement whereby the school issues the citation and the municipal court handles the collection and adjudication. The school then receives a percentage of the court's collections from campus citations.

Organization and Staffing

Most campus parking offices are involved in issuing parking permits as well as collecting fees. A relatively simple and free annual permit system would require minimal staffing. A more complex permit system would require additional staffing to handle multiple renewals or validations each year and various permit prices and eligibility requirements. Many campus parking offices also issue, process, and collect charges from parking and traffic citations on campus. Some also handle the administrative adjudication of appeals from campus parking and traffic citations. Others are involved in staffing the parking garages and information booths at campus entry points. All of these functions require staffing. In addition, a manual system of applications and records normally requires more staff than a computer-based system.

Employees who handle parking monies should be screened by local police, either prior to or concurrent with hiring decisions. Collection of money also requires verifications of amounts before they are deposited. Whether this requires a full-time accounting clerk or someone on a part-time basis depends upon many factors. But there must be verification of daily deposits, and auditing, issuing, and accounting for all prenumbered receipts used by sales clerks and all permits. Supervisors also will need training in recognizing and preventing white-collar crime. The same person should not be allowed to both collect funds and deposit them; another employee not working for the sales clerk should check and verify all amounts.

The cashier function is difficult to quantify in terms of a recommended staffing level. The decision must be based on such factors as how long it takes to handle each transaction, whether cashiers are the only contact with customers, and how many cashier windows or stations are available. It is important not to staff for peak work loads, but rather for average work loads and supplement staff with temporary help when necessary.

Budgeting

Parking operations usually are self-supporting in that they generate sufficient revenues to cover their expenses and receive no state funds. Besides budgeting for the usual annual salaries and maintenance and operating expenses, consideration must also be given to long-term expenses such as vehicle replacement, maintenance of lots and structures, and construction of new parking facilities. These funds should be placed in a dedicated reserve account that cannot be used for any other purpose; under no circumstances should reserve funds be used to cover normal operating expenses.

The various sources of revenue should be identified and categorized: permit fees, citation income, daily fees (including meters and daily permit parking fees), rental income, and any miscellaneous sources of income such as interest on dedicated reserve funds. Will all of these sources be used to cover operating expenses? Or will some be dedicated to capital improvements?

It is prudent to ensure that there is a steady and predictable amount of revenue to cover all routine annual expenses, rather than relying on variable sources of revenue such as citation charges or daily fees to meet fixed expenses. Indexing the parking permit fees to a standard, such as the cost of living index, ensures that annual increases, if needed, are accomplished logically. Annual and daily parking fees should not be allowed to get so far out of line that it takes a dramatic increase to catch up; it will be difficult or impossible to explain why these fees need to double in one year.

Determining Parking Needs

How much parking is required? No overall standard has been developed to answer this question. Various schools have used everything from building square footage to student enrollment with varying degrees of success. Typically, peak demand is experienced on Mondays, Wednesdays, and Fridays between 9:30 a.m. and 2:00 p.m. A survey by Campus Parking Management Associates of many campus parking administrators found that a ratio of from 1.40:1 to 1.50:1 for faculty and staff was acceptable, representing a maximum of 40 to 50 percent more permits than actual spaces. Obviously, the lower the ratio of parkers to spaces the better the parking situation. Commuting student ratios in the 1.80:1 to 2.00:1 range are generally considered reasonable, while resident student ratios should range from 1.10:1 to 1.50:1.

As most faculty and students are not on campus every day (with the exception of resident students), nor is everyone on campus at the same time, the above ratios are generally acceptable. However, whether or not these ratios are satisfactory will vary from one campus to the next. To maximize use of available parking spaces, parking should never be assigned on a one-for-one basis. Parking for handicapped persons, loading and unloading, and service vehicles are variables each campus must address. As a rule, some of these spaces will be needed at each building and in the vicinity of the required entry point. Nothing can replace a well-documented and tailored parking and traffic analysis performed by a competent parking consultant.

Parking should be located next to or between the buildings on campus, as seen at most shopping malls around the country. Each lot should have enough space to handle parking by the building's users based on the ratios explained previously, plus a growth factor. Major problems develop when a parking lot is used as the site for a new facility whose users will create a parking demand often equal to or greater than the original lot's capacity. All new building plans must address this issue and incorporate a plan for parking.

As most campuses already are locked into their own unique situations, the best use must be made of available spaces. A policy statement is needed before a determination can be made as to where the parking should be and how much is needed.

It must be determined whether the campus is primarily a walking campus or a vehicular campus. A walking campus is one in which parking is on the campus fringe and limited or no parking exists in the central core. In a walking campus, individuals walk four to five blocks from their cars to their destination. These campuses often have green belts in the core area and usually have several large parking lots on the edges of the campus. Aside from service vehicles, the only vehicles allowed in the core area are those for handicapped persons and possibly VIP visitors.

In contrast, a vehicular campus gives priority to parking in order to reduce walking to a minimum. As most campuses do not have sufficient parking located in all the desired areas, this often requires detailed programs to ensure that parking spaces are distributed according to some preselected criterion, such as a lottery based on salary or faculty titles. This also requires a greater degree of enforcement, as there seldom is enough parking space to meet demand, especially in the central core area.

Parking Garage Operations

In these days of increasing land costs and shrinking land availability, more colleges and universities are considering multistory parking facilities. Parking garages are quite expensive (more than $5,000 per space exclusive of land costs), and they normally are expected to be self-sufficient for operating costs and debt service. Some colleges may elect to use a revenue bond to finance the cost and then spread this cost over ten to twenty years. This debt service can either be factored into the garage's revenue equation, or it can be spread out over the entire campus. This issue must be addressed early in the planning stage, since the way it is resolved will affect the rates charged to garage users. Other schools have used a private lease arrangement whereby a developer builds and operates the garage for an agreed-upon time period, after which the structure becomes the property of the college.

Before rushing out to build a garage, a good analysis of potential users must be performed. Will the garage cater to one or more groups to the exclusion of another group? Will it be available to users for a daily fee? What is the maximum amount people are willing to pay for parking before seeking other ways to get to campus? What is the local community's experience with a parking garage? Will there be a reduced rate for monthly or semester users?

If the primary users are students, remember that they will be gone when classes are not in session; student attendance is highest in the fall, slightly lower in the spring, and lowest in the summer. When the students are gone, the garage will be virtually empty and generating little or no revenue.

Some colleges and universities feel that visitors should not pay to park, and this can lead to some attempt to subsidize parking rates. Visitors may come to campus more frequently when the students also are on campus, thereby increasing the demand on a limited number of spaces. Visitors generally do not object to paying a reasonable daily parking fee for the sake of availability and convenience. All who park on the campus should reasonably be expected to contribute to the upkeep of the campus parking facilities. Remember that parking is never "free"; there is always a cost to provide it.

It should not be assumed that everyone will know where the garage is. Plan on advertising its location, its advantages, and its hours. In addition, a garage should look like a garage so that people will be able to find it.

If a garage is considered feasible, insist on using a reputable and experienced parking garage design firm. A good firm can help avoid unnecessary expenses as well as ensure a quality product. Most campus construction and maintenance people are not familiar with the techniques and designs used in garages. A parking garage is often a one-of-a-kind facility on campus and mistakes can be costly. The design firm can help sort out the various entry and exit control devices available, and the types and models of cleaning equipment. If there is a mixture of semester and daily users, computerized controls may be desirable that can not only open and close gates but help keep track of utilization rates, revenues, shift costs, and hours actually worked, all of which aid in managing the garage.

Parking and Traffic Policies Committee

The use of a parking and traffic policies committee is an excellent way to involve the principal campus users in campus parking administration. When users are given a voice in recommending policy, compliance usually is much greater. Typically these committees are composed of members of the faculty, staff, and student body who usually serve for two years with a staggered membership. The chairperson is best appointed by the convening authority (usually the president or chancellor) to minimize conflicts. This committee should have advisors from the parking office, the dean of students, and any other offices that can assist. The key is to involve only those who can help, either because they understand the situation or can offer a solution. The purpose of this committee is to advise the president or chancellor on all matters concerning parking and traffic and recommend solutions.

It is essential that the campus parking administrator or manager be an advisor to this committee and able to work with the chairperson on a day-to-day basis. This committee also allows all campus users a way to "appeal to a higher authority" and can help defuse confrontations. In addition, since the committee represents all campus groups, it can lend a balanced perspective to recommendations on parking space allocations, locations, hours, and requests for exceptions.

Summary

Campus parking is primarily a service function in that it must serve the needs of the faculty, staff, and student body. Everyone involved in campus parking must be sensitive to the overall needs. No one group should have priority over any other; all groups are important to the well-being and mission of the college or university.

All visitors should be welcomed and treated with efficiency. Most official visitors are more concerned with finding a reasonably convenient place to park than they are with the short-term costs. Other visitors may be the parents of students or potential students, while still others may be taxpayers who are visiting "their" campus.

Employees of the campus parking program must be made to feel good about the service they are providing. It is true that a well-paying job is important, but money alone does not make an employee happy. Campus parking administrators must see to it that employees feel good about themselves by providing adequate training; providing a safe, attractive, and efficient work environment; and supporting them as much as possible in their decisions. Campus parking employees often work in tense situations; whenever there is insufficient and inconvenient parking, the potential for confrontation exists. With some foresight and planning, these confrontations can be turned into positive improvements.

CHAPTER 56

Auxiliary Enterprises

Richard M. Engle
Associate Vice President for Facilities
Rutgers, the State University of New Jersey

S upporting or servicing auxiliary enterprises, unique campus operations need not present a dilemma to the facilities manager. Instead, by developing both a method of approach and a policy with the budget staff, the ambiguities sometimes associated with auxiliary enterprises can often be relieved.

56.1 GROUPS DEFINED

The National Association of College and University Business Officers (NACUBO) defines auxiliary enterprises as those campus operations that furnish services directly or indirectly to students, faculty, and/or staff and that charge a fee related to—but not necessarily equal to—the cost of the service. At publicly funded institutions, they are sometimes referred to as nonappropriated fund activities because they are not supported with appropriated funds.

Since inspection fees are fixed costs, the auxiliary should be able to accurately budget for this service. Commonly, auxiliary enterprises are funded separately from the education and general funds of an institution and do not necessarily serve all students.

Good examples of auxiliary enterprises are housing, food service, and campus bookstores. Others might include the student union, recreational facilities, campus bus service, intercollegiate athletics department (as distinct from the instructional department of physical education), and campus parking facilities. Certain research facilities, such as nuclear reactors that are self-supporting, may also fall under the rubric of auxiliary enterprises.

Auxiliary directors usually find that it is more convenient and economical to make use of the plant department's facilities engineering, maintenance, and management capabilities than to duplicate those capabilities or use outside consultants and contractors. This creates a unique situation in which physical plant acts as advisor and contractor in furnishing services requested by each enterprise, while also exercising certain authority in matters pertaining to regulations and engineering practices. For example, facilities managers may advise auxiliary enterprise officials on compliance with institutional and government codes and regulations as well as sound engineering practices.

To meet that need, planning and coordination procedures must be developed. The unique status of auxiliary enterprises creates other ramifications for physical plant. For instance, each enterprise is managed as a separate facility with individual cost accounting. Each one has institutional objectives—such as student recruitment and retention or providing essential student services. Beyond these objectives, however, each is managed largely as a commercial enterprise in which the level of service provided is matched to what users are willing to pay. As a result, maintenance and service levels, as well as priorities designated for work projects, may differ from those at facilities directly funded and managed by the physical plant department.

56.2 BUDGET CONTROL

Another way to define an auxiliary enterprise is anything for which physical plant is not budgeted or, in some cases, is provided for separately. If all departments were drawing from the same budget pool, auxiliary facilities would be competing along with classroom and office facilities for maintenance services, adding to budget control problems for the plant director. If, in fact, this is the case at an institution, the facilities director needs to work with the budget director and other departments involved to set up an allocation of available resources. Otherwise, "the squeaky wheel gets the oil" maxim is likely to prevail.

If there is no allocation mechanism for auxiliaries at an institution, a meeting with the budget director is needed in which auxiliary enterprises are clearly identified and resources allocated. Colleges and universities must have cost accounting methods to evaluate, analyze, and control income and expense items of the auxiliary operations, which make it possible to establish appropriate fees and prices. While this may mean adding accounts, it does assure proper resource control and reveals actual costs to the institution. An added advantage to this method is that the process forces each auxiliary service to justify its own budget, rather than require the plant director to do so. If separate allocations are not possible the plant director may find it beneficial to budget the available resources among all the divisions for which he or she is responsible, including auxiliary enterprises. The plan must be shared with the heads of these divisions and their cooperation secured. While this method is not preferable, it is better than taking no action at all.

56.3 ORGANIZATIONAL VARIATIONS

The management of finances and people should be under the control of the auxiliary director who best knows the operation. However, it is not uncommon to have maintenance and custodial personnel assigned to physical plant do the work for the auxiliary enterprise, with the auxiliary getting charged for costs as they occur. Some auxiliaries use a combination system: residence halls may maintain their own custodial and even small maintenance staff, but the facilities department will provide services and assistance that are more specialized—for example, HVAC systems service, elevator repair. and electrical maintenance. This arrangement ensures a certain amount of flexibility and prevents duplication. Where those specialized services are available through the department, auxiliary directors should not call upon outside contractors.

The size of the institution and auxiliary will probably dictate how staffs are assigned. Auxiliaries at smaller schools will tend to use physical plant as their resource pool in order to gain maximum flexibility. As the college expands along with an auxiliary enterprise, it may become not only desirable, but also feasible for an auxiliary operation to financially support its own maintenance staff.

A word of caution: care must be taken to ensure that in areas where plant personnel are providing services, the auxiliary enterprise does not assume supervisory authority; if control of personnel is lost, flexibility and credit for accomplishments will also be lost.

56.4 PROGRAM PLANNING

It is never good to work in a vacuum, and both the facilities and auxiliary enterprise staffs need to work together, particularly during budget preparation time. As stated above, each auxiliary operation needs to draft and justify its own budget. However, the plant director needs to participate in this process and assure agreement by both plant and auxiliary departments on types and levels of services anticipated for the budget period.

A starting point would be to consider the level of service provided in the past as a base and then anticipate new requirements for the coming year. This is easy to do when separate auxiliary accounts are kept. For example, in the past the plant department may have had four work-years of grounds work dedicated to the needs of the intercollegiate athletic department. However, in the upcoming year, with new emphasis being placed on women's sports, the department wants to upgrade the condition of the women's playing fields. Another one-half of a full-time person's services is needed to accomplish the job. Intercollegiate athletics needs to recognize the expanded maintenance needs and, once agreed upon, include them in their budget for the next program year. The plant director, on the other hand, needs to staff for this additional requirement either by reallocating current resources or securing additional positions.

For auxiliaries, one-time major costs or capital improvements require scrutiny. Good examples of typical one-time needs are reroofing a building or replacing a chiller in an auxiliary facility. If the plant department carries out a reliable yearly comprehensive building inspection (in addition to a preventive maintenance program), these capital improvement items can be identified. A special reserve fund for one-time costs should be maintained separately from the annual operations, maintenance, and repair budget. A good preventive maintenance inspection should also identify areas that the building inspection team should examine in detail.

56.5 SPECIAL SERVICES

Facility Planning and Design Assistance

Section V of this manual, Facilities Planning, Design, and Construction, discusses the design and execution of facilities projects with in-house personnel, consultants, and contractors. Auxiliary enterprises usually rely on the plant department to either design and carry out projects with their own crews or to work with outside consultants in the design and execution of projects by contractors.

Facility Evaluations

The effective management of facilities, including the budgeting step, demands advance planning since the task involves projecting fund requirements for a several year span. Auxiliary enterprise directors look to the physical plant for certain technical expertise before assembling their budget figures. For instance, physical plant is often asked to perform evaluations in three general categories:

- Status of compliance with codes and standards, particularly those that are new or changed.

- Current condition of facilities and appraisal of repair requirements.
- Energy efficiency of buildings as well as mechanical and electrical equipment. The evaluation may include recommendations for improvements.

Preventive Maintenance

Preventive maintenance (PM) must not be overlooked in auxiliary facilities. The best way to deal with upkeep is to assign total responsibility for the institution's campus-wide preventive maintenance program, including all auxiliary facilities, to the plant department.

As an alternative approach, the auxiliary enterprise can establish its own preventive maintenance program modeled on the one used by the plant department. If the auxiliary uses its own maintenance staff to do this, the plant director should help them establish a good PM program and show them how to stick to it.

Preventive maintenance inspectors work for the physical plant, but, as we have mentioned, they often inspect auxiliary facilities. On the chargeback, only costs of the actual inspection should be billed to the auxiliary. Since inspection fees are fixed costs, the auxiliary should be able to budget for them fairly easily. An alternate method allocates such costs to each auxiliary using a prorated share based on a common denominator such as square footage. In any case, whatever maintenance and repair items are identified should be handled by the auxiliary maintenance staff, if one exists. If something beyond their capability arises, it should be taken care of by the plant's maintenance shops and billed to the auxiliary on the charge-back system described earlier. It is good business practice to have an agreement on what can be done by the plant department in an auxiliary facility without prior approval from the auxiliary's management. Otherwise, there can be a significant delay in obtaining the necessary approvals to get the work accomplished.

Energy Management and Electric Load Shedding

The physical plant department usually manages energy usage for the entire campus. However, managers of individual auxiliary enterprises, which pay for the energy used, must participate in formulating and executing the energy conservation program for their operations. A major problem area in energy management is electric load shedding. Since rates for purchased electricity include both demand and usage charges, all users must participate in limiting the demand. It is the plant department's job to work with all users to determine peak demand and to establish a load shedding schedule to avoid exceeding the set limit.

56.6 DEFINED RESPONSIBILITIES

Servicing auxiliaries can be challenging, but there is a need for collaboration and well-defined roles. In spite of sometimes having to wear several hats, the facilities manager is the key person to make this cooperative effort successful. By gracefully accepting auxiliary enterprises and serving them skillfully, plant directors serve the overall mission of education at their institutions. At the same time, directors can build a positive reputation and support within the institution for plant employees and the department. The end result is that everyone wins.

CONCLUSION

CHAPTER 57

Toward Excellence in

Facilities Management

Gene B. Cross
Assistant Vice Chancellor
Planning and Facilities Management
University of California at Berkeley

57.1 MANAGING IT ALTOGETHER

This conclusion is intended to place in perspective the professional contribution of facilities management to higher education, and to point the way to greater development and achievement for the facilities management professional.

The previous sections of this manual have dealt with what an institution of higher education needs to do to manage its facilities. This section explores the essential professional and functional elements the physical plant professional needs to bring all the components together in a coordinated and dynamic operation that meets the needs of the campus constituency. The "critical success factors" are examined for those directly and indirectly responsible for the management of the campus physical facilities.

The Role of Facilities Management

Higher education in the United States predates the nation itself, as some eastern schools were established by charter from the King of England. Many were begun in a single building that had often been constructed for other purposes. With them came the responsibility of caring for and maintaining the buildings; thus, facilities management was born, although it was not considered one of the essential elements in the higher educational process. Nonetheless, it was and continues to be a major consideration that has a significant impact on the successful accomplishment of the purposes of higher education.

Within the organizational structure of an institution, the physical plant department is usually the largest in terms of numbers of employees, operating budget, and total campus impact. Every facet of campus life and its functions are affected by the activities for which the physical plant department is responsible. This impact includes recruitment of students and faculty, serving the staff, and maintaining alumni identification with the institution. In a 1984 Carnegie Foundation survey, "How Do Students Choose A College?," 62 percent of high school seniors surveyed indicated they made their final selection on the general appearance of the campus buildings and grounds. (See Ernest Boyer's foreword to this manual.) The environment in which quality faculty and students carry on their educational and research activities is vitally important and justifies equity in the allocation of resources to maximize the potential of any institution. Good faculty, as well as good students, can go to the institution of their choosing. The one they choose will be the one that promises the most enjoyable and compatible environment for their academic pursuits.

National studies have found that the majority of institutions allocate 10 to 12 percent of their operating budgets to the maintenance and operational needs of physical facilities. In addition, an ever-growing fixed cost demand on our campuses exists that is the single largest liability in higher education today. Deferred maintenance amounts to as much as $60 to $70 billion nationwide, according to the 1989 APPA/NACUBO/Coopers & Lybrand study, *The Decaying American Campus: A Ticking Time Bomb.*

Another significant financial requirement is for the purchase of energy to fuel the utility systems. The ever greater demands for close year-round control of interior environmental conditions and escalating costs have made fuels and utilities the single largest cost of most physical plants.

New and more stringent codes, accessibility regulations, the need to adapt facilities to accommodate changes in academic programs, and numerous other requirements necessitate optimum efficiency and economy in the administration of the physical facilities.

The mission and purposes of facilities management could be stated this way: to serve the institution in its pursuit of excellence in the most efficient and economic manner.

Facilities management is a "silent service." If the work is done appropriately, the campus users are not aware of the effort and resources needed to provide the institution the service it needs, wants, and expects in carrying out the three primary purposes of higher education: teaching, research, and public service.

As seen in Figure 57-1, facilities management is the "chassis" of higher education, the framework on which it operates.

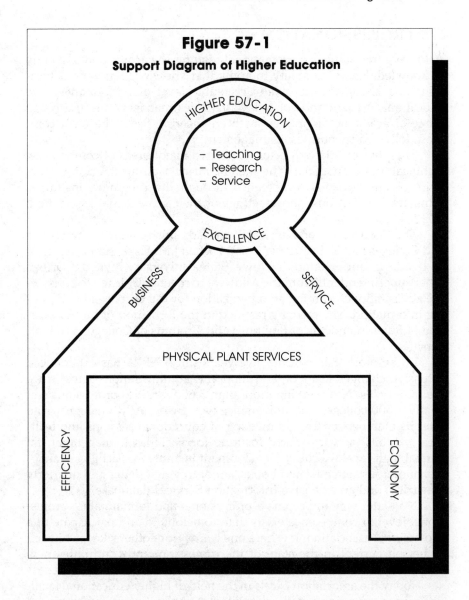

Figure 57-1

Support Diagram of Higher Education

The responsibilities of facilities management touch every member of the campus community—faculty, student, staff, administration, alumni, and visitor—every day. They impact the quality and quantity of the educational experience both physically and financially. In addition, their responsibilities interact directly and indirectly with the local community and can be felt statewide, nationally, and internationally, depending on the individual college or university.

57.2 PROFESSIONALISM

Achieving the status of a professional requires the acquisition of a body of knowledge and the ability to apply that knowledge in various locations and circumstances at an acceptable level of performance. The educational backgrounds of today's facilities managers are in a broad range of academic disciplines, with engineering being the most common, followed by business management.

The physical plant director needs two major areas of competence: technical and managerial. The incumbent or aspiring director can acquire or enhance this competence through the programs, institutes, seminars, publications, and meetings of their professional association, APPA.

The Association of Physical Plant Administrators of Universities and Colleges had its beginning in 1914 when J.M. Fiske, superintendent of buildings and grounds at Iowa State University, invited fourteen other superintendents from the Midwest to meet in Chicago to consider the advisability of forming an organization for the purpose of exchanging information. The meeting resulted in the formation of the Association of Superintendents of Buildings and Grounds of Colleges and Universities.[1]

In the more than seventy-five years since, APPA has experienced extensive changes in its organization and administration—most since the mid-1970s. Now serving more than 3,600 facilities professionals at nearly 1,500 colleges and universities worldwide, APPA has grown to offer its members an annual meeting of educational sessions and technical exhibits, a twice-yearly Institute for Facilities Management, an annual high-level Executive Development Institute for Facilities Managers, numerous seminars and books, a monthly newsletter and quarterly magazine, and an extensive Information Services data base.

No better way to become a professional and to maintain a professional level of competence exists than to belong to and participate in a professional association. It is here one learns from others, keeps himself or herself current in the state of the profession, and contributes new knowledge and techniques to improving professional performance.

Today the association excels in the field of higher educational facilities management, nationally and internationally. Supported by six regional associations that span the North American continent through the United States and Canada, its membership reaches across both oceans.

57.3 PROFESSIONAL GROWTH

What does it take to be an effective physical plant manager? It takes a "person for all seasons." The director of the department must have the ability to manage, lead, technically problem-solve, plan, market, and provide positive customer service for all things and people, at all times, in all circumstances, often with limited resources.

Many physical plant directors come from a technical or engineering background; almost an equal number come from a diverse educational experience. Most have business-oriented training and experience. All successful directors have or acquire the ability to "get the job done" or "make it happen" with people, within complex environments and varying agendas.

When a director's position becomes open at an institution, there are many avenues used to fill the position. The first would be a single promotion with the next senior person. If this is contemplated, it should not be done until a written position description is clearly defined. In this way, any candidate will be able to know the expectations and responsibilities, and the administration will have thought through its expectations for the new director.

A second approach involves a formal search either locally or nationally. First, the administration develops a job specification to be advertised in newspapers and professional publications. *APPA Newsletter* and *Facilities Manager* carry monthly position listings.

A third option is to employ a search firm, or "head hunter." As with any consultant, services, abilities, and fees vary by firm and area; most charge a fee that is a percentage of the annual salary, usually 20 to 30 percent. With the consultant agreement the client must determine what services the consultant is to provide, the fee and what it covers, and which expenses are to be backcharged to the client, such as printing and mailing for job fliers and travel expenses for the consultant and applicants.

A less formal approach is to contact respected people in the profession and ask for recommendations. This method can uncover individuals who are not active in the job market but are doing a good job in the field.

A recruiting institution can appoint a single administrator to handle the recruiting, screening, and selection, or it may set up a representative committee to perform the functions. Because of the encompassing impact of the director's responsibilities on any campus, it is probably better to use a committee approach. This involves faculty, staff, students, the administration, and representatives from principal clients of the physical plant department such as arts and sciences, athletics, housing, food services, and other appropriate units.

Prospective Applicant

What can the prospective applicant do to heighten the potential for consideration and selection?

First, have a qualifying educational background. This educational requirement will usually be stipulated in the position advertisement. It will often stipulate "or comparable qualifying experience." The stipulation benefits the institution and the applicant as a good applicant may have excellent training and experience but no degree.

Second, have adequate or qualifying experience in the direct or related field. It is usually easier to go to a higher position from a larger school to a smaller school or from a comparable position from one school to another. It is also true that those receiving internal promotions receive smaller salary increases than persons recruited from outside the organization or institution.

Third, have an established professional reputation with three to five references who are recognized in the profession or who can attest to your professional competence. The best reference a person can have is to have done an excellent job in previous positions and to have performed in a compatible manner with his or her colleagues and the campus community.

Professional Resume

Most position openings will require a resume or summary that includes educational background, work experience and positions held, committee work, professional affiliations, recognitions and honors, community and service club involvement, and other information regarding capabilities. A resume is an introduction; it informs the reader and "sells" the applicant. Therefore, develop a well-written, accurate, informative, neat, well-organized, and concise document that comprehensively describes you and your qualifications.

A resume's appearance as well as content should impress. Format and style can be acquired from books on the subject, others' resumes, or a professional resume writing agency.

Interviewing

Once a candidate has made it through resume screening to the "short list," usually the top three, he or she will be invited for an interview with an administrator, a committee, and possibly others. A recent response by 153 employers, when asked to list the reasons potential employees were rejected at the interview level, listed the following basic reasons:

1. Poor personal appearance.
2. Lack of interest and enthusiasm.
3. Failure to look at the interviewer when conversing.

4. Late to the interview.
5. No questions about the job.
6. Too overbearing.
7. Know-it-all attitude.
8. Inability to express self clearly.
9. Poor voice, diction, and grammar.
10. Lack of planning for career; lack of purpose and goals.

Therefore, to be well accepted by the interviewer, the antithesis of these points would seem to be:

1. Be well groomed and well dressed but not overly so. The ideal is to find out how the people dress at the organizational level of the position you are applying for and dress appropriately.
2. Show reasonable interest and enthusiasm by asking good questions about the position and its responsibilities. To do this, you have to do your homework for the position. A few well-placed telephone calls are time and money well spent.
3. Always maintain comfortable eye contact.
4. Be a minimum of fifteen minutes early so you are ready when they are ready.
5. Again, do your homework and have a list of substantive questions about the position, its responsibilities, and the employer's expectations. This helps to communicate your knowledge and background.
6. Keep in mind that *you* are being interviewed. That means you are to listen and respond to questions. Your response should be clear and concise. At the end of the interview you should have an opportunity to ask questions.
7. In answering questions always speak to the question and do not stray. Know your limitations and have a plan to supplement your deficiencies.
8. The ability to communicate verbally is normally equated to one's level of intelligence. Practice, take classes, read out loud, make presentations, and give training sessions. Giving training sessions develops your ability to think on your feet and respond to questions. Think through anticipated questions and answers on your own so the answers will come easily and naturally in an interview.
9. Improper grammar and diction are clear indications of limited background, education, or training. Your voice can communicate personality traits, i.e., interest, enthusiasm, confidence, nervousness, incompetence, and boredom.
10. Planning, organization, and preparation for your future communicates your ability and motivation to plan, organize, and prepare your work and responsibilities.

Position Opportunities

Where are the sources of available positions and people? APPA lists position openings for schools that have placed ads in the Job Corner section of *APPA Newsletter* and *Facilities Manager*. *The Chronicle of Higher Education* has an extensive positions available section for all segments of higher education. It also publishes annual salary surveys compiled by the College and University Personnel Association. Some schools use search firms in recruiting. In addition, professional meetings frequently have position openings posted on bulletin boards, and the word-of-mouth system also goes on during these meetings.

57.4 MAKING IT HAPPEN

Lee Iacocca of Chrysler Corporation once said, "To be successful you have to give the people what they want." Therein lies the challenge for the facilities manager—to provide professional services, within limited resources in a manner and to a degree acceptable to the campus customer. Thus, the equation for success is:

Professional Competence + Effective Customer Service = SUCCESS.

To be successful in the management of the physical facilities for an institution of higher education, one must manage resources in an efficient, economical manner while delivering acceptable service to the campus customers, be they administrators, faculty, staff, students, or alumni. Resources are basically of three types: people, time, and money. They should be considered in this order of priority while fully recognizing that all three resources must be consistently well managed for an organization to prosper.

People must be informed of their job responsibilities (job description), communicated with on a frequent timely basis, and given answers to their questions. They should be trained on a regular, minimally monthly, basis to acquire and maintain knowledge and skill about work and responsibilities.

Research has found that, with all the considerations that go into job satisfaction, two elements make the critical difference: feedback and self-determination. People like to know where they stand and how they are doing; even negative feedback is better than none at all. This feedback needs to be on a timely and regular basis. When they do well, recognition should be quick and public (i.e., positive reinforcement). When they make a mistake, feedback should be quick and private, pointing to the problem and not the person, unless the person has actually become part of the problem.

Most people like to have as much latitude as possible in carrying out their responsibilities. They like to exercise their own judgment and initiative. When this type of work environment is created, it generates feelings of commitment as the individual becomes involved in his or her work.

For individuals to be successful, the person must be adequately instructed as to what the responsibilities are, trained to do them with a high degree of proficiency, and evaluated on a regular basis. Outstanding performance should be recognized formally at all levels of the organization.

A physical plant department should have employee recognition programs for performing in highly desirable ways. Many directors develop "employee of the month" (and year) programs. Employees can be recognized for an excellent building, area, or project. This recognition is further complemented if a department has a newsletter where such acknowledgments can be recognized with pictures and articles.

Employees are told to do a good job and they will move up. The better employees should always be rewarded. More people and money should never be added to poor operations. People should be required to do good jobs with what they have, no matter how meager, before they can expect more help. More doesn't make it better, it only provides more resources to do what is being done.

When people are challenged with problems and responsibility, rather than given answers and commands, most will respond positively and try harder. A sure formula for failure is an imbalance in the formula of authority and responsibility. All too often managers will delegate 100 percent of the responsibility for a job but want to retain all or a majority of the authority.

Is it possible to delegate authority and responsibility and retain it at the same time? Yes. For subordinates to have a high potential for success, as well as high job and personal satisfaction, they must be given equal amounts of authority and responsibility for any assigned task. Their superior still retains that authority and responsibility but allows someone else to serve on his or her behalf.

The superior should monitor the progress and approach being used by the subordinate, in an agreed upon manner, and provide guidance and support. Follow-up is the key to successful delegation.

Managing with Less-Than-Adequate Resources

Few, if any, physical plant operations are staffed and funded at a level to meet the total needed planned maintenance program for the campus. Many, if not most, campus physical plant operations are funded and staffed at 50 to 60 percent of known need for a 100 percent planned maintenance program. The balance of the need goes into the ever-deepening bucket of deferred maintenance. This has grown so much as to be the single largest liability in higher education.

How can the facilities manager handle the paradox of the campus' 100 percent expectation with 60 percent capability? It is possible to perform in a positive way that is acceptable to the campus community by doing the important things and laying aside those tasks that are less important.

The 10/90 Postulate

Performing 10 percent of the activities that need doing will accomplish 90 percent of the results toward fulfilling your responsibilities. To be able to consistently prioritize and identify those 10 percent items is a critical factor in success. The less important items pile up and are obvious. The critical success factors have to be searched out and discovered, for example:

- Training. All recognize its importance but relatively few managers set aside regularly scheduled time each month for it.
- Custodial. Floors make the most significant impression as to the cleanliness of a building.
- Communication. No one likes to be surprised with a problem, but almost everyone has great tolerance when forewarned and involved.
- Timeliness. Not communicating creates frustration and anxiety; a timely response with a scheduled plan of action is usually acceptable.

The annual operational budget should be broken down into a planned preventive maintenance program that itemizes what is to be accomplished in each building each year, including ongoing maintenance and operations activities. It is the responsibility of every physical plant director to know, each year, what the total maintenance needs are for the entire campus. To do this the campus buildings and grounds and utility systems must be reviewed or inspected to keep the need list current.

To keep this maintenance work responsive to the campus building occupants, it is vital that this list be reviewed with the deans, directors, or department heads. In this way they are kept informed and have the opportunity to give opinions from the user's point of view. From this interchange comes a prioritized, mutually agreed upon list for the total needs of the building. As sufficient resources do not exist for all the identified needs, the physical plant director must indicate how far down the prioritized list the resources will allow him or her to go. In this way the expectations of the user and the realities of the provider can be brought in line. When expectation is larger than realization, the result is frustration; but when expectation, no matter what degree, is brought in line with reality, the result is some degree of satisfaction.

Through coordination, communication, and cooperation, an agreeable and equitable maintenance and operational level can be achieved and maintained with most building occupants. A physical plant director can promise full knowledge and the best trade-offs available at the time to create and maintain the best environment.

Being Responsive

The response given all too often by many physical plant personnel when confronted with a campus need is either "send me an order to charge it to" or "I don't have the funds to do it" even when the requests are legitimate and they would like to do the work. Every director should have control of some discretionary money, no matter how small, to be able to respond to some of these needs both within the department and for the campus community.

How do you get it? A director finds or creates it by encumbering a designated amount of the department's budget before it is allocated to the department units. A review and allocation process needs to be developed so it can be allocated over the year as special needs arise.

An article in *The Chronicle of Higher Education* (April 13, 1988) dramatized just how important the campus environment is to the success of an institution. The article concerned the efforts to retain a highly prized faculty member. It concluded by saying:

> If there is a lesson for university administrators in all of this
> . . . it is that highly recruited scientists can be kept with two
> things. One is an awful lot of money, but that is No. 2. The
> No. 1 thing is top-notch working conditions. . . . The thing
> that makes the difference is an environment where people
> feel they can get things done.

Those in facilities management create and maintain that campus environment.

57.5 SERVICE DELIVERY

One of the greatest shortcomings of many physical plant operations is the inattention to customer relations. Great attention and care is given to the professional competence (the "what") of the service provided, but little and frequently less-than-adequate emphasis is given to delivery of that service (the "how").

What do customers want?

- A quality service or product.
- Delivered in a timely manner.
- At a reasonable price.
- While being kept appropriately involved and informed.

To provide positive customer service the department staff and customer clientele must be trained and oriented as to what services are available, how they can be delivered, and what limitations exist in providing those services. This can only be done by contact with the work force and customers, in groups and individually, training programs, and observation.

Customer service has to be a well-known, reinforced priority for the organization. Rewards and recognition must be given for those exemplifying the standards of service.

Who Pays?

There is always one major problem in dealing with the campus customer: "who pays?" On most campuses, some services are provided at the expense of the physical plant budget and other services are charged for. What justifies the delineation between the two options? No clear rule exists, but some guidelines or principles can help in developing policies.

The basic guideline is: whoever controls or owns, pays. Three illustrations follow:

1. Normally physical plant paints faculty offices on an eight-year planned maintenance cycle. The department has a new, prominent faculty member coming in and requests the office be painted in July before he arrives. The office was last painted five years ago. Under physical plant control it would be three years before it paints at its own expense. Under the department's control the office would be painted now, but at departmental or "other" expense.
2. The air conditioning unit for the building needs repair and the department has called in the order. The unit was purchased and installed by the institution (not the department) and the equipment was carried on the physical plant department's inventory. Physical plant would fix the unit at its expense.
3. The department had purchased and paid for the installation of a still in a laboratory. A year later it broke, and an order was sent to the physical plant department. Physical plant checked the inventory listing of the equipment and found it was inventoried to the depart-

ment. They then informed the department that it would have to pay for the service.

Not all considerations will fall neatly into the simple test, but the majority will. Whatever policy or guideline is used should be published and communicated to customers and staff for consistent application.

57.6 FACILITIES MANAGEMENT SELF-ASSESSMENT

At its 75th Annual Meeting in July 1988, APPA presented the first Award for Excellence in Facilities Management. The purpose of the Award for Excellence is to recognize excellence in physical plant operations at our colleges and universities. The award recognizes an entire department's effort rather than a single individual or a specific unit or division.

The following are the criteria used in the competitive evaluations of physical plants for the Award for Excellence in Facilities Management.

- Policies and Procedures
  - Mission statement
  - Organization chart
  - Service manual
  - Annual report
  - Work requests
  - Work request system
  - Work scheduling
  - Customer satisfaction feedback
- Quality of Relationships with
  - Faculty
  - Staff
  - Students
  - Visitors
  - Alumni
- Campus Appearance and Condition
  - Maintenance standards
  - Planning
  - Preventive maintenance
  - Deferred maintenance
  - Capital renewal and replacement
  - Work standards
  - Quality and cost control
- Initiative and Innovation

- Campus Planning
  - Architectural guidelines
- Training, Education, and Development
  - Training policy
  - Involvement and activity at regional and national APPA annual meetings, institutes, seminars, and other programs
- Measurement and Success
  - Campus indicators for measuring effectiveness of service delivery.

These are the excellence factors. It is up to the physical plant professional to develop them to best serve their individual campus.

In the first edition of this manual, published in 1984, Terry Suber authored the concluding chapter entitled "Evaluating Plant Management," and described an audit outline and a facilities management profile. These have been widely used since their publication and are included in this text as Appendixes 57-A and 57-B.

In addition to these valuable profile guidelines, there are several others that will help facilities managers and general campus administrators evaluate their physical plant operations. Just as in the book *In Search of Excellence* by Peters and Waterman, which identified common traits of successful companies, the following elements are found most frequently in the successful physical plant departments:

1. The department's mission is clearly defined, widely distributed, and frequently reinforced.
2. The organization is formally outlined and is as simple and as flat as possible while being well understood, consistently applied, and flexible enough to meet change and emergencies.
3. Overall staffing = 1 position for every 10,000 to 15,000 gross square feet.
   - Custodial = 1/20-25,000 gr. sq. ft.
   - Shops = 1/50-70,000 gr. sq. ft.
   - Grounds = 1/3-10 acres.
4. Departmental budgets = 7 to 15 percent of the institutional budget, the majority being 10 to 12 percent.
5. Budget allocation = $3 for salaries/$1 for supplies and equipment.
   - Utilities = 50 percent of department's budget
   - Custodial = 20 percent
   - Shops = 20 percent
   - Grounds = 7 percent
   - Other = 3 percent
   - Per gr. sq. ft. = $2 to $5.

6. A customer service evaluation is conducted to develop a sense of customer satisfaction.

In the final analysis, this manual embodies all the elements required for a successful physical plant operation for the more than 3,400 U.S. institutions of higher education as well as those in other countries. The challenge is up to the individual facilities manager as to how these elements are put to use—the art that brings life to the science.

NOTES

1. For a more complete history of APPA, see Christy Wise's article, "Celebrating APPA's First 75 Years," in the Summer 1988 issue of *Facilities Manager*.

Appendix 57-A

Physical Plant Management Audit Outline

I. Determine purposes and objectives of department.

  A. Review written policies and nonfinancial procedures.

    1. Do objectives communicated to staff agree with objectives as stated by the Board and administration?

    2. Are the written policies and procedures adequate to guide the department?

    3. Are policies and procedures realistic and attainable?

  B. Review significant programs the department handles.

    1. Are the programs clearly defined?

    2. Are goals set for the programs?

  C. Review higher level of authority's agreement with and opinion of the written goals and objectives.

II. Evaluate compliance with significant external regulations.

  A. Determine external regulators.

  B. Compile list of significant regulations with which physical
plant should comply.

  C. Monitor compliance with significant regulations during field work.

III. Evaluate organizational structure and operational procedures.

  A. Organization.

    1. Prepare organization chart; enter names of incumbents.

    2. Examine job descriptions.

    3. Test qualifications of employees. Make general comparisons with written job descriptions.

    4. Evaluate distribution and adequacy of staffing. Review time-and-effort reports.

    5. Is span of command reasonable?

    6. Do supervisors perform physical labor or could they?

    7. Do all administrative positions serve a needed and useful purpose?

     8. Is organization most efficient? Examine proposed organization chart.

     9. Examine employee training programs at all levels.

B. Evaluate internal control.

     1. Perform document and work flow review. Prepare appropriate flow charts.

     2. Review and evaluate adequacy of appropriate financial procedures.

     3. Discuss individual strengths and weaknesses of internal control system and give overall narrative ratings of internal controls.

C. Review architectural and engineering standards development.

     1. What standards are followed by physical plant, e.g., industrial versus commercial? What is the difference?

     2. Are standards comprehensive and adequately documented? Are they applied across-the-board or selectively? Are standards reasonable? What are the criteria for allowing deviations from the standard?

     3. Are standards properly communicated to users, and in what way? When a department wants to remodel space,
do plant personnel explain how standards must be main
tained and the impact on costs?

     4. Select several work projects (in-house and contracted) completed during the fiscal year for review.

        a) Visit departments and determine how standards were
communicated to them.

        b) Determine if the department felt that standards were appropriate, too high, too low.

        c) If exceptions to the standards were allowed, what was the procedure for obtaining exceptions?

        d) Were exceptions documented and approved by appropriate plant personnel?

        e) Was supervision of the project adequate?

     5. Are standards properly enforced?

        a) In-house construction.

(1) What quality controls exist?

(2) What processes assure that actual construction meets design standards?

b) Contracted construction.

(1) How are institutional standards communicated to the vendor? Are standards detailed before the contract is awarded?

(2) How does physical plant assure that the vendors meet standards? Outline the process.

(3) What leverage does the physical plant use to get vendors to correct deficiencies? Is the procedure consistently applied?

D. Review and evaluate decision rules for classifying maintenance work and projects by type and source of funding. Test application of these rules.

E. Evaluate trades operations.

1. Project management.
   a) Evaluate organization.
   b) Are planning, directing, execution, and control adequate?
   c) Evaluate scheduling process.

2. Efficiency/effectiveness measures.
   a) Compare in-house with contractor prices and quality. Determine if proper accountability and market incentives exist.
   (1) Bids/estimates.
      (a) Determine the procedure for developing estimates.
      (b) Determine why estimates are used rather than bids.
      (c) Obtain several estimates. Compare to actual. Note problem areas.
      (d) Trace time reports. What kind of time reporting is required of plant employees?
      (e) Determine break policies—length of breaks, lunch, quitting time? Are breaks, travel time, and returns to shop for tools included in actual labor costs?

(f) What is the basis of contingency fees
in estimates?

(2) Compare physical plant bid to actual
cost when work is contracted.

(3) When vendors are used, identify role of
physical plant in setting standards and
specifications for bids and ensuring that
work is done to specification.

(4) Are plant management costs imposed on
outside contractors reasonable?

b) Is the work force (especially general laborers
and trades helpers) tailored to current conditions to reduce labor expense?

(1) How are the number and qualifications
of people needed on projects
determined?

(2) Do current qualifications meet current
needs?

(3) What proportion of project labor costs is
general (unskilled) labor? What
proportion coul, be?

(4) Is billing done w, actual rather than
appropriate rates?

c) Survey customer satisfaction.

F. Maintenance operations.

1. Evaluate standard-setting process.

2. Review previous consulting study and implementation of recommendations.

3. Evaluate decision rules for determining whether
work is reimbursable or not.

4. Evaluate management of operations.

a) Are planning, directing, controlling, and execution adequate (especially first-line
supervision)?

b) Survey customer/client satisfaction. Do
customers know what service to expect? Is
expected service delivered? How are complaints handled?

5. Arrange with selected building proctors to monitor
custodial services during one month and compare
with established plant standards.

6. Could custodial work begin during the day to
reduce shift differential and allow custodians to
meet people they're helping?

IV. Evaluate budgetary and expenditure control.

A. Identify all financial resources available to the physical plant and the person(s) having expenditure control. Prepare trial balance(s).

B. Determine how the detailed annual budget is developed.
   1. How are revenues estimated?
   2. Is funding allocated to programs? If so, how?
   3. How are expenses estimated?
   4. How are expenses allocated?
   5. Does the budget address *both* current year and long-term objectives of the department?

C. Determine how effectively the budget is executed, controlled, and reported.
   1. Are expenditures and revenues properly coded?
   2. Does financial reporting facilitate budget control?
      a) Identify reports (internal and external to physical plant).
      b) Are reports useful, timely, and accurate?
   3. Is appropriate action taken on variations? Is accountability assigned and maintained?

D. Determine if direct and indirect costs of programs are known and accurately reported. (See V.)
   1. Identify and schedule direct costs.
   2. Identify and schedule indirect costs. Exclude inventories. (See VII.B.)
      a) Determine how the overhead rate was developed.
         (1) Are all items included that should be?
         (2) Are items included that should be a direct charge?
      b) Are the percentages and formulas used reasonable and justifiable?
      c) Examine the adequacy and correctness of the overhead rate.
   3. Are such expenses reasonable and complete?
   4. Analyze financial data.
      a) Prepare and review three-year comparative balance sheet and income statements (standardized).
      b) Prepare and review work order volume by trade.

      c) Prepare and review trends in in-house versus contracted work.

      d) Prepare and review trends in salaries—institution versus local market.

      e) Prepare and review trends in ratio of support staff to workers.

      f) Prepare and review trends in ratio of supervisors to nonsupervisors.

      g) Prepare and review trends in project cost elements (labor, materials, overhead).

      h) Obtain industry statistics on various norms, including work-time standards. Compare with actual operation.

      i) Try to determine how much physical plant-related work may actually be performed by other departments (hidden physical plant costs). Why are these services provided by contractors or in-house staff?

      j) Review rationale for assignment of revenues and expenses to the appropriated resident instruction funds versus the revolving funds.

  5. Utilities.

      a) Review last internal audit report and workpapers.

      b) Evaluate expense distribution methods.

      c) Review and evaluate energy conservation program.

      d) Review long-range plans for providing uninterrupted, cost-effective utilities services.

V. Test revenue and expense transactions. (See IV.D.)

  A. Select a sample of contracts/work orders for examination. Include some projects with multiple bids. (See III.E.2.a)(2).)

    1. Review for proper authorization.

    2. Evaluate reasonableness of financial (and other) details.

VI. Review equipment.

  A. Examine the most recent equipment inventory performed by functional accounting. Are records up to date?

  B. Examine policy on equipment usage (by whom? where? provisions for moving?)

C. Test from floor to records. Are all pieces of equipment properly recorded?

VII. Inventories.

A. Review the most recent functional accounting physical inventory and inventory workpapers.

B. How are inventory items issued and controlled?

1. Identify physical plant storeroom policies and procedures.
2. Determine the overhead rate applied to materials purchased through the storeroom.
3. Follow steps in IV.D.2.
4. Determine the policy, procedures, and charges associated with restocking materials.

C. Are all inventories recorded?

D. Are there any unreasonable overages or shortages? obsolete inventory?

VIII. Travel.

A. Select a sample of travel expenses from the department travel log.

B. Evaluate documentation for compliance and reasonableness.

IX. Investments and obligations.

A. Schedule and review investments and investment income for proper control and effective utilization.

B. Schedule and review long-term obligations and related expense for proper control and effective utilization.

Appendix 57-B

Facilities Management Profile

Levels of Evaluation

Function	Low — Verbal		Medium — Written		High — Formal & Published	
1. Mission of the Department	historical and traditional	verbal to key staff	general guidance	specific guidance	printed and published	plus updating
2. Policies of the Department	**Verbal**		**Incident Generated**		**Detailed Procedures**	
	custom and usage	top-level instructions	general, written instructions	specific, written statements	printed and published	plus updating and contingent guidance
3. Responsibilities and Authority of Director	**Informal**		**Limited Formal**		**Formal**	
	report and act	act and report	written job description	written and detailed	goals and objectives	performance evaluations
4. Functional Organization of Staff	**Unstructured**		**Structured**		**Structured & Controlled**	
	verbal and assumed	individual assignments	general, written guidelines	specific, written guidelines	printed, published & reviewed	printed, plus contingent review
5. Personnel Organization of the Department	**Unstructured with Individual Assignment**		**Structured**		**Structured & Controlled**	
	craft	shop	craft or shop	function	printed chart	charted and written job duties

Function	Stage 1	Stage 2	Stage 3
6. Personnel Training and Career Development	**None** none individual effort	**Informal** on-the-job training	**Formal** formal, classroom career ladder
7. Budgeting	**Informal** assigned record expenditures	**Formal** historical cost basis supported appropriations	**Detailed & Controlled** control forecast for level of maintenance planning, programming, and control
8. Financial Management	**Informal** salaries and expenses record of expenditures	**Formal** general accounting reports cost-center reports	**Detailed & Controlled** management information decision and forecasting data
9. Maintenance	**Verbal** breakdown haphazard	**Written** scheduled by craft plus backlog control	**Formal & Published** comprehensive preventive maintenance plus computerized maintenance nance engineering
10. Work Request	**Family Style** individual worker staff and supervisor	**Informal** departmental verbal request day-shift answering service	**Reception & Control** written record and feedback three-shift receptionist and response
11. Work Identification	**Unplanned** complaints and emergencies routine requests	**Simple Standards** manufacturing and safety standards scheduled inspections	**Planned** planned and scheduled inspections based on standards computerized plus engineering

	Verbal	Informal	Formal Authority
12. Work Authorization	customer · staff or shop	standing or regular work order · supervisors approve specific work orders	specific work order approval by staff · specific work order approval by director

	No Standards	Experience Standards	Formal Standards
13. Planning and Estimating Work	magnitude by foreman · rule of thumb	shop experience · group experience by staff	engineered performance · published standards

	Informal	Partial Formal	Scheduled & Formal
14. Work Scheduling	none · by trade	major work scheduled · preventive maintenance scheduled	in-house force and contract work · scheduling engineering

	Informal	Simple Control	Detailed Evaluation
15. Employee Work Performance	visual · routine checking	supervisors review · staff analysis compared to standards	work sampling and charting · value analysis

	Informal	Formal	Detailed Evaluation
16. Departmental Evaluation and Analysis	complaints · cost based on square footage	written reports · personal involvement	detailed performance analysis · management audit

INDEX

INDEX